CENTRAL AMERICA
ON A SHOESTRING

D0993694

David Zingarelli
Jeff Davis
Conner Gorry
Paul Hellander
Carolyn Miller
Daniel Schechter

LONELY PLANET PUBLICATIONS
Melbourne | Oakland | London | Paris

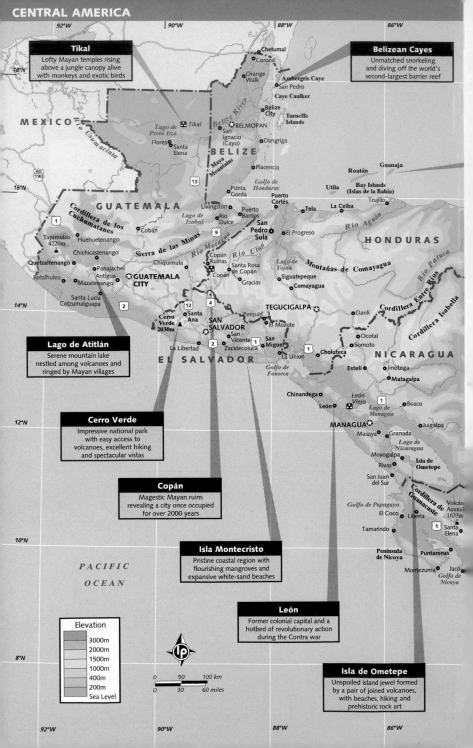

CENTRAL AMERICA

Tikal
Lofty Mayan temples rising above a jungle canopy alive with monkeys and exotic birds

Belizean Cayes
Unmatched snorkeling and diving off the world's second-largest barrier reef

Lago de Atitlán
Serene mountain lake nestled among volcanoes and ringed by Mayan villages

Cerro Verde
Impressive national park with easy access to volcanoes, excellent hiking and spectacular vistas

Copán
Magestic Mayan ruins revealing a city once occupied for over 2000 years

Isla Montecristo
Pristine coastal region with flourishing mangroves and expansive white-sand beaches

León
Former colonial capital and a hotbed of revolutionary action during the Contra war

Isla de Ometepe
Unspoiled island jewel formed by a pair of joined volcanoes, with beaches, hiking and prehistoric rock art

MEXICO

GUATEMALA

BELIZE

HONDURAS

EL SALVADOR

NICARAGUA

Chetumal
Corozal
Orange Walk
Ambergris Caye
San Pedro
Caye Caulker
Belize City
Turneffe Islands
BELMOPAN
San Ignacio (Cayo)
Dangriga
Flores
Santa Elena
Lago de Petén Itzá
Tikal
Maya Mountains
Placencia
Punta Gorda
Golfo de Honduras
Puerto Cortés
Roatán
Guanaja
Utila
Bay Islands (Islas de la Bahía)
Trujillo
Livingston
Puerto Barrios
Tela
La Ceiba
Cobán
Lago de Izabal
Río Dulce
San Pedro Sula
El Progreso
Río Aguán
HONDURAS
Cordillera de los Cuchumatanes
Tajumulco 4220m
Huehuetenango
Chichicastenango
Sierra de las Minas
Río Motagua
Río Ulúa
Chiquimula
Copán Ruinas
Copán
Santa Rosa de Copán
Lago de Yojoa
Montañas de Comayagua
Río Patuca
Quetzaltenango
Panajachel
Antigua
Lago de Atitlán
Gracias
Siguatepeque
Comayagua
Cordillera Entre Ríos
Retalhuleu
Mazatenango
GUATEMALA CITY
TEGUCIGALPA
Danlí
Cordillera Isabella
Santa Lucía Cotzumalguapa
Cerro Verde 2030m
Santa Ana
SAN SALVADOR
Perquín
El Mozote
Ocotal
Somoto
La Libertad
San Vicente
San Miguel
Choluteca
NICARAGUA
EL SALVADOR
Zacatecoluca
La Union
Estelí
Jinotega
Matagalpa
Golfo de Fonseca
Chinandega
León Viejo
León
Boaco
Juigalpa
MANAGUA
Lago de Managua
Masaya
Granada
Lago de Nicaragua
Moyogalpa
Rivas
Isla de Ometepe
San Juan del Sur
Cordillera de Guanacaste
Volcán Arenal 1633m
Golfo de Papagayo
El Coco
Liberia
Santa Elena
Tamarindo
Península de Nicoya
Puntarenas
Montezuma
Jacó
Golfo de Nicoya

PACIFIC OCEAN

Elevation
3000m
2000m
1500m
1000m
400m
200m
Sea Level

0   50   100 km
0   30   60 miles

18°N
16°N
14°N
12°N
10°N
8°N

92°W   90°W   88°W   86°W

MEX 190
1
13
9
12
4
2
2
1
1
1

84°W   82°W   80°W   78°W

JAMAICA   **KINGSTON**

Islas Santanilla (Swan Islands, Honduras)

Bay Islands
Idyllic island haven with protected reefs and plentiful marine life, renowned among divers

16°N

CARIBBEAN

SEA

Laguna de Caratasca

La Mosquitia

Río Coco

Río Wawa

Volcán Arenal
Central America's most active volcano, with spectacular lava flows and eruptions every few hours

14°N

Cayos Miskitos (Nicaragua)

Costa de Miskitos

Puerto Cabezas

Río Grande de Matagalpa

Isla de Providencia (Colombia)

Parque Nacional Corcovado
Pacific coastal rain forest teeming with wildlife, including Costa Rica's largest colonies of scarlet macaws

Laguna de Perlas

Isla de San Andrés (Colombia)

Río Escondido

Rama

Bluefields

Corn Islands (Islas del Maíz, Nicaragua)

12°N

Archipiélago de Bocas del Toro
Deserted beaches, laid-back villages and coral reefs ideal for snorkeling and diving

Bahía Punta Gorda

El Castillo

Panama Canal Zone
One of the world's engineering wonders, bordered by beautiful tropical rain forest

10°N

Volcán Poás 2704m

Tortuguero

Alajuela Heredia [32]

SAN JOSÉ

Puerto Limón

Cartago

Cahuita

Archipiélago de San Blas

COSTA RICA

Puerto Viejo de Talamanca

Cordillera de Talamanca

Bocas del Toro

Colón

Chepo

Cordillera de San Blas

Quepos

San Isidro de El General

Laguna de Chiriquí

Golfo de los Mosquitos

PANAMÁ CITY

Lago Bayano

Río Chucunaque

San Vito [2]

Volcán Barú 3475m

Boquete

Cordillera Central

PANAMA

Bahía de Panamá

Serranía del Darién

Península de Osa

David

Golfo de Chiriquí

Interamericana

Santiago

Penonomé

Chitré

La Palma

Yaviza

Archipiélago de las Perlas

Isla de Coiba

Península de Azuero

Golfo de Panamá

COLOMBIA

84°W   82°W   80°W   78°W

Central America
4th edition – June 2001
First published – February 1992

Published by
Lonely Planet Publications Pty Ltd ABN 36 005 607 983
90 Maribyrnong St, Footscray, Victoria 3011, Australia

Lonely Planet Offices
Australia Locked Bag 1, Footscray, Victoria 3011
USA 150 Linden St, Oakland, CA 94607
UK 10a Spring Place, London NW5 3BH
France 1 rue du Dahomey, 75011 Paris

Photographs
Many of the images in this guide are available for licensing from
Lonely Planet Images.
email: lpi@lonelyplanet.com.au

Front cover photographs
Temple I in Tikal's Great Plaza, Guatemala (Leanne Walker & Andrew
Marshall). Swainson's toucan, Darién rain forest, Panama (Alfredo
Maiquez). Boy in hat, Cuilco, Guatemala (Eric L Wheater).

ISBN 1 86450 186 3

text & maps © Lonely Planet 2001
photos © photographers as indicated 2001

Printed by The Bookmaker International Ltd
Printed in China

Although the authors
and Lonely Planet try
to make the informa-
tion as accurate as
possible, we accept
no responsibility for
any loss, injury or
inconvenience sus-
tained by anyone
using this book.

Contents – Text

2   Contents – Text

BELIZE   253

HONDURAS

305

EL SALVADOR

433

4 Contents – Text

NICARAGUA 497

COSTA RICA 577

6 Contents – Text

PANAMA 685

LANGUAGE 777

GLOSSARY 785

ACKNOWLEDGMENTS 789

INDEX 794

MAP LEGEND 808

Contents – Maps

GUATEMALA

BELIZE

HONDURAS

EL SALVADOR

NICARAGUA

8 Contents – Maps

COSTA RICA

PANAMA

The Authors

David Zingarelli
A California native, David grew up among the redwoods and vineyards of Sonoma County. His first of many encounters with Latin America occurred in 1987, when he set sail for San Cristóbal, Venezuela, for a year that changed everything. The world seemed a lot smaller in the wake of that year, and after taking a break to earn a degree from the University of California at San Diego, David resumed his travels and hasn't stopped since. He spends much of his spare time (and all of his spare change) exploring his favorite corners of the globe and discovering new ones along the way. David most recently contributed to Lonely Planet's *Washington, DC*, and his photography has appeared in a number of other guides. He presently resides in San Francisco and is a senior editor in Lonely Planet's Oakland office.

Jeff Davis
Jeff wrote the Panama chapter. When not traveling and writing, he earns a living as an environmental engineer. He has traveled to Panama and Costa Rica several times to work on air pollution control projects at manufacturing plants. He was born in Alabama, raised in Georgia, with a stint in Puerto Rico, and schooled in Illinois, where he studied music, chemical engineering and writing. He now lives in Cincinnati, Ohio.

Conner Gorry
It all started in Vieques, Puerto Rico, more than 20 years ago. On that seminal trip, it dawned on Conner that there was a world outside of suburban strip malls and prepubescent pap. The Dominican Republic and Culebra followed (islands kick ass!), and it wasn't long before she was hooked. The habit took hold, and between adventures, she got a BA in Latin American Studies and an MA in International Policy. Conner currently lives among all those dot commies in San Francisco with her partner Koch (somebody save us!). Day by day the siren song of Manhattan and Havana grow mightier. She wrote Lonely Planet's *Read This First: Central & South America* and *Guatemala* and has contributed to *South America on a shoestring* and other fabulous LP titles.

Paul Hellander
Paul has never really stopped traveling since he first looked at a map in his native England. He graduated from Birmingham University with a degree in Greek before heading for Australia. He taught modern Greek and trained interpreters and translators for 13 years before throwing it all away for a life as a travel writer. Paul has contributed to over 20 Lonely Planet titles, including *Greece, Cyprus, France, Israel & the Palestinian Territories, Eastern Europe* and *Singapore*. Paul ate and drank his way around the beaches and back roads of Honduras for this edition of *Central America*. He can normally be found attached to his Macintosh. When not traveling with his Mac and Nikons, he lives in Adelaide, South Australia. He was last seen heading for Greece's Dodecanese Islands.

Carolyn Miller

California native Carolyn Miller has been lucky enough to both live and work for travel since graduating from the University of California at Berkeley. She now runs the US marketing department for Lonely Planet and has contributed to a number of the company's projects, including Lonely Planet's *San Francisco*. Happiest in the heat, she has traveled in some of the world's best tropical destinations in Central America, Southeast Asia and the South Pacific. She enjoys scuba diving, hiking and swimming almost as much as reading a good book in a shady hammock. She lives in Oakland with her husband.

Daniel Schechter

A native New Yorker and movie devotee, Daniel C Schechter graduated from NYU's film school, the training ground for such motion picture luminaries as Woody Allen, Martin Scorsese and Spike Lee. Daniel's movie career never got off the ground though, and by 1984, he found himself in front of a classroom of 30 Colombians expecting to learn English. Thus began a career in language teaching that took him from Bogotá to Lisbon to Barcelona to Washington, DC. In 1992, Daniel decided to get serious about his default profession, devoting the next two years to pursuing an MA in teaching English as a second language in a remote corner of Puerto Rico. After moving to Mexico, initially attracted by a position at the Monterrey Technological Institute, he promptly left the field for a minimum-wage job as copy editor at *The News,* Mexico City's English language daily. Daniel worked his way up to assistant managing editor in just a year and a half, but had to leave due to a run-in with a tyrannical editor-in-chief over anachronistic editorial policies. Next came a less chaotic stint at the magazine *Business Mexico,* published by the American Chamber of Commerce Mexico, where as executive editor he had the luxury of approving the publication of his own stories on travel, culture and food. After close to a decade in Latin America, Daniel and wife Myra have transplanted themselves to the moist earth of the Pacific Northwest.

FROM THE AUTHORS

David Zingarelli

Many thanks to my colleagues at Lonely Planet, in particular Laura Harger, for the opportunity to rekindle a dormant passion for a fascinating region of the world; Kate Hoffman, for her healthy doses of wisdom and encouragement; and Wade Fox, for his abundant patience and stalwart professionalism. Thanks also to the other editors, cartographers and designers who wrangled with text and maps and shaped the handsome final product. I'd like to dedicate my efforts on this book to the Familia Macabeo Pinzón, who took me in, treated me as one of their own and then flung the windows of the world wide open, and to my own family, for encouraging me to spread my wings.

Jeff Davis

Thanks to the many Panamanians and fellow travelers who helped me during my journey, especially Marco Gandásegui, Hernán Araúz, Richard Cahill and Jonathan Parish of Ancon Expeditions; Carlos Alfaro and

Wendy Thomas in Guadalupe; Frank Glavas in Boquete; Eric Jackson with *The Panama News*; and Abdiel O'Callaghan in Panama City. Most of all, thanks to my wonderful wife Rina, who provided insightful comments on the Panama chapter. Because of her, coming home is the best part of any journey.

Conner Gorry

I'm feeling pretty blessed right about now, in large part due to my partner/co-conspirator/travel king Koch, who makes life so damn fun and fulfilling I laugh at myself for refusing his first date requests. Thanks baby, for being you and always loving the sometimes intolerable me.

Scores of people work their asses off to make each LP title as hale as possible. Thanks to all of them. I am also indebted to Nancy Keller for her work on the third edition of GBY.

Many people in Guatemala made my work easier, groovier or healthier. In Antigua, great thanks go to Nancy Hoffman and Luis Ramirez of Vision Travel; Gunther Blauth of Germany supplied good info on the 'jungle route.' Tom Lingenfelter in Xela was a terrific help regarding that region. Dr. Bill in Todos Santos (and beyond) kept me healthy in body and spirit. Thanks doc! In Momos, I was graciously hosted by Kermit Frazier and Rigoberto Itzep Chanchavac. Rosie and Bill Fogerty rock on all fronts, and the time we spent at their place in Jaibalito was ethereal. Christine and Aimee (Denmark) saved my sanity in Fray, for which I am truly grateful. Words can barely capture the trial and triumph that was our hike to El Mirador. Gerd Unni Rougnø (Norway) was a paragon of courage, good humor and insight, and the other (better!) half of the first female expedition to ever make that trip. Unni, you're fantastic! Last, but not least, I would like to shout out to our guide Calistro from Carmelita, who taught me an important life lesson with three short words: *poco a poco*.

Paul Hellander

Updating a travel guide is always a collaborative effort and certain people and organizations who contributed to my work in one way or another deserve a mention. They are Alejandra Bravo (Tegucigalpa), Howard Rosenzweig (Copán Ruinas), Warren Post (Santa Rosa de Copán), Alessandro D'Agostino (Tela), Michael Wendling (Pico Bonito), Rick Reno (Utila) and Roland Gassmann (Omoa). Max Libits & Katerina Valtali (Miami) and Dan & Carmen Clay (San Francisco) are thanked for their homes away from home. Wife Stella gets a hats off for her unstinting support and ability to ferret out the oddest photo scenes. Sons Byron and Marcus, as ever, get Dad's blessing once more.

Carolyn Miller

In Belize, thanks for all the help, advice and company from the locals and travelers met along the way. Special thanks to Shakira Oxley and Rudy Borges for setting me off in the right directions, the Crooked Tree folks for showing me all those birds, Allan Forman for talking me into the Blue Hole and Tom Brosnahan for all of the work that went before.

In Oakland, thanks to Kate Hoffman, Mariah Bear and Eric Kettunen for encouraging me to jump the fence, Heather Harrison and the LP marketeers for graciously filling in while I was away, the Matter family for exceptional pet care and Paul Carlstroem for making it so nice to come home. Finally, thanks to Joan and Rich Miller for showing me early on the joys of an open book and an open road.

Daniel Schechter

Mil gracias to the tourism experts at ICT (Costa Rica), Corsatur (El Salvador) and Intur (Nicaragua) for providing resources and contacts. Thanks as well to the scores of Central Americans and resident friends who routinely extended their hospitality and shared their considerable knowledge. I am especially grateful to the following individuals for their support and interest in this project: in El Salvador, Juan Marco Álvarez of SalvaNatura, Roberto Gallardo at the Museo Nacional, Heidi Gómez at the US Embassy, Miguel Huezo at Casa de los Mestizos in Suchitoto, Leslie Schuld of CIS, Lena and Rene at Ximena's Guest House, Maryse Brouwer of CORDES, Sergio & Concha María Camilot at Quechelah in La Palma, and Catherine Berthillier for sharing her insights into the work of Pro-Busqueda; in Costa Rica, Leigh & John Fulbrook, Richard Stern at Casa Agua Buena, Jacques Bertrand at Pensión Santa Elena in Monteverde and Mel Baker at ATEC in Puerto Viejo de Talamanca; in Nicaragua, USDA officer Kelly Preston, Peace Corps volunteer 'Zik' T Chandler, Dr Jeffrey McCrary at Proyecto Ecológico Laguna de Apoyo and Paul Davidson of ONUDI for offering an insider's look at the complexities of the Nicaraguan political scene. Finally, thank you, Myra, as always, for your uncanny critical sense and matchless neck rubs.

This Book

This is the 4th edition of *Central America on a shoestring*. Past authors include Nancy Keller, Tom Brosnahan, Mark Honan, Carolyn Hubbard, Rob Rachowiecki, Barbara Reioux and Stephen Schwartz, and some of their comments and observations were used in this edition.

This book also benefited from the insights of other Lonely Planet authors, whose work on related titles provided a valuable resource for the update of this book. These authors include Scott Doggett, Conner Gorry, Ben Greensfelder, James Lyon, Carolyn Miller, Rob Rachowiecki and John Thompson.

David Zingarelli was the coordinating author of this edition, and he revised and updated the introductory regional chapters. Jeff Davis researched and updated the chapter on Panama; Conner Gorry did the same for Guatemala; Paul Hellander, for Honduras; Carolyn Miller, for Belize; and Daniel Schechter, for Costa Rica, El Salvador and Nicaragua.

FROM THE PUBLISHER

This 4th edition of *Central America on a shoestring* was produced in Lonely Planet's US office, in Oakland, California. Many people contributed their time, energy and talent to this book. Lead editor Wade Fox headed up a diligent team consisting of Rebecca Northen and Vivek Wagle. Senior editor David Zingarelli oversaw the project, and Kate Hoffman pitched in with her usual wisdom. Maps and text were tackled by a star-studded cast of proofers, including Rachel Bernstein, Erin Corrigan, Suki Gear, Gabi Knight, Christine Lee, Rebecca, Paul Sheridan, Jacqueline Volin and Vivek. Ken DellaPenta was the book's ingenious indexer.

Lead designer Margaret Livingston and designer Lora Santiago laid out the book, with guidance from design manager Susan Rimerman. Susan also designed the cover, and Lora created the interior illustrations.

Alex Guilbert and senior cartographer Monica Lepe supervised our crack team of cartographers. Colin Bishop briefly served time as lead cartographer before handing over the reins to Justin Colgan. John Culp, Matthew DeMartini, Molly Green and Tessa Rottiers helped draw the maps. Patrick Bock, Dion Good, Naoko Ogawa, Andrew Rebold, Kat Smith and Eric Thomsen helped with base map edits and edit corrections, among other things.

Foreword

ABOUT LONELY PLANET GUIDEBOOKS

The story begins with a classic travel adventure: Tony and Maureen Wheeler's 1972 journey across Europe and Asia to Australia. Useful information about the overland trail did not exist at that time, so Tony and Maureen published the first Lonely Planet guidebook to meet a growing need.

From a kitchen table, then from a tiny office in Melbourne (Australia), Lonely Planet has become the largest independent travel publisher in the world, an international company with offices in Melbourne, Oakland (USA), London (UK) and Paris (France).

Today Lonely Planet guidebooks cover the globe. There is an ever-growing list of books, and there's information in a variety of forms and media. Some things haven't changed. The main aim is still to help make it possible for adventurous travelers to get out there – to explore and better understand the world.

At Lonely Planet we believe travelers can make a positive contribution to the countries they visit – if they respect their host communities and spend their money wisely. Since 1986 a percentage of the income from each book has been donated to aid projects and human-rights campaigns.

Updates Lonely Planet thoroughly updates each guidebook as often as possible. This usually means there are around two years between editions, although for more unusual or more stable destinations the gap can be longer. Check the imprint page (following the color map at the beginning of the book) for publication dates.

Between editions, up-to-date information is available in two free newsletters – the paper *Planet Talk* and email *Comet* (to subscribe, contact any Lonely Planet office) – and on our website at www.lonelyplanet.com. The *Upgrades* section of the website covers a number of important and volatile destinations and is regularly updated by Lonely Planet authors. *Scoop* covers news and current affairs relevant to travelers. And, lastly, the *Thorn Tree* bulletin board and *Postcards* section of the site carry unverified, but fascinating, reports from travelers.

Correspondence The process of creating new editions begins with the letters, postcards and emails received from travelers. This correspondence often includes suggestions, criticisms and comments about the current editions. Interesting excerpts are immediately passed on via newsletters and the website, and everything goes to our authors to be verified when they're researching on the road. We're keen to get more feedback from organizations or individuals who represent communities visited by travelers.

Lonely Planet gathers information for everyone who's curious about the planet – and especially for those who explore it firsthand. Through guidebooks, phrasebooks, activity guides, maps, literature, newsletters, image library, TV series and website, we act as an information exchange for a worldwide community of travelers.

Research Authors aim to gather sufficient practical information to enable travelers to make informed choices and to make the mechanics of a journey run smoothly. They also research historical and cultural background to help enrich the travel experience and allow travelers to understand and respond appropriately to cultural and environmental issues.

Authors don't stay in every hotel because that would mean spending a couple of months in each medium-size city and, no, they don't eat at every restaurant because that would mean stretching belts beyond capacity. They do visit hotels and restaurants to check standards and prices, but feedback based on readers' direct experiences can be very helpful.

Many of our authors work undercover; others aren't so secretive. None of them accept freebies in exchange for positive write-ups. And none of our guidebooks contain any advertising.

Production Authors submit their raw manuscripts and maps to offices in Australia, the USA, the UK or France. Editors and cartographers – all experienced travelers themselves – then begin the process of assembling the pieces. When the book finally hits the shops, some things are already out of date, we start getting feedback from readers and the process begins again....

WARNING & REQUEST

Things change – prices go up, schedules change, good places go bad and bad places go bankrupt – nothing stays the same. So, if you find things better or worse, recently opened or long since closed, please tell us and help make the next edition even more accurate and useful. We genuinely value all the feedback we receive. Julie Young coordinates a well-traveled team that reads and acknowledges every letter, postcard and email and ensures that every morsel of information finds its way to the appropriate authors, editors and cartographers for verification.

Everyone who writes to us will find their name in the next edition of the appropriate guidebook. They will also receive the latest issue of *Planet Talk*, our quarterly printed newsletter, or *Comet*, our monthly email newsletter. Subscriptions to both newsletters are free. The very best contributions will be rewarded with a free guidebook.

Excerpts from your correspondence may appear in new editions of Lonely Planet guidebooks, the Lonely Planet website, *Planet Talk* or *Comet*, so please let us know if you *don't* want your letter published or your name acknowledged.

Send all correspondence to the Lonely Planet office closest to you:

Australia: Locked Bag 1, Footscray, Victoria 3011
USA: 150 Linden St, Oakland, CA 94607
UK: 10a Spring Place, London NW5 3BH
France: 1 rue du Dahomey, 75011 Paris

Or email us at: talk2us@lonelyplanet.com.au

For news, views and updates, see our website: www.lonelyplanet.com

HOW TO USE A LONELY PLANET GUIDEBOOK

The best way to use a Lonely Planet guidebook is any way you choose. At Lonely Planet, we believe the most memorable travel experiences are often those that are unexpected, and the finest discoveries are those you make yourself. Guidebooks are not intended to be used as if they provided a detailed set of infallible instructions!

Contents All Lonely Planet guidebooks follow the same format. The Facts about the Country chapters or sections give background information ranging from history to weather. Facts for the Visitor gives practical information on issues like visas and health. Getting There & Away gives a brief starting point for researching travel to and from the destination. Getting Around gives an overview of the transport options available when you arrive.

The peculiar demands of each destination determine how subsequent chapters are broken up, but some things remain constant. We always start with background, then proceed to sights, places to stay, places to eat, entertainment, getting there and away, and getting around information – in that order.

Heading Hierarchy Lonely Planet headings are used in a strict hierarchical structure that can be visualized as a set of Russian dolls. Each heading (and its following text) is encompassed by any preceding heading that is higher on the hierarchical ladder.

Entry Points We do not assume guidebooks will be read from beginning to end, but that people will dip into them. The traditional entry points are the list of contents and the index. In addition, however, some books have a complete list of maps and an index map illustrating map coverage.

There may also be a color map that shows highlights. These highlights are dealt with in greater detail later in the book, along with planning questions and suggested itineraries. Each chapter covering a geographical region usually begins with a locator map and another list of highlights. Once you find something of interest in a list of highlights, turn to the index.

Maps Maps play a crucial role in Lonely Planet guidebooks and include a huge amount of information. A legend is printed on the back page. We seek to have complete consistency between maps and text, and to have every important place in the text captured on a map. Map key numbers usually start in the top left corner.

Although inclusion in a guidebook usually implies a recommendation, we cannot list every good place. Exclusion does not necessarily imply criticism. In fact, there are a number of reasons why we might exclude a place – sometimes it is simply inappropriate to encourage an influx of travelers.

Introduction

The seven nations of Central America occupy a land area about a quarter the size of Mexico. Despite its diminutive size, this narrow isthmus is a remarkably varied part of the world, with an array of landscapes, diverse cultural influences and attractions ranging from the ruins of ancient Mayan cities to the Panama Canal, one of the engineering triumphs of the 20th century.

Travelers from all over head to Central America to enjoy its natural attractions, among the most fascinating in the world. Confined within this compact region is an incredible array of ecosystems and habitats, including tropical rain forests, jungle river systems, volcanic lakes and coastal wetlands. Central America's flora and fauna are exceptionally rich and diversified, with hundreds of plant and animal species from the North and South American continents spilling into the isthmus that bridges the gap between them. Many of these species and habitats are represented in the region's ever-expanding network of national parks and biosphere reserves. Ecotourism excursions, including jungle treks, bird watching and river rafting, offer a variety of ways to appreciate Central America's wildlife and

explore the region's landscapes. Hundreds of idyllic Caribbean islands, white-sand beaches and the world's second-largest barrier reef beckon the outdoor and water-sports enthusiast.

Central America's position at the intersection of divergent cultural influences has also provided it with attractions of a different kind. Many travelers visit this region to explore the spectacular Mayan ruins spread across hundreds of kilometers of virgin rain forest. Among the best-known are the archaeological wonders of Tikal, in Guatemala's northern Petén region, and Copán, in western Honduras. The dynamic culture of the indigenous Maya still thrives in the region and is evident in the rich hues of intricately woven tapestries and the lively markets of Guatemala's highlands. The region's Spanish colonial cities are the legacy of a different era; among the best-preserved of these is Antigua Guatemala, known worldwide as a center for language study. The region's urban and cultural centers are fascinating, but some of the most enjoyable and memorable travel experiences happen in small towns and out-of-the-way villages.

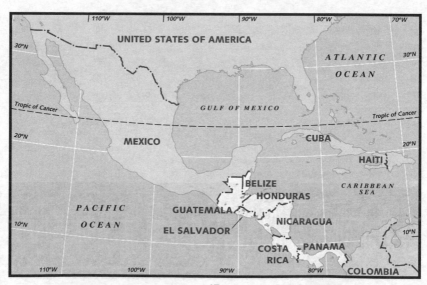

After more than two decades of volatile politics, civil war and guerilla conflict, Central America's nations have emerged into a period of relative peace. As apprehensions about traveling in the region have lessened, so have opportunities for exploration and adventure flourished. In recent years, travelers have gained better and safer access to rarely visited corners of Central America. Once overlooked, El Salvador and Nicaragua are becoming dynamic destinations in their own right, and visitors are more fully able to gain a personal understanding of the people who make this narrow isthmus their home and the conditions they face today.

With all it has to offer, Central America remains an accessible and affordable destination for independent and shoestring travelers. This corner of the world truly offers something for every interest, and opportunities for getting off the beaten track and discovering it for yourself are, now more than ever, virtually limitless.

Facts about Central America

HISTORY
Early Human Settlement

Archaeological evidence indicates that Central America has been heavily populated for many thousands of years. Tracing the origins of the first American peoples to Asia, archaeologists and anthropologists have determined that these peoples migrated across the Bering Strait from Siberia to Alaska during ice ages that caused an increase in glacial ice and a consequent fall in sea levels, leaving a land bridge between the two continents.

A major migration occurred between 20,000 and 25,000 years ago, with populations then fanning out over the North American continent, passing down through Central America and into South America all the way to Tierra del Fuego. The Bering Strait land bridge was inundated by rising sea levels for the last time around 7000 BC.

Some speculate that there could also have been migrations, or at least contact, between the Americas and parts of Africa, particularly Egypt. The pyramids, sculptures, and many other ancient artifacts found in the Western Hemisphere have been cited as evidence of such a contact.

Pre-Hispanic Civilizations

Central America is not only a geographic bridge between North and South America: Historically it has also been an intermediate region between North and South American cultures. The lowlands of Nicaragua and Costa Rica seem to have formed a very loose boundary between the overlapping cultures of indigenous Central and South American peoples.

South of this area were a number of tribes that had cultural contacts ranging into Colombia, Ecuador and down to the Inca Empire of Peru. The languages of these tribes are related to linguistic groups of South America. Tribes living to the north of this intermediate region were more influenced by Mexican cultures, particularly that of the Maya, whose empire stretched through parts of Guatemala, Belize, Chiapas, the Yucatán Peninsula and into the western areas of present-day Honduras and El Salvador.

The Maya are among the three great ancient civilizations of the Americas, along with the Inca of Peru and the Aztec of Mexico. They left behind stone pyramids, sculptures, ceramics and ceramic art and a complex, partly pictorial, partly phonetic writing system that has yet to be fully deciphered. The Maya had a well-established religious and social structure, and they traded throughout their large area of influence. Their architecture, agriculture, mathematics and astronomy were advanced, and they refined a calendar system used by other pre-Hispanic peoples into a tool for the exact recording of earthly and heavenly events.

Though the history of the Maya can be traced back more than 4000 years, the classical period of more advanced Mayan civilization actually began around the 3rd century AD and reached its pinnacle around the 6th to 8th centuries.

After this came a period of decline, but between the 10th and 11th centuries the Maya experienced a renaissance under the influence of the Toltec from Mexico. Some cultural blending also occurred between the Maya and the Aztec.

The Maya were once again in a period of decline by the 14th century, and at the time of the Spanish arrival many of the Mayan cities were deserted. (See the Guatemala chapter for more about the Maya.)

European Contact & Colonization

Christopher Columbus is recognized as the first European to 'discover' America, though his first landfall in 1492 was actually on one of the Caribbean islands, Guanahani in the Bahamas (which Columbus renamed San Salvador Island). It was not until his fourth and final voyage (1502–04) that he reached mainland Central America, exploring the Caribbean coast from present-day Honduras to Panama. Meanwhile, the north coast may have been visited by Alonso de Ojeda in 1499, and Rodrigo de Bastidas certainly sighted Central America when making exploratory trips out from the Gulf of Venezuela in 1501.

Cristóbal Colón, as Columbus is known in Spanish, was not Spanish but Italian. He had unsuccessfully sought Portuguese support for his explorations before Spain's Queen Isabella finally agreed, after six years, to sponsor his voyage. He left Europe looking for a sea route for the spice trade with Asia, and thought at first he had found it; when he landed in the Bahamas, he believed he had reached the Indies, that is, the East Indies. To this day, the Native American peoples are called 'Indians' due to his significant geographical miscalculation.

The first Spanish settlement on the American mainland was on the east side of the Golfo de Urabá, near the present-day border between Colombia and Panama. The settlement was founded in 1509 but was moved the following year to Santa María de la Antigua del Darién, which was an important base for Spanish exploration.

In 1513 Vasco Núñez de Balboa scaled the mountains of the Isthmus of Panama and became the first European to sight the Pacific Ocean. The region's indigenous inhabitants, of course, had known about it for a long time. Panama City was founded on the Pacific side in 1519 by Pedro Arias de Ávila (or Pedrarias, as his Spanish contemporaries called him). The port on the Caribbean side was first located at Nombre de Dios in the Darién but later was moved to Portobelo, which had been explored and named by Columbus. These cities and the isthmus between them became vitally important to the Spaniards.

In 1519, the same year that Panama City was founded, Hernán Cortés was beginning his invasion of Mexico. The Spanish conquest of Central America then radiated outward, from Panama in the south and Mexico in the north.

From the Panama City base, Spanish exploration branched out into the Pacific. The Central American Indians had traded with the Inca, and the Spanish were attracted to Peru by the gold they saw arriving from the south. After Pizarro's conquest of the Inca empire in 1532, gold, pearls and other wealth from Peru began to pass across the isthmus from Panama City to Portobelo, headed for the treasuries of Spain.

Spanish Expansion
From Panama, the Spaniards bypassed Costa Rica and pushed northward to the lowlands of Nicaragua. Two large Indian towns stood on the banks of Lago de Managua and Lago de Nicaragua, where Managua and Granada are today.

These cities had also attracted the Spanish forces that were sent down from Mexico by Cortés. The two Spanish forces, meeting on the plains of Nicaragua, battled against one another. Also in Nicaragua, the city of León was established in 1524 by Fernández de Córdoba. Costa Rica was settled later, in the latter half of the century, mostly by missionary and agricultural Spaniards.

Cortés had also sent his lieutenant, Pedro de Alvarado, out to conquer Guatemala. Alvarado's bloodthirstiness, as well as the bitter fighting between his forces and the Indians of Guatemala, matched the savagery of the Mexican conquest. Alvarado, accompanied by Aztec warriors, crossed the Isthmus of Tehuantepec in 1522, and the decisive battle occurred in the area around Quetzaltenango in 1524. From there, Alvarado went on to conquer all of present-day Guatemala and a good deal of El Salvador.

Honduras, which had been initially claimed for Spain by Columbus, was also conquered by one of Cortés' warriors. Cristóbal de Olid was sent from Mexico at around the same time as Alvarado. He arrived on the Honduran coast and established a base near present-day Trujillo. From there the Spanish invaded the area of present-day Honduras and established settlements at Gracias a Dios, Comayagua, Olancho and Naca.

Colonial Period
Under the Spaniards, the region called Guatemala, which included all of Central America except Panama, was designated a part of the viceroyalty of Mexico, then called Nueva España (New Spain).

Though under Mexico, Guatemala became a captaincy general, reporting directly to the Spanish crown. A capital was established very briefly at an initial location, but in 1527 it was moved to a site on the flanks of the large Volcán Agua. The city was destroyed in 1541, when the aptly named volcano loosed a flood of water pent up in its crater, burying the city under tons of rock and mud.

The capital was moved to the nearby Valle de Panchoy, where La Muy Noble y Muy Leal Ciudad de Santiago de los Caballeros de Guatemala (today called Antigua) was founded as capital on March 10, 1543. The capital flourished there for 233 years until it was destroyed by a great earthquake on July 29, 1773. The capital was moved again, this time to Valle de la Ermita, the present site of Guatemala City, in hopes of escaping further destruction. On September 27, 1775, King Carlos III of Spain signed a royal charter for the founding of La Nueva Guatemala de la Asunción, and Guatemala City was officially born. The former capital became known as La Antigua Guatemala ('the Old Guatemala').

Panama continued to be an important part of the Spanish empire throughout the colonial period. The rest of Central America was no great producer of wealth, so it was not of such vital interest to the Spaniards.

The colonial period lasted until 1821, by which time both Mexico and Guatemala had declared their independence from Spain. In the same year, Colombia, including Panama, also became independent. Panama was a region of Nueva Andalucía, Nueva Granada and finally Colombia until 1903.

Independence

In 1810, a rising tide of disaffection with Spanish rule first erupted into rebellion in Mexico, under the leadership of a parish priest, Miguel Hidalgo. The following year, another priest, José Matías Delgado, together with liberal leader Manuel José Arce, organized a revolt in San Salvador, but it was quickly suppressed by forces from Guatemala City.

The will for independence sprang almost entirely from the criollos – those of Spanish ancestry born in the Americas – and local businesspeople frustrated by Spain's trade restrictions on its overseas dependencies. Together they formed a homegrown middle class, united by their resentment at being excluded from the colony's positions of power, which were reserved for Spaniards (those born in Spain).

Napoleon's invasion of Spain in 1812 boosted the drive for reform in the colonies. In 1821, Mexico's viceroy, Agustín de Iturbide, defected to the rebels and shortly became the self-styled emperor of independent Mexico. In the same year, the last of Guatemala's conservative captains general, Brigadier Don Gabino Gainza, was obliged to sign the first of several acts of independence. The link with Spain was forever severed, but Central America's political tumult had only begun.

The moment Guatemala declared independence, Iturbide sent his troops from Mexico to annex the states of the fledgling republic. Conservatives in many of the smaller states supported union with Mexico. El Salvador, however, under the leadership of Arce and Delgado, held out for months before its defenses were finally broken down by the invaders.

In many respects the forces for change were fiercely divided. A political chasm yawned between the liberals, who sought a more egalitarian state, and the powerful conservatives, who wanted to retain essentially the same kind of authoritarian society but under their control. This made any smooth political change impossible.

The Central American Federation

Iturbide's empire was short-lived. The following year he was overthrown by Mexican republicans, and in 1823 the Central American states declared their independence again, this time from Mexico. They formed a loose federation, the Provincias Unidas del Centro de América, with five constituent states – Guatemala, Honduras, El Salvador, Nicaragua and Costa Rica – and a constitution modeled on that of the United States (unlike the US, however, the Central American federation abolished slavery).

General Arce became the first federation president in 1825, but he had difficulty asserting his authority and finding the right executives. In his home state, he was embroiled in conflict with fellow liberals. Ultimately, he set himself up as a dictator until he was overthrown by an alliance of liberals under Francisco Morazán, a Honduran general. Morazán became the new leader of the federation in 1830. Like Arce before him, his grip on power was tenuous.

In Guatemala, too, the liberal leader was under threat. A cholera epidemic raged and an unpopular new penal code was introduced. The underclass – a vast group of the dispossessed for whom middle-class freedoms meant little – grew increasingly restive.

Under the leadership of the young, charismatic Rafael Carrera, a largely Indian mob marched on Guatemala City in 1837. An unlikely alliance formed between Carrera, the Church and the conservatives, and Carrera was installed as dictator. His victory signaled the end of the liberal era and thus of the federation.

In 1838, the congress passed a resolution permitting states to leave the federation. By 1839 El Salvador was the only state left. Regional rivalries between the now separate countries persisted, but from this time the individual realms pursued their own courses.

The modern history of each of the Central American republics is covered in the corresponding country chapters of this guide.

GEOGRAPHY
Because of the region's political history, the term 'Central America' is sometimes used to mean only the five states of the former federation, which did not include Belize and Panama, but in recent years it has usually been used to refer to all the land between Mexico and Colombia. Central America covers only a small area – the seven countries together comprise around 544,700 sq km, about a quarter of the size of Mexico. Nevertheless, Central America is a strategically important part of the world, as it separates the Pacific Ocean from the Caribbean Sea and the Atlantic Ocean. It also forms a bridge, or a barrier, between North and South America.

The dominant geographical features of Central America are its mountains and volcanoes and its long coastlines. The region has 2379km of Caribbean coast and 3287km of Pacific coast, separated by a landmass that is 280km wide at its widest point (near the border of Honduras and Nicaragua) but only about 60km wide at its narrowest point (the isthmus of Panama).

The relatively narrow strip of land that forms Central America is primarily volcanic in origin, with over 100 major volcanoes and 150 minor ones. Several separate *cordilleras* (mountain chains) stretch for hundreds of

kilometers down through this strip of land. The result is a pattern of mountain ranges and volcanoes, broken by valleys and basins with large, fertile areas of rich volcanic soil.

In the past 300 years a number of major cities have been destroyed by volcanoes and earthquakes: Antigua Guatemala in 1773, Guatemala City in 1917–18 and 1976, Managua in 1931 and 1972, and San Salvador in 1854 and 1986. Another major quake, measuring 7.4 on the Richter scale, rocked Costa Rica and the northwestern corner of Panama in April 1991, and a magnitude 6.7 quake centered near the Costa Rican capital of San José shook the area again in 1999. It may seem strange to find cities at the bases of giant volcanoes, where they are repeatedly threatened by eruptions and earthquakes, but despite these perils there is a compelling motive behind this pattern of settlement – the volcanic soil is excellent for all types of agriculture and can support the greatest concentrations of agricultural people.

A narrow plain runs along both coasts. In most places it's no more than a 15km- to 40km-wide strip between the sea and the mountains. The coastal plain is also fertile, and in some areas there are large, flat plantations of export crops (bananas and pineapples, for example) close to the ports from which the produce is shipped to overseas markets, principally the USA.

GEOLOGY
Geologists believe that the surface of the earth consists of a number of huge tectonic plates that slowly move over millions of years, changing the character of the earth's surface slowly but constantly. With Central America's volcanoes and earthquakes, it's no surprise that it is a geologically volatile area.

There are four tectonic plates in the Central America region. The two most significant are the Cocos and Caribbean Plates. The Cocos Plate, the northeastern edge of which parallels the Pacific coast about 60 to 120 miles offshore, borders the southwestern edge of the Caribbean Plate. The Cocos Plate is moving northeast and crashing into the Caribbean Plate at a rate of around 10cm per year – a thundering speed, geologically speaking. The point of impact between plates is called a subduction zone; in the case of Central America, this zone is where the Cocos Plate is sliding underneath and forcing the edge of the Caribbean Plate to break up and become uplifted, causing earthquakes and volcanic activity.

This process began underwater and has been going on for about five million years. Long ago, North and South America were separated by 3000km of open sea. Consequently, animals and plants developed on the two continents quite independently of one another. Around three million years ago at the end of the Pliocene age, the volcanic activity and uplifting of land caused by the collision of the tectonic plates raised the land bridge that united North and South America, and plants and animals began to spread across.

Central America is the most active volcanic zone in the Americas. Although half of the volcanoes are dormant and a quarter are extinct, the rest are still active. Guatemala's Pacaya and Santiaguito Volcanoes, and Costa Rica's Arenal, Poás, Irazú and Rincón de la Vieja Volcanoes are all glowing and smoking away. Occasionally some flare up, sometimes necessitating evacuation of nearby villages. Other volcanoes classified as still active include Fuego and Santa María in Guatemala, Izalco in El Salvador, and Concepción and Las Pilas-Cerro Negro in Nicaragua. Panama's sole volcano, Volcán Barú, is classified as inactive.

CLIMATE

All of Central America is within the tropics, but there's a lot of variation in climate within this small region. The land rises from sea level to over 4000m, dividing the region into three primary temperature zones according to altitude, but there is little variation in temperature throughout the year.

The lowlands (from sea level to about 1000m) represent the hottest zone; daytime temperatures range from 29°C to 32°C (84°F to 90°F), nighttime temperatures from 21°C to 23°C (70°F to 74°F). Visitors accustomed to a more temperate climate may find the high heat and humidity of these areas oppressive, but most adjust to the conditions after a few days.

The temperate zone (from around 1000m to 2000m) has a pleasant, springlike climate, with daytime temperatures ranging from 23°C to 26°C (74°F to 79°F) and nighttime temperatures from around 15°C to 21°C (59°F to 70°F).

The cold zone (above 2000m) has similar daytime temperatures to the temperate zone but is colder at night, around 10°C to 12°C (50°F to 54°F). The very few areas over 4000m are characterized by an alpine climate.

The main seasons are characterized not by temperature but by amount of rainfall. The rainy season, which runs from around April to mid-December in most of Central America, is called *invierno* (winter). The rest of the year constitutes the dry season and is called *verano* (summer). Thus the seasons are, in name at least, the opposite of their designations in North America. There are some regional variations to the general rule; see the Climate sections of the individual country chapters for details.

The Caribbean side of Central America gets much more rainfall than the Pacific side – often more than twice as much. In Panama, for example, the Caribbean side receives up to 3500mm of rainfall annually, whereas the Pacific side, less than 100km away, averages only about 1800mm. The Caribbean coast receives a lot of rainfall year-round and is always green. On the Pacific side, the landscape dries out and browns in the dry season, and the air can be dusty and smoky with burning vegetation.

Even during the rainy season, it's a rare day when the sun doesn't shine; a typical pattern is sun during the morning, clouding over later in the day and a downpour that might last for an hour or so in the late afternoon or evening. But don't bank on it: It can rain any time of day, and if a tropical storm hits (most likely in September and October on the Caribbean coast), it can rain heavily for days at a time. In most places the rainy season doesn't interfere much with travel, but there are a few notable exceptions. It is too hazardous to go overland through the Darién Gap during the rainy season, and occasional flooding can impede travel on the Caribbean coast of Honduras from December to February. Traveling anywhere on dirt roads can be a thrill in the rainy season, but most of the main routes in Central America are paved.

Hurricane Season

The official hurricane season for the Atlantic Basin (which consists of the Atlantic Ocean, the Caribbean Sea, and the Gulf of Mexico) is from June 1 to November 30. The peak of the season is from mid-August to late October. However, deadly hurricanes can occur anytime during the season and patterns can vary considerably from year to year. The zones in which hurricanes form and the tracks they travel on are generally related to the time of year and the corresponding weather conditions. Consequently, different areas of the Central American region are at greater risk during different months. Belize, for example, has been known to suffer from frequent, devastating hurricanes from September to as late as December.

The 1998 hurricane season proved to be a very deadly and costly one for Central America and the Caribbean. Focusing its fury on Honduras and Nicaragua, Hurricane Mitch caused human loss and property damage on a scale unprecedented in the recorded history of the Western Hemisphere. A month earlier, Hurricane Georges hit the island of Hispaniola, causing severe damage to the Dominican Republic and Haiti.

Hurricanes are generally identified in their formative stages, and researchers have been working on longer-range predictions of hurricane activity. Efforts to predict annual tropical storm and hurricane activity a year or more in the future have showed promise, but the ability to make long-range predictions about the specific locations

High-Velocity Winds

Hurricanes that strike Central America originate off the coast of Africa, forming as winds rush toward a low-pressure area and swirl around it due to the rotational forces of Earth's spin. The storms move counterclockwise across the Atlantic, fed by warm winds and moisture, building up force in their 3000km run toward Central and North America.

A hurricane builds in stages, the first of which is called a 'tropical disturbance.' The next stage is a tropical depression, at which point the storm begins to take on the familiar spiral appearance due to the flow of the winds and Earth's rotation. When winds exceed 64km per hour, the weather system is upgraded to a tropical storm and is usually accompanied by heavy rains. The system is called a hurricane if wind speed exceeds 120km per hour and intensifies around a low-pressure center, the so-called eye of the storm.

Hurricane systems can range from 80km in diameter to devastating giants more than 1600km across. Their energy is prodigious – far more than the mightiest thermonuclear explosions ever unleashed on Earth. The area affected by winds of great destructive force may exceed 240km in diameter. Gale-force winds can prevail over an area twice as great.

The strength of a hurricane is rated from one to five. The mildest, a Category 1 hurricane, has wind speeds of at least 120km per hour. The strongest and rarest hurricane, the Category 5 monster, packs winds that exceed 250km per hour; Hurricane Mitch, which killed more than 10,000 people in Central America and southeastern Mexico in late 1998, was a rare Category 5 hurricane. The category of the storm does not necessarily relate directly to the damage it will inflict, however. Lower category storms (and even tropical storms) can cause substantial damage depending on what other weather patterns they interact with, where they strike and the speed at which they move. Hurricanes travel at varying speeds, from as slowly as 10km per hour to more than 50km per hour. During their life spans, hurricanes can last for more than two weeks over the ocean.

There are two distinct stages of alert: a hurricane watch, issued when a hurricane may strike the area within the next 36 to 48 hours, and a hurricane warning, issued when a hurricane is likely to strike the area. For current tropical storm coverage and tracking, go to the *Miami Herald* Web site (www.herald.com) and scan the menu for hurricane information. Another excellent source is the Web site maintained by the US National Oceanic and Atmospheric Administration (www.noaa.gov/wx.html).

where hurricanes will strike is still well out of reach.

ECOLOGY & ENVIRONMENT
Deforestation

This is happening at such a rate that most of the world's tropical forests will have disappeared by early in the 21st century; loss of other habitats is a less publicized but equally pressing concern. Deforestation is taking place in every Central American country. In some places, the forests have been stripped for export timber. Elsewhere, the native forest has been cleared for subsistence slash-and-burn agriculture, for grazing land or for the planting of crops for export. The UN Food and Agriculture Organization estimates that, between 1990 and 1995, the region lost around 2,284,000 hectares of forest.

In 1950, about 60% of Central America was covered by some form of tropical forest. Today, less than half of that percentage of the region is forested. (Guatemala, Honduras, Nicaragua and Panama all have forest cover figures more than double those for Belize, Costa Rica, or densely populated El Salvador.)

Almost a million known species live in tropical rain forests, and scientists predict that millions of additional plant and animal species remain to be discovered in the world's remaining rain forests. This incredible array of plants and animals cannot exist unless the forest that they inhabit is protected – thus, deforestation is resulting not only in the loss of the rain forest but in the extinction of countless species as well.

Tropical forests, and their variety, are vitally important for pharmaceutical purposes and as a source of genetic diversity in our increasingly monocultural agriculture. In the event of a crop epidemic, scientists look in the forests for disease-resistant wild strains to breed into the commercially raised crops. Deforestation leads not only to species extinction but also to loss of the genetic diversity that may help species adapt to a changing world.

Rain forests are important on a global scale because they moderate climatic patterns worldwide. Destruction of the rain forests is a major contributing factor to global warming. Gases exuded by the great masses of plants in the rain forest are also important in maintaining the delicate balance of gases in Earth's atmosphere.

While conserving rain forests for aesthetic, medicinal, and genetic reasons may be important to travelers, it is even more important to the local indigenous peoples who still survive in tropical rain forests. Miskito in Honduras and Nicaragua, Bribri in Costa Rica and the Choco of Panama are some of the indigenous groups that still live in the rain forest in a more or less traditional manner. Many of these Indian groups still practice shifting agriculture, hunting and gathering as methods of subsistence.

However, any discussion of the rain forests must take into consideration the point of view of the developing nations within whose borders they lie. Clearing of rain forests provides lumber, pastureland, and possible mineral wealth in the short term. Efforts are now under way to show that the long-term economic value of the standing rain forest as a resource of biodiversity, genetic variation and pharmaceutical wealth is greater than the quick profits realized by deforestation.

One proposal for making the tropical forest an economically productive resource is protecting it in national parks and reserves that make it accessible to the public. During the last decade, ecotourism has proven to be an increasingly important element of the economies of all Central American nations. More people are likely to visit a tropical country to see monkeys in the forest than to see cows in the pasture. All the Central American countries have national parks and reserves, and both government and nongovernment organizations are devoted to conserving and protecting the natural environment. Costa Rica, for example, in an attempt to control rapid deforestation and protect its wildlife, has instituted the most progressive national park system in Latin America. An increasing number of tour companies are offering ecotourism excursions, including jungle treks, bird watching, river rafting and other adventures.

In spite of the deforestation, Central America still has some wilderness areas where the forests are largely unexplored. These include parts of Belize, the Mosquitia region of Honduras and Nicaragua, and the Darién region of Panama.

Other Environmental Concerns

Apart from the direct loss of tropical forests and the plants and animals that depend on them, deforestation has led directly or indirectly to other severe environmental problems in the region. The first and greatest issue is that of soil erosion. Forests protect the soil beneath them from the ravages of tropical rainstorms, and after deforestation much of the topsoil is washed away, lowering the productivity of the land and silting up watersheds. Scientists claim that drenched, barren soil exacerbated the massive devastation of Hurricane Mitch in 1998, causing catastrophic flooding and landslides. Some scientists believe that restoring trees and watersheds is the region's only hope for adequate protection against future storm devastation and that expanding the forests of the Central American isthmus, a biological corridor that runs through the region, would create the best defense.

Smog is a problem in most Central American cities, particularly Guatemala City, Tegucigalpa, San Salvador and Managua. Without controls on emissions from vehicles, it's very common to be engulfed in a cloud of oily black exhaust when a bus passes or, when driving on a highway, to be stuck for miles behind a vehicle billowing smoke, a choking and unnecessary experience in an otherwise beautiful countryside.

Trash is another problem. It's common practice for people to throw trash out the windows of vehicles, and often the land along roadsides is turned into impromptu trash dumps. People traveling in boats often toss trash over the side into lakes, rivers and the sea.

FLORA & FAUNA

Central America's flora and fauna are exceptionally rich and diversified, with tens of thousands of species represented. Much of the diversity arises from the region's location bridging the North and South American continents. Hundreds of plant and animal species from both continents spill into Central America, and there are also endemic species in specific areas. Costa Rica has probably the greatest range of accessible flora and fauna in Central America (see that chapter for more details).

Flora

Central America's geographical position, its varying altitudes, wet and dry climates and differing soil types all contribute to the wide variety of plant species found in the region.

There are five major types of vegetation. On the Caribbean coastal plain, up to about 850m, there is tropical rain forest with a canopy of tall trees, a layer of medium-size trees and a lush ground cover of smaller plants.

The Pacific coastal strip and the northern lowlands of Belize are covered with tropical dry forest and savanna. Deciduous trees and shrubs are parched and brown during the dry season but turn green during the rainy season. (Tropical dry forest is characterized by its pronounced dry season, during which trees lose their leaves, as opposed to tropical rain forest, where there is no seasonal leaf loss.)

Higher up, at around 850 to 1650m, there's a cooler climate with a mixed upland forest of evergreen trees and pines, deciduous oaks and broadleaf trees, and a ground cover of shrubs, herbs, grasses and flowering plants.

At around 1650m and above is one of Central America's loveliest terrains, the cloud forest. With close to 100% humidity and a cool climate year-round, the cloud forests are bathed in either clouds or rain, so they never dry out. The canopy of high trees means that direct sunlight rarely reaches the forest floor, which is covered by herbs, ferns and mosses.

Only very small areas of Central America, at elevations over 3000m, have alpine vegetation, with short, coarse grasses, ferns, mosses and flowering herbs. But even at such high elevations there is regional variety. For example, the Andean *páramo* is found in Costa Rica, but the North American bunchgrass landscape occurs in the Guatemalan highlands above the tree line.

A walk through a tropical forest is very different from a stroll through the temperate forests familiar to many readers. Temperate forests tend to have little variety. Tropical forests, on the other hand, have great variety. If you stand in one spot and look around, you'll see scores of different species of trees, and you often have to walk several hundred meters to find another example of any particular species.

This biodiversity is one of the reasons that biologists and conservationists are calling for a halt to the destruction of tropical forests.

Fauna

Central America has thousands of species of mammals, birds, insects, reptiles, amphibians and fishes. Costa Rica and Belize are particularly known for abundant wildlife.

Mammals include jaguars, pumas, ocelots and other cats; spider monkeys, howler monkeys, white-faced capuchin monkeys and squirrel *(tití)* monkeys; agoutis, coatis, kinkajous, and tapirs; two species each of deer, peccary, armadillo and sloth; several species of anteater and squirrel; and scores of bat species. Manatees live in some coastal waters, and dolphins and whales in the sea.

Fish are also abundant in rivers and lakes, and along the Pacific and Caribbean coasts. Reptiles and amphibians include sea, river and land turtles (Costa Rica has some famous nesting sites); crocodiles; frogs (such as tree frogs and the colorful poison-arrow frog); iguanas; and many others. There are many species of snake, including the boa constrictor, but only a few are poisonous, notably the tiny coral snake and the large *barba amarilla* or fer-de-lance.

Central America is a bird-watcher's dream – around 900 species of bird have been recorded in Panama alone. A number of factors combine to account for the incredible diversity of birds. Part of it is due to Central America's geographical position – North American, South American and Caribbean birds are all found here. Migrating birds tend to funnel and concentrate in Central America. Another factor behind the diversity of species is the region's geographical variation – everything from coastal wetland birds to mountain forest birds are represented.

The famous resplendent quetzal (ket-**sal**) is the national bird of Guatemala and an often-used symbol of Central America. Quetzals are about 35cm long – though the male has a very long tail that may add another 60cm – and brilliantly plumed with bright green, red and white feathers. Quetzals live in high-altitude forests all the way from southern Mexico to Panama, but unfortunately, as the forests become threatened, the birds are also endangered.

Quetzals can survive only in the wild – they die in captivity. Locals may know where to spot one; good places to look are Monteverde, in northwestern Costa Rica, and various areas in southern Costa Rica. The March to June breeding season is the easiest time to see them. At other times, they are less active and quite wary.

Other beautiful birds of the region include toucans, macaws, many species of parrot, hummingbirds, hawks, harpy eagles and doves. Striking but common birds are motmots, jacamars, trogons, chacalacas, woodcreepers, puffbirds, manakins, oropendolas and tanagers. It's a rich field for bird watchers.

Not only the quetzal but also many other species are endangered and may be facing extinction. Hunting takes a large toll, but even more critical is the destruction of the forest environments on which so many creatures depend.

Parks & Protected Areas

Central America's ecosystems and habitats include tropical rain forests, cloud forests, jungle river systems, lagoons and coastal wildlife reserves, to name just a few. Many of these are represented in the region's national parks, where visitors find thousands of tropical plant and wildlife species.

Like the national parks, other protected areas in the region – among them wildlife refuges, biological reserves, biosphere reserves and a number of private nature preserves – further the objective of conserving the region's diverse habitats and wildlife, in addition to preserving other valued areas including sites of archaeological or other cultural significance. A few of the best-known national parks and nature reserves are listed below, but there are a great many others that are also worth visiting. Details on these and other parks are contained in the individual country chapters.

Guatemala

One of the most spectacular of the Mayan archaeological sites, Tikal is surrounded by a national park that preserves a lush, tropical jungle full of wildlife. In eastern Guatemala, Parque Nacional Río Dulce protects the canyon of one of the country's most beautiful rivers.

Belize

Mountain Pine Ridge, in the Maya Mountains, is dotted with waterfalls and teems with exotic flora and fauna. Shipstern Nature Reserve protects forest, wetlands and mangrove habitats and is home to a butterfly breeding farm.

Honduras

La Tigra, just a few kilometers from the capital, preserves a lush high-altitude cloud forest. Punta Sal, a coastal national park near Tela, is also popular and accessible and is a sanctuary for migratory and coastal birds. In the remote Mosquitia region, the Río Plátano Biosphere Reserve was the first of such protected areas in Central America; today it's also a Unesco world heritage site.

El Salvador

The remote cloud forest reserve of Parque Nacional Montecristo – El Triunfo is shared by Guatemala, Honduras and El Salvador. Parque Nacional Cerro Verde harbors a forest within the crater of an extinct volcano and is also an important bird sanctuary.

Nicaragua

Visitors to Parque Nacional Volcán Masaya can walk to the summit of this active volcano and peer into its smoldering crater. Reserva Natural Miraflor, named after the serene lake within its expanses, covers a range of habitats, from tropical savanna to dry forest to cloud forest where orchids and begonias bloom amid mossy oaks and tall pines.

Costa Rica

At Parque Nacional Volcán Arenal, visitors can view periodic lava flows and eruptions from the most active volcano in Central America. The national park at Tortuguero is the western Caribbean's most important nesting area for the endangered green sea turtle; it's also a great place for river trips to see exotic birds, crocodiles, lizards and monkeys. Parque Nacional Corcovado offers opportunities for backpacking in pristine rain forest that contains Costa Rica's largest colonies of scarlet macaws.

Panama

In western Panama, Parque Internacional La Amistad is a world heritage site shared by Panama and Costa Rica; it protects a great variety of tropical habitats and is home to a number of indigenous tribes. Parque Nacional Marino Isla Bastimentos, on the Caribbean coast of western Panama in the Bocas del Toro Province, conserves marine and coastal ecosystems as well as more than 200 species of tropical fish. In eastern Panama, Parque Nacional Darién is another world heritage site and contains the largest tropical rain forest wilderness area in Central America.

GOVERNMENT & POLITICS

All seven Central American countries are members of the United Nations (UN) and the Organization of American States (OAS), which was formed in 1948 to link North, Central and South America in a common defense agreement.

Guatemala, Honduras, El Salvador, Nicaragua and Costa Rica are members of the Organization of Central American States (in Spanish, Organización de Estados Centroamericanos, or ODECA), established in 1951 in an effort to bring unity to the region. The organization includes the Central American Court of Justice and executive, legislative and economic councils.

Central American politics are notoriously volatile, not only within the various countries but also occasionally among them. Tensions have eased in recent years, though. Conflict between Honduras and El Salvador, which erupted into the 'Football War' in 1969, festered for more than two decades until a continuing land dispute between the two countries was finally settled by the International Court of Justice in 1992. In the 1980s, the Contra war in Nicaragua and the civil wars in El Salvador and Guatemala affected neighboring countries, as soldiers, rebels and refugees crossed borders. The USA used Honduras and (to a more limited extent) Costa Rica as bases of military operations in the region, increasing tensions with neighboring countries. The US military presence decreased with the end of various civil wars, and tensions arising from US involvement eased.

When Panama's General Manuel Noriega declared war on the US in 1989, US troops once again stepped into the arena and invaded Panama City in a mission called 'Operation Just Cause.' The attack crippled the nation's economy for years and the Panamanian death toll resulting from the invasion was a subject of great controversy. More than a decade later, Panamanian opinion of the US invasion remains divided. (See the Panama chapter for details.)

ECONOMY

Each Central American country has its particular economic structure. By and large this is still considered a 'developing' part of the world, but some countries are doing much better than others. The gross domestic product (GDP; the US dollar value of all final goods and services produced within a nation in a given year) figures for 1999 were as follows:

country	GDP totals	per capita
Guatemala	US$47.9 billion	US$3900
Belize	US$740 million	US$3100
Honduras	US$14.1 billion	US$2050
El Salvador	US$18.1 billion	US$3100
Nicaragua	US$12.5 billion	US$2650
Costa Rica	US$26 billion	US$7100
Panama	US$21 billion	US$7600

Although GDP figures (total and per capita) aid in measuring the material output of a country and the average income of a country's citizens, they do not reveal how equitably income is distributed among all the people. In fact, the great disparity of the distribution of wealth is a problem in all of the Central American republics, some more than others. It's not uncommon for the top 5% to 10% of the population to possess more than half the country's wealth, while the greatest part of the population lives in dire poverty. This substantial gap between the very rich and the very poor is the source of much of the strife and civil conflict that has beset some of these countries for many years, especially Guatemala, El Salvador and Nicaragua.

In 1960, all five member countries of ODECA (Panama and Belize were never members) established the Central American Common Market (CACM; in Spanish, Mercado Común Centroamericano, or MCCA). The purpose of CACM was to promote regional economic development, free trade and economic integration. Despite substantial increases in internal regional trade between 1961 and 1968, the overall benefits fostered by CACM proved to be rather limited. In the mid-1980s, trade among member nations was disrupted owing to internal strife, political instability and mounting debt, and some countries reinstated tariffs and other restrictions on incoming goods from other member nations. The effective demise of CACM reversed the limited progress made toward regional economic cooperation.

In 1993, all of CACM's members except Costa Rica signed agreements creating a new Central American Free Trade Zone, which essentially provided that member nations would gradually reduce their tariffs on interregional trade over a period of several years.

Implemented in 1994, the single-market trade laws of the North American Free Trade Agreement (NAFTA) have had a negative impact on the economies of the Central American nations. Essentially, the failure of the US Congress to approve NAFTA parity for the Caribbean and Central American countries belonging to the Caribbean Basin Initiative has caused a diversion of US trade and investment from this region to Mexico. As a result, the US's smaller neighbors are finding it increasingly difficult to compete with Mexico, which enjoys the privilege of duty-free exports to the US.

Most of Central America experienced several years of economic growth and stability in the late 1990s. In 1998, however, Hurricane Mitch struck a devastating blow to the region's economy. In addition to killing an estimated 10,000 people and leaving millions homeless, Mitch also caused more than US$3 billion in damages in Honduras alone. What compounded this natural disaster was that it came at a time when the nations of Central America were making collective political and economic progress. Despite massive relief and rehabilitation efforts, the economic consequences of the hurricane have been staggering and recovery slow. Hardest hit was the all-important agriculture sector, which is responsible for the majority of exports in countries such as Honduras, Nicaragua and El Salvador. Consequently, trade deficits and inflation rates were adversely affected in spite of the progress made prior to the storm.

Economists speculate that the rate of recovery and reconstruction in the areas of Central America that sustained the most damage – specifically Honduras and Nicaragua – is largely dependent on continuing international aid, and that alleviating these nations' staggering burden of international debt is particularly important. In 2000, Honduras qualified for debt relief totaling more than US$556 million through the Heavily Indebted Poor Countries program administered by the World Bank and the International Monetary Fund. (At the end of 1999, Honduras' total debt was US$3.1 billion.)

Despite the setbacks suffered by Honduras and Nicaragua, most of the Central American nations (particularly Belize,

Costa Rica and Panama) continue to experience steady financial growth and improvements to their economic forecasts at the outset of the 21st century.

Economic Sectors

Agricultural production (including farming, livestock, fisheries and forestry) is the primary economic sector of every Central American country except Panama, where it's surpassed by the services industry (mostly banking, commerce and tourism). In addition to basic subsistence crops, such as maize, beans, vegetables and fruits, several countries also produce export crops including coffee, sugarcane, cotton, tobacco, bananas, citrus fruits, pineapples and coconuts. Forestry and timber industries are important in some countries.

Fishing, including catches of shrimp and lobster, is important on both coasts, especially on the Caribbean, and in the region's lakes and rivers.

The manufacturing industry is developing in some places more than others. San Pedro Sula in Honduras, for example, has experienced rapid growth as a manufacturing center for clothing, shoes and other goods produced in hundreds of local factories. Thanks to its location at an international crossroads, Panama has additional sources of income from the Panama Canal and from duty-free trade and offshore banking.

Tourism, especially ecotourism, is increasingly important to the economies of many Central American nations. Because the tourist and governmental infrastructure for ecotourism is fairly new in some countries, however, the rapid growth in this industry has taken some nations by surprise. The financial opportunities generated by the tourism boom have been promising, but the lack of a comprehensive development plan has meant that growth has often been poorly controlled, and, in some cases, that the very natural resources that attract hoards of international visitors have themselves become threatened. See the Ecology & Environment section, earlier in this chapter, for more on this and other issues concerning the region's environment.

POPULATION & PEOPLE

The majority of the population of Central America is mestizo, that is, of mixed Indian and Spanish descent. Mestizos who speak Spanish are often called 'ladinos.' Each country has its own particular mixture of peoples and cultures.

The Spanish-Indian mixture ranges from almost pure Indian to almost pure European. In Guatemala well over half of the population is Maya Indian, and many mestizos are of predominantly Indian descent. On the other hand, over 95% of Costa Ricans are of wholly or predominantly European descent. Fewer than 1% of the population is Indian; the native populations were almost completely wiped out by European diseases. (Note that the literal translation of Indian is *indio*, which is an insulting term to Costa Rica's indigenous inhabitants. They prefer the term *indígena*, which means 'native inhabitant.') In El Salvador there are very few Indians – around 1% of the nation's inhabitants – but Honduras, Nicaragua and Panama all have significant Indian populations. Coastal Belize is home to a predominantly Creole population, descended from African slaves and the area's early British settlers. Most of the people in the country's interior are either Maya or mestizo.

Native Peoples

Prior to the Spanish conquest, Central America had many different groups of native peoples, and all the Central American countries still have groups, larger or smaller, of indigenous people. The largest surviving groups are the Mayan communities in Chiapas, the Yucatán Peninsula (both of Mexico), Belize and Guatemala. The Guatemalan areas around Chichicastenango, Lago de Atitlán and Todos Santos Cuchamatán are particularly known for the colorfully dressed, traditional Maya Indians who live there.

In Honduras, and spilling over into Nicaragua, are the Tolupanes (Jicaque), Pech (Paya), Tawahka (Sumo), Lenca, Chorti and Miskito peoples. Nicaragua is also home to the Rama Indians. El Salvador has small numbers of Izalco and Pancho Indians, descended from the Pipil. Costa Rica has very few native inhabitants, but they include Bribri, Boruca, Cabecar, Terraba and Guatuso. In Panama there are significant groups of Guaymí, Chocó and Kuna Indians.

After five centuries of contact with the Spaniards, the Indian groups vary in the extent of their assimilation into ladino society. On one end of the spectrum are Indians who wear traditional dress, maintain traditional social and economic systems and speak only their native language. Even some of these groups have been influenced by the Spanish presence in the region. For example, some groups have integrated the beliefs and practices of Catholicism, the state-sponsored religion of the conquering Spaniards, with their own centuries-old religious traditions. At the other extreme, many of the region's Indians are assimilated into modern Central American society, speak only Spanish and are indistinguishable from the mestizo populations around them.

In between are groups of varying degrees of assimilation. In some of these, the men don Western attire and speak Spanish in addition to their Indian language, and the women, more sheltered, still wear traditional dress and speak only their indigenous language. In some groups the older members are more likely to maintain traditional ways, but the young people are becoming more modernized, attending school and learning Spanish.

Social distinctions are often more connected to these visible social factors than to actual bloodlines. People who observe the traditional Indian ways are called Indians, but those of Indian ancestry who speak Spanish and live and work in the towns are often called ladinos. Thus, in some places, the percentage of Indians in census figures appears to be declining, but in reality this may only reflect the fact that fewer people are identifying themselves as Indian.

People of African Descent

Black people inhabit much of the Caribbean coast of Central America; most of them are descended from Africans brought to the West Indies (primarily Jamaica) as slaves. Some slaves were brought to the region by the Spaniards, especially to Panama, but most black people came to Central America from the islands of the Caribbean during the 19th century, not as slaves but as laborers, largely to work on agricultural (especially banana) plantations. Another large group of West Indian blacks came to Panama to work on the canal early in the 20th century.

In many parts of the region, black people speak a Caribbean-accented English. In the Central American countries bordering the Caribbean, blacks constitute a majority in some coastal areas though only a small proportion of the total population. In Belize, however, the country's largest ethnic group is made up of black Creoles, descendants of African slaves and early European (mostly British) settlers. (Note that in most of Latin America, 'Creole,' from the Spanish *criollo,* is used to denote someone of European parentage born in the Americas.)

Garífuna The region's northern Caribbean coast is home to another group of blacks, the Garífuna, who are descended from West African slaves and Carib Indians. They were transplanted from the Caribbean island of St Vincent to the island of Roatán, off the coast of Honduras, by the British in 1797. From there they spread out and established communities that still thrive on the coasts of Guatemala, Belize, Honduras and Nicaragua. (For more about the Garífuna, see the Honduras and Belize chapters.)

ARTS

Latin America's artistic tradition is a centuries-old weave that draws upon the belief systems and musical and visual-arts traditions of Europe, Africa and indigenous America. Although it is common to refer to Latin America as a single cultural entity, most of the artistic traditions have a distinctly national or even regional character. Central America is perhaps best known for its vibrant and ubiquitous folk art. *Artesanías* (handicrafts) are produced in every country and some are world famous, particularly the weaving, embroidery and other textile arts of the highland Maya of Guatemala.

Other enduring artistic traditions in Central America include leatherwork, wood carving, ceramics, basketry and jewelry, hammock and musical instrument making. (See the Arts and Shopping sections in the individual country chapters for more on these art forms.)

Literature

The literary tradition is well established in Central America. In the modern era, the region's most famous artist is probably the innovative Nicaraguan poet Rubén Darío (1867–1916), whose work was a prime influence in the development of modernism in Spanish literature (see the Nicaragua chapter for more on the artist). More recently, Guatemalan writer Miguel Ángel Asturias (1899–1974) won the Nobel Prize in literature (1967) for his thinly veiled vilification of Latin American dictators in *El Señor Presidente*.

The following books by contemporary Central American authors have been translated into English: *And We Sold the Rain: Contemporary Fiction from Central America*, edited by Rosario Santos, a collection of 22 short stories by Central American writers; *Beyond the Border: A New Age in Latin American Women's Fiction*, edited by Nora Erro-Peralta and Caridad Silva-Nuñez; *Clamor of Innocence: Central American Short Stories*, edited by Barbara Paschke and David Volpendesta, a collection of 31 short stories by Central American writers; and *When New Flowers Bloomed: Short Stories by Women Writers from Costa Rica & Panama*, edited by Enrique J Levi.

Music & Dance

Traditional music and dance also have an important place in Central American society, and you're likely to hear live music at any time on streets, plazas or even buses. The music of the xylophone-like marimba is particularly popular and can be heard in much of the region – especially in Guatemala, where many believe it was invented. Indigenous instruments, including the Mayan *chirimía* (related to the oboe) and reed flute, are still played in churches in the Mayan highlands, and music and traditional dances are important parts of the many colorful festivals on the Mayan calendar. Performances honor Christian saints, but in many cases they have pre-Hispanic roots and retain traces of ancient ritual. The Afro-Caribbean sounds and associated dances of reggae, *punta* and *soca* represent another important element of the region's musical tradition and can be enjoyed along the region's Caribbean coast.

SOCIETY & CONDUCT
Traditional Cultures

Most countries of Central America have agrarian economies and cultures tied to the traditions of the land. The family, usually a large, extended entity, is the basic unit of society and the most important thing in the lives of most people.

Though Central America remains primarily rural, many places have seen a significant migration from the countryside to the cities. People come to the cities seeking education, employment, money and a more modern existence – a 'better life.' Even in the cities, though, there are holdovers from rural life – the family remains the principal social unit, and neighborhood churches and large open-air markets like those of the country abound.

Religion is very important in Central America, and much of the culture revolves around it. Every city, town and village has its patron saint, and the annual festival or fair on the saint's day is usually the most important local celebration of the year. Semana Santa (Holy Week; the week preceding Easter Sunday) is generally the most important holiday, with church services, processions through the streets, dramas, dances, fiestas, special foods and other celebrations. Semana Santa is also the time when most people get a weeklong vacation from work. During Semana Santa, people often take a trip to the beach or to a resort or visit faraway family members. Often this is the only time of the year they can do this, so it's a special holiday for secular as well as religious reasons.

Navidad (Christmas), often celebrated not on Christmas Day but on the evening of December 24, is another important holiday, celebrated in different ways in different locales. In Tegucigalpa, for example, lots of people get drunk and many set off fireworks at midnight. After a midnight Mass, people may stay up all night long, going from house to house visiting and having parties, and then spend Christmas Day resting and recovering.

The many ethnic groups of Central America all have their own distinct cultures. In some countries, especially Guatemala and Panama, a number of Indian groups maintain their own language, type of dress and traditional customs. The mestizos are not only racially, but also culturally, a mixture of Spanish and Indian. The Garífunas and other blacks of the Caribbean coast, small groups of immigrant Chinese, North

Americans, Europeans and other groups also all have their own distinctive cultural features, making Central America a patchwork rather than a uniform cultural fabric.

The USA also has a significant influence on Central American life. It's a rare place where you won't find Coca-Cola and Pepsi, blue jeans, mass-produced clothes (often secondhand from the USA), and radios and cassette tape recorders. TV stations from the USA come in by satellite. Many Central Americans have traveled north to the USA seeking work, and many more dream of doing so.

All the Central American countries have radio and TV, and in many rural areas, homes might have a TV even before they have running water. This can lead to some strange sights. For example, in a remote Garífuna fishing village you might see young men with flat-top haircuts. Ask why they wear their hair like that and they'll tell you, 'That's how they wear it in New York!'

'How do you know?'

'We saw it on television!'

Dos & Don'ts

Politeness is a very important element of social interactions in Central America. When addressing someone, even in such routine situations as in a store or on the bus, you should preface your conversation with a greeting to the other person – a simple *buenos días* or *buenas tardes* and a smile, answered by a similar greeting on the other person's part, gets a conversation off to a positive start. When you enter a room, even a public place such as a restaurant or waiting room, it's polite to make a general greeting to everyone in the room – a simple *buenos días* or *buenas tardes* will do. Handshakes are another friendly gesture and are used frequently here.

Pay attention to your appearance when traveling in Central America. Latin Americans on the whole are very conscious of appearance, grooming and dress; it's difficult for them to understand why a foreign traveler, who is naturally assumed to be rich, would go around looking scruffy when even poor people in Latin America do their best to look neat. This doesn't mean that donning your Armani suit will win you favor with the locals, but your relations with them are likely to be smoother if you try to

present as clean an appearance as possible. This is especially true if you're dealing with officialdom (police, border officials, immigration officers), when it's a good idea to look not only clean but also as conservative and respectable as possible.

In recent years standards of modesty in dress have been relaxing somewhat; you may see local women wearing miniskirts, though just a few years ago this would have been unthinkable. Nevertheless, not everyone appreciates this type of attire – many local people still find it offensive. As a foreigner, it's a good idea for you to take particular care not to offend local people with your attire. A general rule of thumb is to notice what the people around you are wearing and dress accordingly.

Shorts are usually worn by both sexes only at the beach and in coastal towns; if you do wear shorts, be sure they are modest. Beachwear should be worn only at the swimming pool or the beach. You'll notice that many local women swim with T-shirts over their swimming suits, and you may want to do the same, or be prepared to receive a lot of male attention. Consult the Women Travelers section in the following chapter for tips specifically for women travelers.

Dress modestly when entering churches, as this shows respect for local people and their culture. Some churches in heavily touristed areas will post signs at the door asking that shorts and tank tops not be worn in church, but in most places it's assumed that everyone knows not to do this.

Also think about safety in connection with your appearance. In many places in Central America, especially the capital cities, the locals will warn you against wearing wedding bands or even cheap imitation jewelry: You could be mugged for it. If you have any wealth, take care not to flaunt it. See the Dangers & Annoyances section in the following chapter for information on basic travel safety.

RELIGION

Roman Catholicism, the religion imposed upon the region's native inhabitants by the Spaniards, is the principal religion of Central America. In Caribbean areas that were colonized or otherwise influenced by the British, Protestant sects are predominant.

Against the background of Catholicism, however, Central America is host to many different religions and sects. Evangelical and Pentecostal Christian denominations have gained wide followings in many areas. Other religious sects include Baptists, Mennonites, Mormons and Seventh-Day Adventists.

In addition, indigenous peoples and other ethnic groups of the Central American region continue to practice and preserve their traditional religions, often fused with the beliefs and practices of Catholicism. The contemporary Mayan practice of Catholicism, for example, is a fascinating fusion of shamanist-animist and Christian ritual. The traditional religious ways are so important that often a Maya will try to recover from a malady by seeking the advice of a shaman-healer rather than a medical doctor. Use of folk remedies linked with animist tradition is widespread in Mayan areas. The Garífuna of the region's Caribbean coastal areas continue to practice their traditional African-based religion, emphasizing the worship of ancestral spirits, in addition to Christianity.

Regional Facts for the Visitor

HIGHLIGHTS

Central America's top sights are among the most fascinating on the planet, but some of the most enjoyable and memorable travel experiences happen in small towns and villages off the beaten track. Just because these lesser-known spots and activities are not mentioned below does not mean they are unworthy of your time. For country-specific highlights and details on any of the following, see the individual country chapters.

Mayan Archaeological Sites

The stone pyramids, temples, hieroglyphics, statues, stone carvings, artwork and mysteriously abandoned cities of the Maya rank them as one of the great ancient civilizations of the world. Guatemala's Tikal is the best-known and most spectacular Mayan archaeological site in Central America, followed closely by Copán, in Honduras just across the border from Guatemala.

If you enjoy having archaeological sites more or less to yourself, consider exploring some of the region's lesser known but nonetheless interesting sites, including Quiriguá, off Guatemala's Carretera al Atlántico, Uaxactún, north of Tikal, and El Puente at La Entrada, in Honduras.

Panama Canal

This engineering marvel is flanked by national parks, spanned by the graceful Puente de las Américas (Bridge of the Americas), and contains the island nature preserve of Isla Barro Colorado in its waters. Visitors can observe the parade of ships waiting at either end of the canal and see how they pass through the locks.

Antigua Guatemala

Among the most beautiful and best-preserved colonial cities in Latin America, Antigua Guatemala is particularly noted as a center for language study. Semana Santa (Holy Week) is an unforgettable spectacle here, with colorful religious processions and other events.

Chichicastenango Handicrafts

The picturesque Guatemalan mountain town of Chichicastenango has been famous for centuries for its traditional Mayan market on Thursday and Sunday, where villagers from the area sell colorful woven cloths and textiles, carved and painted wooden masks (still used in fiestas), pottery and many other beautiful handicrafts. Sololá, near Lake Atitlán, has a Friday market day just as colorful but with fewer handicrafts (and fewer tourists).

National Parks & Wilderness Areas

Central America harbors some of the richest natural beauty on Earth. Endeavoring to preserve these natural wonders, each of the Central American countries has established national parks, wildlife preserves and other protected areas that attract increasing numbers of travelers, bird watchers and scientists from around the world. For an overview of the region's offerings, see Parks & Protected Areas in the Facts about Central America chapter.

For the more adventurous explorer, the region offers a number of rugged wilderness areas, such as the Mosquitia region of Honduras, Darién Province in Panama and the more remote national parks and wildlife sanctuaries of Costa Rica.

Islands & Beaches

Several islands off the Caribbean coast of Central America are wonderful destinations for diving, snorkeling, swimming, fishing and just enjoying sunny, palm-lined, white-sand beaches. Many of these places are designated as national marine parks to protect the coral reefs and hundreds of species of fish and other marine life that inhabit their waters. Numerous shipwrecks from the region's colonial era make diving in the Caribbean additionally exciting.

The barrier reef off the coast of Belize is the second largest in the world (only Australia's Great Barrier Reef is larger). Caye Caulker and Ambergris Caye are the two islands to visit.

Travelers make the pilgrimage to all three Bay Islands (Islas de la Bahía) off the coast of Honduras, but Roatán is favored by most. Neighboring Utila, said to be the cheapest place in the world to get an open water diving certificate, attracts lots of shoestring travelers. Both islands have extensive protected reef areas and are great places for diving.

Nicaragua has the Islas del Maíz (Corn Islands), popular holiday spots that offer excellent diving in beautiful surroundings off the Caribbean coast.

Panama has numerous islands that are ideal for snorkeling and diving. The Archipiélago de San Blas is an off-the-beaten-track chain of lovely Caribbean isles ruled by the Kuna Indians. In western Panama, the Archipiélago de Bocas del Toro is another beautiful spot protected by a national marine park.

Volcanoes

Central America is home to hundreds of volcanoes, some dormant and some active. In several places, you can climb volcanoes and look right into the craters; some even have roads leading right up to the top. Two of the most impressive volcanoes to see are Poás and Irazú, both in Costa Rican national parks that can be visited on day trips from the capital. Visitors to Costa Rica will also find Volcán Arenal, which is constantly in a state of eruption and is easily visited from nearby La Fortuna, and the active Volcán Rincón de la Vieja, which is less accessible but great for hikers and campers.

Perhaps the most famous volcano views in all of Central America are those from Lago de Atitlán and Antigua, both in Guatemala. Several volcanoes are popular for climbing, including Agua (near Antigua), the temperamental Pacaya, San Pedro (beside Lago de Atitlán) and Santa María (near Quetzaltenango). Highest of all is Volcán Tajumulco (4220m), accessible on a two-day trip from Quetzaltenango. Of these, Pacaya and Santiaguito (on the southwestern flank of Santa María) are considered active volcanoes.

With more than 25 extinct volcanoes, El Salvador has a few magnificent specimens to offer. The Volcán de San Salvador, with two prominent peaks, towers over the capital and makes a good day trip. You can also climb Volcán Izalco in the western part of the country; this volcano has been known for more than a century as 'the lighthouse of the Pacific' but is now a dark cone on the landscape.

In Nicaragua, Parque Nacional Volcán Masaya can easily be visited on a day trip from Managua. The Laguna de Xiloá, also near Managua, is a beautiful volcanic crater lake.

Panama's only volcano, the extinct Volcán Barú, is protected as a national park that offers hiking on the volcano's slopes and is home to quetzals and other wildlife.

Lago de Atitlán

Formed from a collapsed volcanic cone, this Guatemalan lake is nestled among volcanoes and surrounded by communities of Maya Indians. The lake is breathtakingly beautiful, and the villages on its shores offer fascinating possibilities for meeting and getting to know the modern Maya.

Cultural Events & Festivals

The cultural events staged by members of the diverse indigenous and immigrant communities of Central America are fascinating; if you get a chance to participate in one, don't miss it. The anniversaries of the arrival of the Garífuna people on Central American shores (April 12, 1797 in Honduras, November 19, 1828 in Belize) are joyfully celebrated by Garífuna communities. Look for performances by Garífuna dance troupes in Honduras and Belize. In Panama, the Kuna Indians are known for their engaging music and dance.

Town fairs, annual festivals, Carnaval and saints' days are magnificent occasions in Central America. Some of the more famous of these are Semana Santa (Holy Week) in Antigua Guatemala; Carnaval in Panama City or the much smaller version in La Ceiba, on the Caribbean coast of Honduras; and Corpus Christi in Las Tablas, Panama. The celebrations commemorating the July 19th anniversary of the revolution are a big event in Managua. Religious pilgrimages take place on occasions such as the day of the Virgen de Suyapa (patron saint of Honduras), near Tegucigalpa (February 2), and on the day of the Virgen de Fátima (May 13), at the Virgin's shrine outside Cojutepeque, El Salvador. On a smaller scale, the cofradías (religious brotherhoods) of highland Guatemalan communities hold street processions on saints' days and festival Sundays, accompanied by a ragtag assortment of drums, trumpets, firecrackers and incense. The repopulated communities in northern El Salvador usually have a celebration on the anniversary of the return of the villagers after the civil war.

River Trips

You can make a number of well-known river-bound excursions within Central America, depending on your time and itinerary. Among the most popular are boat trips on the Río Dulce in Guatemala. This one-day trip starts at Lívingston, on the Caribbean coast, and travels up the Río Dulce through tropical jungle to El Golfete, a lake-like body of water that is home to a reserve for endangered manatees and other wildlife. The ride then continues on to the Castillo de San Felipe, an old Spanish fort on the shores of Lago de Izabal.

In Nicaragua, you can make another river trip along the route from Managua to off-the-beaten-track Bluefields, on the Caribbean coast. This is a relaxing two-day journey, one day by land from Managua to Rama, a small river town on the Río Escondido, and the second day by boat down the river to Bluefields.

The Río San Juan is the base for another popular excursion. The river forms the eastern part of the border between Nicaragua and Costa Rica. Boat trips on the Río San Juan depart from San Carlos on Lago de Nicaragua and travel through the jungle to El Castillo, another old Spanish fort.

Local Food & Drink

Sampling new cuisine is a great part of any travel experience, and you'll no doubt discover some new favorites in Central America. Sample the seafood soups and coconut bread along the Caribbean coast; the strong, rich coffee in Costa Rica; the shaved ice with sweet fruit syrup from street stands in Panama City; and frothy beverages made from an amazing variety of tropical fruits, found everywhere.

SUGGESTED ITINERARIES

Where you go in Central America and how you get there will largely depend on time and money. With unlimited quantities of both, you could travel the entire length of the isthmus and beyond. Needless to say, few travelers are so fortunate, so it's important to decide on what you want to see most

before setting off. For country-specific highlights and suggested itineraries, see the individual country chapters.

Most travelers arrive by air at one of the region's capital cities, as these airports have the most frequent and far-reaching air services. Some people prefer to explore one country in depth, usually flying in and out of the capital and traveling by bus to sites of interest. Others take on more territory and fly into one country and out of another farther down the road. Consider starting in Antigua (Guatemala) or San José (Costa Rica). Both of these cities are abuzz with international backpackers, and buses to anywhere on the isthmus are available.

The so-called Gringo Trail, which links many points that are of interest to foreign backpackers (hence the name), runs from Mexico to Peru and then south through Bolivia, Chile and Argentina. The route can be lengthened or shortened according to your time, budget, mode of travel and desires, but the whole enchilada requires about three months. After visiting the main hot spots of Tikal, Quetzaltenango, Panajachel and Antigua (all in Guatemala), the Belizean cayes, and the ruins of Copán in Honduras, many travelers pass through El Salvador and Nicaragua to Costa Rica, a popular destination in its own right. Many then head to Panama en route to Ecuador and Peru.

La Ruta Maya is something of a mini Gringo Trail, with an emphasis on visiting the major Mayan ruins; the route takes travelers through Guatemala, Belize and the Yucatán Peninsula of Mexico. This itinerary generally begins in Guatemala City and encompasses the main attractions of Tikal, in the northern region of Petén; Copán in Honduras; the beaches, diving and snorkeling in the Belizean cayes; and the major archaeological sites of Palenque and Tulum in Mexico's Yucatán Peninsula. You should allow at least three weeks to a month to see most of these sites, but Tikal, Copán and a short visit to Belize can be squeezed into a well-organized two weeks.

Depending on how much time you have to explore the region, you might want to focus on having a representative variety of experiences. Consider planning an adventure that incorporates cities and towns, Mayan archeological sites, islands and beaches, volcanoes and one or more of Central America's fascinating national parks and wilderness areas.

PLANNING

If this is your first trip to Latin America, you might want to check out Lonely Planet's *Read This First: Central & South America.* It's full of useful predeparture information on planning, buying tickets, visa applications, health issues and what to expect from the region. It also includes a country profile section with full-color maps, highlights and suggested itineraries.

You might also consider having a look at the Lonely Planet video *Central America: Costa Rica & Honduras* for an overview of those countries.

When to Go

Central America is an enjoyable destination at any time of year. On the whole, the region's busiest tourist periods are during the dry season, from around mid-December to April, and again during the North American summer holidays, mostly July and August. There are regional exceptions, of course – the Caribbean islands, for example, have more 'fun and sun' enthusiasts during the North American and European winter.

Weather Precipitation is the distinguishing factor between the wet season (*invierno,* or winter) and the dry season (*verano,* or summer). The winter months tend to be hot and humid, and especially on the coast you can expect rain more often than not, sometimes for days in a row; inland areas tend to stay drier. The summer dry season is the ideal time to travel in the region – for you and everyone else: Be aware that during this period prices may rise, accommodations can become pinched and tourist areas and transportation are likely to be crowded.

Altitude is the other significant variable in climatic differences throughout the region. You can travel practically anywhere in Central America, regardless of the season, with just a few exceptions – during the rainy season, for example, flooding may make some areas hazardous or inaccessible. Hurricane season is another factor worth considering when planning your trip; see Climate in the Facts about Central America chapter for further information.

Travel Periods When planing your arrival and departure dates, remember that the airlines serving Central America offer high-season, low-season and shoulder-season rates based on corresponding travel periods. The more expensive high-season rates are likely to apply around Christmas and Hanukkah, New Year, Easter, Thanksgiving (in the USA) and the North American summer holiday seasons. The off-season travel periods (generally February, May and September to November) are likely to yield the lowest fares. Consult a travel agent for details on when to find the best rates to your destination. (For more on travel periods and fares, see the Air Travel Glossary in the Getting There & Away chapter.)

Special Events Central America is chock-full of exciting festivals and observances; you might want to incorporate some of the region's special events into your itinerary. Semana Santa (Holy Week) in Antigua Guatemala, for example, is an unforgettable spectacle. It is celebrated as a holiday week all over Central America; it is notoriously tough to get a room and travel about during this week, especially at beach resorts and other holiday spots. In planning for any major event, book a room far in advance, anticipate crowded public transportation and arrive at least a couple of days prior to the beginning of the festival. See the country chapters for descriptions of some of the region's more spectacular events.

What Kind of Trip

The kind of trip you take will be determined by how long you plan to travel, your reasons for going and your budget (see Costs under Money, later in this chapter). At the outset, you'll need to decide whether you want to go on an organized tour, travel independently or combine both options.

An organized tour enables you to visit out-of-the-way places with a minimum of hassle. Trips that present logistical difficulties or require specialized equipment can also be facilitated if organized by professionals. Some tour guides also double as interpreters, and many offer expertise in areas such as wildlife observation or natural history. But organized tours tend to be more expensive than traveling independently and are certainly more restricting. Tours that specialize in activities that interest you, such as bird watching or white-water rafting, are more likely to attract like-minded people and create a more rewarding travel experience. (See Organized Tours in the Getting There & Away chapter for tour operator listings.)

Central America is a remote destination for some travelers, and just getting there can be expensive business. Budget travelers often plan to stay for some time – perhaps for several months or more. Others might spend a year in the region and still feel that they'd barely scratched the surface. Good planning, however, can make even a short trip worthwhile.

Travelers go to Central America for a variety of reasons. Many come to pursue special interests: engaging in a thrilling white-water adventure on the region's rivers; exploring the Mayan pyramids and other ruins; diving and snorkeling off the islands of the Caribbean coast; or studying Spanish, particularly in Antigua Guatemala, where one can participate in some of the best and cheapest language courses in the world. Nicaragua and El Salvador draw international visitors interested in the politics and social change that have influenced those areas. Other people come with church or academic study groups or as Peace Corps volunteers. Others contribute to agricultural, social or conservation projects.

Adventure travel and ecotourism are booming in Central America, particularly in countries like Costa Rica where the tourism infrastructure is more developed. Costa Rica leads the way in river adventure sports, with many tour operators available, and Guatemala and Honduras are developing rafting industries of their own. Surfing and kayaking are also popular, especially along the Pacific coast.

Birding and wildlife-watching enthusiasts also flock to Central America to witness the region's incredible diversity of species. A system of national parks, wildlife refuges and biosphere reserves throughout the region facilitates independent wildlife viewing and bird watching, but it's worth considering an organized tour or two to increase your chances of seeing the rarer or more spectacular species.

The possibilities for diverse experiences in Central America are virtually limitless.

Consider weaving lessons in Guatemala, getting a diving certificate in Honduras, working to protect endangered sea turtles in Costa Rica and hiking or cycling anywhere in the region, to name a few options. Volunteer work can also play a dynamic part in your trip; see the Work section, later in this chapter.

Maps

The best map of the region is the 1:1,800,000 *Traveller's Reference Map of Central America,* produced by and available from International Travel Map Productions, 530 W Broadway, Vancouver, BC, Canada V5Z 1E9. This color map shows road, rail, topographical, national park and private reserve information. ITM also publishes separate maps covering each of the Central American countries and various regions of Mexico, as well as several maps of South America. ITM maps are also available through International Travel Maps and Books (☎ 604-687 3320, fax 604-687 5925), 552 Seymour St, Vancouver, BC, Canada V6B 3J6, the South American Explorers (see Useful Organizations, later in this chapter), and from a variety of travel shops worldwide. ITMB also has a Web site at www.itmb.com.

In the USA, Maplink (☎ 805-692 6777, fax 805-692 6787, custserv@maplink.com) is an excellent source for maps of Central America and just about anywhere else in the world. Their address is 30 S La Patera Lane, Unit 5, Santa Barbara, CA 93117, with a Web site at www.maplink.com. A similarly extensive selection of maps is available in the UK from Stanfords Map Centre (☎ 020 7836 1321), 12-14 Long Acre, London WC2E 9LP.

The American Automobile Association (AAA) publishes a decent road map called *Central America;* it's free for AAA members or members of other motor clubs with reciprocal arrangements with AAA. Visit the organization's Web site (www.aaa.com) for office locations in your area.

See the individual country chapters for information on map sources in Central America.

What to Bring

Travel light: Overweight baggage soon becomes a nightmare, especially in hot weather and on public transportation. Most budget travelers prefer backpacks; internal-frame packs are more suitable than those with external frames. If you travel very light, a bag with a shoulder strap is still easy to carry and perhaps more secure – a backpack is vulnerable to a thief with a razor.

A sturdy convertible backpack with zip-away straps is a good compromise. For long, dusty bus trips, carry a large, strong plastic bag or even a lockable duffel for the luggage compartment or roof.

A flashlight will prove useful for walking around at night and in case of a power failure. During the rainy season, carry an umbrella. If you want to trek in rain forests at any time of year, you'll need water-resistant boots and decent rain gear.

If you have a special interest, such as snorkeling, bird watching or fishing, bring your own equipment with you. Binoculars are essential if you intend to do a lot of wildlife observation. You may find such resources available in certain places, but you'll be glad to have them when visiting some of the region's more remote snorkeling spots, bird sanctuaries or wildlife refuges.

Central America is not generally cold, so there's no need to load up with clothing – a windproof jacket, and a warm layer to wear underneath, is necessary in the mountains and should be warm enough for any time of year unless you plan on camping in the high-altitude cloud forests. If you'll be in the highlands of Guatemala in December or January, you will need warmer clothes. Remember that warm clothing is generally available for sale in colder areas, so you can buy something locally rather than carrying around cumbersome bundles during your entire trip.

Don't forget small essentials. A combination pocketknife such as a Swiss Army knife; a needle, cotton and a small pair of scissors; a padlock; and one or two good long novels (English-language books can be hard to come by and are usually expensive in Central America). Most toiletries (toilet paper, toothpaste, shampoo etc) are easily found in large cities and most small towns. If you use prescription medicines, contraceptives or contact-lens solution, bring them along. Tampons are available in the larger cities, but it's best to bring some with you anyway, as often you won't be able to find

the kind you prefer. Virtually every small shop sells packets of washing powder just large enough for a pile of laundry. A 'universal' sink plug is also useful. See the Health section for suggestions for a personal medical kit.

RESPONSIBLE TOURISM

Travelers to Central America should bear in mind that many souvenirs sold in the region are made from endangered plants and animals that have been acquired illegally. By collecting or purchasing these items you aid in their extinction. Avoid purchasing any items made from turtle shell or coral. The sale and purchase of jaguar teeth and pelts, as well as crocodile, ocelot and margay skins, is illegal. Orchids are endemic and are also protected by domestic and international law; view but don't pick. There is also a trend toward serving 'exotic' fare at some restaurants, and this may include endangered or threatened species. Don't contribute to the demise of Central American fauna by ordering these dishes.

Don't take home anything that you pick up at the site of an ancient city or out on a coral reef. Be careful what you touch and where you place your feet when you're snorkeling and scuba diving; not only can coral cut you, but it's extremely fragile and takes years to grow even a finger's length; see the 'Considerations for Responsible Diving' boxed text, later in this chapter.

Many areas in the region have limited water reserves, and in times of drought the situation can become grave. Additionally, wastewater-treatment facilities (where they exist) can't always keep up with the strain placed on them by local residents, let alone tourists. Contamination of groundwater is becoming a serious problem. Do your part to help by keeping water use down, especially in areas that have signs requesting you to do so.

The term 'ecotourism' has been used and abused more than any other word during the huge growth of the tourism industry that Central America has experienced during the last decade. Some developers, hotel owners, and tour operators have jumped on the ecotourism bandwagon, offering a packaged glimpse of nature without making any positive impact on the country. A different class of operators and hoteliers, based in Costa Rica, has arrived at a series of guidelines designed to minimize negative impacts of tourism and emphasize sustainable development of the industry at all levels. These guidelines enable the traveler to make enlightened choices when visiting Central America and can generally be applied to countries worldwide. The guidelines have two main themes: conservation and cultural sensitivity.

Waste Disposal
Don't litter. Patronize hotels with recycling programs. Some hotels will provide towel or sheet changes on request, rather than daily, to minimize unnecessary use of soap and water. Travel with tour operators who provide and use waste receptacles aboard buses and boats and who dispose of trash properly.

Wildlife
Don't disturb animals or damage plants. Stay on trails. Observe wildlife from a distance with binoculars. Follow the instructions of trained naturalist guides. Never feed wild animals. Do not collect or buy endangered animals or plants.

Local Communities
Allow the small communities at your destination to benefit from tourism. Use local guides. Patronize locally owned and operated restaurants and hotels. Buy locally made crafts and souvenirs (though never those made from endangered species such as turtles or black coral).

Cultural Sensitivity
Interact with local people. Speak as much of the local language as you can. Appreciate and learn from the different cultural traditions of the areas you visit.

Education
Learn about wildlife and local conservation, environmental and cultural issues both before your trip and during your visit. Ask questions.

Sustainability
Avoid overcrowded areas unless you really want to see them. Support tourism companies with conservation initiatives and long-term management plans.

TOURIST OFFICES

A number of Central American countries have overseas tourist offices, though most are only represented in one or two countries outside of Latin America. Alternately, consulates usually can provide some semblance of tourist information. To find countries that have tourist offices overseas, go to the Tourism Offices Worldwide Directory Web site (www.towd.com), which has regularly updated contact information for tourist office sites.

VISAS & DOCUMENTS
Passport
See the individual country chapters for destination-specific information on passports and visas. Make sure you know when your passport expires; some countries may not let you in when you're close to the expiration date. If you are traveling the region by private car, you will need motor-vehicle insurance and a valid import permit, as well as a driver's license. See the Getting There & Away chapter for details.

Visas
A visa is an endorsement in your passport, usually a stamp, permitting you to enter a country and remain for a specified period of time. It is obtained from a foreign embassy or consulate of that country. You can often get them in your home country, but it's usually possible to get them en route, which may be better if your itinerary is flexible: Most visas are only good for a limited period after they're issued. Ask other travelers about the best places to get them, since two consulates of the same country may enforce different requirements: The fees might vary; one consular official might want to see your money or an onward ticket and another might not ask; or one office might issue a visa on the spot but another might take days to do so.

If you really need a visa in a hurry, ask nicely and explain your reasons. Consulates can often be very helpful if the officials sympathize and your papers are in order. Sometimes they will charge a fee for fast processing, but don't mistake this for a bribe.

Nationals of most European countries and Japan require few visas, but travelers from the USA need some, and travelers from Australia, New Zealand or South Africa might need quite a few visas. Carry a handful of passport-size photographs for visa applications (though most border towns have a photographer who can do them).

Visa requirements are given in the Facts for the Visitor section of each individual country chapter. Note that if you need a visa for a certain country and arrive at a land border without one, you will probably have to return to the nearest town with a consulate and obtain a visa before being admitted. Airlines will not normally let you board a plane for a country to which you don't have the necessary visa. Also, a visa in itself may not guarantee entry: You may still be turned back at the border if you don't have 'sufficient funds' or an onward or return ticket.

Sufficient Funds Getting visas is generally a routine procedure, but officials may ask, either verbally or on the application form, about your financial resources. If you lack 'sufficient funds' for your proposed visit, officials may limit the length of your stay. (US$500 per month of your planned stay is generally considered sufficient; traveler's checks should qualify toward the total amount.) Once you are in the country, however, you can usually renew or extend your visa by showing a wad of traveler's checks. A credit card or two is often convincing evidence of sufficient funds.

Onward or Return Tickets Several Central American countries require you to have a ticket out of the country – as proof that you will eventually leave – before they will grant you a visa or admit you at the border. The onward or return ticket requirement can be a nuisance for overland travelers who want to fly into one country and travel overland through others. Belize, Costa Rica and Panama all have such laws on the books, though the laws may not be consistently enforced.

Sometimes you can satisfy the return ticket requirement by purchasing an MCO (miscellaneous charge order), a document that looks like an airline ticket but can be refunded in cash or credited toward a specific flight with any International Air Transport Association (IATA) carrier. Check whether consular or immigration officials will accept an MCO as an onward ticket. If not, try to buy a refundable onward or return ticket – ask specifically where you can get a refund, as some airlines will only refund tickets at the office of purchase or at their head office.

Any ticket out of Central America plus sufficient funds might be an adequate substitute for an onward ticket. Having a recognized international credit card or two

might help. A prosperous appearance and a sympathetic official also will improve your chances.

If you are heading to Colombia, Venezuela or another South American country from Panama or elsewhere in Central America, you may need an onward ticket before you'll be allowed entry or even allowed to board the plane out. A quick check with the appropriate embassy will tell you whether the country you're heading to has an onward-ticket requirement.

The only way to avoid the onward-ticket requirement altogether in countries that demand it is to enter the country by private rather than public transportation. If you enter by private vehicle, either your own or one that has picked you up, no onward ticket is required.

Extensions Once you are inside a country, you can always apply for an extension at the country's immigration office. Usually there is a limit on how many extensions you can receive; if you leave the country and reenter, your time starts over again.

Travel Insurance

A travel insurance policy to cover theft, loss and medical problems is a good idea. Some policies offer lower and higher medical-expense options; the higher ones are chiefly designed for countries that have extremely high medical costs, such as the USA. A wide variety of policies are available, so check the small print.

Some policies specifically exclude 'dangerous activities,' which can include scuba diving, motorcycling or even trekking. If such activities are on your agenda, you don't want this sort of policy.

You may prefer a policy that pays doctors or hospitals directly rather than making you pay on the spot and claim later. If you do have to claim later, make sure that you keep all documentation. Some policies ask you to call back (reverse charges) to a center in your home country, where an immediate assessment of your problem is made.

Check that the policy covers ambulances or an emergency flight home.

Driver's License & Permits

Before you start out, check to see if your driver's license from your home country is honored in all the countries you plan to visit. Chances are, if you intend to drive in Central America, you will need an International Driving Permit (IDP), and it's wise to obtain one even if you don't plan to drive your own vehicle. IDPs are issued by automobile associations in your home country for a nominal fee (usually about US$10) when you present a current state or national driver's license. Applicants must be over 18 years of age.

Hostel Cards
Hostelling International-American Youth Hostel (HI-AYH) membership cards are not particularly useful in Central America. With the exception of Costa Rica, where there is a small network of hostels, accredited hostel accommodations in the region are limited and minimal discounts are available to cardholders. Those traveling on to South America, however, might want to invest in the membership, which costs US$25 a year; visit the official HI Web site (www.iyhf.org) for additional information.

Student, Youth & Teacher Cards
The International Student Identity Card (ISIC) is recognized almost everywhere *except* Latin America; this is largely due to a proliferation of forged cards in recent years. Still, the ISIC is useful in some countries for reductions on admission charges to archaeological sites and museums. At times, it will also entitle you to reductions on bus, train and air tickets. One ISIC benefit worth considering is that the card automatically entitles the purchaser to travel insurance (or, in some cases, allows the cardholder to purchase a policy at a very low price). The official ISIC is offered by the International Student Travel Confederation (ISTC), based in Denmark, and costs US$20; to qualify you must present proof of your status as a full-time student. You can apply for the card at accredited travel agencies such as Council Travel and STA Travel, both with offices and affiliates worldwide (see the Getting There & Away chapter). Visit their Web site (www.istc.org) for more information.

ISTC also offers other discount cards, including the International Youth Travel Card (IYTC; formerly the GO 25 Card) and the International Teacher Identity Card (ITIC), both of which offer discounts and benefits similar to those of the student card. The youth card has specific age requirements (12 to 25), and the teacher card requires that you teach full-time at a recognized school; both cost US$20 and can be purchased at the travel agencies named above.

Vaccination Certificates
An international health certificate, listing the type and date of all your vaccinations and immunizations, is a good idea for international travelers but not required for entry into any of the Central American countries. In some countries, health authorities issue the International Certificate of Vaccination (in the USA, order one at ☎ 202-512 1800), otherwise, ask your physician or government health agency for a certificate detailing your vaccination history and carry it with your passport.

Note that, for travelers to and from many parts of South America, proof of vaccination against yellow fever is essential.

Documents for Minors

In some Latin American countries, travelers under 18 years of age not accompanied by one or both of their parents are required to show a notarized consent form signed by both parents or the absent parent. Contact the appropriate embassy or consulate to determine exactly what paperwork you'll need to enter the country.

Even minors traveling with a parent may require special documents. Single parents traveling with underage children have been prevented from boarding planes and from entering Canada, Mexico and several Latin American countries. In an effort to prevent child abductions, US policy will soon require the signature of both parents on a child's passport application. To avoid being stranded, mom, dad or any guardian traveling with a minor should carry notarized letters from both parents authorizing the international travel of their child.

Copies

Before you leave home, you should photocopy all important documents (passport data page and visa page, credit cards, travel insurance policy, air/bus/train tickets, driver's license etc). Leave one copy with someone at home and keep another with you, separate from the originals.

It's also a good idea to store details of your vital travel documents in Lonely Planet's free online Travel Vault in case you lose the photocopies or can't be bothered with them. Your password-protected Travel Vault is accessible online anywhere in the world – create it at www.ekno.lonelyplanet.com.

EMBASSIES & CONSULATES
Your Own Embassy

As a visitor in a Central American country, it's important to realize what your own embassy – the embassy of the country of which you are a citizen – can and can't do.

Generally speaking, it won't be much help in emergencies if the trouble you're in is remotely your own fault. Remember that you are bound by the laws of the country you are in. Your embassy will not be sympathetic if you end up in jail after committing a crime locally, even if such actions are legal in your own country.

In genuine emergencies, you might get some assistance, but only if other channels have been exhausted. For example, if you need to get home urgently, a free ticket home is exceedingly unlikely – the embassy would expect you to have insurance. If you have all your money and documents stolen, it might assist in getting a new passport, but a loan for onward travel is out of the question. Some embassies may repatriate a penniless citizen as a last resort but will probably confiscate your passport until you repay the debt – and it won't be a cheap flight. French embassies don't usually repatriate their citizens, and US embassies rarely do so.

Embassies used to keep letters for travelers or have a small reading room with home newspapers, but these days the mail holding service has been stopped, and even newspapers tend to be out of date.

Central American Embassies & Consulates

In some cases, Central American countries maintain multiple posts in a single foreign host country. Honduras, for example, maintains diplomatic posts in some 18 different US cities in addition to its principal office in Washington, DC. The following listings contain only primary embassies and consulates.

Some consulates mentioned below are actually honorary consulates or consular agencies. These posts can usually issue visas, but they refer more complicated matters to the nearest full consulate or consular section.

For the diplomatic offices of each of the Central American nations in neighboring countries within the region, look under the appropriate host country in the Foreign Embassies & Consulates in Central America section, which follows.

Guatemala The following are Guatemala's diplomatic offices abroad. Note that Guatemala does not maintain embassies in Australia or New Zealand; contact the Guatemalan embassy in Tokyo for travel to those destinations.

Canada (☎ 613-233 7188, 613-233 7237) 130 Albert St, Suite 1010, Ottawa, Ontario K1P 5G4; also consulates in Vancouver and Montréal

France (☎ 14 227 7863, fax 14 754 0206) 73 rue de Courcelles, 75008 Paris; also consulates in Ajaccio, Bordeaux, Le Havre, Strasbourg and Marseilles

Germany (☎ 228 351 579, fax 228 354 940) Zietenstrasse 16, 53173 Bonn; also consulates in Dusseldorf, Hamburg, Munich and Stuttgart

Japan (☎ 3 3400 1830, fax 3 3400 1820) 38 Kowa Bldg, Room 905, 4-12-24 Nichi-Azabu, Tokyo 106; also a consulate in Osaka

Mexico (☎ 5 540 7520, fax 5 202 1142) Avenida Explanada 1025, Colonia Lomas de Chapultepec 11000, Mexico 4, DF

UK (☎ 171 351 3042, fax 171 376 5708) 13 Fawcett St, London SW10 9HN

USA (☎ 202-745 4952, fax 202-745 1908) 2220 R St NW, Washington, DC 20008

Belize The overseas diplomatic affairs of Belize are generally handled by British embassies and consulates. Belize's diplomatic posts abroad include the following:

Canada (honorary consul; ☎ 416-865 7000, fax 416-865 7048) Suite 3800, South Tower, Royal Bank Plaza, Toronto, Ontario M5J 2J7

Germany (honorary consul; ☎ 71 423 925, fax 71 423 225) Lindenstrasse 46-48, 74321 Beitigheim, Bissingen

Mexico (☎ 5 520 1274, fax 5 520 6089) Calle Bernardo de Gálvez 215, Colonia Lomas de Chaptultepec, Mexico, DF 11000

UK (Belize High Commission to London; ☎ 20 7499 9728, fax 20 7491 4139) 22 Harcourt House, 19 Cavendish Square, London W1M 9AD

USA (☎ 202-332 9636, fax 202-332 6888) 2535 Massachusetts Ave NW, Washington, DC 20008

Honduras Visas for travel to Honduras can be obtained at the following Honduran embassies and consulates:

Australia (consulate; ☎ 02 9252 3779) 19/31 Pitt St, Sydney NSW

Canada (☎ 613-233 8900, ☎/fax 613-232 0193) 151 Slater St, Suite 908A, Ottawa, Ontario K1P 5H3

Colombia (☎ 236 0357, fax 616 0774) Carretera 16, No 885 15, Apto 302, Santa Fe de Bogotá

France (☎ 1 47 55 86 45, fax 1 47 55 86 48) 8 rue Crevaux, 75116 Paris

Germany (☎ 228 356 394, ☎/fax 228 351 981) Ubierestrasse-15300 Bonn 2

Mexico (☎ 5 211 5747, fax 5 211 5425) Alfonso Reyes No 220, Colonia Condesa, México DF 06140

UK (☎/fax 171 486 4880) 115 Gloucester Place, London W1H 3PJ

USA (☎ 202-966 7702, fax 202-966 9571) 3007 Tilden St NW, Washington, DC 20008

El Salvador The following are the addresses of El Salvador's embassies and consulates abroad:

Canada (☎ 613-238 2939) 209 Kent St, Ottawa, Ontario K2P 1Z8

France (☎ 331 47 23 98 03, fax 331 40 70 01 95) 12 rue Galilee, Paris 75116

Italy (☎ 396 807 6605) Via Gualtiero Castellini 13, Scala B Int 3, 00197 Rome

Mexico (☎ 525 520 0856, fax 525 520 3698) Monte Altai No 320, Colonia Lomas de Chapultepec, Delegación Miguel Hidalgo, Mexico DF 11000

UK (☎ 171 430 2141, fax 171 430 0484) 5 Gt James St, London WC1N 3DA

USA (☎ 202-387 6511, fax 202-234 3834) 2308 California St NW, Washington, DC 20008

Nicaragua The following are the addresses of Nicaragua's embassies and consulates abroad:

Austria (☎ 403 1839, fax 403 2752, 113350.2341@ compuserve.com) Ebendorferstrasse, 10-3-12, 1010 Vienna

Canada Canadian citizens should contact the US embassy in Washington, DC

France (☎ 1 45 00 41 02, fax 1 45 00 96 81) Avenue Bugeaud, 75116 Paris

Germany (also Switzerland; ☎ 228 362 505, fax 228 354 001) Konstantinstrasse 41, D-53159 Bonn/2

Mexico (☎ 5 540 5625, fax 5 520 6960) Prado de Norte 470, Colonia Lomas de Chapultepec, CP 11000, Delegación Miguel Hidalgo, Mexico DF

Netherlands (☎ 70 306 17 42, fax 70 306 1743) Sumatrastraat 336, 2585CZ The Hague

Spain (☎ 91 555 5510, fax 91 555 5737) Paseo La Castellana 127, 10-B, 28046 Madrid

Sweden (also Denmark, Finland and Norway; ☎ 468 667 1857, fax 468 662 4160) Sandhamnasgatan 40-6 tr, 11528 Stockholm

UK (☎ 171 409 2536, fax 171 409 2593) 36 Upper Brook St, London W1Y 1PE

USA (also Canada; ☎ 202-939 6531, fax 202-939 6532) 1627 New Hampshire Ave NW, Washington, DC 20009

Costa Rica Embassies and consulates for Costa Rica include the following:

Australia (☎ 2 9261 1177, fax 2 9261 2953) 30 Clarence St, 11th floor, Sydney, NSW 2000

Canada (☎ 613-562 2855, fax 613-562 2582) 135 York St, Suite 208, Ottawa, Ontario K1N 5TA

Denmark (☎ 3311 0885, fax 3393 7530) Kvasthusgade 3, 125 Copenhagen

France (☎ 1 45 78 96 96, fax 1 45 78 99 66, embcr@ wanadoo.fr) 78 Avenue Emile Zola, 75015 Paris

Germany (☎ 228 540 040, fax 228 549 053, 100730.1020@compuserve.com) Langenbachstrasse 19, 53113 Bonn

Israel (☎ 2 2566 6197, fax 2 2563 2591, emcri@ netmedia.net.il) Reh ov Diskin 13 No 1, Jerusalem 91012

Italy (☎ 6 4425 1046, fax 6 4425 1048, embcosta@ mix.it) Vía Bartolomeo, Eustacho 22, Interno 6, Rome 00161

Netherlands (☎ 70 354 0780, fax 70 358 4754, Embajada@embacrica.demon.nl) Laan Copes Van Cattenburg 46, 2585 GB The Hague

Spain (☎ 91 345 9622, fax 91 353 3709, contact embajadade.costarica@anit.es) Paseo de la Castellana 164, No 17 A, 28046 Madrid

Switzerland (☎ 31 372 78 87, fax 31 372 7834, Embajada.Costa.Rica@thenet.ch) Schwarztorstrasse 11, 3007 Bern

UK (☎ 171 706 8544, general@embcrlon.demon .co.uk) Flat 1, 14 Lancaster Gate, London W1 3LH

USA (☎ 202-234 2945, fax 202-265 4795, embassy@costarica.com) 2114 S St NW, Washington, DC 20008

Panama Embassies and consulates for Panama include the following:

Canada (☎ 613-236 7177, fax 613-236 5775) 130 Albert St, Suite 300, Ottawa, Ontario K1P 5G4

Colombia (☎ 257 5067, 257 5068, fax 257 5068) Calle 92, No 7-70, Bogotá

France (☎ 1 4783 2332, 1 4566 4244, fax 1 45 67 9943) 145 Avenue de Suffren, 75015 Paris

Germany (☎ 228 36 1036, fax 228 36 3558) Lutzowstrasse 1, 53173 Bonn

Mexico (☎ 5 250 4229, fax 5 250 4045) Schiller 326, 8th floor, Colonia Chapultepec-Morales, CP 11570, Mexico DF

UK (☎ 171 493 4646, fax 171 493 4499) 48 Park St, London W1Y 3PD

USA (☎ 202-483 1407, fax 202-483 8413) 2862 McGill Terrace NW, Washington, DC 20008

Foreign Embassies & Consulates in Central America

When planning a visit to one of the following offices, it's best to call ahead to confirm locations and get directions. Note that the nearest consulates for Australia and New Zealand are in Mexico.

Guatemala All of the following offices are in Guatemala City except where noted. Australia, Ireland and New Zealand do not maintain diplomatic representation in Guatemala.

Belize (☎ 334 5531, 331 1137, fax 334 5536) Avenida La Reforma 1-50, Zona 9, Edificio El Reformador, Office 803

Canada (☎ 333 6102, fax 363 4208) 13a Calle 8-44, Zona 10, Edificio Plaza Edyma, 8th floor

Costa Rica (☎ 331 9604, ☎/fax 332 0531) Avenida La Reforma 8-60, Zona 9, Edificio Galerías Reforma, Office 702

El Salvador (☎ 366 2240, fax 366 7960) 4a Avenida 13-60, Zona 10

France (☎ 337 3639, 337 3180) 16a Calle 4-53, Zona 10, Edificio Marbella, 11th floor

Germany (☎ 337 0028) 20a Calle 6-20, Edificio Plaza Marítima, Zona 10

Honduras (☎ 335 3281, 338 2068, fax 338 2073) 12a Calle 1-25, Edificio Géminis, 12th floor, Zona 10; also a consulate in Esquipulas ☎ 943 2027, 943 1547, fax 943 1371) 2a Avenida in the Hotel Payaquí

Japan (☎ 367 2244, fax 367 2245) Avenida la Reforma 16-85, 10th floor, Zona 10

Mexico (☎ 333 7254) 15a Calle 3-20, Edificio Centro Ejecutivo, 7th floor, Zona 10; also consulates in Guatemala City (☎ 331 8165, 331 9573) 13a Calle 7-30, Zona 9; Huehuetenango, 5a Avenida 4-11, Zona 1; and Quetzaltenango (☎ 763 1312) 9a Avenida 6-19, Zona 1

Netherlands (☎ 367 4761, fax 367 5024, nlgovgua@infovia.com.gt) 16a Calle 0-55, Torre Internacional, 13th floor, Zona 10

Nicaragua (☎ 368 0785, fax 337 4264) 10a Avenida 14-72, Zona 10

Panama (☎ 333 7182, 337 2495, fax 337 2445) 5a Avenida 15-45, Edificio Centro Empresarial, Torre II, Office 702, Zona 10

UK (☎ 367 5425, fax 367 5430, embassy@infovia.com.gt) 16a Calle 0-55, Torre Internacional, 11th floor, Zona 10

USA (☎ 331 1541) Avenida La Reforma 7-01, Zona 10

Belize A number of countries have ambassadors resident in Belize. Many others, however, appoint nonresident ambassadors who are responsible for handling Belizean affairs from offices in their home countries. Unless otherwise noted, all the embassies and consulates listed below are in Belize City.

Denmark (consulate; ☎ 2 72172, fax 2 77280) 13 Southern Foreshore

European Union (Commission of the European Union; ☎ 2 72785, 2 32070) Eyre St at Hutson St

Germany (honorary consul; ☎ 2 24371, fax 2 24375) 31⁄2 Miles, Western Hwy

Guatemala (☎ 2 33150, 2 33314, fax 2 35140) 6A St Matthew St, near Municipal Airport

Israel (honorary consul; ☎ 2 73991, fax 2 30463) 4 Albert St

Italy (honorary consul; ☎ 2 78449, fax 2 73056) 18 Albert St

Mexico (☎ 2 30194, 2 31388, fax 2 78742) 20 N Park St; also an office in Belmopan

Netherlands (honorary consul; ☎ 2 73612, fax 2 75936) 14 Central American Blvd

Norway (honorary consul; ☎ 2 77031, fax 2 77062) 1 King St

Panama (consulate; ☎ 2 34282, fax 2 30653) 5481 Princess Margaret Dr

Sweden (honorary consul general; ☎ 2 30623) 11 Princess Margaret Dr

UK (British High Commission; ☎ 8 22146, fax 8 22761) Embassy Square, Belmopan

USA (☎ 2 77161, fax 2 30802) 29 Gabourel Lane

Honduras Most of the foreign embassies and a number of consulates in Honduras are in Tegucigalpa. Several countries also have consulates in San Pedro Sula. Those countries with offices in Tegucigalpa include the following:

Belize (consulate; ☎/fax 239 1034) in the Hotel Honduras Maya near Avenida República de Chile

Canada (consulate; ☎ 232 4551, fax 232 2767) in the Financiero Banexpo Local Bldg No 3, on Blvd Juan Pablo II

Colombia (☎ 232 1709, fax 232 8133) in the Edificio Palmira, 4th floor, opposite Hotel Honduras Maya

Costa Rica (☎ 232 1768, fax 232 1876) on Blvd Morazán

El Salvador (☎ 236 7344, fax 236 0436) 2a Avenida 205, 1½ blocks from Blvd Morazán

France (☎ 236 6800, fax 236 8051) at 3a Calle and Avenida Juan Lindo, Colonia Palmira

Germany (☎ 232 3161, fax 232 9518) in the Edificio Paysen, 3rd floor, on Blvd Morazán

Guatemala (☎ 232 9704, fax 232 8469) 4a Calle, Arturo López Rodezno, No 2421, Colonia Las Minitas

Japan (☎ 236 6829, fax 236 6100) on Calzada República de Paraguay, between 4a and 5a Calles

Mexico (☎ 232 6471, fax 232 4719) on Avenida República de Mexico, Colonia Palmira

Netherlands (consulate; ☎ 232 7501, fax 232 5009) in the Edificio Festival, on Avenida Principal

Nicaragua (☎ 232 4290, fax 231 1412) Bloque M-1, Calle 11, Colonia Lomas del Tepeyac

Panama (☎ 239 5508, fax 232 8147) in the Edificio Palmira, 2nd floor, No 200, opposite Hotel Honduras Maya

UK (☎ 232 0618, fax 232 5429) in the Edificio Palmira, 3rd floor, opposite Hotel Honduras Maya

USA (☎ 236 9320, fax 236 9037) in the Edificio Embajada Americana, on Avenida La Paz

Embassies in San Pedro Sula include the following:

Belize (consulate; ☎ 551 6191, fax 551 6460) 7a Calle 102, Colonia Bella Vista

Costa Rica (☎ 558 0744, fax 558 1019) in the Hotel Saint Anthony

El Salvador (☎/fax 553 4604) in the River and Cia Bldg

France (☎ 557 4187) in Colonia Zerón

Guatemala (☎ 553 3560) 8a Calle 38

Mexico (☎ 553 2604, fax 552 3293) 20a Avenida SO 205

Nicaragua (☎/fax 550 3394) 23a Avenida 145

UK (☎ 557 2046, fax 552 9764) on 13a Avenida between 10a and 12a Calles SE

El Salvador Corsatur keeps a current listing of all foreign embassies and consulates in San Salvador. Those offices include the following:

Belize (☎ 226 3682) Condominio Médico B, Local 5, Blvd Tutunichapa, Urbanización La Esperanza

Costa Rica (☎ 264 3863) 85a Avenida Sur 4415

France (☎ 298 4260) 1a Calle Poniente 3718

Germany (☎ 263 2088) 77a Avenida Norte 3972

Guatemala (☎ 271 2225, fax 271 3019) 15a Avenida Norte 135

Honduras (☎ 263 2808) 89a Avenida Norte, between 7a and 9a Calles Poniente, Casa 561

Italy (☎ 223 7325) Calle La Reforma 158

Mexico (☎ 243 2037) at Pasaje 12 and Calle Circunvalación

Netherlands (☎ 298 2185) 1a Calle Poniente 3510

Nicaragua (☎ 223 7729) 1a Calle Poniente 164

Panama (☎ 260 5554) 55a Avenida Norte 2838

UK (☎ 263 6527) Paseo General Escalón 4828

USA (☎ 278 4444) near the end of Blvd Santa Elena; take bus or micro No 44

Nicaragua The tourist office and the local telephone book have complete lists of Managua's many embassies and consulates, which include the following:

Costa Rica (☎ 266 3986, fax 266 3955) from Montoya statue, two blocks north, one block east

Denmark (☎ 268 0250) from Rotonda El Güegüense, one block west, two blocks north, a half block west

El Salvador (☎ 276 0712) Avenida del Campo 142, Las Colinas

France (☎ 222 6210, fax 228 1057) 1½ blocks west of El Carmen church

Germany (☎ 266 3918) from Rotonda El Güegüense, 1½ blocks north

Guatemala (☎ 279 9609, fax 279 9610) Carretera a Masaya Km 11.5; also a consulate in León

Honduras (☎ 279 8233, fax 279 8228) Carretera a Masaya Km 12.5

Mexico (☎ 278 4919) Carretera a Masaya Km 4½, one block east

Netherlands (☎ 266 6175) from Canal 2, a half block north, one block west

Panama (☎ 266 8633) from Main Fire Station, one block west, No 93, Colonia Mántica

UK (☎ 278 0014, fax 278 4086) behind Hotel Princess, Colonia Los Robles

USA (☎ 266 6012, 266 6038 after hours) Km 4½, Carretera Sur

Costa Rica The following countries have embassies or consulates in the San José area:

Canada (☎ 296 4149, fax 296 4270) Oficentro Bldg, Sabana Sur

El Salvador (☎ 257 7855) from Toyota dealership on Paseo Colón, 500m north and 50m west

France (☎ 253 5010, fax 253 7027) Carretera a Curridabat, 200m south and 50m west of Indoor Club

Germany (☎ 232 5533, fax 231 6403) 200m north and 75m east of ex-president Oscar Arias' residence, Rohrmoser

Guatemala (☎ 283 2557) Carretera a Curridabat, 500m south and 30m east of Pops

Honduras (☎ 234 9502, fax 253 2209) from Universidad Las Veritas, 250m east, 200m north then another 100m east

Israel (☎ 221 6444, fax 257 0867) Centro Colón, 11th floor, Paseo Colón

Italy (☎ 234 2326, fax 225 8200) Calle 33, Avenidas 8 and 10, Los Yoses

Nicaragua (☎ 222 2373) Avenida Central 2540, Calles 25 and 27, Barrio La California

Panama (☎ 257 3241, fax 257 4864) Calle 38, 250m north of Centro Colón

UK (☎ 258 2025, fax 233 9938) Centro Colón, 11th floor, Paseo Colón

USA (☎ 220 3939, fax 220 2305) Carretera a Pavas opposite Centro Commercial del Oeste

Panama More than 50 countries have embassies or consulates in Panama City, including the following:

Belize (☎ 266 8939) Calle Quinta, Colonias del Prado, Casa 592

Canada (☎ 264 7973) Avenida Samuel Lewis and Calle Gerardo Ortega, Banco Central Hispano Bldg, 4th floor, in front of the Comosa Bldg

Colombia (☎ 264 9266) Calle 53, World Trade Center Bldg, 1802

Costa Rica (☎ 264 4057) Avenida Samuel Lewis; In David (consulate; ☎/fax 774 7725) Calle C Sur between Avenidas 1 and 2 Este

El Salvador (☎ 223 3020) Avenida Manuel E Batista, Metropolis Bldg, 4th floor, behind Iglesia del Carmen

France (☎ 228 7824) Plaza de Francia, Las Bóvedas, Casco Antiguo

Germany (☎ 263 7733) Calles 50 and 53 Este, Bancomer Bldg, 6th floor

Guatemala (☎ 269 3406) Altamira Bldg, 9th floor, Vía Argentina

Honduras (☎ 225 8200, ☎/fax 225 3283) Tapia Bldg, Calle 31 Este, between Avenidas Justo Arosemena and México, 2nd floor

Mexico (☎ 263 5021) Calles 50 and 53 Este, Bancomer Bldg, 5th floor

Nicaragua (☎ 223 0981) Avenida J San Martín, 31 Central

UK (☎ 269 0866) Calle 53 Este, Swissbank Bldg, 4th floor, Marbella district

USA (☎ 227 1777, usembpan@sinfo.net) Avenida Balboa and Calle 37

MONEY

The most useful currency to bring to Central America is US dollars; they can be exchanged everywhere in the region. It's possible to change other currencies in major cities, but outside the capitals you'll inevitably need US dollars, either in cash or traveler's checks.

The three main choices for carrying money are cash, traveler's checks and credit or debit cards. For efficiency and safety, don't rely on just one method. Most experienced travelers carry a combination of all three.

Exchanging Money

Change traveler's checks or foreign cash at a bank or a *casa de cambio* (exchange house). Rates are usually similar, but in general casas de cambio are quicker, less bureaucratic and open longer or have weekend hours. Street money changers, who may or may not be legal, will only handle cash. Sometimes you can also change money unofficially at hotels or in shops that sell imported goods (electronics dealers are an obvious choice). Big cities tend to offer the best exchange rates, so change the money you'll need before heading out into the countryside. Also, try not to change a lot of money at borders, where rates are lower. When looking for the best place to exchange your money, consult your guidebook or other travelers and compare exchange rates and commission fees before you commit. At times you might want to use street money changers, if only because they are so much faster and more convenient than banks (see Black Market, later in this section).

It's usually possible to exchange Central American currencies from one country to the next, though it's easier to do so when you're at or near the border. If you wait until you're far into the next country, you may not find anyone willing to change the leftover money. If you're just about to leave the country, don't change a large-denomination bill or traveler's check, because you'll lose money when you reconvert it into the next country's currency or back into dollars. Try to use up all your local money while you're in the country, and start changing dollars again when you get to the next country.

Cash You should always carry some money in cash US dollars. Small bills are best: They can be changed almost anywhere. It's especially useful to have cash for times when you can't change traveler's checks – in remote places, or when the banks are closed or when the casa de cambio changes cash but not checks. It's also useful to be able to change just a few dollars when you're about to leave a country.

US dollars are also convenient when there's a black market or unofficial exchange rate. In some places, you can exchange US-dollar traveler's checks for US dollars in cash at banks and casas de cambio, in order to stock up on cash from time to time.

Sometimes it's useful to get a relatively large amount of local currency cash in a big city, before venturing into the countryside where facilities may be limited. But if you have too much local cash, it might not be worth much at the border, even less in a neighboring country.

Of course there is a risk in carrying cash rather than traveler's checks – nobody will give you a refund for lost or stolen cash.

Traveler's Checks The safest way to carry money is in traveler's checks. American Express, Visa, Thomas Cook and Citibank are among the best known brands and, in most cases, offer instant replacement in case

of loss or theft. Checks issued by smaller banks with limited international affiliations may be difficult to cash, especially in more remote areas. To facilitate replacement in case of theft, keep a record of check numbers and the original bill of sale in a safe place. Even with proper records, replacement can take time.

Be sure to have some traveler's checks in small denominations, say US$20 or US$50. A little goes a long way in Central America, and if you carry only large denominations, you might find yourself stuck with a large amount of local currency when leaving a country.

In some countries, traveler's checks are more difficult to cash, and banks and casas de cambio charge high commissions. In Nicaragua, for example, you may find it difficult to exchange traveler's checks outside of Managua. Often there is a fixed transaction fee for cashing traveler's checks, regardless of the number and value of the checks, so it can be more economical to change large amounts.

ATMs Automatic teller machines (ATMs) are available in most cities and large towns, and they are usually a convenient, reliable, secure and economical way of getting cash in local currency when you need it. The rate of exchange is usually as good as, or better than, any bank or legal money changer. Many ATMs are connected to the Cirrus or Plus network. If you rely on ATMs, bring two cards in case one is lost or stolen and keep an emergency phone number for your bank in a separate place. Some banks that issue ATM cards charge a fee for international transactions; check the policy before leaving home.

Credit & Debit Cards A credit card is a great thing to have when traveling: It can be handy in emergencies, and it enables you to obtain cash or enjoy an unexpected luxury somewhere along the way. It can also be useful if you're asked to demonstrate 'sufficient funds' when entering a country.

American Express, Visa and MasterCard are the most widely accepted credit cards in Central America. Depending on the country, credit cards can be used to withdraw cash at automatic teller machines (ATMs). Don't expect this to be the norm, however. Machines that can perform these transactions will have network icons displayed that should match one of the icons on the back of your card. For a list of ATMs around the world that service Visa cards, go to www.visa.com; for MasterCard check out www.mastercard.com/atm.

Some travelers rely on cash advances to reduce the need for traveler's checks, but be aware that this isn't always possible. Indeed, cards will be useless in smaller Central American towns. The best strategy is to have some traveler's checks, but to use your credit card for big-ticket or splurge items. Also, inquire about transaction charges for cash advances; in some countries you may be charged a fee in addition to that charged by the card company back home. Some card companies also charge a fee (usually around 2%) for international transactions. Check the policy before you travel.

The amount you actually pay your credit card company will depend on when they bill you and the current exchange rate. If you plan to be on the road for some time, you can avoid the hassle of making monthly payments by paying a sum into your credit card account *before* you take off on your trip, so that you won't have to make any payments or incur any interest until you've used up your initial deposit. On the other hand, some cards require that you pay the full payment at the end of each month – if you're in the middle of a lengthy trip and don't settle up, you'll be hit with serious penalty fees and/or interest.

With a debit card, you can only access money you have previously deposited in your bank account, but otherwise it works like a credit card and can be used for purchases, cash advances and in ATMs.

Keep your cards separate and note the numbers of the cards and the emergency phone numbers of the card companies. Beware of credit card fraud – never let the card out of your sight. Always double-check credit- and debit-card receipts. Review the invoice when you get home and make sure that your purchases are reflected accurately on the bill.

If you run out of money while on the road, you could ask someone back home to deposit some into your credit- or debit-card account rather than sending it by bank transfer. This might save you a lot of anxiety while you're waiting for the money to show up!

International Transfers If you're out of money and don't have a credit card, you can arrange to have your bank at home send money to a local bank. In Central America, Western Union money transfers are the easiest way to go, although they are pricey. The transfer is fast (usually less than 24 hours) and convenient, but there will be a fee of around 7% to 10% for this service. For more information, call Western Union (☎ 800 833833 in the UK or 800-325 6000 in the USA).

For bank money transfers, ask your bank at home to send a draft, specifying the city, the bank and the branch of destination. Cable transfers should arrive in a few days, but you can run into complications, even with supposedly reliable banks. Mail drafts will take at least two weeks and often longer. Some banks delay releasing transferred money because they earn interest on hard currency deposits. Allow as much time as you can for bank transfers, rather than waiting until you're down to your last centavo before starting the process.

Although some countries will let you have your money in US dollars, others will only release it in local currency. Be certain before you arrange the transfer; otherwise, you could lose a fair amount of money if there's a major gap between official and unofficial exchange rates. Regulations change frequently, so ask for the latest information.

Black Market The unofficial exchange rate for the US dollar can be higher than the official bank rate because official rates do not always reflect the market value of local currency. Official rates may be artificially high for political reasons, or they may not be adjusted sufficiently for inflation, which has at times been very high in Central America. The unofficial rate is often known as the *mercado negro* (black market) or *mercado paralelo* (parallel market).

Crossing land borders, you may find that the black market is your only option for obtaining the local currency of the country you're entering and unloading your excess from the country you're leaving. Make sure you know the correct *current* rate or you could be easily ripped off. Better yet, change only enough to last you until you can get to a bank.

If you choose to participate in the black market, observe a few precautions. Be discreet, as it's illegal (though it may be tolerated). Have the exact amount handy, to avoid pulling out large wads of notes. Beware of scams and sleight-of-hand tricks: Insist on personally counting out the notes you are handed one by one, and don't hand over your dollars until satisfied you have the exact amount agreed upon. One common trick is to hand you the agreed amount, less a few pesos, so that, on counting it, you will complain that it's short. They take it back, recount it, discover the 'mistake,' top it up and then hand it back, in the process spiriting away all but one of your largest bills. For certainty, recount it yourself and don't be distracted by supposed alarms such as 'police' or 'danger.'

Security

Everyone has a preferred way to carry money. Some use money belts; others have hidden pockets inside their trousers or leg pouches with elastic bands; and others hang a pouch around their neck. Leather money belts, which appear from the outside to be ordinary belts, seem to be effective, but their capacity is limited. If you use a neck pouch, consider incorporating a length of guitar string into the strap so that it can't be cut without alerting you.

Ideally, have some traveler's checks *and* a stash of US cash *and* at least two pieces of plastic (credit or debit cards), and carry them in two or three separate places. For other suggestions on money security, see the Dangers & Annoyances section, later in this chapter.

Costs

The major factors contributing to your on-the-road costs will be comfort level, how much and by what means you move around and the cost of living in the country you visit. What one traveler considers frugal, another may find extravagant, so remember that all on-the-road costs are open to interpretation. This book focuses on the cheapest ways to travel in Central America while adhering to some minimum standards of hygiene and comfort.

Generally speaking, it will cost less (per person) if you travel as a couple or in a small group, and you will spend less if you travel slowly with long stops. It will cost more if you want comforts like air-conditioning and a private bathroom, if you want to eat in good restaurants, if you plan to do expensive tours of out of the way places or if you indulge in expensive activities like skiing or going to nightclubs.

Trains, planes and automobiles will erode your budget quickly. If you are on a tight budget but have plenty of time, take buses instead. They can be slow, uncomfortable and unpredictable, but they're also guaranteed to be the most interesting form of transportation.

The cost of living varies among the different countries in the region, and your budget should account for some fluctuation in prices. Inflation rates are now much lower than the astronomical levels some countries achieved in the 1980s, but prices can still be unpredictable. A currency devaluation means that local prices drop in relation to hard currencies like the US dollar, but normally local prices soon rise, so dollar costs soon return to previous levels (or higher). These factors make it difficult to quote prices in local currencies, but one thing is certain: If a hotel or restaurant was cheap before price increases, it's still going to be cheap compared to other hotels and restaurants after a price rise. Because prices tend to be more stable in terms of the US dollar, all prices in this guide are quoted in US dollars, based on current prices during research time. Do bear in mind, however, that these prices will change during the life of this book, so plan accordingly. Belize and Panama are the priciest of the Central American countries, but often you'll get a good value, because although prices are higher, quality is better.

Tipping & Bargaining

Practices vary a bit throughout the region, but generally whether you tip – and how much – will be up to you. The exceptions are porters, food servers in restaurants frequented by foreign tourists and guides on long excursions or tours. Some restaurants add a 10% to 20% service charge to the bill; there is no reason to tip again, and the gratuity rate should be noted on the menu.

Otherwise, anything from spare change to 10% of the bill should suffice. A small tip for taxi drivers or for the cleaning staff at your hotel is not necessary, but it's a gesture that will no doubt be much appreciated.

In Central America, probably the only things you'll have to haggle over are long-term accommodations and purchases from markets, especially craft goods, the prices of which are normally very negotiable. Although bargaining in outdoor markets is commonplace (indeed, almost expected), in supermarkets or other indoor shops you'll be expected to pay the marked price. In general, you'll find that bargaining works better in rural areas than urban.

Bargaining definitely requires a technique; indeed, it's almost an art. Of course, the object is to arrive at a price agreeable to both you and the seller. Patience, humor and an ability to speak the local language will make the process more enjoyable and productive. Techniques vary widely, but it's important to have fun and keep things in perspective: Too many travelers feel constantly besieged and victimized by scams, and as a result they tend to haggle over small change in every transaction. Remember that the people you're dealing with are trying to make a living, and although they shouldn't rip you off, you shouldn't expect to come away with something for nothing either. Approach the transaction with fairness and respect.

Aside from haggling in markets, you can sometimes bargain for better rates at hotels and guesthouses, especially at times when business is slow. From the proprietor's point of view, it's better to rent a room at a lower rate than to have it stand empty, but there's no reason to do so if another customer is likely to show up and pay the full price. Often you can get a discount off the nightly rate if you take the room for a few days or a week; ask about this at the time you check in.

Taxes

Several Central American countries have sales taxes that are added onto the price of all purchased items; see the individual country chapters for details. Some countries also have a hotel tax. In Guatemala, for example, the national sales tax is 10%, and the INGUAT (national tourist office) tax is

another 10%, adding a hefty 20% onto the price of hotel rooms. In this book, we've calculated the taxes into the room prices we quote. When you inquire about rates, be sure to ask whether the price includes tax.

POST & COMMUNICATIONS
Postal Services

The quality of postal service varies between countries, and at times it can be very uncertain business. Letters airmailed to Europe and North America typically take 14 days, but don't be surprised if they take longer. Surface mail will likely arrive long after you return from your travels, if at all. Generally, important mail and parcels should be sent by registered or certified service, and if you want something to arrive within a reasonable amount of time, be sure to specify airmail (correo aéreo or por avión). Sending parcels can be awkward, as often a customs officer must inspect the contents before a postal clerk can accept them. Note that the place for posting overseas parcels is sometimes different from the main post office. UPS, FedEx, DHL and other shipping and private courier services are available in some countries, providing an efficient but expensive alternative.

Note that there is a high rate of mail theft in Central America. This is primarily a problem with mail sent from the USA to points in Central America, presumably because many Central Americans live and work in the USA and send money home to their families, but theft can also occur with mail coming from other countries or even with mail being sent out from Central America to other parts of the world. Mail is most likely to reach its destination when it looks like there is no way it could contain money or anything else of value, as with a postcard or a fold-up aerogram.

Each country has its own postal quirks; see the Post & Communications sections in the individual country chapters for rates and other details.

Receiving Mail The simplest way of receiving mail is to have letters sent to you poste restante (general delivery), known in Latin America as lista de correos. See the Post & Communications sections in the individual country chapters for the correct way to address mail to each destination, and details on how long your mail will be held. Note that, Guatemala no longer has poste restante service.

American Express operates a mail service for clients, including those who use American Express traveler's checks. Some embassies will hold mail for their citizens, among them Australia, Canada, Germany, Israel and Switzerland. British and US embassies are very poor in this regard; letters addressed to a British embassy will be sent to the main post office.

To collect mail from a post office, American Express office or an embassy, you need to produce identification, preferably a passport. If expected correspondence does not arrive, ask the clerk to check under every possible combination of your initials, even 'M' (for Mr, Ms etc). There may be particular confusion if correspondents use your middle name, since Latin Americans use both paternal and maternal surnames for identification, with the former listed first.

Local Addresses Many Central American addresses in this book contain a post-office box number as well as a street address. A post-office box is known as an *apartado* (abbreviated to 'Ap' or 'Apto') or a *casilla de correos* ('Casilla,' 'CC').

Telephone & Fax

Traditionally, governments have administered the national and international telecommunications systems, and, traditionally, services have been wretched. Quite a few countries have now privatized their phone systems, choosing high charges over poor service, but sometimes getting both. International calls are particularly expensive, but costs vary from country to country.

Local, long-distance and international telephone, fax and telex services are available at centralized telephone offices in every city and town; these are commonly administered by the telephone company but may be private businesses. In places like Costa Rica, it's possible to place international calls from pay phones using credit cards or phone cards.

Note that it is *not* possible to make collect (reverse-charge) calls to a number of countries from Central America – collect calls will only be accepted in countries having reciprocal agreements with the

country from which you are calling; check with the telephone office. You usually can place them to the USA. It is sometimes cheaper to make a collect or credit-card call to Europe or North America than to pay for the call at the source. Often the best way is to make a quick international call and have the other party call you back (some telephone offices allow this).

Direct lines abroad, accessed via special numbers and billed to an account at home, have made international calls much simpler. There are different access numbers for each telephone company in each country – get a list from your phone company before you leave home.

For country-specific details on making phone calls, refer to the individual country chapters.

Telephone Cards There's a wide range of local and international phonecards. Lonely Planet's eKno Communication Card is aimed specifically at independent travelers and provides budget international calls, a range of messaging services, free email and travel information – for local calls, you're usually better off with a local card. eKno does not yet cover all the countries in this book, though new countries are being added all the time. You can join online at www.ekno.lonelyplanet.com. As we go to print, you can use eKno from Costa Rica and Nicaragua by dialing the following access numbers:

from	to access	alternate
Costa Rica	0800 015 0158	0800 012 0263
Nicaragua	001 800 220 1402	

Check the eKno Web site for joining and access numbers from other countries and updates on super-budget local access numbers and new features.

Email & Internet Access

Public Internet access is available in all Central American countries: Check out www.nctcafeguide.com for an up-to-date list. Many towns and cities have cybercafes or Internet cafes (very few actually serve coffee) that let you use a PC and access the Internet for somewhere between US$0.50 and US$5 per hour. These places have become something of a travelers' scene in themselves, with a bunch of backpackers huddled over keyboards, typing out messages to friends and family back home – even to other travelers on the road.

In addition to mid-range and upper-end hotels, some budget-oriented lodgings now provide economical Internet access for their guests. This book lists Internet access points in many towns and cities, and you can also ask at a tourist office or your hotel. You may also find public Internet access in post offices, libraries and universities. In places frequented by international travelers, private computer and communications offices provide services.

Email is faster, cheaper and usually more reliable than international post and much cheaper than telephone calls or faxes. The most straightforward way to send and receive email while on the road is to open a free eKno Web-based email account online at www.ekno.lonelyplanet.com, or with other providers such as Yahoo! (www.yahoo .com) and Hotmail (www.hotmail.com). You can then access your mail from anywhere in the world from any Internet-connected machine running a standard Web browser.

Traveling with a portable computer is a great way to stay in touch with life back home, but unless you know what you're doing, it's fraught with potential problems. If you plan to carry your notebook or handheld computer with you, remember that the power supply voltage in the countries you visit may vary from that at home, risking damage to your equipment. The best investment is a universal AC adapter for your appliance, which will enable you to plug it in anywhere without frying the innards; a surge protector is also a worthwhile precaution against uneven current.

Also, your PC-card modem may or may not work once you leave your home country – and you won't know for sure until you try. The safest option is to buy a reputable 'global' modem before you leave home, or buy a local PC-card modem if you're spending an extended time in any one country. Keep in mind that the telephone socket in each country you visit may be different from the one at home, so ensure that you have at least a US RJ-11 telephone adapter that works with your modem. You can almost always find an adapter that will convert from RJ-11 to the local variety. For more information on traveling with a portable computer, see www.teleadapt.com or www.warrior.com.

Before starting your trip, check to see whether your computer is covered by an international warranty or your travel insurance. Some policies specifically exclude computers or provide an upper limit of baggage insurance that would not cover the replacement cost of the computer.

INTERNET RESOURCES

The World Wide Web is a rich resource for travelers. You can research your trip, hunt down bargain airfares, book hotels, check on weather conditions and chat with locals and other travelers about the best places to visit (or avoid!).

There's no better place to start your Web explorations than the Lonely Planet Web site (www.lonelyplanet.com). Here you'll find succinct summaries on traveling to most places on earth, postcards from other travelers and the Thorn Tree bulletin board, where you can ask questions before you go or dispense advice when you get back. You can also find travel news and updates for many of our most popular guidebooks, and the subWWWay section links you to the most useful travel resources elsewhere on the Web. The site has destination profiles on all Central American countries, feedback from travelers on the road and links to other sites.

The South American Explorers site (www.samexplo.org) is also an excellent starting point for research on the Web. For background information on every country in the region, check the US CIA Factbook (www.odci.gov/cia/publications/factbook).

For travel advisories and more, visit the US State Dept site (www.travel.state.gov) or the UK Foreign & Commonwealth Office (FCO; http://193.114.50.10/travel). For up-to-date information on safety, political and economic conditions, health risks and costs for all Latin American countries, see the *Latin American Travel Advisor,* a free impartial online information service. Browse their Web site at www.amerispan.com/lata/ or request free headlines by email at LATA@pi.pro.ec.

For country profiles and links to news and information resources on Latin

America and the Caribbean, visit the Latin American Bureau's site at www.lab.org.uk.

Most of the other interesting Internet sites pertaining to Central America are devoted to specific countries within the region – see the individual country chapters for suggestions.

BOOKS

Most books are published in different editions by different publishers in different countries. As a result, a book might be a hardcover rarity in one country but readily available in paperback in another. Fortunately, bookstores and libraries can search by title or author, so your local bookstore or library is the best place to find out about the availability of the following recommendations and those that appear in individual country chapters.

Of the many books on Central America, some are available in general-interest or travel bookstores, but others, particularly older and more specialized titles, will most likely be found in university libraries. Many old titles are still available through Internet booksellers. For a list of books by Central American authors, see the Literature section in the preceding Facts about Central America chapter.

Lonely Planet

Lonely Planet publishes in-depth, regularly updated guidebooks covering several countries in Central America. Look for *Belize, Guatemala & Yucatán,* a detailed guide to the land of the Maya including the Yucatán Peninsula and Chiapas, and individual country guides including *Costa Rica, Guatemala* and *Panama.*

If you're heading north from Central America, LP publishes a comprehensive guide to Mexico, as well as a title covering the Yucatán Peninsula. If you're continuing south, *South America on a shoestring* is that continent's counterpart to this book, and LP also publishes individual guides for nearly all the countries of South America. In the Caribbean, check out LP's guides to the Bahamas, Cuba, Jamaica, Puerto Rico and the Eastern Caribbean.

Other useful titles from Lonely Planet include *Healthy Travel Central & South America,* a guide to minimizing common health risks on the road, and *Read This*

First: Central & South America, a know-before-you-go book that covers trip-planning essentials and provides maps, capsule overviews and suggested itineraries for the each of the countries in the region. Also consider LP's *Latin American Spanish phrasebook* and the *Costa Rica Spanish phrasebook.*

Guidebooks

The Footprint *Mexico & Central American Handbook* contains excellent information, though its format and style is something of an acquired taste. It also has companion volumes covering the Caribbean and South America.

The People's Guide to Mexico, by Carl Franz, has long been an invaluable, amusing resource for anyone on an extended trip. Although the book is mostly about Mexico, its coverage does venture into Central America. It doesn't provide hotel, transportation or sightseeing specifics but does give an all-around general introduction to the region.

Those driving their own vehicle down to Central America from the USA might want to check out *Driving the Pan-American Highway to Mexico and Central America,* by Raymond F and Aubrey Pritchard.

Hiking & Backpacking

If you want to get out and explore the many natural wonders of Central America, *Backpacking in Central America,* by Tim Burford, is an excellent guide with detailed information for long and short treks all over the region (with the exception of Belize).

Diving & Snorkeling

Scuba divers and snorkelers might want to pick up a copy of the diving guide from Lonely Planet's comprehensive Pisces series, *Diving & Snorkeling Roatan & Honduras' Bay Islands*. This excellent diver's companion covers some of the best diving sites in the Caribbean off Honduras' north coast. If Belize is on your itinerary, *Lonely Planet Diving & Snorkeling Belize* is also worth seeking out.

Bicycle Touring

For cycling enthusiasts, *Latin America on Bicycle,* by JP Panet, has chapters on Costa Rica, Guatemala and a few other Latin American countries. *Latin America by Bike:*

A Complete Touring Guide, by Walter Sienko, covers all the Central American countries except El Salvador.

Nature & Wildlife
Tropical Nature: Life and Death in the Rain Forests of Central and South America, by Adrian Forsyth and Ken Miyata, is an entertaining read for the layperson interested in biology, particularly of the rain forest. *A Neotropical Companion,* by John C Kricher and Mark Plotkin, is a readable book, subtitled 'An Introduction to the Animals, Plants, and Ecosystems of the New World Tropics' – which tells you all you need to know. *In the Rainforest,* by Catherine Caulfield, is another good choice; it emphasizes the problems of the loss of the rain forest. Another worthwhile title is *Life above the Jungle Floor: A Biologist Explores a Strange and Hidden Treetop World,* by Donald Perry.

Field Guides
A Field Guide to the Birds of Mexico and Central America, by LI Davis, has plenty to keep bird watchers busy. *Neotropical Rainforest Mammals: A Field Guide,* by Louise H Emmons and François Feer, provides color illustrations for identification. Piet van Ipenburg and Rob Boschhuizen's *Ecology of Tropical Rainforests: An Introduction for Eco-tourists* is a booklet packed with intriguing minutiae about sloths, bats, strangler figs and other rain-forest biota. It's available in the UK from J Forrest, 64 Belsize Park, London NW3 4EH, or in the USA from M Doolittle, 32 Amy Rd, Falls Village, CT 06031.

General History
A Brief History of Central America, by Hector Perez-Brignoli, is a short account of the region's past. John A Crow's *The Epic of Latin America* is an imposing but readable volume that covers nearly the whole of the region from Mexico to Tierra del Fuego, from prehistory to the present. George Pendle's *A History of Latin America* is a readable but very general account of the region since the European invasions.

Mayan Life & Culture
Those interested in Mayan history should find a copy of *Maya: The Riddle and Redis-* *covery of a Lost Civilization,* by Charles Gallenkamp. It's the best available general introduction to Mayan life and culture. Equally good but more scholarly is *The Maya,* by eminent Mayanist Michael D Coe. By the same author, *Breaking the Maya Code* tells the inside story of the deciphering of the ancient Mayan hieroglyphs, a great achievement of recent years.

Prehistoric Mesoamerica, by Richard EW Adams, is a scholarly survey of the history, culture and peoples of Mesoamerica. Another entertaining and academically accurate book is *A Forest of Kings: The Untold Story of the Ancient Maya,* by Linda Schele & David Freidel, a much more detailed look at Mayan history and beliefs.

Politics & Contemporary Issues
The Interhemispheric Resource Center guides (☎ 504-842 8288) are a series of paperback guides on each of the seven Central American countries, covering politics, institutions, economy, environment, international relations and so on; write PO Box 4506, Albuquerque, NM 87196, USA, or visit the Web site (www.irc-online.org) for a free catalog. The *Central America Fact Book,* by Tom Barry and Deb Preusch, examines the economic, political and military role of the USA in Central America, in addition to other issues. *Cocaine Politics: Drugs, Armies and the CIA in Central America,* by Peter Dale Scott and Jonathan Marshall, is a well-researched and documented account focusing on the contradrug connection and provides a new perspective on the US 'war on drugs.' Other interesting and relevant titles include *Inevitable Revolutions: The United States in Central America,* by Walter LaFeber; *Roots of Rebellion: Land and Hunger in Central America,* by Tom Barry; and *Turning the Tide: US Intervention in Central America and the Struggle for Peace,* by Noam Chomsky.

Travel Literature
Peter Ford's *Around the Edge* is the story of the author's travels along the Caribbean coast from Belize to Panama, on foot and by boat. From the Lonely Planet Journeys series, *Green Dreams: Travels in Central America,* by Stephen Benz, explores the myths and realities of ecotourism, taking an

entertaining and thought-provoking look at the dilemma of 'sustainable development' in the region.

The books *Incidents of Travel in Central America, Chiapas and Yucatan,* in two volumes (1969 and later reprints of the original 1841 edition), and *Incidents of Travel in Yucatan,* in two volumes (1963 and later reprints of the 1843 edition), are available in paperback at some bookstores in the region, among other places.

Sweet Waist of America, by Anthony Daniels, is a fine book telling about the author's travels, mostly throughout Guatemala but also in Honduras, El Salvador and Nicaragua.

The Old Patagonian Express: By Train through the Americas, by Paul Theroux, details the author's journey by train from a suburb of Boston all the way to Patagonia. Sadly, many of the train routes he took are no longer in operation, but it's still a great book.

So Far from God: A Journey to Central America, by Patrick Marnham, was the winner of the 1985 Thomas Cook Travel Book Award. It's an insightful and often amusing account of a leisurely meander from Texas down to Mexico City and on into Central America.

Tekkin a Waalk, by Peter Ford, is an entertaining and informative account of a trip by foot and boat along the Caribbean coast from Belize to Panama, including negotiating the Mosquitia jungle in the dying days of the Contra-Sandinista war. Historical anecdotes and personal experiences are combined with insights into the culture of Garífuna and Miskito communities.

Through the Volcanoes: A Central American Journey, by Jeremy Paxman, is the story of a journey through the region in the early 1980s. *Time among the Maya: Travels in Belize, Guatemala, and Mexico,* by Ronald Wright, describes a number of journeys among the modern Maya people and offers an interesting insight into Mayan culture.

NEWSPAPERS & MAGAZINES

The best regular source of Central American news in English is the *Miami Herald,* which publishes an overseas edition available in capital cities and a few other centers throughout Latin America. Look for the paper online at www.herald.com. The *Econ-*

omist and the *International Herald Tribune* also have good coverage of the region.

Some major US newspapers such as *USA Today,* the *Miami Herald* and the *Los Angeles Times* are sold at luxury-hotel newsstands and some big-city and airport bookshops in the region. *Newsweek* and *Time* magazines are also sometimes available, along with the *New York Times* and the *Wall Street Journal.* The better hotel shops also have good selections of European newspapers and magazines in French, German, Italian and Spanish.

The quarterly *Mundo Maya* (Maya World) contains articles in Spanish and English about the Mayan culture and natural attractions found in the Mayan-populated regions of Mexico, Belize, Honduras, Guatemala and El Salvador. The current edition of the magazine can be read online, and back issues and upcoming issues can be ordered via the Internet.

See the individual country chapters for information on the region's major Spanish-language newspapers.

Periodicals

The *Latin American Weekly Report* has about a dozen pages of the latest news from Latin America and the Caribbean. It's available by airmail subscription from Latin American Newsletters (☎ 020 7251 0012, fax 253 8193), 61 Old St, London EC1V 9HX, UK; you can also subscribe online at www.biz-lib.com/ZLAWR.html. Additionally, the organization publishes a range of more specialized newsletters on specific parts of the region.

Other useful periodicals include:

NACLA Report on the Americas (☎ 212-870 3146, fax 212-870 3305, nacla@nacla.org), North American Congress on Latin America, 475 Riverside Dr, Suite 454, New York, NY 10115, USA; published bimonthly in English
Web site: http://www.nacla.org/

South American Explorer (see Useful Organizations, later in this chapter, for details.)

The Tico Times (☎ 506-258 1558, fax 506-233 6378, ttimes@sol.racsa.co.cr) Apdo 4632, San José, Costa Rica or Dept 717, PO Box 025216, Miami, FL 33102, USA; weekly English language newspaper published in Costa Rica on Fridays; covers Costa Rica news in detail and has a page on Central America
Web site: http://www.ticotimes.net/

PHOTOGRAPHY
Film & Equipment

Film is widely available throughout the region, though if you want slide film or a particular type of print film apart from the standard Kodak, Fuji or Agfa color variety, you might do well to bring it from home. It's not uncommon to find film for sale that has an expired use-by date or that has been stored improperly so that your pictures come out looking like junk. It's best to bring a few rolls from home or stock up in the larger cities as you travel. For equipment purchases, the larger cities have specialized camera and photography stores.

Photo processing is relatively expensive, but widely available. E6 slide processing is available in larger centers, but the quality you will receive is unreliable. Have one roll processed and check the results before you hand over your whole collection. It is almost impossible to obtain Kodachrome film or have it processed in Central America. Most professionals take their film home for processing. Avoid mailing unprocessed film – postal authorities use powerful x-rays to screen parcels. Likewise, try to avoid leaving your film in your baggage at airports, as the high-powered x-ray machines can damage it. Carry-on luggage detectors shouldn't affect your film, but to be safe you can ask airport officials to hand-check your film. Be careful to keep film away from excessive sunlight and heat.

Technical Tips

The best times of day for photography are usually in the early morning or late afternoon, when natural light is softest; photos taken at midday can look harsher and flatter. If your interest is wildlife photography, early morning is when you'll spot the most birds and other wildlife.

For the best quality photos, you might consider carrying a couple of different speeds of film: ASA 100 is best for outdoor photography on bright days; ASA 200 is a good all-around speed for varying conditions; and ASA 400 is best for night or dim-light situations. For the low-light conditions of the rain and cloud forests, it's a good idea to carry a few rolls of high-speed (ASA 400) film and a flash. Kodachrome (in ASA 64 and 200) is better at capturing true reds and nearby colors of the spectrum and is often more suitable for deserts and urban areas. Kodachrome and slide film are particularly difficult to come by in Central America, so bring some along with you as needed.

Always protect camera lenses with an ultraviolet (UV) filter. In high-altitude tropical light conditions, the UV filter may not be sufficient to prevent washed-out photos; a polarizing filter can correct this problem.

Restrictions

Some tourist sites charge an additional fee for tourists with cameras. It's unwise and possibly illegal to take photos of military installations or security-sensitive places such as police stations.

Photographing People

Ask for permission before photographing individuals, particularly indigenous people. If someone is giving a public performance (such as a street musician or a dancer), or is incidental to a photograph (in a broad cityscape, for example), this is not usually necessary – but if in doubt, ask or refrain.

In some places, indigenous people may ask for a small payment in exchange for permission to photograph them. This is particularly true of the Kuna Indians of Panama; the fee is usually US$1 per photo.

TIME

All the Central American countries are six hours behind Greenwich mean time (GMT), except for Panama, which is five hours behind GMT.

ELECTRICITY

Electric current almost everywhere in Central America is 110 volts AC, 60 cycles, the same as in the USA, Canada and Mexico. Plugs are the same flat two-prong style as in these countries. It's rare to see a socket with three holes, so if your appliance has the third prong on it, you should bring an adapter.

There is, however, the occasional place in Honduras and Panama that has 220 volt current, as in Europe, Australia and New Zealand. If you use an electric appliance, always ask about the current first, just to be on the safe side. Use a surge protector with computers and other sensitive devices, as current is often very uneven.

WEIGHTS & MEASURES

All of the Central American countries use some combination of metric and imperial measures. For metric-imperial conversions, see the inside back cover of this book.

Lengths and distances are metric (meters, kilometers). The regional *vara* (0.825 meters or 33 inches) is also used in some places.

Land areas are often measured in hectares (a metric measurement), but local measurements are also used, including the *manzana* (0.7 hectares or 1.73 acres) in Honduras and the *cuadra* (about a quarter-acre) in Guatemala.

Weights are often measured in pounds, but occasionally in kilograms. Gasoline is measured in US gallons.

LAUNDRY

Many guesthouses and budget hotels have a place where you can wash your own clothes and lines where you can hang them out to dry, usually for no charge.

Otherwise, most cities have laundries and dry-cleaning shops where you can drop off your clothes and have them cleaned. Often you can have your laundry back in a day; dry cleaning usually takes at least overnight. Locations of convenient laundries are given in this guidebook for each city that has them.

TOILETS

Toilets are generally the same in Central America as in other places. However, the plumbing leaves something to be desired. Nowhere in the region should you deposit toilet paper or anything else in the toilet bowl unless a posted sign specifically says it's OK to do so. Wastebaskets are generally provided for discarding used toilet paper; if there is not a wastebasket provided, people generally drop the toilet paper on the floor near the base of the toilet.

Never assume that because there is a toilet there is paper, since usually this isn't the case. Always carry toilet paper with you when traveling. Occasionally, a public toilet will have an attendant offering paper for a small tip. Most towns and cities have public toilets but they're often few and far between; most bars and restaurants will allow you to use their facilities if you ask politely.

HEALTH

Travel health depends on your predeparture preparations, your daily health care while traveling and how you handle any medical problem that does develop. Although the potential dangers can seem quite frightening, few travelers experience anything more serious than an upset stomach.

Predeparture Planning

Health Insurance Make sure that you have adequate health insurance. If you have health insurance at home, contact your insurer to determine whether you'll be covered by your policy while traveling outside your home country. See Travel Insurance under Visas & Documents, earlier in this chapter.

Immunizations Plan ahead for getting your vaccinations – some of them require more than one injection, and some vaccinations should not be given together. It is recommended you seek medical advice at least six weeks before traveling. Note that some vaccinations should not be given during pregnancy or to people with allergies – discuss with your doctor. The risk of disease is often greater for children and pregnant women.

The number of vaccines subject to international health regulations has been dramatically reduced during the last decade; currently yellow fever is the only vaccine subject to international health regulations. Proof of immunization against yellow fever is a statutory requirement for entry into most Latin American countries if you are traveling from an infected country in Africa or South America. At press time, the Centers for Disease Control and Prevention recommended yellow fever vaccinations for visitors to Panama planning to travel outside urban areas.

A number of immunizations are recommended for travel in various parts of Central America for your own protection, even though not required by law. The risk for malaria exists all year in the rural lowlands and in some urban areas of the region; prevent infection by taking prescription antimalarial drugs and protecting yourself against mosquito bites (see Malaria, later in this section). Most travelers from developed countries will have been immunized against various diseases during childhood, but your doctor may still recommend booster shots against diphtheria-tetanus, measles or polio.

All vaccinations should be recorded in an International Health Certificate, a yellow booklet available from physicians or government health departments (see Visas & Documents, earlier in this chapter).

Yellow Fever Yellow-fever vaccination is a legal requirement for entry into many countries when a visitor is coming from an infected area. Protection lasts 10 years and is recommended for most of the lowland tropical areas of South America, where the disease is endemic. Not many doctors stock this vaccine, so you may have to go to a special yellow-fever vaccination center. Vaccination poses some risk during pregnancy, but if you must travel to a high-risk area, it is advisable. People allergic to eggs may not be able to have yellow-fever vaccination.

Hepatitis A The hepatitis A vaccine (eg, Avaxim, Havrix 1440 or VAQTA) provides long-term immunity (possibly for more than 10 years) after an initial injection and a booster at six to 12 months. Alternatively, an injection of gamma globulin can provide short-term protection against hepatitis A – two to six months, depending on the dose given. It is not a vaccine, but is a ready-made antibody collected from blood donations. It is reasonably effective and, unlike the vaccine, it is protective immediately, but because it is a blood product, there are current concerns about its long-term safety.

Hepatitis B Travelers who should consider a hepatitis B vaccination include health workers, those likely to have sexual contacts, and those visiting countries with many hep B carriers or countries where blood supplies may not be adequately screened. Vaccination involves three injections, the quickest course being over three weeks with a booster at 12 months. A combined hepatitis A and hepatitis B vaccine called Twinrix is also available. Three injections over a six-month period are required, the first two providing substantial protection against hepatitis A.

Malaria This serious disease is spread by mosquito bites and is widespread in tropical South America, where drug-resistant strains of the disease are prevalent. In Central America, main areas of risk are the rural lowlands, along the coasts, in rain forest areas and even in some urban parts of the region; areas above 2500m are safe. In malarial areas, it is imperative to protect yourself against mosquito bites and to take antimalarial drugs. These drugs do not prevent you from becoming infected, but kill the malaria parasites during their development and reduce the risk of serious illness or death. Antimalarial

drugs are not vaccinations as such, but it is important to start taking them up to a week before entering a malarial area. In most parts of Central America, chloroquine is considered the antimalarial of choice. Chloroquine is quite safe for general use; side effects are minimal and it can be taken by pregnant women. However, chloroquine-resistant strains of malaria have been reported in three provinces of Panama: Bocas del Toro in the west and Darién and San Blas in the east. Expert advice on medication should be sought, as there are many factors to consider, including the area to be visited, the risk of exposure to malaria-carrying mosquitoes, the side effects of medication, your medical history and whether you are a child or adult, or pregnant. Travelers to isolated areas in high-risk countries may wish to carry a treatment dose of medication for use if symptoms occur. (See Insect-Borne Diseases, later in this section, for more information.)

Diphtheria & Tetanus Vaccinations for these two diseases are usually combined and are recommended for everyone. After an initial course of three injections (usually given in childhood), boosters are necessary every 10 years.

Poliomyelitis A booster of either the oral or injected polio vaccine is required every 10 years to maintain immunity. More frequent boosters may be needed in tropical areas. Polio is a very serious, easily transmitted disease that still occurs in Latin America.

Typhoid This is an important vaccination to have in areas where hygiene is a problem, recommended if you are traveling for long periods in rural, tropical areas. It is available either as an injection or as oral capsules.

Cholera This disease is usually transmitted by water and is most likely in the presence of unsanitary conditions. Vaccination gives poor protection, lasts only six months, has various side effects and is contraindicated in pregnancy. Though not generally recommended, and not required by international law, cholera vaccination may still be required at some Central American border crossings if you're coming from an infected area.

Meningococcal Meningitis Outbreaks of this disease occur periodically in Latin America. Vaccination is not generally recommended except in special circumstances. The vaccine is not recommended for children younger than two years old.

Rabies Pretravel rabies vaccination requires three injections over 21 to 28 days. It should be considered by those who will spend a month or longer in Latin America, especially if they are handling animals, cycling, caving or traveling to remote areas. Children may not report a bite and are therefore at greater risk than adults. If a vaccinated person is bitten or scratched by an animal, he or she will require two booster injections of vaccine. Those not vaccinated require more.

Tuberculosis TB risk to travelers is usually very low, but the disease is becoming more common in some Latin American cities. The main risk is to those living closely with local people in infected areas for extended periods. Vaccination against TB (BCG) is recommended for children and young adults living in these areas for three months or more. Most healthy adults do not develop symptoms, so a skin test is necessary to determine whether exposure has occurred.

Travel Health Guides If you are planning to be away or traveling in remote areas for a long period of time, you may want to consider taking a more detailed health guide.

Healthy Travel Central & South America, by Dr Isabelle Young (Lonely Planet Publications), is an easy-to-carry guide offering tips on predeparture planning and has everything you'll need to stay healthy on the road.

CDC's Complete Guide to Healthy Travel (Open Road Publishing) contains the US Centers for Disease Control and Prevention's recommendations for international travel.

Staying Healthy in Asia, Africa & Latin America, by Dirk Schroeder (Moon Publications), is one of the best all-around guides to carry; it's compact, detailed and well organized.

Travelers' Health, by Dr Richard Dawood (Oxford University Press and Random House), is comprehensive, easy to read, authoritative and highly recommended, although it's rather large to lug around.

Where There Is No Doctor, by David Werner, is a very detailed guide intended for someone such as a Peace Corps volunteer who is planning to work in an underdeveloped country.

Travel with Children, by Maureen Wheeler (Lonely Planet Publications), includes advice on travel health for younger children.

There are also a number of travel health sites on the Internet. From the Lonely Planet Web site (www.lonelyplanet.com) there are links to the World Health Organization and The Centers for Disease Control and Prevention.

Other Preparations Make sure you're healthy before you start traveling. If you are embarking on a long trip, make sure your teeth are OK; there are lots of places where a visit to the dentist would be the last thing you'd want.

Medical Kit Check List

Following is a list of items you should consider including in your medical kit – consult your pharmacist for brands available in your country.

- ❑ **Aspirin or paracetamol** (acetaminophen in the USA) – for pain or fever
- ❑ **Antihistamine** – for allergies, eg, hay fever; to ease the itch from insect bites or stings; and to prevent motion sickness
- ❑ **Cold and flu tablets, throat lozenges and nasal decongestant**
- ❑ **Multivitamins** – consider taking for long trips, when dietary vitamin intake may be inadequate
- ❑ **Antibiotics** – consider including these if you're traveling well off the beaten track; see your doctor, as they must be prescribed, and carry the prescription with you
- ❑ **Loperamide or diphenoxylate** –'blockers' for diarrhea
- ❑ **Prochlorperazine or metaclopramide** – for nausea and vomiting
- ❑ **Rehydration mixture** – to prevent dehydration, which may occur, for example, during bouts of diarrhea; particularly important when traveling with children
- ❑ **Insect repellent, sunscreen, lip balm and eye drops**
- ❑ **Calamine lotion, sting relief spray or aloe vera** – to ease irritation from sunburn and insect bites or stings
- ❑ **Antifungal cream or powder** – for fungal skin infections and thrush
- ❑ **Antiseptic (such as povidone-iodine)** – for cuts and grazes
- ❑ **Bandages, Band-Aids (plasters) and other wound dressings**
- ❑ **Water purification tablets or iodine**
- ❑ **Scissors, tweezers and a thermometer** – note that mercury thermometers are prohibited by airlines
- ❑ **Sterile kit** – in case you need injections in a country with medical hygiene problems, discuss with your doctor

If you wear glasses, take a spare pair and your prescription. Losing your glasses can be a real problem, although in many places you can get new spectacles made up quickly, cheaply and competently.

If you require a particular medication, take an adequate supply, as it may not be available locally. Take the prescription or, better still, part of the packaging that shows the generic rather than the brand name (which may not be locally available), as it will make getting refills easier. It's a good idea to have a legible prescription or letter from your doctor to show you legally use the medication.

Basic Rules

Care in what you eat and drink is the most important health rule. It's common to experience stomach upsets, especially in the first couple of weeks, but these are usually minor. Don't become paranoid; trying the local food is part of the experience of travel.

Water Be very careful about the water you drink, and this includes ice. If you don't know for certain that the water (or the ice) is safe, assume the worst. Bottled water is widely available, although in some places bottles may be refilled with tap water – make sure the bottle has an intact seal. Some hotels have a container of filtered water available, but this cannot be relied on. Take care with fruit juice, particularly if water may have been added. Milk should be treated with suspicion, as it is often unpasteurized, though boiled milk is fine if it is kept hygienically. Tea or coffee should be OK if the water has been boiled.

The simplest method of water purification is to boil it thoroughly. At high altitudes, water boils at a lower temperature, so germs are less likely to be killed. Boil it for longer in these environments.

Consider bringing a water filter, of which there are two main kinds. Total filters take out all parasites, bacteria and viruses and make water safe to drink. They are often expensive, but can they be more cost effective than buying bottled water. Simple filters (which can even be a nylon mesh bag) take out dirt and larger foreign bodies from the water so that chemical solutions work much more effectively; if water is dirty, chemical solutions may not work at all. Simple filtering will not remove all dangerous organisms, so the water should also be boiled or treated chemically. Chlorine tablets (Puritabs, Steritabs or other brand names) will kill many pathogens, but not some parasites like giardia and amoebic cysts. Iodine is more effective in purifying water and is available in tablet form (such as Potable Aqua). Follow the directions carefully and remember that too much iodine can be harmful.

Food Vegetables and fruit should be washed with purified water or peeled when possible. Beware of ice cream that is sold in the street or anywhere it might have been melted and refrozen. Thoroughly cooked food is safest, but not if it has been left to cool or if it has been reheated. Raw shellfish such as mussels, oysters and clams should be avoided, as should undercooked meat, particularly in the form of mince. Steaming does not make shellfish safe for eating.

If a place looks clean and well run and the vendor also looks clean and healthy, then the food is probably safe. In general, places that are packed with travelers or locals will be fine, but empty restaurants are questionable. The food in busy restaurants is generally cooked and eaten quickly with little standing around and is probably not reheated.

Nutrition If your food is poor or limited in availability, if you're traveling hard and fast and therefore missing meals or if you simply lose your appetite, you can soon start to lose weight and place your health at risk. Make sure your diet is well balanced. Cooked eggs, beans and nuts are all safe ways to get protein. Fruit you can peel (bananas, oranges or mandarins, for example) is usually safe and a good source of vitamins (melons can harbor bacteria in their flesh and are best avoided). Try to eat plenty of grains (including rice) and bread. Food is generally safer if it is cooked well, but overcooked food loses much of its nutritional value. If your diet isn't well balanced or your food intake is insufficient, it's a good idea to take vitamin and iron pills.

In hot climates make sure you drink enough water – don't rely on feeling thirsty to indicate when you should drink. Not needing to urinate is a danger sign, as is very dark yellow urine. Always carry a water bottle with you on long trips. Excessive sweating can lead to loss of salt, and muscle cramping can result. Salt tablets are not a good idea as a preventative, but in places where salt is not used much, adding salt to food can help.

Everyday Health Normal body temperature is 37°C (98.6°F); more than 2°C (4°F) higher indicates a 'high' fever. The normal adult pulse rate is 60 to 80 per minute (children 80 to 100, babies 100 to 140). You should know how to take a temperature and a pulse rate. As a general rule the pulse increases about 20 beats per minute for each degree Celsius rise in fever.

Respiration (breathing) rate is also an indicator of illness. Count the number of breaths per minute: Between 12 and 20 is normal for adults and older children (up to 30 for younger children, 40 for babies). People with a high fever or serious respiratory illness (like pneumonia) breathe more quickly than normal. More than 40 shallow breaths per minute usually indicates pneumonia.

Illnesses ranging from the common cold to cholera have been proven to be easily transmitted through physical contact. Try not to put your hand to your mouth, and wash your hands before meals. Clean your teeth with purified water rather than water straight from the tap. Avoid climatic extremes: Keep out of the sun when it's hot, dress warmly when it's cold. Avoid potential diseases by dressing sensibly. You can get worm infections by walking barefoot. Avoid insect bites by covering bare skin when insects are around, by screening windows or beds and by using insect repellents. Seek local advice: Heed warnings about the presence of jellyfish, piranhas or schistosomiasis. In situations where there is no information, discretion is the better choice.

Medical Problems & Treatment

Self-diagnosis and treatment can be risky, so you should always seek medical help. Although we do give drug dosages in this section, they are for emergency use only. Correct diagnosis is vital. Generic names are given here for medications – check with a pharmacist for brands available locally.

An embassy, consulate or any well-run hotel can usually recommend a good place to go for medical advice. In some places standards of medical attention are so low that for some ailments the best advice is to get on a plane and go somewhere else.

Antibiotics should ideally be administered only under medical supervision. Take only the recommended dose at the prescribed intervals and use the whole course, even if the illness seems to be cured earlier. Stop immediately if there are any serious reactions, and don't use the antibiotic at all if you are unsure that you have the correct one. If you are allergic to commonly prescribed antibiotics, such as penicillin or sulfa drugs, carry this information (eg, on a bracelet) when traveling.

Environmental Hazards

Sunburn In the tropics, the desert or at high altitude you can get sunburned surprisingly quickly, even through cloud cover. Use a sunscreen, hat and barrier cream for your nose and lips. Calamine lotion and aloe vera gel are good for treating mild sunburn. Protect your eyes with good-quality sunglasses, particularly if you will be near water, sand or snow.

Prickly Heat Excessive perspiration trapped under the skin can cause an itchy rash known as prickly heat. It usually strikes people who have just arrived in a hot climate and whose pores have not yet opened sufficiently to cope with greater sweating. Keeping cool, bathing often, using a mild talcum powder or even resorting to air-conditioning may help until you can acclimatize.

Heat Exhaustion Dehydration or salt deficiency can cause heat exhaustion. Take time to acclimatize to high temperatures by making sure that you get sufficient liquids. Wear loose clothing and a broad-brimmed hat, and do not do anything too physically demanding.

Salt deficiency is characterized by fatigue, lethargy, headaches, giddiness and muscle cramps, and in this case salt tablets may help. Vomiting or diarrhea can deplete your liquid and salt levels.

Heat Stroke This serious – sometimes fatal – condition can occur if the body's heat-regulating mechanism breaks down and the body temperature rises to dangerous levels. Long, continuous periods of exposure to high temperatures can leave you vulnerable to heat stroke. Avoid excessive alcohol or strenuous activity when you first arrive in a hot climate.

The symptoms of heat stroke are feeling unwell, not sweating very much or not at all and high body temperature (39°C to 41°C, 102°F to 106°F). Skin becomes flushed and red where sweating has ceased. Severe, throbbing headaches and lack of coordination will also occur, and the sufferer may be confused or aggressive. Eventually the victim will become delirious or convulse. Hospitalization is essential, but meanwhile get the victim out of the sun, remove their clothing, cover them with a wet sheet or towel and then fan the victim continually.

Hypothermia Too much cold is just as dangerous as too much heat, as it may cause hypothermia. You're more likely to encounter too much heat than too much cold in Central America, but at higher elevations temperatures can be much chillier than you'd expect. While the lowlands are baking, nighttime temperatures at high altitudes can drop below freezing. The effects of low temperatures are exacerbated by wind, rain or dampness. If you are trekking at high altitudes or simply taking a long bus trip over mountains, particularly at night, be prepared.

Hypothermia occurs when the body loses heat faster than it can produce it and the core temperature of the body falls. It is surprisingly easy to progress from very cold to dangerously cold due to a combination of wind, wet clothing, fatigue and hunger, even if the air temperature is above freezing. It is best to dress in layers; silk, wool and some of the new artificial fibers are all good insulating materials. A hat is important, as a lot of heat is lost through the head. A strong, waterproof outer layer is essential because keeping dry is vital. Carry basic supplies, including food containing simple sugars, to generate heat quickly, and lots of drinks. A space blanket is something all travelers in cold environments should carry.

Symptoms of hypothermia are exhaustion, numb skin (particularly toes and fingers), shivering, slurred speech, irrational or violent behavior, lethargy, stumbling, dizzy spells, muscle cramps and violent bursts of energy. Irrationality may take the form of sufferers claiming they are warm and then trying to take off their clothes.

To treat mild hypothermia, first get the person out of the wind or rain, remove their clothing if it's wet and replace it with dry, warm clothing. Give them hot liquids – no alcohol – and some high-calorie, easily digestible food. Do not rub victims; instead, allow them to slowly warm themselves. This should be enough to treat the early stages of hypothermia. The early recognition and treatment of mild hypothermia is the only way to prevent severe hypothermia, which is a critical condition.

Fungal Infections These occur more commonly in hot weather and are usually found on the scalp, between the toes or fingers, in the groin and on the body (ringworm). You get ringworm (a fungal infection, not a worm) from infected animals or other people. Moisture encourages these infections to flourish.

To prevent fungal infections wear loose, comfortable clothes, avoid artificial fibers, wash frequently and dry carefully. If you do get an infection, wash the infected area at least daily with a disinfectant or medicated soap and water, and rinse and dry well. Apply an antifungal cream or powder like tolnifate (Tinaderm). Try to expose the infected area to air or sunlight as much as possible and wash all towels and underwear often in hot water and then let them dry in the sun.

Altitude Sickness At altitudes above about 2500m, the lack of oxygen affects most people to some extent until they become acclimatized. The effect may be mild or severe and occurs because less oxygen reaches the muscles and the brain at high altitude, requiring the heart and lungs to compensate by working harder.

Symptoms of acute mountain sickness (AMS) usually develop during the first 24 hours at altitude but may be delayed up to three weeks. Mild symptoms include headache, lethargy, dizziness, difficulty sleeping and loss of appetite. AMS may become more severe without warning and can be fatal. Severe symptoms include breathlessness, a dry, irritative cough (which may progress to the production of pink, frothy sputum), severe headache, lack of coordina-

tion and balance, confusion, irrational behavior, vomiting, drowsiness and uncon-
sciousness. There is no hard-and-fast rule as
to what is too high: AMS has been fatal at
3000m, although 3500 to 4500m is the usual
range at which AMS becomes dangerous.

Treat mild symptoms by resting at the
same altitude until recovery, usually a day
or two. Paracetamol or aspirin can be taken
for headaches. If symptoms persist or
become worse, however, *immediate descent
is necessary*; even 500m can help. Drug
treatments should never be used to avoid
descent or to enable further ascent.

To prevent acute mountain sickness, note
the following:

- Ascend slowly – have frequent rest days,
  spending two to three nights at each rise of
  1000m. If you reach a high altitude by
  trekking, acclimatization takes place gradually,
  and you are less likely to be affected than if
  you fly directly to high altitude.
- If possible, sleep at a lower altitude than the
  greatest height reached during the day. Once
  above 3000m, care should be taken not to
  increase the sleeping altitude by more than
  300m per day.
- Drink extra fluids. The mountain air is dry and
  cold, and moisture is lost as you breathe.
  Evaporation of sweat may occur unnoticed
  and result in dehydration.
- Eat light, high-carbohydrate meals for more
  energy.
- Avoid alcohol as it may increase the risk of
  dehydration.
- Avoid sedatives.

Jet Lag This is experienced when a person
travels by air across more than three time
zones (each time zone usually represents a
time difference of one hour). It occurs
because many of the functions of the
human body (such as temperature, pulse
rate and emptying of the bladder and
bowels) are regulated by internal 24-hour
cycles. When we travel long distances
rapidly, our bodies take time to adjust to
the 'new time' of our destination, and we
may experience fatigue, disorientation, in-
somnia, anxiety, impaired concentration
and loss of appetite. These effects will
usually be gone within three days of arrival,
but to minimize the impact of jet lag, consider doing the following:

- Rest for a couple of days prior to departure.
- Try to select flight schedules that minimize
  sleep deprivation; arriving late in the day
  means you can go to sleep soon after you
  arrive. For very long flights, try to organize a
  stopover.
- Avoid excessive eating (which bloats the
  stomach) and alcohol (which causes
  dehydration) during the flight. Instead, drink
  plenty of noncarbonated, nonalcoholic drinks,
  such as fruit juice or water.
- Avoid smoking.
- Make yourself comfortable by wearing loose-
  fitting clothes and perhaps bringing an eye
  mask and earplugs to help you sleep.
- Try to sleep at the appropriate time for the
  time zone of your destination.

Motion Sickness Eating lightly before and
during a trip will reduce the chances of
motion sickness. If you are prone to motion
sickness, try to find a place that minimizes
movement – near the wing on aircraft, close
to midship on boats, near the center on buses.
Fresh air usually helps; reading and cigarette
smoke don't. Commercial motion-sickness
preparations, which can cause drowsiness,
have to be taken before the trip commences.
Ginger (available in capsule form) and pep-
permint (including mint-flavored sweets) are
believed to be natural preventatives.

Infectious Diseases

Diarrhea Simple things like a change of
water, food or climate can all cause a mild
bout of diarrhea, but a few rushed toilet
trips with no other symptoms are not indicative of a major problem.

Dehydration is the main danger with any
diarrhea, particularly in children or the
elderly. Under all circumstances, *fluid replacement* (at least equal to the volume
being lost) is the most important thing to remember. Weak black tea with a little sugar,
soda water or soft drinks allowed to go flat
and diluted 50% with clean water are all
good. With severe diarrhea, a rehydrating
solution is preferable to replace minerals
and salts lost. Commercially available oral
rehydration salts (ORS) are very useful; add
them to boiled or bottled water. In an emergency you can make up a solution of six tea-
spoons of sugar and a half-teaspoon of salt
to a liter of boiled or bottled water. You
need to drink at least the same volume of

fluid that you are losing in bowel movements and vomiting. Urine is the best guide to the adequacy of replacement – if you have small amounts of concentrated urine, you need to drink more. Keep drinking small amounts often. Stick to a bland diet as you recover.

Lomotil or Imodium can be used to bring relief from the symptoms, although they do not actually cure the problem. Only use these drugs if you do not have access to toilets – if you *must* travel. For children younger than 12, Lomotil and Imodium are not recommended. Do not use these drugs if the person has a high fever or is severely dehydrated.

In certain situations, antibiotics may be required: diarrhea with blood or mucus (dysentery), any fever, watery diarrhea with fever and lethargy, persistent diarrhea not improving after 48 hours and severe diarrhea. In these situations, gut-paralyzing drugs like Imodium or Lomotil should be avoided.

A stool test is necessary to diagnose which kind of dysentery you have, so you should seek medical help urgently. Where this is not possible, the recommended drugs for dysentery are norfloxacin, 400mg twice daily for three days, or ciprofloxacin, 500mg twice daily for five days. These are not recommended for children or pregnant women. The drug of choice for children would be co-trimoxazole (Bactrim, Septrin, Resprim), with dosage dependent on weight. A five-day course is given. Ampicillin or amoxycillin may be given in pregnancy, but medical care is necessary.

Another common cause of persistent diarrhea in travelers is amoebic dysentery, caused by the protozoan *Entamoeba histolytica* and characterized by a gradual onset of low-grade diarrhea, often with blood and mucus. Cramping abdominal pain and vomiting are less likely than in other types of diarrhea, and fever may not be present. It will persist until treated and can recur and cause other health problems.

Diarrhea may also be a symptom of giardiasis, which is caused by a common parasite, *Giardia lamblia*. Symptoms include stomach cramps, nausea, a bloated stomach, watery, foul-smelling diarrhea and frequent gas. Giardiasis can appear several weeks after you have been exposed to the parasite.

The symptoms may disappear for a few days and then return; this can go on for several weeks.

You should seek medical advice if you think you have giardiasis or amoebic dysentery, but where this is not possible, tinidazole or metronidazole are the drugs that are recommended. Treatment is a 2g single dose of tinidazole (known as Fasigyn) or 250mg of metronidazole (Flagyl) three times daily for five to 10 days.

Cholera This is the worst of the watery diarrheas and medical help should be sought. Cholera is caused by bacteria and is transmitted via contaminated food (especially seafood, including crustaceans and shellfish that get infected via sewage) and water. Outbreaks of cholera are generally widely reported, so avoid such problem areas. *Fluid replacement is the most important treatment* – the risk of dehydration is severe, as you may lose up to 20 liters of fluid per day. If there is a delay in getting to a hospital then begin taking tetracycline. The adult dose is 250mg, four times daily. It is not recommended for children under nine years or for pregnant women. Tetracycline may help shorten the illness, but adequate fluids are required.

Although cholera is generally a low risk for most travelers, it is likely to be a problem in Central America for the foreseeable future. Elimination of cholera depends on major improvements in the supply of drinking water and sewage treatment systems.

Hepatitis Hepatitis A is transmitted by contaminated food and drinking water. You should seek medical advice, but there is not much you can do apart from resting, drinking lots of fluids, eating lightly and avoiding fatty foods. Hepatitis E is transmitted in the same way as hepatitis A; it can be particularly serious in pregnant women.

There are almost 300 million chronic carriers of hepatitis B in the world. It is spread through contact with infected blood, blood products or body fluids, for example through sexual contact, unsterilized needles and blood transfusions, or contact with blood via small breaks in the skin. Getting tattoos or body piercings, or even shaving with contaminated equipment can be a risk.

The symptoms of hepatitis B may be more severe than type A, and the disease can lead to long-term problems, such as chronic liver damage, liver cancer or a long-term carrier state. Hepatitis C and D are spread in the same way as hepatitis B and can also lead to long-term complications.

There are vaccines against hepatitis A and B, but there are currently no vaccines against other types of hepatitis. Following the basic rules about food and water (hepatitis A and E) and avoiding risk situations (hepatitis B, C and D) are important preventative measures.

Typhoid Typhoid fever is a dangerous gut infection caused by contaminated water and food. Medical help must be sought.

In typhoid's early stages, sufferers may feel they have a bad cold or flu on the way, as early symptoms are a headache, body aches and a fever that rises a little each day until it is around 40°C (104°F) or more. The victim's pulse is often slow relative to the degree of fever present – unlike a normal fever where pulse increases. There may also be vomiting, abdominal pain, diarrhea or constipation.

In the second week, the high fever and slow pulse continue, and a few pink spots may appear on the body; trembling, delirium, weakness, weight loss and dehydration may occur. Complications such as pneumonia, perforated bowel or meningitis may occur.

The fever should be treated by keeping the victim cool and giving them fluids (watch for dehydration). A dosage of 750mg ciprofloxacin twice a day for 10 days is good for adults.

Chloramphenicol is recommended in many countries. The adult dosage is two 250mg capsules, four times per day. Children between eight and 12 years old should have half the adult dose, younger children one-third the adult dose.

Meningococcal Meningitis This rare but very serious disease attacks the brain and can be fatal. A scattered, blotchy rash, fever, severe headache, sensitivity to light and neck stiffness that prevents forward bending of the head are the first symptoms. Death can occur within a few hours, so immediate treatment is important.

The treatment is large doses of penicillin given directly into the bloodstream, or, if that is not possible, intramuscularly (in the buttocks). Vaccination offers good protection for more than a year, but you should also check for reports of current epidemics.

Tuberculosis TB is a bacterial infection usually transmitted from person to person by coughing or spitting, but it can be transmitted through consumption of unpasteurized milk. Milk that has been boiled is safe to drink, and the souring of milk to make yogurt or cheese also kills the bacilli. Travelers are usually not at great risk, as close household contact with the infected person is usually required before the disease is passed on.

HIV & AIDS HIV (human immunodeficiency virus), develops into AIDS (acquired immune deficiency syndrome), which is a fatal disease. Called SIDA in Spanish, this is still a growing problem in Central America. Any exposure to blood, blood products or body fluids may put the individual at risk. HIV can be spread through infected blood transfusions; most developing countries cannot afford to screen blood for transfusions properly. HIV can also be transmitted through sexual contact or dirty needles – vaccinations, acupuncture, tattooing and body piercing can be potentially as dangerous as intravenous drug use. If you do need an injection, it may be a good idea to buy a new syringe from a pharmacy and ask the doctor to use it. If you plan to engage in sexual activity, the most effective preventative is to practice safe sex using condoms.

Fear of HIV infection should never preclude the treatment of a serious medical condition.

Sexually Transmitted Diseases Gonorrhea, herpes and syphilis are among these diseases; sores, blisters or rashes around the genitals, discharges or pain when urinating are common symptoms. In some STDs, such as wart virus or chlamydia, symptoms may be less marked or not observed at all, especially in women. Syphilis symptoms eventually disappear completely, but the disease continues and can cause severe problems in later years. Although abstinence from sexual contact is the only 100% effective prevention, using condoms can also be effective. Gonorrhea and syphilis are treated with antibiotics. Different sexually transmitted diseases each require specific antibiotics. There is no cure for herpes or AIDS.

Insect-Borne Diseases

Malaria If you are traveling in endemic areas, it is extremely important to avoid mosquito bites and to take antimalaria tablets (see Immunizations, earlier in this section). Symptoms range from fever, chills and sweating, headache, diarrhea and abdominal pains, to a vague feeling of ill health. Seek medical help immediately if malaria is suspected. Without treatment, malaria can rapidly become more serious and can be fatal.

If medical care is not available, antimalaria tablets can be used for treatment. You need to use a tablet that is different from the one you were taking when you contracted malaria. The treatment dosages are mefloquine (two 250mg tablets and a further two six hours later), Fansidar (a single dose of three tablets). If you were previously taking mefloquine (Lariam) and cannot obtain Fansidar, alternatives are Malarone (atovaquone-proguanil; four tablets once daily for three days), halofantrine (three doses of two 250mg tablets every six hours) or quinine sulfate (600mg every six hours). If used with mefloquine, there is a greater risk of side effects with these dosages than in normal use, so medical advice is preferable. Halofantrine is no longer recommended by the World Health Organization (WHO) as emergency standby treatment because of side effects and should only be used if no other drugs are available.

Because antimalaria tablets are not 100% effective, the primary preventative is protection from mosquito bites. The mosquitoes that transmit malaria bite from dusk to dawn, but precautions should be taken at all times:

- wear light-colored clothing
- wear long pants and long-sleeve shirts
- use mosquito repellents containing the compound DEET on exposed areas (prolonged overuse of DEET may be harmful, especially to children, but its use is considered preferable to being bitten by disease-transmitting mosquitoes)
- avoid highly scented perfumes or deodorants
- use a mosquito net impregnated with mosquito repellent (permethrin) – it may be worth taking your own
- impregnate clothes with permethrin to effectively deter mosquitoes and other insects

Malaria can be diagnosed by a simple blood test. Seek examination immediately if there is any suggestion of malaria. Some species of the parasite may lie dormant in the liver, but they can be eradicated using a specific medication. Malaria is curable, as long as the traveler seeks medical help when symptoms occur.

Dengue Fever This serious disease is a rapidly growing problem in tropical Latin America. The *Aedes aegypti* mosquito, which transmits the dengue virus, is most active during the day and is found mainly in urban areas, in and around human dwellings.

Signs and symptoms of dengue fever include a sudden onset of high fever, headache, joint and muscle pains, nausea and vomiting. A rash of small red spots sometimes appears three to four days after the onset of fever. In the early phase, dengue may be mistaken for other diseases, including malaria and influenza. Later it can progress to the potentially fatal dengue hemorrhagic fever (DHF), a severe illness characterized by heavy bleeding. Recovery even from simple dengue fever may be prolonged, with tiredness lasting for several weeks.

If you think you may be infected, seek medical attention quickly. A blood test can exclude malaria and indicate the possibility of dengue fever, for which there is no specific treatment. Aspirin should be avoided, as it increases the risk of hemorrhaging.

There is no vaccine against dengue fever. The best prevention is to avoid mosquito bites at all times, as for malaria.

Yellow Fever This is a viral disease transmitted to humans by mosquitoes; the initial symptoms are fever, headache, abdominal pain and vomiting. Seek medical care urgently and drink lots of fluids. Vaccination against yellow fever is a requirement for travel to and from many parts of South America.

Chagas' Disease This parasitic disease is transmitted by the reduvid bug, locally called the *vinchuca* or *barbeiro*. It infests crevices and palm fronds, often lives in thatched roofs and comes out to feed at night. A hard, violet-colored swelling appears at the site of the bite in about a week. The disease is treatable in the early stages, and the body usually overcomes the disease unaided, but if it continues it can eventually be fatal. Avoid sleeping in thatched-roof huts, or use a mosquito net, insecticides and repellents and check for hidden insects, especially in bedding.

Typhus Spread by ticks, mites or lice, typhus begins with fever, chills, headache and muscle pains, followed a few days later by a body rash. There is often a large painful sore at the site of the bite, and nearby lymph nodes are swollen and painful. Typhus can be treated under medical supervision. Seek local advice about areas where ticks pose a danger and always check your skin (including scalp and hair) carefully for ticks after walking in a danger area such as a tropical forest. A strong insect repellent can help, and serious walkers in tick areas should consider having their boots and trousers impregnated with benzyl benzoate and dibutyl phthalate.

Cuts, Bites & Stings

Cuts & Scratches If you're traveling in areas with poor environmental cleanliness and a lack of clean water, there's a high risk of infection, especially in hot, humid climates. Carry a few antiseptic wipes with you to use as an immediate measure, especially if no water is available. A small wound can be cleaned with an antiseptic wipe (but remember to wipe across the wound just once). Deep or dirty wounds need to be cleaned thoroughly.

Coral cuts are notoriously slow to heal, and if they are not adequately cleaned, small pieces of coral can become embedded in the wound. Avoid coral cuts by wearing shoes if there's a chance that you might step on any coral, and clean any cut thoroughly with an antiseptic. Severe pain, throbbing, redness, fever or generally feeling unwell suggest infection and the prompt need for antibiotics, as coral cuts may result in serious infections.

It's best to seek medical advice for any wound that fails to heal after a week or so.

Insect Bites & Stings Bee and wasp stings are usually painful rather than dangerous. However, in people who are allergic to them, severe breathing difficulties may occur and require urgent medical care. Calamine lotion or Stingose spray will give relief, and ice packs will reduce the pain and swelling. Scorpions often shelter in shoes or clothing, and their stings are notoriously painful. Develop the habit of shaking out your shoes and clothing before putting them on.

Bedbugs & Lice Bedbugs live in various places, but particularly in dirty mattresses and bedding, evidenced by spots of blood on bedclothes or on the wall. Bedbugs leave itchy bites in neat rows. Calamine lotion or Stingose spray may help.

All lice cause itching and discomfort. They make themselves at home in hair (head lice), clothing (body lice) or pubic hair (crabs). You catch lice through direct contact with infected people or by sharing combs, clothing and the like. Powder or shampoo treatment will kill the lice. Infected clothing should then be washed in very hot, soapy water and left out in the sun to dry.

Tetanus This disease occurs when a wound becomes infected by a germ that lives in soil and in the feces of horses and other animals. It enters the body via breaks in the skin, so the best prevention is to clean all wounds promptly and thoroughly and use an antiseptic. Use antibiotics if the wound becomes hot, throbs or pus is seen. The first symptom may be discomfort in swallowing or stiffening of the jaw and neck; this is followed by painful convulsions of the jaw and whole body. The disease can be fatal, but is preventable with vaccination.

Rabies This is a fatal viral infection found throughout Latin America. Many animals can be infected (such as dogs, cats, bats and monkeys), and it is their saliva that is infectious. Any bite, scratch or even lick from a warm-blooded, furry animal should be cleaned immediately and thoroughly. Scrub with soap and running water and then apply alcohol or iodine solution. Medical help should be sought promptly to receive a course of injections to prevent the onset of symptoms and death.

Leeches & Ticks Leeches may be present in damp rain-forest conditions; they attach themselves to your skin to suck your blood. Trekkers often get them on their legs or in their boots. Salt or a lighted cigarette end will make them fall off. Do not pull them off, as the bite is then more likely to become infected. Clean and apply pressure if the point of attachment is bleeding. An insect repellent may keep them away.

Always check all over your body after walking through a potentially tick-infested area, as ticks can cause skin infections and more serious diseases. Adult ticks suck blood from hosts by burying their head into skin, but they are often found unattached and can simply be brushed off. Avoid pulling the rear of the body, as this may squeeze the tick's gut contents through the attached mouth parts into the skin, increasing the risk of infection and disease. To remove an attached tick, use a pair of tweezers, grab it by the head and gently pull it straight out – do not twist it. (If no tweezers are available, use your fingers, but protect them from contamination with a piece of tissue or paper.) Do not touch the tick with a hot object like a match or a cigarette – this can cause it to regurgitate noxious gut substances or saliva into the wound. And do not rub oil, alcohol or petroleum jelly on it. If you get sick in the next couple of weeks, consult a doctor.

Snakes To minimize your chances of being bitten, always wear boots, socks and long trousers when walking through undergrowth where snakes may be present. Don't put your hands into holes and crevices, and be careful when collecting firewood.

Central America has dozens of species of snakes, but most are not poisonous. The most poisonous snake of all is the tiny coral snake, which is actually a land dweller. It is brightly colored with bands of red, yellow and black. Coral snakes are nocturnal and not aggressive. The large fer-de-lance is much more of a danger. Called *barba amarilla* (yellow chin) in Central America, it's recognizable by its lance-shaped head

and the diamond markings on its back. It is often encountered in undergrowth and cane fields and sometimes comes out at night to lie on warm roads and trails. Its venom is extremely toxic. Rattlesnakes are also found in Central America.

Snakebites do not cause instantaneous death, and antivenins are usually available. Immediately wrap the bitten limb tightly, as you would for a sprained ankle, and then attach a splint to immobilize it. Keep the victim still and seek medical help, if possible bringing the dead snake for identification. Don't attempt to catch the snake if there is a possibility of being bitten again. Tourniquets and sucking out the poison are now comprehensively discredited as snakebite remedies.

Jellyfish Local advice is the best way of avoiding contact with these sea creatures, which have stinging tentacles. The stings from most jellyfish are rather painful but not lethal. Dousing skin in vinegar will get rid of the sting and deactivate any stingers that have not 'fired'; this is also useful if you touch fire coral, which causes a stinging skin reaction. Calamine lotion, antihistamines and analgesics may reduce the reaction and relieve the pain.

Women's Health

Gynecological Problems Antibiotic use, synthetic underwear, sweating and contraceptive pills can lead to fungal vaginal infections when traveling in hot climates. Wearing loose-fitting clothes and cotton underwear will help to prevent these infections.

Fungal infections, characterized by a rash, itch and discharge, can be treated with a vinegar or lemon-juice douche, or with yogurt. Nystatin, miconazole or clotrimazole pessaries or vaginal cream are the usual treatment.

Other vaginal problems include a smelly discharge, painful intercourse and sometimes a burning sensation when urinating. These may be sexually transmitted, so sexual partners must also be treated. Medical attention should be sought, and remember that in addition to these diseases, HIV or hepatitis B may also be acquired during exposure. Besides abstinence, the best preventative is to practice safer sex using condoms.

Pregnancy Safe travel in much of Latin America requires vaccinations, and some of these are not advisable during pregnancy. In addition, some diseases, such as malaria, are much more serious during pregnancy and may pose a risk to the fetus. Pregnant women should avoid all unnecessary medication, but medical advice should be sought on vaccination and malaria prophylaxis. Additional care should be taken to prevent illness (eg, avoiding mosquito bites), and particular attention should be paid to diet and nutrition.

Most miscarriages occur during the first three months of pregnancy. Miscarriage is not uncommon and can occasionally lead to severe bleeding. The last three months should also be spent within reasonable distance of good medical care. A baby born as early as 24 weeks stands a chance of survival, but only in a good modern hospital.

WOMEN TRAVELERS

Two women traveling together or a woman traveling alone in the region may experience unwanted sexual advances or insulting and disrespectful comments and behavior. Being prepared for this eventuality and exploring your options before something happens can help you deal with any uncomfortable overtures thrown your way.

Machismo, the myth that stereotypes men as strong and women as dependent and fragile, is alive and well in Latin America. Machista attitudes, stressing masculine pride and virility, are often expressed in boasting and in exaggerated attention toward women. As a woman traveling alone, you can expect to hear whistles, hisses and other obviously sexist sound effects; ignoring these is usually the most effective response. Snappy put-down lines or other caustic responses to unwanted advances may make the man feel threatened, and he may become aggressive. Most women find it more effective to invent a husband and leave the guy with his pride intact, especially in front of others.

It's commonly believed that foreign women without male companions are easy game for local men. Minimize your troubles by dressing conservatively, don't hang out in bars drinking until the wee hours, and don't encourage overtures you have no intention of entertaining. Take all the usual precautions, such as avoiding dark places and lone stretches of beach, and always keep a little extra money on you in case you want to catch a taxi back to your lodging. Wearing a wedding ring can help deflect unwanted attention.

Most importantly, act confident and assertive when you travel. Note that assertive and aggressive are not the same thing – the point is not to antagonize people, but to have them recognize and respect your boundaries.

Safety Precautions

Although there's no need to be paranoid, women travelers should be aware that the possibility of rape, mugging and so on does exist. The greatest risk seems to be in remote or isolated areas, to women trekking or on tours. Some cases have involved tour guides assaulting tour group members, so it's worth double-checking the identity and reputation of any guide or tour operator. Also be aware that women have been drugged, in bars and elsewhere, using drinks, cigarettes or pills. In general, Central American police are not likely to be very helpful in rape cases. Tourist police may be more sympathetic, but it's possibly better to see a doctor and contact your embassy before reporting a rape to police.

What to Wear

Women travelers will get on much better if they dress conservatively. A good general rule is to watch how local women dress and behave, and to follow their example. In places where there's a lot of international tourism, standards of dress tend to be more relaxed.

The definition of appropriate attire varies depending where you are. Modest shorts are fine at the beach and in most beachside communities, but may draw a lot of unwanted attention in cities or up in the mountains, where women virtually never wear them. Long pants are OK everywhere but can be hot unless you're in the mountains. Many women travelers find that loose cotton skirts with hemlines below the knee and a T-shirt or similar modest blouse are the most convenient traveling clothes.

Wherever you are and whatever else you're wearing, always wear a bra, whether or not it's your usual custom. Not doing so in this part of the world is regarded as provocative.

When swimming, many local women wear T-shirts over their swimsuits or shorts. You might want to do the same to avoid unwanted attention.

GAY & LESBIAN TRAVELERS

On the whole, Central America is a pitifully unwelcoming place for gay men, and although lesbians have it a bit better, homosexuality is generally shunned in much of the region. In Nicaragua, there is a statute criminalizing homosexual behavior, and although enforcement is inconsistent, harassment of gays does occur there. The absence of such laws does not prevent official and police harassment elsewhere, however; Guatemala and Panama are noted for being particularly homophobic, and in El Salvador, a series of violent acts against gay men, lesbians and transgender people in 1999 and 2000 has drawn the attention of human-rights groups. Misinformation about homosexuality in general and AIDS in particular has made Latin America that much more inhospitable for gay people. Even Costa Rica, which boasts tolerance and promotes gay- and lesbian-oriented tours, has experienced violent protests against gays visiting from abroad. In general, public displays of affection will not be tolerated, and gay men (and possibly women) could find themselves the target of verbal or physical abuse. Discretion is definitely the rule, especially in rural Central America. Lesbians are generally less maligned than gay men, and women traveling together should have few, if any, problems.

There is usually at least one gay bar in every city, which makes meeting people easier. Gay travelers to several of the region's larger cities can rely on an organized support network and choose from a variety of social venues. See the individual country chapters for information on national and local publications and organizations that can recommend gay-friendly hotels, bars and meeting places.

Despite a growing number of publications and Web sites devoted to gay travel, very few have specific advice about Central American destinations. The gay travel newsletter *Out & About* has occasionally covered Central America; their Web site (www.outandabout.com) offers general information and allows you to order back issues with feature articles on Belize, Costa Rica and Guatemala.

A growing number of gay- and lesbian-oriented tour operators offer package tours and cruises to destinations throughout Central America, most notably Belize and Costa Rica. Visit the Out & About Web site (above) for a comprehensive list of gay and lesbian tour operators and links to their individual sites; you can also find links to other gay travel sites and a list of recommended travel agencies, some of which specialize in Central American destinations.

Organizations & Resources

If your travel plans include Costa Rica, you might want to pick up a copy of the *Women's Traveller* or the *Damron Men's Travel Guide,* both published annually by Damron Company (☎ 415-255 0404, 800-462 6654), PO Box 422458, San Francisco, CA 94142, USA. You can purchase their publications on the Web at www.damron .com. Additional information on gay and lesbian travel in Latin America can be obtained through the US or Australian offices of the International Gay & Lesbian Travel Association (IGLTA; ☎ 800-448 8550 in the USA, iglta@iglta.org), 52 W Oakland Park Blvd No 237, Wilton Manors, FL 33311; in Australia, contact IGLTA Australia/NZ/Asia/Pacific (☎ 2 9818 6669, fax 2 9878 6660, Rhopkins@iglta.org), PO Box 1397, Rozelle NSW Australia 2039. IGLTA is an organization of more than 1200 companies serving travelers worldwide; call for lists of travel agents, tour operators, accommodations and events or contact their Web site (www.iglta .com). Other useful resources include the International Gay & Lesbian Human Rights Commission (IGLHRC; ☎ 415-255 8680, fax 415-255 8662), 1360 Mission St, Suite 200, San Francisco, CA 94103, USA; its Web site (www.iglhrc.org) features 'action alerts' that address human-rights violations against members of gay, lesbian, bisexual and transgender communities worldwide, including several in Latin American countries.

On the Internet, the Arenal Lesbigay homepage (www.indiana.edu/~arenal/ingles .html), in English and Spanish, features articles, news stories and a reading list with links to Amazon.com.

DISABLED TRAVELERS

Latin America generally is not well equipped for disabled travelers. Unfortunately, expensive international hotels are more likely to cater to guests with disabilities than cheap local lodgings; air travel will be more feasible than inexpensive local buses; and well-developed tourist attractions will be more accessible than off-the-beaten-track destinations. Careful planning is essential, but there is little detailed information on Central America for travelers with a disability.

Travelers who use a wheelchair will find it difficult to get around major cities because of street congestion and generally poor road or sidewalk surfaces. Public buses don't have provisions that allow wheelchairs to be carried. Wheelchair-accessible toilet facilities are virtually nonexistent except in five-star hotels. Special phones for hearing-impaired people or signs in Braille are very rare.

Despite the challenges to disabled visitors to the region, there is some progress worth noting: As of the mid-1990s, new or newly remodeled businesses in Costa Rica are required to have a barrier-free entrance for disabled people. See that country chapter for information on local organizations that cater to travelers with a disability.

Organizations & Resources

There are many resources for disabled travelers, offering both general advice and information specific to Latin America. Organizations in the USA include Mobility International (☎ 541-343 1284, fax 541-343 6812), PO Box 10767, Eugene, OR 97440; Access Foundation (☎ 516-887 5798), PO Box 356, Malverne, NY 11565; and the Society for the Advancement of Travel for the Handicapped (SATH; ☎ 718-858 5483), 26 Court St, Brooklyn, NY 11242.

Some Internet resources include the Mobility International Web site (www.miusa .org); the SATH site (http://sath.org/index.html); the Access-Able Travel Source homepage (www.access-able.com), which has useful links and lists travel agents who have experience with people with special needs; the Global Access Web site (www.geocities.com/Paris/1502), offering good tips and personal accounts of travel in Latin America; and Accessible Journeys (www.disabilitytravel.com), which operates escorted trips to Costa Rica and other parts of Latin America and provides resources for independent travelers as well.

Vaya con Silla de Ruedas (Go with Wheelchairs; ☎ 391 5045, fax 454 2810, vayacon@sol.racsa.co.cr) operates tours in Costa Rica and neighboring countries for travelers with a disability. Other services include bilingual guides, hotel reservations, and a van especially designed to transport travelers in wheelchairs. Its Web site (www.gowithwheelchairs.com) has links to other sites of interest to disabled visitors to Costa Rica and Nicaragua.

SENIOR TRAVELERS

Seniors with a reasonably good level of health and fitness should definitely consider Central America for a holiday. Bathroom facilities and public transportation might be more rustic than you are accustomed to at home, but the hospitality of the region will more than compensate for any minor discomforts. In Latin America, older people are generally accorded the respect and courtesy they're due, and traveling seniors will probably receive a similar encouraging welcome.

Although there are few discounts or special deals for older travelers and few facilities for those of limited mobility, it's worth checking out travel bargains offered by organizations dedicated to seniors. In the USA these include the American Association of Retired Persons (AARP; ☎ 800-424 3410), 601 E St NW, Washington, DC 20049, which represents people ages 50 and older (non-US residents can get one-year memberships for $10, three-year memberships for $24). Check out their Web site (www .aarp.org). Grand Circle Travel (☎ 617-350 7500, 800-221 2610;), 347 Congress St, Boston, MA 02210, distributes a useful free booklet, *Going Abroad: 101 Tips for Mature Travelers*. They also have an informative Web site (www.gct.com).

TRAVEL WITH CHILDREN

A small number of foreigners visit Central America with children, and those that do are usually treated with great kindness throughout the region. Though there are few attractions or facilities specifically for kids, transportation, food and lodging are all quite manageable, and a widespread affection for kids throughout Latin America makes them something of a social asset. Children with fair hair and light skin are especially likely to receive attention, and this may become tiresome for them.

In general, civilian airlines let kids younger than 12 fly at half the regular economy fare. Long-distance buses usually charge children full fare if they occupy a seat (but bus fares are usually cheap anyway). Most hotels have some rooms with three or four beds – these rooms cost more, but ask for a special family rate. Restaurants rarely advertise children's meals, but will often offer a child-size serving at a lower price and invariably allow two kids to share an adult meal. For light, cheap meals, bring some cups, plates and utensils and buy cereals, soft drinks and sandwich stuff from a supermarket.

You might find water parks and amusement parks in the more developed countries like Costa Rica, but they are generally uncommon. Kids will enjoy the beaches and perhaps some natural attractions in addition to trains, boat rides and the ubiquitous video arcades. They'll also enjoy outdoor activities such as hiking, white-water rafting, snorkeling, horseback riding and even walking. It's a good idea to alternate adult activities (museums, galleries, shopping, scenic tours) with things that kids will enjoy.

A baby backpack is the best way to carry very young children, but a stroller can be very useful, too. Strollers may be impossible to push on many rough pavements, but they're great as a portable place for sitting and sleeping and carrying kids' stuff. Have your child carry a small bag with a few favorite toys or teddies, some books, crayons and paper.

For a wealth of good ideas, pick up a copy of Lonely Planet's *Travel with Children*, by Maureen Wheeler. For information on the legal aspects of taking your children along, refer to the 'Documents for Minors' boxed text, earlier in this chapter under Visas & Documents.

USEFUL ORGANIZATIONS

Travelers will find a tourist office in the capital city of each country; some countries have them in outlying towns as well. If you're a student, look for student travel agencies in the capital cities of Costa Rica and Panama.

South American Explorers

This very informative nonprofit organization has offices in Cusco, Lima and Quito. The US office (☎ 607-277 0488, fax 607-277 6122, explorer@samexplo.org), 126 Indian Creek Rd, Ithaca, NY 14850, publishes the quarterly magazine, *South American Explorer*, and maintains the Web site (www.samexplo.org).

SAE (formerly the South American Explorers Club) was founded in 1977 and functions as an information center for travelers, adventurers and researchers. It supports scientific fieldwork, mountaineering and other expeditions, wilderness conservation and social development in Latin America. The club's Lima office has an extensive library of books, maps and traveler's reports. The club sells maps, books and other items by mail order, online and at its offices in Lima and Quito.

Membership costs US$40 per person per year (US$70 for a couple) and includes a subscription to *South American Explorer* magazine. Members receive access to the club's information service, library, luggage storage facilities, mail service, book exchange, and discounts at some hotels and travel services. Visit the SAE Web site if you're interested in joining or wish to obtain contact information for the organization's South American offices.

Latin American Bureau

Based in London, the Latin American Bureau (LAB; ☎ 0171 278 2829) is an independent organization engaged in research and publishing on Latin America and the Caribbean. LAB is a particularly good source of information on issues of human rights, social justice, and economic and political development in the region. Most of its publications are available online (www.lab.org.uk) or by mail order; for the book catalog call or write to LAB at 1 Amwell St, London EC1R 1UL, UK.

Environmental Organizations

See the individual country chapters for national and local organizations promoting environmental preservation in Central

America. The following groups may have suggestions for prospective travelers to the region.

Australia
Friends of the Earth (☎ 03 9419 8700) 312 Smith St, Collingwood, PO Box 222, Fitzroy, Victoria 3065
Web site: www.foe.org.au

UK
Friends of the Earth (☎ 020 7490 1555) 26-28 Underwood St, London N1 7JQ
Web site: www.foe.co.uk

Survival International (☎ 020 7242 1441) 11-15 Emerald St, London WC1N 3QL

WWF (☎ 1483 426 444) Panda House, Weyside Park, Godalming, Surrey GU7 1BP

USA
The Rainforest Action Network (RAN; ☎ 415-398 4404), 221 Pine St, Suite 500, San Francisco, CA 94104
Web site: www.ran.org

Conservation International (☎ 202-429 5660) 2501 M St NW, Suite 200, Washington, DC 20037
Web site: www.conservation.org

The Nature Conservancy (☎ 703-841 5300) 4245 N Fairfax Dr, Suite 100, Arlington, VA 22203
Web site: www.tnc.org

DANGERS & ANNOYANCES

Travel in Central America poses a number of potential dangers that demand caution, but don't be put off. Most areas are quite safe, and with sensible precautions, you are unlikely to have any problems.

General Safety

The protracted civil wars in El Salvador and Nicaragua and the 36-year-long guerrilla conflict in Guatemala are over, but these dangers have been replaced by an alarming rise in the general crime rate – particularly in Guatemala, where there have been incidents of rape, assault, bus- and car-jacking and even murder of foreign tourists. These incidents occur at random and are not predictable. Parts of Panama's Darién Province, which borders Colombia, are extremely dangerous because of guerilla activity. Refer to the individual country chapters for specific warnings and trouble areas. Up-to-date travel advisories are available from the US Department of State's Web site at www.travel.state

.gov/travel_warnings.html. Those without Internet access can telephone the department's Office of American Citizens Services at ☎ 202-647 5225. British subjects can contact the UK Foreign Office's Travel Advisory Service (☎ 020 7238 4503) or visit its Web site (http://193.114.50.10/travel).

Will you run into trouble? No one can say. Tens of thousands of foreign visitors enjoy the incomparable beauties of the region and the friendliness of its people every year, the huge majority without untoward incidents of any kind. But then there are the unlucky few.

Your best defenses against trouble are up-to-date information and reasonable caution. You should make the effort to contact your government and inquire about current conditions and trouble spots, then follow the advice offered.

Robbery & Theft

Robbery is a danger in the region's large cities. Theft, particularly pickpocketing and purse snatching, is also not unusual in cities and occurs in beach areas as well. Foreign tourists are particularly singled out for theft as they are presumed to be 'wealthy' and to be carrying valuables.

To protect yourself, take these common-sense precautions:

- Unless you have immediate need of them, leave most of your cash and traveler's checks, your passport, jewelry, airline tickets, credit cards, expensive watch, camera and other valuables in a sealed, signed envelope in your hotel's safe; obtain a receipt for the envelope. Virtually all hotels except the very cheapest provide a safe for guests' valuables. You may have to provide the envelope. Buy some at a *papelería* (stationery store). Your signature on the envelope and a receipt from the hotel clerk will help to ensure the security of your things.

- Leaving valuable items in a locked suitcase in your hotel room is often safer than carrying them with you on the streets.

- Have a money belt or a pouch on a string around your neck; place your remaining valuables in it and wear it *underneath your clothing*. You can carry a small amount of ready money in a pocket or bag.

- Be aware that any purse or bag in plain sight may be slashed or grabbed. Often two thieves work together, one cutting the strap, the other grabbing the bag in a lunge past you, even as you walk along a street or stand at a bus stop. At ticket counters in airports and bus stations, keep your bag between your feet, particularly when you're busy talking to a ticket agent.

- Be wary if anyone points out a foreign substance soiling your clothes. A ploy used increasingly by pickpockets (sometimes operating in teams) in many parts of the world is to distract the victim by 'accidentally' soiling him or her (with mustard, ice cream or the like), then helping to clean the victim off. In a variation on this ploy, a setup person will spit at or throw a noxious substance (such as dog feces) on the victim.

- Do not wander alone down empty city streets or in isolated areas, particularly at night.

- Do not leave any valuables visible in your vehicle when you park it in a city, unless it is in a guarded parking lot.

- On beaches and in the countryside, do not camp overnight in secluded places unless you can be sure it's safe.

- When paying for something, wait until all of the change has been counted out before picking it up. A favorite ruse of dishonest ticket clerks in particular is to hand over the change slowly, bit by bit, in the hope that you'll pick it up and go before you have it all.

There's little point in going to the police after a robbery unless your loss is insured, in which case you'll need a statement from the police to present to your insurance company. Outside of Belize, you'll probably have to communicate with them in Spanish, so if your Spanish is poor, take a more fluent speaker along. Say, *Yo quisiera poner una acta de un robo* (I'd like to report a robbery). This should make it clear that you merely want a piece of paper and aren't going to ask the police to do anything inconvenient like look for the thieves or attempt to recover your goods. With luck, you should get the required piece of paper without too much trouble. You may have to write it up yourself, then present it for official stamp and signature.

Drugs
Marijuana and cocaine are available in many places but illegal everywhere, and penalties are severe. Be aware that drugs are sometimes used to set up travelers for blackmail and bribery. Avoid any conversation with someone who offers you drugs. If you are in an area where drug trafficking is prevalent, ignore it and do not show any interest whatsoever.

Don't accept food, drinks, sweets or cigarettes from strangers on buses, trains or in bars. They may be laced with a powerful sedative drug, and you will be robbed while you're unconscious.

Roll-your-own cigarettes or cigarette papers may arouse suspicion.

Police & Military
Corruption is a very serious problem among Latin American police, who are generally poorly paid and poorly supervised. In many countries, they are not reluctant to plant drugs on unsuspecting travelers or enforce minor regulations to the letter in hopes of extracting *coimas* (bribes).

If you are stopped by 'plainclothes policemen,' *never* get into a vehicle with them. Don't give them any documents or show them any money, and don't take them to your hotel. If the police appear to be the real thing, insist on going to a bona fide police station on foot.

The military often has considerable influence, even under civilian governments. Don't approach military installations, which may display warnings like 'No stopping or photographs – the sentry will shoot.' In the event of a coup or other emergency, state-of-siege regulations suspend civil rights. Always carry identification and be sure someone knows your whereabouts. Contact your embassy or consulate for advice.

Natural Hazards
Central America is prone to a wide variety of natural disasters, including earthquakes, hurricanes, floods and volcanic eruptions. General information about natural disaster preparedness is available via the Internet from the US Federal Emergency Management Agency (FEMA) at www.fema.gov.

Swimming Safety
Hundreds of people drown each year at Central America's beaches – about 200 drownings are recorded annually at Costa Rican beaches alone. Of these, 80% are caused by riptides, which are strong currents that pull the swimmer out to sea. They can occur even in waist-deep water. The best

advice of all: Ask about local conditions before entering the water.

LEGAL MATTERS

Police officers in these countries are sometimes (if not often) part of the problem rather than of the solution. The less you have to do with the law, the better.

Whatever you do, *don't* get involved in any way with illegal drugs: Don't buy or sell, use or carry, or associate with people who do – even if the locals seem to do so freely. As a foreigner, you are at a distinct disadvantage, and you may be set up by others. Drug laws in all of these countries are strict, and though enforcement may be uneven, penalties are severe.

PUBLIC HOLIDAYS & SPECIAL EVENTS

National holidays *(días feriados)* are taken seriously in Central America, and banks, public offices and many stores close. The big national holidays are dictated by the Roman Catholic Church calendar. Christmas and Holy Week (Semana Santa), the week leading up to Easter, are the most important. Hotels are usually booked well in advance of this week, especially in beach areas and in towns that have particularly elaborate and colorful celebrations, such as Antigua, Guatemala. Bus service may be limited or nonexistent on the Thursday afternoon and Friday before Easter, and many businesses are closed for the entire week preceding the holiday. In general, public transportation tends to be tight on all holidays and the days immediately preceding or following them, so book tickets in advance.

See the Facts for the Visitor section in each of the country chapters for a list of national and important local holidays and special events.

ACTIVITIES
Diving & Snorkeling

Some of the top diving sites in Latin America are along the Belizean barrier reef, particularly around Caye Caulker and Ambergris Caye, and around the Bay Islands off the coast of Honduras. For superior snorkeling, try any of the above-mentioned locales, many parts of Costa Rica and the Caribbean coast of Nicaragua and Panama.

The Bay Islands of Honduras are known for their affordable certification; a four-day Professional Association of Diving Instructors (PADI) open-water diving certification course costs around US$250.

If you plan to dive, bring evidence of your certification to show the dive-shop people, and check the rental equipment over carefully before you dive. For safety considerations, see the 'Guidelines for Safe Diving' boxed text in the Bay Islands section of the Honduras chapter.

Surfing

There is no shortage of coastline in Central America, and the region's Pacific coast has several internationally renowned surf breaks, including a perfect left break in Costa Rica's Parque Nacional Santa Rosa. International surfing competitions are held in these parts, most notably at Zunzal in El Salvador.

White-Water Rafting

Some of the best white-water rafting in the tropics can be found in Central America, and rafting is fast becoming popular all over Latin America. Guatemala and Honduras are developing a rafting industry, and a number of rivers there offer anything from frothing Class IV white water to easy Class II floats. See those country chapters for details. Costa Rica leads the pack in river adventure sports, with many tour operators available. Favorites there include the Río Reventazón and the Río Pacuare, both accessible as day trips from the capital.

Wildlife Watching

The wildlife viewing and birding opportunities in Central America are world-class. A system of national parks, wildlife refuges, biosphere reserves and other protected areas throughout the region facilitates independent wildlife viewing and bird watching. Even private areas such as gardens around rural hotels can yield a sampling of birds, insects, reptiles and even monkeys. Early morning and late afternoon are the best times to watch for wildlife activity anywhere.

If you want to splurge, it's worth considering an organized tour or two to increase your chances of seeing the rarer or more spectacular species, such as the elusive quetzal.

Considerations for Responsible Diving

The popularity of diving is placing immense pressure on many sites, particularly on Central America's Caribbean coast. Please consider the following tips when diving, and help preserve the ecology and beauty of reefs:

1. Do not use anchors on the reef, and take care not to ground boats on coral. Encourage dive operators and regulatory bodies to establish permanent moorings at popular dive sites.
2. Avoid touching living marine organisms with your body or dragging equipment across the reef. Polyps can be damaged by even the gentlest contact. Never stand on corals, even if they look solid and robust. If you must hold on to the reef, only touch exposed rock or dead coral.
3. Be conscious of your fins. Even without contact, the surge from heavy fin strokes near the reef can damage delicate organisms. When treading water in shallow reef areas, take care not to kick up clouds of sand. Settling sand can easily smother the delicate organisms of the reef.
4. Practice and maintain proper buoyancy control. Major damage can be done by divers descending too fast and colliding with the reef. Make sure that you are correctly weighted and that your weight belt is positioned so that you stay horizontal. If you have not dived for a while, do a practice dive in a pool before taking to the reef. Be aware that buoyancy can change over the period of an extended trip: Initially, you may breathe harder and need more weight; a few days later, you may breathe more easily and need less weight.
5. Take great care in underwater caves. Spend as little time within them as possible, as your air bubbles may be caught within the roof and thereby leave previously submerged organisms high and dry. Taking turns to inspect the interior of a small cave lessens the chances of damaging contact.
6. Resist the temptation to collect or buy corals or shells. Aside from the ecological damage, taking home marine souvenirs depletes the beauty of a site and spoils the enjoyment of others. The same goes for marine archaeological sites (mainly shipwrecks). Respect their integrity; some sites are even protected from looting by law.
7. Ensure that you take home all your rubbish and any litter you may find as well. Plastics in particular are a serious threat to marine life. Turtles can mistake plastic for jellyfish and eat it.
8. Resist the temptation to feed fish. You may disturb their normal eating habits, encourage aggressive behavior or feed them food that is detrimental to their health.
9. Minimize your disturbance of marine animals. In particular, do not ride on the backs of turtles, as this causes them great anxiety.

Hiking & Backpacking

Pristine natural environments, abundant wildlife and a landscape that's punctuated by hundreds of volcanoes make Central America a place of limitless possibilities for hikers. From the Petén region of northern Guatemala to the slopes of Volcán Barú in Panama, the terrain ranges from cloud and rain forests to lowland jungles, river trails and palm-lined beaches. Jungle trekking can be strenuous, and hikers should be prepared. If you intend to make a holiday of hiking and camping, you might want to bring your own equipment, as hiking and camping equipment may not be available locally or may be of inferior quality.

LANGUAGE COURSES

Spanish language courses are available in most Central American cities, with the most popular language learning centers being Antigua and Quetzaltenango (Guatemala), and to a lesser extent, San José (Costa Rica). Opportunities to learn Mayan languages are available in Quetzaltenango. See the country chapters in this book for more details on language courses. For an online directory of language schools throughout Latin America, visit the Learn Spanish Web site (www.studyspanish.com). AmeriSpan Unlimited (☎ 215-751 1100, 800-879 6640, info@amerispan.com), Box 40007, Philadelphia, PA 19106, USA, arranges courses with homestays in several Central American cities. You can check out their Web site at www.amerispan.com.

WORK

According to law you must have a permit to work in any of these countries. In practice you may get paid under the table or through some bureaucratic loophole, if you can find suitable work. The most plentiful work for native English speakers is teaching their language. Consult the classified advertisements in local newspapers (both English- and Spanish-language ones), browse the bulletin boards in spots where foreigners gather and ask around. Big cities offer the best possibilities. Pay may be low, but it's better than a negative cash flow.

The Council on International Educational Exchange (CIEE; ☎ 888-268 6245, 212-822 2600), 205 E 42nd St, New York, NY 10017, helps individuals interested in working, studying or volunteering outside their home countries. Their work and volunteer programs can be a fascinating way to immerse yourself in the culture and language of your host country. Check their Web site for more information (www.ciee.org).

Transitions Abroad Publishing (☎ 413-256 3414, 800-293 0373, fax 413-256 0373, info@TransitionsAbroad.com), PO Box 1300, Amherst, MA 01004, publishes a bimonthly magazine – highlighting opportunities to work, study or travel abroad – and maintains a Web site (www.transabroad .com). It also publishes *Work Abroad,* a comprehensive guide to finding and preparing for a job overseas.

If you're looking for volunteer work, Spanish is usually essential, and with some organizations you will have to arrange your own meals and lodging. Researching volunteer opportunities before you leave home is a good idea; check the following Web sites.

Amerispan Unlimited (www.amerispan.com/ volunteer) operates a volunteer and internship program with opportunities for various skills in Costa Rica and Guatemala.

Earthwatch Institute (www.earthwatch.org) places volunteers on research teams and projects related to conservation, cultural diversity and health; no special skills are required.

WorldTeach (www.igc.org/worldteach) provides volunteers to teach English and basic skills; ter-

tiary qualification is required, but not specifically in education.

Other opportunities to volunteer involve contributing to local conservation efforts. On the coasts of Panama and Costa Rica, for example, organizations working to protect endangered sea turtles and their eggs during nesting season often take on volunteers. Details on specific programs are provided in the country chapters.

ACCOMMODATIONS

Accommodations range from luxury resort hotels, tourist vacation hotels, budget hotels and motels to *casas de huéspedes* (guesthouses) and simple spots to hang a hammock. Prices vary from place to place; lodgings in Panama and touristy parts of Belize, for example, are more expensive across the board than other countries in the region. In most Central American countries, however, you can get a roof over your head for as low as US$5 to US$10 a night. Accommodations prices cited in this book are year 2000 high-season (roughly Christmas to Easter) rates, and they include applicable national taxes on hotel rooms. All prices quoted in this book are approximate, not guaranteed.

It's worth noting that many establishments (more frequently mid-range and top-end places) are open to negotiation when business is slow. Some hotels might offer walk-in customers large discounts on the posted rates with no prompting. Many others state their rates are negotiable, and some might advertise promotions that include a free breakfast or other perks combined with lowered rates.

Discounts can often be negotiated for multinight stays, groups, and sometimes, at upper-end places, payment in cash. If prices for accommodations seem high, it's always worth asking the proprietor for a discount or *promoción.*

Reservations

It's advisable to reserve a room in advance at particularly popular hotels or if you plan to visit busy areas either during the Christmas–New Year holidays or during July and August. In tourist areas of most Central American countries, it's essential to book ahead for Semana Santa (Easter Week); in addition to foreign guests, many locals head for vacation spots at this time, and prices can double in some places.

You should request a reservation by email, telephone or fax, asking whether a deposit is required and how to send it, and requesting confirmation in writing.

Hammocks & Bungalows

On the beach and in other natural settings in Central America, you can rent hammocks for the night or bring your own to sling between two trees. Usually the space to hang your hammock will be under a thatched-roof or lean-to type structure. Expect to pay between US$2 and US$5 for a rental hammock and space, possibly more depending on location and season.

Another accommodation option on the beach and occasionally in the forest are *cabañas* (also *cabinas*), or bungalows. These can be dirt-floor, thatched-roof arrangements or something more elaborate. Obviously, prices will reflect the type of amenities involved.

Camping

Camping is not a popular pastime among residents of Central America, and organized campsites such as those in the USA or Europe are not commonly found. However, some national parks and reserves (particularly in Costa Rica) offer basic, inexpensive camping facilities or food and accommodations in ranger stations; these facilities are mentioned in the country chapters where relevant. Water, fire pits and toilets or latrines are usually available, but it's advisable to bring your own gear. Wherever facilities are available for campers, expect to pay from US$3 to US$15 per night, depending upon the facilities and the desirability of the location.

It is recommended that you camp only in the designated camping areas of national parks or on someone's land with their permission. Camping in remote wilderness areas and on isolated beaches can be risky; be very aware of your surroundings and do not leave your belongings unattended.

Hostels

Travelers will not find a Hostelling International membership particularly useful in Central America, as there are very few hostels in the region. One exception is Costa Rica, where there's a small network of HI-affiliated youth hostels with dormitory accommodations ranging from US$11 to US$40 per night. Unfortunately, these generally are no cheaper than other types of budget accommodations.

Guesthouses

Hospedajes or *casas de húespedes,* homes converted into guesthouses, are an attractive and inexpensive option in some cities. These generally offer basic, well-maintained and reasonably priced rooms that usually include breakfast in the price.

B&Bs

The bed and breakfast (B&B) concept is a relatively new one in Central America. It began to take hold in the 1990s, particularly in and around San José, Costa Rica, where B&B-style accommodations have become increasingly popular. Unlike their counterparts in the UK, B&Bs in Central America can often be as expensive as mid-range to high-end hotels. These establishments are usually not converted homes; instead they are designed and built as mini hotels that offer a high standard of accommodation, with private facilities, TV, air-conditioning and telephone. Naturally, breakfast is part of the deal.

Hotels

Cheap hotels can be found in almost every town, and although the accommodations are sometimes very basic, they can be a great value. You'll usually have to use communal bathrooms in budget hotels, but you can sometimes find reasonably priced rooms with a private bathroom. Rates vary from country to country, but budget lodgings typically range from US$5 per person to US$20 for a double room. Hotels in the 'mid-range' category usually charge about US$20 to US$40 for a double room, and as much as US$30 to US$80 in countries such as Belize, Costa Rica and Panama. You may pay substantially more for air-conditioning or a private bathroom.

Often the difference in price between a single and a double room is negligible, so if you're sharing with someone else the price per person can drop considerably. Particularly in beach communities, hotels are designed with large families in mind and may have four to six beds in a room – a cheap per-person option if you're traveling in a small group.

Hot water supplies are often erratic, or may only be available at certain hours of the day. Beware of the electric shower, a single cold-water shower head hooked up to an electric heating element. Don't touch the heating unit, or anything metal, while in the shower or you may get a shock – never strong enough to throw you across the room, but unpleasant nevertheless. Cheap hotels may advertise hot water, but if water is supplied by an electric shower, it's usually tepid. Used toilet paper should be placed in the receptacle provided – the plumbing cannot handle the paper.

Before accepting a room, look around the hotel if possible. The same prices are often charged for rooms of widely differing quality. If you don't like the first room they show, you can ask to see another without causing offense. At the other end of the spectrum, hotel staff may want to rent foreign tourists their most expensive suites – ask if they have more economical rooms if you don't want the suite.

As a general rule, breakfast is *not* included in the overnight rate, though it may sometimes be available on the premises.

Homestays

The option of staying with a local family is another relatively recent phenomenon in Central America; these opportunities are generally reserved for travelers enrolled in language courses and the homes offer varying degrees of comfort and authenticity. See the Language Courses sections in the Guatemala and Costa Rica chapters for details.

FOOD

The various cuisines found throughout the region have similarities as well as unique elements. For the particulars of each nation's culinary favorites, look under Food in the Facts for the Visitor section of the country chapters.

Among the staple foods found throughout the region are *tortillas*, thin round patties of pressed corn dough cooked on griddles and wrapped around or topped with various foods; *frijoles* (beans), served boiled, fried, refried, in soups, spread on tortillas or with eggs; *chiles* (peppers), which come in many varieties and are consumed in hundreds of ways; *plátanos*, ripe plantains

cut lengthwise and either fried, boiled, or broiled with butter and served hot; and the ubiquitous *arroz* (rice).

Most restaurants serve *bistec* (beef), *pollo* (chicken) and *pescado* (fish) dishes. Note that, *carne* literally means 'meat,' but in many countries it tends to specifically refer to beef.

Meals

The standard three daily meals are breakfast *(el desayuno),* lunch *(la comida, el almuerzo)* and supper *(la cena).*

The morning meal can be either continental or US-style. A light, continental-style breakfast can be made of sweet rolls or toast, and coffee. US-style breakfasts are available in tourist towns and might include bacon or sausage and eggs, pancakes, cold or hot cereal, fruit juice and coffee.

Lunch is the biggest meal of the day and is served at about 1 or 2 pm. In restaurants that do not cater primarily to tourists, menus might change daily, weekly or not at all. Most cafes and restaurants offer a set bargain meal or daily special *(comida corrida* or *plato del día)* at lunchtime for around US$1 to US$3. Typically it will include rice, beans, eggs or meat (usually chicken, beef or fish), cheese or a dollop of cream, a small salad, tortillas and a cold drink. It may also include soup, dessert and coffee. Another term for comida corrida is *menú,* though in tourist-oriented restaurants using this word may get you the written list of offerings (usually known as *la carta.)*

Served at about 7 pm, *la cena* (supper) is a lighter version of lunch. In beach resorts the evening meal tends to be the big one, as everyone is out at the beach during the day.

Nearly every town has a market with cheap and plentiful fruit and vegetables, some of which you will have never seen before. At street stalls you might sample local cooking and fill your stomach for a dollar or two. Many illnesses are blamed on improper or unhygienic preparation of such food, however, so you should use your judgement when eating on the street. Pay particular attention to salads and unpeeled fruit, which are among the worst culprits for making you sick. (See the Health section, earlier in this chapter, for information on food and waterborne diseases.)

If you tire of sampling the local cuisine, plenty of fast-food options (hamburgers, pizzas etc) can be found in most large towns. Immigrant groups have introduced other possibilities – you can find Chinese, Korean, Japanese, Middle Eastern or Italian food in some surprising places.

Vegetarian

Eating well (or at all) in Central America will depend on the strictness of your vegetarian diet. Problems arise the farther off the beaten track you roam, or if you forego fish or meat by-products such as bullion. On the more popular tourist routes there are numerous vegetarian restaurants, and you should have little trouble finding them. Awareness about vegetarian diets and the benefits of certain local grains (eg, quinoa) and proteins (soya) is on the rise; if you explain your dietary preferences, someone will probably make an attempt to whip something up. It may too often be rice, beans and eggs, so vitamin supplements or your own periodic trips to the market should be incorporated into your travels to avoid deficiencies. Vegans will face tougher hurdles than vegetarians and should anticipate doing a lot of their own cooking while on the road.

DRINKS

Because of the hot climate in many parts of the region, you will find yourself drinking lots of fluids. Indeed, you must remember to drink even if you don't feel particularly thirsty, in order to prevent dehydration and heat exhaustion (see the Health section, earlier in this chapter).

Nonalcoholic Drinks

Water & Soft Drinks Bottled or purified water is widely available in hotels and shops. You can also order safe-to-drink fizzy mineral water by asking for 'soda.'

Besides the easily recognizable and internationally known brands of *refrescos* (soft drinks) such as Coca-Cola and Pepsi, you will find interesting local flavors. Orange-flavored (*naranja*) soda is popular, and grapefruit (*toronja*) is even better, though less readily available. Squirt (eh-**skweert**) is a brand of citrus-flavored soda that is a bit drier than 7-Up.

Coffee, Tea & Cocoa Some of the world's best coffee is grown in Latin America, but the good stuff might be more difficult to find than you'd expect; most of it is exported, and instant coffee is very popular as a result. You can get a cup of percolated coffee in most places, but it may take some time to figure out how to order it – coffee cultures differ from country to country, and you may have to do some explaining to get what you want.

Black tea (*té negro*), usually made from bags (often locally produced Lipton), tends to be a disappointment to devoted tea drinkers. It's best to bring your own supply of loose tea and a tea infuser; then just order *una taza de agua caliente* (a cup of hot water) and brew your own.

Herbal teas are much better. Chamomile tea (*té de manzanilla*), a common item on restaurant and cafe menus, is a specific remedy for a queasy stomach.

Hot chocolate or cocoa was the royal stimulant during the classic period of Mayan civilization, when kings and nobility drank it on ceremonial occasions. Their version was unsweetened and dreadfully bitter. Today it's sweetened and, if not authentic, at least more palatable.

Fruit & Vegetable Juices Fresh fruit and vegetable juices (*jugos*) and shakes (*licuados*) are popular drinks and widely available in Central America. All of the fruits and a few of the squeezable vegetables are used either individually (as in jugos) or in some combination (as in licuados). Fruit drinks can come straight up, mixed with water and sugar or whipped up with milk. If the drink has water in it, make sure it's purified; this can be a concern if you're buying from a street or market vendor.

Alcoholic Drinks

There is no shortage of beer (*cerveza*) in Central America; each country has its national breweries and favorite labels. Most local beers are light lagers, served cold from bottles or cans, but there are also a few flavorful dark beers as well. Imports are available in cities and tourist destinations, but not elsewhere. Local wines are generally scarce and imported wines can be fairly expensive.

Rum and *aguardiente* (sugarcane liquor, also known as *caña*) are among the region's spirits of choice, and though most are of low price and matching quality, some local products are exceptionally fine. Cheaper rums and brandies are often mixed with soft drinks to make potent but cooling drinks, like the *Cuba libre* of rum and Coke.

Other drinks include gin – mixed with tonic water, ice and lime juice to make what many consider the perfect drink for the hot tropics – and whiskey.

Getting There & Away

The easiest approach to Central America, and the one most travelers use, is by air. Approaches by land from North America via Mexico are easy, with fairly good roads and frequent service in comfortable (though not luxurious) buses.

AIR
Airports & Airlines
The region's major international airports are in Guatemala City, Guatemala; Belize City, Belize; Tegucigalpa, Honduras; San Pedro Sula, Honduras; San Salvador, El Salvador; Managua, Nicaragua; San José, Costa Rica; and Panama City, Panama. A limited amount of international traffic also heads for Flores, Guatemala; the island of Roatán, off the north coast of Honduras; and David, in southwestern Panama. Mexico City also receives a large number of flights from all parts of the world, with connecting flights to Guatemala City and points farther south on the isthmus.

The main air connection points in North America for flights to and from the principal Central American cities include Atlanta, Chicago, Dallas/Fort Worth, Houston, Los Angeles, Miami, Newark (New Jersey), New York, San Francisco, Toronto and Washington, DC.

International air routes are structured so that virtually all flights into the region from the rest of the world pass through six 'hub' cities: Dallas/Fort Worth, Houston, Los Angeles, Miami, Mexico City or San Salvador. If you're traveling from North America or elsewhere in the world, you may have to change planes in one of these cities.

A number of airlines connect each Central American country with other countries on the isthmus, South America, North America and the Caribbean. The most frequent and direct flights to any Central American country are likely to be with its national 'flag carrier' airline; the region's national airlines are Aviateca (Guatemala), COPA (Panama), Lacsa (Costa Rica), Nica (Nicaragua) and TACA (El Salvador). A consortium of four of these airlines (all except COPA) is united under the Grupo TACA banner and can be accessed by calling ☎ 800-535 8780 or visiting its Web site at www.grupotaca.com. These airlines have collaborated to offer a series of special fare plans to visitors to the region (see Air Passes in the regional Getting Around chapter).

Following are the contacts for each of the principal international airlines of Central America; all of the principal international airlines have offices in the USA. For airline contact information and office locations within Central America, see the individual country chapters.

Aviateca (Guatemala)	☎ 800-327 9832
COPA (Panama)	☎ 800-359 2672
Lacsa (Costa Rica)	☎ 800-225 2272
Nica (Nicaragua)	☎ 800-831 6422
TACA (El Salvador)	☎ 800-535 8780

Onward-Ticket Requirements
Belize, Costa Rica and Panama officially have an onward-ticket requirement; that is, you cannot enter the country unless you possess an onward ticket to another destination. Although travelers report that immigration officials at land borders and

---

Warning

The information in this chapter is particularly vulnerable to change: Prices for international travel are volatile, routes are introduced and canceled, schedules change, special deals come and go, and rules and visa requirements are amended. Airlines and governments seem to take a perverse pleasure in making price structures and regulations as complicated as possible. You should check directly with the airline or a travel agent to make sure you understand how a fare (and ticket you may buy) works. In addition, the travel industry is highly competitive and there are many lurks and perks.

The upshot of this is that you should get opinions, quotes and advice from as many airlines and travel agents as possible before you part with your hard-earned cash. The details given in this chapter should be regarded as pointers and are not a substitute for your own careful, up-to-date research.

airports rarely enforce the onward-ticket requirement, airlines often do.

If you are aiming to fly into one of these countries, but you don't have a ticket out of the country, it's likely the airline will not even let you board the plane. If you arrive in a country and are refused entry, the airline is responsible for flying you back out again, so they make sure you have the necessary passport, papers and tickets before you board. See Visas & Documents in the Regional Facts for the Visitor chapter for details and options for satisfying this requirement. Note that an open-jaw ticket (see the Air Travel Glossary in this chapter) will suffice.

Buying Tickets

The cost of flying to Central America depends on your point of departure, when you're traveling, your destination, your access to discount travel agencies and whether you are able to take advantage of advance-purchase fares and special offers. Patience and flexibility will get you the best deal. An understanding of some basics will help; see the Air Travel Glossary in this chapter.

Airlines are the best source of information on routes, timetables and standard fares, but they don't usually sell the cheapest tickets.

Start shopping for airfares as soon as you can, because the cheapest tickets have to be bought months in advance, and popular flights sell out early.

The fares quoted in this book are a guide only; they are approximate and based on the rates advertised by travel agents at press time. Quoted airfares do not imply a recommendation for the carrier.

Bucket Shops & Charter Flights Some travel agencies specialize in officially or unofficially discounted air tickets. In the UK, they are unbonded agencies called 'bucket shops.' In the USA, the cheapest fares are available through 'consolidators.'

Bucket-shop tickets often cost less than advance-purchase fares, without advance purchase or cancellation penalties, though some agents have their own penalties. Most bucket shops are well established and honorable, but unscrupulous agents might take your money and disappear before issuing a

ticket or issue an invalid or unusable ticket. Check carefully before handing over the money and confirm the reservation directly with the airline.

From continental Europe, the cheapest airfare may be offered on a charter flight, and some agencies specialize in arranging these. The dates of charter flights are generally fixed.

Buying Tickets Online Most airlines have their own Web sites with online ticket sales, often discounted for online customers. In North America, last-minute specials available online from individual airlines can save you a bundle if your travel dates are flexible. To buy a ticket on the Internet you'll need to use a credit card. Commercial reservation networks offer airline ticketing as well as information and bookings for hotels, car rental and other services, though Central American offerings can be very limited or nonexistent on many booking networks.

CNN Interactive's Travel Guide
www.cnn.com/Travel

Excite Travel by City.Net
http://travel.excite.com

Internet Travel Network
www.itn.net

Microsoft Expedia
www.expedia.com

Travelocity
www.travelocity.com

There are also online travel agents that specialize in cheap fares, but only a few have a good selection of flights to Central America. In North America, try Cheap Tickets, www.cheaptickets.com; in Europe, www.etn.nl; in Australia, www.travel.com.au.

Courier Flights Courier flights are a great bargain if you're lucky enough to find one to your destination. Air-freight companies expedite delivery of urgent items by sending them with you as your baggage allowance. You are permitted to bring along a carry-on bag, but that's all. In return, you get a steeply discounted ticket.

There are other restrictions: Courier tickets are sold for a fixed date, and schedule changes can be difficult to make. If you buy a roundtrip ticket, your schedule is even more rigid. Before you fly, you need to

Air Travel Glossary

Cancellation Penalties If you have to cancel or change a discounted ticket, there are often heavy penalties involved; insurance can sometimes be taken out against these penalties. Some airlines impose penalties on regular tickets as well, particularly against 'no-show' passengers.

Courier Fares Businesses often need to send urgent documents or freight securely and quickly. Courier companies hire people to accompany the package through customs and, in return, offer a discount ticket that is sometimes a phenomenal bargain. However, you may have to surrender all your baggage allowance and take only carry-on luggage.

Full Fares Airlines traditionally offer 1st class (coded F), business class (coded J) and economy class (coded Y) tickets. These days there are so many promotional and discounted fares available that few passengers pay full economy fare.

Lost Tickets If you lose your airline ticket an airline will usually treat it like a traveler's check and, after inquiries, issue you another one. Legally, however, an airline is entitled to treat it like cash and if you lose it then it's gone forever. Take good care of your tickets.

Onward Tickets An entry requirement for many countries is that you have a ticket out of the country. If you're unsure of your next move, the easiest solution is to buy the cheapest onward ticket to a neighboring country or a ticket from a reliable airline that can later be refunded if you do not use it.

Open-Jaw Tickets These are return tickets where you fly out to one place but return from another. If available, this can save you backtracking to your arrival point.

Overbooking Since every flight has some passengers who fail to show up, airlines often book more passengers than have seats. Usually excess passengers make up for the no-shows,

clarify what restrictions apply to your ticket, and don't expect a refund once you've paid.

Reserving a courier ticket takes some effort. They are not readily available, and arrangements have to be made a month or more in advance. You won't find courier flights on all routes, either – just on the major air routes.

Courier flights are occasionally advertised in the newspapers, or you can contact air-freight companies listed in the phone book. You may even have to go to the air-freight company to get an answer – the companies aren't always keen to give out information over the phone.

Travel Unlimited (PO Box 1058, Allston, MA 02134, USA) is a monthly travel newsletter that publishes many courier flight deals from destinations worldwide. A 12-month subscription to the newsletter costs US$25, or US$35 for readers outside the USA.

Another possibility is to join the International Association of Air Travel Couriers (IAATC). The membership fee of US$45 (US$50 outside the USA and Canada) gets members a bimonthly update of air-courier

offerings, access to a fax-on-demand service with daily updates of last minute specials and the bimonthly newsletter *Shoestring Traveler*. For more information, contact IAATC (☎ 561-582 8320) or visit its Web site (www.courier.org). Be aware that joining this organization does not guarantee you'll get a courier flight.

Most courier flights to Central America operate from Miami and go to a variety of destinations within the region, including Guatemala City, San Salvador, Managua and Panama City. One of the major courier services in Miami offering flights to Central America is Trans Air Systems (☎ 305-592 1771, fax 305-592 2927).

Stopovers Flights from North America, Europe, Australia and New Zealand may permit a stopover in Central America on the way to your destination city. This can effectively give you a free air connection within the region and allow you to visit additional countries at no extra cost; usually the fare is the same whether you pick up the next leg at a later date or continue on im-

Air Travel Glossary

but occasionally somebody gets 'bumped' onto the next available flight. Guess who it is most likely to be? The passengers who check in late.

Promotional Fares These are officially discounted fares, available from travel agencies or direct from the airline.

Reconfirmation If you don't reconfirm your flight at least 72 hours prior to departure, the airline may delete your name from the passenger list. Call to find out if your airline requires reconfirmation.

Restrictions Discounted tickets often have various restrictions on them – such as needing to be paid for in advance and incurring a penalty to be altered. Others are restrictions on the minimum and maximum period you must be away.

Round-the-World Tickets RTW tickets give you a limited period (usually a year) in which to circumnavigate the globe. You can go anywhere the carrying airlines go, as long as you don't backtrack. The number of stopovers or total number of separate flights is decided before you set off, and they usually cost a bit more than a basic return flight.

Transferred Tickets Airline tickets cannot be transferred from one person to another. Travelers sometimes try to sell the return half of their ticket, but officials can ask you to prove that you are the person named on the ticket. On an international flight tickets are compared with passports.

Travel Periods Ticket prices vary with the time of year. There is a low (off-peak) season and a high (peak) season, and often a low-shoulder season and a high-shoulder season as well. Usually the fare depends on your outward flight – if you depart in the high season and return in the low season, you pay the high-season fare.

---

mediately. If you're interested in visiting multiple destinations within the region, ask about stopover options when comparing flights.

Student & Youth Fares Full-time students and people under 26 have access to better deals than other travelers. The better deals may not always involve cheaper fares but can include more flexibility to change flights or routes once the ticket has been purchased. You have to show a document proving your date of birth or a valid International Student Identity Card (ISIC) when buying your ticket and when boarding the plane. There are plenty of places around the world where nonstudents can get fake student cards, but if you get caught using a fake card, you could have your ticket confiscated.

Travelers with Special Needs

Most international airlines can cater to people with special needs – travelers with disabilities, people with young children and even children traveling alone.

Travelers with special dietary preferences (vegetarian, kosher, etc) can request appropriate meals with advance notice. If you are traveling in a wheelchair, most international airports can provide an escort from check-in desk to plane when needed, and ramps, lifts, toilets and phones are generally available.

Airlines usually allow babies up to two years of age to fly for 10% of the adult fare, although a few may allow them to fly free of charge. Reputable international airlines usually provide diapers (nappies), tissues, talcum and all the other paraphernalia needed to keep babies clean, dry and happy. For children between the ages of two and 12, the fare on international flights is usually 50% of the regular fare or 67% of a discounted fare.

The USA

American, Continental, Delta, Northwest and United are the US airlines offering the most service to Central America. Aeroméxico, Aeronica, Aeroquetzal, Aviateca, COPA, Lacsa, Mexicana and TACA are the

Latin American airlines with flights connecting the region to the USA.

Dozens of airfares can apply to any given air route. They vary with each company, class of service, season of the year, length of stay, dates of travel, date of purchase and type of reservation. Your ticket may cost more or less depending upon the flexibility you are allowed in changing your plans. The price of the ticket is even affected by how you buy it and from whom. Note that for weekend travel, ticket costs are generally US$20 to US$25 higher per direction.

Travel agents are the first people to consult about fares and routes. Once you've discovered the basics of the airlines flying to your destination, the routes taken and the various discounted tickets available, you can consult your favorite bucket shop, consolidator or charter airline to see if their fares are better. Following are some sample fixed-date roundtrip fares (also called 'excursion fares') from various US hubs to the principal Central American cities.

destination	from	fare
Guatemala City	Chicago	US$420
	Miami	US$385
Belize City	San Francisco	US$520
	Newark	US$530
Tegucigalpa	New Orleans	US$550
	Washington, DC	US$650
San Salvador	New York	US$525
	Los Angeles	US$540
Managua	Houston	US$510
	Miami	US$350
San José	San Francisco	US$580
	Miami	US$320
Panama City	Atlanta	US$600
	New York	US$450

Many package tours from the USA provide roundtrip airfare, transfers and accommodations for a few days or a week. This can be an economical way to visit Central America. Some of these tour packages allow you to extend your stay in order to tour the region on your own.

Package tours change in price and features as the seasons change. For a cheap flight to Central America, read the advertisements in the travel section of your local newspaper and find a package-tour operator or a travel agent who sells such tours. Then call and ask if you can buy 'air only' (just the roundtrip air transportation, not the hotel or other features). Often this is possible, and usually it is cheaper than buying a discounted excursion ticket. Sometimes, though, the difference between air-only and a tour package with hotel is so small that it makes sense just to accept the hotel along with the flight.

Don't overlook the possibility of flying to Mexico first and then traveling overland to Central America. Travel agents and discount houses frequently offer special airfares to Mexico or package tours from the USA at very reasonable prices; ask if you can take the return portion of the ticket at a later date. Cancún, on Mexico's Yucatán Peninsula, is a popular package-tour destination, for example, and it could make a convenient starting point for onward travel to Belize and Guatemala.

Consolidators are organizations that buy bulk seats from airlines at considerable discounts and then resell them to the public, often through travel agents, sometimes directly through newspaper and magazine ads. Though there are some shady dealers, many consolidators are legitimate. Ask your travel agent about buying a consolidator ticket, or look for the consolidator ads in the travel section of the newspaper (they're the ones with tables of destinations and fares and a toll-free number to call). In particular, look for agencies specializing in the region, such as eXito Latin America (☎ 510-655 2154, 800-655 4053, fax 415-704 3255, exito@wonderlink.com), 1212 Broadway, Suite 910, Oakland, CA 94612. Try its Web site at www.wonderlink.com

Council Travel has more than 60 offices in the USA that specialize in student and youth fares. Call its national reservations center (☎ 800-226 8624, 617-528 2091) in Boston for information or try its Web site (www.counciltravel.com). Council's head office (☎ 212-822 2600, 800-226 8624, fax 212-822 2699) is at 205 E 42nd St, New York, NY 10017.

Another popular budget and student travel agent is STA (☎ 310-394 5126, 800-777 0112, fax 310-394 4041), 411 Santa Monica Blvd, Santa Monica, CA 90401. It also has offices in Boston, Chicago, Miami,

New York, Philadelphia, San Francisco, Seattle, Washington, DC, and other cities. Call the 800-number for office locations or try its Web site (www.statravel.com) for more information.

Canada

Most flights from Canada to Central America involve a connection via one of the US gateways. Canada's national student travel agency is Travel CUTS (☎ 416-979 2406, fax 416-979 8167), 187 College St, Toronto, ON M5T 1P7, and at 50 other locations across Canada, including Montréal, Calgary, Edmonton and Vancouver. It has good deals for students and offers services to the general public as well. Check its Web site (www.travelcuts.com) for more information.

South America & the Caribbean

Grupo TACA member airlines (see Airports & Airlines, earlier) and COPA, Panama's national carrier, connect Central American cities to Venezuela, Colombia, Ecuador, Peru, Chile and Argentina. Several US carriers, including American Airlines, Continental, Delta and United, have connections from a number of South American countries. A few South American carriers fly to Central America, but routes change frequently.

Flights from South American countries are generally subject to high tax (often over 10%), and consolidator deals are difficult to come by.

The shortest and cheapest way to fly between Central and South America is between Panama and Colombia. Within these countries, the cheapest routes are those linking Panama City to Cartagena, Barranquilla or Medellín. Flights from Panama City to Bogotá and Cali tend to be slightly more expensive.

Venezuela has some of the cheapest air links to Central America. In Caracas, IVI Tours (☎ 02 993 60 82), residencia La Hacienda, Piso Bajo, Local 1-4-T, Final Avenida Principal de las Mercedes, is the affiliate for STA Travel in Venezuela and often has a range of cheap fares. In Argentina, Asatej Group maintains offices in nine Argentine cities, as well as Santiago de Chile and Montevideo, and offers some good student/youth fares. You can check out

their Web site (www.almundo.com) for more information.

Sample fares to and from Guatemala City start at around US$500 for Caracas, US$550 for Lima, US$1100 for Rio de Janeiro and US$800 for Buenos Aires. One-way and roundtrip fares are much the same.

Roundtrip airfare on COPA between Bogotá and Panama City costs about US$270.

Within Central America, expect to spend at least US$150 on roundtrip airfare to Guatemala City from San José (Costa Rica) and San Salvador. (See the Getting Around chapter for more on air travel within the region.)

Via Isla de San Andrés Several airlines land at San Andrés, an island off the coast of Nicaragua that is actually Colombian territory. From San Andrés you can continue on a domestic Colombian flight to cities such as Barranquilla, Cartagena or Bogotá. From all Central American countries except Panama, it's generally cheaper to fly via San Andrés than to fly directly to the Colombian mainland.

Europe

The cheapest fares are on charter flights, such as those run by Air Europa from Spain and Martinair from Amsterdam. Most of the scheduled airlines' routes take you to one of the US hub cities, where you change to a plane of a US, Mexican, Guatemalan or other Central American airline before reaching your final destination.

The UK For cheap tickets from London, pick up a copy of *City Limits, Time Out, TNT* or any of the other magazines that advertise discount (bucket shop) flights, and check out a few of the advertisers. The *Evening Standard* is also a good resource, and the magazine *Business Traveller* has lots of good advice on airfare bargains. Most bucket shops are trustworthy and reliable, but the occasional shady operator appears – *Time Out* and *Business Traveller* give some useful advice on precautions to take to avoid scams.

Reputable discount ticket agencies in London offering cheap fares to Latin America include the following (all have branches in other cities).

Journey Latin America (☎ 020 8747 3108), 12-13 Heathfield Terrace, London W4 4JE
Web site: www.journeylatinamerica.co.uk

STA Travel (☎ 020 7361 6145), 86 Old Brompton Rd, London SW7 3LQ
Web site: www.statravel.com

Trailfinders (☎ 020 7938 3939), 194 Kensington High St, London W8 7RG
Web site: www.trailfinder.com

Usit Campus (☎ 0870 240 1010,), 52 Grosvenor Gardens, London SW1W 0AG
Web site: www.usitcampus.co.uk

Typical fixed-date return (excursion) fares from London at the time of writing were as follows: Panama City, US$1200; Managua, US$1290; Guatemala City, US$985.

Continental Europe Discount tickets are available at prices similar to London's in several European cities. Amsterdam, Paris and Frankfurt are among the main cheap flight centers. Air France, KLM, Iberia and the Colombian airline Avianca are some of the airlines whose tickets are handled by discount agents. Most flights from Europe originate from Amsterdam, Brussels, Frankfurt, London, Madrid, Paris or Zürich. Roundtrip fares from Europe typically range from US$750 to US$950.

Also investigate the option of flying to Mexico (Cancún or Mexico City); often the fares are lower and charter flights are available. Once in Mexico you can easily fly or travel overland by bus to Guatemala or Belize.

Following were some typical fixed-date return (excursion) fares to Central American cities at the time of writing.

Amsterdam to Tegucigalpa	US$1050
Frankfurt to Panama City	US$850
Paris to San José	US$880

Australia & New Zealand

No direct flights from Australia to the region are available. The cheapest way of getting to Central America is via the USA, particularly Miami or Los Angeles. Discount roundtrip flights from Sydney to Los Angeles cost around US$900 and up. Cheap flights from the USA to the region are hard to find in Australia. The cheapest Los Angeles–Guatemala City fare at the time of writing was US$500 roundtrip, US$385 from Miami (see The USA, earlier). A

typical fare to Panama City from Sydney or Melbourne at the time of writing was US$1750.

Travelers looking to combine a visit to the Mayan region with travel to South America will find that the cheapest roundtrip tickets from Sydney to Lima or Rio de Janeiro cost about US$1200. Santiago and Buenos Aires are cheaper at about US$1000.

Round-the-world tickets with a Mexico/ Guatemala option are sometimes available in Australia.

A number of agents offer cheap air tickets out of Australia. STA Travel, with more than 80 offices around the country, is one of the most popular discount travel agents in Australia. It maintains a Web site (www.statravel.com.au) and also has sales offices or agents in New Zealand and all over the world. Flight Centres International also specializes in cheap airfares and has a Web site (www.flightcentre.com.au) and offices in most capital cities, as well as many suburban branches. It's also worth checking the advertisements in Saturday editions of major newspapers, such as Melbourne's *Age* or the *Sydney Morning Herald*.

Departure Taxes

A departure tax of about US$17 is charged on international flights from Mexico. Departure taxes also apply to all the Central American countries: US$30 from Guatemala; US$15 from Belize; US$25 from Honduras, El Salvador and Nicaragua; US$17 from Costa Rica; and US$20 from Panama. If you buy your ticket in Central America, the tax may be included in your ticket cost; the letters XD on your ticket show that the tax has been paid. If it hasn't, you must pay with cash during airport check-in.

LAND
Border Crossings

For details on land border crossings among the Central American nations and country-specific entry requirements, see the introductory Getting There & Away section in each chapter.

If you fly into Central America, you should have few, if any, hassles. However, if you cross at land border points, you may run into other situations. Border officials in

Latin American countries sometimes request unofficial 'fees' from travelers at the border; these are called *la mordida*, or the 'bite.' There are some things you can try to do to avoid paying, such as scowling quietly and acting important or cosmopolitan (dressing nicely helps). Scowl all you want, but whatever you do, keep everything formal. Never *ever* raise your voice, mumble a curse, get angry or verbally confront a Latin American official. You'll get farther acting quietly superior and unruffled at all times. See Police & Military under Dangers & Annoyances in the Regional Facts for the Visitor chapter for other considerations.

In addition to the usual documents, sometimes a show of cash is required to cross land borders (US$500 per month of your planned stay is generally sufficient; traveler's checks should qualify toward the total amount). If you lack 'sufficient funds' for your proposed visit, officials may limit the length of your stay, but once you are in the country, you can usually renew or extend your visa by showing a wad of traveler's checks.

If you're driving, there are a lot of fees, paperwork and red tape involved in crossing borders within the region. Regulations and costs vary considerably from one country to another, and generally it can be a time-consuming business. At each crossing, you will usually be issued a special permit for your vehicle, which must be renewed at regular intervals, and insurance requirements must also be satisfied.

Bus

All overland routes from the USA and Canada necessarily go through Mexico. If you are traveling overland from North America, you will have to change buses at the US-Mexican border; plans for buses from the interior of the US to the interior of Mexico that would preclude a change at the border have yet to be implemented. Bus companies providing cross-border service include Greyhound (☎ 800-231 2222 in the USA), ADO Trailways (☎ 713-921 3838 in the USA) and El Expreso (☎ 713-650 6565 in the USA). Greyhound has a Web site at www.greyhound.com.

Several international bus routes connect Mexico to Guatemala, Belize, Honduras, El Salvador and points south. Tica Bus (☎ 502 261 1773 in Guatemala, 502 331 4279) has daily service from Guatemala City to San Salvador. From San Salvador, buses continue to all the other Central American capitals except Belize City. When traveling between Guatemala and neighboring countries, you will often have the choice of a direct, 1st-class bus or a series of 'chicken buses.' The latter option usually takes longer, but is always cheaper and infinitely more interesting. Try Tica Bus' Web site (www.ticabus.com) for more information.

For additional information on bus travel within Central America, see the regional Getting Around chapter and the introductory transportation sections in each of the country chapters.

Car & Motorcycle

Traveling overland by car or motorcycle in Central America is not for everyone – you should know some Spanish and have basic mechanical aptitude, large reserves of patience and access to some extra cash for emergencies. You should also note warnings about risk areas for highway robbery (see Dangers & Annoyances in each country's Facts for the Visitor section) and avoid intercity driving at night.

For details on country-specific requirements pertaining to documentation, fees and insurance regulations for private vehicles, see the introductory Getting There & Away section in each country chapter. For information on vehicle purchase and rental, see the Getting Around chapter.

Taking a car is useful for travelers who

- have plenty of time
- plan to go to remote places
- will be camping a lot
- have surfboards, diving equipment or other cumbersome luggage
- will be traveling with a group of four or more

Don't take a car if you

- are on a tight schedule
- have a limited budget
- plan to spend most of your time in urban areas
- will be traveling alone
- want a relaxing trip with minimum risks

Cars are fairly expensive to rent or buy in Central America, so your best option is to take one in from the USA. If that means buying it first, you may need a few weeks to find a good vehicle at a reasonable price. It may also take time at the end of your trip to sell the car.

There are a number of things to consider when deciding whether to take a vehicle to Central America. The most apparent difficulty in driving your own vehicle is that most North American cars now have catalytic converters, which require unleaded fuel. Though unleaded is sold in Mexico, it is not yet widely available in Central American countries, including neighboring Guatemala and Belize. You can arrange to have your catalytic converter disconnected and replaced with a straight piece of exhaust pipe soon after you cross into Mexico (it's illegal to have it done in the USA). Save the converter and have it replaced before crossing the border back into the USA.

Make sure your car is in good condition and that you know a thing or two about repairing it should the need arise. It may be difficult to find mechanics and parts for newer-model US and Canadian cars with sophisticated electronics and pollution-control systems. If your vehicle breaks down in Central America and needs parts, they may have to be ordered from the USA or Canada. Take as many spare parts as you can manage and know what to do with (for example, spare fuel filters are very useful). Tires (including spare), shock absorbers and suspension should be in good condition. For security, have something to immobilize the steering wheel, such as 'the Club'; you should also consider getting a kill switch installed.

If you do drive your own vehicle, consider that driving even major Central American roads at night is not recommended: They are narrow, unlit, rarely painted with a center stripe, often potholed and subject to hazards such as cattle and pedestrians in rural areas.

Security and parking can present problems, and in many places street parking will not be safe. Look for hotels listed in this book with parking facilities. Sometimes this is simply the hotel courtyard, but it's safer than the alternative.

Motorcycling in Central America is not for the faint-hearted. Roads and traffic can be rough, and parts and mechanics hard to come by.

Motor Vehicle Insurance You'd be wise to buy local liability insurance in this region; in case of an accident, no matter whose fault, you could be 'detained' indefinitely until all claims are settled. Regulations concerning vehicle insurance vary considerably from one country to another; rates depend on your vehicle's value. See each country's Getting There & Away section for details.

Sanborn's Insurance (☎ 956-686 0711, fax 956-686 1417), 2009 South 10th St, McAllen, Texas 78503, sells coverage for Mexico and Central America and has offices in several other cities near the US-Mexico border.

Driver's License To drive any motor vehicle in this region, you need a valid driver's license from your home country. Police will be familiar with US and Canadian licenses; those from other countries may be scrutinized more closely, but they are still legal. Obtaining an international driver's permit from an automobile association in your home country is a sensible precaution.

Importing Motor Vehicles The rules for taking a vehicle into this region, outlined below, change from time to time. Check current laws with the American Automobile Association (AAA) and any local consulate or government tourist office.

You will need a temporary import permit if you want to take a vehicle more than 25km into Mexico. The permits are available at the *aduana* (customs) office near border crossings.

In addition to a passport and tourist card, you'll need the following documents, which must be in your own name: a certificate of title or ownership for the vehicle, a current registration card and a driver's license. Have at least one photocopy of each of these documents, as well as the original.

One person cannot bring in two vehicles. If, for example, you have a motorcycle attached to your car, you'll need another adult traveling with you to obtain a permit for the motorcycle, and that person will need to have all the right papers for it. If the motorcycle is registered in your name, you'll need a notarized affidavit authorizing the other person to take it into Mexico.

As a rule, the owner cannot leave Mexico without the vehicle. If it's wrecked completely, you must obtain permission to leave it in the country from either the Registro Federal de Vehículos (Federal Registry of Vehicles) in Mexico City, or a Hacienda (Treasury Department) office in another city or town. If you have to leave the country in an emergency, the vehicle can be left in temporary storage at an airport or seaport or with an aduana or Hacienda office. Similar rules apply in most Central American countries.

Shipping Your Own Vehicle Those traveling overland by car from North to South America, or vice versa, will have to work around the Darién Gap (see South America). This means you'll have to ship your vehicle across it, usually between Panama and Colombia. This is a costly and difficult process, but it can be done.

If you're willing to part with the cash, don't overlook the option of shipping a vehicle from a US port to somewhere in Central America. It's possible, for example, to ship a car from Miami to Costa Rica for about US$770 and up, depending on the car. Contact Latii Express International (☎ 800-590 3789, 305-593 8929, fax 305-593 8786, latiiexpress@prodigy.net) for specifics.

Shipping your car to South America is an option, but it's not cheap and there is a lot of paperwork involved. From North America, it is generally cheaper to ship from Atlantic ports than from Pacific ports. There are many companies specializing in shipping cars and it pays to shop around; look in the phone directory under 'Automobile Transporters.' Expect to pay at least US$1500 to get your car from an eastern US port to Guayaquil (Ecuador) or Barranquilla (Colombia). Shipping your vehicle to Caracas, Venezuela, is another possibility.

If you're shipping a vehicle to South America, you may need a *carnet de passages* or a *libreta de pasos por aduana* in addition to the customs, shipping and other paperwork. Check with the appropriate consulates, particularly for any country where your vehicle will arrive by land or sea. The carnet is a bond guaranteeing that you won't sell your vehicle in South America – you post a bond to get the carnet, and it's partially refunded when you get back and

show that you still have the vehicle. The best source of information is usually the national automobile club in the country where you purchased the car.

You don't need the carnet for travel in Central America, but failure to present one once you've arrived in South America could get you and your vehicle denied entry at any border on the continent.

South America

If you plan to enter Panama overland from South America, it's a good idea to get a visa or tourist card before showing up at the border, as border posts occasionally run out of tourist cards. If a post is out of tourist cards, you'll be prohibited from entering the country. Remember that both Panama and Colombia demand onward tickets, so get a ticket and any visas you need before setting out from either north or south. Many travelers have been turned back for lack of an onward ticket or sufficient funds, especially traveling from Colombia to Panama. (See Onward-Ticket Requirements, earlier, for details.)

Remember that if you want to transport a vehicle between Central and South America, you will have to ship it across the Darién Gap, as the Interamericana stops short of the Colombian border (see Shipping Your Own Vehicle, earlier).

Via the Darién Gap Coming from North America, you can travel overland only as far south as Panama. There is no road connection onward to Colombia: The Carretera Interamericana (Interamerican Hwy) ends in the vast rain-forest wilderness called the Darién, in southeast Panama. Travelers know this roadless area between Central and South America as the Darién Gap – in the past it has been difficult, but possible, to trek across the Darién Gap with the help of local guides. For further details, see the Darién Province section in the Panama chapter.

Warning Since around 1998, the Darién Gap has been prohibitively dangerous because of bandit and guerilla activity, especially on the Colombian side. Particularly treacherous are the areas between Boca de Cupe and Colombia, the traditional path through the Darién Gap, which includes the towns of

Púcuro, Paya, Limón, Balsal and Palo de las Letras. The areas north and east of this are also considered dangerous, including the mountains Altos de Limón, the Río Tuquesa and the trail from Puerto Obaldía. It is still possible to skirt the northern edge of the Darién, trekking and using local boats, but it's not easy or completely safe. It's possible to do in as little as a week, but allow twice this time. Take dried food, drinking water and purification tablets or equipment.

Puerto Obaldía to Capurganá The Panama-Colombia border can also be crossed at a rugged point on the Caribbean coast between rustic Puerto Obaldía (on the Panamanian side) and the resort of Capurganá (on the Colombian side). You can walk or boat between these two points. Walking to the first Colombian village, Sapzurro, takes about 2½ hours, but the track is indistinct in places, and the presence of bandits and smugglers in the area makes boating the better option. From Sapzurro, it's a two-hour walk to Capurganá. Be sure to obtain the entry procedures from the Colombian embassy or consulate in your home country prior to crossing the border.

SEA

A few cruise ships from Europe and the US call on Central American ports, but they are much more expensive than any air ticket. Some cargo ships from ports such as Houston, New Orleans, Hamburg and Amsterdam will take a limited number of passengers to South American ports, but they are also expensive. The standard reference for passenger ships is the *OAG Cruise & Ferry Guide,* published four times a year by Reed Travel Group (☎ 44 1582 600111), Church St, Dunstable, Bedfordshire LU5 4HB, UK. The US office (☎ 800-323 3537, 630-574 6000, fax 630-574 6565) is at 2000 Clearwater Dr, Oak Brook, Illinois 60523. A one-year subscription costs US$237 for US residents.

On the Caribbean side of the isthmus, boats are continually coming and going between all the Central American countries, the Caribbean islands, Mexico, the USA and the north coast of South America. With a lot of luck and good timing, you may be able to arrange passage

with a yacht or a cargo or fishing vessel; ask around the docks at ports and yacht marinas. The Pacific coast yields fewer opportunities for travelers, as there is less sea traffic and most of the boats are larger vessels on defined schedules.

Boat trips from a number of Central American ports can transport you to other countries in the region. For information on regularly scheduled passenger boat service (as well as unofficial options) linking the various countries, see the Getting There & Away sections in the country chapters.

Once in Central America, it may be possible to arrange long-distance passage with cargo or fishing vessels if you pay your way. From the Caribbean coast of Honduras, for example, you can try to find a boat around Puerto Cortés, Tela, La Ceiba, Trujillo or the Bay Islands. The most common international destinations for these boats – in addition to those within Central America – are Caribbean islands including Grand Cayman and Jamaica, and New Orleans and Miami in the USA.

The Panama Canal, one of the world's major shipping crossroads, is a sure place to encounter sea traffic. Some private yachts offer trips, usually at a cost, but sometimes in exchange for serving on the crew or line handling through the canal. Notices are often posted at the Panama Canal Yacht Club in Colón or in pensions such as the Voyager International Hostel in Panama City. Besides possible risks associated with boat safety and smuggling activity, a certain amount of schedule flexibility is necessary.

There's no regular boat service from Colombia to Panama, and the cargo ships that ply the Caribbean from Colón to San Blas and on to the Colombian port of Barranquilla are not very safe or reliable. Nevertheless, some of these ships will take paying passengers, and some will also take motorcycles and even cars; prices are very negotiable. This is a very unofficial (and potentially risky) way to go, but it can be done.

If you arrive or depart from Central America by sea, be sure to clear your paperwork (entry and exit stamps, etc) with the nearest immigration office in both countries at the first opportunity.

ORGANIZED TOURS

Although there are many well-regarded organized tour operators within Central America (see the country chapters for details), travelers with limited time or experience may want to arrange a tour from home. These will almost always be more expensive than a similar package arranged in Central America, however.

Travelers in search of a thematic trip (for example, archaeology or bird watching) led by experts may be interested in organized tours as well. Whatever your reasoning for taking an organized trip, tour operators should be available to answer any questions or concerns you have well before departure and be willing to provide a detailed itinerary upon request. Read the fine print and be aware of exactly what the tour price includes.

Of particular interest to shoestring travelers, Green Tortoise (☎ 800-867 8647, 415-956 7500, fax 415-956 4900), 494 Broadway, San Francisco, CA 94133, USA, offers several budget tours to Central America. Green Tortoise has long been known for its North American tours, on which young-at-heart travelers sleep on bunks in the bus (a sort of communal home-on-wheels) and join in preparing meals. Most of its Central America trips operate during Central America's dry season, but schedules vary. At the time of writing, Green Tortoise was offering a 14-day Costa Rica and Nicaragua loop tour (May departure); a 17-day Costa Rica/Panama Carnaval tour (February departure); and a best-of-Costa Rica loop tour with departures in January, March, April, May, July and November. Each of these tours costs between US$500 and US$550 per person plus US$120 for meals. Check out its Web site at www.greentortoise.com.

The following operators offer tours to Central America.

The USA

Lost World Adventures (☎ 800-999 0558, 404-373 5820, info@lostworldadventures.com), 112 Church St, Decatur, GA 30030. Arranges tours of the highlands, Petén and similar destinations of interest to the general traveler.
Web site: www.lostworldadventures.com

Ecotour Expeditions (☎ 401-423 3377, 800-688 1822, fax 401-423 9630), PO Box 128, Jamestown,

RI 02835. Offers five- to 10-day natural history and highlights tours.
Web site: www.naturetours.com

Ceiba Adventures (☎ 800-217 1060, 520-527 0171, fax 520-527 8127, ceiba@primenet.com), PO Box 2274, Flagstaff, AZ 86003. Offers white-water rafting trips to some of the most inaccessible Mayan ruins in the Petén region of Guatemala.

Canada

GAP (☎ 416-922 8899, 800-465 5600, fax 416-922 0822), 264 Dupont St, Toronto, Ontario M5R 1V7. Lower-priced escorted tours using public transport and inexpensive hotels.
Web site: www.gap.ca

Offbeat Adventures (☎ 905-509 4494, fax 905-509 0444, offbeat@sympatico.ca), 284 Lancrest St, Pickering, Ontario L1V 6N3. Offers tours to ruins, beaches and volcanoes with scuba certification and snorkeling options.
Web site: www.offbeatadventures.com

The UK & Continental Europe

Journey Latin America (☎ 44 208 747 8315, fax 44 208 742 1312, tours@journeylatinamerica.co.uk), 12 & 13 Heathfield Terrace, London W4 4JE, UK, and (☎ 44 161 832 1441, fax 44 161 832 1551, man@journeylatinamerica.co.uk), 2nd Floor Barton Arcade, 51-63 Deansgate, Manchester M3 2BH, UK. Recommended flight, tour and custom-itinerary specialists to Central America, with many years of experience.
Web site: www.journeylatinamerica.co.uk

Yax Pac Tours (☎/fax 41 01 432 62 92, webmaster@yaxpactours.com), contact Susette Isenschmied, Grimselstrasse 28, 8048 Zürich, Switzerland. Runs tours long on adventure, short on comfort; recommended for backpackers who want a little structure.
Web site: www.yaxpactours.com

Australia

Adventure Associates (☎ 02 9389 7466, fax 02 9369 1853), 197 Oxford St, Bondi Junction, Sydney, NSW 2022. Standard one-week tours plus independent travel arrangements.
Web site: www.adventureassociates.com

Contours (☎ 03 9670 6900, fax 03 9670 7558, contours@compuserve.com) 1/84 William St, Melbourne, Victoria 3000. Good variety of Latin American tours at mid-range to lower-top-end prices.

Visit the Central American resources page at the helpful Gorp Travel Web site (www.gorp.com) for more ideas about organized tours.

Getting Around

Buses are the cheapest and most accessible way to get around Central America. Although bus travel gives you the best feel for life in this part of the world, not everyone has the time or patience to ride cheek by jowl with the masses and their produce (vegetable *and* animal). Luckily, domestic air travel is on the rise, with new routes and airports – or at least serviceable airstrips – allowing travelers with more money than time to get to the major sights quickly.

Unfortunately, car rental companies have yet to join this 'easy access' campaign. Rental cars are expensive in Central America, and navigating narrow roads alongside hell-bent drivers is no treat. In most cases, you are not allowed to drive a rental car across the borders of the country in which you rented it. In those cases where you may drive across borders, you'll need permission in writing from the car rental company. Thus, a plan to tour most of the region by rental car often involves different rentals in different countries and bus or air travel in between.

AIR

With the exception of Belize and Honduras, all of the Central American countries have a national airline that offers both domestic and international service. All of these carriers except Panama's COPA have formed a regional alliance called Grupo TACA. (See the Getting There & Away sections of each country chapter for airline contact information within the region.) Member airlines operate cooperatively with one another to avoid overlap of routes; if you buy a ticket with more than one connecting flight, you may find you'll be scheduled on different airlines for the various legs of your itinerary.

In addition to Central America's international carriers, a number of smaller airlines provide domestic service within each country; details on these carriers are provided in the country chapters. Aircraft servicing more remote destinations will most likely be small, two-propeller passenger planes. Most of these planes have a per-passenger baggage limit of about 20lb; you must pay extra for anything over the limit.

Also, expect a minimal domestic departure tax to be levied on domestic flights.

Considering the relatively short distances that separate the region's major population centers, flights among the various Central American countries tend to be expensive; a half-hour flight can easily cost US$100 or more. If your time in Central America is limited, however, air travel can help you avoid some long, laborious overland trips and allow quick access to remote areas. A few popular air routes (with one-way fares) are those linking Belize City with Flores (near Tikal; US$85) and Guatemala City with Flores (US$85) or Copán (US$100). See the transportation sections of each country chapter for additional sample fares among the region's cities, as well as route and schedule information.

Open-jaw itineraries and free stopovers on flights from your home country are some of the ways in which you can save money on air travel within Central America; see the Air section in the preceding Getting There & Away chapter for information.

When planning air travel within the region, avoid scheduling a domestic flight with a tight connection for an international flight. Confirming (and reconfirming) your flight is imperative. Many flights are oversold, and failing to reconfirm your seat 72 hours prior to departure could get you bumped from your flight. Arrive at the airport at least an hour before flight time – several hours in advance if possible – as airlines often hand out boarding passes on a first-come, first-serve basis.

If you buy any type of airline ticket in Central America, pay attention to the currency-exchange rate the airline is using. Often you can pay for the ticket in either the local currency or in US dollars (cash, traveler's checks or credit card). Check the difference between the price quoted in dollars and the price in the local currency – paying in one currency or the other can sometimes make a difference in the cost.

Remember that Belize, Costa Rica and Panama officially have an onward-ticket requirement; that is, you cannot enter the country unless you possess an onward ticket to another destination outside that country.

See Onward-Ticket Requirements in the Getting There & Away chapter.

Air Passes

The member airlines of the regional alliance Grupo TACA, including Aviateca, Lacsa, Nica and TACA, have developed special fare plans for visitors to Central America. Usually these passes must be purchased outside the countries for which they are valid and in conjunction with an international ticket, so you have to consider this option before you leave. An air pass can be an economical way to cover long distances within the region if your time is limited, but some passes are very inflexible with regard to schedule and route changes; be sure to check the restrictions before you purchase the pass.

Through Grupo TACA, you can buy a Mayan air pass or a Visit Central America air pass, either of which allows you to fly from a US gateway (usually Miami, New Orleans or Houston) and visit as few as four regional cities (two in the case of the Central America plan), and as many as eight, for a very competitive fare. For example, a low-season air pass for the following itinerary cost US$770 at the time of writing: Miami to San Salvador; San Salvador to San José; San José to Tegucigalpa; Tegucigalpa to Miami. For details on current pricing, contact Grupo TACA, any of the individual member airlines or a travel agent. (See Airports & Airlines in the Getting There & Away chapter for contact information.)

Another useful resource for arranging Central American air passes is eXito Latin America (☎ 510-655 2154, 800-655 4053, fax 415-704 3255, exito@wonderlink.com), 1212 Broadway, Suite 910, Oakland, CA 94612. Its Web site (www.wonderlink.com) has a calculator that spits out a fare after you enter the destination cities of your choice.

Aerocaribe also offers a Mayan air pass; visit its Web site at www.aerocaribe.com for more information.

BUS

You'll probably spend most of your travel time and money on buses, and this will be an experience in itself. Road transportation, especially by bus, is well developed throughout the region, but road conditions and the quality of the buses vary widely from place to place. Buses in Central America range air-conditioned, 1st-class coaches to former US school buses and converted flatbed trucks with wooden seats. Direct, 1st-class trips are often available between major cities, but in more remote areas, be prepared for a few adventures.

On both local and long-distance routes, bus traffic tends to be most intense in the morning (beginning as early as 4 or 5 am), tapering off by mid- or late afternoon. In many places within the region, no buses run in the late afternoon or evening. Where they do operate, nighttime buses are not recommended for safety reasons. Buses may run every few minutes, on the half hour, hourly or only once or twice a day, depending on the route.

Remote towns and villages may or may not have bus services. If not, pickup trucks serve as de facto buses; you hail the driver and pay them as if they were the real thing. Routes to remote towns and villages serve residents going to market in larger towns. This often means that the only bus departs from the village early in the morning and returns from the larger market town by midafternoon. If you want to visit such a village, you may have to take an afternoon bus and stay the night or hitch a ride back on a pickup, though reverse traffic on market day can be slow.

Luggage may be stored in a lower compartment or be piled on the roof of the bus. Since buses are the principal means of transportation in the region, people carry anything and everything on board: goods to sell at the market, produce bought at the market and occasionally even small farm animals (hence the term 'chicken bus' used among foreign travelers to describe this mode of transportation).

Always keep an eye on your luggage on bus trips, wherever it is stored for the journey (or at least until the point that the bus is ready to depart), and if possible, try to keep your belongings with you. If you're unable to do this, transfer anything valuable or fragile from your backpack to your day pack before the ride. Also watch out for pickpockets on crowded buses and in bus terminals; Managua is particularly notorious for theft. See the Dangers & Annoyances section in the Regional

Facts for the Visitor chapter for suggested precautions.

When making travel plans, don't assume that listed bus departure times are correct, as schedules are particularly vulnerable to change. Sometimes buses only leave once there are enough passengers on board. Before you buy your ticket, ascertain the class and type of bus you'll be traveling on and ask about the approximate length of the trip.

For country-specific details on getting around by bus, and for detailed route and fare information on bus travel among the various countries, see the transportation sections in the individual country chapters.

Bus Terminals

Most major cities and towns have a *terminal de autobuses* (long-distance bus terminal). Often this is outside the center of town, and you'll need a local bus or taxi to reach it. The biggest and best terminals also have restaurants, shops, showers and other services, and the surrounding area is often a good place to look for cheap accommodations and food. Most bus companies have ticket offices at central terminals and information boards showing routes, departure times and fares. Seats are numbered and booked in advance. At holiday times especially, seats on major routes may be hard to come by.

Some cities have several terminals, each serving a different route. In cities like San Salvador, for example, all the westbound buses come and go from one bus station, and all the eastbound buses come and go from another. If you are just passing through the city, you will have to take a local bus between the two stations. In other places, such as Guatemala City, Tegucigalpa and San Pedro Sula, each bus company has its own station. Where this is the case, all major bus stations are listed in this book and shown on the city maps where possible. If the bus stations are spread out in this manner, try asking a taxi driver which station has buses going to your destination. A small, one-company terminal may be nothing more than a parking area and a ticket seller.

You can almost always buy food at bus stations, and sodas and other beverages are generally available as well. It is also quite common for food to be available along the way, with crowds of people running up to sell snacks and drinks through the bus windows at every stop.

Shuttle

Some private companies offer shuttle or minibus services between tourist destinations and the region's major airports; in some cases, they will even pick you up and return you to your hotel of choice. These shuttle services come and go with the seasons and are listed – where they exist – under the various destination sections in each country chapter.

Tourist shuttles typically carry eight to 10 passengers, cost significantly more than the regular bus services and provide faster service than regular buses.

CAR & MOTORCYCLE

Central America is relatively easy to explore by private vehicle. Renting a vehicle or taking your own car is more expensive than taking the bus, however, and infinitely more complicated. See Car & Motorcycle in the Getting There & Away chapter for a list of things to consider when deciding whether to take a vehicle to Central America. Information on documentation, insurance and regulations for importing or shipping motor vehicles is also provided in that chapter.

For details on country-specific requirements pertaining to documentation, fees and insurance regulations for private vehicles, see the introductory Getting There & Away section in each country chapter.

Road Rules

Drivers in Central American countries operate on the right-hand side of the road. Road rules are frequently ignored and seldom enforced, road and driving conditions can be hazardous, and many drivers are reckless. Traffic signs are in Spanish and don't always display an internationally recognized symbol; see the Language chapter for a list of important traffic signs that visiting drivers should become familiar with.

Rental

Car rental is expensive in Central America: Expect to pay around US$50 to US$75 a day, not including gas. Trucks, minivans and 4WD vehicles are also available. Insurance policies accompanying rental cars may not protect you from loss or theft, in which case you can be liable for US$600 to US$1500 or more in damages. Be careful where you park, especially in large cities and at night. Motorcycles can also be rented in some places; check the transportation sections in the country chapters. Although not required by law, safety gear such as a helmet and gloves are recommended for motorcyclists.

To rent a car or motorcycle you need to show your passport, driver's license and a major credit card. Usually, the person renting the vehicle must be 25 years or older. If you are not the holder of a valid credit card, you may be able to leave a large cash deposit. Obviously, an official receipt would be needed in this event.

Major international rental agencies such as Avis, Budget and Hertz have offices in Central American capitals and other major cities, but there are also local agencies. Check the telephone directory under 'Alquiler de Automóviles' and 'Renta de Automóviles.' Car rental costs at airports can be inflated; you often get much better prices by taking the airport transportation into town and renting a car from an agency there.

Whenever you rent a vehicle, particularly from a local operator, always ask about your liability in the event of an accident or breakdown. Some travelers have been faced with big bills for damage that wasn't necessarily their fault.

Purchase & Sale

If you're coming from overseas and wish to travel the region by car, you may want to buy a used car or van in the USA, where they're relatively cheap, and drive through the USA to Mexico and points south on the isthmus. In Central America, the cost of buying a car is prohibitive, and renting a car can be expensive and restrictive if you intend to visit a number of countries. If you do purchase a vehicle in Central America, bc prepared to deal with exasperating bureaucracies. Be certain of the title; as a foreigner, you may find it very useful to get a notarized document authorizing your use of the car, since the bureaucracy may take some time to change the title. In some instances, you may find obstacles to taking a vehicle purchased in Central America across international borders.

If you choose to buy a vehicle in North America and travel overland through Mexico, you may want to allow a few weeks to find a good car at a reasonable price. Again, make sure the title is clean, and get a notarized document authorizing your use of the vehicle. See the Getting There & Away chapter for regulations on importing private vehicles.

In the past, foreign visitors to the region have sought to make money by purchasing used vehicles in the USA, driving them to Central America and selling them there, but in recent years, many readers have reported that this is no longer the profitable venture it once was. If you want to try your luck selling a vehicle in Central America, you should consider it as a possible way to subsidize your trip rather than as a money-making opportunity. Even this is not a guarantee that you will be successful, as Central American governments levy substantial taxes on car sales, and any local who buys a car from you will have to pay a large import tax before the car can be registered. This additional cost reduces the amount you can expect to get when you sell the car.

BICYCLE

Cycling is coming into its own in Central America: Not only can you rent bikes in several cities, you can also take mountain-bike tours or hit the road independently. Long-distance cycling can be dangerous, however, as few drivers are accustomed to sharing the roads with bikes; be aware at all times and equip your bike with the proper mirrors and safety equipment such as reflectors. Be sure to bring with you any spare parts you might need.

In general, traveling within the region's larger cities by bicycle is not wise. The roads tend to be narrow, there are no bike lanes, and bus drivers and motorists drive aggressively. Outside the cities, roads tend to be in decent shape, but many highways – including parts of the Interamericana – are narrow, leaving little room to move aside should a car pass by.

If you're planning a cycling trip, consider the seasons. Unless you like pedaling in the rain, it's wise to plan your trip for the dry season (roughly October to May). Although it doesn't rain constantly during the wet season, dirt roads in the more remote areas may be very muddy. Heat and humidity are other factors worth considering. Temperatures are cooler in the highlands, but in the lowlands the heat can be brutal. Be sure to drink enough water, and if possible, avoid cycling during the midday heat.

See the transportation sections in the individual country chapters for places of particular interest to cyclists and options for equipment rental and sale. For guides on bicycle touring in Central America, see Books in the Regional Facts for the Visitor chapter.

HITCHHIKING

Hitchhiking is never entirely safe in any country in the world, and Lonely Planet does not recommend it. Travelers who decide to hitchhike should understand that they are taking a small but potentially serious risk. People who do choose to hitchhike will be safer if they travel in pairs and let someone know where they are planning to go; women traveling alone are at the greatest risk and should not hitchhike in the region.

In Central America, hitchhiking in the strict sense of the word is not generally practiced because it is not safe. However, in rural areas where bus service is infrequent and few people have private vehicles, hitching is a recognized supplement to existing public transportation (if any), and it's common for the drivers of pickup trucks and other vehicles to transport others in need of a ride. There's no need to wait at the roadside for a lift, unless it happens to be convenient. Almost every town has a central truck park, often in or near the market. Ask around for a truck going in your direction and how much it will cost; be there about 30 minutes before the departure time given by the driver.

Hitchhiking is not necessarily free transportation. In most cases, if you are picked up by a truck, you will be expected to pay a fare similar to that charged on the bus, if there is one. (In some areas, pickup and flatbed stake trucks *are* the 'buses' of the region, and every rider pays.) If you're traveling with other hitchhikers, ask them what they're paying before handing over your money. Your best bet for a free ride is with other foreign travelers who have their own vehicle.

All the usual commonsense precautions apply here. Use your instincts, and don't get into a vehicle if you have any suspicions whatsoever about the driver. The reward of a cheap ride is not worth the potential dangers.

BOAT

Central America has extensive coastlines on both the Caribbean and Pacific sides, hundreds of sea islands, thousands of kilometers of rivers and the Panama Canal, one of the world's most important waterways. Boat trips from a number of Central American ports, and on an array of principal rivers, can provide transportation within each country and connect you to other countries in the region. For information on regularly scheduled passenger boat service (as well as unofficial options) connecting the various countries and boat travel within each country, see the individual country chapters.

Some of the region's more famous boat trips include journeys on the Río Dulce in Guatemala, the Río Plátano in Honduras, the trip from Rama to Bluefields in Nicaragua, various trips on the Río San Juan on the Nicaragua–Costa Rica border and crossings of the Panama Canal. Boats also serve various islands in Lago de Nicaragua, including Ometepe, the Archipiélago de Solentiname and Las Isletas near Granada. White-water rafting and kayaking are on the rise in many countries, too.

Boat trips on the Caribbean include those between Lívingston and Puerto Barrios in Guatemala, between La Ceiba and the Bay Islands in Honduras, between Bluefields and the Corn Islands in Nicaragua, and along the hundreds of islands of eastern Panama's Archipiélago de San Blas.

For information on boat travel to and from Central America, see the Getting There & Away chapter.

ORGANIZED TOURS

The possibilities for organized tours in Central America are virtually limitless. Options range from small group tours using local transportation and inexpensive accommodations to overland journeys in specially equipped vehicles (trucks, vans or buses), with a driver-mechanic-cook-tour leader.

The principal advantage of an organized tour is that it enables you to reach out-of-the-way destinations with a minimum of hassles. Trips that present logistical or bureaucratic challenges if attempted independently can be made smooth if arranged by professionals experienced in the region. Such trips might include excursions to far-flung destinations, places regulated by the government or those requiring specialized equipment (for example, white-water rafting). Tours are usually all-inclusive, and guides often double as translators.

Particularly in Central America, tours that involve specialized activities, such as bird or wildlife watching, archaeology or the exploration of parks and wilderness areas, are often guided by local experts in the field and can be more rewarding and informative than a solo excursion.

The bad news is that organized tours are more expensive than independent travel and certainly more restricting. The region's burgeoning ecotourism industry – particularly in Costa Rica, where over 200 tour operators are recognized by the Costa Rican Tourist Board – has pushed the cost of some specialized tours beyond the reach of most shoestring travelers. That said, there are many affordable and well-regarded tour operators in the region; detailed information on local companies can be found in the Organized Tours sections of each country chapter.

Guatemala

The heart of the Mayan world, Guatemala is a beautiful, mystical land. The highland Maya, living amid breathtaking mountain scenery, closely guard ancient customs and ways of life. Splendid pageantry marks holidays and festivals, and weekly markets blaze with vividly colorful traditional costumes.

But modernity is penetrating Mayan culture, offering advantages and drawbacks alike. Tourism income improves quality of life, education and health, but lures the younger generation away from their roots and toward the raucous, bustling cities.

Distinctions between indigenous and European heritage, and between traditional and modern culture and commerce, have marked the region since the days of the conquistadores. Today they divide Guatemalan society in two, often leading to oppression and bloody conflict.

Traditional and modern values also clash when local farmers and ranchers clear the rain forest to provide for their families. Their method is the traditional slash-and-burn technique; the result is ecological disaster.

However, with its tragic history and modern difficulties, Guatemala remains a fascinating land, its paradoxes fueling its air of inscrutability.

Facts about Guatemala

HISTORY
From conquistadores and earthquakes to death squads and guerrilla cadres, Guatemala has been locked in a centuries-long struggle for tranquility and equality. For colonial Guatemalan history, see the History section in the Facts about Central America chapter.

The country's history since independence in 1847 has been one of struggle between the forces of left and right. Unfortunately, both sides have bolstered the social and economic elite and done little for the people of the countryside, mostly Maya.

The 19th Century
Early in Guatemala's republican history, the liberals, who had been the first to advocate independence, opposed the interests of elite conservatives, who included large landowners and the Church.

During the short existence of the United Provinces of Central America, liberal president Francisco Morazán (1830-39) instituted reforms aimed at correcting three persistent problems: the overwhelming economic, political and social power of the Church; the division of society into a Hispanic upper class and an Indian lower class; and the region's impotence in world markets. This program was echoed by Guatemalan chief of state Mariano Gálvez (1831–38).

Highlights

- Get blown away by the majesty of Lago de Atitlán
- Explore the fascinating history and killer ruins of Antigua
- Experience the energy and excitement of Chichicastenango's Thursday and Sunday markets
- Take in the imperial splendor of Tikal in its lush jungle setting
- Climb volcanoes or just kick back in the Caribbean
- Enjoy a boat trip on the Río Dulce
- Cheer at the baby sea-turtle races in Monterrico

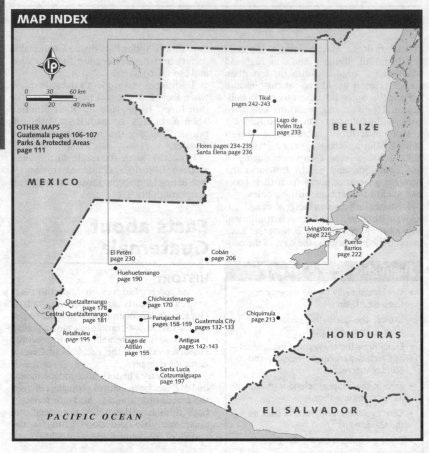

MAP INDEX

But unpopular economic policies, heavy taxes and an 1837 cholera epidemic led to an Indian uprising that brought conservative pig farmer Rafael Carrera to power. Carrera ruled until 1865 and undid much of Morazán's and Gálvez' achievements. His government allowed Britain to take control of Belize in exchange for construction of a road between Guatemala City and Belize City. However, the road was never built, and Guatemala's claims for compensation were never resolved. The dispute between Belize and Guatemala persists and is revived often – usually when one of the nations needs a distraction from domestic problems.

The liberals came to power again in the 1870s under president Justo Rufino Barrios,

a rich, young coffee *finca* (plantation) owner who ruled as a dictator (1873-79). During his tenure, the country made great strides toward modernization, constructing roads, railways, schools and a modern banking system. Unsurprisingly, Barrios also did everything possible to encourage coffee production, including promoting forced relocation and labor. Peasants in good coffee-growing areas were forced off their lands and many Maya were forced to contribute seasonal labor. Most of the policies of the liberal reform movement benefited the finca owners and urban traders. Succeeding governments generally pursued the same policies of control by a wealthy minority and repression of opposition.

The Early 20th Century

From 1898 to 1920, Manuel Estrada Cabrera ruled as a dictator. He fancied himself an enlightened despot, seeking to turn Guatemala into a 'tropical Athens,' while looting the treasury, ignoring education and spending millions on the military.

When Estrada Cabrera was overthrown, Guatemala entered a period of instability that ended in 1931 with the election of General Jorge Ubico. Ubico insisted on honesty, and he modernized the country's health and social welfare infrastructure. Debt peonage was outlawed, but was replaced by a new servitude of labor contributions.

In the early 1940s Ubico dispossessed and exiled the German coffee finca owners. He assumed a pro-Allied stance during the war, but also openly admired Spain's Francisco Franco. In 1944 he was forced into exile.

The 1945 elections brought philosopher Juan José Arévalo to power. Arévalo established the nation's social security system, a bureau of Indian affairs, a modern public-health system and liberal labor laws. His six years as president saw 25 coup attempts by conservative military forces – an average of one attempt every three months.

Arévalo was succeeded in 1951 by Colonel Jacobo Arbenz Guzmán, who looked to break up estates and foster high productivity on small farms. But the US supported the interests of large companies such as United Fruit, and in 1954 (in one of the first documented covert operations by the CIA) the US government orchestrated an invasion from Honduras led by two exiled Guatemalan military officers. Arbenz was forced to step down and land reform never took place. Violence, oppression and disenfranchisement ensued, fueling the formation of guerrilla groups and fomenting discord.

Civil War

During the 1960s and '70s, economic inequality, surging urban migration, and the development of labor unions forced oppression to new heights. Amnesty International has estimated that 50,000 to 60,000 people were killed in Guatemala during the political violence of the 1970s alone. Furthermore, the 1976 earthquake killed about 22,000 people and left about a million

homeless. Most of the aid sent to help the people in need never reached them.

In 1982, General José Efraín Ríos Montt initiated a 'scorched earth' policy that exterminated the populations of over 400 villages. President Ríos Montt, an evangelical Christian, was acting in the name of anti-insurgency, stabilization and anticommunism. An estimated 15,000 people, mostly Maya men, were tortured and massacred; 100,000 refugees fled to Mexico. In response, four guerrilla organizations united to form the URNG (Guatemalan National Revolutionary Unity).

In August 1983 Ríos Montt was deposed in a coup led by General Oscar Humberto Mejía Victores, but the abuses continued. It was estimated that over 100 political assassinations and 40 abductions occurred every month under the new ruler. The US suspended military assistance to the government, which led to the 1985 election of the civilian Christian Democratic candidate, Marco Vinicio Cerezo Arévalo – but not before the military secured immunity from prosecution and control of the countryside.

The 1990s

Cerezo Arévalo was succeeded by Jorge Serrano Elías (1990-93), who reopened dialogue with the URNG. But the talks collapsed, Serrano's popularity declined, and he came to depend more on the army for support. On May 25, 1993, Serrano carried out an *autogolpe* (autocoup), suspending the constitution and ruling by decree. Though supported by the military, the coup was unsuccessful and Serrano was forced into exile. Congress elected Ramiro de León Carpio, the Solicitor for Human Rights and an outspoken critic of the army, to complete Serrano's term.

In March 1995, the USA announced another suspension of aid due to the government's failure to investigate the murder or disappearance of US citizens in Guatemala. These cases included the 1990 murder of Michael Devine, who had operated Finca Ixobel in Poptún, and URNG leader Efraín Bámaca Velásquez, whose wife, US attorney Jennifer Harbury, had been conducting a protest (covered in the international media) since his disappearance in 1992. Eventually it was revealed that he had been murdered. Charges were made

GUATEMALA

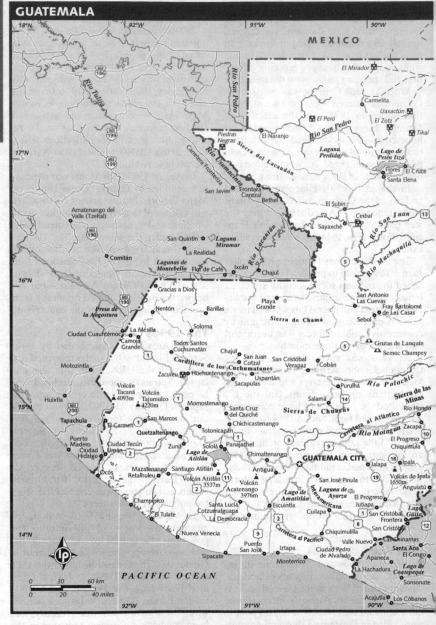

that the CIA had been instrumental in both of the murders, but after investigating the claims, the US government declared them unfounded.

The Signing of the Peace Accords

In 1996, Álvaro Enrique Arzú Irigoyen of the middle-right PAN (Partido de Avanzada Nacional) was elected. In December, he and the UNRG signed peace accords ending the 36-year civil war – a war in which an estimated 200,000 Guatemalans were killed, a million were left homeless and untold thousands 'disappeared.'

The accords called for accountability for the armed forces' human-rights violations and resettlement of one million refugees. They also addressed the identity and rights of indigenous peoples, health care, education and other basic social services, women's rights, the abolition of obligatory military service and the incorporation of the ex-guerrillas into civilian life.

It has been a rocky road since the war's end. Bishop Juan Gerardi, coordinator of the Guatemalan Archbishop's Human Rights Office (ODHAG), was beaten to death outside his home on April 26, 1998, two days after detailing the military's human-rights violations during the civil war. (Three suspects were finally arrested for the murder in January 2000.) And in May 1999, a minuscule 18% of the population came out to vote down referenda that would have permitted constitutional reforms integral to the peace process. On an encouraging note, the country's Maya population has mobilized politically since the signing of the peace accords.

The greatest challenge to peace stems from inequities in the power structure. It's estimated that 70% of the country's arable land is owned by less than 3% of the population. According to a UN report, the top 20% of the population has an income 30 times greater than the bottom 20%.

Discrimination against indigenous people, deeply ingrained in society, results in poverty and misery for most of the population. How the need for economic and social reforms is met may be the most important factor in creating a true and lasting peace.

Guatemala Today

In November 1999, Guatemala held its first peacetime elections in nearly 40 years. In a runoff, conservative and admitted murderer Alfonso Portillo of the FRG (Frente Republicano Guatemalteco) defeated Oscar Berger of the incumbent PAN party.

Portillo promised to be tough on criminals, citing his murders as proof of his ability to defend his people. For many human-rights observers, more disturbing than this muddy logic was that Ríos Montt (executor of the 'scorched earth' massacres) also ran on the FRG ticket and advised Portillo. (Ríos Montt went on to become the leader of Congress.)

Portillo has vowed to clean up the judicial system, crack down on crime, tax the rich and respect human rights. In March 2000, he invited UN observers to stay beyond their targeted December 2000 departure date. However, his recent moves, including bolstering municipal police squads with national troops and sending most of his family to Canada in self-imposed exile, are particularly worrisome.

GEOGRAPHY & GEOLOGY

Consisting primarily of mountainous forest highlands and jungle plains, Guatemala covers an area of 109,000 sq km. The western highlands hold 30 volcanoes, reaching heights of 3800m in the Cuchumatanes range northwest of Huehuetenango. Here land that has not been cleared for Mayan *milpas* (cornfields) is covered in pine forests, though these are dwindling rapidly.

The Pacific Slope holds rich coffee, cacao, fruit and sugar plantations. Down along the shore the volcanic slope meets the sea, yielding vast, sweltering beaches of black volcanic sand.

Guatemala City lies at an altitude of around 1500m. To the north, the Alta Verapaz highlands gradually give way to El Petén, whose climate and topography is like that of Yucatán: hot and humid or hot and dry. Southeast of El Petén is the banana-rich valley of the Río Motagua, dry in some areas, moist in others.

Guatemala is at the confluence of three tectonic plates, resulting in earthquakes and volcanic eruptions. Major quakes struck in 1773, 1917 and 1976. Its dynamic geology includes a tremendous system of above-ground and subterranean caves. This type of terrain – known as karst – riddles the Verapaces region and has made Guatemala a popular spelunking destination. Surface-level caves have been used for Mayan ceremonies since ancient times.

CLIMATE

Although Guatemala is officially the 'Land of Eternal Spring,' temperatures can be freezing at night in the highland mountains, and days can be dank and chill during the rainy season. In the dry season – from late October to May – the highlands are warm and delightful, but even then, nights are never hot.

Guatemala's coasts are tropical, rainy, hot and humid. Temperatures often reach 32°C to 38°C (90°F to 100°F), and the humidity abates only slightly in the dry season. On the Caribbean side, rain is possible anytime. Cobán has only about one month of strictly dry weather (April), though you can catch some less-than-soggy spells between November and March.

The vast jungle lowland of El Petén has a tropical climate that is seasonally hot and humid or hot and dry. December and January are the coolest months, while March and April are like hell on earth.

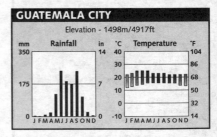

GUATEMALA CITY
Elevation - 1498m/4917ft

ECOLOGY & ENVIRONMENT

Deforestation is a problem in Guatemala, especially in the Petén, where cattle-ranch development destroys jungle at an alarming rate. Returning refugees and Guatemalans migrating from other, more crowded areas also tax the region's resources. Only a few years ago, the government required anyone buying tracts of land in the Petén to clear a certain portion of it – presumably in the name of 'progress.'

Most of the Petén is now officially protected; in addition to the 576-sq-km Tikal

National Park, there's the nearly 2-million-hectare Maya Biosphere Reserve, which includes most of the northern Petén. The reserve is theoretically split into three spheres: the multiple-use zone on the outer fringe permits settlements and slash-and-burn agriculture; the buffer zone allows only minimal-impact activities such as gathering forest products; the smallest is the core zone at the center of the reserve, which allows no human activity other than limited ecotourism. However, even the inner forest is ravaged by poachers, tomb looters and tourists, no matter how ecology-conscious. The only hope for preservation lies with local communities, which are learning to generate income from alternative forest products and activities like ecotourism.

On Guatemala's Pacific side, which holds most of the country's population, the land is devoted to agriculture and industry. Communities here have almost exhausted the forests' trees for heat and cooking purposes.

Another immediate problem is garbage. Open dumps lie outside towns and cities with garbage collection. Elsewhere, people burn everything. What can't be burned is thrown in rivers or along the road. If garbage is ignored long enough, it will become a health, as well as an environmental, issue.

Environmental Organizations

The following organizations in Guatemala City are good resources for finding out more about Guatemala's natural and protected areas:

Asociación Amigos del Bosque (☎ 238 3486), 9a Calle 2-23, Zona 1

Centro de Estudios Conservacionistas de la Universidad de San Carlos (Cecon; ☎ 331 0904, 334 6064, 334 7662), Avenida La Reforma 0-63, Zona 10

Comisión Nacional del Medio Ambiente (Conama; ☎ 334 1708, 331 2723), 5a Avenida 8-07, Zona 10

Consejo Nacional de Areas Protegidas (Conap; ☎ 332 0465, 332 0464), Via 5 4-50, Edificio Maya, 4th floor, Zona 4

Fundación Defensores de la Naturaleza (Defensores; ☎ 334 1885, fax 361 7011, defensores@pronet.net.gt), 14 Calle 6-49, Zona 9; Defensores also maintains an office in El Estor.

Fundación Solar (☎ 360 1172, 332 2548, fax 332 2548, funsolar@guate.net), 15a Avenida 18-78, Zona 13

Fundación para el Ecodesarrollo y la Conservación (Fundaeco; ☎ 472 4268), 7a Calle A 20-53, Zona 11, Colonia El Mirador

The following organizations, all in Flores, concentrate on conservation efforts in the Petén:

Asociación Alianza Verde (☎/fax 926 0718, alianzaverde@conservation.org.gt), north side of plaza

Centro de Información sobre la Naturaleza, Cultura y Artesanía de Petén (CINCAP), north side of plaza

ProPetén (☎ 926 1370, fax 926 0495, propeten@guate.net), Calle Central
Web site: www.conservation.org

FLORA & FAUNA

Guatemala has over 8000 plant species in 19 different ecosystems, ranging from coastal mangrove forests to mountainous interior pine forests to high cloud forests. In addition, the Petén supports a variety of trees, including mahogany, cedar, ramón and sapodilla.

The national flower, the *monja blanca*, or white nun orchid, is said to have been picked so much that it's now rare in the wild. Nevertheless, the country holds around 600 species of orchid, a third of them endemic.

Guatemala also has the perfect climate for *xate* (**sha**-tay), a low-growing palm that thrives in the Petén and is prized in the developed world as flower-arrangement filler. *Xateros* – xate collectors – live in the jungle for months at a time, disrupting its fragile ecosytem. The same type of degradation is perpetuated by *chicleros*, men who harvest chicle for chewing gum (see the boxed text 'Chicle & Chewing Gum').

The country's abundance of animals includes 250 species of mammal, 600 bird species, 200 species of reptile and amphibian, and numerous butterflies and other insects.

The national bird, the resplendent quetzal, is often used to symbolize Central America. Though small, the quetzal is exceptionally beautiful. The males sport a bright red breast, brilliant blue-green across the rest of the body and a spot of bright

GUATEMALA

Chicle & Chewing Gum

Chicle, a pinkish to reddish-brown gum, is the coagulated milky sap, or latex, of the sapodilla tree (Achras zapota), a tropical evergreen native to the Yucatán and Central America. Chicleros enter the forests and cut large gashes in the sapodillas' trunks. The sap runs down the trunk into a container at the base. After being boiled, it is shaped into blocks for shipping. After 10 years, the cuts often kill the tree, and thus chicle harvesting tends to result in the serious depletion of sapodilla forests.

Chicle was first used as a substitute for natural rubber, but by about 1890 chicle was best known as the main ingredient in chewing gum.

As a result of war research for a rubber substitute during the 1940s, synthetic substitutes were developed for chicle. Now chewing gum is made mostly from these substitutes. However, in northern Petén, chicleros still live in the forest for months to harvest. To check out some real chicle gum, visit www.junglegum.com.

– Tom Brosnahan & Conner Gorry

white on the underside of the long tail. The females, alas, are decidedly less dramatic.

Other colorful birds include toucans, macaws and parrots. Boasting the ocellated turkey (or 'Petén turkey') – a large, impressive, multicolored bird reminiscent of a peacock, Tikal is a birding hot spot, with some 300 tropical and migratory species sighted to date. Several woodpecker species, nine types of hummingbirds and four trogon species are just the beginning of the list. Also in the area are large white herons, hawks, warblers, kingfishers, harpy eagles (rare) and a plethora of other feathered creatures.

Although Guatemala's forests host several mammal and reptile species, many remain difficult to observe. Still, visitors to Tikal can enjoy the antics of the omnipresent *pizotes* (coatis) and might spy howler and spider monkeys. Other mammals deeper in the forest include jaguars, ocelots, pumas, peccaries, agoutis, opossums, tapirs, kinkajous, *tepezcuintles*

(pacas), white-tailed and red brocket deer, armadillos, and very large rattlesnakes. Reptiles and amphibians in the rest of Guatemala include at least three species of sea turtle (leatherback, *tortuga negra* and olive ridley) and two species of crocodile (one found in the Petén, the other in the Río Dulce). Manatees also frequent the waters around Río Dulce.

PARKS & PROTECTED AREAS

Guatemala has more than 30 protected areas, including *parques nacionales* (national parks) and *biotopos* (biological reserves). Over 40 more have been proposed. Many protected areas are remote; the ones listed here are the most interesting and easily accessible.

National Parks & Biosphere Reserves

Reserva de la Biósfera Maya – This 1,844,900-hectare reserve is Guatemala's largest protected area. It contains many important Mayan archaeological sites, including Tikal, Uaxactún, El Zotz, El Mirador and Río Azul. Tours and access information are available in Flores.

Reserva de la Biósfera de Sierra de Las Minas – Guatemala's most important cloud forest reserve protects a mountainous area ranging in elevation from 150m to over 3000m. Before entering, visitors must obtain permission from the Fundación Defensores de la Naturaleza (see Ecology & Environment, earlier in this section).

Parque Nacional Tikal – Guatemala's principal tourist attraction, this park within the Maya Biosphere Reserve contains the magnificent Tikal archaeological site as well as 57,600 hectares of pristine jungle. It's also one of the easiest places to observe wildlife in Guatemala.

Parque Nacional Ceibal – This archaeological site tucked in the jungle near Sayaxché is accessible only by boat for most of the year. Ceibal is noted for its carved stelae and has several temples, including a rare circular one. Tours are available from Flores and Sayaxché.

Parque Nacional Río Dulce – In eastern Guatemala, between Lago de Izabal and the Caribbean, this 7200-hectare reserve protects the canyon of the Río Dulce, one of the country's most beautiful rivers. Boat trips on the river can be taken from either Lívingston or the village of Río Dulce.

Parque Nacional Laguna Lachuá – In the northeast of the department of Alta Verapaz, this 10,000-hectare park contains a beautiful,

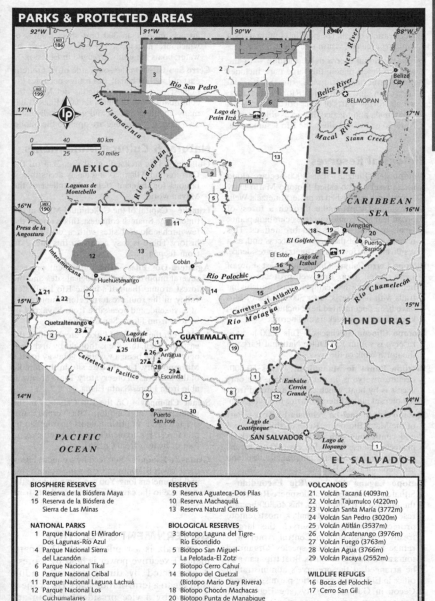

PARKS & PROTECTED AREAS

BIOSPHERE RESERVES
2 Reserva de la Biósfera Maya
15 Reserva de la Biósfera de
    Sierra de Las Minas

NATIONAL PARKS
1 Parque Nacional El Mirador-
   Dos Lagunas-Río Azul
4 Parque Nacional Sierra
   del Lacandón
6 Parque Nacional Tikal
8 Parque Nacional Ceibal
11 Parque Nacional Laguna Lachuá
12 Parque Nacional Los
    Cuchumatanes
19 Parque Nacional Río Dulce

RESERVES
9 Reserva Aguateca-Dos Pilas
10 Reserva Machaquilá
13 Reserva Natural Cerro Bisís

BIOLOGICAL RESERVES
3 Biotopo Laguna del Tigre-
   Río Escondido
5 Biotopo San Miguel-
   La Pelotada-El Zotz
7 Biotopo Cerro Cahuí
14 Biotopo del Quetzal
    (Biotopo Mario Dary Rivera)
18 Biotopo Chocón Machacas
20 Biotopo Punta de Manabique
30 Biotopo Monterrico-Hawaii

VOLCANOES
21 Volcán Tacaná (4093m)
22 Volcán Tajumulco (4220m)
23 Volcán Santa María (3772m)
24 Volcán San Pedro (3020m)
25 Volcán Atitlán (3537m)
26 Volcán Acatenango (3976m)
27 Volcán Fuego (3763m)
28 Volcán Agua (3766m)
29 Volcán Pacaya (2552m)

WILDLIFE REFUGES
16 Bocas del Polochic
17 Cerro San Gil

circular, turquoise-colored lake that is only 5km in surface area but over 220m deep and holds a great variety of fish. The park has hiking trails, a camping area and visitor's center.

Parque Nacional Sierra del Lacandón – In the western Petén region, this large park includes the southern portion of the Sierra del Lacandón and abuts the Río Usumacinta, which forms part of the border between Guatemala and Mexico. It's accessible from El Naranjo or by boat along the Río Usumacinta.

Biological Reserves

Biotopo del Quetzal – This 1000-hectare cloud forest reserve, also called Biotopo Mario Dary Rivera, was established to protect quetzals. Well-maintained trails snake through a forest of broad-leaf and coniferous trees, climbing plants, ferns, mosses, orchids and bromeliads. This reserve is one of the easiest to access and, as a result, has very few (if any) quetzals in residence.

Biotopo Cerro Cahuí – On the northeast shore of Lago Petén Itzá, this well-protected 650-hectare reserve has campgrounds and hiking trails with fine views. Over 300 species of bird have been documented here, including toucans, kingfishers, woodpeckers and herons.

Biotopo Chocón Machacas – This 7600-hectare reserve is within Río Dulce National Park, on the north bank of the river.

Biotopo Punta de Manabique – This 50,000-hectare reserve is on the Caribbean. The only access is by boat, which can be arranged from the piers at either Puerto Barrios or Lívingston.

Biotopo San Miguel-La Pelotada-El Zotz – Part of the Maya Biosphere Reserve, this is west of and contiguous with Tikal National Park. It protects a dense forest, bat caves (*zotz* means 'bat' in many Mayan languages) and the archaeological site El Zotz.

Biotopo Laguna del Tigre/Río Escondido – Situated within the Maya Biosphere Reserve in the northwest of the Petén, this 46,300-hectare reserve is one of Guatemala's most remote protected areas. It conserves the largest freshwater wetlands in Central America, a refuge for countless bird species. Organized tours are available in Flores. Boat trips can also be arranged at the preserve's administration office in El Naranjo, with prior permission from Cecon in Guatemala City (see Ecology & Environment, earlier in this section).

Wildlife Refuges

Bocas del Polochic – On the western side of Lago de Izabal, the Río Polochic forms a marshy delta where it empties into the lake; this is Guatemala's second largest freshwater wetland area. It's especially enticing for birders since it attracts more than 300 bird species, 40% of which are migratory. It's accessible only by water; boats are easily arranged in El Estor.

Cerro San Gil – On the south side of El Golfete, east of Lago de Izabal, this refuge occupies the highest part of the Montañas del Mico, the continuation of the Sierra de las Minas. It has many endemic species and great biodiversity. Two parts of the refuge are open to the public.

Natural & Cultural Monuments

Quiriguá – This archaeological site, 2km off the Carretera al Atlántico and easily accessible, is famous for its giant stelae, the tallest in the Mayan world.

Iximché – Capital of the Cakchiquel Maya at the time of the Spanish conquest, this is one of the few archaeological sites with a documented history. There is easy access to this site, 2km from Tecpán.

Aguateca-Dos Pilas – This monument protects several important archaeological sites and the forest around them. It's in the Río La Pasión valley, in the southwestern Petén municipality of Sayaxché, and accessible from Sayaxché or by tour from Flores/Santa Elena.

Yaxjá – On the shores of Lake Petexbatún in the eastern Petén, this site is thought by archaeologists to have been a vacation getaway for the Maya nobility. The Topoxté site in the middle of the lake was an observatory. Tours are available from Flores/Santa Elena.

Semuc Champey – On the Río Cahabón in the municipality of Lanquín, Alta Verapaz, this site is a series of pristine pools surrounded by rain forest. It's accessible by 4WD vehicles, on foot or by tour from Cobán.

Grutas de Lanquín – Serviced by frequent buses, these caves 61km from Cobán are at least several kilometers long. You can camp outside the entrance to the caves. Tours are available from Cobán.

GOVERNMENT & POLITICS

Guatemala is a republic with 22 departments. Executive power is held by a president elected by direct universal adult suffrage to a term of four years. He or she is assisted by a vice president and an appointed cabinet. The unicameral national congress has 80 members (64 departmental representatives and 16 national seats), also elected to four-year terms. Judicial power rests in a Supreme Court and associated courts.

With a few notable exceptions, such as the administrations of Juan José Arévalo and Jacobo Arbenz Guzmán, Guatemala's government has always been controlled by and for the commercial, military, landowning and bureaucratic classes. Real government often takes place by means of intimidation and secret military activities (see the History section).

ECONOMY

Coffee is the biggest export crop, followed by sugar, cotton, bananas and cardamom. Other exports include fruits, vegetables, natural rubber and flowers. Tourism is the second-largest income producer after coffee.

Similar in sprawl and bustle to Mexico City, Guatemala City is the industrial and commercial center of the country. Like many other Latin American urban centers, it has problems of overcrowding, pollution, congestion and crime.

The Guatemalan highlands are given over to agriculture, particularly corn, with some mining and light industry around the larger cities. The Pacific Slope has large coffee, citrus and sugarcane plantations worked by highland migrant labor, and the Pacific coast has cattle ranches and fishing villages.

The Motagua Valley holds some mining operations, but agriculture – primarily banana and sugarcane plantations – takes precedence. The lush hills of Alta Verapaz have dairy farms, cardamom and coffee plantations and timber-producing forests.

El Petén depends upon tourism and farming. The growth of agriculture and cattle ranching poses a serious threat to its ecology; tourism, however, is a positive factor, providing income that depends upon preservation. Still, not all tour outfits wearing the ecotourism label promote environmentally responsible adventures.

POPULATION & PEOPLE

According to 1999 estimates, Guatemala's population is nearing 12.5 million. Official census statistics list 56% of the population as *ladino* (Indian or mestizo people who speak Spanish) and 44% as indigenous. In fact, Maya probably make up over half of the population, but the survey defines 'indigenous' as only those who wear traditional dress and speak a Mayan language.

Obviously, this excludes all people of direct Maya heritage who speak Spanish and wear jeans.

About 40% of Guatemalans live in cities, the biggest of which are Guatemala City, Quetzaltenango and Escuintla. The Petén and Izabal regions are the most sparsely populated, though internal migration to both those areas is on the rise. On average, the country has a population density of 170 inhabitants per square kilometer. The Guatemalan population is due to double by the year 2020 if it continues to grow at its current rate of 2.68% annually.

EDUCATION

Education in Guatemala is free and compulsory between the ages of seven and 14. Primary education lasts six years; it's estimated that 79% of children of this age are actually in school. Secondary education begins at age 13 and lasts for up to six years, with two cycles of three years each; it's estimated that only 23% of children of this group are in school. Not all secondary education is free – a considerable deterrent to poorer families.

Guatemala has five universities; the University of San Carlos, founded in 1676 in Antigua (and later moved to Guatemala City), was Central America's first.

Overall adult literacy is around 65%, but rates vary widely among different ethnic groups. Some estimates indicate that up to 95% of Guatemala's rural Maya women can't read. Maya children who do migrant work find it difficult to get an education, as the time the families go away to work falls during the school year.

ARTS

The Maya of Guatemala still make various traditional handicrafts. Weavings, embroidery and other textile arts are among the most striking, but their craft art also includes basketry, ceramics and woodcarving.

A number of well-known Maya painters work in a primitivist style depicting scenes from daily life. Known as Tz'utuhil oil painting, this genre is typified by vibrant colors and is centered in Lago de Atitlán. Accomplished artists of this style include Rafael González y González, Pedro Rafael González Chavajay and Mariano González Chavajay. For more on Mayan oil painting, visit the Arte Maya Web site at www .artemaya.com.

Music is a very important part of Guatemalan society, and it is a source of pride that the marimba may have been invented here. (Other possibilities are that this xylophone-type instrument might have existed in Africa before slaves brought it to Guatemala, or have been created/refined in the New World.) The Maya also play traditional instruments including the *chirimía* (of Arabic origin and related to the oboe) and reed flute.

Guatemalan writer Miguel Ángel Asturias won the Nobel Prize in literature in 1967 – another source of national pride. Best known for his thinly veiled vilification of Latin American dictators in *El Señor Presidente*, Asturias also wrote poetry (collected in *Sien de Alondra*, published in English as *Temple of the Lark*). Other celebrated Guatemalan writers include poet Luis Cardoza y Aragón and short-story master Augusto Monterroso.

The ancient Mayan ruins and Spanish colonial structures in Antigua are both impressive works of architecture. Interestingly, Mayan embellishments can be found on many colonial buildings (such as the lotus flowers adorning Antigua's La Merced) – an enduring testament by the Maya laborers forced to carry out European architectural concepts.

SOCIETY & CONDUCT

Guatemalan society is divided between the ladino and Maya peoples. While the ladino culture proceeds into the modern world, in many ways the Maya are holding to their traditional culture and identity despite five centuries of European domination and occupation.

Most noticeable to visitors is the beautiful *traje* (traditional handmade clothing) worn by Maya women. Men typically wear western clothing, but in some places, such as Sololá and Todos Santos Cuchumatán, males also wear traje. Each village has its own unique style of dress. When all of the different variations are taken into account, the Maya have something like 500 distinctive clothing designs, each with its own significance.

Most Maya still speak one of 20 different Mayan languages as their vernacular.

Mayan religion, firmly based in nature, is also still practiced.

Unfortunately, in Guatemala the Maya suffer vicious (and often violent) discrimination. While a tiny minority of Maya are attending university, working in the business world and joining modern society, those continuing the traditional way of life are the poorest sector of Guatemalan society.

The plight of these people has attracted international attention, drawing the aid of global nongovernmental organizations. Travelers can help by patronizing Maya-owned businesses and paying fair prices for traditional Mayan handicrafts.

Ladino culture is most strongly felt in literature, dance and music (particularly mariachi), anything cowboy – from firearms to exquisite leatherwork – and, of course, soccer. A medley of North American and European influences have wended their way into Guatemalan culture over the years; for tourists this will be most evident at the dinner table, where spaghetti and tacos often show up.

Dos & Don'ts

See the Dos & Don'ts section in the Facts about Central America chapter for general tips on conduct in Latin America.

In recent years, stories circulated through Guatemala that some foreign visitors (particularly white women) were kidnapping Maya children, perhaps to sell their organs or raise as their own. Some people are extremely suspicious of foreigners who make friendly overtures toward local children, *especially foreigners who photograph indigenous children.*

While Maya women are extremely eager to sell traditional clothing to foreigners, it is considered bad form for a visitor to wear these things in Guatemala. Save the traje for home.

Also think about safety in connection with your appearance. Particularly in the capital, avoid even cheap imitation jewelry: you could be mugged for it. Avoid flaunting wealth.

RELIGION

Roman Catholicism is Guatemala's predominant religion, but not the only one. Since the 1980s, evangelical Protestant sects, most of them rabidly Pentecostal, have surged in popularity, and now an estimated 30% of Guatemalans are of this faith.

Catholicism never wiped out the traditional Mayan religion. Many aspects of Catholicism easily blended with Mayan beliefs, and the Maya still bring offerings and make sacrifices at many ancient places of worship.

Various saints hold double meanings for the Maya; often the saint's Catholic identity was superimposed over a pre-Hispanic deity or saint. The Maya also have some of their own saints, such as Maximón in Santiago Atitlán and San Simón in Zunil.

LANGUAGE
Spanish is the official national language, but in practice 23 different languages are spoken in Guatemala, including Garífuna, a Pipil-based language spoken by the Xinka people, and 20 Mayan languages. Many Maya people speak Spanish, but some elders, women and children do not. Maya children often start to learn Spanish only after they begin school.

Facts for the Visitor

SUGGESTED ITINERARIES
If you have just a week, assuming you arrive by air in Guatemala City, head straight to Antigua for a day of acclimatization and exploration of that singular colonial city. On day two, hop a bus to Lago de Atitlán, which deserves at least a couple days. Day four can be spent at the market at Chichicastenanago, before heading back to Guatemala City or Antigua for the very early morning flight to Flores. Spend days five and six at Tikal and Lago de Petén Itzú.

With more time you could add on Todas Santos, Río Dulce, Poptún or Cobán; Semuc Champey is sometimes considered a nightlife highlight. With a month or more, add in Spanish lessons while living with a Guatemalan family.

PLANNING
When to Go
There is really no bad time for a Guatemalan adventure, though rain may limit access to certain areas. The rainy season, from May to

October, turns the lowland jungles muddy and brings cold temperatures to the highlands, especially at night. The dry season, from late October or early November through the end of April, means sweltering heat in the Petén, possible rain in the Caribbean and comfortably warm days and cool nights in the highlands.

High tourist season is from the end of December to the beginning of April, with the crunch becoming acute around Christmas, New Year's and Easter. A secondary high season lasts from June to August, when throngs of foreigners descend on Guatemala to study Spanish.

Maps
ITMB Publishing (☎ 604-879 3621, fax 604-879 4521, itmb@itmb.com), 530 W Broadway, Vancouver BC, Canada V5Z 1E9, publishes a good 1:500,000 scale Guatemala map. They're on the Internet at www.itmb.com. INGUAT, 7 Avenida 1-17, Zona 4, Guatemala City, Centro America, publishes the useful *Mapa Vial Turístico*. Write well in advance, or pick the map up in Guatemala at shops or from street vendors (US$2), or order over the Internet at www.amerispan.com/lata/.

The Instituto Geográfico Militar (☎ 332 2611), Avenida Las Américas 5-76, Zona 13, Guatemala City, is the best resource for good topographical maps.

RESPONSIBLE TOURISM
Tourism is a touchy subject in a country just emerging from 36 years of civil war. The Maya have suffered terribly during this period and travelers should refrain from probing into wartime tragedies.

New areas are accessible to tourists since peace broke out, and many companies peg Guatemala as the next ecotourism jewel. While some outfits are running genuinely ecofriendly tours, others are simply exploiting the enthusiasm for low-impact travel. This is a growing problem with some jungle tours, especially those visiting remote areas.

Another unfortunate trend is the serving of 'exotic' fare -including endangered or threatened species – at restaurants. On certain menus you'll find anything from turtle soup to *tepescuintle*. By ordering these dishes you may be contributing to the extinction of endemic fauna.

TOURIST OFFICES

The main outpost of the national tourist office, Instituto Guatemalteco de Turismo (INGUAT; ☎ 331 1333, fax 331 8893, inguat@guate.net), is in Guatemala City at 7a Avenida 1-17, Centro Cívico, Zona 4. Another office is in Zone 9 of the capital. Branch offices are in Antigua, Flores, Panajachel, Quetzaltenango and at the international airports in Guatemala City and Flores/Santa Elena.

In the USA, INGUAT's central information source (☎ 888-464 8281, inguat@ guate.net) is OK for the most basic queries (www.travel-guatemala.org.gt). For more detailed queries, contact a Guatemalan embassy or consulate (see the Regional Facts for the Visitor chapter).

VISAS & DOCUMENTS
Visas

Most travelers can enter Guatemala without a visa. However, if you do need a visa and arrive at the border without one, you will be turned back. You probably won't be allowed to board a plane for Guatemala without having the necessary documents.

As of 2000, citizens of many countries – among them Australia, Canada, France, Germany, Honduras, Ireland, Mexico, the Netherlands, New Zealand, the USA and the UK – do not need a visa or tourist card and may stay up to 90 days in Guatemala after arrival. Ask for the 90-day maximum or you may end up with a 30-day stamp.

Citizens of Belize and a few other countries do not need a visa or tourist card but may stay only up to 30 days after arrival.

Citizens of other countries must obtain a visa; contact a Guatemalan embassy or consulate in your country for information.

If you want to cross into Honduras on a day (or two) pass to visit Copán, Guatemalan immigration officials will usually allow you to return to Guatemala and continue your journey without interrupting your original entry stamp.

Visa Extensions Most foreigners are now permitted a total of 180 days' stay – 90 upon entering and 90 upon renewal. Extensions must be applied for in person at the Dirección General de Migración in Guatemala City (see Information in the Guatemala City section). Plans are afoot to establish another office in Antigua. To apply for an extension you'll need your passport, a recent photo, proof of funds and an onward ticket.

Onward Tickets

Guatemala requires all visitors to show proof of funds and an onward ticket before they're permitted entry. Very rarely will you be asked to produce either. A credit card as proof of funds and an international bus ticket as proof of onward passage suffice.

Minors Traveling Alone

If you are under 18 and alone, to enter Guatemala you technically must have a letter signed by both your parents and witnessed by a Guatemalan consular official.

CUSTOMS

Customs limits are the usual two cartons of cigarettes and three liters of alcohol. Tourists are allowed a US$100 duty-free exemption. International treaties stipulate harsh penalties for trafficking in Mayan artifacts.

MONEY
Currency

Named for the national bird, the Guatemalan *quetzal* (Q) is divided into 100 *centavos,* with coins of one, five, 10 and 25 centavos and notes of 50 centavos, and one, five, 10, 20, 50 and 100 quetzals. In 1999 the government introduced new coins of one and 50 centavos and one quetzal.

Exchange Rates

Currency exchange rates were as follows as this book went to press:

country	unit		quetzals
Australia	A$1	=	Q4.28
Belize	BZ$1	=	Q3.91
Canada	C$1	=	Q5.08
El Salvador	¢1	=	Q0.88
Euro	€1	=	Q7.12
France	FF1	=	Q1.08
Germany	DM1	=	Q3.64
Honduras	L1	=	Q0.51
Japan	¥100	=	Q6.82
Mexico	N$10	=	Q8.02
Netherlands	f1	=	Q3.21
New Zealand	NZ$1	=	Q3.40
UK	UK£1	=	Q11.41
USA	US$1	=	Q7.70

Exchanging Money

Any currency besides US dollars – even those of neighboring countries – will prove difficult to exchange. The banks at the airports in Guatemala City and Flores/Santa Elena are among the few places that exchange other currencies.

Many – but not all – establishments accept US dollars, usually at the bank exchange rate. Carry a stash of small quetzals, as many towns suffer from a change shortage.

Traveler's checks are usually easy to exchange in larger towns. Rates are sometimes slightly lower than for cash.

Automated teller machines (ATMs; *cajeros automáticos*) are available in the biggest cities and tourist towns. Those at the international airport in Guatemala City also accept Visa and MasterCard. The majority are on the Visa/Plus system. Master-Card is useless in most of Guatemala; some banks impose a 500 quetzal (US$65) daily withdrawal limit on MasterCard. Credomatic branches in Guatemala City and Quetzaltenango give cash advances on Visa and MasterCard.

Guatemalan ATMs accept only four-digit personal identification numbers (PINs), so contact your bank to get one.

Costs

Prices are low. Little pensions may charge US$6 for a double, and camping can be even cheaper. Markets sell fruits and snacks for small change, cheap *comedores* offer plate meals for US$2, and bus trips cost less than US$1 per hour. You could spend under US$15 a day in Guatemala. If you want rooms with private showers and meals in nicer restaurants, you could still pay only US$25 per day for room and board. Hook up with other travelers to defray costs.

Prices for everything are higher around Tikal.

Tipping & Bargaining

A 10% tip is expected at restaurants. In comedores, leave spare change. Tip tour guides around 10% (more if they were truly outstanding), especially on longer trips.

For details about bargaining, see the Tipping & Bargaining section in the Regional Facts for the Visitor chapter.

Taxes

Guatemala's IVA (national sales tax) is 10%, and there's a 10% hotel tax to pay INGUAT, so a total tax of 20% will be added to your hotel bill. (In this book, tax is included.) The very cheapest places don't charge tax.

POST & COMMUNICATIONS
Post

The Guatemalan postal service was privatized in 1999. Generally, letters from Guatemala take a week to arrive in the US and Canada and twice that to Europe. Almost every city and town has a post office where you can buy stamps and send mail. A letter sent to North America costs around US$0.40, and to anywhere outside the Americas it costs around US$0.50.

For packages, it's more efficient to use an international shipping service. DHL, Federal Express and International Bonded Couriers have offices in Guatemala.

The Guatemalan postal service no longer holds post restante. The easiest way to receive mail is through a private address; American Express will hold mail for card members, and some travel agencies in Antigua hold mail for clients. Address mail clearly; the last lines should read 'Guatemala – Centro America.'

Telephone

Telgua, the Guatemalan phone system, was also recently privatized and has experienced a jump in reliability, technology and price. Coin-operated phones are nearly obsolete – the newfangled units accept cards only. Phonecards are available in denominations of 20, 30 and 50 quetzals. These cards work domestically and internationally.

A direct-dial local call costs about US$0.12 a minute; long distance is twice that. In smaller cities and towns, you have to go to the Telgua office to make calls. Where there is no Telgua office, there will likely be a *teléfono comunitario* (community telephone) that will place calls. Guatemala's country code is 502. There are no area codes. Directory assistance is ☎ 124.

International Calls The best way to call internationally is through agencies offering phone services. As prices are high (US$0.75 a minute to the USA and US$1.50 to

Europe), have your party call you back. Don't use the phones around tourist towns that say 'Press 2 to call the US free!' This scam ends up costing you US$8 to US$20 per minute.

Sprint, MCI and AT&T have deals for calls to the USA; preface the number listed with 99-99 to receive the reduced rate.

There are also 'direct line' services, such as AT&T's USADirect. Dial 190 and you will be connected with an AT&T operator in the USA who will complete your collect or credit-card call. The following are the direct-line numbers:

Intercity long distance calls	☎ 121
International calls (by operator)	☎ 171
MCI Call USA	☎ 189
USADirect (AT&T)	☎ 190
España Directo	☎ 191
Italia Directo	☎ 193
Sprint Express	☎ 195
Costa Rica Directo	☎ 196
Canada Direct	☎ 198

Cellular Phones Long-term travelers may consider leasing a cellular phone. Read the fine print before signing on. Try Cellular Rent (☎/fax 331 6251), 6a Avenida 6-45, Zona 10 in Guatemala City.

Email & Internet Access
All cities and most tourist towns have Internet capabilities. Cybercafes are popular, and some hotels have email services for their guests. Prices for Internet access range from US$1.50 an hour in Antigua to US$7.75 in Cobán.

INTERNET RESOURCES
The Guatemalan Web Page Directory (http://mars.cropsoil.uga.edu/trop-ag/guatem.htm) stands out for its in-depth cultural information and terrific kids' page. Travelers interested in Mayan ceremonial life should visit www.geocities.com/momostenango. In addition to those and the many other Web sites listed throughout the book, the following are some sites that you might find helpful:

Useful Organizations
BBC World Service
www.bbc.co.uk/worldservice/tuning

La Ruta Maya Online
http://larutamayaonline.com
Radio Canada International
www.rcinet.ca
US Department of Health, Centers for Disease Control & Prevention
www.cdc.gov/travel/travel.html
Voice of America
www.voa.gov/allsked.html

Travel/Transportation
Explore Worldwide Ltd
www.exploreworldwide.com
Journey Latin America
www.journeylatinamerica.co.uk

General
Antigua Pages
www.theantiguajournal.com
Central American Report
www.worldcom.nl/inforpress
Guatemala Web
www.guatemalaweb.com
University of Texas Guatemala Resource Page
http://lanic.utexas.edu/la/ca/guatemala
WWWanderer CA Volunteer guide
www.tmn.com/wwwanderer/Volguide/projects.html

BOOKS
Guatemala in the Spanish Colonial Period, by Oakah L Jones Jr, details 300 years of Spanish dominance. Where this book leaves off, Paul J Dosal's *Doing Business with the Dictators: A Political History of United Fruit in Guatemala, 1899-1944* takes over. *Bitter Fruit: The Story of the American Coup in Guatemala*, by Stephen Schlesinger et al, is a readable analysis of US dirty-pool politics.

I, Rigoberta Menchú: An Indian Woman in Guatemala, by 1992 Nobel Peace Prize laureate Rigoberta Menchú, is highly recommended reading. Almost singlehandedly, Menchú brought the plight of Guatemala's Maya to the world's attention. Her follow-up effort, *Crossing Borders*, was published in 1998. David Stoll shocked the world with the 1999 publication of *Rigoberta Menchú and the Story of All Poor Guatemalans*, in which he contests the veracity of Menchú's first book.

Jennifer Harbury's *Searching for Everardo: A Story of Love, War and the CIA in Guatemala* tells of the search for her husband, a URNG commander who disappeared mysteriously in 1992. Her earlier *Bridge of Courage: Life Stories of the Guatemalan Compañeros and Compañeras* focuses on the guerrilla movement.

Unfinished Conquest: The Guatemalan Tragedy, by Victor Perera, explores the history and present-day conditions of the Maya. A fascinating account of the war's aftermath is presented in *Return of Guatemala's Refugees: Reweaving the Torn*, by Taylor Clark. *Guatemala: A Guide to the People, Politics and Culture*, by Trish O'Kane, is a well-written book on modern Guatemala.

Orchids of Guatemala and Belize, by Oakes Ames and Stewart Donovan, remains one of the best handbooks on orchids available internationally. *Birds of Guatemala*, by Hugh C Land (1970), is a field guide to bird watching in Guatemala. *The Birds of Tikal: An Annotated Checklist for Tikal National Park and Petén, Guatemala*, by Randell A Beavers, is a must-have for birders.

Guatemalan Journey, by Stephen Benz, lends a traveler's eye to an honest and funny account of modern Guatemala. *Bird of Life, Bird of Death*, by Jonathan Evan Maslow, tells of the author's travels in Guatemala, where he went to see the quetzal (the 'bird of life'). What he found instead was the flourishing *zopilote* (vulture), the 'bird of death.'

FILMS

The few Guatemalan films that exist are poignant. *El Silencio de Neto* follows a boy's coming of age during the Arbenz coup. *La Hija del Puma* is a powerful drama about the displacement, torture and genocide suffered by the Maya during the civil war.

Check out *Dirty Secrets: Jennifer, Everardo & the CIA in Guatemala*, the abbreviated story of Jennifer Harbury and her disappeared husband during the civil war, and the great *Todos Santos*, which tells the story of that mountain town.

NEWSPAPERS & MAGAZINES

Among Guatemala's many daily newspapers are *La Prensa Libre*, *El Gráfico*, *La República*, *Siglo Veintiuno*, *El Periódico* and *Al Día*. The weekly *El Regional*, written in both Spanish and Mayan, is read by many Maya. *La Cuerda*, a well-written monthly

discussing women's issues, appears in *El Periódico* and *El Regional*.

English newspapers include two free weeklies distributed in major hotels and tourist spots: the *Guatemala Weekly* (☎ 337 1061, fax 337 1076, gweekly@pronet.net.gt), 14 Calle 3-27, Zona 10, Local 8, Guatemala City, or in the USA, PO Box 591999-F-69, Miami, FL 33159-1999, and *The Siglo News* (☎ 332 8101/2/3, fax 332 8119, sales@sigloxxi.com), 11 Calle 0-65, Zona 10, Edificio Vizcaya, 4th floor, Guatemala City; or in the USA (☎ 888-287 4921), NotiNET SA, Worldbox Gu-0147, PO Box 379012, Miami, FL 33137-9012.

Web site: www.sigloxxi.com

The *Revue* is Guatemala's monthly English-language magazine; you can read it at www.revue.conexion.com.

USA Today, the *Miami Herald* and the *Los Angeles Times*, are sold in luxury hotels and some city and airport bookstores in the region. *Newsweek* and *Time* are also sometimes available.

RADIO & TV

Guatemala has 11 radio stations and five TV stations. Several US stations, including CNN, come in by cable, as do movies and sports in both English and Spanish.

PHOTOGRAPHY

In theory, you are allowed to bring no more than one camera and 12 rolls of film into Guatemala, though this is rarely, if ever, enforced. Ubiquitous film stores and pharmacies sell film. Prices for film are slightly lower than in the USA and Europe, though always check the expiration date. See Photography in the Regional Facts for the Visitor chapter for more details.

Photographing People

Photography is a sensitive subject in Guatemala. You should always ask permission before taking portraits, especially of Maya women and children. Don't be surprised if your request is denied. Indigenous children make a habit of requesting payment in return for posing. This is usually about the equivalent of US$0.15.

In certain places, like the church of Santo Tomás in Chichicastenango, photography is forbidden. Mayan ceremonies

GUATEMALA

(should you be so lucky to witness one) are off limits for photography unless you are given explicit permission to take pictures. If local people make any sign of being offended, you should put your camera away and apologize immediately, both out of decency and for your own safety.

Never take photos of army installations, men with guns or other sensitive military subjects. For more on photo ettiquette, see Dos & Don'ts under the Facts about Guatemala section, earlier in this chapter.

LAUNDRY

Laundries offer wash, dry and fold service for around US$2 per load; you can pick up your laundry a few hours after dropoff. Cheaper lodgings usually have a *lavadero* where you can handwash your clothes, and a clothesline.

HEALTH

Tap water is generally not safe to drink in Guatemala, so you must either purify it or drink bottled water.

Malaria is present, especially in lowland rural areas, but there is no risk in the highlands. Chloroquine is the recommended antimalarial. Dengue fever and cholera are also present in Guatemala. See the Health section in the Regional Facts for the Visitor chapter for more detailed health information.

WOMEN TRAVELERS

Women should encounter no special problems traveling in Guatemala. Modesty in dress is highly regarded by Guatemalans. The catcalls, hisses and howls so frequently directed at women in other parts of Central America are rare in Guatemala – just do as local women and ignore the harassment completely.

See the Women Travelers section in the Regional Facts for the Visitor chapter and Society & Conduct, earlier in this chapter, for more information.

GAY & LESBIAN TRAVELERS

Few places in Latin America are genuinely gay friendly, and that includes Guatemala (where, by the way, homosexuality is legal for persons 18 years and older). Though Antigua has an active, subdued scene, affec-

tion and action are kept behind closed doors; the exception is The Casbah on Thursday nights, which is so hopping it's become more of a mixed crowd than gay crowd. In Guatemala City, Pandora's Box and Eclipso are the current hot spots. In large part though, gay folks traveling in Guatemala will find themselves pushing the twin beds together – a tired but workable compromise.

Toto Tours (☎ 800-565 1241, 773-274 8686, fax 773-274 8695, info@tototours .com), 1326 W Albion Ave, Chicago, IL 60626 USA, runs all-gay-men adventure trips to Guatemala and other parts of Central America. The company's Web site is www.tototours.com.

DANGERS & ANNOYANCES

The war has been replaced by a precipitous rise in the crime rate. Armed thieves roam the highlands; it's best to avoid stopping in desolate places. Guatemala City has seen armed robbery, purse-snatching and carjacking. Don't wander around any city late at night. When driving, keep valuables out of sight and keep your car windows rolled up at least halfway. If approached by carjackers, relinquish your vehicle without resistance.

Tourists have been injured on Volcán Pacaya by flaming rocks and debris. In January 2000, this volcano was upgraded to orange alert status. Keep abreast of developments before you go.

See also the Regional Facts for the Visitor chapter.

EMERGENCIES

Emergency telephone numbers in Guatemala include the following: tourism police, ☎ 110 or 120; fire department, ☎ 122; ambulance, ☎ 125 or 128; and Red Cross (Cruz Roja), ☎ 125.

BUSINESS HOURS

Guatemalan businesses are generally open 8 am to noon and 2 to 6 pm daily. A two-hour siesta is the norm, and hours, however, may be curtailed on Sunday. Government offices keep shorter hours, usually 8 am to 4 pm weekdays. You will find that official business is always better conducted in the morning.

PUBLIC HOLIDAYS & SPECIAL EVENTS

The following are public holidays:

New Year's Day	January 1
Holy Thursday, Holy Friday and Easter Sunday	March/April
Labor Day	May 1
Army Day	June 30
Fiesta de Guatemala City	August 15
Independence Day	September 15
Revolution of 1944	October 20
All Saints' Day	November 1
Christmas Eve	December 24
Christmas Day	December 25
New Year's Eve	December 31

Certain special events throughout the year are well worth experiencing. Semana Santa (the week before Easter) in Antigua is unforgettable. It's celebrated in other places, too – each indigenous group has its own religious and folkloric traditions. See each city's section for details.

Traditional celebrations also take place on All Saints' Day (November 1) and All Souls' Day (November 2). Throughout Guatemala people spruce up graveyards and picnic at the graves of their dearly departed. It's a time for the living to visit with those they miss.

On November 1, thousands come to fly giant, colorful *barriletes* (kites) in the cemeteries of Santiago Sacatepéquez and Sumpango, both near Antigua. It's believed that the soaring kites provide communication with dead loved ones. In Todos Santos Cuchumatán, local men dressed in traditional costumes hurtle through town in the drunken horse race – the culmination of a week of debauchery (October 21 through November 1) that reaches fever pitch the night before.

Each town celebrates its patron saint day with a fiesta. Chichicastenango's fiesta – honoring Santo Tomás – begins December 13 and peaks on December 21 with the *palo volador* derring-do, in which a tall pole is set up in the plaza and costumed *voladores* (fliers) swing around the top of it.

In late July, Q'cqchi' Indians throughout the Verapaces celebrate Rabin Ajau with folkloric festivals. Perhaps the most impressive is in Cobán, where festivities culminate with the traditional Paabanc, a medley of folkloric dances.

Visitors interested in the Mayan life cycle should head to one of the towns still observing the Mayan calendar (eg, Momostenango or Todos Santos) for Wajshakib Batz, the Mayan New Year. It will fall on the following dates: July 23, 2001; April 9, 2002; December 25, 2002; September 11, 2003; and May 28, 2004. However, don't try to join in the sacred ceremonies.

Other interesting festivals include the birthday of San Simón (also known as Maximón and Ry Laj Man) on October 28, celebrated with an all-out party in San Andrés Iztapa, near Antigua, and a fiesta in Zunil; and Quema del Diablo, the Burning of the Devil, celebrated on December 7 throughout the country but particularly noteworthy in Chichicastenango.

ACTIVITIES
Mountaineering

Guatemala is a climber's paradise, but facilities and services are limited. Volcán Tajumulco (at 4220m, Central America's tallest peak) is one of the most challenging ascents in the country. Good climbing can also be found in the Cuchumatanes Range. Popular day trips include hiking Volcán Pacaya or Volcán San Pedro.

Spelunking

Attracting spelunkers from the world over, the Verapaces are riddled with caves. While the caves of Lanquín and Poptún have long been popular, new discoveries such as the Gruta Rey Marcos, the Chicoy Cave and the caves at Candelaria are broadening spelunking opportunities.

Rafting & Kayaking

From placid Class II to raging Class IV rapids, Guatemala has some excellent river rafting and kayaking. The Cahabón River can be run year-round, while the Esclavos, Motagua and Naranjo are rushing from June to October. Kayaking is excellent on the Ríos Lanquín, Sauce and Esclavos in September and October and on the Río

Cahabón year-round. Quality equipment and guides are available.

Wildlife Watching

National parks and biospheres offer excellent wildlife watching opportunities. Sites such as Tikal, El Mirador and the Biotopo Cerro Cahuí have an abundance of wildlife. The Bocas de Polochic on Lake Izabal and the mangroves near Monterrico are among the best birding places. You can see lots of wildlife even on day trips to Lake Chicabal near Xela or the Atitlán Nature Reserve in Panajachel.

LANGUAGE COURSES

Spanish-language courses are extremely popular in Antigua and Quetzaltenango; those cities boast over 100 schools. There are also schools on Lago de Atitlán (in San Pedro La Laguna and Panajachel), on Lago Petén Itzá (in San Andrés and San José) and in Todos Santos, Huehuetenango and Cobán. Schools typically provide one-on-one instruction, family homestays, electives such as dancing or weaving, and volunteer opportunities. Some highland schools also offer instruction in Mayan languages such as Mam and Quiché.

WORK

Work is hard to come by and wages are very low. You might teach English, but don't count on it. Service jobs with hostels, bars and restaurants catering to travelers are easier to find. Xela, Antigua, Monterrico and Panajachel are likely spots. Skilled guides may find work as the tourism industry continues to blossom.

Volunteer Work

Opportunities to volunteer abound, especially for travelers with specific skills. To learn more about volunteer positions in Guatemala visit the AmeriSpan volunteer Web site (www.amerispan.com/volunteer/default.htm).

Most positions require Spanish skills and a time commitment. Volunteers may have to pay for room and board. See the boxed text 'Volunteer Opportunities in Guatemala.'

ACCOMMODATIONS

All accommodations levels are available, from basic pensions to luxury resorts. If studying Spanish, you may prefer a family homestay, a cheap option offered by virtually all Spanish language schools. Camping and hammock-slinging are rock-bottom budget options.

FOOD

Guatemalan food is basic; try to develop a taste for corn tortillas before your trip. Maintaining a vegetarian diet is challenging but not impossible.

Mostly you will encounter *bistec* (tough grilled or fried beef), *pollo asado* (grilled chicken), *chuletas de puerco* (pork chops) and lighter fare such as *hamburguesas* (hamburgers) and *salchichas* (sausages similar to hot dogs). Of the simpler food, *frijoles con arroz* (beans and rice) is cheapest and often best. A few Mexican standards such as enchiladas, guacamole and tamales are usually available as well.

A good source for vegetarian food is Chinese restaurants, present in all the cities and some large towns.

DRINKS

In the tourist towns you can find delicious brewed coffee, but everywhere else it's of the weak, sweet instant variety.

As elsewhere throughout the region, sweetened fruit juice mixed with water (ask if it's purified) is popular and refreshing. Soft drinks are available everywhere.

Delicious *limonadas* are made with lime juice, water and sugar. *Naranjadas* are the same thing made with orange juice. *Jamaica* (hah-**my**-cah) is a refreshing juice made from hibiscus flowers.

The three Guatemalan beers are Gallo (the most popular), Moza and Dorado.

Guatemala grows plenty of sugarcane and makes rum. The dark Ron Zacapa Centenario is said to be the best. Ron Botrán Añejo, another dark rum, is also good. Venado is a light, locally produced rum. Then there's Quetzalteca Especial, a white firewater made of sugarcane.

SHOPPING

Guatemala's brilliantly colorful Mayan weavings and textiles are world famous. Wall hangings, clothing and accessories are good values.

Guatemalan craftspeople make sublime leather goods, including fine briefcases, duffel

Volunteer Opportunities in Guatemala

The following well-established organizations in Guatemala are always in search of volunteers:

Arcas (Asociación de Rescate y Conservación de Vida Silvestre – the Wildlife Rescue and Conservation Association; ☎/fax 591 4731, arcas@pronet.net.gt), 1a Calle 50-37, Zona 11, Colonia Molino de las Flores, Guatemala City (in the USA, write: Arcas, Section 717, PO Box 52-7270, Miami, FL 33152-7270), operates a wildlife rescue center near Flores and a sea turtle hatchery east of Monterrico. See the Monterrico and Flores sections for details. Arcas also has other volunteer projects, including education and health projects.

Asociación Hogar Nuevos Horizontes (☎ 761 2608, fax 761 4328), 3a Calle 6-51, Zona 2, Quetzaltenango, runs a battered women's shelter, legal and medical clinics and a child-care center. The organization is dedicated to ending domestic violence. Men are encouraged to apply. A minimum one-month commitment is required.

Casa Alianza (☎ 253 2965, 251 2569, fax 253 3003, guatemala@casa-alianza.org), 3a Avenida 11-28, 5th floor, Zona 1, Guatemala City, runs a shelter for street children in Guatemala City. Volunteers can work in the shelter or administrative offices. Working in the shelter requires a minimum six-month commitment. Web site: www.casa-alianza.org/en/help/volunteer2.shtml.

Casa Guatemala (☎ 232 5517, casaguatemal@guate.net), 14a Calle 10-63, Zona 1, Guatemala City, helps abandoned, orphaned and malnourished children. A second facility and the main administrative offices (☎/fax 331 9408) are at 5a Avenida 7-22, Zona 10. Programs in Guatemala City include a clinic, food-distribution program and temporary home for teenage orphans and pregnant teens. It also has an orphanage on the Río Dulce (☎ 902 0612, 208 1779, fax 902 0612), in eastern Guatemala. Short-term opportunities are available.

Escuela de la Calle (☎ 761 1521, fax 763 2104, edelac@usa.net), Diagonal 15, 7-61, Zona 5, Quetzaltenango, helps at-risk children in Xela with a variety of programs, including a school and dorm. A two-month commitment is required. In the USA, contact Michael Shorr (☎ 505-820 0114, mhshorr@earthlink.net), 2003 Hopi Rd, Santa Fe, NM 87505-2401. Information is also available at Quetzaltrekkers (☎ 761 2470, quetzaltrekkers@hotmail.com), Diagonal 12 8-37, Zona 1, Quetzaltenango, which donates all its proceeds to Escuela de la Calle. Web site: beef.brownrice.com/streetschool/home.htm.

Kuinik Ta'ik Volunteer Program (email Kermit Frazier at momostenango@conexion.com.gt), has opportunities in the Momostenango area for teachers, medical personnel and agricultural specialists. A minimum commitment of three months is required except for medical personnel, who need only commit to a month; homestays are available. Web site: www.geocities.com/momostenango.

Proyecto Ak' Tenamit (☎/fax 254 1560), 11a Avenida A 9-39, Zona 2, Guatemala City, works with the Q'eqchi' Maya near Río Dulce. Programs include a medical volunteer project, a dental clinic, a school, potable-water projects and a women's cooperative. A one-year commitment is preferred. In Río Dulce call ☎ 902 0608. In the USA, contact the Guatemalan Tomorrow Fund (☎ 407-747 9790, fax 407-747 0901), PO Box 3636, Tequesta, FL 33469.

Red International (email Volunteer Coordinator Alex Morales at redidh@yahoo.com), sends human-rights observers for a three-week minimum to villages in Chiapas, Mexico. Observers conduct interviews with villagers and file reports about the human rights situation in Chiapas. Information is also available at Quetzaltrekkers (☎ 761 2470), Diagonal 12 8-37, Zona 1, Quetzaltenango.

bags, backpacks and belts. Cowboy boots and hats can be custom made in some areas.

Although the finest coffee beans are earmarked for export, some are held back for the tourist trade. Most tourist shops sell overpriced coffee in cute traditional-cloth bags, and some is even sold already ground – java blasphemy! Visit one of the several farms and/or roasters and buy from them directly. Cobán and Antigua produce some of the world's greatest coffee; both towns have growers and roasters. There are also roasters in Xela and Panajachel.

Jade is sold in many markets countrywide and in specialty jade shops in Antigua. Beautiful well-carved stones can cost US$100 or much more.

The largest markets are in Chichicastenango and Panajachel. If you're serious about buying handicrafts, it's worth a trip to one of these places. Many fine textiles are also available in Antigua, but the prices are higher.

All villages also have market days. The weavers of Todos Santos are famed for their vibrant red traje, and Sololá and Santa Catarina Palopó on Lago de Atitlán are great towns in which to buy textiles. Momostenango is famed for its woolen blankets, coveted in many a cold clime.

Getting There & Away

AIR

Guatemala's two major international airports are in Guatemala City and Flores, near Tikal. Limited international service is also provided at the airports in Puerto Barrios and Quetzaltenango.

A US$30 departure tax is charged on all international flights leaving Guatemala.

Airlines

Airline contacts in Guatemala City are as follows:

Aerocaribe – see Mexicana

Aeroméxico – see Mexicana

Aerovías (☎ 332 7470, 361 5703, fax 334 7935), La Aurora International Airport

Alitalia (☎ 331 1276), 10a Calle 3-17, Zona 10
  Web site: www.alitalia.com/english/index.html

American Airlines (☎ 334 7379), Hotel El Dorado, 7a Avenida 15-45, Zona 9
  Web site: www.americanair.com

Aviateca – see TACA

British Airways (☎ 332 7402/3/4, fax 332 7401), 1a Avenida 10-81, Zona 10, Edificio Inexsa, 6th floor
  Web site: www.british-airways.com

Continental Airlines (☎ 335 3341, 366 9985, fax 335 3444), 12a Calle 1-25, Zona 10, Edificio Géminis 10, Torre Norte, 12th floor, office 1210; La Aurora International Airport (☎ 331 2051/2/3/4, fax 331 2055)
  Web site: www.continental.com

COPA (Compañía Panameña de Aviación; ☎ 361 1567, 361 1607, fax 331 8314), 1a Avenida 10-17, Zona 10
  Web site: www.copaair.com

Delta Air Lines (☎ 337 0642, fax 337 0588), 15a Calle 3-20, Zona 10, 2nd floor

Iberia (☎ 334 3816/7, fax 334 3715), Avenida La Reforma 8-60, Zona 9, Edificio Galerías Reforma, Local 204; La Aurora International Airport (☎ 332 5517/8, fax 332 3634)
  Web site: www.iberia.com

LACSA (Líneas Aéreas Costarricenses) – see TACA

Lufthansa (☎ 336 5526, fax 339 2995), Diagonal 6 10-01, Zona 10, Centro Gerencial Las Margaritas, Torre II, 8th floor
  Web site: www.lufthansa.com

Mayan World (☎ 334 2067, 339 1519), 7a Avenida 6-53, Zona 4, Edificio El Triángulo, 2nd floor

Mexicana (☎ 333 6048), 13a Calle 8-44, Zona 10; La Aurora International Airport (☎ 332 1924, 331 3291)
  Web site:www.mexicana.com

Nica – see TACA

TACA (☎ 334 7722 for reservations, 331 8222 main office, fax 334 2775), Avenida Hincapié 12-22, Zona 13; Centro de Servicio (☎ 332 2360, 332 4640), 7 Avenida 14-35, Zona 9; Hotel Ritz Continental (☎ 238 1415, 238 1479), 6a Avenida A 10-13, Zona 1; La Aurora International Airport (☎ 331 8222); Plaza Biltmore (☎ 331 2520, 337 3462), 14 Calle 0-20, Zona 10

Tapsa (☎ 331 4860, 331 9180, fax 334 5572), La Aurora International Airport

Tikal Jets (☎ 334 5631, 334 5568, fax 361 3343), La Aurora International Airport
  Web site: www.tikaljets.centroamerica.com

United Airlines (☎ 332 2995, fax 332 3903), Avenida La Reforma 1-50, Zona 9, Edificio El Reformador, 2nd floor; La Aurora International Airport (☎ 332 1994/5, fax 332 2795)
  Web site: www.ual.com

Destinations

The following flight information includes national as well as international destinations. The flights are from Guatemala City unless otherwise noted.

Belize City – TACA has four flights a week via El Salvador. Tikal Jets flies five days a week via Flores. Aerovías flies three times a week via Flores.

Cancún – Aerocaribe, Aviateca, TACA and Tikal Jets have daily flights.

Chetumal (Mexico) – Aeroméxico has flights four times weekly via Flores.

Flores, El Petén (for Tikal) – Mayan World has three flights daily. Tikal Jets, Racsa, TACA and Aviateca have daily direct flights.

Havana – Aviateca has two direct flights a week. Cubana Air has three a week.

Houston – Continental has two direct flights daily. Aviateca has three direct flights per week. TACA has daily flights via El Salvador and Belize City.

Los Angeles – Aviateca, United and TACA all have daily direct flights. Mexicana has daily flights via Mexico City.

Madrid – Iberia has daily flights via Miami.

Managua – TACA and COPA both have two daily flights via San Salvador.

Mérida – Aviateca has a morning flight three days per week.

Mexico City – Mexicana, United and Aviateca have daily nonstop flights.

Miami – American has three daily flights. Aviateca and Iberia each have one direct flight daily. TACA has daily flights via El Salvador.

New York – TACA has flights daily via Washington, DC. Delta and American have one daily flight.

Palenque – Tikal Jets and Aerocaribe have daily flights from Flores.

Panama City – COPA has three flights daily; two are via San José, Costa Rica.

San Francisco – United and Continental have daily flights via Houston. TACA has direct flights four times weekly.

San José (Costa Rica) – United and COPA have direct flights daily. TACA, Aviateca and LACSA have daily flights.

San Pedro Sula (Honduras) – TACA and COPA have daily flights.

San Salvador – Several daily nonstops by TACA, COPA and Aviateca.

Tapachula (Mexico) – Tikal Jets has daily flights from Guatemala City, some connect through Quetzaltenango.

LAND

Guatemala is linked to Chiapas (Mexico) by two official highway routes and three road-and-river routes; to Belize by one road route and one sea route; and to Honduras and El Salvador by numerous overland routes.

The most popular and easily accessible entry points to Guatemala from Mexico are at Tecún Umán/Ciudad Hidalgo, entering Guatemala's Pacific Slope from the Soconusco region of Chiapas, and at La Mesilla/Ciudad Cuauhtémoc, entering the southwestern highlands of Guatemala from highland Chiapas. More adventurous routes take you by country bus and riverboat from Yaxchilán in Chiapas via the Río Usumacinta or the Río de la Pasión to El Petén. For information on these routes, see the El Petén section. For the routes from Belize, see the Belize chapter.

Most border crossings between Guatemala and neighboring countries are now well trodden, including the so-called jungle route from eastern Guatemala to Honduras and the road-and-river routes between El Petén and Chiapas.

Bus

Several international bus routes connect Guatemala with Mexico, Belize, El Salvador and Honduras. When traveling between Guatemala and neighboring countries, you will often have the choice of a direct, 1st-class bus or a series of 'chicken buses' (with lots of rowdy live animal cargo). The latter option usually takes longer but is always cheaper and infinitely more interesting. International bus routes from Guatemala City include the following:

Belize City (US$55, 12 hours, 684km)
Autopullman Línea Dorada (☎ 232 9658, 220 7990, lineadorada@intelnet.net.gt), 16a Calle 10-55, Zona 1, has Thursday and Sunday departures at 8 pm, leaving Belize City on the return trip Friday and Monday at 4 pm.

El Carmen/Talismán (Mexican border; US$6, five to six hours, 275km)
Transportes Galgos (☎ 232 3661, 253 4868), 7a Avenida 19-44, Zona 1, runs direct along the Pacific Slope road stopping at Escuintla (change for Santa Lucía Cotzumalguapa), Mazatenango, Retalhuleu and Coatepeque at 5:30 and 10 am and 1:30 and 3:30 pm. It also

operates buses going all the way to Tapachula (Mexico); see Tapachula, below.

El Florido/Copán (Honduras; US$3.50, six hours)
Take the bus to Chiquimula (daily departures every 30 minutes; see Bus in the Getting Around section, later in this chapter), where you change buses to continue on to the border at El Florido.

La Mesilla/Ciudad Cuauhtémoc (Mexican border; US$4.50, seven hours, 345km)
Transportes Velásquez, at the intersection of 20a Calle and 2a Avenida, Zona 1, has hourly buses from 8 am to 4 pm.

Managua (US$25, 14 hours, 667km)
Very crowded chicken bus leaves from 9a Avenida 15-10, Zona 1, daily at 1 pm. Get there at least three hours early.

Melchor de Mencos (Belizean border; 10 to 12 hours, 588km)
Buses of Transportes Rosita (☎ 251 7351) leave from 15a Calle 9-58, Zona 1 at 3, 5 and 8 pm (US$8). Autopullman Línea Dorada (☎ 232 9658, 220 7990, lineadorada@intelnet.net.gt), 16a Calle 10-55, Zona 1, has 1st-class buses departing at 8 pm daily to Melchor de Mencos via Santa Elena (US$30). They make the return trip every day at 6 pm.

San Salvador, El Salvador (five hours, 268km)
Melva Internacional (☎ 331 0874), 3a Avenida 1-38, Zona 9, runs buses via Cuilapa, Oratorio and Jalpatagua to the Salvadoran border at Valle Nuevo and onward to San Salvador (US$6.45 one-way) hourly from 5 am to 4 pm. Tica Bus (☎ 261 1773, 331 4279, ticabus@ticabus.com), 11a Calle 2-72, Zona 9, has a daily departure at 1 pm (US$8.50 one-way, US$17 roundtrip); from San Salvador, Tica buses continue to all the other Central American capitals except Belize City.
Web site: www.ticabus.com

Confort Lines (☎ 332 6702), Avenida Las Américas at 2a Calle, Zona 13, Edificio El Obelisco, Nivel 1, has luxury buses daily at 8 am and 2 pm (US$15 one-way, US$25 roundtrip). Transportes King Quality (☎ 331 1761), 7a Avenida 14-44, Zona 9, Edificio La Galería, has luxury buses departing at 6:30 am and 3:30 pm (US$20 one-way, US$35 roundtrip), with connections to Tegucigalpa. Pulmantur (☎ 332 9797) has luxury bus departures at 6:15 am and 3:15 pm daily from the Radisson Suites Villa Magna Hotel, 1a Avenida 12-43, Zona 10 (US$23 one-way, US$45 roundtrip).

Tapachula, Mexico (US$22, seven hours, 291km)
Transportes Galgos (☎ 253 4868, 232 3661), 7a Avenida 19-44, Zona 1, has direct buses at 7:30 am and 1:30 pm. (From Tapachula, they depart for Guatemala City at 9:30 am and 1:30 pm.) These buses cross the border at El Carmen/Talismán and go into Mexico as far as Tapachula, where they connect with Mexican buses.

Tecún Umán/Ciudad Hidalgo (Mexican border; US$4.50, five hours, 248km)
Transportes Fortaleza (☎ 232 3643, 251 7994), 19 Calle 8-70, Zona 1, has 30 daily departures between 1:30 am and 7:15 pm.

Shuttle Minibus
Zippy, comfortable minivans called shuttle buses are becoming increasingly popular as Guatemala begins to attract travelers with more money than time. See the Antigua, Panajachel and Flores sections in this chapter for more information.

SEA & RIVER
On the Caribbean coast, boats leave Punta Gorda (Belize) for Puerto Barrios daily and for Lívingston twice weekly. Passage from Omoa (Honduras) to Lívingston is also possible twice a week, though it may be difficult to arrange in the low season. Generally, sea passage is easiest to and from Puerto Barrios, as this is an active transit point. No car ferries are available.

Three river crossings connect Chiapas, Mexico, to El Petén, Guatemala. These are good alternatives for travelers visiting Palenque and Tikal in one trip. All involve a combination of bus and boat travel. See the El Petén section for details.

If arriving or departing by river or sea, make sure you get your exit and entry stamps at the appropriate immigration offices in both countries.

Getting Around

AIR
During the high season, flights should be available to any of Guatemala's several airports. In addition to the international airports in Guatemala City and Santa Elena/Flores, there are airports in Coatepeque, Cobán, Huehuetenango, Playa Grande, Puerto Barrios, Quetzaltenango, Quiché, Retalhuleu and Río Dulce. You can also fly into an airstrip near Copán in Honduras. For schedules and prices, see the individual regional sections.

A US$0.65 departure tax, payable at the airport, is charged to all passengers on domestic flights.

BUS

The overwhelming majority of Guatemalan buses are resurrected and jam-packed schoolbuses from the USA and Canada. These 'chicken buses' are frequent, crowded and cheap. Expect to pay US$1 or less per hour. Popular routes are served by more luxurious *especial* buses. These may have bathrooms, TVs and food service.

The following bus information should get you from Guatemala City to most places you may want to go within the country:

Amatitlán (US$0.30, 30 minutes, 25km)
Buses depart from 20a Calle at 2a Avenida, Zona 1, every half hour from 7 am to 7 pm. Also see Puerto San José.

Antigua (US$0.50, one hour, 45km)
Transportes Unidos (☎ 232 4949, 253 6929), 15 Calle 3-65, Zona 1, has departures every half hour from 7 am to 7 pm, stopping in San Lucas Sacatepéquez. Other buses depart more frequently, every 15 minutes from around 4 am to 7 pm, from the lot at 18a Calle and 4a Avenida, Zona 1. Several shuttle minibus companies also offer services; see that section below.

Autosafari Chapín (US$1, 1½ hours, 88km)
Delta y Tropical, 1a Calle at 2a Avenida, Zona 4, has buses every 30 minutes via Escuintla.

Biotopo del Quetzal (US$2.20, three hours, 156km)
Escobar y Monja Blanca, 8a Avenida 15-16, Zona 1, has hourly buses from 4 am to 5 pm via El Rancho and Purulhá. (Any bus heading for Cobán will stop here.)

Chichicastenango (US$1.45, 3½ hours, 144km)
Veloz Quichelense, Terminal de Buses, Zona 4, runs buses every half hour from 5 am to 6 pm, stopping in San Lucas, Chimaltenango and Los Encuentros. Many continue to Quiché and beyond.

Chiquimula (US$3, three hours, 169km)
Rutas Orientales (☎ 253 7282, 251 2160), 19 Calle 8-18, Zona 1, runs buses via El Rancho, Río Hondo and Zacapa every 30 minutes from 5 am to 6 pm. Next door, Transportes Guerra has five daily departures (US$2.30). If you're heading for Copán, Honduras, change buses at Chiquimula to continue to the border at El Florido.

Cobán (US$3.60, four hours, 213km)
Escobar Monja Blanca (☎ 251 1878), 8a Avenida 15-16, Zona 1, has deluxe buses hourly from 4 am to 5 pm, stopping at El Rancho, the Biotopo del Quetzal, Purulhá, Tactic and San Cristóbal. Special (US$3.20) and regular (US$2.20) buses are also available.

El Estor (US$7.75, four hours, 216km)
Fuentes del Norte (☎ 238 3894, 251 3817), 17a Calle 8-46, Zona 1, has one daily departure, at 10 am.

Escuintla (US$1.15, one hour, 57km)
See Autosafari Chapín, La Democracia, Monterrico, Puerto San José and Tecún Umán.

Esquipulas (US$3.10, four hours, 222km)
Rutas Orientales (☎ 253 7282, 251 2160), 19a Calle 8-18, Zona 1, has buses every half hour from 5 am to 6 pm, with stops at El Rancho, Río Hondo, Zacapa and Chiquimula.

Flores (Petén; 488km)
Fuentes del Norte (☎ 238 3894, 251 3817), 17a Calle 8-46, Zona 1, runs more than a dozen daily buses departing from the capital and stopping at Río Dulce and Poptún (US$10.30, 12 hours). Its Maya del Oro luxury service (US$19.50, 10 hours) departs at 8 pm daily. Máxima (☎ 232 2495, 238 4032), 9a Avenida 17-28, Zona 1, has buses departing at 4, 6 and 8 pm. Autopullman Línea Dorada (☎ 232 9658, 220 7990, lineadorada@intelnet.net.gt), 16a Calle 10-55, Zona 1, operates three luxury buses daily at 9 am and 8 and 9 pm (US$30, eight hours); buses make stops at Río Dulce and Poptún (buses usually leave Guatemala City and Santa Elena full; anyone getting on midway stands). Transportes Rosita, 15a Calle 9-58, Zona 1, has departures at 3, 5 and 8 pm (US$6.45, 12 hours).

Huehuetenango (US$3.75, five hours, 266km)
Los Halcones, 7a Avenida 15-27, Zona 1, runs three buses a day (7 am and 2 and 5 pm) up the Interamericana to Huehue, stopping at Chimaltenango, Patzicía, Tecpán, Los Encuentros, San Cristóbal and Totonicapán. Buses to La Mesilla also stop here; see La Mesilla.

La Democracia (US$1, two hours, 92km)
Chatla Gomerana, at Muelle Central, Terminal de Autobuses, Zona 4, has buses every half hour from 6 am to 4:30 pm, stopping at Escuintla, Siquinalá (change for Santa Lucía Cotzumalguapa), La Democracia, La Gomera and Sipacate.

La Mesilla/Ciudad Cuauhtémoc (Mexican border; US$4.50, seven hours, 345km)
Transportes Velásquez, 20a Calle at 2a Avenida, Zona 1, has buses going to La Mesilla, on the Interamericana at the border with Mexico, hourly from 8 am to 4 pm. Stops are at Los Encuentros, Totonicapán and Huehuetenango.

Lívingston
See Puerto Barrios.

Monterrico (US$1.50, four hours, 124km)
Transportes Cubanita, at Muelle Central, Terminal de Buses, Zona 4, has buses departing

at 10:30 am and 12:30 and 2:30 pm, stopping at Escuintla, Taxisco and La Avellana.

Panajachel (US$1.70, three hours, 148 km)
Transportes Rébuli (☎ 251 3521), 21a Calle 1-34, Zona 1, departs hourly from 7 am to 4 pm, stopping at Chimaltenango, Patzicía, Tecpán Guatemala (for the ruins at Iximché), Los Encuentros and Sololá. It also has one daily departure from Antigua (US$3.20, two hours, 146km).

Poptún
See Flores.

Puerto Barrios (US$5.15, five hours, 295km)
Transportes Litegua (☎ 232 7578, 253 8169), 15a Calle 10-40, Zona 1, has *especial* buses at 6, 6:30, 7:30, 10, 10:30 and 11:30 am and 12:30, 2, 2:30, 4, 4:30 and 5 pm, with stops at El Rancho, Teculután, Río Hondo, Los Amates and Quiriguá. There are also a dozen regular buses (US$3.85) a day. Boats run from Puerto Barrios to Lívingston until about 5 pm.

Puerto San José (two hours, 106km)
Transportes Esmeralda (☎ 471 0327), Trebol, Zona 12, operates buses every 10 minutes from 5 am to 8 pm, stopping at Amatitlán, Palín and Escuintla.

Quetzaltenango (US$3.60, four hours, 206km)
Transportes Alamo (☎ 253 0219), 21a Calle 1-14, Zona 1, has buses at 8 and 10 am and 12:45, 3 and 5:45 pm. Líneas América (☎ 232 1432), 2a Avenida 18-47, Zona 1, has buses at 5:15 and 9:15 am, noon and 3:15, 4:40 and 7:30 pm. Transportes Galgos (☎ 253 6312, 232 3661), 7a Avenida 19-44, Zona 1, makes this run at 5:30, 8:30 and 11 am and 12:30, 2:30, 5 and 7 pm. All these buses stop at Chimaltenango, Los Encuentros and San Cristobal.

Quiché (three hours, 163km)
See Chichicastenango.

Quiriguá
See Puerto Barrios.

Retalhuleu (US$3.65, three hours, 186km)
See El Carmen (under Bus in the Getting There & Away section, earlier in this chapter) and Tecún Umán.

Río Dulce (US$4.50, five hours, 274km)
Transportes Litegua (☎ 232 7578, 253 8169), 15a Calle 10-40, Zona 1, has daily departures at 6 and 9 am and 1 pm; also see Flores.

Río Hondo
See Chiquimula, Esquipulas and Puerto Barrios.

San Pedro La Laguna (Lago de Atitlán; US$2.65, three to four hours, 170km)
Ruta Méndez, 21a Calle & 5a Avenida, Zona 1, has buses at 10 and 11 am, noon and 1 pm.

Santa Elena
See Flores.

Santa Lucía Cotzumalguapa
See El Carmen (under Bus in the Getting There & Away section, earlier in this chapter), La Democracia and Tecún Umán.

Sayaxché (US$9, 11 hours, 397km)
Fuentes del Norte (☎ 238 3894, 251 3817), 17a Calle 8-46, Zona 1, has one daily departure, at 4:30 pm.

Tecún Umán/Ciudad Hidalgo (Mexican border; US$4.50, five hours, 248km)
Transportes Fortaleza (☎ 232 3643, 251 7994), 19 Calle 8-70, Zona 1, has hourly buses from 1:30 am to 7:15 pm, stopping at Escuintla (change for Santa Lucía Cotzumalguapa), Mazatenango, Retalhuleu and Coatepeque.

Tikal
See Flores.

Shuttle Minibus

Various companies offer minibus services on the main tourist routes (Guatemala City–Aeropuerto La Aurora–Antigua–Panajachel–Chichicastenango). Most of these operators have their offices in Antigua; check that section for contact information. Turansa has an office in Guatemala City (☎ 595 3574, fax 595 3583) in the Supercentro Metro, Carretera Roosevelt Km 15, Zona 11, Local 68-69.
Web site: www.turansa.com

CAR & MOTORCYCLE

Before setting off, consider whether you can make repairs, how you'll secure your vehicle and how comfortable you are driving in a foreign country with screwy road rules, no signs, and the threat of bandits.

Three types of fuel are available in Guatemala. Regular (87 octane) costs around US$1.75 a gallon; Premium or Super (91 octane) costs US$1.90 a gallon; and Diesel fuel, widely available, costs about US$1.25 a gallon.

Rental

Expect to pay around US$50 to US$75 a day plus gas. In addition to cars, there are trucks, minivans and 4WD vehicles available for rent. Insurance policies accompanying rental cars may not protect you from loss or theft, in which case you can be liable for US$600 to US$1500 or more in damages. Motorcycles can be rented in Antigua and Panajachel.

To rent a car or motorcycle you need to show your passport, driver's license and a major credit card. Usually, the person renting the vehicle must be 25 years or older. You may be able to rent by leaving a large cash deposit. Obviously, an official receipt is needed in this event. Guatemala has both international and local rental car companies.

BICYCLE

Cycling is coming into its own in Guatemala. You can join biking tours or take to the hills independently. Bikes can be rented in Antigua, Flores, Panajachel and Quetzaltenango. Remember that few drivers are accustomed to sharing the roads with bikes.

HITCHHIKING

While there are no free lifts in Guatemala, pickup trucks and other vehicles serve as public transportation. Stand by the side of the road, hold your arm out and someone will stop. You are expected to pay the driver as if it were a bus, and the fare will be similar. This is a safe and reliable system used by locals and travelers; get used to severe overcrowding.

BOAT

Speedy motorboats called *lanchas* are becoming the norm for transportation on Lago de Atitlán and between Puerto Barrios, Lívingston and Río Dulce, replacing bigger, cheaper ferries.

A few of Guatemala's natural reserves and archaeological sites are accessible only – or preferably – by water (see Parks & Protected Areas in the Facts about Guatemala section, earlier in this chapter).

LOCAL TRANSPORTATION

Local buses (available only in Guatemala City and Quetzaltenango) are crowded and cheap. Few Guatemalan taxis are metered, and fares are exorbitant. If you don't like the price quote, walk away.

ORGANIZED TOURS

The quantity and quality of locally organized tours reflects Guatemala's growing popularity. The following is a selection of recommended tour operators:

Area Verde Expeditions (☎/fax 832 3383, 832 6506, ☎/fax 719-583 8929 in the USA, anthonyjosh@hotmail.com), 1a Avenida Sur No

15, Antigua, offers white-water rafting trips and general tours of the country.
Web site: www.adventuresports.com/kayak/areaverd/welcome.htm

Aventuras Turísticas (☎ 951 4213, ☎/fax 951 4214), 3a Calle 2-38, Zona 3, Cobán, offers a host of tours in the Verapaces and El Petén, plus custom tours.

AVINSA Tikal Travel (☎ 926 0808, fax 926 0807, info@tikaltravel.com), 4a Calle, Santa Elena, runs horseback riding, hiking and camping trips to the more inaccessible sites in the Petén, including Yaxjá and Nakum. It can also arrange sailing trips from Río Dulce to Belize.
Web site: www.tikaltravel.com

EcoMaya (☎ 926 1363, 926 3321, fax 926 3322, ecomaya@guate.net), Calle 30 de Junio, Flores, runs hardcore adventure trips to the jungle and archaeological sites of El Mirador, El Perú, El Zotz and Tikal.
Web site: www.ecomaya.com

Ecotourism & Adventure Specialists (☎ 361 3104, fax 334 0453, info@ecotourism-adventure.com), Avenida Reforma 8-60, Zona 9, Guatemala City, offers extreme-sports tours and jungle adventures to remote sites. It employs archaeologists and ornithologists as guides and coordinates trips with its offices in Belize, Mexico and Honduras. English, Spanish and Hebrew are spoken.
Web site: www.ecotourism-adventure.com

Guatemalan Birding Resource Center (☎ 767 7339, birdguatemala@latinmail.com), 7a Calle 15-18, Zona 1, Quetzaltenango, offers birding tours to the Pacific coast and the highlands. In the USA contact Anne M Berry (☎ 317-842 1494), 7361 Hawthorne Lane, Indianapolis, IN 46250.
Web site: www.xelapages.com/gbrc

Maya Expeditions (☎ 363 4955, 363 4965, ☎/fax 337 4666, mayaexp@guate.net), 15a Calle 1-91, Zona 10, Local 104, Guatemala City, runs white-water rafting trips. In Antigua, Maya Expeditions is represented by Sin Fronteras (☎ 832 1017, ☎/fax 832 2674), 3a Calle Poniente No 12.

Monkey Eco Tours (☎ 201 0759, fax 926 0807, fax 978-945 6486 in the USA, nitun@nitun.com), run by the Ni'tun Ecolodge, San Andrés, Petén, operates luxury adventure jungle trips with specialist guides including archaeologists, biologists and ecologists.
Web site: www.nitun.com

Old Town Outfitters (☎ 832 4243, trvlnlite@hotmail.com), 6a Calle Poniente No 7, Antigua, specializes in mountain biking, hiking and volcano tours. 'We summit any volcano' is its motto.

Proyecto EcoQuetzal (☎/fax 952 1047, bidaspeq@guate.net), 2a Calle 14-36, Zona 1, Cobán,

arranges full immersion trips to Q'eqchi' villages and builds quetzal-viewing platforms; available from March to June; one month prior reservation required.
Web site: www.granjaguar.com/peq

Quetzalventures (☎ 761 2470, info@quetzalventures .com), Diagonal 12 8-37, Zona 1, Quetzaltenango, offers traditional tours, adventure tours and budget adventures. Options include scuba diving, rafting, bungee jumping, Spanish classes and more. All profits go to Xela's nonprofit Escuela de la Calle.
Web site: www.quetzalventures.com

Vision Travel & Information Services (☎ 832 3293, 832 1962, fax 832 1955, vision@guatemalainfo .com), 3a Avenida Norte No 3, Antigua, offers all manner of tours, both packaged and customized, including trips to the highlands, Tikal, Copán and Lago de Atitlán. In addition, it offers special event tours for Día de Todos los Santos and Easter.
Web site: www.guatemalainfo.com

Guatemala City

pop 2 million

Guatemala's capital city, the largest urban agglomeration in Central America, spreads across a flattened mountain range run through by deep ravines. Its huge chaotic market bursts with dazzling smells, sounds and colors. Rickety buses chug along in clouds of diesel, trolling for ever more passengers, and street urchins eke out a tenuous existence in the city's poverty-stricken outlying areas.

The city's few interesting sights can be seen in a day or two, and many travelers skip 'Guate' altogether, preferring to make Antigua their base. Still, you may need to get acquainted with the capital since it's a transportation and service hub.

HISTORY

On July 29, 1773, an earthquake devastated the Spanish capital of Central America at La Ciudad de Santiago de los Caballeros de Guatemala (known today as Antigua Guatemala or simply Antigua). In hopes of escaping further destruction, the government moved to the present site of Guatemala City. On September 27, 1775, King Carlos III of Spain signed a royal charter for the founding of La Nueva Guatemala de la Asunción, and Guatemala City was officially born.

Unfortunately, colonial planners didn't move the capital far enough; earthquakes in 1917, 1918 and 1976 rocked Guatemala City, reducing buildings to rubble. The 1976 quake killed nearly 23,000, injured another 75,000 and left an estimated one million homeless. The city's comparatively recent founding and its history of earthquakes have left little to see in the way of colonial churches, palaces or quaint neighborhoods.

ORIENTATION
Street Grid System

Guatemala City, like all Guatemalan towns, is laid out according to a logical grid system. Avenidas run north-south; calles run east-west. Streets are usually numbered from north and west (lowest) to south and east (highest); building numbers run in the same directions, with odd numbers on the left side and even on the right as you head south or east. However, Guatemala City is divided into 15 *zonas*, each with its own version of the grid. Thus 14a Calle in Zona 10 is a completely different street several miles from 14a Calle in Zona 1, though major thoroughfares such as 6a Avenida and 7a Avenida cross several zones.

Addresses are given in this form: '9a Avenida 15-12, Zona 1,' which means '9th Avenue above 15th Street, No 12, in Zone 1.' The building will be on 9th Ave between 15th and 16th Sts, on the right side as you walk south. Beware of anomalies, such as diagonal *rutas* and *vías* and wandering *diagonales*.

Short streets may be suffixed 'A,' as in 14a Calle A, running between 14a Calle and 15a Calle.

Landmarks

The ceremonial center of Guatemala City is Plaza Mayor (sometimes called Parque Central). It's at the heart of Zona 1, surrounded by the Palacio Nacional, the Catedral Metropolitana and the Portal del Comercio. To the west is Parque Centenario, the central park. Zona 1 is also the retail district, where shops sell clothing, crafts, film etc. Behind the cathedral, the Mercado Central features lots of crafts. Most of the city's good budget and mid-range hotels are in Zona 1.

Around the Zona 1-Zona 4 border is the Centro Cívico (Civic Center), which holds various government buildings, including the main office of the national tourist bureau. Southwestern Zona 4 is the city's major market district and holds frenetic bus terminals.

South of Zona 4, 10a Avenida becomes Avenida La Reforma and divides Zonas 9 and 10, a pair of tony residential areas boasting several interesting small museums. Zona 10, east of Avenida La Reforma, is the poshest – its Zona Viva (Lively Zone) arrayed around deluxe hotels.

In Zona 9, landmarks include the mini-Eiffel Tower (called the Torre del Reformador), at 7a Avenida and 2a Calle, and the Plazuela España traffic roundabout at 7a Avenida and 12a Calle.

Zona 13 just to the south of Zona 9, holds the large Parque Aurora, several museums and Aeropuerto Internacional La Aurora.

Maps
The INGUAT tourist office sells a useful map with Guatemala City insets for US$1. The Librería de Pensativo (see Bookstores & Libraries under Information, below) sells International Travel Maps' Guatemala map. Detailed topographical maps can be purchased at the Instituto Geográfico Militar (☎ 332 2611), Avenida Las Américas 5-76, Zona 13.

INFORMATION
Tourist Offices
The friendly, helpful tourist office is in the lobby of the INGUAT headquarters (☎ 331 1333, fax 331 8893, inguat@guate.net), 7a Avenida 1-17, Centro Cívico, Zona 4. Look for the blue-and-white sign with the letter 'i' on the east side of the street; it's next to a flight of stairs, a few meters south of the railway viaduct that crosses above 7a Avenida. INGUAT's tourist office is open 8 am to 4 pm Monday to Friday, 8 am to 1 pm Saturday. A second office is at Avenida La Reforma 13-70, Zona 9.

INGUAT's office at La Aurora International Airport (☎ 331 4256 ext 294) is open 6 am to 9 pm daily.

Immigration Offices
Extensions must be applied for in person at the Dirección General de Migración (☎ 634 8476/7/8), 7a Avenida 1-17, Piso 2, INGUAT office, Zona 4. It's open 9 am to 3 pm Monday to Friday.

Money
Banco del Agro, on the south side of Parque Centenario, changes US dollars cash and traveler's checks; it's open 9 am to 8 pm Monday to Friday, 10 am to 2 pm Saturday. More than 100 ATMs dot the city, with the majority accepting Visa cards – look for a Bancared sign.

Credomatic, in the tall building at the corner of 5a Avenida and 11a Calle, Zona 1, gives cash advances on Visa and MasterCard. It's open 8 am to 7 pm Monday to Friday, 9 am to 1 pm Saturday. Inside, you can withdraw a maximum of US$500; the ATM limits transactions to US$100, but places no limit on the number of transactions.

The Banquetzal at the airport is open 7 am to 8 pm Monday to Friday, 8 am to 6 pm Saturday and Sunday. Here you can change US dollars cash or traveler's checks into quetzals, change European currencies into US dollars and buy US dollar traveler's checks. There is a MasterCard ATM here, too. The Banco Industrial at the airport has a Visa ATM.

American Express (☎ 339 2877, fax 339 2882) is in the Centro Gerencial Las Margaritas, Diagonal 6 10-01, Torre II, Zona 10, with Clark Tours. It's open 8:30 am to 5 pm Monday to Friday.

Post & Communications
The city's main post office is at 7a Avenida 12-11, Zona 1, in the huge pink building. It's open 8 am to 7 pm Monday to Friday, 8 am to 4:30 pm Saturday. EMS (Express Mail Service), in the rear of the post office building, is open 9 am to 5 pm Monday to Friday. A branch post office at La Aurora International Airport is open 7 am to 3 pm Monday to Friday.

DHL has a pick-up point at Centro Gerencial Las Margaritas, Diagonal 6, Zona 10, Local 202-B, open 8:30 am to 7 pm Monday to Friday, 8:30 am to noon Saturday.

Telgua's central office is on 7a Avenida, between 12a and 13a Calles, Zona 1, near the main post office. Services are available from 7 am to midnight daily. Other Telgua branches are found around the city; the one in the airport is open 7 am to 7 pm daily. You can also fax to or from Telgua offices.

GUATEMALA

GUATEMALA CITY

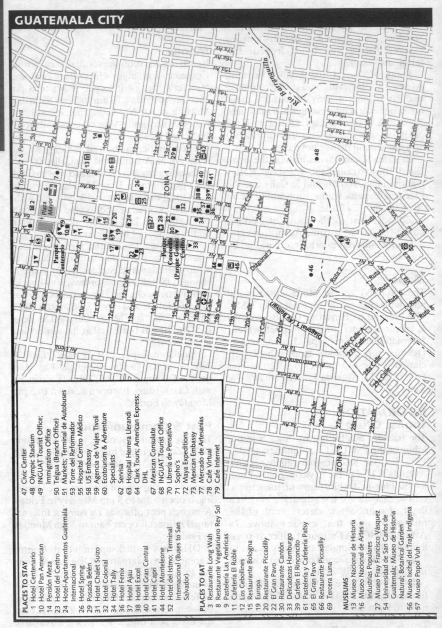

PLACES TO STAY
1 Hotel Centenario
10 Hotel Pan American
14 Pensión Meza
23 Hotel del Centro
24 Hotel-Apartamentos Guatemala
    Internacional
26 Hotel Spring
29 Posada Belén
31 Hotel Chalet Suizo
32 Hotel Colonial
34 Hotel Tally
36 Hotel Fenix
37 Hotel Ajau
38 Hotel Excel
40 Hotel Gran Central
41 Hotel Capri
44 Hotel Monteleone
52 Hotel del Istmo; Terminal
    Internacional (Buses to San
    Salvador)

PLACES TO EAT
3 Restaurante Long Wah
8 Restaurante Vegetariano Rey Sol
9 Pastelería Las Américas
11 Cafetería El Roble
12 Los Cebollines
15 Restaurante Bologna
19 Europa
20 Restaurante Piccadilly
22 El Gran Pavo
30 Restaurante Cantón
33 Delicadezas Hamburgo
39 Cafetín El Rinconcito
61 Pastelería y Cafetería Patsy
65 El Gran Pavo
66 Restaurante Piccadilly
69 Tercera Luna

MUSEUMS
13 Museo Nacional de Historia
16 Museo Nacional de Artes e
    Industrias Populares
27 Museo Fray Francisco Vásquez
54 Universidad de San Carlos de
    Guatemala; Museo de Historia
    Natural; Botanical Garden
56 Museo Ixchel del Traje Indígena
57 Museo Popol Vuh

47 Civic Center
48 Olympic Stadium
49 INGUAT Tourist Office;
    Immigration Office
50 Telgua (Branch Office)
51 Markets; Terminal de Autobuses
53 Torre del Reformador
55 Hospital Centro Médico
58 US Embassy
59 Agencia de Viajes Tivoli
60 Ecotourism & Adventure
    Specialists
62 Servisa
63 Hospital Herrera Llerandi
64 Clark Tours; American Express;
    DHL
67 Mexican Consulate
68 INGUAT Tourist Office
70 Librería de Pensativo
71 Sopho's
72 Maya Expeditions
73 Mexican Embassy
77 Mercado de Artesanías
78 Cafe Virtual
79 Cafe Internet

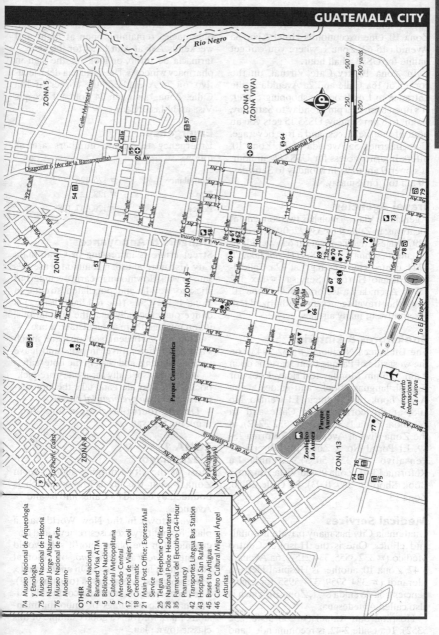

GUATEMALA CITY

GUATEMALA

Río Negro

ZONA 5

ZONA 10
(ZONA VIVA)

Diagonal 6 (Av de la Barranquilla)

ZONA 4

ZONA 9

Parque Centroamérica

ZONA 8

To Pacific Coast

To Antigua &
Kaminaljuyú

To Antigua

Aeropuerto
Internacional
La Aurora

Parque
Aurora

Zoológico
La Aurora

ZONA 13

Plazuela
España

To El Salvador

Blvd Aeropuerto

74 Museo Nacional de Arqueología
y Etnología
75 Museo Nacional de Historia
Natural Jorge Albarra
76 Museo Nacional de Arte
Moderno

OTHER
2 Palacio Nacional
4 Bancared Visa ATM
5 Biblioteca Nacional
6 Catedral Metropolitana
7 Mercado Central
17 Agencia de Viajes Tivoli
18 Credomatic
21 Main Post Office; Express Mail
Service
25 Telgua Telephone Office
28 National Police Headquarters
35 Farmacia del Ejecutivo (24-Hour
Pharmacy)
42 Transportes Litegua Bus Station
43 Hospital San Rafael
45 Buses to Antigua
46 Centro Cultural Miguel Ángel
Asturias

Internet services in Guatemala City are largely limited to expensive cybercafes in Zona 10. One exception is Hotel Ajau, 8a Avenida 15-62, Zona 1, where you can get online for US$3 a half hour.

In Zona 10, try Cafe Virtual, on the corner of 16a Calle and 2a Avenida at the entrance to Los Proceres shopping center. It's open 8 am to 9 pm Monday to Saturday, 10 am to 8 pm Sunday; US$5.15 gets you an hour of Internet access and a free beverage. Cafe Internet, 5a Avenida 16-11, Zona 10, offers Internet access for US$3.85 an hour. It's open 9 am to 9 pm Monday to Saturday, 10 am to 7 pm Sunday.

Travel Agencies
Agencia de Viajes Tivoli has two convenient locations: in Zona 9 (☎ 339 2260/1/2, fax 334 3297, viajes@tivoli.com.gt) at 6a Avenida 8-41; and in Zona 1 (☎ 238 4771/2/3, fax 220 4744, centro@tivoli.com.gt) at 12a Calle 4-55, Edificio Herrera. Servisa (☎/fax 332 7526), Avenida La Reforma 8-33, Zona 10, is another travel agency and authorized representative of many airlines.

Bookstores & Libraries
The Biblioteca Nacional (☎ 232 2443), on the west side of Parque Centenario, is open 9 am to 6 pm Monday to Friday. Look for English-language books and guides at the Arnel bookstore, Edificio El Centro, No 108, at the corner of 9a Calle and 7a Avenida, Zona 1; Sopho's (☎ 332 3242), in the Zona Viva at Avenida La Reforma 13-89, El Portal No 1, Zona 10; Librería de Pensativo (☎ 332 5055), Avenida La Reforma 13-01, Zona 9; and Vista Hermosa Book Shop (☎ 269 1003), 2a Calle 18-50, Zona 15.

Medical Services
Guatemala City has many private hospitals and clinics. One is the Hospital Centro Médico (☎ 332 3555, 334 2157), 6a Avenida 3-47, Zona 10; another is Hospital Herrera Llerandi (☎ 334 5959, 334 5955 for emergencies), 6a Avenida 8-71, Zona 10, which is also called Amedesgua.

Hospital San Rafael (☎ 230 5048, 232 5352), 16a Calle 2-42, is recommended and cheap, though most of its doctors speak only Spanish. The Guatemalan Red Cross (☎ 125) is at 3a Calle 8-40, Zona 1.

Guatemala City uses a duty-chemist (*farmacia de turno*) system with designated pharmacies remaining open at night and weekends. Ask at your hotel for the nearest farmacia de turno, or look for the sign in pharmacy windows. The Farmacia del Ejecutivo, on 7a Avenida at the corner of 15a Calle, Zona 1, is open 24 hours; it accepts Visa and MasterCard.

Emergency
Emergency telephone numbers are as follows:

Ambulance	☎ 125, 128
Fire	☎ 122, 123
Police	☎ 120, 137, 138

Dangers & Annoyances
Street crime is increasing in Guatemala City. Use normal urban common sense. It's safe to walk downtown in early evening, but stick to well-lit and populated streets. In Zona 1, 18a Calle (the red light district) is dangerous, especially near the bus stations; if you must go there at night, take a taxi.

The city's affluent sections are much safer. Even here, travel in pairs and leave your documents and cash in the hotel safe.

All buses, especially local ones, are pickpocket turf. Stay alert and take the more expensive *servicio preferencial* buses.

Despite tourist-brochure claims, don't drink the tap water.

ZONA 1
Plaza Mayor
Most of the city's notable sights are in Zona 1 near the Plaza Mayor, which is bounded by 6a and 8a Calles and 6a and 7a Avenidas.

Every town in the New World had a plaza for military exercises, reviews and ceremonies. On the plaza's north side would be the *palacio de gobierno*, or colonial government headquarters. On another side, preferably east, was a church (or cathedral). The other sides of the square could hold additional civic buildings or imposing mansions. Plaza Mayor is a good example of this classic town plan.

Visit on Sunday, when locals stroll, play in the fountains, gossip, neck and groove to salsa music. Otherwise, try for lunchtime or late afternoon. You'll be besieged by shoeshine boys and sellers of kitsch.

Palacio Nacional

On Plaza Mayor's north side is the magnificent Palacio Nacional, built at enormous cost during the dictatorial presidency of Jorge Ubico (1931-44). It's the third palace to stand here, and it's currently being restored to house a Guatemalan-history museum.

Free tours are given between 9 am and 5:30 pm Monday to Friday and between 8 am and 3 pm Saturday and Sunday. The tour takes you through a labyrinth of gleaming brass, polished wood, carved stone and frescoed arches (painted by Alberto Gálvez Suárez). Notable features include the 2000kg gold, bronze and Bohemian-crystal chandelier in the reception salon and two Moorish-style courtyards.

Catedral Metropolitana

Built between 1782 and 1809 (the towers were finished later, in 1867), the restored Metropolitan Cathedral is not a particularly beautiful building. It's supposedly open 8 am to 7 pm daily.

Mercado Central

Until it was destroyed by the earthquake of 1976, the central market on 9a Avenida between 6a and 8a Calles, behind the cathedral, was where locals bought food and other necessities. Reconstructed in the late 1970s, the new market specializes in touristy items such as cloth, carved wood, worked leather and metal, basketry and other handicrafts. Vegetables and other daily needs have been moved to the surrounding streets. There are better places to buy crafts. Market hours are 7 am to 6 pm Monday to Saturday, 6 am to noon Sunday.

The city's true 'central' food market is in Zona 4.

Museums

Museums in Zona 1 include Museo Fray Francisco Vásquez (☎ 232 3625), Iglesia San Francisco, 6a Avenida at 13a Calle, which houses a Franciscan friar's belongings. It's open 9 am to noon and 3 to 6 pm daily.

The Museo Nacional de Artes e Industrias Populares (☎ 238 0334), 10a Avenida 10-72, is the national popular arts museum,

exhibiting paintings, ceramics, masks, musical instruments, metalwork and gourds. It's open 9 am to 5 pm Monday to Friday.

The collection at the Museo Nacional de Historia (☎ 253 6149), 9a Calle 9-70, is a jumble of historical relics but is strong on photography. The museum is open 9 am to 4 pm Tuesday to Friday, 9 am to noon and 2 to 4 pm Saturday and Sunday. Admission costs US$1.25. This museum may be moved to the Palacio Nacional after that building is restored.

ZONA 2

Zona 2 is north of Zona 1. Though mostly a middle-class residential district, its northern end holds the large Parque Minerva, which is surrounded by golf courses, sports grounds and the buildings of the Universidad Mariano Gálvez.

Parque Minerva

Minerva, goddess of wisdom, technical skill and invention, was a favorite of President Manuel Estrada Cabrera (see History in the Facts about Guatemala section, earlier in this chapter). Her park is a placid place, good for walking among the eucalyptus trees and sipping a cool drink. Watch out for pickpockets and purse-snatchers.

The prime sight here is the Mapa En Relieve, a huge relief map of Guatemala. Constructed in 1904 under the direction of Francisco Vela, the map shows the country at a scale of 1:10,000, but the height of the mountainous terrain has been exaggerated to 1:2000 for dramatic effect. Fully restored in late 1999, the map's in fine shape. Viewing towers afford a panoramic view. This place is odd but fun. Hours are 9 am to 5 pm daily (US$2). Nearby are carnival rides and games for children.

The Mapa En Relieve and Parque Minerva are 2km north of Plaza Mayor along 6a Avenida, but that street is one-way heading south. Catch a northbound bus (No 1, 45 or 46) on 5a Avenida in Zona 1 and take it to the end of the line.

CIVIC CENTER AREA

The Centro Cívico complex, constructed during the 1950s and '60s, lies around the junction of Zonas 1, 4 and 5. Here you'll find the Palace of Justice, the headquarters of the Guatemalan Institute of Social Security

(IGSS), the Banco del Quetzal, city hall and INGUAT headquarters. The Banco del Quetzal building bears high-relief murals by Dagoberto Vásquez depicting the history of his homeland. City hall holds a huge mosaic by Carlos Mérida.

Behind INGUAT is the Olympic Stadium, and across the street from the Centro Cívico on a hilltop is the Centro Cultural Miguel Ángel Asturias, which holds the national theater, a chamber theater, an open-air theater and a small museum of old armaments.

Other than the Civic Center, this area is known mostly for its markets and bus stations, all thrown together in the chaotic southwestern corner of Zona 4 near the railway.

ZONA 10

East of Avenida La Reforma, the posh Zona 10 holds two of the city's most important museums, both in large new buildings at the Universidad Francisco Marroquín, on the east end of 6a Calle.

Museo Ixchel del Traje Indígena (☎ 331 3634, 331 3638) is named for Ixchel, wife of Maya sky god Itzamná and goddess of the moon, women, reproduction, textiles, among other things. Photographs and exhibits of indigenous costumes, textiles and other crafts show the incredible richness of traditional highland art. If you enjoy seeing Guatemalan textiles at all, you must make a visit to this museum. It's open 8 am to 5:50 pm Monday to Friday, 9 am to 12:50 pm Saturday (US$2).

Behind it is the **Museo Popol Vuh** (☎/fax 361 2301), where well-chosen polychrome pottery, figurines, incense burners, burial urns, carved-wood masks and traditional textiles fill several exhibit rooms. Other rooms hold colonial paintings and wood and silver objects. A faithful copy of the Dresden Codex, one of the precious 'painted books' of the Maya, is among the most interesting pieces. This is an important collection, especially given its precolonial emphasis. This museum is open 9 am to 5 pm Monday to Friday, 9 am to 1 pm Saturday (US$2).

The biology department at the Universidad de San Carlos de Guatemala (☎ 476 2010), Calle Mariscal Cruz 1-56, has a **museo de historia natural** and a large

botanical garden. Hours are 8 am to 3 pm Monday to Friday (US$1.25).

ZONA 13

The major attraction in the city's southern reaches is the Parque Aurora, with its zoo, children's playground, fairgrounds and several museums. One of the museums, the Moorish-looking **Museo Nacional de Arqueología y Etnología** (☎ 472 0478), has a collection of Mayan artifacts from all over Guatemala, including stone carvings, jade, ceramics, statues, stelae and a tomb. Models depict the ruins at Tikal and Zaculeu. Exhibits in the ethnology section highlight the various indigenous peoples and languages in Guatemala, with emphasis on traditional costumes, dances and implements of daily life. The museum is open 9 am to 4 pm Tuesday to Friday, 9 am to noon and 2 to 4 pm Saturday (US$4).

Facing it is the **Museo Nacional de Arte Moderno** (☎ 472 0467), which holds a collection of 20th-century Guatemalan art, especially paintings and sculpture. Hours are 9 am to 4 pm Tuesday to Friday, 9 am to noon and 2 to 4 pm Saturday and Sunday (US$1.25).

Nearby is the **Museo Nacional de Historia Natural Jorge Albarra** (☎ 472 0468), whose claim to fame is its large collection of dissected animals. The museaum is open 9 am to 4 pm Tuesday to Friday, 9 am to noon and 2 to 4 pm Saturday and Sunday (US$1.50).

Several hundred meters east of these museums is the city's official handicrafts market, the **Mercado de Artesanías** (☎ 472 0208), on 11a Avenida, just off the access road to the airport. It's a sleepy place where shopkeepers display the same items available in hotel gift shops. It's open 8 am to 6 pm Monday to Saturday, 8:30 am to 2 pm Sunday.

The pleasant **Zoológico La Aurora** (☎ 472 0507) is open 9 am to 5 pm Tuesday to Sunday (US$1 adults, US$0.50 children).

KAMINALJUYÚ

Several kilometers west of the center, in Colonia Kaminaljuyú, Zona 7, lie the extensive ruins of Kaminaljuyú (☎ 253 1570), a late pre-Classic/early Classic Mayan site displaying both Mexican and Mayan influences.

Unfortunately, much of Kaminaljuyú has been covered by urban sprawl. Your time would be better spent looking at the artifacts recovered here that are on display in the city's museums. It's open 9 am to 4 pm daily (US$1.25). Bus Nos 35 and 37 come here from 4a Avenida, Zona 1.

PLACES TO STAY

As you would expect from a capital city, Guatemala City has accommodations for every budget. Prices are higher here than anywhere else in the country. The top-end choices are not listed in this guide, however, the Zona Viva contains many of them.

Budget

Many decent budget hotels and cheap, convenient little restaurants lie several blocks south of the Plaza Mayor, near National Police Headquarters and the post office in an area bounded by 6a and 9a Avenidas and 12a and 16a Calles. Factor in street noise as you look for a room. The places listed below are in Zona 1 unless otherwise indicated.

Hotel Spring (☎ 230 2858, 230 2958, fax 232 0107, 8a Avenida 12-65) is a clean, comfortable old hotel that's often full because of its good location, sunny courtyard and decent prices: US$10/14/20 single/double/triple with shared, hot bath; US$14/20/24 with private bath and cable TV; US$22/28/34 for fancier rooms in the new *anexo*, some wheelchair accessible. The cafeteria serves meals from 6:30 am to 1:30 pm.

Hotel Ajau (☎ 232 0488, 251 3008, fax 251 8097, hotajaugua.gbm.net, 8a Avenida 15-62) is fairly clean and also somewhat cheaper and quieter than many hotels on 8a Avenida. Rooms cost US$7/7.75/9.25 with shared bath; US$11.50/12.50/14.65 with private bath. All rooms have cable TV. Laundry and email services are available.

Hotel Chalet Suizo (☎ 251 3786, fax 232 0429, 14a Calle 6-82) has been a travelers' favorite for decades. The 47 rooms around plant-filled courtyards are comfortable and immaculate. Rates are US$12/16 single/double with shared bath, or US$24/28 with private bath. Book in advance.

Hotel Excel (☎ 253 2709, 230 0140, fax 238 4071, 9a Avenida 15-12) is a bright, modern place with 17 rooms and a cafeteria

on three levels around a courtyard/parking lot. Rooms with bath and cable TV are US$20/23/27. Across the street is the super-budget *Hotel Gran Central* (☎ 232 9514), a sprawling three-story building where cleanish, basic, dark rooms are US$3.50/4.75/6. Hot water may be available. The nearby *Hotel Capri* (☎ 232 8191, 251 3737, 9a Avenida 15-63) has rooms with private bath and cable TV for US$11.50/16.

Pensión Meza (☎ 232 3777, 10a Calle 10-17) has drab rooms but is busy with international backpackers who like the sunny courtyard, camaraderie, helpful proprietor and low prices. Rooms with shared bath are US$6.45/7.75 with one bed, US$8.35 with two beds; dorm bunks are US$4.50 per person. The restaurant serves cheap meals, and there's a good book swap. *Hotel Fenix* (☎ 251 6625, 7a Avenida 15-81) has been one of Guatemala's best cheapies for years due to the friendly atmosphere and clean rooms. Basic rooms with shared, hot bath are US$5.50 single or double, US$9.40/10.80 triple/quad. The hotel has a cafeteria and spacious hangout areas.

The recommended *Hotel Monteleone* (☎ 238 2600, fax 253 9205, 18a Calle 4-63, Zona 1) is across from the Antigua bus stop. Clean rooms in an amicable environment are US$7.50 single or double with shared bath, US$11.75 double with private bath.

If you're arriving by bus from San Salvador, *Hotel del Istmo* (☎ 332 4389, 3a Avenida 1-38, Zona 9), at the Terminal Internacional, is convenient. It's clean and comfortable, with an inexpensive cafeteria. Rooms with private, hot bath are US$10.50/13/15.50.

A couple of good budget hotels near the airport charge US$10 per room. These include the popular *Dos Lunas* (☎/fax 334 5264, lorena@pronet.gt, 21a Calle 10-92, Zona 13, Aurora II), with a Web site at www.xelapages.com/doslunas, and *Economy Dorms* (☎ 331 8029, 8a Avenida 17-74, Zona 13, Aurora I).

Mid-Range

Guatemala City's mid-range lodgings are good values. All are comfortable and some are even charming; they're all in Zona 1.

A converted colonial home, *Posada Belén* (☎ 232 9226, 253 4530, fax 251 3478, pbelen@guatemalaweb.com, 13a Calle A 10-30) is a quiet, quaint hostelry offering 11 rooms with private bath, a dining room serving all meals and laundry service. Rooms cost US$36/43/48/53 single/double/triple/quad.

Hotel Pan American (☎ 232 6807/8/9, fax 251 8749, panamhot@infovia.com.gt, 9a Calle 5-63) was Guatemala City's luxury hotel before WWII. It still attracts many faithful returners who like its faded charm. The 55 pleasant, comfortable rooms, all art deco and Biedermeier, have cable TV, telephone, private bathtub and fan. Avoid rooms facing the noisy street. Rates are US$41/43/46/48; rooms with six beds are US$53. Amenities include a restaurant and many guest services, including email.

Hotel del Centro (☎ 232 5980, 238 1519, fax 230 0208, hotelcentro@guate.net, 13a Calle 4-55) has been dependable for decades. The 55 large, comfortable rooms come with shiny baths and cable TV; some have two double beds. Watch for street noise. Rates are US$42/48/54. The hotel has a restaurant, a bar with music on Friday night and a rooftop terrace.

Hotel Colonial (☎ 232 6722, 232 2955, fax 232 8671, colonial@infovia.com.gt, 7a Avenida 14-19) is a large converted old house with heavy, dark colonial decor. The interior court is inviting and the 42 rooms are clean. Four rooms have shared bath for US$18/24; the rest have private bath for US$24/32/41. A restaurant serves meals from 6:30 am to 2 pm.

Attractive for long stays or families is the convenient **Hotel-Apartamentos Guatemala Internacional** (☎ 238 4441/2, fax 232 4350, 6a Avenida 12-21). Each of its 27 furnished apartments has a TV, telephone and full kitchen. One-bedroom apartments run US$24/30/36 single/double/triple or quad; two-bedroom units are US$27/33/40. A few larger apartments sleep six. Studios (like the apartments but without a kitchen) are US$18/20 single/double.

Hotel Centenario (☎ 230 4005/7, fax 238 2039, 6a Calle 5-33), on the north side of Parque Centenario, has 42 rooms with well-worn but clean showers. Many have a double and a single bed. Prices are US$25/32/40/45.

Hotel Tally (☎ 232 9845, 251 7082, fax 253 1749, 7a Avenida 15-24) is a terrific, convenient new place. Each of its sparkling rooms has a private, hot bath, cable TV and air-con. Prices are US$23/29/33/37. Reservations are recommended.

PLACES TO EAT
Budget
Cheap eats are easily found, as fast-food and snack shops abound. To really save money, head for Parque Concordia, in Zona 1 bounded by 5a and 6a Avenidas and 14a and 15a Calles, whose west side is lined with stalls serving sandwiches and snacks at rock-bottom prices (US$2) from early morning to late evening.

Delicadezas Hamburgo (15a Calle 5-34, Zona 1), on the south side of Parque Concordia, features a long list of sandwiches at lunch and dinner. It's open 7 am to 9:30 pm daily.

Restaurante Cantón (☎ 251 6331, 6a Avenida 14-29, Zona 1), on the east side of the park, is the place for Chinese food – US$5 to US$8 per platter. It's open 9 am to 9:30 pm daily. Other Chinese restaurants lie near the corner of 6a Avenida and 14a Calle.

The city's other rich concentration of Chinese restaurants is west of Parque Centenario along 6a Calle, where you'll find **Restaurante Long Wah** (☎ 232 6611, 6a Calle 3-70, Zona 1) and several other places such as **Palacio Real, Palacio Dorado** and **Jou Jou**.

Along 6a Avenida between 10a and 15a Calles, you'll find dozens of restaurants of all types, cooking up dishes for US$3 to US$4. **Pastelería Las Américas** (6a Avenida 8-52), near Plaza Mayor, is a good place to stop for coffee and a European-style pastry or cake.

Several good little restaurants are on 9a Avenida between 15a and 16a Calles. The **Cafetín El Rinconcito** (9a Avenida 15-74), facing the Hotel Capri, is good for tacos and sandwiches; breakfast, lunch and dinner each cost around US$1.50 to US$2.

Cafetería El Roble (9a Calle 5-46, Zona 1), facing the Hotel Pan American entrance, is a clean little cafe popular with local office workers for all meals (US$1.15 to US$1.65).

Europa (☎ 253 4929, 11a Calle 5-16, Zona 1) is a comfortable restaurant, bar and gathering place for locals and foreigners. A sign on the door says 'English spoken, but not understood.' Inside you'll find cable TV, a book exchange and good, inexpensive food; it's open 8 am to 1 am Monday to Saturday. A block and a half north is *Los Cebollines* *(6a Avenida 9-75, Zona 1)*, a casual, recommended place for Mexican food.

Pastelería y Cafetería Patsy, on the corner of 8a Calle and Avenida La Reforma in Zona 10, is a bustling, popular place. The chicken, pasta, sandwiches and other light meals here are cheap – especially for the Zona Viva.

For coffee in Zona 10, head over to *Tercera Luna* (☎ 362 5030, *1a Avenida 12-70*), with rockin' java and happening art exhibits and poetry readings. *Sopho's* *(Avenida La Reforma 13-89, El Portal No 1, Zona 10)* is a bookstore with a nice outdoor cafe.

Restaurante Vegetariano Rey Sol (8a Calle 5-36), on the south side of Parque Centenario, has a long cafeteria line with a good selection: whole-grain breads, sandwiches, soya products, fruit and vegetable salads, hot foods and more. It's open 7:15 am to 8:45 pm Monday to Saturday.

Restaurante Piccadilly (☎ 230 2866, 253 9223, *6a Avenida 11-01, Zona 1)* is among the capital's most popular eateries, with a multinational menu heavy on Italian fare. Most main courses cost US$3 or less. Another branch is on Plazuela España at 7a Avenida 12-00, Zona 9.

Mid-Range

Most mid-range hotels in Zona 1 offer excellent set lunches for US$6 to US$10. Try *Hotel Del Centro* or the popular *Hotel Pan American*.

The small but attractive *Restaurante Bologna* (☎ 251 1167, *10a Calle 6-20, Zona 1)* serves tasty pizza and pasta for US$3 to US$4. It's open 10 am to 9:30 pm daily, except Tuesday.

El Gran Pavo (☎ 232 9912, *13a Calle 4-41, Zona 1)* is a big place just west of Hotel del Centro's entrance (other branches around town include one at 12a Calle 5-54, Zona 9). The menu seems to include every Mexican dish imaginable, including *hirria*, a spicy-hot soup of meat, onions, peppers and cilantro, served with tortillas – a meal in itself for US$3.75. The restaurant is open 10 am to midnight daily, with mariachi music on Friday and Saturday nights.

ENTERTAINMENT

Many visitors enjoy wining and dining the night away in the pricey Zona Viva. If that's beyond your budget, catch a movie (US$1.50) at one of the cinemas along 6a Avenida between Plaza Mayor and Parque Concordia. Or check out the events at the *Centro Cultural Miguel Ángel Asturias* (☎ 232 4041/2/3/4/5, 253 1743), in Zona 4. Guatemala City has a hopping creative scene, so if you're itching for some urban culture, check out some of the bars and clubs in Zona 1.

GETTING THERE & AWAY
Air

International flights arrive and depart from La Aurora International Airport. Taxis and shuttle buses depart from the lower (arrivals) level. La Aurora is also served by regional and domestic carriers. See the Getting There & Away section, earlier in this chapter.

Bus & Shuttle Minibus

See Getting There & Away, earlier, for information on international buses. Guatemala City has no central bus terminal; if you ask, locals will probably refer you to the Terminal de Autobuses in Zona 4. Ticket offices and departure points are different for each company. Many are near the huge, chaotic market in Zona 4. If the bus you want is here, go to the market and ask until you find it.

Shuttle minibuses serve the most popular international routes. See Antigua, Panajachel and Flores for information.

Car

Major international rental companies have offices at the airport and in the city center. Offices in Guatemala City include the following:

Ahorrent (☎ 361 5661, fax 361 5621), Boulevard Liberación 4-83, Zona 9; Hotel Cortijo Reforma (☎ 332 0712 ext 180), Avenida La Reforma 2-18, Zona 9; La Aurora International Airport (☎ 362 8921/2)

Avis (☎ 332 7744/7, fax 332 7448, avis@guate.net), 6a Avenida 11-24, Zona 9; La Aurora International Airport (☎ 331 0017, 361 5645)

Budget (☎ 332 2491), Avenida Hincapie 11-01, Zona 13; La Aurora International Airport (☎ 331 0273, 360 8639)

Dollar (☎ 232 3446, fax 238 1046), Hotel Ritz Continental, 6a Avenida A 10-13, Zona 1; La Aurora International Airport (☎ 331 7185, fax 362 5393)

Guatemala Rent (☎ 473 1330, rentautos@centroamerica.com), 19a Calle 16-91 (Calle Real de Petapa), Zona 12; La Aurora International Airport (☎ 362 0205/6)

Hertz (☎ 334 2540/1, fax 331 7924, rentauto@guate.net), 7a Avenida 14-76, Zona 9; Hotel Camino Real (☎ 368 0107), Avenida La Reforma at 14a Calle, Zona 10; La Aurora International Airport (☎ 331 1711)

National (Interrent-Europcar-Tilden; ☎ 360 3963, 332 4702, fax 360 1404, national@pronet.net.gt), 12a Calle 7-69, Zona 9; La Aurora International Airport (☎ 331 8365, 361 5618)

Tabarini (☎ 332 2161, 334 5907, fax 334 1925), 2a Calle A 7-30, Zona 10; La Aurora International Airport (☎ 331 4755)

Tally (☎ 232 0421, fax 253 1749), 7a Avenida 14-60, Zona 1; La Aurora International Airport (☎ 332 6063, fax 334 5925)

Thrifty (☎ 332 1130, 332 1220, fax 332 1207), Avenida La Reforma 8-33, Zona 10; La Aurora International Airport (☎ 332 1265)

Tikal (☎ 332 4721, 361 0247), 2a Calle 6-56, Zona 10

GETTING AROUND
To/From the Airport
La Aurora International Airport (☎ 334 7680, 334 7689) is in Zona 13, the southern part of the city, 10 minutes from Zona 1 by taxi, 30 minutes by bus. Car rental offices and taxi ranks are outside the airport.

For the city bus, go upstairs to the departures level and cross the parking lot to the bus stop. Bus No 83 comes every 15 minutes, 6 am to 9 pm (US$0.15), and will take you through Zonas 9 and 4 to Zona 1. From town to the airport, No 83 goes south through Zona 1 on 10a Avenida and through Zona 9 on 6a Avenida, passing by the zoo and the museums on 7a Avenida and stopping right in front of the international terminal.

Taxi fares to various points in the center are negotiable, though high: from the airport to Zona 9 or 10, US$5; to Zona 1, US$7. A tip is expected. Be sure to establish the destination and price before getting in.

Many companies offer shuttle service between the airport and Antigua, with door-to-door service on the Antigua end (US$7). A taxi to Antigua costs around US$20;

bargain hard and hook up with other travelers to cut costs.

Bus & Jitney
Buses are frequent and cheap. In Zona 9, 6a Avenida (southbound) and 7a Avenida (northbound) buses traverse the city; in Zona 1 these buses swing away from the commercial district and travel along 4a, 5a, 9a and 10a Avenidas. The most useful north-south routes are bus Nos 2, 5 and 14. Note that modified numbers (such as 2A or 5-Bolívar) follow different routes. Buses marked 'Terminal' stop at the Terminal de Autobuses in Zona 4.

To get between Zonas 1 and 10, take bus No 82 or 101 from the corner of 10a Avenida between 8a and 12a Calles. The No 82 bus passes the Centro Cívico before turning onto Avenida La Reforma; this one is good for getting to INGUAT and several embassies.

Buses stop running at about 9 pm, and *ruteleros* (jitneys) begin to travel the main avenues, running until buses resume at 5 am. Hold up your hand to stop a jitney or bus.

Taxi
Taxi Amarilla (☎ 332 1515) charges half the price of other taxi companies, and their cabs are metered.

Antigua

pop 30,000
Nestled between three volcanoes, Antigua Guatemala is among the oldest and most beautiful cities in the Americas. Its majestic setting, cobblestone streets, crumbling ruins and sprays of bougainvillea bursting from terra cotta roofs charm even the most wordly traveler. Antigua is one of Guatemala's most kid-friendly cities, with playgrounds, Spanish classes for children and food for the finicky.

The most exciting time to visit Antigua is during Holy Week – especially Good Friday. It takes planning (reserve hotels at least four months in advance), as this is the busiest week of the year. Other busy times are June through August and November to April.

Antigua is cold after sunset, especially between September and March, so bring warm clothes, a sleeping bag or a blanket.

HISTORY

Antigua was founded on March 10, 1543, and served as the colonial capital for 233 years. The capital was transferred to Guatemala City in 1776, after Antigua was razed in the earthquake of July 29, 1773.

The town was slowly rebuilt, retaining its traditional character, architecture and cobblestone streets. In 1944 the Legislative Assembly declared Antigua a national monument, and in 1979 Unesco declared it a World Heritage Site.

Most of Antigua's buildings were constructed during the 17th and 18th centuries, when the city was a rich Spanish outpost and the Catholic church was ascending to power. Many handsome, sturdy colonial buildings remain, and several impressive ruins have been preserved and are open to the public.

ORIENTATION

Volcán Agua is southeast of the city and visible from most points; Volcán Acatenango is to the west; and Volcán Fuego (Fire) – easily recognizable by its plume of smoke and red glow – is to the southwest. These three volcanoes (which appear on the city's coat of arms) provide easy reference points.

Antigua's streets use a modified version of Guatemala City's numbering system (see Orientation in the Guatemala City section, earlier in this chapter). In Antigua, compass points are added to the avenidas and calles. Calles run east-west, so 4a Calle west of Parque Central is 4a Calle Poniente; avenidas run north-south, so 3a Avenida north of Parque Central is 3a Avenida Norte.

Landmarks surrounding Parque Central include the Palacio de los Capitanes, the old headquarters of the Spanish colonial government (recognizable by its double, two-story arcade), on the plaza's south side; the cathedral, on the east side; and the Palacio del Ayuntamiento (Town Hall), on the north side. The **Arco de Santa Catarina**, spanning 5a Avenida Norte between 1a and 2a Calles, is another famous landmark. Built in 1694 (and rebuilt in the 19th century), this arch was one of the few structures in town that withstood the 1773 quake.

Most buses arrive at the Terminal de Buses, a large open lot just west of the market, four blocks west of Parque Central along 4a Calle Poniente.

INFORMATION
Tourist Offices

Antigua's INGUAT tourist office (☎ 832 0763) is on the southeast corner of Parque Central, next to the Palacio de los Capitanes. It's open 8 am to 5 pm daily and has free city maps, bus information and a schedule of Semana Santa events.

The Tourist Police office (☎ 832 4131) is on the corner of 4a Calle Oriente and 4a Avenida Norte. Officers provide free escorts to heretofore dangerous spots such as the cemetery and Cerro de la Cruz at 8:30 and 11 am and 3 pm daily.

El Arco, 5a Avenida Norte 25B, maintains a list of volunteer opportunities in Guatemala. AmeriSpan Guatemala (☎ 832 0164, 832 4846, fax 832 1896, amerispan@ guate.net), 6a Avenida Norte 40A, is another source of information on volunteer projects and Spanish schools.

Visitors should look for the informative *Antigua Guatemala: An illustrated history of the city and its monuments*, by Elizabeth Bell and Trevor Long.

Money

Banco Occidental, on 4a Calle Poniente just off Parque Central's northwest corner, changes US currency and traveler's checks and gives Visa card cash advances; the bank is open 8:30 am to 7 pm Monday to Friday, 9 am to 2 pm Saturday. Banco Industrial, on 5a Avenida Sur next to the Telgua office, is open 8 am to 7 pm Monday to Friday, 8 am to 5 pm Saturday, and has a Visa ATM. Bancafé, 4a Calle Poniente 22, also has a Visa ATM. Banquetzal gives the best exchange rate for dollars; the branch on the park's northwest corner has a MasterCard ATM.

Post & Communications

The post office is at 4a Calle Poniente and Alameda de Santa Lucía, west of Parque Central near the market. To ship packages, try DHL (☎ 832 3718, ☎/fax 832 3732), 6a Avenida Sur 16, open 8 am to 6 pm Monday to Friday, 8 am to noon Saturday; or International Bonded Couriers (☎/fax 832 1696), 6a Avenida Sur 12. They'll pick up, pack and deliver packages door-to-door.

ANTIGUA

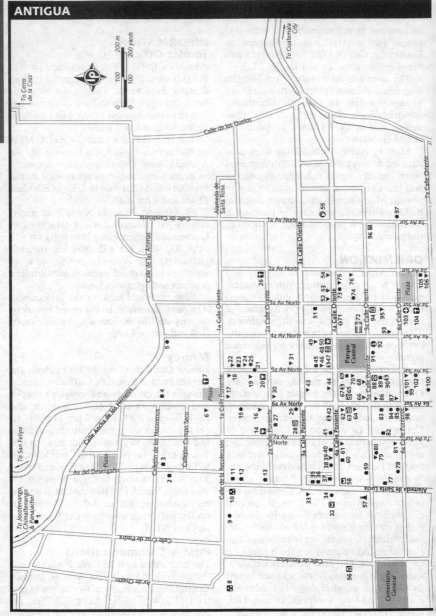

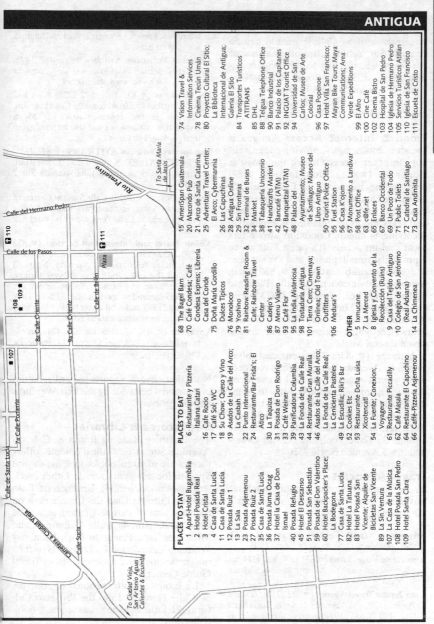

PLACES TO STAY

1 Apart-Hotel Bugambilia
2 Hotel Posada Real
3 Hotel Cristal
4 Casa de Santa Lucía
11 Casa de Santa Lucía
12 Posada Ruiz 1
13 La Sala
23 Posada Asjemenou
27 Posada Ruiz 2
35 Casa de Santa Lucía
36 Posada Juma Ocag
37 Hotel la Casa de Don Ismael
40 Posada Refugio
45 Hotel El Descanso
51 Posada San Sebastián
59 Posada de Don Valentino
60 Hotel Backpacker's Place; La Bodegona
77 Casa de Santa Lucía
82 Hotel La Tatuana
83 Hotel Posada San Vicente; Alquiler de Bicicletas San Vicente
89 La Sin Ventura
107 La Casa de la Música
108 Hotel Posada San Pedro
109 Hotel Santa Clara

PLACES TO EAT

6 Restaurante y Pizzería Italiana Catari
16 Café Rocío
17 Café Sol; WC
18 Su Chow; Queso y Vino
19 Asados de la Calle del Arco; La Casbah
22 Punto Internacional
24 Restaurante/Bar Frida's; El Atico
30 La Taquiza
31 Posada de Don Rodrigo
33 Café Weiner
39 Panificadora Columbia
43 La Fonda de la Calle Real
44 Restaurante Gran Muralla
46 Asados de la Calle del Arco; La Fonda de la Calle Real; La Cenicienta Pasteles
49 La Escudilla; Riki's Bar
53 Restaurante Doña Luisa Xicotencatl
54 La Fuente; Conexion; Voyageur
61 Restaurante Piccadilly
62 Café Masala
66 Restaurante El Capuchino
66 Caffé-Pizzería Asjemenou
68 The Bagel Barn
70 Café Condesa; Café Condesa Express; Librería Casa del Conde
75 Doña María Gordillo Dulces Típicos
76 Monoloco
79 Yoshino
81 Rainbow Reading Room & Cafe; Rainbow Travel Center
86 Cadejo's
87 Menu Viajero
93 Café Flor
95 La India Misteriosa
98 Tostaduria Antigua
101 Tierra Cero; Cinemaya; Onlinea; Old Town Outfitters
106 Medusa's

OTHER

5 Ixmucane
7 La Merced
8 Iglesia y Convento de la Recolección (Ruins)
9 Casa del Tejido Antiguo
10 Colegio de San Jerónimo (Real Aduana)
14 La Chimenea
15 AmeriSpan Guatemala
20 Macondo Pub
21 Arco de Santa Catarina
25 Adventure Travel Center; El Arco; Cybermannia
26 Las Capuchinas
28 Antigua Online
29 Sin Fronteras
32 Terminal de Buses
34 Market
38 Tabaquería Unicornio
41 Handicrafts Market
42 Bancafé (ATM)
47 Banquetzal (ATM)
48 Palacio del Ayuntamiento; Museo de Santiago; Museo del Libro Antiguo
50 Tourist Police Office
55 Fuel Station
56 Casa K'ojom
57 Monumento a Landivar
58 Post Office
63 c@fe.net
65 Enlaces
67 Banco Occidental
69 Un Poco de Todo
71 Public Toilets
72 Catedral de Santiago
73 Casa Andinista
74 Vision Travel & Information Services
78 Cinema Tecún Umán
80 Proyecto Cultural El Sitio; La Biblioteca Internacional de Antigua; Galería El Sitio
84 Transportes Turísticos ATITRANS
85 DHL
88 Telgua Telephone Office
90 Banco Industrial
91 Palacio de los Capitanes
92 INGUAT Tourist Office
94 Universidad de San Carlos; Museo de Arte Colonial
96 Casa Popenoe
97 Hotel Villa San Francisco; Mayan Bike Tours; Maya Communications; Area Verde Expeditions
99 El Afro
100 Cine Café
102 Cinema Bistro
103 Hospital de San Pedro
104 Iglesia de Hermano Pedro
105 Servicios Turísticos Atitlán
110 Iglesia de San Francisco
111 Escuela de Cristo

The Telgua telephone office is just off Parque Central's southwest corner, at the intersection of 5a Calle Poniente and 5a Avenida Sur. You're better off using one of the businesses catering to the communication needs of international tourists (see Email & Internet Access, below).

Don't use the phones imploring you to call the USA for free. They lie.

Email & Internet Access Antigua is awash in businesses supplying cheap, reliable Internet access. One of the oldest is Conexion (☎ 832 3768, fax 832 0082, users@conexion.com), 4a Calle Oriente 14, inside La Fuente courtyard, where you can send and receive phone, fax, email and telex messages. Sending is expensive; receiving is cheap. Conexion also offers local dial-up access. It's open 8:30 am to 7 pm daily. Email, phone and fax services are also available at WC (☎ 832 5666, wwcall@infovia.com), 1a Calle Poniente 9, by Café Sol, opposite La Merced church, and at Maya Communications, 1a Avenida Sur 15, in the Hotel Villa San Francisco, which claims 24-hour access, seven days a week.

Enlaces (☎ 832 0216, enlace@pobox .com), 6a Avenida Norte 1, offers competitively priced email, phone and fax services. It's open 8 am to 7:30 pm Monday to Saturday, 8 am to 1 pm Sunday. Other Internet places include Onlinea, 6a Calle Poniente 7; c@fe.net, 6a Avenida Norte 14; Antigua Online, 3a Calle Poniente 12; and Cybermannia, 5 Avenida Norte 25B.

Travel Agencies
Everywhere you turn in Antigua, you'll see travel agencies. Reputable agencies include the following:

Adventure Travel Center (☎/fax 832 0162, viarealguate.net), 5a Avenida Norte 25-B

Agencia de Viajes Tivoli (☎ 832 1370, 832 4274, fax 832 5690, antigua@tivoli.com), 4a Calle Oriente 10, local 3

Gran Jaguar Travel Agency (☎ 832 2712), 4a Calle Poniente 30, and Alameda de Santa Lucia Sur 3 (☎ 832 3149, 832 3107 evenings); this agency has the cheapest tours to Volcán Pacaya.

Monarcas Travel (☎ 832 4779), 7a Avenida Norte 15-A, and 6a Avenida Norte 60-A (☎ 832 4305); offers trips to Mayan sites and shuttles to Copán.

Rainbow Travel Center (☎ 832 4202/3/4/5/6/7, fax 832 4206, myers@gua.gbm.net), 7a Avenida Sur 8; English, French, German, Italian and Spanish are spoken here.

Servicios Turísticos Atitlán (☎/fax 832 1493, turisticosatitlan@yahoo.com), 2a Avenida Sur 4A. Web site: www.atitlan.com

Sin Fronteras (☎ 832 1017, 832 1226, ☎/fax 832 2674, sinfront@sinfront.com), 3a Calle Poniente 12; this is the representative for Maya Expedition rafting tours and also features many tour packages to Cuba.

Transportes Turísticos ATITRANS (☎ 832 1381, 832 1297, ☎/fax 832 0644, ☎ 832 3371 after 8 pm, atitrans@quick.guate.com), 6a Avenida Sur 7 and 8

Turansa (☎/fax 832 2928), Calle Sucia at Carretera a Ciudad Vieja, in the Hotel Radisson Villa Antigua; and 5a Calle Poniente 11-B (☎/fax 832 3316)

Vision Travel and Information Services (☎ 832 3293, 832 1962/64, fax 832 1955, vision@ guatemalainfo.com), 3a Avenida Norte 3 (behind the cathedral); a guidebook library, shuttles, tours and phone calls are among the well-recommended services offered here. They also hold mail and refill water bottles for cheap. Web site: www.guatemalainfo.com

Voyageur (☎ 832 4237/38, fax 832 4247, info@ travel.net.gt), 4a Calle Oriente 14, inside La Fuente courtyard

Note that, several reports have alleged unprofessional behavior by the Eco Aventuras travel agency.

Bookstores & Libraries
The Rainbow Reading Room & Cafe, 7a Avenida Sur at 6a Calle Poniente, offers thousands of used books in English and Spanish for sale, rent or trade. Other excellent bookstores include Un Poco de Todo and the Librería Casa del Conde, both on the west side of Parque Central, as well as Casa Andinista, 4a Calle Oriente 5, and Monoloco (see Places to Eat). Hamlin y White, 4a Calle Oriente 12A, boasts over 65 magazine titles and a Lonely Planet Travel Guide Center.

La Biblioteca Internacional de Antigua, 5a Calle Poniente 15 in the Proyecto Cultural El Sitio building, has a good book collection.

Medical Services
Hospital de San Pedro (☎ 832 0301) is at 3a Avenida Sur and 6a Calle Oriente.

Ixmucane (☎ 832 5539, houston@conexion.com.gt), 4a Avenida Norte 32, provides a complete range of gynecological services. Herbal supplements are also available; German, English and Spanish are spoken.

Emergency
The National Police are at ☎ 832 0251. If you're robbed, call the helpful Tourism Police at ☎ 832 4131. The municipal fire department is at ☎ 832 1075.

Dangers & Annoyances
Antigua isn't quite as mellow as it seems. Though you probably will never have a problem, be wary at night. Armed robberies (and worse) have occurred on Cerro de la Cruz, on Volcán Pacaya and at the cemetery, which should be considered off-limits unless you are escorted by the Tourist Police. Crime against tourists has dropped precipitously since the formation of this agency (see Tourist Offices).

PARQUE CENTRAL
The gathering place for locals and visitors alike, on most days the plaza is lined with villagers selling handicrafts to tourists; on Sunday it's mobbed and the streets on the east and west sides are closed to traffic. Things are cheapest late Sunday afternoon, when the peddling is winding down.

The plaza's famous fountain was built in 1738. At night, mariachi or marimba bands play in the park.

Palacio de los Capitanes
Built in 1543, the Palacio de los Capitanes has a stately double arcade on its façade, which marches proudly across the park's southern extent. Most of the façade is original, but the rest of the building was reconstructed a century ago. From 1543 to 1773, this building was the governmental center of all Central America, ruling Chiapas, Guatemala, Honduras and Nicaragua.

Catedral de Santiago
On the park's east side, the cathedral was founded in 1542, damaged by earthquakes many times, badly ruined in 1773 and only partially rebuilt between 1780 and 1820. In the 16th and early 17th centuries, Antigua's churches had lavish baroque interiors, but most – including this one – lost this richness

during post-earthquake rebuilding. The cathedral is being restored, but it will never regain its grandeur. Inside, a crypt contains the bones of Bernal Díaz del Castillo, historian of the Spanish conquest, who died in 1581. If the front entrance is closed, you can enter at the rear or on the south side.

Palacio del Ayuntamiento
On the park's north side stands the Palacio del Ayuntamiento, Antigua's town hall, which dates mostly from 1743. In addition to town offices, it houses the **Museo de Santiago**, which exhibits colonial furnishings, artifacts and weapons. Museum hours are 9 am to 4 pm Tuesday to Friday, 9 am to noon and 2 to 4 pm Saturday and Sunday (US$1.25).

Next door are the colonial prison and the **Museo del Libro Antiguo** (Old Book Museum; same hours and admission price as the Museo de Santiago), which has exhibits of colonial printing and binding.

Universidad de San Carlos
This university was founded in 1676. Its main building (built in 1763), 5a Calle Oriente 5, half a block east of the park, houses the **Museo de Arte Colonial** (☎ 832 0429), notable for the Saint Francis series of paintings by colonial artist Cristóbal de Villapando. The museum keeps the same hours as the Museo de Santiago (US$0.75).

CHURCHES
Once glorious in their gilded baroque finery, Antigua's churches have suffered indignities from both nature and humankind. Rebuilding after earthquakes gave the churches thicker walls, lower towers and belfries, and bland interiors, and moving the capital to Guatemala City deprived Antigua of the population needed to maintain the churches in their traditional richness. Still, they are impressive. Most are open 9 am to 5 pm daily; entrance costs under US$2. In addition to those noted below, you'll find many others scattered around town in various states of decay.

La Merced
From the park, walk three long blocks up 5a Avenida Norte, passing beneath the Arco de Santa Catarina. At the north end of 5a Avenida is the Iglesia y Convento de

Nuestra Señora de La Merced, Antigua's most striking colonial church.

La Merced's construction began in 1548. Improvements continued until 1717, when the church was ruined by earthquakes. Reconstruction was completed in 1767, but in 1773 earthquake struck again and the convent was destroyed. Repairs to the church were made from 1850 to 1855; its baroque façade dates from this period. Inside the ruins is a fountain 27m in diameter – said to be the largest in Central America. Admission to the convent costs US$0.25 and is well worth it.

San Francisco

The town's next most notable church is the Iglesia de San Francisco, 7a Calle Oriente at 1a Avenida Sur. It dates from the mid-16th century, but little of the original building remains. Rebuilding and restoration over the centuries have produced a handsome structure; reinforced concrete added in 1961 protected the church from suffering serious damage in the 1976 earthquake. All that remains of the original church is the Chapel of Hermano Pedro (not to be confused with the Iglesia de Hermano Pedro on 3a Avenida Sur), resting place of Hermano Pedro de San José Betancourt, a Franciscan monk who founded a hospital for the poor and earned the gratitude of generations. He died here in 1667; his intercession is still sought by the ill, who pray here fervently.

Las Capuchinas

The Iglesia y Convento de Nuestra Señora del Pilar de Zaragoza, usually called simply Las Capuchinas, 2a Avenida Norte and 2a Calle Oriente, was founded in 1736 by nuns from Madrid. Destroyed repeatedly by earthquakes, it is now a museum, with exhibits on religious life in colonial times. The building has an unusual structure of 18 concentric cells around a circular patio.

Church Ruins

A massive ruin at the west end of 1a Calle Poniente, the Iglesia y Convento de la Recolección, is among Antigua's most impressive monuments. Built between 1701 and 1708, it was destroyed in the 1773 earthquake.

Near La Recolección, at Alameda de Santa Lucía and 1a Calle Poniente, Colegio de San Jerónimo (also called the Real Aduana) was built in 1757 by friars of the Merced order. Because it did not have royal authorization, it was taken over by Spain's Carlos III in 1761. In 1765 it was designated for use as the Royal Customhouse, but was destroyed in the 1773 earthquake. The ruins are open 9 am to 5 pm daily (US$1.25).

OTHER ATTRACTIONS
Casa K'ojom

In 1984, Samuel Franco Arce began photographing Mayan ceremonies and festivals and recording their music. By 1987 he had enough to found Casa K'ojom (House of Music; ☎ 832 3087), Calle de Recoletos 55, a block west of the bus station, a museum dedicated to Mayan music and the ceremonies in which it was used. Besides the fine collection of photographs, Franco has amassed a cleverly displayed collection of musical instruments, tools, masks and figures. Don't miss the Maximón exhibit, featuring the crafty folk-god venerated in several highland towns.

It's open 9:30 am to 12:30 pm and 2 to 5 pm Monday to Friday, 9:30 am to 12:30 pm and 2 to 4 pm Saturday. The admission price of US$0.65 includes a superlative audiovisual show and a live demonstration of the instruments in the collection. The gift shop is worth a stop.

Casa Popenoe

At the corner of 5a Calle Oriente and 1a Avenida Sur stands this beautiful mansion built in 1636 by Don Luis de las Infantas Mendoza y Venegas. Ruined by the 1773 earthquake, the house stood desolate until bought in 1931 by Dr Wilson and Dorothy Popenoe. The couple's painstaking, authentic restoration yields a fascinating glimpse of how an Antiguan royal official's family lived in the 17th century. The house is open 2 to 4 pm Monday to Saturday; a self-guided tour costs US$0.85.

Monumento a Landívar

At the west end of 5a Calle Poniente is the Landívar Monument, a structure of five colonial-style arches set in a little park. The poetry of Rafael Landívar, an 18th-century Jesuit priest and poet, is esteemed as the colonial period's best, even though he wrote much of it in Italy after the Jesuits were expelled from Guatemala. Landívar's Antigua house was nearby on 5a Calle Poniente.

Market
At the west end of 4a Calle Poniente, across Alameda de Santa Lucía, sprawls the market – chaotic, colorful and always abustle. The frenzied mornings are the best time to come. Official market days are Monday, Thursday and Saturday.

Cementerio General
Antigua's cemetery, west of the market and bus terminal, is a beautiful conglomeration of tombs and mausoleums, all decked out with wreaths, exotic flowers and other signs of mourning. Unfortunately, lurking thieves render it dangerous. Go with a Tourist Police escort (see Tourist Offices, earlier) or in a group, though even large groups have been robbed here.

Cerro de la Cruz
On the town's northeast side is the Hill of the Cross, offering fine views over Antigua and south toward Volcán Agua. Don't come here without a Tourist Police escort (see Tourist Offices), it's famous for muggers. The Tourist Police was formed because of robberies at Cerro de la Cruz; reportedly no crime against tourists has taken place on the hill since.

ACTIVITIES
Horseback Riding
Several stables rent horses and arrange day or overnight trips into the countryside. Establo Santiago has been recommended; contact them through the Adventure Travel Center (see Travel Agencies, earlier).

Several readers recommend the Ravenscroft Riding Stables (☎ 832 6229 afternoons), 2a Avenida Sur 3, San Juan del Obispo. It's 3.2km south of Antigua, on the road to Santa María de Jesús; buses leave every half hour from the bus station behind the market. The stables offer English-style riding, with scenic rides of three to five hours in and around Antigua. Reservations and information are available through Hotel San Jorge (☎ 832 3132), 4a Avenida Sur 13.

Another option is La Ronda Stables (☎ 832 1224), which leads two- to six-hour tours for all levels. Reservations and information are also available at The Bagel Barn (see Places to Eat, later).

Cycling
You can rent bicycles at several places, including Alquiler de Bicicletas San Vicente (☎/fax 832 3311), 6a Avenida Sur 6 in Hotel Posada San Vicente, and Aviatur (☎/fax 832 2642), 5a Avenida Norte 35, just north of the arch. Prices are around US$1.35 an hour, US$6 to US$8.35 a day, US$25 a week or US$35 for two weeks. Prices and equipment vary, so shop around.

Mayan Bike Tours (☎ 832 3383, 832 6506, mayanbikeone@conexion.com.gt), 1a Avenida Sur 15, rents bikes and offers several area mountain-bike tours. Tours include gear and cost US$19 for a half day, US$39 for a full day with lunch. They also run hike-and-bike tours to Acatenango (US$49, 12 hours) and Lago de Atitlán (US$175, two days/one night).

Old Town Outfitters (☎ 832 4243, trvlnlite@hotmail.com), 6a Calle Poniente 7, rents high-quality standard bikes (US$7 a day) and premium bikes (US$14). It also offers tours, including a two-day/one-night pedal-and-paddle tour (bike and kayak) to Lago de Atitlán for US$125. You can rent camping gear here as well.
Web site: www.bikeguatemala.com

Climbing the Volcanoes
Although foreigners climbing the volcanoes around Antigua sometimes used to be robbed and even raped or murdered, recent tourist-safety measures have reduced the problem dramatically.

Volcán Pacaya Because of its status as the only active volcano near Antigua, Pacaya attracts the most tourists and most bandits. The situation is improving, however, since each group is now accompanied by a security guard (little comfort when he turns out to be prepubescent). Guards or no, a hike up Pacaya still entails risks. Still, travelers now are more likely to be hurt by flaming rocks and sulfurous fog than criminals. Climbers have suffered serious, even fatal injuries when the volcano erupted unexpectedly while they were near the summit.

In early 2000, the frisky Pacaya was upgraded to orange alert status.

Get reliable safety advice before you climb. Check with your embassy in Guatemala City or with the tourist office in Antigua. If you decide to go, make sure you're with reputable guides, arranged through an established agency.

Wear adequate footwear (volcanic rock can shred shoes), warm clothing and, in the rainy season, some sort of rain gear. Carry snacks, water and a flashlight.

Other Volcanoes The volcanoes nearer Antigua (Agua, Fuego and Acatenango) are inactive and attract fewer tourists. Still, they are impressive and offer magnificent views.

Volcán Agua (3766m) looms over Antigua, south of town. Various outfitters in Antigua can furnish details about the climb. To get to the mountain, follow 2a Avenida Sur or Calle de los Pasos south toward El Calvario (2km), then continue onward via San Juan del Obispo (another 3km) to Santa María de Jesús, a tiny village in the shadow of the volcano. This is the jumping-off point for treks. The main plaza is also the bus terminal. *Comedor & Hospedaje El Oasis*, a tidy little pension, offers meals and beds.

You could also climb the other two volcanoes near Antigua: **Volcán Acatenango** and **Volcán Fuego**. Various companies offer guided tours. Mayan Bike Tours (see Bicycling, earlier) offers hike/bike tours on Acatenango, while Old Town Outfitters will take you to the summit of any volcano.

White-Water Rafting

Area Verde Expeditions (☎/fax 832 3383, ☎/fax 719-583 8929 in the USA, mayanbike@guate.net), 1a Avenida Sur 15, is in the Hotel Villa San Francisco. The company offers a variety of one- to five-day rafting tours year-round.

Maya Expeditions, represented in Antigua by Sin Fronteras (☎ 832 1017, ☎/fax 832 2674), 3a Calle Poniente 12, also leads a variety of day trips and multiday tours on several rivers.

LANGUAGE COURSES

Antigua is world-famous for its many Spanish-language schools. Prices, teacher quality and student satisfaction vary greatly, so shop around. Ask for references and talk to alumni. The INGUAT tourist office has a list of reputable schools, including:

Academia de Español Guatemala (☎ 832 5057, 832 5060, fax 832 5058, aegnow@guate.net), 7a Calle Oriente 15
Web site: www.travellog.com/guatemala/antigua /acadespanol/school.html

Academia de Español Sevilla (☎/fax 832 0442), 1a Avenida Sur 8

Academia de Español Tecún Umán (☎/fax 832 2792, etecun@centramerica.com), 6a Calle Poniente 34
Web site: www.tecunuman.centroamerica.com

Centro de Español Don Pedro de Alvarado (☎/fax 832 4180), 1a Calle Poniente 24

Centro Lingüístico La Unión (☎/fax 832 7337, launion@conexion.com) 1a Avenida Sur 21
Web site: www.launion.conexion.com

Centro Lingüístico Maya (☎ 832 1342, clmmaya@ guate.net), 5a Calle Poniente 20

Christian Spanish Academy (CSA; ☎ 832 3922, fax 832 3760, chspanac@infovia.com.gt), 6a Avenida Norte 15

Don Quijote Spanish Academy (☎ 832 2868, infocentral@donquijote.org), Portal del Ayuntamiento 6, in the Museo del Libro Antiguo on Parque Central
Web site: www.donquijote.org

Escuela de Español San José el Viejo (☎ 832 3028, fax 832 3029, 800-562 6274 in the USA, spanish@guate.net), 5a Avenida Sur 34; in the USA write Section 544, PO Box 02-5289, Miami, FL 33102.
Web site: www.guate.net/spanish

Proyecto Lingüístico Francisco Marroquín (☎/fax 832 2886, info@langlink.com), 7a Calle Poniente 31 and three other locations in Antigua

Classes start every Monday at most schools, though you can usually be placed with a teacher any day of the week. Cost for four hours of one-to-one instruction daily, five days a week, ranges from around US$75 to US$100 per week; you can also enroll for up to seven hours a day. Most schools can arrange room and board with local families for around US$40 to US$60 per week.

Often several foreigners stay with a single family, creating more of a hotel atmosphere. Sometimes, too, students and the family will have separate mealtimes. If you truly want to be totally immersed, inquire about such details.

With so many foreigners here, it takes discipline to converse solely in Spanish. If you think this will bother you, consider studying in Xela or the Petén.

ORGANIZED TOURS

One of the most popular organized tours from Antigua is the day hike up Volcán Pacaya (see Activities, earlier). Though most agencies in Antigua offer this trip, the tours are all subcontracted by Gran Jaguar Travel Agency, which actually provides the transportation, guide and security for the hike. Booking the trip directly with Gran Jaguar costs around US$5, whereas it can be double or even triple elsewhere.

Author and Antigua aficionado Elizabeth Bell leads cultural tours of the town (in English and/or Spanish) on Tuesday, Wednesday, Friday and Saturday at 9:30 am. On Monday and Thursday, groups are led by Roberto Spillari and start at 2 pm. The tours take two hours and cost US$18. Reservations are suggested and can be made at Antigua Tours (☎ 832 0140 ext 341, elizbell@guate.net), in the lobby of the Hotel Casa Santo Domingo, 3a Calle Oriente 28. (See Entertainment, later, for information on Bell's slide shows.)

The Adventure Travel Center offers an interesting three-hour Villages & Farms Tour for US$25. Vision Travel leads a recommended Guatemala City museum tour for US$25. (See Travel Agencies, earlier in this chapter, for contact details.)

Numerous travel agencies offer farther-flung tours to Tikal, Copán-Quiriguá-Río Dulce, Monterrico, Chichicastenango, Panajachel and other places.

SPECIAL EVENTS
Semana Santa

By far the most interesting time in Antigua is Semana Santa (Holy Week), when hundreds dress in violet robes to accompany daily processions in remembrance of the crucifixion. Dense clouds of incense envelop the parade. Streets are covered in breathtakingly elaborate and colorful *alfombras* (carpets) of colored sawdust and flower petals. These fragile works of art are destroyed as the processions shuffle through them, but they're re-created the next morning for another parade.

Traditionally, the most interesting days are Palm Sunday, when a procession departs from La Merced (see Churches, earlier in this section) in midafternoon; Holy Thursday, when a late-afternoon procession departs from the Iglesia de San Francisco; and Good Friday, when an early-morning procession departs from La Merced and a late-afternoon one leaves from the Escuela de Cristo, at the corner of Calle de Belén and Calle de los Pasos. Have ironclad hotel reservations well in advance of these dates, or plan to stay in another town and commute.

The booklet *Lent and Easter Week in Antigua* by Elizabeth Bell gives explanations and a day-by-day schedule of processions, *velaciones* (vigils) and other events throughout the Lenten season, the 40 days before Easter.

On a secular note, beware of pickpockets. It seems that Guatemala City's entire pickpocket population (numbering in the hundreds) decamps to Antigua for Semana Santa. In the press of the emotion-filled crowds, they target foreign tourists especially.

PLACES TO STAY

Antigua's climate, combined with the cement used in building construction, makes for some damp, musty and even moldy hotel rooms. Carpeted and ground-floor rooms seem to fare worse, so try to get a tiled upstairs room.

Budget

When checking out budget hotels, look at several rooms, as some are much better than others.

Posada Refugio (4a Calle Poniente 30) is the backpacker's supercheapie du jour. Basic rooms go for US$2.60/3.25/4 single/double/triple without bath, US$4/8/9.65 with bath. Rooms vary widely. *Posada Ruiz 2 (2a Calle Poniente 25)* is a good deal for the price. Its small rooms go for US$2.20/3.85 single/double with shared bath. Lots of young international travelers stay here, congregating in the central courtyard in the evening. Not as nice is *Posada Ruiz 1 (Alameda de Santa Lucía 17)*, charging US$3.85 per person. A hopping option is *La Sala (☎ 832 6483)* on the corner of Alameda de Santa Lucía and 2a Calle Poniente, where a dorm bed is US$2.30.

The new *Hotel Backpacker's Place* (☎ 832 5023, 4a Calle Poniente 27) is convenient for bus departures and has comfortable beds in spacious, if generic, rooms; US$6.45/7.75 with shared bath, US$7.75/9.65 with private bath. South-facing rooms have views of Volcán Agua. Another great value is the safe, friendly and popular *Hotel la Casa de Don Ismael (3a Calle Poniente 6)*, down the unnamed alley off 3a Calle Poniente, between 7a Avenida and Alameda de Santa Lucía. Clean, comfortable rooms with shared hot bath are US$5.15/7.75; try to get an upstairs room off the terrace. There's also a pretty, compact courtyard.

Posada Juma Ocag (☎ 832 3109, Alameda de Santa Lucía 13) is the superior budget hotel here. It's very quiet, despite being across from the market, and the four spotless, comfortable rooms have great mattresses, traditional appointments and private hot bath. Other amenities include a rooftop patio and small, well-tended garden. Touches like reading lamps and drinking water make this a killer value at US$10.30/12.50 double/triple. Unfortunately, reservations aren't accepted. *Hotel Cristal (☎ 832 4177, Avenida del Desengaño 25)* is also superlative for the price. Its 10 clean rooms surround a beautiful garden; US$6.45/9/11.50 with shared bath, US$9/11.50/13 with private bath. Students receive a discount.

With four locations, *Casas de Santa Lucía* is a mini-hotel chain. All charge US$10.25 double for clean, pleasant, attractive rooms with private hot bath, and all have rooftop terraces with views. Try the newly renovated original, at Alameda de Santa Lucía 9, between 5a and 6a Calles Poniente; *Casa de Santa Lucía No 2 (Alameda de Santa Lucía Norte 21)*; *Casa de Santa Lucía No 3 (6a Avenida Norte 43A)*; or *Casa de Santa Lucía No 4 (Alameda de Santa Lucía 5)*, which has nice rooms but can be loud.

Hotel La Tatuana (☎ 832 1223, 7a Avenida Sur 3) has good, clean rooms with private bath for US$13/15. Try bargaining in the off-season. Similar in price is *Hotel Posada San Vicente (☎/fax 832 3311, 6a Avenida Sur 6)*, which has rooms with private bath for US$13 double; the upstairs rooms are better. Amenities include a pool table and bicycle rentals.

A step up in quality, *Posada de Don Valentino (☎ 832 0384, 5a Calle Poniente 28)* has a nice patio, a garden and bright, clean rooms with private bath for US$12/20/25. Parking is available nearby.

Apart-Hotel Bugambilia (☎/fax 832 2732, Calle Ancha de los Herreros 27) has 10 apartments, each with fully equipped kitchen, two or three double beds, cable TV and private hot bath. Daily rates are US$15/19/23. Discounts are offered for weekly and monthly stays. Amenities include sitting areas, a beautiful patio garden, a fountain and a rooftop terrace.

Avoid the Arizona Hotel (2a Calle Poniente 29A), which has an unsavory reputation.

Mid-Range

Antigua's mid-range hotels allow you to wallow in the city's colonial charms for a moderate cash outlay.

Posada Asjemenou (☎ 832 2670, 5a Avenida Norte 31), just north of the arch, is a beautifully renovated house built around a grassy courtyard with a fountain. It charges US$20/33 single/double for rooms with shared bath, US$26/40 for private bath. Discounts are available for stays of a week or more.

The convivial *Hotel Posada San Pedro (☎ 832 3594, 3a Avenida Sur 15)* comes highly recommended. Its 10 rooms are squeaky clean and nicely appointed; upstairs units have views. Guests have use of a communal kitchen and rooftop patio. This is a good choice at US$20/25 with private bath.

Hotel El Descanso (☎ 832 0142, 5a Avenida Norte 9) is friendly, clean and convenient. Its five rooms cost US$24/30 with private bath. There's a terrace upstairs in the rear. *Hotel Santa Clara (☎/fax 832 0342, 2a Avenida Sur 20)* is quiet, proper and clean, with a relaxing garden. Rooms with terrific hot bath are US$21/25 in high season, US$13/16 in off-season; some large rooms with two double beds are available.

La Sin Ventura (☎ 832 0581, frontdesk@ lasinventura.com, 5a Avenida Sur 8) has a great location just off the park and sparkling rooms for US$19/30. Its Web site is www.lasinventura.com. *Hotel Posada Real (☎ 832 3396, Avenida del Desengaño 24)* is a beautiful colonial hotel. Its nine rooms and suites, all with private hot bath and cable TV, are lovely, and many have fireplaces. Rooms can be noisy, however. Rates are US$25/35/45 single/double/triple.

Posada San Sebastián (☎/fax 832 2621, 3a Avenida Norte 4) is like a museum where you get to spend the night. Each of the eight rooms is packed with Guatemalan antiques and laid with terra cotta tile, giving this place a historic, quirky ambience. The unique rooms, all with private hot bath and cable TV, cost US$36/46/56. Guests have use of the kitchen and rooftop terrace.

La Casa de la Música (☎ 832 0335, fax 832 3690, ginger@guate.net, 7a Calle Poniente 3) is a charming B&B with patios, fountains, gardens and a roof terrace. The five rooms and one suite range from US$125 to US$264 single or double per week, including a fabulous breakfast daily. A one-week minimum stay is required. This place is very kid-friendly. Its Web site is www.lacasadelamusica.centramerica.com.

PLACES TO EAT
Budget
Eating cheaply is easy. Probably the cheapest food in town is the tasty fare served from midmorning to early evening at the stands on 4a Calle Poniente, a block west of the park.

Restaurante Gran Muralla (4a Calle Poniente 18) and *La Estrella* across the street are two options for Chinese food.

One of Antigua's best-known eateries is *Restaurant Doña Luisa Xicotencatl (4a Calle Oriente 12)*, 1½ blocks east of Parque Central. Tables are set around the central courtyard, with more on the upper level. The menu lists a dozen sandwiches (made with handmade bread), yogurt, chili, burgers, stuffed potatoes, cakes and pies, all priced under US$4. Alcohol is served, as is excellent Antiguan coffee. The busy restaurant is open 7 am to 9:30 pm daily. The bakery sells many kinds of breads.

Rainbow Reading Room & Cafe, 7a Avenida Sur at 6a Calle Poniente, is a lending library, bookstore, travelers' club and restaurant all in one. Healthy vegetarian dishes are a specialty, as is close camaraderie. The cafe is open 9 am to 11 pm daily.

Café Condesa, on the plaza's west side (walk through the Librería Casa del Conde bookstore to the rear), is a beautiful restaurant in the courtyard of an opulent Spanish mansion built in 1549. On the menu are excellent breakfasts, coffee, light meals and snacks. The Sunday buffet from 10 am to 2 pm, a lavish spread for US$6, is an Antigua institution. The cafe is open daily. For a quick java fix, hit the *Café Condesa Express*, next door; it's open 6:45 am to 7:45 pm daily.

La Fuente (4a Calle Oriente 14) is another beautiful restaurant in the courtyard of an old Spanish home. The menu features lots of vegetarian selections, good coffee and desserts. Hours are 7 am to 7 pm daily. *Café Sol (1a Calle Poniente 9)*, opposite La Merced church, is a smaller, simpler, inexpensive patio restaurant with decent breakfasts.

Numerous restaurants line 5a Avenida Norte, north of Parque Central. *Asados de la Calle del Arco*, just off the park, has a simple but beautiful atmosphere, with candlelight in the evening and tables both inside and out on the back patio. It serves grilled meats and Tex-Mex food, though portions are small. Hours are 7 am to 10 pm daily. A second branch is farther north up 5a Avenida Norte.

La Fonda de la Calle Real (5a Avenida Norte 5) serves good and varied food in its upstairs dining room. The house specialty is *caldo real*, a hearty chicken soup that makes a filling meal (US$3.50). Grilled meats, *queso fundido* (melted cheese), *chiles rellenos* and nachos are priced from US$3 to US$8. The restaurant is open 7 am to 10 pm daily. Around the corner, *La Fonda de la Calle Real No 2 (3a Calle Poniente 7)* has the same menu and is open noon to 10 pm daily.

La Cenicienta Pasteles (5a Avenida Norte 7) serves mostly cakes, pastries, pies and coffee, but the blackboard menu often features yogurt, fruit, quiche lorraine and quiche chapín (Guatemalan-style) as well. A slice of something and a hot beverage will cost less than US$2. It's open daily. *Cookies Etc*, on 3a Avenida Norte at 4a Calle Oriente, is another good place for sweets; it opens at 8 am daily and serves bottomless cups of coffee with breakfast. *The Bagel Barn*, on 5a Calle Poniente just off the Parque Central, is popular for bagels, soups and coffee.

Near the arch, *Restaurante/Bar Frida's* (☎ 832 0504, 5a Avenida Norte 29) serves good Mexican fare and is jumping most evenings, sometimes with live music. It's open 12:30 pm to midnight daily. Nearby *Punto Internacional* (5a Avenida Norte 35) has been recommended by readers, as has *Su Chow* (5a Avenida Norte 36), a Chinese place open late at night. Also on this strip is *Queso y Vino* (5a Avenida Norte 32), a good choice for Italian food.

The best place in Antigua for breakfast is *Restaurante El Capuchino* (6a Avenida Norte 10), where everything costs US$1.70. Try the omelet made with real cheese, olive oil and bell peppers. To top it off, the restaurant has an all-you-can-drink coffee policy. It's open 7 am to 10 pm Tuesday through Sunday and also serves lunch and dinner. The best coffee in town is at *Tostaduría Antigua* (6a Avenida Sur 12A).

Antigua has an outlet of *Restaurante Piccadilly* (4a Calle Poniente 17), serving up the three p's: pasta, pollo and pizza. Two blocks away is *Cadejo's* (6a Avenida Sur 1A), a popular place for pizza and beer; occasionally it presents live music. Also serving pizza is *Caffé-Pizzería Asjemenou* (5a Calle Poniente 4). Some think this is the best pizza in town. It's open 7 am to 10 pm daily.

One of the current hot spots for food and camaraderie is *La Escudilla* (4a Avenida Norte 4). This place features simple, well-prepared meals and a set special for under US$3. Also here is Riki's Bar (see Entertainment, later in this section). Another leader in the popularity contest is *Menu Viajero* (6a Calle Poniente 14A), which serves big plates of stir-fry or noodles, vegetarian or carnivore style, for as little as US$2.

Café Flor (4a Avenida Sur 1) serves huge portions of delicious food including Thai, Indonesian, Chinese and Indian dishes, each for around US$5. One dish can easily feed two people. Takeout is available. It's open 11 am to 11 pm Tuesday to Sunday; Friday and Saturday until midnight. The *Café Masala* (6a Avenida Norte 14A), near 4a Calle Poniente, has been recommended for Thai and Japanese food. It's open noon to 10 pm daily except Wednesday. Along the same pan-Asian gastronomic lines is *Cafe Rocio* (6a Avenida Norte 34), which has a romantic garden area. It's open 7:30 am to 9:30 pm daily.

La Taquiza (☎ 832 1560, 6a Avenida Norte 19) serves fresh, satisfying meals combining Mexican and Guatemalan flavors. The atmosphere is relaxed and the service friendly. For German food, try *Café Weiner* (Alameda de Santa Lucía Portal 8), which boasts Antigua's only superschnitzel. The cafe makes decent breakfasts and has a patio upstairs.

For Japanese food, head to *Yoshino* (☎ 832 6766, 5a Calle Poniente 17A). Choose from sushi, tempura, teriyaki and more; the daily special includes soup, salad, appetizer and a main dish for US$4. It's open 12:30 to 4:30 pm and 6 to 9:30 pm Tuesday to Saturday, 12:30 to 3:30 pm Sunday.

Tierra Cero (6a Calle Poniente 7) is a casual place set around a courtyard. The menu includes good salads and other veggie options. Also here are a cinema, book exchange, cybercafe and bike rentals. *La India Misteriosa* (3a Avenida Sur 4) is recommended for vegetarian fare.

For Italian food try *Restaurante y Pizzería Italiana Catari* (6a Avenida Norte 52), opposite La Merced church. It's run by well-known chef Martedino Castrovinci. From noon to 4 pm the enormous lunch special is US$3, including beverage. It's open daily.

Monoloco (2a Avenida Norte 6B), an upstairs restaurant/bar, serves tasty burgers, burritos and similar pub food for around US$3.50. This is a popular gathering place, with microbrews on tap and two satellite TVs showing the likes of the Rugby World Cup and the World Series. There's a great book swap, too.

Panificadora Columbia (4a Calle Poniente 34) is a good stop for breads, coffee and breakfast before boarding the 7 am luxury bus to Panajachel (see Getting There & Around, later in this section). Across the street, *La Bodegona* is a full-blown megamarket selling everything from underwear to bottled water.

Mid-Range

The dining room in the *Posada de Don Rodrigo* (☎ 832 0291, 832 0387, 5a Avenida Norte 17) is one of the city's most pleasant places for lunch or dinner. Order the Plato Chapín (a platter of Guatemalan specialties) for US$11. A marimba band plays from noon to 4 pm and 7 to 9 pm daily.

The owners of perennial favorite Frida's have recently opened **Medusa's** (☎ 832 6951, 2a Avenida Sur 12), a ceviche and sushi place. The warm, comfortable restaurant does good seafood and snacks. Happy hour, from 7 to 10 pm daily, features free appetizers with each cocktail.

Antigüenos line up for traditional Guatemalan sweets from **Doña María Gordillo Dulces Típicos** (4a Calle Oriente 11). Local handicrafts are also sold here.

ENTERTAINMENT
Nightlife on weekends can be a bit crazed, as revelers pour in from Guatemala City. Cocktail fans will have no trouble getting a bargain buzz here.

Proyecto Cultural El Sitio (☎ 832 3037) presents cultural events like theater, concerts, video films and art exhibitions.

Bars & Clubs
The town's hottest spot is **Riki's Bar** (4a Avenida Norte 4), which attracts a hip crowd of locals and travelers. The big courtyard, decent food and low-key **Paris Bar Exclusivo** in the rear all make for a good night out. Another spot popular with students and Peace Corps types is **Monoloco** (see Places to Eat).

Other bars include **La Chimenea**, on the corner of 7a Avenida Norte and 2a Calle Poniente; the rougher **Latinos** down the block; **El Atico** (5a Avenida Norte 29), upstairs from Frida's; and the **Macondo Pub** across the street.

For dancing, try **La Casbah** (5a Avenida Norte 30), near Asados de la Calle del Arco restaurant and the Santa Catalina arch. It's open 7 pm to 1 am Wednesday to Saturday. Thursday is gay night – the best time to drop in and boogie. **El Afro** (6a Calle Poniente 9) is the place for salsa dancing. It's open 6 pm to 1 am Tuesday to Sunday, but things don't heat up until around 10 pm.

Cinemas
One of Antigua's most pleasant forms of entertainment is video-watching at cinema houses, where you can see a wide variety of international films (US$1.50). Try one of the following:

Cine Café (7a Calle Poniente 22)
Cinema Bistro (5a Avenida Sur 14)
Cinema Tecún Umán (6a Calle Poniente 34A)
Cinemaya (6a Calle Poniente 7)
Proyecto Cultural El Sitio (5a Calle Poniente 15)

Elizabeth Bell gives a fascinating slide show about Antigua called 'Behind the Walls' from 6 to 7 pm Tuesday at the Christian Spanish Academy (see Language Courses, earlier in this chapter); the cost is US$2.50.

SHOPPING
Vendors flood Antigua to satisfy tourists' desires for colorful Guatemalan woven goods and other handicrafts. The sleepy **Mercado de Artesanías**, on the town's west side by the bus station, has plenty to choose from. A number of shops are on 4a Calle Poniente, in the blocks between Parque Central and the market. And look for outdoor markets at the corner of 6a Calle Oriente and 2a Avenida Sur, and at 4a Calle Poniente at 7a Avenida Norte.

Be aware that prices for handicrafts tend to be much higher in Antigua than elsewhere in Guatemala. For a better selection at cheaper prices, try the markets in Chichicastenango, Panajachel and Guatemala City. Whenever buying handicrafts, be sure to bargain. It's expected and welcome.

Antigua has several shops specializing in jade, including La Casa de Jade, 4a Calle Oriente 3; Jades, SA, 4a Calle Oriente 34; and the Jade Kingdom, 4a Avenida Norte 10. These places offer free tours of the jade factories behind their showrooms. Jades, SA has interesting exhibits and is open daily.

Galería El Sitio, 5a Calle Poniente 15 (at the Proyecto Cultural El Sitio), specializes in paintings by modern Guatemalan artists. Ring the bell for admission. A number of other interesting galleries are along 4a Calle Oriente, in the blocks east of Parque Central.

Nim Po't, 5a Avenida Norte 29, boasts 'the world's largest retail collection of Maya dress,' a claim hard to refute. This sprawling space is packed with traditional *huipiles, cortes, fajas* and more, all arranged according to region, so it makes for a fascinating visit whether you're buying or not. If you're pressed for time, this is a great place for one-stop shopping. It's open 9 am to 9 pm daily. Another intriguing place to buy textiles is Casa del Tejido Antiguo, 1a Calle Poniente 51, which is like a museum, market and workshop rolled into one. It's open 8 am to 5 pm daily (US$0.65).

For coffee, head over to the Tostaduría Antigua, 6a Avenida Sur 12A, where a pound of beans, freshly roasted to your specifications, costs about US$3.

The Tabaquería Unicornio, 4a Calle Poniente 38, sells a variety of fine tobacco, including Cuban cigars, as well as cigarettes and loose tobacco such as Drum and American Spirit.

GETTING THERE & AROUND
Bus
Buses arrive and depart from a large open lot beyond the market, on the town's west side. Connections with Guatemala City are frequent, and one direct bus daily runs to Panajachel. To reach other highland towns such as Chichicastenango, Quetzaltenango and Huehuetenango, or Panajachel at any other time of day, take one of the frequent buses to Chimaltenango, on the Interamericana, and catch an onward bus from there. Or take a bus heading toward Guatemala City, get off at San Lucas Sacatepéquez and change buses there – this takes a little more time, but it's a good road, and since you'll be boarding the bus closer to the capital you're more likely to get a seat (important if you want to avoid the possibility of standing for several hours).

Buses to outlying villages such as Santa María de Jesús (US$0.25, 30 minutes) and San Antonio Aguas Calientes (US$0.20, 25 minutes) depart from the bus area behind the market. It's best to make your outward trip early in the morning, returning by midafternoon, as bus services drop off dramatically as late afternoon appoaches.

Chimaltenango (US$0.30, one hour, 19km)
Buses leave every 15 minutes, 6 am to 6 pm.
Escuintla (US$0.65, 2½ hours, 102km)
Two buses depart daily, 7 am and 1 pm.
Guatemala City (US$0.50, one hour, 45km)
Buses depart every 15 minutes, 4 am to 7 pm, stopping in San Lucas Sacatepéquez.
Panajachel (US$3.25, 2½ hours, 146km)
One *especial* bus departs daily, 7 am, departs from Hotel Backpacker's Place. Or take a bus to Chimaltenango and change there to a bus bound for Los Encuentros, Sololá or Panajachel. One of these buses passes every 20

minutes or so. The entire trip costs US$2.45 and takes longer.

Shuttle Minibus
Numerous travel agencies offer frequent and convenient shuttle services to places tourists go, including Guatemala City, La Aurora International Airport, Panajachel and Chichi. They also go less frequently (usually on weekends) to places farther afield such as Río Dulce, Copán Ruinas (Honduras) and Monterrico. These services cost a lot more than ordinary buses (for example, from US$5 to US$10 to Guatemala City, as opposed to US$0.50 on a chicken bus), but they are comfortable and convenient, with door-to-door service on both ends. For recommendations, see Travel Agencies under Information, earlier in this section.

Car & Motorcycle
Rental companies in Antigua include the following:

Ahorrent (☎ 832 0968, ahorrent@infovia.com.gt), 5a Calle Oriente 11B
Web site: www.infovia.com.gt/ahorrent
Moto Servicio Antigua (☎ 511 8932), Carretera a Ciudad Vieja 90; rents motorcycles only
Sears Motorcycle Rental (☎ 832 6203), 3a Avenida Norte 3
Tabarini (☎/fax 832 3091, tabarini@centramerica .com), 2a Calle Poniente 19A; Hotel Radisson Villa Antigua (☎/fax 832 7450)
Web site: www.centramerica.com/tabarini

Taxi
Taxis congregate at the bus station and on the east side of Parque Central. A ride in town costs around US$1.65.

The Highlands – Lago de Atitlán

Guatemala's most dramatic region, the highlands stretch from Antigua to the Mexican border northwest of Huehuetenango. Here the verdant hills sport emerald green grass, cornfields and towering stands of pine, and every town and village has a story.

The traditional values and customs of Guatemala's indigenous peoples are strongest in the highlands. Mayan dialects are the first language, Spanish a distant second. The age-old culture based on maize is still alive; a sturdy cottage set in the midst of a thriving *milpa* (cornfield) is a common sight, one as old as Mayan culture itself. And on every road you'll see men, women and children carrying burdens of *leña* (firewood), to be used for heating and cooking.

One of the most spectacular locales in Central America, **Lago de Atitlán** is a caldera (collapsed volcanic cone) filled with shimmering waters to a maximum depth of more than 320m. The lake covers an area of 128 sq km and is surrounded by colorful hills. Three powerful volcanoes – Volcán Tolimán (3158m), Volcán Atitlán (3537m),

and Volcán San Pedro (3020m) – loom over the landscape.

The lake is often still and beautiful early in the day. By noon the Xocomil, a southeasterly wind, may have risen to ruffle the surface, sometimes violently, making it a tough crossing for the small motorboats plying the shores.

The topography keeps certain parts of the highlands tucked away. If you visit during the rainy season, May to October, be prepared for some dreary, chilly, damp days; the region's lush vegetation comes from abundant rain. But when the sun comes out, this land is glorious.

If you have only three or four days in the highlands, spend them in Antigua, Panajachel and Chichicastenango. With more time

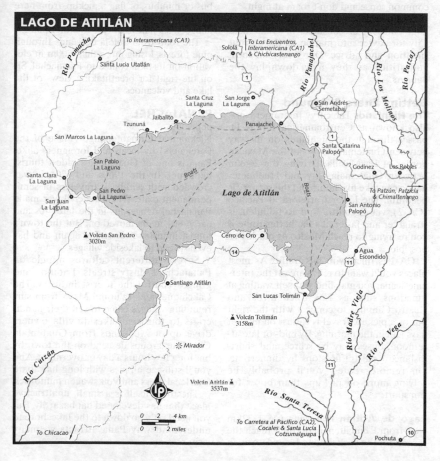

LAGO DE ATITLÁN

you can make your way to Quetzaltenango and nearby sights such as Zunil, Fuentes Georginas, San Francisco El Alto, Momostenango and Totonicapán. Villages high in the Cuchumatanes mountains north of Huehuetenango offer stellar scenery and adventures for intrepid travelers. Huehuetenango and the ruins nearby at Zaculeu are worth a visit if you're passing through or if you have lots of time.

Warning

Though most visitors never experience any trouble, there have been incidents of robbery, rape and murder in the highlands. These have occurred on volcano trails, on the outskirts of Chichicastenango and at desolate spots along roads. Use caution and common sense and don't roam at night.

Before traveling in the highlands, contact your embassy or consulate in Guatemala City for advice information on the current situation and advice. Don't rely on local authorities, as they may downplay the dangers.

Getting There & Around

The Highlands The curvy Interamericana, also known as Centroamérica 1 (CA-1), passes through the highlands on its way between Guatemala City and the Mexican border at La Mesilla. Driving the 266km between Guatemala City and Huehuetenango can take five hours, but the scenery is beautiful. The lower Carretera al Pacífico (CA-2), via Escuintla and Retalhuleu, is straighter and faster; it's the better route if you're trying to reach Mexico as quickly as possible.

CA-1 is thick with bus traffic. As most places you'll want to reach are off the Interamericana, you may find yourself waiting at junctions such as Los Encuentros and Cuatro Caminos to connect with the right bus or a pickup. Travel is easiest on market days and in the morning. By mid- or late afternoon, buses may be scarce, and short-distance local traffic stops by dinnertime. On remote routes, you'll probably be relying more on pickups than buses for transport.

Lago de Atitlán Following CA-1 32km west from Chimaltenango, you'll reach the turnoff for the back road to Lago de Atitlán

via Patzicía and Patzún. The area around these two towns has been notable for high levels of guerrilla and bandit activity in the past, so stay on the Interamericana to Tecpán Guatemala, the starting point for a visit to the ruined Cakchiquel capital of Iximché.

Another 40km west along the Interamericana from Tecpán is the **Los Encuentros** junction. A nascent town serves people waiting to catch buses. The road to the right heads north to Chichicastenango and Santa Cruz del Quiché. From the Interamericana a road to the left descends 12km to Sololá and another 8km to Panajachel, on the shores of Lago de Atitlán.

If you are not on a direct bus, you can get off at Los Encuentros and catch another bus or minibus, or flag a pickup, from here down to Panajachel or up to Chichicastenango; it's a half-hour ride to either place.

The road from Sololá descends through pine forests, losing more than 500m in elevation on its 8km course to Panajachel. Sit on the right for breathtaking views of the lake and volcanoes.

PANAJACHEL
pop 5000

Nicknamed Gringotenango (Place of the Foreigners) by locals and foreigners alike, Pana is one of Guatemala's oldest tourist hangouts. In the 1960s and '70s, it was crowded with laid-back travelers in semipermanent exile. When the civil war made Panajachel dangerous in the late '70s and early '80s, many moved on. But the town's tourist industry is booming again and has even spread to lakeside villages.

Several different cultures mingle on Panajachel's dusty streets. Ladinos and gringos control the tourist industry. The Cakchiquel and Tz'utuhil Maya from surrounding villages come to sell their handicrafts to tourists. Lakeside-villa owners drive up on weekends from Guatemala City. Tour groups descend on the town by bus for a few hours a day or overnight. And you'll still see hippies with long hair, bare feet, local dress and Volkswagen minibuses.

The town itself is a small, unattractive place that has developed haphazardly. But you need only go down to the lakeshore to understand why Pana attracts so many visitors.

Information

Tourist Offices The INGUAT tourist office (☎ 762 1392) is in the Edificio Rincón Sai on Calle Santander. It's supposedly open 8 am to 1 pm and 2 to 5 pm daily.

Money Banco Industrial, on Calle Santander, changes US dollars cash and traveler's checks, gives cash advances on Visa cards and has an ATM. Banco Inmobiliario, at the corner of Calles Santander and Real, is open longer hours. Banco Agrícola Mercantil (BAM), on the same corner, changes money and is an agent for Western Union. The Bancared ATM at Calle Real 0-78 accepts Visa cards.

You can also change cash and traveler's checks at the INGUAT office and Hotel Regis, both on Calle Santander. The hotel gives cash advances on Visa and Master-Card, as does the adjacent Servicios Turísticos Atitlán (☎ 762 2075), for a 10% commission.

Post & Communications The post office is at the corner of Calles Santander and 15 de Febrero. Get Guated Out (☎ 762 0595, fax 762 2015, gguated@quetzal.net), located on Avenida Los Árboles, ships letters and parcels by air freight or by international courier. They will also buy handicrafts for you and ship them for export – which is handy if you can't come to Panajachel yourself. Email services are also available here.

DHL has a drop-off location on Calle Santander in the complex with INGUAT. It's open 9 am to 6 pm weekdays and 9 am to 1 pm Saturday.

The Telgua office on Calle Santander is open daily. Many other places along Calle Santander offer cheaper services. Check the ubiquitous travel agencies for phone, fax and email services.

Many places offer Internet access for about US$1.50 an hour. MayaNet on Calle Santander, across from Hotel Regis, is open 9 am to 9 pm Monday to Saturday, 2:30 to 8 pm Sunday. Just down the block, adjacent to the Telgua office, is c@fe.net, open 9 am to 9 pm daily.

Travel Agencies Several full-service travel agencies offering trips, tours and shuttle buses are strung along Calle Santander.

Bookstores Owner/author Jake Horsley vows to make Xibalba, in the Centro Comercial on Avenida Los Árboles, the best used-book store in Central America. It's open 10 am to 7 pm daily. Located in the same complex is The Gallery Bookstore (☎ 762 0595, fax 762 2015), which also offers telephone/fax and travel services.

Things to See & Do

The **Reserva Natural Atitlán** (☎ 762 2565) is down the spur leading to Hotel Atitlán and makes a good day trip. The well-designed nature reserve has trails, an interpretive center, butterfly farm, small shade coffee plantation, lots of monkeys and an aviary. It's open 8 am to 5 pm daily (US$3).

Lago de Atitlán offers phenomenal **hiking and biking**. You can walk from Panajachel to the lakeside village of Santa Catarina in about an hour, continuing to San Antonio in about another hour; it takes only half as long by bicycle, on hilly roads. Or take a bike by boat to Santiago, San Pedro or another village to start a tour of the lake. Several places along Calle Santander rent bicycles; rates start around US$2.50 per half day. Equipment varies, so check out your bike first.

ATI Divers (☎ 762 2646, santacruz@guate.net), on Calle Santander near INGUAT, leads **dive trips** from Santa Cruz La Laguna (see that section, later). A four-day PADI certification course costs US$160. The best time to dive here is between May and October, when the water is clear. Web site: www.atidivers.com.

Visitors short on time are encouraged to take a **boat tour** around the lake. A typical tour lasts around seven hours and visits San Pedro, Santiago and San Antonio for US$7. To arrange a tour, head to the pier at the foot of Calle del Balneario and start bargaining. Most travel agencies also arrange boat tours.

Language Courses

Spanish courses are available from the Escuela de Español Panajachel (☎ 762 2637, fax 762 0092, nicholas_tr@latinmail.com), on Calle El Chali; the current favorite Jabel Tinamit (☎ 762 0238, spanishschool@hotmail.com), just off Calle Santander before INGUAT; and Panatitlán (☎ 762 0319, panatitlan@yahoo.com), at Calle de la

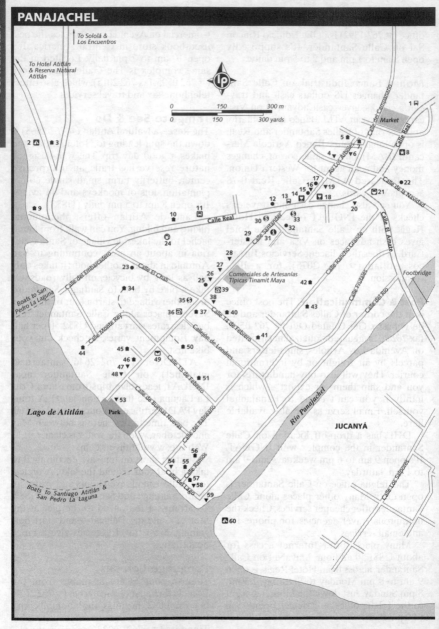

PANAJACHEL

GUATEMALA

To Sololá &
Los Encuentros

To Hotel Atitlán
& Reserva Natural
Atitlán

Market

0   150   300 m
0   150   300 yards

Calle del Campanario
Calle Real
Av Los Árboles
Calle de la Navidad
Calle El Amate
Calle Rancho Grande
Calle Frutales
Calle del Río

Footbridge

Calle Real
Calle Santander
Calle del Embarcadero
Calle El Chalí
Calle Monte Rey
Calle 14 de Febrero
Callejón de Londres
Calle 15 de Febrero
Calle de Buenas Nuevas
Calle del Balneario
Calle Ramos
Calle del Lago

Comerciales de Artesanías
Típicas Tinamit Maya

Boats to San
Pedro La Laguna

Lago de Atitlán   Park

Boats to Santiago Atitlán &
San Pedro La Laguna

Río Panajachel

JUCANYÁ

Calle Los Salpores

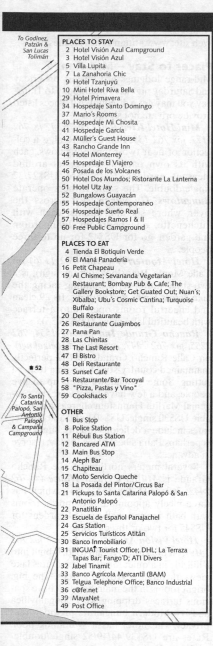

To Godínez,
Patzún &
San Lucas
Tolimán

PLACES TO STAY
2   Hotel Visión Azul Campground
3   Hotel Visión Azul
5   Villa Lupita
7   La Zanahoria Chic
9   Hotel Tzanjuyú
10 Mini Hotel Riva Bella
29 Hotel Primavera
34 Hospedaje Santo Domingo
37 Mario's Rooms
40 Hospedaje Mi Chosita
41 Hospedaje García
42 Müller's Guest House
43 Rancho Grande Inn
44 Hotel Monterrey
45 Hospedaje El Viajero
46 Posada de los Volcanes
50 Hotel Dos Mundos; Ristorante La Lanterna
51 Hotel Utz Jay
52 Bungalows Guayacán
55 Hospedaje Contemporaneo
56 Hospedaje Sueño Real
57 Hospedajes Ramos I & II
60 Free Public Campground

PLACES TO EAT
4   Tienda El Botiquín Verde
6   El Maná Panadería
16 Petit Chapeau
19 Al Chisme; Sevananda Vegetarian
    Restaurant; Bombay Pub & Cafe; The
    Gallery Bookstore; Get Guated Out; Nuan's;
    Xibalba; Ubu's Cosmic Cantina; Turquoise
    Buffalo
20 Deli Restaurante
26 Restaurante Guajimbos
27 Pana Pan
28 Las Chinitas
38 The Last Resort
47 El Bistro
48 Deli Restaurante
53 Sunset Cafe
54 Restaurante/Bar Tocoyal
58 "Pizza, Pastas y Vino"
59 Cookshacks

OTHER
1   Bus Stop
8   Police Station
11 Rébuli Bus Station
12 Bancared ATM
13 Main Bus Stop
14 Aleph Bar
15 Chapiteau
17 Moto Servicio Queche
18 La Posada del Pintor/Circus Bar
21 Pickups to Santa Catarina Palopó & San
    Antonio Palopó
22 Panatitlán
23 Escuela de Español Panajachel
24 Gas Station
25 Servicios Turísticos Atitán
30 Banco Inmobiliario
31 INGUAT Tourist Office; DHL; La Terraza
    Tapas Bar; Fango'D; ATI Divers
32 Jabel Tinamit
33 Banco Agrícola Mercantil (BAM)
35 Telgua Telephone Office; Banco Industrial
36 c@fe.net
39 MayaNet
49 Post Office

52

To Santa
Catarina
Palopó, San
Antonio
Palopó
& Campaña
Campground

Navidad 0-40. Panatitlán will send the teacher to you, so you can study in the lakeside village of your choice. The cost for 30 hours of one-on-one study a week, including a homestay with a local family, is around US$130 per week.

Places to Stay – Budget

Camping A free public campground lies on the beach, east of Río Panajachel's mouth in Jucanyá. The site is basically a dirt patch, and safety can be a problem. A safer alternative is the spacious lakeside lawn at *Hotel Visión Azul* (☎ 762 1426, ☎/fax 762 1419) on the town's western outskirts. It has electrical and water hookups for campers. Costs are US$1.30 per person, plus US$5 per tent and US$2.50 per vehicle.

Better for price and vibe is *Campaña Campground* (☎ 762 2479) on the road to Santa Catarina Palopó. For US$2 you can pitch a tent and use the kitchen. Amenities include a book exchange, luggage storage and pickup from Pana.

Hospedajes & Hotels Budget travelers here will rejoice at the profusion of family-run hospedajes. They're simple – perhaps two rough beds, a small table and a light bulb in a bare boarding room – but cheap. Most provide clean toilets, and some have hot showers.

For a terrific value, head to *Villa Lupita*, on Callejón Don Tino (off Calle del Campanario near the church). Clean, secure rooms with bedside tables and lamps, comfortable beds and shared hot bath cost US$3.20 per person. Another great deal is *Hospedaje El Viajero* (☎ 762 0128) off Calle Santander, a welcoming, clean place with five rooms (with private hot bath) set about 40m back from the street. It's quiet and peaceful, yet you're near everything. Upstairs rooms have more air and light. Rates are US$6.50/9.25 single/double.

Hospedaje Santo Domingo (☎ 762 0236) is an amicable place with a variety of cheap rooms; take the road toward Hotel Monterrey, then follow the signs. It's away from the bustle of Calle Santander. Basic wood-plank rooms with shared bath are US$2/3.50; more attractive upstairs rooms are US$6.45 double. Rooms with private bath are US$7/10.30.

Mario's Rooms (☎ 762 2370, 762 1313) on Calle Santander, is popular with young, adventurous travelers. Rooms cost US$4.25/5.25/7.75 single/double/triple with shared hot bath; US$7.75/10.50/13.25 with private cold bath. *Hospedaje Mi Chosita*, on Calle 14 de Febrero (turn at Mario's Rooms), is tidy and quiet; US$3.35/4.15/5 with shared bath. Similarly priced is the clean *Hospedaje García* (☎ 762 2187, 4a Calle 2-24, Zona 2) east along the same street.

Prices rise close to the beach. Hook a left up the alley called Calle Ramos to *Hospedajes Ramos I & II* (☎ 762 0413), which has simple rooms with private bath for US$4.50/7.75. They claim to have hot water. Fifty meters farther back is *Hospedaje Contemporaneo* (☎ 762 2214), a hospitable place with spare, clean rooms with private bath for US$6.20/9.25. Upstairs rooms have partial lake views. Just beyond is the new and recommended *Hospedaje Sueño Real* (☎ 762 0608), which has tasteful, clean rooms for US$5.15 per person with shared bath; US$7/11.60 with private bath. Bicycle rentals and phone and taxi services are available.

The standout *Hotel Utz Jay* (☎/fax 762 1358, utzjay@atitlan.com) is on Calle 15 de Febrero near Calle Santander. Its four beautifully outfitted rooms are in adobe casitas. Each has a private hot bath, traditional fabrics and touches like candles and drinking water; US$12.90/15.45/18/21 single/double/triple/quad. Other amenities include gardens, hammocks, a communal kitchen and a *chuj*, or traditional Mayan sauna. The owners speak French and English and lead hiking and camping trips around the lake.

The new *Hotel Primavera* (☎/fax 762 2052, primavera@atitlan.com) on Calle Santander, is reader recommended. Upstairs rooms overlooking a lush garden are US$12.25/15.45 in high season; US$6.45/13 in low. *La Zanahoria Chic* (☎ 762 1249, fax 762 2138, Avenida Los Árboles 0-46) has seven clean rooms opening onto a communal sitting area with two shared baths. The rooms are simple but comfortable, and the whole place has a cozy, lived-in feeling (US$3.85/7.75/11.50). The *Posada de los Volcanes* (☎ 762 0244, ☎/fax 762 2367, posadavolcanes@atitlan.com, Calle Santander 5-51) is a beautiful place offering

rooms with private bath and cable TV for US$20/25.
Web site: www.atitlan.com/volcanes.htm

Places to Stay – Mid-Range

Mid-range lodgings are busiest on Friday and Saturday nights. From Sunday to Thursday you may get a discount. All places listed provide private hot showers.

Mini Hotel Riva Bella (☎ 762 1348, 762 1177, fax 762 1353) on Calle Real, is a collection of neat two-room bungalows, each with its own parking place, set around pleasant gardens. Rates are US$27/32 single/double. The same owners operate *Bungalows Guayacán*, just across the river, where six apartments, each with kitchenette, one bedroom, living room and garden, go for US$42 for up to three people.

Hotel Monterrey (☎/fax 762 1126) on Calle Monte Rey (look for the sign), is a two-story motel-style building facing the lake across lawns and gardens. Its 29 clean and cheerful rooms open onto a terrace with beautiful lake views (US$25/35).

Rancho Grande Inn (☎ 762 1554, 762 2255, fax 762 2247, hranchog@quetzal.net), on Calle Rancho Grande, has 12 perfectly maintained country-style villas in a tropical setting. Some bungalows sleep up to five people, and a few have fireplaces. The congenial Marlita Hannstein charges a reasonable US$30 single, US$40 to US$60 double; rates include a delicious full breakfast. This is perhaps Pana's best place to stay; reserve in advance.

Several meters north on Calle Rancho Grande is *Müller's Guest House* (☎ 762 2442, 762 2392, fax 363 1306), which has three nicely appointed, if dampish, rooms with bath around well tended gardens for US$45 for two or three people.

Hotel Visión Azul (☎ 762 1426, ☎/fax 762 1419), on the Hotel Atitlán road, is built into a hillside in a quiet location. It features lake views through a grove of trees. The big, bright rooms in the main building have spacious terraces dripping with bougainvillea and ivy. Modern bungalows provide more privacy. The hotel has a swimming pool. Rates are US$39/44/49/52 single/double/triple/quad.

On the main road out of town, *Hotel Tzanjuyú* (☎/fax 762 1318) has large gardens and a private beach on a beautiful cove. All the rooms open onto small balconies with great lake views and cost US$31/35/39/43. A swimming pool and restaurant are on-site.

Well back from the street, *Hotel Dos Mundos* (☎ 762 2078, 762 2140, fax 762 0127, dosmundos@atitlan.com, Calle Santander 4-72) is an attractive place with 16 bungalows amid tropical gardens. All have cable TV and nice decor; rates are US$45/55/65. Also here are a swimming pool and a good Italian restaurant.

Places to Eat

The cheapest places to eat are down by the beach at the mouth of the Río Panajachel. The cookshacks on the shore have rock-bottom prices, as do the food stalls around the parking lot. Across the street, you can fill up for US$4 at any of several little restaurants, all of which offer priceless lake views. *Pizza, Pastas y Vino* along here is open 24 hours.

At the lake end of Calle Santander, the open-air *Sunset Cafe* has a great lake vista. Meat or vegetarian meals start at US$3; snacks are less. The cafe has a bar with live music on weekends. It's open 11 am to 10 pm daily.

Nearby on Calle Santander, *Deli Restaurante No 2* is a tranquil garden restaurant serving a good variety of healthy, inexpensive foods to the strains of classical music. It's open 7 am to 5:45 pm daily except Tuesday; breakfast is served all day. *Deli Restaurante No 1*, on Calle Real near Calle El Amate, has the same menu and hours, except it's open on Tuesday, closed on Thursday.

El Bistro, on Calle Santander half a block from the lake, is another relaxing restaurant. It offers candlelight dining in the evening and sometimes live music. It's open 7 am to 10 pm daily.

Las Chinitas, on Calle Santander in El Patio complex, serves unbelievably delicious, inexpensive Asian food. Ling, the friendly owner, is from Malaysia via New York and has been in Panajachel for many years.

Nearby on Calle Santander is the popular *Restaurante Guajimbos*, which has scores of menu items but is notable for its bottomless cups of coffee. Grab some bread

or pastries at *Pana Pan*, next door, to go with the all-you-can-drink java.

The Last Resort restaurant/bar, just off Calle Santander on Calle 14 de Febrero, is famous for its good, inexpensive food. All meals on the varied menu are served with soup, salad, bread and coffee for US$3.35 to US$5; the buffet breakfast is US$2. Alcohol is served, there's table tennis in the rear, and on cool evenings the fireplace is a welcome treat. The restaurant is open daily.

The shady streetside patio at *Al Chisme*, on Avenida Los Árboles, is a favorite with locals and Pana regulars. Breakfasts of English muffins, Belgian waffles and omelets cost US$2 to US$4. For lunch and dinner, Al Chisme offers a variety of meat and vegetarian dishes, including Tex-Mex specialties. It's open daily except Wednesday.

Next door is *Sevananda Vegetarian Restaurant*, offering sandwiches and vegetable plates for US$2 to US$4; open daily except Sunday. Next door again is *Bombay Pub and Cafe*, serving all-vegetarian burritos, pastas and stir-fry in a pretty courtyard.

At the *Fly'n Mayan Yacht Club*, near the intersection of Calle Real and Calle Santander, the pizzas (US$3.50 to US$6.50) have a good reputation. It's open daily except Thursday.

Restaurante/Bar Tocoyal, at the beach end of Calle Rancho Grande, is a tidy, modern thatch-roofed place serving good meals (including fish) for about US$8.

El Maná Panadería, on Avenida Los Árboles near La Zanahoria Chic, sells an awesome selection of fresh breads. Across the street, *Tienda El Botiquín Verde* sells organic vegetables, free-range eggs, tofu, nut oils, juices, vitamins and herbal remedies. It's open 9 am to 3 pm weekdays, 9 am to 1 pm Saturday.

Fango'D, on Calle Santander in the complex with INGUAT, serves some of Pana's best coffee. It's open 6 am to 5 pm daily.

The *Ristorante La Lanterna*, at Hotel Dos Mundos, set back from the street on Calle Santander, is an authentic Italian restaurant; diners can use the hotel swimming pool. It's open 7 am to 3 pm and 6 to 10 pm daily.

Upstairs in the same building with the INGUAT tourist office, **La Terraza Tapas Bar** (☎ 762 0041) is a lovely, upmarket open-air restaurant/bar open daily; locals consistently cite this as one of Pana's best restaurants.

Entertainment

Popular venues in Panajachel include **Aleph Bar**, on Avenida Los Árboles; **Sunset Cafe** (see Places to Eat); **El Bistro** (see Places to Eat); and **La Posada del Pintor/ Circus Bar**.

Pana's two discos – **Chapiteau** and **Nuan's** – are both on Avenida Los Árboles. **Ubu's Cosmic Cantina**, next to Nuan's, has a pool table, giant screen TV and couches.

Turquoise Buffalo, on Avenida Los Árboles next to Al Chisme, shows several films in English nightly. At **La Zanahoria Chic** video cafe, on Avenida Los Árboles, you can choose from a list of over a hundred films.

Shopping

You can shop to your heart's content here and have the goods shipped to your door back home. There are even companies here that will do the shopping and shipping for you. Calle Santander is lined with booths, stores and complexes.

One of Guatemala's most extensive handicrafts markets is the local Comerciales de Artesanías Típicas Tinamit Maya, on Calle Santander, selling traditional clothing, jade, leather items, wood carvings and more. You can get good deals if you're patient and bargain. It's open 7 am to 7 pm daily.

Getting There & Away

Bus The town's main bus stop is where Calles Santander and Real meet, across from the Banco Agrícola Mercantil. Rébuli buses depart from the Rébuli office on Calle Real.

Antigua (US$3.25, 2½ hours, 146km)
Rébuli runs one direct deluxe bus at 11 am daily except Sunday. Or take the 10 am deluxe bus (US$1.95) to Chimaltenango and change there. Any Guatemala City bus will get you to Chimaltenango.

Chichicastenango (US$1.65, 1½ hours, 37km)
Mendoza has nine buses 6:45 am to 4 pm daily. Rébuli buses (US$1.30) leave at 6:45 am Thursday and Sunday, Chichi's market days. Or

take any bus to Los Encuentros and change there.

Cocales (Carretera al Pacífico; US$1, 2½ hours, 56km)
Eight buses daily, from 6:30 am to 3 pm.

El Carmen/Talismán (Mexican border)
Via the Pacific route, take the bus to Cocales and change there. Via the highland route, take the bus to Quetzaltenango and change there.

Guatemala City (US$2.60, 3½ hours, 148km)
Rébuli has 10 daily departures, 5:30 am to 3 pm. Or take a bus to Los Encuentros and change there.

Huehuetenango (3½ hours, 159km)
Take the bus to Los Encuentros and wait there for a bus bound for Huehue or La Mesilla (see the Getting Around section, earlier in this chapter). Or catch a Quetzaltenango bus and change at Cuatro Caminos. Buses run hourly from these junctions.

La Mesilla (Mexican border; seven hours, 241km)
See Huehuetenango.

Los Encuentros (US$0.50, 35 minutes, 20km)
Take any bus heading toward Guatemala City, Chichicastenango, Quetzaltenango or the Interamericana.

Quetzaltenango (US$1.55, 2½ hours, 99km)
There are six buses daily, 5:30, 6:15, 7:30, 10 and 11:30 am and 2 pm. Or take a bus to Los Encuentros and change there.

San Antonio Palopó (US$0.40, 45 minutes, 9km)
There are daily buses via Santa Catarina Palopó, or grab one of the many pickups leaving from the corner of Calles Real and El Amate.

San Lucas Tolimán (US$1, 1½ hours, 24km)
There are two buses daily, 6:45 am and 4 pm, or take any bus heading for Cocales, get off at the crossroads to San Lucas, and walk about 1km into town.

Santa Catarina Palopó (US$0.25, 20 minutes, 4km)
There are daily buses, or get a pickup at the corner of Calles Real and El Amate.

Sololá (US$0.15, 10 minutes, 8km)
There are frequent direct local buses, or take any bus heading to Guatemala City, Chichicastenango, Quetzaltenango or Los Encuentros.

Shuttle Minibus Tourist shuttle buses usually take about half as much time as local buses. See Travel Agencies for companies offering shuttles.

Car & Motorcycle Dalton Rent A Car (☎/fax 762 1275, 762 2251) has an office on Avenida Los Árboles. Moto Servicio

Queche (☎ 762 2089), just past the intersection of Avenida Los Árboles and Calle Real, rents bicycles and off-road motorcycles.

Boat Passenger boats depart from the public beach at the foot of Calle del Balneario. The big, slow ferries have largely been discontinued in favor of fast, frequent lanchas. Boats stop running around 6 pm.

One-way passage *anywhere* on Lago de Atitlán costs US$0.65, but the *lancheros* will quote a price quadruple that. Generally, foreigners end up paying around US$1.30. You can hold out for the US$0.65 fare, but you may have to let a few boats go by.

The trip to Santiago Atitlán takes less than an hour. Another boat route stops in Santa Catarina Palopó, San Antonio Palopó and San Lucas Tolimán, though it's cheaper to go by bus to these nearby towns.

Another route goes counterclockwise around the lake, stopping in Santa Cruz La Laguna (15 minutes), Jaibalito, Tzununá, San Marcos La Laguna (30 minutes), San Juan La Laguna and San Pedro La Laguna (40 minutes). After departing Panajachel from the Calle del Balneario dock, the boats stop at another dock at the foot of Calle del Embarcadero before heading out (or vice versa, when arriving at Panajachel).

SANTA CATARINA PALOPÓ & SAN ANTONIO PALOPÓ

Four winding kilometers east of Panajachel lies Santa Catarina Palopó. Here narrow streets paved in stone blocks run past adobe houses with roofs of thatch or corrugated tin, and the gleaming white church commands the center of attention. Chickens cackle, dogs bark and the villagers go about their daily life dressed in beautiful clothing.

Except for appreciating village life and enjoying the stunning views, there's little to do. This is one of the best places to buy the luminescent indigo *huipiles* you see around Lago de Atitlán. Look for vendors on the path to the shore, or pop into one of the simple wooden storefronts. Several little *comedores* on the main plaza sell refreshments, and you can get a reasonably priced meal at the open-air *Restaurante Laguna Azul* on the lakeshore.

The road continues past Santa Catarina 5km to San Antonio Palopó, a larger but similar village where men and women in traditional clothing tend their terraced fields and clean mountains of scallions by the lakeshore.

See Panajachel for transportation details. From Panajachel, you can walk to Santa Catarina in about an hour, continuing to San Antonio in another. Bicycling is another option.

SANTIAGO ATITLÁN

South across the lake from Panajachel, on the shore of a lagoon squeezed between the volcanoes of Tolimán and San Pedro, lies Santiago Atitlán. Though the most visited village outside Panajachel, it clings to the traditional lifestyle and clothing of the Tz'utuhil Maya. The best days to visit are market days (Friday and Sunday, with a lesser market on Tuesday).

Santiago reveres Maximón (mah-shee-**mohn**; see the boxed text 'A God is a God is a God'), who is paraded around during Semana Santa – a good excuse to head this way during Easter. The rest of the year, Maximón resides with a caretaker, receiving offerings. Local children will take you to see him for a small tip.

As you disembark, children greet you selling clay whistles and little embroidered strips of cloth. They can act as guides, find you a taxi or lead you to a hotel, for a tip.

Boats to Santiago from Pana take about an hour; from San Pedro La Laguna 20 minutes.

Orientation & Information

Walk to the left from the dock along the shore to reach the street into town. It's lined with shops selling woven cloth and other handicrafts.

Near the dock is the office of the Grupo Guías de Turismo Rilaj Maam, a guide cooperative offering trips to many nearby places, including the volcanoes and the Chutinamit archaeological site. The office is open 8 am to 5 pm daily. Martin Tzina is a recommended guide.

Santiago has a post office, a Telgua telephone/fax office and a bank where you can change US dollars and traveler's checks.

Things to See & Do

At the top of the slope is the main square, flanked by the town office and a huge centuries-old **church**. Within are wooden

A God Is a God Is a God

The Spanish called him San Simón, the ladinos named him Maximón, and the Maya knew him as Ry Laj Man (rhee-la-mohn). By any name, he's the deity revered throughout the Guatemalan highlands. Assumed to be a combination of Mayan gods, Pedro de Alvarado (the fierce conquistador of Guatemala) and the biblical Judas, San Simón is an effigy to which Guatemalans of every stripe make offerings and ask for blessings. He's usually cared for and housed by a cofradía member (town elder). The name, shape and ceremonies associated with this deity vary from town to town, but encountering him will be memorable regardless of where that happens to occur. For a small fee, photography is usually permitted. Offerings of cigarettes, rum or candles are always appreciated.

In Santiago Atitlán, locals worship a wooden figure draped in colorful scarves smoking a fat cigar. His favorite gifts are Payaso cigarettes and Venado rum, but he often has to settle for the cheaper Quetzalteca Especial. Each year, Maximón is moved to a new home. This is a custom that anthropologists speculate was established to periodically redistribute the balance of power.

In Nahualá between Los Encuentros and Quetzaltenango, Maximón is a god à la Picasso: a simple wooden box with a cigarette protruding out of it. Still, the same offerings are made and simple blessings asked for. In Zunil, near Xela, the deity is known as San Simón, but is similar to Santiago's Maximón.

San Jorge La Laguna, on Lake Atitlán, is a very spiritual place for the Maya; here they worship Ry Laj Man. It is possible that the first effigy was made near here, carved from the palo de pito tree that spoke to the ancient shamans, telling them to preserve their culture, language and traditions by carving Ry Laj Man. Although the flowers of the palo de pito can be smoked to induce hallucinations, don't try this at home. The effigy in San Jorge looks like a joker, with an absurdly long tongue.

The residents of San Andrés Itzapa, near Antigua, also worship Ry Laj Man. Here he has a permanent home and is brought out on October 28 and paraded about in an unparalleled festival. This is an all night, hedonistic party where cosmic dancers grab the staff of Ry Laj Man to harness his power and receive magical visions. San Andrés is less than 10km south of Chimaltenango, so you can easily make the party from Antigua.

statues of the saints, each of whom gets new handmade clothes every year. On the carved pulpit, note the figures of corn (from which humans were formed, according to Mayan religion), as well as a literate quetzal bird and Yum-Kax, the Maya god of corn. A similar carving is on the back of the priest's chair.

A memorial plaque at the back commemorates Father Stanley Francis Rother, a missionary priest from Oklahoma; beloved by the local people, he was murdered in the church by ultrarightist 'death squads' in 1981.

Among the several good **hikes** around Santiago is a four-hour walk to San Pedro. Take the path veering right just beyond the Posada de Santiago and continue around the San Pedro volcano saddle; get the last lancha back in the early afternoon. You can also catch a pickup to the small village of Cerro de Oro, between Santiago and San Lucas Tolimán. The village has a pretty church, and the eponymous hill provides great views. Pickups leave from in front of Hotel Chi-Nim-Yá.

A challenging 10km roundtrip hike to the **Mirador**, south of Santiago, is rewarding, taking you through cloud forest filled with parakeets, curassows, swifts and other birds. The path starts 1km beyond the Posada de Santiago (veer left at the fork) and leads to a lookout point with beautiful panoramic views. Plan on about five hours roundtrip, and start early to avoid clouds. A guide costs US$13.

Language Courses

Recommended Spanish classes are offered by Cecilia and Rosa Archila (☎ 703 2562, fax 762 2466); in the USA write to PO Box 520972, Miami, FL 33152-0972. Follow signs from the dock or ask at the Grupo Guías office for more information.

Places to Stay & Eat

Near the dock, the simple *Hotel Chi-Nim-Yá (☎ 721 7131)* has 22 clean rooms around a central courtyard. Rates are US$2.60/4 single/double with shared bath; US$6.60/8 with private bath. The nicest room is No 106. Nearby, *Restaurante Regiomontano* is open 7 am to 7 pm daily.

Hotel y Restaurante Tzutuhil (☎ 721 7174) about three blocks uphill on the road from the dock, is an incongruously modern five-story building. Many of the rooms have large windows with decent views; some have cable TV. Rooms vary widely, so look before committing. Clean rooms are US$2 per person with shared hot bath, US$3.25 per person with private bath – a good deal. Go up on the rooftop for great sunsets. The restaurant here is open 6 am to 10:30 pm daily.

Restaurant Santa Rita, a few steps from the plaza's northeast corner, past Distribuidor El Buen Precio, boasts *deliciosos pays* (delicious pies).

One of the most charming lakeside hotels is *Posada de Santiago (☎ 721 7167, posdesantiagoguate.net)*. Its half dozen bungalows and two suites, all with stone walls, fireplaces, porches and hammocks, are set around beautiful gardens stretching uphill from the lake. Rates are US$30/40/50/60/70 single/double/triple/quad/suite. Walk 1km out of town on the road past the Hospedaje Rosita, and keep walking along the lakeside road. The restaurant at the Posada de Santiago is special, too, with well-prepared food and cozy ambience.

SAN PEDRO LA LAGUNA

The next most popular lakeside town is San Pedro La Laguna, heavily populated with bohemian travelers who liked it here so much they stayed.

You'll see coffee being picked and spread out to dry on wide platforms at the beginning of the dry season. Marijuana is also grown here; before long you'll smell the telltale blue smoke and be fielding purchase offers. Accommodations in San Pedro are among the cheapest in Guatemala. Try bargaining for longer stays and during the off season.

Orientation & Information

San Pedro has two docks. The one on the south side of town serves boats going to/from Santiago Atitlán. Another dock, around on the east side of town, serves boats going to/from Pana. At either, walk uphill to reach the center of town. Alternatively, from the Santiago dock, you can take your first right past the Ti Kaaj and follow the beaten path for about 15 minutes to the other side of town. Along this path are several hospedajes and simple eateries. To take this route coming from the Panajachel dock, take your first left and then a right into the little alley across from the Hospedaje Casa Elena; a sign painted on the wall says 'to El Balneario.'

San Pedro has a post office, a Telgua telephone/fax office and a Banrural that exchanges US dollars and traveler's checks. The folks at Thermal Waters offer email but no Internet access.

Most of the hotels, restaurants and other businesses here don't have telephones. To reach them, you can phone the community telephone at Telgua (☎ 762 2486) and give them a time when you'll call back; the business will send someone over to receive your call.

Things to See & Do

When you arrive by boat from Panajachel, boys will greet you, asking if you want a guide to ascend the **Volcán San Pedro**, on foot or horseback. Guides are worth it; the cost is around US$3 per person for the hiking trip, slightly more on horseback. It takes around four hours to hike. Bring water and snacks.

Thermal Waters (☎ 206 9658), right on the lakeshore between the two docks, has individual open-air solar-heated pools with great views. Reservations are a good idea. The cost is US$2.60 per person. Antonio from California, the eccentric horticulturist inventor who built and operates Thermal Waters, also runs an organic vegetarian restaurant and a sweat lodge here.

Several **walks** between San Pedro and neighboring villages make terrific day trips. You can walk west to San Juan La Laguna (30 minutes), San Pablo La Laguna (1½ hours), San Marcos (three hours), Jaibalito (five hours) and finally, Santa Cruz (all day). From the last three you can easily hail a lancha back to San Pedro until around 3 pm. Walking southeast over and around the saddle of Volcán San Pedro, you can make it to Santiago Atitlán in around four hours.

Language Courses
Casa Rosario, a Spanish-language school, is operated by Professor Samuel Cumes, a well-known San Pedro teacher. It's very economical at US$55 per week for instruction and lodging. You can arrange weaving classes here as well. Another option is the San Pedro Spanish School, between the two docks.

Places to Stay & Eat
When you arrive at the dock serving boats to/from Pana, head up the main street and make your first right, walking along the trash-strewn path for about 75m to reach *Hotel & Restaurante Valle Azul* (☎ 207 7292) This cement behemoth has seen better days. Small, basic rooms with shared bath are US$1.95 per person (plus US$0.50 per shower). The restaurant is a great, inexpensive little place open 7 am to 10 pm daily.

Continue through the small cornfield for about five minutes to get to *Café Luna Azul*; most boat drivers will drop you there if you ask. This place reputedly has the best omelet-and-hash-browns breakfast going (US$2). The cafe also serves lunch.

Nearby, *Restaurante Nick's* is the vortex of the traveler scene. It hosts free movies nightly. Upstairs, *D'Noz* is another backpacker restaurant.

Make a left just beyond Nick's to reach *Hospedaje Casa Elena*, a popular, family-run pension; rates are US$2.50/3.35 single/double with shared bath. Farther on is a simple comedor, *El Paisaje*. Take a right there and you'll see *Hospedaje Xocomil*, which rents quiet rooms around a cement courtyard for US$1.30 per person.

Continue to the alley opposite Hospedaje Casa Elena to reach several more pensions en route to the Santiago dock; follow the signs for Casa Rosario. Make two lefts to reach *Hospedaje Posada Xetawal* and *Posada Casa Domingo*; both have rooms for about US$1 a night. If you continue straight instead, toward the Santiago dock, you come to *Restaurant Pinocchio*, which serves good, homemade pastas and cakes; the breakfast here is a good value.

Next is the recommended *Hotelito El Amanecer Sak'cari*, which has rooms with private hot bath for US$4.50/9. Just past here the path takes a left and then a quick right to the friendly *Comedor Mata Hari*, a local place serving wholesome, cheap food.

Finally, you'll reach *Ti Kaaj*, a popular, inexpensive place with hammocks around the gardens and basic rooms with shared bath for US$1.55/2.80/4 single/double/triple. It has a restaurant, disco and bar. From the Santiago dock, make your first right to get here.

Along and just off the road leading uphill from the Santiago dock are several more lodgings, including *Hospedaje Villa Sol*, *Hotel San Pedro*, *Hospedaje San Francisco* and *Hotel San Francisco*; all offer rooms for around US$2 to US$4 per person.

Heading left from the Santiago dock is the laid-back *Las Milpas* (*lasmilpas@atitlan.com*), which rents private bungalows for US$6.45/7.75; rooms with shared bath for US$9.30/14 (or simpler versions for US$6.45 per person); and larger rooms with private bath for US$20/24 double/triple. You can also camp, and all guests have use of the hot tub, sauna and gardens.

Cafe Arte, on the road leading uphill from the Santiago dock, is a good, inexpensive cafe serving meat, fish and vegetarian dishes. It's operated by the family of internationally known primitivist artist Pedro Rafael González Chavajay; his paintings, and those of his students, are exhibited here. The cafe is open 7 am to 11 pm daily.

Getting There & Away
Unless you want to bring a vehicle, it's easiest to reach San Pedro by passenger boats, which come here from Panajachel and from Santiago.

SAN MARCOS LA LAGUNA
San Marcos is a peaceful place with houses set among shady coffee plants near the lakeshore. The shore is beautiful, with several little docks for swimming.

The town's greatest claim to fame is **Las Pirámides** meditation center (☎ 205 7302, 205 7151), on the path heading inland from Posada Schumann. Every structure on the property is built in a pyramid shape and oriented to the four cardinal points. Among the many physical (eg, yoga, massage) and metaphysical (eg, Tarot readings, channeling) offerings is a one-month lunar meditation course that begins every full moon and covers the four elements of human development (physical, mental, emotional and spiritual). Most sessions are held in English. The last week of the course requires fasting and silence by participants. Nonguests can come for meditation or Hatha yoga sessions Monday to Saturday (US$3.90).

Accommodations in pyramid-shaped houses are available for US$10/9/8 per day by the day/week/month. This includes the meditation course, use of the sauna and access to a fascinating multilingual library. A restaurant serves vegetarian fare. The best chance to get a space is just prior to the full moon. Las Pirámides has a private dock; all the lancheros know it and can drop you here.

Places to Stay & Eat

Just to the left of the public dock is the comfortable *Hotel & Restaurante Arco Iris* (☎ *306 5039, arcoiris@atitlan.com*), with good beds in clean rooms for US$5.15 per person. Hammocks are hung around the manicured grounds, and a restaurant overlooks the lake. Italian, English, French and German are spoken.

To get to the other hotels, walk for a few hundred meters along the inland street running parallel to the lake. Turn left onto the dirt path (look for the Posada Schumann sign).

The first hotel you reach is *Hotel Paco Real* (*fax 762 1196*) with nice gardens and simple, tastefully decorated rooms. Charming bungalows each with a loft bed, porch and shared bath are US$10.50 for two people. Clean rooms with tiled floors and shared bath are US$4.50/10.50/15 single/double/triple. Some rooms are musty. Also here, is a restaurant run by a French chef; it's open 7 am to 9 pm daily.

Next on the strip is the mellow *Hotel La Paz* (☎ *702 9168*), which offers basic little bungalows on rambling grounds that also hold organic gardens, a vegetarian restaurant and a traditional Mayan sauna. Each bungalow sleeps five people dorm-style and costs US$3.20 per person. One private double is available for US$9. Camping is allowed, and a common room above the restaurant has musical instruments and books. Gardeners,

chefs, carpenters, masseurs and other folks good with their hands may have luck bartering.

Unicornio Rooms is another attractive place, with beautiful gardens, a sauna and a communal kitchen (but no electricity). Three small, thatch-roofed, A-frame bungalows with shared cold bath cost US$2.60/5.15. One large two-story bungalow with private kitchen and bath is also available.

Right on the lakeside, *Posada Schumann* (☎ *202 2216, in Guatemala City 360 4049, 339 2683, fax 473 1326*) has three stone bungalows – each with kitchen and private bath – a restaurant and a sauna. The bungalows run US$12/24; cheaper rooms are also available, US$7.75/15.50. You can save by renting weekly or monthly. Posada Schumann has a private pier for those arriving by lancha.

Getting There & Away

You can drive to San Marcos from the Interamericana; the turnoff is at Km 148. See Hiking in the San Pedro section, earlier, if you're interested in walking. The walk or drive between Santa Clara La Laguna and San Marcos is incredible.

See Panajachel for information on passenger boats.

JAIBALITO

Accessible only by boat or on foot, Jaibalito is remarkable for Guatemala's most magical hotel. Perched on a secluded cliff, *La Casa del Mundo Hotel & Cafe* (☎ *204 5558, fax 762 1092, casamundo@ yahoo.com*) was designed and built by husband-and-wife team Bill and Rosie Fogarty. It has gorgeous gardens, swimming holes and a hot tub overhanging the lake. Rooms with private bath are US$16.75 double; rooms with shared hot bath are US$6.50 per person. All rooms have views and are impeccably outfitted with comfortable beds, *típico* fabrics and fresh flowers. The restaurant is fantastic. You can rent kayaks or bikes here. Reservations are advisable.

SANTA CRUZ LA LAGUNA

Another peaceful lakeside village, Santa Cruz features a vibe somewhere between the party scene of San Pedro and the spiritual feel of San Marcos. The main part of the village is up the hill from the dock; the hotels are on the shore.

See Panajachel for details on passenger boats.

Activities

ATI Divers (☎ 762 2646, fax 762 1196, santacruz@guate.net) offers a four-day PADI open-water diving certification course (US$160), as well as a PADI high-altitude course and fun dives. It's based at La Iguana Perdida hotel.

Good walks from Santa Cruz include the beautiful lakeside walking track between Santa Cruz and San Marcos, about four hours one way. You can stop for a beer and a meal at La Casa del Mundo en route (see Jaibalito, earlier). Or you can walk up the hill to Sololá, a 3½-hour walk one way.

Places to Stay & Eat

Three pleasant lakeside hotels provide accommodations and meals. Although electricity is available up the hill, the shoreside hotels have none. In the evening, guests eat by candlelight and lantern light.

None of the following hotels has a telephone, but you can fax them at 762 1196 or try their email. It can take a few days to hear back from them.

Arca de Noé (thearca@yahoo.com) is recommended for its excellent food and beautiful lake views from its dense, colorful gardens. Standard rooms with shared bath go for US$5.95/10 single/double; plush rooms with private bath are US$20/21.75; dorm beds are US$3.50.

Popular with the backpacking set, *La Iguana Perdida (santacruz@guate.net)* has a restaurant and a variety of accommodations. Rates are US$2.35 per person for a dorm bed; US$5.40/7.75 for a private room; US$7.75/9.50 for a small cabaña with shared bath. Meals are served family-style; a three-course dinner is US$4.50, and a vegetarian choice is always available. There's also a sauna. The friendly managers, Deedle Denman (from the UK) and Mike Kiersgard (from Greenland), also operate ATI Divers.

Posada Abaj Hotel (abaj@atitlan.com) also on the lakefront, is a nice big place that also has a restaurant. Rooms with shared bath are US$5 per person; bungalows with private bath are US$16.75 for two people.

Spanish classes are offered and a sauna is on the nicely maintained grounds.

SOLOLÁ
pop 9000

Sololá lies along trade routes between the *tierra caliente* (Pacific Slope 'hot lands') and *tierra fría* (the chilly highlands). All the traders meet here, and Sololá's Friday market – a local, rather than a tourist, affair – is one of the highlands' best. The plaza next to the cathedral comes ablaze with the colorful costumes of people from a dozen surrounding villages, and neatly arranged displays of meat, vegetables, fruit, housewares and clothing occupy every available space.

Every Sunday morning the officers of the traditional religious brotherhoods *(cofradías)* parade ceremoniously to the cathedral for their devotions. On other days, Sololá sleeps.

It's a pleasant walk from Sololá down to the lake, whether on the highway to Panajachel (9km) or on the path to Santa Cruz La Laguna (10km).

IXIMCHÉ

Off CA-1 near the small dusty town of Tecpán Guatemala lie the ruins of Iximché (**eesh**-im-chay), capital of the Cakchiquel Maya. Set on a flat promontory surrounded by steep cliffs, Iximché (founded in the late 15th century) was easily defended against attack by the hostile Quiché Maya.

When the conquistadores arrived in 1524, the Cakchiquel formed an alliance with them against the Quiché and the Tz'utuhils. The Spaniards set up headquarters next door to the Cakchiquel capital at Tecpán Guatemala, but Spanish demands for gold and other loot soured the alliance; the Cakchiquel were defeated in the ensuing battles.

Entering Tecpán, you'll see signs for the unpaved road leading less than 6km south to Iximché. You can walk, see the ruins and rest, then walk back to Tecpán in around three hours. Go in the morning so you can return to the highway by early afternoon, before bus traffic dwindles.

The archaeological site has a small museum, four ceremonial plazas surrounded by grass-covered temple structures and ball courts. Some of the structures have been cleaned and maintained; on a few, the original plaster coating is still in place, and traces of the original paint are visible. The site is open 9 am to 4 pm daily (US$3.25).

Tecpán has a couple of basic hotels and small eateries. Transportes Poaquileña runs buses between Tecpán and Guatemala City (1½ hours, 87km) every half hour, from 3 am to 5 pm eastbound and from 5 am to 7:30 pm westbound.

The Highlands – Quiché

The department of Quiché is famous mostly for the town of Chichicastenango, with its bustling Thursday and Sunday markets. Beyond Chichi to the north is Santa Cruz del Quiché, the capital of the department; on its outskirts lie the ruins of K'umarcaaj (or Gumarcaah), also called Utatlán, the last capital city of the Quiché Maya.

See The Highlands – Lago de Atitlán section, earlier in this chapter, for introductory information on the highlands, including a Warning.

Getting There & Away
The road to Quiché leaves the Interamericana at Los Encuentros, winding its way north through pine forests and cornfields, down into a steep valley and up the other side. Women sit in front of their roadside cottages weaving gorgeous pieces of cloth on their simple back-strap looms. From Los Encuentros, it takes half an hour to travel the 17km to Chichicastenango.

CHICHICASTENANGO
pop 8000
Surrounded by valleys, with nearby mountains looming overhead, Chichicastenango seems isolated from the rest of Guatemala. When its narrow cobbled streets and red-tiled roofs are enveloped in mists, it seems magical.

Chichi is a beautiful, interesting place with shamanistic and ceremonial undertones despite gaggles of camera-toting tour groups. *Masheños* (citizens of Chichicastenango) are famous for their adherence to

pre-Christian religious beliefs and ceremonies. You can readily see versions of these old rites in and around the church of Santo Tomás and at the shrine of Pascual Abaj on the outskirts of town.

Chichi has always been an important trading town, and its Sunday and Thursday markets remain fabulous. If you have a choice of days, come on Sunday, when the *cofradías* (religious brotherhoods) often hold processions.

History
Once called Chaviar, this was an important Cakchiquel trading town long before the Spanish conquest. Just prior to the conquistadores arrival, the Cakchiquel and the Quiché (based at K'umarcaaj near present-day Santa Cruz del Quiché, 20km north) went to war. The Cakchiquel abandoned Chaviar and moved to Iximché, which was easier to defend. The conquistadores came and conquered K'umarcaaj, and many of its residents fled to Chaviar, which they renamed Chugüilá (Above the Nettles) and Tziguan Tinamit (Surrounded by Canyons). These names are still used by the Quiché Maya, although everyone else calls the place Chichicastenango, a foreign name given by the conquistadores' Mexican allies.

Information
Direct questions to staff at the museum on the plaza or ask at one of the hotels. You'll find the Mayan Inn, on 8a Calle A at 3a Avenida, is among the most helpful and best informed.

All the banks here are open Sunday. Most change US dollars and traveler's checks; Bancafé, on 5a Avenida between 6a and 7a Calles, gives cash advances on Visa cards and has a Bancared ATM. The Hotel Santo Tomás, 7a Avenida 5-32, will change traveler's checks for guests and nonguests, at a lower rate than the banks.

The post office is at 7a Avenida 8-47, 3½ blocks south of Hotel Santo Tomás on the road into town.

The Telgua telephone office is on 6a Calle between 5a and 6a Avenidas

Acses Computación, on 6a Calle in the same complex as Hotel Girón (see Places to Stay, later in this section), offers email and Internet access when its network is up and running.

GUATEMALA

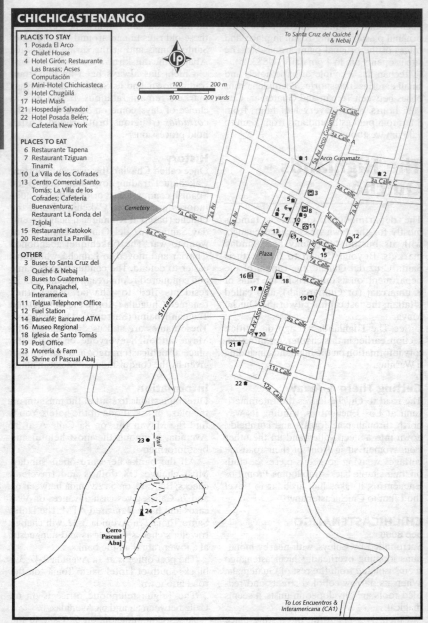

CHICHICASTENANGO

PLACES TO STAY
1 Posada El Arco
2 Chalet House
4 Hotel Girón; Restaurante
   Las Brasas; Acses
   Computación
5 Mini-Hotel Chichicasteca
9 Hotel Chugüilá
17 Hotel Mash
21 Hospedaje Salvador
22 Hotel Posada Belén;
   Cafetería New York

PLACES TO EAT
6 Restaurante Tapena
7 Restaurant Tziguan
   Tinamit
10 La Villa de los Cofrades
13 Centro Comercial Santo
   Tomás; La Villa de los
   Cofrades; Cafetería
   Buenaventura;
   Restaurant La Fonda del
   Tzijolaj
15 Restaurante Katokok
20 Restaurant La Parrilla

OTHER
3 Buses to Santa Cruz del
   Quiché & Nebaj
8 Buses to Guatemala
   City, Panajachel,
   Interamerica
11 Telgua Telephone Office
12 Fuel Station
14 Bancafé; Bancared ATM
16 Museo Regional
18 Iglesia de Santo Tomás
19 Post Office
23 Morería & Farm
24 Shrine of Pascual Abaj

To Santa Cruz del Quiché
& Nebaj

Cemetery

Plaza

Stream

trail

Cerro
Pascual
Abaj

To Los Encuentros &
Interamericana (CA1)

The cemetery on the town's western edge is a decidedly unsavory place to wander, even in groups. There have been several reports of tourists being robbed at gunpoint.

Market

Maya traders from outlying villages come to Chichi on Wednesday and Saturday evenings in preparation for one of Guatemala's largest indigenous markets. You'll see them carrying bundles of long poles up the narrow cobbled streets to the square, then laying down their loads and spreading out blankets to cook dinner and sleep in the arcades surrounding the square.

Just after dawn on Sunday and Thursday, the poles are erected into stalls, which are hung with cloth, furnished with tables and piled with goods for sale. In general, the tourist-oriented stalls sell carved-wood masks, lengths of embroidered cloth and garments; these stalls are around the market's outer edges in the most visible areas. Behind them, the center of the square is devoted to things the villagers want and need: vegetables and fruit, baked goods, macaroni, soap, clothing, spices, sewing notions and toys. Cheap cookshops provide lunch for buyers and sellers alike.

Most of the stalls are taken down by late afternoon. Prices are best just before the market breaks up, as traders would rather sell an item cheap than carry it back with them.

Arriving in town the day before the market to pin down a room is highly recommended. In this way, too, you'll be up early for the action. One traveler wrote to say it's worth being here on Saturday night to attend the Saturday night mass. Otherwise, you can always come by bus on market day itself, or by shuttle bus; market day shuttle buses come from Antigua, Panajachel and Guatemala City, returning in early afternoon. The market starts winding down around 3 or 4 pm.

Iglesia de Santo Tomás

Though dedicated to the Catholic rite, this simple church, at the corner of 5a Avenida and 8a Calle, dating from about 1540, is more often the scene of rituals that are only slightly Catholic and more distinctly Mayan. The front steps of the church serve much the same purpose as did the great flights of

stairs leading up to Mayan pyramids. For much of the day (especially on Sunday), the steps smolder with copal incense, while indigenous prayer leaders called *chuchkajaues* (mother-fathers) swing censers containing *estoraque* (balsam) incense and chant magic words in honor of the ancient Mayan calendar and of their ancestors.

It's customary for the front steps and door of the church to be used only by important church officials and by the chuchkajaues, so you should go around to the right and enter by the side door.

Inside, the floor of the church may be spread with pine boughs and dotted with offerings of corn, flowers and bottles of liquor; candles are everywhere. Many local families can trace their lineage back centuries, some even to the ancient kings of Quiché. The candles and offerings on the floor are in remembrance of the ancestors, many of whom are buried beneath the church floor just as Mayan kings were buried beneath pyramids. Photography is not permitted in this church.

Museo Regional

In the arcade facing the square's south side is the Museo Regional, which holds exhibits of ancient clay pots and figurines, flint and obsidian arrowheads and spearheads, copper ax heads, metates and a jade collection. Hours are 8 am to noon and 2 to 5 pm Wednesday to Monday (US$0.10).

Shrine of Pascual Abaj

Before you have been in Chichi very long, some village lad will offer to guide you (for a tip) to a pine-clad hilltop on the town's outskirts to have a look at Pascual Abaj (Sacrifice Stone), which is the local shrine to Huyup Tak'ah, the Mayan earth god. Said to be hundreds – perhaps thousands – of years old, the stone-faced idol has suffered numerous indignities at the hands of outsiders, but locals still revere it. Chuchkajaues come here regularly to offer incense, food, cigarettes, flowers, liquor and Coca-Cola to the earth god. They may even sacrifice a chicken – all to express their thanks and hope for the earth's continuing fertility. The site also offers nice views of the town and valley.

Tourists have been robbed walking to visit Pascual Abaj, so the best plan is to go in a large group. To get there, walk down the hill on 5a Avenida from the Santo Tomás church, turn right onto 9a Calle and continue downhill along this unpaved road, which bends to the left. At the bottom of the hill, when the road turns sharply right, bear left and follow a path through the cornfields, keeping the stream on your left. Signs mark the way. Walk to the buildings just ahead, which include a farmhouse and a workshop where masks are made. Greet the family here. If the children are not in school, you may be invited to see them perform a local dance in full costume on your return from Pascual Abaj (a tip is expected).

Walk through the farm buildings to the hill behind, then follow the switchbacking path to the top and along the ridge of the hill. Soon you'll reach a clearing and see the idol in its rocky shrine. The idol looks like something from Easter Island. The squat stone crosses near it have many levels of significance for the Maya, only one of which pertains to Christ. The area of the shrine is littered with past offerings, and the bark of nearby pines has been stripped away in places to be used as fuel in the incense fires.

Special Events

December 7 is Quema del Diablo, the Burning of the Devil, when residents burn their garbage in the streets to release the evil spirits within. Highlights include a marimba band and a daring fireworks display that has observers running for cover. The following day is the Feast of the Immaculate Conception; don't miss the early-morning dance of the giant cartoon characters in the plaza.

The Feast of Santo Tomás starts on December 13 and culminates on December 21, when pairs of brave (or maniacal) men fly about at high speeds suspended from a pole in the *palo volador*.

Places to Stay

As Chichi has few accommodations, arrive early on Wednesday or Saturday if you want to secure a room before market day.

The clean *Hotel Girón* (☎ 756 1156, fax 756 1226, 6a Calle 4-52) surrounds a courtyard/parking lot and offers reasonable value. Rooms cost US$5.50/7.75 single/double with

shared cold bath, US$12.35/15.45 with private hot bath.

Mini-Hotel Chichicasteca (☎ 756 1008, 5a Calle 4-42) is a good budget choice popular with locals. Rooms with shared bath are US$3.90 per person.

Hospedaje Salvador (☎ 756 1329, 5a Avenida 10-09), two blocks southwest of the Santo Tomás church, is a large, maze-like building with 48 rooms on three floors. Rates are US$4/6.45/9 single/double/triple with shared bath, US$9.65 double with private bath. Bargain hard.

Hotel Mash is a classic cheapie on 5a Avenida a half block from the plaza. Enter through the black door under the Tienda El Tzijhola sign and walk through the alley, past the simple residences to the staircase with the potted plants. Big, wood-plank rooms with shared bath are US$4 a night. This is about as close as you'll get to Guatemalan living, short of a homestay.

Hotel Posada Belén (☎/fax 756 1244, 12a Calle 5-55) is up a hill away from the market hubbub. Clean, comfortable rooms are US$4.50/7.75 with shared bath, US$6.45/10.30 with private bath. The showers aren't great, but the owners are friendly and the views excellenct. You can pay US$1.65 more to get cable TV, and there's laundry service.

Posada El Arco (☎ 756 1255, 4a Calle 4-36), near the Arco Gucumatz, is a sweet guesthouse where you can relax in the rear garden and enjoy a great view north toward the mountains of Quiché. All the rooms are spacious and spotless, with attractive decor and private hot bath. Upstairs rooms (US$15.50 for one or two people) have fireplaces; downstairs rooms (US$13.15 for one or two people) are larger. The friendly owners, Emilsa and Pedro Macario, speak English and Spanish. Reservations are a good idea.

Another charming, recommended place owned by a friendly husband-and-wife team is *Chalet House* (☎ 756 1360, 3a Calle C 7-44). Cozy rooms with good beds and nice touches are US$14.15 double in high season, US$10.30 in low season. Breakfast is available.

Hotel Chugüilá (☎ 756 1134, fax 756 1279, 5a Avenida 5-24) is pretty and a decent value. All of the 36 colonial-style rooms have private bath; some have a fireplace. A few two-room suites and a restaurant are available. For what you get, the price is reasonable: US$31/36/40 single/double/triple. Certain rooms are noticeably better than others, as mildew has beset some.

Places to Eat

On Sunday and Thursday, eating at the *cookshops* set up in the center of the market is the cheapest way to go. Don't be deterred by the fried-food stalls crowding the fringe – dive in to the center for wholesome fare. On other days, look for the little *comedores* near the post office on the road into town.

Restaurant La Fonda del Tzijolaj, upstairs in the Centro Comercial Santo Tomás on the plaza's north side, has everything: good views, nice decor, decent food and reasonable prices – US$2 to US$3 for breakfast, twice that for lunch or dinner. It's closed Tuesday. Several other restaurants with portico tables are in the Centro Comercial; at *La Villa de los Cofrades* you can while away the hours with checkers/draughts, backgammon and the best coffee in town. It's a popular place, with breakfast for around US$2.50, lunch or dinner around US$4.

The inner courtyard of the Centro Comercial Santo Tomás is a vegetable market on market days, a basketball court the rest of the time. Upstairs, *Cafetería Buenaventura* is clean and economical.

La Villa de los Cofrades No 2, upstairs at the corner of 6a Calle and 5a Avenida (enter from 6a Calle), has tables inside and out on the balcony, overlooking the market street. It has good coffee and delicious food. An ample lunch or dinner with several courses and big portions costs around US$4 to US$6; simpler meals cost less. Down the block is the similar *Restaurante Katokok*, where pasta and meat dishes cost between US$4 and US$7. The coffee here is also good.

Restaurant Tziguan Tinamit, at the corner of 6 Calle and 5a Avenida, takes its name from the Quiché Maya name for Chichicastenango. It's popular with locals and foreigners for pizza, pasta and meat dishes; open daily.

On 6a Calle, upstairs from Hotel Girón, is *Restaurante Las Brasas*, which is open earlier than other places in Chichi. The breakfast here is a good value.

Restaurante Tapena, on 5a Avenida across the street from Hotel Chugüilá, is a gregarious, family-owned place with huge portions of tasty food for cheap. The service is very attentive.

Restaurant La Parrilla, at the corner of 5a Avenida Arco Gucumatz and 10a Calle, is a good, economical restaurant specializing in charcoal-grilled meats. Hearty meals of your choice of meat, served with rice, salad and soup are US$3 to US$5; breakfasts are cheaper.

Nearby, *Cafetería New York* is upstairs from Hotel Posada Belén; the owner is a Guatemalan who spent 14 years in New York and speaks English. Beans, rice and chicken are staples here.

Hotel Chugüilá (see Places to Stay, earlier) is one of the most pleasant places to eat. Main-course plates are priced at US$5.

Getting There & Away

Chichi has no bus station. Buses heading south to Guatemala City, Panajachel, Quetzaltenango and all other points reached from the Interamericana arrive and depart from 5a Calle at 5a Avenida Arco Gucumatz, Zona 1, one block south of the arch. Buses heading north to Santa Cruz del Quiché and Nebaj arrive and depart from around the corner on 5a Avenida Arco Gucumatz. Any bus heading south can drop you at Los Encuentros, where you can catch a bus to your final destination.

Antigua (3½ hours, 108km)
Take any bus heading for Guatemala City and change buses at Chimaltenango.

Guatemala City (US$1.45, 3½ hours, 144km)
Buses leave every 20 minutes, 3:30 am to 6 pm.

Los Encuentros (US$0.35, 30 minutes, 17km)
Take any bus heading for Guatemala City, Panajachel, Quetzaltenango and so on.

Nebaj (US$2.50, 4½ hours, 103km)
Two buses depart daily, or take a bus to Santa Cruz del Quiché and change buses there.

Panajachel (US$1.65, 1½ hours, 37km)
Eleven buses depart daily (approximately hourly), 4:30 am to 2:30 pm, or take any bus heading south and change buses at Los Encuentros.

Quetzaltenango (US$1.50, three hours, 94km)
Seven buses leave daily, mostly in the morning, or take any bus heading south and change at Los Encuentros.

Santa Cruz del Quiché (US$0.50, 30 minutes, 19km)
Buses depart every 20 minutes, 6 am to 9 pm.

On market days, minibuses arrive around midmorning, park in front of Hotel Santo Tomás and depart for the return trip around 2 pm. If you're in Chichi, you can usually catch a ride out on one of these.

SANTA CRUZ DEL QUICHÉ
pop 13,000

The capital of the department, Santa Cruz – usually called 'El Quiché' or simply 'Quiché' – is 19km north of Chichicastenango. The small, dusty town is quieter and more typical of the Guatemalan countryside than Chichi. Few tourists come here, but those who do come are treated well.

K'umarcaaj

The ruins of the ancient Quiché Maya capital are 3km west of El Quiché. Start out of town along 10a Calle and ask the way frequently. No signs mark the way and no buses ply the route. You can hire a taxi in town at the stand by the bus terminal; roundtrip fare, plus waiting time while you explore the ruins, is around US$6.50. Consider yourself lucky if you succeed in hitching a ride with other travelers. Admission to the site costs a few cents.

The kingdom of Quiché was established in Late Postclassic times (about the 14th century) from a mixture of indigenous people and Mexican invaders. Around 1400, King Gucumatz founded his capital here at K'umarcaaj and conquered many neighboring cities. Eventually, the kingdom of Quiché extended its borders to Huehuetenango, Sacapulas, Rabinal and Cobán, even coming to influence the peoples of the Soconusco region in Mexico.

Pedro de Alvarado led his Spanish conquistadores into Guatemala in 1524, and it was the Quiché, under their king, Tecún Umán, who organized the defense of the territory. In the decisive battle fought near Quetzaltenango on February 12, 1524, Alvarado and Tecún locked in mortal combat. Alvarado won. The defeated Quiché invited the victorious Alvarado to visit their capital, where they secretly planned to kill him. Smelling a rat, Alvarado enlisted the aid of his Mexican auxiliaries and the anti-Quiché Cakchiquel, and together they captured the Quiché leaders, burnt them alive and destroyed K'umarcaaj (called Utatlán by his Mexican allies).

The history is more interesting than the ruined city, of which little remains but a few grass-covered mounds. Still, the site – shaded by tall trees and surrounded by defensive ravines (which failed to save the city from the conquistadores) – is a beautiful place for a picnic. It's also used by locals as a religious ritual site; a long tunnel beneath the plaza is a favorite spot for prayers and chicken sacrifices.

Places to Stay & Eat

The safe, clean *Hotel San Pascual* (☎ 755 1107, 7a Calle 0-43, Zona 1), a block south of the church, is run by a dynamo señora. It's a friendly place, with guests gathering to watch TV in the evening. Rooms with private hot bath are US$5.15/6.45/9 single/double/triple.

Hotel Rey K'iche (☎ 755 0824, 8a Calle 0-39, Zona 5) is two blocks from the bus terminal, toward the plaza. It's a clean, modern place with rooms with shared bath for US$5.15/7.75 single/double; rooms with private bath (some with color TV) are US$9/13. It also has a decent restaurant, open daily until 9 pm.

Comedor Fliper (1a Avenida 7-31), 1½ blocks south of the church, is inexpensive, small, clean and friendly. Guests from Hotel San Pascual often walk around the corner to eat here. It's open 7 am to 9 pm daily.

Restaurante El Torito Steak House, on 4a Calle half a block west of the plaza, serves breakfast for US$2; burgers or sandwiches are the same. The house specialty, filet mignon, is US$4.50 for breakfast, US$6 for a full dinner with soup and more. It's open daily. *La Casona*, on 2a Calle between 4a and 5a Avenidas, a few blocks northwest of the church, is also popular.

Getting There & Away

Grupo TACA (☎ 334 7722 for reservations, fax 334 2775) offers flights between Guatemala City and El Quiché.

Many buses from Guatemala City to Chichicastenango continue to El Quiché (look for 'Quiché' on the signboard). The last bus from El Quiché headed south to Chichi and Los Encuentros leaves in midafternoon, so don't tarry.

El Quiché is the transportation hub for the sparsely populated and remote northern reaches of Quiché Department, which extends all the way to the Mexican border.

The bus station is about five blocks south and two blocks east of the plaza. Buses include the following:

Chichicastenango (US$0.50, 30 minutes, 19km)
Take any bus heading for Guatemala City.

Guatemala City (US$1.65, 3½ hours, 163km)
Buses depart every 20 minutes, 3 am to 4 pm.

Nebaj (US$1.30, four hours, 84km)
Buses depart at 8 and 10 am and 12:30, 1 and 3:30 pm. Or take a bus to Sacapulas and change there.

Sacapulas (US$1, 1½ hours, 50km)
There are hourly buses from 9 am to 4 pm, or take any bus heading for Nebaj or Uspantán.

Uspantán (US$2, six hours, 90km)
Buses depart at 10 and 11 am, noon and 1 pm. Or take a bus to Sacapulas and change there; one bus a day leaves Sacapulas, at 10 am.

NEBAJ
pop 9000

High among the Cuchumatanes are the Ixil Maya villages of Nebaj, Chajul and Cotzal. The scenery is breathtakingly beautiful, and the local people, removed from modern influences, proudly preserve their ancient way of life. They make excellent handicrafts, mostly textiles, and the Nebaj women wear beautiful huipiles.

Nebaj's remote location has been a blessing and a curse. The Spaniards found it difficult to conquer, and they laid waste to the inhabitants when they finally did. In more recent times, guerrilla forces made the area a base of operations, drawing strong measures from the army to dislodge them – particularly during the short, brutal reign of Ríos Montt. The few surviving inhabitants of these villages either fled across the border into Mexico or were herded into 'strategic hamlets.' Refugees are still making their way back home here.

Travelers come to Nebaj for the scenery, local culture, excellent handicrafts, market (Thursday and Sunday) and, during the second week in August, the annual festival honoring La Virgen de la Asunción.

Bancafé is at 2a Avenida 46; it changes US dollars and traveler's checks. The post office is on 4a Calle; it's open 8:30 am to 5:50 pm Monday to Friday.

Hiking

Hiking in this area is breathtaking. Ask around for the location of nearby waterfalls and head off on your own, or track down Gaspar Terraza Ramos, a recommended local guide who knows the area and its history well. The hikes start at US$3 an hour – you'll also be asked to donate to refugee programs championed by Gaspar. He usually hangs about the bus station or plaza trying to drum up business.

Places to Stay & Eat

The new **Posada de Don Pablo** (*6a Avenida 5-15*) is the most comfortable place in town; rooms with private hot bath are US$6.45/9/9.70 single/double/triple. The current budget favorite is the friendly **Hotel Ixel**, where simple, clean rooms with shared bath are set around two courtyards. Each room is different. Rates are US$2.35/4/5.80; for something a bit more upscale, ask about the nearby *anexo,* where rooms with private warm bath are US$4.80 per person.

Pasabien, at the bus terminal, has garnered rave reviews from inveterate travelers for great food, ample portions and low prices. It's open for dinner only. Near the plaza, **Comedor Irene** offers filling, nutritious dinners for just over US$1. *Maya-Inca*, on the plaza, serves reasonably priced Guatemalan and Peruvian dishes. A burgeoning cottage industry has developed around local women cooking meals for tourists.

Getting There & Away

Buses come to Nebaj from Quiché, Huehue, Sacapulas and Cobán. More frequent pickup trucks provide transportation for the same fare. The earlier you're up and at 'em in this part of Guatemala, the better.

Coming from Cobán (9½ hours), you have to change buses several times, and it is nearly impossible to make it to Nebaj in one day. It's easier to reach Nebaj from Huehuetenango or from El Quiché, going via Sacapulas, as buses are more frequent.

Buses leave Nebaj for Quiché via Sacapulas (US$1.35) at 6 and 11:30 am and 2 pm daily. If you're headed toward Cobán, you must be on that first one to have any chance of making the connection to Uspantán in Sacapulas that same day. Sacapulas has a good hospedaje and restaurant.

SACAPULAS TO COBÁN

Heading east out of Sacapulas, the road winds its way up sadly deforested slopes before reaching the village of **Uspantán**. Rigoberta Menchú, the 1992 Nobel Peace Prize laureate, grew up a five-hour walk from Uspantán. Be aware that Menchú is not universally loved around here.

If you're headed to Cobán by bus, you'll be spending the night in Uspantán, as the single daily eastbound bus leaves at 3 am (US$1.30, 4½ hours); this bus fills up fast, so get to the stop by 2:30 am. It can get very cold here. *Pensión Galindo (5a Calle 2-09)* three blocks from the plaza, charges US$2 per person and is a fine place to stay. A Banrural on the plaza will change US dollars.

Along with the Huehue to Sacapulas leg of the same highway (see East toward Cobán under Around Huehuetenango, later in this chapter), the Uspantán to Cobán road is one of the most gorgeous rides in Guatemala. Sit on the right for views.

Western Highlands

The areas around Quetzaltenango, Totonicapán and Huehuetenango are more mountainous and less frequented by tourists than regions closer to Guatemala City. The scenery here is just as beautiful and the indigenous culture as fascinating. Travelers going to and from the border post at La Mesilla find these towns welcome breaks, and the area offers some interesting excursion possibilities.

See The Highlands – Lago de Atitlán section, earlier, for introductory information on the highlands, including a Warning.

CUATRO CAMINOS

Heading westward from Los Encuentros, the Interamericana twists and turns ever higher into the mountains, bringing increasingly dramatic scenery and cooler temperatures. After 59km you come to the important highway junction known as Cuatro Caminos (Four Roads), where you can continue north (straight on) to Huehuetenango (77km),

turn east to Totonicapán (12km) or turn southwest to Xela (13km). Buses pass through Cuatro Caminos about every half hour from 6 am to 6 pm, on their way between Totonicapán and Quetzaltenango.

TOTONICAPÁN
pop 9000

San Miguel Totonicapán is a pretty Guatemalan highland town with few tourists. Buses between Totonicapán and Quetzaltenango (passing through Cuatro Caminos) run frequently throughout the day. Placards in the bus window say 'Toto.' The ride from Cuatro Caminos is along a beautiful pine-studded valley.

Flanking Totonicapán's *parque* (as the plaza is called) are the requisite colonial church and a wonderful municipal theater, built in 1924 in the neoclassical style and restored in recent years. Buses drop you right at the parque.

Market days are Tuesday and Saturday; it's a locals' market, not a tourist affair, and it winds down by late morning. After that, you might want to check out Agua Caliente hot springs, a popular local bathing place 2km from the parque.

Casa de la Cultura Totonicapense

This cultural center (☎/fax 766 1575, kiche78@hotmail.com), 8a Avenida 2-17, Zona 1, to the left of Hospedaje San Miguel, holds displays on indigenous culture and crafts. It also administers a wonderful 'Meet the Artisans' program that allows tourists to meet artisans and local families, observing how they live, work and play. Cost for the program ranges from US$42 per person for four people to US$20 per person for 15 to 20 people; the money goes directly to the artists involved. An extended program includes a one-night stay with a local family for US$15 per person, including meals.
Web site: http://larutamayaonline.com/aventura.html

The Casa de la Cultura also offers a tour of Totonicapán-area workshops, community projects, schools and Mayan ceremonial sites (US$5 to US$13 per person) and leads guided hikes to local hot springs and altars. Reservations are requested; all tours are conducted in Spanish.

Special Events

Totonicapán celebrates the Fiesta de Esquipulas on January 15 in Cantón Chotacaj, 3km from the parque; the festival of the Apparition of the Archangel Michael on May 8, with fireworks and traditional dances; the Festival of Traditional Dance on the last Sunday in June; and the Feria Titular de San Miguel Arcángel (Name-Day Festival of the Archangel Saint Michael) September 24 to 30, with the principal celebration being on September 29.

Places to Stay & Eat

On the way into town, one block before the parque, on the left is *Hospedaje San Miguel* (☎ *766 1452, 3a Calle 7-49, Zona 1*). It's reasonably tidy and good for the price. Rooms cost US$3.90/7.75 single/double with shared hot bath, US$5.35/9.75 with private bath. Next door, *Cafe and Comdeor Alex* is a clean and friendly place serving a hearty lunch for US$1.30. Continue on 3a Calle for a block toward the parque to *Restaurante La Hacienda*, which features steaks.

QUETZALTENANGO (XELA)

pop 101,000

Almost everyone calls Quetzaltenango by its Quiché Maya name: Xelajú, or simply Xela (**shay**-lah). The commercial center of southwestern Guatemala, Xela is Guatemala's second-largest city and the center of the Quiché Maya people. Towering over the city to the south is the 3772m Santa María volcano, with the active 2488m Santiaguito volcano on its southwestern flank.

Xela's good selection of hotels makes it an excellent base for day trips to hot springs, lakes and traditional villages. In recent years, Xela has built a worldwide reputation for its Spanish-language schools. Many students prefer them over those in Antigua because the environment here more closely approaches the total-immersion ideal of language study.

History

Quetzaltenango came under the sway of the Quiché Maya of K'umarcaaj in the 14th century. Before that it had been a Mam Maya town. See K'umarcaaj in the Santa Cruz del Quiché section, earlier, for more on this period.

With the mid-19th-century formation of the Federation of Central America, Quetzaltenango initially decided on federation with Chiapas and Mexico instead of with Central America. Later, the city switched alliances and joined the Central American Federation, becoming an integral part of Guatemala in 1840.

The late-19th-century coffee boom augmented Quetzaltenango's wealth. Plantation owners came to buy supplies, and coffee brokers opened warehouses. The city prospered until 1902, when a dual calamity – an earthquake and a volcanic eruption – brought mass destruction.

Still, Xela's position at the intersection of the roads to the Pacific Slope, Mexico and Guatemala City guaranteed it some degree of affluence. Today it's again busy with commerce.

Orientation

The heart of Xela is the Parque Centroamérica, which is shaded by old trees, graced with neoclassical monuments and surrounded by the town's important buildings. Most of the city's lodgings are within a couple of blocks.

Quetzaltenango has several bus stations. The largest and busiest is the 2nd-class Terminal Minerva, on 6a Calle in Zona 3 (on the western outskirts near Parque Minerva, next to the market). City bus Nos 2, 6 and 10 run between the terminal and Parque Centroamérica – look for 'Terminal' and 'Parque' signs in the front windows of the buses.

First-class bus lines have their own terminals. For locations, see Getting There & Away, later in this section.

INGUAT has free maps of Xela. Alfa Internacional (see Post & Communications, below) sells decent country maps.

Information

Tourist Offices The INGUAT tourist office (☎/fax 761 4931) is in the Casa de la Cultura (also called the Museo de Historia Natural), at the southern end of Parque Centroamérica. It's open 8 am to 1 pm and 2 to 5 pm weekdays, 8 am to noon Saturday, and has free maps and limited information about the town and the area, in Spanish and English.

QUETZALTENANGO (XELA)

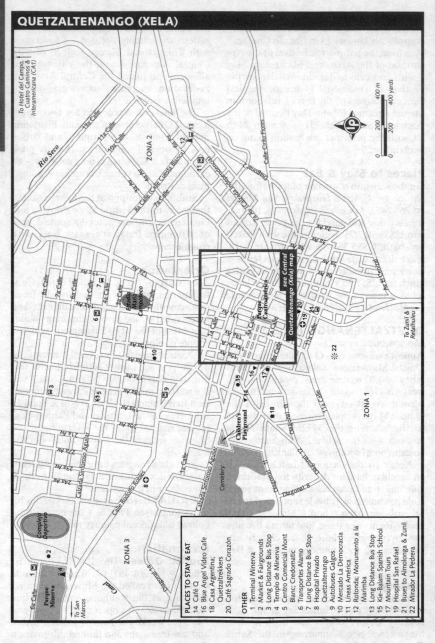

PLACES TO STAY & EAT
14 Café Q
16 Blue Angel Video Cafe
18 Casa Argentina;
    Quetzaltrekkers
20 Café Sagrado Corazón

OTHER
1 Terminal Minerva
2 Market & Fairgrounds
3 Long Distance Bus Stop
4 Templo de Minerva
5 Centro Comercial Mont
    Blanc; Credomatic
6 Transportes Alamo
7 Long Distance Bus Stop
8 Hospital Privado
    Quetzaltenango
9 Autobuses Galgos
10 Mercado La Democracia
11 Lineas América
12 Rotonda; Monumento a la
    Marimba
13 Long Distance Bus Stop
15 Kie-Balam Spanish School
17 Mountain Tours
19 Hospital San Rafael
21 Buses to Almolonga & Zunil
22 Mirador La Pedrera

Money Parque Centroamérica is the place for banks. Banco de Occidente, in the beautiful building on the plaza's north side, and Construbanco, on the east side, both change cash and traveler's checks and give cash advances on Visa cards. Banco Industrial, also on the east side, has a Visa ATM. A Bancared Visa ATM is adjacent to the Banrural on 12a Avenida, facing the park.

Credomatic (☎ 763 5722), in the Centro Comercial Mont Blanc, 4a Calle 18-01, Zona 3, gives cash advances on Visa and MasterCard. Banquetzal, on 14a Avenida, usually has the best exchange rate for US dollars.

Post & Communications The post office is at 4a Calle 15-07, Zona 1. The Telgua telephone office is nearby, upstairs in the shopping center at the corner of 15a Avenida and 4a Calle. It's open daily. For shipping packages, try International Bonded Couriers, 8a Avenida 6-23, Zona 1.

Several other places offer phone, fax, email and Internet services, including the following:

Alfa Internacional, 15a Avenida 3-51, Zona 1; open 9 am to 6 pm daily except Sunday

Alternativos, 16a Avenida 3-35, Parque Benito Juárez, Zona 3

Arytex, below Casa de la Cultura, Parque Centroamérica, Zona 1

Casa Verde, 12a Avenida 1-40, Zona 1

International Speed Calls, 15a Avenida 5-22, Zona 1

Marketing Communications, on 4a Calle next to the post office; open 9 am to 10 pm daily

Maya Communications, Bar/Salon Tecún, Pasaje Enríquez, just off Parque Centroamérica, Zona 1; open 8 am to midnight daily

Medical Services Hospital San Rafael (☎ 761 4414, 761 2956), 9a Calle 10-41, Zona 1, has 24-hour emergency service; Dr Oscar Rolando de León there speaks English. Hospital Privado Quetzaltenango (☎ 761 4381), Calle Rodolfo Robles 23-51, Zona 1, is another option. The Red Cross (Cruz Roja; ☎/fax 761 2746) is at 8a Avenida 6-62, Zona 1.

Emergency Call the national police at ☎ 761 2569, the municipal police at ☎ 761 5805, and the fire department at ☎ 761 2002.

Parque Centroamérica

This plaza and its surrounding buildings are pretty much all there is to see in Xela proper. At its southeast end, the Casa de la Cultura holds the **Museo de Historia Natural**, which has exhibits on the Maya, the liberal revolution in Central American politics and the Estado de Los Altos, of which Quetzaltenango was the capital. Marimbas, weaving, taxidermy and other local lore also claim places here. It's fascinating because it's funky. Hours are 8 am to noon and 2 to 6 pm weekdays, 9 am to 1 pm Saturday (US$1).

Continuing counterclockwise around the plaza, the once-crumbling **cathedral** has been rebuilt in the last few decades and was still being renovated at the time of writing. Up the block, the **Municipalidad** (Town Hall) follows the grandiose neoclassical style so favored as a symbol of culture and refinement in this wild mountain country. On the plaza's northwest side, the palatial **Pasaje Enríquez**, between 4a and 5a Calles, was built to be lined with elegant shops, but as Quetzaltenango has few elegant shoppers, it has suffered decline.

At the plaza's southwest corner, the **Museo del Ferrocarril de los Altos**, 12a Avenida at 7a Calle, is a museum focusing on the railroad that once connected Xela and Retalhuleu. Upstairs you'll find an **art museum** (mostly modern art) and schools of art, dance and marimba. Hours and admission are the same as at the Museo de Historia Natural.

Other Attractions

Walk north on 14a Avenida to 1a Calle to see the impressive neoclassical **Teatro Municipal**, which hosts regular performing-arts productions, from international dance recitals to the crowning of La Señorita Quetzaltenango.

Mercado La Democracia, in Zona 3, is about 10 blocks northwest of the plaza. To get there, walk along 14a Avenida to 1a Calle (to the Teatro Municipal), turn left, turn right onto 16a Avenida and cross the major street called Calle Rodolfo Robles; the market will be on your right. It's an authentic urban market with fresh produce and meat, foodstuffs and necessities.

Farther northwest, near the Terminal Minerva, is **Parque Minerva**. The neoclassical

Templo de Minerva here was built to honor the classical goddess of education and inspire Guatemalan youth to new heights of learning.

The **Mirador La Pedrera**, a 15-minute walk (or $4 taxi ride) from the center, offers a fine view of the city. A small store at the top sells snacks and drinks.

Activities

Hiking Volcán Tajumulco (4220m) is the highest point in Central America and a challenging two-day hike from Quetzaltenango. Volcán Santiaguito (2488m) and Volcán Santa María (3772m) can also be ascended from Xela. Quetzaltrekkers (☎ 761 2470, quetzaltrekkers@hotmail.com), Diagonal 12 8-37, Zona 1, is a recommended outfit specializing in these ascents. The Tajumulco trek costs US$35. All profits go to nonprofit Escuela de la Calle, which works with street children in Xela.
Web site: http://beef.brownrice.com/streetschool

Cycling Cycling is a great way to explore the surrounding countryside or commute to Spanish class. Fuentes Georginas, San Andrés Xequl and the steam vents at Los Vahos (see Around Quetzaltenango (Xela), later) are all attainable day trips. Vrisa Bicicletas (☎ 761 3862), 15a Avenida 0-67, Zona 1, rents mountain and town bikes for US$2.60 a day, US$9.65 a week.

Dance Lessons Salsa and merengue lessons are popular here. Two recommended places for dance offering one-on-one instruction are Latin Dance Lessons (☎ 763 0271), at the Casa Verde, 12a Avenida 1-46, Zona 1, and Latin Rhythm Dance Studio (☎ 761 2707, ☎ 767 2104 in the evenings, latinrhythm@latinmail.com), inside the Diego Rivera Café, 15a Avenida 5-31, Zona 1. An hour of instruction costs from US$2 to $4.50; slightly more for couples or groups.

Language Courses

In recent years, Xela has become well known for its Spanish-language schools. Unlike Antigua, Xela is not overrun with foreigners, but it does have a small student social scene. The Xela Pages Web site, www.xelapages.com/schools.htm, has information on many of the schools here.

Most of the city's Spanish schools participate in social-action programs with the local Quiché people and provide students an opportunity to get involved. The standard price is around US$110/120/130 per week for four/five/six hours of daily instruction, weekdays, including room and board with a local family, or around US$85 per week without homestay. The following are among the many reputable schools:

Academia Latinoamericana Mayanse (ALM; ☎ 761 2877), 15a Avenida 6-75, Zona 1 (Apdo Postal 375)

Casa Xelajú (☎ 761 9954, fax 761 5953, office@casaxelaju.com), Callejón 15, Diagonal 13-02, Zona 1; in the USA ☎ 512-416 6991 or write to PO Box 3275, Austin, TX 78764-3275; classes in Quiché and literature available
Web site: www.casaxelaju.com

Celas-Maya (☎/fax 761 4342, celasmaya@yahoo.com), 6a Calle 14-55, Zona 1; also offers classes in Quiché

Centro Bilingüe Amerindia (CBA; ☎ 761 1613, fax 761 8773, cba@guate.net), 7a Avenida 9-05, Zona 1 (Apdo Postal 381); in the USA ☎ 508-896 7589 or write to c/o Martha Holden, 37 Run Hill Rd, Brewster MA 02631-2331; classes in Mayan languages offered

Centro de Estudios de Español Pop Wuj (☎/fax 761 8286, popwujxelpronet.net.gt,), 1a Calle 17-72, Zona 1 (Apdo Postal 68); http://members.aol.com/popwuj/main.html; in the USA ☎/fax 707-869 1116, popwuj@juno.com, or write to PO Box 11127, Santa Rosa, CA 95406

Centro Maya de Idiomas (CMI; ☎ 767 0352, info@centromaya.org), 21 Avenida 5-69, Zona 3; classes offered in Quiché, Mam, Q'anjob'al and Tz'utuhil
Web site: www.centromaya.org

Desarrollo del Pueblo Spanish Language Institute (☎/fax 761 4624, desapu@hotmail.com), Diagonal 12 6-28, Zona 1

English Club International Language School (☎ 763 2198), Diagonal 4 9-71, Zona 9; classes in Spanish, Quiché and Mam

Escuela de Español Sakribal (☎/fax 761 5211), 10a Calle 7-17, Zona 1 (Apdo Postal 164); in the USA contact Kimberly Mueller (k_mueller@yahoo.com), 360 S Pleasant St No 2, Amherst, MA 01002

Guatemalensis Spanish School (☎/fax 765 1384, gssxela@infovia.com.gt), 19a Avenida 2-14, Zona 1 (Apdo Postal 53)
Web site: www.infovia.com.gt/gssxela

Instituto de Estudios de Español y Participación en Ayuda Social (INEPAS; ☎ 765 1308, fax 765 2584, iximulew@guate.net), 15a Avenida 4-59,

CENTRAL QUETZALTENANGO (XELA)

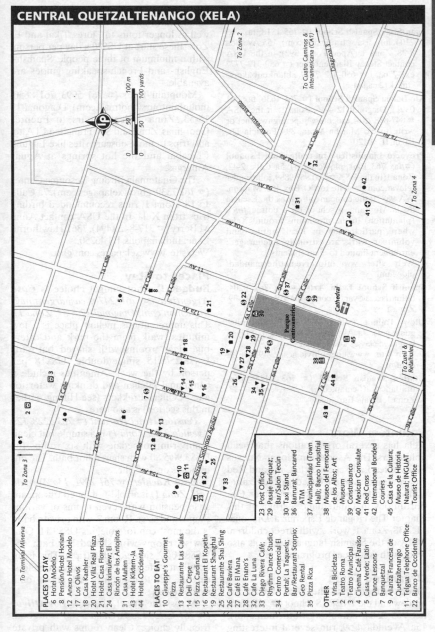

To Terminal Minerva

To Zona 3

To Zona 2

To Cuatro Caminos & Interamericana (CA1)

Diagonal 3

To Zona 4

Parque Centroamérica

Cathedral

To Zunil & Retalhuleu

100 m
100 yards

PLACES TO STAY
6   Hotel Modelo
8   Pensión/Hotel Horiani
12 Anexo/Hotel Modelo
17 Los Olivos
18 Casa Kaehler
20 Hotel Villa Real Plaza
21 Hotel Casa Florencia
24 Casa Iximulew; El
    Rincón de los Antojitos
31 Casa Mañen
43 Hotel Kiktem-Ja
44 Hotel Occidental

PLACES TO EAT
10 Giuseppe's Gourmet
    Pizza
13 Restaurante Las Calas
14 Deli Crepe
15 Pizza Cardinali
16 Restaurant El Kopetin
19 Restaurant Shanghai
25 Restaurante Shai Shing
26 Café Baviera
27 Café El Mana
28 Café Enano's
32 Café La Luna
33 Diego Rivera Café;
    Rhythm Dance Studio
34 Centro Comercial El
    Portal; La Taquería;
    Bar/Restaurant Scorpio;
    Geo Rental
35 Pizza Rica

23 Post Office
29 Pasaje Enriquez;
    Bar/Salon Tecún
30 Taxi Stand
36 Banrural; Bancared
    ATM
37 Municipalidad (Town
    Hall); Banco Industrial
38 Museo del Ferrocarril
    de los Altos; Art
    Museum
39 Construbanco
40 Mexican Consulate
41 Red Cross
42 International Bonded
    Couriers
45 Casa de la Cultura;
    Museo de Historia
    Natural; INGUAT
    Tourist Office

OTHER
1   Vrisa Bicicletas
2   Teatro Roma
3   Teatro Municipal
4   Cinema Café Paraíso
5   Casa Verde; Latin
    Dance Lessons
7   Banquetzal
9   Alianza Francesa de
    Quetzaltenango
11 Telgua Telephone Office
22 Banco de Occidente

Zona 1; in the USA contact Elliott Brown (☎ 607-273 8471); English and French spoken

Juan Sisay Spanish School (☎ 765 1318, fax 763 2104, info-sisay@trafficman.com), 15a Avenida 8-38, Zona 1 (Apdo Postal 392); in the USA contact Stacey Blankenbaker (☎ 650-312 7777 ext 7763, fax 650-312 7779, sblankenbaker@ sfmc.k12.ca.us)

Kie-Balam Spanish School (☎ 761 1636, fax 761 0391), Diagonal 12 4-46, Zona 1; in the USA ☎ 847-888 2514, moebius@superhighway.net or write to c/o Martha Mora, 894 Patricia Dr, Elgin, IL 60120

Proyecto Lingüístico Quetzalteco de Español (☎/fax 763 1061, plq@c.net.gt), 5a Calle 2-42, Zona 1; in the USA ☎ 800-963 9889, johnson@ televar.com or write to PO Box 452, Manson, WA 98831; the company also runs the Escuela de la Montaña, a school on a coffee *finca* (plantation) in the mountains around Xela, where participation in local culture and volunteer work are strongly encouraged; enrollment limited to eight students
Web site: www.infoserve.net/hermandad/ plqe.html

Spanish School Latin Arts (☎/fax 761 0204, latinartsxela@yahoo.com), 10a Avenida C-09, Zona 1

Ulew Tinimit (☎/fax 761 6242, utinimit@ guate.net), 7a Avenida 3-18, Zona 1; Mayan language classes also offered
Web site: www.unet.univie.ac.at/~a9509611/ ut.html

Utatlán Spanish School (☎ 763 0446, info-utatlan@trafficman.com), 12a Avenida 4-32, Zona 1, Pasaje Enríquez

Volunteer Work

Xela has several organizations that need volunteers. The Asociación Hogar Nuevos Horizontes, La Escuela de la Calle and Red International are all based in Quetzalte-nango. See the boxed text 'Volunteer Opportunities in Guatemala,' earlier in this chapter. The Hogar de Esperanza, Diagonal 11 7-38, Zona 1, works with street children. Many of the Spanish-language schools also work with volunteer programs.

Organized Tours

Thierry Roquet and the folks at Casa Ix-imulew and the INEPAS school (☎ 765 1308, fax 765 2584, iximulew@trafficman.com), 15a Avenida 4-59, run several interesting tours. Half-day tours include Fuentes Georginas, Los Vahos and San Francisco El Alto (US$32 for two people). Also offered

are camping trips to Lake Atitlán and the Santa María and Santiaguito volcanoes, as well as longer tours to Flores, Tikal and El Zotz; these start at US$20 a day per person, with a minimum of three people. Spanish-, English- and French-speaking guides are available.

Mountain Tours (☎ 761 5993, 761 8650, mountaintours@hotmail.com), Diagonal 13 15-53, Zona 1, leads tours to Fuentes Georginas, Zunil and San Francisco El Alto, and trips to more obscure sites like Laguna Chicabal and the hot springs at Aguas Amargas.

The Guatemala Birding Resource Center (☎ 767 7339, gbrc@xelapages.com), 7a Calle 15-18, Zona 1, runs recommended birding trips from Xela. In the USA contact Anne M Berry (☎ 317-842 1494), 7361 Hawthorne Lane, Indianapolis, IN 46250.
Web site: www.xelapages.com/gbrc

Places to Stay

Budget The hot budget choice is *Casa Argentina* (☎ 761 2470, casaargentina@ trafficman.com, Diagonal 12 8-37, Zona 1). This unpretentious, mellow place is a few minutes' walk from the park and offers big, clean rooms with shared bath for US$3.25/5.15 single/double, US$18 per person by the week. Amenities include a communal kitchen and drinking water for guests. Quetzaltrekkers (see Hiking, earlier in this section) is also here.

Pensión/Hotel Horiani (☎ 763 5228, 12a Avenida 2-23, Zona 1) is a simple but clean family-run hospedaje with six rooms for US$3.90/5.80 with shared hot bath. The entrance is on 2a Calle.

Casa Kaehler (☎ 761 2091, 13a Avenida 3-33, Zona 1) is an old-fashioned European-style pension with seven rooms of various shapes and sizes. Room 7, with private bath, is the most comfortable; it's US$9/11. Otherwise, rooms with shared hot bath are US$8/10/12 single/double/triple. This is an excellent, safe place for women travelers; ring the bell to gain entry. Ask about tours in the region.

Across the street, the new *Los Olivos* (☎ 761 0215, 13a Avenida 3-32) is a good, friendly choice. Clean rooms with private hot bath, cable TV, towels and drinking water are US$13/19.30/24/28 single/double/ triple/quad.

Casa Iximulew (☎ *765 1308, fax 765 2584, iximulew@trafficman.com, 15a Avenida 4-59, Zona 1*) has one clean, spacious room with shared warm bath for US$4.65/6.60 for one/two people or US$5.80/8.10 including breakfast at its adjoining restaurant, El Rincón de los Antojitos (see Places to Eat). The Casa also rents apartments, about a 10-minute walk from the town center, for US$70/235 a week/month furnished. Each has two bedrooms, a fully equipped kitchen, living room, courtyard and cable TV. Unfurnished apartments rent for US$150 a month. The busy Casa also offers tours and runs the INEPAS Spanish school. French, English and Spanish are spoken.

The friendly *Hotel Occidental* (☎ *765 4065, 7a Calle 12-23, Zona 1*) is right off the park and a good value. Clean and quiet rooms with quality beds are US$5.15/8.40 with shared hot bath, US$7/10.30 with private bath.

Southwest of the park is the huge old *Hotel Kiktem-Ja* (☎ *761 4304, 13a Avenida 7-18, Zona 1*). The 20 rooms, all with private bath and eight with fireplace, are on two levels around the courtyard, which also serves as a parking lot. Rooms hold one to eight people (US$15/20/25).

For long-term stays, check out *Hospedaje Tecún* (☎ *765 1203, 761 2382, 4a Calle 10-55, Zona 3*), about a 10-minute stroll from the center. This house has a kitchen, garden and communal space; private rooms rent for US$65 a month. Ask at the Bar/Salon Tecún (see Places to Eat) for information. You could also contact Señora Lidia de Mazariegos (☎ *761 2166, 4a Calle 15-34, Zona 1*), who rents fully furnished apartments with cable TV and free gas for the first month.

Mid-Range If you want to spend a little more for a lot more comfort, head straight for the family-run *Hotel Modelo* (☎ *761 2529, 763 0216, fax 763 1376, 14a Avenida A 2-31, Zona 1*). Pleasant small rooms with bath, cable TV and phone are US$25/28/31 single/double/triple in the main hotel (where three of the rooms have a fireplace) or US$17/20/24 in the equally comfortable *anexo* (☎ *765 1271*). The hotel's good dining room serves breakfast, lunch and dinner. Parking is available.

Hotel Casa Florencia (☎ *761 2326, 12a Avenida 3-61, Zona 1*), a few steps from the plaza, is run by a pleasant señora who keeps everything spotless. The nine spacious rooms, all with bath, cable TV and carpet, are US$20/25/30.

The comfortable *Hotel Villa Real Plaza* (☎ *761 4045, 761 6036, fax 761 6780, 4a Calle 12-22, Zona 1*) is half a block west of the park. Its 60 large, airy rooms, all with bath, cable TV and phone, are US$32/36/41. Amenities include a restaurant, bar, sauna and parking.

Casa Mañen (☎ *765 0786, fax 765 0678, casamannen@xela.net.gt, 9a Avenida 4-11, Zona 1*) is a quiet place with a romantic atmosphere, beautifully outfitted rooms, tranquil gardens and distinguished service. All nine rooms have traditional appointments, hand-carved furniture, tile floors, TV and private bath. Some rooms have a fireplace, and upstairs units have balconies and views. The standard rooms are US$35/45 single/double; two suites go for US$50. Breakfast is available and there's a rooftop terrace.

The *Hotel del Campo* (☎ *263 1665, fax 263 0074*), Km 224, Camino a Cantel, is Xela's most modern hotel. Its 96 rooms have showers and TV and are decorated in wood and red brick. The hotel also boasts an all-weather swimming pool. Rooms on the lowest floor can be dark, so get a room numbered in the 50s. Prices are reasonable: US$25/31/37. The hotel is 4.5km (a 10-minute drive) east of the town center, a short distance off the main road between Quetzaltenango and Cuatro Caminos; watch for signs for the hotel and for the road to Cantel.

Places to Eat

As with hotels, Quetzaltenango has a broad selection of places to eat. Cheapest are the food stalls in and around the small market to the left of the Casa de la Cultura, where snacks and substantial main-course plates are sold for US$1 or less.

An excellent place for Guatemalan home cooking is *Café Sagrado Corazón*, on 9a Avenida at 9a Calle, Zona 1. The gregarious mother-daughter team here serves delicious breakfast, lunch and dinner and always offers a vegetarian option. Lunch plates start at US$1.55. It's open 9 am to 9 pm Monday to Saturday, 9 am to 3 pm Sunday.

Cafe Baviera, on 13a Avenida at 5a Calle, is a European-style cafe serving good coffee roasted on the premises. Breakfast and other meals, pastries, snacks and alcoholic beverages are also served. It's open daily. Across the street, the friendly *Café El Mana* serves cheap and hearty breakfasts, lunches and dinners. Down the block on 5a Calle and in the same vein is the recommended *Café Enano's*. Here you can dig in to economical, big meals in a family atmosphere.

A popular spot with good food is *El Rincón de los Antojitos*, on 15a Avenida at 5a Calle, Zona 1. The menu is mostly Guatemalan, with a few concessions to international tastes and a variety of vegetarian dishes. The house specialty is *pepián* (chicken in a sesame sauce), a typical indigenous Guatemalan dish (US$5). Nearby, *Giuseppe's Gourmet Pizza (15a Avenida 3-68)* makes tasty and filling pizza and pasta at reasonable prices. It's open noon to 10 pm daily. Another place for pizza is the well-regarded *Pizza Rica (13a Avenida 5-42)*.

Cafe La Luna, on 8a Avenida at 4a Calle, Zona 1, is a welcoming little place to hang out, drink coffee, write letters and socialize. Similar is *Diego Rivera Café (☎ 761 2707, 15a Avenida 5-31, Zona 1)*, a laid-back place for coffee or a meal.

Popular with students, *Blue Angel Video Cafe (7a Calle 15-22, Zona 1)* offers a good variety of excellent, healthy foods at economical prices. All the salads and veggies are sterilized. Alcohol is served. It's open 2 to 11:30 pm daily (see Entertainment, later). Nearby, *Café Q (Diagonal 12 4-46)* has an interesting menu featuring vegetarian options like falafel, soy burgers and lentil soup. It's open 1 pm to 'late,' Monday to Saturday.

The *Bar/Salon Tecún*, in Pasaje Enríquez, is another popular gathering spot for foreigners. It offers good Italian food, along with plenty of drinking and socializing, from noon to 3 pm and 5 pm to 1 am daily.

Pizza Cardinali (14a Avenida 3-41, Zona 1) serves savory pizza and pasta dishes. In the same block, *Restaurant El Kopetin* has a family atmosphere and a long and varied menu ranging from Cuban-style sandwiches to filet mignon. An average full meal costs around US$5; alcohol is served. Both are open daily. A few doors down is *Deli Crepe*,

serving good portions of tasty food at great prices. Tacos, crepes, burritos and *licuados* come in an infinite variety here. Check out this place if you're traveling with children, as the atmosphere and food are kid-friendly.

A couple of other decent restaurants are in the Centro Comercial El Portal, 13a Avenida 5-38, Zona 1. *La Taquería* is a bright, cheerful Mexican restaurant with excellent prices; full meals are US$2 to US$4. *Bar/Restaurant Scorpio* has lunch specials or burgers for US$2.65, main dishes for US$4. The big fireplace is pleasant in the evening. Both have tables inside and out on the patio.

Restaurant Shanghai (4a Calle 12-22, Zona 1) features Guatemalan Chinese cuisine: *pato* (duck), *camarones* (shrimp) and other Chinese specialties cost about US$3.35 to US$5 per plate. Passable, cheap Chinese food is also served at *Restaurante Shai Shing (4a Calle 14-25)*.

The new *Restaurante Las Calas (14a Avenida A 3-21)* is heaven sent, serving some of the best meals around. Satisfying portions of chicken, fish or beef are well prepared and cost US$3. Also featured are paella and four types of flan. The service is top notch and there's an art gallery through the courtyard. Hours are 8 am to 9:30 pm daily. Don't be surprised if the restaurant's prices rise with its popularity.

The dining room of *Hotel Modelo (14a Avenida A 2-31)* serves breakfast and has good set lunches and dinners (US$5.50).

Entertainment

The Parque Central is a softly lit, pleasant (though chilly) place for an evening stroll.

Casa Verde (☎/fax 763 0271, 12a Avenida 1-40, Zona 1) is a happening venue for concerts, theater, poetry readings, films and other activities. Wednesday night features salsa dancing. It also offers board games and a restaurant/bar. Hours are 4 pm until around midnight, Tuesday to Saturday.

Performances and cultural events are also presented at the beautiful *Teatro Municipal*, on 1a Calle, and at *Casa de la Cultura (☎ 761 6427)* on the plaza's south side.

The *Blue Angel Video Cafe* (see Places to Eat, earlier in this section) is popular for evening socializing and shows nightly videos. Other places to catch a flick are *Cinema Café Paraíso* (*14a Avenida A 1-04*); *Alianza Francesa de Quetzaltenango* (*☎/fax 761 4076, 15a Avenida 3-64, Zona 1*); and *Teatro Roma*, on 14a Avenida A facing the Teatro Municipal.

For cocktails and carousing, head to the ever popular *Bar/Salon Tecún*, in Pasaje Enríquez (see Places to Eat, earlier).

Getting There & Away

Air Grupo TACA flies between Xela and Guatemala City.

Bus For 2nd-class buses, head to Terminal Minerva, on 6a Calle in Zona 3 (on the western outskirts near Parque Minerva, next to the market). Bus Nos 2, 6 and 10 run between the terminal and Parque Centroamérica (look for 'Terminal' and 'Parque' signs in the bus window). You can catch the city bus (US$0.05) to the terminal from 8a Calle at 12a Avenida or from 13a Avenida at 4a Calle in the town center.

The city bus drops you off a short walk from where the long-distance buses depart. To get there, you must cross through the market; keeping the park and taxis on your left, head toward the market stalls. A passage leads to the other side of the busy bus terminal.

Buses that depart from Terminal Minerva headed for the Interamericana also pick up passengers at bus stops at the corner of 19a Avenida and 7a Calle, Zona 3, at the corner of 13a Avenida and 4a Calle, and at the corner of 7a Avenida (Calzada Independencia) and 8a Calle (Calle Cuesta Blanca) at the *rotonda* (traffic circle) and the Monumento a la Marimba. You can board the buses at any of these stops, though your chances of getting a seat are much better if you board at the terminal.

Transportes Alamo, Líneas América and Autobuses Galgos, three 1st-class lines operating buses between Guatemala City and Quetzaltenango, each have their own terminals. Transportes Alamo (☎ 761 2964) is at 4a Calle 14-04, Zona 3. Líneas América (☎ 761 2063, 761 4587) is at 7a Avenida 13-33, Zona 2. Autobuses Galgos (☎ 761 2248) is at Calle Rodolfo Robles 17-43, Zona 1.

The following buses depart from Terminal Minerva, unless otherwise noted:

Almolonga (for Los Vahos; US$0.35, 10 minutes, 6km)
Buses depart every 15 minutes from 5:30 am to 5 pm, with a possible stop for additional passengers in Zona 1 southeast of the park.

Chichicastenango (US$1.50, three hours, 94km)
Buses depart at 6, 8:30, 9:30, 10:15 and 11 am and 12:30, 1:30, 2:30 and 4 pm. Or change at Los Encuentros.

Ciudad Tecún Umán (Mexican border; US$1.95, 2½ hours, 129km)
Buses leave every half hour, 5:30 am to 4:30 pm.

El Carmen/Talismán (Mexican border)
Take a bus to Coatepeque and change there for a bus to El Carmen. From Coatepeque it's two hours to El Carmen (US$1.65).

Guatemala City (US$3.60, four hours, 206km)
First-class buses with Transportes Alamo leave five times daily, with Líneas América six times daily and with Autobuses Galgos eight times daily, each departing from its own terminal (see above). First-class buses stop at Totonicapán, Los Encuentros (change for Chichi or Pana) and Chimaltenango (change for Antigua). Second-class buses (US$1.80) depart from Terminal Minerva every half hour, 3 am to 4:30 pm; these make many stops and take longer.

Huehuetenango (US$1, two hours, 90km)
Buses depart every half hour, 5:30 am to 5:30 pm.

La Mesilla (Mexican border; US$1.80, 3½ hours, 170km)
Buses depart every half hour, 5:30 am to 5:30 pm. Or take a bus to Huehuetenango and change there.

Momostenango (US$0.45, 45 minutes, 35km)
There are hourly buses, 6:30 am to 5 pm.

Panajachel (US$1.55, 2½ hours, 99km)
Buses depart at 5, 6 and 8 am, noon, 3 and 4 pm. Or take any bus bound for Guatemala City and change at Los Encuentros.

Retalhuleu (US$0.80, 1½ hours, 67km)
Buses depart every 20 minutes, 4:30 am to 6 pm. Look for 'Reu' in the bus window.

San Andrés Xequl (US$0.15, 40 minutes)
There are hourly buses, 6 am to 3 pm, or take any bus to San Francisco El Alto or Totonicapán, disembark at the Esso station at the Moreiria junction and flag a pickup from there.

San Francisco El Alto (US$0.25, one hour, 17km)
Buses depart every 15 minutes, 6 am to 6 pm.

San Martín Chile Verde (Sacatepéquez; US$0.25, 45 minutes, 25km)
Xelajú buses depart every 30 minutes, 6:30 am to 4 pm. Placard in the bus window will say 'Colomba' or 'El Rincón.'

Totonicapán (US$0.25, one hour, 30km)
Buses depart every 15 minutes, 6 am to 5 pm.

Zunil (US$0.25, 15 minutes, 10km)
Buses leave every half hour, 7 am to 7 pm, departing from Terminal Minerva, with a possible additional stop in Zona 4, southeast of the park.

Shuttle Minibus Pana Tours (☎/fax 763 0606), at 12a Avenida 12-07, Zona 1, operates shuttle service from Xela to Fuentes Georginas, Zunil, Guatemala City, Antigua, Chichicastenango, Panajachel and various other places around Guatemala.

Car Rental car companies in Xela include Geo Rental (☎ 763 0267), in the Centro Comercial El Portal, 13a Avenida 5-38, Zona 1; and Tabarini (☎/fax 763 0418), 9a Calle 9-21, Zona 1.

Getting Around
INGUAT has information on city bus routes. Taxis wait at the stand on the north end of Parque Centroamérica. Cab fare between Terminal Minerva and the city center is around US$3.

AROUND QUETZALTENANGO (XELA)
The beautiful volcanic countryside around Quetzaltenango makes for exciting day trips. The natural steam baths at Los Vahos are primitive; the baths at Almolonga are basic, cheap and accessible; and the hot springs at Fuentes Georginas are idyllic.

You can feast your eyes and soul on the wild church at San Andrés Xequl, hike to the shores of Laguna Chicabal from Xela, or simply hop on a bus and explore the myriad traditional villages that pepper this part of the highlands. Market days in the surrounding towns include Sunday in Momostenango, Monday in Zunil, Tuesday and Saturday in Totonicapán and Friday in San Francisco El Alto.

Los Vahos
Hikers will enjoy a trip to the rough-and-ready sauna/steam baths at Los Vahos (The Vapors), about 3.5km from Parque Centroamérica. To get there take a bus headed for Almolonga and ask to get out at the road to Los Vahos, which is marked with a small sign reading 'A Los Vahos.' From here

it's a 2.3km uphill walk (around 1½ hours) to Los Vahos. The views are remarkable. It's open 8 am to 6 pm daily (US$1.30).

San Andrés Xequl
About 10km northwest of Xela is San Andrés Xequl. Surrounded by fertile hills, this small town boasts perhaps the most bizarre church anywhere; Technicolor saints, angels, flowers and climbing vines share space with whimsical tigers and monkeys on its shocking-yellow façade. The village has no visitor facilities.

Take a northbound bus from Xela and get off at the Esso station at the Moreiria crossroads, then hail a pickup or walk the 3km uphill to town. Alternatively, you could cool your heels in Xela's terminal until a direct bus is ready to leave. Buses returning to Xela leave from the plaza until about 3 pm.

Zunil
pop 6000
Zunil is a pretty agricultural market town in a lush valley framed by steep hills and dominated by a towering volcano. As you approach from Quetzaltenango, you will see it framed as if in a picture, with its white colonial church gleaming above the red-tiled and rusted-tin roofs of the low houses.

On the way to Zunil the road passes **Almolonga**, a vegetable-growing town 6km from Quetzaltenango. Just over 1km beyond Almolonga is **Los Baños**, an area with natural hot sulfur springs. Several little places along here have bath installations; most are decrepit, but if a cheap hot bath is your desire, you may want to stop. Tomb-like enclosed concrete tubs rent for a few quetzals per hour.

Zunil, founded in 1529 as Santa Catarina Zunil, is a typical Guatemalan highland town. The cultivated plots, divided by stone fences, are irrigated by canals; you'll see the indigenous farmers scooping up water from the canals with a shovel-like instrument and throwing it over their plants. Women wash clothes near the river bridge, in pools of hot water that emerges from the rocks.

Things to See & Do Another attraction of Zunil is its particularly pretty **church**; the ornate façade, with eight pairs of serpentine columns, is echoed inside by a richly worked silver altar. On market day (Monday) the plaza in front of the church is bright with the predominantly red traditional garb of local people buying and selling goods.

Half a block downhill from the church plaza, the **Cooperativa Santa Ana** is a handicrafts cooperative in which over 500 local women participate. Handicrafts are displayed and sold here, and weaving lessons are offered. The cooperative operates 8:30 am to 5 pm Monday to Saturday, 2 to 5 pm Sunday.

While you're in Zunil, visit the image of **San Simón**, an effigy of a local Maya hero venerated as a (non-Catholic) saint. The effigy is moved each year to a different house; ask anyone where to find San Simón (local children will take you for a small tip). You'll be charged a few quetzals to visit him and take pictures. See the boxed text 'A God Is a God Is a God' in the Santiago Atitlán section, earlier in this chapter.

The festival of San Simón is held each year on October 28, after which the image is moved to a new house. The festival of Santa Catarina Alejandrí, official patron saint of Zunil, is celebrated on November 25. Almolonga celebrates its annual fair on June 27.

Getting There & Away From Zunil, which is 10km from Quetzaltenango, you can continue on to Fuentes Georginas (8km), return to Quetzaltenango via the Cantel road (16km), or alternately, take the jungle-bound toll road down the mountainside to El Zarco junction and the Carretera al Pacífico. Buses depart every 10 minutes, 6 am to 6:30 pm, for the return trip to Quetzaltenango (US$0.25, one hour).

Fuentes Georginas

This is the prettiest natural spa in Guatemala. Here, pools of varying temperatures are fed by hot sulfur springs and framed by a high wall of tropical vines, ferns and flowers. Fans of Fuentes Georginas were dismayed when a massive landslide caused by 1998's heavy October rains destroyed several structures (including the primary

bathing pool) and crushed the Greek goddess that previously gazed upon the pools. After restoration, spa regulars realized the landslide had opened a new vent. As a result, the water is hotter than ever. Though the setting is intensely tropical, the mountain air keeps it deliciously cool all day.

The site has a restaurant and three sheltered picnic tables with cooking grills (bring your own fuel). Down the valley a few dozen meters are seven rustic *cottages* that rent for US$4.50/5.80/7 single/double/triple. Each cottage has a shower, a BBQ area and a fireplace to ward off the nighttime chill (wood and matches are provided). Big-time soakers will want to spend the night, as cottage rates include all-day, all-night pool access.

Trails here lead to two nearby volcanoes: Volcán Zunil (three hours each way) and Volcán Santo Tomás (five hours each way). Going with a guide is essential. They're available (ask at the restaurant) for US$10 for either trip, whatever the number of people in the group.

Fuentes Georginas is open 8 am to 6 pm daily (US$1.30), bathing suits required.

Getting There & Away Take any bus to Zunil, where pickups wait to take you 8km up to the springs (30 minutes). Negotiate the price. They'll probably tell you it's US$4 roundtrip, but when you arrive at the top they'll say it's US$4 *each way*. If there are many people in the group, they may charge US$1 per person. Unless you want to walk back down the hill, arrange a time for the driver to return to pick you up.

You can walk from Zunil to Fuentes Georginas in about two hours. If you're the mountain goat type, you may enjoy the strenuous 8km climb.

Hitchhiking is not good on the Fuentes Georginas access road. You might luck out on weekends.

If you're driving, walking or hitching, go uphill from Zunil's plaza to the Cantel road (about 60m), turn right and go downhill 100m to a road on the left marked 'Turicentro Fuentes Georginas, 8km.' This road (near the bus stop on the Quetzaltenango-Retalhuleu road – note that there are three different bus stops in Zunil) heads off into the mountains; the baths are 9km from Zunil's plaza.

San Francisco El Alto

pop 3000

High on a hilltop overlooking Quetzalte-nango stands San Francisco El Alto, Guatemala's garment district. Every inch is jammed with vendors selling sweaters, socks, blankets, jeans and more. Bolts of cloth spill from overstuffed storefronts, and this is on the quiet days! On Friday the town explodes as the real market action kicks in. The large plaza, sur-rounded by the church and Municipalidad and centered on a cupola-like *mirador* (lookout), is covered in goods. Stalls crowd into neighboring streets, and the press of traffic is so great that a special system of one-way roads is established. Vehicles en-tering the town on market day must pay a small fee.

This is regarded as the country's biggest, most authentic market, but it's not nearly as heavy with handicrafts as are the markets in Chichicastenango and Antigua. Beware of pickpockets and stay alert.

Around midmorning when the clouds roll away, panoramic views can be had throughout town, but especially from the church roof. The caretaker will let you up.

Most people come to San Francisco as a day trip from Quetzaltenango, 17km away. This is just as well, since the lodging situa-tion here is dire. The big, new *Hospedaje Los Altos*, at 1a Avenida and 6a Calle, is your best bet. It charges US$6.45 per person for a room with private bath, and it has parking. For food try *Comedor San Cristóbal*, near the Hospedaje San Fran-cisco de Asís. A Banco de Commercio on the corner of 2a Calle and 3a Avenida changes dollars and traveler's checks.

The town's annual festival day is October 5.

Momostenango

pop 7500

Beyond San Francisco El Alto, 35km from Quetzaltenango, Momostenango is Guate-mala's famous center for *chamarras* – thick, heavy woolen blankets. The villagers also make ponchos and other woolen garments. As you enter the plaza, you'll see signs invit-ing you to watch blankets being made and to purchase the finished products. The best time to do this is market day, Sunday; haggle like mad. A basic good blanket costs around

US$13, perhaps twice as much for an extra-heavy 'matrimonial.'

Momostenango is also noted for its ad-herence to the ancient Mayan calendar and traditional rites. Ceremonies coordinated with the important dates of the calendar round take place in the hills about 2km west of the plaza. It's not easy to witness these rites, though Rigoberto Itzep Chanchavac (see Things to See & Do, later in this section) hosts ceremonial workshops.

Picturesque *diablo* (devil) dances are held in the plaza a few times a year, notably on Christmas Eve and New Year's Eve. The homemade devil costumes can get elabo-rate; all have masks and cardboard wings, and some go whole hog with fake fur suits, heavily sequined outfits and more. Dance groups gather in the plaza, dancing to a five-to 13-piece band and drinking alcoholic re-freshments during the breaks – they're most entertaining around 3 pm, but the festivities go on late into the night.

Information The Banrural on the plaza's south side changes dollars and traveler's checks. It's open 8:30 am to 5 pm weekdays, 9 am to 1 pm Saturday. The post office is across the park on the eastern corner. Medical services are available at the hospi-tal, on 1a Calle and 3a Avenida, near the bus stop.

For information on volunteer opportuni-ties, see that boxed text, earlier in this chapter.

Things to See & Do Momostenango's **Los Riscos** (The Crags) are peculiar geological formations on the edge of town. The eroded pumice spires rise into the air like some-thing from Star Trek. To get there, take the left heading downhill from the bus stop at the Artesanía Palecom; look for the sign that says 'Entrada.' At the first intersection, you'll see another sign hanging from a corner store reading 'A Los Riscos.' Cross the bridge and head uphill about 50m and take a right onto 2a Calle, continuing about 120m to the formations.

The Takliben May (Misión Maya) Waj-shakib Batz' (ritzep@hotmail.com), 3a Avenida A 6-85, Zona 3, at the entrance to town, teaches classes in **Mayan ceremonies**. Its director, Rigoberto Itzep Chanchavac, is a Maya priest who does horoscopes

(US$3.50 to US$7) and private consultations and hosts ceremonial workshops. His traditional Mayan *tuj* (sauna) is open 2 to 5 pm Tuesday and Thursday; advance notice required.

Web site: www.geocities.com/momostenango

Kieb Noj Language School (☎ 736 5196), 4a Avenida 4-49, Barrio Santa Isabel, offers **Spanish and Quiché classes.** Twenty five hours of instruction a week costs US$100, including a homestay and three meals a day.

Places to Stay & Eat Four blocks downhill from the bus stop, the *Hotel Estiver (1a Calle 4-15, Zona 1)* has eight rooms sharing two large bathrooms for US$2.60 per person, and two rooms with private bath for US$3.25 per person.

Other places are basic. The serviceable *Comedor y Hospedaje Paclom*, on 1a Calle just off the plaza, charges US$5.25 double for rooms sharing a hot bath. Next door, *Comedor Santa Isabel* has been recommended for its good cooking. Of the several basic comedores on the plaza, *Comedor Aracely*, below the church, has received high marks.

Getting There & Away You can catch an early bus from Quetzaltenango's Terminal Minerva, or at Cuatro Caminos, or at San Francisco El Alto. There are five or six buses daily; the last one back leaves Momostenango by about 4 pm.

Another bus route departs from the plaza's west side and goes through Pologuá, which might be an advantage to travelers heading for Huehue or La Mesilla.

Laguna Chicabal

This magical lake is nestled in a crater of the Chicabal Volcano (2712m). The 'Center of Maya-Mam Cosmovision,' Laguna Chicabal is an intensely sacred place and a hotbed for Mayan ceremonies. Mayan priests come from all over to make offerings here, especially around May 3. Visitors are definitely not welcome at this time. *Do not visit Laguna Chicabal the first week of May.*

The lake is a two-hour hike from San Martín Chile Verde (also known as San Martín Sacatepéquez), a friendly, interesting village about 25km from Xela and notable for the traditional dress worn by the village men. To get to the lake, head down from the highway toward town and look for the sign on your right (you can't miss it). Hike 45 minutes uphill through fields and past houses until you crest the hill. Continue hiking downhill for 15 minutes to the ranger station, where you pay a US$1.30 entrance fee. From here, it's another 30 minutes uphill to a mirador and then a whopping 615 steep steps down to the edge of the lake. Start early for the best visibility; clouds and mists envelop the volcano and crater by early afternoon.

The thick vegetation ringing the lake hides picnic tables and sublime campsites. Treat the lake with the utmost respect.

Xelajú buses leave Quetzaltenango every 30 minutes until 4 pm for San Martín Chile Verde; hail a pickup to get back.

HUEHUETENANGO
pop 20,000

Separated from the capital by mountains and a twisting road, Huehuetenango has that self-sufficient air exuded by many mountain towns. Coffee growing, mining, sheep raising, light manufacturing and agriculture are the region's main activities.

The lively Indian market is filled daily with traders who come down from the Cuchumatanes Mountains (highest in Central America). Surprisingly, the market area is about the only place you'll see traditional costumes in this town, as most of its citizens are ladinos wearing modern clothes.

For travelers, Huehue (**way**-way) is usually a leg on the journey to or from Mexico – the logical place to spend your first night in Guatemala. Though unattractive, the town is the perfect staging area for forays deeper into the Cuchumatanes or through the highlands on back roads.

Orientation & Information

The town center is 5km north of the Interamericana. The bus station and new market are 3km from the highway along the road to the town center (6a Calle).

Almost every service of interest to tourists is in Zona 1 within a few blocks of the plaza. The old market, bordered by 1a and 2a Avenidas and 3a and 4a Calles in Zona 1, is still the busy one, especially on Wednesday, market day.

GUATEMALA

HUEHUETENANGO

PLACES TO STAY	**PLACES TO EAT**	**OTHER**	23 Taxis
3 Hotel Zaculeu	5 La Cabaña del Café	1 Xinabajul Spanish	24 Church
4 Todos Santos Inn	6 Especialidades Doña Estercita	Academy	26 Multibanco; Bancared ATM
7 Hospedaje El Viajero	Cafetería y Pastelería	2 Fuel Station	28 Mexican Consulate;
8 Hotel Central	10 Steak House/Restaurante Las	13 Buses to Zaculeu	Farmacia del Cid
9 Hotel Gobernador	Brasas	16 Municipalidad (Town	29 Shuttle buses to Bus
12 Hotel Mary	11 Panadería Pan Delis; Cafetería	Hall)	Terminal
14 Hotel Lerri Colonial	Mary	17 Toilets	30 Toilets
20 Hotel Casa Blanca	15 Pizzería/Restaurante La Fonda	18 Post Office	31 Telgua Telephone Office
27 Hotel y Restaurante La	de Don Juan	19 Police	(Temporary)
Sexta	22 Mi Tierra Café; Internet Access	21 Interhuehue	
	25 Pan del Trigo		

A Bancared ATM accepting Visa cards is at the Multibanco branch at 4a Calle 6-81. Huehue has several other banks; most are also Western Union agents.

The post office is at 2a Calle 3-54, opposite Hotel Mary, half a block east of Parque Central. The Telgua office is at the Edificio Triángulo, 4a Avenida 6-54, four blocks south of Parque Central; this is its temporary address while the regular office next to the post office is being remodeled.

Just inside Mi Tierra Café (see Places to Eat, later in this chapter) is a business that offers Internet access for US$1.70 for 15 minutes. The cafe is open 9 am to 12:30 pm and 2:30 to 7 pm weekdays, 8 am to noon and 3 to 7 pm Saturday. Interhuehue, 3a

Calle 6-65B, offering access for the same price. It's open 8 am to 12:30 pm and 2 to 6 pm daily.

The Mexican consulate is on 5a Avenida 4-11, near the corner of 4a Calle, in the same building as the Farmacia del Cid; it's open 9 am to noon and 3 to 5 pm weekdays.

Parque Central

Huehuetenango's main plaza is shaded by nice old trees and surrounded by the town's imposing buildings: the Municipalidad (with its band shell on the upper floor) and the huge colonial church. The plaza has its own little relief map of Huehuetenango Department.

Zaculeu

The late Postclassic religious center of Zaculeu occupies a strategic defensive location. Surrounded by natural barriers – ravines and a river – on three sides, the site served its Mam Maya inhabitants well until 1525, when Gonzalo de Alvarado and his conquistadores laid siege to it, starving out the defenders.

The buildings in this park-like archaeological zone show a great deal of Mexican influence and were probably designed and built with little innovation. Visitors accustomed to seeing archaeological sites with ruddy bare stones and grass-covered mounds may find the stark tidiness of Zaculeu unsettling. Some of the construction methods used in the restoration were not authentic to the buildings, but the work goes further than others in trying to re-create the city's look from its glory days.

When Zaculeu flourished, its buildings were coated with plaster (Zaculeu means 'white earth' in the Mam language). In an attempt to be true to the original, the pyramids, ball courts and ceremonial platforms are today likewise covered in (thick and graying) plaster. But missing is the fresco decoration that the Mam no doubt applied to the wet plaster.

Zaculeu is 4km north of Huehuetenango's main plaza. It's open 8 am to 5 pm daily; admission is free. Cold soft drinks and snacks are available. You're allowed to climb on the restored structures but not on the grassy mounds that await excavation.

From Huehue, jitney trucks to Zaculeu depart from in front of the school, on 2a Calle near the corner of 7a Avenida, every 30 minutes (or possibly hourly), 7:30 am to 7:30 pm (US$0.13, 20 minutes). Or you can take a taxi from the central plaza for US$5 roundtrip, with a half hour to spend at the ruins. To walk all the way from the main plaza takes about 45 minutes.

El Mirador

This lookout up in the Cuchumatanes, 12km from town, offers a great view of Huehuetenango and the entire region. A beautiful poem, *A Los Cuchumatanes*, is mounted on plaques here. Getting to El Mirador is easiest with a private vehicle; a taxi from town costs around US$30 roundtrip.

Language Courses

The Xinabajul Spanish Academy (☎/fax 964 1518), 6a Avenida 0-69, offers one-to-one Spanish courses and homestays with local families.

Special Events

Special events in Huehue include the Fiestas Julias (July 13 to 20), held in honor of La Virgen del Carmen, Huehue's patron saint; and the Fiestas de Concepción (December 5 and 6), honoring the Virgen de Concepción. The Carrera Maratón Ascenso Los Cuchumatanes, a 12km run from Huehue's central plaza up to El Mirador, is held each fall and attracts hundreds of runners.

Places to Stay

Half a block northwest of the plaza, *Hotel Central* (☎ 764 1202, 5a Avenida 1-33) has 11 large, simple and well-used rooms with shared bath. Rates are US$2.30/3.90/5.40/6.95 single/double/triple/quad. The hotel's comedor serves cheap, hearty meals (US$1.55) daily except Sunday. It opens for breakfast at 7 am.

Hotel Lerri Colonial (☎ 764 1526, 2a Calle 5-49), near the plaza, has 21 superbasic rooms in a convenient location. Rates are US$2.60 per person with shared bath, $3.25 with private bath. The courtyard holds a comedor and parking. Across the street, *Hospedaje El Viajero* (2a Calle 5-30) is not as good, but it's cheap. Rooms cost US$1.95 per person with shared bath with cold showers.

Hotel y Restaurante La Sexta, on 6a Avenida near 4a Calle, has a restaurant, parking, international phone service and decent rooms arranged around a courtyard; US$3.90 per person with shared bath, US$7.80/9.65/19.30 single/double/triple with private hot bath.

A block east of the plaza, *Hotel Mary* (☎ 764 1618, 2a Calle 3-52) is a cut above the other places. Its 25 small rooms have bedspreads and other nice touches. Rooms cost US$6.45 single or double with shared bath; US$6.45/9.65/11.60 with private bath and cable TV. Hot water is available only three hours a day. A good cafeteria is attached.

Nearby, the friendly *Hotel Gobernador* (☎/fax 769 0765, 4a Avenida 1-45) is a good budget choice, with rooms for

US$3.75/5.30/7.75 with extra-hot shared bath, US$5.30/8.40/12.25 with private bath. Some rooms are less damp than others. A decent cafeteria here serves breakfast, lunch and dinner.

Todos Santos Inn (☎ *764 1241, 2a Calle 7-64*) is among Huehue's best budget hotels. Simple rooms with nice touches such as towels, bedside tables and reading lamps are US$3.25 per person with shared bath or US$5.15 with private bath. There's hot water sometimes.

Hotel Zaculeu (☎ *764 1086, fax 764 1575, 5a Avenida 1-14*), half a block northwest of the plaza, is a colonial-style place with a lovely garden courtyard, a good dining room, laundry service and 37 rooms, all with private bath and cable TV. Rooms in the older downstairs section (US$14.85/22/30/37) open onto the courtyard and are preferable to those at the back of the hotel. Rooms in the newer upstairs section are US$28/37/47.

Hotel Casa Blanca (☎/*fax 769 0775 to 0781, 7a Avenida 3-41*) is such a bright, pleasant hotel that it's tempting to say it's the best place in town. The 15 rooms, all with private bath and cable TV, cost US$23/29/35. Private parking is provided, and the hotel's two lovely restaurants are open 6 am to 10 pm daily.

Places to Eat

On 2a Calle, a block west of the plaza, is *Especialidades Doña Estercita Cafetería y Pastelería*, a tidy, cheerful place serving pastries and meals. Down the block, *La Cabaña del Café* serves Huehue's best coffee and is a popular dinner spot for pasta and other Italian fare. It's open 7 am to 9 pm daily.

Cafetería Mary and *Panadería Pan Delis* are next to Hotel Mary, at 2a Calle 3-52. Another good bakery is *Pan del Trigo* (*4a Calle 3-24*), which usually has wholegrain breads; the cafetería here offers breakfasts and dinners for US$2; open daily.

Mi Tierra Café (*4a Calle 6-46*) is a casual, upbeat place serving tasty food in the Western vein. Breakfast features croissants, omelets, pancakes and good coffee. Dinner tends towards Tex-Mex.

The *Pizzería/Restaurante La Fonda de Don Juan* (*2a Calle 5-35*), a few steps from the park, is a clean, reliable place serving pizza and a variety of other dishes. It's open daily.

One of Huehue's best restaurants is *Steak House/Restaurante Las Brasas*, on 4a Avenida just off 2a Calle, half a block from the park. A full meal of Chinese food or steak (the specialties here) will cost about US$7. Alcohol is served, and it's open daily.

For lovely surroundings, you can't beat the two restaurants at *Hotel Casa Blanca* (see Places to Stay, earlier). Breakfasts are around US$3.35, burgers and sandwiches US$2, and steaks under US$6. Both are open 6 am to 10 pm daily.

Getting There & Away

TACA offers one daily flight between Guatemala City and Huehue via Quiché.

The bus terminal is in Zona 4, 2km southwest of the plaza along 6a Calle. To reach Antigua, take any bus going to Guatemala City and change in Chimaltenango; for Lago de Atitlán, take the same bus and change at Los Encuentros. Buses serving this terminal include the following:

Aguacatán (US$0.65, 1½ hours, 22km)
    A dozen buses depart daily, starting at 6 am.
Cuatro Caminos (US$1, 1½ hours, 77km)
    Take any bus heading for Guatemala City or Quetzaltenango.
Guatemala City (US$3.75, five hours, 266km)
    Buses depart at 2, 3, 8:30, 9:30 and 10 am.
La Mesilla (Mexican border; US$1.15, two hours, 79km)
    Buses depart every half hour, 3:30 am to 5 pm.
Nebaj (US$1.70, six hours, 77km)
    There is one daily departure, at 11:30 am, via Aguacatán and Sacapulas.
Quetzaltenango (US$1, two hours, 90km)
    There are hourly buses, 4 am to 6 pm.
Sacapulas (US$1.05, four hours, 50km)
    Buses depart at 11 am and 12:30 pm; sometimes there's a 9:30 am departure, which is convenient if you're going to Cobán via Uspantán.
Soloma (US$1.55, four hours, 69km)
    Transportes Alicia has departures at 10:15 and 11 am.
Todos Santos Cuchumatán (US$0.90, 2½ hours, 40km)
    Buses depart at 11:30 am and 12:30, 1 and 4 pm; sit on the left for views.

Buses between the terminal and the center of town operate from 2 am to 11 pm; they depart from the corner of 4a Calle and 4a Avenida every five minutes in daytime, every half hour at night and before sunrise (US$0.06). Inner-city buses let you off two covered markets away from where the long-distance buses depart; walk through the markets to reach the terminal's other side. A taxi between the bus terminal and town center costs US$2.

Tabarini Rent A Car (☎ 764 1951, fax 764 2816) has an office in Hotel Los Cuchumatanes, Zona 7. Amigos Rent-A-Car (☎ 769 0775), 7a Avenida 3-41, is in Hotel Casa Blanca.

AROUND HUEHUETENANGO
Todos Santos Cuchumatán
pop 2000

The picturesque mountain town of Todos Santos Cuchumatán is one of the few Guatemalan towns in which the Mayan *tzolkin* calendar is still remembered and (partially) observed and both men and women still wear traditional Mayan clothing.

Saturday is market day, with a smaller market on Wednesday. Hiking is good in the local hills, and the town is home to a couple of language schools: La Hermandad Educativa, Proyecto Lingüístico (☎/fax 763 1061 in Xela, proylingts@hotmail.com, ☎ 800-963 9889 in the USA, johnsond@televar.com); and Nuevo Amanecer (mitierra@c.net.gt). There's a bank here.

Todos Santos is famous for the annual **horse races** held on the morning of November 1, which cap a week of festivities and follow an all-night drinking spree. Traditional foods are served throughout the day, and mask dances take place. **Christmas posadas** are held on each of the 10 days leading up to Christmas.

If you're coming to Todos Santos in winter, bring warm clothes.

Places to Stay & Eat Friendly, family-owned *Hospedaje Casa Familiar*, 30m south of the plaza, is clean but rustic. There's hot water and a sauna. The rooms have plenty of blankets, windows and a fine view; cost is US$2.60 per person. For a similar price, you can try the new *Hotelito Todos Santos*, on the road leading east from the plaza. Villagers often rent rooms in their homes; ask around.

Comedor Karin, downhill from the plaza, serves tasty, wholesome meals for US$1.30. *Comedor Katy* is another decent choice. For gringo-style food, head to *Restaurant Cuchumatan* on the main road into town. Nearby, *Restaurant Tzolkin* is another bar/restaurant serving pancakes, pizza and other Western fare.

Getting There & Away Buses operate between Huehuetenango and Todos Santos four times daily (US$0.90, 2½ hours, 40km). Ride on the top of the bus, if you like – the views are spectacular.

East Toward Cobán

The road from Huehuetenango to Cobán is rarely traveled, often rugged and always inspiring. It takes nearly three days of challenging travel and several transfers to make the 150km trip by bus, but it's well worth it for the views and tableaux of highland life. Adventure types craving more can continue the odyssey via the Cobán to Poptún route.

Starting high in the Cuchumatanes Mountains, you climb out of Huehuetenango en route to **Aguacatán**, from where you'll have panoramic views of pine-pocked slopes and the fertile valleys below. The road then snakes down through the Río Blanco valley to **Sacapulas**, along the Río Negro. This makes a good stopover. For more on the eastward continuation of this route, see Sacapulas to Cobán in the Quiché section, earlier.

LA MESILLA

Four kilometers separate the Mexican and Guatemalan immigration posts at La Mesilla/Ciudad Cuauhtémoc, and you'll have to drive, walk, hitch or take a collective taxi (US$1) between them. The strip in La Mesilla leading to the border post has a variety of services including a police station, post office and a Banrural.

Money changers at the border give a good rate if you're exchanging your dollars for their pesos or quetzals, a terrible one if you want dollars for your pesos or quetzals.

If you get marooned in La Mesilla, try *Hotel Mily's*, which has doubles with fan, cable TV and private hot bath for US$13. Though relatively pricey, this is the best place to bed down between here and Comitán (Mexico), some 85km down the road. Farther down the hill is the super-basic *Hotel El Pobre Simón*. A place to lay your head for the night here is US$1; the attached comedor is very popular with locals.

Good onward connections are available from the border post east to Huehuetenango and northwest to Comitán.

The Pacific Slope

Guatemala's steamy Pacific Slope is lush and tropical, with rich volcanic soil good for growing coffee at the higher elevations and palm oil seeds and sugarcane lower down. Along the coast, the temperature and humidity are uncomfortably high – day and night, rainy season and dry – and endless spoiled stretches of dark volcanic sand remind the visitor that beautiful beaches are not Guatemala's strong suit.

The Carretera al Pacífico (CA-2) runs from the border crossings at Ciudad Hidalgo/Tecún Umán and Talismán/El Carmen to Guatemala City. The 275 kilometers between the Mexican border at Tecún Umán and Guatemala City takes about four hours by car, five by bus – much less than the Interamericana between La Mesilla and Guatemala. If speed is your goal, CA-2 is your route.

Most of the towns along the Carretera al Pacífico are muggy and chaotic, and most of the beach villages are hot and dilapidated. Still, visitors willing to hopscotch around will find a few places worth checking out.

Retalhuleu, a logical stopping place if you're coming from Mexico, is pleasant and fun. Nearby is the active archaeological dig at Abaj Takalik. East of Retalhuleu, the pre-Olmec stone carvings at Santa Lucía Cotzumalguapa (8km west of Siquinalá) and La Democracia (9km south of Siquinalá) are unique.

The small beach village of Monterrico, with its nature reserve and wildlife preservation project, is buzzing with foreigners, who come from Antigua on weekends. Otherwise, the port town of Iztapa and its beach resort of Likín are fine if you simply must get to the beach.

CIUDAD TECÚN UMÁN
This is the preferable and busier of the two Pacific Slope border crossings; a bridge links Ciudad Tecún Umán (Guatemala) with Ciudad Hidalgo (Mexico). The border posts are open 24 hours a day, and banks change dollars and traveler's checks. Several basic hotels and restaurants are available, but you'll want to cross the border and get on your way as soon as possible.

Minibuses and buses run frequently between Ciudad Hidalgo and Tapachula, 38km to the north. From Ciudad Tecún Umán, frequent buses head east along the Carretera al Pacífico, stopping at Coatepeque, Retalhuleu, Mazatenango and Escuintla before climbing into the mountains toward Guatemala City. If you don't find a bus to your destination, take any bus to Coatepeque or, preferably, Retalhuleu, and change there.

EL CARMEN
Though you can cross at El Carmen, you will encounter much less hassle and expense if you cross at Tecún Umán.

A toll bridge across the Río Suchiate connects Talismán (Mexico) and El Carmen (Guatemala). The border posts are open 24 hours. Minibuses and trucks run frequently between Talismán and Tapachula, 20km away.

The few services that exist are basic. Buses run regularly from El Carmen to Malacatán, on the San Marcos-Quetzaltenango road, and to Ciudad Tecún Umán, 39km to the south. Fairly frequent 1st-class buses run to Guatemala City along the Carretera al Pacífico (US$6, five to six hours, 275km). Transportes Galgos (☎ 232 3661, 253 4868) is one company operating along this route. It runs five buses daily from El Carmen, stopping at Ciudad Tecún Umán, Coatepeque, Retalhuleu, Mazatenango and Escuintla (change for Santa Lucía Cotzumalguapa). Rutas Lima has a daily bus to Quetzaltenango via Retalhuleu and El Zarco junction.

EL ZARCO JUNCTION
About 40km east of the brash, ugly and chaotic commercial center of Coatepeque (many services if you get stuck) and 9km east of the turnoff for Retalhuleu on the Carretera al Pacífico is El Zarco, a major road

junction. The toll road (under US$1) heading north from here climbs more than 2000m in its 47km run to Quetzaltenango.

RETALHULEU
pop 40,000
The Pacific Slope is a rich agricultural region, and Retalhuleu – known simply as Reu (**ray**-oo) to most Guatemalans – is its clean, attractive capital. The balmy tropical air and laid-back attitude are restful, and the region's wealthy coffee traders come here to relax – splashing in the pool at the Posada de Don José or sipping a drink in the bar. The rest of the citizens get their kicks strolling through the palm-shaded plaza between the whitewashed colonial church and the wedding-cake government buildings. Tourists are something of a curiosity in Reu and are treated well.

Orientation & Information
The town center is 4km southwest of the Carretera al Pacífico along a grand boulevard lined with towering palms. The bus station is on 10a Calle between 7a and 8a Avenidas, Zona 1, northeast of the plaza. To

find the plaza, look for the twin church towers and walk toward them.

Most services are within blocks of the plaza. There is no official tourist office, but people in the Municipalidad, on 6a Avenida facing the church, will do their best to help.

Banco Occidente, on 6a Calle at 6a Avenida, and Banco Industrial, on 6a Calle at 5a Avenida, both change US dollars and traveler's checks and give cash advances on Visa cards. Banco del Agro, on 5a Avenida facing the park, changes US dollars and traveler's checks and gives cash advances on MasterCard.

The post office is on 6a Avenida between 5a and 6a Calles. Telgua, at 5a Calle 4-50, is half a block from the park.

Things to See & Do
The town's small **Museo de Arqueología y Etnología**, on 6a Avenida opposite the church, features archaeological relics. Upstairs are historical photos and a mural showing locations of 33 archaeological sites in Retalhuleu Department. It's open 8 am to 1 pm and 2 to 5 pm Tuesday to Sunday (US$0.15).

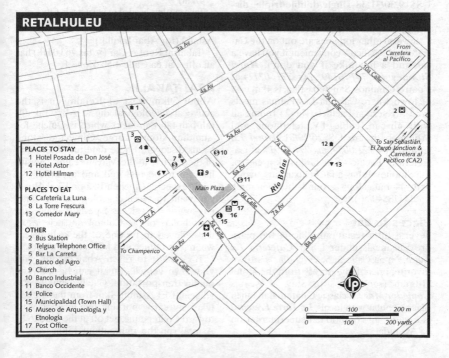

RETALHULEU

PLACES TO STAY
1 Hotel Posada de Don José
4 Hotel Astor
12 Hotel Hilman

PLACES TO EAT
6 Cafetería La Luna
8 La Torre Frescura
13 Comedor Mary

OTHER
2 Bus Station
3 Telgua Telephone Office
5 Bar La Carreta
7 Banco del Agro
9 Church
10 Banco Industrial
11 Banco Occidente
14 Police
15 Municipalidad (Town Hall)
16 Museo de Arqueología y
   Etnología
17 Post Office

Nonguests can swim in the pools at the Siboney and La Colonia Hotels (see Places to Stay, below). Cost is US$0.65 at the Siboney, US$1.65 at the Colonia (which also has a poolside bar and food service).

Places to Stay

For a real cheapie, try *Hotel Hilman (7a Avenida 7-99)*, which has simple rooms with private bath and fan for US$3.25 per person.

Half a block west of the plaza, the remodeled *Hotel Astor (☎ 771 0475, 771 2780, fax 771 2562, 5a Calle 4-60, Zona 1)* has a charming courtyard and 27 well-kept rooms, each with ceiling fan, private bath and cable TV. The upstairs rooms are new; the downstairs ones have more atmosphere. Rates are US$13/23 single/double; parking is available.

The nicest place is *Hotel Posada de Don José (☎ 771 0963, 771 0841, ☎/fax 771 1179, 5a Calle 3-67, Zona 1)*, across the street from the railway station and two blocks northwest of the plaza. On weekends Don José is often filled; at other times you can get an air-conditioned room with cable TV, telephone and private bath for US$19.30/31/38 single/double/triple; discounts may be offered. Amenities include a swimming pool, cafe and restaurant.

Several other lodgings are out on the Carretera al Pacífico – convenient if you have a car and a hot hike if you don't. *Hotel Siboney (☎ 771 0149, fax 771 0711)*, at Cuatro Caminos, San Sebastian, is 4km east of town where Calzada Las Palmas meets the Carretera al Pacífico. The 25 rooms, all with air-con, cable TV, telephone and private bath, are US$26/29/31. *Hotel La Colonia (☎ 771 0054, fax 771 0191)*, at Carretera al Pacífico Km 178, is 1km east of the Siboney. It has a fairly luxurious layout, with 44 bungalows around the swimming pool (US$40/50).

Places to Eat

Several little restaurants facing the plaza provide meals under US$3. *Cafetería La Luna*, on 5a Calle at 5a Avenida, is a town favorite; open daily. Across from the Hotel Hilman (see Places to Stay, above) is *Comedor Mary*, a classic Guatemalan lunch place popular with locals. *La Torre Frescura* is a giant, air-conditioned supermarket on 5a Avenida.

For the best meal in town, try *Hotel Posada de Don José* (see Places to Stay, above), where the pleasant restaurant offers beef and chicken plates for US$4 to US$6 and a big, full meal for US$7 to US$10. Breakfast is served here as well.

For cocktails, check out *Bar La Carreta (5a Calle 4-50)*, next to the Hotel Astor.

Getting There & Away

There are daily TACA flights (☎ 334 7722 for reservations) between Guatemala City and Reu.

As Reu is the most important town on the Carretera al Pacífico, transport is easy. Most buses stop at the city's bus station, on 10a Calle between 7a and 8a Avenidas, Zona 1, about 400m northeast of the plaza. Long-distance buses include the following:

Ciudad Tecún Umán (US$1.65, 1½ hours, 78km)
   Buses depart every 20 minutes, 5 am to 10 pm.
Guatemala City (US$3.65, three hours, 186km)
   Buses depart every 15 minutes, 2 am to 8:30 pm.
Quetzaltenango (US$0.80, 1½ hours, 67km)
   Buses depart every 15 minutes, 3 am to 7 pm.
Santa Lucía Cotzumalguapa (US$2.60, two hours, 97km)
   Take any bus headed to Guatemala City.

Local buses go to Champerico and El Asintal (for Abaj Takalik).

Tabarini Rent A Car (☎/fax 763 0418) has an office at 6a Calle 4-50, Zona 1.

ABAJ TAKALIK

About 30km west of Retalhuleu is the active archaeological dig at Abaj Takalik (ah-**bah**-tah-kah-**leek**), which is Quiché for 'standing stone.' Large 'Olmecoid' stone heads discovered here date the site as one of the earliest in the Mayan realm. The site has yet to be restored and prettified, so don't expect a Chichén Itzá or Tikal. But if you want to see archaeology as it's done, pay a visit. This site is especially important for scholars of pre-Columbian societies as it's believed to be one of the only places where the Olmec and Maya lived together.

It's easiest to reach Abaj Takalik with your own vehicle, but it can be done by public transportation. Catch a bus to the village of El Asintal, 4km from the site. Or take any early morning bus heading west toward Coatepeque, get off at the road to El Asintal (on the right, about 15km west of

Retalhuleu along the Carretera al Pacífico), and walk the 5km to the village (you may have some luck hitching). Pickups at El Asintal provide transportation to Abaj Takalik. Spanish-speaking guides are available at the site entrance.

CHAMPERICO

Built as a coffee-shipping point during the late 19th century, Champerico, 38km southwest of Retalhuleu, is a tawdry, sweltering, dilapidated place that sees few tourists. Despite this ickiness, it's one of the easiest beaches to access on a day trip from Xela, and beach-starved foreigners still try their luck here. The town has several cheap hotels and restaurants.

SANTA LUCÍA COTZUMALGUAPA

pop 24,000

About 100km east of Retalhuleu is the unexciting but historically important town of Santa Lucía Cotzumalguapa. In the sugarcane fields and fincas near town stand great stone heads carved with grotesque faces and fine relief scenes. Who carved these ritual objects, and why, remains a mystery.

The people are descended from the Pipil, an Indian culture known to have historic, linguistic and cultural links with the Nahuatl-speaking peoples of central Mexico. In early Classic times, the Pipil grew cacao, the currency of the time. They were obsessed with the Mayan/Aztec ball game and with the rites and mysteries of death. Pipil art, unlike the flowery, almost romantic Mayan style, is cold, grotesque and severe, but it's finely done. How these 'Mexicans' ended up in the midst of Maya territory remains unexplained.

Orientation

Santa Lucía Cotzumalguapa is northwest of the Carretera al Pacífico. In its main square, several blocks from the highway, are copies of some of the region's famous carved stones. A few basic hotels and restaurants are available in town.

The main archaeological sites to visit are Bilbao, a finca right on the outskirts of town; Finca El Baúl, a large plantation farther from town, at which there are two sites (a hilltop site and the finca headquarters); and

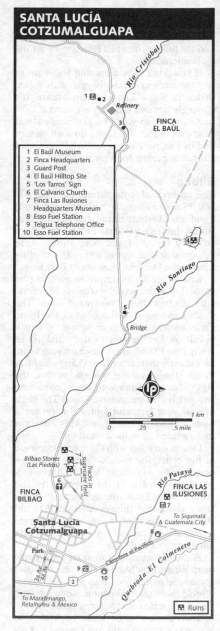

SANTA LUCÍA COTZUMALGUAPA

1 El Baúl Museum
2 Finca Headquarters
3 Guard Post
4 El Baúl Hilltop Site
5 'Los Tarros' Sign
6 El Calvario Church
7 Finca Las Ilusiones Headquarters Museum
8 Esso Fuel Station
9 Telgua Telephone Office
10 Esso Fuel Station

Finca Las Ilusiones, which has collected most of its findings into a museum near the finca headquarters. Of these sites, Bilbao and the hilltop site at El Baúl are by far the most interesting.

If you don't have a car and you want to see the sites in a day, haggle with a taxi driver in Santa Lucía's main square. It's cloyingly hot and the sites are several kilometers apart, so you'll be glad you rode at least part of the way. If you do it all on foot and by bus, pack a lunch; the hilltop site at El Baúl is perfect for a picnic.

Bilbao

This ceremonial center flourished about AD 600. Plows have unearthed (and damaged) hundreds of stones during the last few centuries; thieves have carted off many others. In 1880 many of the best stones were removed to museums abroad, including nine in the Dahlem Museum in Berlin.

Known locally as simply *las piedras* (the stones), this site actually consists of several sites deep within a sugarcane finca. The fields come right to the edge of the town. From Santa Lucía's main square, go north uphill on 3a Avenida to the outskirts of town. Pass El Calvario church on your right, and shortly thereafter turn sharply right. A hundred meters along, this road veers to the right but an unpaved road continues straight; follow the unpaved road. The fields are on your left, and you will soon see a path cut into the cane. Local kids will show up to guide you in for a small tip.

One stone is flat with three figures carved in low relief; the middle figure's ribs show prominently, as though he were starving. A predatory bird is in the upper left-hand corner. Holes in the middle-right part of the stone show that thieves attempted to cut the stone. Another stone is an elaborate relief showing cacao bean pods, fruit, birds, animals and a ball game.

Although some of the stones are badly worn, others bear Mexican-style circular date glyphs and more mysterious patterns that resemble those used by people along the Gulf Coast of Mexico near Villahermosa.

To continue to El Baúl, backtrack to where you turned right just beyond El Calvario church. Buses to El Baúl pass this point every few hours; you can also hitch-

hike. If driving, you'll have to return to the town center along 4a Avenida and come back out on 3a Avenida, as these roads are one-way.

Finca El Baúl

Just as interesting is the hilltop site at El Baúl, an active place of worship for locals. Some distance from the site on another road, next to the finca headquarters, is the finca's private museum of stones uncovered on the property.

El Baúl is 4.2km northwest of El Calvario church. From the church (or the intersection just beyond it), go 2.7km to a fork in the road just beyond a bridge; look for the 'Los Tarros' sign – buses will go up to here. Take the right fork (an unpaved road). From the Los Tarros sign it's 1.5km to the point where a dirt track crosses the road; on your right is a tree-covered 'hill' in the midst of flat fields. It's actually a great, unrestored temple platform. Make your way across the field and around the hill's south side, following the track to the top. If you have a car, you can drive to within 50m of the top. If you visit on a weekend, you may find worshipers here; people have been coming to pay homage to the idols for over 1400 years.

Of the two stones here, the great grotesque half-buried head is the more striking. The elaborate headdress, 'blind' eyes with big bags underneath, beaklike nose and shit-eating grin seem at odds with the blackened face and its position, half-buried in the ancient soil. The head is stained with candle wax, liquor and the smoke and ashes of incense fires – all part of worship. The other stone is a relief carving of a figure surrounded by circular motifs that may be date glyphs. A copy of this stone is in Santa Lucía's main square.

From the hilltop site, backtrack 1.5km to the fork with the Los Tarros sign. Take the other fork this time, and follow the paved road 3km to the headquarters of Finca El Baúl. (If you're on foot, you can walk from the hilltop site back to the unpaved road and straight across it, continuing on the dirt track. This will eventually bring you to the asphalt road that leads to the finca headquarters. When you reach the road, turn right.) Buses trundle along this road every

GUATEMALA

few hours, shuttling workers between the refinery and the town center.

Approaching the finca headquarters (6km from Santa Lucía's main square), cross a narrow bridge. Continue uphill and you will see the entrance on the left, marked by a machine-gun pillbox. Beyond, you pass workers' houses and a sugar refinery on the right and finally come to the headquarters, guarded by several men with rifles. Ask permission to visit the museum and a guard will unlock the gate.

Within the gates, sheltered by a palapa, are numerous sculpted figures and reliefs found on the plantation, some of which are very fine. Unfortunately, nothing is labeled.

Finca Las Ilusiones

The third site is very close to Bilbao – indeed, this is the finca that controls the Bilbao cane fields – but, paradoxically, access is more difficult. Your reward is the chance to view hundreds of objects that have been collected from the fields over the centuries.

Leave the town center heading east along Calzada 15 de Septiembre, which joins the highway at an Esso station. Go northeast for a short distance, then take an unpaved road on the left (just before another Esso station); this road leads 1km to Finca Las Ilusiones and its museum. If the key-keeper isn't around, you're limited to the many stones collected around the outside of the museum.

Getting There & Away

Esmeralda 2nd-class buses shuttle between Santa Lucía Cotzumalguapa and Guatemala City (4a Avenida at 2a Calle, Zona 9) every half hour or so between 6 am and 5 pm, charging US$1.50 for the 90km, two-hour ride. You can also catch any bus traveling along the Carretera al Pacífico between Guatemala City and such points as Mazatenango, Retalhuleu or the Mexican border.

To travel between La Democracia and Santa Lucía, catch a bus running along the Carretera al Pacífico toward Siquinalá (8km) and change there for La Democracia.

Between Santa Lucía and Lago de Atitlán you will probably have to change buses at Cocales junction, 23km west of Santa Lucía and 58km south of Panajachel.

LA DEMOCRACIA
pop 4200

South of Siquinalá, 9.5km along the road to Puerto San José, is La Democracia, a nondescript Pacific Slope town that's always hot. Like Santa Lucía Cotzumalguapa, La Democracia is in the midst of a region populated from early times – according to some archaeologists – by cultures with mysterious connections to Mexico's Gulf Coast.

At the Monte Alto archaeological site, on the outskirts of La Democracia, huge basalt heads have been found. Though cruder, the heads resemble those carved by the Olmec near Veracruz several thousand years ago.

Today these heads are arranged around La Democracia's main plaza. As you come into town from the highway, follow signs to the museo, which will lead you left, then left again, and left yet again.

Facing the plaza, along with the church and the modest Palacio Municipal, is the small, modern Museo Rubén Chevez Van Dorne, with other fascinating archaeological finds. The star is an exquisite jade mask. Smaller figures, 'yokes' used in the ball game, relief carvings and other objects make up the rest of this important small collection. On the walls are overly dramatic paintings of Olmecoid scenes. A rear room has more paintings and lots of potsherds only an archaeologist could love. The museum is open 8 am to noon and 2 to 5 pm (US$0.50).

Places to Eat

La Democracia has no places to stay and only a few basic and ill-supplied eateries; it's best to bring your own food and buy drinks at the plaza. *Café Maritza*, next to the museum, is a picture-perfect hot-tropics hangout with a *rockola* (jukebox) blasting music and a small crew of locals sipping beers.

Getting There & Away

Chatla Gomerana, Muelle Central, Terminal de Buses, Zona 4, Guatemala City, has buses every half hour from 6 am to 4:30 pm (US$1, two hours, 92km). Buses stop at Escuintla, Siquinalá (change for Santa Lucía), La Democracia and Sipacate.

ESCUINTLA

Surrounded by rich, green foliage, Escuintla should be a relaxed tropical idyll. But it's actually a hot, dingy, dilapidated industrial city that's important to the Pacific Slope's economy but not to travelers, except to change buses. Inhabited by Pipils before the conquest, it's now solidly ladino. If you're stranded, try *Hotel Costa Sur* (☎ 888 1819, *12a Calle 4-13*), two blocks north of the bus terminal. Rooms with private hot bath are US$7.75/9.65 single/double. There's a restaurant and parking.

Most people know Escuintla for its bus terminal, in the southern part of town; this is where you catch buses to Antigua, at 7 am and 1 pm (US$0.65, three to four hours), Puerto San José, Pueblo Viejo and Iztapa. Buses for Guatemala City leave frequently from the main plaza. Most buses to the border with El Salvador go through Chiquimulilla.

AUTOSAFARI CHAPÍN

Autosafari Chapín (☎ 363 1105, fax 337 1274), at Carretera al Pacífico Km 87.5, is a drive-through safari park and animal conservation project. Species include white-tailed deer, peccaries, macaws and nonnative species such as lions, rhinos and leopards. The park has a restaurant and pool; admission is US$4.50. Guatemala City's Delta y Tropical, 1a Calle at 2a Avenida, Zona 4, has buses every 30 minutes via Escuintla (US$1, 1½ hours, 88km), or you can take any bus going from Escuintla to El Salvador. By car, the Autosafari is about 30km from Escuintla (toward Taxisco) on the Carretera al Pacífico.

PUERTO SAN JOSÉ,
LIKÍN & IZTAPA

Puerto San José, Guatemala's most important seaside resort, leaves much to be desired. If you're eager to get into the Pacific surf, head south from Escuintla 50km to Puerto San José and neighboring settlements.

Puerto San José (population 14,000) was Guatemala's most important Pacific port in the latter half of the 19th century and well into the 20th. Now superseded by Puerto Quetzal to the east, the city languishes. Its beach, inconveniently located across the Canal de Chiquimulilla, is reached by boat. You'd do better to head west along the coast 5km to Balneario Chulamar, which has a nicer beach and a suitable hotel or two.

About 5km east of Puerto San José is **Balneario Likín**, Guatemala's only upmarket Pacific resort, beloved by well-to-do families from Guatemala City.

Another 12km east of Puerto San José is **Iztapa**, Guatemala's first Pacific port, used by none other than Pedro de Alvarado in the 16th century. When Puerto San José was built in 1853, Iztapa's reign as the port of the capital city came to an end, and the city relaxed into a tropical torpor from which it has yet to emerge.

Iztapa has gained notoriety as a premier **deep-sea fishing** spot. World records have been set here and enthusiasts can fish for marlin, sharks and yellowfin tuna, among others. Aside from fishing, lounging is the prime pastime. The town has a post office but no bank.

Should you want to stay, check out *Sol y Playa Tropical* (☎ 881 4365/6, *1a Calle 5-48)*, which has a pool, restaurant and clean, airy rooms with fans and bath for US$10.65/21 single/double. Rates are lower in the off season. *Hotel Posada María del Mar* (☎ 881 4055), across from the post office, rents rooms for US$6.45 double without bath, US$11 with private bath.

The bonus about Iztapa is that you can catch a Transportes Pacífico bus from the market in Zona 4 in Guatemala City all the way here (four hours), or pick it up at Escuintla (one hour) or Puerto San José. You can also get to Monterrico from here by catching one of the frequent *lanchas* (US$0.50) across the Canal de Chiquimulilla to Pueblo Viejo and transferring to a bus.

MONTERRICO

The coastal area around Monterrico is a totally different Guatemala. Life here is imbued with a sultry, tropical flavor that's more relaxed and inviting than anywhere else on the Pacific Slope. The architecture, too, is different; wooden slat walls and thatched roofs prevail over the cement walls and corrugated-tin roofs common elsewhere.

Monterrico is probably the best spot in Guatemala for a weekend beach break. Quiet on weekdays, on weekends and holidays it teems with families. It's also becoming popular with foreigners. The village has a post office (on Calle Principal) but no bank.

A few small, inexpensive hotels front the beach, which is dramatic here; powerful surf and riptides collide at odd angles. Swim with caution. Behind the beach, on the other side of town, is a large network of mangrove swamps and canals, part of the 190-km Canal de Chiquimulilla. Also in the area are a large wildlife reserve and a center for the hatching and release of sea turtles and caimans.

Things to See & Do

A big attraction here is the **Biotopo Monterrico-Hawaii**, a 20-km-long nature reserve of coastal mangrove swamps filled with bird and aquatic life. The reserve is a breeding area for endangered leatherback and ridley turtles, who lay their eggs on the beach in many places along the coast.

Canals lace the swamps, connecting 25 lagoons hidden among the mangroves. Boat tours of the reserve, going through the swamps and visiting several of the lagoons, take around two hours and cost US$8 for two passengers. It's best to go early in the morning, when you'll see the most wildlife. Bring binoculars.

To arrange a boat tour, stop by the **Tortugario Monterrico** visitor's center, a short walk east (left, if you're facing the sea) down the beach from the Monterrico hotels. Other villagers also offer boat tours, but the guides who work at the Tortugario are particularly concerned with wildlife. At the visitor's center, you'll learn about the endangered species raised here, including leatherback, olive ridley and green sea turtles, caimans and iguanas. Also here is an interesting interpretive trail. The center is open 8 am to noon and 2 to 5 pm daily.

The **Reserva Natural Hawaii** is operated by the Asociación de Rescate y Conservación de Vida Silvestre (Arcas; Association to Rescue and Conserve Wildlife), which operates a sea turtle hatchery on the beach 8km east of Monterrico. Volunteers are welcome year-round, but hatching season is from June to November, with

A Race to the Sea

Every Saturday from September to January, a delightful ritual takes place at sunset on Monterrico's beach. Workers from the Tortugario Monterrico walk out on the beach carrying big plastic tubs and two long ropes. They lay one rope out along the beach at a certain distance from the waterline and lay the other parallel to the first, several yards away. Tourists from the beach hotels gather around; come up to see what's going on and you'll find out the plastic tubs are full of baby sea turtles!

Pick a likely looking turtle out of the tub, make a small donation (less than US$2) to support the *tortugario* (turtle hatchery), and line up behind the rope farthest from the waves. It's an amazing feeling to hold the baby sea turtle in your hand. On the count of three, everyone releases their turtles, which make a frantic scramble toward the sea. If yours is the first to reach the rope closer to the waves, you'll win a free meal for two at one of the Monterrico hotels. Eventually, all the turtles reach the water and are washed away by the waves as the sun sinks.

The race is not only a fun chance to win a free dinner, it's also poignant, as you consider the fate of 'your' little sea turtle. The turtles are released two to three days after they hatch. They're released in a group to give them a better chance of survival. Scientists say that on this race across the sand to the sea, the tiny turtles are being imprinted with information about their place of birth (the components of the sand, the water etc). This enables them to return to this exact spot to lay eggs when they are adults. Most of them won't make it to adulthood. But the efforts of conservation groups such as the tortugario are giving the endangered turtles a better chance.

– Nancy Keller

August and September being the peak months. Volunteers are charged US$25 for a room; homestay options are available. See the boxed text 'Volunteer Opportunities in Guatemala' in the Facts for the Visitor

section, earlier in this chapter, for more about Arcas.

Places to Stay & Eat

Monterrico has several simple hotels near the beach, most with restaurants. From where you alight from La Avellana boat (see Getting There & Away, below), it's about a 15-minute walk through the village to the beach and hotels. Alternatively, if you take the bus from Pueblo Viejo, you'll have a five-minute walk down Calle Principal to the beach. If you brought a vehicle across on a car ferry, you can park it at any of the hotels. Coming from Calle Principal, head left to reach the following cluster of hotels, most of which offer discounts for stays of three nights or more.

Hotel Baule Beach (☎ 473 6196) is an insanely popular hotel run by former Peace Corps volunteer Nancy Garver. Throngs of foreign students choke the place on weekends, so if you want to party with other travelers, head here. Ragged, cleanish rooms with private bath, right on the beach, cost US$7.50/12.60/17 single/double/triple; bigger rooms accommodate up to six people. Meals are reasonably priced. Current transportation schedules are posted here.

The next place over is the new *Hotel El Mangle* (☎ 369 7631), where the clean, comfortable rooms have fans, mosquito nets, private baths and quality beds – a good value at US$15.45 double. There's space for hanging out and it's quiet.

A favorite of vacationing Guatemalan families, *Johnny's Lodging* (☎ 337 4191, 633 0321) has clean rooms with fan and private bath for US$7.75 per person. It also has seven bungalows, each with two bedrooms, a living room, private bath and fully equipped kitchen, for US$50 for four people. Two bungalows share a barbecue and small swimming pool (a second pool is available for the other guests).

Nearby, *Kaiman Inn* (☎ 334 6214, ☎/fax 334 6215) has eight rooms, each with fan, mosquito nets and private bath, for US$6.45 per person during the week, US$7.75 on weekends; rooms hold two to five people. The restaurant serves excellent Italian cuisine and seafood.

Down the beach is *Hotel La Sirena*, which you'll know by the travelers lounging in the hammocks. This is one of Monterrico's best values, with a variety of rooms. Big, bare rooms with private bath, fan and three beds are US$11.60; rooms sleeping four with bath, refrigerator, stove and dining area are US$20; and simple rooms with shared bath are US$5.15 for one or two people. The hotel has a pool, and the restaurant here has the usual fish dishes that every other hotel on the beach is serving, but at half the price.

Nearby is *Pig Pen Pub*, an open-air beachfront bar with good music and atmosphere. It's open from 8 pm 'until you're done drinking.' The gregarious expat owner knows the area well. Ask him about birding and mangrove tours.

Set back from the beach on the little paths that circumscribe the town are two recommended places. The first is *Guest House*, a new hostel with four cozy, rustic rooms with mosquito nets, fans and shared bath for US$3.25/5.15 single/double. Stay here now while this introductory price lasts. You'll pass it if you're coming from La Avellana; from the beach, make a left at the first alley. Nearby, *Restaurant Neptune* garners rave reviews from repeat diners, and though it's not the cheapest place in town, it's worth a splash out.

Getting There & Away

There are two ways to get to Monterrico. You can take a bus to Iztapa (four hours from Guatemala City), catch a lancha across the canal to Pueblo Viejo and switch to another bus to Monterrico (US$0.65, one hour). This is the longer alternative, but it's a pretty journey that allows you to experience local life at a sane pace.

The other option is to head to La Avellana, where lanchas and car ferries depart for Monterrico. About 10 direct buses daily run from Guatemala City to La Avellana (US$1.50, four hours, 124km); buses run hourly from La Avellana to Guatemala City between 4 am and 4:30 pm. Or you can change buses at Taxisco, on CA-2 – buses operate hourly between Guatemala City and Taxisco (US$1.65, 3½ hours, 106km) and hourly between Taxisco and La Avellana (US$0.40, 20 minutes, 18km).

Shuttle buses also serve La Avellana. You can take a shuttle from Antigua for US$12 one-way on weekdays, US$10 on weekends. From Antigua it's a 2½-hour trip. The Adventure Travel Center in Antigua (see Travel Agencies in the Antigua section, earlier in this chapter) comes over every Saturday and returns every Sunday; other shuttle services also make the trip. Shuttle services depart from La Avellana for Antigua at 2:30 pm on Saturday and Sunday. Phone the Hotel Baule Beach (see Places to Stay & Eat, above) in Monterrico to check the current schedule for buses and shuttles. During the week, Hotel Baule Beach runs its own shuttle to Antigua (US$15 per person, minimum two people).

From La Avellana, *colectivo* lanchas charge US$0.35 per passenger for the half-hour trip along the Canal de Chiquimulilla, a long mangrove canal. They start at 4:30 am and run every half hour. Car ferries (US$7) leave when a car and passengers are ready to go.

Those wishing to check out the Biotopo Monterrico-Hawaii can take a new road between Monterrico and the Biotopo; one bus a day runs between the two.

The Verapaces

North and east of Guatemala City, the topography ranges from misty, pine-covered mountains to hot, dry-tropic lowlands and coastal regions. Leaving the capital heading northeast on Carretera al Atlántico (CA-9), you'll climb into the mountains and get a tease of cool temperatures before descending into the Río Motagua Valley, where dinosaurs once roamed. A turnoff at the valley's west end will lead you north into the Verapaces.

This mountainous region is home to the Rabinal Maya, once noted for their warlike habits and merciless victories. The Rabinals battled the powerful Quiché Maya for a century but were never conquered. When the conquistadores arrived, they too had trouble defeating the Rabinals. It was Fray Bartolomé de Las Casas who convinced the Spanish authorities to give peace a chance. Armed with an edict forbidding Spanish soldiers from entering the region for five years, the friar and his brethren succeeded in pacifying and converting the Rabinals. The area was renamed Verapaz (True Peace) and is now divided into the depart-

ments of Baja Verapaz, with its capital at Salamá, and Alta Verapaz, centered on Cobán.

The scenic asphalt road to the two capitals wends from the hot, dry Río Motagua valley into the mountains through long stretches of coffee-growing country. The region holds many intriguing Rabinal villages, where the people remain dedicated to ancient traditions. On the way to Cobán is one of Guatemala's premier nature reserves, the Biotopo del Quetzal. Beyond Cobán, along rough unpaved roads, are the country's most famous caverns. Farther back still, on roads left to the whims of nature, are rarely traveled routes to El Petén.

SALAMÁ
pop 11,000

Highway 17, also marked CA-14, leaves the Carretera al Atlántico at El Rancho, 84km from Guatemala City. It heads west through a dry, desert-like lowland area, then turns north and ascends into the forested hills. After 47km is the turnoff for Salamá.

Services here are grouped around or near the plaza. The Bancafé across from the church changes traveler's checks at a poor rate and gives cash advances on Visa. The Banrural on the plaza may offer better rates. The Telgua telephone office is across from the Hotel Tezulutlán, and a police station is on the corner of 5a Calle and 9a Avenida.

Things to See & Do

Salamá is an attractive town with a bustling Sunday market and reminders of colonial rule. The main plaza boasts an ornate **church** with gold encrusted altars and a pulpit with rococo carvings; there are only two such pulpits in Latin America (the other is in Lima, Peru). Don't miss Jesus lying in his glass coffin, his stigmata stuffed with cotton bunting and droplets of blood seeping from his scalp.

The local, experienced naturalists at EcoVerapaz (☎/fax 940 0294), 8a Avenida 4-77, Zona 1, offer a variety of interesting tours throughout Baja Verapaz. Caving, birding, hiking, horseback riding and orchid trips are among their specialties. The guides speak English. One-day tours start at US$40 per person for a group of five or more.

Places to Stay & Eat

In the block directly behind the church, the unmarked *Hospedaje Juárez (☎ 940 0055, 10a Avenida 5-55, Zona 1)* is a clean, safe and friendly place to stay. All 15 rooms have private hot bath and cost US$5.15 per person. The family runs a cheaper place with the same name on the corner of 5a Calle, just down the block; rooms with shared bath there are US$3.90 per person.

Hotel Tezulutlán (☎/fax 940 0141), just off the main square behind the Texaco station, has 15 rooms arranged around a garden courtyard. All have cable TV and private bath (four rooms have hot water); rates are US$11/14/17 single/double/triple. Two other rooms with shared bath are US$6.45 double. Next door, *Restaurant Happy Ranch* offers entire roasted chickens for US$3.25. Across the street, *Hotel San Ignacio (☎ 940 0186)* is a clean, family-run place where rooms cost US$4/5 single/double with shared bath, US$5/7.75 with private cold bath; *Cafetería Apolo XI* is in the same building.

The new *Hotel Real Legendario (☎ 940 0187, 8a Avenida 3-57, Zona 1)* is a good value. Its clean, secure rooms with private hot bath and cable TV cost US$8.40/13.50/18. Travelers with children may want to check out the spacious *Turicentro Las Orquídeas (☎ 940 0142)*, at Carretera a Salamá Km 147, which has a pool, a restaurant and open spaces slung with hammocks.

A few doors from the plaza, *Cafe Deli-Donas* is a hospitable coffee shop serving light meals, sweets and Salamá´s best coffee; it's open daily. Nearby, *Cafetería Central* offers savory, filling lunches for US$3.25. At *Restaurante El Ganadero*, a half-block off the main square on the road out of town, lunch might cost US$4 to US$6, a sandwich much less. On the plaza, clean and friendly *Pollo to Go* serves burgers and chicken.

Getting There & Away

Buses bound for Guatemala City depart hourly, 3 am to 4 pm, in front of the Municipalidad (US$2, three hours, 151km). Buses originating in Guatemala City continue west from Salamá to Rabinal (US$1, one hour, 19km) and 15km farther to Cubulco. Buses for San Jerónimo leave from in front of the church every half hour from 6 am to 4 pm (US$0.25, 20 minutes).

In Guatemala City, buses to Salamá depart hourly, 5 am to 5 pm, from the office of Transportes Unidos Baja Verapacenses (☎ 253 4618), 17a Calle 11-32.

AROUND SALAMÁ

Ten kilometers along the road to Salamá from the Cobán highway, you come to the turnoff for **San Jerónimo**. Behind the town's beautiful church, a former sugar mill is now a museum with a decent collection of unlabeled artifacts and photographs; admission is free. On the town plaza are some large stones carved in ancient times.

Nine kilometers west of Salamá along Hwy 5 is **San Miguel Chicaj**, known for its weaving and traditional fiesta (September 25 to 29). Continue along the same road another 10km to reach the colonial town of **Rabinal**, founded in 1537 by Fray Bartolomé de Las Casas as a base for proselytizing. Rabinal has gained fame as a center for pottery-making (look for the hand-painted chocolate cups) and citrus-growing (the harvest is in November and December). Rabinal is also known for its adherence to pre-Columbian traditions. Try to make the annual fiesta of Saint Peter, between January 19 and 25 (things reach a fever pitch on January 21), or Corpus Cristi. Market day is Sunday. Two small hotels, *Pensión Motagua* and *Hospedaje Caballeros*, can put you up.

It's possible to continue from Rabinal another 15km west to **Cubulco** or about 100km south to Guatemala City. Hwy 5 to Guatemala City passes through several small villages en route. It's best to tackle this road with a 4WD vehicle. Buses ply this remote route very slowly. Along the way you can visit the **ruins of Mixco Viejo**, near San Juan Sacatepéquez, about 25km from Guatemala City.

BIOTOPO DEL QUETZAL

Along the main highway (CA-14) 34km north of the turnoff for Salamá is the Biotopo Mario Dary Rivera reserve, commonly called the Biotopo del Quetzal; it's at Km 161, near the village of Purulhá (no services). The ride along here is sobering: Entire hillsides are deforested and covered in huge sheets of black plastic meant to optimize growing conditions for *xate*, a green palm exported for use in floral arrangements.

If you intend on seeing a quetzal, Guatemala's national bird, you'll likely be disappointed – the birds are rare and elusive, and their habitat is almost destroyed. The best time to see them is between February and September. However, it's still worth a visit to explore their lush, high-altitude cloud forest habitat.

The two well-maintained trails that wind through the reserve pass several waterfalls, most of which cascade into swimmable pools. Deep in the forest is Xiu Ua Li Che (Grandfather Tree), some 450 years old, which was alive when the conquistadores fought the Rabinals in these mountains.

Trail maps in English and Spanish can be purchased at the visitor's center for US$0.50. They contain a checklist of 87 birds commonly seen here. Other animals include spider monkeys and *tigrillos*, similar to ocelots. Good luck.

The reserve is open 6 am to 4 pm daily (you must be in by 4 pm, but you can stay longer); admission costs US$5. Drinks (but no food) are available.

Camping is currently not allowed, though this may change. Services in the area include *Hotel y Comedor Ranchito del Quetzal* (☎ 953 9235), a rustic budget hospedaje with a restaurant, just north of the reserve; the more comfortable and expensive *Posada Montaña del Quetzal* (☎ 208 5958), at Km 156.5, which has a restaurant and swimming pool and *Biotopín Restaurant*, at Km 160.5, a recommended place to eat.

The road between the Biotopo and Cobán is good – smooth and fast (though curvy). As you ascend into the evergreen forests, you'll still see tropical flowers here and there.

COBÁN

pop 20,000

Cobán was once a stronghold of the Rabinal Maya. In the 19th century, German immigrants moved in, founding vast coffee and cardamom fincas and giving Cobán the look and feel of a German mountain town. The era of German cultural and economic domination ended during WWII, when the USA prevailed upon the Guatemalan government to deport the powerful finca owners, many of whom supported the Nazis.

Today Cobán is a pleasant town, despite the chilly, rainy weather. You can count on sunny days in Cobán for only about three weeks in April. In the midst of the 'dry' season (January to March) it can be misty and rainy, or bright and marvelously clear.

Guatemala's most impressive indigenous festival, the folkloric festival of Rabin Ajau, takes place in late July or early August.

Information

Most services of interest to travelers are within a few blocks of the plaza. The heart of Cobán is built on a rise, so unless what you're looking for is in the dead center, you'll be trudging uphill and down.

The Casa D'Acuña and Hostal de Doña Victoria (see Places to Stay) both have loads of information.

Banco Occidente, on the plaza, changes US dollars cash and traveler's checks and gives cash advances on Visa cards. Banco G&T, behind the cathedral, also changes money and gives MasterCard cash advances. Banco Industrial, on 1a Calle, Zona 1, changes money and has a Visa ATM. Bancafé, 1a Avenida 2-66, Zona 2, also has a Visa ATM.

The post office is a block from the plaza at the corner of 2a Avenida and 3a Calle, Zona 3. The Telgua telephone office is on the plaza. Access Computación (☎ 951 4040, intercafe@c.net.gt), 1a Calle 3-13, Zona 1, offers expensive email service (US$7.75 an hour).

Templo El Calvario

You'll get a fine view over town from this church atop a long flight of stairs at the north end of 7a Avenida, Zona 1. Indigenous people leave offerings at shrines and crosses in front of the church. You can walk behind the church to enter the Parque Nacional Las Victorias, though this is not the park's main entrance.

Parque Nacional Las Victorias

This forested 82-hectare national park, right in town, has trails, ponds, barbecue/picnic areas, children's play areas, a lookout point and camping (US$1.30). It's open 8 am to 4:30 pm daily; admission is US$0.80. The entrance is at 9a Avenida and 3a Calle, Zona 1. Or you can enter by walking around to the rear of Templo El Calvario.

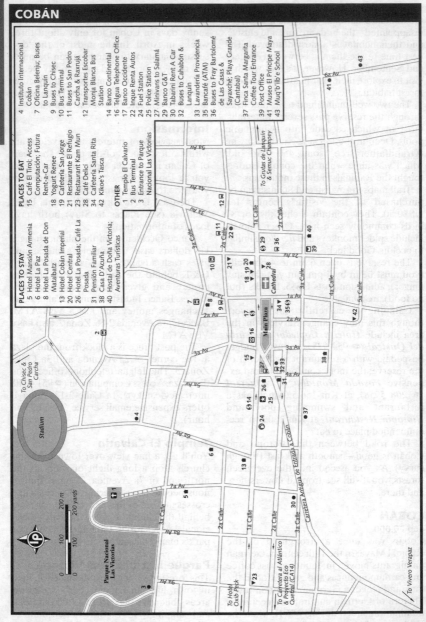

COBÁN

PLACES TO STAY
5   Hotel Mansión Armenia
6   Hotel La Paz
8   Hotel La Posada de Don Matabalz
13 Hotel Cobán Imperial
20 Hotel Central
26 Hotel La Posada; Café La Posada
31 Pensión Familiar
38 Casa D'Acuña
40 Hostal de Doña Victoria; Aventuras Turísticas

PLACES TO EAT
15 Café El Tirol; Access Computación; Futura Rent-a-Car
18 Yogurt Renee
19 Cafetería San Jorge
21 Restaurante El Refugio
23 Restaurant Kam Mun
28 Café Delici
34 Cafetería Santa Rita
42 Kikoe's Tasca

OTHER
1   Templo El Calvario
2   Bus Terminal
3   Entrance to Parque Nacional Las Victorias
4   Instituto Internacional Cobán
7   Oficina Belenjú; Buses to Lanquín
9   Buses to Chisec
10 Bus Terminal
11 Buses to San Pedro Carcha & Raxrujá
12 Transportes Escobar Monja Blanca Bus Station
14 Banco Continental
16 Telgua Telephone Office
17 Banco Occidente
22 Inque Renta Autos
24 Fuel Station
25 Police Station
27 Minivans to Salamá
29 Banco G&T
30 Tabarini Rent A Car
32 Buses to Cahabón & Lanquín
33 Lavandería Providencia
35 Bancafé (ATM)
36 Buses to Fray Bartolomé de Las Casas & Sayaxché; Playa Grande (Cantabal)
37 Finca Santa Margarita Coffee Tour Entrance
39 Post Office
41 Museo El Príncipe Maya
43 Muq'b'ilb'e School

Vivero Verapaz

Orchid lovers mustn't miss a chance to see the many thousands of species at this famous nursery (☎ 952 1133). The rare *monja blanca*, or white nun orchid (Guatemala's national flower), grows here, as do hundreds of miniature orchid species, some so small you need a magnifying glass to see them. The owners will take you on a tour for US$0.65. The national orchid show is held here each December.

Vivero Verapaz is on the Carretera Antigua de Entrada a Cobán, about 2km from the town center. It's a 20-minute walk southwest from the plaza on the heavily trafficked Carretera; you might prefer taking a taxi (US$1.50). Hours are 9 am to noon and 2 to 5 pm Monday to Saturday.

Finca Santa Margarita

Finca Santa Margarita (☎ 952 1286), 3a Calle 4-12, Zona 2, is a working coffee farm offering stellar guided tours. From propagation and planting to roasting and exporting, the 45-minute tour will tell you all you ever wanted to know about these beans. You can purchase beans for as little as US$3 a pound. Tours in English or Spanish are available 8 am to 12:30 pm and 1:30 to 5 pm weekdays and 8 am to noon Saturday (US$2).

Museo El Príncipe Maya

This private museum (☎ 952 1541), 6a Avenida 4-26, Zona 3, features an impressive collection of pre-Columbian artifacts, with an emphasis on jewelry, other body adornments and pottery. The displays are well designed and maintained. It's open 9 am to 6 pm Monday to Saturday (US$1.30).

Language Courses

The Muq'b'ilb'e School (☎ 951 2459), 6a Avenida 5-39, Zona 3, is run by Oscar Macz and is well recommended for Spanish and Q'eqchi' instruction. The Instituto Internacional Cobán (INCO), ☎/fax 951 3113), 6a Avenida 3-03, Apdo 22, Zona 1, also offers Spanish classes.

Organized Tours

Aventuras Turísticas (☎ 951 4213, ☎/fax 951 4214), 3a Calle 2-38, Zona 3, in the Hostal de Doña Victoria, leads tours to Laguna Lachuá, the Rey Marco and Candelaria caves, Semuc Champey and Lanquín, Tikal, Ceibal and beyond. The company employs French, English and Spanish-speaking guides and will custom design itineraries for you.

The Casa D'Acuña (☎ 951 0482/84, fax 952 1547, uisa@infovia.com.gt), 4a Calle 3-11, Zona 2, also offers tours to Semuc Champey, the Grutas de Lanquín and other places farther afield.

The folks at Access Computación (see Information, earlier in this section) offer day trips and overnight camping excursions to an idyllic lagoon and waterfall on Río Sachicha. The trips are not cheap (US$20 each for a day trip; US$27 for camping), but the river is on private land and not accessible to independent travelers. The company also runs cave tours and trips to El Salto waterfall.

Proyecto EcoQuetzal (☎/fax 952 1047, bidaspeq@guate.net), 2a Calle 14-36, Zona 1, is a recommended outfit offering ethnotourism trips. Participants hike to nearby villages nestled in the cloud forest, where they stay with a Q'eqchi' family. The price of US$11 per day includes three meals, lodging and guided hikes to interesting spots (the men of the host families serve as the guides, providing alternative income for their families). Reservations are required at least one day in advance. The office is open 8:30 am to 1 pm and 2 to 5:30 pm Monday to Friday. Participants should speak some Spanish. Web site: www.granjaguar.com/peq

Places to Stay

Camping is available at Parque Nacional Las Victorias, right in town. Facilities include water and toilets but no showers.

One of the cheapest places in town is *Pensión Familiar*, at the intersection of 2a Calle and the Carretera de Entrada a Cobán, Zona 2. Basic rooms with saggy beds are US$2.60 per person

Casa D'Acuña (☎ *951 0482/84, fax 952 1547, uisa@infovia.com.gt, 4a Calle 3-11, Zona 2*), down a steep hill from the plaza, is a clean, copacetic European-style hostel. Cost is US$4.50 per bunk, in rooms with two or four beds and shared bath (with incredible hot shower). One private room with shared bath is available for US$9 double. Amenities include a good restaurant, gift shop, laundry service and reasonably priced local tours.

Popular with Guatemalan families, the old but clean *Hotel Cobán Imperial* (☎ 952 1131, 6a Avenida 1-12, Zona 1) is 250m from the plaza. Rooms with private bath are US$5.80/9/12.25 single/double/triple.

Convenient for odd-hour bus travel is *Hotel La Posada de Don Matalbatz* (☎/fax 951 0811, 3a Calle 1-46, Zona 1). This friendly place has big, clean rooms facing a pretty courtyard. Rooms with private hot bath and cable TV are US$8.40 per person. Rooms with clean, shared bath and little balconies are US$6.20 per person. Some rooms are mildewy, so sniff a few first. The hotel has a pool table, restaurant and parking, and you can make international calls here.

Hotel La Paz (☎ 952 1358, 6a Avenida 2-19, Zona 1) is cheerful, clean and an excellent deal: US$3.10/6.20 with shared bath, US$4.65/9 with private bath. It has many flowers, courtyard parking and a good cafeteria next door. It claims to have hot water.

Hotel Central (☎ 952 1118, ☎/fax 951 1442, 1a Calle 1-79, Zona 4) is tidy, with rooms, each with private bath, around a flowered courtyard. Rates are US$7/12.50/18 without TV, US$9.25/14.85/20 with TV. Cafetería San Jorge is also here.

The comfortable *Hotel Mansión Armenia* (☎ 951 4284, 951 0978, 7a Avenida 2-18, Zona 1), one block from Templo El Calvario, is clean, quiet and modern, with parking and a cafeteria. Rooms with private bath and cable TV are US$11/20/27.

Hotel Oxib Peck (☎ 951 3224, fax 952 1039, 1a Calle 12-11, Zona 1) is 12 blocks (750m) west of the plaza on the road out of town. The rooms are clean and pleasant, and the hotel has a dining room, laundry service and parking. Rooms with private bath and cable TV are US$15/22/29.

Hostal de Doña Victoria (☎ 951-4213/4, 3a Calle 2-38, Zona 3) is in a restored mansion over 400 years old. Comfortable rooms with private bath surround a central courtyard that has plants and a restaurant/bar. Prices are US$17/24/30/33 single/double/triple/quad.

Best in town is the colonial-style *Hotel La Posada* (☎ 952 1495, 951 0588, 1a Calle 4-12, Zona 2), just off the plaza in the very center of town. Its colonnaded porches are draped with tropical flowers and furnished with lounge chairs and hammocks from which you can enjoy the mountain views. The rooms have private baths, nice old furniture, fireplaces and wall hangings of local weaving; rates are US$23/29/34.

Places to Eat

Most of Cobán's hotels have restaurants. The one at *Casa D'Acuña* is among the town's best, offering authentic Italian and other continental dishes in an attractive setting. Dinners start at around US$5. The restaurant opens at 7 am for breakfast. Also recommended is the restaurant at *Hostal de Doña Victoria*.

Tiny *Café Delici*, on 1a Calle at 2a Avenida, just behind the cathedral, serves awesome coffee, espresso and other java drinks in a friendly atmosphere. Try some pastries or the set lunch (US$1.30).

Café El Tirol, near the Hotel La Posada, advertises 'the best coffee' (try the specials) and offers several types of hot chocolate. It's a cozy little place to enjoy pastries and coffee for US$1 to US$2. Breakfast and light meals are served as well. It's closed on Sunday.

Café La Posada, at the Hotel La Posada on the plaza's west end, has tables on a verandah, overlooking the plaza. Inside is a comfortable sitting room with couches, coffee tables and a fireplace. All the usual café fare is served. Also facing the main square, *Cafetería Santa Rita* is small, tidy and popular with locals. Good typical Guatemalan meals go for around US$2.

Cafetería San Jorge, on 1a Calle between 1a and 2a Avenidas, Zona 4, near the cathedral, has a varied menu and a dining room with views through large windows. Substantial meat dishes are offered (US$3), along with a variety of sandwiches (US$1 to US$2). Next door, *Yogurt Renee* makes delicious fruit yogurts and ice cream.

Restaurante El Refugio, at the corner of 2a Avenida and 2a Calle, Zona 4, has rustic wooden decor and a menu with lots of game, seafood and meat options (grilled steaks are US$3 to US$8), as well as Mexican dishes.

Almost 500m from the plaza on the road out of town, *Restaurant Kam Mun* (1a Calle 8-12, Zona 2) serves Chinese fare in clean and pleasant surroundings. Full meals costs US$5 to US$8. *Kikoe's Tasca*, on the southern part of 2a Avenida, Zona 2, near the Casa D'Acuña, is a bar in the Bavarian vein. Cocktails, beer and bar food are served; it opens at 5 pm daily.

In the evening, food trucks park around the plaza, offering some of the cheapest dining in town. Some serve safe food, others don't.

Getting There & Away
Air TACA (☎ 334 7722 for reservations) offers one daily flight each way between Guatemala City and Cobán.

Bus The CA-14/Carretera al Atlántico route is the most traveled circuit between Cobán and the outside world, but buses also serve other off-the-beaten-track routes. Consider taking the phenomenal route between Cobán and Huehuetenango (see East Toward Cobán under Around Huehuetenango in the Western Highlands section). Or head from Cobán to El Estor, on Lago de Izabel, or to Poptún in the Petén on the backdoor route via Fray Bartolomé de Las Casas.

Many buses leave from Cobán's new bus terminal, southeast of the stadium. Buses to Guatemala City, Salamá, Lanquín and many other destinations depart from completely different stations. Bus stops are shown on the map. From Cobán, buses include the following:

Biotopo del Quetzal (US$1, one hour, 58km)
Any bus heading for Guatemala City will drop you at the entrance to the Biotopo.
Cahabón (US$2, 4½ hours, 85km)
Same buses as to Lanquín; more than a dozen departures daily.
Chisec (1½ hours, 66km)
Six buses a day leave from the corner of 1a Avenida and 2a Calle between 6 am and 3 pm. The last bus returns to Cobán from Chisec at 12:30 pm.
El Estor (US$2.30, 7½ hours, 166km)
Brenda Mercedes and Valenciana buses depart from the bus terminal 12 times daily; the first departure is at 4 am, the last at 3 pm.
Fray Bartolomé de Las Casas (US$2, 5½ hours, 101km)
Several buses depart daily, starting at 5 am. You can catch this bus on 2a Avenida, Zona 3, near Banco G&T.
Guatemala City (US$2.20 to US$3.60, four hours, 213km)

Transportes Escobar Monja Blanca (☎ 251 1878), 2a Calle 3-77, Zona 4, has buses leaving for Guatemala City every half hour from 2 to 6 am, then hourly from 6 am to 4 pm.
Lanquín (US$1.15, 2½ hours, 61km)
Buses depart at 6 am, noon, 1 and 3 pm from Oficina Belenju on 3a Calle, Zona 1. The return buses depart Lanquín at 5 am, 7 am and 3 pm. Rutas Nicte Amely buses leave at 5:15 am and 12:15 pm, returning at 4:30 am and 2 pm. You can catch these buses from 2a Calle, Zona 2, across from the Lavandería Providencia.
Playa Grande (sometimes called Cantabal; US$3, four hours, 141km)
A few buses leave daily from 2a Avenida, Zona 3, near the Banco G&T; the first is at 4:30 am.
Puerto Barrios (6½ hours, 335km)
Take any bus headed to Guatemala City and change at El Rancho junction. Do the same to get to Río Dulce, but transfer again at La Ruidosa junction (169km past El Rancho).
Salamá (US$1.15, one hour, 57km)
Frequent minivans leave from 2a Calle, across the street from the Lavandería Providencia.
San Pedro Carcha (US$0.10, 20 minutes, 6km)
Buses depart every 10 minutes, 6 am to 7 pm, from 2a Calle between 2a and 3a Avenidas, Zona 4.
Sayaxché (US$5, seven hours, 184km)
One daily departure, at 4:40 am, leaves from 2a Avenida near the Banco G&T.
Uspantán (US$1.30, 4½ hours, 94km)
Two buses daily, at 10 am and noon from the bus terminal south of the stadium.

Car Cobán's small car rental places may not always have every type of vehicle; make reservations. If you want to go to the Grutas de Lanquín or Semuc Champey, you'll need a 4WD. Companies include the following:

Futura Rent-a-Car (☎ 952 2059), 1a Calle 3-13, Zona 1, in the same building as the Café El Tirol, in the rear right corner of the courtyard
Inque Renta Autos (☎ 952 1994, 952 1172), 3a Avenida 1-18, Zona 4
Ochoch Pec Renta Autos (☎ 951 3474, 951 3214), opposite La Carrita el Viaje at the entrance to town
Tabarini Rent A Car (☎ 952 1504, ☎/fax 951 3282), 7a Avenida 2-27, Zona 2

AROUND COBÁN
Cobán (indeed all of Alta Verapaz) is becoming a hot destination for adventure travel. Not only does the area hold scores of villages where you can find traditional

Mayan culture in some of its purest extant form, it also harbors caves, waterfalls, pristine lagoons and many other undiscovered natural wonders.

San Juan Chamelco

About 16km southeast of Cobán is the village of San Juan Chamelco, with swimming at the Balneario Chio. The church here, which dates back to the colonial period and may have been the first church in Alta Verapaz, sits at the top of a small rise and has awesome views of the villages below. Mass is still held here in Spanish (Sunday 5 pm) and Q'eqchi' (Sunday 7 and 9:30 am).

In Aldea Chajaneb, Jerry Makransky (everyone knows him as 'Don Jerónimo'; sbrizuel@c.net.gt) rents comfortable, simple bungalows for US$25 per person (US$45 per couple) per day. Included with the bungalow are three ample, delicious vegetarian meals fresh from the garden and many activities: tours to caves, to the mountains, inner tubing on the Río Sotzil and more. Jerry dotes on his guests, and the atmosphere is friendly.

To get there, take a bus from Cobán to San Juan Chamelco. From there, take a bus or pickup toward Chamil and ask the driver to let you off at Don Jerónimo's. Take the footpath to the left for 300m, cross the bridge and it's the first house on the right. Alternatively, you can hire a taxi from Cobán for about US$6.

Grutas de Lanquín

If you don't mind bad roads, the best excursion from Cobán is to the caves near Lanquín, a pretty village 61km east. If you get this far, make sure to visit Semuc Champey as well.

The Grutas de Lanquín are a short distance northwest of the town and extend several kilometers into the earth. You must first stop at the police station in the Municipalidad (Town Hall) in Lanquín, pay the US$1.30 admission and ask them to open the caves; there is no attendant at the caves. The caves have lights, but bring a powerful flashlight anyway. You'll also need shoes with good traction, as it's slippery inside.

Though the first few hundred meters of cavern has been equipped with a walkway and electric lights, most of this subterranean system is untouched. If you're a neophyte spelunker, think twice about wandering too far – the entire extent of this cave has yet to be explored, let alone mapped. Aside from funky stalactites and stalagmites, these caves are crammed with bats; at sunset, they fly out of the mouth of the cave in dense, sky-obscuring formations. Sit at the entrance while they exit for a dazzling display of navigation skills. The river here gushes from the cave in clean, cool and delicious torrents; search out the hot pockets near the shore.

Camping is permitted near the cave entrance. In Lanquín, *La Divina Providencia* has simple rooms for about US$2 per person. *El Recreo* (☎ 952 2160), between the town and the caves, is more attractive and more expensive; US$15/20 single/double. The new *El Retiro* is a recommended place popular with backpackers. The four rooms all share a bath and cost US$2.60 per person. Meals are available for around US$1.50. *Comedor Shalom* is also good for a meal.

Semuc Champey

Ten kilometers southeast of Lanquín along a rough, bumpy, slow road is Semuc Champey, famed for a natural wonder: a great limestone bridge 300m long, on top of which is a stepped series of pools of refreshing, flowing water good for swimming. The pools are fed by mountain stream runoff, while the powerful Río Cahabón rushes beneath the bridge underground. Though this bit of paradise is difficult to reach (and describe!), the gorgeous setting and the perfection of the pools, ranging from turquoise to emerald green, make it all worth it. Some consider this the most beautiful spot in all Guatemala.

It's possible to camp at Semuc Champey, but only in the upper areas, as flash floods are common down below. Don't leave anything unattended, as it might get stolen. Solo travelers may feel uncomfortable in such a secluded spot.

Tours to the Grutas de Lanquín and Semuc Champey, offered in Cobán for around US$35 per person, are the easiest way to visit these places. On your own, if you're driving, you'll need a four-wheel-drive vehicle.

Several buses daily run between Cobán and Lanquín, continuing to Cahabón. Buses leave Lanquín on the return to Cobán at 4:30, 5 and 7 am and 2 and 3 pm. Since the last return bus departs so early, you should probably plan to stay the night. Occasional buses and trucks make the run from Lanquín to Semuc Champey; your chances of catching a ride to Semuc Champey are better in the early morning. Otherwise, you're in for a long, hot walk. Admission to the site is US$1.

BACKDOOR PETÉN ROUTES

The **Cobán to Poptún** route via Fray Bartolomé de Las Casas used to be a desolate dirt road. Nowadays, plenty of buses and pickups ply the decent roads. This route is a great opportunity for you to get off the Gringo Trail and into the heart of Guatemala.

The hospitable town of **Fray Bartolomé de Las Casas**, often referred to as 'Fray' (pronounced 'fry'), is sizable for the middle of nowhere. You can't make it from Cobán to Poptún in one shot, so you'll be spending the night here. The friendly *Hotel y Restaurante Diamelas*, near the plaza, is the best place to stay in town. Its five rooms with private bath cost US$3.25 per person. The restaurant serves a terrific set lunch. Around the corner is *Hospedaje Ralios*, but it's not as good. Here, dark, basic rooms around a neglected courtyard are US$2.35. (Note that a solo female traveler was harassed at Hotel & Restaurant Fontana, down the road to the market, so steer clear if you fall into that category.) The town has a bank, post office and police station.

One bus departs daily from the plaza at 3 am for Poptún (US$3.90, five hours, 100km). Buses for Cobán leave at 5, 6, 8, 10 and 11 am (US$2, 5½ hours, 101km).

Another backdoor trip you could take would be from **Cobán to Sayaxché and El Ceibal** – either by getting the one daily direct bus from Cobán (4:40 am) or one of the several departures to Chisec, where you transfer. See Getting There & Away in the Cobán section, earlier. You can also go via Raxrujá (many services), west of Fray Bartolomé de Las Casas. One bus daily leaves Fray for Sayaxché at 10 am (4½ hours, 117km).

Zacapa & Chiquimula

From the Río Motagua valley on the Carretera al Atlántico, continuing east takes you to the department of Zacapa. This area and its neighboring department to the south, Chiquimula, hold myriad interesting destinations and provide access to the first-rate Mayan ruins at Copán, just across the border in Honduras. Highlights of the region include the paleontology museum at Estanzuela; the great basilica at Esquipulas, famous throughout Central America; and Copán itself (see the Honduras chapter).

RÍO HONDO

Río Hondo (Deep River) lies at the junction of CA-9 and CA-10, 42km east of El Rancho Junction and 126km from Guatemala City. The center of town is northeast of the highway junction. By car, it's an hour from here to Quiriguá, half an hour to Chiquimula and 1½ hours to Esquipulas.

Places to Stay & Eat

Río Hondo motels are used as weekend resorts by locals and Guatemala City residents, so they may be full on weekends. All are modern, with well-equipped bungalows (with cable TV and private bath), spacious grounds and good restaurants. All except the Hotel Santa Cruz have giant swimming pools.

The following four motels are all near one another at Km 126 on the Carretera al Atlántico.

Cheapest is *Hotel Santa Cruz* (☎ 934 7112, ☎/fax 934 7075), where rooms in duplex bungalows are US$9.65 per person with fan, US$12 with air-con. The popular restaurant here is cheaper than some of the others. Four apartments with kitchen are also available.

Hotel El Atlántico (☎ 934 7160, fax 934 7041) is probably the most attractive, with large, well-equipped bungalows, a large swimming pool, beautiful expansive grounds and a good restaurant. Rates are US$16/27/32 single/double/triple. Reservations are wise.

Across the highway, *Hotel Nuevo Pasabién* (☎ /fax 934 7201, 934 7073/4) has large rooms with air-con for US$19.50/34 single/double, as well as less expensive rooms with fan.

GUATEMALA

Opposite the Hotel Santa Cruz and behind the 24-hour Shell gas station, *Hotel Longarone* (☎ 934 7126, fax 934 7035) is the old standard in this area. Some rooms are in a long row, others are in duplex bungalows. Simple rooms are US$24/30/36, or US$30/36/42 with cable TV and refrigerator; all have air-con. The hotel has two large swimming pools, two smaller ones for children and a tennis court.

Valle Dorado (☎ 941 2542, 933 1111, fax 941 2543), at Carretera al Atlántico Km 149, 14km east of the CA-10 junction and 23km from the other Río Hondo hotels, is an enormous complex that includes an aquatic park with giant pools, waterslides, toboggans and other entertainment. Rooms are US$45 for one to four people, or US$72 for six. Make reservations on weekends, when it fills up with families.

Many people prefer to stay at one of the other Río Hondo hotels and come to Valle Dorado for the day. Day use costs US$6/5 for adults/children on weekends, US$4.50/3.65 during the week. The park is open from 8 am to sunset daily.

ESTANZUELA
pop 10,000
Traveling south from Río Hondo along CA-10 takes you to the midst of the Río Motagua valley, a hot, 'dry tropic' area that once supported a great number and variety of dinosaurs. Three kilometers south of the Carretera al Atlántico you'll see a small monument on the right (west) side of the road commemorating the terrible earthquake of February 4, 1976.

Less than 2km south of the monument is the small town of Estanzuela, with its **Museo de Paleontología, Arqueología y Geología Roberto Woolfolk Sarvia**. This interesting museum holds bones of dinosaurs, a giant ground sloth some 30,000 years old and a prehistoric whale. Also on display are early Mayan artifacts. The museum is open 8 am to noon and 1 to 5 pm daily; admission is free. To get there, go 1km west from the highway directly through town, following the small blue *museo* signs; anyone you see can help point the way.

CHIQUIMULA
pop 24,000
Capital of its namesake department, Chiquimula lies in a mining and tobacco-growing region on CA-10, 32km south of the Carretera al Atlántico. Though small, it's a major market town for eastern Guatemala. It's also a transportation point and overnight stop for those en route to Copán in Honduras; this is the reason most travelers stop here. Among other things, Chiquimula is known for its sweltering climate and decent budget hotels.

Information
Many banks will change US dollars cash and traveler's checks. Banco G&T, at 7a Avenida 4-75, changes both and also gives cash advances on Visa and MasterCard; it's open 9 am to 8 pm weekdays, 10 am to 2 pm Saturday. Bancor, at 3a Calle 8-30, has longer Saturday hours, from 9 am to 6 pm. Bancafé, at 3a Calle and 7a Avenida, has a Visa ATM.

The post office, on 10a Avenida between 1a and 2a Calles, is in the dirt alley, around the building opposite the bus station. The Telgua telephone office is on 3a Calle, a few doors downhill from the plaza (Parque Ismael Cerna). The Hotel Hernández offers phone services and email for US$0.15 a minute. The Hotel Victoria, 2a Calle at 10a Avenida, has phone service, too. The busy market is near Telgua.

Viajes Tivoli (☎ 942 4915/33, fax 942 2258), 8a Avenida 4-71, can help you deal with any travel arrangements.

Places to Stay
On the north side of the plaza is *Hotel Chiquimulja* (☎ 942 0387, 3a Calle 6-51). It was being remodeled at the time of writing, but will reopen with rooms with private bath and air-con.

Hotel Hernández (☎ 942 0708, 3a Calle 7-41) is clean, friendly and a great value; the owner speaks English, Spanish and a litle bit of French. The hotel has parking and a sparkling swimming pool, and the rooms have fans and good beds. Rates are US$3.90/6.20 single/double with shared hot bath; US$7.75/10 with private bath and cable TV. Some of the rooms have air-conditioning.

Hospedaje Río Jordan (☎ 942 0887, 3a Calle 8-91), a block farther downhill, has parking, a simple restaurant and rates of US$2 per person for rooms with shared bath, US$3.25 per person with private bath.

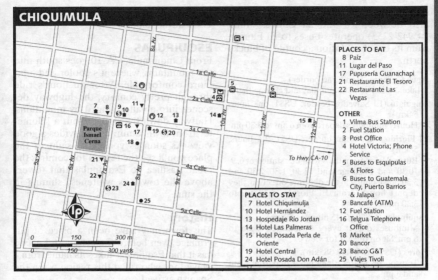

CHIQUIMULA

PLACES TO EAT
8   Paíz
11 Lugar del Paso
17 Pupusería Guanachapi
21 Restaurante El Tesoro
22 Restaurante Las
    Vegas

OTHER
1   Vilma Bus Station
2   Fuel Station
3   Post Office
4   Hotel Victoria; Phone
    Service
5   Buses to Esquipulas
    & Flores
6   Buses to Guatemala
    City, Puerto Barrios
    & Jalapa
9   Bancafé (ATM)
12 Fuel Station
16 Telgua Telephone
    Office
18 Market
20 Bancor
23 Banco G&T
25 Viajes Tivoli

PLACES TO STAY
7   Hotel Chiquimulja
10 Hotel Hernández
13 Hospedaje Río Jordan
14 Hotel Las Palmeras
15 Hotel Posada Perla de
    Oriente
19 Hotel Central
24 Hotel Posada Don Adán

Ncarby is friendly ***Hotel Central*** (☎ 942 6352, 3a Calle 8-30, 2nd floor), which has five clean rooms with private bath, air-con, cable TV and small balconies overlooking the action; US$7.75/12.50/15.50/18.50 single/double/triple/quad.

Near the bus station, ***Hotel Las Palmeras*** (☎ 942 4647, fax 942 0763, 10a Avenida 2-00) is a clean, family-run place that has rooms with private bath, cable TV and good beds for US$6.50/13 with air-con, US$4/7.75 with fan.

Hotel Posada Perla de Oriente (☎ 942 0014, fax 942 0534, 12a Avenida 2-30), entrance on 2a Calle, has a small swimming pool and a restaurant. Simple rooms with private bath, fan and cable TV cost US$12/21/30/41.

Hotel Posada Don Adán (☎ 942 3924, 8a Avenida 4-30) is spotless. It's run by a friendly, efficient señora who charges US$13/17.40/22 for rooms with private bath, telephone, cable TV, fan and air-con.

Places to Eat

Chiquimula has lots of cheap little places to eat. Try ***Pupusería Guanachapi***, on 3a Calle between 7a and 8a Avenidas, or ***Lugar del Paso***, around the corner on 8a Avenida, which serves reasonably priced grilled meats, burgers and chicken dishes and has a full bar. ***Restaurante El Tesoro***, on the main plaza, serves Chinese food at fair prices.

For a step up in quality, try ***Restaurante Las Vegas*** (7a Avenida 4-40), half a block from the plaza. It's perhaps Chiquimula's best, with fancy plants, jazzy music, a well-stocked bar and full meals for around US$6 (sandwiches are less). It's open 7 am to midnight daily.

The ***Paíz*** grocery store on the park is huge. Stock up here for a picnic and enjoy the air-con. The ***panadería*** next door to the Hotel Hernández opens at 5:30 am – perfect for predawn bus departures.

Getting There & Away

Chiquimula is more a transit point than destination. Your goal is probably the fabulous Copán, just across the Honduran border from El Florido. The turnoff to Copán lies just south of Chiquimula. Beyond that, the road splits at Padre Miguel Junction. Take the left (east) branch to reach Esquipulas and Nueva Ocotepeque (Honduras); the right branch leads to Anguiatú, a remote border crossing into El Salvador.

Several companies operate buses to Guatemala City and Puerto Barrios; all arrive and depart from the bus station area on 11a Avenida, between 1a and 2a Calles. Minivans to Esquipulas and buses to Flores arrive and depart from the bus station area a block away, on 10a Avenida also between 1a and 2a Calles. Vilma (☎ 942 2253) operates buses to El Florido from its own bus station a couple of blocks north.

Agua Caliente (Honduran border)
  Take a minibus to Esquipulas and change there.

Anguiatú (El Salvador border; US$1, one hour, 54km)
  Hourly minibuses depart from 6 am to 3:30 pm.

El Florido (Honduran border; US$1, 2½ hours, 58km)
  Buses depart from the Vilma bus station at 6, 9, 10:30 am and 11:30 am and 12:30, 1:30, 2:30 and 3:30 pm. Coming in the opposite direction, they depart hourly from El Florido, 5:30 am to 3:30 pm.

Esquipulas (US$0.80, 45 minutes, 52km)
  Minibuses depart every 10 minutes, 4 am to 8 pm. Sit on the left for views.

Flores (US$7, 10 hours, 385km)
  Transportes María Elena buses depart at 6 am and 3 pm.

Guatemala City (US$3, three hours, 169km)
  Rutas Orientales, Transportes Guerra and Guatesqui operate buses departing every half hour, 3 am to 4:30 pm.

Puerto Barrios (US$2.50, 4½ hours, 192km)
  Buses every 30 minutes, 4 am to 3 pm; take this bus for Quiriguá (US$1.30, two hours, 103km) and Río Dulce (change at La Ruidosa junction; US$2, three hours, 144km).

Quiriguá
  See Puerto Barrios.

Río Dulce
  See Puerto Barrios.

Río Hondo (US$1, 35 minutes, 32km)
  Minibuses depart every half hour, 5 am to 6 pm. Or take any bus heading for Guatemala City, Flores or Puerto Barrios.

PADRE MIGUEL JUNCTION & ANGUIATÚ

Between Chiquimula and Esquipulas is Padre Miguel Junction, the turnoff for Anguiatú (the El Salvador border, which is 30 minutes and 19km away). Minibuses pass frequently, coming from Chiquimula, Quezaltepeque and Esquipulas. The crossroads has a guard house, a bus stop shelter and little else.

The border at Anguiatú is open 6 am to 6 pm daily, though you might be able to get through on 'extraordinary service' until 9 pm. Across the border, buses run hourly to San Salvador, passing through Metapán,

12km from the border, and Santa Ana, 47km farther along.

ESQUIPULAS

From Chiquimula, CA-10 goes south into the mountains, where it's cooler and a bit more comfortable. After an hour's ride through pretty country, the highway descends into a valley ringed by mountains. Halfway down the slope, about a kilometer from town, a mirador provides a good view. As soon as you catch sight of the place you'll see the reason for coming: the great Basílica de Esquipulas that towers above the town, its whiteness shining in the sun.

History

This town may have been a place of pilgrimage even before the conquest. Legend has it that Esquipulas takes its name from a Maya lord who ruled this region when the Spanish arrived.

With the arrival of the friars, a church was built, and in 1595 an image of Christ carved from black wood was installed. The steady flow of pilgrims to Esquipulas became a flood after 1737, when Pedro Pardo de Figueroa, Archbishop of Guatemala, came here on pilgrimage and went away cured of a chronic ailment. Delighted with this development, the prelate commissioned a huge new church to be built on the site. It was finished in 1758, and the pilgrimage trade has been the town's livelihood ever since.

Esquipulas is assured a place in modern history, too. Beginning here in 1986, President Vinicio Cerezo Arévalo brokered agreements with the other Central American leaders on economic cooperation and conflict resolution. These became the seeds of the Guatemalan Peace Accords, which were finally signed in 1996.

Orientation & Information

The church and adjacent park are the center of everything. Most of the good cheap hotels are within a block or two, as are numerous small restaurants. The highway does not enter town; 11a Calle, also sometimes called Doble Vía Quirio Cataño, comes in from the highway and is the town's 'main drag.'

A number of banks change US dollars cash and traveler's checks. Bancafé, 3a Avenida 6-68, Zona 1, changes both, gives cash advances on Visa and MasterCard and is the town's American Express agent.

The post office is at 6a Avenida 2-15, about 10 blocks north of the center. The Telgua telephone office, on 5a Avenida at 9a Calle, is open daily. You can use phone cards in public telephones.

Basilica

A massive pile of stone that has resisted earthquakes for almost 2½ centuries, the basilica is approached through a pretty park and up a flight of steps. The impressive façade and towers are floodlit at night.

Inside, the devout approach El Cristo Negro with extreme reverence, many on their knees. Incense, the murmur of prayers and the scuffle of sandaled feet fill the air. When throngs of pilgrims are here, you must enter the church from the side to get a close view of the famous Black Christ. Shuffling along quickly, you may get a good glimpse before being shoved onward by the press of the crowd. On Sunday, religious holidays and (especially) during the festival around January 15, the press of devotees is intense. Otherwise, you may have the place to yourself.

Cueva de las Minas

The Centro Turístico Cueva de las Minas has a 50m-deep cave (bring your own light), grassy picnic areas, and the Río El Milagro, where people come for a miraculous dip. The cave and river are half a kilometer from the entrance gate, which is behind the basilica's cemetery, 300m south of the turnoff into town on the road heading toward Honduras. It's open 6:30 am to 4 pm daily (US$0.35). Refreshments are available.

Places to Stay

Esquipulas has an abundance of accommodations. On holidays and during the annual festival, every hotel in town is filled, whatever the price; weekends are fairly busy as well, with prices substantially higher. On non-festival weekdays, ask for a *descuento* (discount).

The area north of the basilica holds many cheap lodgings. The family-run *Pensión Santa Rosa* (☎ 943 2908), on 10a Calle at 1a Avenida, is typical of these small places. It charges US$2.60 per person with shared bath, US$4 with private bath. Several others are on 10a Calle as well.

Hotel Monte Cristo (☎ 943 1453, fax 943 1042, 3a Avenida 9-12) is clean and OK, with parking and a restaurant. Rooms run US$6.20/11 single/double with shared bath, US$13/19.50 with private bath.

Hotel El Peregrino (☎ 943 1054, 943 1859, 2a Avenida 11-94), on the southwest corner of the park, has simple rooms with private bath for US$6.45 per person, plus a new section in the rear where larger, fancier rooms with cable TV are US$23 double. Next door, *Hotel Los Angeles* (☎ 943 1254, 2a Avenida 11-94) has 20 rooms arranged around a bright inner courtyard. All have private bath, fan and cable TV. Rates are US$7.75/15. Both places have restaurants and parking.

In the same block, *Hotel Payaquí* (☎ 943 2025, fax 943 1371) is a large, attractive hotel with 55 rooms, all with private bath, cable TV, telephone and refrigerator. Rooms are US$19.50/32, with or without air-con. It has two restaurants, one in the rear by the swimming pool and one in front with a view of the park.

Hotel Villa Zonia (☎ 943 1133, 10a Calle 1-84) is a bright hotel with 15 rooms, all with private bath and cable TV. Rates are US$22 for one double bed, US$25 for two double beds. Parking is available.

The clean *Hotel Internacional* (☎ 943 1131, 943 1667, 10a Calle 0-85) has a small swimming pool, sauna, restaurant and parking. The 49 rooms, all with private bath, cable TV and phone, are US$15/19.50 with fan, US$19.50/23 with air-con.

Hotel Posada del Cristo Negro (☎ 943 1482, fax 943 1829), at Carretera Internacional a Honduras Km 224, is 2km from the church, out of town on the way to Honduras. Nice touches include broad green lawns, a pretty swimming pool and a large dining room. Comfortable rooms with private bath, refrigerator and TV cost US$14/20/27/33 single/double/triple/quad. Two or three children (up to age eight) stay free.

Places to Eat

Restaurants are more expensive here than in other parts of Guatemala. Budget restaurants are clustered at the park's north end, where hungry pilgrims can find them readily; ask in advance the price of each food item and add up your bill carefully.

Many small eateries lie along 3a Avenida, the street running north opposite the church. **Comedor Rosy No 2** is tidy and cheerful, with meals for around US$2.50 and big bottles of pickled chiles on the tables. Across the street, **Restaurante y Cafetería Victoria** is a bit fancier, with tablecloths, plants and higher prices. In the same block, **Comedor y Cafetería Beato Hermano Pedro** advertises set meals for around US$2.

On the park's west side, **Jimmy's** is a bright and clean cafeteria with big windows looking out onto the park. Prices are reasonable, and the menu is varied. Roast chicken is one of the specialties; you can get a whole chicken for US$6, or a quarter chicken with fries, salad and tortillas for US$2.

At **La Rotonda**, on 11a Calle opposite the Rutas Orientales bus station, chairs surround a circular open-air counter under a big awning. It's breezy, clean and welcoming. The menu of the day, with soup, a main course, rice, vegetables, dessert and a drink is US$4, and plenty of other selections are available, including pizza, pasta and burgers.

All these places are open from around 6 am until 9 or 10 pm daily.

Getting There & Away

Buses to Guatemala City arrive and depart from the Rutas Orientales (☎ 943 1366) bus station on 11a Calle at 1a Avenida, near the entrance to town. Minibuses to Agua Caliente arrive and depart across the street; taxis also wait here. The taxis charge the same as the minibuses, and they leave when they have five passengers.

Minibuses to Chiquimula and to Anguiatú depart from the east end of 11a Calle; you'll see them hawking for passengers along the main street. Transportes María Elena operates buses to Flores from the far east side of town, beyond the market.

Agua Caliente (Honduras border; US$0.70, 30 minutes, 10km)
Minibuses depart every half hour, 6 am to 5 pm.

Anguiatú (El Salvador border; US$1, one hour, 33km)
Minibuses depart every half hour, 6 am to 4 pm.

Chiquimula (US$0.80, 45 minutes, 52km)
Minibuses depart every 10 minutes, 5 am to 5 pm.

Flores (US$7.75, 11 hours, 437km)
Transportes María Elena buses depart at 4:20 am and 1:30 pm.

Guatemala City (US$3.10, four hours, 222km)
Rutas Orientales' *servicio especial* buses depart at 6:30 and 7:30 am and 1:30 and 3:30 pm; ordinary buses depart at 3:30, 5, 6:30, 7:30, 8:15 and 11:30 am and 1, 1:30, 3, 3:30 and 5:30 pm.

Izabal

About 60km east of Estanzuela is the department of Izabal, which holds the marvelous Mayan stelae and zoomorphs at Quiriguá; beautiful Lago de Izabal, the country's largest lake; the jungle waterway of Río Dulce; and Guatemala's only stretch of Caribbean coastline.

The Carretera al Atlántico passes near Lago de Izabal and ends at Puerto Barrios, Guatemala's Caribbean port. If you're not done moving yet, you can catch a boat here to Lívingston, a laid-back Garífuna hideaway.

QUIRIGUÁ

Quiriguá's archaeological zone is famed for its intricately carved stelae – gigantic sandstone monoliths up to 10.5m tall – that rise like ancient sentinels in a quiet tropical park. Visiting the ruins is easy if you have your own transportation, more difficult if you're traveling by bus. From the Río Hondo junction it's 67km along the Carretera al Atlántico to Los Amates, which has a couple of hotels, a restaurant and a bank. The village of Quiriguá is 1.5km east of Los Amates, and the turnoff to the ruins is 1.5km farther east. Following the access road south from the Carretera al Atlántico, it's 3.4km through banana groves to the archaeological site.

History

Quiriguá's history parallels that of Copán, of which it was a dependency during much of the Classic period. The location lent itself to the carving of giant stelae. Beds of brown sandstone in the nearby Río Motagua had cleavage planes suitable for cutting large pieces. Though soft when first cut, the sandstone dried hard. With Copán's expert artisans nearby for guidance, Quiriguá's stonecarvers were ready for greatness. All they needed was a leader to inspire them – and to pay for the carving.

That leader was Cauac Sky (725-84), who decided that Quiriguá should no longer be subject to Copán. In a war with his former suzerain, Cauac Sky took Copán's King 18 Rabbit prisoner in 737 and later had him beheaded. Independent at last, Cauac Sky commissioned his stonecutters to go to work; for the next 38 years they turned out giant stelae and zoomorphs dedicated to his glory.

In the early 1900s all the land around Quiriguá was sold to the United Fruit Company and turned into banana groves. The company is gone, but the bananas and Quiriguá remain. In 1981, Unesco declared Quiriguá a World Heritage Site.

Ruins

Despite the sticky heat and bothersome mosquitoes, this beautiful park-like archaeological zone is a wonderful place. The giant stelae on the Great Plaza are all much more worn than those at Copán, but they still inspire awe.

Seven of the stelae, designated A, C, D, E, F, H and J, were built during the reign of Cauac Sky and carved with his image. Stela E is the largest Mayan stela known, standing some 8m above ground, with another 3m or so buried in the earth. It weighs almost 60,000 kg. Note the exuberant, elaborate headdresses; the beards on some of the figures (an oddity in Mayan art and life); the staffs of office held in the kings' hands; and the glyphs on the stelae's sides.

At the far end of the plaza is the Acropolis, far less impressive than the one at Copán. At its base are several zoomorphs, blocks of stone carved to resemble real and mythic creatures. Frogs, tortoises, jaguars and serpents were favorite subjects. The low zoomorphs can't compete with the towering stelae in impressiveness, but are superb as works of art, imagination and mythic significance.

Quiriguá is open 7:30 am to 5 pm daily (US$0.65). A small stand near the entrance sells cold drinks and snacks, but you'll be better off bringing your own picnic.

Places to Stay & Eat

In the center of the village of Quiriguá, 700m south of the Carretera al Atlántico, *Hotel y Restaurante Royal* is simple, clean and quiet. Rooms with shared bath are US$4/6.50 single/double; larger rooms with

private bath and five beds are US$6/9/13/17/20 for one to five people. The restaurant serves meat and vegetarian meals. Most guests here are international travelers visiting the archaeological site.

At Los Amates, on the Carretera al Atlántico 3km west of Quiriguá village, is a 24-hour Texaco fuel station. Behind the Texaco station, *Hotel y Restaurante Santa Mónica* has eight rooms with private bath for US$6.50/9/11 single/double/triple. About 100m east of the Texaco station is the *Ranchón Chileño*, the area's best restaurant, where you can get good, filling meals for about US$6 and light meals for half that.

Comedor y Hospedaje Doña María, at Carretera al Atlántico Km 181, is at the east end of the Doña María bridge, 20km west of Los Amates. The 10 rooms here, all with private bath, rent for US$6 per person; they're old but clean, lined up along an open-air walkway beside the river. Across the river is a large, grassy camping area with coconut palms and fruit trees, covered picnic tables and campsites for US$4 per vehicle or tent. Ask at the hotel and they'll open the gate for you. The open-air restaurant, open 6 am to 9 pm daily, has a great view of the river, and the swimming is good. Ask permission before crossing the footbridge for a picnic.

Getting There & Away

The turnoff to Quiriguá is 205km (four hours) northeast of Guatemala City, 70km northeast of the Río Hondo junction, 43km southwest of the road to Flores in El Petén, and 90km southwest of Puerto Barrios.

Buses running Guatemala City–Puerto Barrios, Guatemala City–Flores, Esquipulas-Flores or Chiquimula-Flores will drop you off or pick you up at the turnoff to Quiriguá town. Better yet, they'll drop you at the turnoff to the archaeological site if you ask.

The transportation center in this area is Morales, about 40km northeast of Quiriguá. It's not pretty, but it's where the bus for Río Dulce originates. If a seat isn't important to you, skip Morales and wait at the La Ruidosa junction for the Río Dulce bus.

Getting Around

From the turnoff on the highway, it's 3.4km to the archaeological site. Buses and pickups provide transportation between the turnoff and the site for US$0.25 each way. If you don't see one, don't fret; it's a nice walk on a dirt road through banana plantations to get there.

If you're staying in the village of Quiriguá or Los Amates and walking to and from the archaeological site, you can take a shortcut along the railway branch line from the village through the banana fields, crossing the access road near the site entrance.

LAGO DE IZABAL

This largest Guatemalan lake, north of the Carretera al Atlántico, is starting to register on travelers' radars. Most visitors stay at Río Dulce village, north of the bridge where CA-13, the road to Flores and Tikal, crosses the lake's east end. East of this bridge is the beautiful Río Dulce, which opens into El Golfete before flowing into the Caribbean at Lívingston; a river trip is one of the highlights of a visit to eastern Guatemala.

Other lake highlights include El Castillo de San Felipe (an old Spanish fortress) and the Bocas del Polochic river delta. Many undiscovered spots in this area await exploration.

Río Dulce

East of Quiriguá at Km 245 on the Carretera al Atlántico (near the town of Morales) is La Ruidosa junction, where CA-13 turns north en route to Flores. About 34km up CA-13 from the junction, the road crosses the Río Dulce, an outlet of Lago de Izabal. Straddling the river are a pair of villages: the village of Río Dulce, sometimes called Fronteras, on the bridge's north side, and El Relleno on the south side. The communities both harbor a sizable population of foreign yachties – folks sailing around the world or some part thereof.

The minute you alight from the bus, young men will approach you to put you on a motorboat to Lívingston. This may be exactly what you want to do. However, you can also spend some relaxing days around the lake. For details of Río Dulce boat trips, see the Around Lívingston section, later.

Orientation & Information Unless you're staying at Hotel Backpacker's (see Places to Stay & Eat) or volunteering at the adjacent Casa Guatemala, get off the bus on the north side of the bridge near the Río Bravo Restaurant. Otherwise you'll find yourself trudging over what is purported to be Central America's longest bridge – it's a steamy 30-minute walk.

Tijax Express, right by the river near where the bus drops you, is Río Dulce's unofficial tourist information center. Bus, boat, hotel and other travel details are available here. It's open daily and English is spoken.

If you need to change money or traveler's checks, head for the Banrural or Banco de Comercio in town.

Cap't Nemo's Communications (☎ 902 0616, rio@guate.net), beside Bruno's on the river, offers email and international phone/fax services. It's open 8 am to 6 pm Monday to Saturday, 9 am to 5 pm Sunday. It caters to contact-starved yachties, so it isn't cheap.

Organized Tours ATI Divers (santacruz@guate.net) offers seven-day excursions to Belize's barrier reef aboard the company's trimaran. The tours feature the same laid-back style that has made famous their Iguana Perdida hostel on Lago de Atitlán (see Santa Cruz La Laguna in the Highlands section). Trips include all taxes and meals; snorkeling costs US$370 and scuba diving starts at US$490. The ATI office is at Bruno's (see Places to Stay & Eat).

Places to Stay & Eat The *Hacienda Tijax* (☎ 902 0858, 367 5563 in Guatemala City, tijax@guate.net), a 500-acre hacienda a two-minute boat ride across the cove from the Río Bravo Restaurant, is a special place to stay. Activities include horseback riding, hiking, birding, sailboat trips and tours around the rubber plantation. Small private rooms over the hacienda's restaurant are US$6/10 single/double. New cabañas built over the river with fans, nets and shared bath run US$13/17/22 single/double/triple. Thai-style thatch-roofed houses, each with private hot bath and kitchen, are US$50 single or double. You can pitch a tent in the camping area for US$2 per person. Access is by boat or by a road that turns off the highway about 1km north of the village. The folks here speak Spanish, English, Dutch, French and Italian, and they'll pick you up from across the river; ask at the Tijax Express office. The hacienda has a restaurant. Day passes are US$1.30. Some travelers might be uncomfortable with the isolation of this place. You can call them on VHF channel 09.

Web site: www.tijax.com

Just up from the dock is *Las Brisas Hotel*, offering acceptable rooms for US$4.50 single with shared bath, US$6.45 per person with private bath and fan, US$10.75 with private bath and air-con.

Alongside the bridge, you'll see a path leading to *Bruno's* (☎ /fax 902 0610, rio@ guate.net), a riverside hangout for yachties. Rooms with private hot bath and air-con are comfortable, clean and cost US$23 double. Cheaper rooms, also clean and comfortable, with a sink, fan and shared bath are US$7.75/15.45. A fully equipped apartment that sleeps five is available for US$75.

Other places to stay in the village include: *Riverside Motel*, a simple place on the highway offering basic rooms with shared bath and fan for US$4 single or double; *Hotel Don Paco*, a yellow building with no sign, renting simple rooms with shared bath for US$4/7 single/double; and *Hotel Portal del Río*, among the better hotels in the village (which isn't saying much), offering rooms for US$5.15 with private bath and fan, US$13 to add air-con and cable TV.

Across the bridge is *Hotel Backpacker's*, (☎ 208 1779, casaguatemala@guate.net), a business run by Casa Guatemala and the orphans it serves. Foam dorm beds are US$4.50 with bath or US$3.90 without; space to hang your hammock is US$2, plus US$2.60 if you need to rent one; and basic private rooms are US$9.65 per person with bath, US$6.45 without – go for one overlooking the river. The hotel has a restaurant and bar right on the water and offers lancha, laundry, phone, fax and email services (US$5.15 an hour). If you're coming by lancha, ask the boat pilot to let you off here to spare yourself the walk across the bridge.

The best place to dine is *Restaurant Río Bravo*, which has an open-air deck over the lake, just on the north side of the bridge. Its menu offers a good variety of seafood (including ceviche) and pasta dishes; cocktails are available. Simple lunch and dinner plates start at US$4; you can get a good breakfast for US$1.30.

Nearby, *Bruno's*, another open-air place beside the water, is a restaurant/sports bar with satellite TV and video. *Cafetería La Carreta*, off the highway on the road toward San Felipe, is often recommended by locals. *Hacienda Tijax* has a restaurant with a full bar and good coffee.

Getting There & Away Grupo TACA flies three times a week each way between Guatemala City and Río Dulce.

Beginning at 7 am, eight buses a day head north along a paved road to Poptún (US$3.90, three hours, 99km) and Flores (US$6.45, five hours, 208km). The 8:30 and 10:30 pm departures continue all the way to Melchor de Mencos (US$9) on the Belize border. In the other direction, buses go to Guatemala City (US$4.50, five hours, 274km) 15 times a day. To get to Puerto Barrios, take any bus heading for Guatemala City and change at La Ruidosa.

The Atitlán Shuttle minibus operates from an office on the highway, near Tijax Express. Shuttles to Antigua cost around US$35.

Dilapidated Fuentes del Norte buses leave for El Estor (US$1.30, 1½ hours, 43km) from the highway in the middle of town, across from Restaurant Costa Libre. They depart several times daily between 7:30 am and 4 pm. This bus does *not* go to San Felipe; take one of the pickup trucks to get there.

Colectivo motorboats go down the Río Dulce to Lívingston whenever a minimum of six to eight people want to go. With plenty of stops, the trip takes about three hours and costs around US$7.75 per person (bargain for a fair price). Boats usually leave in the morning, but they may leave throughout the day.

The Road to Flores

North across the bridge is the road into El Petén, Guatemala's vast jungle province. It's 208km to Santa Elena and Flores, and another 71km to Tikal.

The entire stretch of road from the Carretera al Atlántico to Santa Elena has been recently paved, so it's a smooth ride all the way from Río Dulce to the Tikal ruins. You can make it there in a snappy five hours.

The forest here is disappearing at an alarming rate, falling to the machetes of subsistence farmers. Sections are felled and burned off, crops are grown for a few seasons until the fragile jungle soil is exhausted, then the farmer moves deeper into the forest to slash and burn anew. Cattle ranchers have contributed to the damage, as has the migration of Guatemalans from the cities to the Petén.

Mariscos

This is the principal town on the lake's quiet south side. *Denny's Beach*, 10 minutes by boat from Mariscos, is a good place to get away from the tourist bustle. It offers cabañas (US$5 per person), tours, hiking and swimming and hosts full moon parties. You can camp here or sling a hammock for US$2 per person. Denny's is operated by Dennis Gulck and his wife, Lupe. When you arrive in Mariscos (or Río Dulce), you can radio them on VHF channel 63 – many people and businesses in the area use radios, so it isn't hard to find one – and they'll come pick you up. Otherwise, hitch a *cayuco* (dugout canoe) at the Mariscos market for US$0.65. *Karlinda's* and *Marinita* are other places to stay in Mariscos; both have restaurants and offer lake tours.

El Castillo de San Felipe

The fortress and castle of San Felipe de Lara, about 3km west of the bridge, was built in 1652 to keep pirates from looting the villages and commercial caravans of Izabal. Though it deterred the buccaneers a bit, a pirate force captured and burned the fortress in 1686. By the end of the next century, pirates had disappeared from the Caribbean and the fort's sturdy walls served as a prison. Eventually, the fortress was abandoned and became a ruin. The present fort was reconstructed in 1956.

Today, the castle is protected as a park and is one of the lake's principal tourist attractions. In addition to the fort itself, the site has a large park, with barbecue/picnic areas, and you can swim in the lake here. It's open 8 am to 5 pm daily (US$1).

Near the Castillo, *Hotel Don Humberto* offers simple but clean rooms with private bath for US$4/7/10.50 single/double/triple. The hotel has a restaurant, or you could try *Cafetería Selva Tropical*.

On the lakeshore, about a 10-minute walk from El Castillo, *Rancho Escondido*

(☎/fax 369 2681 in Guatemala City) is a pleasant little hotel and restaurant. Downstairs rooms with shared bath are US$5/9 single/double; more attractive upstairs rooms with private bath are US$6.45/12.25, or you can stay in a hammock for US$2.50 per night. Amenities include laundry service, good food, swimming in the lake and other activities. The owners will pick you up when you arrive in Río Dulce; ask at the Tijax Express and they'll radio for you.

San Felipe is on the lakeshore, 3km west of Río Dulce. It's a beautiful 45-minute walk between the two. Colectivo pickups provide transportation between the towns for US$0.35, running about every half hour. In Río Dulce, pickups stop at the corner of the highway and the road to El Estor, across from Restaurant Costa Libre; in San Felipe they stop in front of Hotel Don Humberto, at the entrance to El Castillo.

Boats coming from Lívingston will drop you in San Felipe if you ask them. The Río Dulce boat trips usually come to El Castillo, allowing you to get out and visit the castle. Or you can come over from Río Dulce by private launch for US$5.

Finca El Paraíso

On the lake's north side, between San Felipe and El Estor, the Finca El Paraíso is a popular day trip from Río Dulce and other places around the lake. At the finca, which is a working ranch, you can walk to an incredibly beautiful spot in the jungle where a wide, hot waterfall drops about 12m into a clear, deep pool. You can bathe in the hot water, swim in the cool pool or duck under an overhanging promontory and enjoy a jungle-style sauna. Also on the finca are several interesting caves and good hiking; admission is US$0.65. You can rent bungalows for US$20 double.

To get to the finca, take the El Estor bus from Río Dulce (US$1, one hour). The last bus in either direction passes at around 5 pm, so don't dawdle past then unless you plan on spending the night.

El Estor

The major settlement on the northwest shore is El Estor. Once a nickel-mining town, it is now growing in popularity as a way station for intrepid travelers on the

Cobán-Lago de Izabal route through the beautiful Panzós Valley. El Estor is also the jumping-off point for explorations into the Bocas de Polochic, an area of extreme biodiversity supporting more than 300 bird species and many varieties of butterflies and fish (visit now, before it attains ecotourism mecca status).

El Estor is an easily negotiable, friendly, somnolent town. Banrural on 3a Calle at 5a Avenida changes US dollars; the Corpobanco across the street is a Western Union agent. The police station is on 1a Calle at 5a Avenida, near the lakeshore. Phone calls can be made from Comedor Dalila No 1 (see below).

An office of the Fundación Defensores de la Naturaleza (☎ 949 7237, defensores@pronet.net.gt) is next to the police station. Visitors interested in exploring the Reserva de la Biósfera de Sierra de las Minas or the Bocas del Polochic should stop in here. Ask for permission to stay at the foundation's scientific research station near Río Zarquito; the cost for transportation, a bunk and three meals a day is around US$15 per person.

Overlooking the lake, *Hotel Vista al Lago* (☎ 949 7205, 6a Avenida 1-13, Zona 1) is airy and clean. Built between 1825 and 1830, the building was once a general store owned by an Englishman and a Dutchman; 'the store' gave the town of El Estor its name. The 21 rooms here, each with private bath and fan, are US$9/11/15 single/double/triple. The present owners can arrange tours and guides.

Hotel Santa Clara (☎ 949 7244, 5a Avenida 2-11) has clean rooms with private bath on the upper level for US$4.65/6.20/7.75 and worse rooms downstairs without bath for US$1.95 per person. *Hotel Villela* (6a Avenida 2-06) is another good place to stay, with clean, simple rooms arranged around a courtyard. Rooms with private bath and fan are US$3.25 per person.

Comedor Dalila No 1, across from Transportes Valenciana, is a clean, cheap place serving huge plates of standard Guatemalan food. On the road into town, *Restaurante Centenario* has been locally recommended, as has *Ranchón Tipico Chaabil*, which is probably El Estor's best restaurant. It's across the street from the Fuentes del Norte bus office on the park.

Hugo's Restaurant serves simple meals and has information about tours around the lake and cabañas on the Río Sauce.

Brenda Mercedes and Transportes Valenciana buses operate between El Estor and Cobán (US$2.30, 7½ hours, 166km) several times daily. The first departure is at 5 am. The route is slow going but very beautiful. Fuentes de Polochic has three morning departures to Guatemala City (US$7, four hours, 216km), as does Fuentes del Norte. This company also has hourly buses to Río Dulce and Puerto Barrios from 6 am to 5 pm.

No public boat services operate between El Estor and other lake destinations. Private lanchas can be contracted, though this can be pricey, especially for solo travelers. Ask at your hotel or the Defensores office about hiring a boat or guide.

PUERTO BARRIOS
pop 35,000
Heading east from La Ruidosa junction toward Puerto Barrios, the country becomes even more lush, tropical and humid. The powerful United Fruit Company owned vast plantations in the Río Motagua valley and many other parts of the country. It built railways to ship produce to the coast, and built Puerto Barrios early in the 20th century to put that produce onto ships sailing for New Orleans and New York. Laid out as a company town, Puerto Barrios has long, wide streets arranged neatly on a grid. Many of its Caribbean-style wood-frame houses are on stilts.

When United Fruit's power and influence declined in the 1960s, the Del Monte company became successor to its interests. But the heyday of the imperial foreign firms was past, as was that of Puerto Barrios. A new, modern, efficient port was built a few kilometers to the southwest, at Santo Tomás de Castilla, and Puerto Barrios settled into tropical torpor.

For foreign visitors, Puerto Barrios is little more than the jumping-off point for boats to Punta Gorda (Belize) or Lívingston. As the Lívingston boats leave at odd hours, you may find yourself staying the night in this rough, unfriendly town. While the ships and sailors may have left, the dive bars and brothels remain. Most travelers will want to move on fast.

GUATEMALA

PUERTO BARRIOS

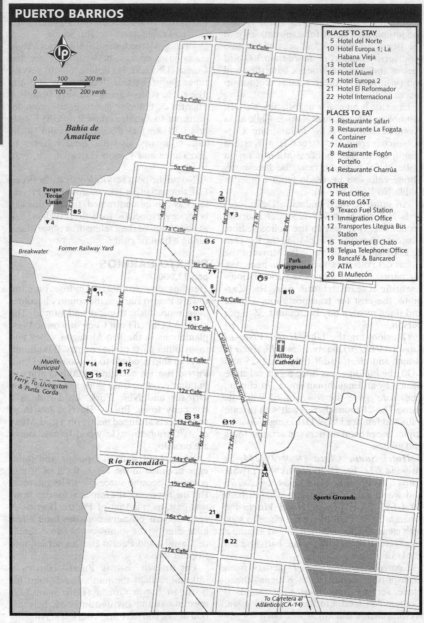

PLACES TO STAY
5   Hotel del Norte
10 Hotel Europa 1; La
    Habana Vieja
13 Hotel Lee
16 Hotel Miami
17 Hotel Europa 2
21 Hotel El Reformador
22 Hotel Internacional

PLACES TO EAT
1   Restaurante Safari
3   Restaurante La Fogata
4   Container
7   Maxim
8   Restaurante Fogón
    Porteño
14 Restaurante Charrúa

OTHER
2   Post Office
6   Banco G&T
9   Texaco Fuel Station
11 Immigration Office
12 Transportes Litegua Bus
    Station
15 Transportes El Chato
18 Telgua Telephone Office
19 Bancafé & Bancared
    ATM
20 El Muñecón

1a Calle
2a Calle
3a Calle
4a Calle
5a Calle
6a Calle
7a Calle
8a Calle
9a Calle
10a Calle
11a Calle
12a Calle
13a Calle
14a Calle
15a Calle
16a Calle
17a Calle

Bahía de
Amatique

Parque
Tecún
Umán

Breakwater   Former Railway Yard

Muelle
Municipal

Ferry To Livingston
& Punta Gorda

Río Escondido

Park
(Playground)

Hilltop
Cathedral

Sports Grounds

To Carretera al
Atlántico (CA-14)

Orientation & Information

It's 800m from the Transportes Litegua bus terminal to the Muelle Municipal (Municipal Boat Dock) at the foot of 12a Calle, from which boats depart for Lívingston and Punta Gorda. If you're in town just to take a boat, select a hotel near the dock. However, avoid getting there via 9a Calle, which is crawling with ruffians.

El Muñecón, at the intersection of 8a Avenida, 14a Calle and the Calzada Justo Rufino Barrios, is a statue of a *bananero* (banana worker); it's a favorite monument in the town.

Many banks change US dollars cash and traveler's checks. Banco G&T, on 7a Calle between 5a and 6a Avenidas, changes both and gives cash advances on MasterCard and Visa; it's open 9 am to 8 pm Monday to Friday, 10 am to 2 pm Saturday. The Bancafé on 13a Calle near 6a Avenida has a Bancared ATM that accepts Visa cards.

The post office is on 6a Calle at 6a Avenida. Telgua is on 13a Calle, between 5a and 6a Avenidas.

The immigration office (☎ 948 0802, 948 0327) is at 9a Calle and 2a Avenida, a couple of blocks from the dock. Be sure to get your entry or exit stamp if you're entering or leaving the country.

In the evening, the noisy bars and brothels along 9a Calle really get going.

Places to Stay

A couple of good, clean hotels are on 3a Avenida between 11a and 12a Calles, one block from the dock. Both have rooms with private bath and fan arranged around a central courtyard. *Hotel Europa 2* (☎ 948 1292), perhaps the slightly more attractive, has rooms for US$4.65 per person; at *Hotel Miami* (☎ 948 0537) rooms are US$5.15/10 single/double, or US$15 with air-con. If you need a safe place to leave your car while you visit Lívingston, park in the courtyard of either place for US$2.50 per day.

The original *Hotel Europa 1* (☎ 948 0127), on 8a Avenida between 8a and 9a Calles, is 1½ blocks from the cathedral (look for the openwork cross on top of the steeple). Fairly clean, comfortable and quiet, it has rooms with bath for US$4.65/9.30.

Hotel Lee (☎ 948 0685), on 5a Avenida around the corner from the Litegua bus terminal, is a friendly, family-owned place offering great value. The rooms are a bit cramped but have private bath, good beds and fans for US$4.50 per person. A restaurant and bar are attached.

In a class by itself, the old *Hotel del Norte* (☎ 948 2116, ☎/fax 948 0087), on 7a Calle at 1a Avenida, is at the waterfront end of 7a Calle, 1.2km from the dock (you must walk around the railway yard). In its airy dining room overlooking the Bahía de Amatique, you can almost hear the echoing conversation of turn-of-the-century banana moguls and smell their pungent cigars. Spare, simple and agreeably dilapidated, this is a real museum piece. Rooms with sea view, private bath and air-con are US$13/19.50/26 single/double/triple; less agreeable interior rooms with fan are US$9/14. Meals are served in the dining room; other amenities include a bar and two seaside swimming pools. Service is refined, careful and elegantly old-fashioned, but the food can be otherwise.

South of the streambed and west of the main road (Calzada Justo Rufino Barrios) are two fancier, more comfortable hotels. The 48-room *Hotel El Reformador* (☎ 948 0533, 948 5489, fax 948 1531, 7a Avenida 159), at 16a Calle, is a modern place offering rooms with TV and private bath for US$14/24 with fan, US$23/29 with air-con. Better located rooms with bath, air-con and TV are US$33/51. The hotel has its own restaurant. Around the corner, *Hotel Internacional* (☎ 948 7719/20), on 7a Avenida between 16a and 17a Calles, has a swimming pool, restaurant and parking. Rooms with private bath and TV are US$9/14 with fan, US$14/25 with air-con.

Places to Eat

The town's most enjoyable restaurant is *Restaurante Safari* (☎ 948 0568), on a thatch-roofed dock right over the water at the north end of 5a Avenida, about a kilometer from the town center. Locals and visitors alike love to eat here, catching the fresh sea breezes while mariachis stroll from table to table. Seafood meals of all kinds are the specialty (US$6 to US$10); burgers, sandwiches and chicken are also served. It's open 10 am to 9 pm daily.

Restaurante La Fogata, on 6a Avenida between 6a and 7a Calles, is another fancy place, specializing in charcoal-grilled steaks and seafood. It offers a set lunch for US$3.50 and live music most nights.

Simpler places include *Restaurante Fogón Porteño*, opposite the bus station, which features charcoal-grilled chicken, steak and seafood; *Maxim*, a funky Chinese place on 6a Avenida at 8a Calle; and *La Habana Vieja*, attached to the Hotel Europa 1, with a full bar and tasty grilled meats, seafood and pasta dishes at reasonable prices.

Perhaps the oddest eatery in town is *Container*, a cafe and drinks stand at the foot of 7a Calle, near the Hotel del Norte. It's made of two steel shipping containers, and the chairs and tables set out in the street afford a fine bay view.

Restaurante Charrúa, at the Muelle Municipal, serves filling and cheap Guatemalan fare for breakfast, lunch and dinner.

Getting There & Away

Air The airport at Puerto Barrios receives a limited number of international flights, but it's served often by TACA (☎ 334 7722 for reservations) from Guatemala City and Santa Elena/Flores.

Bus The Transportes Litegua bus station (☎ 948 1172, 948 1002) is near the corner of 6a Avenida and 9a Calle. This is also the terminal for most other buses. Express buses to Guatemala City (US$5.15, five hours, 295km) leave at 1, 1:30, 2, 3, 7, 7:30 and 10 am, noon and 4 pm. Ordinary buses take several hours longer and leave more frequently.

Buses for Chiquimula (US$2.50, 4½ hours, 192km) leave every hour. Take this bus for Quiriguá and Río Dulce. You have to transfer at La Ruidosa.

You can store your luggage at the terminal for about US$0.25 per piece, per day.

Boat All boats depart from the Muelle Municipal at the foot of 12a Calle. Get to the dock at least 30 or 45 minutes prior to departure for a seat.

A ferry departs for Lívingston at 10 am and 5 pm daily (US$1.35, 1½ hours). On the Lívingston side, it departs for Puerto Barrios at 5 am and 2 pm daily; if everything goes smoothly, the last ferry arrives in Puerto Barrios at 3:30 pm and the last bus to Guatemala City leaves at 4 pm, so you'll have to rush from the dock to the bus station. Colectivo lanchas depart from both sides whenever 12 people are ready to go; they take 30 minutes and cost US$2.60. Especially in low season, don't count on 12 people getting together late in the day.

Small lanchas depart Puerto Barrios for Punta Gorda, Belize, at 10 am on Monday, Wednesday, Thursday and Saturday and at 8 am on Tuesday and Friday. Boats return from Punta Gorda at 4 pm Monday to Saturday; these take 50 minutes and cost US$7.75. Transportes El Chato (☎ 948 5525), at the Muelle Municipal in Puerto Barrios offers this service. You may also be able to contract a colectivo to Punta Manabique, north of Puerto Barrios.

The boats to Punta Gorda no longer stop in Lívingston. If you take one of these boats, you must pass through Guatemalan customs and immigration before boarding. Allow some time, and have your passport handy.

Overland to Honduras Information on this route – from Puerto Barrios to Puerto Cortés, Honduras – is based on letters from Camille Geels and Anja Boye (Denmark), Peter Kúgerl (Austria) and Matthew Willson (UK) and conversations with Gunther Blauth (Germany).

Whereas this route used to be off-limits to all but the most adventurous travelers, new roads and bridges make it a fairly easy trip. You can make it in one day, but some people prefer to break the journey at Omoa.

The trip takes about four hours. The first thing you need to do is get your Guatemalan exit stamp from the immigration office in Puerto Barrios (you may want to get it the day before). If you're coming from Lívingston, the trade-off here is you have to overnight in Puerto Barrios. Otherwise, take the 5 am ferry from Lívingston to Puerto Barrios and cool your heels until the immigration office opens.

After arranging your paperwork, take the bus from the market in Puerto Barrios to Finca La Inca (US$0.50), the last station on the bus line; the buses depart hourly, starting at 7 am. At Finca La Inca, get off the bus and switch to a pickup that will take you over a new bridge spanning the Río

Motagua and into Honduras. Here you get your passport stamped, pay US$2 and continue on the pickup to Tegulcigalpita (US$1, one hour). From Tegulcigalpita, buses go to Omoa, Puerto Cortés and beyond. If you miss the chance to get your passport stamped before Tegucigalpita, be sure to take care of that at the immigration office in Puerto Cortés or Omoa.

Presumably, the same thing can be done in reverse if you're coming to Guatemala from Honduras.

LÍVINGSTON
pop 5500

As you come ashore in Lívingston, which is reachable only by boat, you'll meet black Guatemalans who speak Spanish and their traditional Garífuna language; some also speak the musical English of Belize and the islands. Lívingston is an interesting anomaly, with a laid-back, Belizean way of life, groves of coconut palms, gaily painted wooden buildings and an economy based on fishing and tourism.

The Garífuna (Garinagu, or Black Carib) people of Lívingston and southern Belize are the descendants of Africans brought to the New World as slaves. They trace their roots to the Honduran island of Roatán, where they were settled by the British after the Garífuna revolt on the Caribbean island of St Vincent in 1795. From Roatán, the Garífuna people spread out along the Caribbean Coast of Central America, from Belize to Nicaragua. Intermarrying with

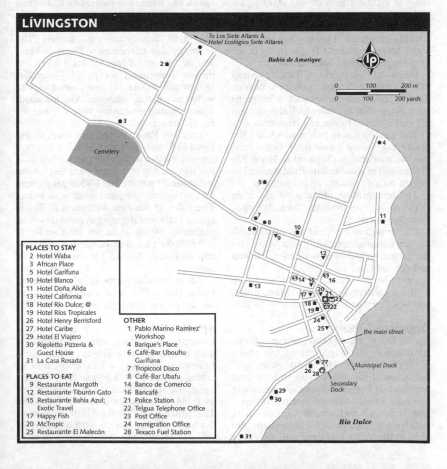

LÍVINGSTON

To Los Siete Altares &
Hotel Ecológico Siete Altares

Bahía de Amatique

0   100   200 m
0   100   200 yards

Cemetery

the main street

Municipal Dock

Secondary
Dock

Río Dulce

PLACES TO STAY
2 Hotel Waba
3 African Place
5 Hotel Garífuna
10 Hotel Blanco
11 Hotel Doña Alida
13 Hotel California
18 Hotel Río Dulce; @
19 Hotel Ríos Tropicales
26 Hotel Henry Berrisford
27 Hotel Caribe
29 Hotel El Viajero
30 Rigoletto Pizzería &
    Guest House
31 La Casa Rosada

PLACES TO EAT
9 Restaurante Margoth
12 Restaurante Tiburón Gato
15 Restaurante Bahía Azul;
    Exotic Travel
17 Happy Fish
20 McTropic
25 Restaurante El Malecón

OTHER
1 Pablo Marino Ramírez'
   Workshop
4 Barique's Place
6 Café-Bar Ubouhu
   Garífuna
7 Tropicool Disco
8 Café-Bar Ubafu
14 Banco de Comercio
16 Bancafé
21 Police Station
22 Telgua Telephone Office
23 Post Office
24 Immigration Office
28 Texaco Fuel Station

Carib Indians as well as with Maya and shipwrecked sailors of other races, they've developed a distinct culture and language incorporating African, Indian and European elements.

Other people in Lívingston include the indigenous Q'eqchi' Maya, ladinos and a smattering of international travelers.

Beaches here are largely disappointing, as the jungle comes down to the water's edge. Those beaches that do exist are often clogged with vegetation and unsafe for swimming due to contaminated water. Safe swimming is possible at Los Siete Altares (see Around Lívingston, later in this chapter).

Orientation & Information

After half an hour you'll know where everything is. Exotic Travel (☎ 947 0049/51, fax 947 0136, kjchew@hotmail.com), based at the Bahía Azul restaurant on the main street in the center of town, offers free maps and information about things to do in the area (see Organized Tours, below).

Banco de Comercio and Bancafé change US dollars cash and traveler's checks. Several private businesses do, too, including Restaurante Bahía Azul, which also changes the currencies of Belize and Honduras.

The post office is half a block off the main road. Telgua is next door. Email services are available at (adjacent to Hotel Río Dulce) and at Restaurante El Malecón. The former is more reliable and expensive.

The immigration office is on the main street coming up from the dock. It's open 7 am to 9 pm daily.

Use mosquito repellent and other sensible precautions, especially if you go out into the jungle; mosquitoes here carry malaria and dengue fever.

Pablo Marino Ramírez has a workshop by the sea where he makes Garífuna drums and woodcarvings. You're welcome to visit.

Organized Tours

Exotic Travel, based at Restaurante Bahía Azul, offers various tours of the area's natural wonders. The Ecological Tour walks you through town, up to a lookout spot and on to the Río Quehúeche, where you take a half-hour canoe trip downriver and then a jungle walk to Los Siete Altares (Seven Altars). From there you head to the beach and hang out, then walk down the beach back to Lívingston. The trip leaves from the Bahía Azul restaurant at 9 am daily and arrives back around 4 pm; the cost is US$7.75, which includes a boxed lunch. This is a great way to see the area, and the friendly local guides give you a good introduction to the Garífuna people.

The Playa Blanca tour goes by boat first to the Seven Altars, then to the swimmable Río Cocolí, and then on to Playa Blanca (the area's best beach) for two or three hours. The trip goes with a minimum of six people and costs US$7.75 per person. The Casa Rosada hotel offers the same trip for US$12.50, including a picnic lunch.

Exotic Travel also offers day trips to the Cayos Sapodillas, well off the coast in southern Belize, where the snorkeling and fishing are great. The cost is split among the people going (if eight people go, it's US$19.50 each, plus US$10 to enter the cayes). The company also offers trips to Punta de Manabique biological reserve for US$13 per person (minimum six people). Smaller groups can do any of these tours if they're willing to pay the difference. Also ask about a new mountain-biking tour offered by Exotic Travel.

La Casa Rosada organizes tours to the Finca El Paraíso on Lago de Izabal (see that section, earlier in this chapter). It's a long day trip, leaving at around 6 am and returning around 7 pm; it costs US$20 per person, maximum nine people. Lunch is included. The folks at Rigoletto Pizzería & Guest House run tours stopping in eight different, picturesque spots, including the Castillo de San Felipe on Lago de Izabal. It's an all-day trip and costs US$15 for three or more people.

All of the above trips are also organized by the Happy Fish restaurant (☎ 902 7143), but not on any fixed schedule.

Special Events

Lívingston is packed with holidaymakers during Semana Santa. The day of San Isidro Labrador, who was a cultivator, is celebrated on May 15 with people bringing their agricultural products to a mass in the morning, followed by a street procession. The national day of the Garífuna is celebrated on November 26 with a variety of cultural events. The day of the Virgin of

Guadalupe, Mexico's patron saint, is celebrated on December 12.

Places to Stay

When you arrive by boat, you may be met by local boys offering to take you to a hotel and carry your luggage (there are no taxis). They'll lead you to place after place until you find one you like. They expect a small tip, and also get a commission from the hotel. It isn't safe to sleep on the beach.

Several places to stay are right beside the river, to the left of the boat dock. *Hotel Caribe* (☎ 947 0053), a minute's walk along the shore, is one of the cheapest in town: US$2.35/4.70 single/double with shared bath, US$3.10/6.20 with private bath. Look before you rent, as quality varies. *Hotel El Viajero* is another basic place along here, with singles for US$2.35 with shared bath, US$3 with private bath.

Even cheaper is scruffy *Hotel Blanco*, which has basic rooms, all with shared bath, on two floors. Upstairs units are US$2.60 per person; downstairs they're US$1.95. This place is uphill past the center of town and popular with hardcore budget travelers.

Hotel Río Dulce, an authentic Caribbean two-story wood-frame place uphill from the dock on the main street, is another cheapie. Upstairs rooms with shared bathrooms in the backyard are US$3.25 per person; three rooms with private bath are US$6.50. The rooms here are none too clean, and you may hear mice at night. Still, many shoestring travelers like this funky old place. The breezy wide balcony overlooking the street is great for people watching.

Next door, *Hotel Ríos Tropicales* (☎ 947 0158) is a good deal, with big, clean rooms with private bath and fan around a patio for US$5.80 per person. Rooms with shared bath are US$4.50. The hotel has hammocks and a restaurant, and you can hand-wash clothes. *Hotel California* is a clean, fine place with 10 simple rooms with private bath for US$5/8.

A few blocks from the center of town, *Hotel Garífuna* (☎ 947 0183, fax 947 0184) offers rooms with private bath for US$5.15/7.75/10.30 single/double/triple. It has international phone and fax service.

African Place (☎ 948 0218/21), a large white building with Moorish arches, is an old favorite in Lívingston. The 25 rooms are clean and rent for US$4/6/7 with shared bath, US$6/10/12.50 with private bath. The hotel has a big flower-filled garden in back and a good restaurant. On the down side, it's a longish walk from town (10 or 15 minutes) and there have been reports of security problems (don't leave valuables in your room).

Turn right at the African Place for *Hotel Waba* (☎ 947 0193), where clean rooms with private bath are US$5.15/7.75. Two rooms with shared bath are US$2.60 per person. The balcony has a sea view, and an open-air palapa restaurant in the yard serves affordable meals.

For homey, friendly atmosphere, you can't beat *Rigoletto Pizzería & Guest House*, beside the river 300m left of the dock. Clean, simple rooms sharing a clean bathroom are US$10.50 double, and all three meals are served (the owner is a great cook). Other amenities include laundry and a riverside garden with tables and chairs. Boats will drop you off here if you ask.

Beside the river, *Hotel Henry Berrisford* (☎/fax 948 1568) has clean, comfortable rooms with private bath and TV. Beware, though: The swimming pool is not always clean. Rooms with fan are US$7.50 per person, or US$10 per person with breakfast; with air-con and breakfast they are US$14 per person.

Hotel Doña Alida (☎/fax 947 0027), beside the sea a few blocks from town center, has a beautiful beach, a restaurant and terraces with sea views. Doubles with shared bath are US$13; extra-large triple rooms with private bath, some with sea view, are US$39; a double bungalow is US$28. Breakfast is available.

La Casa Rosada (☎ 947 0303, fax 947 0304) is an attractive place right on the river, 800m to the left of the dock; boats will drop you here if you ask. Ample riverside gardens, a dock with a gazebo and refreshments available anytime all contribute to the relaxed, friendly ambience. For US$8 a person you can enjoy one of 10 freestanding, thatch-roofed bungalows, each with fan, screens and mosquito nets and sharing three clean bathrooms. Also available are laundry, daily tours and one of the town's best restaurants.

Hotel Ecológico Siete Altares (☎ *332 7107, fax 478 2159, sietealtares@hotmail.com*) is a welcoming cluster of riverside bungalows about an hour's walk from Lívingston. The rustic thatch bungalows have fans, sleep two, four or six people and cost US$10 per person.

You can take a lancha from the dock in Lívingston or follow the shore north toward Siete Altares for an hour. A restaurant is nearby.

Places to Eat

Food in Lívingston is expensive because most of it (except fish and coconuts) must be brought from elsewhere. *Tapado,* a rich stew made from fish, shrimp, crab other seafood, coconut and plantain, and spiced with coriander, is the local specialty.

The main street is lined with little *comedores*. It may be best to choose the currently most popular place. At the time of writing, *Restaurante Tiburón Gato* was the title holder.

Restaurante Margoth has a full bar and offers filling, well-prepared fish and meat dishes at reasonable prices. Service can be slow. *Restaurante Bahía Azul* is a popular gathering spot in relaxed surroundings. It has good food, reasonable prices and live music some evenings. It's open 7 am to 10 pm daily.

Other popular places on the main street include *Restaurante El Malecón*, just up the hill from the dock, on the left, where Caribbean-inspired fare goes for US$4 to US$7; the *McTropic*, a bit farther up the hill on the right side, which is half restaurant, half shop and is favored by the thriftiest crowd; and *Happy Fish*.

African Place (see Places to Stay) serves a variety of exotic and local dishes. Full meals, including tapado, are available for US$6 or less.

On the road beside the river are a couple of other good restaurants. *Rigoletto Pizzería* (see Places to Stay) has Italian, South Asian, Chinese and other dishes, with many meat and veggie selections. The pizzas are made in a real pizza oven and are available for take-out.

Farther along, the restaurant at *La Casa Rosada* is another enjoyable riverside spot. All three meals are served, with good, ample dinners for around US$6 to US$8;

dinner reservations are advisable. The coffee here is probably the best in town.

Entertainment

Garífuna people have a distinctive form of music and dance. The traditional Garífuna band, composed of three large drums, a turtle shell, maracas and a big conch shell, produces throbbing, haunting rhythms and melodies. The chanted words are like a litany, with responses often taken up by the audience. The dance is the *punta*, which features lot of gyrating hip movements.

Lívingston is about the only place in Guatemala where Garífuna music and dance are accessible to visitors. *Restaurante Bahía Azul* has live music weekends and sometimes other evenings. *Café-Bar Ubafu* has live Garífuna music and dancing most evenings; it's liveliest on weekends. Across the street, *Café-Bar Ubouhu Garífuna* is another popular nightspot.

The disco *Barique's Place*, by the sea on the town's north side, is open weekends. This is a moonlit, beachy type of place thick with locals, where the liquor flows freely and things can get rough. It might not be the best place for travelers. *Tropicool Disco*, on the other hand, is usually packed with foreigners getting down to disco beats. It's next to the Café-Bar Ubafu and liveliest on weekends.

Getting There & Away

The only way to get to Lívingston is by boat, which come frequently from Río Dulce and Puerto Barrios; see those sections for details. Boats also come here from Honduras and Belize.

Exotic Travel, based at Restaurante Bahía Azul, operates boats to Omoa (Honduras) and Punta Gorda (Belize). They run on a schedule, but will also go at any other time with a minimum of six people. Be sure to get your passport entry and exit stamps at the immigration offices on both ends of the journey.

The boats to Omoa depart Lívingston at 7 am Tuesday and Friday, arriving about 10 am. In Omoa, the boat docks near the bus stop, where you can catch a bus to Puerto Cortés, San Pedro Sula or La Ceiba. The boat leaves Omoa for the return trip around noon or 1 pm, arriving back in Lívingston around 3:30 pm. Cost is US$35 from

Lívingston to Omoa, US$25 from Omoa to Lívingston. The captain will take you to get your exit and entry stamps on both ends of the journey.

The boats to Punta Gorda (Belize) also leave Lívingston at 7 am Tuesday and Friday. This is a shorter trip, taking just 45 minutes; cost is US$13 each way. The boats depart Punta Gorda for the return trip at 9 am. Get your own exit stamp from the immigration office in Lívingston; the captain will take you to get your entry stamp in Punta Gorda.

Trips to Punta Gorda, Omoa and other places can also be arranged at the Happy Fish restaurant (☎ 902 7143).

AROUND LÍVINGSTON
Río Dulce Cruises

Lívingston is the starting point for boat rides on the Río Dulce. Passengers enjoy the tropical jungle scenery, swim and picnic, and explore the Biotopo Chocón Machacas, 12km west along the river.

Almost anyone in Lívingston can tell you who's organizing trips upriver. Exotic Travel makes trips daily, as do La Casa Rosada hotel and the Happy Fish restaurant (see Lívingston, earlier). Or you can simply walk to the dock and arrange a trip, thereby supporting the many local boat captains.

Shortly after you leave Lívingston headed upriver, you'll enter a steep-walled gorge called **Cueva de la Vaca**, its walls hung with great tangles of jungle foliage and bromeliads. The humid air is noisy with the cries of tropical birds. Just beyond is **La Pintada**, a graffiti-covered rock escarpment. Farther on, a thermal spring forces sulfurous water out at the base of the cliff, providing a delightful place for a swim.

Emerging from the gorge, the river eventually widens into **El Golfete**, a lake-like body of water that presages the even vaster Lago de Izabal.

On the north shore of El Golfete is the **Biotopo Chocón Machacas**, a 7600-hectare reserve established to protect the beautiful river landscape, the valuable mangrove swamps and, especially, the manatees that inhabit the waters. A network of 'water trails' (boat routes around several jungle lagoons) provide ways to see the reserve's flora and fauna. A nature trail begins at the visitor's center and winds its way through forests of mahogany, palms and rich tropical foliage. Jaguars and tapirs live in the reserve, though seeing one is unlikely. The walrus-like manatees are even more elusive. These huge mammals can weigh up to a ton, yet glide effortlessly beneath the river.

From El Golfete and the nature reserve, the boats continue upriver to the village of Río Dulce, where the road into El Petén crosses the river, and to the Castillo de San Felipe on Lago de Izabal (see the Lago de Izabal section, earlier in this chapter).

The trip is also offered from Río Dulce; ask at the Tijax Express office. Fare is US$7.75 one-way or US$13 roundtrip. Trips are organized by La Casa Rosada and Rigoletto Pizzería in Lívingston.

Los Siete Altares

The Seven Altars is a series of freshwater falls and pools about 5km (1½-hour walk) northwest of Lívingston along the shore of Bahía de Amatique. It's a pleasant goal for a beach walk and a good place for a picnic and swim. Follow the shore northward to the river mouth. Ford the river and walk along the beach until it meets the path into the woods (about 30 minutes). Follow this path all the way to the falls. If you'd rather not do the ford, find a boat at the river mouth to ferry you across for a few quetzals.

Boat trips go to the Seven Altars, but locals say it's better to walk there to experience the natural beauty and the Garífuna people along the way. Although robberies were common in the past, Lívingston has beefed up its police force, so you should have an enjoyable, safe walk. The falls can be disappointing in the dry season, however.

Finca Tatin

This wonderful B&B and Spanish school is at the confluence of the Ríos Dulce and Tatin. Finca Tatin (☎ 902 0831, fincatatin@ centramerica.com) was built by husbandwife team Carlos and Claudia Simonini. A program of 20 hours of instruction in an open thatch bungalow overlooking the river, including room, is US$120 a week. Kitchen facilities are available, or meals can be made for you (US$2.60, or cheaper vegetarian options). You can skip the classes and just relax here; basic rooms in bungalows with shared bath are US$5 a day. There are trails, waterfalls and endless river tributaries that you can explore with one of the cayucos available for guest use. Or ask for suggestions on area camping. This is not a place for phobics of bugs or creeping fauna.

Finca Tatin is easiest to reach by lancha from Lívingston (30 minutes). Hire a lanchero or call the Finca and they'll come pick you up (US$3.90). Spanish, English, French and Italian are spoken.

Web site: www.centramerica.com/fincatatin

El Petén

In the dense jungle cover of Guatemala's vast northeastern department of El Petén, you may hear the squawk of parrots, the chatter of monkeys and the rustlings of strange animals moving through the bush. The landscape here is utterly different from that of Guatemala's cool mountainous highlands or steamy Pacific Slope.

The monumental ceremonial center at Tikal is among the most impressive Mayan archaeological site. Though it is possible to visit Tikal on a single-day excursion by plane from Guatemala City, travelers are strongly encouraged to stay at least one night, whether in Flores, El Remate or Tikal itself. A day trip simply cannot do the place justice. The ruins of Uaxactún and Ceibal aren't as easily accessible, which makes them more exciting to visit. Several dozen other great Mayan cities hidden in El Petén, previously only accessible to archaeologists

(or artifact poachers) with aircraft, are now being opened for limited tourism.

In 1990 the Guatemalan government established the 1-million-hectare Maya Biosphere Reserve, which includes most of northern El Petén. The Guatemalan reserve adjoins the vast Calakmul Biosphere Reserve in Mexico and the Río Bravo Conservation Area in Belize, forming a multinational reserve of over 2 million hectares.

Many travelers linger in Poptún, a small town 113km southeast of Santa Elena that has been a popular backpacker layover for many years.

Warning

In years past, robbery of luxury and tourist buses on roads in El Petén was a concern, especially between Río Dulce and Flores and around the Belizean border at Melchor de Mencos/Benque Viejo del Carmen. Fortunately, things have quieted down considerably, and the overwhelming majority of visitors enjoy safe visits. Still, contact your embassy or consulate in Guatemala City for current information on road safety in the region; query other travelers as well.

Getting There & Around

The roads leading into El Petén have now all been paved, so travel is fast and smooth. Unfortunately, improved access has encouraged the migration of farmers and ranchers from other areas, increasing the pressure on resources and leading to even more deforestation in a region whose forests had already been falling at an alarming rate.

The Guatemalan government long ago decided to develop the adjoining towns of Flores, Santa Elena and San Benito, on the shores of Lago de Petén Itzá, into the region's tourism base. Here you'll find an airport, hotels and other services. A few small hotels and restaurants are right at Tikal, but other services there remain limited.

POPTÚN

pop 8000

Diminutive Poptún is about halfway between Río Dulce and Flores, and makes a good stopover en route to Tikal, especially if you're coming via Fray Bartolomé de Las Casas.

Several banks line 5a Calle. Bancafé gives cash advances on Visa cards. The Telgua office is behind the police station near the market. Email services are sporadically available at Fonda Ixobel II restaurant from 11 am to 1 pm daily (US$2.60 a half hour).

Places to Stay & Eat

The 400-acre *Finca Ixobel* (☎/fax 927 7363, *fincaixobel@conexion.com.gt*) is a friendly, relaxed spot for meeting other travelers from all parts of the globe. For several decades Carole DeVine has offered tent sites, *palapas* for hanging hammocks, beds and good homemade meals with veggie options galore. Swimming, horseback riding, camping trips, inner tubing on the river and a famous, thrilling cave trip (which even includes bodysurfing rapids) are all organized on a daily basis, for a reasonable charge.

Web site: http://fincaixobel.conexion.com

Accommodations run the gamut: Camping or hammock space costs US$2.10 per person; dorm beds are US$3; tree houses are US$5.80/7 single/double; a private room with shared bath is US$6.45/9/10.30 single/double/triple; a bungalow with private bath is US$11.60/16/21; and a big, private villa with bath is US$14.15/19.30/24. Meals offer stellar value, particularly the eat-all-you-like buffet dinner for US$4.50. You can cook in the campground, but bring all your own food as the finca has no store.

Volunteer opportunities exist for bilingual English-Spanish speakers; volunteers get free room and board. If you want to help/hang out for a month minimum, ask about volunteering.

Finca Ixobel also owns the Tierra Grande protected area and sanctuary, 16km from Poptún. This patch of rain forest supports a variety of tropical flora and fauna, and trips here are a valuable introduction to the jungle. Visitors sleep in hammocks, cook on an open fire and bathe in the river. Good-value multiday camping trips (starting at US$64.50, including transportation, guide, food and equipment) can be arranged at the finca or by calling ahead. Volunteers are also needed here to reintroduce captive animals into the wild. If you would like to help, a two-week minimum commitment is required.

The turnoff for the finca is marked on the highway, 5km south of town. In the daytime, ask the bus driver to let you off there; it's a 15-minute walk to the finca. At night, get off the bus in town and go to the Fonda Ixobel II restaurant, near the bus stop. They will radio for a taxi to the finca (US$1 per person). It's important not to walk at night, as robberies have occurred on the way. Robberies have also been attempted in daylight, so solo travelers might want to use the taxi service.

Serviceable hotels in town include the good *Hotel Posada de los Castellanos* (☎ 927 7222), where clean rooms (some dark) with fan and private bath arranged around a leafy courtyard are US$4.50/5.80/7.75/9.25 single/double/triple/quad; and *Pensión Izalco*, which has rooms with shared bath for US$3.25 single with fan, US$2.60 without.

Beyond Poptún, *Camping Cocay* (☎ 927 7024, *birgitleistner@compuserve.com*), 7km north of town and then 700m from the highway, is a primitive campground in the forest beside the river, which is good for swimming, inner tubing and fishing. The prices of US$2.60 per person in a tent or hammock, US$3.25 in a dorm, include breakfast; dinner is available for US$3.25. Area activities are offered. This place is primitive, remote and right in the jungle. Bring plenty of mosquito repellent.
Web site: http://ourworld.compuserve.com/homepages/birgitleistner

Getting There & Away

All the Guatemala City-Flores buses stop in Poptún; see Getting There & Away in the Flores & Santa Elena section, below, and the Getting Around section, earlier in this chapter, for bus details.

Buses also travel the remote route between Poptún and Fray Bartolomé de Las Casas on the way to Cobán. From Poptún it's five hours to Fray and another 5½ hours to Cobán.

Flores (US$2.60, two hours, 113km)
Several buses leave daily. The first departures at 8 and 10:30 am do not pass Finca Ixobel (you must travel into town to catch the early buses).

Fray Bartolomé de Las Casas (US$3.90, five hours, 100km)
One bus leaves at 11:30 am daily.

Guatemala City (US$7.75, eight hours, 373km)
Buses leave at 9 and 10:30 am, noon, 1 and 4 pm

daily, with an additional deluxe departure at 10 pm (US$16.75).

Melchor de Mencos (Belize border; US$3.90, four hours, 199km)
Transportes Rosita (☎ 927 7413) buses leave at midnight, 2 and 4 am.

Río Dulce (US$3.90, three hours, 99km)
Take any bus heading for Guatemala City.

If you're driving, fill your fuel tank before leaving Flores or Río Dulce, take some food, drink and a spare tire, and get an early start. The road is good in both directions, so drivers should have no problem between Poptún, Flores and Tikal.

FLORES & SANTA ELENA
pop 2000 & 17,000

Flores is built on an island in Lago de Petén Itzá. A 500m causeway connects it to the lakeshore town of Santa Elena. Adjoining Santa Elena to the west is San Benito (population 22,000).

As the departmental capital, Flores is a dignified place. Its church, small government building and municipal basketball court surround the plaza, which sits atop a hill in the island's center. The narrow streets are lined with charming, red-roofed houses. Santa Elena is a disorganized town of dusty unpaved streets, and San Benito is even more disorganized, but its honky-tonk bars keep it lively.

The three towns form one large settlement usually referred to simply as 'Flores.' All have numerous small hotels and restaurants.

History

Flores was founded on an island (*petén*) by the Itzáes after their expulsion from Chichén Itzá. They named the place Tayasal. Hernán Cortés peaceably dropped in on King Canek of Tayasal in 1524 on his way to Honduras. Only in March 1697 did the Spaniards finally bring Tayasal's Maya forcibly under their control.

At the time of conquest, Flores was perhaps the last major functioning Mayan ceremonial center; it was covered in pyramids and temples, with idols everywhere. The God-fearing Spanish soldiers destroyed these buildings, and no trace remains.

Tayasal's Maya fled into the jungle and may have started anew, giving rise to stories of a 'lost' Mayan city; some believe this is

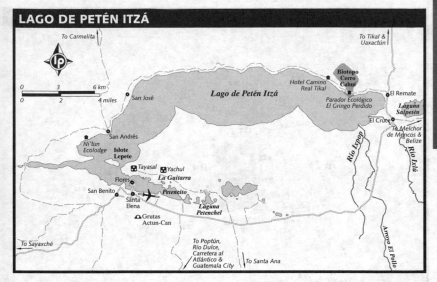

LAGO DE PETÉN ITZÁ

To Carmelita

0   3   6 km
0   2   4 miles

San José

Lago de Petén Itzá

To Tikal &
Uaxactún

Hotel Camino
Real Tikal

Biotopo
Cerro
Cahuí

Parador Ecológico
El Gringo Perdido

El Remate

Laguna
Salpetén

El Cruce

To Melchor
de Mencos &
Belize

San Andrés

Ni'tun
Ecolodge   Islote
Lepete

Tayasal   Yachul
La Guitarra

Flores

San Benito

Santa
Elena

Petencito

Laguna
Petenchel

Grutas
Actun-Can

Río Ixpop

Río Ixlú

Arroyo El Pollo

To Sayaxché

To Poptún,
Río Dulce,
Carretera al
Atlántico &
Guatemala City

To Santa Ana

El Mirador, near the Guatemala-Mexico border.

Orientation

The airport is on Santa Elena's eastern outskirts, 2km from the causeway connecting Santa Elena and Flores. Each bus company has its own terminal in Santa Elena. All buses drop passengers in Santa Elena, so if you want to stay in Flores, you'll have to walk, hire a taxi or hop a lancha across the lake to get there.

Santa Elena's 'main drag' is 4a Calle. All the important hotels, restaurants and banks are on or just off this street.

Information

Tourist Offices INGUAT staffs tourist information desks at the airport (☎ 926 0533) and on the plaza in Flores (☎ 926 0669). The offices are open 7:30 to 10 am and 3 to 6 pm daily.

Money Hotels and travel agencies in Flores change cash and traveler's checks at terrible rates.

Banks in Santa Elena are on 4a Calle. Banco Industrial has an ATM and gives cash advances on Visa cards. Bancafé changes cash, traveler's checks and gives cash advances on Visa cards; it's open 8:30 am to 7 pm weekdays, 9 am to 1 pm

Saturday. Banoro changes cash and traveler's checks; it's open 8:30 am to 8 pm weekdays, 9 am to 4 pm Saturday. Banquetzal has good rates and gives cash advances on MasterCard. San Juan Hotel Tours & Travel in Santa Elena gives cash advances on Visa, MasterCard and American Express, as does EcoMaya in Flores (see Organized Tours, later in this section).

Currencies of the USA, Mexico and Belize can be changed at the Banquetzal at the airport, which also gives cash advances on MasterCard. It's supposedly open 8 am to noon and 2 to 5 pm daily.

Post & Communications In Flores, the post office is just off the plaza; Martsam Travel Agency, EcoMaya and Cahuí International Services offer domestic and international telephone and fax facilities; and both TikalNet, on Calle Centroamérica, and café.net, on Avenida Barrios, offer reasonably priced Internet service.

In Santa Elena, the post office is on 2a Calle at 7a Avenida; the Telgua telephone office is on 5a Calle and open daily; and Educomsa Petén (☎ 926 0765) is at 4a Calle 6-76, Local B, Zona 1, and offers email and computer services.

Travel Agencies In Flores, Martsam Travel Agency (☎/fax 926 0493), next to

GUATEMALA

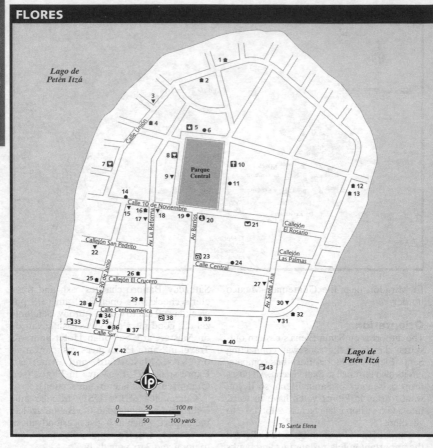

FLORES

Lago de
Petén Itzá

Parque
Central

Calle Unión

Calle 10 de Noviembre

Av La Reforma

Av Barrios

Callejón San Pedrito

Calle 30 de Junio

Callejón El Crucero

Calle Centroamérica

Calle Sur

Av Santa Ana

Callejón
El Rosario

Callejón
Las Palmas

Calle Central

Lago de
Petén Itzá

0   50   100 m
0   50   100 yards

To Santa Elena

Restaurante y Hotel La Jungla, and Cahuí
International Services (☎/fax 926 0494),
next to Hotel Santana, offer travel agency
and telephone/fax services, tours, currency
exchange and bicycle rental. EcoMaya has
similar services, plus international newspapers and magazines, a small book exchange
and a message board; the company also
runs organized tours to several jungle archaeological sites.

Most of Flores' travel agencies lead trips
to the more accessible sites such as Tikal,
Uaxactún and Ceibal. Places that offer trips
include Hotel Guayacán (see Places to Stay,
later in this section) and Martsam. Shop and
ask around.

San Juan Hotel Tours & Travel in Santa
Elena and the San Juan de Isla Hotel &

Travel Agency in Flores provide pricey
shuttle services to various destinations.

Useful Organizations The Centro de Información sobre la Naturaleza, Cultura y
Artesanía del Petén (CINCAP), on the
north side of the plaza in Flores, sells regional handicrafts and has exhibits on
natural resources and forest conservation.
It's open 9 am to 1 pm and 2 to 7 pm
Tuesday to Saturday. Sharing the space is
the Asociación Alianza Verde (☎/fax 926
0718, alianzaverde@conservation.org.gt), an
organization dedicated to responsible
tourism. It's open 9 am to noon and 2 to
6 pm weekdays, 9 am to noon Saturday.

The Asociación de Rescate y Conservación de Vida Silvestre (Arcas) has a

PLACES TO STAY		30	Restaurante & Pizzería
1	Hotel Sabana		Picasso
2	Hospedaje Doña Goya	31	Restaurante/Bar Posada
4	Hotel Posada Tayazal		El Tucán
12	Posada Tucán No 2	41	Restaurante
13	Mirador del Lago		Chal-tun-ha
16	Hotel Isla de Flores	42	Restaurante Don
25	Hotel Petén		Quijote
26	Hotel y Restaurante La		
	Mesa de los Mayas		OTHER
28	Hotel Santana; Cahuí	5	Police Station
	International Services	6	CINCAP & Asociación
29	Hotel y Restaurante		Alianza Verde
	Posada El Peregrino	7	Kayuko's
32	Hotel Villa del Lago	8	El Balcón del Cielo
34	Hotel y Restaurante La	10	Church
	Jungla; Martsam Travel	11	Gobernación
	Agency		Departamental
35	Hotel Santa Rita		(Departmental
37	Hotel Guayacán		Government Building)
39	Hotel y Restaurante La	14	EcoMaya
	Canoa	19	Municipalidad (Town
40	Petenchel Hotel		Hall)
		20	INGUAT Tourist Office;
PLACES TO EAT			Public Telephones
3	Restaurante La Unión	21	Post Office
9	El Mirador	23	café.net
15	La Luna	24	ProPetén
17	Sala Maya	33	Boats to San Andrés &
18	Mayan Princess Café,		San José
	Bar & Cinema	36	San Juan de Isla Hotel
22	Restaurante Gran Jaguar		& Travel Agency
27	Restaurante/Bar Las	38	TikalNet
	Puertas	43	Boats to Santa Elena

forest communities to promote tourism and other alternative resource utilization. To this end, they've organized and trained Comites Comunitarios de Ecoturismo (Community Ecotourism Committees), which take visitors into the jungle to El Zotz (with an optional Tikal leg), El Perú and El Mirador. None of these trips can be made independently; travelers wishing to arrange for guides through the Comites directly (rather than through an agency) should contact ProPetén.

Emergency The national police can be reached at ☎ 926 1365; the national hospital, at ☎ 926 1333.

Grutas Actun-Can

The limestone cave of Actun-Can, also called La Cueva de la Serpiente (Cave of the Serpent), holds no serpents, but the cavekeeper may give you the rundown on the cave formations, which suggest animals, humans and various scenes. Bring a flashlight and adequate shoes – it can be slippery. Explorations take 30 to 45 minutes. It's open 8 am to 5 pm daily (US$1.15). At the cave entrance is a shady picnic area.

Actun-Can makes a good goal for a long walk from Santa Elena. Head south on 6a Avenida past the Telgua office. About 1km from the center of Santa Elena, turn left, go 300m and turn right at the electricity generating plant. Go another 1km to the site. A taxi costs US$2.

wildlife rescue center about 12km east of Santa Elena, near Laguna Petenchel. Animals include macaws, parrots, jaguars, howler and spider monkeys, kinkajous and coatis that have been rescued from smugglers. The animals are rehabilitated for release back into the wild. Ask permission before visiting (☎/fax 591 4731 in Guatemala City). Volunteers are welcome to stay at the center, paying US$50 per week for room and board and volunteering any amount of time. Contact Arcas (see the boxed text 'Volunteer Opportunities in Guatemala' in the Facts for the Visitor section, earlier in this chapter) for details.

The Proyecto Petenero para un Bosque Sostenible (ProPetén; ☎ 926 1370, fax 926 0495, propeten@guate.net) works with

Organized Tours

Travel agencies in Flores offer a number of interesting, though expensive, tours to remote parts of the Petén region. Agencies include EcoMaya (☎ 926 1363, 926 3321, fax 926 3322, 800-429 5660 in the USA, ecomaya@guate.net), on Calle 30 de Junio; Web site: www.ecomaya.com; Avinsa Tikal Travel (☎ 926 0808, fax 926 0807, info@tikaltravel.com), on 4a Calle in Santa Elena; Web site: www.tikal.com; and Monkey Eco Tours (☎ 201 0759, fax 926 0808, fax 978 945 6486 in the USA, nitun@nitun.com), based at the Ni'tun Ecolodge on the lake's northwest side; Web site: www.nitun.com.

Locals offering boat rides around the lake are often freelance agents who get

SANTA ELENA

Islote Santa Bárbara

FLORES

see Flores map

PLACES TO STAY
2 Hotel Sac-Nicté
5 Casa Elena Hotel
13 Hotel Posada Santander
28 Hotel Fiesta
29 Hotel Continental

PLACES TO EAT
3 Embajada Maya
4 Tienda y Comedor Jennifer
8 Restaurante Petenchel; La Fonda de Don Diego
9 Restaurante El Rodeo
16 Restaurante Mijaro

Lago de Petén Itzá

SAN BENITO

1a Calle
2a Calle
3a Calle
4a Calle
4a Calle A
4a Calle

Calzada Virgilio Rodríguez Macal

SANTA ELENA

Parque

Cemetery

Airport

To Airport Entrance, Tikal & Belize

To Grutas Actun-Can

OTHER
1 Boats for Flores & Trips on Lake
6 San Juan Hotel Tours & Travel; Transportes Pinita Buses
7 INGUAT Tourist Office
10 Parque Central
11 Post Office
12 Avinsa Tikal Travel
14 Linea Dorada Bus Station
15 Banquetzal
17 Super 24 (24-hour supermarket)
18 Fuel Station
19 Banoro
20 Bancafé
21 Transportes María Elena Bus Station; Banco Industrial

22 Fuentes del Norte
23 Market
24 Autobuses Máxima & Rosita Bus Stations
25 Educomsa Petén
26 Telgua Telephone Office
27 Fuel Station
30 Arcas Office
31 Fuel Station
32 Electricity Generating Plant

0   200   400 m
0   200   400 yards

commissions; talk with the boat owner directly. Inspect the boat and bargain, or ask at the Restaurante/Bar Las Puertas in Flores; Carlos, the owner, offers boat trips around the lake and across to the other side, where he has land and a private dock for swimming and sunning.

There's good birding on the Río Ixpop, which runs into the east side of the lake. Boat trips on the river start from El Remate, on the lake's east side.

Places to Stay – Budget
Santa Elena The spotless *Hotel Posada Santander* (☎ 926 0574), on 4a Calle, is a simple hostelry in a convenient, but loud, location. The friendly family-run establishment offers ample rooms with private bath

and two good double beds for US$5.15/6.45 single/double. Rooms with shared bath are US$3.25/3.90. The family also operates Transportes Inter Petén, a minibus service to Tikal and other places.

Nearer the lake, *Hotel Sac-Nicté* (☎ 926 0092) has clean, large upstairs rooms with private bath, balcony and views across the lake to Flores for US$10.50. Viewless downstairs rooms cost US$7.75. The hotel has a restaurant, parking and transportation service.

The large *Hotel Continental* (☎ 926 0095), on 6a Avenida at Calzada Virgilio Rodríguez Macal, is relatively removed from everything. Rooms are US$2.60 per person with shared bath, US$3.90 with private bath. Amenities include a restaurant and courtyard parking. Better is *Hotel Fiesta*, next door, which also has a restaurant.

Flores One of the town's best budget choices, *Hospedaje Doña Goya* (☎ 926 3538), on Calle Unión, is often full. Spotless rooms with comfortable beds and shared hot bath are US$3.90/6.45; doubles with private bath are US$7.75. The rooftop terrace has hammocks, lounge chairs and lake views. Solo women travelers should head here first.

Beside the lake, cheerful, family-run *Hotel Villa del Lago* (☎/fax 926 0629) is much nicer inside than its exterior would suggest. Simple rooms with private bath are US$6.45 double. Bigger, nicer units with bath and TV are US$15.50 with fan, US$19.50 with air-con.

Facing the causeway is the new *Petenchel Hotel* (☎ 926 3359). This is a good value, with clean (sometimes dark) rooms with private hot bath and comfortable beds for US$6.45/9.

Next door is an entrance to the friendly *Hotel y Restaurante La Canoa* (☎ 926 0852/3). Rooms with private hot bath are US$3.90 per person; upstairs rooms are airier, and downstairs triples can be crowded. Two rooms with shared bath are available for US$2.60 per person. There's a good, popular restaurant here.

Hotel Guayacán (☎ 926 0351) has simple, serviceable rooms with shared bath for US$2.60 per person. *Hotel Posada Tayazal* (☎ 926 0568), on Calle Unión, has decent, cleanish doubles with private hot bath and fan for US$7.75. The hot upstairs rooms have partial lake views.

The simple but clean *Posada Tucán No 2* (☎ 926 1467) is OK. Rooms are US$4.50/5.15 with shared bath. Some rooms have lake views. Next door, the *Mirador del Lago* is a decent value, with rooms with private bath for US$7.75 double. The roof terrace has lake views.

Hotel Santa Rita (☎ 926 0710) is clean, friendly and family run; it's an excellent deal at US$5.80/9 with private bath. The adjacent *Hotel y Restaurante La Jungla* (☎ 926 0634) has clean, generic rooms with private cold bath for US$10/14/18 single/double/triple; credit cards are accepted.

Hotel y Restaurante Posada El Peregrino, on Avenida La Reforma, has reasonable rooms for US$6.45 double with shared bath, US$9 with private hot bath and TV. The restaurant is terrific.

Hotel y Restaurante La Mesa de los Mayas (☎/fax 926 1240) is lovely, very clean and well kept. Doubles with private bath are US$15 with fan, US$20 with air-con; US$20/25 triple/quad for larger units with fan. The hotel accepts Visa and MasterCard.

Places to Stay – Mid-Range
Santa Elena The new *Casa Elena Hotel* (☎ 926 2238/39, fax 926 0097, ☎ 472 4045 in Guatemala City, fax 472 1633), on the first block over the causeway, has characterless but comfortable rooms with private hot bath, cable TV and telephone for US$35/45 single/double. Some have park views, while others overlook the pool. Amenities include a bar, restaurant and roof terrace.

Flores On the island's north side, *Hotel Sabana* (☎/fax 926 1248) has a restaurant and sundeck over the water. Rooms with private bath, fan, air-con and cable TV are US$20/30/40 single/double/triple.

Hotel Petén (☎/fax 926 0692, lacasona@ guate.net) has a small courtyard with tropical plants, a pleasant lakeside terrace and restaurant and an indoor swimming pool. The 19 comfy-if-plain rooms, all with private bath, air-con and fan, are US$25/30/40 from April to June and September to November; all other times they're US$30/35/45. Try to get a top-floor room with a lake view.

At *Hotel Santana* (☎ 926 0491, ☎/fax 926 0662), most of the rooms have great lake views and large balconies; each has private bath, cable TV, air-con and fan; rates are US$30/45/55/65 single/double/triple/quad. The restaurant has a lakeside terrace.

Hotel Isla de Flores (☎ 926 0614, 476 8775 in Guatemala City, fax 476 0294, reservaciones@junglelodge.com) is clean and attractive. The rooms are large and well equipped, with cable TV, air-con, ceiling fan, telephone and private bath with tub. Many have private balconies with a view of the lake. Rates are US$35/40.
Web site: www.junglelodge.guate.com

Places to Eat
As with hotels, the restaurants in Santa Elena tend to be cheaper than in Flores. All

keep long hours. Beer, drinks and even wine are served, and most places offer a variety of local game, including *tepezcuintle* (paca or cavy, a rabbit-sized jungle rodent), *venado* (deer), armadillo and *pavo silvestre* (wild turkey).

Santa Elena Hotel Sac-Nicté, Hotel Fiesta, Hotel Continental, the Embajada Maya and the Casa Elena Hotel all have restaurants.

Restaurante El Rodeo, on 2a Calle at 5a Avenida, is recommended by locals. It's open 11 am to 9 pm daily. In the same block, *Super 24* is a 24-hour supermarket. In the next block of 2a Calle, *Restaurante Petenchel* and *La Fonda de Don Diego* are also popular. *Restaurante Mijaro*, a simple comedor on the main road, is also locally recommended; it's open 7 am to 9 pm daily. *Tienda y Comedor Jennifer* is a simple place near the causeway with good food, cold beer and great people watching. A big plate of fried chicken with French fries costs US$2.

Flores A popular hangout is *Restaurante/ Bar Las Puertas*, which has decent, pricey food and an interesting clientele.

The small *Restaurante Chal-tun-ha* has an open and fresh decor, and a terrace with fine lake views. The menu offers a good selection of inexpensive dishes. It's open 9 am to 7:30 pm daily. *Restaurante Don Quijote*, in a small boat docked on the southern shore, serves affordable lunch and dinner.

Restaurante/Bar Posada El Tucán, next to the Villa del Lago, has a breeze-catching lakeside terrace. Set breakfasts cost US$2 to US$3, lunches and dinners US$5 to US$8. Across the street is the recommended *Restaurante & Pizzería Picasso*, offering fairly priced pizza, pasta and salads. Cheaper, plainer *Restaurante La Canoa*, on Calle Centroamérica, appeals to budget travelers. Don't miss the killer tortillas.

Hotel y Restaurante La Mesa de los Mayas serves good traditional foods and local game. A mixed plate goes for US$9, a vegetarian plate is US$5, and chicken costs even less. It's open 7 am to 11 pm daily.

Restaurante Gran Jaguar is locally recommended. It has a good variety of reasonably priced dishes, attractive decor and bar service. Hours are 11 am to 10 pm Monday to Saturday. *Restaurante La Unión*, on the

northwestern bend of the island, serves chicken, pasta and seafood dishes at decent prices. The real reason to come here is the lakeside location.

Mayan Princess Café, Bar & Cinema, on Calle 10 de Noviembre at Avenida La Reforma, serves surprisingly good traveler food like chicken florentine and pesto ravioli. Prices are reasonable (around US$4), though the portions are smallish and the service spotty. Across the street is the very local, friendly *Sala Maya*, serving set and a la carte meals at rock-bottom (for Flores!) prices. Try the *limonada con soda* on a hot day.

Another place serving delicious food at great prices is *Hotel y Restaurante Posada El Peregrino*, on Avenida La Reforma. For US$3.25 you can dine on succulent roasted chicken and fries, salad and rice. A similar place long on atmosphere is *El Mirador*, on the plaza's west side. Here you can get a big set lunch for US$1.50 while enjoying lake views.

At *La Luna*, on the corner of Calles 30 de Junio and 10 de Noviembre, the food is delectable, with innovative chicken, fish and beef dishes the likes of which you'll be hard-pressed to find anywhere else in Guatemala. Expect to pay around US$8 for a meal, not including drinks. It's open for lunch and dinner Tuesday to Sunday.

Entertainment

Flores has only a couple of hangouts. Local bars include *Kayuko's*, on Calle Unión; *El Balcón del Cielo*; and *La Luna*.

The *Mayan Princess Café, Bar & Cinema* shows free movies (some of dubious quality) at 4 and 9 pm in its dining room.

Getting There & Away

Air The airport at Santa Elena (usually called 'the airport at Flores') is busy these days. International flights include those to/ from Belize City with Tikal Jets, Tropic Air, Island Air, Grupo TACA, Racsa, Tapsa and Aerovías; to/from Palenque, Chetumal, Cancún and Havana with Aerocaribe; and to/from Cancún with Aviateca (four times a week) and Grupo TACA (daily). There are also services to and from Guatemala City and Puerto Barrios.

When you arrive at the airport in Flores you may be subjected to a cursory customs and immigration check, as this is a special customs and immigration district. You have to pay a US$30 departure tax if you're leaving Guatemala, US$0.65 if you're flying within the country.

Bus Travel by bus is fast and comfortable, except on the Bethel and Sayaxché routes. Each company has its own office. Transportes Pinita buses depart from the San Juan Hotel in Santa Elena (☎ 926 0041/2). The Transportes María Elena office (☎ 926 0574) is across the street from the Hotel Posada Santander in Santa Elena. Other Santa Elena companies include Fuentes del Norte (☎ 926 0517), Linea Dorada (☎ 926 0070, 926 1817, lineadorada@intelnet.net.gt), Autobuses Máxima (☎ 926 0676) and Transportes Rosío. The chicken bus is always slower and cheaper than the tourist shuttle.

Belize City (US$20, five hours, 222km)
San Juan Hotel runs a daily shuttle that will pick you up from your hotel around 5 am and arrive in Belize City around 10 am (theoretically in time to connect with the boat to Caye Caulker and San Pedro, Ambergris Caye). Or take local buses from Santa Elena to Melchor de Mencos and change there (see Melchor de Mencos below).

Bethel (Mexico border; US$3.25, four hours, 127km)
Transportes Pinita buses depart at 5 and 8 am and 1 pm; this is a rough road.

Ceibal
See Sayaxché.

Chetumal, Mexico (US$35, seven hours, 350km)
A special direct 1st-class San Juan bus departs from the San Juan Hotel and Hotel Continental in Santa Elena daily at 5 am, bypasses Belize City and goes straight to Chetumal. At Chetumal it connects with buses heading north along the coast to Tulum, Playa del Carmen and Cancún. Cheaper are Rosita buses leaving Santa Elena for Melchor de Mencos on the Belize border (see below), with a connection at the border to Chetumal.

El Naranjo
See El Petén to Chiapas, later in the chapter.

El Remate/Puente Ixlú (40 minutes, 35km)
Tikal-bound buses and minibuses (see Tikal) will drop you here. Buses to/from Melchor de Mencos will drop you at Puente Ixlú/El Cruce, less than 2km south of El Remate.

Esquipulas (US$7.75, 11 hours, 437km)
Two daily Transportes María Elena buses

depart at 6 am and 2 pm. This bus goes via Chiquimula (US$6.45, 10 hours).

Guatemala City (US$10.30, 12 hours, 488km)
Fuentes del Norte operates buses all day from 7:30 am to 9:30 pm. Linea Dorada luxury buses (US$30, eight hours) depart at 10 am and 8 and 10 pm. Autobuses Máxima runs deluxe buses at 7 and 8 pm.

La Ruidosa (crossroads to Puerto Barrios; US$6, eight hours, 242km)
Take any bus bound for Guatemala City.

Melchor de Mencos (Belize border; US$2, two hours, 100km)
Second-class Transportes Pinita buses depart at 5, 8 and 10:30 am. Rosita buses at 5, 7:30 and 11 am and 2, 4 and 6 pm. On the Belize side, buses (US$0.50) and share-taxis (US$2) leave for Benque Viejo and San Ignacio (30 minutes) every hour or so.

Palenque, Mexico
See El Petén to Chiapas, later in the chapter.

Poptún (US$2.60, two hours, 113km)
Take any bus heading for Guatemala City.

Río Dulce (US$6.45, five hours, 208km)
Take any bus heading for Guatemala City.

San Andrés (US$0.65, one hour, 20km)
Transportes Pinita buses leave at 5:30 am and noon, departing San Andrés for the return trip at 7 am and 1:30 pm. Boats make this trip more frequently (US$0.40, 30 minutes), departing from San Benito, on the west side of Santa Elena, and from Flores beside the Hotel Santana.

Sayaxché (US$1.30, two hours, 61km)
Second-class Transportes Pinita buses leave at 5:30, 7, 8, 9 and 10:30 am and 1 and 3:30 pm. There are also tours from Santa Elena via Sayaxché to the ruins at Ceibal, departing from the San Juan Hotel and Hotel Continental at 8 am, returning at 4 pm (US$30).

Tikal (US$1.30, two hours, 71km)
One Transportes Pinita bus leaves daily at 1 pm, continuing to Uaxactún. It departs Tikal for the return trip at 6 am. It's quicker and more convenient to take a shuttle minibus to Tikal (see below).

Uaxactún (US$2.50, three hours, 94km)
A Transportes Pinita bus leaves at 1 pm. It departs from Uaxactún for the return trip at 5 am.

Shuttle Minibus Minibuses bound for Tikal pick up passengers in front of their hotel (5, 6, 8 and 10 am) and from the airport (meeting all flights). Any hotel can arrange a trip for you. The fare is US$5.15 per person roundtrip; the trip takes one to 1½ hours.

GUATEMALA

Return trips generally depart from Tikal at 2, 4 and 5 pm. Drivers will anticipate that you'll want to return to Flores that same afternoon; if you know which return trip you plan to be on, they'll hold a seat for you or arrange a seat in a colleague's minibus. If you go out to Tikal and decide to stay overnight, it's a good idea to reserve a seat early the next morning for that afternoon's return trip; talk to one of the minibus drivers as soon as they arrive from Flores. Don't wait until departure time and expect to find a seat.

A taxi from Flores/Santa Elena or the airport to Tikal costs US$40 roundtrip (for up to four people).

Getting Around

Bus Buses and minibuses bound for the small villages around the lake and nearby depart from Santa Elena's market area.

Car Several hotels, car rental companies and travel agencies offer rentals, including cars, 4WDs, pickups and minibuses. Rental car companies are in the arrivals hall at the airport:

Garrido	☎ 926 0092
Hertz	☎ 926 0332, 926 0415
Koka	☎ 926 0526, 926 1233
Los Compadres	☎ 926 0444
Los Jades	☎ 926 0734
Nesa	☎ 926 0082
Tabarini	☎/fax 302 5900

The travel agency at the San Juan Hotel in Santa Elena (☎ 926 0041/2, fax 926 0514) also has rental cars and there is a Hertz office in the lobby of the Hotel Camino Real Tikal (☎ 929 0206 ext 2).

Bicycle In Flores, you can rent bicycles from Cahuí International Services (☎/fax 926 0494) for US$0.85 per hour or US$6.65 per day; or from Hotel Guayacán (☎ 926 0351) for US$0.65 an hour. Around the lake in El Remate, Casa Mobego (☎ 926 0269) also rents bicycles.

Boat Lanchas ferrying passengers between Santa Elena and Flores depart from both ends of the causeway (US$0.15, five minutes). Motor launches making tours around Lago de Petén Itzá depart from the

Santa Elena end. Colectivo boats to San Andrés and San José, villages across the lake, depart from San Benito, on the west side of Santa Elena and alongside the Hotel Santana in Flores (US$0.40 if the boat is full, US$8 for one passenger). You can also contract the lancheros for lake tours; bargain hard.

EL REMATE

Once little more than a few thatched huts 35km northeast of Santa Elena on the Tikal road, El Remate keeps on growing, thanks to the tourist trade. Halfway between Flores and Tikal, it allows you to be closer to Tikal but still on the lake.

El Remate is known for its wood carving. Several handicrafts shops on the lakeshore opposite La Mansión del Pájaro Serpiente sell local handicrafts and rent canoes, rafts and kayaks.

From El Remate an unpaved road snakes around the lake's northeast shore to the Biotopo Cerro Cahuí, the luxury Hotel Camino Real Tikal and on to the villages of San José and San Andrés, on the northwest side of the lake. It's possible to go all the way around the lake by road.

With their newfound prosperity, *remate-cos* have built a *balneario municipal* (municipal beach) just off the highway; several cheap pensions and small hotels have opened here as well.

Biotopo Cerro Cahuí

At the northeast end of Lago de Petén Itzá, about 43km from Santa Elena and 3km from the Flores-Tikal road, the Biotopo Cerro Cahuí covers 651 hectares of subtropical forest. Within are mahogany, cedar, ramón, broom, sapodilla and cohune palm trees, as well as many species of lianas and epiphytes, including bromeliads, ferns and orchids. The hard sapodilla wood was used in Mayan temple door lintels, which have survived from the Classic period. Chicle is still sapped from the trees' innards.

Among the many animals within the reserve are spider and howler monkeys, ocelots, white-tailed deer, raccoons, armadillos, numerous species of fish, turtle and snake, and *Crocodylus moreleti* – the Petén crocodile. Depending upon the season and migration patterns, you might see kingfishers, ducks, herons, hawks, parrots, toucans, woodpeckers and the beautiful ocellated (Petén) turkey, which resembles a peacock.

A network of loop trails starts at the road and goes uphill, affording a view of the lake and Lagunas Salpetén and Petenchel. A trail map is at the entrance.

Entrance to the reserve costs US$2.60 per person. The gate is usually open 6 am to 4 pm (once in, you can stay as late as you like). If it's closed, go to the administration center and they'll let you in. You can camp here for an additional US$2.60; toilets and showers are available, but El Remate is the closest place to get food and other necessities.

Places to Stay & Eat

El Remate has several small hotels and pensions, and more are opening all the time.

Offering terrific value is *Casa de Don Luis*, on the east side of the Flores-Tikal road. This friendly, family-owned place has two spotless rooms with comfortable beds, fan and shared bath for US$6.45/7.75/9 for one/two/three people. It has no sign, but look for the slatted gate just before *Casa de Juan*, which has super basic rooms for US$1.95 per person. Rooms do have fan and nets, and the restaurant is pretty good.

Nearby on the path to the lake is *Hotel Sun Breeze*, where simple, clean cement rooms with shared bath are US$2.60 per person. One or two comedores are nearby.

A couple of other decent places on the Flores-Tikal road offer great lake views. At *Mirador del Duende* (☎ 926 0269, fax 926 0397) you can camp with your own hammock or tent for US$1.30 a person, sleep in a shelter for US$2.60 or stay in a bungalow for US$4.50. Economical vegetarian food is served. Forest hiking tours are offered, and you can rent horses (US$10 a day) and canoes (US$4 a day).

A couple of other good places are about 3km west of El Remate on the road around the lake's north side, near the Biotopo Cerro Cahuí. First you'll come to a couple of laid-back cheapies, both with lake views. *Casa de Doña Tonita* has six beds in a thatch *rancho* for US$3.25 per person. It has a restaurant. Nearby *Casa Mobego* (☎ 926 0269) has simple bungalows with outside bathrooms for US$4 per person. US$9 per person covers accommodations, dinner and

breakfast. A swimming dock is in front, and you can rent mountain bikes.

Farther along, right on the lakeshore, is *Parador Ecológico El Gringo Perdido* (☎ /fax 334 2305 in Guatemala City). Shady, rustic hillside gardens hold a restaurant, bucolic camping area and simple but pleasant bungalows and dormitories. Per-person rates are US$3 to camp, US$6 for a camping bungalow with roof, beds and mosquito netting, US$10 for a dorm bunk and US$14 for rooms with private bath. Four-person bungalows, each with its own patio with hammocks and a small private lakeside dock, are US$25 per person, breakfast and dinner included. Two luxury bungalows with air-con are US$50. Overall cost is cheaper if you get a room-and-meals package. Activities include swimming, fishing, windsurfing, volleyball, basketball, bicycling and boat trips on the lake.

Getting There & Away

Any bus or minibus going north from Santa Elena to Tikal can drop you at El Remate. Taxis from Santa Elena or the airport will cost US$20. Once you are in El Remate, you can hail any passing bus or minibus on the Flores-Tikal road to take you to Tikal or Flores, but traffic is light after midmorning.

TIKAL

Towering pyramids rise above the jungle canopy to catch the sun. Howler monkeys swing through the branches of ancient trees as bright parrots and toucans dart from perch to perch. When the complex warbling song of some mysterious bird tapers off, the buzz of tree frogs provides background noise.

Certainly Tikal's most striking feature is its architecture. But Tikal is different from Chichén Itzá, Uxmal, Copán and most other great Mayan sites because it's nestled in the jungle. Its many plazas have been cleared of trees and vines, its temples uncovered and partially restored, but as you walk between buildings you pass beneath the rain forest canopy. Rich smells of earth and vegetation, peacefulness and animal noises contribute to an experience offered by no other readily accessible site.

If you visit from December to February, expect cool nights and mornings. March and April are the hottest and driest months. The rains begin in May or June, and with them

TIKAL

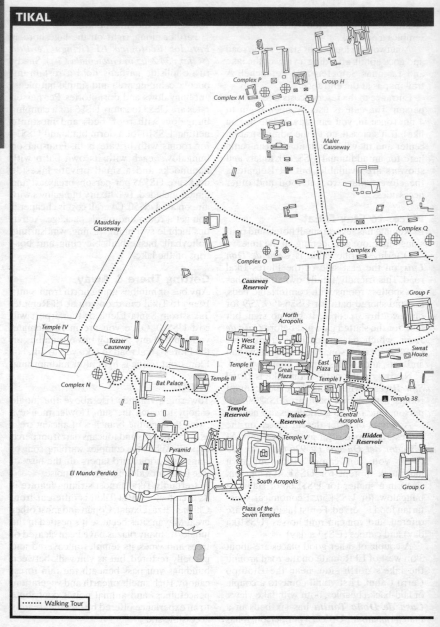

Complex P

Complex M

Group H

Maler Causeway

Complex Q

Complex R

Group F

Maudslay Causeway

Complex O

Causeway Reservoir

Temple IV

North Acropolis

Sweat House

Tozzer Causeway

West Plaza

Temple II

East Plaza

Complex N

Bat Palace

Temple III

Great Plaza

Temple I

Templo 38

Temple Reservoir

Palace Reservoir

Central Acropolis

Pyramid

Temple V

Hidden Reservoir

El Mundo Perdido

South Acropolis

Group G

Plaza of the Seven Temples

········· Walking Tour

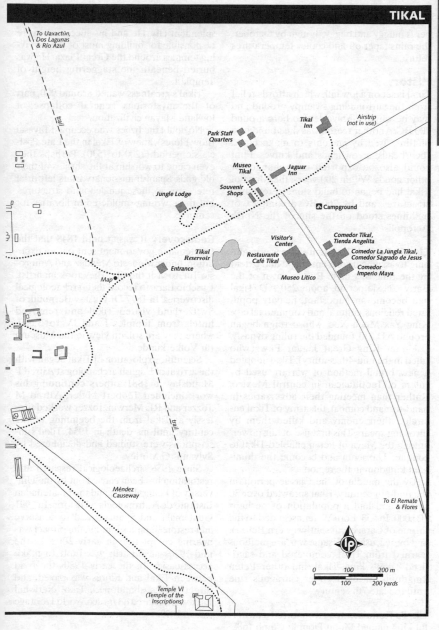

To Uaxactún,
Dos Lagunas
& Río Azul

trail

Park Staff
Quarters

Tikal
Inn

Airstrip
(not in use)

Museo
Tikal

Jaguar
Inn

Jungle Lodge

Souvenir
Shops

Campground

Tikal
Reservoir

Entrance

Visitor's
Center

Comedor Tikal,
Tienda Angelita

Restaurante
Café Tikal

Comedor La Jungla Tikal,
Comedor Sagrado de Jesus

Map

Museo Lítico

Comedor
Imperio Maya

trail

Méndez
Causeway

To El Remate
& Flores

0   100   200 m
0   100   200 yards

Temple VI
(Temple of the
Inscriptions)

come the mosquitoes – bring rain gear, repellent and a mosquito net. July to November is muggy and buggy, though by October, the rains taper off and cooler temperatures return.

History

Tikal is set on a low hill, which affords relief from the surrounding swampy ground and may be why the Maya settled here around 700 BC. Another reason was the abundance of flint, used by ancients to make clubs, spearheads, arrowheads and knives. Flint could also be exported in exchange for other goods. Within 200 years, the Maya of Tikal had begun to build stone ceremonial structures, and by 200 BC a complex of buildings stood on the site of the North Acropolis.

Classic Period The Great Plaza was beginning to assume its present shape and extent by the time of Christ. By the dawn of the Early Classic period, about 250 AD, Tikal had become an important, heavily populated religious, cultural and commercial city. King Yax Moch Xoc, whose reign began around AD 230, founded the ruling dynasty.

Under King Great Jaguar Paw (who ruled in the mid-4th century), Tikal adopted a new, brutal method of warfare used by rulers of Teotihuacán in central Mexico. Rather than meeting their adversaries in hand-to-hand combat, the army of Tikal encircled their enemy and killed them by throwing spears. This first use of 'air power' among the Maya of Petén enabled Tikal to conquer Uaxactún and become the dominant kingdom in the region.

By the middle of the Classic period, in the mid-6th century, Tikal sprawled over 30 sq km and had a population of perhaps 100,000. In 553, Lord Water ascended to the throne of Caracol (in southwestern Belize), and by 562, using the same warfare methods learned from Tikal, conquered and sacrificed Tikal's king. Tikal and other Petén kingdoms suffered under Caracol's rule until the late 7th century.

Tikal's Renaissance Around 700 a powerful king named Moon Double Comb (682-734), also called Ah Cacau (Lord Chocolate), 26th successor of Yax Moch Xoc, ascended the throne of Tikal. He restored not only its military strength, but also its primacy as the Mayan world's most resplendent city. He and his successors were responsible for building most of the surviving temples around the Great Plaza. He was buried beneath the staggering height of Temple I.

Tikal's greatness waned around 900, part of the mysterious general collapse of lowland Mayan civilization.

No doubt the Itzáes, who occupied Tayasal (now Flores), knew of Tikal in the Late Postclassic period (1200 to 1530). Perhaps they even came to worship at the shrines of their old gods. Spanish missionary friars left brief references to these junglebound structures, but these writings moldered in libraries for centuries.

Rediscovery It wasn't until 1848 that the Guatemalan government sent out an expedition, under Modesto Méndez and Ambrosio Tut, to visit the site. They took an artist, Eusebio Lara, to record their archaeological discoveries. In 1877 Dr Gustav Bernoulli of Switzerland visited Tikal and removed lintels from Temples I and IV to Basel, where they are still on view in the Museum für Völkerkunde.

Scientific exploration of Tikal began with the arrival of English archaeologist Alfred P Maudslay in 1881; others continuing his work included Teobert Maler, Alfred M Tozzer and RE Merwin. Tozzer worked tirelessly at Tikal from the beginning of the century until his death in 1954. Tikal's inscriptions were studied and deciphered by Sylvanus G Morley.

Since 1956, archaeological research and restoration has been carried out by the University of Pennsylvania and the Guatemalan Instituto de Antropología e Historia. In 1991 Guatemala and Spain agreed to conserve and restore Temples I and V; the project was nearing completion in early 2000. In the mid-1950s an airstrip was built to make access easier. In the early 1980s the road between Tikal and Flores was paved, and direct flights abandoned. Tikal National Park was declared a Unesco World Heritage Site in 1979.

Orientation & Information

The ruins lie within Tikal National Park, a 576-sq-km preserve containing thousands of ancient structures. The city's central area occupied about 16 sq km and held more than 4000 structures.

The road from Flores enters the park about 15km south of the ruins. When you enter you must pay US$6.45 for the day; if you enter after about 3 pm, you can have your ticket validated for the following day as well. Multilingual guides are available at the visitor's center for US$20 for a half-day tour.

The area around the visitor's center includes three hotels, a camping area, several small comedores, a post office, a police station, two museums and the abandoned airstrip. From the visitor's center it's a 20- to 30-minute walk southwest to the Great Plaza.

The walk from the Great Plaza to the Temple of the Inscriptions is over 1km; from the Great Plaza to Complex P, it's 1km in the opposite direction. To visit all the major complexes you must walk over 10km.

For complete information on the monuments, pick up *Tikal – A Handbook of the Ancient Maya Ruins*, by William R Coe, widely available in Flores and at Tikal. *The Birds of Tikal* by Frank B Smithe (Natural History Press, 1966), available at the Tikal museums, is a good resource.

The ruins are open 6 am to 5 pm daily. You may be able to stay until 8 pm by applying to the Inspectorería to the west of the visitor's center. Carry a flashlight if you stay after sunset or arrive before dawn.

Wear shoes with good traction – the ruins here can be slick, especially during the wet season. Also, bring adequate water, as dehydration is a real danger.

Great Plaza

Follow the signs to reach the Great Plaza. The path enters the plaza around Temple I, the Temple of the Grand Jaguar, built for King Moon Double Comb. The king may have worked out the plans himself, but it was erected above his tomb by his son, who succeeded to the throne in 734. Burial goods included 180 beautiful jade objects, 90 pieces of bone carved with hieroglyphs, and pearls and stingray spines, used for ritual bloodletting. At the top of the 44m-high temple is a small enclosure of three rooms covered by a corbeled arch. The lofty roof comb was originally adorned with reliefs and bright paint, perhaps symbolizing the 13 realms of the Mayan heaven.

Since at least two people tumbled to their deaths, the stairs up Temple I have been closed. Don't fret: The views from Temple II just across the way are nearly as awe-inspiring. Temple II was once almost as high as Temple I, but now measures 38m without its roof comb.

The North Acropolis, while not as impressive as the twin temples, is of great significance. Archaeologists have uncovered about 100 structures, the oldest of which dates from before the time of Christ, with evidence of occupation as far back as 400 BC. The Maya rebuilt on top of older structures, and the many layers, combined with the elaborate burials, added sanctity and power to their temples. Look for the two huge, powerful wall masks, uncovered from an earlier structure. The final version of the Acropolis, as it stood around AD 800, had more than 12 temples atop a vast platform, many of them the work of King Moon Double Comb.

On the plaza side of the North Acropolis are two rows of stelae. Though hardly as impressive as those at Copán or Quiriguá, these served the same purpose: to record the great deeds of the kings of Tikal, to sanctify their memory and to add 'power' to the surrounding temples and plazas.

Central Acropolis

On the south side of the Great Plaza, this maze of courtyards, little rooms and small temples is thought by some to have been a residential palace for Tikal's nobility. Others believe the tiny rooms may have been used for sacred rites, as graffiti found within suggests. Over the centuries the room configuration was repeatedly changed, indicating perhaps that this 'palace' was in fact a residence changed to accommodate different groups of relatives. A century ago, one part of the acropolis, called Maler's Palace, provided lodgings for archaeologist Teobert Maler when he worked at Tikal.

West Plaza

The West Plaza is north of Temple II. On its north side is a large Late Classic temple. To the south, across the Tozzer Causeway, is Temple III, 55m high. Yet to be uncovered, it allows you to see a temple the way the last Tikal Maya and first explorers saw them. The causeway leading to Temple IV was one of several sacred ways built among the complexes, no doubt for astronomical as well as aesthetic reasons.

South Acropolis & Temple V

Due south of the Great Plaza is the South Acropolis. Excavation has just begun on this two-hectare mass of masonry. The palaces on top are from Late Classic times, but earlier constructions probably go back 1000 years.

Temple V, just east of the South Acropolis, is 58m high and was built around AD 700. Unlike the other great temples, this one has rounded corners and one tiny room at the top. The room is less than a meter deep, but its walls are up to 4.5m thick. Restoration of this temple was started in 1991.

Plaza of the Seven Temples

This plaza is on the other side of the South Acropolis. The little temples, clustered together, were built in Late Classic times, though the structures beneath go back at least a millennium. Note the skull and crossbones on the central temple (the one with the stela and altar in front). On the plaza's north side is an unusual triple ball court; another, larger version in the same design stands just south of Temple I.

El Mundo Perdido

About 400m southwest of the Great Plaza is El Mundo Perdido (The Lost World), a complex of 38 structures surrounding a huge pyramid. Unlike the rest of Tikal, where Late Classic construction overlays earlier work, El Mundo Perdido holds buildings of many different periods. The large pyramid is thought to be Preclassic with some later repairs and renovations, the Talud-Tablero Temple (or Temple of the Three Rooms) is an Early Classic structure, and the Temple of the Skulls is Late Classic.

The pyramid, 32m high and 80m along its base, had huge masks flanking each stairway but no temple structure at the top. Each side displays a slightly different architectural style. Tunnels dug by archaeologists reveal four similar pyramids beneath the outer face; the earliest (Structure 5C-54 Sub 2B) dates from 700 BC, making the pyramid the oldest Mayan structure in Tikal.

Temple IV & Complex N

Complex N, near Temple IV, is an example of the 'twin-temple' complexes popular

among Tikal's rulers during the Late Classic period. These complexes are thought to have commemorated the completion of a *katun*, or 20-year cycle in the Mayan calendar. This one was built in 711 by King Moon Double Comb to mark the 14th katun of Baktun 9. The king is portrayed on Stela 16, one of Tikal's finest.

Temple IV, at 64m, is Tikal's highest building. It was completed about 741, in the reign of King Moon Double Comb's son. A series of steep wooden steps and ladders take you to the top. If you stay up here for the sunset, climb down immediately thereafter, as it gets dark on the path quickly.

Temple of the Inscriptions (Temple VI)

Compared to Copán or Quiriguá, Tikal sports relatively few inscriptions. The exception is this temple, 1.2km southeast of the Great Plaza. On the rear of the 12m-high roof comb is a long inscription; the sides and cornice of the roof comb bear glyphs as well. The inscriptions give us the date AD 766. Stela 21 and Altar 9, standing before the temple, date from 736. Badly damaged, the stela has now been repaired.

Warning The Temple of the Inscriptions is remote, and there have been incidents of robbery and rape of single travelers and couples in the past. Though safety has been greatly improved at Tikal, ask a guard before you make the trek out here, or come in a group.

Northern Complexes

About 1km north of the Great Plaza is Complex P. Like Complex N, it's a Late Classic twin-temple complex that probably commemorated the end of a katun. Complex M, next to it, was partially torn down by Late Classic Maya to provide material for the causeway – now named after Alfred Maudslay, who is most widely known for his photographs of Central American ruins – that runs southwest to Temple IV. Group H had some interesting graffiti within its temples.

Complexes Q and R, about 300m due north of the Great Plaza, are Late Classic twin-pyramid complexes. Complex Q is perhaps the best example of the twin-temple type, as it has been mostly restored. Stela 22 and Altar 10 are excellent examples of Late Classic Tikal relief carving, dated 771.

Complex O, due west of these complexes on the west side of the Maler Causeway, has an uncarved stela and altar in its north enclosure. The point of stelae was to record happenings – why did this one remain uncarved?

Museums

Tikal has two museums. **Museo Lítico**, the larger, is in the visitor's center. It houses several stelae and carved stones from the ruins. Outside is a large relief map showing how Tikal would have looked during the Late Classic period, around AD 800. Admission is free.

The smaller **Museo Tikal** has fascinating exhibits, including the burial goods of King Moon Double Comb, carved jade, inscribed bones, shells, stelae, ceramics and other recovered items. Admission is US$1.30.

Both museums are open 9 am to 5 pm Monday to Friday, 9 am to 4 pm Saturday and Sunday.

Birding

Around 300 bird species (migratory and endemic) have been recorded at Tikal. Early morning is the best time to go; even amateurs will have their share of sightings. Ask at the visitor's center about early-morning and late-afternoon tours led by accomplished birder Luis Antonio Oliveros. Bring binoculars, tread quietly and be patient and you will probably see some of the following birds:

- tody motmots, four trogon species and royal flycatchers around the Temple of the Inscriptions

- two oriole species, keel-billed toucans and collared aracaris in El Mundo Perdido

- great curassows, three species of woodpecker, crested guans, plain chachalacas and three tanager species around Complex P

- three kingfisher species, jacanas, blue herons, two sandpiper species and great kiskadees at the Tikal Reservoir near the entrance; tiger herons in the huge ceiba tree along the entrance path

- red-capped and white-collared manakins near Complex Q; emerald toucanets near Complex R

Trails

The Sendero Benilj'a'a, a 3km trail with three sections, begins in front of the Jungle Lodge. Ruta Monte Medio and Ruta Monte Medio Alto (both one hour) are accessible year-round. Ruta Monte Bajo (35 minutes) is accessible only in summer. A short interpretive trail called *El Misterio de la Vida Maya* (The Mystery of Maya Life) leads to the Great Plaza.

Organized Tours

All the hotels can arrange guided tours of the ruins, as well as tours to other places in the region.

Places to Stay

Intrepid visitors used to convince park guards (with a US$5 'tip') to let them sleep atop Temple IV, but this is extremely rare now, as safety is a major concern. If you are caught in the ruins after hours, you'll be escorted out. Nowadays, the best way to catch solitude and get an early glimpse of the wildlife is to camp at the entrance.

Other than camping, there are only three places to stay at Tikal. Most are booked in advance by tour groups. In recent years, travelers have logged numerous complaints of price gouging, unacceptable accommodations and 'lost' reservations at these hotels. And the value you get compared to hotels in the rest of the country is laughable. It may be best to stay in Flores or El Remate and visit Tikal on day trips.

On the other hand, staying at Tikal enables you to relax and savor the dawn and dusk, when most of the jungle fauna can be observed. If this appeals to you, the easiest way is to forget about making reservations, and take a tour. Any travel agency can arrange one including lodging, meals, a guided tour of the ruins and airfare. The Adventure Travel Center (☎/fax 832 0162, viarealguate.net), 5a Avenida Norte 25-B, near the arch in Antigua, is one; there are plenty of others. Reservations aren't necessary if you want to camp.

Camping Cheapest of Tikal's lodgings is the official camping area by the entrance road and airstrip. Set in a shaded lawn, it has tent spaces on the grass and also on concrete platforms under palapas; you can hang a hammock here, too. Water for the toilets and showers is pretty dependable. Camping is US$4.50 per person. The Restaurant Café Tikal, across the way near the museum, rents camping equipment at reasonable rates.

The Jaguar Inn (see below) has a smaller camping area with bathroom and shower facilities. Camping is US$3.25 per person with your own tent or hammock; they don't rent gear.

Hotels The largest and the most attractive of these hotels is the *Jungle Lodge (in Guatemala City ☎ 476 8775, 477 0754, fax 476 0294, reservaciones@junglelodge .guate.com)*, built originally to house the archaeologists excavating and restoring Tikal. Rooms have private hot bath and two double beds, for US$48/60/70/80 single/ double/triple/quad. In an older section are 12 much less attractive rooms with shared bath for US$20/25 single/double. Amenities include a swimming pool, large garden grounds and a restaurant/bar with breakfast for US$5, lunch or dinner for US$10. Web site: www.junglelodge.guate.com

Tikal Inn (☎/fax 594 6944 or 926 0065) is the next best choice. It has 17 rooms in the main building, as well as bungalows, plus gardens, a pool and restaurant. The simple rooms have private hot bath and ceiling fan; US$27/35 in the main building, US$55/82 in the bungalows. Electricity operates only from 11 am to 10 pm.

Jaguar Inn (☎ 926 0002, solis@quetzal.net) has nine bungalow rooms with private bath and ceiling fan for US$30/48/66/78 in high season; US$20/32/44/52 in low. Dorm beds are US$10 per person. The restaurant serves breakfast for US$3, lunch and dinner for US$6.

Places to Eat

As you arrive in Tikal, look on the right side of the road for the comedores: *Comedor Imperio Maya* (seemingly the favorite), *Comedor La Jungla Tikal, Comedor Tikal, Comedor Sagrado de Jesus* and *Tienda Angelita*. All are rustic and serve huge, cheap plates of fairly tasty food. The meal of the day is usually roast chicken, rice, salad and fruit (enough to feed two people) for US$4. All are open from around 5 am to 9 pm daily.

Across the street from the comedores, *Restaurant Café Tikal*, in the visitor's center, serves fancier food at fancier prices.

Picnic tables beneath shelters lie just off Tikal's Great Plaza; itinerant soft-drink peddlers stand by, but no food is sold anywhere at the ruins.

Getting There & Away

See the Flores & Santa Elena section, earlier, for transportation details from there. Coming from Belize, you can get off the bus at El Cruce/Puente Ixlú. Wait for a northbound bus or minibus – or hitch with an obliging tourist – to take you the remaining 35km to Tikal. Note that there is very little northbound traffic after lunch. If you come to Puente Ixlú in the afternoon, you should continue to Flores or El Remate for the night rather than risk being stranded at El Cruce.

You don't need a car to get to Tikal, but a 4WD vehicle of your own can be useful for visiting Uaxactún. Fill your fuel tank in Flores; no fuel is available at Tikal or Uaxactún.

UAXACTÚN

Uaxactún (wah-shahk-**toon**), 23km north of Tikal along a poor, unpaved road through the jungle, was Tikal's political and military rival in Late Preclassic times. It was eventually conquered by Tikal's King Great Jaguar Paw in the mid-4th century, and was subservient to its great southern sister for centuries thereafter.

When you arrive, sign your name at the guard's hut (at the edge of the derelict airstrip). About halfway down the airstrip, roads go off to the left and to the right to the ruins.

Villagers in Uaxactún live in houses lined up along the airstrip. They make a living by collecting chicle, *pimienta* (allspice) and *xate* (**sha**-tay; a frond exported for floral arrangements) from the surrounding forest.

Ruins

The pyramids at Uaxactún were uncovered and stabilized to prevent further deterioration; they were not restored. White mortar is the mark of the repair crews, who patched cracks to keep out water and roots. Much of the work on the famous Temple E-VII-Sub was done by Earthwatch volunteers in 1974.

Turn right from the airstrip to reach Groups E and H, a 15-minute walk. Perhaps the most significant temple here is E-VII-

Sub, among the earliest intact temples excavated, with foundations going back perhaps to 2000 BC. It lay beneath much larger structures, which have been stripped away. On its flat top are sockets for the poles that would have supported a wood-and-thatch temple.

About a 20-minute walk to the northwest of the runway are Groups A and B. At Group A, early excavators sponsored by Andrew Carnegie cut into the temple sides indiscriminately, looking for graves, occasionally using dynamite. This destroyed many temples, which are now being reconstructed.

The ruins are always open and accessible, and no admission is charged. However, the turnoff onto the Uaxactún road is inside the gate to Tikal, so you must pay the US$6.45 admission fee there.

Tours to Uaxactún can be arranged at the hotels in Tikal.

Places to Stay & Eat

If you have your own gear, you can camp at one of several places. *Eco Camping*, at the entrance to the larger group of ruins, is an organized campground with basic cabins.

Posada y Restaurante Campamento El Chiclero, near the airstrip, is a primitive place with seven musty thatch-roofed rooms – US$4.50 per person, or you can pitch a tent. Bathrooms are shared, and there's no electricity. It's a 10-minute walk from the ruins. Trips can be arranged here to elsewhere in the area, including Parque Nacional El Mirador–Dos Lagunas–Río Azul, La Muralla, Nakbé and Manantial.

Getting There & Away

During the rainy season (from May to October), you may find it difficult to get to Uaxactún. At other times of the year, ask in Flores or Tikal about the road's condition. You may be advised to make the hour-long drive only in a 4WD vehicle.

A bus operates daily between Santa Elena and Uaxactún, stopping at Tikal. The cost is US$2.50 from Santa Elena (three hours) or US$1 from Tikal (one hour). The bus departs Uaxactún daily at 6 am and departs Santa Elena at 1 pm for the return trip.

If driving, fill your fuel tank in Flores; no fuel is available at Tikal or Uaxactún. You

might also want to pack some food and drink. You can hire a taxi from Flores to Uaxactún for about US$50; bargain hard.

From Uaxactún it's another 104km to the Río Azul ruins, or 88km to San Andrés.

EASTWARD TO BELIZE

It's 100km from Flores/Santa Elena east to Melchor de Mencos, on the border with Belize. You can take a bus there from Santa Elena and transfer to the Belizean side. Alternatively, the San Juan Hotel shuttle bus (see Getting There & Away in the Flores & Santa Elena section, earlier in this chapter) leaves Santa Elena at 5 am and goes all the way to Belize City, connecting with the boat to Caye Caulker and Ambergris Caye. This enables travelers to avoid spending the night in seedy Belize City.

The road from Flores to El Cruce/Puente Ixlú is good and fast. From Tikal, start early in the morning and get off at El Cruce to catch a bus or hitch a ride east. For the fastest, most reliable service, however, it's best to be on that 5 am bus.

East of El Cruce the road goes to Melchor de Mencos; the trip takes two hours. In the past, there was guerrilla and bandit activity along here. There's an extremely remote chance that your bus could be stopped and your valuables robbed – it's been a long time since this has happened.

At the border you must pay a small fee (around US$1.30) before proceeding to Benque Viejo in Belize, about 3km from the border. At the border, buses wait to continue to Benque Viejo, San Ignacio, Belmopan and Belize City. If you arrive in Benque Viejo early enough in the day, you may have sufficient time to visit the Mayan ruins of Xunantunich on your way to San Ignacio.

EL PETÉN TO CHIAPAS (MEXICO)

Three routes currently cut their way through the jungle from Flores to Palenque (Mexico). Whichever way you go, make sure you clear customs and get your passport exit and entry stamps on both sides of the border.

Via El Naranjo & La Palma

The traditional route is via bus to El Naranjo, then by boat down the Río San

Pedro to La Palma, then by colectivo and bus to Tenosique and Palenque.

Transportes Pinita buses to El Naranjo depart from San Juan Hotel in Santa Elena daily at 5, 7, 8, 9 and 11 am and 1 and 3:30 pm; cost is US$2.60 for the rough, 125km, five-hour ride. Rosío buses depart for the same trip at 4:45, 8 and 10:30 am and 1:30 pm. San Juan Hotel offers a Santa Elena to Palenque transportation package via El Naranjo and La Palma for US$30 per person; departures at 5 am daily.

From El Naranjo, a hamlet with an immigration post and basic lodgings, you must catch a boat on the river around midday for the four-hour cruise to the border town of La Palma (US$20, bargain *hard*). From La Palma you can go by colectivo or bus to Tenosique (1½ hours), then by bus or combi to Emiliano Zapata (one hour, 40km) and from there by bus or combi to Palenque.

In the reverse direction, Palenque travel agencies offer to get you from Palenque to La Palma by minibus in time to catch the boat to El Naranjo, which departs between 8 and 9 am. You then catch the bus for the dreadful five-hour ride to Flores, arriving around 7 pm the same day. The cost is about US$55 per person. However, you can do it yourself by taking the 4:30 am bus from the ADO terminal to Tenosique, then a taxi (US$10) to La Palma to catch the 8 am boat. If you catch a later bus, you can stay at one of the basic hotels in Tenosique or hang your hammock in La Palma.

Via Bethel & Frontera Corozal

A faster route is by early morning bus on dilapidated roads from Flores via La Libertad and the crossroads at El Subín to the hamlet of Bethel (US$3, four hours) on the Río Usumacinta, which forms the Guatemala-Mexico border.

The early bus should get you to Bethel before noon, but if you're stuck you can spend the night at *Posada Maya*, beside the river in the forest 1km from Bethel. Lodging and meals are available, and it's not expensive; you can rent a cabin or sling a hammock. Food is grown in the organic garden. Activities include swimming in the river and tours to nearby places such as Yaxchilán, a natural spring and a lookout point. The friendly owners can arrange transportation including boats and horses.

Frequent boats make the half-hour trip downriver from Bethel to Frontera Corozal on the Mexico side, charging US$4 to US$12 for the voyage, depending on your bargaining power and number of passengers.

Frontera Corozal (formerly Frontera Echeverría) has a restaurant and primitive accommodations, but you're better off taking one of the colectivos that wait for passengers to Palenque. The last colectivo leaves around 2 or 3 pm. San Juan Hotel in Santa Elena also offers an all-inclusive transportation package to Palenque.

From Frontera Corozal, a chartered boat to the Yaxchilán archaeological site might cost US$60, but sometimes you can hitch a ride with a group for US$10 or so; this is tough in the off-season. Buses from Frontera Corozal go to Palenque (US$5, 4½ hours).

Coming from Palenque, you can take a bus to Frontera Corozal (US$4, three hours), then a boat upstream (25 minutes to the Posada Maya, 35 minutes to Bethel), staying overnight at the Posada Maya or continuing on a bus to Flores.

In Palenque, travel agencies may insist that you must sign up for their US$30 trip – and that there is no place to stay overnight at the border. Not so! These organized trips save you some hassle, but you can do the same thing for half the price. Just be sure to hit the road as early as possible in the morning.

Via Sayaxché, Pipiles & Benemérito

From Sayaxché, you can negotiate a ride on one of the cargo boats for the eight-hour trip (US$6.45) down the Río de la Pasión via Pipiles (the Guatemalan border post) to Benemérito, in Chiapas. These boats leave when they have sufficient cargo and people. From Benemérito, proceed by bus or boat to the ruins at Yaxchilán and Bonampak, then onward to Palenque. There are also buses that run directly between Benemérito and Palenque (US$12, 10 hours).

SAYAXCHÉ & CEIBAL

The town of Sayaxché, 61km south of Flores through the jungle, is the closest settlement to a half dozen Mayan archaeological sites, including Aguateca, Altar de Los Sacrificios,

Ceibal, Dos Pilas, El Caribe, Itzán, La Amelia and Tamarindito. Of these, Ceibal on the Río de la Pasión, is the best restored and most interesting, partly because of its monuments and partly because of the river voyage and jungle walk necessary to reach it.

Dos Pilas, presently under excavation, is not equipped to receive overnight visitors without camping gear. However, in good weather, you can make the trek in four hours on foot. From Dos Pilas, the minor sites of Tamarindito and Aguateca may be reached on foot and by boat, but they are unrestored, covered in jungle and of interest only to the very intrepid. Campgrounds are available at all these sites.

Sayaxché itself is of little interest, but its few basic services allow you to eat and stay overnight in this region.

Orientation & Information

The bus from Santa Elena drops you on the north bank of the Río de la Pasión. The main part of town is on the south bank. Frequent ferries cross the river (US$0.15).

The Banoro on the main street changes cash and traveler's checks at a weak rate. A block up the hill and to your right is a Banrural that changes money. The post office is way off the main drag near the radio station; head for the radio tower and ask passersby for directions.

Ceibal

Unimportant during the Classic Period, Ceibal grew rapidly thereafter, attaining a population of perhaps 10,000 by AD 900. Much of the growth may have been due to immigration from what is now Chiapas, in Mexico, because the art and culture of Ceibal seems to have changed markedly during this period. The Postclassic period saw the decline of Ceibal, after which its low ruined temples were quickly covered by a thick jungle carpet.

Today, Ceibal is not one of the most impressive Mayan sites, but the journey to Ceibal is among the most memorable. A two-hour voyage on the jungle-bound Río de la Pasión brings you to a primitive dock. After landing, you clamber up a rocky path beneath gigantic trees and vines to reach the archaeological zone.

Smallish temples, many still (or again) covered with jungle, surround two principal plazas. In front of a few temples, and standing seemingly alone on jungle paths, are magnificent, intact stelae. Exploring the site takes about two hours.

Organized Tours

Viajes Don Pedro (☎/fax 928 6109), on the riverbank, is run by the affable Pedro Mendéz. He can arrange transportation to any of the area sites. Viajes Turísticos & Restaurant La Montaña (☎ 928 6169/14, fax 928 6168), just up from Banoro, is another outfit running tours to Ceibal and Aguateca.

Places to Stay & Eat

The *Hotel Guayacán* (☎ 926 6111), just up from the dock on the south side of the river in Sayaxché, is serviceable. Rooms cost US$13 single or double with shared bath, US$16 with private bath. *Hotel Mayapán*, up the street to the left, has cell-like rooms for US$2 per person. Upstairs are much better, cleanish rooms with private bath and fan for US$5.15/9 single/double.

Hotel Posada Segura is the best budget option. Clean rooms with good beds, fan and shared bath are US$3.90 per person, US$7.75 with private bath. To get there, take your first right up from the river, follow this road until it dead ends, then hook a left.

Restaurant La Montaña serves tasty roasted chicken and other simple dishes at reasonable prices. Around the corner, dark and funky *El Botanero Restaurant Café-Bar* serves a variety of beef, chicken and seafood dishes starting around US$3.25. There's a full bar. *Restaurant Yaxkin* is typical of the other few eateries in town: basic, family-run and inexpensive.

Getting There & Away

Day trips to Ceibal are organized by various agencies and drivers in Santa Elena, Flores and Tikal; cost is about US$30 per person roundtrip. It can be done cheaper, and less conveniently, on your own.

Transportes Pinita buses depart from Santa Elena at 5:30, 7, 8, 9 and 10:30 am and 1 and 3:30 pm for Sayaxché (US$1.30, two hours). From here you can arrange a tour with an agency or strike a deal with one of the lancheros by the river. From the river, it's less than 30 minutes' walk to the Ceibal site. You should hire a guide, as some of the finest stelae are off the plazas in the jungle.

Most lancheros conveniently also serve as guides.

Buses leave Sayaxché for Flores from across the river at 5, 6 and 11 am and 1 pm. There is also a Fuentes del Norte departure to Guatemala City at 11 am (US$9, 14 hours).

REMOTE MAYAN SITES

Several sites of interest to archaeology buffs and adventure travelers are open for limited tourism. Few can be visited without a guide, but many businesses in Flores and Santa Elena offer trips to sites deep in the jungle (see Organized Tours in the Flores & Santa Elena section, earlier in this chapter). Few of these tours offer anything approaching comfort, and you should be prepared for buggy, basic conditions.

The ceremonial site of **Yaxjá**, on the lake of the same name, is about 48km east of El Remate. Scholars believe it may have been a vacation spot for Maya nobility during the Classic period. The ruins here include a large plaza and two temples. A ruined observatory sits on Topoxté island in the middle of the lake.

El Zotz is about 25km west of Tikal. Zotz means 'bat,' and you'll encounter plenty on a trek here. Among the many unexcavated mounds and ruins is Devil's Pyramid, which is so tall that from its summit you can see to

the temples of Tikal. Trips to El Zotz can be extended to include a trek to Tikal.

El Perú, 62km northwest from Flores, lies along the Scarlet Macaw Trail. The trek starts in Paso Caballos and continues by boat along the Río San Pedro. Several important structures here have been dated to between AD 300 and 900. Archaeologists believe El Perú was an important commercial center.

El Mirador is buried within the farthest reaches of the Petén jungle, just 7km from the Mexican border. A trip here involves an arduous 60km trek in primitive conditions. The metropolis at El Mirador flourished between 150 BC and AD 150, when it was abandoned for mysterious reasons. The site holds the tallest pyramid ever built in the Mayan world: El Tigre is over 60m high, and its base covers 18,000 sq meters. It's twin, La Danta (Tapir), though technically smaller, soars higher because it's built on a rise. There are hundreds of buildings at El Mirador, but almost everything is still hidden beneath the jungle.

This trip is not for the faint of heart. For more on this incredible site, see the September, 1987 *National Geographic* article 'An Early Maya Metropolis Uncovered: El Mirador.' This is the most thorough mainstream investigative report ever written about the site.

Belize

This English-speaking tropical country embraces a beguiling mixture of Caribbean and Latin cultures. The people are friendly, open and relaxed – everyone here seems to know how to have a good time. Belizeans readily offer visitors help and advice, and they're committed to avoiding the pitfalls of mass-market tourism.

Belize is a tiny country. Its entire population numbers only about 250,000 (the size of

Highlights

- Take in the colonial architecture and cooling sea breezes of Belize City's Fort George district
- Visit the ruins at Altun Ha, the most-visited Mayan site in Belize, yet surprisingly tranquil
- Dive and snorkel off the barrier reef or head farther out to sea to find unmatched diving through pristine coral fields
- Enjoy the freewheeling, sun-dappled Caribbean lifestyle at Ambergris Caye or at Caye Caulker, a laid-back and budget-oriented hideout
- Take the picturesque river tour to the ruins of Lamanai, one of the Mayan world's most famous ancient centers
- Enjoy the easy international beach life in Placencia
- Spend some time soaking up Garífuna culture in Dangriga, Hopkins or Sittee

a small city in Mexico, Europe or the USA), and its 23,300-sq-km area is only slightly larger than that of Wales or Massachusetts. Yet despite its diminutive size, the country offers a variety of terrain and plenty of opportunity for adventure. You can go snorkeling and diving in the cayes; hiking and caving inland; bird and wildlife viewing in the country's robust network of unspoiled national parks; or exploring at any of several Mayan ruins, which you're likely to have to yourself outside peak tourism hours.

Many visitors divide their time between the cayes or the beach at Placencia and the mountainous regions of Cayo. Travelers who wish to get off the beaten track need only travel a couple of hours out from Belize City, heading north to, say, Corozal or south to Punta Gorda. The country is an independent traveler's dream – an efficient network of buses making frequent runs in all directions means that it's easy to get from point to point without much waiting around or advance planning.

Facts about Belize

HISTORY

In the opinion of its Spanish conquerors, Belize was a backwater, good only for its harvestable logwood, which was used to make dye. The country had no obvious riches to exploit and no great population to convert for 'the glory of God' and the profit of the conquerors. Far from being profitable, Belize was dangerous, because the barrier reef tended to tear the keels from Spanish ships attempting to approach the shore.

The lack of effective government and the safety afforded by the barrier reef attracted English and Scottish pirates to Belizean waters during the 17th century. They operated mostly without serious hindrance, capturing Spanish galleons heavily laden with gold and other riches taken from Spain's American empire. In 1670, however, Spain convinced the British government to clamp down on the pirates' activities. Most of the pirates, now unemployed, went into the logwood business.

of the Castes during the mid-19th century. The war also brought a flood of refugees to Belize. First came the whites and their mestizo lieutenants, driven out by the wrath of the Maya; then came the Maya themselves when the whites regained control of Yucatán. The Maya brought farming skills that were of great value in expanding the horizons and economic viability of Belizean society.

In 1862, while the USA was embroiled in the Civil War and unable to enforce the terms of the Monroe Doctrine, which closed the Western Hemisphere to colonization, Great Britain declared Belize its colony, calling it British Honduras. The declaration encouraged people from many parts of the British Empire to settle in Belize, which accounts for the country's present-day ethnic diversity.

The Belizean economy worsened after WWII, leading to agitation for independence from the United Kingdom. Democratic institutions and political parties were formed over the years, and self-government eventually became a reality. On September 21, 1981, the colony of British Honduras officially became the independent nation of Belize.

In the 1780s the British actively protected the former pirates' logging interests, at the same time assuring Spain that Belize was indeed a Spanish possession. This was a fiction. By this time, Belize was already British by tradition and sympathy, and it was with relief and jubilation that Belizeans received the news, on September 10, 1798, that a British force had defeated the Spanish armada off St George's Caye. Belize had been delivered from Spanish rule, a fact that was ratified by treaty some 60 years later.

The country's new status did not bring prosperity, however. Belize was still essentially one large logging camp, not a balanced society of farmers, artisans, merchants and traders. When the logwood trade collapsed, killed by the invention of synthetic dyes, the colony's economy crashed. It was revived by the trade in mahogany during the early 19th century, but this collapsed, too when African sources of the wood brought fierce price competition.

Belize's next trade boom was in arms, ammunition and other supplies sold to the Maya rebels in Yucatán who fought the War

GEOGRAPHY & CLIMATE

Belize is mostly tropical lowland, typically hot and humid for most of the year. Rainfall is lightest in the north, heaviest in the south. The southern rain forests receive almost 4m of precipitation annually, making the south the country's most humid region.

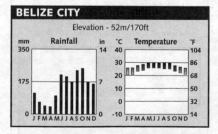

BELIZE CITY

Elevation - 52m/170ft

An exception to Belize's low-lying topography and hot, sticky climate can be found in the Maya Mountains, which traverse western and southern Belize at elevations approaching 1000m. The mountains enjoy a more pleasant climate than the lowlands – comfortably warm during the day, cooling off a bit at night.

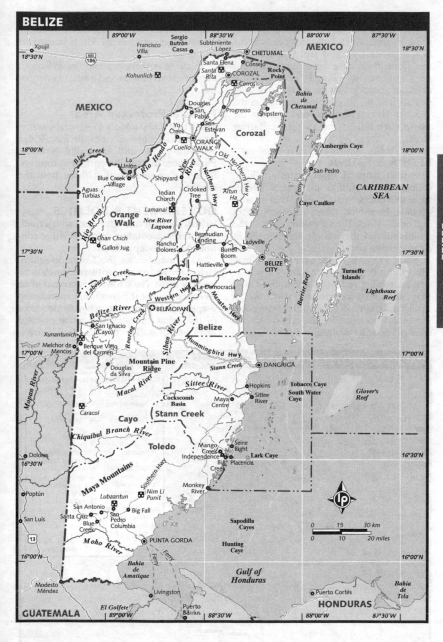

The country's coastline and northern coastal plain are largely covered in mangrove swamp, which indistinctly defines the line between land and sea. Offshore, the limestone bedrock extends eastward into the Caribbean for several kilometers at a depth of about 5m. At the eastern extent of this shelf is the longest barrier reef in the Western Hemisphere, second longest in the world (behind Australia's Great Barrier Reef).

FLORA & FAUNA

The lush tropical forests contain huge ceiba trees as well as mahogany, guanacaste and cohune palms, all festooned with orchids, bromeliads and other epiphytes and lianas vines. The shorelines of both the mainland and the islands are cloaked in dense mangrove.

Baird's tapir is Belize's national animal. The gibnut or paca *(tepezcuintle),* a rabbit-size burrowing rodent, is abundant. Other tropical animals include the jaguar, ocelot, howler monkey, peccary, vulture, stork and anteater. Watch out for the occasional boa constrictor or fer-de-lance.

Belize's birdlife is varied and abundant, with hummingbirds, keel-billed toucans, woodpeckers and many kinds of parrots and macaws.

In the seas there are lobsters, manatees, occasional crocodiles and a great variety of fish.

Parks & Protected Areas

Much of the Maya Mountain forest south of San Ignacio is protected as the Pine Ridge Forest Reserve and Chiquibul National Park. There are smaller parks and reserves, including marine reserves, throughout the country.

GOVERNMENT & POLITICS

British colonial rule left Belize with a tradition of representative democracy that continued after independence.

As a member of the Commonwealth, Belize recognizes the British monarch as its head of state. The Crown is represented on Belizean soil by the governor-general, who is appointed by the monarch with the advice of the prime minister, the actual political head of Belize. The Belizean legislature is

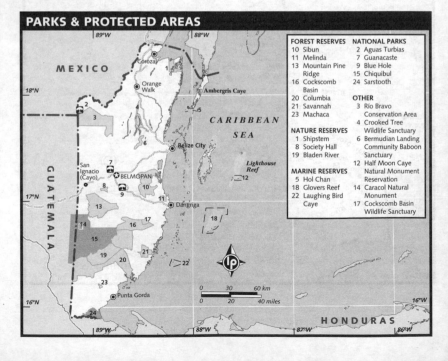

bicameral, with a popularly elected House of Representatives and a nominated Senate similar in function to the British House of Lords.

In 1996 George Price, who had been prime minister for most of Belize's independence, announced his retirement as head of the People's United Party (PUP), opening the way to a noisy power struggle among his lieutenants. Said Musa won the struggle and led the PUP to a stunning sweep of town board seats in the March 1997 by-elections. The PUP and Said Musa now have control of the central and local governments.

ECONOMY

Belize has never been a rich country. Its economic history in the past hundred years has been one of getting by, benefiting from economic aid granted by the UK and the USA, money sent home by Belizeans living and working abroad and the foreign currency generated by its small agricultural sector.

In the lands west and south of Belize City, cattle ranching is a prime economic component, along with farming and, in the Maya Mountains, forestry. In the north, cattle ranches share the land with large sugarcane plantations and their attendant refineries. The cayes depend on tourism and fishing for their income.

The government has invested heavily in foreign public-relations campaigns while working to improve the travel infrastructure on the home front. Because of these efforts, the country has seen record increases in visitors and tourist dollars.

POPULATION & PEOPLE

For such a tiny country, Belize enjoys a fabulous, improbable ethnic diversity. Creoles – descendants of the African slaves and British pirates who first settled here to exploit the country's forest riches – make up the country's largest ethnic group. Racially mixed and proud of it, Creoles speak a fascinating, unique dialect of English that, though it sounds familiar at first, is not easily intelligible to a speaker of standard English.

Fully one-third of Belize's people are mestizos, or persons of mixed European and Central American Indian ancestry,

some of whose ancestors immigrated from Yucatán during the 19th century.

The Maya of Belize make up about 10% of the population and are divided into three linguistic groups. The Yucatec live in the north near the Yucatán border, the Mopan live in western Belize around the border town of Benque Viejo del Carmen, and the Kekchi inhabit far southern Belize in and around Punta Gorda. In recent years, political refugees coming in from Guatemala and El Salvador have added to Belize's Maya population.

Southern Belize is the home of the Garífuna (or Garinagus, also called Black Caribs), who account for less than 10% of the population. The Garífuna are of South American Indian and African descent. They look more African than Indian, but they speak a language that's much more Indian than African and their unique culture combines aspects of both peoples.

Other ethnic groups in Belize include small populations of Europeans, North Americans, Chinese and East Indians.

RELIGION

Belize's mixture of religions follows its ethnic composition. Anglicans, Buddhists, Catholics, Hindus, Muslims, Mennonites and evangelical Protestants are all represented, and some communities still observe traditional Mayan rites.

LANGUAGE

Belize is officially English-speaking, but the Creoles (over half of the population) speak their own dialect as well as standard English flavored with the Caribbean's musical lilt. Spanish is the first language in the north and in some towns in the west.

Facts for the Visitor

SUGGESTED ITINERARIES

If you've got one week in Belize, a good option is to spend half of your time on the Caribbean Sea and half of your time exploring the inland region. There's a well-worn track between Cayes Caulker and Ambergris and the mountainous Cayo region, the location of San Ignacio and the

Mountain Pine Ridge – some call this the surf and turf holiday. The cayes are terrific for diving and snorkeling, but if you're really yearning for a good beach on which to sit a spell, consider Placencia. It's more rustic, and less expensive than the cayes. Cayo in Western Belize has something for everyone – San Ignacio is a lively base to explore the region, or if you want to get away from it all consider retreating to a rustic jungle lodge.

If you've got up to two weeks, you can add some time in the north – check out Lamanai, Corozal and surroundings and use the extra time to explore farther out to sea or deeper into the Mountain Pine Ridge. It's easy to arrange a one- or two-day trip over the Guatemalan border to Tikal.

With two or more weeks consider heading down to the relatively untouristed Punta Gorda, Belize's southernmost region, or setting sail to one of the southern cayes.

PLANNING
When to Go
The busy winter season is from mid-December to April, and a second peak occurs June through August. The dry season (November to May) is the best time to travel, however, prices are lower and lodgings on the cayes are easier to find in summer (July to November). If you do visit in summer, be aware that this is hurricane season. Belize City was badly damaged by hurricanes, with heavy loss of life, in 1931, 1961 and 1978.

Maps
If you're driving, pick up a copy of Emory King's annual *Driver's Guide to Beautiful Belize*, sold in bookstores and gift shops in Belize City. The guide has basic maps and detailed route descriptions – helpful since road markers in Belize are few and far between.

The various British Ordnance Survey maps (1:750,000 to 1:1000) are the most detailed and accurate of the country. In North America, order them from OMNI Resources (☎ 910 227 8300, fax 910 227 8374), PO Box 2096, Burlington, NC 27216; or Map Link (☎ 805 692 6777, fax 805 692 6787), 30 South La Patera Lane, Unit 5, Santa Barbara, CA 93117.

More readily accessible in Belize is the *Belize Facilities Map* issued by the Belize Tourism Board, PO Box 325, Belize City. Derived from the Ordnance Survey maps, it has plans of all major towns in Belize, a road map, plans of the archaeological sites at Altun Ha and Xunantunich and a list of facts about Belize. If you write to the Board in advance you may be able to get one free; in Belizean shops the map is sold for US\$4.

TOURIST OFFICES
The Belize Tourism Board (☎ 2 31910, 2 31913, fax 2 31943, btbb@btl.net) is headquartered in the Central Bank Building on Gabourel Lane in Belize City. It also maintains a branch in Germany: (☎ 711 233 947), Bopserwaldstrasse 40-G, D-70184, Stuttgart. Web site: www.travelbelize.org

The Belize Tourism Industry Association (☎ 2 75717, 2 71144, fax 2 78710, btia@btl.net), 10 N Park St, Belize City, is Belize's private-sector tourism organization. This association publishes *Destination Belize*, a helpful visitor's guide available from information kiosks and hotels throughout the country.

VISAS & DOCUMENTS
Citizens of many countries (among them Australia, Canada, France, Germany, Ireland, Italy, Mexico, New Zealand, the UK, the USA and many Caribbean nations) do not need to obtain a Belizean visa in advance, provided they have a valid passport and an onward or roundtrip airline ticket. A visitor's permit valid for 30 days will be stamped in their passport at a border crossing or at the airport. Details on visa requirements for other visitors are available from any Belizean embassy or consulate (see Embassies & Consulates in the Regional Facts for the Visitor chapter).

If you plan to drive in Belize, you'll need to bring a valid driver's license from your home country.

MONEY
Currency
The Belizean dollar (BZ\$) is divided into 100 cents. Coins come in denominations of one, five, 10, 25 and 50 cents, and one dollar; bills (notes) are all of the same size but differ in color and come in denominations of two, five, 10, 20, 50 and 100 dollars. Be sure to have small denominations if you're heading off the tourist trail.

The Belizean dollar's value has been fixed for many years at US$0.50. Prices are generally quoted in Belizean dollars, written as '$30 BZE,' though you will also occasionally see '$15 US.' To avoid surprises, be sure to confirm with service providers whether they are quoting prices in US or Belizean dollars.

Exchanging Money

Most businesses accept US currency in cash without question. They usually give change in Belizean dollars, though they may return US change if you ask for it. Many also accept US-dollar traveler's checks.

Canadian dollars and UK pounds sterling are exchangeable at any bank, although non-US-dollar traveler's checks are not consistently accepted by Belizean banks. It is difficult if not impossible to exchange other foreign currencies in Belize.

Moneychangers around border-crossing points will change your US cash for Belizean dollars legally at the standard rate of US$1=BZ$2. If you change money or traveler's checks at a bank, you may get only US$1=BZ$1.97; they may also charge a fee of BZ$5 (US$2.50) to change a traveler's check.

ATMs & Credit Cards ATMs for Belizean banks are becoming common, but they don't yet accept foreign ATM cards. If you depend upon your ATM card for money, stock up on cash in Mexico or Guatemala before entering Belize.

Major credit cards such as Visa and MasterCard are accepted at all airline and car rental companies and at the larger hotels and restaurants everywhere; American Express is often accepted at higher-end places and is becoming more common among the smaller establishments. Most businesses add a surcharge (usually 5%) to your bill when you pay by credit card.

Belize has Western Union offices where you can arrange wire transfers.

Costs

Though a poor country, Belize is more expensive than you might anticipate. A fried-chicken dinner that costs US$3 in Guatemala costs US$5 in Belize. A very basic, waterless pension room, cheap in Guatemala and Mexico, costs US$8 to US$10 per person on Caye Caulker. Budget travelers will find it difficult to spend less than US$15 per day for a room and three meals; US$20 is a more realistic bottom-end figure, and US$25 makes life a lot easier. Mid-range travelers will be fine on US$50 to US$60 a day.

Tipping & Bargaining

In highly touristed areas, tipping tour leaders, dive operators and waitstaff is becoming more common, but this should be done only if you feel the service warrants it. Tips need go no higher than 10%.

Bargaining is not a huge part of the culture in Belize, because shops generally have set prices on goods.

Taxes & Refunds

Belize levies an 8% value-added tax (VAT) on retail sales, as well as a 7% tax on hotel rooms, meals and drinks. The rates listed in this book for accommodations in Belize do not include the 7% room tax. If you stay in a small hotel or guesthouse just one night and don't insist on a receipt, you may not be charged the hotel tax. Foreign visitors do not get a refund of the VAT.

POST & COMMUNICATIONS

By airmail to Canada or the USA, a postcard costs BZ$0.30, a letter BZ$0.60. To Europe it's BZ$0.40 for a postcard and BZ$0.75 for a letter.

Address poste restante (general delivery) mail to: (name), c/o Poste Restante, (town), Belize. To claim poste restante mail, present a passport or other identification; there's no charge.

The country's telephone system is operated by Belize Telecommunications Ltd (BTL), with offices in major towns (open 8 am to noon and 1 to 4 pm Monday to Friday and 8 am to noon Saturday).

Local calls cost BZ$0.25. Telephone debit cards are sold in denominations of BZ$10, BZ$20 and BZ$50.

The country code is 501. To call one part of Belize from another, dial 0 (zero), then the one- or two-digit area code (which is listed in the text under the headings for the towns), then the four- or five-digit local number. You must also dial 0 and the area code when you're making a local call with a phone card.

BELIZE

BELIZE

The following are some useful numbers:

Directory assistance	☎ 113
Local & regional operator	☎ 114
Long-distance (trunk) operator	☎ 110
International operator	☎ 115
Fire & ambulance	☎ 90
Police	☎ 911

The large American long-distance companies provide international service as well. Their rates may not be much different than BTL's, however. AT&T's USADirect and WorldConnect services can be requested through the international operator.

Fax service is available at many hotels and businesses. BTL provides Internet access to local residents with accounts, charging by the hour. Most hotels will send email messages for guests. Cybercafes are starting to crop up in Belize's tourist centers; rates average around US$3 for 15 minutes. CompuServe and America Online do not have nodes in Belize at the time of this writing.

INTERNET RESOURCES
Several helpful Web sites offer information for travelers to Belize. The best starting points are www.belizetravel.org, the Belize Tourism Board's official Web site, and www.belizenet.com, which provides excellent travel and accommodations information as well as links to regional Web sites. Belizenet.com operates the Belize Forums, a top-notch travelers' bulletin board offering discussion topics and monitored by Belize travel experts who can help answer your trip-planning questions.

The entertaining www.belizeans.com offers a quirky look at Belizean lifestyle and culture, with content provided by both resident and expat Belizeans.

NEWSPAPERS & MAGAZINES
Most Belizean newspapers are supported by one political party or another, and as a consequence, much space is devoted to political diatribe. The PUP-leaning Amandala (www.belizemall.com/amandala) has the largest circulation in the country. Belize Times (www.belizetimes.com) represents the opposition UDP perspective. The Reporter (www.reporterbelize.com) appears to present the most neutral coverage.

Belize First Magazine has information of interest to travelers as well as retirees and other expats. Especially helpful are the reader recommendations on lodging, restaurants and tours. An online version is available at www.turq.com/belizefirst. The print version is published quarterly and sold for US$29 per year. To order, fax a request to 828 667 1717, email bzefirst@aol.com, or write to Equator Travel Publications/Asheville, 280 Beaverdam Rd, Candler, NC 28715 USA.

RADIO & TV
Love-FM serves as the national radio station. Showing up at various spots on the radio dial, it's a charming mix of local news, public-service announcements and the world's best love songs.

Channel 5 is Belize's primary TV station. Programming consists mainly of rebroadcast US satellite feeds and a few hours of local content. Most hotels with TVs in their guest rooms provide cable service with several dozen channels.

WEIGHTS & MEASURES
Despite its claim to use the metric system, Belize's road signs are marked in miles, and motor fuel is sold in US gallons.

WOMEN TRAVELERS
Men in Belize can be forward and at times aggressive with comments about women's appearance. This can be uncomfortable and embarrassing, but shouldn't be considered threatening (although commonsense rules for women travelers should be followed). Do as your mother probably told you in elementary school: Ignore them, and they'll go away. And (you may have heard this from mom, too), the more modestly you're dressed, the less attention you'll receive.

BUSINESS HOURS
Banking hours vary, but most banks are open 8 am to 1:30 pm Monday to Thursday and 8 am to 4:30 pm Friday. Most banks and many businesses and shops close on Wednesday afternoon. Shops are usually open 8 am to noon Monday to Saturday and 1 to 4 pm Monday, Tuesday, Thursday and Friday. Some shops have evening hours from 7 to 9 pm on those days as well. Most businesses, offices and city restaurants close

on Sunday. Note that in smaller towns, the popular Belizean restaurants usually close before 6 pm.

ACTIVITIES
Snorkeling and diving are best on the cayes. Boats depart Ambergris and Caulker on day and overnight voyages to the best spots.

Horseback riding, canoeing and kayaking, hiking, bird watching and archaeology are best in the Cayo District of western Belize.

ACCOMMODATIONS
Lodgings in Belize are generally more expensive and of lower comfort than in neighboring countries. Some have great charm and are well worth the cost; most are just places to stay.

FOOD
Belize has never developed an elaborate native cuisine. Recipes are mostly borrowed – from the UK, the Caribbean, Mexico and the USA. Each community has its own local favorites, but Garífuna and Mayan dishes and traditional favorites such as *boil-up* rarely appear on restaurant menus. Even so, there is some good food to be had, especially the fresh fish options near the sea.

Rice and beans prevail on Belizean menus and plates. They're usually served with other ingredients – chicken, pork, beef, fish, vegetables, even lobster – plus some spices and condiments such as coconut milk. 'Stew beans with rice' is stewed beans on one side of the plate, boiled rice on the other side and chicken, beef or pork on top.

Some restaurants serve wild game such as armadillo, venison and the guinea-pig-like gibnut (also called 'paca'). Conservationists frown on this practice. Lobsters are in season from mid-June to mid-February (to discourage poaching, don't order them the rest of the year), and conch season begins when lobster season ends.

SHOPPING
Some useful and valuable goods made in Belize can be picked up for souvenirs. Among these are Rainforest Remedies (a line of all-natural health products produced by IxChel farms in San Ignacio); Marie Sharp's hot sauce; and Rasta Pasta spice

packets, for creating traditional Belizean dishes at home. Books and recordings by Belizean artists can be purchased from Cubola Productions (cubolabz@btl.net, www.belizemall.com/cubola).

Getting There & Away

AIR
Major airlines serving Belize include American (from Miami and Dallas), Continental (from Houston) and Grupo TACA (from Los Angeles). Most international air routes to Belize City go through these gateways.

Grupo TACA also offers direct flights between Belize City and Guatemala City (Guatemala), San Salvador (El Salvador), and Roatán and San Pedro Sula (Honduras), as well as connecting flights from Panama, Nicaragua and Costa Rica. Mexicana Airlines (☎ 800-531 7921 in the USA, no ticket agent in Belize) flies between Cancún (Mexico) and Belize City on Thursday, Saturday and Sunday.
Web site: www.mexicana.com.

Departure taxes and airport fees of BZ$30 (US$15) are levied on non-Belizean travelers departing Goldson International Airport in Belize City for foreign destinations.

Flights to Tikal (Guatemala)
Tropic Air offers day and overnight tours by air from San Pedro on Ambergris Caye to Tikal in Guatemala. The tours leave at 8 am and 2 pm Monday to Friday, stopping at Goldson International Airport at 8:30 am and 2:30 pm and leaving Flores on the return trip at 9:30 am and 3:30 pm. A one-way flight with no tour services costs US$85.

LAND
Several companies operate direct buses from Chetumal (Mexico) to Belize City. Other companies, including Novelo's, run between Belize City and Benque Viejo del Carmen on the Guatemalan border, connecting with Guatemalan buses headed for Flores. Some of these lines arrange connections so that you can travel between Flores and Chetumal directly, with only brief stops in Belize to change buses.

BELIZE

Exit tax at Belizean land border-crossing points is US$7.50.

SEA

The *Gulf Cruza* runs between Belize City and Puerto Cortés (Honduras), with stops in Placencia and Big Creek, every Friday, returning Monday morning.

Scheduled boats and occasional small passenger boats ply the waters between Punta Gorda in southern Belize and Lívingston and Puerto Barrios in eastern Guatemala. Refer to the Southern Belize section for details. These boats can usually be hired for special trips between countries, and if enough passengers split the cost, the price can be reasonable.

Getting Around

AIR

Belize City has two airports. All international flights use Philip SW Goldson International Airport (BZE), 9 miles (16km) northwest of the city center. The Municipal Airport (TZA) is 1.5 miles (2.5km) north of the city center, on the shore. Most local flights will stop and pick you up at either airport, but fares are almost always lower from Municipal, so unless you're connecting to an international flight, use that one.

Two airlines operate along two principal domestic air routes: Belize City–Caye Caulker–San Pedro–Corozal; and Belize City–Dangriga–Placencia–Punta Gorda. Sometimes planes will not stop at a particular airport if they have no passengers to drop off or pick up, so be sure to reserve your seat in advance whenever possible. Tickets for both airlines can be booked through most of the hotels and tour agencies within the country.

Local Belizean airlines include:

Maya Island Air (☎ 2 31140 in Belize City, miatza@btl.net, 26 2435 in San Pedro, miaspr@btl.net, 800-521 1247 in the USA and Canada) Web site: www.mayaairways.com

Tropic Air (☎ 26 2012 and fax 26 2338 in San Pedro, ☎ 800-422 3435 in the USA and Canada, tropicair@btl.net) Web site: www.tropicair.com

Fares for the individual legs of the routes average about US$30.

BUS

Most Belizean buses are used US school buses, although a few 1st-class services are available. The larger companies operate frequent buses along the country's three major roads. Smaller village lines tend to be run on local work and school schedules: Buses run from a smaller town to a larger town in the morning, and then they return in the afternoon. Fares average about US$1.50 per hour's ride.

Each major bus company has its own terminals. Outside Belize City, bus drivers will usually pick up and drop off passengers at undesignated stops if requested.

Visit www.belizetravel.org for an automated bus schedule.

Pilferage of luggage has been a problem, particularly on the Punta Gorda route. Give your luggage only to the bus driver or conductor, and watch as it is stored. Be there when the bus is unloaded and retrieve your luggage at once.

CAR

Belize has three good paved two-lane roads: the Northern Hwy between the Mexican border near Corozal and Belize City; the Western Hwy between Belize City and the Guatemalan border at Benque Viejo del Carmen; and the Hummingbird Hwy from Belmopan to Dangriga. Most other roads are narrow one- or two-lane dirt roads; many are impassable after heavy rains. The Southern Hwy is paved in patches but remains slow going.

Sites off the main roads may be accessible only by 4WD vehicles, especially between May and November. After heavy rains in Belize, you can get profoundly stuck in floodwaters or mud even with 4WD, and getting winched out is expensive. Wet conditions aren't the only challenge; in mountain regions the dry soil is loose and rocky, making it hard to keep traction on steep roads.

Mileposts and highway signs record distances in miles and speed limits in miles per hour, although many vehicles have odometers and speedometers that are calibrated in kilometers.

Road Rules

Although Belize is a former British colony, cars drive on the right side of the road here.

Except in the Cayo District in western Belize, road signs pointing the way to towns and villages are few and far between. Keep track of your mileage so you know when your turnoff is approaching, and don't be afraid to ask people for directions. Watch out for sudden changes in road conditions, especially in the south; an overly quick transition from pavement to dirt could cause you to lose control of your vehicle. Be prepared to slow down for speed bumps (called 'sleeping policemen') at the approaches to towns and intersections.

Consider driving with your headlights on during the day so that you'll be visible to oncoming traffic. And if you're in any doubt about whether you have room to pass, don't take a risk – there will always be other opportunities.

When making a left turn, you must pull over to the right, let oncoming cars pass and make your turn when traffic is clear in both directions.

Use of seat belts is required. If you are caught not wearing yours, the fine is US$12.50.

Rental

Generally, renters must be at least 25 years old, have a valid driver's license and pay by credit card or leave a large cash deposit. You must obtain a release from the car rental agency if you plan to drive a rental out of Belize.

Most car rental companies have representatives at Belize City's Goldson International Airport; many will also deliver or take return of cars at Belize City's Municipal Airport. Rates are around US$80 to US$88 per day (US$482 to US$498 per week), 15% tax included, with unlimited mileage. A Loss Damage Waiver (LDW, loosely known as 'insurance') costs an additional US$14 per day, tax included.

Budget Rent-a-Car (☎ 2 32435, 2 33986, 800-283 4387 in the USA, jmagroup@btl.net), 771 Bella Vista, Belize City. Most of its Suzuki and Vitara cars have 4WD, AM-FM radio and air-con.

Crystal Auto Rental (☎ 3 31600, crystal@btl.net), 1½ miles, Northern Hwy. Offers good prices on 2WD pickups as well as 4WDs. You can arrange for pick-ups or drop-offs from your hotel or the airports.

National Rental Car (☎ 2 31587, 2 31650), 12 N Front St, Belize City.

Insurance

Liability insurance is required in Belize, and you must have it for the customs officer to approve the temporary importation of your car into Belize. You can usually buy the insurance from booths at the border for about US$1 per day. Note that the booths are generally closed on Sunday; if you're crossing the border with a car, try to do it on a weekday morning.

BOAT

Fast motor launches zoom between Belize City, Caye Caulker and Ambergris Caye frequently every day.

Be sure to bring sunscreen, a hat and clothing to protect you from the sun and the spray. If you sit in the bow, there's less spray, but you bang down harder when the boat goes over a wave. Sitting in the stern will give you a smoother ride, but you may get dampened.

Schedules

The Belize Marine Terminal (☎ 2 31969), on Front St at the north end of the Swing Bridge in Belize City, is the main dock for boats to the northern cayes.

The efficient Caye Caulker Water Taxi Association (☎ 2 31969 in Belize City, 22 2992 on Caye Caulker, 26 2036 in San Pedro) operates fast, frequent launches between Belize City, Caye Caulker and San Pedro on Ambergris Caye, with stops on request at Caye Chapel and St George's Caye. Against the wind, the trip to Caulker takes 30 to 45 minutes. The San Pedro ride takes 45 minutes to an hour. See the Cayes section for details.

Slightly cheaper is a ride from Triple J Boating Service (☎ 2 33464, fax 2 44375), which runs boats to Caye Caulker and San Pedro from the Court House Wharf behind the Supreme Court building.

Belize City

☎ 2 • pop 80,000

Colorful, ramshackle and alive with Caribbean-style hustle and bustle, Belize City is a great place to explore. Here, unlike in more tourist-oriented areas, you'll have a good opportunity to meet Belizeans going about their everyday lives.

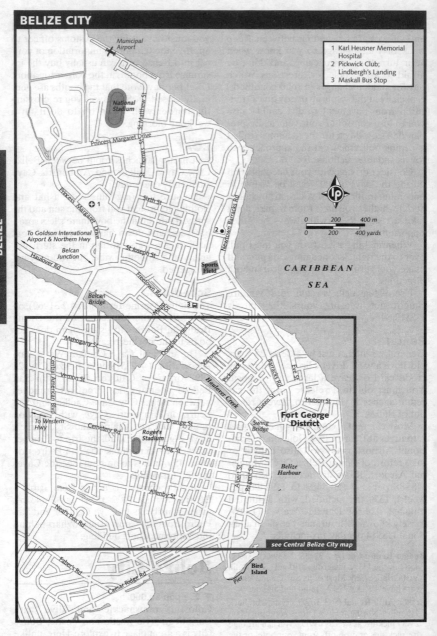

BELIZE CITY

1 Karl Heusner Memorial
   Hospital
2 Pickwick Club;
   Lindbergh's Landing
3 Maskall Bus Stop

Municipal
Airport

National
Stadium

St Matthew St

Princess Margaret Drive

St Thomas St

Sixth St

⊕ 1

Newtown Barracks Rd

To Goldson International
Airport & Northern Hwy

Belcan
Junction

Haulover Rd

St Joseph St

2 ●

Freetown Rd

Belcan
Bridge

Sports
Field

3 🚏

BEL St

CARIBBEAN

SEA

0   200   400 m
0   200   400 yards

Mahogany St

Central American Blvd

Vernon St

Douglas Jones St

Yelemie St

Pickwood St

Barracks Rd

Eve St

Haulover Creek

Queen St

Hutson St

Fort George
District

To Western
Hwy

Cemetery Rd

Roger's
Stadium

Orange St

King St

Swing
Bridge

Albert St

Regent St

Belize
Harbour

Allenby St

Neal's Pen Rd

Faber's Rd

Caesar Ridge Rd

Pier

Bird
Island

see Central Belize City map

History

Originally the nation's capital, Belize City was built on landfill on the site of a Mayan fishing village. After the city was ravaged by Hurricane Hattie in 1961, the government moved inland to Belmopan, the country's current capital. That said, the prime minister still lives in Belize City, and most events and announcements of nationwide significance still originate here.

Orientation

Haulover Creek, a branch of the Belize River, runs through the middle of the city, separating the commercial center (bounded by Albert, Regent, King and Orange Sts) from the slightly more genteel residential and hotel district of Fort George to the northeast.

The Swing Bridge joins Albert St with Queen St, which runs through the Fort George district and its pleasant King's Park neighborhood. The bridge, a product of Liverpool's ironworks, was built in 1923 and is the only known working bridge of its type in the world. Its operators manually rotate the bridge open at 5:30 am and 5:30 pm daily, just long enough to let tall boats pass and to bring most of the traffic in the city center to a halt.

The Belize Marine Terminal, used by motor launches traveling to Caye Caulker and Ambergris Caye, is at the bridge's north end.

Each of Belize's bus companies has its own terminal. Most are on the west side of W Collett Canal St, near Cemetery Rd. This is a rundown area not good for walking at night; take a taxi.

Information

Tourist Offices The Belize Tourism Board (BTB; ☎ 31910/13, fax 31943, btbb@btl.net), in the Central Bank Building on Gabourel Lane, is open 8 am to noon and 1 to 5 pm Monday to Friday (until 4:30 pm on Friday).

The Belize Tourism Industry Association (☎ 75717, 71144, fax 78710, btia@btl.net), 10 N Park St, on the north side of Memorial Park in the Fort George district, can provide information about its members, including most of the country's hotels, restaurants, tour operators and other travel-related businesses. Hours are 8:30 am to noon and 1

to 4:30 pm Monday to Friday (until 4 pm on Friday).

Money Scotiabank (☎ 77027), on Albert St at the intersection with Bishop St, is open 8 am to 1 pm Monday to Friday and 3 to 6 pm on Friday afternoon.

Nearby, the Atlantic Bank Limited (☎ 77124), 6 Albert St at King St, is open 8 am to noon and 1 to 3 pm Monday, Tuesday and Thursday, 8 am to 1 pm Wednesday and 8 am to 4:30 pm Friday.

Also on Albert St you'll find the prominent Belize Bank (☎ 77132), 60 Market Square (facing the Swing Bridge), and Barclay's Bank (☎ 77211), 21 Albert St.

Post & Communications The main post office is in the Paslow Building at the north end of the Swing Bridge, at the intersection of Queen and Front Sts. Hours are 8 am to noon and 1 to 5 pm Monday to Saturday.

You can check your email at Angelus Press (☎ 35777), 10 Queen St, for US$5 an hour.

Travel Agencies Belize Adventures (☎ 77257, fax 75213, bzeadventure@btl.net), 41 Albert St, is an experienced agency that works with the major airlines. You might also try G&W Holiday Tours (☎ 52461, fax 52645, gholiday@btl.net) at Goldson International Airport.

Bookstores Books are sold at Angelus Books, 10 Queen St, and Thrift & Book Town, 4 Church St (the book department is upstairs).

Laundry Stan's Laundry, at 22 Dean St, between Albert and Canal, charges US$5 per load. Most hotels can arrange laundry service for you at similar prices.

Medical Services Karl Heusner Memorial Hospital (☎ 31548) is on Princess Margaret Dr in the northern part of town.

Emergency Belize City's emergency police number is ☎ 911. For the fire department or ambulance call ☎ 90.

Dangers & Annoyances Yes, there is petty crime in Belize City, but it's not as bad as some doomsayers will tell you. Take the

BELIZE

same commonsense precautions that you would in any major city. Don't flash wads of cash, expensive camera equipment or other signs of wealth. Don't leave valuables in your hotel room. Don't use or deal in illicit drugs. Don't walk alone at night, and avoid deserted streets, even in daylight.

It's always better to walk in pairs or groups and to stick to major streets in the city center, Fort George and King's Park. Especially avoid walking along Front St south and east of the Swing Bridge; this is a favorite area for muggers. Ask your hotel operator or a shopkeeper for advice on the safety of a particular neighborhood or establishment, and when in doubt, take a cab.

If you're hassled or scammed, report any incidents to the BTB so its staff will be aware of trouble spots and patterns.

Walking Tour

In a few hours it's possible to take in many of the city's sights and sounds.

Central Belize City Starting at the Swing Bridge, first take in the **Maritime Museum** (☎ 31969), in the Belize Marine Terminal, where exhibits focus on fishing, boats, the reef and other sea-related topics. It's open 8 am to 5 pm daily (US$4, US$2 for students with ID).

From the Marine Terminal, cross the Swing Bridge and walk south along Regent St, one block inland from the shore. The large, modern **Commercial Center** to the left, just off the Swing Bridge, replaced a ramshackle market dating from 1820. The ground floor holds a food market; offices and shops are above.

As you continue down Regent St, you can't miss the prominent **Court House**, built in 1926 as the headquarters for Belize's colonial administrators. It still serves administrative and judicial functions.

Battlefield Park is on the right across from the Court House. Always busy with vendors, loungers, con artists and other slice-of-life segments of Belize City society, the park offers welcome shade in the sweltering midday heat.

Turn left just past the Court House and walk one long block to the waterfront street, called Southern Foreshore, to find the **Bliss Institute** (☎ 72458). Baron Bliss was an Englishman with a happy name and

a Portuguese title who came here on his yacht to fish. When he died – not too long after his arrival – he left the bulk of his wealth in trust to the people of Belize. Income from the trust has paid for roads, market buildings, schools, cultural centers and many other worthwhile projects over the years.

The Bliss Institute is open 8:30 am to noon and 2 to 8 pm Monday to Friday, 8 am to noon Saturday. Belize City's prime cultural institution, it is home to the National Arts Council, which stages periodic exhibits, concerts and theatrical works. The Institute also houses the **National Library** (upstairs) and a small display of artifacts from the Mayan archaeological site at Caracol.

Continue walking south to the end of Southern Foreshore, then south on Regent St to reach the **House of Culture** (☎ 73050), built in 1814. Formerly called the Government House, this was the residence of the governor-general until Belize attained independence within the British Commonwealth in 1981.

Today it holds the tableware once used at the residence, along with exhibits of historic photographs and occasional special exhibits. It's open 8:30 am to 4:30 pm Monday to Friday (US$5). The admission price is a bit steep to look at old crockery, but you can stroll around the pleasant grounds for free.

Down beyond the House of Culture you'll come to **Albert Park**, which gets nice sea breezes and has a well-maintained playground, and **Bird Island**, a recreation area with a basketball court (US$2.50 per hour) and an open-air restaurant that serves snacks and cool drinks.

Inland from the House of Culture, at the corner of Albert and Regent Sts, is **St John's Cathedral**, the oldest Anglican church in Central America, dating from 1847.

A block southwest of the cathedral is **Yarborough Cemetery**, whose gravestones outline the turbulent history of Belize going back to 1781.

Walk back to the Swing Bridge northward along Albert St, the city's main commercial thoroughfare. Note the unlikely little **Hindu temple** between South and Dean Sts, with offices for Amerijet and FedEx on its 1st floor.

Northern Neighborhoods Cross the Swing Bridge heading north and you'll come face-to-face with the wood-frame **Paslow Building**, which houses the city's main post office. Go straight along Queen St to see the city's quaint wooden **central police headquarters**. At the end of Queen St, look left to see the old Belize prison, rumored to be the future site of a national museum, and then turn right onto Gabourel Lane.

Down Gabourel you'll pass the **US embassy**, set among some pretty Victorian houses. A left at Hutson St will take you to the sea, where if you head south (a right turn) on Marine Parade you'll pass **Memorial Park**, the Chateau Caribbean Hotel and the Radisson Fort George Hotel. At the southern tip of the peninsula you'll reach the **Baron Bliss Memorial**, next to the Fort George lighthouse. A small park here offers good views of the water and the city.

Walking back to the Swing Bridge along Fort St (which eventually turns into Front St) you'll pass the **Belize Audubon Society** (☎ 35004), 12 Fort St, offering information on national parks and wildlife reserves throughout the country. The **Image Factory Art Foundation** (☎ 34151), 81 N Front St, near the Marine Terminal, displays work by Belizean artists.

Places to Stay

A 7% lodging tax will be added to the cost of your room. In addition, some hotels will tack on a service charge, often around 10%. Prices listed here (and throughout the Belize chapter of this book) are base prices, exclusive of tax and service charge; when settling on the cost of a room, be sure to ask about additional charges.

Budget The BTB keeps an eye on the city's lowest-budget lodgings and occasionally shuts down those it deems unworthy. Travelers on a flophouse budget should call first to make sure the place they're thinking of staying is open for business.

Seaside Guest House (☎ 78339, fax 71689, jself@ucb.edu.bz, 3 Prince St) is operated by Friends Services International, a Quaker service organization. The six clean, simple rooms share baths and rent for US$16.50/24/33 single/double/triple. A bunk in the seven-bed dorm room costs US$10.

Breakfast is available, as is valuable information on travel in Belize City and beyond. This is the most popular budget guesthouse in Belize City, and it's usually necessary to book well in advance.

Freddie's Guest House (☎ 33851, 86 Eve St) is well run, quiet and on a pleasant residential street. Two rooms share one bath and cost US$21 double; a third room with private bath costs US$23. *Isabel Guest House* (☎ 73139, 3 Albert St) is at the intersection of Albert, Regent, and Water above Matus Store, but it's entered by a rear stairway; walk around the Central Drug Store to the back and follow the signs. A family-run place, it offers three double rooms with shower for US$24. *Glenthorne Guesthouse* (☎ 44212, glenthorneguesthouse@btl.net, 27 Barracks Rd) is a nice Victorian house which has a small garden, high ceilings and eclectic furnishings. The eight rooms rent for US$28/35 single/double, and breakfast is included. Guests are welcome to use the kitchen.

The best of the ultra-low-priced hotels are clustered on N Front St, east of Pickstock St. They're dreary affairs but are relatively clean and secure.

The eight-room *North Front Street Guest House* (☎ 77595, 124 N Front St) is a favorite of low-budget travelers. Breakfast and dinner are served if you order ahead. Next door, the *Bonaventure Hotel* (☎ 44248, 122 N Front St) has nine rooms, while across the street, the *Mira Rio Hotel* (☎ 34147, 59 N Front St) has seven rooms, each with in-room sink and non-partitioned toilet. All three charge US$8.50/13, with shared bath.

Mid-Range You'll find the best deal in town at the charming *Colton House* (☎ 44666, fax 30451, coltonhse@btl.net, 9 Cork St), near the Radisson Fort George Hotel. The graciously restored wooden colonial house was built in 1928. Rooms rent for US$50/60/70, and each has a fan, private bath and private access from the wraparound porch. Morning coffee is served, but meals aren't. A garden apartment with kitchenette, air-con and cable TV rents for US$75.

Just up the street, the *Fort Street Guest House* (☎ 30116, fax 78808, fortst@btl.net, 4 Fort St) has six comfortable guest rooms with fan and shared bath for US$65,

BELIZE

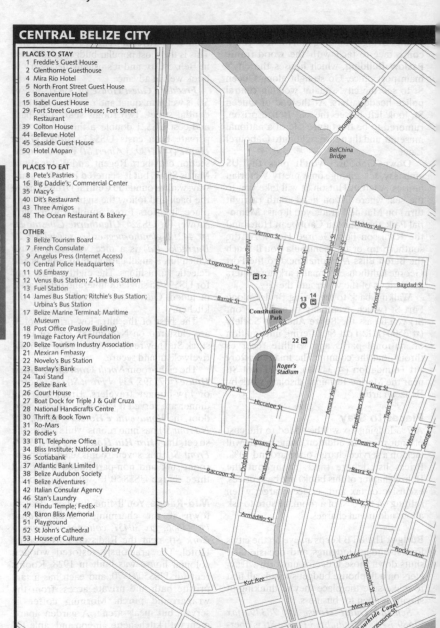

CENTRAL BELIZE CITY

PLACES TO STAY
1 Freddie's Guest House
2 Glenthorne Guesthouse
4 Mira Rio Hotel
5 North Front Street Guest House
6 Bonaventure Hotel
15 Isabel Guest House
29 Fort Street Guest House; Fort Street Restaurant
39 Colton House
44 Bellevue Hotel
45 Seaside Guest House
50 Hotel Mopan

PLACES TO EAT
8 Pete's Pastries
16 Big Daddie's; Commercial Center
35 Macy's
40 Dit's Restaurant
43 Three Amigos
48 The Ocean Restaurant & Bakery

OTHER
3 Belize Tourism Board
7 French Consulate
9 Angelus Press (Internet Access)
10 Central Police Headquarters
11 US Embassy
12 Venus Bus Station; Z-Line Bus Station
13 Fuel Station
14 James Bus Station; Ritchie's Bus Station; Urbina's Bus Station
17 Belize Marine Terminal; Maritime Museum
18 Post Office (Paslow Building)
19 Image Factory Art Foundation
20 Belize Tourism Industry Association
21 Mexican Embassy
22 Novelo's Bus Station
23 Barclay's Bank
24 Taxi Stand
25 Belize Bank
26 Court House
27 Boat Dock for Triple J & Gulf Cruza
28 National Handicrafts Centre
30 Thrift & Book Town
31 Ro-Mars
32 Brodie's
33 BTL Telephone Office
34 Bliss Institute; National Library
36 Scotiabank
37 Atlantic Bank Limited
38 Belize Audubon Society
41 Belize Adventures
42 Italian Consular Agency
46 Stan's Laundry
47 Hindu Temple; FedEx
49 Baron Bliss Memorial
51 Playground
52 St John's Cathedral
53 House of Culture

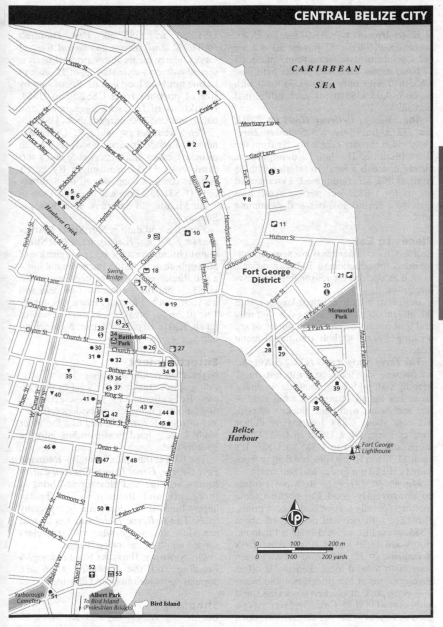

CARIBBEAN
SEA

Haulover Creek

Fort George
District

Memorial
Park

*Belize
Harbour*

Fort George
Lighthouse
49

Albert Park
To Bird Island
(Pedestrian Bridge)   Bird Island

Yarborough
Cemetery 51

BELIZE

Castle St
Lovely Lane
Craig St
Mortuary Lane
Gaol Lane
Eve St
Hutson St
Keyhole Alley
Gabourel Lane
Pinks Alley
Handyside St
Bideri Lane
Queen St
N Front St
Front St
Swing
Bridge
Water Lane
Orange St
Glynn St
Church St
Church St
Bishop St
King St
Prince St
Dean St
South St
Simmons St
Palm Lane
Rectory Lane
Wagner St
Berkeley St
Albert St
Albert St
West St
Victoria St
Cradle Lane
Usher St
Price Alley
Pickstock St
Petticoat Alley
Hydes Lane
Barracks Rd
Daly St
New Rd
Curt Lane
Frederick St
Regent St W
Richard St
Blue St
Canal St
Canal St
W Canal St
Albert St
Regent St
Southern Foreshore
Marine Parade
N Park St
S Park St
Eyre St
Cork St
Dredger St
Dredger St
Fort St
Fort St

0   100   200 m
0   100   200 yards

breakfast included. The restaurant is one of the best in town.

Hotel Mopan (☎ 73356, 77351, fax 75383, hotelmopan@btl.net, 55 Regent St) is a big old Caribbean-style wood-frame place. Its 12 basic rooms, each with private bath, cost US$30/40 with only a fan, US$40/50 with air-con. Add US$10 for each additional person.

The 35-room **Bellevue Hotel** (☎ 77051, fax 73253, fins@btl.net, 5 Southern Foreshore) is in the city center not far from the Bliss Institute. The hotel's unimpressive facade conceals a modern interior with 35 comfortable, air-conditioned, TV-equipped rooms for US$33 per person. Amenities include a restaurant, bar and swimming pool.

Places to Eat

Belize City's restaurants present a well-rounded introduction to Belizean cuisine, as well as options for reasonable and tasty foreign meals.

Belizeans usually eat their large meal in the afternoon, so later in the day you may find that restaurants have run out of, or are no longer serving, their traditional menu items.

The Three Amigos (☎ 74378, 2-B King St) is a favorite with travelers for its tasty food, friendly staff and clean, comfortable dining areas. For lunch, a burger or a big plate of rice and beans with beef, chicken or pork will cost about US$4. Imaginative dinner courses range from US$8 to US$14, and soups and salads run US$5 to US$6. It's open 11:30 am to 2:30 pm and 5:30 to 9 pm daily (until 10 pm Friday and Saturday).

Macy's (☎ 73419, 18 Bishop St) offers up consistently good Caribbean-Creole cooking, friendly service and decent prices. Fish fillet with rice and beans costs about US$5, armadillo or wild boar a bit more. Hours are 11:30 am to 10 pm daily. **Dit's Restaurant** (☎ 33330, 50 King St) is a homey place with a loyal local clientele. It offers huge portions at low prices; rice and beans with beef, pork or chicken costs US$3, and burgers are US$1.75. Cakes and pies make a good dessert at US$1 per slice. Dit's is open 8 am to 9 pm daily.

A good bet for Chinese is **Ocean Restaurant & Bakery** (☎ 70597, 46 Regent St), where the chef/proprietor makes his own

noodles, eschews lard and serves delicious stir-fries, and rice and noodle dishes for US$3.50 to US$7.50. **Big Daddie's** (☎ 70932, 2nd floor, Commercial Center) serves hearty meals at low prices. Lunch is served cafeteria-style starting at 11 am and lasting until the food is gone. Prices vary by size of portions from US$2.50 to US$4. Breakfasts of fry jacks, eggs, beans and bacon are US$3.50, burgers about US$2.

Pete's Pastries (☎ 44974, 41 Queen St), near Handyside St, serves good pies (of fruit or meat), cakes and tarts. A slice and a soft drink costs US$1. You might try Pete's famous cowfoot soup, served on Saturday only (US$1.75). Pete's is open 8:30 am to 7 pm Monday to Saturday, 8 am to 6 pm Sunday.

For high-end dining, **Fort Street Restaurant** (☎ 2-30116, 4 Fort St), at the Fort Street Guest House, offers the best combination of atmosphere and cuisine. Prices are not low – a full dinner with wine or beer might cost US$30 – but the setting can't be beat and it's your best bet for the money. Open daily 7 to 10 am for breakfast, 11 am to 2 pm for lunch, 5:30 to 10 pm for dinner. No lunch on Sunday.

Entertainment

Nightfall in Belize City brings lots of interesting action, much of it illegal or dangerous. Be judicious in your selection of nightspots. If drugs are in evidence, there's lots of room for trouble, and as a foreigner you'll have a hard time blending into the background.

The bars at the upscale hotels – **Radisson Fort George, Great House, Chateau Caribbean** – are safe and pleasant and bring in foreigners and Belizeans alike. Friday happy hour at the Radisson is especially lively. The **Bellevue Hotel Bar** has a great sea view and is popular with travelers staying south of the Swing Bridge.

On Newtown Barracks Rd, **Lindbergh's Landing** and the **Pickwick Club** are popular spots for music and dancing.

Shopping

Brodie's, 2 Albert St, and Ro-Mars, 27 Albert St, are good places to load up on groceries and other supplies. Brodie's has some English-language books and magazines. For a good selection of Belizean crafts, visit the National Handicrafts Centre (☎ 33636), 3 Fort St.

Getting There & Away

Buses, boats and planes are available to take you from Belize City to any other part of the country, and car rentals are available. See the Getting Around section, earlier in this chapter, for details.

Below is information on buses from Belize City to major destinations. Travel times are approximate, as the length of a ride depends upon how many times the driver stops to pick up and drop off passengers along the way.

Belmopan (one hour, 52 miles)
See Benque Viejo del Carmen.

Benque Viejo del Carmen (three hours, 81 miles)
Novelo's operates daily buses from Belize City to Belmopan, San Ignacio and Benque Viejo del Carmen on the hour and half hour from 11 am to 9 pm. Returning from Benque/Melchor, buses to San Ignacio, Belmopan and Belize City start at 11:30 am; the last bus leaves at 4 pm.

Chetumal, Mexico (four hours, 100 miles)
Twelve southbound buses from Chetumal's Nuevo Mercado run from 4 am to 6:30 pm. Venus Bus Lines has buses departing from Belize City for Chetumal at 11:30 am and 1, 2, 3, 4, 5:20, 6:30 and 7 pm; departures from Chetumal are on the hour from 5 to 10 am.

Corozal (three hours, 96 miles)
All Venus buses to and from Chetumal stop in Corozal. Venus runs additional southbound buses on the half hour from 4 to 11:30 am.

Dangriga (three to four hours, 195 miles)
Z-Line has hourly buses from Belize City to Dangriga from 8 am to 5 pm. Most buses go via Belmopan and the Hummingbird Hwy, although some take the shorter but unpaved Manatee Hwy. James Bus Service has a daily 7 am Belize City–Belmopan–Dangriga–Punta Gorda route. A northern bus returns through Dangriga at 9:30 am Monday, Wednesday, Thursday and Saturday; 4 pm Tuesday and Friday; and 11 am Sunday. Ritchie's Bus Service has Belize City–Dangriga runs at 2:30 and 4:30 pm, and Dangriga–Belize City runs at 5:15 and 8:30 am.

Flores, Guatemala (five hours, 146 miles)
Take a bus to Melchor de Mencos (see Benque Viejo del Carmen) and transfer to a Guatemalan bus. Some hotels and tour companies organize minibus trips, which are more expensive but much faster and more comfortable.

Melchor de Mencos, Guatemala (3¼ hours, 84 miles)
See Benque Viejo del Carmen.

Orange Walk (two hours, 58 miles)
See Chetumal and Corozal schedules. Escalante's makes six runs from Belize City to Orange Walk from 4:15 to 5:30 pm and six southbound runs between the cities from 5 to 6:30 am. Urbina's runs hourly from noon to 6 pm between Belize City and Orange Walk, and at 6:30, 7, 7:30 and 8 am between Orange Walk and Belize City.

Placencia (four hours, 161 miles)
Take a morning Z-Line bus to Dangriga, then catch the connector bus to Placencia. A bus returns from Placencia to Dangriga at 5:30 and 8 am; there may be others as well, depending upon the number of customers. Ritchie's bus leaves Belize City at 2:30 pm. Northern routes leave Placencia at 5:30 and 6 am. The 5:30 am bus stops in Hopkins.

Punta Gorda (eight to 10 hours, 210 miles)
Z-Line has buses from Belize City to Punta Gorda at 6 and 8 am and 3 pm, northern routes at 5 and 9 am, noon and 3 pm. James Bus Service has a daily 7 am Belize City–Belmopan–Dangriga–Punta Gorda route. A northern bus leaves at 4:30 am on Monday, Wednesday, Thursday and Saturday; 11 am on Tuesday and Friday; 6 am on Sunday.

San Ignacio (2½ hours, 72 miles)
See Benque Viejo del Carmen.

Getting Around

To/From the Airport The taxi fare to or from the international airport is US$15. You might want to approach other passengers about sharing a cab to the city center.

It takes about half an hour to walk from the air terminal 2 miles (3km) out the access road to the Northern Hwy, where it's easy to catch a bus going either north or south.

Taxi Trips by taxi within Belize City (including to and from Municipal Airport) cost US$2.50 for one person, US$6 for two or three and US$8 for four. Be aware that if you phone for a cab instead of hailing one on the street, the price may go up, as it will if you're going outside the city center. Secure the price in advance with your driver and, if in doubt, check with hotel staff about what the cost should be before setting out.

The Cayes

Belize's 180-mile-long barrier reef is the eastern edge of the limestone shelf that underlies most of the Mayan lands. To the west of the reef the sea is very shallow – usually not much more than 15 feet (around 5m) deep – which allows numerous islands called cayes (pronounced 'keys') to bask in warm waters.

Of the dozens of cayes, large and small, that dot the blue waters of the Caribbean off the Belizean coast, the two most popular with travelers are Caye Caulker and Ambergris Caye. Caulker is commonly thought of as the low-budget island, where hotels and restaurants are less expensive than on resort-conscious Ambergris, though with Caulker's booming popularity its residents are fighting to keep the distinction.

Water sports are the name of the game on both islands, especially on Ambergris. The streets of San Pedro tend to be deserted in early afternoon, filling up again after the dive and snorkeling boats return in late afternoon. These cayes aren't so much about hanging out at the beach – Placencia's for that. Visitors here tend to stay active and scheduled during the day, but return home smiling and ready for more fun.

CAYE CAULKER
☎ 22 • pop 800

Caye Caulker (called Hicaco in Spanish, sometimes Corker in English) lies some 20 miles (32km) north of Belize City and 15 miles (24km) south of Ambergris Caye. The island is about 4 miles (6.5km) long from north to south and there are only about 650 yards (600m) at its widest point. Mangrove covers much of the shore and coconut palms provide shade. The village is on the southern portion of the island. Actually Caulker is two islands, since Hurricane Hattie split the island just north of the village. The split is called, simply, the Split (or the Cut). It has a tiny beach, with swift currents running through it. North of the Split is mostly undeveloped land, and part of it has just been declared a nature reserve.

Orientation & Information

The village has two principal streets: Front St to the east and Back St to the west. The distance from the Split in the north to the village's southern edge is little more than a half mile (0.8km).

South of the village is the Belize Tourism Industry Association office, on the site of the **Caye Caulker Mini Reserve** (☎ 2251).

Here you can get information on what to see and do on the island, then stroll an interpretive trail identifying the island's flora and fauna. Call first, as hours are irregular.

Atlantic Bank, on Back St, is open 8 am to 2 pm Monday to Friday and 8:30 am to noon Saturday.

Caye Caulker has its own Web site (www.gocayecaulker.com). A cybercafe on the dock street charges US$1.50 for 15 minutes. Mike's Movie House, on the east shore, screens videos for US$7.50 for one to three people and offers Internet access at US$2.50 for 15 minutes.

Water Sports

The surf breaks on the barrier reef, easily visible from the eastern shore of Caye Caulker. Don't attempt to swim out to it, however – the local boaters speed their powerful craft through these waters and are completely heedless of swimmers. Swim only in protected areas.

A short boat ride takes you out to the reef to enjoy some of the world's most exciting snorkeling, diving and fishing. Boat trips are big business on the island, so you have many operators to choose from. Virtually all of the island residents are trustworthy boaters, but it's still good to discuss price, number of people on the boat (they can become crowded), duration, areas to be visited and the seaworthiness of the boat. Boat and motor should be in good condition. Even sailboats should have motors in case of emergency (the weather can change quickly here).

Several places in town rent water-sports equipment. Snorkeling gear and beach floats each cost around US$5 per day, sit-on sea kayaks US$20 per half day, and a Hobie Cat sailboat US$20 per hour or US$50 per half day.

Organized Tours

A variety of inland trips can be arranged from the cayes. The most popular is the Altun Ha river trip, which stops at Maruba Resort for lunch, swimming and horseback riding. Cost is US$60.

Nature, mangrove and bird-watching tours can be arranged through Ellen McRae at CariSearch/Galleria Hicaco (☎ 2178) or Dorothy Beveridge at Seaing is Belizing (☎ 21 2079). Cost is US$13. Beveridge starts

BELIZE

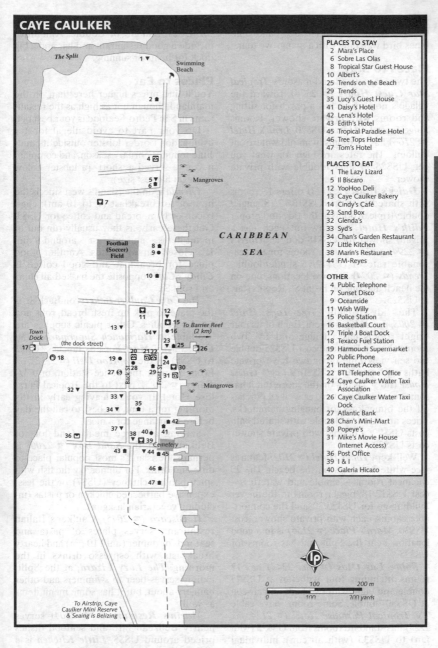

CAYE CAULKER

The Split

Swimming Beach

Mangroves

CARIBBEAN SEA

Football (Soccer) Field

To Barrier Reef (2 km)

Town Dock

(the dock street)

Mangroves

Cemetery

To Airstrip, Caye Caulker Mini Reserve & Seaing is Belizing

0   100   200 m
0   100   200 yards

PLACES TO STAY
2 Mara's Place
6 Sobre Las Olas
8 Tropical Star Guest House
10 Albert's
25 Trends on the Beach
29 Trends
35 Lucy's Guest House
41 Daisy's Hotel
43 Lena's Hotel
43 Edith's Hotel
45 Tropical Paradise Hotel
46 Tree Tops Hotel
47 Tom's Hotel

PLACES TO EAT
1 The Lazy Lizard
5 Il Biscaro
12 YooHoo Deli
13 Caye Caulker Bakery
14 Cindy's Café
23 Sand Box
32 Glenda's
33 Syd's
34 Chan's Garden Restaurant
37 Little Kitchen
38 Marin's Restaurant
44 FM-Reyes

OTHER
4 Public Telephone
7 Sunset Disco
9 Oceanside
11 Wish Willy
15 Police Station
16 Basketball Court
17 Triple J Boat Dock
18 Texaco Fuel Station
19 Harmouch Supermarket
20 Public Phone
21 Internet Access
22 BTL Telephone Office
24 Caye Caulker Water Taxi Association
26 Caye Caulker Water Taxi Dock
27 Atlantic Bank
28 Chan's Mini-Mart
30 Popeye's
31 Mike's Movie House (Internet Access)
36 Post Office
39 I & I
40 Galeria Hicaco

with the interpretive trail at the Caye Caulker Mini Reserve (☎ 2251) and combines bird watching with a mangrove tour.

Places to Stay

The two-story wood-and-masonry *Tropical Star Guest House* (☎ 2374), toward the village's north side, has a porch for sitting and rooms with private shower. Rooms range from US$15 to US$20. *Lena's Hotel* (☎ 2106) has 11 rooms in an old waterfront building. The rates are high for what you get: US$25/30 single/double with private shower.

Daisy's Hotel (☎ 2123) offers 11 rooms with shared bath for US$10/13/18 single/double/triple. Rooms at the tidy and proper *Edith's Hotel* are tiny, but each has a private shower for US$18 double. *Albert's* (☎ 2294) rents six clean rooms for the reasonable rate of US$12/16 single/double. *Trends* (☎ 2094) has two locations, one on the beach and one on Front St. Rooms start at US$25.

The tidy, friendly *Tree Tops Hotel* (☎ 2008, fax 2115) is a gem. Each of its four bright rooms has a fridge and TV. Two rooms share a bath and cost US$25 double (no sea view); the other two have private baths and rent for US$30. *Lucy's Guest House* (no ☎) is not on the shore, but it has some trees and gardens, as well as porches off the bungalows for hanging hammocks. Prices are good: A double with shared bath costs US$22; a double with private shower costs US$32.

Well-kept *Tom's Hotel* (☎ 2102) features nice white buildings on the beach. The 20 cheapest rooms – simple and waterless – cost US$12/18; bigger rooms in the newer building go for US$23/30; and the comfortable cabins, each with private shower, cost US$30. *Mara's Place* (☎ 2156) is in a good location near the Split and has rooms for US$25.

Sobre Las Olas (☎ /fax 2243) has 12 rooms, including four with fan at US$25 double and eight with two beds and air-con at US$30 double. Some rooms have cable TV. *Tropical Paradise Hotel* (☎ 2124, fax 2225) has standard rooms from US$25 (with fan) to US$35 (with air-con); individual cabins – tightly packed together – for US$40 (fan) to US$50 (air-con and cable

TV); and suites with air-con and cable TV for US$70, single or double. Amenities include a good restaurant and bar and a big dock for boats or sunning.

Places to Eat

You'll find prices higher here than on the mainland, though not as high as the restaurants in San Pedro. Seafood is your best bet.

Do your part to avoid illegal lobster fishing: don't order lobster outside its mid-June to mid-February season, and complain if you're served a 'short' (a lobster below the legal harvest size).

Glenda's, on the island's west side, is the in spot for breakfast (7 to 10 am): eggs, bacon or ham, bread and coffee for US$3. Get there early, as they usually run out of menu items – and interest – around 9 am. It's closed on weekends. Another good place for breakfast and good coffee is *Cindy's Café* , opposite the basketball court on Front St.

The *Caye Caulker Bakery*, on Back St, is the place to pick up fresh bread, rolls and similar goodies. Other picnic supplies are available at *Harmouch Supermarket* and *Chan's Mini-Mart*. For box lunches (US$3 to US$5) try the *YooHoo Deli* (☎ 2232), on Front St near the police station, or *FM-Reyes* (☎ 2125), next to the Tropical Paradise Hotel. If you're leaving early in the morning for a tour, it's best to call the day before to arrange for a meal.

Serving all three meals (and lots of Belikin beer), the *Sand Box* (☎ 2200) is perhaps the island's most popular place to dine and drink. For dinner, try the fish with spicy banana chutney (US$7) or the less-expensive barbecued chicken or pastas (including vegetarian lasagna).

Il Biscaro (☎ 2045), Caulker's Italian restaurant, serves plates of pasta and seafood for dinner (until 10 pm) and hearty breakfasts with espresso drinks in the morning. *The Lazy Lizard*, at the Split, mainly serves the beer to swimmers and other hangers-about, but it has some menu items as well.

Marin's Restaurant (☎ 2104) serves hearty Belizean fare and seafood dishes priced around US$5. *Little Kitchen* is a slightly cheaper alternative. *Syd's* is popular for seafood and Mexican dishes. Try a couple of tostadas for lunch (US$0.50 each) or the steamed fish for dinner (US$4). *Chan's Garden Restaurant* serves reasonably authentic Chinese food at moderate prices.

The restaurant at the *Tropical Paradise Hotel* is busy all day because it serves the island's most consistently good food in big portions at decent prices. The light, cheerful dining room serves breakfast 8 am to noon, lunch 11:30 am to 2 pm and dinner 6 to 10 pm. You can order curried shrimp or lobster for US$12 or many other things for less.

Entertainment

I&I is the happening reggae bar, the *Oceanside* often hosts live bands, and the *Sand Box*, *Wish Willy* and *Popeye's* attract their fair share of thirsty travelers. The *Sunset Disco*, on the west side of the island, has weekend dances and a rooftop bar with snacks.

Getting There & Away

Maya Island Air (☎ 2012) and Tropic Air (☎ 2040) offer regular flights between Caye Caulker, Ambergris Caye and the Belize City airports.

The Caye Caulker Water Taxi Association (☎ 2992, 2-31969 in Belize City) runs boats from Caulker to Belize City at 6:30, 7:30, 8:30 and 10 am, noon and 3 pm (also at 5 pm on weekends and holidays). Boats leave Belize City's Marine Terminal for Caye Caulker at 9 and 10:30 am, noon, 1:30, 3 and 5 pm. The ride takes 30 to 45 minutes, depending on the weather. Fare is US$7.50 one-way, US$12.50 roundtrip.

Boats to San Pedro on Ambergris Caye run at 7, 8:30 and 10 am and 1 and 4 pm, returning at 8, 9:30 and 11:30 am and 2:30 pm (also 4:30 pm on weekends and holidays). The ride takes 20 to 30 minutes. Fare is US$7.50 one-way, US$12.50 roundtrip.

Water taxis also run to St George's Caye and Caye Chapel.

Getting Around

Caulker is so small that most people walk everywhere. If need be, you can rent a bicycle or golf cart or use the golf-cart taxi service, which costs US$2.50 for a one-way trip anywhere on the island.

AMBERGRIS CAYE & SAN PEDRO

☎ 26 • pop 2000

The largest of Belize's cayes, Ambergris (pronounced am-*ber*-griss) lies 36 miles (58km) north of Belize City. It's about 25 miles (40km) long, and its northern side almost adjoins Mexican territory.

Most of the island's population lives in the town of San Pedro, near the southern tip. The barrier reef is only a half mile (0.8km) east of San Pedro.

San Pedro started life as a fishing town but is now Belize's prime tourist destination. More than half of the tourists who visit Belize fly straight to San Pedro and use it as their base for excursions elsewhere. Even so, San Pedro is certainly no Cancún, though there has been some small-scale development in recent years.

Orientation

San Pedro has three main north-south streets, which used to be called Front St (to the east), Middle St and Back St (to the west). Now these streets have tourist-class names – Barrier Reef Dr, Pescador Dr and Angel Coral Dr – but some islanders still use the old names.

The river at the end of Pescador Dr is as far as you can go by car. From there, you can cross the river by taking a hand-drawn ferry to reach a bike and golf-cart trail that runs north all the way to Journey's End resort. Most travelers take the road only as far as Sweet Basil (☎ 3870) for lunch, or the Palapa Bar for drinks, before heading back to San Pedro.

Minivan taxis cost US$2.50 for a one-way trip anywhere. The far north resorts are accessed by water taxi.

Information

Tourist Offices The BTB office (☎ 2605) is at the smallish Ambergris Museum, in the Island Sun Shopping Center at Barrier Reef Dr and Pelican St. (Admission to the museum is US$2.50.) Tourist information is also available on the caye's own Web site (www.ambergriscaye.com).

Money You can change money easily in San Pedro, and US cash and traveler's checks are accepted in most establishments.

SAN PEDRO (AMBERGRIS CAYE)

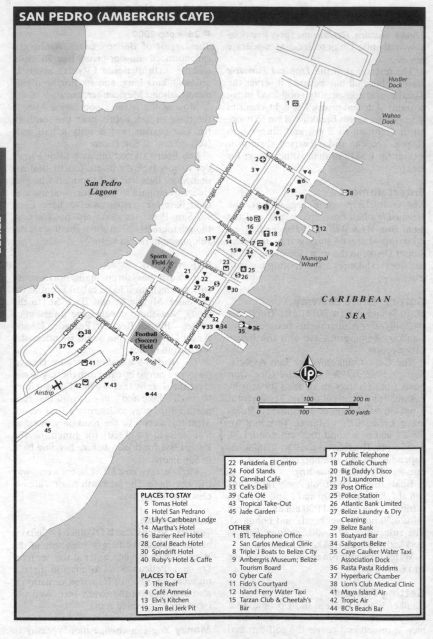

22 Panadería El Centro	17 Public Telephone
24 Food Stands	18 Catholic Church
32 Cannibal Café	20 Big Daddy's Disco
33 Celi's Deli	21 J's Laundromat
39 Café Olé	23 Post Office
43 Tropical Take-Out	25 Police Station
45 Jade Garden	26 Atlantic Bank Limited
	27 Belize Laundry & Dry
PLACES TO STAY	Cleaning
5 Tomas Hotel	29 Belize Bank
6 Hotel San Pedrano	31 Boatyard Bar
7 Lily's Caribbean Lodge	34 Sailsports Belize
14 Martha's Hotel	35 Caye Caulker Water Taxi
16 Barrier Reef Hotel	Association Dock
28 Coral Beach Hotel	36 Rasta Pasta Riddims
30 Spindrift Hotel	37 Hyperbaric Chamber
40 Ruby's Hotel & Caffe	38 Lion's Club Medical Clinic
	41 Maya Island Air
PLACES TO EAT	42 Tropic Air
3 The Reef	44 BC's Beach Bar
4 Café Amnesia	
8 Elvi's Kitchen	**OTHER**
19 Jam Bei Jerk Pit	1 BTL Telephone Office
	2 San Carlos Medical Clinic
	8 Triple J Boats to Belize City
	9 Ambergris Museum; Belize
	Tourism Board
	10 Cyber Café
	11 Fido's Courtyard
	12 Island Ferry Water Taxi
	15 Tarzan Club & Cheetah's
	Bar

Atlantic Bank Limited (☎ 2195), on Barrier Reef Dr, is open 8 am to noon and 1 to 3 pm Monday, Tuesday and Thursday; 8 am to 1 pm Wednesday; 8 am to 1 pm and 3 to 6 pm Friday; and 8:30 am to noon Saturday. Across the street and one block down from Atlantic Bank Limited is Belize Bank, open 8 am to 3 pm Monday to Thursday, 8 am to 1 pm and 3 to 6 pm Friday and 8:30 am to noon Saturday.

Post & Communications The post office is on Buccaneer St off Barrier Reef Dr. Hours are 8 am to noon and 1 to 5 pm weekdays (until 4:30 pm on Friday). It's closed on Saturday and Sunday.

Cyber Café (☎ 3015), 25 Barrier Reef Dr, provides customers with free cookies and coffee while they're using the equipment. Rates are US$0.75 for five minutes, US$10 per hour or all day, with in-and-out privileges.

Laundry Several Laundromats lie at the southern end of Pescador Dr, among them Belize Laundry & Dry Cleaning and J's Laundromat.

Medical Services San Carlos Medical Clinic, Pharmacy & Pathology Lab (☎ 2918, 3649, 14 9251 for emergencies), on Pescador Dr just south of Caribeña St, treats ailments and does blood tests.

The Lion's Club Medical Clinic is across the street from the Maya Island Air terminal at the airport. Right next door is the island's hyperbaric chamber for diving accidents.

Water Sports

Ambergris is good for all water sports: scuba diving, snorkeling, sailboarding, boating, swimming, deep-sea fishing and sunbathing. Many island hotels have their own dive shops, which rent equipment, provide instruction and organize diving excursions. In fact, just about any local can put you in touch with someone organizing water-sports trips.

Snorkeling and picnicking excursions cost about US$40. The going rental rate for a snorkel, mask and fins is US$8. Manatee-watching off Goff's Caye can be added to a snorkeling trip (US$75). Sailsports Belize (☎ 14 8070) rents sailboards for US$20 per hour and sailboats for US$30 per hour; lessons are available.

All beaches are public, and most waterside hotels and resorts are generous with their lounge chairs on slow days. While sandy beaches are plentiful, protected sea grass at the waterline makes entry from shore not terribly pleasant, so you'll be swimming from piers. Swimming is best off the pier at Ramon's Village, south of town on Coconut Dr.

Organized Tours

The *Winnie Estelle* (☎ 2394), a 66-foot island trader moored at the Paradise Resort Hotel pier, at the north end of Barrier Reef Dr, goes out on daily snorkeling trips to Caye Caulker.

The *Reef Seeker* glass-bottom boat, based at the San Pedro Holiday Hotel, also on Barrier Reef Dr, makes daily reef trips for US$20 per adult (half price for kids). The aptly named *Rum Punch II*, a wooden sailboat, runs sunset cocktail cruises for US$20.

Tours are available to the Mayan ruins at Altun Ha (US$75) and Lamanai (US$125) or beyond to the Belize Zoo, Xunantunich, Crooked Tree Bird Sanctuary, the Baboon Sanctuary, Mountain Pine Ridge and Tikal (Guatemala). Any hotel, travel agency or dive shop can fill you in on tours, or contact Excaliber Tours (☎ 3235), Seaduced by Belize (☎ 2254) or Hustler Tours (☎ 4137).

Places to Stay

Wherever you stay, you'll never be more than a minute's walk from the water. All but the cheapest hotels accept major credit cards, usually for a 5% surcharge. Listed below are winter, peak-season rates. Rates usually drop 15% to 20% May through November, although some hotels may consider June through August high season as well, since it coincides with summer break for North American schools.

Competition for guests on San Pedro is fierce, and taxi drivers are often rewarded commissions for bringing guests to hotels. Often this commission is tacked on to the cost of your room, so you're likely to save money if you make reservations in advance or show up unescorted.

Budget Right on the water, *Ruby's Hotel* (☎ 2063, fax 2434), at the south end of

BELIZE

Barrier Reef Dr, attracts return visitors year after year. Five of the nine rooms have a private shower. Rates are US$15/20 single/double with shared bath and US$25 to US$45 double with private bath. The choice waterfront rooms must be reserved in advance.

Tomas Hotel (☎ 2061), on Barrier Reef Dr, offers a very good value. This family-run place offers eight light, airy rooms with private bath (some with tub) for US$25 double, or US$35 with air-con.

Martha's Hotel (☎ 2053, fax 2589), on Ambergris St at Pescador Dr, has 16 rooms, all with private bath. Rates are US$24/35/47/59 single/double/triple/quad.

Hotel San Pedrano (☎ 2054, fax 2093, sanpedrano@btl.net), on Barrier Reef Dr at Caribeña St, has six rooms, all with private bath and three with air-con. Most rooms don't have ocean views, but you can always sit out on the wraparound porch. Fan-only rooms rent for US$25/30/38/43. Add US$10 per room for air-con.

Mid-Range Note that some of these hotels charge an additional 10% or 15% for service along with the 7% government room tax.

Coral Beach Hotel (☎ 2013, fax 2864), on Barrier Reef Dr, is a simple diver's hotel charging US$45/65/85 for air-conditioned rooms. They also offer good-value dive packages.

Lily's Caribbean Lodge (☎ 2059, fax 2673), off the east end of Caribeña St, faces the sea and offers 10 clean, pleasant rooms with air-con; several (especially those on the top floor) have good sea views. Rates are US$45/50/60.

Spindrift Hotel (☎ 2018, 2174, fax 2251), on Buccaneer St at Barrier Reef Dr, has a good location right in the center of town on the beach. It's a modern concrete affair with 30 rooms of various sizes. Each of the small rooms has one double bed, a ceiling fan and a view of the street (US$47 double). Larger ones have two double beds, air-con and sea views (US$83). Several apartments are also available (US$110).

The **Barrier Reef Hotel** (☎ 2075, fax 2719, barriereef@btl.net), on Barrier Reef Dr in the center of town, is a landmark, its attractive Caribbean wood-frame construction captured by countless tourist cameras

daily. The hotel's eight guest rooms are not in this structure, however, but in a newer and less charming concrete-block addition at the back. Rates are US$55/75/85 with air-con and cable TV.

Places to Eat

Several small cafes in the center of town serve cheap, simple meals. The best places for low-budget feasting are the stands in front of the park, where you can pick up a plate of stewed chicken with beans and rice, barbecue and other delicacies for under US$2.

Ruby's Caffe, next to Ruby's Hotel on Barrier Reef Dr, is a tiny place with good cakes and pastries but unpredictable hours. For simpler take-out pastries and bread, try the **Panadería El Centro**, on Buccaneer St at Pescador Dr. **Celi's Deli**, on Barrier Reef Dr just north of the San Pedro Holiday Hotel, serves food to go – fried chicken, sandwiches, ice cream and their own banana bread – at prices ranging from US$1.50 to US$5.

Café Olé, across from the airport, has a deli offering olive oils, cheeses and wine, and it's open for all three meals. **Tropical Take-Out**, across the street from the Tropic Air terminal at the airport, has daily specials as well as the usual list of sandwiches and light meals. Taco plates are US$2.50, and most other meals are US$4.

Hotel staff will recommend **Elvi's Kitchen** (☎ 2176), on Pescador Dr near Ambergris St, for seafood and traditional Belizean dishes. You can spend US$5 for a hamburger or as much as US$30 for a full lobster dinner with wine. Mixed drinks are available but expensive. Be sure to ask about items not priced on the menu – they're sometimes out of scale and you may get a surprise.

If you're yearning for traditional Belizean fare at traditional prices, try **The Reef**, on Pescador Dr between Pelican and Caribeña Sts. Meals run around US$5 to US$7 at this thatched-roof place with sand-covered floors. **Jade Garden** (☎ 2506), on Coconut Dr, a 10-minute walk south of the airport, is San Pedro's Chinese restaurant, with a long menu and prices from US$5 to US$18.

Jam Bei Jerk Pit, next to Big Daddy's disco, serves spicy hot Jamaican dishes at reasonable prices. It also has a nice rooftop patio. The beachside *Cannibal Café*, on Barrier Reef Dr at Black Coral St, serves moderately priced breakfasts, lunches and early dinners. *Café Amnesia* (☎ *2806*), located at the north end of Barrier Reef Dr, serves an imaginative amalgam of European and Caribbean cuisines in a cozy, candlelit dining room. Pizza specials are served daily.

Entertainment
Rasta Pasta Riddims, on the wharf at the east end of Black Coral Dr, frequently presents live reggae. *Fido's Courtyard Bar*, on Barrier Reef Dr near Pelican St, is the landlubbers' favorite.

BC's Beach Bar, on the beach in a *palapa* between Ramon's Village and the Sea Breeze Hotel, stays open late and is usually filled with sun-crisped expatriates enjoying Jimmy Buffett on the jukebox. The Sunday afternoon barbecue is a favorite with travelers. The fun starts at noon and continues until the food runs out, usually around 2:30 pm.

Big Daddy's Disco, right next to San Pedro's church, is a hot nightspot, often featuring live reggae, especially during winter. Across Barrier Reef Dr, the *Tarzan Club & Cheetah's Bar*, a jungle-themed bar, is often closed off-season, but it rocks in winter. The recently opened *Barefoot Iguana*, on Coconut Dr south of the airstrip, is giving the older establishments a run for their money.

The *Boatyard Bar* is west of the airstrip on the lagoon in an enormous palapa. Wednesday night is ladies' night, but the whole town tends to show up.

Shopping
One of the best shopping spots is Belizean Arts (☎ 3019), in Fido's Courtyard, which sells ceramics, woodcarvings and paintings alongside affordable and tasteful knick-knacks. Also in Fido's Courtyard is Amber (☎ 3101), selling handmade jewelry produced on the island.

Getting There & Away
Maya Island Air (☎ 2435) and Tropic Air (☎ 2012) offer several flights daily between San Pedro and the Belize City airports and to Corozal.

The Caye Caulker Water Taxi Association (☎ 2036, 22-2992 in Caye Caulker) runs boats between San Pedro, Caye Caulker and Belize City. Boats to Belize City via Caye Caulker leave from the Rasta Pasta Riddims dock in San Pedro at 8, 9:30 and 11:30 am and 2:30 pm (also 4:30 pm on weekends and holidays). Boats leave Belize City for San Pedro at 9 am, noon and 3 pm. Cost is US$12.50 one-way, US$23 roundtrip. Boats leave Caye Caulker for San Pedro at 7, 8:30 and 10 am and 1 and 4 pm; fare is US$7.50 each way, US$12.50 roundtrip.

Getting Around
You can walk to town from the airport in 10 minutes or less, and the walk from the boat docks is even shorter. A taxi from the airport costs US$2.50 to any place in town, US$5 to the hotels south of town.

The Island Ferry (☎ 3231) operates an Ambergris-only water taxi service north and south from the Fido's Courtyard dock.

Northern Belize

The northern Belize most commonly seen by visitors is farmland. Sugarcane fields grow alongside the paved, swift Northern Hwy, and off on the side roads, Mennonites, Maya and mestizos tend efficient multipurpose farms. Head deeper into the region and you'll hit jungle in the hilly west and mangrove swamp along the convoluted Caribbean shoreline.

Orange Walk and Corozal are the region's major towns. Orange Walk is the commercial center for area farming, and it is also the starting point for river tours to the Mayan ruins of Lamanai.

Corozal is Belize's northernmost town of appreciable size and is a gateway for travelers going to and from Mexico's Yucatán Peninsula. It's a pleasant seaside town offering a nice combination of Mayan, Mexican and Caribbean cultures, and its sea breezes are a refreshing escape from the area's inland heat.

The north has several significant biosphere reserves. Largest is the Río Bravo Conservation Area, around 400 sq miles (1000 sq km) of tropical forests, rivers, ponds and Mayan archaeological sites in the western part of the Orange Walk District.

BERMUDIAN LANDING COMMUNITY BABOON SANCTUARY

In 1985 local farmers organized to help preserve the endangered black howler monkey and its habitat. Care is taken to maintain the forests along the banks of the Belize River, where the black howler, found only in Belize, feeds, sleeps and – at dawn and dusk – howls (loudly and unmistakably).

At the Community Baboon Sanctuary (☎ 21 2181), in the village of Bermudian Landing, you can learn all about the black howler and the 200 other species of wildlife found in the reserve.

A guided nature walk is included with your price of admission (US$5), arranged at the visitor's center. Tours of villages surrounding the sanctuary are available for US$20, as are canoe trips and night hikes. For further information about the reserve, check with the Belize Audubon Society (☎ 2 35004, fax 2 34985, base@btl.net), 12 Fort St, Belize City.

Places to Stay & Eat

Rustic accommodations are available at the reserve but are best arranged in advance. Camping (US$5 per person) and village homestays (US$12.50) can be arranged at the visitor's center.

Nature Resort (☎ 2 33668, fax 21 2197, naturer@btl.net), adjacent to the visitor's center, rents refurbished cabañas for US$25 double with shared bath, US$35 with private bath, US$50 with private bath and kitchenette.

The *Howler Monkey Resort* (☎ 21 2158, jungled@btl.net), formerly the Jungle Drift Lodge, rents cabañas for US$12.50 per person, but appears to be more interested in catering to group tours than individuals.

Getting There & Away

The Community Baboon Sanctuary is 26 miles (42km) west of Belize City in the village of Bermudian Landing – an easy day trip from Belize City or the cayes.

If you're driving, turn west off the Northern Hwy at the Burrell Boom turnoff (Mile 13). From there it's another 12 miles (20km) of dirt road to the sanctuary.

Russell's and McFadzean's both operate bus routes to Bermudian Landing, but the schedules are such that it's necessary to spend the night and leave early the next morning. Another option is to catch one of the frequent northern highway buses heading to the Mexican border, get off at Burrell Boom and hitch the 13 miles (8km) into the sanctuary.

ALTUN HA

Northern Belize's most famous Mayan ruin is Altun Ha, 34 miles (55km) north of Belize City along the Old Northern Hwy. The site is near the village of Rockstone Pond, 10 miles (16km) south of Maskall.

Altun Ha (Mayan for 'Rockstone Pond') was undoubtedly a small but rich and important Mayan trading town, with agriculture also playing an essential role in its economy. Altun Ha had formed as a community by at least 600 BC, perhaps several centuries earlier, and the town flourished until the mysterious collapse of classic Mayan civilization around AD 900.

Of the grass-covered temples arranged around the two plazas here, the largest and most important is the Temple of the Masonry Altars (Structure B-4), in Plaza B. The restored structure you see dates from the first half of the 7th century and takes its name from altars on which copal was burned and beautifully carved jade pieces were smashed in sacrifice.

In Plaza A, Structure A-1 is sometimes called the Temple of the Green Tomb. Deep within it was discovered the tomb of a priest-king dating from around AD 600. Tropical humidity had destroyed the king's garments and the paper of the Mayan 'painted book' that was buried with him, but many riches were intact: shell necklaces, pottery, pearls, stingray spines used in bloodletting rites, jade beads and pendants, and ceremonial flints.

Altun Ha is open 9 am to 5 pm daily (US$2.50). Modern toilets and a drinks shop are on site.

Places to Stay & Eat

Camping, though not strictly legal, is sometimes permitted; ask at the site.

Mayan Wells Restaurant (☎ 21 2039), on the road to Altun Ha, is a popular stop for lunch or refreshments. Traditional Belizean lunches of rice, beans and stewed chicken are served for US$5 in a pleasant outdoor setting. Camping is allowed on the premises for US$5; bathroom and shower facilities are available.

Getting There & Away

The easiest way to visit Altun Ha is on one of the many tours running daily from Belize City or San Pedro on Ambergris Caye.

To get there in your own vehicle, take the Northern Hwy 19 miles (31km) northwest from Belize City to the town of Sand Hill, where the highway divides – the new paved highway continues northwest and the old one heads northeast to the ruins. The old road is narrow and potholed, passing through jungle and the occasional village. The ruins are about 2 miles (3km) west off the road, 10.5 miles (17km) from the junction. Note that the Old Northern Hwy is not busy; a breakdown could be problematic, and hitchhiking is usually disappointing.

If you're firmly committed to public transportation, you can catch an afternoon bus departing from Douglas Jones St (see the Belize City map) for the town of Maskall, north of Altun Ha.

CROOKED TREE WILDLIFE SANCTUARY

Midway between Belize City and Orange Walk, 3.5 miles (5.5km) west of the Northern Hwy, lies the fishing and farming village of Crooked Tree. In 1984 the Belize Audubon Society succeeded in having 5 sq miles (12 sq km) around the village declared a wildlife sanctuary, principally because of the area's wealth of bird life. The best time of year for wildlife watching is in May, when the water in the lagoon drops to its lowest level and the animals must come farther out into the open to reach their food supply.

Day trips to Crooked Tree are possible, but it's best to stay the night so you can be here at dawn, when the birds are most active. Trails weave through the villages and you can spot plenty of species on your own, but you'll get farther and see more on a guided tour. In fact, for those interested in viewing birds and other wildlife, a guided nature tour of this sanctuary is among the most rewarding experiences in Belize.

Admission to the sanctuary is US$5. Tours cost US$60 to US$70 for groups of four (less per person for larger groups) and

usually include a boat trip through the lagoon, a walk along the elevated boardwalk and viewing time atop the observation towers. Arrangements can be made through the visitor's center or your hotel. More information can be obtained from the Belize Audubon Society (☎ 2 35004, fax 2 34985, base@btl.net), 12 Fort St, Belize City.

Places to Stay & Eat

Sam Tillett's Hotel & Tour (☎ 21 2026, *samhotel@btl.net*) rents one budget room with shared bath for US$10, rooms with private bath for US$20/30 single/double and the luxury Jabiru Suite for US$50. Meals are available. Sam's bird tours are in demand – he's known throughout the country as the 'king of birds.'

Also enjoying a considerable reputation among birders is the Crawford family, owners of the *Paradise Inn* (☎ 25 2535, fax 25 2534). The inn rents simple cabañas with lagoon views and private baths for US$35/45, and the restaurant gets high marks with travelers. Breakfast is US$3, lunch US$4, dinner US$10.

In Crooked Tree village, *Bird's Eye View Lodge* (☎ 2 32040, birdseye@btl.net) faces the lagoon. Rooms, all of which have private baths, cost US$40/60/70 single/double/triple. Meals are available, as are campsites.

Getting There & Away

The road to Crooked Tree village is 30 miles (48km) up the Northern Hwy from Belize City, 25 miles (40km) south of Orange Walk. The village is 3.5 miles (5km) west of the highway via a causeway over Crooked Tree Lagoon.

If you want to take a bus roundtrip to Crooked Tree, you'll have to spend the night there. Jex Bus offers service daily departing Belize City for Crooked Tree village at 10:30 am and 4:30 and 5:30 pm daily; return trips leave Crooked Tree at 6, 6:30 and 7 am.

If you start early from Belize City, Corozal or Orange Walk, you can bus to Crooked Tree Junction and walk the 3.5 miles (5.5km) to the village (about an hour).

RÍO BRAVO CONSERVATION AREA

Protecting 240,000 acres of tropical forest and its inhabitants, the Río Bravo Conservation Area is the flagship project of the Programme for Belize (PFB).

BELIZE

In addition to the wealth of plant and animal life here, over 60 Mayan sites have been discovered on the land. The preeminent site is **La Milpa**, the third-largest Mayan site in Belize, believed to have been founded in the late preclassic period.

La Milpa Field Station is near Gallon Jug on the road to Chan Chich Lodge. Visiting and transportation arrangements must be made in advance through Programme for Belize (☎ 2 75616, fax 2 75635, pfbel@ btl.net), 1 Eyre St, Belize City. Cost for a cabaña is US$90 per person, meals and two guided tours included.

LAMANAI

By far the most impressive site in this part of the country is Lamanai, in its own archaeological reserve on the New River Lagoon near the settlement of Indian Church. Though much of the site remains unexcavated and unrestored, the trip to Lamanai, by motorboat up the New River, is an adventure in itself.

Take a sun hat, sunblock, insect repellent, shoes (rather than sandals), lunch and a beverage (unless you plan to take a tour that includes lunch).

History

As with most sites in northern Belize, Lamanai ('Submerged Crocodile,' the original Mayan name of the place) was occupied as early as 1500 BC, with the first stone buildings appearing between 800 and 600 BC. Lamanai flourished in late preclassic times, growing into a major ceremonial center with immense temples long before most other Mayan sites.

Unlike many other sites, Maya lived here until the coming of the Spanish in the 16th century. British interests later built a sugar mill, now in ruins, at Indian Church. The archaeological site was excavated by David Pendergast in the 1970s and '80s.

New River Voyage

Most visitors opt to reach Lamanai on a spectacular boat ride up the New River from the Tower Hill toll bridge south of Orange Walk. On this trip, you motor 1½ hours upriver, between riverbanks crowded with dense jungle vegetation. En route, your skipper/guide points out the many local

birds and will almost certainly spot a crocodile or two. Along the way you pass the Mennonite community at Shipyard. Finally you come to New River Lagoon – a long, broad expanse of water that can be choppy during the frequent rainshowers – and the boat dock at Lamanai.

Touring Lamanai

A tour of the ruins takes 90 minutes minimum, more comfortably two or three hours. Of the 60 significant structures identified here, the grandest is Structure N10-43, a huge, late-preclassic building rising more than 111 feet (34m) above the jungle canopy. It's been partially uncovered and restored. Not far from N10-43 is Lamanai's ball court, a smallish one, partially uncovered.

To the north along a jungle path is Structure P9-56, built several centuries later, with a huge stylized mask of a man in a crocodile-mouth headdress 13 feet (4m) high emblazoned on its southwest face.

Near this structure are a small temple and a ruined stela that once stood on the temple's front face. Apparently some worshipers built a fire at the base of the limestone stela and later doused the fire with water. The hot stone stela, cooled too quickly by the water, broke and toppled. The stela's bas-relief carving of a majestic figure is extremely fine.

A small museum near the boat landing exhibits some interesting figurative pottery and large flint tools.

Lamanai is open from 9 am to 5 pm daily; admission is US$2.50.

Getting There & Away

Though the river voyage is much more convenient and enjoyable, Lamanai can be reached by road (36 miles/58km) from Orange Walk via Yo Creek and San Felipe. Bus service from Orange Walk is available but limited (it's primarily for village people coming to town for marketing); buses depart Orange Walk on Tuesday at 3 pm and Thursday at 4 pm.

ORANGE WALK

☎ 3 • pop 10,000

The agricultural and social center of northern Belize, Orange Walk is 58 miles (94km)

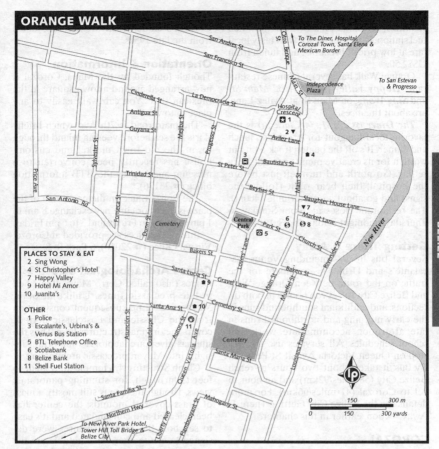

ORANGE WALK

To The Diner, Hospital,
Corozal Town, Santa Elena &
Mexican Border

To San Estevan
& Progresso

Independence
Plaza

Hospital/
Crescent

PLACES TO STAY & EAT
2 Sing Wong
4 St Christopher's Hotel
7 Happy Valley
9 Hotel Mi Amor
10 Juanita's

OTHER
1 Police
3 Escalante's, Urbina's &
   Venus Bus Station
5 BTL Telephone Office
6 Scotiabank
8 Belize Bank
11 Shell Fuel Station

Central
Park

Cemetery

Cemetery

New River

To New River Park Hotel,
Tower Hill Toll Bridge &
Belize City

0   150   300 m
0   150   300 yards

BELIZE

north of Belize City. It's not highly developed for tourism but does have a few
modest hotels and good restaurants.

The Northern Hwy, called Queen Victoria
Ave in town, serves as the main road. The
center of town is shady Central Park, on the
east side of Queen Victoria Ave. The town
hospital is in the northern outskirts, readily
visible on the west side of Northern Hwy.

Places to Stay

Juanita's (☎ 22677, 8 Santa Ana St), popular
for its restaurant, rents five basic but clean
and sunny rooms, all with shared bath, for
US$8.50 single or double.

St Christopher's Hotel (☎ 21064, 10 Main
St) is simple, relatively quiet and decently

priced. Rooms with fan, private bath and
cable TV cost US$23/28/33/38 single/
double/triple/quad. Rooms with air-con
start at US$35. The riverside rooms are the
nicest.

Hotel Mi Amor (☎ 22031, fax 23462, 19
Queen Victoria Ave) has doubles for US$25
with fan, US$38 with TV and air-con. A
noisy disco is on the ground floor.

New River Park Hotel (☎ 23987), on the
east side of the Northern Hwy, 4 miles
(7km) south of Orange Walk, just north of
the Tower Hill toll bridge, is convenient if
you're taking the boat trip to Lamanai.
Double rooms cost US$25 with fan, US$50
with air-con. The terrace restaurant offers
meals from US$4 to US$9.

Places to Eat

Juanita's, on Santa Ana St near the Shell fuel station, is a simple place with tasty local fare at low prices; breakfast and lunch from US$2.50.

Orange Walk has several Chinese restaurants. *Happy Valley* (☎ 22554, 32 Main St) and *Sing Wong*, on Main St at Avilez Lane, are about the nicest.

The Diner (☎ 22131, 34 Clark St) is the favorite local hangout for breakfast, lunch and dinner. It's off the beaten track a bit but worth it for its creative menu and cool, leafy setting. Go north and turn left just before the hospital, then bear right (follow the signs) and go about a quarter mile (400m). The restaurant closes at 10pm Sunday to Thursday, midnight Friday and Saturday.

Getting There & Away

Several bus lines – including Venus, Escalante's and Urbina's – compete for the traffic on the route between Orange Walk and Belize City. Buses run hourly in both directions, and additional southbound runs in the early morning and northbound runs in late afternoon accommodate work and school schedules. All services use the bus stop on Queen Victoria Ave at St Peter St. By bus, it takes about two hours to reach Belize City (58 miles/92km) and an hour to get to Corozal (41 miles/66km). For more details see the Belize City Getting There & Away section, earlier in this chapter.

COROZAL

☎ 4 • pop 9000

Corozal is a prosperous farming town blessed with fertile land and a favorable climate for agriculture (sugarcane is the area's leading crop). It's a popular stop with travelers busing their way to or from Mexico.

History

Though Maya have been living around Corozal since 1500 BC, modern Corozal dates from only 1849. In that year, refugees from the War of the Castes in Yucatán fled across the border to safe haven. They founded a town and named it after the cohune palm, a symbol of fertility. For years it had the look of a typical Caribbean town, until Hurricane Janet roared through in 1955 and blew away many of the old

wooden buildings on stilts. Much of Corozal's cinderblock architecture dates from the late 1950s.

Orientation & Information

Though founded by the Maya, Corozal is now arranged around a town square in the Mexican style. You can walk easily to any place in town.

The main road is 7th Ave, which briefly skirts the sea before veering inland through town. The old town market and customhouse has recently been converted to a museum and houses the BTB information office (☎ 23176).

The Belize Bank on the north side of the plaza is open for currency exchange 8 am to 1 pm Monday to Friday and 3 to 6 pm Friday.

Internet services are provided at Corozal Virtual Office (☎ 22010), 6 Park St S.

Cerros Archaeological Site

Cerros (also called Cerro Maya) flourished in late preclassic times. Unlike at other Mayan sites, little subsequent construction from the Classic and Postclassic periods covers the original structures here. Thus the site has given archaeologists important insights into Mayan preclassic architecture.

Climb Structure 4, a temple more than 65 feet (20m) high, for stunning panoramic views. Though the site is still mostly a mass of grass-covered mounds, the center has been cleared and consolidated and it's easy to see how the plaza structures were designed to fit together. Also notable are the canals that ring the site, which have remained mysteriously clear of vegetation through the ages.

Tours can be arranged through your hotel. You can also charter a boat (US$50) or arrange for a fisherman to take you over to the site to explore independently. The boat trip takes about 15 minutes; then you walk 10 minutes to the site.

Places to Stay

On 7th Ave (the main road), the *Hotel Maya* (☎ 22082, fax 22827, hotelmaya@btl.net), between 9th and 10th Sts S, is the longtime budget favorite. The 17 aged but clean rooms with private shower cost US$25 double with fan, US$30 with fan and TV and US$43 with air-con and cable TV. Good, cheap meals are served in the adjoining eatery.

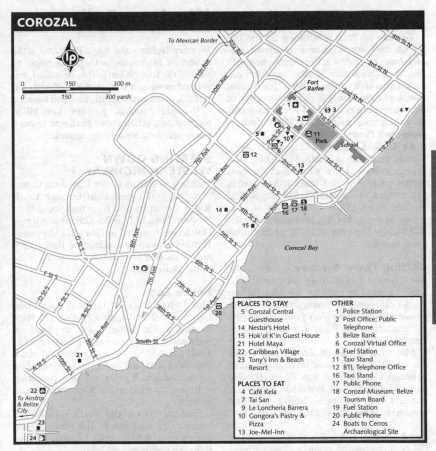

COROZAL

To Mexican Border

Fort Barlee

Park

School

Corozal Bay

PLACES TO STAY
5 Corozal Central Guesthouse
14 Nestor's Hotel
15 Hok'ol K'in Guest House
21 Hotel Maya
22 Caribbean Village
23 Tony's Inn & Beach Resort

PLACES TO EAT
4 Café Kela
7 Tai San
9 Le Lonchería Barrera
10 Gongora's Pastry & Pizza
13 Joe-Mel-Inn

OTHER
1 Police Station
2 Post Office; Public Telephone
3 Belize Bank
6 Corozal Virtual Office
8 Fuel Station
11 Taxi Stand
12 BTL Telephone Office
16 Taxi Stand
17 Public Phone
18 Corozal Museum; Belize Tourism Board
19 Fuel Station
20 Public Phone
24 Boats to Cerros Archaeological Site

To Airstrip & Belize City

BELIZE

Corozal Central Guesthouse (☎ 22335, cghczl@yahoo.com, 22 6th Ave), which is a short walk from the plaza, is simpler and cheaper than the Hotel Maya, with waterless rooms going for US$15 double. Bonuses include a cooking area and a large common area.

Caribbean Village (☎ 22752), south of town across the main road from the sea, has large swaths of lush grass shaded by coconut palms. Basic palapas rent for US$15/20 single/double. Campsite rates are US$2.50 per person for a tent.

Nestor's Hotel (☎ 22354, 125 5th Ave S) makes most of its money from its restaurant-bar and video machines. Rooms are cheap at US$15/18, but they suffer greatly from bar noise.

The *Hok'ol K'in Guest House* (☎ 23329, fax 23569), on 4th St S at 4th Ave, is a small, modern hotel with a nice dining room and patio. The comfortable rooms are designed to catch sea breezes, and each has two double beds, a bathroom and cable TV. At US$32/44, this is the best value in town.

About a mile (1.6km) south of the plaza on the shore road is *Tony's Inn & Beach Resort* (☎ 22055, fax 22829, tonys@btl.net), with its own swimming lagoon, cable TV, restaurant and bar. The 26 rooms come with fan or air-con and cost US$65 to US$70 double.

Places to Eat
The *Hok'ol K'in Guest House*, *Hotel Maya* and *Tony's Inn & Beach Resort* have

decent restaurants. *Nestor's Hotel* is a popular watering hole for travelers.

Tai San, on Park St between 1st and 2nd Sts S, is the favored Chinese restaurant. *Joe-Mel-Inn*, on 4th Ave at the intersection with 2nd St S, serves terrific Belizean food but isn't open for dinner. Also for lunch, *Lonchería Barrera*, off the west corner of the square, offers delicious Mexican dishes at unbeatable prices. Just next door is *Gongora's Pastry & Pizza*.

Le Café Kela (☎ 22833, 37 1st Ave), blends traditional Belizean dishes with French cuisine. Here you'll find the best crepes in Belize. Belizean dishes, pastas and crepes are around US$4; steak and seafood run US$6 to US$8. With 24-hour notice you can get a traditional cassoulet (US$4.50). The restaurant is open for all three meals.

Getting There & Away

Air Corozal has its own airstrip (CZL) south of the town center, reached by taxi (US$4). It is only an airstrip, with no shelter or services, so there's no point in arriving too early for your flight. Taxis meet all incoming flights.

Maya Island Air (☎ 22874) and Tropic Air (☎ 20356) each have three flights daily between Corozal and San Pedro (US$30 one-way, 20 minutes). From San Pedro you connect with flights to Belize City and onward to other parts of the country.

Land Corozal is 8 miles (13km) south of the border-crossing point at Santa Elena/ Subteniente López. Most of the frequent buses that travel between Chetumal (Mexico) and Belize City stop at Corozal. Otherwise, hitch a ride or hire a taxi (expensive at US$12) to get to Santa Elena. From Subteniente López, minibuses shuttle the 7 miles (12km) to Chetumal's Minibus Terminal all day. You'll have to pay a tourist fee of around US$18.50 to cross into Mexico.

Buses leave Corozal and head south via Orange Walk for Belize City at least every hour from 4 am to 7:30 pm, with extra buses in the morning. Likewise, buses run from Belize City to Corozal hourly (2¼ to 2¾ hours, 96 miles/155km), with extra runs in the afternoon to accommodate work and school schedules.

Western Belize

Western Belize – the Cayo District – is the country's highlands, with peaks rising to over 3000 feet (900m). This beautiful, unspoiled mountain terrain is dotted with waterfalls, caves and Mayan ruins and teeming with wild orchids, parrots, keel-billed toucans and other exotic flora and fauna – prime territory for adventure seekers.

STARTING DOWN WESTERN HIGHWAY

Heading west from Belize City along Cemetery Rd, you'll pass right through Lords Ridge Cemetery and soon find yourself on Western Hwy. In 15 miles (25km) you'll pass Hattieville, founded in 1961 after Hurricane Hattie wreaked destruction on Belize City, and in another 13 miles (21km) you'll come to the Belize Zoo.

Belize Zoo

The Belize Zoo & Tropical Education Centre (☎ 92 3310), Mile 29, Western Hwy, displays native Belizean wildlife in natural surroundings on 29 acres (12 hectares). On a self-guided tour (45 to 60 minutes) you'll see over 125 native animals, including jaguars, ocelots, howler monkeys, peccaries, vultures, storks, crocodiles, tapirs and gibnuts.

The zoo is on the north side of the highway (a sign marks the turnoff) and open 8 am to 4:30 pm daily (closed on major Belizean holidays; US$7.50).

Competing for customers just west of the zoo on Western Hwy are *Cheer's* (☎ 14 9311), Mile 31.25 (Km 50) Western Hwy, and *JB's Watering Hole* (☎ 14 8098), Mile 32 (Km 52) Western Hwy. Each serves Belizean, Mexican and American dishes accompanied by ice-cold Belikins, all at moderate prices.

Guanacaste National Park

Farther west down the highway, at the junction with Hummingbird Hwy, is Guanacaste National Park, a small 52-acre (21-hectare) nature reserve at the confluence of Roaring Creek and the Belize River.

A hike along the park's 2 miles (3km) of trails will introduce you to the abundant and colorful local bird life. After your hike,

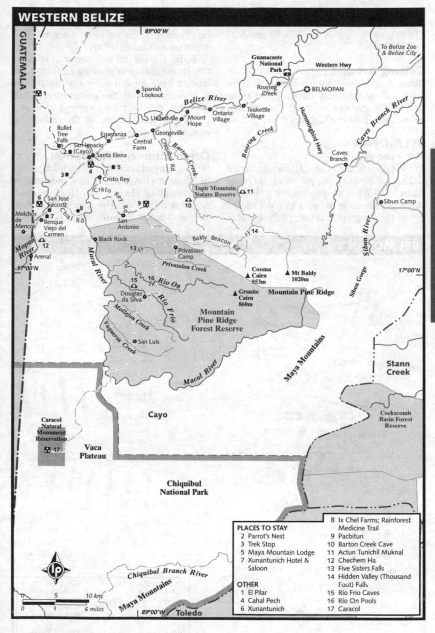

WESTERN BELIZE

GUATEMALA

89°00'W

To Belize Zoo
& Belize City

Guanacaste
National
Park

Western Hwy

BELMOPAN

Belize River

Roaring
Creek

Spanish
Lookout

Unitedville
Mount
Hope

Ontario
Village

Teakettle
Village

Hummingbird Hwy

Caves
Branch

Caves Branch River

Bullet
Tree
Falls

Esperanza

Central
Farm

Georgeville

Chiquibul Rd

Barton Creek

Roaring Creek

Sibun Camp

San Ignacio
(Cayo)

Santa Elena

Cristo Rey

Sibun River

San José
Succotz

Cristo Rey Rd

Tapir Mountain
Nature Reserve

11

Melchor
de
Mencos

Benque
Viejo del
Carmen

Chial Rd

San
Antonio

10

Sibun Gorge

Mopan
River

Arenal

Black Rock

Baldy Beacon Rd

14

17°00'N

Macal River

13

Privassion
Camp

Privassion Creek

Cooma
Cairn
953m

Mt Baldy
1020m

17°00'N

Río On

Granite
Cairn
860m

Mountain Pine Ridge

Douglas
da Silva

Río Frio

Mollejon Creek

Mountain
Pine Ridge
Forest Reserve

Maya Mountains

Stann
Creek

Vaqueros Creek

San Luis

Macal River

Cayo

Cockscomb
Basin Forest
Reserve

Caracol
Natural
Monument
Reservation

17

Vaca
Plateau

Chiquibul
National Park

LP

0   5   10 km
0   3   6 miles

Chiquibul Branch River

Maya Mountains

89°00'W   Toledo

BELIZE

PLACES TO STAY
2 Parrot's Nest
3 Trek Stop
5 Maya Mountain Lodge
7 Xunantunich Hotel &
   Saloon

OTHER
1 El Pilar
4 Cahal Pech
6 Xunantunich

8 Ix Chel Farms; Rainforest
   Medicine Trail
9 Pacbitun
10 Barton Creek Cave
11 Actun Tunichil Muknal
12 Chechem Ha
13 Five Sisters Falls
14 Hidden Valley (Thousand
   Foot) Falls
15 Río Frio Caves
16 Río On Pools
17 Caracol

you can head down to the Belize River for a dip in the park's good, deep swimming hole. The reserve is open 8 am to 4:30 pm daily (US$2.50).

Getting Around

Buses run at least hourly along Western Hwy and upon request will drop you at the zoo, by Guanacaste National Park or anywhere else along the highway.

BELMOPAN
☎ 8 • pop 4000

In 1961, Hurricane Hattie all but destroyed Belize City. Many people were skeptical when in 1970 the government of Belize declared its intention to build a model capital city in the geographic center of the country.

But certain that killer hurricanes would come again and that Belize City could never be properly defended from them, the government decided to move.

Today the capital has begun to come to life. Its population is growing and some embassies have moved here. But unless you have business with the government, you'll probably stay only long enough to have a snack or a meal at one of the restaurants near the bus stops.

Orientation & Information

Belmopan, just under 2.5 miles (4km) south of Western Hwy and about a mile east of Hummingbird Hwy, is a small place easily negotiated on foot. The regional bus lines stop at Market Square, which is near the

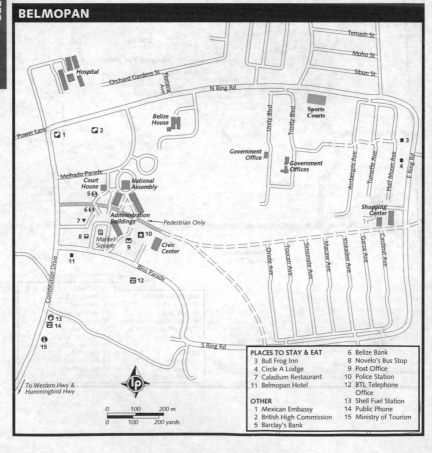

BELMOPAN

PLACES TO STAY & EAT
3 Bull Frog Inn
4 Circle A Lodge
7 Caladium Restaurant
11 Belmopan Hotel

OTHER
1 Mexican Embassy
2 British High Commission
5 Barclay's Bank

6 Belize Bank
8 Novelo's Bus Stop
9 Post Office
10 Police Station
12 BTL Telephone Office
13 Shell Fuel Station
14 Public Phone
15 Ministry of Tourism

post office, police station, market and telephone office.

Places to Stay & Eat

Belmopan is a town for bureaucrats and diplomats, not one for budget travelers. The 14-room *Circle A Lodge* (☎ 22296, fax 23616, 35-37 Half Moon Ave) is perhaps the town's oldest hotel, but it's still serviceable at US$25 double with fan or US$30 with air-con.

The neighboring *Bull Frog Inn* (☎ 22111, fax 23155, bullfrog@btl.net, 25 Half Moon Ave), also with 14 rooms, is Belmopan's nicest place to stay. Its cheerful air-conditioned rooms, each with bathroom and cable TV, cost US$48/63 single/double. The restaurant here is one of the town's best; dinners are around US$7, breakfast and lunch US$3 to US$4.

The 20-room *Belmopan Hotel* (☎ 22130, fax 23066, 2 Bliss Parade) is convenient to the Market Square bus stops. Rooms with air-con, TV and private bath cost US$44/50.

Caladium Restaurant (☎ 22754), on Market Square just opposite the Novelo's bus station, offers daily special plates for US$4. Another option is the market, which features plenty of snack carts selling tasty, low-cost munchies.

Getting There & Away

Thanks to its location near a major highway intersection, Belmopan is a stop for virtually all buses operating along Western and Hummingbird Hwys. That makes it easy to get in and out of the city. See the Belize City Getting There & Away section, earlier in this chapter, for details.

SAN IGNACIO (CAYO)
☎ 92 • pop 8000

San Ignacio, also called Cayo, is a prosperous farming and holiday center in the lovely, tropical Macal River valley. Together with Santa Elena across the river, this is the chief population center of the Cayo District. That said, it's still small, and during the day it's quiet. At night the quiet disappears and the jungle rocks to music from the town's bars and restaurants.

There's nothing much to do in town, but San Ignacio is a good base from which to explore the natural beauties of the Mountain Pine Ridge area.

With a selection of hotels and restaurants, it's also the logical place to spend the night before or after you cross the Guatemalan border.

Orientation

San Ignacio is west of the river; Santa Elena is to the east. Two bridges join the towns and are usually both one-way – the newer, northernmost bridge leads traffic into San Ignacio, and Hawkesworth Bridge, San Ignacio's landmark suspension bridge, leads traffic out of town. During the rainy season, however, the new bridge often floods, and traffic is diverted to Hawkesworth Bridge. Burns Ave is the town's main street. Almost everything in town is accessible on foot.

Information

The town's traditional information exchange is Eva's Restaurant & Bar (see Places to Eat, below). The BTB office (☎ 9 32318) is in the visitor's center at Cahal Pech.

Belize Bank, on Burns Ave, is open 8 am to 1 pm Monday to Thursday, 8 am to 1 pm and 3 to 6 pm Friday. Atlantic Bank is also on Burns Ave.

The post office is on the upper floor of Government House, near the bridge. It's open 8 am to noon and 1 to 5 pm Monday to Friday and 8 am to 1 pm Saturday.

Eva's Restaurant and Bar offers Internet access for US$2.50 for 15 minutes, US$9.50 per hour. Down the street, Posters & Print, 30 Burns Ave, above Tropicool Hotel, charges US$7.50 per hour.

The basic San Ignacio Hospital (☎ 2066) is up the hill off Waight's Ave, west of the center. Across the river in Santa Elena is the Hospital La Loma Luz (☎ 2087, fax 2674).

Archaeological Sites

Two Mayan ruin sites make good excursions from San Ignacio. **Cahal Pech** is right on the edge of town, and **El Pilar** is a short distance to the northwest.

Mayan for 'Tick City,' Cahal Pech (not its original name) was a city of some importance from around 900 BC through AD 800. The 34 buildings here are spread over 6 acres (2.4 hectares) and grouped around seven plazas. Plaza B, about 500 feet (150m) from the museum building and parking area, is the site's largest plaza and also the most

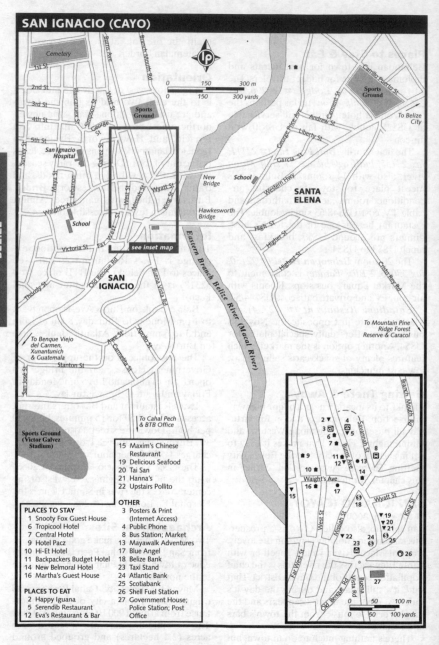

SAN IGNACIO (CAYO)

15 Maxim's Chinese
    Restaurant
19 Delicious Seafood
20 Tai San
21 Hanna's
22 Upstairs Pollito

OTHER
3 Posters & Print
   (Internet Access)
4 Public Phone
8 Bus Station; Market
13 Mayawalk Adventures
17 Blue Angel
18 Belize Bank
23 Taxi Stand
24 Atlantic Bank
25 Scotiabank
26 Shell Fuel Station
27 Government House;
   Police Station; Post
   Office

PLACES TO STAY
1 Snooty Fox Guest House
6 Tropicool Hotel
7 Central Hotel
9 Hotel Pacz
10 Hi-Et Hotel
11 Backpackers Budget Hotel
14 New Belmoral Hotel
16 Martha's Guest House

PLACES TO EAT
2 Happy Iguana
5 Serendib Restaurant
12 Eva's Restaurant & Bar

impressive. It's surrounded by some of the site's most significant buildings. Off Plaza A, Structure A-1 is the site's tallest pyramid.

Cahal Pech is about a mile (under 2km) from Hawkesworth Bridge off Buena Vista Rd. Hours are 9 am to 4:30 pm (US$2.50).

About 12 miles (19km) northwest of San Ignacio, 7 miles (11km) northwest of Bullet Tree Falls, El Pilar is perched almost 900 feet (275m) above the Belize River. El Pilar has been left largely uncleared, and five archaeological and nature trails meander among the jungle-covered mounds.

Places to Stay

San Ignacio A good option is *Martha's Guest House* (☎ 2732, marthas@btl.net, 10 West St), a modern home with a family atmosphere. Rooms rent for US$17.50 double with shared bath and fan, US$20 with private bath. Some rooms have cable TV. Amenities include a Laundromat(US$5 per load) and a ground-floor cafe serving good food.

Hotel Pacz (☎/fax 2110, 402 Far West St) rents five basic but sparkling clean rooms for US$10/17.50/20 single/double/triple; bathrooms are shared.

Hi-Et Hotel (☎ 2828, 12 West St), at Waight's Ave, is a rickety old house with thinly partitioned rooms, clean beds and rates of US$5/10 single/double for rooms with shared bath.

New Belmoral Hotel (☎ 2024, 17 Burns Ave), at Waight's Ave, has 11 rooms with private bath and cable TV for US$12.50/20 with fan or US$30/40 with air-con.

Tropicool Hotel (☎ 3052, 30A Burns Ave) has pleasant ground-floor rooms facing a garden for US$10/12.50 with shared bath.

Central Hotel (☎ 2253, 24 Burns Ave) is among the town's cheapest hotels at US$8/12 for rooms without running water. The neighboring *Backpackers Budget Hotel* competes fiercely for the same clientele.

Around San Ignacio The tidy *Snooty Fox Guest House* (☎ 2150, fax 3556, 64 George Price Ave), just across the river in Santa Elena, has clean rooms with shared bath for US$20 double, cabins with private bath for US$35 and an apartment with two bedrooms and kitchen for US$50.

The *Trek Stop* (☎ 9 32265, susa@btl.net), Mile 71 (Km 114), Western Hwy, 6 miles (10km) west of San Ignacio, is ideal for backpackers. Basic cabins rent for US$10 per person. A campsite costs US$3.50 with your tent (or no tent), US$6 with their tent. Meal packages are available for US$15 per day, and kitchen facilities are available.

The *Parrot's Nest* (☎ 9 37008, 14 6083 cellular, parrot@btl.net), 3 miles (5km) northwest of San Ignacio, near Bullet Tree Falls, is aptly named: guests stay in treehouselike thatched cabins built high on stilts. Baths are mostly shared, but there's electricity all the time and the price is right: US$25 to US$28 double; one cabin with private toilet for US$33. The site is beautiful, surrounded by the river on three sides. Hiking, canoeing and horseback riding are available, and shuttles to San Ignacio can be arranged.

Maya Mountain Lodge (☎ 2164, fax 2029, jungle@mayamountain.com, 9 Cristo Rey Rd) is just over 1.5 miles (3.5km) from San Ignacio. The six rooms and eight thatched cottages all have fan and private bath with hot water. Delicious meals are served in the verandah restaurant. Rates are US$49 to US$89 single or double. Homestyle meals cost US$8 at breakfast and lunch, US$16 at dinner.

Places to Eat

Eva's Restaurant & Bar (☎/fax 2267, evas@btl.net, 22 Burns Ave) is the information and social center of the expatriate set – temporary and permanent – in San Ignacio. Daily special plates at US$4 to US$6 are the best value.

The popular terrace cafe at *Martha's Guest House* (10 West St) serves all three meals. You can get breakfast for US$4 to US$5, pizzas for US$9 to US$11 and sandwiches for US$2 to US$3.

Happy Iguana (27 Burns Ave) has a cheerful patio setting and serves stewed chicken, burgers and sandwiches for US$3 to US$5. *Upstairs Pollito*, on Missiah St, is another popular spot with travelers for cheap, good cats.

Maxim's Chinese Restaurant, at the intersection of Far West St and Waight's Ave, is recommended by the locals. Prices range from US$2.50 to US$5. The small, dark restaurant is open 11:30 am to 2:30 pm and

BELIZE

5 pm until midnight. Other choices for Chinese food are *Tai San* and *Delicious Seafood*, both on Burns Ave.

Across Burns Ave from Eva's and a short distance north is the *Serendib Restaurant*, serving – of all things – Sri Lankan dishes. The service is friendly, the food is good, and the prices are not bad, ranging from US$3.50 for the simpler dishes up to US$10 for steak or lobster. Lunch is served 9:30 am to 3 pm, dinner 6:30 to 11 pm.

Hanna's (☎ *3014, 5 Burns Ave*) serves Indian, Belizean and vegetarian dishes priced from US$4.50 to US$6. It's open 6:30 am to 3 pm and 6:30 to 10 pm daily.

Entertainment

The *Blue Angel*, on Waight's Ave, regularly has big-name live music on weekends. The *Cahel Pech Bar* sometimes schedules weekend dances. Benque Viejo del Carmen, the small town just east of the Guatemala border, often holds weekend dances attracting people from all over the country. Ask in San Ignacio to see if anything's on for the weekend.

Getting There & Away

Buses run to and from Belize City, Belmopan and Benque Viejo del Carmen nearly every half hour.

The taxi stand for the Cayo Taxi Drivers Association (☎ 2196) is located on the traffic circle opposite Government House. Rates can be surprisingly high for short trips out of town (a trip of a few miles can easily cost US$5 to US$10), but a jitney cab ride to Benque Viejo del Carmen costs only US$1.50.

MOUNTAIN PINE RIDGE AREA

South of Western Hwy, between Belmopan and the Guatemala border, the land begins to climb toward the heights of the Maya Mountains, which separate the Cayo District from the Stann Creek District to the east and Toledo District to the south.

In the heart of this highland area – land of macaws, mahogany, mangoes and jaguars – over 300 sq miles (777 sq km) of tropical pine forest has been set aside as the **Mountain Pine Ridge Forest Reserve**. The reserve and its surrounding area are full of rivers, pools, waterfalls and caves to explore.

Rainforest Medicine Trail

This herbal-cure research center is at **Ix Chel Farms** (☎ 92-3870), 8 miles (13km) southwest of San Ignacio up Chial Rd.

Dr Eligio Pantí, who died in 1996 at age 103, was a healer in San Antonio village who used traditional Mayan herb cures. Dr Rosita Arvigo, an American, studied medicinal plants with Dr Pantí, then began several projects to spread the wisdom of traditional healing methods and to preserve the rain forest habitats, which harbor an incredible 4000 plant species.

One of her projects was the establishment of the Rainforest Medicine Trail, a self-guiding path among the jungle's natural cures. It's open 8 am to noon and 1 to 5 pm daily (US$5).

Caves

The **Río Frio Caves** are the region's most famous and visited caverns, but gaining in popularity is **Barton Creek Cave**, accessible only by tour prearranged with Barton Creek Ranch. One of the more popular day trips offered out of San Ignacio, the cave holds spooky skulls and bones and pottery shards from the ancient Maya. To see them you'll have to negotiate some very narrow passages.

Chechem Ha is a Mayan cave complete with ancient ceremonial pots. Members of the Morales family, who discovered the cave, act as guides, leading you up the steep slope to the cave mouth, then down inside to see what the Maya left. A fee of US$25 pays for one to three people. Take water and a flashlight. You can also camp at Chechem Ha or sleep in one of the simple bunks.

The latest cave system to be opened for tours is **Actun Tunichil Muknal**. In an effort to prevent looting of the Mayan bones and artifacts within, and to keep general wear and tear to a minimum, only a couple of tour operators are allowed to run tours here at this point. To arrange a tour (around US$65 per person), check with your hotel or with Mayawalk Adventures (☎ 92 3070, 14 4352 cellular), 19 Burns Ave in San Ignacio.

Pools & Waterfalls

At Río On Pools, small waterfalls connect a series of pools that the river has carved out of granite boulders. Some of the falls double as water slides. The pools at tranquil Five Sisters Falls, accessible by an outdoor-elevator ride (small charge, usually US$2) at Five Sisters Lodge, are connected by five falls cascading over a short drop-off.

The region's aquatic highlight is Hidden Valley (or Thousand Foot) Falls, southeast of San Antonio. Hiking trails surround the falls and a viewing platform at the top of the cascade is a great spot for catching a Mountain Pine Ridge vista. The falls actually are around 1500 feet high, but they aren't spectacular in the dry season.

Archaeological Sites
The highlands here hold two Mayan ruins of interest, one small and one huge.

Pacbitun, a small site, 12 miles (20km) south of San Ignacio via Cristo Rey Rd, near San Antonio, seems to have been occupied continuously through most of Mayan history, from 900 BC to AD 900. Today only lofty Plaza A has been uncovered and partially consolidated. Structures 1 and 2, on the east and west sides of the plaza, respectively, are worth a look. Within them, archaeologists discovered the graves of noble Maya women buried with a variety of musical instruments, perhaps played at their funerals.

Some 53 miles (86km) south of San Ignacio via Chiquibul Rd lies **Caracol**, a vast Mayan city hidden in the jungle. The site encompasses some 35 sq miles (88 sq km), with 36,000 structures marked so far.

Caracol was occupied in the postclassic period from around 300 BC until AD 1150. At its height, between AD 650 and 700, Caracol is thought to have had a population of 150,000 – not much less than the entire population of Belize today.

Highlights of the site include Caana (Sky-Palace) in Plaza B, Caracol's tallest structure at 138 feet (42m); the Temple of the Wooden Lintel, dating from AD 50, in Plaza A; the ball court with a marker commemorating Caracol's defeat of rivals Tikal in AD 562 and Naranjo in AD 631; and the central acropolis, containing a royal tomb.

Places to Stay
The forests and mountains of the greater Mountain Pine Ridge area are dotted with small inns, lodges and ranches offering accommodations, meals, hiking, horseback

trips, caving, swimming, bird watching and similar outdoor activities.

A few lodges are for the budget traveler; the rest are expensive, though they offer a good value for the money. Most of the lodges have Web sites that are accessible through www.belizenet.com.

WEST TO GUATEMALA
From San Ignacio it's another 10 miles (16km) southwest down Western Hwy to the Guatemala border.

Xunantunich
Belize's most accessible Mayan site of significance, Xunantunich (soo-**nahn**-too-neech) is reached via a free ferry crossing at San José Succotz, on Western Hwy about 7 miles (12km) west of San Ignacio. From the ferry it's a 1-mile-walk (2km) uphill to the ruins.

The site's dominant structure, El Castillo (Structure A-6), rises 130 feet (40m) above the jungle floor. The stairway on its northern side – the side you approach from the courtyard – goes only as far as the temple building. To climb to the roofcomb you must go around to the southern side and use a separate set of steps. On the temple's east side, a few of the masks that once surrounded the structure have been restored.

Xunantunich is open 9 am to 5 pm (US$2.50). Guides can be hired for a one-hour tour for US$13, but the site can easily be navigated independently. The *Xunantunich Hotel & Saloon*, across the road, is a good stop for lunch and refreshments. It also rents rooms at rates ranging from US$20 double (fan, shared bath) to US$63 (air-con, private bath).

Buses on their way between San Ignacio and Benque Viejo del Carmen will drop you at the ferry for the fare of US$0.50. Jitney taxis shuttling the same route cost US$1.50. Ferry hours are 8 am to noon and 1 to 5 pm; crossing is on demand and free for both foot passengers and cars.

Benque Viejo del Carmen
A sleepy town 2 miles (3km) east of the Guatemalan border, Benque Viejo del Carmen holds few services for travelers, and you're better off eating and sleeping in San Ignacio. The town stirs from its normal tropical

somnolence in mid-July, when the Benque Festival brings three days of revelry.

Crossing the Border

Cross early in the morning to have the best chance of catching buses onward. Get your passport (and, if applicable, your car papers) stamped at the Belizean station, then cross into Guatemala. The border station is supposedly open 24 hours a day, but most travelers try to cross during daylight hours. If you need a Guatemalan visa or tourist card (see Visas & Documents in the Facts for the Visitor section of the Guatemala chapter), obtain it before you reach the border. Be prepared to pay a US$3.75 Protected Areas Conservation Trust fee when crossing the border. This fee is valid for 30 days if you cross another border from Belize.

Two banks at the border will change money, but the itinerant moneychangers often give you a better deal – for US cash. The rates for exchanging Belizean dollars to Guatemalan quetzals and vice versa are poor. Use up your local currency before you get to the border, then change hard foreign currency, preferably US dollars.

Both Transportes Pinita and Transportes Rosalita buses westward to Santa Elena (Guatemala) depart town early in the morning. Sometimes available are more comfortable – and more expensive – minibuses (US$10 per person); many travelers feel this is money well spent.

To go on to Tikal, get off the bus at El Cruce (Puente Ixlu), 22 miles (36km) east of Flores, and wait for another bus, minibus or obliging car or truck to take you the final 21 miles (35km) north to Tikal.

Southern Belize

If you want to explore off the tourist track, southern Belize is the place to do it. The region's biggest draw is Placencia, attracting beach-loving budget travelers for whom life in the cayes is just too hectic. Dangriga, the main town of the Stann Creek District, is a lively seaside town and the center of Garífuna culture in Belize. Out to sea you'll find Tobacco and South Water Cayes and Glover's Reef, offering divers nearly virgin reef to explore.

Southern Hwy – long, bumpy and dusty – carries travelers through the region to its final destination, the Toledo District. Toledo's main town, Punta Gorda, is a wild mixture of all the cultures of Belize and lies near several unrestored ruins and natural wonders. This is the most remote, least explored part of the country and getting around can be an expensive hassle, but it's a wonderland for the truly adventurous.

HUMMINGBIRD HIGHWAY

Heading south from Belmopan, Hummingbird Hwy stretches 49 miles (79km) to the junction of Southern Hwy and the turnoff to Dangriga. It is almost entirely paved, but be prepared to slow for roadwork or sudden transitions to dirt road.

Blue Hole National Park

The Blue Hole – focus of the like-named national park – is a cenote (water-filled limestone sinkhole) some 328 feet (100m) in diameter and 108 feet (33m) deep. Fed by underground tributaries of the Sibun River, it's deliciously cool on the hottest days and makes an excellent swimming hole.

The park visitor's center is about 11 miles (18km) south of Belmopan on Hummingbird Hwy. At the center is the trailhead to **St Herman's Cave**, a large cavern once used by the Maya during the classic period. This is one of the few caves in Belize you can visit independently, although a guide is required if you wish to venture in farther than 150 yards. Also here are a series of nature trails and an observation tower.

The trail to the Blue Hole itself starts at a parking area about a mile farther down the highway. (Break-ins have been reported here, so be careful with your belongings.) You don't have to stop at the visitor's center if you're just going for a swim; an attendant is posted at the trail to the Blue Hole to collect your money. The park is open 8 am to 4 pm daily (US$4).

Five Blues National Park

Twenty-two miles (36km) south of Belmopan is the turnoff to Five Blues National Park, a primitive community-managed reserve surrounding five (blue) lakes. Turn left off the highway and you'll see a visitor's center, where you'll be asked to pay an entry fee of US$4. Be sure to pick up a map from the visitor's center attendant. The park's features – a series of nature walks, a diving platform, and a couple of small caves – are not clearly marked. The park is about 4 rough miles (6.5km) from the visitor's center and is difficult to reach without your own transportation.

DANGRIGA
☎ 5 • pop 10,000

Dangriga (see map on next page) is the largest town in southern Belize. It's much smaller than Belize City, but it's friendlier and quieter. There's not much to do here except spend the night and head onward – unless it's November 19, Garífuna Settlement Day, a frenzy of dancing, drinking and celebration of the Garífuna's heritage. Eight miles (13km) northwest of town on Melinda Rd is Marie Sharp's Factory (☎ 22370), the source of Belize's beloved hot sauce. Casual tours, often led by Marie herself, are offered during business hours.

Orientation & Information

Stann Creek empties into the Gulf of Honduras at the center of town. Dangriga's main street is called St Vincent St south of the creek and Commerce St to the north. The bus station is at the southern end of St Vincent St just north of the Shell fuel station. The airstrip is a mile (2km) north of the center, near the Pelican Beach Resort. The Riverside Café serves as the unofficial water taxi terminal where you can arrange trips out to the southern cayes with local fishermen or tradespeople. It's best to stop in by 10 am to find out when boats will be leaving.

Barclay's and Scotiabank have branches here; hours for both are 8 am to 1 pm Monday to Thursday, 8 am to 4:30 pm Friday.

You can get your clothes washed and check your email at the same time at Val's Laundry (☎ 23324), 1 Sharp St at Mahogany. A load costs US$5, as does a half hour on the Internet.

Places to Stay & Eat

Pal's Guest House (☎/fax 22095, 868-A Magoon St) is spartan but clean, with a sea breeze and the sound of the surf. You pay US$15 double for a room with shared bath, US$30 for one with private bath, TV and

sea view. The *Bluefield Lodge* (☎ 22742, 6 Bluefield Rd) has seven tidy rooms with fan for US$12.50/14.50 single/double with shared bath, US$17.50 double with private bath.

Chaleanor Hotel (☎ 22587, 35 Magoon St) has clean, comfortable rooms with private baths for US$30 double. The rooftop deck offers views of the Caribbean.

The *Riverside Café*, on S Riverside Dr just east of the North Stann Creek Bridge, serves up three tasty meals daily at budget to moderate prices. This is a good place to ask about fishing and snorkeling trips out to the cayes or treks inland.

The locals favor *Ritchie's Dinette*, on Commerce St, for Belizean food. Most of the other restaurants along Commerce St are Chinese: *Sunrise*, *Starlight* and *Silver Garden* serve full meals for about US$6.

Getting There & Away

Maya Island Air and Tropic Air serve Dangriga on flights also stopping at Placencia, Punta Gorda and Belize City.

Z-Line runs five buses daily from Belize City (four hours via Hummingbird Hwy, three hours via Coastal Hwy). Also operating to and from Belize City are Ritchie's Bus Service (two buses daily) and James (one bus daily). Most buses continue south to Placencia and Punta Gorda.

TOBACCO CAYE, SOUTH WATER CAYE & GLOVER'S REEF
☎ 5

Tobacco Caye, South Water Caye and the resorts of Glover's Reef are accessed by boat from Dangriga. Their distance from Belize City has kept casual visitors away, protecting the reef from much human impact. Dolphins, manta rays and manatees are commonly sighted, and the quantity and variety of coral on display is incredible. Good snorkeling and diving can be had right off the shore from the cayes.

Tobacco Caye is a 5-acre (2-hectare) island catering to travelers on a low to moderate budget. Diving, fishing, snorkeling and hammocking are the favorite pastimes here. The caye was hit hard by Hurricane Mitch in October 1998, and it's still in the process of rebuilding.

Lodging possibilities include *Lana's* (☎ 22571, 14 7451 cellular), which has 10

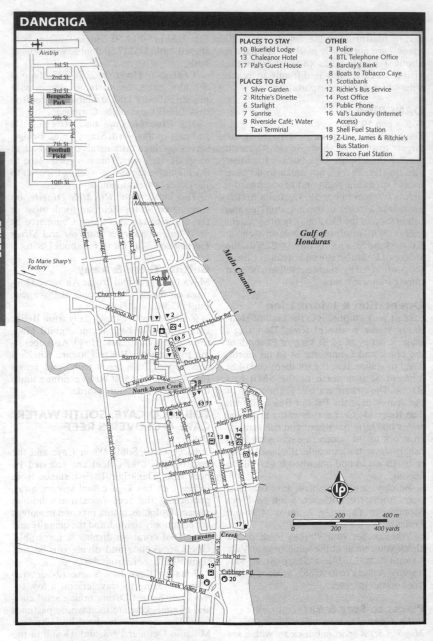

DANGRIGA

PLACES TO STAY
10 Bluefield Lodge
13 Chaleanor Hotel
17 Pal's Guest House

PLACES TO EAT
1 Silver Garden
2 Ritchie's Dinette
6 Starlight
7 Sunrise
9 Riverside Café; Water
  Taxi Terminal

OTHER
3 Police
4 BTL Telephone Office
5 Barclay's Bank
8 Boats to Tobacco Caye
11 Scotiabank
12 Richie's Bus Service
14 Post Office
15 Public Phone
16 Val's Laundry (Internet
  Access)
18 Shell Fuel Station
19 Z-Line, James & Ritchie's
  Bus Station
20 Texaco Fuel Station

Airstrip
1st St
2nd St
3rd St
Benguche Park
5th St
7th St
Football Field
10th St
Benguche Ave
Pen Rd
Cumnagur St
Savar St
Yampa St

Monument

To Marie Sharp's Factory

School

Church Rd
Melinda Rd
Coconut Rd
Ramos Rd

Front St
Main Channel

Gulf of Honduras

Court House Rd
Commerce St
Plum St
Doctor's Alley

N Riverside Drive
North Stann Creek
S Riverside Drive
S Foreshore

Bluefield Rd
Chatuye St

Ecumenical Drive
Cedar St
Canal St
Moho Rd
Madre Cacao Rd
Salmwood Rd
Yemeri Rd

Mahogany Rd
Tuberose St
S Vincent St
Magoon St
Sharp St
Alejo Beni Ave

Mangrove Rd

Havana St
Havana Creek
Isla Rd
Unity St
Stann Creek Valley Rd
Cabbage Rd

0   200   400 m
0   200   400 yards

spartan rooms with shared baths for US$30 double; and *Gaviota's* (☎ 22294, 14 9763 cellular), about the same price. Double-occupancy rates for all lodges include meals for two.

Passage to Tobacco Caye can be arranged along the river near the Riverside Café in Dangriga. The cost is around US$15 one-way.

Five miles south of Tobacco Caye is **South Water Caye**, a much more exclusive island, with dive resorts offering packaged accommodations.

Named for the pirate John Glover, **Glover's Reef** holds a handful of secluded lodges, each on its own atoll.

Glover's Atoll Resort (☎ 12016, 14 8351 cellular, glovers@btl.net), on Northeast Caye, offers budget accommodations on a 9-acre (3.6-hectare) atoll about 20 miles (32km) from the mainland. Weekly rates are US$80 for camping, US$99 for a dorm bunk and US$149 double for a cabin. Facilities are rustic, but the 360-degree Caribbean view can't be beat. It's a good deal for budget travelers, but extras – water, food, equipment – can add up. A sailboat departs for the island every Sunday morning at 8 am from the Sittee River Guesthouse (see the Southern Highway section, below). The trip costs US$30 and takes three to four hours, depending on the weather.

SOUTHERN HIGHWAY
☎ 5

South of Dangriga, this highway is mostly unpaved and can be rough, especially in the rainy months, but along the way are some great opportunities for experiencing off-the-beaten-track Belize.

Hopkins
pop 1100

The farming and fishing village of Hopkins is 4 miles (7km) east of Southern Hwy, on the coast. Most of its people are Garífuna, living as the coastal inhabitants of Belize have lived for centuries.

A handful of thatch cabaña lodges lie south of town. The best is *Sandy Beach Lodge* (☎ 37006, t-travels@btl.net), owned and operated by the Sandy Beach Women's Cooperative. Its six simple, dorm-style rooms rent for US$9/10 single/double with shared bath. Cabins with private bath cost

US$13/18. North of the town center, the *Swinging Armadillo*, a cheery restaurant and bar, also has bunks available for US$10 per person.

Sittee River

Another small coastal village where you can get away from it all is Sittee River. *Sittee River Guesthouse* rents bunks for US$5 a night (not worth a penny more). The boat to Glover's Reef picks up passengers here. Next door is the more gracious, good-value *Toucan Sittee* (☎ 37039), offering riverside rooms at US$8 to US$12 per person (shared bath), as well as two apartments at US$40 and US$55 double.

Cockscomb Basin Wildlife Sanctuary

Almost halfway between Dangriga and Independence is the village of Maya Centre, where a track goes 6 miles (10km) west to the Cockscomb Basin Wildlife Sanctuary (sometimes called the Jaguar Reserve), a prime place for wildlife watching. The varied topography and lush tropical forest within the 98,000-acre (39,000-hectare) sanctuary make it an ideal habitat for a wide variety of native Belizean fauna.

Visitor facilities at the reserve include a *campsite* (US$2.50 per person), several simple shared *rental cabins* with solar electricity (US$15 per person, kitchen use US$1 per person), a visitor's center and numerous hiking trails. The walk through the lush forest is a pretty one, and though you cannot be assured of seeing a jaguar, you will certainly enjoy seeing many of the hundreds of other species of birds, plants and animals in this rich environment. No public transportation to the reserve is available.

For information, contact the Belize Audubon Society (☎ 2 35004, fax 2 34985, base@btl.net), 12 Fort St, Belize City, or the Cockscomb Basin Wildlife Sanctuary, PO Box 90, Dangriga.

At the start of the road into the reserve, in Maya Centre, are the *Nuch Che'il Cottages* (☎ 12021), Mile 14 (Km 23) Southern Hwy, and the Hmen Herbal Center Medicinal Trail (entrance fee US$2). Bunks in the cheery dorm cost US$8, and rooms are US$18/20 single/double. Three meals a day are served (not included in rates).

PLACENCIA

☎ 6 • pop 600

Perched at the southern tip of a long, narrow, sandy peninsula, Placencia is 'the caye you can drive to.' Not too long ago, the only practical way to get here was by boat from the mainland. Now a road runs all the way down the peninsula and an airstrip lies just north of town. But Placencia still has the wonderful laid-back ambience of the cayes, along with varied accommodations and friendly local people. The palm-lined beaches on its east side attract an international crowd looking for sun and sand, and they make low-key pastimes such as swimming, sunbathing and lazing-about the preferred 'activities' for many visitors.

Orientation & Information

The village's main north-south 'street' is actually a narrow concrete footpath about 3 feet (1m) wide that threads its way among simple wood-frame houses (some on stilts) and beachfront lodges. An unpaved road skirts the town to the west, ending at the peninsula's southern tip, which is the bus stop.

An easy walk takes you anywhere in town. From the airstrip, it's a half mile (0.8km) south to the village and a mile (1.6km) farther to the peninsula's southern tip.

At the south end of town you'll find the wharf, fuel station, bus stop and icehouse. Atlantic Bank, also on the south end of town, is open 9 am to 2 pm Monday to

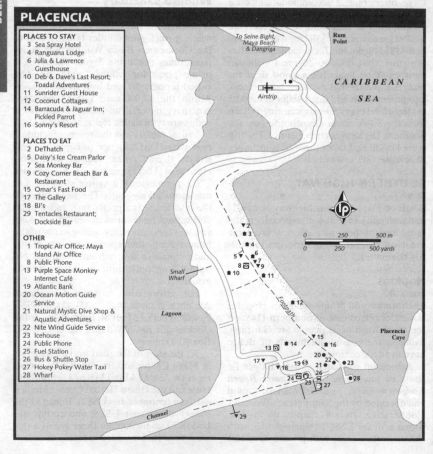

PLACENCIA

PLACES TO STAY
3 Sea Spray Hotel
4 Ranguana Lodge
6 Julia & Lawrence
   Guesthouse
10 Deb & Dave's Last Resort;
   Toadal Adventures
11 Sunrider Guest House
12 Coconut Cottages
14 Barracuda & Jaguar Inn;
   Pickled Parrot
16 Sonny's Resort

PLACES TO EAT
2 DeThatch
5 Daisy's Ice Cream Parlor
7 Sea Monkey Bar
9 Cozy Corner Beach Bar &
   Restaurant
15 Omar's Fast Food
17 The Galley
18 BJ's
29 Tentacles Restaurant;
   Dockside Bar

OTHER
1 Tropic Air Office; Maya
   Island Air Office
8 Public Phone
13 Purple Space Monkey
   Internet Café
19 Atlantic Bank
20 Ocean Motion Guide
   Service
21 Natural Mystic Dive Shop &
   Aquatic Adventures
22 Nite Wind Guide Service
23 Icehouse
24 Public Phone
25 Fuel Station
26 Bus & Shuttle Stop
27 Hokey Pokey Water Taxi
28 Wharf

To Seine Bight,
Maya Beach
& Dangriga

Rum
Point

Airstrip

CARIBBEAN
SEA

Small
Wharf

Lagoon

Footpath

Placencia
Caye

Channel

0   250   500 m
0   250   500 yards

Thursday, 9 am to noon and 1 to 4 pm Friday. Check your email at The Purple Space Monkey Internet Café (☎ 24094) for US$2.50 for 15 minutes, US$6 for one hour. It's open 7 am to midnight and has an espresso machine.

Laundry service is available from most of the hotels and guesthouses on the peninsula for US$5 a load.

Organized Tours

Vying to sign up customers for tours of the region are Ocean Motion Guide Service (☎ 23363, 23162) and Nite Wind Guide Service (☎ 23487, 23176), both operating out of small offices near the boat dock. Next door, offering dive trips, is the Natural Mystic Dive Shop & Aquatic Adventures (☎ 23182).

For inland tours, check with Toadal Adventure (☎ 23207, fax 23334), operating out of Deb and Dave's Last Resort, or with Kitty's Place (☎ 23227, kittys@btl.net).

Places to Stay

Placencia has lodgings in all price ranges. Budget and mid-range accommodations are in the village (you're likely to get a beach-side cabaña, but your neighbor will be just a couple of feet away).

The *Julia & Lawrence Guesthouse* (☎ 23478) is central and clean. Rooms with shared bath go for US$13/18 single/double; ones with private baths are a bit more. *Sunrider Guest House* (☎ 23486) has good, clean rooms with private bath for US$16/21/25 single/double/triple. The rooms face a beach with shady palms.

Deb & Dave's Last Resort (☎ 23297, fax 23334, debanddave@btl.net) has rooms with shared bath for US$16/22. It's on the lagoon side of the peninsula and stays quieter than the beach places.

To the south, *Sonny's Resort* (☎ 23103, fax 2 32819) has well-spaced but expensive rooms with cable TV for US$22 double. A restaurant and bar are on site. *Barracuda & Jaguar Inn* (☎ 23330, fax 23250, wende@btl.net) rents two hardwood cabañas with refrigerator and coffeemaker for US$45, light breakfast included. *Coconut Cottages* (☎ /fax 23234) has cottages on the beach for US$28.

Sea Spray Hotel (☎ 23148), right in the village center on the beach, has rooms and cabins with shared or private bath (and hot water) priced from US$25 to US$40 double. The more expensive rooms are larger and have porches and sea views. *Ranguana Lodge* (☎/fax 23112) has attractive, good-sized mahogany cabins, but they're packed tightly together; US$50 to US$60 double with private shower. Each room has a fan, refrigerator, coffeemaker and balcony. The more expensive rooms have beach views.

Places to Eat

Omar's Fast Food offers homemade food at low prices. Try the cheap, good burritos or higher-priced menu items like conch steak (US$9). It's open 7 am to 10 pm. A good stop for low-priced Belizean food is *BJ's*, in the south part of town off the main road. *Daisy's Ice Cream Parlor*, in the center of town, west off the central pathway, serves meals as well as desserts and has a pleasant patio area. Burgers cost US$2; meals run from US$7 to US$10.

The best of the beachside places is *Sea Monkey Bar* (☎ 24060), where the staff is friendly and the setting simple and comfortable. The menu is limited, but the offerings are delicious, with bar snacks such as nachos and black bean chili for US$2 to US$3.

Nearby, the *Cozy Corner Beach Bar & Restaurant* (☎ 23280) is open for lunch and dinner daily and stays open for drinks until around 10 pm (later on weekends). Another good place to hang out late is the *Pickled Parrot*, the restaurant and bar at the Barracuda & Jaguar Inn. *DeThatch* (☎ 24011) is a small bar on the beach serving drinks and some meals. Fish burritos cost US$3.50.

The Galley, west of the main part of the village, is a favorite for long dinners with good conversation. A full meal with drinks costs about US$10 to US$15. *Tentacles Restaurant* (☎ 23333) is another evening favorite – a breezy, atmospheric place with its popular *Dockside Bar* built on a wharf out over the water.

Getting There & Away

Maya Island Air and Tropic Air offer daily flights linking Placencia with Belize City and Dangriga to the north and Punta Gorda to the south. The village begins a half mile (0.8km) south of the airstrip; taxis meet most flights.

Ritchie's and Z-Line each run two buses from Belize City to Placencia via Dangriga.

Daily except Sunday, the *Hokey Pokey Water Taxi* (US$5) departs Placencia at 10 am for Mango Creek, and departs Mango Creek at 2:30 pm for the return trip. The water taxi departs Placencia again at 4 pm. Many boats will do a charter run to/from Mango Creek for US$20 for up to six persons.

The *Gulf Cruza* (☎ 2 24506) makes a Belize City–Placencia–Big Creek–Puerto Cortés (Honduras) run on Friday, leaving Placencia at 9:30 am, arriving at Puerto Cortés at 11 am. It takes the same route north on Monday, leaving Placencia at 2:30 pm, arriving at Belize City at 5 pm. The boat takes passengers only, no vehicles.

Getting Around

Placencia Shuttle Service makes six daily runs in each direction between Maya Beach, Seine Bight and Placencia from 6 am to 8 pm, stopping at the resorts along the way. Schedules are posted at most hotels and restaurants en route.

You can rent bicycles for US$15 a day at the Purple Space Monkey (☎ 24094) or call John (☎ 14 4087) for a bike.

PUNTA GORDA
☎ 7 • pop 3000

Southern Hwy ends at Punta Gorda, the southernmost town in Belize. Rainfall and humidity are at their highest and the jungle at its lushest here in the Toledo District. Prepare yourself for at least a short downpour almost daily and some sultry weather in-between.

Known throughout Belize simply as 'PG,' this sleepy town was founded for the Garífuna who emigrated from Honduras in 1832. Though still predominantly Garífuna, PG is also home to the usual bewildering variety of Belizean citizenry: Creoles, Kekchi Maya, and expat Americans, Brits, Canadians, Chinese and East Indians.

Orientation & Information

The town center is a triangular park with a bandstand and a distinctive blue-and-white clock tower. Saturday is market day, when area villagers come to town to buy, sell and barbecue. It's a fascinating and colorful mix-up.

Nature's Way Guest House (☎ 22119), 65 N Front St, is the unofficial information center for travelers. The Belize Tourism Board office (☎ 22531) and the Toledo Visitors' Information Center (☎ 22470), run by the BTIA, are off Front St and open 9 am to 1 pm Monday to Wednesday, Friday and Saturday.

Belize Bank, at Main and Queen Sts across from the town square, is open 8 am to 1 pm Monday to Thursday, 8 am to 4:30 pm Friday. The Punta Gorda Laundry is at 2 Prince St and charges US$1.50 per pound.

Places to Stay

Punta Gorda's lodging is resolutely budget-class, with only a few places rising above basic shelter.

Nature's Way Guest House (☎ 22119, 65 Front St) is the intrepid travelers' gathering place and charges US$8/13/18 single/double/triple in rooms with clean shared showers.

St Charles Inn (☎ 22149, 23 King St) offers a good value for the money. Clean and well kept, it has rooms with private bath and fan for US$15/20 single/double. Small groups sometimes fill it. *Pallavi's Hotel* (☎ 22414, 19 N Main St) has rooms for US$11 double.

Punta Caliente Hotel (☎ 22561, 108 José María Núñez), near the Z-Line bus station, has a good restaurant on the ground floor and rooms above. Each room has good ventilation as well as a fan and private bath for US$20/25.

The *Tidal Waves Retreat* (☎ 22111, bills_tidalwaves@yahoo.com), on the sea at the south edge of town, rents two rooms for US$19/24, including access to a kitchenette. A cabaña rents for US$49, including breakfast. Camping is available for US$5 per person, US$9 with breakfast.

The *Sea Front Inn* (☎ 22300, fax 22682, seafrontinn@btl.net), north of the town center on Front St, is Punta Gorda's newest hotel but nonetheless a ramshackle arrangement of wood and stone, towering above the rest of the town's buildings. The rooms have private baths and cable TV and cost US$50 double.

Places to Eat

The restaurant at the *Punta Caliente Hotel* serves stew pork, fish fillet, beans and rice

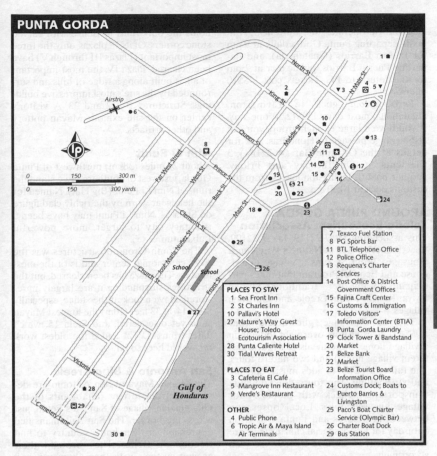

PUNTA GORDA

PLACES TO STAY
1 Sea Front Inn
2 St Charles Inn
10 Pallavi's Hotel
27 Nature's Way Guest
   House; Toledo
   Ecotourism Association
28 Punta Caliente Hotel
30 Tidal Waves Retreat

PLACES TO EAT
3 Cafeteria El Café
5 Mangrove Inn Restaurant
9 Verde's Restaurant

OTHER
4 Public Phone
6 Tropic Air & Maya Island
   Air Terminals
7 Texaco Fuel Station
8 PG Sports Bar
11 BTL Telephone Office
12 Police Office
13 Requena's Charter
   Services
14 Post Office & District
   Government Offices
15 Fajina Craft Center
16 Customs & Immigration
17 Toledo Visitors'
   Information Center (BTIA)
18 Punta Gorda Laundry
19 Clock Tower & Bandstand
20 Market
21 Belize Bank
22 Market
23 Belize Tourist Board
   Information Office
24 Customs Dock; Boats to
   Puerto Barrios &
   Livingston
25 Paco's Boat Charter
   Service (Olympic Bar)
26 Charter Boat Dock
29 Bus Station

Gulf of Honduras

with chicken and similar dishes for US$3.50 to US$5, and it's all good.

Cafeteria El Café is a tidy place open for breakfast and lunch. *Verde's Restaurant*, on Main St, offers standard Belizean family cooking and good breakfasts.

Mangrove Inn Restaurant (☎ 39910) serves daily fresh-fish specials, good Mexican food and quite possibly the best fried chicken to be had in all of Belize for US$6 to US$8.

Entertainment
The *PG Sports Bar*, West and Prince Sts., is a good bet for live music on weekends. It's a good-sized, fairly standard bar, incongruously enhanced by a staggering collection of US sports photos and posters.

Shopping
Fajina Craft Center, on Front St next door to the post office, is a good place to pick up local Mayan handicrafts such as jipijapa baskets, slate carvings and embroidered shirts, dresses and hangings.

Getting There & Away
Punta Gorda is served daily by Maya Island Air and Tropic Air. Ticket offices are located at the airport. If you plan to fly out of PG, be at the airstrip at least 15 minutes before departure time, as the planes sometimes leave early.

James Bus offers one run daily each way between Belize City and Punta Gorda; Z-Line offers four runs in each direction daily.

Requena's Charter Services (☎ 22070), 12 Front St, operates the *Mariestela*, with boats departing Punta Gorda daily at 9 am for Puerto Barrios (Guatemala), and departing Puerto Barrios' public pier at 2 pm for the return to PG. Tickets cost US$10 one-way.

Paco's Boat goes to Lívingston, Guatemala, most days; US$12.50 one-way. If you have a large enough group, you can also arrange passage to Honduras. Ask for details at the Olympic Bar (☎ 22164), 3 Clements St. On Tuesday and Friday, another boat to Lívingston leaves from the customs dock at 10:30 am.

AROUND PUNTA GORDA
Toledo Ecotourism Association
This association (☎ 7-22119, fax 7-22199, ttea@btl.net), based at Nature's Way Guest House, 65 Front St, runs a Village Guesthouse and Ecotrail Program that takes participants to any of 13 traditional Mopan Maya, Kekchi Maya, Creole and Garífuna villages.

The basic village guesthouse tour (US$43) gives visitors overnight lodging in a village home, three meals (each at a different village home) and two nature tours. The full tour (US$88) adds music, dancing and storytelling. The tours don't include transportation; check with the TEA for village bus schedules. Local buses run between the villages and Punta Gorda on Saturday for US$5; special charter trips are very expensive – around US$80 – so plan accordingly.

More than 85% of the tour fee stays in the village with the villagers, helping them achieve a sustainable, ecofriendly economy as an alternative to traditional slash-and-burn agriculture.

Lubaantun
The Mayan ruins at Lubaantun (Fallen Stones), 1 mile (1.6km) northwest of the village of San Pedro Columbia, have been excavated to some extent but not restored. The many temples are still mostly covered with jungle, so you will have to use your imagination to envisage the great city that once thrived here.

Archaeologists have found evidence that Lubaantun flourished until the late 8th century AD, after which little was built. The site covers a square mile (3 sq km) and holds the only ruins in Belize with curved stone corners. Of its 18 plazas, only the three most important (Plazas III through V) have been cleared. Plaza IV, the most important of all, is built along a ridge of hills and surrounded by the site's most impressive buildings: Structures 10, 12 and 33. A visitor's center on the site exhibits Mayan pottery and other artifacts.

Nim Li Punit
About 24 miles (38km) northwest of Punta Gorda, just west of Southern Hwy, stand the ruins of Nim Li Punit (Big Hat). Named for the headgear worn by the richly clad figure on Stela 14, Nim Li Punit may have been a tributary city to larger, more powerful Lubaantun.

The South Group of structures was the city's ceremonial center and is of the most interest. The plaza has been cleared, but the structures surrounding it are largely unrestored. Have a look at the stelae, especially Stela 14, at 33 feet (10m) the longest Mayan stela yet discovered, and Stela 15, which dates from AD 721 and is the oldest work recovered here so far.

San Antonio & Blue Creek
The Mopan Maya of San Antonio are descended from former inhabitants of the Guatemalan village of San Luis Petén, just across the border. The San Antonians fled oppression in their home country to find freedom in Belize. They brought their ancient customs with them, however, and you can observe a traditional lowland Mayan village on a short visit here. If you are here during a festival, your visit will be much more memorable.

About 4 miles (6km) west of San Antonio, near the village of Santa Cruz, is the archaeological site of **Uxbenka**, which has numerous carved stelae.

About 12 miles (20km) south of San Antonio lies the village of Blue Creek, and beyond it the **nature reserve** of Blue Creek Cave. Hike into the site (less than 1 mile/1.6km) along the marked trail and enjoy the rain forest around you and the pools, channels, caves and refreshingly cool waters of the creek system.

Guided nature walks – including a canopy walk and a climb to an observation deck accessed by rope ladder (you must wear helmet and harness for your protection) – are available for about US$15 per hour.

International Zoological Expeditions (☎ 14 3967, bluecreek@btl.net) operates a *guesthouse* on the site. Its seven cabins rent for US$45 per person, including meals.

Getting There & Away
Village buses serve the sites listed above, but the schedules are somewhat erratic.

Honduras

The second largest of the Central American countries, Honduras has a cool, mountainous interior and a long, warm Caribbean coastline. Travel is easy, enjoyable and inexpensive. Among the better-known Honduran attractions are the spectacular Mayan ruins at Copán near the Guatemalan border, with its pyramids, temples and intricately carved stelae (standing stone monuments). Also popular with travelers are the Bay Islands (Islas de la Bahía), the idyllic Caribbean islands just off the north coast. Roatán is the most popular and probably most beautiful of the islands, but the smaller island, Utila, also has many aficionados. The coral reefs here are a continuation of the barrier reef off Belize, which is the second-largest barrier reef in the world. These reefs are excellent for diving and snorkeling.

Several of the Caribbean beach towns, most notably Omoa and Tela, have fine beaches, plenty of coconut palms, wonderful seafood, lots of opportunities for walking and interesting places to visit nearby. The capital city, Tegucigalpa, in the central highlands, is surrounded by pine-clad mountains and has a temperate climate.

Less well known are the national parks and nature reserves. La Tigra, just a few kilometers from the capital, is a lush, cool cloud forest. Several other cloud forests are also protected in national parks – La Muralla, Celaque, Cusuco and Pico Bonito are the most accessible for visitors.

Coastal and marine parks protect coastlands, wetlands and lagoons inhabited by manatees and other wildlife and birdlife. The Río Plátano Biosphere Reserve, a world heritage site, protects a pristine river system flowing through tropical rain forest in the Mosquitia region, one of Central America's large wilderness areas.

Highlights

- Visit the magnificent Mayan ruins at Copán
- Explore the cloud forests, coastal wetlands and lagoons and other beautiful natural features protected in Honduras' numerous national parks and nature reserves
- Dive and snorkel in the Bay Islands
- Enjoy the museums in Tegucigalpa, San Pedro Sula and Copán

Facts about Honduras

HISTORY
Pre-Columbian History

The remnants of one of the earliest examples of civilization in Honduras can be seen at the ruins of Copán in western Honduras, near the border with Guatemala. The ruins indicate settlement there beginning at least around 1200 BC. At its highest glory, during the classical period from around AD 250 to 900, Copán was the most southeasterly of the great Mayan city-states that extended from present-day western Honduras and El Salvador throughout Guatemala and Belize and well up into Mexico.

Western Honduras, including the large, fertile Sula and Comayagua Valleys, was a heavily settled, rich agricultural area in pre-Columbian times. It was also an area of intense contact and trade between the Mesoamerican zone, which extended halfway up into Mexico, and the Central American zone, which extended south from Honduras and El Salvador throughout Central America and into Colombia, Venezuela and Ecuador.

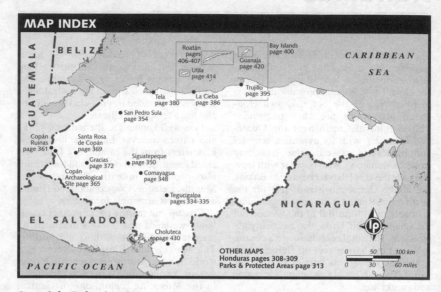

Spanish Colonization

Columbus, on his fourth and final voyage, sailed from Jamaica and first landed on American mainland soil near present-day Trujillo, Honduras, on August 14, 1502. He named the place Honduras ('depths' in Spanish) after the deep waters off the north coast.

The town of Trujillo, founded in 1525 near where Columbus landed, was the first capital of the Spanish colony of Honduras, but the Spanish soon became more interested in colonizing the cooler highlands of the interior. In 1537, Comayagua, in the geographical center of Honduras, replaced Trujillo as the capital. Comayagua remained the political and religious center of Honduras for over three centuries (until the capital was transferred to its present location at Tegucigalpa in 1880).

In the early days, fighting in the colony was commonplace. Various Spaniards tried to assert their individual power, with some Spanish infighting even as Indians resisted the Spanish invaders. By some accounts, the Indians nearly succeeded in driving the Spanish from their land. In 1537, Lempira, a chief of the Lenca tribe, led 30,000 Indians against the Spanish. He was treacherously murdered at a peace talk arranged with the Spanish in 1538, and by the following year the Indian resistance

was largely crushed. Today Lempira is a national hero, and the currency of Honduras bears his name.

British Settlement

While the Spanish focused their settlement in the interior of Honduras, the British settled the Bay Islands and the Caribbean coast. The British were attracted to the Honduran Caribbean coast, as they were to Belize, by stands of mahogany and other hardwoods. The British brought black settlers from Jamaica and other West Indian islands to work in the timber industry.

On April 12, 1797, following an uprising on the Caribbean island of St Vincent, the British brought a large group of black people from that island and dumped them off at Port Royal on the island of Roatán. These people, the ancestors of Honduras' Garífuna people, survived, prospered and multiplied; they crossed over to the mainland and eventually fanned out in small fishing settlements all along the Honduran coast.

Following an appeal to the British by chiefs of the Miskito Indians, a British protectorate was declared over the entire Mosquitia region, extending from Honduras far into Nicaragua.

Spain was never happy with the British control of the coast, but the British ruled the territory until 1859, when they relinquished the lands to Honduras. The British influence is still evident today, especially on the Bay Islands, where English is the principal language.

Independence

After independence from Spain in 1821, Honduras was briefly part of independent Mexico and then a member of the Central American Federation. The Honduran liberal hero General Francisco Morazán was elected president of the United Provinces in 1830. The union was short-lived, however, largely due to continuing conflicts between liberals and conservatives, and Honduras declared its independence as a separate nation on November 5, 1838.

The liberal and conservative factions continued to wrestle for power in Honduras after independence. Power alternated between the two factions, and Honduras was ruled by a succession of civilian governments and military regimes. (The country's constitution would be rewritten 17 times in the years between 1821 and 1982.) Government has officially been by popular election, but Honduras has experienced literally hundreds of coups, rebellions, power seizures, electoral 'irregularities' and other manipulations of power since achieving independence from Spain.

The 'Banana Republic'

In the 1850s, William Walker, an American, attempted to take over Central America and in fact did gain control of Nicaragua for a time. He made his final ill-fated attack on Central America at Trujillo. His campaign ended in defeat, and he was captured and executed by firing squad. Where William Walker failed to gain control of Honduras for the USA, free enterprise succeeded. Around the end of the 19th century, US traders took an interest in bananas produced on the fertile north coast of Honduras, just a short sail from the southern USA. With the development of refrigeration the banana industry boomed, and new markets opened up in the USA and Europe. US entrepreneurs who wanted to buy land for growing bananas were offered generous incentives to do so by a succession of Honduran governments. The three major companies were the Vaccaro brothers (later to become Standard Fruit), which operated around La Ceiba; the Cuyamel Fruit Company near the Río Cuyamel and Tela; and after 1912, United Fruit, to the east, which by 1929 had swallowed up Cuyamel. The three companies owned a large part of northern Honduras, and by 1918, 75% of all Honduran banana lands were held by US companies.

Bananas provided 11% of Honduras' exports in 1892, 42% in 1903 and 66% in 1913. The economic success of the banana industry made the banana companies extremely powerful within Honduras, with policy and politicians controlled by banana company interests. Cuyamel Fruit Company allied itself with the Liberal Party, United Fruit with the National Party, and the rivalries between banana companies shaped Honduran politics.

Honduras failed to develop an indigenous landholding elite, unlike Guatemala, El Salvador and Nicaragua. Instead the economy and politics of the country became controlled by US banana interests.

20th-Century Politics

Along with economic involvement came increasing influence from the USA in various sectors of Honduran affairs, especially in the military. In 1911 and 1912, when it appeared that the US banana interests were threatened by Honduran political developments, US president William Howard Taft sent the Marines into Honduras to 'protect US investments.'

During the worldwide economic depression of the 1930s, in the midst of civil unrest, General Tiburcio Carías Andino was elected president, establishing a virtual dictatorship that lasted from 1932 until 1949.

In 1954, the USA and Honduras signed a military pact that promised military training and equipment to Honduras in return for unlimited US access to raw materials should the need arise. In 1957, a new constitution put the military officially out of the control of civilian government, and the military then entered politics as an independent power.

Various elections and coups have come and gone, but whether the government has been civilian or military, the military has maintained much control. In 1963, Colonel Osvaldo López Arrellano led a military

HONDURAS

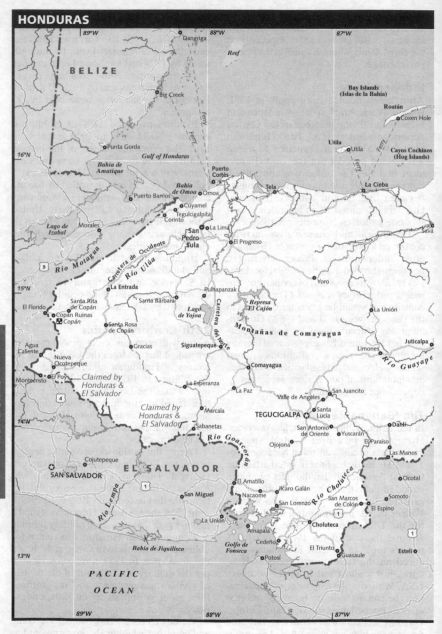

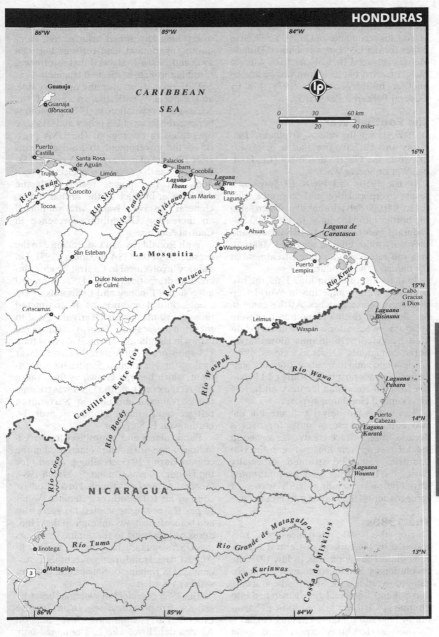

coup and ruled as president until he was forced to resign because of a scandal involving his acceptance of US$1.25 million in bribes from a US company, United Brands. He was replaced by Colonel Juan Alberto Melgar Castro, but he in turn was ousted by another military coup in 1978, led by General Policarpo Paz García.

The Football War

In 1969, during the rule of Arrellano, Honduras and El Salvador had a brief war known as the Guerra de Fútbol (the Football War or Soccer War).

In the 1950s and 1960s, El Salvador's severe overpopulation and economic crisis led to 300,000 Salvadorans illegally crossing the border into Honduras. In 1969, 500 Salvadorans were sent back to El Salvador, and they were followed by a wave of 15,000 Salvadoran refugees alleging mistreatment at the hands of the Hondurans.

In the midst of this, in June 1969, the two countries were competing in World Cup qualifying soccer matches. At the game in San Salvador, visiting Honduran fans were attacked by Salvadorans. Honduras retaliated by evicting thousands more Salvadoran immigrants. El Salvador closed off its borders, and amid more allegations of abuse against Salvadorans in Honduras, El Salvador invaded Honduran territory on July 14 and bombed Honduran airports.

The war lasted only 100 hours, but the two countries were at odds for over a decade, until a peace treaty was signed in 1980. However, relations between the two countries remained strained, especially during the 1980s, when El Salvador erupted into civil war, sending fresh waves of refugees across the border into Honduras.

The 1980s

During the 1980s, Honduras was surrounded by the turmoil of Central American political developments. In July 1979, the revolutionary Sandinista movement in Nicaragua overthrew the Somoza dictatorship, and Somoza's national guardsmen fled into Honduras. Civil war broke out in El Salvador in 1980 and continued in Guatemala.

Though Honduras experienced some unrest, Honduran politics were far more conservative. This can be attributed largely to the strong US influence, which helped direct the course of Honduran politics and created a strong Honduran military capable of crushing any armed insurrection. Honduran government land reforms between 1962 and 1980 also showed that reform was possible through established channels.

With revolutions erupting on every side, and especially with the success of the Nicaraguan revolution in 1979, Honduras became the focus of US policy and strategic operations in the region. The USA pressured the government to hold elections after 17 years of military rule. A civilian, Dr Roberto Suazo Córdova, was elected president, but real power rested with the commander-in-chief of the armed forces, General Gustavo Álvarez, who supported an increasing US military presence in Central America.

With Ronald Reagan's ascendance to the presidency of the USA in January 1981, US military involvement in Central America increased dramatically. The USA funneled huge sums of money and thousands of US troops into Honduras as it conducted provocative maneuvers clearly designed to threaten Nicaragua. Nicaraguan refugee camps in Honduras were used as bases for a US-sponsored undeclared covert war against the Nicaraguan Sandinista government, which became known as the Contra war. At the same time the USA was training the Salvadoran military at Salvadoran refugee camps inside Honduras, near the border with El Salvador.

Public alarm and opposition to the US militarization of Honduras increased in the country during 1983, creating problems for the Honduran government. In March 1984, General Álvarez was toppled in a bloodless coup by his fellow officers. General Walter López Reyes was appointed his successor, and before long it was announced that Honduras was planning to reexamine its role as the USA's military base in the region. In August, the Honduran government suspended US training of Salvadoran military within its borders.

The 1985 presidential election, beset by serious irregularities, was won by the Liberal Party candidate José Simeón Azcona del Hoyo, who had obtained only 27% of the votes. Rafael Leonardo Callejas Romero of the National Party, who had obtained 42% of the votes, lost.

Despite growing disquiet in Washington after the revelations of the Iran-Contra Affair in 1986, the Contra war escalated. In 1988 around 12,000 Contras operated from Honduras. Public anger in Honduras increased – anti-US demonstrations drew 60,000 demonstrators in Tegucigalpa and 40,000 in San Pedro Sula – forcing the Honduran government to declare a state of emergency. Finally, in November 1988, the Honduran government refused to sign a new military agreement with the USA, and President Azcona said the Contras would have to leave Honduras. With the election of Violeta Chamorro as president of Nicaragua in 1990, the Contra war ended and the Contras were finally out of Honduras.

The 1990s

Elections in 1989 ushered in Rafael Leonardo Callejas Romero of the National Party, who had lost in 1985, to the presidency in Honduras; he won 51% of the votes and assumed office in January 1990. Early that year, the new administration instituted a severe economic austerity program, which provoked widespread alarm, unrest and protest.

Callejas had promised to keep the *lempira* stable, but instead, once he was in office, the lempira was devalued. During his four years in office, the lempira's value went from about two lempiras to the US dollar to eight to the dollar. Prices in lempiras rose dramatically to keep pace with the US dollar, but salaries did not rise, so the Honduran people became continuously poorer and poorer – a trend that continues today. Callejas kept assuring the public that the economy had to be tightened temporarily due to the national debt and that soon everything would be better.

In the elections of November 1993, the National Party candidate was convincingly beaten by Carlos Roberto Reina Idiaquez of the center-right Liberal Party, who campaigned on a platform of moral reform, promising to attack government corruption and reform state institutions, including the judicial system and the military. Reina took office in January 1994.

When Reina became president, he assumed control of an economically suffering country. After he took office, the lempira continued to devalue: By 1996 it had slid past 12 lempiras to the US dollar and was heading for 13. Prices in lempiras kept rising to keep pace with the dollar, while salaries continued to be frozen, and the country as a whole was extremely concerned about where it would all end. At press time the US dollar was worth around 14.5 lempiras.

On January 27, 1998, Carlos Roberto Flores Facusse took office as Honduras' fifth democratically elected president. A member of the Liberal Party, like his predecessors, he was elected with a 10% margin over his nearest rival – National Party

In the Eye of the Hurricane

On October 27, 1998, an enormous tropical storm, which had formed over a period of only a few days in the Caribbean Sea, smashed into settlements along the north coast of Honduras and the offshore Bay Islands. Hurricane Mitch, as the storm came to be known, caused untold damage within a nightmarish 48-hour period. The hurricane was the largest known by this impoverished country since 1974, when Hurricane Fifi roared in. Reaching wind speeds of up to 180mph and classed, at its peak, as a Category 5 storm, Mitch caught most people unprepared for the intensity of the battering it delivered. The devastation was all the more savage because, instead of lessening in intensity once it hit the coast, the vicious winds continued to wreak havoc as far inland as Tegucigalpa. Here floodwaters from the swollen Choluteca River reached the second floor of some city buildings. Worst hit was the island of Guanaja, which the hurricane hit directly, and towns along the north coast such as Trujillo, La Ceiba and Tela also took a severe battering. In all, an estimated 10,000 people throughout Honduras and neighboring countries lost their lives to Mitch, and many more were made homeless. Today, the devastation is less evident, but broken palm trees, rutted roads and rivers still without proper bridges are visible reminders that another hurricane could strike at any time, without warning and without discrimination.

nominee Nora de Melgar – in elections that were considered fair and clean. He has, to date, instigated a program of reform and modernization of the economy. This task was compromised by the arrival of devastating Hurricane Mitch in November of that same year. The hurricane caused considerable damage to Honduras' already fragile economy, causing an estimated US$3 billion in damages. Honduras' gross domestic product (GDP) shrank by 2% the following year.

By mid-2000 much of the infrastructure damaged in Mitch had been repaired or was still being repaired and the all-important tourism industry had almost recovered fully. Much welcome foreign aid helped to a large degree in the country's recovery, but at the same time increased the nation's foreign debt to unwelcome heights.

GEOGRAPHY

Honduras is the second-largest country in Central America (after Nicaragua), with an area of 112,090 sq km. This includes 288 sq km of territory formerly disputed with El Salvador and added to Honduras in the September 1992 judgment of the International Court of Justice. Honduras is bordered on the north by the Caribbean Sea, on the west by Guatemala, on the south by El Salvador and the Golfo de Fonseca, and on the east and southeast by Nicaragua. The Caribbean coast is 644km long, but the Pacific Coast on the Golfo de Fonseca is only 124km. Honduras possesses many islands, including the Bay Islands and Swan Islands in the Caribbean and a number of other islands in the Golfo de Fonseca.

Honduras is a mountainous country; around 65% to 80% of the total land area is composed of rugged mountains ranging from 300m to 2850m high, with many highland valleys. Lowlands exist only along both coasts and in several river valleys.

CLIMATE

The mountainous interior is much cooler than the coastal lowlands. Tegucigalpa, at an elevation of 975m, has a temperate climate, with maximum/minimum temperatures varying from 25/14°C in January to 30/18°C in May. The coastal lowlands are much warmer and more humid year-round, the Pacific coastal plain near the Golfo de

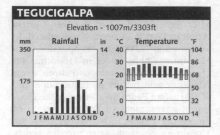

Fonseca being hot indeed. December and January are the coolest months.

The rainfall also varies in different parts of the country. The rainy season runs from around May to October. On the Pacific side and in the interior, this means a relatively dry season from around November to April. However, the amount of rain and when it falls varies considerably from year to year.

On the Caribbean coast, it rains year-round, but the wettest months are from September to January or February. During this time floods can occur on the north coast, impeding travel and occasionally causing severe damage (400 people died in floods in November 1993).

Hurricane season is June to November. See the Hurricane Season section in the Facts about Central America chapter for more information.

ECOLOGY & ENVIRONMENT

Deforestation is a problem in Honduras; it proceeds at a rate of 300,000 hectares (3000 sq km) a year. At this rate, the country could become completely deforested within 20 years. However, in Honduras, as in other Central American countries, conservationists and a number of ecology-minded organizations are working to halt this trend, set aside protected areas and increase public awareness of conservation. Honduras now has 40 protected areas – mainly national parks and wildlife refuges – and more areas have been proposed for reserves.

Still, conservation is a tense subject, since in many places the wishes of conservationists and government decrees seeking to protect natural areas come into direct conflict with a growing population that wants to settle and plant virgin lands. Conflicts have also arisen between conservationists and moneyed interests that want to fund large-scale tourist developments, as happened at Punta Sal near Tela, resulting in the 1995 murder of conservation activist Jeannette Kawas. The area was finally declared a national park in her honor.

FLORA & FAUNA

Honduras is rich in both flora and fauna. The country has a number of different life zones at various elevations, ranging from low-elevation tropical rain forests to high-altitude cloud forests, with each zone comprising its own complex system of flora and fauna. The dominant vegetation of the mountainous interior of the country is pine-and-oak forest.

Some of Honduras' most interesting animals are becoming endangered, primarily due to loss of habitat. The national bird, the *guara roja* or scarlet macaw, is on the endangered species list, as are some species of *loras* (parrots), manatees, jaguars and others. Nevertheless, there's still plenty of wildlife to see in Honduras, especially in the national parks, wildlife reserves and other protected areas, where wildlife abounds. As more areas become protected, populations of depleted species may be saved from early extinction.

Honduras is excellent for birding, and bird watching is becoming a popular activity. See the Bird Watching section in Facts for the Visitor later in this chapter for hints on where to see birds.

Parks & Protected Areas

Honduras has 40 protected areas, including 20 national parks and a number of important wildlife refuges, biological reserves, an anthropological reserve and a biosphere reserve. The following is a list of some of the more important national parks, which are discussed at length later in this chapter:

Celaque is an elevated plateau, with four peaks over 2800m above sea level, including the highest peak in Honduras, at 2827m above sea level. The park is made up of cloud forest, with great biodiversity. Access is easy, as the ranger station is only 7.5km east of Gracias by 4WD vehicle; other access is through Belén Gualcho, Ocotepeque.

Cusuco is cloud forest, with a large population of quetzals. It has interpretive trails, guides and a visitors center. The highest peak is Cerro Jilinco,

PARKS & PROTECTED AREAS

NATIONAL PARKS
5 Cusuco
6 Punta Sal
10 Pico Bonito
11 Capiro-Calentura
13 Cerro Azul
14 Santa Bárbara
15 Cerro Azul Meambar
16 Pico Pijol
17 Montaña de Yoro
18 La Muralla
19 Sierra de Agalta
22 Montecristo-Trifinio
24 Celaque
25 Montaña de Comayagua
26 La Tigra
27 Patuca

OTHER
1 Barbareta
2 Sandy Bay/West End
3 Turtle Harbour
4 Cayos Cochinos (Hog Islands)
7 Lancetilla Botanical Gardens
8 Punta Izopo
9 Cuero y Salado
12 Laguna de Guaimoreto
20 Río Plátano
21 Laguna de Caratasca
23 Guisayote
28 Lagunas de Invierno

at 2242m above sea level. The park can be reached all year with 4WD vehicle; it's 25km northeast by gravel road from to the park ranger station, a two-hour drive from San Pedro Sula. The office is in San Pedro Sula.

La Muralla is a cloud forest park, with a visitors center, marked trails and campsites. The park has very diverse wildlife, including a large quetzal population. It's 15km north of La Unión, 200km from Tegucigalpa, with easy access by road.

Pico Bonito is a very diverse park, with six Holdridge life zones represented, including lowland tropical rain forest, pine and pine-oak forest and cloud forest at higher elevations. The park has high biodiversity and many waterfalls. Montaña de Yoro is the highest peak, at 2436m. The park is 5km south of La Ceiba, but access to the interior is difficult due to steep slopes. The best access is along Río Cangrejal or Río Zacate, where there's easy access to a waterfall; access is also good along Río Bonito and Río Santo.

Punta Sal has various habitats, including mangrove forests and swamps, a small tropical forest, offshore reefs, several coves and the rocky point itself. The park has a large number of migratory and coastal birds. The office is in Tela, and the easiest access is by tour from Tela.

La Tigra, near Tegucigalpa, this protects a beautiful cloud forest, as well as the city's water supply. It was Honduras' first national park, established in 1980. It has interpretive trails and visitors centers at both entrances, and dormitories, houses and camping are available. Access is from Tegucigalpa.

Some of the more accessible national marine parks include the following:

Cayos Cochinos (Hog Islands) are a protected reserve and proposed national marine park. Thirteen cays, two of them large, with beautiful coral reefs, well-preserved forests and fishing villages make up the reserve. Access is by motorized canoe from the town of Nueva Armenia, one hour's drive east of La Ceiba.

Sandy Bay/West End, on northwestern end of Roatán in the Bay Islands, has coral reefs and easy access and is visited frequently by divers.

Turtle Harbour, on the northwestern side of Utila in the Bay Islands, is another marine reserve and proposed national marine park visited frequently by divers.

Some of the more important wildlife refuges include the following:

Cuero y Salado is the largest manatee reserve in Central America. It's 30km west of La Ceiba.

Access is easy, but arrange a visit in advance with the Fucsa (Fundación Cuero y Salado) office, in La Ceiba. Boats are available.

Laguna de Guaimoreto has mangrove forest and high coastal biodiversity, especially coastal birds. It's 5km east of Trujillo by road.

Punta Izopo is made up of tropical wet forest, mangrove forest and wetlands. It has many migratory and coastal birds, a beautiful rocky point and white-sand beaches. It's 16km by highway and dirt road from Tela to Triunfo de la Cruz, a one-hour walk on beach or a one-hour canoe ride. Tours also come from Tela.

Some of the more important biological reserves include the following:

Guisayote is a highly disturbed (by roads and other human intrusions) cloud forest. Sixteen kilometers north on paved road from Nueva Ocotepeque, the park has the easiest access of any Honduras cloud forest. The highest paved road in Honduras passes through this reserve.

Lancetilla Botanical Gardens is a botanical garden with over 700 plant species and 365 species of bird. It has the largest collection of Asiatic fruit trees in the Western Hemisphere.

Honduras has one biosphere reserve:

Río Plátano (5251 sq km) is a world heritage site and the first biosphere reserve in Central America. Large and mostly well-preserved, it consists of lowland tropical rain forest, with remarkable natural, archaeological and cultural resources. Access to the southern zone is through Olancho by road beyond Dulce Nombre de Culmí; access to the northern zone is by plane from La Ceiba to Palacios and then by motorized canoe to other destinations. The central zone is very remote and seeing it requires long expeditions.

Honduras also has an anthropological reserve:

Tawahka, a tropical rain forest, is the last homeland of the Tawahka (Sumo) people, one of the most threatened indigenous groups in Honduras. The landscape is beautiful, and the people live closely with the land, but all of it is threatened by uncontrolled colonization. Access is by plane to Wampusirpi then by boat to Krausirpi and Krautara.

GOVERNMENT & POLITICS

The government of Honduras is a constitutional democracy with three tiers: executive, legislative and judicial. All citizens over 18 can vote. The president is elected by popular vote to a four-year term that cannot be renewed. The legislature consists of the National Congress, with 132 elected legislators. The judiciary consists of the Supreme Court, appointed by the president, which controls all branches of the lower courts, including the appointment of justices.

Honduras is divided into 18 departments, each with a governor appointed by the president. The departments are divided into municipalities, which are further divided into *aldeas* or villages. Rural areas have *caserios,* which are subdivisions of aldeas. Each locality can elect its own council, legal representative and mayor.

Honduras has several political parties, but the two major ones are the Partido Liberal and the Partido Nacional.

ECONOMY

Honduras is a poor country, with one of the lowest gross national products (GNPs) in Latin America; only Haiti and Nicaragua are poorer. It's estimated that 50% of the population lives below the poverty level. Close to 30% of the workforce is unemployed or underemployed; the country has a large foreign debt; and it imports more than it exports. Inflation in 1993 was around 12%, double that of 1992 but much lower than in 1991. By 1996, inflation had soared to around 30% but had dropped to around 14% again by 2000.

Agriculture employs 60% of the workforce and provides 80% of the country's exports. The main products are corn, bananas, coffee, cattle, dry beans, sugarcane, cotton, sorghum and tobacco. Other main industries, listed here in descending order based on percentage of GNP, are forestry, hunting, fishing, manufacturing, trade, services, transportation and communications. Tourism is an increasingly important sector of the economy.

In 2000, coffee provided the largest export income, followed by bananas. The European Union was the biggest purchaser of Honduran products (around 65%, twice as much as the USA), particularly of bananas. The European banana quota introduced in the 1990s is bound to affect Honduras adversely. Exports of nontraditional Honduran exports such as melon and shrimp are expanding, but the nation remains vulnerable to the volatile prices of bananas and coffee.

The USA was traditionally Honduras' principal trading partner, and economic ties remain very strong. Two giant US companies, United Fruit and Standard Fruit, hold a large part of the country's agricultural land and grow the majority of the banana crop. Aid from the USA also forms a large part of the Honduran economy, though it's much less than in the 1980s.

POPULATION & PEOPLE

The population of Honduras grew by about 3.4% per annum in the 1980s. Estimates put the total population at around 6,249,598 by July 2000. Honduras is experiencing the most rapid urbanization in Central America: The urban population was 44% in 1990, but the percentage of the population in cities is expected to hit 59% in 2010.

About 90% of the population are mestizo, a mixture of Spanish and Indian. Another 7% or so are pure Indians living in pockets around the country, each group with its own language and culture; 2% are black; and 1% are white.

The Tolupanes (also called Jicaque or Xicaque) live in a swath of territory sweeping from San Pedro Sula southeast to Montaña de la Flor. The Lenca live in southwestern Honduras; they hold markets in the towns of La Esperanza, Marcala and Tutule. Chorti live near the Guatemala border, about a quarter of the way up from the border's southern point.

Miskito live in the Mosquitia region in northeastern Honduras, on the coast and along the Río Coco, which forms the border between Honduras and Nicaragua. A dark people, Miskito are believed to be a mixed race of indigenous Indians and black Caribs, themselves a mixture of Africans and Carib Indians.

Pech (also called Paya) live in the interior river regions of the Mosquitia. Tawahka (also called Sumo) live in the interior of the Mosquitia in the area around the Río Patuca.

Garífuna are a mixture of African, Carib and Arawak Indians and make up around 2.5% of the population of Honduras. They were transported by the British to the island of Roatán from the Caribbean island of St Vincent in 1797. Today, Garífuna

HONDURAS

settlements are found all along the northern coast of Honduras.

Other black people on the north coast and in the Bay Islands are descendants of Jamaicans and other West Indians who came to Honduras with the British or to work on the banana plantations. They often speak Caribbean-accented English in addition to Spanish and are Protestant rather than Catholic.

EDUCATION
Primary education is free and compulsory, beginning at seven years of age and lasting for six years. Beyond that, education is not compulsory; secondary education, beginning at age 13, lasts for up to five years, with one cycle of three years and a second cycle of two years. Around 93% of children of primary school age are enrolled; the figure drops to only around 30% in the secondary age group. Adult literacy is around 72.7%. Honduras has six universities, including the Universidad Nacional Autónoma de Honduras (UNAH) in Tegucigalpa.

ARTS
Honduras is not as renowned for its arts as are nearby Guatemala and El Salvador, but it does have some interesting art forms. Wood carving is a popular art; many items are made of carved wood, including intricately carved (sometimes also painted) boxes and chests. Other popular arts include basketry, embroidery and textile arts, leather goods and ceramics; the Lencas of western Honduras are especially known for their ceramics.

Honduras' most characteristic style of painting depicts scenes of typical mountain villages, with cobblestone lanes winding among houses with white adobe walls and red tile roofs. This style of painting was made internationally famous by Honduran artist José Antonio Velásquez (1906–1983) and is still very popular today.

Theater is popular in the larger cities; plays are presented at the Teatro Nacional in Tegucigalpa and at the Centro Cultural Sampedrano (San Pedro Cultural Center) in San Pedro Sula. The national symphony is based in Tegucigalpa.

Dance is another popular art form. The Garífuna people of the north coast are especially known for their distinctive dance; if you get a chance to see the Ballet Folklórico Garífuna perform, don't miss it. The troupe is based in Tegucigalpa. The Garífuna's style of popular dance, the *punta*, is easy to see if you travel on the north coast.

The Garífuna also have their own distinctive music, musical instruments and handicrafts. Their traditional band is a combination of three large drums, a turtle shell (hit with a stick) and a large conch shell (blown into). The band usually plays accompanied by song.

SOCIETY & CONDUCT
Honduras is becoming a modern society; you won't see Indians dressed in traditional costume, as in Guatemala or Panama. Also see Society & Conduct in the Facts about Central America chapter.

Facts for the Visitor

SUGGESTED ITINERARIES
With a week on your hands you would be advised to fly into San Pedro Sula and head directly for Copán Ruinas, 177km to the southwest of the city. Spend at least three nights here visiting the famous Mayan ruins and perhaps engaging in some horseback riding in the countryside. Head back to San Pedro Sula and fly to either Roatán for beach life and diving or Utila, if you are just keen on diving.

With an extra week at your disposal, you can make your way to Tegucigalpa from Copán Ruinas via the colonial towns of Santa Rosa de Copán and Gracias in Honduras' outback West. From the nation's capital head for the north coast with stops at say, Omoa and Tela with its vibrant Garífuna community before choosing a Bay Island (Utila, Roatán or Guanaja) for swimming and diving.

PLANNING
When to Go
The most popular time to visit Honduras, especially the beach areas on the Caribbean coast and the Bay Islands, is from around February to April, during the North American winter but after the Honduran rainy season. This is an excellent time to visit, but

outside this time you will find fewer tourists and prices may be lower.

As elsewhere in Central America, the rainy season brings extra humidity to the lowlands, making it feel especially hot.

Maps

The Instituto Geográfico Nacional in Tegucigalpa publishes a tourist map with the country of Honduras on one side and city maps of Tegucigalpa, San Pedro Sula, La Ceiba and the Bay Islands on the other side. In Tegucigalpa the map is sold at the post office, at the Instituto Hondureño de Turismo (Honduran Institute of Tourism) office and at the institute itself. Tourist maps are also available from some gas stations for about the same price.

The Instituto Geográfico Nacional also publishes excellent color topographical and regional maps, which are available at their office (see the Maps part of the Tegucigalpa section later in this chapter).

ITM publishes an excellent 1:750,000 color map of Honduras, showing the geographical features (mountains, lowlands, rivers), cities, towns and national parks and reserves. It also publishes an excellent 1:1,800,000 color map of Central America as a whole. See Maps in the Regional Facts for the Visitor chapter for information on where to obtain ITM publications.

What to Bring

On the north coast, the Bay Islands and in the Mosquitia, be sure to bring insect repellent against the mosquitoes and sand flies. A mosquito net is also a good idea. Be sure to bring antimalaria pills, as malaria is endemic to the region (chloroquine is easily available in most Honduran cities). Since tap water is not safe to drink, carry your own means of purifying water. Bottled water is usually easy to find, but you don't want to be caught short. See What to Bring in the Regional Facts for the Visitor chapter.

TOURIST OFFICES
Local Tourist Offices

The office of the Instituto Hondureño de Turismo is in Tegucigalpa. They used to have more offices in other parts of the country; since those were closed, various other businesses connected with tourism are filling the gap. We've mentioned these places in the various towns in the Information section.

Tourist Offices Abroad

The Instituto Hondureño de Turismo has an office in the USA at 299 Alhambra Circle, Suite 510, Coral Gables, FL 33134 (☎ 305-461 0600, 305-461 0601, fax 305-461 0602).

VISAS & DOCUMENTS

Citizens of most western European countries, Australia, Canada, Japan, New Zealand, the UK and the USA can stay for up to 30 days without a visa if they are visiting as tourists. Upon arrival you will fill out a short immigration form, the yellow portion of which will be stapled into your passport. Do not lose it! This form will be collected when you depart, and it will be stamped if you seek an extension to your stay. Once inside Honduras, you can apply for an extension every 30 days, for a total stay of up to six months. After that you may have to leave the country for three days and reenter.

To extend your stay, take your passport to any immigration office and ask for a *prórroga*; you'll have to fill out a form and pay around US$1 to US$2, depending on your nationality. Practically every city and town in Honduras has an immigration office *(migración)* where you can do this. Most are open Monday to Friday 8:30 am to 4:30 pm; some may have additional hours on Saturday mornings.

The regulations seem to change quite frequently, so check the current situation at a Honduran embassy or consulate before you arrive at the border.

CUSTOMS

Customs regulations allow the usual 200 cigarettes, 100 cigars or half a kilogram of tobacco, and 2 liters of alcohol to be brought into the country. Archaeological items, wildlife and religious relics may not be removed from Honduras.

MONEY
Currency

The unit of currency is the lempira. Notes are of one, two, five, 10, 20, 50, 100 and 500 lempiras.

There are 100 *centavos* in a lempira; coins are of one, two, five, 10, 20 and 50 centavos.

HONDURAS

Centavos are virtually worthless, except for occasional use on urban bus routes.

Exchange Rates

These were the currency exchange rates at the time of publication:

country	unit		lempira
Australia	A$1	=	L8.9
Canada	C$1	=	L10.04
El Salvador	¢1	=	L1.73
Euro	€1	=	L14.18
Germany	DM1	=	L7.25
Guatemala	Q1	=	L1.93
New Zealand	NZ$1	=	L7.03
UK	UK£1	=	L23.30
United States	US$1	=	L14.72

Exchanging Money

The US dollar is the only foreign currency that is easily exchanged in Honduras; away from the borders you will even find it difficult to change the currencies of Guatemala, El Salvador or Nicaragua. Lloyd's Bank in Tegucigalpa also changes the Canadian dollar, the British pound sterling and the German Deutschmark.

Cash Cash usually receives the same rate as traveler's checks. Other than US dollar the only other cash you can easily convert is the British pound, though it may be easier to convert other European currencies in Tegucigalpa and San Pedro Sula.

Traveler's Checks Traveler's checks can be changed in all of the major towns. Not all banks will cash traveler's checks, though the major ones such as Banco Atlántida and Banco de Occidente will. They will usually take a commission, and you will need your passport to cash the checks.

ATMs ATMs are few and far between in Honduras, and where they do exist, they tend to be either inside banks or in the immediate vicinity of banks. One or two hotels in Tegucigalpa and San Pedro Sula also have them.

Credit Cards Cash advances on Visa are available at Credomatic offices and at Atlántida and Bancresa banks. Some other banks will take MasterCard, which is less

widely accepted than Visa. Check the credit-card exchange rate, as it can be unfavorable compared to the rate for cash or traveler's checks. There's no transaction charge on the Honduran end for Visa or MasterCard cash advances.

Visa cards and American Express cards can be used widely throughout the country, including major supermarkets, retail stores, hotels and car rental agencies.

International Transfers Money transfers are usually best handled through a respectable outfit like Western Union. Branch offices can usually be found in major towns and cities.

Costs & Inflation

In recent years, inflation in Honduras has been running at about 14.5% a year, with prices in lempiras rising accordingly. This has been tough for local people: While prices in lempiras have soared, salaries have remained the same, and many people have slid further into poverty. The minimum legal wage in Honduras, which many people earn, is about US$95 per month.

Prices given in US dollars are somewhat more stable. A few places, hotels for example, are starting to calculate their prices in terms of US dollars and translate them into lempiras at the daily rate, keeping the US dollar price steady. Prices for items like food and drink vary considerably depending on where you eat and drink. A basic meal at a street *comedor* can cost as little as US$1.50. At a beachside restaurant on Roatán, an average menu dish will be in the region of US$8 or more. A beer from a *pulpería* in Gracias may cost you US$0.55, but the same beer at a waterside bar in Utila will cost US$1.40.

In this guide we're giving all prices in US dollars, based on current prices during research time, but do bear in mind that these prices will change during the life of this book, so plan accordingly once you have worked out by how much prices may differ.

Black Market There is no real black market as such, and the advantages gained from changing money with street dealers have more to do with convenience than gain. The black-market rate for cash and traveler's checks is only slightly higher than – or even the same as – the official exchange rate.

Money Changers Money changers are commonly found at both Tegucigalpa and San Pedro Sula airports, as well as in the city center of both places. There is nothing sinister about changing money with them, but exchange only the money you wish to change and keep the rest well hidden from observers' sight.

Security

Keep your money in a secure place on your person and never put your wallet or purse in a back pocket. Avoid fanny packs – they scream 'tourist' – and choose instead a loose bag that fits around your neck and under your clothing. Money belts are also good but are a pain to get money out of in the street, and your money and documents have a tendency to get soggy if you wear the belt for any length of time in the muggy heat.

Do not carry cameras or wear expensive watches in risky downtown areas of major cities. Dress down, dress simply and walk and act in a businesslike manner, like a local, if you wish to avoid drawing attention to yourself. Do not walk on remote beaches alone in the evening.

Many shops and businesses and nearly all banks sport armed guards. Even supermarkets have one or two armed security guards. Do not be alarmed: incidents are rare because the security is there.

Costs

The cost of living in Honduras *can* be cheap for foreigners, though it is certainly not cheap for the average Honduran. If you stay at backpacker hostels, eat at street *comedores* (snack bars) and travel on 'chicken run' buses you can survive on less than US$15 a day. If you desire a modicum of comfort in accommodations, eat at established restaurants and use air-conditioned buses to get around the country, your daily costs can easily jump to a minimum of US$50 per day.

Tipping & Bargaining

Most Hondurans do not tip. In places with a lot of tourist and foreign influence, tipping is more common, from a little loose change up to 10% of the bill.

As for bargaining, watch to see what the local people are doing. Bargaining is not as common in Honduras as in some other places in Central America. Usually you should bargain at open markets and on the streets; prices at indoor stores are fixed. Even taxis often have a fixed rate, which you can sometimes bargain down a lempira or two.

Taxes & Refunds

A 12% sales tax will be added to the price of just about every transaction you make in Honduras, including hotels and restaurants. An additional 4% tourism tax is added to all hotel bills as well.

POST & COMMUNICATIONS

Post offices in most Honduran towns are open Monday to Friday 8 am to 5 pm (often with a couple of hours off for lunch between noon and 2 pm) and on Saturday 8 am to noon. In large cities they may be open longer hours.

Postal Rates

The postal service in Honduras is not the best, but these are the rates and theoretical delivery times:

To the USA	US$0.70	ten to 14 days
To Europe	US$0.84	14 days
To Australia	US$0.92	22 days

Despite the apparent long delivery times for postal items, Honducor, the Honduran postal service, is considered to be at least reliable in comparison to other developing nations. Travelers from Nicaragua or Guatemala are advised to hang on to their postcards until they reach Honduras and mail them from here.

Sending & Receiving Mail

You can receive poste restante (general delivery) mail, known in Latin America as *lista de correos,* at any post office; have it directed to you at '(Name), Lista de Correos, (town and department), República de Honduras, Central America.'

HONDURAS

Honduras is notorious for problems with receiving incoming mail from the USA, since Hondurans working in the USA send money to their families back home, and a certain amount of the mail arriving from that country never reaches its destination. Other times there can be inexplicable delays. Most mail, however, does manage to get through. It seems to have a better chance if there is no way it could even *appear* to have money in it; aerograms (which can't contain enclosures) or postcards are two such options. Outgoing post is more reliable.

Express Mail Service (EMS) courier service offers a faster and safer alternative to the regular mail system for both incoming and outgoing mail, though it's more expensive. EMS has offices in every city and major town in Honduras, usually beside or near the post office. In Tegucigalpa, Aerocasillas offers a direct connection to the US mail system.

Several other courier services also operate in Honduras, including Urgente Express and DHL.

Telephone & Fax

International telephone, telegraph, telex and fax services are offered at almost all Hondutel offices in every city and town. Hondutel offices are open 24 hours every day in Tegucigalpa, San Pedro Sula and La Ceiba. In smaller towns, they're open 7 am until around 9 or 10 pm daily. Fax services are available during more limited hours, usually 8 am to 4 pm Monday to Friday.

International calls are still comparatively expensive. At press time, a minimum three-minute call costs US$6.50 to Europe, US$6.50 to Australia, US$4.58 to the USA and US$2 to Costa Rica, but prices are slowly falling. International calls to the USA and Central America are about 20% cheaper between 7 pm and 7 am daily. There are no discount rates for phone calls to other countries.

An interesting quirk in the Honduran phone system is that you can send a fax much cheaper than you can phone; sending a one-page fax costs US$2 to the UK and Europe, US$2.50 to Australia and US$1.45 to the USA or Canada. You can also receive faxes at Hondutel offices; the cost is US$0.08 per page. However, it has been reported that Hondutel frequently loses incoming faxes. Consider using a free Internet fax service for those vital messages and pick up and print your fax at a more secure Internet cafe. Check out www.efax.com for further details.

You can find public telephones outside Hondutel offices and often in public places such as parks and on busy corners. You need a 20 centavo coin for a three-minute local call or a 50 centavo coin for a six-minute local call; keep putting in coins, or you'll get cut off when your time is up. These are the only two coins the public phones will accept. Domestic long-distance calls cost two lempiras. If you still have time remaining when your call is finished, you can push the 'A' button on the phone, receive a dial tone and make another call: Two local calls can be made with a 20 centavo coin or five local calls with a 50 centavo coin. If you hang up, the phone takes your coin, and your time is up.

Most public phones now accept phone cards as well as coins. Phone cards valued at 50 lempiras and 100 lempiras are sold at Hondutel offices.

To reach a domestic long distance operator, dial 191; for local directory assistance, dial 192; for directory assistance for government telephone numbers, dial 193; for an international operator, dial 197. A direct connection to an operator in the USA is available by dialing ☎ 800 0121 for Sprint, ☎ 800 0122 for MCI WorldCom and ☎ 800 0123 for AT&T.

Mobile phones brought from countries using the GSM 900/1800 protocol, which include Europe, Australia, New Zealand and many Asian countries, will not work in Honduras, which uses the North American GSM 1900 protocol.

The country code when calling Honduras from abroad is 504. When calling Honduras from abroad note that there are no specific area codes in the country: Thus the format is the international access code plus the Honduran country code plus the local number.

Email & Internet Access

A growing number of Internet centers or cafes are springing up all around the country. All major tourist centers will have at least one or two places where you can access the Internet. Access on the mainland is generally very good to excellent and is priced moderately. Access from an Internet cafe in Tegucigalpa or La Ceiba costs between US$4 and US$5 an hour, and from Roatán or Utila, access costs as much as US$15 an hour. Access from the Bay Islands can be patchy – thanks to generally poor phone connections to the mainland.

If you are in Honduras for any length of time and have your own laptop PC or palm-held computer, it may be worthwhile to take out a temporary account with one of the main Internet service providers (ISPs) in Honduras. Two good ISPs are Globalnet and Hondutel. (See Internet Resources for details). With a Hondutel account you do *not* pay long distance connect time from a private or hotel phone line (worth noting if you plan to access the Net over long distances – but try convincing a hotel of that valuable piece of information).

INTERNET RESOURCES

A quick search on any decent Internet search engine will also bring you a host of hits on Honduras. Try the following links that we have dug up for you. They will inevitably lead you to other interesting sites.

www.marrder.com/htw – the official site of Honduras This Week, Honduras' only English-language newspaper.

www.in-honduras.com – a comprehensive page of links and information on Honduras.

www.hondurastips.honduras.com – the Web site of the free tourist magazine Honduras tips.

www.tela-honduras.com – the Web page of the Tela Chamber of Tourism, with excellent links and information on things to do on the north coast.

www.bayislands.com – the Web site of the Coconut Telegraph, the Bay Islands magazine dealing mainly with Roatán.

www.roatanonline.com – a comprehensive guide to Roatán, from property investment to tourism.

www.globalnet.hn and **www.hondutel.hn** – the two Web sites of Honduras' major Internet service providers. While the basic data is in Spanish you should be able to get in touch with both ISPs in English if you are thinking about opening a local account.

BOOKS
Lonely Planet

Lonely Planet's *Latin American Spanish phrasebook* will go a long way to helping

you get around Honduras linguistically, and the *Guatemala, Belize & Yucatan* guide is an excellent detailed companion to the book you are holding, if you are planning to explore farther afield.

Scuba divers and snorkelers might want to pick up a copy of the diving guide from the comprehensive LP Pisces series, *Diving & Snorkeling Roatan & Honduras' Bay Islands*. This excellent diver's companion covers some of the best diving sites in the Caribbean off Honduras' north coast.

Guidebooks

An excellent book with an ecotourism twist is *Honduras Adventures in Nature,* by James D Gollin and Ron Mader. This guidebook looks at travel to the country with a view to preserving its natural resources and enjoying its considerable nature reserves. It's great on background and full of interesting asides, but a bit thin regarding places to stay and eat.

Live Well in Honduras: How to Relocate, Retire, and Increase Your Standard of Living, by Frank Ford, is aimed at people considering settlement or retirement in Honduras and covers everything from money matters to legal issues.

History & Politics

The following books should be useful for understanding social, political and economic developments in Honduras. *Honduras: The Making of a Banana Republic,* by Alison Acker, is an informative and gripping account of what made Honduras become a 'banana republic.'

Honduras: State for Sale, by Richard Lapper, is now out of print but is worth tracking down. *Honduras: Portrait of a Captive Nation* (Praeger Publishers), edited by Nancy Peckenham & Annie Street, is a series of essays offering readers a complete overview of Honduras' fascinating and complex history, and a timely and well-informed picture of the present situation. This title may be out of print.

Reinterpreting the Banana Republic, by Darío A Euraque, explores the relations of Honduras' various regions, agriculture, and the development of the Honduran government from 1870 to 1972.

The United States in Honduras, by Jack R Binns, a former ambassador to Honduras, is

HONDURAS

a comprehensive look at US involvement during the turbulent Contra-racked years of 1980 to 1981. *Don't Be Afraid Gringo,* by Elvia Alvarado, a poignant look at the oppressed life of the Honduran peasant, is worth a read for a look at the other side of life in this often difficult country.

Fiction

On a lighter note, Guillermo Yuscarán (William Lewis, in his former incarnation as a professor of Hispanic studies in Santa Barbara, California), who writes mostly in English and now lives near Tegucigalpa, is one of Honduras' most wonderful painters and writers. His books, all in paperback, include (in chronological order) *Blue Pariah, Points of Light: Honduran Short Stories, Conociendo a la Gente Garífuna* (The Garífuna Story), *Beyond Honduras: Tales of Tela, Trujillo and Other Places, El Gran Hotel, Northcoast Honduras: Tropical Karma and Other Stories* and *Gringos in Honduras: The Good, the Bad, and the Ugly. Velasquez: The Man and His Art,* also by Yuscarán, is the first and only biography to be published on the life of Honduras' most acclaimed primitivist painter.

All of Guillermo Yuscarán's books are available in Tegucigalpa at Shakespeare & Co, Metromedia, and the gift shop of the Hotel Honduras Maya; at the Luces del Norte restaurant and the Hotel Tela in Tela; and at the Casi Todo bookshops on Roatán.

Photography Books

Vicente Murphy is an amazing photographer, probably the best photographer in Honduras. If you're in Honduras for long, you'll start to notice his photographs everywhere. *Honduras Al Natural,* an annual weekly agenda/datebook, is published every year, with a Vicente Murphy photograph for each week. The photos are exquisite color prints, mostly of Honduran wildlife and outdoor scenes.

You can find the datebooks for sale in many places, including Metromedia in Tegucigalpa. Or you could order one from Ecoarte, Apdo Postal 163, Tela, Atlántida, Honduras. *Honduras* is a coffee table book of brilliant photos and text, with photos by Vicente Murphy and David W Beyl.

NEWSPAPERS & MAGAZINES

Honduras has five daily newspapers. *El Heraldo* and *La Tribuna* are published in Tegucigalpa, *La Prensa, El Tiempo* and *El Nuevo Día* in San Pedro Sula. *El Tiempo* and *La Prensa* are on the Web.

Honduras This Week is a very useful weekly English-language newspaper published in Tegucigalpa. It comes out every Saturday and can be found in major hotels and English-language bookshops in Tegucigalpa, San Pedro Sula, La Ceiba, Roatán and Utila. You can read the paper online at www.marrder.com/htw/ or get in touch with the publishers regarding subscriptions at Apdo Postal 1312, Tegucigalpa, MDC, Honduras (☎ 239 0285, fax 232 8818, hontweek@ hondutel.hn).

Honduras Tips is a bilingual (English/ Spanish) and biannual magazine indispensable for anyone traveling in Honduras. It gives lots of information on things to see and do and places to stay and eat, with maps and photos. The magazine is available free in Honduras and can be found in many places frequented by travelers. Or you can contact the publisher at Apdo Postal 2699, San Pedro Sula, Honduras (☎ 552 5860, fax 552 9557, hondurastips@honduras.com). Visit their Web site at www.hondurastips .honduras.com for further details.

RADIO & TV

Over 150 radio stations and six television stations broadcast in Honduras. Movies and news in English come from the USA by cable TV. Many bars in tourist areas will have direct transmissions of major sporting events in the USA.

VIDEO SYSTEMS

Honduras uses the American standard NTSC video system. Any videos bought in Honduras can only be played back on NTSC or multisystem video systems.

PHOTOGRAPHY & VIDEO

Color film costs around US$2.80/3.50 for 24/36 exposures; color slide film costs US$4.20/5.85 for 24/36 exposures. Kodak, Fuji and Agfa film are available, as is video film. Larger cities have one-hour photo processing shops. In general, it's better to wait for processing until you get to a more developed country. See Photography & Video in the Regional Facts for the Visitor chapter for more information.

LAUNDRY

Most hotels have somewhere you can wash your clothes; ask to use the *lavadero*. Expensive hotels usually have an expensive laundry service, but in cheaper places you can offer chamber staff a few lempiras to wash your clothes for you. Laundries in most towns offer a wash, dry and fold for around US$4 for 10lb of laundry.

TOILETS

Public toilets are few and far between in Honduras, so you are advised to take your 'rest breaks' at your hotel or at convenient restaurants. Regular western-style toilets are the norm.

HEALTH

No vaccinations are required to enter Honduras, but you should be vaccinated against typhoid and tetanus.

Tap water is not safe to drink in Honduras. Most restaurants and hotels provide purified drinking water, but be sure it really is purified before you drink it, and of course, watch out for ice cubes. Bottled purified water is available almost everywhere, but it's a good idea to carry your own method of purifying water, just in case. Raw salads (lettuce, cabbage) are suspect if they have been washed with unpurified water.

Digestive problems such as stomachache and diarrhea are likely, especially if you eat from street stands; pharmacies are well equipped with medicines and can often cure whatever ails you. In larger towns there is usually a *farmacia de turno* open at all hours.

Malaria-carrying mosquitoes are a problem on the north coast, the Bay Islands and in the aptly named Mosquitia; be sure to follow a regimen of antimalarial medication. Dengue fever is also present. Since both are carried by mosquitoes, it's best to avoid being bitten (see the Health section in the Regional Facts for the Visitor chapter).

Over 1000 cases of cholera (resulting in 49 deaths) have been diagnosed in Honduras since an epidemic broke out in October 1991. The most recent cases were reported in Tegucigalpa and in the departments of Choluteca, Cortés, Santa Bárbara,

Valle and El Paraíso. Be vigilant about the hygiene standards of what you eat and drink everywhere in Honduras. Don't rely on a cholera vaccination to protect you, as it is ineffective.

In early 1997, Honduran health officials announced that 65,000 people in the country were in the late stages of Chagas' disease and would die from the parasitic illness during the next few years. They estimated that around 300,000 people (around 5% of the population) were infected with some stage of the disease (see Chagas' Disease in the Health section in the Regional Facts for the Visitor chapter).

Over 8200 cases of AIDS have been diagnosed in Honduras since 1985, and the World Health Organization estimates that almost 2% of adult Hondurans have the HIV virus. The north coast and San Pedro Sula have the highest concentration of AIDS cases. Apart from abstinence, the most effective preventative is to practice safe sex using condoms.

WOMEN TRAVELERS

Honduras is basically a good country for women travelers. As elsewhere, you'll probably attract less attention if you dress modestly. On the Bay Islands, where lots of beachgoing foreign tourists tend to congregate, standards of modesty in dress are much more relaxed, though topless bathing is most definitely frowned upon. (The suggestions in the Women Travelers section of the Regional Facts for the Visitor chapter apply throughout Honduras.)

Cases of rape against foreign tourists have been reported in a few places along the north coast. As peaceful and idyllic as the coast looks – and usually is – be wary of going to isolated stretches of beach alone, and don't walk on the beach at night. The issue of rape takes on an added dimension here, when you consider the high rate of AIDS.

GAY & LESBIAN TRAVELERS

Honduras is very much 'in the closet,' so it's refreshing to find Grupo Prisma (☎/fax 232 6058, prisma@sdnhon.org.hn), PO Box 4590, Tegucigalpa, Honduras, a gay and lesbian group in Tegucigalpa that holds BBQs, parties, camping trips and other gay and lesbian get-togethers. They also hold

HONDURAS

discussions and consciousness-raising meetings for women (Wednesday evenings) and men (Thursday evenings), in which many different topics are discussed.

Colectivo Violeta (☎ 237 6398, violeta@hondudata.com) is an organization that caters mainly to transvestites. Contact them directly for address details.

DISABLED TRAVELERS

Disabled travelers will find few facilities designed for their convenience, other than in more expensive hotels and resorts. Wheelchair-bound visitors will find it difficult to get around major cities like Tegucigalpa or San Pedro Sula, because of street congestion and generally poor road or sidewalk surfaces. Even smaller villages are difficult to negotiate, since the road surfaces are either unpaved or made up of cobblestones. Toilets for the disabled are virtually nonexistent, other than in four- or five-star hotels.

SENIOR TRAVELERS

Senior travelers will find things a little rough at times, particularly with transportation. Planes to and from the Bay Islands, for example, are small and cramped and may be difficult to board and exit. Other than the luxury buses between major cities, bus travel can be cramped and uncomfortable. The humid and hot climate in the north may be difficult for some travelers not used to tropical weather.

TRAVEL WITH CHILDREN

Although children can adapt to travel more easily than most of us, there are few children-specific activities in Honduras to keep them occupied. Larger hotels usually have swimming pools, and the safest beach swimming is probably at West Bay, on Roatán in the Bay Islands. Horse riding at Copán Ruinas is one possibility for older children, and children of all ages may enjoy organized jungle walks, such as those offered at the Lodge at Pico Bonito (see the Northern Honduras section of this chapter).

DANGERS & ANNOYANCES
Crime

Crime is on the increase in Honduras. Tegucigalpa and San Pedro Sula are the worst places for street crime; walking downtown in the daytime and early evening is fine, but locals will tell you it's dangerous to walk in the downtown streets past 9 pm or so. The 'better' districts are much safer. Comayagüela is worse than the rest of Tegucigalpa: Don't *ever* walk through the market area of Comayagüela after dark.

In general, small towns are much safer than the big cities. Watch yourself on the north coast, though, as several travelers have reported muggings, thefts and rapes there. It's not safe to walk on the north coast beaches after dark, and you should use caution even in daytime, especially in isolated places.

Nevertheless, there's no need to be overly paranoid about visiting Honduras. Using normal caution, most travelers travel in Honduras easily with no problems. See the Regional Facts for the Visitor chapter for helpful hints on safe traveling. You can avoid most problems before they occur just by the way you conduct yourself.

Critters

Malaria-carrying mosquitoes and biting sand flies on the north coast, the Bay Islands and the Mosquitia are definitely an annoyance, and along with unpurified water can be the greatest threat to your well-being. Also watch out for jellyfish and stingrays, which are present on both the Caribbean and Pacific Coasts.

If you go hiking through wild places, beware of poisonous snakes, especially the *barba amarilla* or fer-de-lance *(Bothrops asper)*; the coral snake is also present. Crocodiles and caimans live in the waterways of the Mosquitia, in addition to the peaceful manatee and much other wildlife. Honduras also has scorpions (not lethal), black widow spiders, wasps and other stinging insects. You probably will never see a dangerous animal, but do be aware that they exist. If you encounter a potentially dangerous animal or poisonous insect, above all stay calm and remove yourself as quietly and quickly from the danger as possible. If you are bitten or stung, see Cuts, Bites & Stings in the Regional Facts for the Visitor chapter.

BUSINESS HOURS

Business hours are normally 9 am to noon and 2 to 4:30 or 5 pm Monday to Friday, and often also 9 am to noon Saturday. Bank hours are generally 9 am to 3 pm Monday to Friday, usually with additional Saturday morning hours. Most government offices are open 8:30 am to 4:30 pm Monday to Friday, sometimes with a lunch break that may last from noon to 1 or 2 pm.

For post office and Hondutel hours, see the Post & Communications section earlier in this chapter.

PUBLIC HOLIDAYS & SPECIAL EVENTS

As you will find elsewhere in Central America, just about every city, town and village in Honduras has a patron saint and celebrates an annual festival or fair in the days around their saint's day. Some are big events, attracting crowds from far and wide.

One such fair is the Carnaval at La Ceiba, celebrated during the third week in May; the third Saturday is the biggest day, with parades, costumes, music and celebrations in the streets.

The fair at San Pedro Sula, which is held in the last week of June, is another popular celebration. The fairs at Tela (June 13), Trujillo (June 24), Danlí (last weekend in August) and Copán Ruinas (March 15 to 20) are also good, and there are many others.

The fair for the Virgen de Suyapa, patron saint of Honduras, is celebrated in Suyapa, near Tegucigalpa, from around February 2 to 11; February 3 is actually the saint's day. The services and festivities bring pilgrims and celebrants from all over Central America.

The Feria Centroamericana de Turismo y Artesanía (FECATAI), an all-Central-American international tourism and crafts fair, is held every year from December 6 to 16 in Tegucigalpa. Another annual all-Honduras artisans' and cultural fair is held in the town of Copán Ruinas from December 15 to 21.

If you get a chance to attend a fair or presentation of any of Honduras' indigenous groups, do so. Several Garífuna music and dance troupes give presentations throughout the country, including the excellent Ballet Folklórico Garífuna. April 12, the anniversary of the arrival of the Garífuna people in Honduras in 1797, is a joyful

occasion celebrated in all the Garífuna communities.

Honduran public holidays include:

New Year's Day	January 1
Day of the Americas	April 14
Holy Week	Thursday, Friday and Saturday before Easter Sunday
Labor Day	May 1
Independence Day	September 15
Francisco Morazán Day	October 3
Columbus Day	October 12
Army Day	October 21
Christmas Day	December 25

ACTIVITIES
Walking & Hiking

National parks are great places for hiking. Several of the parks offer well-maintained trails, visitors centers for information and orientation and even guides. Going with a guide is a good idea, as you will learn more about the environment (cloud forest, tropical rain forest or whatever) and see more wildlife than if you go on your own. The park trails usually vary in length and level of difficulty. See the Parks & Protected Areas section earlier in this chapter for more details.

Along the north coast are unlimited opportunities for beach walks along white sandy beaches fringed by coconut palms and other tropical vegetation – it's said you could walk along the beach just about all the way along the entire coast, with just a few detours for rocky outcrops and points. Or you can have some fine times just walking in local areas, wherever you happen to be.

Diving & Snorkeling

The Bay Islands are great for diving and snorkeling. The reef is magnificent, and many diving operators offer diving or snorkeling tours, as well as diving certification courses. Utila is said to be the cheapest place in the world to get diving certification. Snorkeling gear can be rented or bought, or you can bring your own – Utila boasts many excellent places where you can just jump off the beach into the water and enjoy great snorkeling, and it doesn't cost a cent if you have your own gear.

HONDURAS

Kayaking, Canoeing & Small-Boat Tours

Small-boat tours are a good way to visit a number of national parks, wildlife refuges and nature reserves along the north coast, including Punta Sal and the Laguna de los Micos near Tela, Cuero y Salado near La Ceiba and the Laguna de Guaimoreto near Trujillo. Kayaking tours of the Refugio Punta Izopo near Tela let you slip silently among the canals of the mangrove forests, where you'll see plenty of wildlife.

The Mosquitia region, though more remote, is easily accessible by airplane and offers many more possibilities for canoe and boat trips on rivers and lagoons. The Mosquitia is a pristine, unspoiled area with plenty of wildlife.

Canoeing and 'soft rafting' is available on the Río Copán from the Hotel Hacienda de Jaral, an ecotourism resort near Copán Ruinas.

White-Water Rafting

White-water rafting is popular on the Río Cangrejal near La Ceiba; several companies in La Ceiba offer rafting tours on this river. One of these, Ríos Honduras, also offers rafting trips farther afield on the Río Sico in Olancho.

Bird Watching

Birding is becoming a popular activity in Honduras, where you can spot hundreds of species. It's difficult to name the most impressive birds, as there are so many; quetzals, toucans, scarlet macaws (Honduras' national bird) and brilliant green and green-and-yellow parrots are all contenders. National parks and wildlife refuges have been established to protect many environments good for seeing birds – for example, cloud forests, tropical rain forests and coastal wetlands. Quetzals are seen in many of the cloud forest national parks, including Cusuco, Celaque, La Muralla and La Tigra.

Migratory birds are present along the north coast during the North American winter months from November to February. Good places for birders to see them are in the lagoons, national parks and wildlife refuges, and at Lancetilla Botanical Gardens near Tela. Each December 14 and 15 the Audubon Society does a 24-hour bird count at Lancetilla and other places nearby. The record for Lancetilla so far is 365 species counted in a 24-hour period. You can participate in the bird count if you like; further information is available at the Foundation for the Protection of Lancetilla, Punta Sal and Texiguat (Prolansate) office in Tela (☎ 448 2042). Even at other times of year when the migratory birds are not around, Lancetilla is still an excellent spot for birding.

The Lago de Yojoa is another excellent place for birding – 375 species have been counted here so far. The Lodge at Pico Bonito (see the Northern Honduras section) offers a couple of viewing platforms for its guests, as well as guided tours of the Pico Bonito jungle.

In some places you can go on birdwatching tours. A couple of companies in Copán Ruinas offer birding tours in the local area and farther afield, such as to the Lago de Yojoa. Also near Copán Ruinas at the Hacienda de Jaral is a lagoon visited by thousands of migratory herons from November to May.

Horseback Riding

Horseback riding is a popular activity at Copán Ruinas. Horseback tours are also conducted into Parque Nacional Pico Bonito near La Ceiba and at West End on Roatán Island.

LANGUAGE COURSES

Honduras is not as famous for language courses as Guatemala, but you can take Spanish language courses at a few schools around the country; see the Copán Ruinas and La Ceiba sections.

ACCOMMODATIONS
Camping

Camping is not a vacation activity followed by many Hondurans and organized campsites such as those in the USA or Europe do not exist. Camping, however, is allowed in several national parks and reserves and is mentioned in the text wherever it is relevant. Water and toilets or latrines are usually available, and sometimes even kitchens, but generally you should bring your own gear. In Gracias, the Restaurante Guancascos rents camping gear for camping in the Parque Nacional Celaque.

Hostels

There is no network of HI hostels in Honduras as such, but there is a large network of backpacker and traveler-friendly hostels throughout the country, though these tend to be concentrated in major traveler destinations like Copán Ruinas, Utila, Roatán, Omoa and Tela. Naturally, some places are better than others, and many are truly excellent. Prices range from US$5 for a basic bed in a dorm to US$20 for a basic private room.

B&Bs

Unlike the B&B establishments in the UK, which offer cheap alternatives to often expensive hotel accommodations, B&Bs in Honduras can often be as expensive as hotels. These establishments are usually not homes that have been converted to B&Bs. They are usually designed and built as mini hotels that offer a high standard of accommodations, with private facilities, TV, air-conditioning and telephone. Naturally, breakfast is part of the deal. Prices start at around US$35 and reach an upper limit of about US$65. They are often advertised in local publications like *Honduras Tips* or *Honduras This Week* (see the Internet Resources section earlier in this chapter for site details) and are often contactable via email.

Hotels

Economical accommodations are available just about everywhere in Honduras. The cheapest places have a shared cold bath; these can range from truly awful to fine places that would pass the white glove test. If you're traveling on a shoestring and going to the cheapest places, it's a good idea to get into the habit of asking to see a room and its facilities before you pay for it.

When you ask the price for a room, low-priced hotels will usually give you the price *including* the tax, and higher-priced hotels will usually give the price *without* the tax, meaning you'll have to pay a 12% service tax plus a further tourist tax.

A room with a private cold bath is a step up. Hot showers are considered a luxury by Central American standards, and you will pay more for them. You'll also often pay more for two beds than for one – you can save money by sleeping with a friend.

The same goes for air-conditioning, only more so. Air conditioners are expensive to operate, and electricity costs have gone sky high, so it's an expensive luxury – but available almost everywhere. In general, you can get whatever level of comfort you're willing to pay for almost everywhere in Honduras.

Many hotels have restaurants, which are pleasant and handy for that first cup of coffee or early morning breakfast before you head out into the world. Many of the more expensive hotels also have bars or restaurant/bar combinations.

'Theme hotels' are relatively new to Honduras. They include diving resorts in the Bay Islands and at least one new 'eco-tourism ranch' on the mainland, notably the Lodge at Pico Bonito in the buffer zone of the Pico Bonito National Park.

FOOD

The *plato típico* (typical meal) in Honduras usually includes beans, rice, tortillas, chicken or meat (on the coast often fried fish), fried bananas, potatoes or yucca, cream, cheese, and a cabbage and tomato salad, or some combination of these. Most restaurants have the plato típico on the menu, and it's usually the cheapest and most filling meal, whether for breakfast, lunch or dinner.

Most places also offer a *comida corrida* or *plato del día* at lunchtime – usually a good, large, cheap meal.

Baleadas – white flour tortillas folded over a filling of refried beans, cream and crumbled cheese – are a good, filling snack. They usually cost around US$0.75; a couple of them with a soft drink for another US$0.75 will fill you up for a while. Another good snack is *tortillas con quesillo,* two crisp fried corn tortillas with melted white cheese between them. *Enchiladas* in Honduras are not what they are in Mexico. They are what a *tostada* is in Mexico: a crisp fried tortilla topped with spicy meat, which is then topped with salad and crumbled cheese. Fried chicken is another common favorite in Honduras.

On the coasts and around the Lago de Yojoa, the fish is fresh and cheap. Commonly it's fried, though you can find it prepared in other ways, too. On the Caribbean coast, fish and seafood soups, including *sopa de caracol* (conch soup made with coconut), are delicious, as is fish cooked in coconut sauce. Another specialty of the Caribbean coast, *pan de coco* (coconut bread), is also very tasty.

On Sundays, *sopa de mondongo* (tripe soup) is eaten everywhere in Honduras. As in some other parts of the world, it's said to be the best medicine for a hangover.

Tajaditas, crispy fried banana chips, are sold in little bags on the streets, as are sliced green mangos sprinkled with a mixture of salt and cumin. But be cautious about the cleanliness of preparation of any type of food on the street, especially hot foods, which should be *kept* hot, or you could end up with amoebas.

DRINKS

Soft drinks are everywhere, with all the usual brands in evidence, plus a few local flavors, including banana. *Licuados* (milk blended with fruit) are always good; watch out for added ice, which might not have been purified. *Frescos,* fruit drinks blended with water and sugar, are a favorite everywhere, but remember they could have been made with unpurified water, and the ice could be suspect, too. Many places do use purified water to make frescos and ice; ask before you drink.

Four brands of beer are made in Honduras: Salva Vida, Port Royal Export, Nacional and Imperial. Various brands of *aguardiente* rum are also made in Honduras, including Ron Flor de Caña, Ron Plata and the national favorite, Yuscarán. Yuscarán, fondly called the 'aguardiente nacional de Honduras,' is used as the base for drinks typical of various parts of the country. In the Copán department, *timochenko* is Yuscarán mixed with aromatic plants of the region. On the north coast, the Garífuna people mix Yuscarán with various aromatic and marine plants, resulting in *guífiti.* In the town of Yuscarán, where the aguardiente is made, it is mixed with fermented mamey juice to make *mameyazo.*

Cave, a coffee liqueur, is made in San Juancito, a small village near Tegucigalpa. You can find it in markets and even at the airport, in bottles decorated with woven fibers.

ENTERTAINMENT

There's plenty of nightlife in Honduras – concentrated in Tegucigalpa and San Pedro

Sula, of course. La Ceiba also has plenty to do in the evening, with a number of discos and a couple of places with traditional Garífuna music groups and dancing. Trujillo also has pleasant nightlife – plus dances on the beach at Cocopando on weekends and a children's dance on Sunday afternoons. In Tela, the Garífuna museum hosts a fun Saturday night party.

You will find cinemas in the big cities and in smaller towns. Some tourist places have video evenings, or even a mini surround-sound theater to show movies.

Most towns have somewhere pleasant to go for a drink in the evening. Often they are sociable places where you can meet both locals and other travelers. Places that come to mind are the Tunkul Bar in Copán Ruinas, the Expatriates Bar & Grill in La Ceiba and a whole bunch of places in Roatán and Utila.

SPECTATOR SPORTS

As elsewhere in Latin America, in Honduras, *fútbol* (soccer) is the national passion. The professional soccer season runs from around September to March; the National Stadium in Tegucigalpa and the large stadium in San Pedro Sula are the venues for the biggest professional games. But soccer is much more than a professional sport. It's played in every city, town and village in the country, year-round. You can always see a soccer game, especially on Sunday afternoons.

Basketbol (basketball) and *beisbol* (baseball) are up-and-coming spectator sports; boxing is also popular. Cockfights have been banned in Tegucigalpa, but they are still held in San Pedro Sula and Choluteca.

SHOPPING

Honduras produces a number of typical handicrafts, including wood carving and wooden musical instruments, woven *junco* basketry, embroidery and textile arts, leather goods and ceramics. Colorful woven baskets and hats are the specialty at Santa Bárbara. Brightly painted ceramics (especially depicting roosters) are for sale along the road from El Amatillo to Nacaome. Ceramics are also a specialty of the Lenca people of western Honduras.

Paintings of typical mountain villages, with cobblestone lanes winding among houses with white adobe walls and red tile roofs, can be found in many places, including Tegucigalpa, Valle de Angeles and San Pedro Sula. For more details about this style of painting, see Arts in the Facts about Honduras section. Excellent replicas of Mayan carvings can be bought very cheaply in Copán Ruinas. See that section for details. All these things can be found not only in the places they're made, but also in Tegucigalpa and San Pedro Sula.

Tobacco is grown in Honduras, and Honduran cigars are said to be some of the finest. Danlí has several cigar factories where you can buy good hand-rolled cigars. In Santa Rosa de Copán, the La Flor de Copán cigar factory also makes excellent hand-rolled cigars. Ask for a free tour to see the cigars being made.

Getting There & Away

AIR
Frequent direct flights connect Honduras with all the other Central American capitals and many destinations in North America, the Caribbean, South America and Europe. Most international flights arrive and depart from the airports at Tegucigalpa and San Pedro Sula; there are also direct flights between the USA and Roatán, coming from Houston and Miami.

All the Central American airlines, as well as American, Continental, Iberia and KLM, have regular flights serving Honduras. American Airlines' flights connect through Miami; Continental's flights connect through Houston. TACA and Lacsa offer flights connecting Honduras with Houston (US$503 to US$588), Los Angeles (US$670 to US$755), Miami (US$504 to US$589), New Orleans (US$506 to US$591), New York (US$647 to US$679), San Francisco (US$667 to US$698) and Washington, DC (US$647 to US$679), in addition to all the other Central American capitals. These ballpark prices are for roundtrip tickets from the USA – including all taxes – and range from low-season midweek fares to high-season weekend fares.

The lowest possible fare between Amsterdam and Tegucigalpa is with Martinair,

which charges US$585 roundtrip for a ticket valid up to three months. Iberia charges US$671 for the same route.

From Madrid to San Pedro Sula, Air France has a very good deal for US$497 roundtrip, with a three month maximum stay. For the same route, Iberia and American charge US$671.

If you fly out of Honduras, you must pay a hefty US$25 departure tax at the airport.

LAND
Border Crossings
Most Honduran border crossings are open 7 am to 5 pm daily. Everyone leaving or entering is usually charged around US$5. In theory, this is an overtime payment only applicable between noon and 2 pm and after noon on Saturday; in practice it's charged almost any time. It's best to pay up unless the amount demanded is excessive.

To Guatemala, the main crossings are at El Florido (Guatemala), Agua Caliente and El Corinto. To El Salvador, the main crossings are El Poy and El Amatillo; there is also a crossing at Sabanetas, south of La Esperanza. The crossings to Nicaragua are at, Las Manos (Honduras), El Espino and Guasaule (Nicaragua).

Bus
Frequent buses serve all of these border crossings. Most buses do not cross the border, meaning you have to cross on foot and pick up another bus on the other side. The exceptions are international buses. Tica Bus (☎ 220 0590, fax 220 0579), on 16a Calle between 5a and 6a Avenidas in Comayagüela, just across the river from Tegucigalpa, has a bus leaving the capital every morning at 9 am, heading for Panama City via Managua and San José. The bus arrives in Managua (US$20) at 6 pm that same afternoon and continues on the following day to San José leaving at 6 am and arriving at 4 pm (US$35 from Tegucigalpa). On the third day it departs San José for Panama City (US$60 from Tegucigalpa) at 10 pm and arrives at 4 pm on the fourth day.

Another international bus is the King Quality (☎ 225 5414, fax 225 2600), which operates one bus daily between Tegucigalpa and San Salvador; see the Tegucigalpa section for details. If you're traveling between Tegucigalpa and Guatemala City by bus, King Quality makes it possible to make the trip all in one day (you change buses at the station in San Salvador). On Tica Bus, this trip takes two days: one day from Tegucigalpa or Guatemala City to San Salvador, an overnight there, and then one more day on the bus.

Car & Motorcycle

If you're driving, there are a lot of fees, paperwork and red tape involved in bringing a car into Honduras; you will be issued a special permit for your vehicle that must be renewed at regular intervals. Still, it can be done, and you will quite often see Texas- or California-registered vehicles in the most unlikely places.

You need full, clear title on the vehicle and a valid driver's license from your country of origin. An international driver's permit is not required. Generally, your passport will be endorsed with a notation of the vehicle, requiring you to take the vehicle with you when you leave Honduras or pay the import duty.

Normally, customs will issue a 90-day permit that can be renewed for another 90 days. After that, you are forced to take the car out of the country and must wait 72 hours before reentering the country. The fee for the permit is about 400 lempiras. If your car has Central American plates, you don't pay anything, and you are issued a CA-4 document, which allows you to drive throughout the country. In this case, your passport will not be stamped with a notation of the vehicle; however, you still need proof of ownership of the vehicle.

SEA

The only regularly scheduled passenger boat service between Honduras and another country is the small boat that runs twice weekly between Puerto Cortés and Dangriga (Belize). Otherwise, it may be possible to arrange passage with cargo or fishing vessels if you pay your way. Don't waste time negotiating with an ordinary crewmember: Speak to the captain. On the Caribbean coast, you can try to find a boat around Puerto Cortés, Tela, La Ceiba, Trujillo or the Bay Islands. The most common international destinations for these boats are Puerto Barrios (Guatemala), Belize, Puerto Cabezas (Nicaragua), Caribbean islands including Grand Cayman and Jamaica, and New Orleans and Miami in the USA. Private yachts occasionally signal ahead their intention to pick up passengers from the Bay Islands for trips to places like Guatemala or Belize, but you will need to check locally.

On the Pacific side, the Golfo de Fonseca is shared by Nicaragua, Honduras and El Salvador, so you may be able to get a ride on boats sailing between the three countries. San Lorenzo is the main Honduran port town in the gulf.

If you arrive or depart from Honduras by sea, be sure to clear your paperwork (entry and exit stamps, and so on) immediately with the nearest immigration office.

Getting Around

AIR

Domestic air routes have proliferated in Honduras recently; it's now easy to fly to any of the Bay Islands from La Ceiba, Tegucigalpa and San Pedro Sula, and to fly among these three major cities. (Flights to the Bay Islands from Tegucigalpa and San

Sample Domestic Airfares	
flight route	fare
La Ceiba–Palacios	US$3
La Ceiba–Puerto Lempira	US$44
La Ceiba–Roatán	US$14
La Ceiba–Trujillo	US$17
La Ceiba–Utila	US$17
San Pedro Sula–Guanaja (via La Ceiba)	US$43
San Pedro Sula–La Ceiba	US$21.50
San Pedro Sula–Roatán (via La Ceiba)	US$35
San Pedro Sula–Tegucigalpa	US$32
San Pedro Sula–Utila (via La Ceiba)	US$43
Tegucigalpa-Guanaja (via La Ceiba)	US$66.50
Tegucigalpa–La Ceiba	US$45
Tegucigalpa-Roatán (via La Ceiba)	US$60
Tegucigalpa-Utila (via La Ceiba)	US$53

Pedro Sula may connect through La Ceiba.) More air routes into the Mosquitia region are also making that remote area more accessible.

TACA offers flights twice daily between Tegucigalpa and San Pedro Sula. Isleña, Sosa and Rollins Air domestic airlines all offer flights connecting the north coast and the Bay Islands for the same rates. Isleña operates flights connecting Tegucigalpa with the north coast and the Bay Islands. Isleña, Sosa and Rollins Air operate flights connecting La Ceiba with the Mosquitia region. Travel agents have information on all flights, or you can phone the airline offices. Local telephone numbers for all the domestic airlines are given in the individual city sections. Rollins Air has offices in La Ceiba, Tegucigalpa, Roatán and Guanaja.

Airfares are especially subject to change, so check current prices; it's quite likely they'll be higher than the fares listed here. When fuel prices fluctuate, so do airfares. Prices in the adjacent table are for one-way fares (double for roundtrip).

BUS

Buses are an easy and cheap way to get around in Honduras, as buses run frequently to most places in the country. The first buses of the day often start very early in the morning; the last bus often departs in the late afternoon. Buses between Tegucigalpa and San Pedro Sula run later.

On major bus routes, you'll often have a choice between taking a *directo* or a regular bus. When this is the case, the regular bus will make stops all along the way, wherever someone wants to get on or off. On a long trip, it can start to feel like it will take you forever to get where you're going. The directo buses cost a few cents more but only make very brief stops at the major towns.

Ejecutivo (executive) or express buses offer faster deluxe service between Tegucigalpa and San Pedro Sula, and now on to La Ceiba, in modern air-conditioned buses with movies and soft drinks. Most other buses are not air conditioned. Ejecutivo buses are generally about 50% more expensive than directo buses.

In addition to long-distance buses operating between cities and towns, buses also operate on shorter routes connecting major towns with the small villages nearby. Often these long-distance buses are old school buses from the USA.

Shuttle Bus

Some private companies offer shuttle services between tourist destinations and major airports. These come and go with the seasons and are listed – where they exist – under the various destination sections. One useful service is that offered by Garífuna Tours (see the Tela section), linking Tela with San Pedro Sula and its airport and Copán Ruinas.

TRAIN

The only passenger train in Honduras is the one that runs twice a week between Puerto Cortés and Tela. See the Puerto Cortés section for details.

CAR & MOTORCYCLE

The main highways are, for the most part, excellent paved roads. Away from the highways, the roads may be paved or unpaved, with their condition ranging from excellent to disastrous. Nonetheless, driving is easy enough, though extra care should be exercised when driving in Tegucigalpa and San Pedro Sula, where the interpretation of the highway code by local drivers tends to be rather 'elastic.'

Rental cars are available in Tegucigalpa, San Pedro Sula, La Ceiba and on Roatán, but they are not cheap.

Motorcycles can be rented in Trujillo and on Roatán.

BICYCLE

In theory there is no reason why cycling should not be a viable option for getting around. In practice, bicycle rental outlets are few and far between, so you are better off bringing you own bike if you plan on any long distance riding. The north coast is flatter and more cyclist-friendly, and any north-south routes will invariably involve steep to gut-busting gradients somewhere along the way.

A bicycle would be useful on the Bay Island of Roatán, though less useful on the other Bay Islands of Guanaja (no roads as such) and Utila (only dirt tracks outside the main settlement). Cycling between San Pedro Sula and Copán Ruinas would be a good route, since traffic is not excessive and gradients not too taxing for a suitably geared machine.

BOAT

A comfortable air-conditioned passenger ferry, the MV *Galaxy II* (☎ 442 0780 in La Ceiba, 445 1795 in Roatán), operates between La Ceiba, Roatán and Utila. The service is convenient, and it's also considerably cheaper than flying. The trip takes about two hours between La Ceiba and Roatán and about an hour between La Ceiba and Utila.

The schedule has changed a bit over the years but seems to have settled into the following simplified one. Do check before you plan to travel.

route	one-way	roundtrip
La Ceiba–Roatán	US$12.40	US$23.20
La Ceiba–Utila	US$10	US$18.80
Roatán-Utila	US$16.60	US$32

The boat leaves Roatán at 7 am daily and arrives in La Ceiba at 9 am. It then leaves La Ceiba at 9:30 am and arrives in Utila at 10:30 am. The boat then reverses course, leaving Utila at 10:45 am and arriving back in La Ceiba at 11:45 am. It leaves La Ceiba at 3 pm and arrives back in the home port of Coxen Hole on Roatán at 4 pm. Note that the ferry terminal on Roatán is likely to be moved from Coxen Hole to French Harbour some time in 2001.

There's always a chance of catching a ride on cargo boats or even fishing boats. Cargo boats operate frequently between the Caribbean coast and the Bay Islands. To try your luck catching a ride, just go down to the docks and ask around to see what boats are going and when. Cargo boats leave Trujillo for Guanaja and the Mosquitia every couple of days or so; you can also find cargo and fishing boats at the docks in Puerto Cortés, La Ceiba and Tela, as well as on all the Bay Islands.

Boats are also a good way to see some of the natural wonders of the Caribbean coast. Small-boat trips are popular for visiting Parque Nacional Punta Sal, the Laguna de los Micos and the Refugio Punta Izopo, all near Tela; the Cuero y Salado Wildlife Refuge near La Ceiba; and the Laguna de Guaimoreto Wildlife Refuge near Trujillo.

Tour companies organize trips to all of these places, or you could probably arrange a boat trip on your own.

In the Mosquitia, where there is just one road, almost all transportation is along the waterways. Boat trips on the Río Plátano, in the Río Plátano Biosphere Reserve, allow you to see a lot of wildlife; boat trips can also be made on other rivers and lagoons in the Mosquitia, and in this remote area, you'll see plenty of wildlife just about everywhere. See the Mosquitia section later in this chapter for more details on boat trips in this area.

Boat trips on the Lago de Yojoa are also a pleasant pastime; it's only a short hop by boat from the hotels on the north shore of the lake to Los Naranjos archaeological site. Bird watching is also excellent on and around the lake.

LOCAL TRANSPORTATION

Bus

Buses service major towns and cities along a network of local and suburban routes. These are often on old school buses from the USA. On most routes, buses run every day very frequently – every five minutes or so – and cost about US$0.05.

Taxi

Numerous taxis operate in most towns in Honduras. Fares can start as low as US$1.30, which may be charged either as a flat rate for the destination or per person; this would be the normal fare for an average ride in a small or medium-size town. You can expect longer journeys in a major city to cost around US$4. In the major cities, *colectivos* (shared taxis) ply a number of prescribed routes, costing around US$1.30 per passenger.

Taxis are not metered in Honduras, so be sure to negotiate the fare before you take off.

Bicycle

Bicycles are the main way that people get around in some of the medium-size towns; Tela, in particular, is full of people riding bikes.

Rental bicycles are available in only a few places in Honduras, and they are usually at traveler destinations like the Bay Islands, Omoa, Tela or Copán Ruinas.

ORGANIZED TOURS

Organized tours are a good way to visit some of the more out-of-the-way areas. You'll find information on local tour operators in the Tegucigalpa, San Pedro Sula, Copán Ruinas, Tela, La Ceiba and Mosquitia sections of this chapter. Most of the operators offer tours in their own local areas and places farther afield.

Tegucigalpa

pop 1 million

Tegucigalpa, the capital of Honduras, is a busy, noisy city nestled in a bowl-shaped valley surrounded by a ring of mountains. At an altitude of 975m, it has a fresh and pleasant climate, much cooler than the coasts. The surrounding mountainous region is covered in pine trees.

The name Tegucigalpa is a bit of a mouthful; Hondurans often call the city Tegus (TEH-goos) for short. The name, meaning 'silver hill' in the original local Nahuatl dialect, was bestowed when the Spanish founded the city as a silver and gold mining center in 1578, on the slopes of Picacho. Tegucigalpa became the capital of Honduras in 1880, when the government seat was moved from Comayagua, 82km to the northwest.

In 1938 Comayagüela, on the opposite side of the river from Tegucigalpa, became part of the city.

Orientation

The city is divided by the Río Choluteca. On the east side of the river is Tegucigalpa, with the city center and the more affluent districts. Plaza Morazán, usually called Parque Central, with its beautiful cathedral, is at the heart of the city.

On the west side of Parque Central, Avenida Miguel Paz Barahona has been turned into a pedestrian shopping street, extending four blocks from the plaza to Calle El Telégrafo; this section has been renamed Calle Peatonal, and it's a busy thoroughfare with many shops, restaurants and banks.

Across the river from Tegucigalpa is Comayagüela, which is generally poorer and dirtier than the east side of the river, with a sprawling market area, lots of long-distance bus stations, cheap hotels and comedores.

The two areas are connected by a number of bridges.

Maps The tourist map published by the Instituto Geográfico Nacional is for sale for US$1.65 at the tourist office or for US$2.10 at the post office. Unfortunately, the city map has only a few street names on it. At the instituto itself, you can buy excellent color topographical and regional maps. The office (☎ 233 7166, fax 225 2759) is in the SECOPT building, in Comayagüela, just across the river from Tegucigalpa. It's open 8 am to 4 pm Monday to Friday.

Information

Tourist Offices The Instituto Hondureño de Turismo (☎ 222 2124, fax 222 6621, ihturism@hondutel.hn) is on the 5th floor of the Edificio Europa at the corner of Avenida Ramon Ernesto Cruz and Calle República de México. The building is between Blvd Morazán and Avenida La Paz; Lloyd's Bank is on the ground floor. The office is open 8:30 am to 4:30 pm Monday to Friday. However the staff is not really geared to handling walk-in travelers, so don't expect too much in the way of service. You'll also need ID to get past the armed security guard at the entrance. From the downtown area, take any Lomas, Tiloarque Sosa or Hospital San Felipe bus, or take a San Felipe colectivo. If you manage to connect with a member of the staff, they may sell you a city map (see the Maps section). Also available are several free tourist publications. A special office has information on ecotourism in Honduras, including national parks and wildlife refuges.

The national office of the Corporación Hondureña de Desarrollo Forestal (CO-HDEFOR) in Colonia El Carrizal has information on all of Honduras' national parks, wildlife refuges and other protected areas. Ask for the Departamento de Areas Protegidas (☎/fax 223 4346); it's open 8 am to 4 pm Monday to Friday.

Immigration Offices You can extend your visa at the immigration office (Migración; ☎ 222 7711) on Avenida Máximo Jeréz between Calle Las Damas and Calle Dionicio Gutierrez, in the large office building beside the Hotel Rondo. It's open 8:30 am to 4:30 pm Monday to Friday.

TEGUCIGALPA

PLACES TO STAY
- 2 Hotel MacArthur
- 3 Hotel Granada No 3
- 4 Hotel Granada No 2
- 5 Hotel Granada No 1
- 14 Linda Vista B&B
- 19 Hotel Honduras Maya;
     Belizean Consulate
- 23 Hotel Portal del Angel
- 35 Hotel Colonial; Cafe Colonial
- 38 Hotel San Pedro
- 39 Hotel Ticamaya
- 55 Hotel Fortuna
- 56 Hotel Goascoran
- 59 Nuevo Hotel Boston
- 62 Hotel Iberia

PLACES TO EAT
- 6 Café Paradiso
- 20 Theo's
- 34 Pizza Hut
- 41 Lean Chou
- 42 Restaurant Lizeth
- 43 D'Barro
- 63 La Terraza de Don Pepe
- 68 Pizza Hut
- 75 Restaurante Al Natural

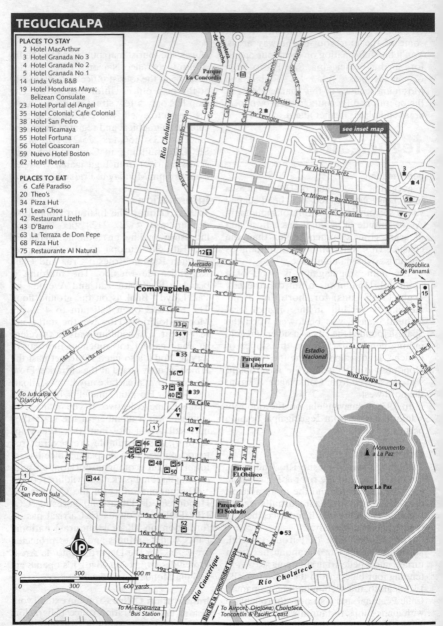

HONDURAS

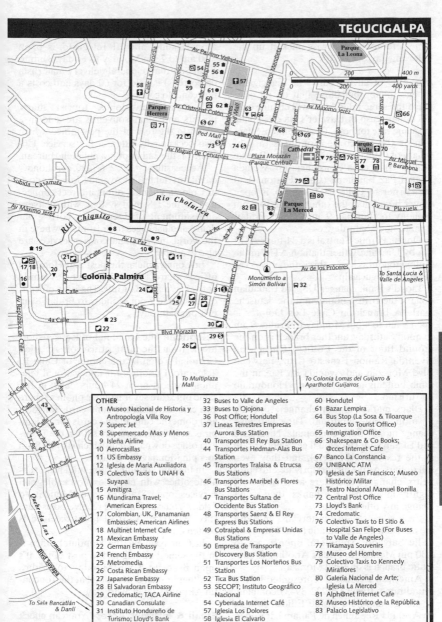

TEGUCIGALPA

Av Paulino Valladares
Parque La Leona
0 — 200 — 400 m
0 — 200 — 400 yards

Parque Herrera
Av Cristobal Colón
Ped Mall
Av Máximo Jérez
Calle Las Damas

Ped Mall
Calle Peatonal
Av Miguel de Cervantes
Plaza Morazán (Parque Central)
Cathedral
Parque Valle
Av Miguel P Barahona

Río Choluteca
Parque La Merced

Subida Casamata
Av Máximo Jérez
Río Chiquito
Av La Paz
Colonia Palmira
Av de los Próceres
To Santa Lucía & Valle de Angeles

Monumento a Simón Bolívar
To Colonia Lomas del Guijarro & Aparthotel Guijarros

Blvd Morazán
To Multiplaza Mall

Quebrada Los Lomas
Blvd Suyapa
To Sala Bancatlán & Danlí

HONDURAS

OTHER

1 Museo Nacional de Historia y Antropología Villa Roy	32 Buses to Valle de Angeles	60 Hondutel
7 Superc Jet	33 Buses to Ojojona	61 Bazar Lempira
8 Supermercado Mas y Menos	36 Post Office; Hondutel	64 Bus Stop (La Sosa & Tiloarque Routes to Tourist Office)
9 Isleña Airline	37 Lineas Terrestres Empresas Aurora Bus Station	65 Immigration Office
10 Aerocasillas	40 Transportes El Rey Bus Station	66 Shakespeare & Co Books; @cces Internet Cafe
11 US Embassy	44 Transportes Hedman-Alas Bus Station	67 Banco La Constancia
12 Iglesia de Maria Auxiliadora	45 Transportes Tralaisa & Etrucsa Bus Stations	69 UNIBANC ATM
13 Colectivo Taxis to UNAH & Suyapa	46 Transportes Maribel & Flores Bus Stations	70 Iglesia de San Francisco; Museo Histórico Militar
15 Amitigra	47 Transportes Sultana de Occidente Bus Station	71 Teatro Nacional Manuel Bonilla
16 Mundirama Travel; American Express	48 Transportes Saenz & El Rey Express Bus Stations	72 Central Post Office
17 Colombian, UK, Panamanian Embassies; American Airlines	49 Cotraipbal & Empresas Unidas Bus Stations	73 Lloyd's Bank
18 Multinet Internet Cafe	50 Empresa de Transporte Discovery Bus Station	75 Credomatic
21 Mexican Embassy	51 Transportes Los Norteños Bus Station	76 Colectivo Taxis to El Sitio & Hospital San Felipe (For Buses to Valle de Angeles)
22 German Embassy	52 Tica Bus Station	77 Tikamaya Souvenirs
24 French Embassy	53 SECOPT; Instituto Geográfico Nacional	78 Museo del Hombre
25 Metromedia	54 Cyberiada Internet Café	79 Colectivo Taxis to Kennedy Miraflores
26 Costa Rican Embassy	57 Iglesia Los Dolores	80 Galería Nacional de Arte; Iglesia La Merced
27 Japanese Embassy	58 Iglesia El Calvario	81 Alph@net Internet Cafe
28 El Salvadoran Embassy		82 Museo Histórico de la República
29 Credomatic; TACA Airline		83 Palacio Legislativo
30 Canadian Consulate		
31 Instituto Hondureño de Turismo; Lloyd's Bank		

If you bring your passport in the morning before 10 am, you can usually get it back the same afternoon; otherwise, pick it up the following day.

Money Not all the banks in Tegucigalpa change money, but those that do all offer much the same rates. Most will change only US dollars cash or traveler's checks, giving the same rate for both. Try the Banco Atlántida or the Banco de Honduras (a subsidiary of Citibank), both located on Parque Central. Banco La Constancia on Avenida Miguel Paz Barahona (Calle Peatonal), at the corner of Calle El Telégrafo, is open longer hours than the others: 9 am to 5 pm Monday to Thursday, 9 am to 6 pm Friday, 9 am to noon Saturday.

On the Parque Central is a 24-hour ATM run by Unibanc. Other than an ATM in the Hotel Honduras Maya, this is the only ATM in central Tegucigalpa.

Lloyd's Bank changes US and Canadian dollars, the British pound and the deutsche mark. A branch on Calle Los Dolores is open 9 am to 4 pm Monday to Friday, 9 am to noon Saturday; another branch is on the ground floor of the Edificio Europa on Avenida Ramon Ernesto Cruz, between Blvd Morazán and Avenida La Paz, in the same building as the Instituto Hondureño de Turismo.

Black-market money changers operate all along Calle Peatonal. They will also change money from Guatemala, Nicaragua and El Salvador (but you'll get a better rate at the respective borders), and they even sell dollars. At the airport, private entrepreneurs change US dollars at a rate only slightly lower than the banks; they won't change any other currency.

Cash advances on MasterCard and Visa are available at Credomatic (☎ 222 0380) on Calle Salvador Mendieta, open 8 am to 5:30 pm Monday to Friday. Another Credomatic branch is on Blvd Morazán.

American Express is represented by the Mundirama Travel (☎ 232 3943) company on the ground floor of the Edificio Ciicsa, on Avenida República de Panamá. It's open 8 am to noon and 1 to 5 pm Monday to Friday, 8 am to noon Saturday. If you have an American Express card or traveler's checks, the office will hold your mail for you indefinitely.

Post The central post office, on the corner of Avenida Miguel Paz Barahona (Calle Peatonal) and Calle El Telégrafo, is open 7:30 am to 7 pm Monday to Friday, 8 am to 1 pm Saturday. General delivery mail (lista de correos) is held for 60 days and costs a few cents to collect.

Postcards, envelopes, tourist maps, posters and other souvenirs are sold in a booth in the rear of the post office, which also occasionally offers a fax service. Upstairs on the 2nd floor is a philatelic bureau.

Aerocasillas (☎/fax 236 7420, aerohond@ david.intertel.hn), at Avenida Juan Lindo 4, in Colonia Palmira, offers a direct connection to the US mail system, with delivery and shipment of documents, correspondence and packages to or from anywhere in the world. International courier services are also available.

In Comayagüela, the post and Hondutel offices share a building on 6a Avenida between 7a and 8a Calle. The post office is open 8 am to 7 pm Monday to Friday, 8 am to 1 pm Saturday.

Telephone The Hondutel office is a short block from the post office, on Avenida Cristóbal Colón at the corner of Calle El Telégrafo. The office for international telephone calls is open 24 hours daily; in the same office are several public phones, where you can use coins or phone cards for local and domestic calls. Phone cards for 50 lempiras and 100 lempiras are sold in the Tesorería office down the hall, which is open 8 am to 4 pm Monday to Friday.

In the same building, Hondutel has a separate office with fax, telex and cablegram services, open 8 am to 4 pm Monday to Friday. You can send and receive faxes here (fax 237 9715); a list of faxes received is posted on the window.

In Comayagüela, the Hondutel office is in the same building as the post office; it's open 8 am to 8 pm Monday to Friday. Another branch of Hondutel at the Toncontín Airport is open every day.

Email & Internet Access You can check your email, and you can surf the Net at one of four downtown Internet centers. The @ccess Internet Cafe (☎ 220 5182, access@ honduras.com), on Avenida Máximo Jeréz, is open 8 am to 7 pm Monday to Friday and

8 am to 5 pm Saturday. The Multinet Internet Cafe (adaer@yahoo.com), opposite the Hotel Honduras Maya, is open 9 am to 6 pm every day except Sunday. Popular with students, the Alph@net Internet Cafe, tucked away in a courtyard off Avenida Miguel de Cervantes, keeps similar hours to the other cafes. All three cafes charge around US$2 per 30 minutes.

The Cyberiada Internet Café (☎ 220 4056, cyberiada@interdata.hn), also on Avenida Máximo Jeréz, is open 24 hours a day, seven days a week, and charges US$2.40 for 30 minutes access time.

One more Internet center, in the Multiplaza Mall (see the Shopping section), keeps similar opening hours and access charges.

Travel Agencies Mundirama Travel (see the Money section, earlier), the agent for American Express, offers card services as well as travel agency services. Check in the telephone directory yellow pages under 'Agencias de Viajes' for other travel agencies; you'll find dozens scattered around the city.

Bookstores Shakespeare & Co Books (☎ 237 3909), on Calle Paz Barahona, carries a wide selection of new and used books in English, German, French and other languages. It sells used books at half the cover price and will trade used books. The store also offers trips to nearby sights (see the Organized Tours section).

Metromedia (☎/fax 232 7108) in the Edificio Casa Real on Avenida San Carlos, is the new incarnation of the old Book Village, which has sold English-language books, newspapers and magazines for many years. The new store, which is four times bigger than the old one, offers books, magazines, videos and music, and it runs a cafe. It's open 10 am to 8 pm Monday to Saturday, noon to 5 pm Sunday. There is also a branch in the Multiplaza Mall (see the Shopping section).

The weekly English-language newspaper, *This Week in Honduras*, is available at the English-language bookshops and in many hotels; you can pick it up for free at the Hotel Plaza, on Calle Peatonal near the corner of Calle El Telégrafo. See also its Web site at www.marrder.com/htw.

Cultural Centers The Instituto Hondureño de Cultura Interamericana (IHCI; ☎ 237 7539), on Calle Real de Comayagüela, offers cultural events relating to all the Americas. It also has a small English-language library.

Alianza Francesa (Alliance Française; ☎ 239 1529), in Colonia Las Lomas del Guijarro, offers cultural events, French classes and weekly French films. Centro Cultural Alemán (The German Institute; ☎ 237 1555), at Calle La Fuente 1465, offers German cultural events and literature, courses in Spanish (for foreigners) and German languages and a German-Honduran cultural exchange.

Laundry At Superc Jet (☎ 237 4154), on Avenida Juan Gutemberg in Barrio Guanacaste, you can have laundry washed, dried and folded for US$0.50 per pound. Drop it off in the morning, and it will be ready that afternoon; dry-cleaning service is also available. It's open 8 am to 6:30 pm Monday to Saturday.

Medical Services Tegucigalpa has several hospitals and clinics; look in the yellow pages of the telephone directory under 'Hospitales.' You might want to ask your hotel or embassy for a recommendation.

Pharmacies are numerous around the city. There's always a *farmacia de turno* on duty – the pharmacies take turns staying open 24 hours. A schedule for the farmacias de turno is published in the major daily newspapers. For simple ailments, it's often unnecessary to go to a doctor; pharmacists can often give you the medicine you need to fix you up.

Emergency In case of emergency, call one of the following numbers:

Ambulance (Red Cross)	☎ 237 2240
Fire	☎ 198, 256 8790, 256 6180
Hospital	☎ 232 2322, 232 3021
Paramedics	☎ 239 9999
Police (FUSEP)	☎ 199, 252 3128, 252 3171
Policía Femenina	☎ 237 2184

The policía femenina are a branch of the police dealing in crimes against women, such as domestic violence and rape.

HONDURAS

Things to See

At the center of the city is the fine **cathedral** and, in front of it, the **Plaza Morazán**, often called Parque Central. The domed 18th-century cathedral (built between 1765 and 1782) has an intricate baroque altar of gold and silver and lots of other fine art. Parque Central, with its statue of Morazán on horseback, is the hub of the city. Opposite the cathedral's south side is the **Alcaldía** (City Hall).

Three blocks east of the cathedral on Avenida Miguel Paz Barahona is the **Parque Valle**, with the old **Iglesia de San Francisco**, the first church in Tegucigalpa, founded in 1592 by the Franciscans. The building beside it was first a convent, then the Spanish mint; it now houses the **Museo Histórico Militar**, with exhibits on Honduras' military history (open 7:30 am to 4 pm Monday to Friday).

Across the street on the south side of the church, the **Museo del Hombre** occupies the former supreme court building, the Antiguo Edificio Corte Suprema de Justicia. Cultural events and exhibitions are held here; the museum is only open when there's something going on. (The entrance is on Avenida Miguel de Cervantes, around the block.)

From Parque Central, head two blocks south to another major plaza, Parque La Merced. The unusual modern building on stilts is the **Palacio Legislativo**, where Congress meets. Next to it in striking contrast is the Antiguo Paraninfo Universitario building, which now houses the **Galería Nacional de Arte** (☎ 237 9884), the impressive national art gallery (open 8 am to 5 pm Tuesday to Sunday). In the same building is the 18th-century **Iglesia La Merced**. In 1847, the convent of La Merced was converted to house Honduras' first university; the national gallery was established there in 1996. The well-restored building is just as interesting as the paintings in the gallery – the building, too, is a work of art.

One block west of Parque La Merced is the **Museo Histórico de la República** (☎ 237 0268), on the corner of Paseo Marco Aurelio Soto and Calle Salvador Mendieta. This museum holds exhibits on the history of Honduras from the winning of independence to the present. Just as interesting as the exhibits is the building itself, which was the Casa Presidencial (the Presidential Palace) from 1920 until 1992. It's open 8:30 am to

noon and 1 to 4 pm Wednesday to Sunday; admission is US$2.50 for foreigners, free for children under seven, and free for everyone on the last Thursday of each month.

Head west from Parque Central along Avenida Miguel Paz Barahona. This lively pedestrian-only section, which is also called Calle Peatonal, has many street vendors. It stretches four blocks west from the plaza to Calle El Telégrafo.

Three blocks west along Calle Peatonal from Parque Central, turn right on Calle Los Dolores and head to another fine colonial church, **Los Dolores** (1732), with a plaza out front and religious art inside. On the front of Los Dolores are figures representing the Passion of Christ – his unseamed cloak, the cock that crowed three times – all crowned by the more indigenous symbol of the sun.

On Avenida Miguel Paz Barahona, two blocks west of Calle Telégrafo, is Parque Herrera, another pleasant plaza. There stands the national theater, **Teatro Nacional Manuel Bonilla**, dating from 1912; its interior was inspired by the Athens Theatre of Paris. Performances are still given in the theater; during the daytime you're welcome to go in and have a look. Also on this park is a peaceful 18th-century church, **El Calvario**.

Walking north for four long blocks from El Calvario on Calle La Concordia, you reach **Parque La Concordia**, an interesting park full of reproductions of the Mayan ruins at Copán, including a pyramid and many stone carvings.

A couple of blocks northeast, way up on a hill, is the **Museo Nacional de Historia y Antropología Villa Roy** (☎ 222 3470), the national museum of anthropology and history. The grand building was the personal home of Julio Lozano, one of Honduras' former presidents. It now contains salons with displays on anthropology, archaeology and the pre-Hispanic history of Honduras, the 'moment of contact' when the Spanish arrived, the colonial period and an interesting section on ethnography, with displays on Honduras' eight indigenous groups showing where and how they live. The museum is open 8:30 am to 3:30 pm Wednesday to Sunday.

About five blocks east is **Parque La Leona**, an attractive park with a fine view over the city. From there you can make your way down the steep streets and into the city center.

Parque La Paz

Near the river and opposite the Parque El Obelisco is Parque La Paz, a wooded hill with a large monument to peace at its summit that commands a sweeping view of the entire city; you can walk or drive up here for a magnificent view. Nearby is the enormous **Estadio Nacional**, the national stadium, where soccer matches are played.

Sala Bancatlán

The headquarters of Bancatlán on Blvd Miraflores, southeast of the center in Miraflores, has the Sala Bancatlán, with a coin collection and an archaeological collection of Mayan statues, vessels and artifacts from Copán and other sites, plus explanatory maps and photos. It's open 9 am to 3 pm Monday to Friday; admission is free. Take bus No 5 (Carrizal-Miraflores) from the center.

El Picacho

On this peak on the north side of Tegucigalpa is the **Parque de las Naciones Unidas** (United Nations Park), established to commemorate the UN's 40th anniversary. There are also a soccer field where games are held on Sunday, several lookout points for excellent views over the city and a zoo. Food and drink are available.

The zoo is not extravagant, but it does have some interesting local wildlife. It's open 9 am to 3 pm weekdays, 9 am to 4 pm weekends; admission is US$0.80.

Buses to Picacho run only on Sunday; take bus No 9 from the bus stop outside the Farmacia Santa Bárbara, behind Iglesia Los Dolores. Be sure you get on the right bus; several other No 9 buses also stop here. The last bus leaves at 5 pm for the return trip to town. A taxi from the center costs US$5.

Organized Tours

Shakespeare & Co Books (see the Bookstores section earlier) offers trips to nearby attractions, including Parque Nacional La Tigra, Valle de Angeles and Santa Lucía, Ojojona and Yuscarán.

La Moskitia Ecoaventuras (☎/fax 237 9398), Apdo Postal 3577, and Adventure Expeditions (☎/fax 237 4793), 1020 Altos de la Hoya, offer trips to the Mosquitia region and other destinations.

Some of the travel agencies also offer tours of the local area; ask the tourist office for details.

Special Events

The Feria de Suyapa (February 2 to 11) is held every year in Suyapa, 7km southeast of Tegucigalpa, to honor the Virgen de Suyapa, Honduras' patron saint. Her day is February 3, but the fair lasts for an entire week, attracting pilgrims and celebrants from all over Central America.

Good Friday is commemorated with processions through the streets. Participants bear religious figures over pathways carpeted with intricate designs of colored sawdust. A similar procession takes place in Comayagua (see the Comayagua section) on the morning of Good Friday; in Tegucigalpa it starts at around noon and continues until around 1 am. As in Comayagua, people work through the night to create the fragile, colored sawdust carpets, and you're welcome to join them.

Places to Stay

Most decent places to stay are on the Tegucigalpa side of the river. You can find a number of basic cheap places to stay in Comayagüela, but they should only be used when the budget is running very low. Comayagüela is not a safe place at night (definitely don't go in the market area), and the few hotels mentioned here are better reached by taxi if you plan on coming home late.

Budget The 90-room *Hotel San Pedro* (☎ 222 8987), on 6a Avenida between 8a and 9a Calles, is popular with shoestring travelers on the Comayagüela side; it's clean and functional. Rooms with one bed are US$3.50 with general bath, US$5.20 with private bath; with two beds they're US$4.20/6. It's handy to the El Rey and Aurora bus stations for buses to San Pedro Sula or Juticalpa, and it has an inexpensive cafe.

Opposite this is the *Hotel Ticamaya* (☎ 237 0084), which charges US$3.20/6 for singles/doubles with general bath, and US$5.50/7.50 for one or two people with private bath.

A row of basic *hospedajes* beside Iglesia Los Dolores provide some of the most inexpensive accommodations in town. They are not flashy, and they don't really cater to backpackers, but they will do in case of need. On the rear corner is the *Hotel Fortuna*, which has singles/doubles with general bath for US$4/5; rooms with private bath are US$6.50/8. A couple of doors down, *Hotel Goascoran* (☎ 238 1903) has rooms for US$4 with general bath or US$6 with private bath. Both of these places are very basic, and the showers are cold, but they're relatively clean, and shoestring travelers do stay at them.

Three hotels all sporting the same name – Granada – are close to each other just outside the main downtown area. They are generally clean, modern and a bit impersonal, but they're a good deal. They are in a district with restaurants, movies and stores, not far from the city center. First up is *Hotel Granada No 1* (☎ 222 2654, Avenida Juan Gutemberg 1401), in Barrio Guanacaste. Lots of Peace Corps workers and other volunteers stay here. Singles/doubles go for US$13.80 with private bath, and the hotel has some larger rooms with two or three beds.

A block away, at *Hotel Granada No 2* (☎ 237 7079, fax 238 4438, Subida Casamata 1326), all the rooms have telephone and private bath, and there's a hotel restaurant, free wake-up service and free coffee. The rates are US$14 for two/three beds. Color cable TV is optional and costs another US$4.15. Across the street, *Hotel Granada No 3* (☎ 237 0843) is the newest of the three Hotel Granadas, with singles/doubles for US$14.50.

The *Hotel Iberia* (☎ 237 9267), upstairs on Calle Los Dolores in front of Iglesia Los Dolores, has singles/doubles for US$13.50 with private bath. Windows open onto an inside sitting area.

Much more pleasant, the *Nuevo Hotel Boston* (☎ 237 9411, fax 237 0186, Avenida Máximo Jeréz 321), in Barrio Abajo, is an excellent place to stay, very clean and well kept, with a comfortable sitting room. Free coffee and purified water are always available. Street-facing rooms, though noisy, are especially large and have doors opening onto a small balcony; these are US$22 for singles/doubles. Quieter, smaller interior

rooms cost US$17. All have private hot baths.

Hotel Colonial (☎ 237 5785), located on 6a Calle between 6a and 7a Avenidas in Comayagüela, is more cheerful, clean and modern; 15 singles/doubles with private hot bath go for US$6/7.50. The clean and inexpensive Cafe Colonial is on the ground floor.

If you are really at the end of your economic rope, you'll come across plenty of other hotels that are a few cents cheaper, but most of them are a lot less pleasant than those listed above.

Mid-Range A pleasant mid-range choice is *Hotel MacArthur* (☎ 237 5906, Avenida Lempira 454), where large, attractive, clean singles/doubles with telephone and private hot bath are US$40.50 with air-con and color cable TV.

The very comfortable *Linda Vista* (☎ 231 0099, fax 232 4294, alvaagui@itsnetworks .net, Calle las Acacias 1438) is a B&B in the more prestigious Colonia Palmira area. Six tastefully decorated, large and well-equipped rooms go for US$55/70 for singles/doubles including breakfast. Each room has cable TV and an Internet phone connection.

Top End Longer-term residents might look to *Aparthotel Guijarros* (☎ 235 6851, fax 235 8767, sales@guijarros.com, Calle Roma 3929), in Colonia Lomas del Guijarro, where very comfortable rooms with all facilities can be had for US$70 or, for an extra US$20, you have access to a spacious lounge and kitchen. Room rates include breakfast and transportation to and from the airport.

Tegucigalpa's classiest boutique hotel has to be the discrete *Hotel Portal del Angel* (☎ 239 6538, fax 235 8839, hpangel@ david.intertel.hn, Avenida República del Perú 2115). Enormous rooms, each decorated differently with Honduran artifacts and sporting two large queen-sized beds, go for US$100 per night.

Hotel Honduras Maya (☎ 220 5000, fax 220 6000), near Avenida República de Chile, is no longer Tegucigalpa's most prestigious hotel, but it is very centrally located. Single/double rooms are available for US$120/130.

Places to Eat

Tegucigalpa Most of the good restaurants are on the Tegucigalpa side of the river.

La Terraza de Don Pepe (☎ 237 1084) an upstairs restaurant on Avenida Cristóbal Colón two blocks west of Parque Central, is 'a tradition in Honduras,' the sign announces. It's a popular place, open 10 am to 10 pm daily, with good prices, a family atmosphere and live music in the evenings. While you're here, take a look at the unusual shrine to the Virgin of Suyapa, whose figure was once abducted from the Basilica de Suyapa and later turned up here, in the men's rest room. The rest room is now a shrine, with newspaper clippings and photos of the event.

Directly behind the cathedral, *Restaurante Al Natural* is lovely and relaxing, removed from the hubbub of the city, with tables set around a lush covered garden. The food is good and fresh, with a large menu to select from, and it's not expensive. It's open 8 am to 7 pm Monday to Friday, 8 am to 3 pm Saturday, closed Sunday.

A popular air-conditioned *Pizza Hut* is on the corner of Avenida Cristóbal Colón and Paseo La Leona, half a block west of Parque Central. You can fill up at the salad bar as many times as you like for US$3.20; lunchtime specials featuring pizza or pasta, with one trip to the salad bar and unlimited soda, are served 11 am to 4 pm Monday to Friday for US$3 to US$4. It's open 9 am to 10 pm daily.

Coffeehouse lingerers will like the *Café Paradiso* (*Avenida Miguel Paz Barahona 1351*), a coffeehouse/gallery near El Arbolito; it's open 9 am to 8 pm weekdays, 9 am to 6 pm Saturday. For live Honduran music on weekends, poetry readings or short theatrical productions look no further than the arty *D'Barro* (☎ 239 6905) on Avenida Manuel Gálvez. This place is one of the few restaurants in Tegucigalpa that does genuine Honduran dishes. The place is low-key, the food excellent and very cheap. It's open 9:30 am to 8 pm Monday to Thursday (closed on Tuesday), 9:30 am to midnight Friday and Saturday, 11:30 am to 9 pm Sunday.

The Colonia Palmira district is home to a number of excellent restaurants, of which *Theo's*, on Avenida República del Perú, is worth a look for a culinary night out.

Mediterranean dishes are the specialty, with Spanish tapas also featured.

Comayagüela Comayagüela has plenty of Chinese restaurants where you can eat for US$2 or less; *Lean Chou*, at 6a Avenida and 10a Calle, has huge portions. At *Restaurant Lizeth*, on 5a Av between 10a and 11a Calles, smaller portions are offset by very low prices; breakfasts are around US$1 to US$1.80. *Pizza Hut* has a branch on 6a Avenida between 5a and 6a Calles.

Entertainment

It's especially pleasant to sit in Parque Central at sunset, when the loud cacophony of flocks of *zanates* in the trees practically drowns out the sounds of the city and traffic. You can buy some *tajaditas* (fried banana chips) or sliced mangoes on the plaza and spend an enjoyable hour sitting and listening to the zanates and watching the pigeons on the ancient façade of the cathedral and the people lounging in the plaza or scurrying to catch buses. The exuberant zanates are quiet at night, sleeping in the trees, but they crank up again at dawn.

Tegucigalpa has a couple of districts with lots of choices in nightlife. Among the better-known nightspots are the *Tropical Port Disco* on Blvd Miraflores, *Confettis* and *Alejandro's Disco* on Blvd Morazán and *Oui*, a combination bar, disco and karaoke bar on Blvd Juan Pablo II.

Gays and lesbians have a couple of gay-friendly bars to head for. *Ouch*, on Centro Comercial D'Arco in Colonia Alameda, is a bar/discoteque that is open Thursday to Saturday only. The *Rock Castle*, on Blvd Juan Pablo II, is a gay-friendly and straight disco opposite the Pollo Campero fast chicken restaurant, open Wednesday to Saturday.

The *Teatro Nacional Manuel Bonilla* (☎ 222 4366), on Parque Herrera, hosts a variety of performing arts, and it's a very enjoyable place to attend a performance.

Cinemas can be found everywhere you turn in Tegucigalpa, and several are on the Comayagüela side, too. Most of the hotels mentioned under Places to Stay have at least one cinema nearby; entry is around US$2. You can often find films in English, with Spanish subtitles, in the theaters. Check the daily newspapers for movie listings.

Shopping

Honduran handicrafts are sold at many places around town. On the west side of Iglesia Los Dolores plaza, on the corner of Avenida Máximo Jeréz, Bazar Lempira (☎ 237 9436) is a handicrafts shop with a good selection of leatherwork, wood carvings, paintings and souvenirs. Best of all is their collection of handmade wooden musical instruments of all shapes and sizes. Most of the instruments are not expensive; you could purchase a guitar, violin or mandolin for as little as US$30. Tikamaya Souvenirs on the corner of Avenida Miguel de Cervantes and Calle Salvador Corletto also has handicrafts and souvenirs.

The Multiplaza Mall is the capital's flashiest shopping spot. You could easily be in suburban Miami here, with its boutique shops, eateries, banks and large supermarket. The mall is in the Colonia Florencia district, about 3km southeast of downtown Tegucigalpa. It is best reached by taxi.

In Comayagüela, you can find just about anything for sale in the sprawling blocks of the Mercado San Isidro, from vegetables to secondhand clothing to some excellent leatherwork and other crafts.

For higher quality handicrafts, it's worth making a trip to Valle de Angeles (see the Around Tegucigalpa section).

Getting There & Away

Air Domestic and international flights arrive and depart from Toncontín International Airport (☎ 233 1111) on the southern outskirts of Tegucigalpa. TACA (☎ 239 0148, fax 231 1517) offers two flights daily between Tegucigalpa and San Pedro Sula. The main office is on Blvd Morazán not far from the main tourist office. Isleña (☎ 237 3370, fax 233 1894), in Edificio Galería La Paz, on Avenida La Paz half a block west of the US embassy, connects Tegucigalpa with La Ceiba, Roatán, Guanaja and Utila. See the Honduras Getting Around section for details on domestic fares, and see the Honduras Getting There & Away section for information on international flights; both are earlier in this chapter.

Bus Excellent bus services connect Tegucigalpa with other parts of Honduras; however, the buses do not depart from a central bus station. Each bus line has its own station, most of them in Comayagüela. Refer to the Tegucigalpa map for the location of each individual company's bus station. The frequency of departures is generally hourly for destinations closer to Tegucigalpa, with up to six or more departures daily for destinations farther afield.

The free tourist magazine *Honduras Tips* has a very helpful section on bus routes and bus company contact addresses. See the Honduras Getting There & Away section for further information on Tica Bus international services. See the 'Long-Distance Buses from Tegucigalpa' boxed text for additional information on bus travel from the capital.

Direct international buses to neighboring countries include the following:

Guatemala City, Guatemala (US$42, 14 hours, 589km) The King Quality (see San Salvador) bus to San Salvador connects with a bus to Guatemala City at 3 pm, arriving in the Guatemalan capital at 8 pm.

Managua, Nicaragua (US$20, eight hours, 391km) Tica Bus (☎ 220 0590, fax 220 0579), 16a Calle between 5a and 6a Avenidas, in Comayagüela, has a bus that departs every day at 9 am. This same bus connects with services to San José (Costa Rica) and Panama City (Panama). See the Honduras Getting There & Away section for details on Tica Bus.

San Salvador, El Salvador (US$25, 7½ hours, 321km) King Quality (☎ 225 5415, fax 225 2600), on Blvd Communidad Economica Europea near 6a Avenida, has a bus once daily, departing at 6 am and arriving in San Salvador at 1:30 pm. Cruceros del Golfo (same station as King Quality) has daily service to San Salvador (US$15, 7½ hours) departing at 1 pm and arriving at 8:30 pm.

Getting Around

To/From the Airport Toncontín International Airport is 6.5km south of the center of Tegucigalpa. Local Loarque buses Nos 1 and 11 stop frequently right outside the entrance to the airport; these run 5:30 am to 9 pm daily. The cost is US$0.50. To go to the airport from the city center, catch the Loarque buses on Avenida Jerez.

A taxi to the airport costs about US$8; from the airport to town, colectivo taxis are cheaper.

Bus An excellent system of city buses operates every day from 5:30 am to 9 pm daily.

Long-Distance Buses from Tegucigalpa

destination	bus line	phone	fare	type	duration
Catacamas	Aurora	237 3647	US$2.32	normal	3¾ hours
Choluteca	Mi Esperanza	225 2863	US$1.76	normal	3 hours
Comayagua	El Rey	237 1462	US$1.15	normal	2 hours
Danlí	Discua Litena	230 0470	US$1.20	normal	2 hours
Danlí	Discua Litena	230 0470	US$1.90	direct	1¾ hours
El Paraíso	Discua Litena	230 0470	US$1.36	normal	2½ hours
El Paraíso	Discua Litena	230 0470	US$2.03	direct	2 hours
Juticalpa	Aurora	237 3647	US$1.90	normal	3 hours
La Ceiba	Viana Clase Oro	235 8184	US$13.56	ejecutivo	7 hours
La Entrada	Sultana de Occidente	237 8101	US$5.76	normal	6 hours
La Paz	Flores	237 3032	US$1.15	normal	1¾ hours
Las Manos	Discua Litena	230 0470	US$1.69	normal	3 hours
San Marcos de Colon	Mi Esperanza	225 2863	US$2.24	normal	4 hours
San Pedro Sula	El Rey Express	237 8561	US$4.34	direct	3½ hours
San Pedro Sula	El Rey y Saenz	237 1462	US$2.78	normal	4 hours
San Pedro Sula	Hedman Alas	237 7143	US$4.34	direct	3½ hours
San Pedro Sula	Norteños	237 0706	US$2.78	normal	4 hours
San Pedro Sula	Saenz Ejecutivo	233 4229	US$10.17	ejecutivo	4 hours
San Pedro Sula	Hedman Alas	237 7143	US$5.42	direct	3½ hours
San Pedro Sula	Viana Clase Oro	235 8184	US$8.30	ejecutivo	3½ hours
Santa Rosa de Copan	Sultana de Occidente	237 8101	US$6.10	normal	7 hours
Siguatepeque	Empresas Unidas y Maribel	222 2071	US$1.36	normal	2½ hours
Tela	Cristina	220 0117	US$6.71	normal	5 hours
Tela	Etrucsa	222 6881	US$6.10	normal	5 hours
Trujillo	Cotraipbal	237 1666	US$8.81	normal	8 hours

Buses are frequent and cost US$0.20. However buses are no longer allowed in to the city center, so all stop or start several hundred meters short of the Parque Central.

Car At all the rental-car companies, you have the best chance of getting one of the cheapest cars if you reserve it about three days (or more) in advance. As always, prices vary considerably, so it pays to shop around. Budget proved to be the most efficient company when this LP researcher needed a car for a couple of weeks. Rental car companies in Tegucigalpa include the following:

Avis (☎ 232 0088, 233 9548 at the airport, fax 239 5710), Edificio Palmira Planta Baja

Budget (☎ 235 9528, fax 231 1810, ☎/fax 233 6927 airport, covesa.brac@datum.hn), Blvd Suyapa

Hertz (☎ 239 0772, 234 3784 at the airport, fax 232 0870), Centro Comercial Villa Real, Colonia Palmira

Maya (☎ 232 0682, fax 232 6133), Avenida República de Chile, Colonia Palmira

Molinari (☎ 237 5335, 233 1307 at the airport, fax 237 4091), at 1a Avenida and 2a Calle, Comayagüela

Thrifty (☎ 235 6077, 233 0922 at the airport, fax 235 6078, thrifty@david.intertel.hn), Colonia Prado Universitarios

Taxi Taxis cruise all over town, giving a little honk to advertise when they are available. A ride in town costs around US$2. You can also phone for a taxi (☎ 222 3304, 222 0533,

HONDURAS

222 3748, 222 0418). Rates for cabs booked by phone are US$3.40 around town.

AROUND TEGUCIGALPA

Suyapa

La Virgen de Suyapa is the patron saint of Honduras; in 1982 a papal decree made her the patron of all Central America. On the Suyapa hillside, about 7km southeast of the center of Tegucigalpa, the huge Gothic **Basílica de Suyapa** dominates the landscape. The construction of the basilica, which is famous for its large, brilliant stained-glass windows, was begun in 1954, and finishing touches are still being added.

La Virgen de Suyapa herself is a tiny painted wooden statue, only 6cm tall. Many believe she has performed hundreds of miracles. She is brought to the large basilica on holidays, especially for the annual Feria de Suyapa beginning on the saint's day (February 2) and continuing for a week; the celebrations attract pilgrims from all over Central America. Most of the time, however, the little statue is kept on the altar of the very simple old church of Suyapa, built in the late 18th and early 19th centuries. It's on the plaza a few hundred meters behind the newer basilica.

The basilica of Suyapa is just up the hill from the **Universidad Nacional Autónoma de Honduras** (UNAH). The campus is called Ciudad Universitaria and houses several museums (history, anthropology, biology, fauna, entomology and herbalism), all open 9 am to 4 pm Monday to Friday.

Getting There & Away You can get from Tegucigalpa to Suyapa by catching either a bus (US$0.50) or a colectivo taxi (US$0.80) from a colectivo stop near the river (see the Tegucigalpa map), taking it to the university and walking the short distance from there. The No 31 Suyapa-Mercado San Isidro bus, departing from the San Isidro market in Comayagüela, also goes to Suyapa.

Santa Lucía

pop 5410

Santa Lucía is a charming old Spanish mining town on a hill. Lots of lanes and walkways wind around the hillside. The town has great views of the pine-covered hills and Tegucigalpa away in the valley. The 18th-century church perched on a hillside is especially beautiful; inside are many old Spanish paintings and the Christ of Las Mercedes, given to Santa Lucía by King Felipe II in 1572. If the doors of the church are closed, walk around to the office at the rear and ask to have them opened for you.

Santa Lucía is an attractive and peaceful town for walking around in the fresh mountain air. Many possible walks lead out of town and into the hills, which are sprinkled with many little farms. An old mule trail leads down to the capital, a hike of several hours; unfortunately we've recently heard this mule trail has become dangerous due to young thugs. Ask locals for current advice.

There are no hotels in Santa Lucía.

Places to Eat The *Restaurante Miluska* (☎ 231 3905) is a favorite, with tables indoors and outdoors on a pleasant covered patio. A 'European corner in the heart of Honduras,' it serves German and Czech dishes in addition to typical Honduran fare; it's open 10 am to 8 pm Tuesday to Sunday. It's well signed from the highway. On the road coming into town from the highway, *Restaurante Donde El Francés* is another little European corner.

Getting There & Away Santa Lucía is 14km east of Tegucigalpa, 2.5km off the road leading to Valle de Angeles and San Juancito. A direct bus to Santa Lucía departs Tegucigalpa every 45 minutes, 7 am to 6 pm, from Mercado San Pablo in Colonia Reparto (US$0.70). Bus route No 6, Carrizal–El Sitio, departing from Parque Central, travels to Mercado San Pablo (US$0.60); colectivo taxis (US$1.40) also go there, departing from the corner of Calle Miguel Paz Barahona and Calle Adolfo Zuniga, two blocks behind the cathedral.

Or you can take the Valle de Angeles bus from the stop on Avenida La Paz, get off at the crossroads and walk or hitch the 2.5km into town.

Valle de Angeles

pop 8740

Eight kilometers past Santa Lucía, Valle de Angeles is another beautiful, historic Spanish mining town. It's been declared a tourist zone, and much of Valle de Angeles has been restored to its original 16th-century appearance. In front of the town's old church is an attractive shady plaza. The annual fair takes place on October 4.

Artisan shops and souvenir emporiums line the streets in Valle de Angeles, where you can find excellent Honduran *artesanías* that are marginally cheaper and of better quality than in Tegucigalpa. Wood carvings, basketry, ceramics, leatherwork, paintings, dolls, wicker and wood furniture and other items are featured. Avoid the weekend crowds.

Places to Stay & Eat Most people come to Valle de Angeles as a day trip from Tegucigalpa, but it would be a quiet, relaxing place to stay over. The only time it gets busy is on weekends and holidays; otherwise, the town is quiet.

About three blocks north of the church, the *Posada del Angel* (☎ 766 2233) is a beautiful place with a restaurant and clean single/double rooms with private hot bath for around US$10 per person, all facing onto a large grassy courtyard.

Valle de Angeles has a great number of small, simple restaurants serving typical Honduran fare. On the main square, you will find *Restaurante Jalapeño* and *El Anafre*, with its English-speaking owner, for good Honduran dishes. *Rudy's Snack Bar* is another English-speaking place, located a block behind the church. It's open 9 am to 8 pm Wednesday to Sunday. You can hardly miss the huge street banner of *Il Pomodoro Pizza* on the south side of the town. Call in here for good pizza and pasta dishes. *Restaurante Turistico* is on the outskirts west of town and has a pleasant terrace overlooking Valle de Angeles. It is signposted on the main road in from Tegucigalpa.

Getting There & Away A bus bound for Valle de Angeles departs every 45 minutes, 7 am to 5 pm, from a stop just off Avenida La Paz in Tegucigalpa, half a block south of the Hospital San Felipe (US$0.75). The Lomas and San Felipe buses departing from the corner of Avenida Cristóbal Colón and Calle Salvador Mendieta in Tegucigalpa will drop you at Hospital San Felipe.

Parque Nacional La Tigra

La Tigra is one of the most beautiful places in Honduras, preserving a lush cloud forest. Only 11km from Tegucigalpa, at an altitude of 2270m, this pristine 238 sq km reserve was Honduras' first national park. The forest is home to a great abundance of wildlife – ocelots, pumas, peccaries, white-tailed deer, armadillos, opossums, agoutis, pacas, toucans, quetzals and other bird life and much more. It is also a botanist's delight, with lush trees, vines, lichens and large ferns, colorful mushrooms, bromeliads, orchids and other flowering plants. Even when it's not cloudy in a cloud forest, the sun rarely shines on the ground because of the canopy of trees, so it's always damp.

Six trails, all well maintained and easy to follow, have been cut through the forest. It is a very rugged, mountainous area, and the damp ground can give way unexpectedly off the trails, so you should stay on them. People have also been lost for days in the dense forest when they wandered off the trails. Most of the trails are on the Juticalpa side of the park, but one, the 9.5km La Cascada Trail, goes all the way from one park entrance to the other, passing a waterfall on the way. It's easiest to do this trail from Juticalpa to El Rosario, as that way it's mostly downhill. The trails vary in length and difficulty, taking half an hour to six hours to traverse. On the El Rosario side of the park, you can see many old mine shafts.

On weekends, guides are available to take you along the trails, pointing out features of the forest and its wildlife. Though not required, a guide doesn't cost much, maybe around US$3 for one of the longer trails, and you'll learn a lot more about the forest if you go with one. On weekdays, the park rangers will guide you along the trails. You can walk from one entrance to the other in a couple of hours by the old disused road (no vehicles allowed), but you see more if you take La Cascada Trail.

The climate at La Tigra is fresh and brisk; in fact it's often quite cold – bring plenty of warm clothes with you. At night the temperature can drop to around 5°C. Long pants and long sleeves are best, as the forest has many mosquitoes. It's also advisable to bring sturdy tennis shoes or hiking boots, mosquito repellent and your own drinking water and food.

The park is open 8 am to 5 pm Tuesday to Sunday, closed Monday. The entrance fee is US$10 to visit the park (US$3 for children under 12, seniors and disabled people).

Information Amitigra (☎ 232 6771), in the Edificio Italia, 4th Floor, Office No 6, Colonia Palmira, Tegucigalpa, has information and manages overnight visits to the park. It's open 8:30 am to 5:30 pm Monday to Friday.

Places to Stay To stay overnight in the park, you must first get written permission from Amitigra. At the park entrance at El Rosario, there are a visitors center with displays on the wildlife and plants in the park, dormitories, houses, camping spots and a cafeteria. A ranger is always there. You can stay in dormitories for US$5 per person; there are 10 rooms, each with six beds. Bring your own bedding and warm clothes. There's no place for you to cook, but there is a cafeteria. Or you can buy simple meals at the white house at the bend, 300m down from the visitors center, but only till about 6 pm.

Also at El Rosario are several houses, for three to five persons, which come complete with kitchen and cost US$50 per night; you still must provide your own bedding. There are also two campsites, with water and latrine, available for US$5 per person. Children up to 12 years old pay half price for all accommodations.

On the Jutiapa side of the park, the visitors center does not have overnight facilities, but you can camp there. Bring everything you'll need.

Getting There & Away La Tigra has two entrances. The western entrance to the park, above Jutiapa, is the closest to Tegucigalpa, 22km away. There's a visitors center at the entrance, where rangers are always on duty. This entrance is reached by taking a turnoff from the top of El Picacho and passing through the villages of El Hatillo, Los Limones and Jutiapa.

Buses depart from Parque Herrera in Tegucigalpa and go as far as Los Limones; from there it's 5km, about a 1½-hour uphill walk, to the park gate. If you don't fancy the walk, it's easy to hitch on weekends – if you go on a weekday, you may be the only person on the road. If there are enough passengers, the bus may continue on 2km to Jutiapa, still leaving you 3km from the park gate, but you can't count on this bus. The bus leaves Parque Herrera four times daily,

around 6:30 am, 9 am, 2 pm and 5 pm, and takes about an hour to reach Los Limones (US$0.70). Buses returning to town leave Los Limones at approximately 8 am, noon and 3 pm.

The eastern park entrance is at El Rosario, a 'ghost town' mining settlement of old wooden houses about 4km up the hill from the village of San Juancito It's a very steep climb up a dirt road from San Juancito to El Rosario; any passing vehicle would probably give you a lift up, but unless you go on a weekend, you may be the only person on the road. A 4WD vehicle is needed.

Western Honduras

Western Honduras is the most settled part of the country and holds some of Honduras' principal attractions, most notably the Mayan ruins of Copán. Other attractions include Honduras' principal lake, the Lago de Yojoa, a couple of national parks, and Comayagua, Honduras' historic first capital.

Also here is San Pedro Sula, the second-largest city in the country. The road between San Pedro Sula and the capital is probably the most traveled in Honduras, connecting as it does the country's two major cities and the southern, western and northern regions.

TEGUCIGALPA TO SAN PEDRO SULA

It's 241km along Honduras' Hwy 1 (Carretera del Norte) from Tegucigalpa to San Pedro Sula, about a four-hour bus trip. The route passes Comayagua, Siguatepeque, the Lago de Yojoa and several archaeological sites. The beautiful Pulhapanzak waterfall is about 30 minutes' drive west of the highway.

This region, called the Valle de Comayagua, was well settled in pre-Columbian times; the Valle de Comayagua formed a cultural 'corridor' between the Valle de Sula (the valley where San Pedro Sula is today) and the Pacific Coast of El Salvador and Nicaragua. Agriculture has been practiced in the Valle de Comayagua for at least 3000 years.

Fourteen archaeological sites have been identified in the department of Comayagua;

apparently one or another of the sites was the primary center of settlement at various times in history. Pottery, jewelry and stone carvings of various styles have been unearthed from the sites.

Based on styles of pottery, archaeologists have identified three major periods in the history of the region. During the preclassic period (600 BC to AD 300), figures of animals and humans formed much of the basis of design, and the agricultural society became increasingly highly organized, shifting from an agrarian society to the organized villages of urban living. During the classic period (AD 300 to 1000) the style of pottery changed, with geometric figures predominating. Apparently, around AD 1000, fighting or warfare occurred, and the organized social structure became more disintegrated until the time of the Spanish conquest in the 16th century.

Between Tegucigalpa and the Lago de Yojoa you'll find three archaeological sites: **Yarumela** (near Comayagua), **Tenampua** (near Siguatepeque) and **Los Naranjos** (near Lago de Yojoa). Yarumela and Tenampua are not developed archaeological parks like Copán Ruinas, but Los Naranjos was opened to the public as an archaeological park in 1998. All of the sites are easy to visit.

COMAYAGUA
pop 85,280
Comayagua, 84km northwest of Tegucigalpa, is the historic first capital of Honduras. The town's colonial past is evident in several fine old churches (including the famous cathedral), three plazas and two interesting museums.

A few kilometers from town is the Honduran military base Sotocano. During the 1980s, when the US was waging the Contra war in Nicaragua, up to 10,000 US soldiers were stationed here, and the base was called Palmerola; since then, it's been converted to a Honduran base, but about a thousand American soldiers are still stationed there. You'll see plenty of signs around town written in both English and Spanish.

Comayagua was founded as the capital of the colonial province of Honduras in 1537 by Spanish Captain Alonso de Cáceres, fulfilling the orders of the Spanish governor of Honduras to establish a new settlement in the geographic center of the territory. The town was initially called Villa de Santa María de Comayagua; in 1543 the name was changed to Villa de la Nueva Valladolid de Comayagua.

Comayagua was declared a city in 1557, and in 1561 the seat of the diocese of Honduras was moved from Trujillo to Comayagua because of its more favorable conditions, central position and closer proximity to the silver- and gold-mining regions.

Comayagua was the center for the political and religious administration of Honduras; for over three centuries, it was the capital city, until the capital was shifted to Tegucigalpa in 1880.

Orientation
Like most Honduran towns, life and essential services focus around the parque central, which is three blocks to the east of the main approach road from the Tegucigalpa–San Pedro Sula highway. Unlike in most Honduran towns, Comayaqua's streets are nearly all paved and airy, and the parque central has been tastefully refurbished with gardens, benches and even piped-in music.

Information
Most banks, including the Banco de Occidente, which is friendlier to travelers than most banks, are clustered around the parque central. The post office and Hondutel office are together behind the cathedral. The bus stop is down by the main highway, a 1km walk or short taxi ride south on El Boulevard.

Churches
The **cathedral** in the center of town is a gem of colonial style. It was built from 1685 to 1715 and is abundantly decorated. It contains much fine art, both inside and out. The altar is similar to that of the Tegucigalpa cathedral: Both were made by the same artist. The clock in the church tower is one of the oldest in the world and is probably the oldest in the Americas. The Moors built it over 800 years ago, for the palace of Alhambra in Granada.

Comayagua's first church was **La Merced**, built from 1550 to 1558. Other fine churches are **San Francisco** (1584) and **La Caridad** (1730). **San Sebastián** (1585) is farther from the center, on the south end of town. All are

COMAYAGUA

PLACES TO STAY
1 Hotel Quan Anexo
2 Hotel Quan
10 Hotel Halston
12 Hotel Libertad; Palmeras
16 Hotel America Inc

PLACES TO EAT
3 Restaurante Mang Ying
11 Comida Rapida Venecia
14 Villa Real
15 Tati's Pizza

OTHER
4 Iglesia La Caridad
5 Museo Regional de Arqueología
6 Iglesia San Francisco
7 Banco de Occidente
8 Cathedral
9 Post Office; Hondutel
13 Museo Colonial
17 Iglesia La Merced
18 Texaco Station; Main Bus Stop
19 Iglesia San Sebastián

worth seeing. Another colonial church, San Juan de Dios (1590), was destroyed by an earthquake in 1750, but samples of its artwork, along with artwork from all the other churches, are on display in the Museo Colonial (see Museums).

If you can read Spanish, look for a small book entitled *Las Iglesias Coloniales de la Ciudad de Comayagua*, which contains an interesting history of Comayagua and its churches. It's available at both museums.

Museums

The first university in Central America was founded in 1632, in the Casa Cural, the building across 4a Calle NO from the cathedral that now houses the **Museo Colonial**; priests have occupied this building since 1558. The university operated there for almost 200 years.

The museum is small but remarkable. Totally renovated in 1990, it contains artwork and religious paraphernalia culled from all the five churches of Comayagua, spanning the 16th to the 18th centuries. In one salon is a display of jewels and ornaments that people gave to the statues in the churches, including pearls and emeralds the size of a thumbnail.

This museum, opened in 1962, was the first in Honduras. The well-informed curator can give you an interesting tour, explaining (in Spanish) the history of each piece. The museum is open 9:30 am to noon and 2 to 4:30 pm daily; admission costs US$1.40.

A block north of the cathedral, the **Museo Regional de Arqueología** (☎ 772 0386) has displays of Honduran archaeological discoveries, including pottery, metates (stone tools used to grind grain), stone carvings, petroglyphs and mastodon bones. It's open 8 am to 4 pm Wednesday to Friday, 9 am to 4 pm Saturday and Sunday, closed Monday and Tuesday. Admission is US$1.40.

Special Events
On the morning of Good Friday, religious images are carried through the streets in a procession over intricate carpets of colored sawdust. Watching the sawdust designs being made the night before the procession is as interesting as the procession itself; you may even be able to join in. Comayagua is the best place in Honduras for visitors to witness Easter celebrations

Places to Stay
About the cheapest place in town is the **Hotel Libertad** (☎ 772 0091), on the parque central. Rooms with one/two/three/four beds are US$3/5/6/7. The rooms share a common cold bath, and they have no windows; they encircle a quiet courtyard containing hammocks and plants.

The **Hotel Halston** (☎ 772 0755), at 3a Calle NO and 2a Avenida NO, is a small upstairs hotel where rooms with private bath and fan are US$9.50 for one or two people. **Hotel America Inc** (☎ 772 0360, fax 772 0009), at 1a Calle NO and 1a Avenida NO, has air-conditioned rooms for around US$14.

Hotel Quan (☎ 772 0070, fax 772 0070, hquan@hondutel.hn), on the north side of town, is in a quiet residential area. It has a variety of rooms, both in the main building and in the newer annex across the street. Room rates vary slightly but average around US$26.50 for an air-conditioned room with TV.

Places to Eat
Comayagua has a few good eating places, including the easy to find **Palmeras**, on the parque central. The oldest restaurant in Comayagua, it has been in operation since 1963. Ask for the *plato del día* for some good, typical Honduran food. It's open for breakfast, lunch and dinner. A couple of blocks away is **Comida Rapida Venecia**, a modern fast-food joint in an old colonial-style building. It's cheap, clean and tasty and does good fresh fruit frescos and desserts.

For pizza, head to **Tati's Pizza**, on El Boulevard, for reputedly the best pizza in town. It's upstairs in the Multicentro Plaza and is open 11:30 am to 10 pm daily except Monday. On weekends it becomes a disco.

For Chinese food, you can't beat the beautiful **Restaurante Mang Ying**, near Hotel Quan. It's a large, attractive Chinese restaurant open 10 am to 10 pm daily. Good food is served in huge portions, with most dishes costing around US$3 to US$4.50.

Perhaps the best restaurant in town is the cozy and atmospheric **Villa Real**, to the southeast of the cathedral. International and Honduran cuisine is the basis of the menu, and prices are mid-range for Honduras. Dine in a relaxing garden and unwind.

Getting There & Away
Comayagua is about 1km east of the highway. Any Tegucigalpa–San Pedro Sula bus will drop or pick you up at the crossroads where El Boulevard meets the Carretera del Norte; you can walk the 1km into town or take a taxi for US$1.40. To Tegucigalpa, express buses cost US$2.50 and take about 1½ to two hours. Catch them at the Texaco gas station.

AROUND COMAYAGUA
Yarumela
This site on the Río Humuya, between Comayagua and La Paz, consists of two major archaeological mounds. The larger one is about 60 feet high; from the top of it you can get a view of the whole Valle de Comayagua.

To the untrained eye, both of the mounds could look simply like hills covered with brush. However, the smaller mound, right beside the river, has been reconstructed on one side, revealing a step pyramid with several platforms and a stairway going up the middle. The other half of the mound has been left in its original state.

To get there, take a bus to La Paz – buses come from Tegucigalpa, or you could pick the bus up from the Tegucigalpa–San Pedro Sula highway at the turnoff for La Paz. In La Paz, you can ask any taxi driver to take

HONDURAS

you to the Zona Arqueológica Yarumela and to pick you up in a couple of hours; the ride takes about 15 or 20 minutes and costs about US$10 roundtrip.

If you have a private vehicle, you can get there from Comayagua in about 15 minutes. From the highway, take the turnoff for La Paz and go over the Río Humuya. Just before you come to a traffic roundabout, there's a dirt road taking off to the right; following this, you will come to the large mound on the right side of the road. The smaller, half-excavated mound is nearby beside the river.

SIGUATEPEQUE
pop 55,120

Siguatepeque is about halfway between Tegucigalpa (117km) and San Pedro Sula (124km), about a two-hour drive from either. There's no real reason to stop in Siguatepeque, though it's not a bad place to break up a journey.

Orientation

At the heart of town is the shady parque central, with lots of trees, a dry fountain and the church and city hall. Three blocks to the west is Plaza San Pablo, with basketball courts, the market and the Empresas Unidas bus station. This is the park you'll see first if you're coming in from the highway, which is 2km from the center of town. Around and between the two plazas are several good places to stay and eat. South of the town is the turnoff for La Esperanza and Marcala.

Places to Stay

Hotel pickings are a bit thin these days but *Hospedaje Elena* (☎ 773 2210), a block west of Plaza San Pablo, is a simple but clean little place with 12 rooms with shared cold bath for US$3 per person.

On the parque central, the *Boarding House Central* (☎ 773 2108) has single/double rooms with private hot bath and cable TV for US$8/10, plus a restaurant and a parking garage in the rear.

Hotel Gomez (☎ 773 2868), on Calle 21 de Junio, is a clean, modern motel with courtyard parking, a cafeteria, cable TV, fans in the rooms and hot water. Singles/doubles go for US$10/13 with TV and private bath.

That's about it as far as accommodations go. Unless you're really keen to stay overnight, move on to Comayagua or to Lake Yojoa.

Places to Eat

Between and around the two plazas, and also in the market, are several comedores where you can get basic meals. Between the

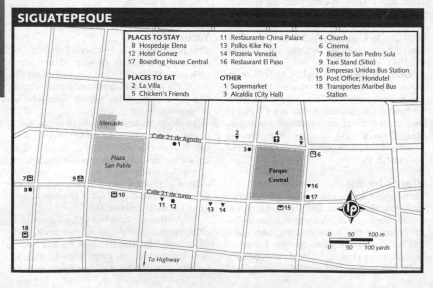

SIGUATEPEQUE

PLACES TO STAY		
8	Hospedaje Elena	
12	Hotel Gomez	
17	Boarding House Central	

PLACES TO EAT	
2	La Villa
5	Chicken's Friends

11 Restaurante China Palace
13 Pollos Kike No 1
14 Pizzería Venezia
16 Restaurant El Paso

OTHER
1 Supermarket
3 Alcaldía (City Hall)

4 Church
6 Cinema
7 Buses to San Pedro Sula
9 Taxi Stand (Sitio)
10 Empresas Unidas Bus Station
15 Post Office; Hondutel
18 Transportes Maribel Bus Station

two plazas, *Restaurante China Palace* serves Chinese and international food, with dishes for around US$3.50 to US$4.50.

Just off the parque central are the *Pizzería Venezia* for pizza, *Pollos Kike No 1* next door for chicken, and *La Villa* Mexican restaurant. On the southeast side of the parque, *Restaurant El Paso* offers simple Honduran dishes. On the northeast side of the parque central, *Chicken's Friends* does fast chicken dishes.

Getting There & Away
Any bus going between Tegucigalpa and San Pedro Sula will drop you at the crossroads at the entrance to Siguatepeque. From there you can walk the 2km into town or take a taxi for US$1.50.

Empresas Unidas (☎ 773 2149) and Transportes Maribel (☎ 773 0254) operate direct buses between Tegucigalpa and Siguatepeque. The Empresas Unidas bus station is on the south side of Plaza San Pablo; the Transportes Mirabel station is a couple of blocks away. Each company offers seven buses daily; between the two, there's a bus leaving for Tegucigalpa roughly every hour, from 4 am to 5 pm (US$2.50, 2½ hours, 117km).

Buses to San Pedro Sula (US$3, 2¾ hours, 124km) depart from an open lot opposite the Hospedaje Elena, a block west of Plaza San Pablo.

AROUND SIGUATEPEQUE
Tenampua
This site was constructed much later than Yarumela, around AD 1000 to 1100. It sits on top of a large hill with a sweeping view overlooking the entire valley. Features include a ball court, walls and archaeological mounds; though ball courts are typical of the Maya, whose area was farther to the west, by this period the ball court had filtered over to this region.

Apparently Tenampua was constructed when warfare was occurring in the valley. The site is well protected and would have been easy to defend; from up here you could easily see anyone approaching the site. The ascent is very steep on three sides; on the fourth side, the people constructed a high, massive wall about 2m thick.

The site is near Siguatepeque, just off the Tegucigalpa–San Pedro Sula highway. Any bus will drop you off at the Restaurante Tenampua, on the east side of the highway at the foot of the Tenampua hill. The people at the restaurant will show you how to hike up the hill to the site; it's a steep climb and takes about one or 1½ hours, but it's worth visiting.

When you're ready to leave, you can flag down a bus on the highway. If you have a private vehicle, you could get here from Comayagua in about half an hour.

LA ESPERANZA
pop 7175
Buses go from Siguatepeque to La Esperanza, 66km to the southwest. A quiet colonial town with an attractive church, La Esperanza is best known for its traditional Lenca Indian market on Sunday. The area is good for walks in the hills, and here are two hotels: *La Esperanza* and the *Hotel Solis*

There is an unpaved road from La Esperanza to Gracias and on to Santa Rosa de Copán; see the Gracias section later in this chapter for more on this route.

CUEVAS DE TAULABÉ
On the highway about 25km north of Siguatepeque and 20km south of the Lago de Yojoa is the entrance to the Cuevas de Taulabé (Caves of Taulabé). There's an entrance fee of US$1.20, and if you like, you can hire a guide to take you on a cave tour. So far, the caves have been explored to a depth of 12km, still without coming to the end.

The first 400m of the cave have been made easier with the addition of lights and a pathway with steps; the pathway can be slippery, so wear adequate shoes. If you want to explore farther into the cave, you must bring your own gear and let the guards at the entrance know of your intentions. Serious explorations into the cave require a permit from the mayor of the town of Taulabé.

LAGO DE YOJOA
The Lago de Yojoa, about three hours (157km) north of Tegucigalpa and one hour (84km) south of San Pedro Sula, is a popular recreation area and highway stopover.

This is a large and beautiful lake, attracting abundant bird life. Bird watchers like to make expeditions to Lago de Yojoa in the early morning; over 375 species of birds have been counted. One morning while sitting on the terrace at the hotel Agua Azul, a birder was surprised to count 37 different species in a single tree.

Fishing on the lake is also good, especially for black bass. Bring your own tackle, as it may not be available locally. All the hotels around the lake can arrange boat and fishing trips.

On the northwest corner of the lake is **Los Naranjos** archaeological site. It was first occupied around 600 or 700 BC. Features include a moat and several archaeological mounds. Plans for the site include opening it as an archaeological park, with a nature trail and interpretive trail. Hurricane Mitch, however, delayed these plans, and the completion date is uncertain. You can get there by taking a small boat from the hotel Agua Azul or one of the other hotels on the north side of the lake.

Two national parks are near the lake: **Santa Bárbara** on the north side and **Cerro Azul Meambar** on the south. Both are cloud forest parks but somewhat difficult to access. Guided tours may be available; ask at the hotel Agua Azul.

Places to Stay & Eat

The highway passes by the lake, but only a few places have direct lake access. Right on the highway, on the south side of the lake, *Hotel Los Remos* (☎ 557 8054) has rooms for US$21 and has a pleasant restaurant overlooking the lake. Any regular bus between Tegucigalpa and San Pedro Sula will drop you there.

About 1km north of the Hotel Los Remos, a row of about thirty restaurants and small comedores serving fried fish fresh from the lake stretches along the highway. The lake is famous for its tasty black bass. A meal of fried fish, salad and tortillas will cost US$2 to US$4, depending on the size and kind of fish. *Rancho Iris* had tasty fried fish, chips, salad and two beers for US$4.

On the north side of the lake, a road taking off to the west toward La Guama and Peña Blanca provides access to several good hotel/resorts on the north shore. The turnoff is marked with a large sign advertising the Hotel Brisas del Lago. This is also the turnoff for the Pulhapanzak waterfall.

The first resort you come to is the *Agua Azul* (☎ 991 7244), a beautiful, peaceful resort 4.5km in from the highway. It's right on the lake and has a dock for small boats, a swimming pool, restaurant and bar. Rooms in duplex cabins with private hot bath are US$23 for one, two or three people. Boat trips on the lake, horse riding and trips to Parque Nacional Azul Meambar can be arranged.

Only Bass, a restaurant about half a kilometer along the lake, is often recommended. Farther along the lake is the larger and more expensive *Hotel Brisas del Lago* (☎ 557 819), with 72 rooms for US$52 per night. Still farther along, the *Finca Las Glorias* (☎ 566 0461) is a luxurious, private and peaceful resort on a large coffee plantation right on the lake, with rooms for US$43.

PULHAPANZAK

Pulhapanzak, a magnificent 443m waterfall on the Río Lindo, can be visited as a stop along the route from Tegucigalpa to San Pedro Sula or as a day trip from San Pedro or the Lago de Yojoa – it's about 17.5km from the lake. Near the waterfall is a very pleasant park and places to swim in the river. It's a popular spot and can be crowded on weekends and holidays. You can camp here if you have your own gear. Entry to the area costs US$0.70.

From San Pedro, Pulhapanzak is 60km (about one hour) south on the highway to Tegucigalpa, then another hour on an unpaved road heading west from the highway; take the La Guama/Peña Blanca turnoff from the highway. Buses reach the waterfall from San Pedro Sula every 40 minutes (see the San Pedro Sula bus section later in this chapter).

SANTA BÁRBARA

pop 30,160

About 53km west of the Lago de Yojoa, Santa Bárbara, capital of the department of the same name, is a small town known for its woven junco handicrafts. The *Boarding House Moderno* (☎ 643 2203) has rooms for US$10 to US$15.

Roads connect Santa Bárbara with the Tegucigalpa–San Pedro Sula highway, and also with the San Pedro Sula–Nueva Ocotepeque highway running along the western side of Honduras. If you're driving between Tegucigalpa and western Honduras, you can cut about 1½ hours off your driving time by making a shortcut through Santa Bárbara, rather than going all the way north to San Pedro Sula.

You can get a bus directly from Tegucigalpa to Santa Bárbara (202km), though the buses run infrequently. Buses run every half hour between Santa Bárbara and San Pedro Sula (US$1 to US$1.25, 1½ to two hours, 94km).

SAN PEDRO SULA
pop 434,936
The second-largest city in Honduras, San Pedro Sula (often called simply San Pedro) is the major industrial, commercial and business center of the country. It is also the major center for the agricultural products of the fertile lowlands surrounding the city.

San Pedro is the transportation hub for the western half of Honduras and for travel to the north coast. The city doesn't have many sights or attractions for visitors, but there are always travelers passing through.

San Pedro is extremely hot and humid for much of the year; the town lies in a valley just 76m above sea level, with little movement of air. January and February are the coolest months, and October to March may be bearable, but from around April to September, San Pedro sizzles. The rainy season runs from May to November.

In the last week of June, San Pedro celebrates a large festival and fair in honor of its founding and the day of San Pedro.

History
The Valle de Sula, hot, rich and fertile, has been heavily settled for thousands of years by various groups. Many archaeological sites have been found in the area, dating from various periods.

San Pedro Sula was founded by Pedro de Alvarado in June 1536. The original name of the town was San Pedro de Puerto Caballos, and it was founded in the nearby Valle de Chooloma (also known as Valle de los Pájaros, or Valley of the Birds). The Spaniards later moved the town to its present location, which was the site of Azula, an Indian village beside the Río Las Piedras. The name San Pedro Sula is a mixture of the names of the two towns.

During the 20th century, San Pedro experienced a rapid boom. The population, at 5000 in 1900 and 21,000 in 1950, had increased to 150,000 by 1975, and to 430,000 by 2000. Much of the recent growth is due to the establishment of over two hundred modern factories. The city continues to grow at a rate of about 5% to 6% each year.

In San Pedro's recent history, rapid growth has also brought crime, air pollution and AIDS. San Pedro bears the unfortunate distinction of being the AIDS capital of Central America; while Honduras has only 16% of Central America's population, it has 60% of its AIDS cases, and a third of these are in San Pedro Sula.

San Pedro has experienced various disasters, including fire and flooding. Despite its long history, nothing is left to see of its colonial past.

Orientation
Downtown San Pedro is flat, with avenidas running north-south and calles running east-west. Primera (1a) Avenida crosses 1a Calle, forming the beginning of the street numbering system; from that point, the numbered avenidas and calles extend out in every direction.

Every address in the center is given in relation to a numbered calle and avenida, and it is further specified by the northeast (noreste, or NE), northwest (noroeste, or NO), southeast (sureste, or SE) or southwest (suroeste, or SO) quadrant of the city.

The center is surrounded by a highway bypass, the Circunvalación, which reduces traffic in the center; an even wider circunvalación is being built, farther from the city center, to reroute even more traffic. Nevertheless, streets are still congested. Most streets in the center are one-way streets.

Information
Tourist Offices There is no government tourist office in San Pedro, but Servicios Culturales y Turísticos (SECTUR; ☎/fax 552 3023) is a private tourist information office selling maps, posters and tourist information. The office is on 4a Calle between 3a and 4a Avenidas NO, Office 304 on the 3rd floor of the building housing the DHL courier service on the ground floor. It's open 8 am to 4 pm Monday to Friday, 8 am to noon Saturday.

HONDURAS

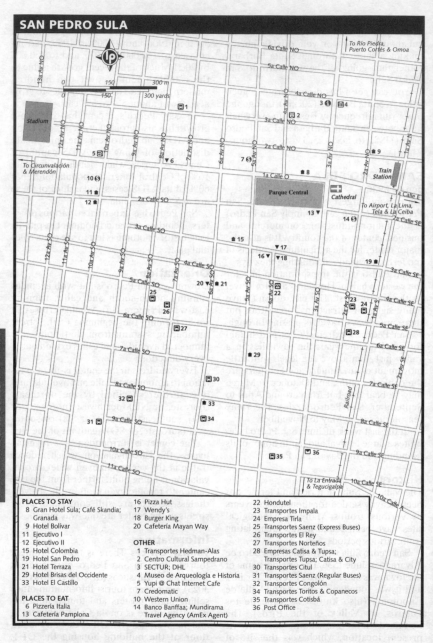

SAN PEDRO SULA

PLACES TO STAY
8   Gran Hotel Sula; Café Skandia;
    Granada
9   Hotel Bolívar
11 Ejecutivo I
12 Ejecutivo II
15 Hotel Colombia
19 Hotel San Pedro
21 Hotel Terraza
29 Hotel Brisas del Occidente
33 Hotel El Castillo

PLACES TO EAT
6   Pizzería Italia
13 Cafetería Pamplona

16 Pizza Hut
17 Wendy's
18 Burger King
20 Cafetería Mayan Way

OTHER
1   Transportes Hedman-Alas
2   Centro Cultural Sampedrano
3   SECTUR; DHL
4   Museo de Arqueología e Historia
5   Yupi @ Chat Internet Cafe
7   Credomatic
10 Western Union
14 Banco Banffaa; Mundirama
    Travel Agency (AmEx Agent)

22 Hondutel
23 Transportes Impala
24 Empresa Tirla
25 Transportes Saenz (Express Buses)
26 Transportes El Rey
27 Transportes Norteños
28 Empresas Catisa & Tupsa;
    Transportes Tupsa; Catisa & City
30 Transportes Citul
31 Transportes Saenz (Regular Buses)
32 Transportes Congolón
34 Transportes Toritos & Copanecos
35 Transportes Cotisbá
36 Post Office

Money Banco Banffaa, by the cathedral, changes traveler's checks. Cash advances on Visa and MasterCard are available at Credomatic (☎ 557 4350) on 5a Avenida between 1a and 2a Calles NO. It's open 8 am to 7 pm Monday to Friday, 8 am to 2 pm Saturday.

The Mundirama travel agency (☎ 552 3400), in the Edificio Martinez Valenzuela (just south of the cathedral), is the agent for American Express; they will hold mail for six months for AmEx card and check users.

Western Union maintains an office on 10a Avenida SO for money transfers to and from Honduras.

Post & Communications The post office is at 9a Calle and 3a Avenida SO. It's open 7:30 am to 8 pm Monday to Friday, 7:30 am to 12:30 pm Saturday. Maps, posters, cards and postcards are sold here, but only until 2:30 pm.

The Hondutel office on the corner of 4a Calle and 4a Avenida SO is open for domestic and international telephone calls 24 hours, every day. Fax service is available 8 am to 4 pm Monday to Friday.

Internet services are provided by Yupi @ Chat Internet Cafe (☎ 550 8365) at 1a Calle and 10a Avenida NO. It is open 10 am to 8 pm Monday to Saturday and 10 am to 2 pm Sunday. Access to one of its 10 modern terminals costs US$3.50 per thirty minutes.

Bookstores There's a small selection of books and magazines in English, as well as the *Miami Herald* and *New York Times* newspapers, at the tobacco shop of the Gran Hotel Sula on the north side of the parque central.

Things to See & Do
The large **cathedral**, facing onto a large shady plaza, is the central feature of San Pedro Sula. It was built during the 1950s.

The **Museo de Arqueología e Historia** (☎ 557 1496) at 3a Avenida and 4a Calle NO, is a large and excellent museum exhibiting hundreds of archaeological artifacts in excellent condition from the Valle de Sula. It illustrates the changes over time of civilization in the valley and the connections between this region and others in pre-Columbian times. Another section features large paintings illustrating the Spanish conquest and life and events of the colonial era, with exhibits on into modern times. It's open 10 am to 4:15 pm Tuesday to Sunday; admission is US$1.

The **Mercado Guamilito** is on the northwest side of town, in the block between 8a and 9a Avenidas, 6a and 7a Calles NO. In addition to the usual fruits, vegetables, household goods and comedores, it houses the **Mercado de Artesanías Guamilito**, a section of the market with a large number of stalls displaying a wide selection of arts and handicrafts from all over Honduras, Guatemala and El Salvador. The market is open 7 am to 5 pm Monday to Saturday, 7 am to noon Sunday.

The main **mercado** is in the southeast section of town, in the block between 6a and 7a Calles, 4a and 5a Avenidas SE. There are stalls in the streets spreading out for blocks around the market. This is a distribution center, and you can sometimes see meters-high piles of green bananas and other produce.

Organized Tours
Mesoamérica Travel (☎ 557 8447, fax 557 8410, info@mesoamerica-travel.com) is an incoming tour operator with its head office in San Pedro Sula. They organize and manage trips for individual travelers or small groups. Their trips vary in length and focus, from one-day adventures and tours to longer, all-terrain and multihabitat itineraries. Check out their informative Web site (www.mesoamerica-travel.com) for further details. They can be found at the Picadelli Bldg, 3a Avenida, at 11a Calle SO.

Places to Stay
Budget San Pedro has many cheap places to stay, but they are not all that savory. They tend to be clustered close to the (disused) railway line and nearby street markets and are a little intimidating and not all that geared to backpackers. In this city, you are advised to settle for something a little more expensive (say around US$20) for better security and peace of mind.

If you really want a budget hotel, there are at least four that just about pass muster. The *Hotel Brisas del Occidente* (☎ 552 2309), on 5a Avenida between 6a and 7a Calle SO, is popular with Peace Corps volunteers. The building is old but clean; all the

HONDURAS

rooms have a fan and shared bath and cost US$5 per room, with one or two beds. Be wary at night in the neighborhood; it's not the most appealing.

The *Hotel El Castillo* (☎ 553 1490), at 6a Avenida SO and 8a Calle SO, close to most of the bus stations, has OK rooms with shared bath for US$8/9, often with a sink in the room. Rooms with private bath cost US$12/13.

The *Hotel Colombia* (☎ 553 3118), on 3a Calle between 5a and 6a Avenida SO, is a little more expensive, at US$17/20, but it is central and in a reasonable part of town. The *Hotel San Pedro* (☎ 550 1513), on 3a Calle SE near 1a Avenida N, is large and offers several types of rooms with hot showers. Room rates are around US$26 for private facilities, though cheaper rooms with shared facilities are available for around US$17.

Mid-Range A budget businessman's hotel and a decidedly better midtown choice, *Hotel Terraza* (☎ 553 3108), on 6a Avenida between 4a and 5a Calle SO, has single/double rooms with private hot bath, telephone, cable TV and one or two beds for US$20. It also has a sports restaurant and bar, and the location is very convenient and safe.

The twin hotels *Ejecutivo I* (☎ 552 4289, fax 552 5868), at 2a Calle SO and 10a Avenida NO, and *Ejecutivo II* (☎ 552 4289, fax 552 5868) on the opposite side of the street offer good to better rooms a little way out of the crush of the city center. Ejecutivo I is a little less plush and somewhat cheaper than Ejecutivo II, which has rooms for US$33.

Hotel Bolívar (☎ 553 3224, fax 553 4823), at the intersection of 2a Avenida and 2a Calle NO, is also upmarket, with a swimming pool, bar and restaurant and private parking. All the rooms have air-con, private hot bath, cable TV and phone and cost US$32 per night.

Top End If you really want to live it up, the *Gran Hotel Sula* (☎ 552 9999), on the plaza, is one of the most luxurious places in town, with 117 rooms priced around US$100. For high rollers, the *Hotel Princess* (☎ 556 9600, fax 550 6143, hotelprincess@globalnet.hn), on 10a Calle SO near the Circunvalación,

will shave a mere US$135 off your daily budget for a luxury room.

Places to Eat

San Pedro Sula has a wide range of excellent eating places catering to all budgets and a surprisingly broad range of cuisines. Many more upmarket places, as well as US fast-food franchises, are on the Circunvalación.

One of the most enjoyable places to eat or just hang out in San Pedro is the *Café Skandia*, the cafeteria of the Gran Hotel Sula on the north side of the parque central. It's air-conditioned, open 24 hours and inexpensive; you can get breakfast, sandwiches or burgers for around US$3.50. It also has lots of foods you don't normally see in Central America, such as waffles, onion rings and apple pie. There are tables beside the swimming pool, and it's an easy place to meet foreigners or locals. Upstairs is a fancier restaurant, the *Granada*, with buffets at breakfast and lunch and a la carte service at dinner.

On the opposite side of the parque central, *Cafetería Pamplona* is another popular, air-conditioned restaurant, open 7 am to 8 pm daily.

Pizza Hut, *Wendy's* and *Burger King* all have air-conditioned branches at the corner of 3a Calle and 4a Avenida SO, a block south of the plaza. All are open 7 am to 10 pm daily. Pizza Hut and Wendy's both have safe salad bars; Pizza Hut's weekday lunchtime special, served from noon to 4 pm, is a good deal, with an individual pizza, a trip to the salad bar and unlimited soft drinks for US$3.

The *Pizzería Italia*, at 1a Calle and 7a Avenida NO, serves good, inexpensive pizza and pasta. It's open 10 am to 10 pm Tuesday to Sunday. For typical Honduran dishes, there's the *Cafetería Mayan Way*, on 6a Avenida SO near 5a Calle SO, where a choice of three lunch specials (including soup) is just US$1.50.

Several other good restaurants are on the southwest side of the Circunvalación, called the Zona Viva for its restaurants and nightspots. *Las Tejas*, Calle 9a SO, and *Restaurante La Tejana*, Calle 9a SO, are often recommended for their seafood and beef. *Restaurante Mexiquense*, at 14a Avenida and 10a Calle SO, is good for Mexican food. *Chef Marianos*, on 16a Avenida between 9a and 10a Calles SO, serves typical Garífuna, Honduran and international dishes.

On the outskirts of town on the Blvd del Sur, the highway heading toward Tegucigalpa, *Shauki's Place* is a pleasant open-air family restaurant and bar where mariachis wander from table to table in the balmy evening air. Come for a meal (they specialize in beef dishes) or just for a drink and a snack. It's open Monday to Saturday from 4 pm on.

Entertainment

Shauki's Place (see the Places to Eat section) is a bar with good music, a pleasant place to go in the evening. *Frogs*, on Blvd Los Próceres between 19a and 20a Calles SO, has three different bars, beach volleyball, mini soccer, pool tables, giant TV screens and a snack bar. It's open 5 pm until after midnight daily.

Discos popular with young people include *Confetis* and *Henry's* both on the Circunvalación. They usually have a cover charge of about US$5. *El Quijote*, on 11a Calle between 3a and 4a Avenidas SO, attracts a bit older crowd and is considered San Pedro Sula's most exclusive disco.

San Pedro doesn't have many gay nightspots, but members of Grupo Prisma in Tegucigalpa (see the Gay & Lesbian Travelers part of the Honduras Facts for the Visitor section) have suggested *Three World*, a bar for gays and lesbians behind the Multiplaza Mall next to the BAMER Autobank; it's open Tuesday to Saturday.

Getting There & Away

Air San Pedro Sula is an air transportation hub. It is served by daily direct flights to all of the major cities in Central America; to Houston, Los Angeles, Miami, New Orleans, New York and San Francisco in the USA; to Mexico City and Cancún in Mexico; and, within Honduras, to Tegucigalpa, La Ceiba and all the Bay Islands.

International airlines serving San Pedro include:

American Airlines (☎ 558 0518, 668 3241 at the airport, fax 558 0527), Blvd Los Andes 16

Continental (☎ 557 4141, 668 3208 at the airport, fax 557 4146), at the Plaza Versalle, Avenida Circunvalación

COPA (☎ 550 5583, 668 6776 at the airport, fax 552 9766), beneath the Gran Hotel Sula

Grupo TACA (☎ 550 5222, 668 3333 at the airport, fax 550 5269), Avenida Circunvalación 13

Iberia (☎ 550 2530, 668 3217 at the airport, fax 550 4162), in the Edificio Quiroz, 2a Calle 2a Avenida SO

Lufthansa (☎ 557 2459, fax 557 1218), in the Edificio Los Alpes, on 8a Calle between 15a and 16a Avenidas NO

Domestic airlines serving San Pedro include:

Isleña (☎ 552 8322, ☎/fax 668 3333 at the airport), in Edificio Trejo Marlón at 1a Calle and 7a Avenida SO

Sosa Airlines (☎/fax 550 6548, 668 3223 at the airport), in the Edificio Roman, on 8a Avenida between 1a and 2a Calles

See the Honduras Getting Around section for domestic fares.

Bus San Pedro is also a land transportation hub, with many bus lines and routes departing in all directions. Buses of different categories travel to most places. The 'direct' or 'express' *(servicio directo)* buses cost slightly more than the normal *(servicio a escala)* buses but will get you there faster, without dozens of stops along the way. The luxury class *(ejecutivo)* buses to major cities like Tegucigalpa and La Ceiba are very well appointed and make no stops. They are about twice as expensive as the direct bus.

As in Tegucigalpa, each bus company operates from its own terminal, most in central San Pedro Sula within walking distance of each other. The exception is the Viana Clase Oro bus station, which is near Wendy's on the Circunvalación.

Refer to the San Pedro Sula map for the location of each individual company's bus station. The frequency of departures is generally hourly for destinations closer to San Pedro Sula, with up to six or more departures daily for destinations farther afield. The free tourist magazine *Honduras Tips* has a very helpful section on bus routes and bus company contact addresses.

Some of the major routes and transport companies are listed in the 'Long-distance Buses from San Pedro Sula' boxed text.

Train The train station (☎ 553 4080) is in the center of town, on the corner of 1a

HONDURAS

Long-Distance Buses from San Pedro Sula

destination	bus line	phone	fare	type	duration
Agua Caliente	Transportes Congolón	553 1174	US$5.40	normal	6 hours
Agua Caliente	Transportes Congolón	553 1174	US$6.50	direct	5 hours
Copán Ruinas	GAMA	552 2861	US$4	direct	3 hours
La Ceiba	Catisa Tupsa	552 1042	US$2.50	normal	3 hours
La Ceiba	Viana Clase Oro	556 9261	US$8.30	ejecutivo	2½ hours
Puerto Cortés	Transportes Citul	553 0070	US$0.85	normal	1½ hours
Puerto Cortés	Transportes Citul	553 0070	US$1.10	direct	1 hour
Puerto Cortés	Transportes Impala	553 0070	US$0.85	normal	1½ hours
Puerto Cortés	Transportes Impala	553 0070	US$1.10	direct	1 hour
Santa Rosa de Copán	Transportes Torito & Copanecos	553 4930	US$2	normal	3 hours
Santa Rosa de Copán	Transportes Torito & Copanecos	553 4930	US$3.50	direct	2½ hours
Tegucigalpa	El Rey Express	550 8355	US$4.34	direct	4 hours
Tegucigalpa	El Rey y Saenz	553 4969	US$2.78	normal	4 hours
Tegucigalpa	Hedman Alas	553 1361	US$4.34	direct	4 hours
Tegucigalpa	Norteños	552 2145	US$2.78	normal	4 hours
Tegucigalpa	Saenz Ejecutivo	553 4969	US$10.17	ejecutivo	4 hours
Tegucigalpa	Hedman Alas	553 1361	US$5.42	direct	3½ hours
Tegucigalpa	Viana Clase Oro	556 9261	US$8.30	ejecutivo	3½ hours
Tela	Catisa Tupsa	552 1042	US$2	normal	2 hours
Tela	Viana Clase Oro	556 9261	US$6	ejecutivo	1½ hours
Trujillo	Cotraipbal	557 8470	US$1.10	normal	5 hours
Trujillo	Cotuc	557 3175	US$1.10	normal	5 hours

Calle and 1a Avenida. Passenger trains no longer operate from San Pedro; there's only one passenger train route in the whole country, operating between Puerto Cortés and Tela. However, the office here in San Pedro is the national train office (the Ferrocarril Nacional de Honduras); you can get current information about this one train route.

Getting Around
To/From the Airport Villeda Morales Airport is about 15km east of town. There is no direct bus to the airport, but you can get on any El Progreso bus, alight at the airport turnoff, and walk for 10 minutes. You'll need to ask the driver to let you off. Taxis cost about US$8 from the airport to town but US$7 going the other way (the average taxi ride in town costs around US$2).

Bus The fare on local buses to the suburbs is US$0.05.

Car San Pedro Sula is a good place to rent a car, particularly if you are looking to pick up a car at the airport.

Car rental agencies in San Pedro Sula include:

Avis (☎ 553 0888, 668 1064 at the airport, fax 553 3718), at 1a Calle and 6a Avenida NO

Budget (☎ 552 2295, 668 3179 at the airport, fax 553 3411), at 1a Calle and 7a Avenida NO

Maya (☎ 552 2670, 668 3168 at the airport, fax 552 7255), 3a Avenida 51 NO

Molinari (☎ 553 2639, 668 6178 at the airport, fax 552 2704), at the Gran Hotel Sula

Thrifty (☎ 668 3153, fax 668 3154, thrifty@ david.intertel.hn), at Villeda Morales Airport

Toyota (☎ 556 2666, 668 3174 at the airport), on 3a Avenida between 5a and 6a Calle

PARQUE NACIONAL CUSUCO

Parque Nacional Cusuco, 20km west of San Pedro Sula in the impressive Merendón mountain range, is a cloud forest park. Its highest peak (Cerro Jilinco) is 2242m. The park has abundant wildlife, including a large population of quetzals and many other tropical birds, among them toucans and parrots. Quetzals are spotted most frequently from April to June.

At the park there are a waterfall, swimming hole, interpretive forest trails of various lengths, a visitors center with exhibits and an audiovisual center. A guide will take you along the trails for around US$4; you'll see more wildlife with a guide. The best time of day to spot wildlife is early in the morning. The park is open 8 am to 4:30 pm daily; admission costs US$15 for foreigners.

Access is easiest with a 4WD vehicle, especially during the rainy season. To get there, take the highway out of San Pedro as if going to Tegucigalpa; at the Chamelecón intersection, take the western highway (marked 'Occidente'). After 30km (about 30 minutes), take the turnoff toward Cofradía; from Cofradía, it's about 25km to the park by a gravel road. Go through Cofradía, and after about an hour, you'll come to Buenos Aires, the last place where food and drink are available. When the road divides, take the left fork and ascend for about 20 more minutes to reach the park visitors center.

Getting there by public transportation is more of a challenge, but it can be done. Buses to Cofradía are operated by Empresa Etica, opposite the cemetery on Avenida Los Leones in San Pedro Sula; they depart every 20 minutes and take about an hour to reach Cofradía. From Cofradía, you can take a pickup (US$1.50) to Buenos Aires; pickups provide public transportation between the two towns, but they don't go every day. You could probably hitch a ride to Buenos Aires if no pickups are going.

Accommodations are available near the park at a small two-bedroom cabin in the village of Buenos Aires, fifteen minutes' walk from the park's visitors center. The cost is US$12 per person; each bedroom has two beds, complete with bedding, and there's a kitchen. Camping is also possible in the park at no cost. For further informa-

tion, ask at the Fundación Ecologista (☎ 552 1014, fax 557 6620, fundeco@netsys.hn), in San Pedro Sula upstairs over the Pizzería Italia at the corner of 1a Calle and 8a Avenida NO. It's open 8 am to noon and 1 to 5 pm Monday to Friday. The staff also has general park information, including maps and a bird checklist.

CARRETERA DE OCCIDENTE

From San Pedro Sula, the Carretera de Occidente runs southwest, roughly parallel with the Guatemalan border, though rather far into the Honduran side. At La Entrada, 124km southwest of San Pedro Sula, the road forks. One fork heads west to Copán Ruinas and the Guatemalan border, the other south to Santa Rosa de Copán, Nueva Ocotepeque and the two borders of Agua Caliente (Guatemala) and El Poy (El Salvador).

LA ENTRADA

La Entrada is a crossroads town with several places to stay and eat; lots of buses and traffic pass through on the way northeast to San Pedro Sula, south to Santa Rosa de Copán and Nueva Ocotepeque, and southwest to Copán Ruinas. You never have to wait long for a bus in La Entrada. That said, it's not a particularly enticing place to stay so it's probably better to plan to move on to your next stop without lingering too long.

Parque Arqueológico El Puente

The town's major attraction is this archaeological park with 210 archaeological structures, a museum and cafeteria. It is estimated that around a thousand Mayan people lived on this site from around AD 650 to 900, when it was a town linked culturally and administratively with Copán, which was the regional capital. The turnoff for the park is 5km from the crossroads at La Entrada on the road heading to Copán; the archaeological park is another 6km from the turnoff. It's open 8 am to 4 pm daily; admission costs US$5.

Places to Stay & Eat

If you do plan to overnight in La Entrada, there are a couple of places you might consider. Right at the crossroads, *Hotel y Restaurant El San Carlos* (☎ 651 4187) is a reasonable enough place to stay. All the rooms have private hot bath, color cable TV, telephone and fan; rooms are around US$13 for two people. The hotel has a restaurant/bar open 7 am to 10 pm daily.

Two blocks north of the crossroads, *Hotel Tegucigalpa* (☎ 651 4046) is a clean hotel with a relaxed, homey feel. All the rooms have private cold bath and color cable TV. Rooms with fan are US$11 with one/two beds or US$14 with air-con. There's parking in the central courtyard, where there's also a simple cafeteria open 6 am to 8 pm daily.

Several small comedores are near the bus stop at the crossroads. For more upmarket dining, *La Terraza Steak House* is recommended by many travelers; it's two blocks north of the crossroads, upstairs beside the Hotel Tegucigalpa.

Getting There & Away
Buses pass through La Entrada frequently in all directions, stopping at the crossroads. These include:

Copán Ruinas (US$2, 2¼ hours, 61km)
Buses depart every 45 minutes from 5 am to 4:30 pm.
Nueva Ocotepeque (US$2.20, 3½ hours, 123km)
Buses depart every 20 minutes from 6 am to 8:30 pm.
San Pedro Sula (regular: US$1.80, 2½ hours; express: US$2.20, two hours, 124km)
Express buses leave at 9 am and 3 pm. Regular buses depart every 20 minutes from 5 am to 7:30 pm.
Santa Rosa de Copán (US$1, 1¼ hours, 28km)
Same buses as to Nueva Ocotepeque.

COPÁN RUINAS
pop 6000
The town of Copán Ruinas, also sometimes simply called Copán, is about 1km from the famous Mayan ruins of the same name. It is a beautiful little village with cobblestone streets, white adobe buildings with red-tile roofs and a lovely colonial church on the plaza. This valley was inhabited by the Maya for around two thousand years, and an aura of timeless peace fills the air. Copán has recently become a primary tourist destination, but this hasn't disrupted the peace to the extent one might expect.

The town's annual festival is celebrated from March 15 to 20.

Orientation
The parque central, with the church on one side, is the heart of town. The parque has been tastefully renovated and is a popular meeting place. The town is very small, and everything is within a few blocks of the parque. The ruins are 1km outside of town, on the road to La Entrada – a pleasant 15-minute stroll along a footpath to one side of the highway. Las Sepulturas archaeological site is 1km farther along.

Information
Banco de Occidente, on the parque central, changes US dollars (maximum US$100 per day) and traveler's checks, Guatemalan quetzals and Salvadoran colones, and it gives cash advances on Visa cards only. The dollar exchange rate is not so good here, so you are advised to use Banco Atlántida and Bancreser, which are also on the parque central. These banks do not exchange traveler's checks, but they do give cash advances on Visa cards. All banks are open 8 am to noon and 2 to 4:30 pm Monday to Friday, 8 am to 11:30 am Saturday.

The post office is a few doors west from the parque central, and Hondutel is a few doors south.

Three Internet cafes service the needs of travelers to Copán Ruinas. Copán Net (☎ 651 4460), a couple blocks south of the parque central, is open 8 am to 8 pm, has six terminals and charges US$4.10 an hour. There are two branches of Maya Connections (☎ 651 4077, fax 651 4315, mayaconn@ hondutel.hn), and each offers similar opening times and access charges as Copán Net. One is part of the Hotel Los Gemelos; the other is one block south of the parque central.

The Justo A Tiempo laundry offers a laundry service, an English-language book exchange and operates a cafe with yummy home-baked goodies. The family at Hotel Los Gemelos also operates a laundry service.

Things to See & Do
Of course, the number one attraction is the Copán archaeological site, 1km outside of town on the road to La Entrada (see the Copán Archaeological Site section). Other fine places to visit in the area are covered in the Around Copán Ruinas section later in

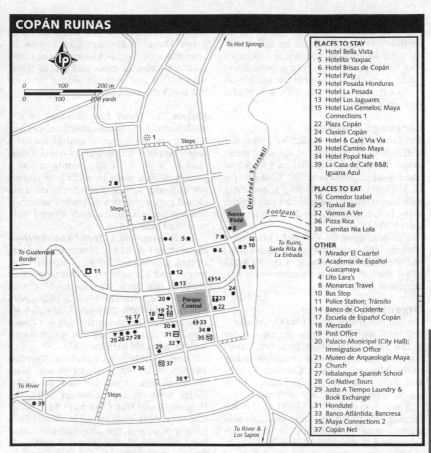

COPÁN RUINAS

PLACES TO STAY
2 Hotel Bella Vista
5 Hotelito Yaxpac
6 Hotel Brisas de Copán
7 Hotel Paty
9 Hotel Posada Honduras
12 Hotel La Posada
13 Hotel Los Jaguares
15 Hotel Los Gemelos; Maya
    Connections 1
22 Plaza Copán
24 Clasico Copán
26 Hotel & Cafe Via Via
30 Hotel Camino Maya
34 Hotel Popol Nah
39 La Casa de Café B&B;
    Iguana Azul

PLACES TO EAT
16 Comedor Izabel
25 Tunkul Bar
32 Vamos A Ver
36 Pizza Rica
38 Carnitas Nia Lola

OTHER
1 Mirador El Cuartel
3 Academia de Español
    Guacamaya
4 Lito Lara's
8 Monarcas Travel
10 Bus Stop
11 Police Station; Tránsito
14 Banco de Occidente
17 Escuela de Español Copán
18 Mercado
19 Post Office
20 Palacio Municipal (City Hall);
    Immigration Office
21 Museo de Arqueología Maya
23 Church
27 Ixbalanque Spanish School
28 Go Native Tours
29 Justo A Tiempo Laundry &
    Book Exchange
31 Hondutel
33 Banco Atlántida; Bancresa
35 Maya Connections 2
37 Copán Net

Map labels: To Hot Springs; Steps; Quebrada Sesesmil; Steps; Soccer Field; Footpath; To Ruins, Santa Rita & La Entrada; To Guatemala Border; Parque Central; To River; Steps; To River & Los Sapos

HONDURAS

this chapter. In town, the **Museo de Arqueología Maya** (☎ 651 4437), on the parque central, is well worth a visit. It contains the original Stela B, portraying King 18 Rabbit, the great builder-king who unfortunately lost his head to the king of Quiriguá. The museum also has interesting and informative exhibits of painted pottery, carved jade, Mayan glyphs, a calendar round and the Tumba del Brujo, the tomb of a shaman or priest who died around AD 700 and was buried with many items under the east corner of the Plaza de los Jaguares. The museum is open 8 am to 4 pm daily; admission is US$2.

About four blocks north of the plaza is the **Mirador El Cuartel**, the old jail, with a magnificent view over town. A pleasant,

easy walk on the road on the south side of town provides a fine view over the corn and tobacco fields surrounding Copán. It's also a pleasant walk to the river, also on the south side of town.

Horseback Riding
You can rent a horse in Copán Ruinas to go out to the archaeological site or make other excursions. Horses can be arranged by either of the town's tour companies or by most hotels. More than likely you will be accosted by young children offering you horseback tours. Better avoid these avid mini-salespersons and opt for booking a tour through your hotel or local tour office.

The Hacienda San Lucas (☎ 651 4106, sanlucas@honduras.com) is possibly your best, most hassle-free horse riding option. Visit their guest center a couple of blocks north of the parque central for full details. They are located out of town at Los Sapos (the Toads), one of the more popular horse riding areas. The *sapos* are in fact old Mayan stone carvings in a spot with a beautiful view over town.

Language Courses

The Ixbalanque Spanish School (☎/fax 651 4432, ixbalan@hn2.com), on the same street as the Tunkul Bar, offers 20 hours weekly of one-on-one instruction in Spanish for US$185 per week, including a homestay with a local family that provides three meals a day. Instruction only, for 20 hours a week, costs US$125.

The Academia de Español Guacamaya (☎ 651 4360, guacamaya@latinmail.com) and the Escuela de Español Copan (☎ 651 4390) also offer hands-on courses for foreigners at similar rates.

Organized Tours

Go Native Tours (☎ 651 4432, ixbalan@ hn2.com), with an office on the same street as the Tunkul Bar, offers both local tours and ecological tours farther afield, including to the Mosquitia region, Celaque, Cusuco and Punta Sal. It also organizes bird-watching tours to the Lago de Yojoa.

Xukpi Tours (☎ 651 4435, 651 4503 in the evening), operated by Jorge Barraza, also offers a number of ecological tours both locally and farther afield. His ruin and bird-watching tours are justly famous; some of the locals call him the *hombre pájaro* (bird man) for his enthusiasm and knowledge about birds. He offers ecological tours to all parts of Honduras (including the Mosquitia region and all the national parks) and to Quiriguá in Guatemala. He is quite an ebullient, knowledgeable, capable and wonderful guide.

Places to Stay – Budget

Hostels The neatest place to stay in town is the *Iguana Azul* (☎ 651 4620, fax 651 4623, casadecafe@mayanet.hn), next door to La Casa de Café B&B. It is owned and run by experienced Honduras hand and writer Howard Rosenzweig and his Honduran wife, Angela. It has two four-bunk bedrooms (US$4.50 per person) and three

single or double rooms for US$7/10 with shared hot bath in a colonial-style ranch home. There's a pleasant garden, and the common area has books, magazines, travel guides, laundry facilities and lots of travel information. It is on the far side of the town but worth the extra hike.

Hotels The *Hotel Los Gemelos* (☎ 651 4077, fax 651 4315, maricela@hondutel.hn), a block east of the parque central, is a long-time favorite with budget travelers. Operated by a very friendly family, it has a garden patio, a place to wash your clothes (or a laundry service if you prefer) and enclosed parking; coffee is always available. Singles/doubles/triples with shared cold bath are US$5/7/10.

In the same block, *Hotel Posada Honduras* (☎ 651 4082) has 13 simple rooms encircling a courtyard full of mango, mamey, lemon and coconut trees, with enclosed parking out back. Singles/doubles with shared cold bath are US$3.50/4.20; with private cold bath they are US$4.20/8.40. Also on the same street, the simple *Clasico Copán* (☎ 651 4040) has renovated rooms with private cold bath for US$14.50

Other simple places include *Hotelito Yaxpac* (☎ 651 4025), with just four plain rooms, all with private hot bath, for US$7. Fairly new on the scene in 2000, the Belgian-owned *Hotel Via Via* (☎ 651 4652) has very neat single/double rooms in a garden adjoining the attached restaurant for US$10.50/14. The *Hotel La Posada* (☎ 651 4070), half a block from the parque central, has double rooms with shared cold bath for US$14.

The *Hotel Popol Nah* (☎ 651 4095) is a clean place with seven rooms for US$17, all with private hot bath. The *Hotel Paty* (☎ 651 4021), near the entrance to town, has rooms around a courtyard, all with private hot bath, for US$15.

Places to Stay – Mid-Range

Copán also has a number of more upmarket places. One of the most attractive is *Hotel Brisas de Copán* (☎ 651 4118), near the entrance to town. Attractive upper rooms with cable TV, shared terraces and plenty of light are US$24. Cheaper rooms are also available; all the rooms come with private hot bath.

Another possibility, **Hotel Bella Vista** (☎ 651 4502), is up on a hill overlooking town, four blocks from the plaza. It has a beautiful view; large, comfortable rooms for US$17 with private hot bath, cable TV and phone; and parking in the courtyard.

For B&B accommodations, look no further than **La Casa de Café** (☎ 651 4620, fax 651 4623, casadecafe@mayanet.hn), four blocks from the plaza. Operated by the same owners as the Iguana Azul hostel, it's a beautiful place in a beautiful setting; there's an outdoor area with tables and hammocks with a view over cornfields to the mountains of Guatemala. Five rooms with private hot bath are US$30/38 for one or two people. All prices include a hearty breakfast.

Other, more expensive places in town include **Hotel Los Jaguares** (☎ 651 4451), with rooms for US$36.50/40; **Hotel Camino Maya** (☎ 651 4646, fax 651 4517, hcmaya@david.intertel.hn), with rooms for US$45; and the very central **Plaza Copán** (☎ 651 4508, fax 651 4039), with a swimming pool, restaurant/bar and rooms for US$43/50. All of these places are beautiful, luxurious and right on the parque central.

Places to Eat

The **Tunkul Bar** (☎ 651 4410), two blocks from the parque central, is the main gathering spot in town. It's an attractive covered-patio bar/restaurant with good food, good music, good company and a book exchange. A variety of meat and vegetarian meals all cost around US$4. The Tunkul is open daily from noon to midnight.

Another pleasant spot is the **Vamos A Ver** cafeteria and restaurant, half a block from the parque central. It's a pleasant little covered-patio place with good, inexpensive foods that you don't always see while traveling in Central America: good homemade breads, a variety of international cheeses, good soups, fruit or vegetable salads, good coffee, fruit licuados, a wide variety of teas and always something for vegetarians. It's open 7 am to 10 pm daily.

On the same street as the Tunkul Bar, **Comedor Izabel** is a cheap, typical comedor with decent food. It's open 6:30 am to 9 pm daily. Also nearby is the **Cafe Via Via** (☎ 651 4652) (see the Places to Stay section), where you can feast on Belgian

pommes frites, Greek salads or excellent chili con carne. This place is also open at 7 am for breakfast.

Pizza Rica (☎ 651 4016) is probably the best place in Copán Ruinas for pizzas. The pizzas are very large, and the American owner even does home deliveries, in case you can't be bothered moving from your hammock.

On the south side of town, **Carnitas Nia Lola** (☎ 651 4196) is a very pleasant restaurant with a beautiful view over corn and tobacco fields toward the mountains. It's a relaxing place with simple and economical food; the specialties are charcoal-grilled chicken and beef and anafres, a kind of gooey, cheese-and-beans fondue. It's open 11am to 10 pm daily.

Entertainment

The **Tunkul Bar** is the happening spot in the evening. This is where most travelers in town hang out to drink beer and margaritas during happy hour (8 to 9 pm). There's a notice board with travelers' tips and a selection of tourist brochures from other places in Honduras and Guatemala, and the Tunkul is a generally buzzing place to be.

Shopping

Items to look out for are leatherware, woven baskets, textiles from Guatemala and tobacco. Some fine cigars can be bought at tobacco shops around town. Perhaps the most enticing souvenirs are replica Mayan carvings made by a local man called Lito Lara (☎ 651 4138). He doesn't have a shop and his house is not marked, so ask around. He'll be happy to show you is genuinely high-quality Mayan carvings. He doesn't speak English himself, but his daughter does.

Getting There & Away

All the buses and pickups serving Copán Ruinas depart from the bus stop along the street at the entrance to town.

To/From San Pedro Sula Direct buses to San Pedro Sula (US$4, 4½ hours, 169km) depart at 6 and 7 am and 3 pm. If you want to leave at another time, you can easily take a bus to La Entrada (US$2, 2¼ hours, 61km) and transfer there to a bus heading to San Pedro. Buses to La Entrada depart every 40 minutes from 4 am to 5 pm.

The GAMA express bus (US$4) departs every morning at 6 am, arriving in San Pedro Sula at 9 am. It departs San Pedro Sula for the return trip at 3 pm, from a parking lot across the street from the Norteño bus line at 6a Avenida. The Casasola bus (US$4) leaves Copán Ruinas at 7 am and returns from San Pedro Sula at 2pm – at the same bus stops.

Go Native Tours (see the Organized Tours section) offers shuttle service to San Pedro Sula for US$12, but not every day; check to see when they're going.

Border Crossing Copán Ruinas is about 12km (30 minutes) from the Guatemalan border at El Florido (see the Guatemala chapter). The border crossing is open 7 am to 6 pm daily. The approach road on the Honduran side is being gradually improved, as is the approach road on the Guatemalan side.

Pickups depart for the border from the bus stop in Copán Ruinas every 40 minutes from 6 am to 6 pm and charge US$1.50. Make sure you are charged the correct price – ask around beforehand to find out what the price should be. From the border, regular buses leave for Chiquimula on the Guatemala side (US$25, 8km, 2½ hours).

The money changers at the border sometimes offer a very unfavorable rate. Before you arrive at the border, find out what the rate of exchange should be.

Monarcas Travel (☎/fax 651 4361) runs a daily shuttle service in a mini-bus from Copán Ruinas to Antigua and Guatemala City in Guatemala. The bus departs from Copán at 3 pm, arriving in Antigua at 9 pm. From Antigua, the bus departs at 4 am. The one-way fare is US$25.

AROUND COPÁN RUINAS
Hot Springs
There are some hot springs 24km north of town, about an hour's drive or hitchhike along a beautiful mountain dirt road through lush, fertile mountains with many coffee plantations. Take the road heading out of town (see the Copán Ruinas map) and just keep going for 24km. A small white sign at the entrance says 'Agua Caliente;' it's on the right-hand side, but it's a small sign

so watch out for it. Admission is US$1. There are a couple of artificial pools, or you can sit in the river, where the boiling hot spring water mixes with the cool river water. Bring warm clothes if you come in the evening.

COPÁN ARCHAEOLOGICAL SITE
Designated by Unesco as a world heritage site, the Copán archaeological site is about 1km outside of town on the road from Copán Ruinas to La Entrada – a pleasant 15-minute stroll along a footpath to one side of the highway. Las Sepulturas archaeological site is a couple of kilometers farther along.

The archaeological site is open 8 am to 5 pm daily. The Museum of Sculpture, also at the site, closes an hour earlier. Admission to the ruins costs US$10 for foreigners and includes entry to Las Sepulturas. Admission to the museum costs US$5 and a further (steep) US$10 to enter the two tunnels that visitors can now explore.

At the entrance to the ruins, the *centro de visitantes* (visitors center) houses the ticket seller and a small exhibition about the site and its excavation. Nearby are a cafeteria and souvenir and handicrafts shops. Cheaper food is available across the road at the Comedor Mayapán. There's a picnic area along the path to the Principal Group of ruins. A *sendero natural* (nature trail) entering the forest several hundred meters from the visitors center passes by a small ball court.

Pick up a copy of the booklet *History Carved in Stone: A Guide to the Archaeological Park of the Ruins of Copán,* by William L Fash and Ricardo Agurcia Fasquelle, available at the visitors center for US$1.65. It will help you understand and appreciate the ruins. It's also a good idea to go with a guide who can help to explain the ruins and bring them to life.

History
Pre-Columbian History Ceramic evidence shows that people have been living in the Copán valley since at least around 1200 BC and probably before that. Copán must have had significant commercial activity since early times; graves showing significant Olmec influence have been dated to around 900 to 600 BC.

COPÁN ARCHAEOLOGICAL SITE

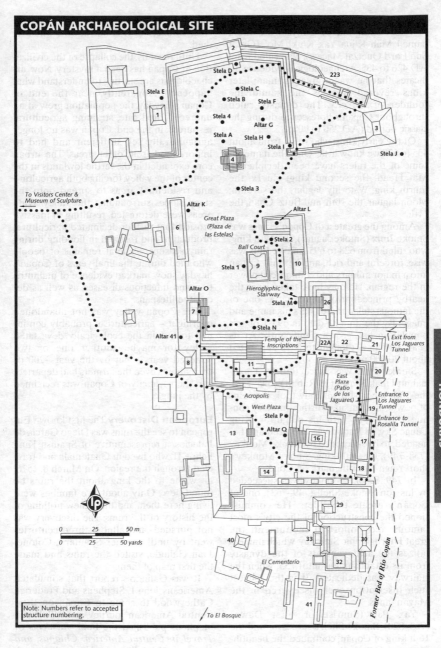

Stela D

223

Stela E

Stela C

Stela B   Stela F

1

Stela 4

Altar G

Stela A   Stela H

Stela I

2

3

Stela J

4

Stela 3

To Visitors Center &
Museum of Sculpture

Altar K

Altar L

Great Plaza
(Plaza de
las Estelas)

6

Stela 2

Ball Court

Stela 1   9   10

Altar O

Hieroglyphic
Stairway

Stela M   26

7

Stela N

A

Altar 41

Temple of the
Inscriptions

22A   22   21

Exit from
Los Jaguares Tunnel

8

11

20

East
Plaza
(Patio
de los
Jaguares)

Acropolis

West Plaza

Stela P

Entrance to
Los Jaguares
Tunnel

19

Entrance to
Rosalila Tunnel

13   Altar Q   16   17

14   18

29

N

0   25   50 m
0   25   50 yards

40   33   30

32

El Cementerio

Former Bed of Río Copán

41

To El Bosque

Note: Numbers refer to accepted
structure numbering.

HONDURAS

Around AD 426, one royal family came to rule Copán, led by a mysterious king named Mah K'ina Yax K'uk' Mo' (Great Sun Lord Quetzal Macaw), who ruled from AD 426 to 435. Archaeological evidence indicates that he was a great shaman; later kings revered him as the semidivine founder of the city. The dynasty ruled throughout Copán's florescence during the classic period (AD 250 to 900).

Of the early kings who ruled from about 435 to 628 we know little. Only the names of some of the rulers have been deciphered: Mat Head, the second king; Cu Ix, the fourth king; Waterlily Jaguar, the seventh; Moon Jaguar, the 10th; and Butz' Chan, the 11th.

Among the greatest of Copán's kings was Smoke Imix (Smoke Jaguar), the 12th king, who ruled from 628 to 695. Smoke Imix was wise, forceful and rich, and he built Copán into a major military and commercial power in the region. He may have taken over the nearby princedom of Quiriguá, as one of the famous stelae there bears his name and image. By the time he died in 695, Copán's population had grown significantly. At its peak, Copán is thought to have supported about 20,000 people.

Smoke Imix was succeeded by Uaxaclahun Ubak K'awil (18 Rabbit) (695–738), the 13th king, who willingly took the reins of power and pursued further military conquest. In a war with his neighbor, King Cauac Sky, 18 Rabbit was captured and beheaded, to be succeeded by Smoke Monkey (738–749), the 14th king. Smoke Monkey's short reign left little mark on Copán.

In 749, Smoke Monkey was succeeded by his son Smoke Shell (749–763), one of Copán's greatest builders. He commissioned the construction of the city's most famous and important monument, the great Hieroglyphic Stairway, which immortalizes the achievements of the dynasty from its establishment until 755, when the stairway was dedicated. It is the longest such inscription ever discovered in the Mayan lands.

Yax Pac (Sunrise or First Dawn) (763–820), Smoke Shell's successor and the 16th king of Copán, continued the beautification of Copán, though it seems that the dynasty's power was declining and its subjects had fallen on hard times. The final aspirant to the throne, U Cit Tok', became ruler in 822, but it is not known when he died.

Until recently, the collapse of the civilization at Copán has been a mystery. Now, archaeologists are starting to understand what happened. Apparently, near the end of Copán's heyday, the population grew at an unprecedented rate, straining agricultural resources; in the end, Copán was no longer agriculturally self-sufficient and had to import food from other areas. The urban core expanded in the fertile lowlands in the center of the valley, forcing both agriculture and residential areas to spread onto the steep slopes surrounding the valley. Wide areas were deforested, resulting in massive erosion that further decimated agricultural production and resulted in flooding during rainy seasons. Skeletal remains of people who died during the final years of Copán's heyday show marked evidence of malnutrition and infectious diseases, as well as decreased lifespans.

The Copán valley was not abandoned overnight – agriculturists probably continued to live in the ecologically devastated valley for maybe another one or two hundred years – but by the year 1200 or thereabouts even the farmers had departed, and the royal city of Copán was reclaimed by the jungle.

European Discovery The first known European to see the ruins was Diego García de Palacios, a representative of Spanish King Felipe II, who lived in Guatemala and traveled through the region. On March 8, 1576, he wrote to the king about the ruins he found here. Only about five families were living here then, and they knew nothing of the history of the ruins. The discovery was not pursued, and almost three centuries went by until another Spaniard, Colonel Juan Galindo, visited the ruins and made the first map of them.

It was Galindo's report that stimulated Americans John L Stephens and Frederick Catherwood to come to Copán on their Central American journey in 1839. When Stephens published the book *Incidents of Travel in Central America, Chiapas, and Yucatán* in 1841, illustrated by Catherwood, the ruins first became known to the world at large.

Today The history of the ruins continues to unfold today, as archaeologists continue to probe the site. The remains of 3450 structures have been found in the 24 sq km surrounding the Principal Group, most of them within about half a kilometer of the Principal Group. In a wider zone, 4509 structures have been detected in 1420 sites within 135 sq km of the ruins. These discoveries indicate that at the peak of Mayan civilization here, around the end of the 8th century, the valley of Copán had over 20,000 inhabitants – a population not reached again until the 1980s.

In addition to examining the area around the Principal Group, archaeologists are continuing to explore and make new discoveries at the Principal Group itself. Five separate phases of building on this site have been identified; the final phase, dating from AD 650 to 820, is what we see today. But buried underneath the visible ruins are layers of other ruins, which archaeologists are exploring by means of underground tunnels. This is how the Rosalila temple was found, a replica of which is now in the Museum of Sculpture; below Rosalila is yet another, earlier temple, Margarita.

Museum of Sculpture

The newest addition to the ruins at Copán is this magnificent museum, opened in August 1996. Entering the museum is an impressive experience by itself: You enter through the mouth of a serpent and wind through the entrails of the beast before suddenly emerging into a fantastic world of sculpture and light. While Tikal is celebrated for its tall temple pyramids and Palenque is renowned for its limestone relief panels, Copán is unique in the Mayan world for its sculpture.

The highlight of the museum is a true-scale replica of the Rosalila temple, discovered in nearly perfect condition by archaeologists in 1989 by means of a tunnel dug into Structure 16, the central building of the Acropolis. Rosalila, dedicated in AD 571 by Copán's 10th ruler, Moon Jaguar, was apparently so sacred that when Structure 16 was built over it, Rosalila was not destroyed but was left completely intact.

The original Rosalila temple is still in the core of Structure 16. Under it is a still earlier temple, Margarita, built 150 years before, as well as other earlier platforms and tombs.

The Principal Group

The Principal Group is a group of ruins about 400m beyond the visitors center, across well-kept lawns, through a gate in a strong fence and down shady avenues of trees.

Stelae of the Great Plaza The path leads to the Great Plaza and the huge, intricately carved stelae portraying the rulers of Copán. Most of Copán's best stelae date from AD 613 to 738, during the reigns of Smoke Imix (628–695) and 18 Rabbit (695–738). All seem to have originally been painted; a few traces of red paint survive on Stela C. Many stelae had vaults beneath or beside them in which sacrifices and offerings could be placed.

Many of the stelae on the Great Plaza portray King 18 Rabbit, including Stelae A, B, C, D, F, H and 4. Perhaps the most beautiful stela in the Great Plaza is Stela A (AD 731); the original has been moved inside the Museum of Sculpture, and the one outdoors is a reproduction. Nearby, and almost equal in beauty, are Stela 4 (AD 731); Stela B (AD 731), depicting 18 Rabbit upon his accession to the throne; and Stela C (AD 782), with a turtle-shaped altar in front. This last stela has figures on both sides. Stela E (AD 614), erected on top of Structure 1 on the west side of the Great Plaza, is among the oldest stela.

At the northern end of the Great Plaza, at the base of Structure 2, Stela D (AD 736) also portrays King 18 Rabbit. On its back are two columns of hieroglyphs; at its base is an altar with fearsome representations of Chac, the rain god. In front of the altar is the burial place of Dr John Owen, an archaeologist with the expedition from Harvard's Peabody Museum who died during the work in 1893.

On the east side of the plaza is Stela F (AD 721), which has a more lyrical design, with the robes of the main figure flowing around to the other side of the stone, where there are glyphs. Altar G (AD 800), showing twin serpent heads, is among the last monuments carved at Copán. Stela H (AD 730) may depict a queen or princess rather than a king. Stela 1 (AD 692), on the structure that runs along the east side of the plaza, is of a person wearing a mask. Stela J, farther off to the east, resembles the stelae of

Quiriguá in that it is covered in glyphs, not human figures.

Ball Court & Hieroglyphic Stairway South of the Great Plaza, across what is known as the Central Plaza, is the ball court (Juego de Pelota; AD 731), the second-largest in Central America. The one you see is the third one on this site; the other two smaller ones were buried by this construction. Note the macaw heads carved at the top of the sloping walls. The central marker in the court was the work of King 18 Rabbit.

South of the ball court is Copán's most famous monument, the Hieroglyphic Stairway, the work of King Smoke Shell. Today it's protected from the elements by a roof. This lessens the impact of its beauty, but you can still get an idea of how it looked. The flight of 63 steps bears a history – in several thousand glyphs – of the royal house of Copán; the steps are bordered by ramps inscribed with more reliefs and glyphs. The story inscribed on the steps is still not completely understood, because the stairway was partially ruined and the stones jumbled.

At the base of the Hieroglyphic Stairway is Stela M (AD 756), bearing a figure (probably King Smoke Shell) in a feathered cloak; glyphs tell of the solar eclipse in that year. The altar in front shows a plumed serpent with a human head emerging from its jaws.

Beside the stairway, a tunnel leads to the tomb of a nobleman, a royal scribe who may have been the son of King Smoke Imix. The tomb, discovered in June 1989, held a treasure trove of painted pottery and beautiful carved jade objects that are now in Honduran museums.

Acropolis The lofty flight of steps to the south of the Hieroglyphic Stairway is called the Temple of the Inscriptions. On top of the stairway, the walls are carved with groups of hieroglyphs. On the south side of the Temple of the Inscriptions are the East Plaza and West Plaza. In the West Plaza, be sure to see Altar Q (AD 776), among the most famous sculptures here; the original is inside the Museum of Sculpture. Around its sides, carved in superb relief, are the 16 great kings of Copán, ending with the altar's creator, Yax Pac. Behind the altar was a sacrificial vault in which archaeologists discovered the bones of 15 jaguars and several macaws that were probably sacrificed to the glory of Yax Pac and his ancestors.

Tunnels In 1999, archaeologists opened up to the public two tunnels that allow visitors to get a glimpse at preexisting structures below the visible structures. If you don't mind the steep (US$10 – ouch!) extra entry fee, amateur archaeologists may appreciate the tunnels. There are now two tunnels open: The first and longest is Los Jaguares tunnel, 700m in length and running along the foundations of Temple 22. This tunnel exits on the outside of the main site, so you must walk around the main site to get back in again. The second tunnel, the Rosalila tunnel, is much shorter and takes only a few visitors at a time. This tunnel also shows you the foundations of Temple 16. Both entrances are in the East Plaza. While undoubtedly fascinating, it is hard to justify the steep entrance fee for what is in essence a fairly short-lived pair of highlights.

Las Sepulturas

Excavations at El Bosque and Las Sepulturas have shed light on the daily life of the Maya of Copán during its golden age.

Las Sepulturas, once connected to the Great Plaza by a causeway, may have been the residential area where rich, powerful nobles lived. One huge, luxurious residential compound seems to have housed some 250 people in 40 or 50 buildings arranged around 11 courtyards. The principal structure, called the House of the Bacabs (officials), had outer walls carved with the full-size figures of 10 males in fancy feathered headdresses; inside was a huge hieroglyphic bench.

To get to the site, you have to go back to the main road, turn right, then right again at the sign (2km).

SANTA ROSA DE COPÁN
pop 25,000

Santa Rosa de Copán is a small, cool, very Spanish mountain town, with cobbled streets and a lovely colonial church beside the parque central. It doesn't have any world-class tourist sights like Copán Ruinas, a few hours away; consequently, it doesn't have as many tourists. It's just a quiet, beautiful little town with a fresh climate and friendly people. The annual festival day is August 30.

Orientation & Information

The town is up on a hill, about 1km from the bus station on the highway.

The immigration office is one block from the parque central. There's no tourist information office, but Warren Post at Pizza Pizza (see the Places to Eat section) is happy to help with information about the town and the area. Max Elvir at the Hotel Elvir, operator of both the hotel and Lenca Land Trails, is another helpful source of information.

Santa Rosa has eight banks, but the Banco Bancahsa and Banco Atlántida on the parque central are the best ones for foreign travelers wishing to exchange currency. There is even a very rare ATM outside the Banco Atlántida. Most banks will do Visa credit card advances.

The post office and Hondutel are side by side on the west side of the parque central.

You can check your email at Pizza Pizza (☎ 662 1104, wpost@hondutel.hn), on Calle Real Centenario, or at Computec (computec@hondutel.hn) on the second floor of a large, yellow commercial building on 2a Avenida NE, between 1a Calle SE and 2a Calle SE. Access charges at both places are around US$2 per half hour.

Check out the Web (http://sites.netscape .net/srcopan/) for the latest information on the town.

Things to See & Do

La Flor de Copán Cigar Factory (☎ 662 0185), 2km out of town, is an interesting place to visit. Ask for a free tour – you'll learn how the hand-rolled cigars are made. The factory is open 7 am to noon and 1 to 5 pm Monday to Friday, 7 am to noon Saturday.

Organized Tours

Lenca Land Trails (☎ 662 0805, fax 662 0103, lenca@hondutel.hn), at the Hotel Elvir, offers tours to places in the area, such as Parque Nacional Celaque, the hot springs, the fort at Gracias and Belén Gualcho.

Places to Stay

Several places in town offer simple lodgings. The **Hotel Copán** (☎ 662 0265), at 1a Calle NE and 3a Avenida NE, has clean if small single/double rooms for US$17. Private parking is available. Half a block away, **Hotel El Rosario** (☎ 662 0211), on 3a Avenida NE, is another simple place; rooms with private bath are US$10.

The **Hotel Blanca Nieves** (☎ 662 1312), on 3a Avenida NE next door to the El

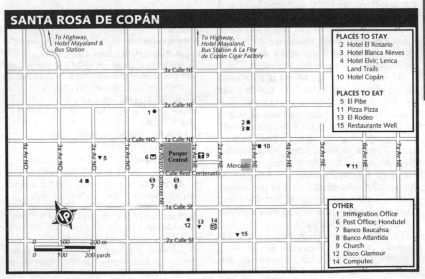

SANTA ROSA DE COPÁN

To Highway, Hotel Mayaland & Bus Station

To Highway, Hotel Mayaland, Bus Station & La Flor de Copán Cigar Factory

3a Calle NE
2a Calle NE
1a Calle NO   1a Calle NE
Parque Central
Calle Real Centenario
Mercado
1a Calle SE
2a Calle SE

1a Av NO
3a Av NO
2a Av NO
Av Alvaro Contreras NE
1a Av NE
2a Av NE
3a Av NE
4a Av NE
5a Av NE
6a Av NE
7a Av NE

PLACES TO STAY
2 Hotel El Rosario
3 Hotel Blanca Nieves
4 Hotel Elvir; Lenca Land Trails
10 Hotel Copán

PLACES TO EAT
5 El Pibe
11 Pizza Pizza
13 El Rodeo
15 Restaurante Well

OTHER
1 Immigration Office
6 Post Office; Hondutel
7 Banco Baucahsa
8 Banco Atlantida
9 Church
12 Disco Glamour
14 Computec

0   100   200 m
0   100   200 yards

HONDURAS

Rosario, is probably the best value for the budget traveler. A double with shared cold water bath costs US$5. Private parking is available.

Down on the highway, 1km from town, is a place that offers more comfortable accommodations. The *Hotel Mayaland* (☎ 662 0233, fax 662 0147), on the highway opposite the bus station, is a clean and modern motel with double rooms for US$29. All the rooms have TVs and private hot bath and are set around a grassy courtyard. The hotel has a restaurant, and there are many cheap comedores along this stretch of the highway.

The fancy place to stay in Santa Rosa is *Hotel Elvir* (☎/fax 662 0103), on Calle Real Centenario two blocks west of the parque central. Rooms are US$36, all with private hot bath, TV and phone. It was remodeled in 2000 with lovely colonial architecture throughout and has both a restaurant and cafeteria.

Places to Eat

Pizza Pizza (☎ 662 1104), on Calle Real Centenario near 6a Avenida NE, offers pizza and other dishes; operated by a North American–Honduran family, it's also a haven for travelers. Warren Post, the knowledgeable and friendly North American owner, is a great source of information on the town and the area. There's also an English-language book exchange here, and they will hold messages and letters for travelers (address mail to [Name], R/do Pizza Pizza, Santa Rosa de Copán, Honduras). It's open 11:30 am to 9 pm every day except Wednesday. Visa cards are accepted.

Another good place to eat is *El Rodeo* on 1a Avenida NE between 1a and 2a Calle SE. It's a covered-patio restaurant with typical Honduran dishes and lots of steaks on the menu; it has good food, good music and an enjoyable atmosphere. You can get a meal, a snack or just a drink; it's a popular place to hang out in the evening, when the bar does a lively business. *El Pibe*, on 2a Avenida NO two blocks west of the parque central, serves only chicken, but it's good, cheap and tasty and is served with *tajaditas* (crispy fried banana chips).

The *Restaurante Well*, on 2a Calle SE between 2a and 3a Avenidas SE, is Santa Rosa de Copán's best Chinese restaurant and is open daily for lunch and dinner. The house specialty, *arroz Well*, makes a very filling meal. The *Hotel Elvir* (see the Places to Stay section) has both a restaurant and cafeteria. Both are pleasant, clean and inexpensive.

Entertainment

The *El Rodeo* restaurant/bar is a good place to go for a drink in the evening, with a jovial, relaxed atmosphere and good music. In the same block, *Disco Glamour* attracts mostly a young crowd; discos are held on Friday and Saturday nights and on Sunday afternoons. Otherwise, you can sit in the plaza and count the stars.

Getting There & Away

Buses from Santa Rosa de Copán come and go from the Terminal de Transporte (☎ 662 0076) on the main highway opposite the Hotel Mayaland, about 1km from the center of town. Sultana (☎ 662 0940) buses to Tegucigalpa and Agua Caliente depart from a separate terminal three blocks west of the main bus station. Taxis wait at the bus station and charge US$0.55 for a ride up the hill into town.

If you're going to San Pedro Sula, it's much better to catch one of the direct buses, which makes only one stop (at La Entrada). The regular buses go more frequently, but they make many stops.

Buses serving Santa Rosa include:

Agua Caliente, Guatemala (US$2.50, 2¾ hours, 110km)
   Seven departures daily via Nueva Ocotepeque.

Copán Ruinas (US$2, three hours, 107km)
   Buses leave at 11:30 am and 12:30 pm, or take any bus heading to San Pedro Sula, get off at La Entrada and take another bus from there.

Gracias (US$1, 45 minutes, 47km)
   Buses at 7:15, 8:30, 10 and 11:45 am; 1:15, 2:15, 4 and 5:30 pm.

La Entrada (US$0.60, 1¼ hours, 28km)
   Same buses as to San Pedro Sula.

Nueva Ocotepeque (US$2, 2½ hours, 95km)
   Buses at 6, 9 and 11:30 am; 1, 3 and 4:45 pm.

San Pedro Sula (regular buses: US$2, 3½ hours; express buses: US$3.50, 2½ hours, 152km)
   Regular buses leave every 30 minutes from 4:20 am to 5:15 pm; express buses at 9:30 am, 2 and 3:30 pm.

Tegucigalpa (US$6, 7½ hours, 393km)
   Buses leave at 4 and 9:45 am, departing from a house marked 'Torito,' on the highway two blocks south of the bus station.

AROUND SANTA ROSA DE COPÁN

A quiet country park with a pond and picnic tables, **La Montañita** is about 15 minutes from Santa Rosa on the road to Gracias; any bus heading for Gracias will drop you at the entrance on request. Entry costs US$0.70. Privately owned **Doricentro**, next door, is perhaps a better option. Spend the whole day on the water toboggan and burn yourself to a crisp. Farther away, **Gracias, Las Tres Jotas** and the **Parque Nacional Celaque** also make popular outings from Santa Rosa.

The **Reserva del Guisayote** is a biological reserve in a cloud forest that can be visited from Santa Rosa; see the Nueva Ocotepeque section.

GRACIAS

pop 24,000

Gracias is a small, attractive mountain town 47km southeast of Santa Rosa de Copán. A colonial Spanish town, it still retains its Spanish character, with cobblestone streets and colonial churches and buildings. Gracias is quiet, slow and peaceful, and it feels like it hasn't changed in centuries.

Gracias has a long history. It was founded in 1526 by Spanish Captain Juan de Chavez; its original name was Gracias a Dios. The Audiencia de los Confines, the governing council for all Central America, was established here on April 16, 1544; the buildings that the council occupied are still here. The town was important and grew for several years, but it was eventually eclipsed in importance by Antigua Guatemala and Comayagua.

The area around Gracias is mountainous and beautiful. Much of it is forested. The town makes a good base for exploring Parque Nacional Celaque. While you're here, don't miss a trip to the hot springs.

Orientation & Information

Gracias is a small town, and everything is within walking distance.

If you need information, go to the Hotel y Restaurante Guancascos. Owner Frony Miedema, who speaks English, Dutch and Spanish, has lots of information about the town and the surrounding area. Information about the Parque Nacional Celaque is available here and at the COHDEFOR office.

The post office and Hondutel are side by side, a block south of the parque central.

Things to See & Do

On a hill about five blocks west of the parque central, **Castillo San Cristobal** is worth the walk for its fine view of the town. It's open 7 am to 5 pm daily. Gracias has several **colonial churches**: San Marcos, Las Mercedes and San Sebastián. Next door to the Iglesia de San Marcos, the **Sede de la Audiencia de los Confines**, important in the town's history, is now the *casa parroquial*, the residence for the parish priest.

Most of the town's other attractions, including a fine hot springs and the Parque Nacional Celaque, are a few kilometers out of town (see the Around Gracias and Parque Nacional Celaque sections).

Places to Stay

There are about a dozen places to stay in Gracias. They range in price from US$6 to US$20.50. A block north of the parque central, family-run *Hotel Erick (☎/fax 656 1066)* is a good place to stay; it's clean, friendly and inexpensive. All the rooms have private bath, some with hot water, and range from US$6 to US$9 in price. Enclosed parking is available. You can leave your luggage here if you stay overnight in the national park.

Hotel y Restaurante Guancascos (☎ 656 1219, fax 651 1273), four blocks west of the plaza, is another good place to stay. Owned and operated by Friesian-born Frony Miedema, it has just nine comfortable rooms, all with private hot bath. The hotel has a garden and is very private. Singles/doubles are US$14/17.

The *Hotel Colonia (☎ 656 1258)* has 26 smallish rooms half a block west of the parque central. All have private bath, hot water and some have TV and cost US$6/12.

The Morales Cruz family of *Posada y Cafetería Fernando's (☎ 656 1231)* offers a number of clean rooms equipped with fans and private bathrooms, around a cool and welcoming garden. Rates are US$3/4.75 without hot water and US$3.20/5.50 with hot water. You can have a big Honduran breakfast here for an extra US$1.75.

For around US$20.50 you can get a comfortable room at *Apart Hotel Patricia (☎ 656 1281)*, right in the middle of town.

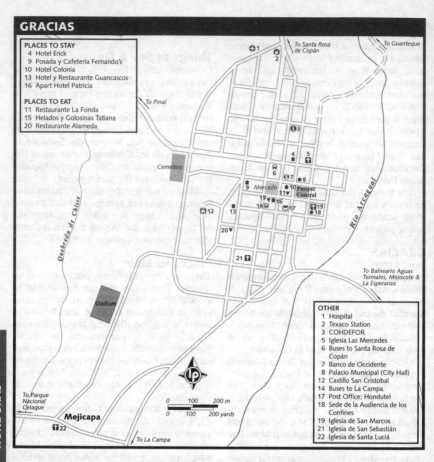

GRACIAS

PLACES TO STAY
4 Hotel Erick
9 Posada y Cafetería Fernando's
10 Hotel Colonia
13 Hotel y Restaurante Guancascos
16 Apart Hotel Patricia

PLACES TO EAT
11 Restaurante La Fonda
15 Helados y Golosinas Tatiana
20 Restaurante Alameda

OTHER
1 Hospital
2 Texaco Station
3 COHDEFOR
5 Iglesia Las Mercedes
6 Buses to Santa Rosa de Copán
7 Banco de Occidente
8 Palacio Municipal (City Hall)
12 Castillo San Cristobal
14 Buses to La Campa
17 Post Office; Hondutel
18 Sede de la Audiencia de los Confines
19 Iglesia de San Marcos
21 Iglesia de San Sebastián
22 Iglesia de Santa Lucía

To Santa Rosa de Copán
To Guanteque
To Pinal
Cemetery
Quebrada de Chisle
Río Arcenal
Mercado
Parque Central
Stadium
To Balneario Aguas Termales, Mejocote & La Esperanza
To Parque Nacional Celaque
Mejicapa
To La Campa

0   100   200 m
0   100   200 yards

Right at the boundary of Parque Nacional Celaque is *Cabaña Villa Verde*, a house with two bedrooms, four beds and a fully equipped kitchen. It is available for US$17.50 per night. Bungalow tents are also available, and there are campsites; you can camp with your own gear, or the Hotel y Restaurante Guancascos has camping gear available for rent. Information about all of these is available from the Hotel y Restaurante Guancascos.

Places to Eat

Part of the hotel of the same name, *Restaurante Guancascos* is the place to go for good food, good company and good information about the area. You can get lunch and dinner here and enjoy the best views in town. It's open 7 am to 10 pm daily.

Other good restaurants in town, serving typical Honduran fare, are *Restaurante La Fonda*, on the parque central, and *Restaurante Alameda*, five blocks southwest of the parque central. *Helados y Golosinas Tatiana*, south of the mercado, is good for ice cream and snacks.

Getting There & Away

The winding mountain road between Santa Rosa de Copán and Gracias is very scenic. The turnoff for Gracias is on the highway 2km north of Santa Rosa de Copán; from the turnoff, it's 45km to Gracias.

Buses to Santa Rosa de Copán (US$1, 45 minutes, 47km) leave from a bus stop two blocks from the parque central in Gracias at 5:30, 6:30, 7:30, 8:30 and 10:15 am and noon,

2 and 4 pm. See the Santa Rosa de Copán section for details on buses coming from Santa Rosa to Gracias.

Buses to La Campa (US$0.90, 1¼ hours, 16km) depart once a day, around noon, when the road is OK; they depart from another stop, two blocks from the parque central in Gracias. The same buses continue on to San Nauel Colohete, which is 16km beyond La Campa.

An unpaved road continues southeast from Gracias to La Esperanza (83km), and from there northeast to Siguatepeque on the Tegucigalpa–San Pedro Sula highway. On the map this looks like a shortcut from Santa Rosa de Copán to Tegucigalpa; however, it's a very winding (though also very beautiful) mountain road, and it takes at least four hours, or so, to get from Gracias to La Esperanza. The road is being improved one section at a time; when it is finally finished, travel time will be much shorter. The worst section of road is currently at the La Esperanza end. Check for current information locally if you're thinking of taking this route. No buses currently service this route.

AROUND GRACIAS

The hot springs at **Balneario Aguas Termales**, 6.5km east of town along the La Esperanza road, are one of Gracias' main attractions. The hot springs have several pools at various temperatures, including a big, cold pool for swimming; inner tubes and towels are available for rent. There is also a restaurant here. The springs are open 6 am to 8 pm daily; admission is US$0.85.

Several small towns near Gracias are also worth a visit, if you have time. The people in this area, mostly Lencas, produce distinctive handicrafts, especially pottery. **La Campa**, a scenic little town 16km south of Gracias, is known for its pottery; it also has a fine colonial church. **San Manuel Colohete**, 16km farther, past La Campa, is another attractive little mountain town with a beautiful colonial church.

Belén Gualcho is another beautiful little town in the area. A colonial town clinging to the side of a mountain at 1600m above sea level, it's cool and fresh. Attractions include an interesting church and a Lenca Indian market on Sunday. There's an entrance to Parque Nacional Celaque here, and although access to the park is easier from the Gracias side, people sometimes walk all the way through the park from Gracias to Belén Gualcho. Buses connect Belén Gualcho and Santa Rosa de Copán.

A bus runs from Gracias once a day to La Campa and on to San Manuel Colohete; you might also be able to catch a lift with a pickup truck. Or the route from Gracias out to the villages could make a fine walk. You could walk from Gracias to La Campa, on to San Manuel, then on to **San Sebastián** and on to Belén Gualcho. From there you could catch a bus to Santa Rosa de Copán.

Each of the villages is about a four- to five-hour walk from the previous one; there are no hotels, but if you wanted to stay overnight, you could arrange to stay with a local family. Ask around at the local café.

PARQUE NACIONAL CELAQUE

Seven kilometers uphill from Gracias is an entrance to Parque Nacional Celaque. Another entrance is at Belén Gualcho, on the park's western side, with accommodations available in the town, but access is better from the Gracias side, which has more facilities and more pristine forest.

Celaque (which means 'box of water' in the local Lenca dialect) is one of Honduras' most impressive national parks. The Montaña de Celaque, at 2827m above sea level, is the highest peak in Honduras and is covered by a lush cloud forest. The park contains the headwaters of 11 rivers, a majestic waterfall visible from the entire valley and very steep slopes, including some vertical cliffs that are a challenge even to expert mountain climbers.

The park is rich in plant and animal life, including several rare or endangered species; jaguars, pumas, ocelots, quetzals and much other wildlife can be seen. A number of endemic species are also found here, due to the geographical isolation. Most wildlife can be seen very early in the morning.

Temperatures in the park are much chillier than down in Gracias, so bring some warm clothes and adequate hiking boots. Also be prepared for dampness and rain – it's always damp in a cloud forest, and the park gets around 2000 to 4000mm of annual precipitation.

It's a steep walk from Gracias along the Río Arcagual up into the park; it takes around 1½ hours to walk from town to the entrance and another half hour from there to reach the park visitors center. You can drive to the visitors center if you have a 4WD vehicle; if not, rather than walking, you might want to arrange a lift up the hill to the park entrance, saving your time and energy for hiking in the park itself. The folks at the Restaurante Guancascos in Gracias will take you up there; the cost is US$10 per load, for as many people as can fit in the 4WD. (Their cabin, Cabaña Villa Verde, is just outside the boundary of the park; see Places to Stay in the Gracias section, earlier.)

At the visitors center, there are bunks for 15 people (bring your own bedding), a kitchen, water, a shower and latrines. Entrance to the park costs US$1; it's another US$1 to stay overnight. The warden's mother will cook you a simple meal for another US$1 if you ask. Near the visitors center is a river that's great for swimming.

From the visitors center, the next cabin, called Campamento Don Tomás, at 2050m above sea level, is about a two- to three-hour uphill walk along a well-marked forest trail. This cabin is smaller and much more basic than the accommodations at the visitors center, but it does have a few bunks, running water and a latrine (no kitchen).

Full information on hiking in the park is available from the Restaurante Guancascos on the plaza in Gracias; the owners also rent camping gear. The COHDEFOR office in Gracias also has information; it's open 8 am to 4:30 pm Monday to Friday.

NUEVA OCOTEPEQUE
pop 15,000
In the southwest corner of Honduras, Nueva Ocotepeque is a crossroads town, with a lot of traffic to and from the nearby borders at Agua Caliente (Guatemala) and El Poy (El Salvador). There's not much to the town, but it's a convenient place to stay overnight before or after crossing the border.

There's not much to do in Nueva Ocotepeque. A reader wrote to recommend going for a swim in the river; he said you can get any of the local children to show you the way. The **Reserva del Guisayote** is a biological reserve in a cloud forest that is the easiest to access of any cloud forest in Honduras. Sixteen kilometers north of Nueva

Ocotepeque on a paved road, it is a good place to see wildlife, including the quetzal.

Places to Stay & Eat
All the places to stay and eat in Nueva Ocotepeque are on or near the main highway through town, within about five blocks of one another. Basic, cheap places to stay include the *Hospedaje San Antonio* (☎ 663 3072), a few doors west of the highway; it's basic but a good value, with single/double rooms for US$3/3.75 with shared bath, or US$5/8.60 with private cold bath. There's enclosed parking in the courtyard. Across the highway, a block from where the buses to El Poy and Agua Caliente are parked, the *Mini Hotel Turista* is another basic place; singles/doubles with shared bath are US$3/5.50, or US$4/7.50 for rooms with private bath. The *Hotel y Comedor Congolón* is on the highway half a block south of the plaza, 3½ blocks south of most of the bus stations. It's a basic, family-run place that includes the hotel, a tiny restaurant and the bus station for the Congolón buses. All the activity can make it a little loud, but the rooms are clean, and all have windows opening onto a central courtyard; they share a common cold bath, and the price is right at US$4.25 per room.

Much more upmarket, *Hotel Maya Chortis* (☎ 653 3377, fax 653 3217) is east of the highway, three blocks behind the bus stop for the buses to El Poy and Agua Caliente. It's an excellent place to stay; the rooms are clean and attractive, and all have private hot bath, color cable TV, telephone and two double beds. Rooms are all around US$20/23. The equally good *Hotel Sandoval* (☎ 653 3098) has marginally more expensive rooms with cable TV, and a pool, sauna and Jacuzzi. Both hotels have a restaurant and bar.

Many simple restaurants are on the highway in the blocks near the bus station. For more upmarket dining, try *Restaurante Don Chepe* at the Hotel Maya Chortis, or *Restaurante Sandoval* at the expensive Hotel Sandoval, one block east of the highway and one block south of the buses to El Poy and Agua Caliente.

Getting There & Away
Nueva Ocotepeque is served by frequent buses. They include:

Agua Caliente, Guatemalan border crossing (US$0.90, 30 minutes, 22km)
Buses depart every half hour from 6 am to 6 pm, leaving from the same bus stop on the highway as for El Poy.

El Poy, Salvadoran border crossing (US$0.35, 15 minutes, 9km)
Buses leave every half hour, 6 am to 8 pm, departing from a bus stop on the highway. Colectivo taxis also go to El Poy for US$0.45.

La Entrada (US$2.25, 3½ hours, 123km)
Same buses as to San Pedro Sula.

San Pedro Sula (US$3.25, five to six hours, 247km)
Toritos & Copanecos buses to San Pedro Sula depart from Agua Caliente at 7:30, 9:30 and 11:30 am, 1:30 and 3:30 pm; the same buses depart half an hour later from Nueva Ocotepeque. They also have one express bus (US$5.40), departing Nueva Ocotepeque at midnight and making no stops along the way. The Toritos & Copanecos bus station is a few doors from the highway in Nueva Ocotepeque. Congolón buses depart from the Hotel Congolón, on the highway half a block south of the plaza and 3½ blocks south of the other bus stops. Buses depart at 1, 7:30 and 10 am, noon, 2 and 4 pm.

Santa Rosa de Copán (US$1.60, 2½ hours, 95km)
Transporte San José buses depart Nueva Ocotepeque at 6, 8, 9:30 and 10:45 am, 1 and 3 pm. Or you can take any bus heading toward San Pedro Sula to get to Santa Rosa de Copán.

EL POY & AGUA CALIENTE

Near Nueva Ocotepeque are the border crossings of El Poy (to El Salvador) and Agua Caliente (to Guatemala). The El Poy crossing is open from around 6 am to 6 pm daily. The Agua Caliente crossing is open a little later, until around 8 pm. The nearest place to stay is at Nueva Ocotepeque.

Northern Honduras

The Caribbean coast of Honduras is probably the most attractive and enticing region of mainland Honduras. The vegetation is classically tropical and greener than elsewhere; the beaches are sandy, languid and inviting; palm trees abound; and life is just that little bit more laid-back and stress free. Travelers come to northern Honduras to enjoy its relaxed ambience, to use it as a stepping-stone to the Bay Islands or to venture further afield into the vast and largely untouristed Mosquitia region to the east.

For the most part, northern Honduras consists of a narrow coastal plain backed by mountains. These plains are among Honduras' most fertile and productive agricultural areas: It is here that Standard and United Fruit grow bananas and pineapples for export to the USA. The two companies own a large part of northern Honduras, and several of the towns, ports, railways, roads and banks in the area were established by the banana companies.

The Caribbean coast has an interesting mixture of races. In addition to the mestizos found everywhere in Honduras, there are many black people descended from Jamaicans and other West Indians who came during the years when the British occupied the Caribbean coast.

A very interesting north coast people are the Garífuna, a mixture of African and Carib Indian peoples, brought by the British from the island of St Vincent to the island of Roatán in the late 18th century. From Roatán, they spread out along the coast and now have small coastal fishing villages all the way from Belize to Nicaragua. Their language has a strong West African sound and is a mixture of several languages – Arawak, French, Yoruba and perhaps others as well. The Garífuna have their own religion, music, dance, foods and other cultural patterns.

The principal towns of the north coast are Puerto Cortés, Tela, La Ceiba and Trujillo. All of them have their attractions, but probably the most enjoyable for travelers is Tela, with the small village of Omoa, near Puerto Cortés, rapidly becoming a popular backpacker destination as well. La Ceiba is Honduras' party town and a popular jumping-off point for travel to the Bay Islands.

The coast fills up with tourists during Semana Santa, when Hondurans have their one week of holiday, beachgoing and merrymaking. If you're on the coast at this time, make sure you've secured a place to stay in advance. Hotels fill up for this week and prices double. The rest of the time, you probably won't see too many tourists.

Safety on the North Coast

Though this researcher never had any problems on the north coast, a number of travelers have, and a considerable number have

HONDURAS

written to urge LP to warn travelers about crime. The problem seems to have been associated with the beaches near to Tela, La Ceiba and Trujillo. Gangs of youths have in the past accosted lone travelers walking these beaches and robbed them of their belongings, both during the day and, more commonly, in the evening. The simple solution is not to walk the beaches without company and certainly never to walk them after dusk, no matter how tempting a moonlight stroll may seem. When swimming off any beach, never leave your valuables unguarded. There is a high chance that they will 'walk.' In the towns, exercise the normal safety sense that you would in any strange town. Honduran towns are no more risky than towns in other foreign countries, but the unsuspecting or unwary will always fall victim to scams. There is no cause for paranoia but every good reason to be sensible and exercise normal caution.

The north coast has a very high rate of HIV infection. Keep this in mind in your relations with others – be vigilant against exposing yourself to it.

PUERTO CORTÉS
pop 82,160

Puerto Cortés, 64km north of San Pedro Sula, is the westernmost of Honduras' major Caribbean towns. It is also the country's most important port, as it's the only port in the country that can handle big cargo containers. Puerto Cortés handles over half of Honduras' export shipping trade. It's just a two-day sail from the USA, with frequent cargo ships sailing to New Orleans and Miami laden with bananas, pineapples and other produce. The docks, right in the town, are the town's focal point and raison d'être. Other than that, it's not a particularly enticing pace to stay. It's a gritty, workaday port – like ports the world over – and does little to entice a tourist crowd

At least a few beaches are close to Puerto Cortés. Playa de Cieneguita, a good stretch of beach a few kilometers from town on the road to Omoa, is a white sandy beach with a couple of beachside hotel/restaurants where you can get meals and snacks. Other beaches are at Travesía and Baja Mar and are accessible by local bus. It takes only an hour by bus to reach Puerto Cortés from

San Pedro Sula, so the beaches around the area are popular day trips for visitors from that city.

In practice, the only real reason for coming to Puerto Cortés is its twice-weekly boat service to Belize – this is the only regularly scheduled boat transportation between the two countries. The only passenger train in Honduras also departs from Puerto Cortés, operating twice a week between here and Tela.

Puerto Cortés' annual fair is held on August 15.

Places to Stay & Eat
Accommodations options in Puerto Cortés are not all that attractive, and you would be better advised to base yourself in Omoa (18km to the west) rather than sit it out in town. The only advantage of staying in Puerto Cortés is to get a head start on catching the train to Tela, which leaves at 7 am, or the ferry to Belize that departs at 8 am.

Still, if you do plan to stay in Puerto Cortés, there is at least one hotel that has been given the thumbs up by an LP reader. *Mr Ggeerr Hotel Internacional* (☎ 665 0444, fax 665 0750), at 3a Avenida and 9a Calle, is a modern property with air-conditioned, carpeted rooms with TV. A double room goes for around US$24.

On Playa de Cieneguita, the nice stretch of beach a few kilometers from town on the road to Omoa, there are some good beach-front hotels, but they're more expensive. The cheapest of the lot is *Hotel Los Arcos* (☎ 665 1889), opposite the beach, with rooms for US$23.50 per night. *Hotel Playa* (☎ 665 0453, fax 665 2287), a fancier place right on the beach, is more expensive, with doubles for a cool US$65.

There are lots of restaurants around the wide and modern central plaza, including a flashy-looking *Pizza Hut*. Look out also for *El Torito* for meat dishes and *Playa Azul* for fish.

Getting There & Away
Bus Buses operate frequently between Puerto Cortés and San Pedro Sula (US$0.75, 1½ hours, 56km).

Two companies operate along this route. Transportes Citul (☎ 665 0456), on 5a Calle Este near 2a Avenida, has direct buses every half hour from 6 am to 6:30 pm. Transportes

Impala (☎ 665 0606), on 3a Avenida near 4a Calle Este, has direct buses every half hour from 4:30 am to 9 pm.

See the Travesía & Baja Mar and Omoa sections for information on buses to those areas.

Train A passenger train operates between Puerto Cortés and Tela on Fridays and Sundays. On both days it departs from Puerto Cortés at 7 am, arriving in Tela at 11 am. It leaves Tela for the return trip at 1 pm, arriving back in Puerto Cortés around 6 pm. The cost is US$0.82. In Puerto Cortés, you can catch the train from a stop a couple of blocks behind the Hotel Formosa; in Tela it departs from the train station. By taking the train, you avoid the loop south and back north again via San Pedro Sula, where you will also have to change buses. You may not gain much in time, but the route is definitely more picturesque.

You might want to check the train schedule before making any travel plans. If you can't get information locally (which is quite possible), stop by or phone the office of the Ferrocarril Nacional de Honduras (☎ 663 4080) at the old train station in San Pedro Sula.

Boat Twice a week, a small 20-passenger boat makes a trip between Puerto Cortés and Dangriga, Belize. It departs Puerto Cortés on Wednesday and Saturday at 9 am (in theory), arriving in Dangriga around 12:30 pm. However, departure is often delayed by an hour or so. The cost for the trip is around US$35. You must come with your passport the day before travel to sign up for the trip. The office is about 3km outside of Puerto Cortés town, in La Laguna at the beginning of the causeway that leads into town. Contact Gulf Cruz (☎ 665 1200) for information and tickets.

TRAVESÍA & BAJA MAR

Just to the east of Puerto Cortés, Travesía and Baja Mar are two seaside Garífuna villages with good beaches and lots of palm trees. The road from Puerto Cortés runs along the sea, first through Travesía and on into Baja Mar; the two villages form a continuous row of wooden houses beside the sea, with small fishing boats lining the shore. The beach is lovely along the whole stretch.

There are one or two restaurants in each village for beachgoers.

Places to Stay & Eat

Right on the beach in Travesía, *Hotel Frontera del Caribe* (☎ 665 5001) is the most pleasant place to stay near Puerto Cortés if you're on a budget. Six upstairs rooms, all with private cold bath and ceiling fan, are US$14.50 per room (sleeping up to three people); the rooms are simple but clean and pleasant. Downstairs is an inexpensive beachside restaurant where all three meals are served. The bus coming from Puerto Cortés stops just outside the door.

Getting There & Away

The bus from Puerto Cortés to Travesía and Baja Mar departs from 5a Calle Este, in the block southeast of the plaza. From Puerto Cortés it departs at 6, 8 and 11 am, 1 and 3 pm; for the return trip, it departs from the end of the line at Baja Mar at 9 am, 12:30, 3 and 5 pm. Cost is US$0.20 to Travesía (about 20 minutes from Puerto Cortés) or US$0.35 to the end of the bus line at Baja Mar (a 45-minute ride). The bus runs less frequently on Sunday. Otherwise you can take local bus Ruta 2, get off where it swings round for the return leg (at Comaguey), and walk along the coast road for 20 minutes.

A taxi will take you between Puerto Cortés and Travesía in about five minutes for US$3.40.

OMOA

pop 2,500

Omoa is a quiet, sleepy village by the sea, 18km west of Puerto Cortés, that nestles round a curving bay with soft, sloping sand. Villagers always greet other villagers and strangers with a friendly '¡hola!' It's the kind of place that makes you want to linger, and its beach is pretty decent. Omoa is frequented on weekends by local visitors from San Pedro Sula and is rapidly becoming a popular backpacker port of call for travelers heading to and coming from nearby Guatemala. Travelers Tracie Eagles and Andy Dodd of Chiswick, England wrote to LP: 'After traveling through Honduras during September this year, I felt compelled to write about a lesser-mentioned place in the LP guide – Omoa. We stopped here initially for one day on our way to Tela, but

HONDURAS

ended up staying three weeks!' Seafood restaurants have sprung up like mushrooms all along the seafront, and there are accommodations options to meet all budget needs. You can easily miss Omoa if you are not looking for it. The beach and restaurants are about 1km from the main junction on the highway, which is indicated by an untidy jumble of small buildings that passes for the village center.

Information
Buses to and from Omoa all stop on the main highway. There are a few small *pulperias* on the highway, but no supermarket as such, so bring any supplies that you can't do without. There is a Banco GBA bank just off the main highway, but no post office. Omoa's annual festival is held on May 30.

Things to See & Do
Omoa's claim to historical fame lies with its Spanish fortress, the **Fortaleza de San Fernando de Omoa**. It was built between 1759 and 1777 under orders from King Fernando VII of Spain to protect the coast from rampant piracy, but in 1779 the fortress was captured by the British after only a four-day battle. Still in good shape, the fort is maintained by the Instituto Hondureño de Antropología e Historia. It is open 8 am to 4 pm Monday to Friday and 9 am to 5 pm Saturday and Sunday; admission is US$1.40.

If you tire of swimming in warm Caribbean waters, there are a couple of cool, refreshing waterfalls in the area. They are a 45- and 60-minute walk respectively from Omoa. The good thing about the spot, apart from the falls, is the associated rock pools where you can take a cooling dip after your walk. Ask Roli at Roli's Place (see below) for details.

Places to Stay & Eat
The best budget lodging in Omoa is **Roli's Place** (☎/fax 658 9082, RG@yaxpactours .com), on Blvd La Playa, run by Swiss national Roland Gassmann. Roli has a large shaded and grassy compound with room for tents (US$2 per person) and open ventilated dormitories (mosquito nets required) for US$3.50 per bed. Private double rooms cost US$8.20. There is also an outside communal kitchen, Internet access for US$3.10 per 30 minutes and bikes and kayaks for

free use by guests. Roli has all the latest data on getting to Guatemala from Omoa.

New in 2000, **Pia's Place** (☎ 658 9076) is not as well established as Roli's, but Pia is working on renovating the wooden structure and adding some more facilities and should be looking more presentable by the time you read this. There are three double rooms for US$7 and beds in a small dorm for US$3.10. Pia often meets buses at the main road in Omoa and offers travelers a lift to her place.

Next door is the more upmarket **Bahía de Omoa** (☎ 658 9076), also run by Pia, where very comfortable double rooms with air-conditioning and private facilities go for US$20.50. You can also rent bikes and sailing gear here, and Pia offers a laundry service.

Hospedaje Julita (☎ 658 9174), on the east side of the village, is another good choice. One of the 10 double rooms here goes for US$13.80.

You will not be short of places to eat in Omoa. You can spend a week here and still not eat at all of them. Take a local tip and head for **La Galera de Capo**. Turn left after **El Paraiso de Stanley's** – another possible eating option – and look for it hidden away to your left next to the beach. Fresh fish is your best bet. It's low-key and somewhat cheaper than the other flashier places. On the main street itself, the **El Botín Suizo**, run by Swiss Ulrich Lang, also offers good seafood by the beach. Readers recommend **La Macarela** and **Cayaquitos**, both easy to find and within a couple of minutes of each other.

Getting There & Away
Bus Buses to Omoa depart from Puerto Cortés every half hour from 6:20 am to 8 pm from the Transportes Citral depot (☎ 655 0888) on 3a Calle Este, one block west of the plaza (US$0.50, one hour, 18km). They let you off on the highway, a short walk from the fort. From Omoa back to Puerto Cortés, the buses depart every half hour from 4:30 am to 6:30 pm.

If you are heading for Guatemala, you can take a through bus from Omoa to Corinto (US$1.10). Corinto is the border town where you must get your exit stamp (US$1.80). There are also money changers here. From Corinto, you will find pickup trucks to take you the last 3km to the border, where a paved road leads on into Guatemala.

The road on the Honduras side is still a bit rough and unpaved in parts but is completely paved on the Guatemalan side and is slowly being upgraded on the Honduras side. In case of wet weather, traveling the Honduran road can be tricky, as buses must traverse a couple of bridgeless rivers.

The old 'Jungle Trail' is a thing of the past, and once the roadworks are completed in Honduras, this will be the main Guatemala-Honduras border crossing in this part of the country. In a similar vein, boats that used to run between Omoa and Livingstone in Guatemala have now virtually ceased, so you are now committed to an increasingly easier land crossing.

TELA
pop 89,440

Tela is many travelers' favorite Honduran Caribbean beach town; it's small and quiet, with superb seafood, several good places to stay and some fine white-sand beaches. This is a great place for relaxing on the beach and enjoying the simple life. Pleasant excursions can also be made to several places nearby (see the Around Tela section).

Tela is somnolent most of the year, but it's quite another story during Holy Week before Easter (Semana Santa), when the town fills up with Honduran vacationers. During Holy Week, hotel rates can double, and advance bookings are essential if you want to get a room. In July and August, North American and European travelers descend upon the town and things get busy, though room rates are unchanged. Tela's annual fiesta day is June 13.

Orientation

Tela is divided into two sections: Tela Vieja, the 'old town,' on the east bank of Río Tela where the river meets the sea, and Tela Nueva, on the west side of the river, where the Hotel Villas Telamar hugs some of the best stretch of beach. The town can be covered easily on foot.

Information

There's no tourist information office in Tela. Filling the gap, Garífuna Tours (see the Or-

ganized Tours section) is the place to come for information about the town and the area. Prolansate (☎ 448 2042), on 9a Calle NE (Calle del Comercio) between 2a and 3a Avenidas NE, has information on Lancetilla Botanical Garden and Punta Sal.

The Casa de Cambio La Teleña, on 4a Avenida NE, changes US dollars in traveler's checks and cash, giving a slightly better rate for cash. It's open 8 am to 11:45 am and 1 to 4:30 pm Monday to Friday, 8 am to noon Saturday. Cash advances on Visa and MasterCard are available from the Banco de Occidente on 6a Avenida NE, which is also the Western Union agent in Tela.

The post office and Hondutel are beside one another on 4a Avenida NE. Email services are available at Garífuna Tours (see the Organized Tours section), where access costs US$3 per hour on one of their six machines, or at the Maya Vista restaurant (see the Places to Eat section), where access to their one machine costs US$4.50 an hour. There is a rather good Web site set up by the local tourist community (www.tela-honduras.com).

The Lavandería El Centro, on 4a Avenida NE, charges about US$2 to wash, dry and fold 12lb of clothes.

Things to See & Do

Tela's main attraction is its **beaches**, which stretch around the bay for several kilometers on either side of the town. The beach right in front of the town is sandy, but not the best. The beach just over the bridge in Tela Nueva, in front of the Hotel Villas Telamar, is much better; its pale, powdery sand and shady grove of coconut trees and the lawn just behind it are kept clean. Beaches farther afield, while much better, can be risky for solo travelers or after dusk (see Safety on the North Coast, earlier in this section).

The **Garífuna Museum**, at the river end of 8a Calle NE, is an interesting cultural museum with exhibits on many aspects of daily life in the Garífuna villages along the north coast of Honduras. Garífuna paintings and handicrafts are for sale; you can also eat a traditional Garífuna meal here (see the Places to Eat section). The museum is open 8 am to 5 pm Monday to Saturday; admission is free.

TELA

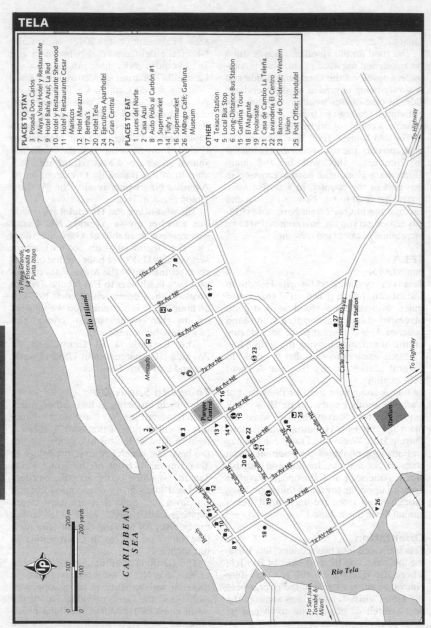

PLACES TO STAY
3 Posada Don Carlos
7 Maya Vista Hotel y Restaurante
9 Hotel Bahía Azul; La Red
10 Hotel y Restaurante Sherwood
11 Hotel y Restaurante Cesar
   Mariscos
12 Hotel Marazul
17 Bertha's
20 Hotel Tela
24 Ejecutivos Aparthotel
27 Gran Central

PLACES TO EAT
1 Luces del Norte
2 Casa Azul
8 Auto Pollo al Carbón #1
13 Supermarket
14 Tuty's
16 Supermarket
26 M@ngo Café; Garifuna
   Museum

OTHER
4 Texaco Station
5 Local Bus Stop
6 Long-Distance Bus Station
15 Garifuna Tours
18 El Magnate
19 Prolansate
21 Casa de Cambio La Teleña
22 Lavandería El Centro
23 Banco de Occidente; Western
   Union
25 Post Office; Hondutel

To Playa Grande,
La Ensenada &
Punta Izopo

Río Hiland

10a AV NE
9a AV NE
8a AV NE
7a AV NE
6a AV NE
5a AV NE
3a AV NE
2a AV NE
1a AV NE

Mercado

Parque
Central

Calle José Trinidad Reyes

Train Station

To Highway

To Highway

Stadium

CARIBBEAN
SEA

11a Calle NE
10a Calle NE
9a Calle NE
8a Calle NE
7a Calle NE
6a Calle NE
5a Calle NE
4a Calle NE

Beach

Río Tela

To San Juan,
Tornabé &
Miami

200 m
0
100
200 yards
0
100

Garífuna Tours (see below), near the southwest corner of the plaza, rents mountain bikes for US$3.75 per half day or US$5 per day. They also offer tours to natural reserves in the area.

You can learn Spanish at the M@ngo Cafe Spanish School (mango@honduras .com). The cost is US$60 for three hours of daily instruction over five days.

Organized Tours

Garífuna Tours (☎/fax 448 2904, garifuna@ hondutel.hn), on 9a Calle NE near the south corner of the plaza, offers all-day boat excursions to Parque Nacional Marino Punta Sal (US$19); morning bird-watching excursions to Los Micos Lagoon (US$20); and morning kayak excursions to the Refugio Punta Izopo (US$16). All tours are given in English and Spanish. Their office is open 7:30 am to 7 pm daily. Also see their Web site (www.garifuna-tours.com).

The Hotel Bahía Azul (see below) also offers trips around the local area and to Punta Sal. They also organize fishing, diving and snorkeling trips. Prolansate also offers occasional trips to Punta Sal (see the Around Tela section later in this chapter).

Places to Stay

The best of the cheapies is *Hotel Marazul* (☎ 448 2313), at 11a Calle NE and 4a Avenida NE. It's a simple but clean little place with 13 rooms around a sandy courtyard. It has a *lavadero* where you can wash your clothes (there's also laundry service), and you can use the kitchen if you ask nicely. One single room with outdoor bath is US$4; the other 12 rooms, all with private cold bath, are US$8.50.

The *Hotel Tela* (☎ 448 2150), on 9a Calle NE at 4a Avenida NE, has a large rooftop terrace and clean, spacious rooms with private cold bath for US$16, plus a restaurant and parking. *Bertha's* (☎ 448 1009), on 8a Calle NE between 8a and 9a Avenidas NE, is another recommended budget hotel that you may want to check out. Each of its 20 rooms go for US$17 for two persons. Similarly the *Posada de Don Carlos* (☎ 448 1820) has six comfortable, air-conditioned rooms for US$24 each.

Several hotels are right on the beach. The cheapest of these is *Hotel Bahía Azul* (☎ 448 2381), on 2a Avenida NE. It has a

good beachfront restaurant/bar, but the rooms themselves don't face the beach. All rooms have private bath and cost US$15.50 with fan (some with cable TV), US$24.50 with air-con and TV.

The *Hotel y Restaurante Sherwood* (☎ 448 1065, fax 448 2294), on Calle Peatonal, has a beachfront swimming pool and attractive beachfront rooms with all the amenities for US$31. Directly opposite, the *Hotel y Restaurante Cesar Mariscos* (☎ 448 1934, fax 448 2083, cesarmariscos@hotmail .com), also on the beach, has six airy rooms, all with air-con, private hot bath and cable TV; rates are US$48 for two people.

The *Ejecutivos Aparthotel* (☎ 448 1076), at 8a Calle NE and 4a Avenida NE, offers luxurious studio apartments with fully equipped kitchens, air-con, two double beds, color cable TV, hot bath and other amenities (including enclosed parking and 24-hour vigilance) for US$27.50 for one or two people.

The *Maya Vista Hotel y Restaurante* (☎ 448 1497, fax 448 1928, mayavista@ hotmail.com), at 10a Avenida NE and 8a Calle NE, commands probably the best and breeziest views in the whole of Tela. This French Canadian–run establishment has excellent double rooms for US$29 and boasts a classy and popular restaurant (see the Places to Eat section).

Right opposite the train station is the brightly painted *Gran Central* (☎ /fax 448 1099, grancentral@hotmail.com), with five plushly furnished colonial-style apartments with fully equipped kitchens. Rates are a very reasonable US$34.50 per apartment, one of the best deals in town for what you get.

Places to Eat

Seafood is plentiful, delicious and inexpensive around Tela. Seafood soups are a particular delicacy of the town; fish, shrimp, lobster and *caracol* (conch) are all found in many restaurants. Another specialty of the town is *pan de coco* (coconut bread); you'll see Garífuna women or their children walking around town selling it. Try it – it's delicious. There are two centrally located **supermarkets** where you can stock up on jungle rations.

Half a block from the beach, *Luces del Norte* is popular with backpackers and has a

HONDURAS

casual atmosphere. Breakfasts are good, but it serves any meal any time. It's open 7 am to 10 pm daily. Near the parque central, *Tuty's* is a pleasant, clean, inexpensive little place for pastries, simple meals and a variety of fruit cocktails, fruit drinks and ice cream. The lunchtime buffet is a great deal for US$2.50. It's open from 6 am to 10 pm daily.

Cesar Mariscos is a bustling and breezy open-air bar/restaurant with great fresh seafood, including seafood soups for around US$4. This is regarded as one of the town's best restaurants. It is open 7 am to 11 pm daily.

The *Maya Vista* (see the Places to Stay section) is a great little restaurant with the best lunchtime view in town. There are pasta dishes for around US$4, as well as well-prepared chicken and fish dishes. It's open for meals 9 am to 9 pm daily

La Red, at the Hotel Bahía Azul, is another good beachfront place with a beach terrace. It serves general continental cuisine, but service can be very slow. *Auto Pollo Al Carbón #1* is a simple open-air chicken shack with good roast chicken, just a wishbone's throw from the beach.

For good international fare, head for *Casa Azul*, a pleasant little bar/restaurant housed in a converted traditional home half a block from the beach, with good food, good atmosphere and good music.

Italian food is offered at *M@ngo Cafe*, behind the Garífuna Museum at the west end of 8a Calle NE. It's not expensive, and different foods are featured each day; try the specialty, *el Pirate Morgan* – fish with salad and wine for US$5 – or *tapado,* a typical Garífuna soup with coconut and *casabe,* for US$4.50. It's open 3 to 11 pm Monday to Saturday.

Entertainment

Tela has many discos. You can hardly miss them, as most are clustered on 11a Calle NE, but some of them can get rough. Ask around for current advice if you want to go dancing. The *El Magnate* in town and the *Disco Delfín* at the Telamar Hotel 1km west of town were both recommended as being better options at the time this chapter was being researched.

The outdoor bar under protective palm fronds at the *Maya Vista* restaurant (see the Places to Eat section) is probably as good and cool as it gets for a lingering evening beer or frozen margarita and is a popular hangout for travelers in search of quality chill-out time. Alternatively, the *Casa Azul* and the *M@ngo Cafe* are other places with a lively night scene.

The *M@ngo Cafe* also shows cult movies each day at 5 pm. Admission is US$1 per person.

Getting There & Away

Bus The long-distance bus station is on the corner of 9a Calle NE and 9a Avenida NE, three blocks northeast of the plaza. Buses depart from Tela bound for La Ceiba every half hour from 4 am to 6 pm (US$1.10, 2½ hours, 103km).

There are no direct buses between Tela and San Pedro Sula; the only way to get a direct bus to San Pedro is to catch one on the highway, as it comes through from La Ceiba. From the bus station in town, you have to catch a bus to El Progreso and change buses there. Regular, stopping buses to El Progreso leave every half hour from 4:30 am until 6 pm (US$0.80, two hours, 63km); direct buses leave for El Progreso twice daily, in the morning on weekdays and in the afternoon on weekends (US$1.10, one hour). From El Progreso to San Pedro Sula it's another hour's ride; the buses leave about every five minutes, with the last bus at 9 pm.

Local buses to the Garífuna villages near Tela depart from the east side of the market; see the Around Tela section for details.

Garífuna Tours runs a shuttle service from Tela to San Pedro Sula (US$11), La Ceiba (US$14) and Copán Ruinas (US$30)

Train A passenger train operates between Puerto Cortés and Tela on Friday and Sunday. See the Puerto Cortés section earlier in this chapter for details.

Boat There are no scheduled boat services out of Tela to anywhere. If you have a group, Garífuna Tours can get you to Utila for US$20 per person for a minimum group of six people.

Getting Around

Tela has many taxis; a ride in town costs US$0.55. A taxi to Lancetilla or San Juan is

HONDURAS

about US$4; to Triunfo de la Cruz, La Ensenada or Tornabé, the fare is also about US$4. Mountain bikes can be rented at the M@ngo Cafe (☎ 448 2856) (see the Places to Eat section) for US$3 for half a day and US$5 for a full day.

AROUND TELA
Lancetilla Jardín Botánico
The Lancetilla Botanical Garden and Research Center is famous throughout Honduras. The United Fruit Company founded Lancetilla in 1926 for the purpose of experimenting with the cultivation of various tropical plants in Central America; some of the plants that were first planted here are now important crops in Central America. Of its 1680 hectares, some protecting natural forest forming the watershed for Tela, 78 hectares contain the arboretum, with open public access; 321 hectares are planted with experimental plants and endangered species, mainly of interest to scientists; and 1281 hectares are a biological reserve, which you can tour with a guide if you reserve in advance.

The garden features fruit trees from every continent, cacao, fine timber plantings, nuts and palms, and a long tunnel formed by an arch of bamboo. There is a swimming hole on the Río Lancetilla at the far end of the park, about 1.5km from the visitors center.

Another attraction of Lancetilla is its bird life. The various plantings have created habitats for over 365 recorded species of birds. A bird checklist is available at the visitors center. Birders frequently come here, and each year on December 14 and 15 the Audubon Society conducts a 24-hour bird count; you can participate if you're here at that time. Migratory species are present from November to February. Bird watching is best in the early morning or late afternoon; even though the entrance gate closes at 2:30 pm, you can stay later to see the birds at dusk.

Lancetilla is about 5km southwest of the center of Tela. There's a ticket kiosk on the highway about 2km from Tela, and the park is another 3.5km inland. The best way to get here is by bike, which you can rent in Tela. However, you can usually hitch a lift with any vehicle passing the ticket booth entrance. There's a visitors information center

where the park begins, and an explanatory map in English is available.

Lancetilla is open 7:30 am to 2:30 pm daily; foreigners pay a rather steep US$7 entry fee. Free guided tours of the garden are given every half hour, taking about an hour; four-hour tours of the biological reserve are also given but must be arranged in advance (usually the day before is fine). Or you can do a self-guided tour; a map and self-guided tour brochure are available in either English or Spanish for US$0.70. Further information is available from Prolansate in Tela (see Information in that section, earlier).

Parque Nacional Jeanette Kawas
Standing on the beach at Tela, you can look out and see a long arc of land curving out to the west to a point almost in front of you. This point, Punta Sal, is the site of the Parque Nacional Marino Punta Sal.

Within this national marine park are various habitats, including mangrove forests and swamps, a small tropical forest, offshore reefs, several coves and the rocky point itself. On the east side of the park, the Laguna de los Micos (Lagoon of the Monkeys) contains extensive mangrove forests. It's a habitat for hundreds of species of birds (especially from November to February, when migratory species are here) and for the monkeys that the lagoon is named for.

Completely unspoiled and undeveloped, this park makes a fine outing from Tela. All-day tours including hiking, snorkeling, swimming and lunch are given by Garífuna Tours and the Hotel Bahía Azul (see the Tela section), or there are morning bird-watching trips to the Laguna de los Micos. Information about the park is available at the Prolansate office and at Garífuna Tours.

The park was named in honor of Jeanette Kawas, the director of Prolansate who was murdered in 1995 during a bitter struggle with big-money interests who wanted to develop the area.

Refugio de Vida Silvestre Punta Izopo
Standing on the beach at Tela and looking to the east, you can see another point: Punta Izopo, with the Punta Izopo Wildlife Refuge. The Ríos Plátano and Xicaque

HONDURAS

flowing through the wildlife refuge spread out into a network of canals passing through mangrove forests. These are home to abundant wildlife, including monkeys, crocodiles, turtles and many species of birds, including toucans and parrots.

Garífuna Tours in Tela offers kayak trips to the refuge. Gliding silently through the mangrove canals in a kayak, you can get close to the wildlife without disturbing it.

Garífuna Villages

Several Garífuna villages are within easy reach of Tela. All of them are right on the coast, with splendid beaches, simple houses shaded by coconut trees, fishing canoes resting on the sand and tiny restaurants serving delicious Garífuna food; the specialties are seafood soups and fish cooked in coconut. Although you can, in theory, quite easily walk to all these villages along the beaches, it is recommended that you do not, but rather take a guided tour or a taxi along the access roads (see the Dangers & Annoyances following).

The larger villages may hold dances on the weekends, and attending a Garífuna dance is a great experience. San Juan and El Triunfo de la Cruz have cultural dance troupes that have performed in many places.

The closest village is **La Ensenada**, 3km east along the arc of the beach from Tela, just before you reach the point, Punta Triunfo, crowned by the Cerro El Triunfo de la Cruz. La Ensenada is a lovely little village with seafood restaurants (although most are only open on the weekend), places for a drink and a great beach.

The larger village of **El Triunfo de la Cruz** can be reached by regular buses from Tela, departing from the corner on the east side of the market. Another beautiful spot, this village was the site of the first Spanish settlement in Honduras.

Another Garífuna village, 8km west of Tela, is **Tornabé**. It is a largish village and quite lovely. Past Tornabé, the beach road becomes rougher and can only be negotiated by 4WD vehicles. It continues for several more kilometers to **Miami**, a beautiful but basic Garífuna village on a narrow sandbar between the Caribbean Sea and the Laguna de los Micos. Miami is more primitive than the other villages: the houses are all made of traditional materials, and there's

Garífuna Dancing

While you're on the north coast, try to catch some live Garífuna music and dancing. The traditional Garífuna band is composed of three large drums, a turtle shell, some maracas and a big conch shell, producing throbbing, haunting rhythms and melodies. The chanted words are like a litany, to which the audience often responds. The dance is the punta, a Garífuna dance with a lot of hip movement. Often the dancers are in costume, with the women in long, loose colorful skirts.

You can attend a Garífuna dance at a number of places along the north coast; Garífuna people live all along here, and they like to have a good time, especially on weekends. In Tela, the Garífuna Museum has a Saturday night party with traditional music and dance at which visitors will feel very comfortable. In La Ceiba, a couple of places in Barrio La Isla have Garífuna dances on weekends.

In Trujillo, the Los Menudos group used to play in Cocopando, but since they became world famous and began touring in places like Europe and Japan, they perform less often locally. Still, if you go to a dance in Cocopando, you'll see plenty of punta dancing. Los Menudos sometimes play in Trujillo at special events.

The smaller Garífuna villages along the coast also often have music and dancing on weekends. Another good option is attending a Garífuna cultural event, if one happens to be held while you're visiting. All the towns and villages have annual fiestas, and cultural events and gatherings of one kind or another take place throughout the year. Garífuna Day (April 12), a big holiday for all the Garífuna communities, commemorates the day in 1797 when the Garífunas arrived in Honduras.

The national Ballet Folklórico Garífuna, based in Tegucigalpa, is a first-rate dance troupe that has performed around the world; if you get a chance to attend a performance, don't miss it.

no electricity. In Miami you can arrange for a boat trip on the Laguna de los Micos, or you can take a tour coming from Tela.

Dangers & Annoyances In recent years a fair number of travelers have been accosted on Tela beaches by armed local youths who have threatened and subsequently robbed them. While the problem now seems to have largely abated, it is still not advisable to walk alone or after dusk along the beaches away from Tela town. Use local transportation wherever possible and take along a friend for safety. While for the most part Garífuna villagers are friendly and welcoming, exercise common sense in case you encounter the fringe rowdy elements that may take an unreasonable shine to your belongings.

Places to Stay & Eat

With the possible exception of Miami, all the villages have places to stay and at least a couple of restaurants beside the beach specializing in seafood (of course).

In La Ensenada, *Budari* is run by a friendly Italian-Garífuna family. It has four rooms with private bath for US$7 per room, plus several other cabins made of traditional Garífuna materials. Also here is the *Comedor Budari*, serving traditional Garífuna and Italian foods. Also in La Ensenada, *Hotelito Mirtha* has simple rooms for US$5/6 with shared/private bath, plus some newer, larger cabins. Both places are on the road just behind the beach road; many places to eat are nearby on the beach.

Triunfo de la Cruz is the largest of the Garífuna villages. It's more developed, and all in all it doesn't have as much of the peaceful, somnolent feeling of the other villages. Still, there are places to stay here. Professor Margarito Colón has three *rooms* with private bath, plus another room made of traditional materials, all right on the beach, costing US$8.

One upmarket place here is the *Caribbean Coral Inn* (☎ 994 9806, fax 448 2942, caribcoral@globalnet.hn), which offers beachside, rustic cabins with private bathrooms for US$40/45 for one/two persons per night, including breakfast.

Getting There & Away

You can, in theory, walk along the beach from Tela to any of the villages. It only takes about half an hour to walk to La Ensenada, longer to reach the others. However, read Dangers & Annoyances previously and act accordingly.

Local buses to the Garífuna villages depart from the east side of the market in Tela. There are two routes: one heading west through San Juan and on to Tornabé, another heading east to Triunfo de la Cruz. Buses on both routes depart hourly from around 6 am to 5 pm; the fare is about US$0.50, and it takes about half an hour to 45 minutes to reach the villages.

If you're driving or cycling, you can get to San Juan on the beach road heading west from Tela and continue on to Tornabé. Be careful where you cross the sandbar at the Laguna de los Micos between San Juan and Tornabé; vehicles regularly get stuck in the sand here. You need a 4WD vehicle to get past Tornabé to Miami. Or you can get to Tornabé from the highway; the turnoff, 5km west of Tela, is marked by a sign directing you to 'The Last Resort.' To drive to La Ensenada or Triunfo de la Cruz, take the highway to the turnoff for Triunfo de la Cruz, 5km east of Tela. About 1km down this road, the road forks and goes left to La Ensenada, right to Triunfo de la Cruz.

LA CEIBA
pop 113,360

La Ceiba is the largest of Honduras' Caribbean port towns, though Puerto Cortés actually takes the lead as the busiest port. Situated on the narrow coastal plain between the towering Cordillera Nombre de Dios mountain range and the Caribbean, it's surrounded by pineapple and banana plantations, which are mostly owned by Standard Fruit, and it's rich in both fishing and agriculture.

La Ceiba is not a particularly attractive town, and there's not much to see in the town itself, but the butterfly museum is worth a visit, and a number of enjoyable excursions can be made in the surrounding area (see the Around La Ceiba section). La Ceiba has plenty of good places to stay and eat, and it's served by convenient air and bus routes, as well as boats to the Bay Islands.

Thousands of visitors descend on La Ceiba for Carnaval (see Special Events later in this section), but other than that,

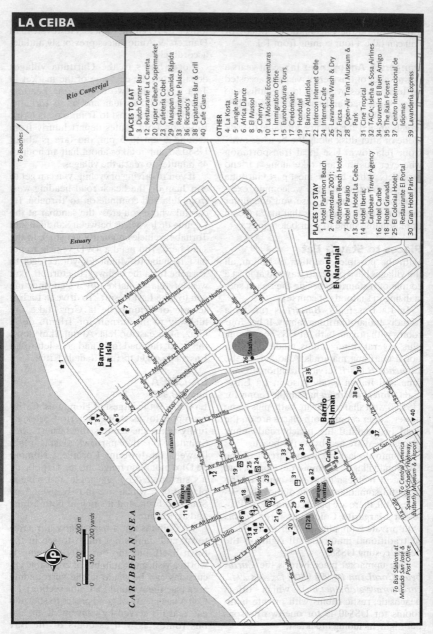

LA CEIBA

PLACES TO EAT
3   Dutch Corner Bar
12 Restaurante La Carreta
20 Super Ceibeño Supermarket
23 Cafetería Cobel
29 Masapan Comida Rápida
33 Restaurante Palace
36 Ricardo's
38 Expatriates Bar & Grill
40 Cafe Giare

OTHER
4   La Kosta
5   Jungle River
6   Africa Dance
8   El Mussol
9   Cherrys
10 La Moskitia Ecoaventuras
11 Immigration Office
15 Eurohondduras Tours
17 Credomatic
19 Hondutel
21 Banco Atlántida
22 Intercon Internet C@fe
24 Internet Cafe
26 Lavandería Wash & Dry
27 Fucsa
28 Open-Air Train Museum &
    Park
31 Cine Tropical
32 TACA; Isleña & Sosa Airlines
34 Souvenirs El Buen Amigo
35 The Rain Forest
37 Centro Internacional de
    Idiomas
39 Lavandería Express

PLACES TO STAY
1   Hotel Partenon Beach
2   Amsterdam 2001;
    Rotterdam Beach Hotel
7   Hotel Paraíso
13 Gran Hotel La Ceiba
14 Hotel Iberia;
    Caribbean Travel Agency
16 Hotel Caribe
18 Hotel Granada
25 El Colonial Hotel;
    Restaurante El Portal
30 Gran Hotel Paris

most travelers have traditionally come to La Ceiba because it's the jumping-off point for visits to the Bay Islands. Nowadays, you can fly to the Bay Islands from San Pedro Sula or Tegucigalpa, but all flights are routed via La Ceiba, with the exception of some direct international flights to Roatán from the US. However, the cheapest way to get from the mainland to Roatán and Utila is a ferry leaving from La Ceiba.

La Ceiba got its name from a very large *ceiba* tree that used to stand on the coast near where the pier is now. Boats would pull in near this spot, and people would congregate to meet, buy and sell in the shade of the big tree.

Orientation
The heart of La Ceiba is its attractive, shady parque central, with the cathedral on one corner. Avenida San Isidro, running from the east side of the plaza to the sea, is La Ceiba's main drag. A block or two over, Avenida 14 de Julio is another major commercial street. Avenida La República, running to the sea from the opposite side of the plaza, has railway tracks down its center that were used to transport fruit and cargo to the pier at the foot of this street.

When you cross the bridge over the estuary, you're in Barrio La Isla. Many Garífuna people live on this side, and there are a couple of decent backpacker places to stay, many simple restaurants and several popular discos, including a couple of places for live Garífuna music and dance. Farther east, about 1km from the center of town where the Río Cangrejal meets the sea at several sandbars, there are pleasant beaches that are cleaner than those in the center.

Information
The immigration office is on Avenida 14 de Julio, on the second floor of a small office block off Parque Bonilla. It's open 8 am to midday and 2 to 4 pm.

There's no tourist office in La Ceiba, but the folks at the Expatriates Bar & Grill (see the Places to Eat section) are good resources for information about the town. Fucsa (Fundación Cuero y Salado; ☎/fax 443 0329), the organization responsible for the Refugio de Vida Silvestre, is in the Edificio Ferrocarril Nacional in Zona Mazapan.

Many banks in the center will change traveler's checks. Banco Atlántida, on Avenida San Isidro, changes all types of traveler's checks and gives cash advances on Visa cards. Cash advances on Visa and MasterCard are available from Credomatic (☎ 443 0668), on Avenida San Isidro opposite the Hotel Iberia.

The post office is southwest of the parque central on Avenida Morazán near the corner of 13a Calle.

Hondutel is back from the road on Avenida Ramón Rosa, between 5a Calle and 7a Calle. It's open for domestic and international telephone calls 24 hours every day. Fax service is available 8 am to 4 pm Monday to Friday.

There are two Internet centers in La Ceiba. The Internet Cafe (☎ 443 4152, fax 443 0904, hondusof@laceiba.com) is in the Centro Comercial Panayotti. The Intercon Internet C@fe (☎ 440 1431, fax 440 1430, intercon@honduras.com) is on the second floor of the Plaza del Sol building on Avenida San Isidro. Both are open 8 am to 8 pm, and rates are about US$2 per half hour.

Lavandería Express, near Expatriates Bar & Grill, and Lavandería Wash & Dry, near the stadium, both offer wash, dry and fold (10lb of laundry for US$2.50).

Things to See & Do
La Ceiba's parque central, the hub of the city's activity, has plenty of shady trees and a crocodile and turtle enclosure. A block away, historic railway cars are displayed in an open-air **train museum** in a grassy park belonging to Standard Fruit. It's open to the public and free.

The **Museum of Butterflies & Other Insects** (☎ 442 2874) in Colonia El Sauce is worth a visit. You'll be given a guided tour (in English or Spanish) of the collection of over five thousand butterflies and moths and a thousand other insects, most of them collected in Honduras by schoolteacher Robert Lehman, all with notes telling where they were found. The largest moth in the world, with a 30cm (1 foot) wingspan, and the most iridescent butterfly in the world are highlights of the museum's collection (both were found in Honduras). There's a 25-minute video about insects. The museum is open 8 am to noon and 2 to 5 pm Monday to Saturday, evenings by appointment (closed Wednesday afternoons); admission is US$1 (students US$0.70). It's on Calle Escuela Internacional in Colonia El Sauce, Segunda Etapa, Casa G-12, about a 20-minute walk from the center of town.

The seawater is not too clean at La Ceiba, but you can find better beaches on either side of the center. **Playa La Barra** is the most popular, near the sandbars where the Río Cangrejal meets the sea, and there's also **Playa Miramar**, about 1km in the opposite direction, west of the center of town. There are plenty more good, cleaner beaches a few kilometers from town. However, exercise caution at all times and especially after dusk, since there have been reports of occasional armed muggings.

There's a **view** of La Ceiba, the coastline and the Bay Islands from Colonia La Merced (go up the road that ascends the hill behind the golf course; it's about an hour's walk). Alternatively, take the 'La Merced' bus from near the southwest corner of the central plaza. A taxi from town costs US$0.60. Bring binoculars if you have them.

Language Courses

The Centro Internacional de Idiomas (☎/fax 440 1557, cii@laceiba.com), on Avenida 14 de Julio between 11a Calle and 12a Calle, offers courses in Spanish, English and Garífuna languages and in Garífuna folklore and dance.

The Central America Spanish School (☎/fax 440 1707, cass@laceiba.com), on Avenida San Isidro, offers language classes five days a week, four hours a day. Students stay with local families, and the US$220 fee includes all meals, course tuition and study materials.

Organized Tours

Several tour companies operate in La Ceiba, offering trips to sights near La Ceiba and farther afield.

Eurohonduras Tours (☎ 443 3874, fax 443 3875, eurohonduras@caribe.hn), at Avenida La República and 6a Calle, provides local tours, including a Scenic Overview tour (to Río Cangrejal, Río María and Sambo Creek), a Forest Waterfall & City Tour, Cuero y Salado, Pico Bonito, white-water rafting on Río Cangrejal and tours farther afield. German, French, English and Spanish are spoken.

Jungle River (☎/fax 440 1268, jungle@laceiba.com), in Barrio la Isla half a block south of Hotel Rotterdam, has white-water rafting trips on Río Cangrejal, hiking in Pico Bonito National Park, and canoe trips to Cacao Lagoon, a monkey and bird refuge, with lunch in the Garífuna village of Corozal.

La Moskitia Ecoaventuras (☎ 442 0104, moskitia@laceiba.com), on Avenida 14 de Julio near the corner of 1a Calle, has local trips to Pico Bonito, Cuero y Salado, white-water rafting on Río Cangrejal, and trips into the Mosquitia region.

Omega Tours (☎ 440 0334, omegatours@laceiba.com) has white-water rafting, kayaking, horse riding, jungle and river hiking tours.

Ríos Honduras (☎ 995 6925, fax 443 1360, rios@hondurashn.com) can be contacted via the Caribbean Travel Agency, on Avenida San Isidro near Hotel San Carlos. It offers tours to Cuero y Salado and white-water rafting trips on the Río Cangrejal and rivers farther afield.

Special Events

Visitors from far and wide descend on La Ceiba for its annual Carnaval, held during the week of May 15, which is the day of San Isidro, the town's patron saint. People dress up in costumes and masks and dance themselves silly; it's a great time.

Places to Stay

Town Center *Hotel Caribe* (☎ 443 1857), on 5a Calle between Avenida San Isidro and Avenida Atlántida, has some quite spacious and sunny rooms up on the 3rd floor that share a wide balcony. All the rooms have private baths and cost US$20 for two persons.

Hotel Iberia (☎ 443 0401, fax 443 0100), on Avenida San Isidro between 5a and 6a Calle, has a welcoming inner courtyard and large, clean, comfortable rooms with private hot bath and cable TV, plus enclosed parking. Rooms cost US$12.50/16.70 with one/two double beds. Next door, the *Gran Hotel La Ceiba* (☎ /fax 443 2737) has singles/doubles with all the same amenities, plus air-con, for US$18/25.50. The *Hotel Granada* (☎ 443 2451), on Avenida Atlántida between 5a and 6a Calle, has been recommended by a few travelers who described it as being 'clean, friendly, with hot water, fan…safe.' A double room here goes for around US$12.40.

If you want to spend up, La Ceiba has some fancier places. *El Colonial Hotel*

(☎ 443 1953, fax 443 1955), on Avenida 14 de Julio between 6a and 7a Calle, has a rooftop bar, Jacuzzis and saunas and a good air-conditioned restaurant/bar. The 50 rooms, all with air-con and cable TV, are US$36/38 with one/two double beds; you may get a 20% discount if you ask for it.

On the north side of the parque central, the **Gran Hotel Paris** (☎ 443 2391, fax 443 1614, hotelparis@psinet.hn) has a swimming pool, air-con, color cable TV and a breakfast cafeteria; singles/doubles are US$30/33.

Barrio La Isla Near the beach in Barrio La Isla, **Amsterdam 2001** (☎ 443 2311) has been a haven for backpackers for many years. Upstairs is a dorm room with a wide sea-view porch; downstairs around the garden are five rooms, each sleeping three people for US$3 per person. There are some private double/triple rooms with cold bath and good beds for US$7/9 per room. Owner Jan van Halderen, an old Dutch sailor who speaks several languages, and his charming wife, María, are like a 'mom and pop' to travelers.

Next door, the **Rotterdam Beach Hotel** (☎ 440 0321) is newer and more upmarket, with eight clean, comfortable rooms opening onto a grassy garden, with private cold bath and fans. It's a great deal for US$10 per room.

Hotel Paraíso (☎ 443 3535, fax 443 3536), on 4a Calle three blocks from the beach, is another newer place. All the rooms have air-con, private hot bath, phone and color cable TV; also the hotel has a cafeteria and enclosed parking. Singles/doubles cost US$20/25.

A bit more pricey but right on the beach in Barrio La Isla, **Hotel Partenon Beach** (☎ 443 0404, fax 443 0434) is a luxurious place with a swimming pool, restaurant, nightclub, casino and Jacuzzi; all rooms have air-con, cable TV and phone. Rooms are US$24 with one bed, or US$32.50 with two beds.

Places to Eat
Town Center You'll find a large **Super Ceibeño Supermarket**, on 7a Calle opposite the park with the small train museum, where you can stock up on adventure rations. **Masapan Comida Rápida**, at 7a Calle and Avenida La República, is popular

and inexpensive. It's air-conditioned and has a long cafeteria buffet. **Cafetería Cobel**, on 7a Calle, is another popular place that's always packed with locals. Try their comida típica or bocadillos.

Restaurante Palace (☎ 443 0685), on Avenida 14 de Julio near 8a Calle, is a large air-conditioned restaurant with good Chinese food. **Restaurante La Carreta**, at 4a Calle and Avenida Ramón Rosa, is a pleasant open-air restaurant specializing in al carbón (grilled) meat dishes. **Cafe Giarre**, at Avenida San Isidro and 13a Calle, is a European-style sidewalk cafe and is relatively new in town. This is the place to come for espresso and cappuccino as well as Italian cakes and tropical cocktails. It's open 1 to 11 pm daily, closed Tuesdays.

El Portal, upstairs in the El Colonial Hotel (see Places to Stay, earlier), is another fine restaurant/bar, with plush decor, air-con and good service; the excellent and extensive menu includes Thai cuisine. Prices are not as high as you'd expect, with main dishes from US$3.50 to US$11.50. It's open 7 am to 10 pm daily.

The **Expatriates Bar & Grill** (☎ 443 2272), at the end of 12a Calle in Barrio El Imán, is upstairs on the roof of the Refricon refrigeration shop. The bar and some tables under a high thatched roof, and others out under the stars, all catch any breeze that comes by. It's great for vegetarians and meat eaters alike. Their specialty is barbecued chicken wings, for around US$4.50. It's open every day but Tuesday and Wednesday from 4 pm to midnight.

Ricardo's (☎ 443 0468), at Avenida 14 de Julio and 10a Calle, is a shade more expensive than La Ceiba's other options, but it's reputed to be one of the finest restaurants in northern Honduras. Seating is inside in an air-conditioned section or outdoors in the garden patio. It's open 11 am to 1:30 pm and 5:30 to 10 pm Monday to Saturday.

Barrio La Isla Many inexpensive open-air seafood restaurants line the beach, all the way from the estuary on the west side to the estuary and Playa La Barra on the east side.

Close by the beach is the **Dutch Corner Bar**, run by the same family that owns the Rotterdam Beach Hotel and Amsterdam 2001. It is open for breakfast and snacks

HONDURAS

throughout the day and drinks in the evening.

Entertainment

La Ceiba has several popular dance clubs, most of them in Barrio La Isla – 1a Calle in Barrio La Isla is known as the 'Zona Viva' for its nightlife. Popular clubs include *Africa Dance*, with live Garífuna music and occasional *punta* dancing, and *La Kosta*, both on 1a Calle beside the beach. There are plenty of others in the area. *Cherrys*, open 8 pm till dawn (cover charge on weekends), and *El Mussol* offer upmarket entertainment and tight security. El Mussol has a cover charge after 9 pm, and it's open from Thursday to Saturday.

The *Cine Tropical* cinema is on 8a Calle between Avenida San Isidro and Avenida 14 de Julio.

The *Expatriates Bar & Grill* (see the Places to Eat section) is a very popular watering hole and attracts a good mix of foreigners and locals.

Shopping

Souvenirs El Buen Amigo, a souvenir shop on Avenida 14 de Julio between 8a and 9a Calles, has a good selection of souvenirs and postcards. Cigar buffs need look no further than the humidors of the Expatriates Bar & Grill, where you can get a wide range of local and imported cigars, including Expatriados, Santa Rosa and Camacho brands. The Rain Forest, on Calle la Julia, has good quality wooden artifacts, pottery, paintings and jewelry.

Getting There & Away

Air TACA (☎ 443 1915), Isleña (☎ 443 0179, 443 2683 at the airport) and Sosa (☎ 443 1399, fax 443 2519, aerosoa@caribe.hn) all have offices on the east side of the parque central. Rollins Air (☎/fax 443 3206) is next to the Hotel Principe and also has an office at the airport.

Frequent flights connect La Ceiba with San Pedro Sula, Tegucigalpa, the Bay Islands, Trujillo and various places in the Mosquitia region. See the Getting Around section earlier in this chapter for details on domestic flights.

The TACA office represents all five of the Central American airlines (TACA, Lacsa, COPA, Nica and Aviateca). It offers

direct international flights to Miami daily and to New Orleans and New York five days a week. International flights to many other places connect through San Pedro Sula. Isleña offers two flights weekly from La Ceiba to Grand Cayman Island for US$200 one-way, US$350 roundtrip.

Bus The bus station is at Mercado San José, about 2km west of the center of La Ceiba. A local bus runs between the bus station and the central plaza (US$0.10), or you can take a taxi (US$1.30). The Viana Clase Oro (☎ 441 2330) express bus station is another 500m farther west along the same street, at the Servicentro Esso Miramar.

Buses go from La Ceiba to the following locations:

El Porvenir (US$0.70, 45 minutes, 15km) Same buses as to La Unión.

La Unión (US$0.50, 1½ hours, 20km)
Monday to Saturday, hourly buses depart from 8:30 am to 5:30 pm; Sunday, hourly buses from 9 am to 5 pm.

Nueva Armenia (US$0.90, 2½ hours, 40km)
One bus daily leaves Nueva Armenia at 5 am, arriving in La Ceiba at 8 am, then leaves La Ceiba at 11:30 am for the return trip, arriving at Nueva Armenia at 2 pm.

San Pedro Sula (US$1.90, three hours, 202km)
Catisa-Tupsa (☎ 441 2539) operates hourly direct buses, with one stop at Tela, 10 times daily from 5:30 am to 6 pm. Cotuc (☎ 441 2199) has service between Trujillo and San Pedro Sula but picks up passengers in La Ceiba four times daily.

Tegucigalpa (US$6, 8½ hours, 397km)
Cristina (☎ 441 2028) has six buses daily between 6:15 am and 3:30 pm; Etrucsa (☎ 441 0340) has direct buses at 3 and 10 am and 2 pm. Viana Clase Oro runs luxury express, air-conditioned buses twice a day at 6:30 am and 3:30 pm (US$13.80, seven hours) via San Pedro Sula.

Tela (US$1.90, 1½ hours, 103km)
Same buses as to San Pedro Sula for same price.

Trujillo (US$2.20, four hours, 171km)
Seven buses run daily from 9:30 am to 7 pm.

Boat Boats operate from the Muelle de Cabotaje, which is about a 20-minute drive (8km) east of town. Taxis will take you there for US$3.50 per person. Be there an hour before departure to buy your ticket. The turnoff is not well posted. Look for the Copena gas station and turn left toward the sea.

The MV *Galaxy II* (☎ 442 0780 in La Ceiba, 445 1795 in Roatán) is a comfortable, air-conditioned ferry sailing between La Ceiba and Roatán and La Ceiba and Utila every day. From La Ceiba it takes about two hours to reach Roatán and about an hour to reach Utila. Departure for Utila is at 9:30 am and for Roatán at 3 pm. (See also the Getting Around section earlier in this chapter for more details and fares.)

You could ask around the Muelle de Cabotaje for boats to other destinations. Captains of cargo and fishing boats *might* be persuaded to take along a passenger, but the practice is now officially discouraged so don't count on it.

Getting Around

To/From the Airport La Ceiba's airport, the Aeropuerto Internacional Golosón, is 10km west of La Ceiba on the highway to Tela. Any bus heading west could drop you there. A slow local bus goes from the central plaza to near the airport, but taking a colectivo from the southwest corner of the plaza is a more reliable option (US$0.60). A normal taxi costs about US$3.50. Oddly, the airport is not posted from the main road. Look for the 'Oficina Golosón' sign and turn here.

Coming from the airport, don't take one of the taxis right at the airport door, which charge about US$3 per person for the ride into town; walk out to the main road and flag down a taxi there, which will take you into town for around US$1.30 per person.

Car Rental agencies include Dino's (☎ 443 0434) at the Hotel Partenon Beach; Maya (☎ 443 3079) at the Hotel La Quinta; Molinari (☎ 443 0055) at the Gran Hotel Paris; Budget (☎ 441 1105) on the airport road; and Toyota (☎ 443 1976) on Avenida San Isidro. Budget proved to be very helpful. The average rate is about US$65 per day.

Taxi Taxis in La Ceiba are easy to find – they will normally find you – and a ride anywhere in town costs US$1.30.

AROUND LA CEIBA

Parque Nacional Pico Bonito (see the following section) lures many visitors just outside the city, but there are plenty of other nearby attractions as well.

Beaches

A number of good beaches are only a few kilometers from La Cciba. East toward Trujillo, there are **Boca Vieja**, 5km from La Ceiba and 2km from the highway; the popular **Playa Peru**, 6km from La Ceiba and 1km from the highway; and **Villa Nuria**, 16km from La Ceiba and 1km from the highway. At **Cuyamel**, 17km from La Ceiba and 1.5km from the highway, there's a small admission fee, and you can purchase barbecued fish by the beach and the river, especially on Sunday. *Las Sirenas*, at Cuyamel, offers camping on the beach for US$8 per tent. See also the following Garífuna Villages section.

Dantio is 6km west toward Tela from La Ceiba; it has a beach, estuary and fresh fish for sale. **El Porvenir** is 15km from La Ceiba; it boasts a beach, river and typical Garífuna food.

Garífuna Villages

Corozal, 15km east of La Ceiba, and **Sambo Creek**, 6km farther east, are two seaside Garífuna fishing villages that are easy to reach from La Ceiba. They are enjoyable places, offering good beaches and fresh seafood. Both villages have Garífuna musical groups, and dances are held on weekend nights.

The annual fair at Corozal, held from around January 6 to 18, is a big event that attracts people from far and wide, especially on the weekends of the fair, when you'll find dancing, partying, games and competitions, lots of fun on the beach and good seafood. The annual fair at Sambo Creek is held in June.

Local buses connect both villages with La Ceiba; see the La Ceiba section earlier in this chapter for transportation details.

At Sambo Creek, *Hotel Hermanos Avila* is opposite the beach, beside the Río Sambo, at the end of the beach road and the end of the bus line. It has a number of rooms ranging in price from US$3 to US$5. However one reader warned that there was no water available, so ask before checking in. They also have a small restaurant where meals cost around US$1.50 to US$2.50, and there are other restaurants nearby. You can rent a dugout canoe (US$1) for exploring on the river. You can also arrange a motorboat ride (US$5) out to Cayos Cochinos

HONDURAS

from Sambo Creek; the crossing takes about an hour.

At Corozal, **Hospedaje David** is in a quiet spot several blocks from the beach. It has eight simple rooms, with fan and shared bath, for US$2.50 per room.

River Balnearios

On the **Río Maria**, 7km east of La Ceiba on the highway to Trujillo, about eight blocks from the highway, is a delightful freshwater *balneario* with pools in the tropical forest, a waterfall and a viewpoint from which you can see the Bay Islands. Any eastbound bus from La Ceiba or any taxi can drop you on the highway here, and you can walk the 15 minutes up to the balneario; local children can show you the way. Euro Honduras Tours (see the Organized Tours part of the La Ceiba section) also comes here.

Los Chorros, 10km east of La Ceiba, is another pleasant balneario.

Villa Rhina 14km east of La Ceiba, right on the highway, is another pleasant riverside balneario. There's no charge to swim in the refreshing, cool pools, but you're expected to spend a minimum of US$2 at the restaurant/bar. You can also stay at the **Hotel de Montaña** (☎ 443 1222, fax 443 3558, villarhina@honduras.com), in one of their eight log cabins, for US$35.

Several other balnearios and riverside beaches are along the Río Cangrejal.

Río Cangrejal

You can take an attractive scenic drive along the Río Cangrejal, starting about 3km east of La Ceiba on the highway to Trujillo. The riverside road is the Old Highway to Olanchito (Antigua Carretera a Olanchito), also called La Culebra because it is such a snakelike, winding road. The road passes waterfalls, rapids and several balnearios, including **Playa de Venado**, 8km from La Ceiba; **Playa de los Lobos**, 2km farther on; and **Balneario Las Mangas**, with its iron bridge, 16km from La Ceiba. The route passes through a lovely forest of precious woods and has some good views.

Several companies now operate **whitewater rafting trips** on this river, classified Class III and IV. Operators include Ríos Honduras, Euro Honduras, La Moskitia Ecoaventuras and Tropical Jungle Tours

(see the Organized Tours part of the La Ceiba section).

If you come on a rafting tour, the company will provide transportation to and from La Ceiba. Otherwise, buses depart hourly from the La Ceiba bus terminal (US$0.40) and go as far as Balneario Las Mangas. Bring your lunch along, as there's nowhere to buy food here; fishing is also good.

There's an important archaeological site in this area, at **La Colorada**. It is unexcavated as yet, but there are around 60 mounds. Experts speculate that the site may one day rank among the important Honduran ruins. Unlike at Copán, the people who built this site were not Maya, but Macrochibcha people.

Refugio de Vida Silvestre Cuero y Salado

On the coast about 30km west of La Ceiba, the Cuero y Salado Wildlife Refuge takes its name from two rivers, the Cuero and Salado, that meet at the coast in a large estuary. This estuary, now a reserve, protects varied and abundant wildlife, including howler and white-faced monkeys, jaguars, ocelots, anteaters, sloths, agoutis, peccaries, iguanas, boa constrictors, otters, manatees, river and sea turtles, crocodiles, caimans, fish and 196 species of birds, including toucans, parrots, herons, pelicans, kingfishers and eagles. Migratory birds are here from around August/September to April/May.

To see the most wildlife, visit the reserve early in the morning or late in the afternoon. During the heat of the day, the animals are hiding from the sun. Bring food, water, sunscreen and insect repellent.

You can visit the reserve on a one-day tour from La Ceiba; La Moskitia Ecoaventuras, Ríos Honduras and Euro Honduras Tours all offer tours (see La Ceiba's Organized Tours section). Fundación Cuero y Salado (Fucsa), the organization running the reserve, arranges group tours from its office in La Ceiba.

Or you can come on your own; Fucsa or Ríos Honduras will help you organize your trip.

To get to the reserve, take a bus (1½ hours) or drive (30 minutes) from La Ceiba to La Unión, past El Porvenir; a taxi to get out there from La Ceiba could cost around

US$8. At La Unión the road meets some old railway tracks. From this point, you take a *burra*, a small rail car propelled by poles, half an hour out to the reserve; the cost for the burra is around US$6.65 to US$10, depending on the number of people in the group (up to eight). Alternatively, if you reserve in advance with Fucsa, you can hire a *motocarro* train for US$5 to take you in. If you walk along the railway tracks, it takes 1½ hours to reach the reserve at a brisk pace (it's about 8km).

When you reach the reserve, there is an entry fee of US$10. Inside are houses and offices belonging to Fucsa and to Standard Fruit. You can tour the reserve by canoe or motorboat. A two-hour boat trip with guide costs about US$11; make a reservation in advance with Fucsa, to ensure that a boat will be available.

You can visit the park all in one day (the last bus leaves La Unión to return to La Ceiba at around 4 pm), or you can allow a couple of days for a leisurely visit. Fucsa is building overnight accommodations in the park; ask them for details. Or you can camp in the park if you have all your own gear. It doesn't cost anything, but you must first obtain permission from Fucsa.

You can get more information from the Fucsa office (☎/fax 443 0329) in the Edificio Ferrocarril Nacional, Zona Mazapan, La Ceiba (see the La Ceiba map). It's open 8 am to 11:30 am and 1:30 to 4:30 pm Monday to Friday, Saturday 8 am to 11:30 am. They have a large wall map that will make all the above directions crystal clear.

Cayos Cochinos

Cayos Cochinos (the Hog Islands), 29km from La Ceiba and just 17km from the shore, can be visited as a day trip or camping trip from La Ceiba. The Hog Islands and the waters and reefs around them are designated a biological marine reserve – it is illegal to anchor on the reef, and commercial fishing is prohibited. Consequently, the reefs are pristine and fish abundant. Diving and snorkeling are excellent around the islands, with black coral reefs, wall diving, cave diving, seamounts and a plane wreck.

You can hire a boat to go out to the small cays, and there are some interesting nature walks. The islands are also known for their unique pink boas.

PARQUE NACIONAL PICO BONITO

Pico Bonito, a few kilometers south and inland from La Ceiba, is one of Honduras' best-known national parks, with an unexplored core area of 500 sq km. It was already the largest national park in Honduras when additional forest territory was included in July 1992. It has magnificent and varied types of forests at different elevations, rivers, waterfalls and abundant wildlife, including jaguars, armadillos, wild pigs, tepescuintes, squirrels, monkeys, doves, toucans, insects and more.

The Pico Bonito itself, at 2436m, is very difficult to ascend; climbers need ropes and mountain-climbing experience. Few groups have succeeded in climbing it, and the ascent and descent would take several days. However, easier walks around the fringes of the park are possible. From the hacienda at the Río Bonito entrance to the park, an easy 1km trail leads to a good swimming hole where the Río Bonito and Río Quebrada meet. From here, there's also a three-hour loop trail, La Guatusa, which goes up to a lookout point.

To get to the park, take a local bus (the Colonia 1 de Mayo-Parque Bonilla route; catch it in La Ceiba at Parque Bonilla), which will bring you to the Aldea Armenia Bonita; from there it's about a 20-minute walk to the park entrance. Anyone can point you in the right direction. If you're driving, take the highway west from La Ceiba for about 8km and then turn toward the mountains on the road just beyond the Honduras Armed Forces camp, which is immediately after the airport. To reach the park entrance, follow this road for 4.5km through the village, taking a right just after the soccer field. You'll cross the Río Bonito just before you reach the entrance.

Alternatively, you could leave the highway and walk up the Río Bonito 4.5km to the park entrance. About 10km west of La Ceiba on the highway to Tela, opposite the Posta de Tránsito, you can walk through La Piñera, the Standard Fruit pineapple plantation, to the river.

About 300m past the park entrance is the hacienda, where a visitors center is being built. A ranger is usually on duty. There are plans for upgrading interpretive trails and providing guides, probably in 2001. When all this is in place, it will cost US$6 to enter the park; until then, the entrance fee is US$2.50.

At the hacienda is a house where you can sleep overnight. There's no kitchen or bedding, so bring along everything you'll need. You can also camp at the hacienda if you have your own gear.

You can easily visit the park in one day if you stay on the trails near the hacienda. You could see more of the forest, however, if you allowed two days or more, one for the ascent and one for the descent.

The Río Bonito entrance is the most accessible entrance to the park, but it's a large park and there are other entrances, including one beside the Río Cangrejal.

If you really want to see the park in some degree of comfort, your best bet is to stay at **The Lodge at Pico Bonito** (*☎ 440 0388, fax 440 0468, picobonito@caribe.hn*). Opened amidst much fanfare in May 2000, this is Honduras' first dedicated eco-lodge, tastefully built in the buffer zone of the park about 3km off the main highway from the village of El Pino. Consisting of discretely hidden and luxuriously equipped individual lodges (no TVs, though, to distract you from nature), the Pico Bonito Lodge caters to discerning travelers. There's a relaxed, colonial-style restaurant and bar for guests (which was ceremoniously christened by this author). A superb four-hour guided and at times strenuous walk through the rain forest will show visitors a good cross-section of the park's diverse fauna and flora. Check the Web site (www.picobonito.com) for full details and current rates, which begin at around US$100 per night in the low season.

For more information on the park, contact the park office in La Ceiba, which shares office space with Fucsa (see the Refugio se Vida Silvestre Cuero y Salado section). They will be offering tours into the park by 2001. Several of the tour companies in La Ceiba also offer trips into the park (see the Organized Tours part of the La Ceiba section).

TRUJILLO
pop 36,000
Capital of the department of Colón, Trujillo sits on the wide arc of the Bahía de Trujillo.

The town is famous for its lovely beaches with coconut palms and gentle seas. Though it's known as one of Honduras' most attractive Caribbean coastal towns, it is not usually full of tourists, except during the celebration of Semana Santa and the annual fair of the town's patron saint, San Juan Bautista, in the last week of June (June 24 is the exact day, but the festival goes on for a week).

History
Trujillo suffered a cruel blow at the hands of Hurricane Mitch in 1998, with much of the north coast in and around the town being badly affected by the hurricane's devastating winds. The town has not really recovered, and tourism has taken something of a back seat ever since. Language schools that existed prior to Mitch have relocated to other towns, and there is a general sense of malaise about Trujillo now. Tourists may eventually drift back, but the process may take longer than hoped for.

Trujillo is not a large town, but it has played an important part in the history of Central America. It was near Trujillo, on August 14, 1502, that Columbus first set foot on the American mainland, having sailed from Jamaica on his fourth (and final) voyage. The first Catholic mass on American mainland soil was said on the spot where he and his crew landed.

Founded on May 18, 1525, Trujillo was one of the earliest Spanish settlements in Central America. The first Spanish town in the colonial province of Honduras, it was the provincial capital until the seat was shifted to Comayagua in 1537. The Catholic bishop's see remained in Trujillo until 1561, when it too was moved to Comayagua.

The Spanish used the port at Trujillo to ship out gold and silver from the interior of Honduras, an activity that attracted pirates to the bay. The Bahía de Trujillo was the scene of several great battles when the town was attacked by pirates, including van Horn, Aury and Henry Morgan.

The Spanish built several fortresses, the ruins of which are still visible; the ruins of the fort of Santa Bárbara lie near the plaza in town. Despite the fortifications, the buccaneers prevailed, and after a sacking by Dutch pirates in 1643, the town lay in ruins for over a century until it was resettled in 1787.

Orientation

Trujillo is a small town, and you can easily walk everywhere you need to go, though there are also taxis. Several good restaurants, a couple of hotels and the best beaches are near the airstrip, which is a few kilometers east of town; you can get there by walking about 20 minutes east along the beach.

Information

There's no tourist information office in Trujillo, but the folks at Café Oasis are very helpful with information about the town.

The immigration office is on the west end of 2a Calle.

The Banco de Occidente changes traveler's checks, gives cash advances on both Visa and MasterCard and represents Western Union. It's open 8 am to noon and 2 to 5 pm Monday to Friday, 8 to 11:30 am Saturday. Right on the plaza, Banco Atlántida changes traveler's checks and gives cash advances on Visa cards.

The post office and Hondutel are side by side, three blocks inland from the plaza. Hondutel is open for domestic and international phone calls from 7 am to 9 pm Monday to Friday, from 8 am to 4 pm Saturday and Sunday. Fax service is available 7 am to 5 pm Monday to Friday, 7 to 11 am Saturday.

Laundry service is available next door to the Restaurante, Bar & Disco Horfez. The shop is open 7 am to 5:30 pm Monday to Friday, 7 am to noon Saturday.

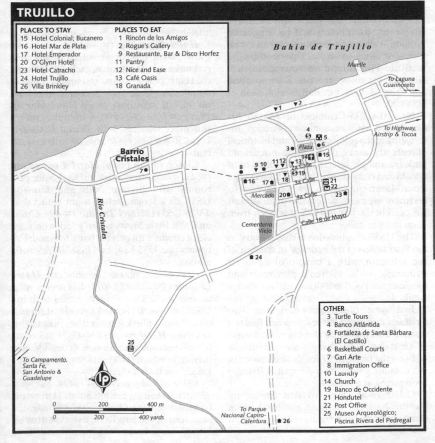

TRUJILLO

PLACES TO STAY
15 Hotel Colonial; Bucanero
16 Hotel Mar de Plata
17 Hotel Emperador
20 O'Glynn Hotel
23 Hotel Catracho
24 Hotel Trujillo
26 Villa Brinkley

PLACES TO EAT
1 Rincón de los Amigos
2 Rogue's Gallery
9 Restaurante, Bar & Disco Horfez
11 Pantry
12 Nice and Ease
13 Café Oasis
18 Granada

OTHER
3 Turtle Tours
4 Banco Atlántida
5 Fortaleza de Santa Bárbara
   (El Castillo)
6 Basketball Courts
7 Gari Arte
8 Immigration Office
10 Laundry
14 Church
19 Banco de Occidente
21 Hondutel
22 Post Office
25 Museo Arqueológico;
   Piscina Rivera del Pedregal

Bahia de Trujillo

Muelle

To Laguna Guaimoreto

To Highway, Airstrip & Tocoa

Barrio Cristales

Plaza

Rio Cristales

Mercado

Cementerio Viejo

Calle 18 de Mayo

To Campamento, Santa Fe, San Antonio & Guadalupe

0   200   400 m
0   200   400 yards

To Parque Nacional Capiro-Calentura

HONDURAS

Things to See & Do

Trujillo is best known for its attractive white-sand beaches. Some of the best are near the airstrip, a 20-minute walk east along the beach from town; several beach-side open-air thatched-roof restaurant/bars provide shade, food and a cool drink for beachgoers and keep the beaches clean. This isn't the only good beach, however. White-sand beaches stretch for several kilo-meters around the bay – you can walk along the beach in either direction from town and pick your spot.

The ruins of the 17th-century Spanish fortress, properly named the Fortaleza Santa Bárbara de Trujillo but usually called El Castillo, are in the center of town near the plaza, behind the basketball courts and overlooking the sea. The fort contains several old cannons and other relics, a plaque marking the place where North American adventurer/would-be conqueror William Walker was executed and an excel-lent view along the coast. Operated by the Instituto Hondureño de Antropología e Historia, the ruins are open 8 am to noon and from 1 to 4 pm daily; admission is US$0.70.

Near the Río Cristales, the Museo Arqueológico has a fascinating collection: Interesting archaeological relics and historical objects are arrayed alongside household junk (seemingly selected on the basis of 'if it's old and rusty, display it'!). Exhibits range from Mayan carvings to mangled typewrit-ers; there are even the remains of an aircraft wrecked in the bay in 1985. It is open from 7 am to 5 pm daily.

The US$0.85 admission includes entry to the Piscina Rivera del Pedregal at the rear of the museum, with a couple of open-air swimming pools, children's' play areas and picnic areas. Food and drink are not always available.

Just west of town, where the Río Cristales flows into the sea, you can find the district Cocopando, in the Garífuna barrio of Cristales. Several open-air restaurants right on the beach offer meals and snacks; in the evening, this is the best spot in Trujillo for dancing and music.

Other good places to visit (including Parque Nacional Capiro-Calentura) are a short distance from town; see the Around Trujillo section.

Organized Tours

Turtle Tours (☎ 434 4444, fax 434 4431) offers tours to places in the area, including Capiro-Calentura, Laguna Guaimoreto, the crocodile reserve and Garífuna villages. It also organizes snorkeling at Cayos Blancos and a Trujillo city tour, and it conducts tours into the Mosquitia region. German, English and Spanish are spoken. The office is at the hotel Villa Brinkley; information about tours is also available in the restaurant on the west side of the central plaza.

Trujillo Ecotours (☎ 434 4101) offers tours to all the same places as Turtle Tours, plus a few more. Information about their tours is available at Chino's Bar, on the beach near the airstrip.

Places to Stay

Trujillo has a number of good places to stay. During Semana Santa you should book ahead.

Hotel Catracho (☎ 434 4438), on 4a Calle, has a row of nine simple wooden rooms built in the garden, each with private cold bath, plus a bar and restaurant. Singles/doubles are US$5.50/6. A couple of blocks up the hill from the plaza is *Hotel Mar de Plata* (☎ /fax 434 4458), a friendly, family-run place. Rooms with shared bath are US$4.50/6.60, or US$6.65/8.20 with private bath.

Closer to the plaza, *Hotel Emperador* (☎ 434 4446) offers small but well-equipped rooms with private bath and fan for US$7.85; a larger, better room with cable TV is US$11. *Hotel Trujillo* (☎ 434 4202), on Calle 18 de Mayo, is also good, with very clean rooms with private bath, fan, and TV; rooms are US$9/14, or US$13/17.25 with air-con.

Beside the plaza, the modern *Hotel Colonial* (☎ /fax 434 4011) has rooms with air-con, cable TV and private cold bath for US$22.40; you'll also find a good restaurant/bar. Three blocks from the plaza, the *O'Glynn Hotel* (☎ /fax 434 4592) has com-fortable rooms with air-con, cable TV and private hot bath for US$18 for one person, US$25 for two or three.

Villa Brinkley (☎ 434 4444, fax 434 4269), perched on the hill about 1km south from the center of town, enjoys a magnifi-cent view of the bay. Rooms start at around US$33 for a room with air-con. All have private hot bath; children 17 and under are free. Amenities include a bar, two restaurants, a swimming pool and a recreation room.

Near the airstrip, a couple of kilometers from town, the *Trujillo Bay Hotel* (☎ /fax 434 4732) has large, comfortable singles/doubles with air-con, cable TV and private hot bath for US$30/32 It's on the land side of the airstrip; just across the airstrip are several good beachside restaurant/bars on one of the finest stretches of beach in the area.

Places to Eat

There are several good inexpensive restaurants in town. *Café Oasis*, on 2a Calle, is a pleasant little place with an outdoor patio and good vegetarian or meat meals and snacks. The foods are different from what you see at most other places, and they also make a variety of fruit drinks. There's an international book exchange and a message board for travelers. Natalie and Daniel, the Canadian-Honduran proprietors, are friendly and helpful with information about the town. It's open from 9 am Monday to Saturday, from 4 pm Sunday, and stays open until around 11 pm or midnight.

Other good restaurants in town include the *Granada*, the *Pantry* and the *Bucanero*, the last at the Hotel Colonial near the plaza. All have air-con and bars, and all serve much the same selection of seafood, meat, soups, sandwiches and burgers, breakfasts and so on at much the same prices; the Pantry also serves pizza. Try *Nice and Ease* for fruit drinks, ice cream and pastries.

Restaurante, Bar & Disco Horfez is an open-air spot with lots of plants; it's open Tuesday to Sunday from 4 pm on. Discos are held here on Friday, Saturday and Sunday nights.

The restaurants at the *Villa Brinkley* up on the hill have an excellent view. They serve a pleasant breakfast for US$2, dinners for around US$5 to US$7. The menu is varied and includes seafood prepared in many styles.

On the beach just below the plaza, there's a row of thatch-roof open-air seafood restaurant/bars. The *Rincón de los Amigos* has excellent seafood, Cajun food and Spanish paella; it's a pleasant, friendly place, with tables, hammocks and the bar. Once or

twice a week there's live Garífuna music and dancing. It's open from around 9:30 am to 11 pm daily. Also along here, *Rogue's Gallery* has seafood, a bar, cable TV, an English-language book exchange, catamaran and boat rentals and 'the best bathrooms on the beach,' owner Jerry from California proudly proclaims. 'Jerry's' is open 7 am to 10 pm daily.

Several other pleasant open-air beachfront restaurant/bars are on a fine stretch of beach near the airport, a couple of kilometers east of town (coming from town, walk east along the beach for about 20 minutes). They include the *Bahía Bar*, *Chino's Bar* and the *Gringo Bar*. Walk along and take your pick. Each has its own special features (hammocks, a volleyball net, boats or water sports for rent). All are open from around 7 am until 10 pm or later daily.

Entertainment

At Cocopando, on the beach in Barrio Cristales where the Garífuna residents live, dances are held Thursday to Sunday nights. Weekend nights are very lively. On Sunday afternoons, local children have a dance – children that barely reach up to your waist are already quite skillful at dancing the punta – and it's a happy time for all.

Once or twice a week, the *Rincón de los Amigos*, on the beach below the plaza, has a dance with a traditional Garífuna band.

In town, *Restaurant, Bar & Disco Horfez* is a popular open-air nightspot with disco dancing on Friday, Saturday and Sunday evenings.

Shopping

In Barrio Cristales, Gari Arte (☎ 434 4207) offers a selection of Garífuna handicrafts, music and souvenirs.

Getting There & Away

Air Trujillo has a small airstrip a few kilometers west of town. Isleña (☎ 434 4965) has a daily (except Sunday) flight between La Ceiba and Palacios that stops at Trujillo; from Trujillo it's US$27 to La Ceiba, US$31 to Palacios.

Bus Buses arrive and depart from Trujillo's central plaza. Direct buses to San Pedro Sula (US$6, five to six hours, 373km) from Trujillo, operated by the Cotuc and

Cotraipbal companies, depart at 2, 3, 5, 6:30 and 8 am. These buses are the quickest and most painless way to get to La Ceiba (2½ hours) and Tela (3½ hours). Otherwise, buses making plenty of stops depart from Trujillo every day for La Ceiba at 2, 3, 4, 5, 6:30, 7:30, 8:30 and 10 am and at noon, 1 and 2 pm (US$2.60, four to 4½ hours, 171km). Minibuses to Tocoa, along the way to La Ceiba, also depart frequently.

There are two inland routes to Tegucigalpa. A direct bus departs at 4 am daily and goes over the mountains via La Unión; it's about a nine-hour trip. Another bus departs at 9 am for the same route, though you have to change buses in the mountains.

Local buses go from Trujillo to the Garífuna villages of Santa Fe, San Antonio and Guadalupe to the west, and to Puerto Castilla across the bay. Buses to Santa Fe, San Antonio and Guadalupe depart four times a day. Ask when they're leaving, and be careful not to miss the bus; they don't always run on schedule, but may depart whenever they're full.

Motorcycle Turtle Tours (see the Organized Tours section) rents Suzuki 350cc motorcycles for US$35 per day.

Boat Boats depart from the *muelle* (pier) at Trujillo for various destinations, including the Bay Islands, the Mosquitia region, the Nicaraguan coast, some Caribbean islands (including the Cayman Islands and Jamaica) and the US (usually New Orleans, four days away by boat). None of these are scheduled departures; you just have to walk down to the pier, see what boats are there and try your luck. They are usually fishing or cargo boats, but you can often pay passage.

Cargo boats usually depart from this pier for Guanaja every couple of days; the passage takes about five hours and should cost you around US$10 or US$12 – much cheaper than flying. Cargo boats also depart every couple of days for the Mosquitia region.

Also check for boats at Puerto Castilla, round the bay.

AROUND TRUJILLO
Parque Nacional Capiro-Calentura
The mountain behind Trujillo, called Cerro Calentura, 1235m above sea level at the summit, is part of the Capiro-Calentura National Park. It can be most easily accessed by heading straight up the hill from town; take the road going up past the Villa Brinkley hotel and just keep on going. The gravel road goes all the way up to the summit, which is 10km from town. Though a 4WD vehicle would be best, you could make it in a regular car (you could also walk it). Turtle Tours and Trujillo Ecotours (see the Organized Tours part of the Trujillo section) also make trips up there.

On the way up the hill, you pass through a couple of distinct vegetation zones. At around 600m to 700m the vegetation changes from tropical rain forest to subtropical low-mountain rain forest, and you find yourself in a zone of giant tree ferns, with lush forest, large trees, vines and flowering plants. There's plenty of wildlife in the park, too, including many species of tropical birds and butterflies, reptiles, monkeys and more.

About a third of the way up, a couple of trails take off from the road to the left, leading to a waterfall and a tiny reservoir; they're not marked, but you can see them distinctly from the road.

It can be sunny, clear and warm in Trujillo, and cloudy and much cooler at the top of the hill. If the weather isn't cloudy, you can get a great view from the summit over the beautiful Valle de Aguán, along the coast as far as Limón, and across to Roatán, Guanaja and the Cayos Cochinos (Hog Islands). There is a radar station is at the summit.

Information about the park is available from the visitors center, which is just beyond the entrance to the park on the road that passes the Villa Brinkley, or from the office of the Fundación Capiro-Calentura Guaimoreto (FUCAGUA; ☎/fax 434 4294), on the second floor of the kiosk building in the middle of the central plaza; it's open 8 am to noon and 2 to 4:30 pm Monday to Friday. Entry to the park costs around US$10.

Laguna Guaimoreto
Five kilometers east of Trujillo, past the airstrip and the Río Negro, Laguna Guaimoreto is a large lagoon with a natural passageway onto the bay. About 6km by 9km, the lagoon is a protected wildlife

refuge; its complex system of canals and mangrove forests is home to abundant animal, bird and plant life, including thousands of migratory birds from around November to February.

Information about the lagoon is available from the FUCAGUA office in the central plaza (see the Parque Nacional Capiro-Calentura section, earlier in this chapter). Turtle Tours and Trujillo Ecotours (see Organized Tours in the Trujillo section) both offer tours on the lagoon.

A less expensive option is to walk out here along the beach from Trujillo to the old bridge between Trujillo and Puerto Castilla. Sometimes you can hire a boat from here to take you to the lagoon.

Garífuna Villages

Several Garífuna villages, all with houses stretching along the beach, are west of Trujillo. **Santa Fe**, the largest village, is 10km west of Trujillo. A couple of kilometers farther are the smaller Garífuna villages of **San Antonio** and then **Guadalupe**.

Santa Fe's annual fair is on July 16.

Places to Stay & Eat A simple *hospedaje* is in Santa Fe about a block past the Comedor Caballero. Rooms are around US$5 per night. There's no sign, but anyone can tell you where it is.

In Guadalupe, *Hotel Franklin* is a simple little place near the beach with just five clean rooms, each with fan and private bath. Singles/doubles are US$5/6.50 per night, with cheaper weekly rates. Nikolasa, the friendly owner, will cook meals for you, and there's also a little shop and other places to eat nearby.

If you go to Santa Fe, eat at *Comedor Caballero*. Meals start at US$2.50, but as Sr Caballero is thought by many to be the best cook in northern Honduras, it's worth splashing out on his *especial carte*, with dishes starting at US$5. It's open from around 8 am to 6 pm daily.

Getting There & Away A dirt road runs out to these villages from Trujillo, and buses connect with Trujillo four times a day (see the Getting Around part of the Trujillo section). You can walk along the beach to reach any of the villages; don't walk on the beach at night, though.

Bay Islands

About 50km off the north coast of Honduras, the three Bay Islands (Islas de la Bahía) – Roatán, Utila and Guanaja – are prime attractions for visitors, who come from around the world to dive and snorkel on the extensive reefs teeming with colorful fishes, corals, sponges, lobsters and lots of other marine life. These reefs, a continuation of the Belize reefs, are the second-largest barrier reef in the world after Australia's Great Barrier Reef.

Utila is known as the cheapest place in the world to take a scuba-diving certification course. Several dive schools on Roatán, a larger and more varied island, offer diving courses for not too much more. Both islands offer great diving, and both have many aficionados. Diving is also good on Guanaja, though this island is not a tourist destination on the same scale as the others.

The Bay Islands Conservation Association (BICA) works to protect and preserve the reef. Reefs in several parts of the islands are now protected areas awaiting designation as national marine parks.

The island economy is based mostly on fishing and shrimp and lobster catching. Many islanders also work as merchant seafarers. All the island settlements hug the Caribbean Sea, and the culture is as much oriented toward the sea as toward land. Nowadays, tourism is becoming an ever-more-important element of the island economy.

History

Ruins on all three of the Bay Islands indicate that they were inhabited well before the Europeans arrived. Apparently human habitation began around AD 600, though evidence is slim until after around AD 1000. The early settlers might have been Maya; there are also caves that may have provided shelter for groups of Pech (Paya) Indians, and there seem to have been Nahuatl-speaking people here (Nahuatl was the language of the Aztecs in Mexico).

Christopher Columbus, on his fourth and final voyage to the New World, landed on the island of Guanaja on July 30, 1502. He encountered a fairly large population of Indians, whom he believed to be cannibals.

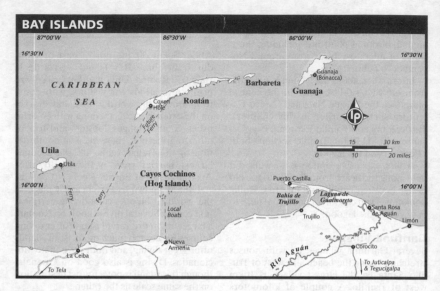

The Spanish enslaved the islanders and sent them to work in the plantations of Cuba and in the gold and silver mines of Mexico. By 1528, the islands were completely depopulated.

They didn't stay empty for long, however. English, French and Dutch pirates established settlements on the islands and raided the cumbersome Spanish cargo vessels laden with gold and other treasures from the New World. The English buccaneer Henry Morgan established his base at Port Royal on Roatán in the mid-17th century; at that time, as many as 5000 pirates were ensconced on the island.

In March 1782, after many vain attempts, the Spanish waged a successful land attack against Port Royal, killing most of the pirates and selling the rest off as slaves. Then once again, the islands were left uninhabited – once again not for long.

In 1795, a Garífuna uprising on the Caribbean island of St Vincent was quickly quelled by British troops. The survivors were rounded up, and those that didn't die of fever were shipped by the British to Roatán; some 3000 were dumped at Port Royal on April 12, 1797.

From Roatán, the Garífuna migrated to the mainland, eventually setting up small fishing and agricultural villages along the coast all the way from Belize to Nicaragua, but mostly along the north coast of Honduras. There is still one settlement of Garífuna people located at Punta Gorda on Roatán.

The Bay Islands, along with the large Mosquitia territory in northeastern Honduras, remained in the hands of the British until 1859, when Great Britain signed a treaty ceding the Bay Islands and the Mosquitia to Honduras. Only in the last few decades, however, when the Honduran school system decided that Spanish must be spoken in all the country's schools, did the islanders begin to speak Spanish. English, spoken with a broad Caribbean accent, remains the preferred language of the islanders.

The orientation of the islands is still, in many ways, more toward England and the US than toward the Honduran mainland just 50km away; many islanders are more likely to have visited the US than their own capital, Tegucigalpa, and many have relatives in the US.

Climate

The rainy season on the islands runs roughly from October or November to February. March and August are the hottest months; at other times the sea breezes temper the heat. Tropical storms are possible in September.

Population & People

The population of the Bay Islands is very diverse. Most Isleñas are blacks whose heritage includes African and Carib Indian, European and other groups. English is the dominant spoken language, and Spanish is a second language. On Roatán there is a Garífuna settlement at Punta Gorda, where Garífuna, English and Spanish are all spoken.

There are still some white descendants of early British settlers. You may meet people who look like they just got off the boat from England, Scotland or Ireland, though actually their ancestors came here over a century ago.

More recently, there has been a large influx of Latinos from the mainland, especially to Roatán, which attracts Hondurans looking for work because it is economically better off than the mainland. The Latino migration is changing the language on the island; you will hear much more Spanish spoken here now than even just a few years ago.

There is also a small population of foreign whites, mostly from Europe and the US. Many of them work for the dive shops and other tourist-oriented businesses; in most dive shops you can be instructed in a variety of languages, including English, Spanish, German, Italian, French and Hebrew, to name a few.

Costs

The Bay Islands are more expensive than the mainland. Guanaja tends to be the most expensive of the three islands, followed by Roatán. Food is more expensive than on the mainland, and the average accommodations are more expensive, too. Still, you can find a few cheap places to stay on Roatán, especially in West End, the most popular part of the island for tourism. Prices are cheaper in Utila, where costs are about the same as on the mainland.

Still, visiting the islands doesn't have to send you to the poorhouse. Hiking, swimming and sunning cost nothing, and if you bring your own snorkeling gear, you can enjoy the reefs just offshore without paying a cent.

Dangers & Annoyances

The islands are generally safer than the mainland, but the mosquitoes and sand flies are voracious, especially during the rainy season. You'll need plenty of repellent, which you can bring along or buy on the islands. Off! or Cactus Juice, two of the most popular repellents on the islands, are effective against both sand flies and mosquitoes. You can also use a mixture of coconut oil or baby oil and repellent; it must be applied copiously, so that the sand flies will get stuck in the oil and drown. The sand flies are only about the size and color of a grain of sand, but their bite is even itchier than that of the mosquitoes. If you go hiking through the jungle on the islands, you must also protect yourself against the numerous ticks.

It's very important that you take antimalarial medication, as malaria is endemic on the islands along with the mosquitoes. Mosquitoes also carry dengue fever.

In the water, keep an eye out for spiny sea urchins and beware of unseen stinging critters in the marine grass. If something stings you, douse yourself with vinegar, and the sting will go away. Don't touch, walk or stand on coral: It damages the reef and will probably cut or sting you, too.

When swimming or snorkeling, don't leave unattended valuables on the beach. There have been reports of thefts from West Bay in Roatán and from the airport beach in Utila.

Diving

Diving is by far the most popular tourist activity on the Bay Islands, and dive shops have proliferated in the last few years. Prices have come down, and it's now one of the cheapest places in the world to get a diving qualification. Most dive shops offer a range of options, from an introductory resort course (basic instruction plus a couple of dives) to a full PADI certification course qualifying you to dive worldwide. Though most dive shops are affiliated with PADI, SSI courses are also available and are preferred by some divers. An open-water diving certification course lasts 3½ to four days and includes two confined water and four open-water dives. Advanced courses are also available. Despite the low cost, safety and equipment standards are reasonable.

Utila is the cheapest island for diving certification courses and scuba diving in general. Though the dive shops on both

Guidelines for Safe Diving

Diving has become a big industry in the Bay Islands. On Utila it's the main activity for visitors. There's only one small town on the island, but about 15 dive shops. Roatán and Guanaja also have a variety of diving businesses, ranging from small, simple outfits to luxurious dive resorts.

Because Utila is known as one of the cheapest places in the world to be certified as a diver, it attracts many visitors looking for a bargain. But simply finding the cheapest dive school or shop doesn't necessarily get you the best school or diving experience. In the competition to offer the lowest prices, some dive schools may skimp in undesirable ways, such as having too high a ratio of students to instructors or divers to divemasters or not having or properly maintaining some important equipment.

A magnificent sport, diving enables you to enter another world, but diving safety must be taken seriously. Needless deaths have resulted when safety measures were skimped on or when underwater supervision was inadequate. The majority of diving accidents involve beginners with fewer than 25 dives, and these types of accidents can often be fatal or cause permanent injury.

When choosing a dive school or diving operator, here's what to look for:

- There should be no more than eight students per instructor. The more individualized the instruction is, the better.
- The school should have experienced diving instructors. Ask to see the instructor's card and make sure it has a validation sticker for the current year. Ask how long the instructor has been teaching diving and how much experience he or she has as a dive guide or divemaster. Ask how many students the instructor has personally certified. Generally, the more you know about the instructor and the more experience he or she has, the better your experience will be. You can also ask to see the instructor's dive logbook. Someone with 100 dives or less is still relatively new to diving; someone with 500 dives has been around for a while.

Someone with no diving experience is unlikely to know what to check for in diving equipment. Here are some tips:

- Scuba units must have two mouthpieces (a primary and a backup), a depth gauge, a pressure (air supply) gauge and a hose to put air into the buoyancy control device (BCD). A timer is also desirable.
- Buoyancy control devices (which resemble lifejackets) should look clean and not be patched or glued.
- Take the dust cover off of the silver 'yoke' on the regulator and look inside. There should be a silver or dark gray filter. If it looks oily, rusty or has white powder, do not trust the shop to have clean air. Also ask to taste and smell the air in the tanks. Any oily smell or odor like car

Roatán and Utila have gotten together to standardize a reasonable price for their courses and dives, competition is fierce and prices can fluctuate – when one shop drops its prices, the other shops may respond in kind, igniting a price war. When comparing diving prices, check whether tax and the certificate are included. Prices listed for Roatán usually include the diving certificate; in Utila you might have to add from US$14 to US$20.

But don't make the mistake of selecting a course purely on the basis of price. Assess the experiences of other travelers, talk to the instructors and inquire about the structure of the course, the size of the class (the smaller the better) and the standard of the equipment (see the 'Guidelines for Safe Diving' boxed text).

Qualified divers also have plenty of options, including fun dives, 10-dive packages, night dives, deep dives, wreck diving, customized dive charters and dives to coral walls and caves. There is a great variety of fish and marine life present, and the visibility is great. The waters between Roatán and Utila are among the best places in the world to view whale sharks,

Guidelines for Safe Diving

exhaust means the air in the tanks is probably bad. Do not dive with a shop with bad air. Leave immediately.

Whether you are looking for a dive school or – after you're certified – a diving operator to take you on a dive, look for the following:

- Small groups in the water – no more than about eight divers per group.
- Good, well-maintained equipment.
- Commitment to safety. Every boat should have someone on board while the divers are underwater; each boat should also have oxygen, a medical first-aid kit and a two-way radio.
- Dive sites appropriate to the diver's level of experience. Accidents happen when inexperienced divers go too deep. The first dive should not exceed 40 feet, and the second dive should not exceed 60 feet. Inexperienced divers should not be diving on a deep wall. Buoyancy is a problem for beginners. On wall dives, a guide should be leading the way, with a divemaster following behind.

Actively monitor your own safety:

- Accept responsibility for your own safety on every dive. Always dive within the limits of your ability and training.
- Evaluate the conditions before every dive. Be sure the conditions fit your personal capabilities.
- Be familiar with and check your equipment both before and during every dive. Don't ever dive with suspicious equipment.
- Use and respect the buddy system. It saves lives.
- Do not surface if you hear a boat motor, unless you are pulling yourself slowly up by the dive-boat mooring line. Many accidents have occurred when boats collided with divers who were on the surface or just under it.
- Do not go into caves. Go through tunnels and 'swim-throughs' only with qualified guides.
- If you feel unsure of a diving operator, don't dive with that company. Your life and health are at risk. 'When in doubt, turn about.'
- Don't ever drink or do drugs and dive. This seems like a very obvious point, but we've heard that some operators permit these activities. Don't go with one of these operators, and don't risk your life by doing this.
- If you haven't dived for a while, consider taking a refresher course before you jump into deep water. It takes about an hour and only costs around US$15. It's much better to discover that you remember all your diving skills in four feet of water than to realize you don't in 40.

HONDURAS

which are here from approximately May to September.

Equipment for dives is provided by the dive shops. If you have your own gear, you might be able to negotiate a small discount.

Getting There & Away

Air Planes fly to all the islands from La Ceiba (most flights are less than 25 minutes); see the Getting Around section earlier in this chapter for details on domestic flights and fares. There are also daily flights connecting Roatán with San Pedro Sula and Tegucigalpa. Through these two

cities, flights connect with all the other major Central American airports, the US and other international destinations. It's quite easy to come from the USA and be in the Bay Islands in a few hours.

TACA (☎ 445 1387 on Roatán) offers direct flights between Roatán and New Orleans (Friday), Houston (Saturday) and Miami (Sunday). It also offers flights to Guatemala City, Los Angeles, Managua, Panama City and San José, all connecting through San Salvador.

Isleña (☎ 445 1833/4 on Roatán, 445 4208 on Guanaja) offers eight flights daily between Roatán and La Ceiba, and flights several times a week connect Roatán with Tegucigalpa and San Pedro Sula.

Sosa (☎ 445 1154 on Roatán, 445 3161 on Utila, 445 4359 on Guanaja) offers four flights daily between Roatán and La Ceiba. It offers two flights between La Ceiba and Utila (US$18) every day except Sunday.

Isleña and Sosa offer daily flights between La Ceiba and Guanaja (Sosa does not fly on Sunday). Sosa's flights, and some of Isleña's, go via Roatán, making it possible to fly directly between Roatán and Guanaja. Fares are US$21 between Guanaja and Roatán, US$26 between Guanaja and La Ceiba.

Boat The MV *Galaxy II,* run by Safeway Maritime Transportation Company SA (☎ 445 1795) offers a fast, comfortable ferry service every day between Roatán and La Ceiba and La Ceiba and Utila. The boat then returns to Roatán the same way. The trip to and from Roatán takes two hours and to and from Utila one hour. See the Getting Around section at the beginning of this chapter for schedule and fares.

No scheduled passenger boats serve Guanaja. Cargo and fishing boats sail between Guanaja and Roatán (three hours), and between Guanaja and Puerto Castilla or Trujillo (four hours), but there is no set schedule; you might spend days waiting for a boat. You could always try to hitch with private yacht owners.

There are occasional ad-hoc yachts from Utila to Belize, or Livingstone in Guatemala, but these are subject to the whims of yacht owners. Normally yacht owners advise a dive shop in Utila beforehand if they are planning a visit (see the Getting There & Away part of the Utila section).

Getting Around
Rudy at Rudy's Coffee Stop in West End village on Roatán (☎ 445 1794, fax 445 1205) occasionally offers charter boat trips to Utila whenever there are eight to 10 people wanting to go. The trip takes two hours and costs US$20 per person.

ROATÁN
pop 15,000
Roatán is the largest and most popular of the Bay Islands. It is about 50km off the coast of Honduras from La Ceiba. About

50km long and just 2 to 4km wide, the island is surrounded by over 100km of living reef, making it a paradise for divers and snorkelers. Parts of Roatán, especially the West End and West Bay beaches, are as idyllic as the most tempting tourist brochure, with clear turquoise water, colorful tropical fish, powdery white sand and coconut palms.

Orientation
Coxen Hole is Roatán's main town; the airport is about a five-minute drive east of here. The best place to stay on the island is West End village, with nearby Sandy Bay a good second option.

Information
There's no tourist office on Roatán, but Coxen Hole's Casi Todo Bookstore provides information about the island. Information on Roatán can also be obtained from the Web sites www.bayislands.com or www.roatanonline.com. The free *Lucky Lempira* magazine (☎/fax 445 1647, papagayos@globalnet.hn) can also be found circulating on Roatán. While the magazine is mainly a listing of various island services, there's an occasionally useful want-ads listing, as well as information on things to do and ads for rooms and apartments for longer-term rental, cars for sale and employment opportunities.

Dangers & Annoyances
Sand flies and mosquitoes are the most annoying things on the island. Take measures to keep yourself from being bitten and take antimalarial medication. Five types of malaria have been identified on the island, and dengue fever is present as well.

When swimming, beware of riptides that can pull you out to sea (see the Swimming Safety section in the Regional Facts for the Visitor chapter), especially at West End.

A traveler wrote to warn that taxi drivers in Roatán can be a bit shifty: They have been known to drive off with people's gear on board, or they may claim they have no change. When taking you from the airport to Coxen Hole, they may tell you the bus no longer runs to West End.

Things to See & Do
Diving, snorkeling, swimming, boating, kayaking, fishing, hiking, meeting the locals

and other travelers and just lazing around on the beach are all popular activities on Roatán. There are some excellent dining opportunities, and the beach at West Bay is the best on the island, with soft sand lapped by an azure, classically Caribbean sea.

In Sandy Bay, the Institute for Marine Sciences and the Roatán Museum, both at the Anthony's Key Resort, are worth a visit, as is the Carambola Botanical Gardens.

The Sandy Bay/West End Marine Reserve, extending offshore from Sandy Bay all the way to the western tip of the island, is a protected reserve awaiting formal status as a national marine park. Diving and snorkeling are excellent here – you can snorkel just offshore from any beach along here and see some magnificent coral, sponges and marine life.

The eastern end of the island, from Punta Gorda in the north around to Port Royal in the south, including the islands of Morat, Barbareta, Santa Helena and the mangrove swamps, has been declared a national marine park. This area is also good for diving and snorkeling, but it doesn't attract as many divers as the developed resorts in the West End, because it's more remote and undeveloped.

Averyl Muller, of the Casi Todo Bookshop (☎ 445 1944, fax 445 1946, casitodo@globalnet.hn) in Coxen Hole, offers island tours to out-of-the-way places not reachable by public transportation. The tours take about five hours and cost US$25.

Getting There & Away

It takes only 20 minutes to fly between La Ceiba and Roatán. La Ceiba is the cheapest and fastest place from which to fly to Roatán, but there are other possibilities. Arriving by boat is the most common way to get to Roatán. See the Bay Islands Getting There & Away section.

Getting Around

To/From the Airport Bus No 1 stops at the airport. The cost is US$0.70 from the airport to Coxen Hole; a taxi costs about twice that. If you're arriving at the airport and going to the west end of the island, go to Coxen Hole (10 minutes from the airport) and catch a bus from there; a shared taxi from the airport to West End will cost around US$4.

Bus Roatán has two bus routes, both originating in Coxen Hole. The bus stop is in front of the small park beside the HB Warren supermarket in the center of town. The buses operate every day.

Bus No 1 goes east from Coxen Hole past the airport to French Harbour, past Polly Tilly Bight, through Punta Gorda and on to Oak Ridge. The bus departs every half hour from 6 am to 5:30 pm; the cost is US$0.70 to French Harbour, US$1 to Punta Gorda or Oak Ridge. The trip takes about 10 minutes from Coxen Hole to the airport, another 20 minutes to French Harbour, and another hour from French Harbour to Oak Ridge.

Bus No 2 goes west from Coxen Hole through Sandy Bay to West End. Minibuses depart every 15 minutes from 6 am to 6 pm. The cost is US$0.80 to go to West End; it's a 25-minute ride on a good road.

Car & Motorcycle Car-rental agencies on Roatán include Sandy Bay Rent-A-Car (☎ 445 1710), Avis (☎ 445 1568), Bay Island Rent-A-Car (☎ 445 1815), and Toyota (☎ 445 1936). As always, it pays to shop around. The cheapest prices on the island at the time of this writing were US$45 per day or US$75 for two days, with unlimited mileage.

Captain Van's in West End rents motorcycles (US$20) and mopeds (US$15).

Taxi Plenty of taxis operate around the island. Most are colectivos during the day and don't charge much more than buses; from Coxen Hole a colectivo to West End is US$1.70 or to French Harbour it's US$1. If you are the first passenger, let them know you want to go colectivo, as this is cheaper than a private ride. As everywhere in Honduras, always clarify the price of the ride before you start.

Bicycle Captain Van's in West End also rents bicycles for about US$5 per day.

Boat The settlements on Roatán all hug the seashore, and the islanders are very much a sea-oriented people. Anywhere there are people, someone will have a boat. You can easily hire someone to take you in a motorboat almost anywhere you could want to go.

ROATÁN

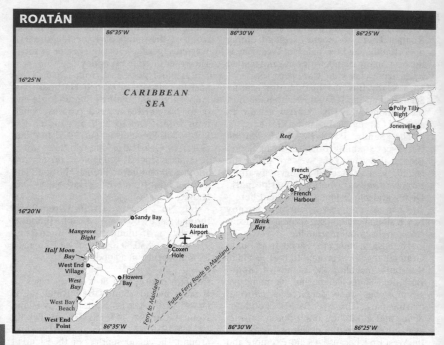

Hitchhiking Hitchhiking is easy on Roatán in the daytime. It's much more difficult to get a ride at night.

Coxen Hole

Coxen Hole may be small, but it's the largest town on Roatán. The government and shipping offices are here, as are the post office and Hondutel, and people come here from around the island to go to the supermarket, HB Warren, which has the island's lowest food prices. Otherwise, Coxen Hole is not an attractive town – it's rather small and dusty, and though it's right beside the sea, there is no beach here. It's probably better to avoid walking around Coxen Hole at night, as discos and bars can get a bit rowdy. Coxen Hole currently is the home port for the *Galaxy II* ferry to La Ceiba, but plans are afoot to relocate that to French Harbour, possibly in 2001.

Orientation The commercial section of Coxen Hole is only a few short blocks. The HB Warren supermarket, with the tiny city park beside it, is at the center of town; everything of interest is nearby or on the

road leading into town. Buses and taxis arrive and depart from in front of the city park. Osgood Cay is just across the water from town, and the airport is a 10-minute drive to the east. The main through road in Coxen Hole is one-way (west to east). Be careful if you are driving a rented car, as there are no signs telling you that the street is one-way.

Information The post office is open 8 am to noon and 2 to 5 pm Monday to Friday, 8 am to noon Saturday.

Hondutel is up the narrow passageway opposite the post office; it's open for domestic and international phone calls from 7 am to 9 pm daily. Fax service is available 8 am to 4 pm Monday to Friday.

Banffaa, Banco Sogerin and Banco GBA all have offices in Coxen Hole. All change US dollars and traveler's checks, and Banco GBA gives cash advances on Visa cards. Credomatic, also in the center of town, gives cash advances on both Visa and MasterCard.

The Casi Todo Bookstore (☎/fax 445 1944), on the road leading into town, carries new and used books in English (buy or

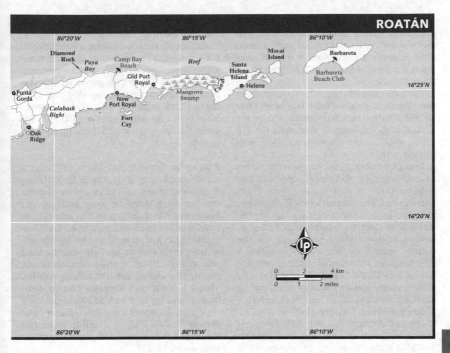

ROATÁN

trade). It's a good place to come for information about the island, or just to hang out at the ¿Qué Tal? Café, which shares the same space and has Internet service.

Internet access is also provided by Paradise Computers (☎ 445 1394, paradise@ globalnet.hn), at the entrance to Coxen Hole, in the blue building in front of the Nazareno wood shop. It is open 8 am to 5 pm Monday to Friday and 8 am to noon Saturday. Access charges are US$7.50 per thirty minutes at one of their six terminals.

Places to Stay Most visitors don't stay in Coxen Hole but rather in more attractive places around the island. Still, the town does have a couple of decent hotels. *Bella Vista* (☎ 445 1036) has six rooms with private bath and fan for US$30 for doubles. It's on the road leading into town, a couple of blocks from the town center. The *Hotel Cay View* (☎ 445 1222) is similar and also has doubles for US$30; its restaurant/bar looks across the water to Osgood Cay.

Places to Eat The cafeteria in the *HB Warren supermarket* has low prices, a selec-

tion of meals and snacks, great ice cream and some of the best fried chicken on the island. The cafeteria and the supermarket are open 7 am to 6 pm Monday to Saturday.

The *¿Qué Tal? Café* (☎ 445 1007) at the Casi Todo Bookstore, on the road leading into town a couple of blocks from the town center, has good coffee, salads, sandwiches and baked goods. Food is served Monday to Friday from around 7 am to 3 pm.

The bar/restaurant at *Hotel El Paso* has a pleasant patio looking over the water to the palm-covered Osgood Cay nearby. The specialty of the house is the *super sopa marinera* (super seafood soup), with lobster, shrimp, crab, conch, fish and squid, for US$12.50. Other seafood dishes are around US$7 to US$12. It's open from around 8 am to 9:30 pm daily.

Several other cheap eateries are around Coxen Hole. *Rolando's*, a tiny comedor located in the center of town, is recommended by locals for good, cheap meals.

French Harbour

French Harbour is the second-largest town on Roatán. An important port town, it's home to a large fishing, shrimp and lobster fleet. While it's a bustling little town and looks a lot better organized than Coxen Hole, it is not a major tourist trap. It does boast a couple of the island's better restaurants, though.

Places to stay in French Harbour include the clean and comfy *Hotel Harbour View* (☎ 445 5390), which has double rooms for US$24, and the simpler *Gabriela* (☎ 455 5365), with double rooms for US$18 with private bath.

French Harbour also has several places to eat. *Gio's* (☎ 455 5214), opposite the Banffaa Bank, is well known for its crabs and steaks. *Casa Romeo's* (☎ 455 5518) has a beautiful wooden deck overlooking the water and does top-class pasta dishes as well as seafood. Both places are on the slightly pricey side, but worth the treat. A cheaper place for a quick breakfast or lunch stop is *The Daily Grind*. Great coffee and bagels, soups and carrot cake are some of the items served here to hungry travelers.

Just past French Harbour at French Cay, Sherman Arch operates an **iguana farm** that you're welcome to visit. The best time to visit is at noon during the dry season, when he feeds the iguanas; iguanas of all shapes and sizes emerge from the greenery and come running for their feeding when he calls them. Baby iguanas up to about two years old are nursed in cages until they are large enough to be released into the wild without danger.

Oak Ridge

On Roatán's eastern side is another port town, Oak Ridge, a more attractive town than French Harbour or Coxen Hole. It's known officially as José Santos Guardiola, but almost no one calls it by its Spanish name. With old-fashioned wooden houses nestled around the sea, it looks like it could be on Cape Cod as easily as on the Caribbean. The tiny town consists of the port facilities and lots of colorful boats, a long row of wooden houses stretching in an arc around a point of land and a town on a small cay just a two-minute motorboat ride from shore.

Water Taxi Tours Water taxis take passengers across to the cay for about US$0.75; they dock in front of the bus stop. Oak Ridge is the end of the line for buses coming east from Coxen Hole.

In Oak Ridge you can hire a water taxi to take you on a pleasant tour through mangrove canals to Jonesville, a small town on a nearby bight. There's no public transportation serving Jonesville, so don't get off there – just return to Oak Ridge. A one-hour boat tour will cost around US$10 for up to four people, or US$15 for up to eight people.

Places to Stay & Eat There are several small, simple places to stay in Oak Ridge, both on land and on the cay. However the smaller places tend to come and go, and Hurricane Mitch put an end to one or two comfortable places that welcomed travelers in the past. Ask around at the harbor for which places may be available on the land side of Oak Ridge. On the cays, there are one or two places that rent rooms. Ask for Teresa Cooper and Romelia Dilbert, who have rooms for around US$20 a night.

Across the water from town, *Hotel Blue Bayou* (☎ 445 2161) is a simple place, but it's expensive; rooms with shared/private bath go for US$17/21.

On the cay, the *Reef House Resort* (☎ 445 2142, 445 2297) is an expensive place to stay, but you can spend the day at the restaurant/ bar on a terrace right over the water and snorkel just offshore – there's a shallow reef here and the Reef House Wall, a good spot for diving. You can rent snorkeling gear from the resort's dive shop or bring your own; ask them about diving.

Near the Reef House, *Hotel San José* (☎ /fax 445 2328) is a simple hotel with six rooms for US$15/20 with shared/private bath. Also nearby, Redell Foutz (☎ 445 2271) rents out a *two-bedroom house* for US$20 per night, but the price is probably going to rise.

Set up on the hill overlooking the harbor is *BJ's Backyard*, a pleasant restaurant/bar where you can eat, hang out and ask about the town and the area. Several other places to eat are also along the footpath leading to BJ's.

One of the most locally popular eating places is only accessible by boat. The *Hole in the Wall*, just west of Jonesville along the mangroves, is a US$3.50 water taxi ride away from Oak Ridge. Take a cold beer at the bar on the water or sample their deliciously fresh shrimp, which are served up for US$10.

West End

On a turquoise bay laced with coconut palms, West End is a small but exceptionally lovely village on the west end of the island. It's without a doubt the most beautiful part of the island. West End is the area to which most backpacking travelers and divers flock. Cheap accommodations are rarer than mid-range to expensive options, but you can still get a decent deal if you look around.

If you're in West End, be sure to also check out Sandy Bay, a long walk but only a short bus ride away.

Information The Hondusoft Internet Cafe (☎ 445 1548, hondusof@hondutel.hn), opposite Fosters Inn, is open 10 am to 6 pm daily and charges an expensive US$8 for 30 minutes or a slightly more advantageous US$15 per hour. Connections are subject to the often unpredictable vagaries of the local phone system, and opening times tend to be erratic. You may also make overseas phone calls from here. Sample per-minute rates are US$2.40 to the US, US$3 to Australia and US$3.10 to Europe.

Phone calls at somewhat higher rates may also be made from the El Sueño del Mar dive shop, situated prominently on the second of the two jetties.

Beaches & Hikes The beach at West Bay, about 4km south of West End village, is the most beautiful beach on Roatán. It's a lovely 40-minute stroll down the beach from West End (bring repellent for the sand flies), or you can take a motorboat from Fosters Inn restaurant for US$1.40 each way – it operates every 15 minutes or so, 9 am to 9 pm, and the trip takes about 10 minutes. The beach is fringed by palm trees, houses and cabins, and there are a couple of restaurants (see the Places to Eat section). There's good snorkeling and diving at West Bay; the reef here is protected.

You can hike across the island from West End to Flowers Bay; it's about a 3km walk. When you reach the ridge, you can look out over both sides of the island. A loop from West End to Flowers Bay then south almost to the tip of the island, over the ridge to West Bay and back up the beach to West End, makes a good five- or six-hour hike. The Flowers Bay side of the island looks quite different from the West Bay side. Be sure to bring fresh water and adequate repellent against the numerous ticks.

Snorkeling There's good snorkeling just offshore at West End. Stop by Ocean Divers (see below) for a map of the reef. It's protected all the way from Sandy Bay to the western tip of the island. The Blue Channel, directly off the small pier at the south end of West End, is an especially beautiful spot, and the section of beach at the far western end of West Bay, called the Black Rocks, is another popular spot. Half Moon Bay is also very good. Snorkeling gear can be rented from the dive shops for around US$5 per day or bought for an average price of US$80 to US$100 for mask, snorkel and fins.

Diving West End has several dive shops offering a variety of dives and courses. The dive shops usually stick to small groups and offer friendly, relaxed, personalized instruction in several languages (see the 'Guidelines for Safe Diving' boxed text). Prices are pretty standard among the shops: A four-day PADI open water diving certification course costs around US$250; one-day resort courses are US$75; and a half-day diving refresher course is US$31. A variety of more advanced courses are also available. Fun dives for those already certified cost US$31 or US$130 for a five-dive package.

Among the dive shops in the center of West End village is the easy to spot and very conveniently located Sueño del Mar (☎ 445 1717, suenodelmar@globalnet.hn), on the first of the two long jetties. Ocean Divers (☎/fax 445 1005) offers diving and accommodations packages at their hotel, the Sunset Inn. Tyll's Dive Shop (☎/fax 445 0020) is a long-established shop that can also help you arrange accommodations. West End Divers (☎/fax 445 1531) is another centrally located shop.

Native Sons Water Sports (☎ 445 1335, mermaid@globalnet.hn) is tucked away at the far end of the village, in a beautifully relaxed location among palm trees right on the beach. Local Roatánian Alvin Jackson is the owner and is a very experienced dive

HONDURAS

Don't Touch the Coral!

Coral comes in many shapes, sizes and colors, especially in the Bay Islands. Some coral, such as fan coral, resembles a plant. Other coral, such as brain coral, looks more like a rock.

Coral is neither a plant nor a rock, however. It is an animal.

'Don't touch the coral' is a refrain you will often hear in the Bay Islands, where thousands of inexperienced divers and snorkelers come every year to explore the magnificent reefs just a few yards offshore.

Coral is so fascinating and beautiful that it tempts you to touch it, especially if you're seeing it for the first time. Even if you resist the temptation, you might accidentally bump against it with a fin as you swim past. If you're learning to dive, you might accidentally rub up against it as you struggle to maintain neutral buoyancy.

But avoiding such contact is really extremely important. You can kill the coral just by touching it. A huge mass of coral can be killed by only one diver touching it in one spot.

Coral has an invisible covering of slime that protects it, much the same way that our outer layer of skin protects us. If you touch the coral, you make a lesion in the animal's protective covering, exposing it to infection and disease. Humans can die as result of only one cut; the same is true of the coral.

The coral ecosystem is very fragile. Coral grows at only about one centimeter (less than half an inch) per year under ideal conditions; the fastest growing sponges grow at about one inch per year. The coral and sponge formations you see here in the Bay Islands are the result of centuries of growth.

Only recently have the islands been inundated with divers and snorkelers, many of them firsttimers. If every diver and snorkeler touched the coral only once, the delicate reef and the abundance of life it supports would soon be destroyed.

Another good reason not to touch the coral is that it will sting you. Fire coral is the most famous for this – you'll feel like you're on fire if you touch this coral. But many types of coral sting – especially corals that are a rich mustard color.

If you are stung by coral, apply vinegar where you were stung, and the stinging sensation will stop. The coral, however, has nothing it can apply for the injury you've inflicted.

So enjoy the reef – but be sure that you don't touch the coral.

instructor. The Seagrape Plantation Dive Center (☎/fax 445 1717, 445 1428) is on the far end of West End village, beyond the road to Coxen Hole; diving and accommodations packages are available at the Seagrape Plantation.

Sea Kayaking Jaye's Sea Breeze (☎ 445 1548, hondusof@hondutel.hn), opposite the Internet Café, rents out sea kayaks and other water sports equipment for between US$3 and US$6 per hour, or US$10 to US$16 per half day. They also do guided half-day tours for a minimum of four persons for US$50.

Other Activities You can take an underwater trip on the *Underwater Paradise*, a semisubmarine and glass-bottomed boat

that does three trips daily out of the Half Moon Bay Cabins. Cost is US$20 per person. The *Coral Reef Explorer* is another semisubmerged vessel, which operates out of West Bay beach and does a reef tour at 11 am and another at 2 pm. Cost per person is also US$20.

Captain Steve Jazz, from Rick's American Cafe (see the Places to Eat section), runs half-day fly-fishing trips for small groups (maximum four persons) in the coral lagoons off Sandy Bay. Cost is US$150 per person.

Keifito's Plantation Retreat (see the Places to Stay section) rents horses for beach rides or inland tours of the island.

Places to Stay Whatever type or standard of accommodations you're looking for, you can find it in West End. This is the part of the island to which most tourists flock. Even though there are so many places to stay, they can still fill up, especially during the busy tourist seasons during July–August and from mid-December to Easter. At these times, book ahead to get the place you want.

Starting with the budget options, *Sam's Lodge* (☎ 445 1335), operated by Sammy Miller, is at the far southern end of West End. It's a fairly basic place with rooms for US$5 to US$8, though all rooms have mosquito screens and fans.

A longtime favorite among backpackers, *Valerie's* (*paradise@globalnet.hn*), beside Tyll's Dive Shop, has two six-bed dorm rooms for US$5 a bunk, three rooms at US$15 for one or two people or more comfortable, air-conditioned double rooms with kitchenette for US$35.

Anderson's Place (☎ 445 1171) has several small oceanside cabins. Each has two rooms that share one bathroom and a pleasant porch. These are some of the coolest rooms in West End, built with good insulation – you'll appreciate this if you're here in hot weather. They cost US$15 per room. One cabin with private bath costs US$25.

About a 10-minute walk south along the beach past Sam's Lodge, *Keifito's Plantation Retreat* (☎ 445 1252) is in a quiet location, away from town. Cabins here are US$20, or US$30 with a stove and two beds; it also has a restaurant/bar, hiking trails, and horses for rent.

At *Chillies* (☎/fax 445 1214, *mermaid@globalnet.hn*), a very neat budget accommodations option, there are about seven rooms, each taking up to three persons, with shared bathroom and kitchen but no hot water, for around $7.50 per person. There are also two cabins with private bathroom and kitchen for US$40. A 20% discount applies to bookings of over a month.

The *Sunset Inn* (☎/fax 445 1005) has 19 rooms, ranging from US$22 for rooms with fans and shared cold bath up to US$48 for an apartment for up to six people with kitchen. Ocean Divers is in the same building; dive and accommodations packages come out cheaper than getting them both separately.

Pinocchio (☎ 445 1466, *pinocchio69@bigfoot.com*) has four airy rooms accommo-

dating up to four people each. All have fans and private bathrooms. Pinocchio is up on the hill back from the main road, ideally placed to catch the cool afternoon breezes. Prices are around US$35 per room.

Georphi's Tropical Hideaway (☎ 445 1794, fax 445 1205), owned by Rudy of Rudy's Coffee House (see the Places to Eat section), has a variety of attractive cabins stretching up the hill. They range in price from US$45 to $60 for air-conditioned double cabins.

Fosters Inn (☎ 445 1124) has bungalows opposite its restaurant for US$50, US$60 and US$80, each with two double beds, fan, private bath, a small fridge and a porch.

Pura Vida (☎/fax 445 1141, *puravida@hondutel.hn*) is run by Italians Giacomo and Adriana and offers 12 comfortable rooms with either fan or air-conditioning, cable TV, private facilities and a handy in-house restaurant for around US$60 per double/triple room.

Half Moon Bay is a beautiful little bay with fewer tourists than West End, just a short walk from West End village, beyond the road leading to Coxen Hole. In Half Moon Bay, the *Half Moon Bay Cabins* (☎/fax 445 1075) has duplex cabins for US$74 for up to three people, with air-conditioning. They provide free snorkeling gear, kayaks and paddleboats; offer snorkeling classes for children; and have an excellent waterside restaurant and bar. Dive/accommodations packages are also available.

Also on Half Moon Bay, at the junction between the West End village road and the road to Coxen Hole, the *Coconut Tree Restaurant & Cabins* (☎ 445 1648) has cabins, most with kitchen, for US$35 to US$40 for singles, US$50 to US$60 for doubles. The cabins have one, two or three bedrooms.

Walk a little farther beyond Half Moon Bay to Mangrove Bight, and you'll find three more places to stay, all with ample grounds. This is a peaceful, quiet, family area – just a short walk from the tourist-oriented businesses at West End but without as many people. On Mangrove Bight, *Burke's Place* (☎ 445 1252) has a variety of duplex cabins with private bath and kitchen for US$20 to US$25. One larger cabin sleeping four people is US$35, and a small one for one person is US$15. Nearby, *Casa Calico* (☎/fax 445 1171) has three ample, attractive upstairs rooms with kitchen, front and back porch, and private bath for US$45 for one or two people; each one can sleep four. The *Seagrape Plantation Resort* (☎/fax 445 1428) is more expensive. Dive/accommodations packages are US$344 for four nights, US$599 for a week, including three meals and three boat dives every day, a night dive and unlimited shore diving.

Cabins on West Bay Beach tend to be more expensive than those in West End village. *Foster's Beach House* (☎ 445 1124), in West End village, has cabins on West Bay Beach for US$80, each with three double beds, private bath, kitchen and a big porch. The *Coconut Tree* (☎ 445 1648) in West End also has cabins on West Bay Beach for US$70. *Bananarama* (☎ 445 1271) and *West bay Lodge* are about the cheapest options, with cabins for US$45 and US$40, respectively.

Places to Eat Food in West End tends to be a bit expensive. Count on spending a minimum of around US$2 for breakfast, and US$4 to US$8 each for lunch and dinner, possibly more. If you stay at a place where you can do your own cooking, you'll save money on food, especially if you go into Coxen Hole to shop at the supermarket or bring your own food from the mainland.

A great place for a quick breakfast of coffee and croissants for US$2 is the *Boulangerie*, which is open from 6:30 am to 2 pm.

Rudy's Coffee Stop is also a popular place to come for breakfast. Good banana pancakes ('the best in the world,' Rudy exclaims modestly) cost US$1.25; the coffee is decent here, too. Lunch is also served, and dinner is served on demand. It's a pleasant place to hang out, with tables spaced around a shady garden.

Cindy's Place makes typical island food, and it's not expensive. Chicken burritos and beer make a quick and cheap lunch.

Pinocchio (see the Places to Stay section) is one of the best places to eat dinner in West End. Owner Patricia, from Italy, offers an eclectic menu of Italian and local dishes in a relaxing, open-air ambience. It's a popular spot, so grab your table

before 8 pm. Pinocchio is closed on Wednesday. Prices are mid-range.

Papagayos, next door to the Sunset Inn, offers lunch and dinner and does some excellent crab dishes, and *Pura Vida* (see the Places to Stay section) is open all day for breakfast, lunch and dinner and does good pizzas and pasta. Good pizza can also be found at the slightly out-of-the-way *Punta dell'Ovest*, signposted as 'wood oven pizza' from the main street. It's a 10-minute (signposted) walk along a winding path leading to the back end of West End.

In West Bay, *The Bite on the Beach* (☎ 445 1466) has a great location built on a wooden deck overlooking the water. Open only from midday to 8 pm Wednesdays to Saturdays (Sundays to 5 pm only), this is *the* place to eat in West Bay. Choose from a wide range of salads for US$5 to US$6, or Asian stir-fry dishes for US$6. Nurse a cold beer at the bar and watch the sun set, if you don't feel like eating.

Entertainment The best spot to watch the sun go down is on the deck of *Eagle Ray's*, where a long happy hour makes it even more worthwhile. Eagle Ray's is above the Sueño del Mar dive shop. The *Twisted Toucan*, a minuscule bar with seats all around, is the spot to hang out after dark. Learn all the local gossip and sip frozen margaritas for US$2. Happy hour runs from 4 to 7 pm. *Fosters Inn* does a Friday night disco party (with cover charge), and the *Reggae Bar* on the beach at the west end of West End is the place to go to get mellow. It's open 1 pm to 1 am Monday to Saturday.

Sandy Bay

About 4km before you reach West End is Sandy Bay, a quiet little community strung out along on the seashore. It's not as developed as West End, and it doesn't have a village center as such – it's just a long settlement along several kilometers of beach.

The beach here is not as good as the one at West End or West Bay – and it's a little shallow for swimming – however, the Sandy Bay community passed an ordinance many years ago protecting its reef as a nature reserve, so it's an excellent place to snorkel, offering lots of marine life. In more recent years, the reserve has been extended all the way past West End village and West Bay to the western tip of the island.

There's a nature trail on Bailey's Cay, opposite Anthony's Key Resort (which has good snorkeling). Across the road from Anthony's Key Resort, the Carambola Botanical Gardens has nature trails, orchids, spice plants and an 'iguana wall.'

At Anthony's Key Resort, the **Institute for Marine Sciences** (☎ 445 1327, fax 445 1329) is a research and educational facility working with dolphins. There are several dolphin-training demonstrations every day, which you are welcome to attend; you can also go for a swim with the dolphins, but this is expensive (US$75, or US$65 for hotel guests). A classroom has videos and educational material about dolphins, coral reefs and other sea life. Also here is the small but interesting **Roatán Museum**, with displays on the archaeology, history, geology and wildlife of the islands and the sea. The museum is open every day except Wednesday, from 8:30 am to 5 pm; admission is US$3.

Places to Stay On a hill overlooking Sandy Bay, *Beth's Hostel* (☎ 445 1266) is not far from the sea. Two single and two double rooms face onto a comfortable kitchen-dining-sitting room. Beds are US$12 per person, US$75 per week or US$250 per month from mid-November to April; from May to mid-November it's US$10 per night, or US$60 per week. Reduced rates are offered for Peace Corps or other volunteers, and snorkeling gear is available for US$5 per day. Nonsmokers only.

The *Caribbean Seashore B&B* (☎ /fax 445 1123), on the beach half a mile west of Anthony's Key Resort, offers five rooms in a two-story house for US$30/35 for singles/doubles. There's good swimming here, it's peaceful and quiet, and they serve breakfast, lunch and dinner.

Also on the beach west of Anthony's Key Resort, *Judy's Fantasea* (☎ 445 1349) has four rooms upstairs, sharing two bathrooms, and one room downstairs. Rooms here are US$20 per day, US$100 per week or US$300 per month. There's a bar and store, and they'll prepare food if you like. On the beach, but in a different part of Sandy Bay, Miss Effie (☎ 445 1233) has two *rooms* without kitchen for US$25 each and one room with kitchen for US$30.

Near the dolphin enclosure at Anthony's Key Resort, the *Oceanside Inn* (☎ 445 1552) is beside the water, though there is no beach here. It has eight rooms, each with ceiling fan and lots of windows; the cost is US$30/45 for the room only, or you can arrange for a room plus meals – a restaurant is also here.

Anthony's Key Resort (☎ 445 1003, akr@gate.net) is one of the major diving resorts on the island, with facilities for diving, underwater photography and so on. It's expensive at US$135, but that includes all meals and diving.

Places to Eat Up the hill from the main road, *Rick's American Cafe* (☎ 445 0123) has a fine view, superb steaks and hamburgers and an international menu. The house specialty is the baby back ribs (US$11.50). Food is served 5 to 9:30 pm daily, with a happy hour from 5 to 6 pm; the bar stays open until 11:30 pm. Look out for Fluffy the parrot. He likes to visit diners at their table.

You can see the dolphins from the deck restaurant at *Anthony's Key Resort*, open from Thursday to Sunday. Nearby, the *Oceanside Inn* (see the Places to Stay section) also has a deck restaurant overlooking Anthony's Key and Bailey's Key. It's recommended for its lobster dishes.

UTILA
pop 6000

Utila is a welcoming place, where the locals always have time to shout a friendly greeting. The pace of life on the island is very slow. Most visitors come here to dive, so if you are looking for a beach vacation, forget it, go to West Bay on Roatán. Utila is the cheapest of the three Bay Islands to visit but offers a variety of food and accommodations for all budgets. Before settling in though, read some sound advice from Utila diving instructor Jamie Monk, who wrote to Lonely Planet:

As you arrive on the ferry, as most travelers do, you can turn left or right for dive shops or head straight up the hill where there are some hotels. At the moment there seems to be a kind of traveler myth that you should turn right for the best accommodation and diving schools, while some of best hotels and more diving schools are to the left. The best bet is to first find a place to stay then look for the dive shops.

UTILA

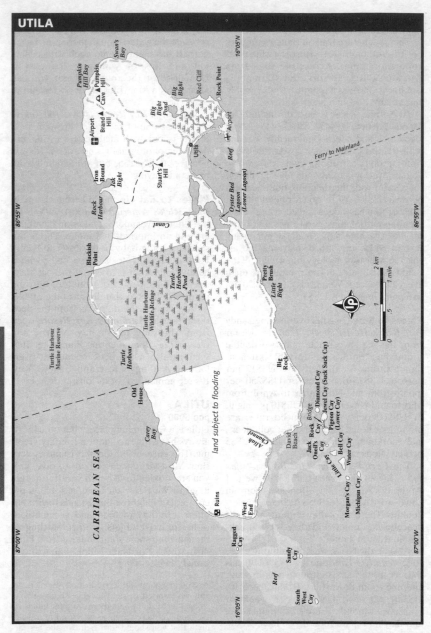

HONDURAS

CARIBBEAN SEA

Turtle Harbour Marine Reserve

Turtle Harbour Wildlife Refuge

Turtle Harbour Pond

Blackish Point

Canal

Rock Harbour

Iron Bound

Jak Bight

Stuart's Hill

Airport
Brand Hill
Pumpkin Cave Hill
Pumpkin Hill Bay

Swan's Bay

Big Bight

Big Bight Pond

Red Cliff

Rock Point

Airport

Utila

Red

Ferry to Mainland

Oyster Bed Lagoon (Lower Lagoon)

Pretty Brush

Little Bight

Big Rock

land subject to flooding

Turtle Harbour

Old House

Carey Bay

Ruins

West End

Ragged Cay

Sandy Cay

Reef

South West Cay

Allub Channel

Rock Bridge

David Beach

Jack O'neill's Cay

Little Cay

Morgan's Cay

Michigan Cay

Water Cay

Bell Cay (Lower Cay)

Pigeon Cay

Jewel Cay (Suck Suck Cay)

Diamond Cay

16°05'N

86°55'W

87°00'W

2 km
1 mile
0   .5   1

Utila is a small island, about 13km long and 5km wide, with several tiny cays on the south side. The closest island to La Ceiba, just 29km away, Utila is practically flat, with only one small hill. The population lives almost entirely in one settlement on a curving bay; another small settlement is on a cay about a 20-minute boat ride away.

Orientation

There's only one town on Utila, and it has only one main road. At one end of the main road is the airport, just a few hundred meters from the 'center' of town. Along this road are houses, places to stay, restaurants, bars, small food shops, a disco and two banks. A new airport is being built on the northern side of the island.

The public jetty, where the MV *Galaxy II* ferry arrives and departs, meets the main road at the intersection of Cola de Mico Rd, which heads inland. A couple of blocks up this road are several places to stay and eat.

At the foot of the jetty, Captain Morgan's Dive Center passes out free town maps, and they'll let you leave your pack or luggage there while you go to look for a place to stay.

The main road leads along the shore all the way to Oyster Bed Lagoon, also called Lower Lagoon, about a 20-minute walk west of the dock. This part of the road, called Sandy Bay Rd, has several more places to stay and eat along it. Henderson's Supermarket, the island's main supermarket, and Hondutel are also along here. The post office is at the foot of the public dock.

The Bay Islands Conservation Association (BICA; fax 425 3260), on the main road, sells a good map of the island, showing the surrounding reefs and dive spots, for US$1. Also pick up a copy of their free brochure, *Utila's Reef and You*. BICA works hard to protect the island's reefs, and it's good to give them your support. Write to them at The Bay Islands Conservation Association, Utila, Bay Islands, Honduras, 34201.

Information

Immigration Offices There's an immigration office on the first floor of the Palacio de Municipio building next to the public jetty.

Money Banco Atlántida and Banco GBA are the two banks on Utila. Banco GBA changes traveler's checks and gives cash advances on Visa cards. Banco Atlántida does not change traveler's checks, but they, too, give cash advances on Visa cards. Henderson's Supermarket changes traveler's checks, usually for a better rate than the bank. The Bundu Cafe (see the Places to Eat section) also cashes British pounds (cash only) and US dollars and traveler's checks.

Post & Communications The post office is at the foot of the public dock. Hondutel, on Sandy Bay Rd, is open for domestic and international telephone and fax service 7 am to 5 pm Monday to Friday, 7 to 11 am Saturday. Electricity on the island shuts off between midnight and 5 am, so you cannot receive a fax at this time.

Two well-equipped Internet cafes serve the island. On Sandy Bay Rd, the Internet Cafe (☎ 425 3124, bicomput@hondutel.hn) has a stable of Macintosh computers. Access charges are US$7 for 30 minutes, and you can connect your own PC for a rather overpriced US$3.50 'setup fee' plus online connection charges. It is open 9 am to 5 pm daily (closed Sunday).

On the main road, Howell's Internet (☎ 425 3317, howell@psinet.hn) offers access at similar rates and is open 8 am to 5:30 pm daily (closed Saturday, open to midday on Sunday).

Bookstore The Bundu Café, on the main road, has a fine selection of books in English and other languages, including a range of pre-loved LP titles.

Medical Services The Utila Community Clinic on Sandy Bay Rd is run by a duty nurse and occasional visiting doctors. It's open 8 am to noon Monday to Friday. The Bay Islands College of Diving (☎ 425 3143, fax 425 3209, bicdive@hondutel.hn) has a recompression chamber, the only one on Utila.

Dangers & Annoyances Utila's sand flies are a force to be reckoned with, and mosquitoes can be a nuisance. They are both worse during the rainy season than at other times of year. Off! or Cactus Juice repellent, sold at general stores in town, keeps away both sand flies and mosquitoes; mosquito coils are also sold. Be sure to take a regimen of antimalarial medication.

Electricity shuts off in Utila from midnight to 5 am, though most of the better hotels have their own electricity generators, so if you are depending on that fan to keep the insects away from you, forget it. Check beforehand. Bring your own mosquito net.

The Cays
A visit to Utila is incomplete without making a trip to the cays on the southwest side of the island. The cays have beautiful beaches, sunsets and fantastic snorkeling. And the cays have no mosquitoes or sand flies!

Water Cay is a beautiful little island with great snorkeling. The island is uninhabited, but there's a caretaker who keeps it clean and charges US$1.25 per visitor for the upkeep of the island. Pigeon Cay is completely covered by a village; it's actually two tiny cays connected by a bridge, with an even smaller little cay off to one side.

There are several ways of traveling to the cays. A snorkeling trip departs every morning from the Bundu Cafe (when at least four people want to go). It costs US$6.50 roundtrip. Gunter's Dive Shop runs trips for US$6 roundtrip.

Other Attractions
Most of Utila's coast is rocky, but there's a sandy beach on Pumpkin Hill Bay about a 3km walk across the island from town. Nearby Pumpkin Hill has some caves; one is supposed to have been a hideout for the pirate Henry Morgan.

Gunter's Driftwood Gallery (☎ 425 3113) is a couple of blocks inland, off Cola de Mico Rd. Turn left after you pass the Monkey Tail Inn and walk past Tony's Place; you'll see the sign on your right. Gunter displays his artwork here, and there's a small museum. He also offers tours to remote places around the island, including a stalactite cave and Indian sites.

Shelby McNab (☎ 425 3275) is a good source of stories and history of Utila; he sometimes offers guided tours of historical places.

Durell Cooper offers dory trips to Rock Harbour via the mangrove canal and to

other places. He also offers guided hikes on the nature trail leading to Turtle Harbour Marine Reserve & Wildlife Refuge. He stops at mangrove lagoons, caves, Indian burial grounds, tropical vegetation and birds. Contact him at the Seven Seas Restaurant.

Ask at the Bahía del Mar Restaurant about glass-bottom-boat trips and fishing trips. Windsurfing equipment may also be available on the island; just ask around.

Diving
Diving is Utila's biggest industry. The island is said to be the cheapest place in the world to learn to dive, and it attracts travelers on all kinds of budgets from everywhere. The warm Caribbean waters are crystal clear, and the tropical fish, corals, sponges and other marine life are abundant and colorful. Magnificent whale sharks can be seen frequently off the coast of Utila.

There are many excellent diving spots around Utila, and many diving operators to help you explore them (at last count there were 12 dive shops on the island). Most shops start a course just about every day of the week, and all offer instruction in a number of languages.

PADI open-water dive courses take four days and cost around US$159. A complete spectrum of more advanced courses is also available. Fun dives cost around US$30 for two dives or US$125 for a 10-dive package; special trips such as night dives and deep dives are also available. Many operators offer discounts on accommodations when you dive with them or throw in a couple of extra dives.

However, don't let your desire to find the cheapest price outweigh your need for safety, especially if you are a beginner. Because the diving situation on Utila is so competitive, some dive shops skimp in undesirable ways – by not having or properly maintaining all their safety equipment or by having too many divers per instructor. Take this seriously: Any accident or mishap while diving is potentially fatal, and deaths occur every year. You will do better to choose a dive shop on the basis of safety rather than price (see the 'Guidelines for Safe Diving' boxed text earlier in this chapter).

Dive shops in Utila include the Bay Islands College of Diving (☎ 425 3143, fax

425 3209, bicdive@hondutel.hn), the best school and currently the only five-star rated PADI training facility. They also cater to Nitrox divers and now have a recompression chamber, the only one on the island.

Other operations are Gunter's Dive Shop (☎/fax 425 3350, ecomar@hondutel .hn), the Utila Watersports Center (☎/fax 425 3239), the Utila Dive Centre (☎ 425 3326, fax 425 3327, info@utiladivecentre .com), Captain Morgan's Dive Center (☎/ fax 425 3161, captm@hondutel.hn), the Cross Creek Dive Center (☎ 425 3134, fax 425 3234, scooper@hondutel.com), Paradise Divers (☎ 425 3148, fax 425 3348), and Underwater Vision (☎ 425 3195, fax 425 3103).

Snorkeling
There's excellent snorkeling on the reef by the airport. The easiest approach to the coral is from the east end of the runway. There's also great snorkeling on the south side of Water Cay, about a half-hour boat ride from town.

Another fine snorkeling spot is at the point of land beside Oyster Bed Lagoon, in front of the Hotel & Restaurant Blue Bayou, a pleasant 20-minute walk west of town on a dirt road running beside the sea. The Blue Bayou charges US$1.50 for use of its hammocks, beach and dock and rents snorkeling gear for US$1.75 per hour.

The dive shops are cheaper, however. They rent snorkeling gear for about US$2.50 per day.

Kayaking & Canoeing
You can kayak to Rock Harbour by going into Oyster Bed Lagoon and then into Lower Lagoon and along the mangrove canal. There's a good beach at Rock Harbour, and it's very private, since the only way to get there is by boat or by hiking across the island. A roundtrip from town, with time at the beach, takes about four hours.

Another option is to kayak under the bridge separating town from the airport, into the lagoon and then up the channel to Big Bight Pond.

Kayaks can be rented from Gunter's Dive Shop for US$4 for half day, or US$6.50 for a day; double kayaks are double the price. Kayaks allow you to reach some out-of-the-way snorkeling spots and are a good form of activity for nondivers.

Places to Stay
Utila has some great deals on cheap accommodations. It doesn't take long to walk around and find something that suits you. Many of the dive shops offer discounted accommodations if you take a diving course with them.

Though there are so many places to stay, it can still be hard to get a good room during the busy tourist seasons (July to August and mid-December to Easter). Reservations are advisable at these times.

Main Road Several good places to stay are along the main road between the public dock and the airport. *Rubi's Inn (☎ 425 3240)* is a clean, simple little place that has a kitchen where you can cook your own meals; singles/doubles are US$5.50/7.50, all with shared bath. *Hotel Celena (☎ 425 3240)* is a clean, pleasant place with rooms with private bath for US$5/7. *Cooper's Inn (☎ 425 3184)* has rooms for US$4.50; under the house, Delany's Island Kitchen specializes in pizza and lasagna.

Trudy's (☎ 425 3195, fax 425 3103) has been around for a while; it has power and water 24 hours, screens on the windows, a waterside terrace and friendly management. Rooms are US$20 with private bath. Across the street, *Hotel Laguna del Mar* is run by the same people and charges US$10.20.

On the airport side of the little bridge is the excellent *Freddy's Place (☎ 425 3142)*. This airy lodging by the water consists of four two-room apartments, each with its own kitchen and bathroom facilities. Single/ double rooms are US$12.50 and have hot water and 24-hour electricity. For two people, this is one of the best deals in town.

Sandy Bay Road About a five-minute walk along Sandy Bay Rd from town, the *Margaritaville Beach Hotel (☎ 425 3366)* is an attractive hotel where spacious, clean rooms with private bath and two double beds cost US$11.50. The *Bayview Hotel (☎ 425 3114)* is an attractive place right on the water, with a private dock and swimming area, hammocks, pleasant porches and 24-hour power and water. The rooms have good screens and good ventilation, and windows are on both sides to catch the sea breezes. Rooms cost US$14.50 with private

HONDURAS

bath, or US$17 for larger rooms with two double beds and private bath.

The **Sea Side Inn** (☎ 425 3150) also has everything you need. Downstairs rooms with shared bath are US$7, upstairs rooms with private bath are US$10. The **Hotel Utila** (☎ 425 3340, fax 425 3140) is more luxurious and more expensive, with doubles for US$43.50.

The best hotel in Utila town is the **Utila Lodge** (☎ 425 3143, fax 425 3209, ulodger@ hondutel.hn). This place has spacious and airy wooden-floored rooms over the water, each with a private balcony and hammock. There's a large restaurant and bar area next to a jetty used by the associated Bay Islands College of Diving. This place caters mainly to prebooked dive packages, but they may have a room if you call or email ahead. Rates are US$50/75.

Inland A couple of blocks inland from the main road are several more good places to stay. The cheapest places to stay on the island are on the road that runs inland from the public dock. **Blueberry Hill** (☎ 445 3141), on Cola de Mico Rd, is run by a friendly older couple, Norma and Will. Rooms with screen, fan and shared bath are US$3.50. Some of the rooms share a kitchen where you can cook your own meals.

Also up here is the **Loma Vista** (☎ 445 3243), with 10 rooms sharing bath and kitchen; all have screens, and there's laundry service and 24-hour power. Rooms are US$4.50/5.50. Other cheap hotels up this way include **Selly's Hotel**, **Tony's Place** and the **Monkey Tail Inn**, all offering beds for around US$3.50 per person.

The **Countryside Inn** (☎ 425 3216), on Mamey Lane Rd, has a quiet, country location three blocks from Sandy Bay Rd, removed from the hubbub of town. It offers a variety of well-equipped rooms with 24-hour power and good screens. Simple rooms with shared bath and kitchen are US$7.50. The owners, Woody and Annie, are friendly and helpful.

The Cays Staying on the Cays is a possibility, but you will need to take along your own food and water supplies. To make it worthwhile, there will need to be at least three or four of you to share the cost of renting a house. On Sandy Cay, a very small cay, you can rent a house that holds five or six people for US$75 per day. Ask about it on Pigeon Cay – the owner lives there.

Places to Eat

There's a good selection of eating places for such a small settlement. In addition, several of the places to stay provide kitchens where you can cook. Fruits and vegetables are scarcer and more expensive on the island than on the mainland, so you might want to bring some over when you come.

Thompson's Bakery, on Cola de Mico Rd, is popular for breakfast and baked goods. **Bundu Cafe**, on the main road, is also popular for breakfast and brews the best coffee in town. **Munchies**, on Sandy Bay Rd next to the Internet cafe, sells cheap snacks such as tacos, baked potatoes and suchlike.

The exotic-looking **Jade Seahorse Restaurant**, on Cola de Mico Rd, is popular for all meals, offering both seafood and vegetarian dishes, good fresh fruit licuados and shakes.

The air-conditioned **Bahía del Mar Restaurant/Bar**, near the airport, is good for all meals. Some people say the breakfasts here are the best on the island; there's also a good selection of other dishes, such as pizza, lasagna, steaks, seafood, BBQ, salads and vegetarian meals.

Delany's Island Kitchen, on the main road, specializes in pizza and pasta. **Mermaid's Corner** is the largest restaurant on the island and also makes pizza, pasta and salads. For typical Honduran Caribbean foods, try the **Island Cafe**, on Sandy Bay Rd, or **Las Delicias** on Cola de Mico Rd.

The **Mango Inn**, in the hotel of the same name, is popular for breakfast, has a good selection of vegetarian alternatives, does a fun Sunday BBQ and is closed on Monday.

Entertainment

The **Coco Loco Bar**, perched on a rather rickety-looking jetty out over the water, is the current hot spot to hang out in. Drink cheap beer for US$0.70 during happy hour (5 to 7 pm) or hang loose in an aerial netting perch with a margarita. Watch your step or else you'll get a dunking. The **Bar in the Bush** is also popular, but can get rowdy. This drinking hole is at the back of town, along Cola de Mico Rd. Lone travelers should take care at night, since the pathway to the bar is unlit. The *Las Delicias Bar* on Cola de Mico Rd, run by German Hans Grauer, is another nightspot favored by local expats. It offers live music once a week. Look out for 'Full Moon' or 'Black Moon' parties, when most bars make an extra effort to be just that little bit crazier.

The *Reef Cinema*, on the main road, offers late release movies for only US$2 a ticket. The *Bundu Cafe* shows movies each night in its surround-sound theater, which accommodates up to 27 movie buffs at a time; admission is also US$2.

Getting There & Away

Air The flights between Utila and La Ceiba take about 15 minutes (see the Getting Around section earlier in this chapter for schedule and fares). There are currently only two flights a day, by Sosa Airlines, to and from the mainland. Services may be disrupted by weather or strikes, so leave plenty of leeway to get off the island if you have an ongoing connection. Upon arrival in Utila *always* reconfirm your flight back to the mainland, or your seat may be sold. Make sure any onward domestic connections (to San Pedro Sula or Tegucigalpa) are also confirmed, or you may find yourself stuck in La Ceiba

Mermaid's Travel Agency (☎ 425 3260), on the main road, can give you current details about flights serving the island.

Boat Most travelers come to Utila via the efficient and modern *Galaxy II*. It currently leaves La Ceiba at 9:30 am and arrives in Utila at 10:30 am, departing Utila for La Ceiba at 10:40 am. The one-way tickets cost US$9. Occasional charter boats go to the mainland or to Roatán, but they can be expensive and run on no set schedule. Don't depend on them.

Gunter's Dive Shop (see the Diving section earlier) keeps tabs on private yachts in the Caribbean and can occasionally put travelers in touch with yachts heading for Livingstone in Guatemala. One-way fares are around US$90.

Getting Around

One or two beat-up taxis run up and down the main road and Sandy Bay Rd, charging a standard US$1 for any distance. Bicycles can be rented at several places in town for US$2 per day. Most facilities are all within walking distance. From the airport to the middle of the settlement is only a 15-minute walk.

GUANAJA
pop 5500

Easternmost of the three Bay Islands, Guanaja is a small island, roughly 18km long and 6km wide at its widest point. The highest of the three Bay Islands, Guanaja is covered in a forest of Caribbean pine; when Christopher Columbus came to the island in 1502, he named it the Isla de Pinos (Isle of Pines). About 90% of the island has been declared a national forest reserve and marine park.

Many kilometers of coral reefs encircle the island and the 15 or so cays around it; the reefs and some sunken ships make Guanaja attractive for snorkeling and diving. Though several dive resorts have appeared on the island, the diving and tourist boom that has hit Roatán and Utila has yet to arrive on Guanaja.

There are a few tiny settlements on the main island, including one on Savannah Bight and another on Mangrove Bight, but the island's principal town, Guanaja, called Bonacca by the locals, is on a small cay just off the island's east coast. Every inch of the cay has been built on: Wooden houses with sloping roofs stand on stilts at all different heights. There are no cars on the cay and no roads; walkways wind around among the houses, and narrow canals allow the residents to pull their boats right up to the houses. Guanaja town is known as the Venice of Honduras.

Guanaja was badly hit by Hurricane Mitch in 1998 and at the time of research for this edition was still feeling the effects of the devastation. While tourist services are all up and running and life is as normal as it can be, damage from Mitch is still evident, and it will be a while until the islands are 100% back to normal.

Information
Banco GBA changes traveler's checks and gives cash advances on Visa cards.

Things to See & Do
Snorkeling, diving and visits to the cays and beaches are the activities on Guanaja (see

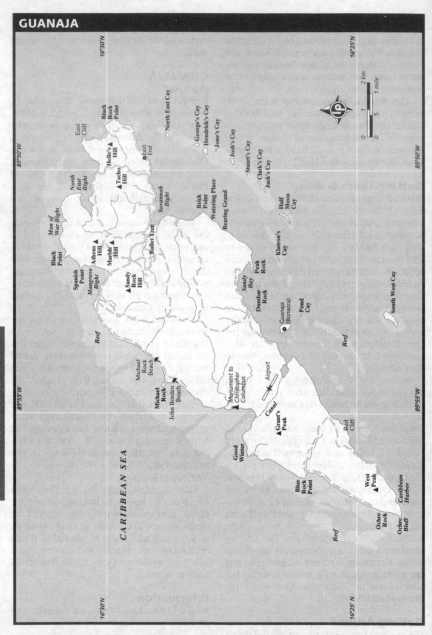

GUANAJA

HONDURAS

CARIBBEAN SEA

16°30'N
16°25'N

85°50'W
85°55'W

Black Rock Point
East Cliff
North East Cay
George's Cay
Hendrick's Cay
Helle's Hill
East End
Jone's Cay
Tacho Hill
Josh's Cay
North East Bight
Savannah Bight
Stuart's Cay
Man of War Bight
Butter Tree
Brick Point
Watering Place
Clark's Cay
Bearing Grand
Jack's Cay
Black Point
Athens Hill
Half Moon Cay
Marble Hill
Spanish Point
Mangrove Bight
Sandy Rock Hill
Klatron's Cay
Sandy Bay
Peak Rock
Dunbar Rock
South West Cay
Pond Cay
Guanaja (Bonacca)
Reef
Michael Rock Beach
Michael Rock
Monument to Christopher Columbus
John Borden Beach
Airport
Canal
Good Winter
Grant's Peak
Red Cliff
Blue Rock Point
West Peak
Caribbean Harbor
Ochre Rock
Ochre Bluff
Reef

0   1   2 km
0   .5   1 mile

the 'Guidelines for Safe Diving' boxed text earlier in this section). You can snorkel right off the town cay; the Hotel Alexander beside the water is a good place to start. There's good snorkeling around South West Cay and several other cays, at Michael Rock Beach on the main island and at many other places. Surprisingly, though, snorkeling gear is not readily available on the island; you should bring your own.

On the main island are a number of hiking trails and a waterfall. You can hire a boat to take you across if you're staying in town. Diving trips can be arranged through the dive resorts on the main island.

Places to Stay & Eat

There are places to stay both in Guanaja town and on the main island. In town, **Hotel Miller** (☎ 453 4327, fax 453 4202) offers singles/doubles with ceiling fan and shared bath for US$15/20; rooms with private bath are US$20/25 or US$25/30 with air-con and cable TV. The hotel also has a restaurant, where meals cost US$3. The Millers own half of Southwest Cay, and you can make trips there to snorkel, BBQ and swim.

Nearby, **Hotel Rosario** (☎/fax 453 4240) has five clean, modern rooms with private bath and cable TV for US$22 with fan, US$34 with air-con. You can arrange boat trips and other activities.

The **Hotel Alexander** (☎ 453 4326, fax 453 4369), looking across the water toward Pond Cay and Southwest Cay, is very comfortable, with lots of amenities. Rooms are US$35/40; a larger penthouse apartment is available. Children under 12 stay for free. You can snorkel right off the dock here, and they can make arrangements for diving.

More places to stay are on the main island, but if you stay on the main island, bring plenty of insect repellent. On the waterside beside the airport, the **Airport Hillton** (☎ 453 4299) has three rooms for US$20 per person, for overnight only, or US$50 per person, including accommodations, three meals, laundry service, fishing, snorkeling and 'honky-tonking' around the island. All the rooms have private bath, two beds, fan and satellite TV. It's run by the famous Captain Al, who can make arrangements for anything you could want to do on the island.

The dive resorts around the island tend to be expensive. All offer diving, accommodations and meals; some also offer activities such as hiking, horseback riding and various water sports.

On Sandy Bay are two small dive resorts, the **Nautilus** (☎ 453 4389, nautilus@caribe.hn) and the **Manatee** (☎ 453 4182), which charge US$117 and US$100 respectively. The **Bayman Bay Club** (☎ 453 4179), on the island's west side, and **Posada del Sol** (☎/fax 453 4186, info@posadadelsol.com), on the east side, are more upscale resorts and have all-inclusive packages for US$200 and US$120 respectively.

The **West Peak Inn**, on the southwest side of the island near West Peak, is 'an island getaway for the not so rich and famous.' Situated on 3 miles of pristine, secluded beach, it has a restaurant and bar and a hiking trail to the top of West Peak with a view of Barbareta and Roatán. Accommodations are in tents, with all camping gear and facilities provided; the cost of US$35 per day includes all meals. Sea kayaking, diving, snorkeling and fishing can all be arranged.

Places to eat in town include **Restaurante El Portal** on the town's main walkway and **Little Pino's Palace Restaurant** opposite the Baptist church. **Ashley's restaurant** is also recommended.

Getting There & Away

Air Flights from La Ceiba take 25 minutes (see the Getting There & Away section in the introduction to the Bay Islands).

There's a dock near the airport where a motorboat meets incoming flights. The five-minute ride to town costs US$2.50. For departing flights, the boat meets the passengers at the dock by the airline office in town to take them back to the airport. If you're staying at one of the resorts around the island and they know you are coming, they will be at the airport to meet you.

Boat No scheduled passenger boats serve Guanaja. Cargo and fishing boats sail between Guanaja and Roatán (three hours) and between Guanaja and Puerto Castilla or Trujillo (four hours), but there is no set schedule. You might spend days waiting for a boat. You could always try to hitch with private yacht owners.

HONDURAS

Getting Around

If you stay in town, you can take boat rides to the main island and to the cays; almost everyone on the island has a motorboat. The standard price for any boat trip is not low, however, at around US$23 per trip out and back. Economically it works out better if you get a group together; the boats hold up to 10 people, and the price is charged by the trip, not by the number of passengers. You may be able to find a boat to take you for as little as US$10 if you're lucky.

Eastern Honduras

The eastern part of Honduras, including the entire department of Gracias a Dios and the eastern sides of Olancho and Colón, is a vast, sparsely inhabited area of rivers and forests. The easternmost part of Honduras is known as the Mosquitia, through which there is just one minor road.

Only two major roads traverse the area northeast of Tegucigalpa. Both run between Tegucigalpa and Trujillo, and both are traversed by bus routes. One goes via Limones, La Unión, Olanchito, Savá and Tocoa; it climbs the mountains west of Juticalpa and can be driven in about eight hours. The other, longer, route goes via Juticalpa (three hours), where you have to change buses; it's another seven hours to Trujillo.

La Unión and Juticalpa are both pleasant towns for an overnight stop. La Unión is the gateway for the Parque Nacional La Muralla, which is beautiful, with its cool cloud forest.

LA UNIÓN

La Unión is a small, typical Honduran mountain town, nestled into a valley surrounded by pine-covered mountains. It's the gateway to beautiful Parque Nacional La Muralla and a convenient stopover on the way between Tegucigalpa and Trujillo.

Places to Stay & Eat

Hotel La Muralla and *Hotel Karol* are both clean little places, each with 10 rooms and shared toilet and showers. Singles/doubles at Hotel La Muralla are US$3/6; at Hotel Karol they're US$3.25/6.50.

La Unión has several comedores where you can get simple meals. *Cafetería La Muralla* is a good place to eat and get information about the national park – one of the park guides lives here. *Auto Pollos*, on the outskirts of town, makes rotisserie chicken (eat there or take out), as does the *Cafetería El Oasis*. Other comedores in town include *Comedor Cindy* and *Café y Naranja*.

Getting There & Away

All the buses between Tegucigalpa and Trujillo stop at La Unión; by bus it's about 4½ to five hours from either place. If you're coming from La Ceiba, you can catch one of these buses at Savá or Olanchito. In La Unión the bus stop is in front of Auto Pollos on the outskirts of town. By private vehicle, it takes about three to four hours to drive to La Unión from Tegucigalpa (200km), La Ceiba (200km) or San Pedro Sula (175km).

AROUND LA UNIÓN

Of course, the number-one attraction is the Parque Nacional La Muralla, but there are also a couple of other enjoyable places to visit near La Unión. Near town, the road heading toward La Muralla crosses a small river, the Río Camote. Following the river toward town from this crossing, you come to **El Chorrón** in less than 150m, a pleasant and refreshing waterfall, about 6m high, with a fine swimming hole at the bottom.

You can make a pleasant 4km hike from La Unión to the nearby village of **Los Encuentros**, where many of the houses are decorated with interesting hand-painted designs. The old wooden *trapiches* (ox-driven sugar mills) are used only during sugarcane harvest, which is around the month of March, but they are interesting to see any time.

PARQUE NACIONAL LA MURALLA

This national park protects a beautiful virgin cloud forest. Since it's rather remote, it isn't overrun with tourists, yet it's easily accessible through La Unión.

A visitors center at the park entrance provides plenty of information. Several well-maintained trails start near the visitors center, including an easy 1km loop trail and several longer trails. Toucanettes and quetzals can be seen from certain spots on the trails; two of the trails have campsites. To camp in the park, bring all your own gear. Otherwise, it's easy to stay in La Unión.

The visitors center has a map and information on all of the trails. Guides are available and charge about US$5 per trail. It's highly recommended you go with a guide, as you will see more wildlife and learn more about the forest. Be sure to bring along a sweater or jacket, good hiking boots and rain gear; it's quite cool in the park. You'll see the most wildlife if you come early in the morning.

Information
The COHDEFOR office in La Unión, three blocks south of the church on the central plaza, has information on the park; it's open 8 am to 5 pm Monday to Friday. You must stop here to register before going up to the park. If you arrive on a weekend, go to the information office across the plaza to get information and to register.

The COHDEFOR office in Tegucigalpa (☎ 223 4346) also has information on the park; ask for the Departamento de Areas Protegidas.

Sr Hubert Argueta at the Cafetería La Muralla in La Unión also has information on the park; he is one of the park guides.

Getting There & Away
A good dirt road leads from La Unión into the park, 14km uphill from town. There's no public transportation into the park, but you can probably arrange a ride in La Unión or hitch. An ordinary vehicle can make the trip; it's not necessary to have 4WD.

JUTICALPA
pop 96,720
The only major town in northeastern Honduras is Juticalpa, the capital of the department of Olancho. There's nothing much to see, but it's a pleasant, friendly town in which to spend a night. The annual festival is held on December 8.

Information
The post office is right on the plaza. Hondutel is one block north of the plaza.

Places to Stay & Eat
On the corner of 1a Avenida NE and 6a Calle SO, between the bus station and the central plaza, *Hotel El Paso* (☎ 885 2311) is

quiet, spacious and clean, with enclosed parking and rooms around a grassy courtyard. It has a small shop, and there are restaurants in the same block. Singles/doubles, all with private bath, overhead fan and wood decor, are US$5.40/9.20.

Hotel Antunez (☎ 885 2250), a block from the plaza, is a large hotel with various types of rooms priced according to the amenities you choose (TV, fan, fridge and so on). Rooms with shared bath are around US$5/7; with private bath they are US$7/9. *Hotel Antunez Anexo* (☎ 885 2034), half a block away, is simple but clean and has rooms for US$5 per person with shared bath, or US$7.50 per person with TV and private bath.

There are several simple comedores around the plaza. Behind the church, *Restaurante El Rancho* is a covered outdoor patio with wooden picnic tables and a good selection of food; it's open 9 am to 11:30 pm daily. *Restaurant El Tablado*, four blocks from the plaza on the entrance road into town, is a fancier restaurant with a bar.

Getting There & Away
The bus station is about 1km from town on the entrance road from the highway. Plenty of taxis run between town and the station (US$0.80).

Transportes Aurora (☎ 885 2237) operates several bus routes:

Catacamas (US$0.90, one hour, 40km)
Buses leave at 9:15 am and then hourly from 12:30 to 6:30 pm.
La Ceiba (US$6.50, eight hours, 345km)
One bus leaves daily at 3 am.
San Esteban (US$3.25, three hours, 125km)
Two buses leave daily at 8 am and noon.
Tegucigalpa (US$2.80, three hours, 170km)
Hourly buses leave from 5 am to 6 pm.
Tocoa (US$5.50, seven hours, 235km)
One bus leaves daily at 5 am.
Trujillo (US$5.50, seven hours, 278km)
One bus leaves daily at 4 am.

The road from Juticalpa to Trujillo passes from pine-forested mountains down to coastal lowlands covered in jungle and coconut palms. Along the way are cattle ranches and lots of cowboys. One direct bus a day runs from Juticalpa to Trujillo, departing at 4 am. If you don't want to get up so early, it's possible to do this journey via bus and minibus, with changes at San Esteban and Tocoa. Ask about connections, or you may have to overnight in San Esteban.

CATACAMAS
pop 75,000
Catacamas, 40km northeast of Juticalpa (about 45 minutes by bus), is a more attractive town than Juticalpa. This is a simple but traditional place, not a tourist center. There are only a couple of basic hotels. The **Hotel Central** is clean and simple, with a courtyard boasting a mango tree, and has rooms for about US$10. **Hotel Colina**, on the parque central, is the better of the two. Rooms go for about US$11 here and have hot water and TVs. Eating is limited to a few comedores or the **Rodeo** on the main street in town. Catacamas is the end of the line for buses coming from Tegucigalpa; many of the Tegucigalpa-Juticalpa buses continue to Catacamas, and additional buses go just between these two towns. From Catacamas, other buses traverse the dirt road to the small town of Dulce Nombre de Culmí.

THE MOSQUITIA
The Mosquitia region, comprising the entire northeast portion of the country, is very different from the rest of Honduras. There are no roads going through the vast area, and most of the region is uninhabited. Those people who do live there – mostly Miskito Indians, with isolated groups of Pech (Paya) and Tawahka (Sumo) Indians in the interior – have their own distinct cultures.

The settlements of the Mosquitia are remote and a little backward; if you go there, don't expect city life. The Mosquitia is mainly worth visiting for its pristine natural beauty. Manatees and much other wildlife live in the eastern lagoons. Monkeys visit the forested areas along the rivers early in the morning, and there is abundant bird life, including toucans, macaws, parrots, egrets, herons and many others. Crocodiles can be seen in many of the waters, especially at night and especially in the mangrove-lined rivers; if you're traveling by water, keep your hands inside the boat.

Most travelers who make it to the region are highly enthusiastic about what they find. All the towns mentioned have inexpensive accommodations for visitors (and some-where to eat), whether in formal hospedajes or with families who rent rooms; some provision will always be made. You can also camp out.

Fish dishes are magnificent in the Mosquitia; other food has to be imported into the region and can be scarce or expensive. If you intend to get really off the beaten track, bring as much food with you as you can, as you'll end up sharing meals with families. Be sure to bring along a method of water purification.

Mosquitoes and sand flies are a major irritation; bring insect repellent, a mosquito net and antimalaria pills. It can rain any time, so rain gear is a good idea, as is a flashlight, since many places have no electricity. Bringing toilet paper is a good idea, too.

As the place is so remote, and accommodations and transportation are relatively unstructured, a working knowledge of Spanish is more important here than elsewhere in Honduras. Such mandatory interaction with the locals make a visit all the more of an adventure.

It may seem tempting to get into Nicaragua through the Mosquitia and avoid backtracking to Tegucigalpa. However, the trouble you will go to may not be worth the effort.

Río Plátano Biosphere Reserve
The Río Plátano Biosphere Reserve is probably the most magnificent nature reserve in Honduras. A world heritage site established jointly in 1980 by Honduras and the United Nations, it is home to abundant bird, mammal and aquatic life, including a number of exotic and endangered species in the river and surrounding jungle.

A good trip on the Río Plátano might start in Palacios, at the northwestern edge of the reserve (see the Palacios section), where there are flights to La Ceiba and Trujillo and places to stay and eat. The best time of year to do this trip is from November to July, and the best time for seeing birds is during February and March, when many migratory birds are here.

From Palacios, take a *cayuca* (a dugout) down the Río Negro and across the Laguna Ibans to Belén, near Cocobila. The trip takes about 1½ hours and costs around US$2 per person.

On the way to Belén, you'll pass Plaplaya, a lovely Garífuna village about half an hour's boat ride from Palacios. Giant leatherback sea turtles nest here; volunteers are needed to help during the turtles' nesting season, which is usually from around April to June (talk to Bonnie Larsen).

Nearer to Belén is Cocobila, and between Cocobila and Belén, Raista. Be sure to check out the butterfly farm at Raista, where 12 different kinds of butterfly are raised, each in their own type of tree. Cocobila, Raista and Belén are all small villages on a narrow strip of land between Laguna Ibans and the sea. From Belén it's about a 2½-hour walk along the beach to Barra Plátano.

At Barra Plátano, where the Río Plátano meets the sea, there's a *hospedaje*, operated by Morgan, where beds are about US$4.50 per person. At Barra Plátano, you can arrange for a cayuca to take you up the Río Plátano to Las Marías, which is about eight hours upriver. Morgan has a cayuca, as do many others; most of these cayucas are large cargo and passenger boats that can hold about eight to 10 people and all their gear.

As you head upriver from Barra Plátano, you'll see much wildlife, including crocodiles, howler and white-faced monkeys, tapirs, macaws, parrots, toucans, herons and about 250 other kinds of birds, especially early in the morning – you'll want to get an early start.

At Las Marías, a village of about 200 or 300 people right in the center of the biosphere reserve, there are two places where you can spend the night: the *Hospedaje Ovidio* and *Hospedaje Mariano*, both of which charge around US$4 per bed, and another US$3.50 per meal. The village is bicultural, with Pech people living at one end and Miskitos at the other; a Peace Corps volunteer is also stationed here.

Starting out again from Las Marías the next day, you can take a boat trip about five hours farther upriver to view some ancient petroglyphs. You can camp overnight at the petroglyphs (bring all your own gear) or return to Las Marías – from the petroglyphs it takes about two hours to get back downriver to Las Marías. From Las Marías it takes about another five hours to get back downriver to Cocobila.

If you stay in Barra Plátano on the way up, you might like to stay in Cocobila on the way back. Rubén Balladares has a *hospedaje* there with rooms for US$4.50. Rubén has two boats, and he'll take you back to Palacios the next day in time to catch the flight back to Trujillo or La Ceiba. The flight leaves at around 11 am, and the boat trip from Cocobila to Palacios only takes an hour (around US$2). Rubén is the Isleña agent in Cocobila; when you arrive, have him radio to Palacios to reserve you a seat on the airplane if you haven't already done so, as the flight often fills up.

Everything about this trip is very affordable, except for one leg: the boat trip upriver from Barra Plátano. This will cost between US$85 and US$125; you can bargain the price down to a point, but don't count on getting it for much less than this. If you can get a few people together to split the cost, it's much more affordable. Several tour companies also make this trip.

A more affordable option than taking the boat trip upriver from Barra Plátano is hiking through the jungle to Las Marías. From the south (inland) side of Laguna Ibans, the hike takes about six hours. It's worth paying a local guide to take you; one might do so for about US$5. Once you reach Las Marías, you can organize a boat trip upriver from there to see the petroglyphs; it would cost about US$30 to US$55.

Palacios

A small town with only about a hundred houses, Palacios is the most accessible place from which to visit the Río Plátano, with regular flights coming in from La Ceiba and Trujillo. From Palacios you can easily arrange boat trips on the river or across the lagoon to the Garífuna village of Batalla.

The best place to stay is the 12-room *hotel* operated by Don Felix, next door to the Isleña office. It has a view of the river, and the rooms, all with private bath, cost around US$7. *Trek* is a cheaper and more basic place, with rooms for around US$6. Don Felix operates a restaurant serving inexpensive meals. He is also the agent for Isleña airline. Reserve in advance with him for your flight leaving Palacios to go back to Trujillo or La Ceiba. These flights often fill up, and if you just show up at the airport, you may not get a seat.

Brus Laguna
pop 1400

Beside the lagoon of the same name at the mouth of the Río Patuca, Brus Laguna is a small Mosquitia town. There is a friendly *hospedaje* for accommodations. You can cook there if you have your own food. Boat trips can be taken on the lagoon and upriver on the Río Patuca, where there's much wildlife.

Ahuas

Ahuas, a small town with a population of under a thousand, is inland from the coast about two hours' walk from the Río Patuca. From here you can take boat trips upriver to the village of Wampusirpi or downriver to Brus Laguna. At certain times of year, however, the river may not be navigable, due to too much water (rainy season) or too little (dry season). Check current conditions before you go.

Puerto Lempira
pop 34,000

Puerto Lempira, the largest town in the Mosquitia, is situated on the inland side of the Laguna de Caratasca. Connecting with several sublagoons, the lagoon is very large but not deep; its average depth is about 3m, with deeper pockets in a few places.

Because the depth clearance over the sandbar forming the entrance to the lagoon is only about 2m, large vessels cannot enter, and only small boats ply the waters. There is a lot of small boat traffic, especially between Puerto Lempira and Cauquira, a village on the lagoon's north side, from which you can easily walk to the sea.

Manatees, birds, fish and other wildlife are in abundance in the lagoon. Mopawi, a tiny place outside of town, has a water buffalo farm that you can ask permission to visit.

If you must stay in Puerto Lempira, ask at the *cafeteria* across from the parque central. The lady who runs it also rents *rooms*.

Organized Tours

Several travel companies undertake organized tours into the Mosquitia region, providing an easy (if more expensive) way to get a taste of the Mosquitia. All of the fol-lowing ones have been recommended. Information on each company is given under the town where its office is located.

Tegucigalpa
La Moskitia Ecoaventuras, Adventure Expeditions

La Ceiba
La Moskitia Ecoaventuras, Euro Honduras Tours

Trujillo
Turtle Tours

Copán Ruinas
Go Native Tours, Xukpi Tours

Getting There & Away

Air La Ceiba is the hub for flights to the Mosquitia, with services to Palacios, Puerto Lempira, Ahuas and Brus Laguna. Isleña, Sosa and Rollins Air all have flights from La Ceiba to the Mosquitia. Isleña's La Ceiba–Palacios flight stops in Trujillo on the way, making Trujillo another viable starting point. See the Getting Around section at the beginning of the Honduras chapter for details on domestic flights.

Boat There are no regularly scheduled boats to the Mosquitia, but cargo and fishing boats go frequently from La Ceiba, Trujillo and Guanaja, and may take passengers. Just go down to the docks in any of these places and ask around for a boat.

Getting Around

Air Most of the flights from La Ceiba to the Mosquitia return directly, so there's not much of a network of flights within the region. An exception is Sosa's (☎ 443 1399 in La Ceiba, fax 443 2519, aerosoa@caribe.hn) twice-weekly flight (La Ceiba-Brus Laguna-Ahuas-La Ceiba).

Alas de Socorro airline, a small enterprise in the Mosquitia for missionaries and hospitals, will take passengers, but space is not always available. They serve the mission hospital in Ahuas and several other places; fares are around US$25. They are available for charter flights within the Mosquitia. Their base is in Ahuas. If you need air transportation within the Mosquitia, fly a scheduled airline to Ahuas from La Ceiba and make a deal with the Alas pilot on duty there. The pilot is Jorge Goff. He can be reached via shortwave radio by asking for him by name.

Boat Ground-level transportation is almost entirely by boat, on the lagoons and rivers as well as the sea, though prices can be high. Flat-bottomed *pipante* boats, propelled by poles or paddles, are the main transportation used on rivers and in the lagoons. Cayucas, with more angular hulls, are the principal transportation in the sea, and they also enter the lagoons. Cayucas are propelled by poles, paddles, or small engines; the motorized canoes are called 'tuk-tuks,' taking their name from their sound. Cayucas are more stable in the sea, but pipantes are more stable in the lagoons and rivers.

The rainy season in the Mosquitia is normally from June to December. At this time too much water (sometimes to the point of flooding) and flotsam in the water can occasionally impede navigation of rivers; during the dry season, some waterways can become too shallow to navigate. The most dangerous times for boat travel are during the driest time of year (April) and the wettest (October). Most of the time, though, there is no problem getting around by boat. Locals say that here, as elsewhere in the world, patterns of rainfall have been less predictable in recent years.

Southern Honduras

Honduras touches the Pacific with a 124km coastline on the Golfo de Fonseca. Bordered by the gulf on the seaward side and by hills on the land side, the strip of land here is part of the hot coastal plain that extends down the Pacific side of Central America through several countries. It's a fertile agricultural and fishing region; much of Tegucigalpa's fish, shrimp, rice, sugarcane and hot-weather fruits (like watermelon) come from this area. Honduras' Pacific port is at San Lorenzo.

Southern Honduras is a much-traveled region; it is where the Interamericana crosses Honduras, carrying all the north- and southbound traffic of Central America, and also where the highway branches north from the Interamericana toward the rest of Honduras.

TEGUCIGALPA TO NICARAGUA
The most direct route from Tegucigalpa to Managua is via **El Paraíso**. It's only 122km from Tegucigalpa to the border going this way (US$1.10, 2½ hours by bus). You can make it from Tegucigalpa to Managua in a day if you get an early start.

The border crossing is at **Las Manos**, near El Paraíso. Coming from Tegucigalpa, take a bus to El Paraíso and then change buses to continue on the half-hour journey to the border station (US$0.30), which is open 7 am to 5 pm daily.

There are several interesting stopovers along this route. About 40km east of the capital at Zamorano, there's a turnoff for **San Antonio de Oriente**, an attractive Spanish colonial mining village about 5km north of the highway. This is the village immortalized by Honduran primitivist painter José Antonio Velásquez.

Farther east is a turnoff south to **Yuscarán**, 66km from Tegucigalpa. Capital of the department of El Paraíso, it is another pleasant Spanish colonial mining village. Its annual fair is held on December 8.

Danlí (population 126,000), 92km east of Tegucigalpa and 19km from El Paraíso, is the largest town along this route. An attractive town, Danlí is the center of an agricultural area producing sugarcane and tobacco; the town also has several cigar factories where you can buy good hand-rolled cigars. The annual festival at Danlí, the Festival del Maíz in the last weekend in August, is a big event and attracts people from far and wide. The Laguna de San Julian, 18km north of Danlí, is a manmade lake popular for outings.

There are several places to stay in Danlí. The *Gran Hotel Granada* (☎ 883 2499, fax 883 2774), with 36 rooms at US$13 per person, is one option, and the *Hotel Ebenezer* (☎ 883 2655), with cheaper rooms at US$9, is another. El Paraíso also has accommodations. The *Quinta Ave Hotel-Restaurante* (☎ 893 4298), in El Paraíso on 5a Avenida, is recommended; single/double rooms with private hot bath are around US$5/6. It also offers Mexican food and secure parking.

TEGUCIGALPA TO THE PACIFIC
Highway CA 5 heads south about 95km from Tegucigalpa until the highway meets the

Interamericana at Jícaro Galán, winding down from the pine-covered hills around the capital to the hot coastal plain. From the crossroads at Jícaro Galán, it's 40km west to the border with El Salvador at **El Amatillo**, passing through the town of Nacaome 6km west of Jícaro Galán, or it's 115km east to the Nicaraguan border at **El Espino**, passing through Choluteca 50km from Jícaro Galán.

If you are traveling along the Interamericana, crossing only this part of Honduras in transit between El Salvador and Nicaragua, you can easily make the entire crossing in a day; from border to border it's only 150km (three hours by bus).

If, however, you want to stop off, there are a few possibilities. The border stations close at 5 pm, so if you can't make it by that time, you'll have to spend the night.

GOLFO DE FONSECA

The shores of Honduras, El Salvador and Nicaragua all touch the Golfo de Fonseca; Honduras has the middle and largest share, with 124km of coastline and jurisdiction over nearly all of the 30-plus islands in the gulf. A ruling of the International Court of Justice in September 1992 eased previous tensions by ruling that sovereignty in the gulf must be shared by the three nations, barring a 3-mile maritime belt around the coast. Of the islands in the gulf, sovereignty was disputed by Honduras and El Salvador in three cases. The court found in favor of Honduras regarding the island of El Tigre, but El Salvador prevailed on Meanguera and Meanguerita.

The European discovery of the Golfo de Fonseca was made in 1522 by Andrés Niño, who named the gulf in honor of his benefactor, Bishop Juan Rodríguez de Fonseca. In 1578, the buccaneer Sir Francis Drake occupied the gulf, using El Tigre as a base as he made raids as far afield as Peru and Baja California. There is still speculation that Drake may have left a hidden treasure, but it has never been found.

El Salvador has a major town on the gulf (La Unión), but Honduras doesn't; on the Honduran part of the coastline, there are only small settlements, and the highway never meets the sea except on the outskirts of San Lorenzo. The Golfo de Fonseca is an extremely hot region.

San Lorenzo
pop 29,120

The Interamericana touches the Golfo de Fonseca only on the outskirts of San Lorenzo. San Lorenzo is the Pacific port town of Honduras, but there's not much to the town, which is small, sleepy and hot. San Lorenzo is in a deep inlet, the Bahía de San Lorenzo, so although you can get to the water and jump in for a swim, there's no view out into the gulf.

From the bus stop on the highway, it's about 10 blocks to the water on a road that passes the market, church and plaza. At the end, beside the shrimp-packing plant, *Hotel Miramar* (☎ *881 2138*) has a restaurant and bar, with a large deck hanging over the water. Rooms cost US$27 for a single/double. Meals, mostly seafood, are about US$6. Canoes and small boats pass by in the channel, and there's a small, muddy beach of sorts beside the hotel. Buses plying the Interamericana all stop at San Lorenzo, some at the bus stop on the highway, some coming the few blocks into town to the market.

Cedeño & Punta Ratón

These are the two principal swimming beaches on the Golfo de Fonseca. Cedeño is the more popular; it has very basic places to stay and eat. The turnoff from the Interamericana is about halfway between Choluteca and San Lorenzo. Buses come from both towns, but only a few times a day; it takes about one to 1½ hours to get to the beaches from either town. There are also buses that run directly between Cedeño and Tegucigalpa.

Amapala
pop 10,000

Amapala is a quiet fishing village on the island of El Tigre, an inactive volcanic island 783m high. Founded in 1833, Amapala was once Honduras' Pacific port town, before the port was moved to the mainland at San Lorenzo. Visitors come here for holidays during Semana Santa, but otherwise the place is very quiet. A view of Amapala is on the back of the 2 lempira note.

There are a few places to stay and eat in Amapala, and some good hikes around the island; from El Vijía, about 100m up, there's a good view of the gulf and its islands. El

Tigre also has several good beaches: Playa Grande, with the Cueva de la Sirena (Mermaid Cave), and Playa Negra, with tranquil shores. Other beaches are Caracolito and El Caracol. The island's seafood is very good.

Places to Stay & Eat The *Hotel Internacional* has been recommended; you can see it on the 2 lempira note, right at the foot of the pier. The downstairs rooms are hot and dark, but the upstairs rooms are large and airy, facing the sea. From the upstairs rooms, doors open onto a large balcony with plenty of room for hammocks. This is an old, cheap hotel; rooms might cost around US$6 or US$8 per night. The *Villas Playa Negra* (☎ 232 0632), around the island on Playa Negra, is more luxurious and expensive, with rooms for around US$45. Both hotels have restaurants.

Getting There & Away Small boats and a car ferry depart from Coyolito, 30km from the Interamericana; the boat trip takes about 20 minutes. Buses go to Coyolito infrequently from San Lorenzo; you could also hitch. There are no overnight facilities at Coyolito.

CHOLUTECA
pop 118,560

Choluteca, capital of the department of the same name, is the largest town in southern Honduras. The town is built near the Río Choluteca, the same river that runs through Tegucigalpa.

There's not much to do in Choluteca; it's principally a commercial center for the agricultural region and a stopping-off point between the borders. It is a pleasant, though very hot, town. The annual festival day is December 8.

Orientation

The streets in Choluteca are laid out in a straightforward grid, with calles running perpendicular to avenidas. The city is divided into quadrants; all the calles and avenidas are numbered sequentially and designated as NO *(noroeste,* northwest), NE *(noreste,* northeast), SO *(suroeste,* southwest) or SE *(sureste,* southeast).

The old market (Mercado Viejo San Antonio) is the center of activity, and prac-

tically everything you need is near it. The new market (Mercado Nuevo La Concepción) is five blocks south. The bus stations are nine blocks east on Blvd Carranza, the main east-west road, which runs two blocks south of the old market.

Information

There's a Nicaraguan consulate (☎ 882 0127) on 4a Calle NO, about a block from the Mercado Viejo, in the center of town. It's open Monday to Friday from 7 am to noon and from 2 to 4 pm.

The post office is on the corner of 2a Calle NO and 3a Avenida NO, three blocks east of the old market. Next door, Hondutel is open for domestic and international telephone calls 7 am to 9 pm daily; fax service is available 8 am to 4 pm Monday to Friday.

Places to Stay

The quiet, clean and pleasant *Hotel Pacífico* (☎ 882 0838), on 4a Avenida NE one block south of Blvd Choluteca, is in the residential neighborhood near the bus stations. There's a courtyard with hammocks and cable TV in the tiny lounge area. All rooms have private bath and fan; singles/doubles are US$4.50/6.75, or US$7.90 with two beds. Rooms with air-con and cable TV cost US$11/13.50. Across the street, the newer *Hotel Pacífico Anexo* (☎ 882 3249) has rooms for the same prices and operates a comedor.

Several other places to stay are near the old market, which in Choluteca is a fine area and not somewhere to be avoided as in some other cities. *Hotel Santa Rosa* (☎ 882 0355), facing the old market on the western side, is comfortable and clean. All the rooms have private bath and overhead fan and face onto a colorful courtyard full of plants and hammocks. They cost US$4.50/9 for singles/doubles.

Around the corner to the north, *Hotelito Don Paco No 2* (☎ 882 2778) is a similar place, only smaller; it's clean and well kept, with a cable TV in the little patio sitting area. Rooms with shared bath are US$3.50, US$4.50 with private bath, or US$7.90 with private bath and TV.

Nearby, *Hotel Mi Esperanza* (☎ 882 0885) offers simple rooms with private bath for US$3.40/5.60; the Esperanza has some larger rooms for US$8/10 for three/four

CHOLUTECA

To San Marcos de Colón, El Espino & Guasaule
To Hotel Centro America
To Tegucigalpa & El Amarillo

5a Av NE
4a Av NE
3a Av NE
2a Av NE
1a Av NE
Blvd Choluteca
1a Av NO
2a Av NO
3a Av NO
4a Av NO
5a Av NO
6a Av NO
7a Av NO
Blvd Choluteca
Av Bojorque
9a Av NO

2a Av SE
1a Av SE
Blvd Carranza
1a Av SO
2a Av SO
3a Av SO
4a Av SO
5a Av SO
6a Av SO
7a Av SO
Blvd Carranza
Av Bojorque
9a Av SO

4a Calle NE
3a Calle NE
2a Calle NE
1a Calle NE
4a Calle NO
3a Calle NO
2a Calle NO
1a Calle NO
4a Calle NO
3a Calle NO
2a Calle NO
1a Calle NO

1a Calle SE
2a Calle SE
3a Calle SE
1a Calle SO
2a Calle SO
3a Calle SO
4a Calle SO

Mercado Viejo San Antonio

Mercado Nuevo La Concepción

0   100   200 m
0   100   200 yards

PLACES TO STAY
3 Hotel Pacífico; Comedor Pacífico
4 Hotel Pacífico Anexo
6 Hotel Mi Esperanza
7 Hotelito Don Paco No 2
8 Hotel Santa Rosa

PLACES TO EAT
5 Comedor Mi Esperanza

OTHER
1 Nicaraguan Consulate
2 Esso Gas Station
9 Post Office; Hondutel
10 Mi Esperanza Bus Station
11 Royeri Bus Station & Others

HONDURAS

people. You can park in the interior court-yards of both places.

Handy for travelers coming from the El Espino border post with Nicaragua, the **Hotel Centro America** (☎ 882 3940) is on the northwest side of Blvd Choluteca. Rooms are somewhat expensive here, at US$27 for a single/double.

Places to Eat
Lots of small comedores line the streets bordering the old market. The **Comedor Mi Esperanza** offers breakfast, lunch or dinner, each for US$2. The new market has a cheap eating area in the center. The Hotel Pacífico has its own comedor, with other places to eat nearby.

Getting There & Away
Royeri and several other companies share a bus station on Blvd Carranza, at the corner of 3a Avenida NE. There are small come-dores and shops in the bus station. Some buses stop by the old market after leaving the station. Buses departing from this station include:

El Amatillo, Salvadoran border crossing (US$1.20, two to 2½ hours, 85km)
Buses leave every half hour, 4 am to 5:30 pm.

Guasaule, Nicaraguan border crossing (US$0.80, one hour, 44km)
Buses leave every half hour from 5 am to 6 pm.

San Marcos de Colón, Nicaraguan border crossing (US$0.65, one to 1½ hours, 58km)
Buses leave every 45 minutes from 6 am to 6 pm.

Tegucigalpa (US$1.80, three hours, 133km)
Buses leave every half hour from 6 am to 6 pm.

Mi Esperanza has its own bus station (☎ 882 0841), on 3a Avenida NE, 1½ blocks north of the other station. Mi Esperanza is one of .the main companies doing the Tegucigalpa-Choluteca-San Marcos de Colón route, and their buses are both more direct and more comfortable than some of the others; people at the Royeri terminal will advise you to take a Mi Esperanza bus if you're going to Tegucigalpa. Mi Esperanza's buses include:

Tegucigalpa (regular bus: US$1.80, three hours; especial bus: US$5.40, two hours, 133km)
12 regular buses depart daily from 4 am to 6 pm. Saturday and Sunday buses are more frequent, leaving about every 15 or 20 minutes. The especial bus departs at 6 and 10 am, 2 and 6 pm.

San Marcos de Colón, Nicaraguan border crossing (US$0.65, one to 1½ hours, 58km)
Five buses depart daily from 6:30 or 7 am to 7 pm.

Local buses connect Choluteca with other places in the south, around the Golfo de Fonseca.

Border Crossings
El Salvador El Amatillo, the border cross-ing between Honduras and El Salvador, is open 7 am to 5 pm daily. It is a relaxed border post; Honduran *campesinos* cross the border here every day to go to market in Santa Rosa de Lima, 18km from the border on the El Salvador side. There are places to stay at Santa Rosa de Lima, or you could press on to San Miguel or La Unión, each a two-hour bus ride from El Amatillo. There's also a basic hospedaje at El Am-atillo on the Honduran side.

From El Amatillo, buses leave frequently for Tegucigalpa (US$1.60, three hours, 130km) and Choluteca (US$1.20, two to 2½ hours, 85km). At Choluteca you can con-tinue to the Nicaraguan border.

Nicaragua The border crossing at **Gua-saule** is open 8 am to 5 pm daily.

Buses operate every half hour between Guasaule and Choluteca (US$0.80, one hour, 44km). On the Nicaraguan side, buses go to both Chinandega and León.

SAN MARCOS DE COLÓN
pop 23,920
San Marcos de Colón is the closest town to the Nicaraguan border at El Espino. It is a small, pleasant mountain town, cool at night, with several places to stay and eat. Some families here offer comfortable ac-commodations in private homes; you may be approached by their children at the bus station. It's easy to change money in San Marcos.

Honduran buses to the border go only as far as San Marcos. From San Marcos, colec-tivo taxis will take you the 7km to the border station at **El Espino** (open 7 am to 5 pm daily) for US$0.40. If you need a visa for either country, be sure you already have it before you reach the border.

If it's getting late in the day, you may want to stay over in Choluteca or San Marcos and make the crossing the following

HONDURAS

day. The choice of accommodations is better here than on the Nicaraguan side near the border. There is no place to stay at El Espino.

Crossing the border in the other direction, you can catch direct buses from San Marcos to Tegucigalpa (US$2.20, 4½ hours, 191km) and Choluteca (US$0.65, one to 1½ hours, 58km); the last bus of the day leaves San Marcos at around 4:45 pm. Choluteca has connecting buses to El Amatillo on the Salvadoran border.

El Salvador

El Salvador's name evokes images of the chaotic civil war fought from 1980 to 1992 in the tangle of mountains and quilts of farmland. But the war has been over for a few years now, and this small but varied country is doing its best to distance itself from its sordid past.

The landscape remains the most turbulent aspect of El Salvador. Volcanoes arise from flat valleys, and lakes fill ancient craters. The Pacific Ocean slams the coast and mixes with the fresh waters of the many rivers slithering through the country.

El Salvador isn't as geared to backpack tourism as neighboring countries, but a trip affords the experience of watching a country redefine itself. Nongovernmental organizations (NGOs) from the USA, Australia and Europe are helping to put the country's pieces back together. Observing or participating in these developments and talking to locals about their experiences and hopes can be the most fulfilling part of a trip.

Efforts to preserve El Salvador's natural wonders have taken root, and the national archaeological museum has finally been renovated. Inexpensive guesthouses are cropping up in mountain areas, opening new possibilities for shoestringers, but traveling here remains a challenge. Tourism infrastructure is still woefully lacking in many areas. Vast social inequities remain: A tour of the capital reveals gleaming shopping malls next to areas of utter squalor. Don't come to El Salvador for a relaxing vacation. Come if you want to know how people in Central America live.

Highlights

- Gaze at the still-smoking black cone of Volcán Izalco from the trails of Cerro Verde National Park
- Watch birds and beachcomb at Isla Montecristo, a peaceful community on a Pacific peninsula
- Soak up colonial splendor in Suchitoto, site of El Salvador's premier cultural festival
- Hike El Imposible, a precious vestige of original forest and haven for an extraordinary variety of wildlife
- Relax in La Palma, a mountain retreat and handicraft center near the Honduran border
- Surf at La Libertad and the Costa del Bálsamo
- Travel the Ruta de las Flores, through scenic coffee country dotted with refreshingly cool mountain villages

Facts about El Salvador

HISTORY

The Olmec people lived in El Salvador at least as early as 2000 BC. The Olmec Boulder, a sculpture of a giant head found near Chalchuapa in western El Salvador, testifies to an early Olmec presence or influence.

The step pyramid ruins at Tazumal and San Andrés show that the Maya lived in western El Salvador for over 1000 years, alongside the Pokomam ethnic group. The eastern region was inhabited by Lenca people.

When the Spanish arrived in the 16th century, the country was dominated by the Pipil, descendants of Nahuatl-speaking Toltecs and Aztecs, both Mexican tribes. The Pipil probably came to central El Salvador in the 11th century, just after the Maya dynasty collapsed. They called the land Cuscatlán, which means Land of Jewels, and

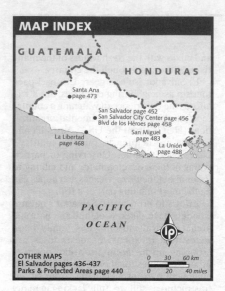

MAP INDEX

GUATEMALA

HONDURAS

Santa Ana
page 473

San Salvador page 452
San Salvador City Center page 456
Blvd de los Héroes page 458

San Miguel
page 483

La Libertad
page 468

La Unión
page 488

PACIFIC

OCEAN

OTHER MAPS
El Salvador pages 436–437
Parks & Protected Areas page 440

0   30   60 km
0   20   40 miles

made what is now Antiguo Cuscatlán, outside San Salvador, the capital. Their culture was similar to that of the Aztec, with heavy Maya influences and a maize-based agricultural economy that supported several cities and a complex culture including hieroglyphic writing, astronomy and mathematics. They spoke Nahua, a dialect related to Nahuatl. Tazumal, San Andrés and Joya de Cerén all show signs of Pipil life.

Spanish Rule & Independence
In El Salvador, the Spanish developed plantations of cotton, balsam and indigo. Throughout the 1700s, agriculture soared, with indigo leading as the No 1 .export. The elite Europeans (namely 14 families) maintained control of most of the land. As elsewhere, they enslaved the indigenous peoples in return for their 'conversion' to Christianity. Slaves from Africa were also used; according to one report, at least 2000 were brought in, but after an uprising in 1625, blacks were restricted access into the country.

El Salvador gained independence from Spain on September 15, 1821. The same wealthy families held tight to their land and continued to push locals off it. Anastasio Aquino led an unsuccessful indigenous rebellion in 1833, setting down his own laws and annulling all debts; he is still a national

hero. In 1841, following the dissolution of the Central American Federation, El Salvador adopted a constitution as a sovereign independent nation.

In Comes Coffee
In the late 19th century, synthetic dyes undermined the indigo market, and coffee took main stage. A handful of wealthy landowners expanded their properties, displacing more indigenous people. Coffee became the most important cash crop and *cafetaleros* (coffee growers) earned purses full of money that was neither taxed nor distributed at reasonable wages to the workers. By the 20th century, 95% of El Salvador's income derived from coffee exports, but only 2% of Salvadorans controlled that wealth.

The 20th Century
Intermittent efforts by the poor majority to redress El Salvador's social and economic injustices were met with severe repression, and the government vigorously eradicated any union activity in the coffee industry during the 1920s.

In January 1932, Augustín Farabundo Martí, a founder of the Central American Socialist Party, led an uprising of peasants and indigenous people. The military responded by systematically killing anyone who looked Indian or supported the uprising. In all, 30,000 people were killed in what became known as La Matanza (the Massacre). Martí was arrested and killed by firing squad. His name is preserved by the Frente Farabundo Martí para la Liberación Nacional (FMLN).

During the 1970s, El Salvador suffered from landlessness, poverty, unemployment and overpopulation. In government, the polarized left and right tangled for power through coups and electoral fraud. In 1972, José Napoleon Duarte, cofounder of the Christian Democrat Party (PDC), ran for president supported by a broad coalition of reform groups. His victory was denied amid allegations of fraud. Subsequent protests and a coup attempt were averted by the military and Duarte was exiled. Guerrilla activity increased and the right wing responded with the creation of 'death squads.' Thousands of Salvadorans were kidnapped, tortured and murdered.

In 1979, a junta of military and civilians overthrew President Carlos Humberto Romero and promised reforms. When these promises were not met, opposition parties banded together as the Frente Democrático Revolucionario (FDR) and allied with the FMLN, a revolutionary army composed of five guerrilla groups. The successful revolution in Nicaragua in 1979 encouraged many Salvadorans to seek reforms and consider armed struggle the only means of change.

On March 24, 1980, Archbishop Oscar A Romero was assassinated while saying Mass in the chapel of the San Salvador Divine Providence Cancer Hospital. His murder ignited an armed insurrection that same year.

Civil War

The rape and murder in late 1980 of four US nuns performing relief work in El Salvador prompted the Carter administration to briefly suspend military aid to the Salvadoran government, but the Reagan administration, unnerved by the success of Nicaragua's socialist revolution, pumped huge sums into the moribund Salvadoran military (over US$500 million in 1985). This effectively prolonged the conflict. Guerrillas gained control of areas in the north and east, and the military retaliated by decimating villages. In 1981, the US-trained Atlacatl Battalion exterminated some 900 men, women and children in El Mozote, Morazán. As many as 300,000 citizens fled the country.

In 1982, Major Roberto D'Aubisson, founder of the extreme-right ARENA party, became president of the legislative assembly, and enacted a law granting the legislative body power over the national president. D'Aubisson created death squads that sought out trade unionists and others who supported the PDC-proposed agrarian reform. The FMLN continued its offensive by blowing up bridges, cutting power lines, destroying coffee plantations and killing livestock – anything to stifle the economy. When the government ignored an FMLN peace proposal, the rebels refused to participate in the 1984 presidential elections, in which Duarte was elected over D'Aubisson. For the next few years the PDC and FMLN engaged in peace talks unsuccessfully. Death squads continued their pillaging, and the guerrillas continued to undermine the military powers and jeopardize municipal elections.

Nearing the End of the War

Hope for peace appeared in 1989, when the FMLN offered to participate in elections if the government agreed to a postponement, to ensure the polls were democratically run. Their calls were ignored; in March Alfredo Cristiani, a wealthy ARENA businessman, was elected president. The FMLN responded by intensifying its attacks and, on November 11, launched a major offensive on the capital. In retaliation, the military killed an estimated 4000 'leftist sympathizers.' Among these enemies of the state were six Jesuit priests, their housekeeper and her

The Search Goes On

When government forces razed villages during the civil war, they didn't always kill everyone. On some occasions, children were spared. Some were taken from their mothers' arms by force. Others were found helpless among the dead bodies on the killing field. Those children who survived were whisked away in helicopters and either divvied up as prizes among military officers or exported abroad for adoption in the USA and Europe. A few were fortunate enough to grow up in loving households.

Many of these children grew up not knowing who their families were or even that they were adopted. Some have the desire to know more about who they are and where they came from. Right after the war ended, their surviving family members may have been reluctant to request an official search, fearing for their own safety. The government did little to make amends. Filling the vacuum is the organization Pro-Búsqueda. Its aim is to find these orphans of the conflict and connect them to their original families, sometimes on the child's request, in other cases on the initiative of the Salvadoran family. Through a combination of family accounts, adoption files and newspaper reports, Pro-Búsqueda has managed to link 98 kids with their blood relatives. But the search goes on: Over 400 cases are still pending.

To find out more about Pro-Búsqueda, phone ☎ 226 9372 or email probusqueda@salnet.net.

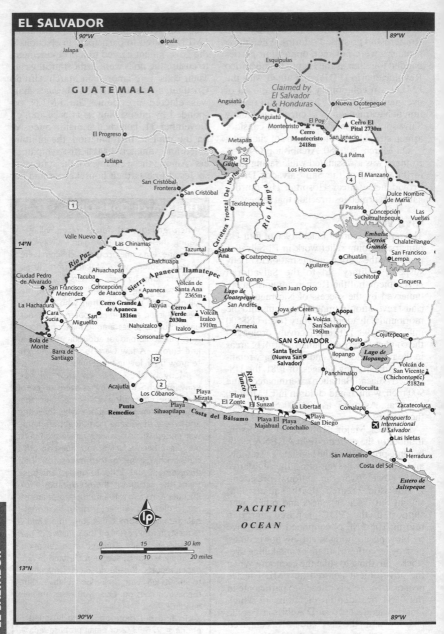

EL SALVADOR

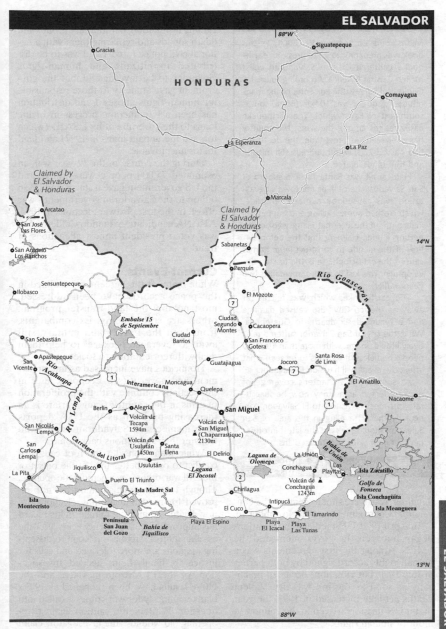

88°W

Gracias

Siguatepeque

HONDURAS

Comayagua

La Esperanza

La Paz

*Claimed by
El Salvador
& Honduras*

Arcatao

Marcala

San José
Las Flores

*Claimed by
El Salvador
& Honduras*

14°N

San Antonio
Los Ranchos

Sabanetas

Sensuntepeque

Perquín

Río Goascorán

Ilobasco

El Mozote

7

*Embalse 15
de Septiembre*

Ciudad
Segundo
Montes

Cacaopera

San Sebastián

Ciudad
Barrios

San Francisco
Gotera

Apastepeque

Santa Rosa
de Lima

San
Vicente

*Río
Acahuapa*

Guatajiagua

Jocoro

7

1

El Amatillo

Interamericana

Moncagua

Nacaome

Berlín

Quelepa

Alegría

San Miguel

Volcán de
Tecapa
1594m

Volcán de
San Miguel
(Chaparrastique)
2130m

San Nicolás
Lempa

Volcán de
Usulután
1450m

Santa
Elena

Carretera del Litoral

Río Lempa

San
Carlos
Lempa

El Delirio

*Laguna de
Olomega*

La Unión

*Bahía de
la Unión*

La Pita

Jiquilisco

Usulután

*Laguna
El Jocotal*

Conchagua

Playitas

Las

Isla Zacatillo

*Isla
Montecristo*

Puerto El Triunfo

Isla Madre Sal

Chirilagua

2

Volcán de
Conchagua
1243m

*Golfo de
Fonseca*

Isla Conchagüita

Corral de Mulas

Intipucá

Isla Meanguera

**Península
San Juan
del Gozo**

*Bahía de
Jiquilisco*

El Cuco

Playa El Espino

Playa
El Icacal

El Tamarindo

Playa
Las Tunas

13°N

88°W

2001 Earthquake

Midmorning on January 13, 2001, as this book was preparing to go to press, an earthquake centered off the Salvadoran coast rocked Central America. According to the US Geological Survey, the epicenter of the magnitude 7.6 quake was 104km (65mi) southsouthwest of San Miguel. The earthquake easily ranges among the worst the country has ever seen. At press time, the death toll had passed 700, with hundreds still missing and thousands injured.

Hardest hit was Santa Tecla, a suburb of San Salvador. The bulk of the town's devastation was caused by a major landslide, which crushed homes, killing and trapping all in its path. In the aftermath, angry voices are getting louder, claiming that the deforestation of the hillside to construct large homes caused the catastrophe (a battle to stop development was lost by environmentalists two years earlier).

The earthquake, which was felt as far away as Mexico City, also caused damage and a recorded six deaths in Guatemala. While the city of San Salvador suffered relatively little damage, with more than 100,000 people homeless, it remains to be seen what effect the event will have on El Salvador.

As some of this chapter's coverage of quake-affected areas may now be inaccurate, prospective visitors to El Salvador, particularly those traveling in the area of San Salvador, should seek out the latest information before making any travel plans.

daughter, who were shot to death at the Universidad Centroamericana on November 16.

In April 1990, UN-mediated negotiations began between the government and the FMLN. Among the first agreements was a human-rights accord signed by both parties in July 1990, but violations occurred practically as soon as the ink was dry. Violent deaths actually increased in 1991, the year that a UN mission arrived in the country to monitor human rights.

Finally, on January 16, 1992, the agreement – or rather compromise – was signed. The ceasefire took effect on February 1. The FMLN became an opposition party, and the government agreed to various reforms, including dismantling paramilitary groups and death squads and replacing them with a national civil police force. Land was to be distributed to citizens and human-rights violations to be investigated, but the government gave amnesty to those responsible for human-rights abuses. Land distribution has been a bureaucratic process involving loans to the government by USAID (which forgave the unpaid loans in 1997) and land that is uncultivable.

During the course of the 12-year war, an estimated 75,000 people were killed, and the US government gave a staggering US$6 billion to the Salvadoran government's war effort. In the first postwar elections in 1994, ARENA candidate Armando Calderón Sol was voted president amidst allegations of fraud.

Current Events

While many of the agreements outlined in the peace accords have been addressed, most notably the land-transfer program, others are still pending. Ex-combatants, from both the FMLN and military, still await a 'severance package' to help them deal with reorientation to society.

Homicides have increased as unemployment and poverty (see Economy, later in this section) combine with the proliferation of arms in the country. Gang warfare is an increasing problem as the USA deports gang members of Salvadoran origin, who transfer their operations back home.

While many consider the root causes of conflict to be no better than at the outset of the civil war, others see a democratic opening. Though the economic situation has not improved for most Salvadorans, elections are now legitimate and the human rights record has improved. In 2000, twenty years after the assassination of Archbishop Romero, dissenting opinions are more tolerated and calls for justice are finally being heeded. Investigations of the El Mozote massacre and the UCA Jesuits have been reopened as 1993's blanket amnesty for war crimes is called into question. While some caution against 'reopening old wounds,' the investigators claim to be driven not so much by a desire for revenge as to set the record straight. Without a proper accounting of the damage done, they say, there can be no reconciliation.

Though ARENA held on to the presidency in 1999, with the election of Francisco Flores, local and national elections in March 2000 reflected the ascendance of the FMLN. For the first time, the leftist party won the largest single block in the legislative assembly, gaining 31 seats compared to ARENA's 29 out of 84. The FMLN won mayoral elections in 78 of 262 municipalities, primarily in the larger towns; it now governs over 65% of the population. The popular Hector Silva, a 'new left' moderate, was reelected mayor of San Salvador.

Flores, the young US-educated president, campaigned as a centrist, but he appears to have swung to the right since taking office and has remained unresponsive to the press. A Sai Baba disciple, he has peppered his speeches with quotes from the guru, though he was pressured into professing Catholic beliefs toward the end of the political campaign. The next presidential elections are scheduled for 2004.

GEOGRAPHY
El Salvador is the smallest country in Central America, with a total area of 20,688 sq km (about the size of the US state of Massachusetts). It is bordered by Guatemala to the west, Honduras to the north and east, and the Pacific Ocean to the south.

More than 25 extinct volcanoes dot the country, the largest being Santa Ana, San Vicente, San Miguel and Cerro Verde.

CLIMATE
The wet season *(invierno)* is from May to October, and the dry season *(verano)* is from November to April.

In San Salvador, the maximum temperature varies from 30°C in November to 34°C in March and April; the minimum nighttime temperatures range from 16°C in January and February to 20°C in March. The coastal lowlands are the hottest region. San Salvador, at a medium elevation (680m above sea level), has a moderate climate compared to the other parts of the country, but you'll sweat all the same.

ECOLOGY & ENVIRONMENT
With the highest level of environmental damage in the Americas, El Salvador runs the risk of losing its beauty. Six percent of the country is forest or woodland, only 2% of that original growth. High population density remains the principal obstacle to the regeneration of ecosystems.

The Río Lempa, an important watershed, suffers from pollution, as do many other rivers and lakes. Uncontrolled vehicle emissions will test your respiratory functions in any metropolitan area. The most visible problem is trash. A circle of soaring vultures usually indicates where a new load of trash has been dumped by the side of the road.

Industrial development and construction of hotels are current threats to the environment. A national environmental law was enacted in 1998 requiring industries to implement cleaner technologies, but until certain key regulations are approved by the president, it remains inoperative.

Private organizations protect such areas as Bosque El Imposible in Ahuachapán and La Montañona in Chalatenango. They also establish reforestation campaigns and sponsor clean drinking-water projects. If you'd like to get involved contact SalvaNatura (see Tourist Offices in the San Salvador section, later in this chapter), UNES (☎ 260 1736), or ASACMA (Salvadoran Association for Conservation of the Environment; ☎ 263 7279, asacma@yahoo.com).

Hurricane Mitch whipped El Salvador in 1998. Though its effects were not as catastrophic as in neighboring Honduras and Nicaragua, Mitch did leave over 200 Salvadorans dead and 70,000 homeless. Damages were most acute in the lower Río Lempa region.

FLORA & FAUNA
With so much of the land cultivated, few of the original plants still exist. Small stands of balsam trees survive along the Costa del Bálsamo, and mangroves line the many estuaries. Bosque Montecristo and El

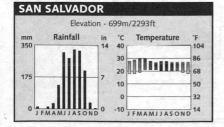

SAN SALVADOR
Elevation - 699m/2293ft

Imposible harbor the greatest variety of indigenous plants in their small areas, and Cerro Verde has a good variety of vegetation. Plants in these areas include mountain pine, fig, maguey and ferns.

Around the Bosque Montecristo, there are quetzals, toucans, white-tailed deer and a couple of species of monkey. In the coastal areas, herons, kingfishers, brown pelicans, egrets, parakeets and sandpipers can all be spotted. Around 400 species of bird exist throughout the country. Butterflies of all colors and sizes frolic everywhere at all elevations.

In all, about 90 species are in danger of extinction. Endangered animals include marine turtles and armadillos.

Parks & Protected Areas

El Salvador has only four official national parks, but you can visit a number of locally or privately administered reserves, some of which are detailed below.

Parque Nacional Montecristo–El Trifinio is a cloud forest reserve in the northern mountains, where the borders of El Salvador, Honduras and Guatemala converge. Giant ferns, orchids and bromeliads are in abundance. The park is only open half the year to humans, to leave the animals in peace during their breeding season. Permits are required.

Parque Nacional El Imposible, near El Salvador's western limit, harbors one of the last remnants of original tropical forest, as well as numerous endangered plant and animal species. Though the park is still largely inaccessible, sections are open to visitors.

Parque Nacional Cerro Verde is a beautiful expanse of forest within the crater of an extinct volcano. Amazing views of nearby Izalco and Santa Ana Volcanoes can be enjoyed from lookout points inside the park, and both volcanoes are near the park.

Parque Nacional Walter T Deininger consists of dry tropical forest on the Pacific Coast, near La Libertad port. It is the habitat for 87 bird species and numerous endangered mammals.

Cerro El Pital, El Salvador's tallest peak, is near La Palma. Torogoz (motmots) and quetzals can be observed on its piney slopes.

Barra de Santiago is a remote bar of mangrove-fringed estuaries and beaches on the Pacific Coast west of Acajutla.

Laguna de Alegría is an emerald green lake fed by hot springs, in the crater of the dormant Volcán

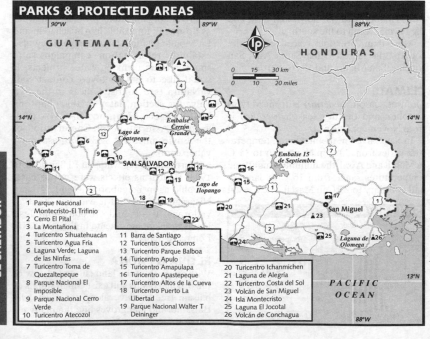

PARKS & PROTECTED AREAS

1 Parque Nacional Montecristo-El Trifinio
2 Cerro El Pital
3 La Montañona
4 Turicentro Sihuatehuacán
5 Turicentro Agua Fría
6 Laguna Verde; Laguna de las Ninfas
7 Turicentro Toma de Quezaltepeque
8 Parque Nacional El Imposible
9 Parque Nacional Cerro Verde
10 Turicentro Atecozol
11 Barra de Santiago
12 Turicentro Los Chorros
13 Turicentro Parque Balboa
14 Turicentro Apulo
15 Turicentro Amapulapa
16 Turicentro Apastepeque
17 Turicentro Altos de la Cueva
18 Turicentro Puerto La Libertad
19 Parque Nacional Walter T Deininger
20 Turicentro Ichanmichen
21 Laguna de Alegría
22 Turicentro Costa del Sol
23 Volcán de San Miguel
24 Isla Montecristo
25 Laguna El Jocotal
26 Volcán de Conchagua

de Tecapa, in Usulután Department. Agoutis, ocelotes and coatis are among wildlife inhabiting primary growth forest surrounding the lake.

Laguna El Jocotal, off Carretera del Litoral east of Usulután, is an important sanctuary for migratory birds from October to March.

Turicentros

The Instituto Salvadoreño de Turismo (ISTU) created 14 of these recreational complexes from the late 1950s to the 1970s, the majority near lakes and natural springs or in forests. Most have swimming pools. Cabins hold little more than a picnic table and chairs, often painted in primary colors. As turicentros are all close to a main town, they are crowded on weekends. The price is the same for all: US$0.80 to get in, US$0.70 to park, US$4 to use a cabin (not for overnighting). All are open 8 am to 4 pm. Only Los Chorros is worth a trip in itself; the rest are good for relaxing during the week.

ISTU runs Sunday excursions to most turicentros for a minimal fee, departing at 7:30 am from Plaza Barrios in front of the cathedral in San Salvador. Call for the current destinations (see Tourist Offices in the San Salvador section, later in this chapter).

GOVERNMENT & POLITICS

El Salvador's government has three divisions. Executive power is held by a president, elected by popular vote to a five-year term. Legislative power is vested in the National Assembly, with 84 members elected to a three-year term. The 13-member Supreme Court is elected by the National Assembly. The country is divided into 14 departments.

Francisco Flores, of the right-wing Nationalist Republican Alliance (ARENA) party, was elected president in 1999. In addition to ARENA, the Farabundo Martí National Liberation Front (FMLN), the Christian Democratic Party (PDC), the Center Democratic Union (CDU), the National Conciliation Party (PCN) and the National Action Party (PAN) all hold seats in the National Assembly.

ECONOMY

El Salvador has one of the stronger economies in Central America and has maintained an average growth rate of 4% to 5% a year since 1990. However, it is estimated that only 2% of the population could be described as upper class, with the relatively new middle class (mostly in the towns) accounting for another 20%. Almost half the population is considered poor. Unemployment is 8%, but underemployment is at 30%, and an estimated one-third of Salvadorans make a living off the so-called informal economy, without any benefits or job security.

Exports in 1999 were marginally deterred by rough global market conditions caused by the Asian crisis, but total exports stood at US$2.4 billion and have grown 300% in the past decade. Leading exports include coffee, sugar, textiles and people. Over one million Salvadorans living in the US sent close to US$1.4 billion in dollar transfers to relatives in El Salvador in 1999, making them the country's top foreign exchange earner. In 1999 the maquila industry, in which foreign-owned factories use cheap local labor to make export products, grew by 11% over the previous year. While such industry creates jobs, the minimum wage for maquila workers is still US$125 per month, well below the US$500 deemed necessary for a family of five to survive.

POPULATION & PEOPLE

The population, as of 2000, is 6,123,515. Of that 90% are mestizo (a mixture of Spanish and indigenous), 1% indigenous and 9% of European ancestry. At the current estimated growth rate of 1.9%, El Salvador's numbers will swell almost half again by 2025.

Women fought alongside guerrillas during the war, and when it ended, many refused to reintegrate into the old ways. Women have made inroads into politics and business.

Over a third of the population is under 15; and a third of those work to bring money to the family. The elderly are in no better shape: A third of the country's senior citizens live in extreme poverty. And malnutrition affects all: A 1999 United Nations Development Project report showed 19.5% of the population don't get the required caloric intake.

EDUCATION

Education is free through the ninth grade, but nearly a fifth of school-age children do not attend classes. An estimated 25% of Salvadoran adults are illiterate.

Universidad de El Salvador and the Jesuit Universidad Centroamericana José Simeón Cañas (UCA), in San Salvador, are the main universities.

ARTS

The village of La Palma in the department of Chalatenango has become famous for a school of art started by Fernando Llort, who also maintains his own gallery, El Arbol de Dios, in San Salvador.

Poetry is very popular in El Salvador; the movement first took its inspiration from the Nicaraguan Rubén Darío. Roque Dalton is an iconoclastic poet whose political agenda led to his exile. His *Taberna y Otros Lugares* (1969) has been cited as a mature expression of his political vision through verse. The work of Claudia Lars, El Salvador's foremost female poet, has been praised for its bold eroticism.

Salvador Efraín Salazar Arrué, writing under the pen name of Salarrué, is one of El Salvador's most famous writers. His *Cuentos de Barro* (Tales of Mud), published in 1933, is said to mark the beginning of the modern Central American short-story genre.

SOCIETY & CONDUCT

El Salvador's indigenous traditions are not as openly expressed as in other Central American countries, due to the legacy of repression against its indigenous inhabitants. Though pockets of indigenous peoples do survive in isolated villages, don't expect friendly locals dressed in colorful robes posing for photos. On the other hand, Salvadorans do welcome visitors and lack the sort of cynicism toward foreigners found in more visited areas. You're more likely to be associated with relief organizations than with package tour groups and may be treated more respectfully than elsewhere. In addition, Salvadorans are remarkably conversant on all kinds of subjects. If you start a conversation, it is likely to go on for a while.

Recent years have seen a broadening in the kind of political discussion that is tolerated, though it is wise to tread delicately in a place where views are so strongly held. Stay gracious and relaxed, and the charms of the people will win you over. The pace is slow,

and you'll be expected to follow that rhythm.

RELIGION

El Salvador is predominantly Roman Catholic. However, during the war the government targeted the Catholic Church for its 'communist' tendency to sympathize with the poor. Many fled the religion, either fearing for their lives or unhappy with the Church's affiliation with the opposition. Protestantism, especially Evangelism, offered a welcome alternative, and between 1976 and 1985, individuals registered in Assemblies of God increased from 65,000 to 200,000 (150%). Recent polls by the UCA show one-fifth of the population claim Evangelism as their affiliation.

LANGUAGE

Spanish is the national language. Only in a few indigenous villages do people still speak the Nahua language of the Pipil, but there is some academic interest in preserving it. Many Salvadorans have picked up some English working in the USA, Australia and elsewhere, and English speakers pop up in the unlikeliest places.

Facts for the Visitor

THE BEST & WORST

Hands down, the best of El Salvador is its people. Most locals you meet will be friendly and helpful. Many people, after they know you, will tell of their experiences during the war and their opinions about the country's state of affairs. Children are polite, curious and quick with a smile.

Another plus is El Salvador's unpopularity: With so few visitors, there is virtually no competition for services. Other highlights are the volcanoes (climbing them or just admiring them), the sobering memorial in El Mozote, misty mornings in La Palma, the mangroves and beaches around Isla Montecristo, cheap lobsters and an ice-cold Pilsener.

Things that could make you weary fast are the trash dumps and circling buzzards overhead, thick exhaust from buses careening through city streets, loud TVs and radios, guard dogs that take their job too seriously and guns everywhere.

PLANNING

Refer to Useful Organizations, later in this section, for places that can line up volunteer work; Language Courses in the San Salvador section to sign up for classes and homestays; Accommodations, later in this section, for information on *centros obreros*, were you can stay free; and Tourist Offices in the San Salvador section for visiting Parque Nacional El Imposible.

When to Go

The dry season is an easier time to go: Roads are in better condition; Bosque Montecristo is open; you won't get drenched every evening; and more cultural festivals take place. In the rainy season, however, prices are lower, beaches less crowded and the evenings slightly cooler after the storms.

Maps

Corsatur (see Tourist Offices) hands out small maps of El Salvador and the capital. You can find a more user-friendly map for US$3 at the Instituto Geográfico Nacional (IGN) in the Centro Nacional de Registros building at 1a Calle Poniente and 43a Avenida Norte (behind Metrosur) in San Salvador, open 8 am to 12:30 pm, 2 to 5 pm weekdays. Regional topo maps (1:25,000 and 1:50,000) of the country are also available from IGN for US$5.75. Maps of other cities and regions are hard to find outside San Salvador.

What to Bring

Take clothes that dry fast (rayon, woven cotton, polyester) and allow your skin to breathe. A mosquito net and a bedsheet are musts if you plan on staying at centros obreros or along the coast. During the rainy season, take a poncho and sandals that dry fast. Some travelers like to take incense to cover up the smelly bathroom fumes. A water bottle is handy.

TOURIST OFFICES

El Salvador's nascent tourism industry is handled by two offices, the Corporación Salvadoreña de Turismo (Corsatur) and the Instituto Salvadoreño de Turismo (ISTU). Corsatur, which is privately run, serves international visitors; government-run ISTU looks after Salvadorans. ISTU is responsible for the development and maintenance of the turicentros (see Parks & Protected Areas, earlier in this chapter) and some national parks. In fact, ISTU is more useful for practical travel information such as bus routes and local festivals, which seems outside Corsatur's purview.

No tourist offices exist outside the capital. However, the Casa de Cultura in most towns can often provide useful information; alternatively, some *alcaldías* (city halls) maintain an information office.

VISAS & DOCUMENTS

Citizens of the USA, Canada, Australia and New Zealand don't need a visa, but must buy a US$10 tourist card (payable in US dollars or colones) upon entering the country. You can request up to 90 days in the country, though the length of your stay is at the discretion of the immigration official. Each time you enter, you must buy another card, even if your reentry is within your allotted time. Citizens of the UK, Germany, the Netherlands, France and Japan need only present a valid passport.

No vaccinations are required unless you are coming from an area infected by yellow fever (some are recommended, however; see Health, later in this section).

CUSTOMS

As in most Central American countries, you can expect less investigation at the airport than if you arrive overland, since people arriving by plane are presumed to have money.

Importation of fruit, vegetables and plant and animal products is restricted, and questionable articles may be confiscated or fumigated. You can bring in three cartons of cigarettes, or 1kg of tobacco, and two bottles of liquor.

MONEY
Currency

In January 2001, El Salvador changed its official currency to the US dollar, although the old currency, the colón, is still in circulation and still may be used. The colón is exchanged at a fixed rate of 8.75 colones to the US dollar and all banking transactions are in dollars. There are 100 centavos in a colón.

Coins are of one colón (¢1) and five, 10, 25 and 50 centavos value. Notes are in denominations of ¢5, ¢10, ¢25, ¢50, ¢100 and ¢200.

Exchange Rates

As of early 2001 exchange rates were as follows:

country	unit		colones
Australia	A$1	=	¢4.86
Canada	C$1	=	¢5.80
Euro	€1	=	¢8.19
France	FF1	=	¢1.25
Germany	DM1	=	¢4.19
New Zealand	NZ$1	=	¢3.86
UK	UK£1	=	¢12.99
USA	US$1	=	¢8.75

Exchanging Money

US dollars are the only currency that you can be sure of always exchanging. Change any extra colones before you leave El Salvador; you may have to resort to the black market.

Few banks exchange traveler's checks readily and easily, and policy is often decided by the individual branch rather than the bank. One exception is Banco Cuscatlán, all of whose branches exchange traveler's checks. You are normally required to show both a passport and receipts for the checks in order to compare signatures (which, of course, you are supposed to keep *separate* from the checks).

Credit Cards & ATMs

Any Credomatic bank can give you a cash advance on a Visa or MasterCard but beware of finance charges. Credomatic branches are found in shopping malls in San Salvador, Santa Ana, San Miguel, Sonsonate and Ahuachapán.

ATMs can be found in banks, shopping malls and the international airport. These only function with cards on the Plus network.

Costs

Accommodations and food are more expensive than in neighboring countries, but bus transportation is cheap, both in cities and long distance. Be prepared to pay admission to archaeological sites and national parks.

Taxes & Tipping

A value-added tax (IVA) of 13% should apply on all goods and services in El Salvador; make sure you know whether this is already included in prices or will be added later. You will mainly find that it is already included, or not charged, except in more expensive hotels, where it is added to your final bill.

A 10% *propina* (tip) is added to the check in pricier restaurants. Elsewhere you should leave the equivalent.

POST & COMMUNICATIONS

There are three rates for sending mail: surface, airmail and express mail. Letters sent by airmail to the USA should arrive in 10 days (US$0.50), to Europe and Australia in up to 15 days (US$0.65). Letters sent by express mail to the USA should take five days (US$1), to Europe and Australia 10 days (US$1.20).

General delivery mail should be addressed to Correos de El Salvador, Centro de Gobierno, Lista de Correos, San Salvador, El Salvador. Mail will be held for five weeks.

The country code when calling El Salvador from abroad is 503. There are no internal area codes.

You can surf the Web or send and receive email at cybercafes in El Salvador's three biggest towns.

INTERNET RESOURCES

The following Web sites may be useful in planning a trip to El Salvador.

The El Salvador Web and Internet Guide (www.search-beat.com/ elsalvador.htm) and Lanic (www.lanic.utexas.edu/la/ca/salvador) contain comprehensive lists of Salvadoran sites, arranged by topic. The former Web site includes a search engine. Corsatur's Web site (www.elsalvadorturismo.gob.sv/) is theoretically helpful but takes a very long time to load.

Punta Mango (www.puntamango.com.sv), the Web site of Mango's Lounge surf shop in La Libertad, tells you where to find the best waves in El Salvador. SalvaNatura's site (www.salvanatura.org/) describes the NGO's conservation efforts in Parque Nacional El Imposible. You can check El Salvador's daily news at La Prensa Gráfica's site (www.laprensa.com.sv/).

¿Aló?

Since Antel, the national telephone company was purchased by French Telecom and private competition opened up, callers now have a bewildering array of options. Chip card phones have been installed in all the larger towns and in many smaller ones. Three competing companies each have their own card, which can only be used in its corresponding phone. Yellow Publitel phones (Telecom) are the most widely available, but green Telefónica phones are also seen in many places. Publitel cards, available at Telecom offices and many stores, are in denominations of 25 and 75 colones, while Telefónica offers a wider range of options. A third company, Comunitel, has its own phones and phone cards. It is the least commonly seen type of phone, but often pops up in out-of-the-way places. Some Salvadorans collect 'em all, carrying three different cards to be prepared to make a call from any public phone.

To use a Telecom or Telefónica phone, simply insert the card into the slot; a window displays the quantity of the card and the time remaining. Comunitel phones are accessed in one of two ways: by passing the card through a scanner or by first dialing a code that is revealed by scratching the back of the card. Though less convenient, it's slightly cheaper than the other cards. Each of these types of phones requires a different access code for international calls; the code is posted beside the phone.

Another kind of phone, Multitel, is coin operated.

At Telecom offices – new plastic signs have been placed in front of the old Antel buildings but people still refer to them as Antel – you can make operator-assisted calls, use card phones where they've been installed, or send faxes. Larger towns also now have a Telepunto office, the Telefónica equivalent. These are similar to the Telecom offices but instead of having an operator connect you, you purchase a card with a scratch-off code, input the code and dial your call direct. All this competition can translate into some good deals – Telefónica was offering weekend rates of US$0.12 a minute on calls to the USA at the time of writing.

BOOKS & FILMS

If you plan on staying any length of time in El Salvador, find a copy of *On Your Own in El Salvador,* by Jeff Brauer, Julian Smith and Veronica Wiles, a very informative travel guide to the country, with maps of many towns. Another good read and is *Salvador,* by Joan Didion.

Witness to War: An American Doctor in El Salvador, by Charles Clements, MD, is the personal story of a Quaker American doctor who worked in the war zone of Chalatenango in 1982 and 1983. It has become a classic, and a film was made from the book. *Oscar Romero: Memories in Mosaic,* by María López Vigil, is a recommended account of the clergyman's life and political conversion told by those who knew him. *When the Dogs Ate Candles,* by Bill Hutchinson, is an anecdotal history of the conflict based on interviews with refugees.

See the films *Romero,* produced by Ellwood Kieser in 1988, and *Salvador,* directed by Oliver Stone, for Hollywood's insights into the civil war.

NEWSPAPERS & MAGAZINES

San Salvador's main newspapers are *La Prensa Gráfica* and the conservative *El Diario de Hoy;* check them for entertainment listings. *El Mundo* and *El Latino* are thinner afternoon papers. *Más,* another afternoon paper, caters to the Salvadoran masses, with heavy coverage of crime and sports. *Revue,* a free English-language magazine based in Guatemala, includes an El Salvador section with articles on lesser-known destinations. It's available at many of the guesthouses and restaurants mentioned in the San Salvador section.

TOILETS

Private bathrooms in cheap hotels permit you to sit on the toilet and shower at the same time. Off the beaten track, dry composting latrines are commonly used, especially where relief work has been done.

EL SALVADOR

Texaco and Esso stations generally have clean facilities with toilet paper. Throw paper in the wastebasket instead of the toilet.

HEALTH

Recommended immunizations include hepatitis A. Take a course of malaria pills if you'll be heading off the beaten track. Take along mosquito *(zancudos)* repellent or a mosquito net.

Your safest bet for staying healthy is watching what you eat. Eating food from street vendors is risky. Hep A and cholera outbreaks spread like wildfire in the cities.

Don't drink the tap water and always make sure ice or any juices are made with purified water *(agua purificada)* or *agua cristal* – a brand of bottled water.

WOMEN TRAVELERS

Foreign women may be approached more often than at home, but such behavior is generally harmless. Although traveling alone here presents a challenge, solo women are unlikely to encounter any dangerous situations if they take ordinary precautions. Ignore the hissing sounds – to acknowledge them is to ask for more unwanted attention.

Follow the example of women around you and dress moderately and conservatively. Pack skirts and T-shirts rather than dresses, to allow access to your money pouch. Don't go out at night unless escorted or in large groups, and then only to safe, well-lit areas.

GAY & LESBIAN TRAVELERS

Little tolerance is given to openly gay men or women. Two women traveling together will not be as scrutinized as two men, but in either case, avoid public displays of affection. In San Salvador, the area around Blvd de los Héroes has cultural centers and clubs that, being more bohemian, are also more tolerant. Entre Amigos (☎ 225 4213) offers a support network for gay men.

USEFUL ORGANIZATIONS

Centro de Intercambio y Solidaridad (CIS; ☎ 226 2623, cis@netcomsa.com), Blvd Universitario 4 in San Salvador, manages logistics for educational and political groups, but they can also put individuals in touch with NGOs and set up volunteer opportunities in human rights work, health care and education. CIS also organizes trips to repopulated communities and indigenous villages. It runs a Spanish-language school and an English school (volunteer English teachers receive scholarships to study Spanish) as well as a crafts shop.

Dozens of political and cultural groups flourish in San Salvador. Contact these groups for information about the following subjects or CIS can make arrangements:

Development
FUNDE (National Foundation for Development; ☎ 264 4938) or Ciudanía y Desarrollo (☎ 274 7339, ciudania.desarrollo@salnet.net)

Human Rights
Tutela Legal (☎ 226 2085)

Repopulated Communities
Fundación Segundo Montes (☎ 226 3717)

Women's Rights
MAM (Mélida Anaya Montes Women's Movement; ☎ 225 6864)

DANGERS & ANNOYANCES

El Salvador has the unfortunate reputation of being a violent country. It has suffered not only a chaotic civil war but all the problems that plague post-war countries. The military presence has been replaced by a civilian police force that is too small and too young to deal with the country's immediate problems. Unemployment, severe poverty and US gang culture contribute to the high crime rate, which in turn engenders a siege mentality and the proliferation of firearms.

Despite all that, violent crime is a pretty rare occurrence among travelers. After dark, streets in the larger cities and some beach communities are deserted and exude a tangible sense of menace, though the danger is probably more from rifle-toting security guards and attack dogs than from actual criminals. Certain volcano trails have a reputation for crime, so ask locals about the current situation. Some forest reserves provide security to accompany you on the riskier hikes.

The main problem for travelers is petty theft. Tourists are an easy target, so carry as little as possible during day trips. Some locals will advise against taking public buses, but as long as you do so during daylight and keep one eye open, all should be OK.

EMERGENCIES
For emergencies, dial ☎ 121 from anywhere in the country.

BUSINESS HOURS
Businesses generally operate 9 am to 6 pm weekdays, while government offices have an 8 am to 4 pm schedule. Some offices close at lunchtime, between noon and 2 pm, but this practice is fading. Banks are open 8 am to 5 pm weekdays; most are open Saturday morning as well. Restaurants serve dinner early, and 4 pm is the *pupusa* hour (see Food, later in this section).

PUBLIC HOLIDAYS & SPECIAL EVENTS
The festival day of El Salvador del Mundo, patron of the country, is August 6. Celebrations are held in San Salvador on this day and the previous week. Other celebrations are held during Semana Santa (Holy Week) and on December 12, the day of the Virgen de Guadalupe. Each city, village and town has a festival for its patron saint during the year.

Public holidays are as follows:

New Year's Day	January 1
Semana Santa	Holy Thursday to Easter Sunday
Labor Day	May 1
Mother's Day	May 10
Festival of El Salvador del Mundo	August 1 to 5
Independence Day	September 15
Día de la Raza (Columbus Day)	October 12
All Souls' Day	November 2
Christmas	December 25 to 31

ACTIVITIES
Diving
Schools of jack and angelfish, eagle mantas, green turtles and other marine life can be observed diving in the coastal waters of western El Salvador; the best time for diving is October to February. Another popular pastime is crater diving in Lago Ilopango and Lago de Coatepeque, where unusual volcanic rock formations make up a different kind of underwater environment. Both Oceanica Diving School (☎ 263 6931, oceanica@ salnet.net) and Salvador Tours (☎ 264 3110, fax 263 6687, saltours@es.com.sv) offer PADI-approved instruction, charging US$300 for a basic diving course, and lead crater dives, day or night.

Surfing
El Salvador is regarded as a new frontier by surfers attracted by its varied breaks, including the much-sought-after 'hollow waves.' Punta Roca, considered the country's finest wave, is at the port of La Libertad, easily accessible from the capital, while La Bocana and El Sunzal, west of there, are renowned for their left waves. The eastern coast from Playa El Cuco to El Tamarindo is also considered pristine territory. The peak season is March to December. Punta Mango (☎ 264 3110, fax 263 6687, info@puntamango.com.sv) conducts surf tours and offers surfing classes.

ACCOMMODATIONS
You get what you pay for. If you want to spend only US$6 a night, your lodging will be near a bus terminal, and the rooms may be rented out by the hour more often than by the night. You pay more for security and the ability to leave after dark. *Casas de húespedes,* homes turned into guesthouses, are an attractive option in the capital. Recently, *hostales rurales* (rural hostels) have opened around western El Salvador. These are simple, well-maintained and reasonably priced houses that usually include breakfast in the price.

Double rooms have two beds, usually a double and single, and coastal establishments may have a hammock where an additional person could sleep.

The best deal is at government workers' centers *(centros de obreros)*, where you can stay free of charge, but there are only four – at Lago de Coatepeque, El Tamarindo, La Palma and just outside La Libertad. These large compounds are developed for government workers to catch up on their R&R and to house school groups on the weekends, but they are virtually empty during the week. You can stay at any as long as you

EL SALVADOR

Queso, Frijoles, Revuelta...

Ask anyone where to get the best pupusas and a heated discussion will no doubt ensue. Pupusas are simple and filling – a cornmeal mass stuffed with farmer's cheese, refried beans (or a mixture of both), chicharrón (fried pork fat), or all three *(revuelta)*. Ordering just one or two will elicit a look of shock from the woman making the pupusas. Surely you would need more than that, and more often than not, even if you order two, a couple more will appear on your plate. The big jar of salad on the table is called *curtido* – a mixture of pickled cabbage, beets and carrots. Drop some of that on the pupusas with a bit of hot sauce, and you've got a meal. While most are made of corn, pupusas made with rice flour, Olocuilta style (after their village of origin), are highly acclaimed and worth checking out. The texture is lighter and a bit crispier.

like, subject to availability, but to do so you must get written permission from the Ministerio de Trabajo (see Tourist Offices in the San Salvador section, later in this chapter). Sheets are not normally provided, so take some along.

FOOD
Eating a big breakfast and lunch is the cheapest way to get through the day, as dinner in restaurants can be overpriced. Eggs, *casamiento* (rice and beans mixed together), fried plantains, a couple of tortillas and coffee get the day going. Or head for a *panadería* for a decent selection of morning cakes and coffee.

Almuerzo (lunch) is the largest meal of the day. Every town has restaurants with *comida a la vista*, a cafeteria/buffet setup. This is a saving grace for the Spanish-impaired, since you get to see the items before choosing. Usually available are meat, chicken and vegetable dishes, as well as several salads, rice and tortillas. From 4 pm till about 9 or 10 pm is *pupusa* time (see the boxed text 'Queso, Frijoles, Revuelta…').

Also popular in the evening are *panes,* French breads sliced open and stuffed with chicken or turkey *(chumpipe),* salsa, salad

and pickled vegetables. Pizza and fried chicken joints are found everywhere.

DRINKS
Licuados (fruit drinks), coffee and *gaseosas* (soft drinks) are easily had. A great refresher is *agua de jamaica,* a sweet red iced tea made from flowers. A common pupusa chaser is *horchata de cebada,* a sweet barley-based beverage spiced with cinnamon. An *ensalada* is a mixed fruit juice served with a spoon for the fruit salad floating on top, sangria style.

Local beers include Pilsener, the most popular, and Suprema, a lighter brew. In some places, you get free *bocas* (little appetizers) with your Pilsener. Guinness is also widely available. *Aguardiente,* firewater made from sugarcane, is very strong but low quality; Tres Puentes and Torito are some of the brand names.

SHOPPING
El Salvador's crafts are not as varied as those of Guatemala or Honduras, but high-quality work is available. Hammocks are beautiful and well made. Wooden boxes and knickknacks painted with designs inspired by the art of Fernando Llort are produced in La Palma. The village of Guatajiagua in Morazán Department produces unique black pottery, and Ilobasco is known for its *sorpresas,* intricate scenes encased in ceramic shells. All of these can be purchased

Típica or Pícara?

Sorpresas (surprises) are tiny, detailed scenes and figures in little oval shells about the size of a walnut. The outside may be designed as a walnut, egg, apple, orange or anything round. Open one up to view the *'típica'* (traditional), a delightful little scene of daily life around a village. An artist in Ilobasco got smart and added a new dimension to the surprise: a naked couple in the throes of sexual passion (or at least in that position). Even though the priest in town condemns the making of these and at one point made the stores remove their heathen goods, the *'pícara'* (sinful) sorpresas still sell, albeit tightly wrapped in paper.

at San Salvador's Mercado de Artesanías or more cheaply in the towns where they're produced.

Organic mountain-grown coffee is sold at the crafts markets; Pipil is a good brand.

Getting There & Away

AIR
El Salvador's international airport is at Comalapa, 44km south of San Salvador. There's a US$25 departure tax to fly out of the airport payable in colones or US dollars.

TACA (☎ 267 8222, 800-535 8780 in the USA), the national airline, has daily flights to/from Los Angeles, New York, Miami, Houston, Toronto and San Francisco. US carriers provide daily service to and from Miami (United), Los Angeles, (Continental), Houston (American) and Atlanta (Delta). See the San Salvador Getting There & Away section for airline office locations. The cost of flights from New York, Los Angeles or San Francisco range from US$450 to US$600 depending on the season. From Miami expect to pay US$350 to US$550.

Grupo TACA, comprised of four Central American carriers, has daily flights to and from all the other Central American capitals. No-frills one-way fares are in the US$125 to US$250 range. See Air Passes in the Getting Around chapter for information on discount Visit Central America passes.

LAND
Car & Motorcycle
If you drive into El Salvador, you must show a driver's license (an international driving permit is accepted) and proof that you own the car. You must also fill out extensive forms. Car insurance is available and advisable but not required. Vehicles may remain in El Salvador for 30 days. Those travelers wishing to stay longer should leave the country and drive back in rather than attempt to deal with the Transport Ministry.

Border Crossings
Border crossings to Guatemala are La Hachadura, Las Chinamas, San Cristóbal

and Anguiatú. The main border crossings to Honduras are El Amatillo and El Poy. There is a crossing at Sabanetas, north of Perquín, but the actual borderline is still in dispute.

Avoid arriving late in the afternoon, especially if crossing on national buses. Visitors of some nationalities must buy a tourist card (see Visas & Documents in the Facts for the Visitor section, earlier in this chapter). Though not required, small payments to those offering to help you through will make for a more expedient crossing. Border crossings are open between 4 am and 8 to 10 pm.

Guatemala
In San Salvador, buses to and from Guatemala operate from two terminals and various hotels. International bus services can also be picked up in Santa Ana; see that section, later in this chapter, for details.

Terminal Puerto Bus TACA, La Vencedora, Melva, Galgos and Pezzarossi bus lines all share the route to Guatemala City, departing hourly from 4:30 am to 4:30 pm daily (US$8, five hours). Deluxe King Quality buses, featuring air-con, movies and an attendant, also use this terminal; departures are at 5:45 am and 2:45 pm (US$23.50/41 one-way/roundtrip). Terminal Puerto Bus (☎ 222 2158) is on Alameda Juan Pablo II at 19a Avenida Norte. Take city buses 29, 101D, 7C or 52.

Terminal de Occidente National bus route No 498 goes to the Guatemalan border at San Cristóbal (five departures daily) and No 200 goes to La Hachadura at 12:30 pm only. Both cost around US$1.25 one-way and take about three hours. To get to Las Chinamas, take bus No 202 to Ahuachapán and pick up a No 263 bus from there; to Anguiatú, take bus No 201 to Santa Ana and transfer to No 235A.

Hotel San Carlos Tica Buses leave for Guatemala City at 5:30 am (US$8/16, five hours). The hotel (☎ 222 4808) is on Calle Concepción between 10a and 12a Avenidas Norte.

Hotel San Salvador Marriott Pullmantur buses (☎ 243 1300) for Guatemala City leave at 8:30 am and 3 pm daily and take at least four hours (US$45 roundtrip). You can buy tickets at the hotel.

Centro Comercial Basilea King Quality buses (☎ 271 3330) leave for Guatemala City from this shopping center in the Zona Rosa at 6:30 am and 3:30 pm (US$23.50 one-way), stopping at the Terminal Puerto Bus. Comfort Lines makes the same journey, departing at 8 am and 2 pm (US$18.25). Take city bus No 30B.

Honduras
In San Salvador, buses to and from Honduras operate from two terminals. International buses can also be picked up in San Miguel; see that section, later in this chapter, for details.

Terminal Puerto Bus Air-conditioned King Quality buses leave every day for Tegucigalpa at 6 am (US$25.50, seven hours).

Terminal de Oriente Bus No 119 goes to El Poy (Honduras border) via La Palma (US$1.25, four hours), departing every half hour from the terminal. At the border, you can pick up a colectivo to Nueva Ocotepeque and continue by bus from there.

To go to El Amatillo, transfer in San Miguel. From San Salvador take bus No 301 to San Miguel (US$1.75, three hours) and then take No 330 to the border (US$0.50, two hours). After crossing the border, you can transfer directly onto a bus to Tegucigalpa or Choluteca.

Nicaragua, Costa Rica & Panama
A Tica Bus leaves the Hotel San Carlos at 5 am and arrives in Managua, Nicaragua, at 5 pm (US$25). If continuing on, spend the night and leave the following morning at 6 am. The bus arrives in San José, Costa Rica, at 3 pm (US$35). It then leaves at 10 pm for Panama (US$60), where you arrive at 4 pm the following day, making for a grand total of three days of bus travel.

SEA
Ask around at the Golfo de Fonseca for boat rides to Honduras and Nicaragua. Owners will be happy to comply for the right price.

Getting Around

BUS
Intercity buses are old American school buses adorned with vivid multicolored designs. Bus terminals are chaotic and dirty, and information is never posted. All stations have an office with someone who can usually point you to the right platform. Avoid getting information from the boys shooing you on to their buses, since they are more interested in getting passengers than providing accurate information. There are no ticket offices; purchase your ticket on the bus after you're seated.

Buses run frequently to points throughout the country and are very cheap (US$0.40 to US$3). Weekend fares increase up to 25%. Routes to some eastern destinations have different categories: *ordinario*, *especial* and *super especial*. The last two options cost more, but they get you where you want to go faster and more comfortably. The last bus of the day usually departs in time to reach its destination at or soon after dark.

Cross-country bus trips take patience. Anyone over 5 feet tall will wish for kneepads to soften the blows from the seat in front. If traveling with a backpack that takes up a seat, you'll be charged twice. This, however, is preferable to putting your pack on the roof.

CAR & MOTORCYCLE
Driving around the country allows you to see more in less time and offers opportunities to see small villages not serviced by buses, but navigating through areas where roads and turnoffs are not marked can be frustrating. Gas is not cheap either. A gallon of regular unleaded is about US$1.90.

Road Safety
Of the 10,000km of highway in the country, only 2000 are paved, and most of those are riddled with potholes. However, roadwork is going on constantly and more sections are well paved and marked than before – particularly San Salvador to Santa Ana and between San Miguel and Santa Rosa de Lima – and most major bridges that had been damaged in the war have been rebuilt.

During the rainy season, constant downpours damage roads and repairs aren't made until the weather clears.

Get in the habit of lightly honking, especially when passing or before turning a curve. Watch out for cows, dogs, chickens, children and oncoming traffic. Also watch for signals from other cars, usually a hand waving for you to pass them or for them to cut you off.

Police set up checkpoints, especially on roads to border crossings. Carjacking is a problem, as are parts stolen off parked cars. Don't drive alone in areas of ill repute and park in safe places. Car insurance is a good idea, but not required.

Rental

If you decide to drive around, rent a car in San Salvador. Avis (☎ 261 1212) and Budget (☎ 263 5583) have offices at the international airport and in town, but their prices are high (US$40 to US$50 a day). The price usually reflects unlimited mileage *(kilometraje libre)*.

Cheaper companies include Euro Rent-Cars (☎ 235 5232), at 7a Avenida Norte 1622 in Colonia Layco, with rates from US$26 per day (three-day minimum rental); Superior (☎ 222 9111), at 3a Calle Poniente and 15a Avenida Norte, with rates of US$29 a day, US$185 a week; and Inter (☎ 263 7499), Paseo Escalón 4357, with rates from US$35 a day, including insurance.

The cheapest rates, however, are for cars that will be unfit for some of the roads. Four-wheel drive (4WD) costs quite a bit more, from US$60 a day. Tropic (☎ 279 3235, tropic@es.com.sv), Avenida Olímpica 3597, rents out 4WD vehicles at competitive rates, especially when renting for longer periods. Corsatur has a list of other rental car companies.

ORGANIZED TOURS

Considering the rudimentary infrastructure of some of El Salvador's most appealing destinations, you might join a tour group at some point. A Pie El Salvador (El Salvador on Foot; ☎ 226 1600, afoot@sal.gbm.net) specializes in walks focusing on ecological, cultural and archaeological themes. Prices are US$17 to US$30 per person per day. SET Adventours (☎ 279 3235, set.adventours@salnet.net), Avenida

Olímpica 3597 in San Salvador, leads 4WD caravan expeditions combined with kayaking, rafting, mountain biking and other activities for around US$45 per day. Participants can either rent their own 4WD vehicle or join other drivers. Alligatours (☎ 262 0348, adventure@alligatour.com) coordinates one-day kayaking tours around the islands of the Estero de Jaltepeque and the aviary wonderland of Laguna de Jocotal (US$70 per person including transportation and lunch), and two- to five-day hiking trips through the western volcano chain and the northern war zones. Ximena's Guest House (see Places to Stay in the San Salvador section) offers a variety of informative group excursions, with English-speaking guides, to out-of-the-way destinations like Tacuba and Barra de Santiago.

San Salvador

pop 485,845 • metropolitan area 2,007,267
San Salvador is the largest city in El Salvador and the nation's principal crossroads. It takes only a few hours to get from the capital to any point in the country, so San Salvador makes a convenient base for travelers. Bus fumes, guns and poverty make it one of the least attractive Latin American capitals, but it is a mandatory stop for anyone obtaining park permits, arranging excursions or contacting NGOs. Aside from its logistical importance, the capital is the country's political, commercial and cultural center, and it has a few worthwhile attractions of its own.

The declining economy during the war set off an internal migration from the countryside to the city, which expanded with new urban poor. Over a quarter of the population of El Salvador inhabit the metropolitan area of the capital. Though San Salvador produces nearly 65% of the national GDP, unemployment is high and people do whatever they can to get by. Everywhere people are trying to sell things, from lottery tickets to armloads of T-shirts to Velcro gun holsters. Some districts, such as San Benito and Colonia Escalón are as luxurious as their counterparts in wealthier countries; other areas of the city are colonies of shacks made of corrugated tin

SAN SALVADOR

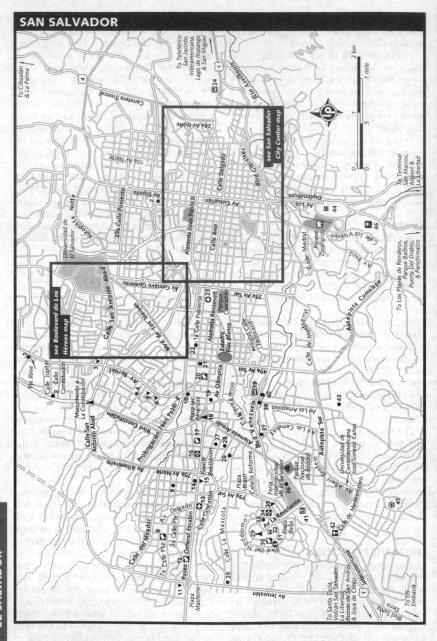

SAN SALVADOR

PLACES TO STAY
1 Hotelito Casa Antigua
2 Casa de Huespedes Maya
21 Hotel Occidental; Hotel Shadai
37 La Posada Guest House
38 Hotel Roma
40 Hotel Pasadena

PLACES TO EAT
3 Olocuilta No 3
4 Restaurant Hey!
5 Pupusería Nelly's
6 Pupusería Vista Hermosa
11 Kalapataru
15 Delicatessen Kreef; Cybermannia
35 La Panetiére; Mario's; Manías; Mango's

OTHER
7 Cuscatlán Escuela de Idiomas

8 Honduras Embassy
9 SalvaNatura Office
10 Yascuas; Milenio
12 British Embassy
13 Hospital de la Mujer
14 Budget Car Rental
16 Galerías Escalón; Café Internet Grupo Ejje; Grupo TACA; United Airlines
17 Nicaragua Embassy
18 El Salvador del Mundo Monument
19 American Airlines
20 Panama Embassy; Copa Airlines
22 Instituto Geográfico Nacional
23 Hospital Rosales
24 Terminal de Oriente
25 El Arbol de Dios
26 American Express/El Salvador Travel Service

27 SET Adventours; Tropic Car Rental
28 Ministerio de Trabajo
29 Monumento a la Revolución
30 Mexico Embassy
31 Corsatur
32 Hotel San Salvador Marriott (Pullmantur Buses)
33 Eutopia
34 Centro Comercial Basilea
36 Mercado Nacional de Artesanías
39 Terminal de Occidente
41 Museo Nacional de Antropología David J Guzmán
42 Iglesia La Ceiba de Guadalupe
43 Estadio Cuscatlán
44 Casa Presidencial
45 Jardín Botánico La Laguna
46 Parque Saburo Hirao; Museo de Historia Natural

and mud, balancing precariously on the edges of polluted rivers.

Despite San Salvador's long history, it has few historic buildings. The city has been destroyed several times – by earthquakes in 1854 and 1873, by the most recent eruption of Volcán San Salvador in 1917 and yet again by floods in 1934. The earthquake of October 10, 1986, also caused considerable damage, and the most recent on January 13, 2001, contributed its share (see the boxed text '2001 Earthquake'). After years of re-construction, the scaffolding is finally coming down on the elegant Palacio Nacio-nal; the central plaza has been given a face-lift; and the national cathedral has been completed. The national anthropology museum has reopened at last; its superb col-lection is essential viewing for those seeking a historical perspective.

Though the center is still a menacing place to be at night, the Blvd de los Héroes area shows signs of rebirth as a zone of pubs and cafes.

History

San Salvador was founded in 1525 by the Spanish conqueror Pedro de Alvarado, about 30km to the northeast of where it now stands, near Suchitoto. Three years later, it was moved to its present site. It was declared a city in 1546.

San Salvador was the capital of the colo-nial province of Cuscatlán. It was here, in 1811, that Father José Matías Delgado made the first call for the independence of Central America. From 1834 to 1839, San Salvador was the capital of the United Provinces of Central America. It has been the capital of El Salvador since 1839.

Orientation

San Salvador follows the same grid as most Central American cities. Unfortu-nately, signage is sparse in the central area, and someone forgot to repaint the names on the street curbs. From the zero point at the cathedral, Avenida España goes north and Avenida Cuscatlán south; Calle Arce runs to the west and Calle Delgado to the east.

Avenida España leads up to 29a Calle Poniente, which heads west to the Universi-dad de El Salvador at the intersection of Blvd de los Héroes and Calle San Antonio Abad. Avenida Cuscatlán crosses Blvd Ve-nezuela, which links the east and west bus terminals, and continues south to Parque Balboa and Puerta del Diablo, crossing the airport highway along the way.

From the city center, 1a Calle Poniente and Calle Rubén Darío, to the north and south of Arce respectively, are the main roads to the wealthier west.

EL SALVADOR

Information

Tourist Offices The office of Corsatur (☎ 243 7835, corsatur@salnet.net) is inconveniently located at Blvd del Hipódromo 508. No bus goes there, so you have to walk 1km uphill. It's open 8 am to 12:30 pm and 1:30 to 5:30 pm weekdays. Corsatur gives out maps, brochures on suggested itineraries and a glossy magazine containing some useful information. They also have an office at the international airport, open 10 am to 5:30 pm. The ISTU office (☎ 222 8000, istu@mh.gob.sv), 619 Calle Rubén Darío between 9a and 11a Avenidas Sur, is in the center of San Salvador. It is open 8:30 am to 12:30 pm and 1:10 to 4 pm Monday to Saturday.

To get permission to stay at one of the four government-run workers' vacation centers, take your passport to the Ministerio de Trabajo (☎ 298 8739), on Calle Nueva 2 just off Alameda Araujo. You can apply to stay at only one center at a time, but you can get around this by getting permission for two to stay at one place and having a travel buddy do the same for another place. The office is open 8 am to 12:30 pm and 1:10 to 4 pm weekdays.

For permission to visit Parque Nacional El Imposible, head to SalvaNatura (☎ 263 1111, salvanatura@saltel.net), 77a Avenida Norte 304.

Immigration Offices Visa renewal and other immigration matters are handled at the Oficina de Migración (☎ 222 5000) in the federal building in the Centro Gobierno, open 8 am to 12:30 pm and 1:30 to 4 pm weekdays.

Money Banco Cuscatlán, on Avenida Cuscatlán a block south of Plaza Barrios, exchanges traveler's checks, with a passport and receipt. Another branch is at Avenida Izalco and San Antonio Abad, next to Centro Comercial San Luis.

Several casas de cambio are along Alameda Juan Pablo II by Parque Infantil. You'll find black-market money changers in this area as well, but their rates for cash are no better than the casas, and rip-offs are a danger. Terminal Puerto Bus has a couple of casas de cambio.

For cash advances on Visa or MasterCard, Banco Credomatic, in Metrocentro and Centro Comercial San Luis, is the one. Don't forget to bring your passport.

Post & Communications The central post office, in the Centro Gobierno complex is open 7:30 am to 5 pm weekdays, 8 am to 12 pm Saturday. A smaller branch is in Metrocentro by the Blvd de los Héroes entrance. EMS, the post office's international courier service, has branches at both locations.

El Salvador Travel Service (☎ 279 3844), in Centro Comercial Mascota on Calle La Mascota, is an American Express agent that holds mail for card and check holders.

Telecom's main office is in the center, at the corner of Calle Rubén Darío and 5a Avenida Sur. Open 8 am to 5 pm daily, it sells cards for its bank of Publitel phones, from which you can make local or international calls. You can also make operator-assisted calls (more expensive) and send faxes here.

Metrocentro and Galerías Escalón have branches of Café Internet Grupo Ejje, open 9 am to 8 pm Monday to Saturday, 10 am to 6 pm Sunday. These state-of-the-art facilities are equipped with big-screen PCs and air-conditioning, but they charge a hefty US$5 an hour, US$3 a half hour. Both El Atico, on Calle San Antonio Abad near Avenida Santa Victoria, and Cybermannia, 3949 Paseo Escalón, are more reasonably priced, and the latter offers discounts for longer blocks of time.

Bookstores Eutopia, with a branch at Avenida La Capilla 258 in Colonia San Benito, stocks an excellent collection of English and Spanish fiction, including some used books. For English magazines, paperback bestsellers in English, and travel books (including Lonely Planet guidebooks), go to Bookmarks in Centro Comercial Basilea. CIS sells books published by Equipo Maíz, which specializes in Salvadoran history from a revolutionary perspective.

Laundry Lavapronto, on Calle Los Sisimiles, charges US$3.25 per load. It's open 7 am to 7 pm weekdays, 7 am to 5 pm Saturday.

Medical Services Hospital de Diagnóstico (☎ 226 5111), at Diagonal Dr Luis Vásquez

429, is considered the country's best hospital, though its services are relatively inexpensive. The US Embassy recommends Hospital de la Mujer (☎ 263 5111), on Calle Juan José Cañas between 81a and 83a Avenidas Sur.

Dangers & Annoyances Crime remains a problem, especially involving gangs and firearms. The central area, in particular, is considered unsafe for walking after 8 pm. More well-to-do districts tend to be deserted after dark, except for guards bearing assault weapons – definitely not conducive to strolling. If you're out late at night, spring for a taxi (buses stop running at 9 pm).

The biggest annoyance is pollution. Smoke emitted from buses is like oily air that gets into your eyes, nose and mouth. Sunglasses provide good protection from those nasty particles. A scarf is handy, too, for wiping off sweat and breathing into when you see smoke rising.

Crossing the street can be hazardous. Cars do not give pedestrians the right of way.

Things to See & Do

City Center A wander through central San Salvador can feel like a descent into the maelstrom, with crowds scurrying through sprawling markets, music blaring from every direction and buses zipping around at breakneck pace, engines roaring. But it's more interesting than the sterile suburbs, and long-term makeovers are finally bearing fruit.

Look for the dome of the **Catedral Metropolitana**, which marks the center of the city's street grid. Completed in 1999 after years of renovation, the cathedral stands on the site of an earlier version that burned in 1956. Flanked by a pair of bell towers, the façade of the beige building is decorated with the colorful *campesino* motifs of La Palma painter Fernando Llort. Underneath is Archbishop Oscar A Romero's tomb. Across the street is **Plaza Barrios**, dedicated to a former president and crusader for the separation of church and state. Sullen men gather around his statue beside a sea of green Telefónica phones. At the north end, a post is occupied by friendly civil police who are happy to orient you.

Headquarters of the government before the devastation of the 1986 earthquake, the

Guns for Sale

Visitors to El Salvador are likely to see more guns in a day than they may see all year back home. Posted in front of banks, hotels and ice cream shops are bored-looking men packing M16 rifles and 9mm pistols (currently, 18,000 security guards are employed in El Salvador). Nor is it uncommon to see a Glock 45 resting on the seat beside the driver of a pickup truck. The war is long over, but the idea that a gun is standard equipment remains in this security-obsessed country.

Around a million illegal guns are currently in circulation by some estimates. But the black market is only one source of firearms in El Salvador. Sharing shopping malls with clothing boutiques and video game rooms, gun shops often seem as ubiquitous as pupuserías in the capital. Men and women over the age of 17 can stride in and pick up a Berretta before breakfast. Gun shoppers must only present a couple of IDs and a clean police record.

ornate **Palacio Nacional** occupies the west side of the plaza. Built of Italian marble in the early 20th century, the Palacio displays the classical style fashionable at the time. Gardens occupy a central patio in the shape of a Greek cross. Upon completion of renovations, it will house the national history museum. The imposing **Biblioteca Nacional** is on the plaza's south end.

From the rear of the cathedral, go east along Delgado to the city's gem, the **Teatro Nacional**. Originally erected in 1917, it languished as a moviehouse for 50-odd years before being renovated in opulent style, with ornate gilt boxes and trimmings, lots of lush red velvet and a sensuous ceiling mural. The theater faces the small **Plaza Morazán**, usually hopping in the late afternoon.

Two blocks east of Plaza Barrios is the recently renovated **Parque Libertad**. The winged statue of Liberty in its center faces what looks like a dilapidated airline hangar (actually a church called **El Rosario**). It's worth a look inside – the building has a surprisingly effective interior adorned only with recycled scrap metal and stained glass panels set into an arched roof. The father of

EL SALVADOR

SAN SALVADOR CITY CENTER

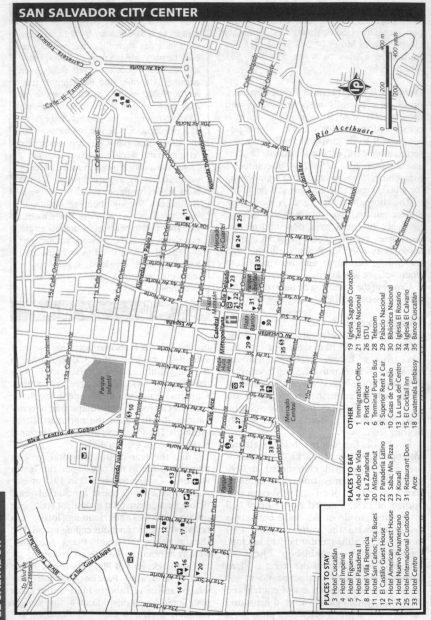

PLACES TO STAY
3   Hotel Cuscatlán
4   Hotel Imperial
5   Hotel Figueroa
7   Hotel Pasadena II
8   Hotel Villa Florencia
11 Hotel San Carlos; Tica Buses
12 El Castillo Guest House
17 Hotel American Guest House
24 Hotel Nuevo Panamericano
25 Hotel Internacional Custodio
33 Hotel Centro

PLACES TO EAT
14 Arbol de Vida
16 La Zanahoria
20 Mister Donut
22 Panadería Latino
23 Saba; Mía Pizza
27 Koradi
31 Restaurant Don
    Arce

OTHER
1   Immigration Office
2   Post Office
6   Terminal Puerto Bus
9   Superior Rent a Car
10 Casas de Cambio
13 La Luna del Centro
15 El Cocktail Inn
18 Guatemala Embassy
19 Iglesia Sagrado Corazón
21 Teatro Nacional
26 ISTU
28 Telecom
29 Palacio Nacional
30 Biblioteca Nacional
32 Iglesia El Rosario
32 Iglesia El Calvario
35 Banco Cuscatlán

Central American independence, Padre Delgado, is buried here.

West down 6a Calle Poniente, you'll see the Gothic towers of the decaying **Iglesia El Calvario** beside the stalls of the huge **Mercado Central**. Just south of the church are vendors of various natural medicines, from magic good luck potions to armadillo skins to cure flu.

West of the Center Calle Rubén Darío heads west out of the center, changing names a couple of times along the way. Bus No 52 rumbles down the entire length of this road. When the street is Alameda Roosevelt, it passes **Parque Cuscatlán**, an unkempt spot of green. Farther along, it passes Estadio Flor Blanca, the national stadium, where soccer games and an occasional rock concert are held. At 65a Avenida, you come to the **Plaza Las Américas**, with the statue **El Salvador del Mundo**. This symbol of the country depicts Jesus standing on top of the world.

West beyond this plaza the road becomes Paseo General Escalón, going through the **Colonia Escalón**, one of San Salvador's higher rent districts. Farther west you hit Plaza Masferrer.

At Plaza Masferrer, turn south onto Avenida Jerusalén and go four long blocks to **El Arbol de Dios**, the gallery and restaurant of La Palma artist Fernando Llort. This gallery houses an extensive collection of his work, with excellent sculptures and canvases unlike his simpler and better-known wood paintings. The gallery is open 9 am to 7 pm Monday to Saturday.

Southwest of the Center Bus No 42 travels this way from the center. Heading southwest from Plaza Las Américas, Alameda Araujo goes past the international fairgrounds, with the **Mercado Nacional de Artesanías**. Opposite the fairgrounds across Avenida La Revolución is the **Museo Nacional de Antropología David J Guzmán**. Designed to create an alternative vision of Salvadoran culture, it is one of the highlights of a visit to the capital. Most of the country's notable archaeological finds are on display here in five thematically arranged exhibit halls: settlements, agriculture, craft production, religion and communication. Temporary expositions are held in a separate space.

Prehistoric rock carvings are in an adjacent garden. All explanations are in Spanish. The museum is open 9 am to 12 pm and 1 to 5 pm Tuesday to Sunday (US$3).

Venture up Avenida La Revolución to the **Zona Rosa**, San Salvador's ritzy and exclusive restaurant and nightlife district. You'll recognize it by the plush Blvd del Hipódromo, lined with manicured lawns and street lamps indiscreetly advertising Coca-Cola, MasterCard and Levi's. Up Avenida La Revolución from Blvd del Hipódromo is the larger-than-life stone mosaic **Monumento a la Revolución**.

At Universidad Centroamericana José Simeón Cañas ('La UCA') on Autopista Sur, **Centro Monseñor Romero** (☎ 273 4508) is a well-organized museum that pays homage to the martyred archbishop. One room contains disturbing photos of the six Jesuits as they were found after being slain by military forces on the campus in 1989. The Jesuits are buried in the chapel just a few meters away. UCA students give tours. To get there, take the road to the left and up after passing the guard. It's open 8 am to noon and 2 to 6 pm weekdays, 8 to 11:30 am Saturday; admission is free.

Farther southwest on the Interamericana is the elegant white **Iglesia La Ceiba de Guadalupe**, an attractive church and a welcome refuge from the heat and smoke of the road. Round stained-glass windows rotate to let air circulate.

If it's time to breathe some oxygen, head to the **Jardín Botánico La Laguna**, also called Plan de La Laguna, a lovely botanical garden at the bottom of a volcanic crater. The garden is shady and cool even on a hot day and has a pleasant cafeteria next to a pond. Hours are 9 am to 5:30 pm Tuesday to Sunday (US$0.50). It's near Antiguo Cuscatlán on the outskirts of San Salvador. Take bus No 44 from the center; the driver will let you off at the right spot, from which it's a 1km downhill walk to the garden.

Boulevard de los Héroes From the center, take bus No 29 or 30 to this wide US influenced boulevard, replete with fastfood chains, gas stations, video stores and lots of neon signs. North of the boulevard is a residential area where quite a few internationals live and where the majority of casas de huéspedes are found. You'll also

BOULEVARD DE LOS HÉROES

PLACES TO STAY
1 Oasis Guest House
3 El Torogoz
4 International
   Guest's House Hotel
5 Alexa's Guest House
23 Ximena's Guest
   House

PLACES TO EAT
2 Salvatore's
6 Las Fajitas
7 Pizza Nova
9 Sol y Luna
10 Los Chumpipes
16 La Ventana
17 Casablanca Café
21 La Luna Casa y Arte
27 La Hola Beto's
28 Hang Ly

Av Santa
Av Aguilares
Av Sucre
Av Juarez
Av José Marti
Av Bolivar

Av José Manos Obrado
Av Washington
Av libertad
Calle los Pinos
Calle Los Lirios
Calle Los Lirios
3a Av Norte
3ra Av Norte
Av Central
2a Av Norte
25a Av Norte
3
4

Calle Las Violetas
Av Los Cedros
5

Universidad de
El Salvador

Calle las Palmas

Boulevard universitario
6
8
11
7 9 10
Blvd Universitario

14 Pasaje 2a
12 Parque
13 San José
Park
Calle 4a
Calle 2a

Autopista Norte

15 16
17
18
Calle El Quetzal
Av San José
Calle San Antonio Abad
19

Av Italo
Av Alvarado
Av Santa
Av Italo
Pje Italia
Victoria
20

Calle Aurora
25a C Poniente
Av Gustavo Guerrero
23a Av Norte

Calle Chabela Mistral
Calle Centro America
Calle Guatemala
Calle San Salvador
Calle Managua
Mejillishuat
21
23a Calle Poniente

Av 3 de Mayo
Calle Berlin
Pje Plat
2 1a Calle Poniente
25a Av Norte
27 Av Norte
23a Av Norte

Av Los Stumles
22
Calle Talahanca
Pje Carmelo
Av Cortes
Pje Los Angeles
23
24
Calle Gabriela Mistral
25
Diagonal 2

Zona
Real
28 26
27
Calle Lantialtepec
Pasaje San Carlos
Pasaje Las Palmeras
29
30
Blvd de Los Héroes
Boulevard Tutunichapa

31
Tercera Septima

OTHER
8 CIS; Mélida Anaya Montes
   Spanish Language School
11 Cine Reforma
12 Centro Comercial San Luis;
   Banco Credomatic
13 Banco Cuscatlán
14 El Arpa
15 Las Celtas
18 Las 3 Diables
19 El Atico
20 El Corral
22 Lavapronto
24 Esso Station
25 Hospital de Diagnóstico
26 Hotel Camino Real
29 Continental Airlines
30 Metrocentro
31 Metrosur

EL SALVADOR

find some interesting cultural centers, a good variety of restaurants and decent nightspots. The **Universidad de El Salvador** is near the corner of Blvd de los Héroes and Calle San Antonio Abad.

Opposite Hotel Camino Real Intercontinental are a pair of megamalls, **Metrocentro** and **Metrosur**, with multiplex cinemas, food courts, a post office, an Internet cafe and a supermarket, along with scads of card phones, all in close proximity.

South of the Center Sights of interest south are quite far away but worth the trip. Those traveling with kids should visit the **Teleférico de San Jacinto**, an amusement park on a hill southeast of the city. Its main attraction is getting there. A gondola takes you to the top of the hill as the city's immensity spreads out before you, affording amazing vistas of the surrounding volcanoes and lakes. The amusement park is uncommonly clean and full of vintage rides and restaurants with a view. It's open 9 am to 6 pm Thursday to Sunday (US$2.30 including roundtrip gondola ride); last ride to the top is at 5:30 pm. Bus No 9 takes you to the entrance.

South on Avenida Cuscatlán, the **Parque Zoológico** is open 9 am to 4 pm Wednesday to Sunday. Continuing south on Avenida Cuscatlán, you pass the **Casa Presidencial**, the presidential palace. Farther south, **Parque Saburo Hirao**, open 9 am to 4 pm Wednesday to Sunday, has the **Museo de Historia Natural** with unexceptional exhibits. Take bus No 2 from the center.

Keep going for Los Planes de Renderos, Parque Balboa, Puerta del Diablo and Panchimalco (see South of San Salvador, later in this section).

Language Courses

Mélida Anaya Montes Spanish Language School operates out of the Centro de Intercambio y Solidaridad (CIS; ☎ 226 2623, cis@netcomsa.com). The school is named after a prominent Salvadoran educator who became an FMLN commander amid growing government repression, and the program encourages political involvement, utilizing the CIS's extensive contacts with social justice organizations. Language classes, taught by Salvadoran instructors, meet for four hours daily and cost US$100

per week, plus an administration fee of US$12.50 during the first month. Should you wish to be placed with a family, room and board is US$60 a week, including two meals per day.

The Cuscatlán Escuela de Idiomas (☎ 235 0776, cuzcatlanls@hotmail.com), at 1a Avenida Norte and 19 Calle Poniente, offers 20 hours of lessons a week for US$110 and can arrange lodging with a family for US$83. Three-day cultural/political trips cost US$44. Take bus No 2 from the center, get off at Mercado San Miguelito and walk two blocks.

Organized Tours

Eco-Mayan Tours (☎ 298 2844) can show you around the capital, including a morning in the city center followed by a pupusa break at Los Planes de Renderos and a visit to the outlying indigenous village of Panchimalco. The tour costs US$25 per person. SET Adventours (☎ 279 3235) offers a similar itinerary for US$35.

Places to Stay

While there is no shortage of hotels around San Salvador, you may need to do some thinking about what you are willing to pay. Many cheap hotels can be found around the two main bus terminals, but the neighborhoods necessitate caution, especially for women traveling alone. You can find better service and safety in a whole slew of guesthouses above Blvd de los Héroes. These cost US$15 to US$20 a night on average but offer safety, clean sheets and more freedom to go out at night.

City Center If braving the city center is for you, one of the best deals is the large, clean *Hotel Internacional Custodio* (☎ 221 5810, *10a Avenida Sur 109)*, near the Mercado Ex-Cuartel. Rooms here are US$9.25 per person with private bath, US$4.75 without. You can ask to do laundry. *Hotel Nuevo Panamericano* (☎ 222 2959, *8a Avenida Sur 113)* is smaller and shabbier, with 18 rooms around a central courtyard/parking area; rooms are US$8/10.50 single/double with private bath.

North from the center, *Hotel San Carlos* (☎ 222 4808, *Calle Concepción 121)* is convenient if you're taking Tica buses early in the morning, but the neighborhood is not conducive to longer stays. Rates for small, clean rooms with private bath are US$10 per person.

Close to the mercado central, *Hotel Centro* (☎ 271 5045, *9a Avenida Sur 410*) is a clean, safe, efficient place catering mainly to couples. All rooms have cable TV, telephone and private bath and cost US$14.50 for 12 hours, US$20 for 24 hours. You can climb a ladder to reach the 'roof garden.' Secure parking is available.

Near the Puerto Bus terminal on 3a Calle Poniente, you'll find a pair of decent places, *Hotel Pasadena II* (☎ 221 4786, *3a Calle Poniente 1037*) and *Hotel Villa Florencia* (☎ 221 1706, *3a Calle Poniente 1023*). Both charge US$10.50/15/18.50 for single/double/triple rooms with private bath, and both are quite clean and hospitable. Avoid the front rooms if you're planning to get any sleep.

Two more good options are down 17a Avenida Norte. *El Castillo Guest House* (☎ 221 2435), on 17 Avenida Norte at 1 Calle Poniente, is rather rundown but clean and retains traces of former elegance. Rooms with private bath and TV are US$11.50/14.50/17.25. *Hotel American Guest House* (☎ 271 0224, *17 Avenida Norte 119*) has a homey atmosphere, with antique furniture, pictures and plants in the hallway. It charges US$17.25/20.75 with fan, TV and hot shower, or $11.50/14 including use of moldy shared bathrooms. The restaurant in the front prepares all meals.

About a 10-minute walk from the Terminal de Oriente, you'll find a cluster of cheap hotels on Calle Concepción, a seedy area whose streets turn mean after dark. The best of the bunch is *Hotel Figueroa* (☎ 222 1541), at No 653. Tidy, freshly painted singles/doubles along a peaceful courtyard are US$7/8. All rooms come with private bath. *Hotel Imperial* (☎ 222 4920), at No 659, charges US$7 per person for big rooms that have two beds, fan and private bath or US$4 with shared bath. *Hotel Cuscatlán* (☎ 222 3298), at No 675, has single or double rooms with private bath for US$7, slightly more with color TV. Rooms with three beds cost US$10.50.

Boulevard de los Héroes During the war, a few FMLN-supporters who lived around Universidad de El Salvador began opening their houses to people who wanted to learn more about their ideologies. Today, these guesthouses lodge visiting NGOs, election observers and other progressively minded groups, but they're open to all. Rates are often negotiable for longer stays. Space may be limited when groups are in town, so call ahead. The main area is between the university and Blvd Constitución. Buses No 26 and No 30 run frequently between here and the center. One block east, four blocks north of Cine Reforma is the pleasant *International Guest's House Hotel* (☎/fax 226 7343, *35a Avenida Norte 9 Bis*). Narrow, tidy rooms with ceiling fans cost US$17/30, all with private bath and breakfast. Next door, *El Torogoz* (☎/fax 235 4173, eltorogoz@vianet.com.sv, *35a Avenida Norte 7B*) offers well-maintained rooms for US$15/25; singles with private bath are US$20. All rooms have cable TV, and breakfast is included. Both places accept Visa and MasterCard but tack on an 8% charge for the service, and both offer Internet access at US$4 an hour. *Alexa's Guest House* (☎ 225 1422), at Calle Las Violetas and 37a Avenida Norte, is in a well-worn suburban home. Rooms are US$15/25 with bath, or US$10 per person without.

Head north on 39a Avenida Norte and bear right at Avenida Morazán to get to *Oasis Guest House* (☎ 226 5983, oasis@es.com.sv), at Pasaje Santa Marta. The lodging isn't *lujoso*, but it's only US$10 per person.

A longtime favorite with backpackers, *Ximena's Guest House* (☎ 260 2481, ximenas@navegante.com.sv, *Calle San Salvador 202*) is in a quiet residential area near the Blvd de los Héroes. It charges US$4 to US$7.50 for bunk beds in several dormitory rooms of varying size and comfort. Otherwise, you pay a rather steep US$22/41 for single/double rooms with private bath and cable TV. Granola, fruit salads and other meals are available on the premises.

Around Town Near the Terminal de Occidente, *Hotel Pasadena* (☎ 223 7905, *Blvd Venezuela 3093*) has rooms for US$7/12.75, all with unpleasant private bathrooms. A few doors west is a marginally better option, *Hotel Roma* (☎ 245 3363, *Blvd Venezuela 3145*). Rooms with one or two beds and private bath go for US$11.50 (US$10 without bathroom).

Worth the extra cash, *La Posada Guest House* (☎ 298 7240, laposada@hotmail.com,

Avenida Las Camelias 2) is 1km farther west along Blvd Venezuela. Attractively furnished, air-conditioned rooms with private bath, cable TV, phone and Internet access start at $25 a night. Complimentary breakfast is served alongside a charming patio. It is a bit out of the way, though, and you'll need to catch a taxi home at night.

A pair of reasonably priced hotels stand side-by-side along a traffic-jammed stretch of 49a Avenida Norte north of Roosevelt. *Hotel Occidental* (☎ 260 5274), at No 171, offers worn-out but clean rooms with battered furniture, tiny TVs and adequate bathrooms for US$14.50/17.25/23. *Hotel Shadai* (☎ 260 5747), at No 161, is better maintained and a pretty good deal at US$17.25/20/23 for rooms with fans, cable TV and sparkling bathrooms.

In the north part of town are a couple of excellent guesthouses. *Hotelito Casa Antigua* (☎ 274 5267, mgonzal@netcomsa. com, Avenida Cuchumatanes 12)* is about 1km north of Blvd Universitario, off Avenida Bernal (take bus No 30-B). Rates including breakfast are US$12 per person in comfortable rooms with fans or US$15 with private bath. *Casa de Huespedes Maya* (☎ 274 4438, Pasaje Leo 6E), near Blvd Constitución, is slightly higher – $15 per person or $20 with private bath; breakfast is extra. To get there, take bus No 30. Both places have spacious lounging areas, shops and good service.

Places to Eat

City Center There are plenty of places to eat in the center, but few standouts. Breakfast is served from 6 am at *Restaurant Don Arce*, on the southeast corner of Plaza Barrios. Take a booth by the window of the large upstairs hall to enjoy views of the activity in the plaza. The *Mister Donut* chain is another good bet for breakfast; there's one on Calle Arce near 21a Avenida Sur.

At lunchtime, follow the crowds to *Panadería Latino*, next door to the Teatro Nacional, offering the supreme comida a la vista. Servers fill your plate from trays of lasagna, beef in salsa, steamed veggies and so on, then fill your cup from pails of tamarind, cashew and melon juice. A big plate of food goes for under US$2. OK Chinese food can be found at the basement-

level *Saba*, on 4a Avenida Sur just below Delgado, a grimy working-class joint with soy sauce on the tables. A large plate of chicken chow mein costs US$3. *Mía Pizza*, upstairs from Saba, offers pizzas from US$2.75, submarine sandwiches and beer on tap.

Vegetarians have several options. *Koradi*, on 9a Avenida Sur near 4a Calle Poniente, serves tamales and cheese pupusas for breakfast and inexpensive veggie comida a la vista for lunch. *Arbol de Vida*, in the Plaza Real shopping center on 21a Avenida Norte near Calle Arce, serves up a great variety of meatless entrees from noon to 3 pm Monday to Saturday. Around the corner on Arce, *La Zanahoria* has salads, soy-based main dishes and a good juice bar. Lunches cost about US$1.75. It's open 9 am to 8 pm weekdays, till 2 pm on Saturday.

After 4 pm, many locals head for *Plaza Hula Hula* for beer and snacks. Stalls serving hamburgers, hot dogs and Pilsener ring the plaza, but cleanliness is not a priority. Pupusa vendors are clustered around the markets.

For dinner there isn't much choice around the center, since everything shuts down early. However, *chupaderos* (see Bars & Clubs under Entertainment, later) serve tacos, sandwiches and fries until late.

Boulevard de los Héroes If you've got a hankering for a burger, you have your choice along this strip of Wendy's or McDonald's, and there's a Pizza Hut restaurant; all are guarded by guys with rifles.

In Metrosur is *El Ranchón*, a large open-air food court with Mexican, Chinese, Salvadoran and other varieties of food. A couple restaurants stand out among the dozen beer/snack/sports TV joints on Calle Lamatepec behind the Camino Real, an area called the Zona Real. *La Hola Beto's*, on the left end, specializes in seafood, with shrimp cocktails for US$5 and oysters on the half shell for US$2.50 a dozen. *Hang Ly* is a cut above the average Salvadoran Chinese restaurant, serving exotic fare such as fish balls in curry sauce. Main courses cost US$3 to US$5.

At *La Luna Casa y Arte* (☎ 260 2921, Calle Berlín 228) you can order good grilled sandwiches, soups (US$2.50), salads (US$2.50 to US$5) and various meatless meals. Daily lunch specials, including salad, drink and a creatively prepared main course cost US$2.50.

Coffee aficionados will appreciate *La Ventana* (☎ 225 6893) across from Centro Comercial San Luis on Calle San Antonio Abad, serving a variety of caffeinated fare along with the *New York Times*. The menu features new options daily, with a sandwich, salad and pasta of the day for about US$5.25 each (closed Monday). Next door is the pleasant, clean *Casablanca Café*, offering an excellent lunch special, comida a la vista style, for under US$2.

Several restaurants are clustered around the corner of 39a Avenida Norte and Blvd Universitario. At *Pizza Nova*, you can get a *pizza personal* and a beer for US$3.50. *Las Fajitas* serves Mexican; quesadillas cost around US$2, enchiladas US$4.50.

Down Blvd Universitario, you come to *Sol y Luna*, open 8 am to 8:30 pm. The vegetarian restaurant offers fruit salad and granola for breakfast, combination plates for lunch (US$2) and pupusas in the evening. Across the road is *Los Chumpipes*, specializing in messy turkey sandwiches costing around US$1.50.

In the guesthouse district on 35a Avenida Norte, the upstairs restaurant *Salvatore's* serves good pizzas (from US$6 for a large pie) and big plates of pasta (from US$3.75).

Avenida Bernal *Olocuilta No 3*, at Blvd Universitario and Avenida Bernal, is a popular pupusa stop in the evening. There's a grill in front where girls slap out rice pupusas (US$0.50), and big jars of chopped cabbage and marinated onions are on the tables. There are other pupuserías along Bernal, including the excellent *Pupusería Nelly's*, just below Calle Toluca. It's open till 9:30 pm nightly except Monday. Farther down is *Pupusería Vista Hermosa*, a bright and airy place on an upper level terrace that is popular with families.

Restaurant Hey! (☎ 260 1499, Pasaje Palmeral 31), west of Avenida Bernal in Colonia Toluca, serves wonderful Chilean food. Entrees are not cheap, but the quality is consistently high.

Colonia Escalón & Zona Rosa To keep your expenses down in this high-rent district, try the food court of Galerías Escalón,

which contains the usual fast-food options. A few blocks up Paseo Escalón is *Delicatessen Kreef*, offering pastrami sandwiches and knockwurst with sauerkraut for under US$3.

In the Zona Rosa, have a café latte with San Salvador's cosmopolitan set at *La Panetiére*. The sidewalk cafe serves excellent coffee with fresh pastries, crepes (US$3) and bagel sandwiches (US$4). On the other side of Blvd Hipódromo, inside the Centro Comercial Basilea, is an equally good coffee shop, *Shaw's*, with seating on a pleasant terrace overlooking the zone.

Kalapataru, on Avenida Masferrer just north of the plaza of the same name, has vegetarian specials, either a la carte or buffet-style, for lunch and dinner. And they serve pupusas with spinach, broccoli and garlic stuffings.

Entertainment

Performances The *Teatro Nacional* (☎ 222 5689) stages contemporary and folk dance programs, as well as theater and opera, and there are chamber music concerts in the recital hall. Tickets cost about US$3 and can be purchased at the box office before the show. Check *Revue* magazine for the current program or phone the theater.

Cinemas The usual Hollywood lineup, shown in the original language with subtitles, dominates the screens of *Cine Reforma* on Blvd Universitario and the multiplex cinemas of *Galerías Escalón* and *Metrocentro*. Tickets are around US$3. Alternatively, *La Luna Casa y Arte* screens less mainstream fare Monday and Tuesday evenings (see Bars & Clubs). Check *Revue* magazine for listings.

Bars & Clubs The city comes alive on weekends. Paseo Escalón, between Plaza Masferrer and Fuente Beethoven, and the Zona Rosa are the most active zones. Among the myriad themed clubs in the Zona Rosa, *Mango's* is the most stylish and *Manías* the most manic. *Mario's* (☎ 223 6068), opposite the Hotel Princess on Blvd del Hipódromo, is one of the trendier dance clubs, but the dress code will challenge backpackers. Live salsa and cumbia bands heat up the dance floor at *El Corral*, on Blvd de los Héroes, Friday and Saturday nights from 8 pm (US$5 cover).

La Luna Casa y Arte is the coolest club in the city, with live jazz, *rock latino* and salsa, as well as movies and guest chefs. The cover ranges from free to US$5. The food is good, and you can order from a whole range of mixed drinks. *La Luna del Centro (☎ 221 2016, 1a Calle Poniente 822)*, between 13a and 15a Avenidas Norte, is a bold attempt by the club to bring its cultural mix to the central grid. Rock, blues and folk concerts are on Friday and Saturday afternoons.

The NGO hood north of Blvd de los Héroes has a cluster of hip clubs and pubs. *La Ventana* (see Places to Eat) is a lively hangout where you can down Belgian ales and German beers for around the same price as local brews. The cultural space provides a welcome blend of intriguing art and good music. It's open till 1 am Tuesday to Thursday, later on weekends. A block east, *Les 3 Diables* attracts a younger crowd. Beer and rock and roll are the main attractions, but there's good cheap food, too. *El Arpa* (the Harp), alongside the Parque San José, is a popular pub run by Irish national Jerry Monaghan. People of all political persuasions come here to relax and converse. The atmosphere is welcoming, and the Irish stew is tasty. Another pub, *Las Celtas*, is Scottish-run; it's on Calle Principal around the corner from La Ventana.

Yascuas, in Condominios Juan Pablo II on Prolongación Juan Pablo II, is a gay-oriented bar, open Thursday to Saturday nights. In the same building is the gay disco *Milenio*.

Chupaderos are found around the city. You can identify these beer gardens by large advertisements for either Pilsener or 'Mi Barrilito.' One such, *El Cocktail Inn*, is on 21a Avenida Norte between Arce and 1a Calle Poniente. It's open till 9 or 10 pm nightly, with live music from 5 pm Wednesday to Saturday. This is definitely a guys' place to drink; an unescorted woman is likely to be the focus of excessive male attention.

El Salvador legalized gambling in 1999, so you can now shoot craps in public. Hotel Colonial and Hotel Siesta house gaming halls.

Spectator Sports

In San Salvador, soccer games are held in Estadio Cuscatlán (☎ 273 2231), just off Autopista Sur, and Estadio Flor Blanca (☎ 223 7238) on 49a Avenida Sur. General admission seats are around US$3.

The baseball season is from December to March. San Salvador's Parque Nacional de Béisbol (☎ 279 2476) is southwest of the center on the Interamericana.

Shopping

See Shopping in the Facts for the Visitor section for a rundown on what to buy. The Mercado Nacional de Artesanías is on the grounds of the Feria Internacional. Though more expensive than other markets, the quality is consistently high. Mercado Ex-Cuartel, three blocks east of the Teatro Nacional along Calle Delgado, has a mixture of handicrafts, as well as clothing and towels. Prices are lower here than at other markets, lower still if you bargain, but the vendors are pushy. If it's hammocks you're after, you'll find vendors át Avenida Cuscatlán and 6a Calle Oriente, a block south of Plaza Barrios.

Both CIS (☎ 226 2623), Blvd Universitario 4, and the NGO Crispaz (☎ 226 0829), 23 Calle Oriente 430 at 10a Avenida Norte, sell quality crafts, jewelry and clothing purchased directly from a number of cooperatives.

Getting There & Away

Air Airline offices in San Salvador include American Airlines (☎ 298 0777) in Edificio La Centroamericana on Alameda Roosevelt, United Airlines (☎ 279 3900) and Grupo TACA (☎ 298 5055) in Galerías Escalón, Continental (☎ 260 2180) in Metrocentro, Delta (☎ 298 4422) in Centro Comercial Atrium Plaza on Blvd Santa Elena and Panama's Copa Airlines (☎ 260 3399) at Alameda Roosevelt and 55a Avenida Norte.

Bus San Salvador has three main terminals for national long-distance buses. See the Getting There & Away section, for information on international buses leaving from the hotels and Terminal Puerto Bus.

Buses serving all points east and a few northern destinations arrive and depart from the Terminal de Oriente (☎ 221 5379), on the eastern side of the city. Buses serving all points west, including the Guatemalan border, arrive and depart from the Terminal de Occidente (☎ 279 3548), on Blvd Venezuela near 49a Avenida Sur.

Bus Terminal San Marcos (also called Terminal del Sur), in the south of the city, serves destinations to the southeast, such as Costa del Sol and Usulután.

EL SALVADOR

The following buses depart from Terminal de Oriente (take bus No 9, 29 or 34 from city center, 52 from Blvd de los Héroes):

destination	bus no	duration
Chalatenango	125	2 hours
El Poy*	119	4 hours
Ilobasco	111	1½ hours
La Palma	119	3 hours
La Unión	304	4 hours**
San Miguel	301	3 hours**
San Sebastián	110	1½ hours
San Vicente	116	1½ hours
Suchitoto	129	1½ hours

*Honduran border
**Faster especial service available

From Terminal de Occidente (take bus No 27 or 34 from city center, No 44 from Blvd de los Héroes):

destination	bus no	duration
Ahuachapán	202	2 hours
Cerro Verde	201 to El Congo, then 248	2 hours
Joya de Cerén	108 (to San Juan Opico)	1 hour
La Hachadura	205 to Sonsonate, then 259A	3½ hours
Lago de Coatepeque	201 to El Congo, then 220	1½ hours
Las Chinamas	202 to Ahuachapán, then 263	2½ hours
Los Cóbanos	205 to Sonsonate, then 257	2½ hours
Metapán	201A	2¾ hours
Ruinas de San Andrés	201	40 mins
Santa Ana	201	1½ hours
Sonsonate	205	1½ hours

From Terminal San Marcos (take bus No 26 or microbus No 11B from city center):

destination	bus no	duration
Costa del Sol	495	2 hours
Puerto El Triunfo	302 to Usulután, then 363 from Jiquilisco turnoff	2¼ hours
Usulután	302	2½ hours*
Zacatecoluca	133	1 hour

*Faster especial service available

Getting Around

To/From the Airport A ride with Taxis Acacya (☎ 271 4937) to or from the airport costs about US$15. They also run colectivo vans between the airport and the capital, a trip of about 40 minutes (US$3). From San Salvador, they depart from the corner of 19a Avenida Norte and 3a Calle Poniente, behind the Puerto Bus terminal, at 6, 7 and 10 am and 2 pm; from the airport at 9 am and 1 and 5:30 pm.

No 138 microbuses travel to and from Terminal del Sur (Terminal San Marcos) every 10 minutes; No 400 travels to and from the Plaza Barrios in the center every half hour (US$0.60). From the airport terminal, go through the parking lot, past a shopping center and out to the road where there's a bus shelter.

Bus San Salvador's extensive bus network can get you just about anywhere. City buses are red and white and cost US$0.20. Microbuses cost US$0.25 and run roughly the same routes but go into more residential areas where the large buses don't fit. While buses only let passengers on and off at bus stops, often spaced far apart, microbuses will try to grab people anywhere en route and consequently take longer and drive more recklessly.

Buses run frequently from 5 am to 7:30 pm daily; fewer buses run on Sunday. Between around 7:30 and 8:30 pm, they become less frequent and finally stop; the microbuses run later, until around 9 pm. After 9 pm, you'll have to take a taxi.

You're better off boarding outside the central grid, since traffic in the center is hopelessly snarled most of the time.

Some key routes include the following:

Bus 9 goes down 29a Avenida Norte alongside the Universidad de El Salvador. Then it turns east toward city center, heading past the cathedral and up Independencia past Terminal de Oriente.

Bus 26 goes east along Calle Constitución, eventually turning south on 39a Avenida Norte. At Calle San Antonio Abad, it turns east again, following Autopista Norte; then it turns down 5a Avenida Norte and continues south along Avenida España/Cuscatlán, past Parque Zoológico, Parque Saburo Hirao, ending up at the Terminal San Marcos.

Bus 30B goes south on Avenida Bernal, east on San Antonio Abad, then southwest down Blvd de los Héroes to Metrocentro. From there, it goes west along Alameda Roosevelt, past the Salvador del Mundo monument and continues west along Paseo Escalón past Galerías mall. It then turns south at 79a Avenida and continues along Blvd del Hipódromo through the Zona Rosa and down to Plaza Italia (two blocks from Corsatur office), where it swings around and returns.

Bus 42 goes west along Calle Arce from the cathedral and continues along Alameda Roosevelt. At Salvador del Mundo, it heads southwest along Araujo, passing the Mercado de Artesanías and Museo Nacional Guzmán and continues down the Interamericana, passing La Ceiba de Guadalupe.

Bus 44 goes down 29a Avenida from Plaza Zacamil then south on Blvd de los Héroes past Metrocentro and down 49a Avenida. Then it turns west on Blvd Los Proceres and south at Avenida La Sultana, past the pedestrian entrance of UCA and into Antiguo Cuscatlán.

Car Signage is improving, but in the center, you may have to decipher street names from eroded paint on the curb. Once you get the system of even/odd, north/south, avenida/calle down, you'll fare better, but there's no way of guessing which road is one-way in which direction. Your best bet is to leave the car in a safe lot and take the bus. Carjackings are on the rise, so stay cautious.

Taxi In San Salvador, taxis are plentiful, though not metered, so negotiate an acceptable price before you climb in. A ride in town should cost about US$3 during the day; late at night the rates are about 50% higher. If you don't spot a taxi passing by at the moment you want one, phone one of the following radio taxi services: Taxis Acacya (☎ 271 4937), Radio Taxis Latinos (☎ 264 0417) or Acontaxis (☎ 270 1176).

EAST OF SAN SALVADOR
Lago de Ilopango
In about the 2nd century AD, a volcano exploded 15km east of San Salvador, just beyond what is now San Salvador's Ilopango Airport. El Salvador's largest lake, 15km long, 8km wide and 248m deep, formed in the volcanic crater. Another eruption in early 1880 formed the Cerros Quemados (Burnt Hills) Islands in the middle of the lake, accessible by boat (US$4).

At the village of Apulo, there's a turicentro. Restaurants serve fresh fish and crayfish, but the lake is said to be polluted by heavy metals discharged from the enterprise zone on the shore. To reach the lake from the city, take bus No 15 from 3a Avenida Sur at Plaza Hula Hula.

NORTH OF SAN SALVADOR
Cihuatán
An immense urban area, possibly the largest pre-Columbian city between Guatemala and Peru, grew up beside the Río Guazapa and thrived for 100 years before being burned to the ground and abandoned in the 10th century AD. It was probably occupied by Mayas, Lencas and other groups. Excavated by US archaeologist Stanley Boggs in the 1950s, Cihuatán shows evidence of two separate ceremonial centers and hundreds of buildings, though much remains to be explored. A pair of ball courts and a large mound where a pyramid once stood, all surrounded by a low defensive wall, have been uncovered in the western center.

Cihuatán is open 9 am to 4 pm Tuesday to Sunday. From the Terminal de Oriente, take bus No 119 toward Chalatenango and get off about 4km beyond Aguilares; ask the driver to let you off at Las Ruinas. It's an 800m walk to the site.

WEST OF SAN SALVADOR
Boquerón
Quezaltepeque (Volcán San Salvador) has two peaks. The higher peak, at 1960m, is called Picacho. The other, Boquerón (Big Mouth), is 1893m high and has a second cone within its crater – 45m high and perfectly symmetrical – formed in 1917. The beauty of this place lies not only in the panoramic views, but also in the immensity of the crater and its lush foliage. Though parts of it are fenced off for television antennas, you can still hike around the rim; it takes two to three hours. From the parking lot, a small path on your left leads to the trail. The road itself continues on to the gate of Channel 12. Skirt around the fence to get to two nice viewing areas. Once on the trail you can follow another trail down 543m into the crater itself.

Paths can be slippery and dangerous in places – hire one of the local kids offering to act as a guide for US$3 or US$4. Muggings have been reported along the trail; it's less risky to attempt the hike on a weekend when more people are around.

Get an early start if you want to hike, as getting there by bus from San Salvador takes a couple of hours. From Parque Cuscatlán, take bus No 101A or B to Santa Tecla. From there, bus No 103 departs from 6a Avenida Sur. The bus is sporadic, but pickups depart from the same place. It's an 11km trip uphill to the village of Boquerón, from which it's a 1km walk up a plastic-bag-paved road to the crater. Some buses only go as far as the crossroads, a 30-minute walk below the village. Be sure to find out when the last bus returns to San Salvador.

Ruinas de San Andrés

In 1977 a step pyramid and a large court-yard with a subterranean section were un-earthed in this site inhabited by Maya between AD 600 and 900. Named after the hacienda on which it was discovered, the monumental center was surrounded by ex-tensive residential areas that are estimated to have had over 12,000 inhabitants. Experts believe the regional capital held sway over the Valle de Zapotitán and possibly the neighboring Valle de las Hamacas where San Salvador is now situated.

The principal structures rest atop a plat-form called the Acropolis. The main pyramid, sometimes called the Campana San Andrés owing to its bell shape, may contain the tombs of rulers, but it hasn't been excavated yet. The unexcavated area to the north is pre-sumed to have been a playing field or market area. A ditch in front of Estructura 3 shows how the platform was built with hundreds of thousands of adobe bricks.

Quite a bit of restoration has been per-formed to protect the original structures, and protective walls cover the original bricks. The pyramids mark the entrance to this site. Past them is the Río Sucio and, on the other side, the village now known as Joya de Cerén. Another 15 mounds are yet to be unearthed.

A fine museum displays pre-Columbian and colonial objects. Outside the building are the extensive remains of a Spanish indigo production facility, uncovered during the excavation of the museum's foundation. There's a small replica of the indigo works inside. The site is open 9 am to 5 pm Tuesday to Sunday; admission is US$3.

The ruins are about 300m north of the highway, 33km west of San Salvador in the Valle Zapotitán. Take the Santa Ana bus (No 201) from San Salvador's Terminal de Occidente and get off at km 33, where there's a small black sign for the ruins, near a ceiba tree. Turn right (north) down this road to get to the ruins.

Joya de Cerén

When the Laguna Caldera volcano erupted in AD 600, a small Maya settlement was buried under 4 to 6m of volcanic ash. The intense heat (between 100°C and 500°C) and blankets of ash from the eruption pre-served not only the structures, but pottery, plants, seeds and animal remains (see the boxed text 'Evidence of a Better Past').

So far, 10 of the 18 identified buildings in three separate compounds have been un-covered. The compounds are closed off, but you can look at two of them from viewing areas. This is the only site that gives clues on how people lived back then: their intricate farming techniques, gardens of flowers and vegetables, storerooms and kitchens. The on-site museum has a good collection of ar-tifacts and models of the villages, but the in-formation is in Spanish. It is open 9 am to 5 pm Tuesday to Sunday (US$3).

The site is 36km west of San Salvador; take bus No 108 from Terminal de Occi-dente and get off after crossing the bridge over the Río Sucio.

SOUTH OF SAN SALVADOR
Los Planes de Renderos

Within this district you will find **Parque Balboa**, one of the most popular parks around San Salvador. Close to 28 hectares are preserved for family fun; you'll find a few trails to take some quick walks, a skating rink, playgrounds and some pre-Columbian-style sculptures. The best time to come is on a Saturday or Sunday afternoon, when you can really see how people enjoy their time here. Admission is US$0.80. The park is 12km from the city center.

A couple of kilometers past Parque Balboa is **Puerta del Diablo** (the Devil's Door). Two towering boulders, reputedly once a single stone split in two, form this ominous lookout (during the war this place was an execution point, the cliffs offering easy disposal of the bodies). When it's clear, the view is fantastic, and when the fog starts up in the afternoon and rolls through like

Evidence of a Better Past

The Laguna Caldera Volcano erupted some 1400 years ago, sending ash spewing in all directions. Between 4m and 6m of that ash settled on a farming village. The intense heat from the eruption (between 100°C and 500°C) preserved not only the structures, but pottery, plants, seeds and animal remains.

The village was accidentally discovered in 1976. While no human remains were found (it is believed residents fled prior to the explosion), archaeologists dug up tools, seeds and polychrome pots. They discerned what crops were planted – corn, beans, squash, cacao and chiles – and what meat the people ate. Medicinal plants and maguey (still used to make twine) were growing in the gardens. Houses had thick walls and firm structures, with separate rooms for the kitchen and sleeping areas. This site, now called Joya de Cerén (Jewel of Cerén, named after the Spanish family that owned the land) is right outside San Salvador where thousands of descendants of this community now live in leaking corrugated iron shacks and subsist on little more than rice and beans.

smoke, well, it's positively surreal. Meander along the trails that wind up and around the boulders, but forewarn any lovebirds of your presence.

Take the No 12 'Mil Cumbres' bus from the east side of the Mercado Central, at 12a Calle Poniente. If you're driving, head down Avenida Cuscatlán until you see the signs.

Panchimalco

Toltec immigrants founded this quiet, culturally proud town, situated in a lush valley. The baroque church, built in the mid-18th century by indigenous craftsmen, has some interesting woodwork inside. A pair of cultural centers along 1a Avenida display ceramics and dance costumes and have some literature; the one by Calle Arce has a great mural.

Panchimalco is renowned for its religious festivals, particularly Palm Sunday, when residents march through the streets bearing decorated palm fronds. The spring festival in

early May features more palm artistry, folk dancing and fireworks.

Microbus and bus No 17 depart for Panchimalco from Avenida 29 de Agosto on the south side of the Mercado Central in San Salvador.

Western El Salvador

LA LIBERTAD
pop 45,644

If you surf, you've probably already heard of this place. If you don't surf, you'll have to seek out other attractions in or around the port. The pier is interesting, full of fish – dried and diced, alive and dead – all emitting a pungent, salty smell. Also note the shark oil ointments, seahorses and turtle eggs.

Information

Banco Desarrollo, on Barrios east of the market, changes traveler's checks. It's open 8:30 am to 5 pm weekdays, 8:30 am to 12 pm Saturday. There's a Telecom office on 2a Calle Oriente and a Telepunto branch the next block over.

Gang activity and public drunkenness can make the streets menacing after dark. And be cautious about what you eat – a cholera epidemic hit the port in early 2000.

Beaches

The closest beach to the capital, La Libertad fills up with city dwellers on weekends. In winter (March to October), the beach is rocky, covered with large black boulders, and the riptide, along with sewage, makes the water uninviting. In summer, the rocks get covered in sand, but the boulders are still whipped by the waves.

Surfers consider Punta Roca the best wave in El Salvador. Mango's Lounge surf shop (☎ 335 3782), at the corner of 5a Avenida Norte and Calvario, rents boards and paraphernalia, plus diving and fishing gear. Open 10 am to 10 pm daily, it also functions as a snack bar and all-around surfer cultural center. Surfing lessons can be arranged. Check out their Web site (www.puntamango.com.sv).

If you just want to frolic in the waves, head west to the Costa del Bálsamo or east to sandy Playa San Diego. Fisherman's Club (☎ 264 3110), at Playa Las Flores east of

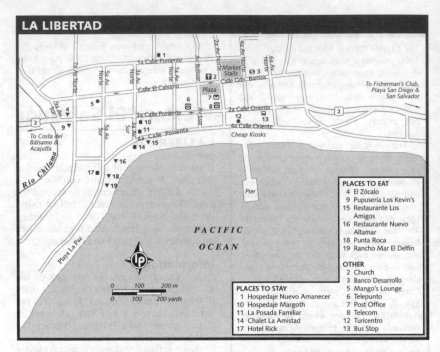

LA LIBERTAD

To Fisherman's Club,
Playa San Diego &
San Salvador

To Costa del
Bálsamo &
Acajutla

PACIFIC
OCEAN

Pier

Playa La Paz

Río Chilama

0   100   200 m
0   100   200 yards

PLACES TO EAT
4   El Zócalo
9   Pupusería Los Kevin's
15 Restaurante Los
    Amigos
16 Restaurante Nuevo
    Altamar
18 Punta Roca
19 Rancho Mar El Delfín

OTHER
2   Church
3   Banco Desarrollo
5   Mango's Lounge
6   Telepunto
7   Post Office
8   Telecom
12 Turicentro
13 Bus Stop

PLACES TO STAY
1   Hospedaje Nuevo Amanecer
10 Hospedaje Margoth
11 La Posada Familiar
14 Chalet La Amistad
17 Hotel Rick

town, has pools, tennis courts, hammocks and beach access for US$5.75/1.75 adults/kids.

Places to Stay

Some hotels in La Libertad charge for 12 hours at a time, so be sure you clarify what you're paying for when checking in. The prices listed below are for 24 hours.

Three blocks from the beach, *Hospedaje Nuevo Amanecer*, on 1a Calle Poniente opposite a fetid creek, charges US$5.75/11.50 for fairly clean single/double rooms. Another cheapie is *Hospedaje Margoth*, on 3a Avenida Sur. It's extremely basic but not bad at US$3.50/7; toilets and showers are downstairs. Just down the street is *La Posada Familiar* (☎ 335 3252), popular with foreign surfers. Rooms around a pleasant central courtyard/parking lot with plenty of hammocks are US$11.50/14.50 including private bath, or US$9.25 without. The restaurant in front serves seafood. Continuing toward the beach, you'll find *Chalet La Amistad*. It charges US$5.75/7 for boxlike rooms, one of which has a window facing the sea.

Several hotels and restaurants line 5a Avenida Sur where it branches off the grid

on its way out to Playa La Paz. *Hotel Rick* (☎ 335 3033) has clean if spartan rooms, all with private bath, for US$11.50/17.25. The staff will watch your luggage if you take off for a few days.

Places to Eat

Start the day at *Rancho Mar El Delfín*, where you can look at the waves and enjoy a good cheap *típico* breakfast consisting of eggs, black beans, plantains, fresh juice and coffee for around US$2.

Pricey restaurants line the beach, all offering fresh fish, shrimp cocktails and *mariscada* (bouillabaisse overflowing with seafood) for lunch or dinner. Of these, *Nuevo Altamar* and *Los Amigos* are the most recommended. A meal with drinks at either one will cost US$8 to US$12. *Punta Roca*, with superb views of the beach, has a varied menu and is less expensive. You can order half a mariscada for US$4.75. Restaurants shut down early, so plan accordingly.

Cheap kiosks of variable cleanliness abound near the pier, serving up fish soup at US$1.75 a bowl and lunch plates for US$1.50. If you can coerce someone to let you use their kitchen, buy some fish out on the pier and some fresh veggies at the town market. Most of the hotels are willing to cook up meals for guests.

Pupusería Los Kevin's, near the corner of 2a Calle Poniente and 9a Avenida Sur, gets crowded with surfers and locals in the evening. Across the street the inexpensive **El Zócalo** offers Mexican *tortas*, tacos and fajitas.

There are more places east of town at Playa Flores (coming from San Salvador, turn left at the T). **La Curva de Don Jere** has nice beach views. Roving combos provide a varied musical menu along with your *mariscada especial*. Just east, **La Dolce Vita** specializes in seafood pastas (from US$5.75).

Getting There & Away

Bus No 102 goes to and from San Salvador (US$0.45, one hour). In San Salvador, catch it on 4a Calle Poniente beside Parque Bolívar. If you're driving from San Salvador, go toward Santa Tecla; the turnoff will be to your right, just after the overpass. When you get to the end of the road (about a 45-minute drive), turn right into the town center.

Buses to Costa del Bálsamo (No 102) and Playa San Diego leave from the bus stop on 2a Calle Oriente.

From La Libertad, bus No 80 covers the coast on either side of the port from Playa El Sunzal to Playa San Diego. Surfers note: You can take boards on the buses. To Sonsonate, take bus No 287 at 1:45 pm (2½ hours, frequent stops) or No 192 to Playa Mizata at 6 am or 1 pm and change. All buses leave from near the intersection of 4a Avenida Norte and 2a Calle Oriente.

PARQUE WALTER T DEININGER

This protected area, east of La Libertad along the Comalapa road, was named after the German settler who donated his lands to El Salvador. It consists of two types of forest: *caducifolio*, which sheds its leaves in summer, and *galería*, which retains its foliage year-round. A well-maintained 18km trail skirts the park; you must be accompanied by a ranger. Signs point out trails to the Río Amayo, 'the Mystery Cave' and a lookout point offering views of the whole park down to the sea that fringes the forest. Deer, raccoons and the endangered

paca *(tepezcuintle)* can be spotted in the park, as well as many bird species, including the blue-crowned motmot *(torogoz)*, El Salvador's national bird.

To visit the Parque Deininger, you must obtain a permit from ISTU (☎ 222 8455) in San Salvador five days ahead of time. The park is open daily, but there's no entry between noon and 1 pm; admission is US$0.80. It's a 15-minute ride from La Libertad along the Comalapa road; catch bus No 187 in front of the market.

Beyond Parque Deininger is Estero de Toluca, currently being developed as a turtle reserve.

LA COSTA DEL BÁLSAMO

The coastal expanse between La Libertad and Sihuapilapa to the west derives its name from the balsam trees from which dyes were once extracted. Today only a handful of trees remain, and the main industry is cotton.

From Libertad, the road winds west above a rocky coast with many sheltered coves and sandy beaches (most are private). Weekend hordes head for Playas Conchalío and El Majahual, the latter a wide swath of black sand bordered by endless seafood shacks and parking lots, and surfers favor Playas El Tunco ('the best left break in El Salvador'), El Sunzal ('the longest point break') and El Zonte, 16km west of La Libertad. Of these, Sunzal is the most attractive, particularly from October to February when the water is calm enough for snorkeling. Still farther west are Playas Mizata and Sihuapilapa.

Buses No 192, 107 and 80 run along the coast. Just tell the driver where you want to get off. Beaches farther west are better accessed from Sonsonate.

Places to Stay & Eat

At Playa Conchalío is the free **Centro Obrero Dr Humberto Romero Alvergue**, right on a picturesque expanse of rocky beach. Rooms are equipped with four flimsy cots – bring your own sheets. One block is serviced by a bathhouse; another has acceptable private bathrooms. The main compound has a pool. Meals are available at shacks beside the beach gate or go to La Libertad, but arrange with the guard to let you back in after 7 pm. To stay here, you need prior written permission from the Ministerio de Trabajo in San Salvador (see Tourist Offices in that section, earlier in this chapter).

At Playa El Tunco, the brand new *Tortuga Surf Lodge* (☎ 298 2986, 888 6225, rob.gal@vianet.com.sv) is arguably the best budget hotel along this coast. Cool, tidy double rooms with outside/private bath are US$15/20. There's a bar and a kitchen serving breakfast and lunch. Owner Roberto Gallardo, a passionate surfer and archaeologist with the national anthropology museum, leads tours in English of the main archaeological sites for US$20 per person. More places are clustered near the Río El Tunco, a center of surfer culture. Overlooking the river, *Hotel del Surfeador* (☎ 826 5347) has five simple, freshly painted singles with fans for US$9.25 and one bathroom. A quieter place, set back from the beach, *El Tubo* (☎ 827 6083) has rooms for US$4.75/7 single/double (US$2 more on weekends) with basic shared toilets and showers. *La Bocana* is the best of several restaurants here.

West past a pair of private beach clubs is *Kilimanjaro*. It is magnificently located a few steps from the waves of Playa El Sunzal, but it is not well-maintained. The beachfront block has several large doubles with private bath and nonfunctional fans for US$17.25, some moldy smaller rooms with shared bath for US$11.50 and a dormitory at US$5.75 per person. Kitchen facilities include a cooler and an unreliable propane stove.

Another recent entry along this coast is *Horizonte Surf Camp*, on Playa El Zonte 16km west of La Libertad. Secure and well-designed, it offers four neat thatched cabañas with hammocks and fans; showers and toilets are separate. There's a pool and *palapa* bar. The camp's an extraordinary deal: US$4.75 per person. Nearby, a few beachfront huts serve seafood. Take bus No 192, 107 or 287 from La Libertad and get off about 3km past Atami Beach Club.

LAGO DE COATEPEQUE

On the eastern slope of the Volcán de Santa Ana, Lago de Coatepeque is a clean, sparkling blue volcanic crater lake, 6km wide and 120m deep, surrounded by green slopes. The Cerro Verde, Izalco and Santa Ana volcanoes loom above the lake. It's a popular weekend retreat for San Salvador's well-to-do, many of whom have private homes that obstruct public access to most of the lake. But there are a few cheap hotels here, and during the week it is a peaceful, quiet oasis. The bus takes you along the northeast side of the lake to an area with hotels and public access. For a small fee, usually around US$2.50 or the price of a meal, you can hang out for the day at one of the hotels listed below.

Places to Stay & Eat

The best deal on the lake is the deserted *Centro de Obreros Constitución*, where you can stay for free with written permission from the Ministerio de Trabajo in San Salvador (see Tourist Offices in that section, earlier in this chapter). The government workers' center has lake access, but the water here is murky; alternatively, you can swim in one of several pools. Recently remodeled cabins contain four single beds, a table and a perfectly good bathroom. Bring a mosquito net, as windows don't have screens. You can get food when the restaurant is open. The compound is on the right, shortly after the bus loops round to circle the lake.

A couple of kilometers farther down is *Amacuilco Guest House* (☎ 441 0608). This laid-back but well-maintained place is popular with backpackers and Peace Corps volunteers. It's a full service facility, offering guided hikes, Spanish classes, a foreign-language library and visits to the local community. It's also the cheapest hotel around, charging US$16/20 for pleasant singles/doubles with private bath and overhead fan or US$8.75/11.50 with use of clean shared bathrooms; beds in dorm-style rooms are US$7.50.

Another 500m down the road, *Hotel Torremolinos* (☎ 441 6037) has the best restaurant on the lake, with dining on the back terrace and out on the pier and live music Sunday afternoon. But the rather drab accommodations are overpriced: US$28.75/40 for rooms with two/three beds and private bath. A much better deal is the ornate *Hotel del Lago* (☎ 446 9511), in a quieter area another 1.5km around the lake near where the bus stops. Old Spanish-style double rooms with high ceilings and wooden shutters are US$18.50, newer rooms are US$30. An elegant terrace overlooks the lake, a small muddy beach and a swimming pool. You can have lunch on the terrace or at the end of the pier for an additional cost, presumably because the waiters have to walk farther. *Comedor Patricar* at the curve in the road just past the Hotel Torremolinos has similar fare for less.

Getting There & Away

From El Congo, on the Interamericana between San Salvador and Santa Ana, a road goes southwest and splits at the lake to skirt the north and south sides. The 'El Lago' bus (No 220) from Santa Ana takes the north branch, then doubles back and down a partially paved stretch to the hotel area. From San Salvador take bus No 201 heading to Santa Ana, then at El Congo pick up the 220. The last bus back to Santa Ana leaves the lake at 4:45 pm.

CERRO VERDE & VOLCÁN IZALCO

One of the gems of the country, Cerro Verde is a national park on top of an old volcano with incredible views of Lago de Coatepeque below and the still smoking **Volcán Izalco**. Before February 1770, Izalco's present site was nothing but a hole in the earth from which columns of black sulfuric smoke would rise. Then a cone began to form where the smoke fumed. Within a short time the cone had grown to a prodigious size – today it stands 1910m high.

Izalco continued to erupt into the 20th century, sending out smoke, boulders and flames – an impressive sight by night or day – earning it a reputation as 'the lighthouse of the Pacific.' In 1957, after erupting continuously for 187 years, Izalco stopped. The only time it's been heard from since was a small burp in 1966, but it's still classified as active. Today, the perfect cone, black and bare, stands devoid of life in an otherwise fertile land.

In addition to being a spectacular national park, **Cerro Verde** is also a major bird sanctuary, with many migratory species passing through, including emerald toucanets, jays, woodpeckers and motmots and 17 species of hummingbird. Knowledgeable park rangers will be more than happy to point out these and other local wildlife. It's

clearest early in the morning; later on, a thick fog bank tends to envelop the area with fleeting glimpses of the peaks emerging from the mist. It can get chilly and wet here, but most of the time it's refreshingly cool.

The park is open 8 am to 5 pm daily. Admission is US$0.80, plus US$0.70 for parking; it's an additional US$0.50 to get into the hotel area.

Hiking

This is the place to climb a couple of volcanoes. To ascend Izalco, take the marked path 100m before the park entrance. The rocky two-hour hike to the top takes you past graffiti-covered rocks on a not-so-ecotouristy trail. Park police advise that you not ascend alone. They will accompany you on request. If you prefer to admire Izalco from a distance, the best viewpoint is from the Hotel de Montaña (see Places to Stay & Eat), which at 2030m above sea level allows you to look down on the volcano.

A short, 40-minute circular trail starting from the parking lot is studded with not terribly informative signs in Spanish. Along the way observation points give stunning views of the lake and Volcán de Santa Ana, also called Ilamatepec (2365m). From there a well-used path branches off to the top of the volcano (three hours roundtrip).

Places to Stay & Eat

You can camp near the picnic areas in Cerro Verde at no charge apart from the entrance fee. Otherwise, stay at one of three ISTU-administered *cabins* beside the National Civil Police building. They charge $23/29 for two/three beds and bathrooms with hot showers. You can just show up or call ISTU in San Salvador to make a reservation (☎ 222 8000). Two comedores are above the cabins.

As the legend goes, *Hotel de Montaña* was built to provide an ideal vantage point from which to observe Izalco erupting, but a day before the hotel's completion, in 1957, the volcano turned itself off. Since 1996, the hotel's been officially shut. Corsatur took over and various grandiose plans are underway, including one to make it El Salvador's showcase eco-lodge. It costs US$0.50 to enter the complex, which houses a bar that serves meals, pupusas and drinks (closed Monday, open till 5 pm other days), a crafts shop and well-cared-for gardens.

Getting There & Away

Cerro Verde is 37km from Santa Ana. Bus No 248 from Santa Ana leaves at least five times daily. The first departure is at 7:30 am (US$0.75, two hours); the last bus back is at 5:30 pm. Verify these times beforehand.

From San Salvador, take buses to Santa Ana and disembark at El Congo on the Interamericana; walk uphill to the overpass and catch bus No 248. The trip from El Congo to Cerro Verde is incredibly scenic but driven at a snail's pace. Santa Ana–Sonsonate No 209 buses (marked 'Cerro Verde') skirt the lake, so you can get off at the Cerro Verde turnoff and hop on a pickup up the 14km hill.

If you're driving, Cerro Verde is 67km from San Salvador along the Sonsonate route or 77km by the more scenic Interamericana toward Santa Ana.

SANTA ANA
pop 253,037

The second-largest city in El Salvador and the capital of the department of the same name, Santa Ana was originally named Cihuatehuacán, which is Nahua for 'Place of Holy Women.' More pleasant than San Salvador, it's worth considering as a base for exploring the western and northwestern corners of the country. It also retains far more evidence of its colonial past. However, Santa Ana's streets are poorly lit and deserted after dark, so you won't want to linger.

Information

Banco Cuscatlán changes traveler's checks. Banco Credomatic, in Metrocentro, handles cash advances on credit cards.

Telecom is at the corner of 5a Avenida Norte and Calle Libertad Oriente, and a Telepunto branch is on Avenida Independencia Sur. Alecom Computer (& Variedades Michel), 10a Avenida Sur, has a row of fast PCs alongside the shelves of toy trucks and shampoo. Open 8 am to 12 pm and 2 to 6 pm Monday to Saturday, 8 am to 12 pm Sunday, it charges US$2.50 an hour for Internet access. Get a map of the city at La Curacao department store.

Things to See & Do

The most notable sight in Santa Ana is its large neo-Gothic cathedral. Ornate moldings cover the church's entire front, and the inside

has a sense of high-arched spaciousness and peace. Inside is a figure of the city's patron saint, who is feted in late July. On the square west of the cathedral is the **Teatro de Santa Ana**, whose construction was funded by taxes on coffee exports. Renovation is scheduled for completion in 2002 (a process that's taken twice as long as its original construction), but key sections are finished. Inquire in the office for a peek inside. Other attractive colonial buildings are on the streets east of Parque Menéndez and north of the cathedral, many with less lofty functions. Check out the superb but badly worn building kittycorner from Telecom, now a pool hall.

On the outskirts of town is a much-used turicentro, **Sihuatehuacán**. Past the towering ceiba tree at the entrance are tennis courts, snack bars and several large pools with a new waterslide. Take local bus No 51A from 4a Calle Poniente and Independencia.

Places to Stay

The **Hotel Livingston** (☎ 441 1801), on 10a Avenida Sur between 7a and 9a Calles Poniente, is the best budget choice in Santa Ana. Two new wings were built in 1999, and the new rooms are spiffy, if sterile, while the old rooms remain shabby. Singles/doubles in the new section are US$17.25/$23, and those in the old block are US$14.50. All rooms have private bath and TV.

Built around a big tiled courtyard, **Hospedaje San Miguel** (☎ 441 3465), on 7a Calle Poniente near Delgado, charges US$5.75 for rooms with an attached bathroom, US$4 without. The **Hotel Libertad** (☎ 441 2358) is centrally placed on 4a Calle Oriente, but renovations are long overdue. Rooms with private bath, fan and TV go for US$11.50/18.50/25.50 single/double/triple. Secure parking is available.

Six blocks east of the center, **Hotel Maya** (☎ 441 3612) won't win any awards for aesthetics, but it does have adequate rooms with private bath, fan and TV for US$14.50/17.25.

Right beside the stop for Guatemala-bound buses on 25a Calle Poniente is **Hotel La 25**, with clean but stuffy rooms for US$11.50/15. There's only one bathroom. A block west is **Internacional Hotel-Inn** (☎ 440 0804). Its small threadbare rooms with private bath go for US$15.50/26/37.50. Rooms facing the street are noisy. The

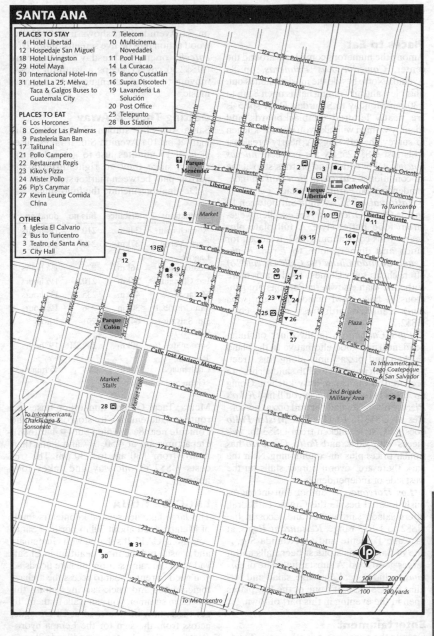

SANTA ANA

PLACES TO STAY
4 Hotel Libertad
12 Hospedaje San Miguel
18 Hotel Livingston
29 Hotel Maya
30 Internacional Hotel-Inn
31 Hotel La 25; Melva,
   Taca & Galgos Buses to
   Guatemala City

PLACES TO EAT
6 Los Horcones
8 Comedor Las Palmeras
9 Pastelería Ban Ban
17 Talitunal
21 Pollo Campero
22 Restaurant Regis
23 Kiko's Pizza
24 Mister Pollo
26 Pip's Carymar
27 Kevin Leung Comida
   China

OTHER
1 Iglesia El Calvario
2 Bus to Turicentro
3 Teatro de Santa Ana
5 City Hall

7 Telecom
10 Multicinema
   Novedades
11 Pool Hall
14 La Curacao
15 Banco Cuscatlán
16 Supra Discotech
19 Lavandería La
   Solución
20 Post Office
25 Telepunto
28 Bus Station

Parque
Menéndez

12a Calle Poniente
10a Calle Poniente
8a Calle Poniente
6a Calle Poniente
4a Calle Poniente
2a Calle Poniente
Libertad Poniente
1a Calle Poniente
3a Calle Poniente
5a Calle Poniente
7a Calle Poniente
9a Calle Poniente
11a Calle Poniente
Calle José Mariano Méndez
13a Calle Poniente
15a Calle Poniente
17a Calle Poniente
19a Calle Poniente
21a Calle Poniente
23a Calle Poniente
27a Calle Poniente

Parque
Libertad

Cathedral
To Turicentro

Libertad Oriente
1a Calle Oriente
2a Calle Oriente
3a Calle Oriente
4a Calle Oriente
5a Calle Oriente
7a Calle Oriente
9a Calle Oriente

To Interamericana,
Lago Coatepeque
& San Salvador

11a Calle Oriente
13a Calle Oriente
15a Calle Oriente
17a Calle Oriente
19a Calle Oriente
21a Calle Oriente
23a Calle Oriente

Plaza

2nd Brigade
Military Area

Parque
Colón

Market
Stalls

To Interamericana,
Chalchuapa &
Sonsonate

Market

Los Tanques del Molino

To Metrocentro

0   100   200 m
0   100   200 yards

EL SALVADOR

attached Casino San Remo is open 6:30 pm to 4 am.

Places to Eat

Among the numerous comedores around the center, **Comedor Las Palmeras**, on 8a Avenida Norte beside the market, stands out. This pleasant, airy dining hall is open 8 am to 3:30 pm Monday to Saturday. Daily specials are neatly lettered on blackboards, and friendly women will take you into the kitchen to survey the offerings. A hearty breakfast costs just US$1.25; try the excellent *huevos rancheros*. For coffee and pastries, stop at the air-conditioned **Pastelería Ban Ban** on Independencia near Parque Libertad.

Talitunal, on 5a Avenida Sur between 1a and 3a Calles Oriente, serves excellent vegetarian food buffet style. A full plate plus hearty rolls costs about US$2. It's open for lunch and dinner, noon to 7 pm. **Kevin Leung Comida China** (*9a Calle Oriente 16*) offers cheap, tasty Chinese food that is more authentic than elsewhere. Portions are generous: A huge bowl of noodle soup (*sopa min*) crammed with fresh veggies costs US$2.75.

Pip's Carymar, a family diner on Independencia, is a good alternative to the bland chicken and pizza joints along this street. Snacks from pupusas to club sandwiches are prepared in the clean, busy kitchen. Going up Avenida Independencia you'll find **Kiko's Pizza**, offering a salad bar and pizzas personales at US$3.75 to US$4.75. **Mister Pollo** does KFC-style chicken from US$3 for two pieces with sides, and **Pollo Campero** has similar prices plus air-conditioning. Near the park there are several burger stalls on the west side of Independencia.

Los Horcones, a bamboo hut incongruously located beside the Gothic cathedral, offers salads, sandwiches and tacos in the US$2 to US$3 range. **Restaurant Regis**, at 9a Calle Poniente and 6a Avenida Sur, is one of Santa Ana's oldest beer halls and serves good food. A substantial plate of *carnitas* includes steak, sausage, salad and tortillas for US$2.50. It's one of the few places open in the evening in this part of town.

Entertainment

Despite the ongoing renovations, the **Teatro de Santa Ana** hosts concerts and ballet and indigenous dance performances. Stop by for the current program. **Multicinema Novedades**, a block east of Parque Libertad on 3a Avenida Sur, shows mostly Hollywood action fare on five screens. **Supra Discotech**, open Wednesday to Saturday (US$2.50 cover), keeps a youthful crowd moving to rock, merengue and 'romantic' music.

Getting There & Away

Santa Ana's bus station is adjacent to the market on 10a Avenida Sur. It takes buses at least 15 minutes just to get out of the station since they go right through the narrow path between market stalls.

Destinations include the following:

destination	distance	bus no	duration
Ahuachapán	34km	210	1¼ hours
Cerro Verde	37km	248	2 hours
Lago de Coatepeque	16km	220	1¼ hours
Las Chinamas*	57km	210A	1½ hours
Metapán	45km	235	1½ hours
San Cristóbal*	30km	236	1½ hours
San Salvador (directo)	64km	201	1 hour
Sonsonate	40km	209, 216	1½ hours
Tazumal, Chalchuapa	14km	218	45 minutes

*Guatemalan border

Melva, Taca, Galgos and other buses en route to Guatemala City stop on 25a Calle Poniente near 8a Avenida Sur (☎ 440 1608). Departures are at 4:50, 6, 7 and 8 am, then hourly from 9:30 am to 3:30 pm. The trip costs US$7.50 one-way and takes four hours.

LAGO DE GÜIJA

This large lake lies several kilometers south of Metapán and about 30km north of Santa Ana along CA12. It's shared with Guatemala and considered the most beautiful in El Salvador. In the rainy season the lake floods, so you need to rent a boat to access the archaeological sites and rock carvings along the shores; in summer, you can walk to them. To get there, turn off the road at El Desagüe, across from the sign for the Lempa hydroelectric project. A gravel road leads 2km to the lake and the tiny community on its shores.

PARQUE NACIONAL MONTECRISTO–EL TRIFINIO

The borders of El Salvador, Honduras and Guatemala converge at this cloud forest reserve. The highest point in the park (2418m) is referred to as El Trifinio. This is the most humid region in the country, with 2000mm annual precipitation and 100% average relative humidity. Oak and laurel trees grow to 30m, where leaves intertwine to form a canopy impenetrable to sunlight. The forest floor provides a habitat for abundant exotic plant life including orchids, mushrooms, lichens and mosses and tree ferns up to 8m tall. The temperature averages between 10°C and 15°C.

For anyone interested in botany or animals, the park is a great place to visit. Animals seen (albeit rarely) include spider monkeys, two-fingered anteaters, porcupines, spotted and hooded skunks, pumas, red and gray squirrels, wild pigs, opossums, coyotes and agoutis. The forest is also home to at least 87 bird species, including quetzals, green toucans, woodpeckers, hummingbirds, nightingales, white-faced quail and striped owls.

Getting there, however, is a challenge. While officially protected by the Salvadoran government, the park's sheer inaccessibility, especially from the bordering two countries, is its best protection.

Ideally, make the journey by 4WD, but if you can't manage that, first get to Metapán. From there hitch a ride in one of the pickups that goes to and from the community of Majadita in the park. The road to the main gate (5km) branches off the highway at Hotel San José. You could walk to the gate if you wanted, but you can't *walk* into the park – that's the rule.

Three kilometers beyond the gate is a turnoff to the Casco Colonial, a restored foundry built in 1783. Clean whitewashed walls, red-tile roofs, brick floors and warm patios lined with hanging plants make this a pleasant stop.

Climbing up the road, you'll pass the community of Majadita. Another 12km up the road brings you to Los Planes, where a soccer field lies in the cup of the lush hill rising up to El Trifinio. A few landscaped gardens and a small store detract from the wildness, but plenty of hiking trails lead to vistas of the multi-hued lands below or to

the tangle of jungle above. To access the cloud forest, hike up the road right by the entrance to Los Planes. It's 7km to El Trifinio.

Information

The area above Los Planes is closed from May to November, the breeding season of the local fauna. The remainder of the park is open the rest of the year, but you can only venture a few kilometers up the road.

To take full advantage of the park when it's open, you'll need to spend the night. Los Planes has camping sites and firepits; Casco Colonial has a couple of ill-kept rooms with cots from US$7. To stay at either place you need advance permission from the National Parks and Wildlife Service at the Ministerio de Agricultura in San Salvador (☎ 294 0566 ext 72); the office, open 8 am to 4 pm weekdays, is on Calle El Matazano, Colonia Santa Lucia (bus No 33A from the city center). Getting permission is usually no problem, except for weekends.

Take your own food, warm clothes and waterproof gear. The guards at the front gate sell firewood. Make sure to arrive before 3 pm if you want to camp. Admission to the park is US$2 for locals, US$5.75 for foreigners, plus US$1.15 to US$2.30 for a vehicle.

RUINAS DE TAZUMAL

The Maya ruins of Tazumal, considered the most important in El Salvador, are in the town of **Chalchuapa**, 13km west of Santa Ana on the way to Ahuachapán. In the Quiché language Tazumal means 'pyramid where the victims were burned.'

Archeologists estimate that the first settlements in the area were around 5000 BC. Part of a 10-sq-km zone, much of it still buried under the town, the excavated ruins on display span a period of over 1000 years. Even though these are some of the most important ruins in El Salvador, they pale in comparison to those in neighboring countries. Restoration with drab concrete didn't help either, but there's a good view from the top.

The museum displays artifacts taken from the site, which provide evidence of ancient and active trade with places as far away as Panama and Mexico. Pieces are abundantly described in English. Other finds, including the Estela de Tazumal, a 2.65m-high basalt monolith inscribed with hieroglyphics, are at the Museo Nacional Davíd G Guzmán in San Salvador.

Tazumal is open 9 am to 5 pm Tuesday to Sunday (US$3). Bus No 218 comes from Santa Ana, 14km (45 minutes) away. A sign on the main road through Chalchuapa points toward the ruins, about a five-minute walk from the highway. If driving from Santa Ana, stay right at the fork in the road, continuing toward Ahuachapán, then turn left at the Texaco station in Chalchuapa. The ruins are at the end of the road.

AHUACHAPÁN
pop 110,129

Ahuachapán sits in a geothermically active area, and the plant here supplies over 15% of the country's electrical power. Just 16km from the Guatemalan border, it makes a pleasant enough first stop, but there isn't much to do. Otherwise, you could forge on to Santa Ana, 34km to the east.

Activity revolves around Parque Menéndez by the market and bus station. Six blocks south is Plaza Concordia, with a kiosk at the base of a clocktower and the Nuestra Señora de Asunción Church, recently renovated but still retaining its 18th-century wood columns.

Banco Credomatic, at 1a Avenida Norte and Calle Barrios, gives cash advances on Visa cards and changes traveler's checks. The Telecom office is on Plaza Concordia.

Places to Stay & Eat

Hotel Casa Blanca (☎ 443 1505), at 2a Avenida Norte and Calle Barrios, offers affordable luxury. Large, attractively furnished singles/doubles with private bath and hot water cost US$16/26.50, or US$23/31.75 with air-conditioning. Have a drink or dine under the stars in the tranquil central courtyard. *Hotel San José* (☎ 413 1908) is inside an enclosed compound that blocks out the noise from the adjacent Parque Menéndez. It charges US$7/14 for tidy rooms with private bath; rooms with air-con are US$9.25/18.50.

La Estancia, in a colonial-style house on 1a Avenida Sur between Calle Barrios and 1a Calle Oriente is a charming place to enjoy breakfast or lunch for under US$2. The popular *Restaurant Mixta 'S,'* on 2a

Avenida Sur just south of 1a Calle Poniente, serves *mixtas* – pita bread stuffed with pickled veggies, salsa and meat or cheese (US$1.50) – and good fruit shakes. *Pizza Attos*, at Menéndez and 2a Calle Oriente, has better-than-average pizzas from US$2.50 to US$9.25, plus a salad bar and beer on tap. It's open till 8 pm as is Mixta 'S.'

Getting There & Away

The bus 'station' is on the north side of town. Buses to Santa Ana, Tacuba and San Salvador depart from the west side of the Santa Ana highway. Buses to Sonsonate via Apaneca wait along the Sonsonate turnoff on the opposite side of the road; Apaneca microbuses depart when they're full. Buses for the Guatemalan border leave from the west side of Parque Menéndez.

destination	distance	bus no	duration
Las Chinamas	16km	263	30 minutes
San Salvador	100km	202	2 hours
Santa Ana	34km	210	1½ hours
Sonsonate via Juayúa	36km	249	2 hours
Tacuba	14km	264	1 hour

TACUBA

The pleasant village of Tacuba lies 14km west of Ahuachapán in an area lushly endowed with varied vegetation and exuberant bird life. You can explore the ruins of a colonial church destroyed in the 1773 quake that hit Antigua, Guatemala. Manolo González leads hikes to the Río Paz and some 30m waterfalls. He can also show you a 600-year-old tree jammed with parrots at dusk – the noise is almost deafening. Full-day tours including transportation, and meals are US$11.50 to US$17.50 per person. Manolo can be reached at ☎ 443 1911 ext 258, or inquire at Ximena's Guest House in San Salvador.

RUTA DE LAS FLORES

The 36km stretch of the CA8 linking Sonsonate and Ahuachapán has been named for the abundant wildflowers that decorate the region from October to February. It traverses the heart of El Salvador's coffee country, and in May white coffee blossoms coat the volcanic slopes of the plantations.

The route takes in several interesting mountain towns.

North of Sonsonate, **Nahuizalco** is an indigenous Pipil village specializing in wicker baskets and furniture. Occasionally you see a woman in traditional Pipil clothing, a colorful wraparound skirt. Nahuizalco holds an unusual night market, illuminated by candles in baskets, until 11 pm.

Salcoatitán, another 9km north, features an 18th-century church and an orchid nursery. From there, a road branches east to **Juayúa**, a tranquil town with a turbulent past, while the main route continues northwest, crossing into the Ahuachapán Department before reaching **Apaneca**, with plenty of opportunities for hiking. Colorful textiles are produced in **Concepción de Ataco**, 14km north of Apaneca.

Juayúa
pop 33,000

Juayúa is a clean, refreshingly cool mountain village set amid volcanoes and coffee-dominated hillsides. An attractive plaza with a fountain and ample foliage fronts a fine white church dating from 1957. Though busy with *capitalinos* on weekends, it's placid during the week, and rooms are yours for the asking.

Juayúa's happy vibe – people actually walk around or ride bikes after dark – contrasts with the events of the not-so-distant past. It was in Juayúa, Salcoatitán and Izalco that indigenous uprisings ignited the revolutionary movement of 1932. The ill-organized insurrection was brutally put down by government forces backed by the coffee elite.

Coffee remains the source of the town's relative prosperity. Most of its agriculturally productive land is given over to the bean. Its plantations – recognizable by the neat rows of *copalchín* trees that serve as windbreaks – produce 11% of the country's coffee exports.

A splendid half-hour hike takes you to **Los Chorros de Calera**, a series of falls forming large pools – actually dikes used to generate hydroelectric power. To get there, take 6a Calle Oriente east. At the end of the street, turn left and take the first right. Follow this trash-strewn trail east alongside coffee fields, over a bridge and through an archway. You'll find yourself above a deep chasm, where high waterfalls are fed by the Río Santa Lucía. Beyond this are three sets of falls, the last of which is the smallest and loveliest, abundantly adorned with impatiens blossoms. It's practically deserted during the week but beware of outlaws. Inquire at Doña Mercedes (see Places to Stay & Eat) for a guide.

Bus No 249 to Apaneca and Ahuachapán departs every 15 minutes from the plaza (US$0.25).

Places to Stay & Eat A pair of excellent new hostels make an extended stay in Juayúa an appealing option. *Casa de Huespedes Doña Mercedes* (☎ 452 2287), at 2a Avenida Sur and 6a Calle Oriente, offers immaculate, tasteful double rooms with firm beds for US$19 or US$23 including private bath. The house features a comfortable lounge and secure parking. From the bus stop, go downhill past the orange bakery; at the end of the street turn left and go two blocks. *Alojamiento Turístico Las Azaleas* (☎ 452 2383, 6a Avenida Norte 2-5), near 3a Calle Oriente, is a bit simpler and cheaper but neat and comfortable. On a quiet street, the little blue house has a lounge and four bedrooms. The price is US$14.50 for one or two beds, US$17.25 for three beds. Inquire at the Pollo Rico.

Across the street from Doña Mercedes is *Doña Cony*, serving fine pupusas. *Pollo Rico* is primarily a chicken takeout business, but there are several pleasant dining rooms and some tables beside a leafy patio. Two-piece chicken dinners are US$3.25. *Café Restaurante La Calera*, a cozy hangout on the plaza, serves coffee from its own plantation and good pastries. Breakfast (US$3) is served weekends only.

Apaneca
pop 8420

Situated in the Sierra Apaneca Ilamatepec, Apaneca, the highest town in El Salvador, seems even more remote and peaceful than Juayúa. The 400-year-old Iglesia San Andres Apóstol dominates a central plaza filled with bird activity in late afternoon. Local craftsmen produce furniture from cypress and coffee wood, and there are quite a few flower and plant nurseries.

Come here to enjoy the cool mountain air and to hike on extinct volcanoes. The

EL SALVADOR

crater lakes **Laguna de las Ninfas** and **Laguna Verde**, north and northeast of town, are within hiking distance. The latter is deep and cold, the former swampy and full of reeds and lily pads. You can camp on the **Cerro Grande de Apaneca** (Chichicaste-peque), which at 1816m affords outstanding views of the region. Arévalo Service (☎ 433 0326), across from the church, arranges excursions to these destinations accompanied by tourist police. The cost is US$17.25 for groups of up to 10 people.

Intriguing evidence of Mayan influence is found on the **Finca Santa Leticia** coffee plantation just south of town. Three pot-bellied figures carved from huge basalt boulders rest where they were found by the plantation's owner. The heaviest weighs in at 24,000 pounds. Experts speculate that the 2000-year-old sculptures were created by an early Maya group, possibly in deference to their rulers. The finca charges US$1.75 to visit the archaeological park.

Minibuses from Apaneca to Ahuachapán (US$0.35, 40 minutes) depart from the plaza.

Places to Stay & Eat The best budget choice is *Hostal Rural Las Orquídeas* (☎ 433 0061), on 4a Calle Poniente near Avenida Central Sur. It offers clean, brightly painted singles/doubles with large bathrooms for US$11.50/23. *Hostal Rural Las Ninfas* (☎ 433 0059), three blocks north of the plaza at the end of 1a Avenida Norte, is similar but homier. It charges US$23/29 for two-/three-bed rooms with spacious bathrooms, but may reduce the price for a single traveler.

While Juayúa is quaint, Apaneca is primitive, so it isn't so easy to find locally oriented restaurants or cafes. Pupusas and other cheap eats are available along the edge of the market but even this winds down by 7 pm. *Comedor Carmela*, on Avenida Central Norte between 1a and 3a Calles Poniente, has been recommended and it's open every day.

At the Hotel Santa Leticia, *Restaurante La Finca* serves the plantation's own world-class java, as well as toothsome local fare. It's not cheap but the portions are generous and the setting is lovely. Overstuffed sandwiches are around US$6 and meat platters are US$8 to US$9.50. Similar in style,

Restaurante Las Cabañas de Apaneca, in the hotel of the same name, has very good country cooking till 5 pm daily. Main courses run US$5.75 to US$10.50 and snacks are in the US$3 range. *La Cocina de Mi Abuela*, near the plaza, is another place serving *comida típica*, but only on Saturday and Sunday.

SONSONATE
pop 98,976

Not much of a destination in itself, Sonsonate can be a base for exploring the western beaches or nearby indigenous villages. This hot and humid city holds one of the country's most vivid Semana Santa celebrations, during which residents decorate the streets with elaborate carpets made of colored sawdust.

The village of **Izalco**, 8km northeast at the foot of Volcán Izalco, was the site of an indigenous revolt in 1932. The Nahua language is still spoken by some inhabitants. Nearby is **Atecozol**, a turicentro with the usual swimming holes, kiosks and gardens. Around the grounds are stone sculptures by Agustín Estrada, including one of Atonatl, the indigenous warrior who shot an arrow through the leg of the conquistador Pedro de Alvarado here in 1524.

The University of El Salvador brings groups to the outlying indigenous villages of Santa Caterina Masahuat and Santo Domingo de Guzmán; inquire at CIS (See Useful Organizations in the Facts for the Visitor section, earlier in this chapter).

Coastal points accessible from here include **Los Cóbanos**, a prime diving destination, and **Barra de Santiago**, a protected mangrove forest reserve where canoes can be hired for estuary tours.

Places to Stay & Eat

Among the cheap hotels in the seedy area around the bus station, *Hotel Sagitario* (☎ 451 1174), on 18a Avenida Sur, is the least dilapidated, with singles/doubles that cost US$5.75/9.25. A better value is the *Hotel Modelo* (☎ 451 1679), at 10a Avenida Norte and Marroquín, in the middle of a chaotic market area. It's easy to spot – look for a little waterfall cascading over an aquamarine wall. The Modelo offers nicely furnished, air-conditioned one-bed rooms with cable TV and spacious bathrooms for a mere

US$14.50. You might also consider *Hotel Agape* (☎ 451 1456, ramon@intradec.com), on the highway north of town along the 53A bus route to Izalco. Founded by Padre Flavián Mucci, a Franciscan priest from Boston, the hotel funds social programs, such as a hospital for undernourished kids. Set amid peaceful gardens populated by retirees and lawn gnomes, the Agape charges US$16/22.50 for air-conditioned rooms with private bath and cable TV. There's a small pool and a restaurant.

Getting There & Away

Bus The bus station on the east side of town is typically grimy and anarchic. Key destinations include the following:

destination	distance	bus no	duration
Ahuachapán via Juayúa and Apaneca	36km	210	2 hours
La Hachadura*	58km	259A	1¾ hours
La Libertad	76km	287	3 hours
La Perla	51km	261	1¼ hours
Los Cóbanos	24km	257	½ hour
Santa Ana	40km	216	1¼ hours

*Guatemalan border

Bus No 53A to Izalco and No 53D to Nahuizalco depart from the north side of the central plaza. Bus No 252 to Acajutla leaves from the Caja de Crédito building on 10a Avenida Sur. Bus No 285 goes to Barra de Santiago at 4:45 pm; otherwise, take No 259A toward the border and hitch a ride from the turnoff.

Train El Salvador's only passenger train travels to Armenia, an hour to the east. It leaves at 6:10 and 9:10 am, and 12:10 and 3 pm. Get your ticket at the station, at Marroquín and 8a Avenida Sur, half an hour before departure. Even if you don't take the train, the old station house is worth a look, with a revolving piece of track that turns the train around, and the trainmen are glad to talk about these antiques.

PARQUE NACIONAL EL IMPOSIBLE

Decreed a national park in 1989, El Imposible is a tropical mountain forest between 300m and 1450m above sea level in the Apaneca Ilamatepec mountain range, near the towns of Concepción de Ataco, Tacuba and San Francisco Menéndez. The park is named for the perilous gorge through which coffee growers once labored to move their crop from the northern fincas to the port of Acajutla. Many mules and crews fell to their deaths attempting to cross the gorge via makeshift tree-trunk bridges until a bridge was built over the treacherous gorge in 1968.

The majority of the park is original forest, the remains of a threatened ecosystem and habitat for an extraordinary variety of plant and animal life. Nearly 400 kinds of trees grow in the area, and endangered animals such as puma, tigrillo, wild boar, king hawk and black-crested eagle are protected here. Eight rivers flow through Imposible, providing the watershed for Barra de Santiago and other mangrove forests along the coast.

The San Benito entrance is on the park's east side, via the hamlet of San Miguelito. To visit, you must get written permission for a fee of US$5.75 from SalvaNatura, the environmental group responsible for protecting the reserve (see Tourist Offices in the San Salvador section, earlier in this chapter). A western entrance at San Francisco Menéndez was scheduled to open by 2001 (no permit required).

The best time to visit is October to February, as the rainy season hinders travel. Hiking trails meander throughout the park. A well-graded 1km trail leads to an observation point with excellent views of the Guayapa Valley. From there, branch trails lead to Cerro León (four hours) and Los Enganches, the confluence of two rivers, where you'll find prehistoric rock carvings (three hours). You'll be assigned an authorized guide, a member of the local community who's been trained to identify plants and animals. You should leave a US$4 or US$5 tip, as the guides do not receive a salary.

The solar-powered visitor's center/ranger station at San Benito features exhibits on local history and the park's flora and fauna, enhanced by videos and computers that play birdsongs.

Two camping areas with toilets and showers are inside the park but no fires are allowed. It's possible to stay in San Miguelito, however infrastructure is still rudimentary. There are a couple of stores selling food, water, T-shirts and camping gear; a few comedores; and a dirt-floor hut with cots and a latrine called a hospedaje (US$3.50 per person). Local craftsman Martín Hipólito González paints eagles and other park creatures on mahogany keychains and paperweights. He also has field guides on birds and animals of the area that he'll share with you. These local businesses get credit backing from SalvaNatura.

From Sonsonate catch a 259A Frontera bus (frequent) and get off at Cara Sucia, where you can find crowded pickup trucks to San Miguelito (US$0.90, one hour). Alternatively, you can get off at the Desvío Ahuachapío and hike or hitch from there (13.5km). You'll go through the villages of Ahuachapío and Refugio before reaching San Miguelito.

Eastern El Salvador

The eastern corners of El Salvador, especially the northeast, have always been poor. The people in these regions do what they can to live off what little land they have. The FMLN gained control in this region by rallying many of those people to fight for land reform. Some towns remained ambivalent but were affected nonetheless.

Since the war ended, the region has been slowly rebuilding itself. Two bridges over the Río Lempa that had been blown up by rebel forces, the Puente Cuscatlán and the Puente de Oro, are finally back in operation. And the long-moribund port of La Unión is making a comeback thanks in part to Japanese investment.

Traveling east, you are unlikely to find much tourist competition, but be prepared for more primitive conditions. Untrammeled beaches, towering volcanoes and offshore islands await, but tourism infrastructure is minimal. Hurricane Mitch had its greatest impact on the lower Lempa, which is still being resettled.

There are two ways to travel east – along the Interamericana or along the Carretera del Litoral (CA2); the latter accesses the beaches, and the former the northern reaches. For full coverage of the area, you could make a roundtrip from San Salvador using both roads.

THE INTERAMERICANA

The Interamericana goes east from San Salvador to San Miguel, on to La Unión and up again to the Honduran border at El Amatillo. Despite the importance of the road, you'll still be playing roulette with the potholes if you're driving and it's a bumpy ride in a bus. Highway CA7 is a shorter, more direct connection between San Miguel and El Amatillo.

A few towns of interest lie between San Salvador and San Vicente on the Interamericana. **Cojutepeque**, 32km east of San Salvador, is a small town best known for the Cerro Las Pavas (Hill of the Turkeys), which has an outdoor shrine to the Virgen de Fátima brought here from Portugal in 1949. The shrine attracts religious pilgrims, especially on Sunday and on May 13, El Día de la Virgen. In San Salvador, catch Bus No 113 from the Reloj de Flores, just west of the Terminal de Oriente; it's about a 45-minute ride.

Farther along the highway (54km from San Salvador or 22km from Cojutepeque) is the turnoff to **Ilobasco**, a town known for ceramics. Right after the entrance to the town is a string of *artesanía* shops along Avenida Carlo Bonilla. Taller y Escuela de Cerámicas Kiko (☎ 332 2324), open 8 am to noon and 1 to 5 pm weekdays, gives tours and offers pottery classes. The annual crafts fair runs September 24 to 29. Take bus No 111 or No 142 from the Terminal de Oriente or from Cojutepeque.

Another 8.5km heading east along the Interamericana is the road to **San Sebastián**, known for woven hammocks and textiles. The difference here is that most of the weavers are male. January 17 to 25 is the annual fair. Bus No 111 goes there, or catch a bus in Cojutepeque.

Cruising farther down the Interamericana you'll spot **San Vicente**, a town of 51,000, by the Río Acahuapa at the foot of the twin-peaked 2182m Chichontepec Volcano. The town's landmark is an unusual white clock tower in the main plaza; climb up for a view. Also of note is El Pilar, the colonial church built in the 1760s. Near San Vicente are two swimming holes: Amapulapa, an overused turicentro, and the cleaner Laguna Apastapeque. Take bus No 177 and No 156, respectively, from San Vicente's plaza.

CARRETERA DEL LITORAL

The Carretera del Litoral (Hwy CA2) runs from San Salvador southeast through Zacatecoluca and Usulután, eventually coming to a crossroads with routes heading north to San Miguel and south to the Pacific coast.

The first town of any size southeast of San Salvador is **Zacatecoluca** (57km), near the largest turicentro in El Salvador, Ichanmichen. From there, the Litoral is a well-marked four-lane highway with shoulders, until you get to the Río Lempa, spanned by the recently completed Puente de Oro. Beyond the bridge, the road narrows but is still in decent shape. Another 27km to the east is the departmental capital of Usulután.

The highway then skirts a rugged range to the south. The turnoff for **Playa El Espino** is just past El Tránsito, 10km east of Usulután. You'll need a four-wheel drive to navigate the bumpy, windy road. It takes close to two hours to get there, but you are rewarded with your very own beach. **Laguna El Jocotál**, farther east, is a migratory bird sanctuary best visited in early morning, before the water-lily islands disperse.

The road then winds up into lava hills until the roundabout at El Delirio. From there, it's a straight shot north to San Miguel or south to Playa El Cuco and the eastern beaches.

ISLA MONTECRISTO

Where the Río Lempa meets the Pacific Ocean, mangroves flourish, brown pelicans glide, egrets pose gracefully and fish skip over the river's surface. This natural spot is still undeveloped and more pristine than the accessible beaches around it.

During the war, the island and its cashew plantation were abandoned and taken over by the FMLN. After 1992, it was settled by migrants from Zacatecoluca and elsewhere, who took advantage of the post-war land transfer program. The community was again evacuated in 1998 when Hurricane Mitch flooded the lower Lempa. It is now inhabited by about 22 families practicing subsistence agriculture; they also grow organic cashews as an export crop.

You could spend a pleasant day or two here simply admiring the big river coursing by, watching birds and getting to know the islanders. Juan Lobo leads canoe tours through the mangrove canals and to the mouth of the Lempa (US$14). He can also ferry you to the beach (US$5 per boat), a broad, clean, usually uninhabited strip of sand, though only strong swimmers will want to plunge into these rough waters. Horseback tours are a good way to explore the cashew plantation and get to know the island's community.

If you'd like to spend the night, there are several comfortable thatched-roof *cabañas* with a couple of cots each for US$9.25, plus a hammock hut for lounging by the river. Mosquito nets and sheets are provided. There's no running water, but you can wash up by the well. Hospitable hosts Juan and Carmen Sulim have a store where they serve meals for about US$2. Beer and soft drinks are available.

The NGO CORDES (☎ 235 8262, 883 4825, cordes.ses@salnet.net), whose aim is to help people in rural areas find new livelihoods, can help you arrange a stay on Isla Montecristo. They have an office in San Carlos Lempa on the way to the island. Otherwise, contact Carmen on the island: Call her beeper at ☎ 298 1122, ask for unit 337-525 and leave a message saying when you're planning to come.

It takes about two hours to get from San Salvador to La Pita, the embarkation point for the island. Take bus No 302 toward Usulután and get off at San Nicolás Lempa, just before the Río Lempa bridge. Look for the right turnoff by the Texaco station. Pickup trucks shuttle passengers down this road every half hour, some of which make the 13km journey to La Pita. Bus No 158 leaves San Nicolás for La Pita at 5 am and 2 pm, returning at 5:30 am and 3 pm. Drivers note: Beyond the village of San Carlos Lempa, the road challenges any 4WD expert in the rainy season.

From La Pita, lanchas (US$14 round-trip) or canoes (US$2.50 one-way) can take you to the island – during the verano months, they only cross at high tide. Phone CORDES or Carmen the day before to ensure a boat can take you across.

On the way down, you could have a look at San Carlos Lempa, a well-organized community with programs in education, self-sufficient agriculture and an EU-financed cashew processing facility. CORDES can arrange tours.

USULUTÁN
pop 69,511

Situated at the foot of Volcán de Usulután (1450m), this busy departmental capital makes a suitable base for trips to the **Bahía de Jiquilisco**, Playa El Espino and Laguna El Jocotal. Another possible day trip is to **Laguna de Alegría**, a jade-green lake fed by sulfurous springs in the crater of Volcán de Tecapa (1594m). It's a half-hour hike from the town of Alegría, northwest of Usulután.

Among the handful of hotels scattered around town, the best option is *Hotel Florida* (☎ 662 0540), a very clean establishment with a helpful staff. Singles/ doubles with fans and private bath cost US$6.50/11.50 or US$13/15 with air-con. All meals are served on the premises. *Posada del Viajero* (☎ 662 0216) is another good deal with comfortable rooms for US$5.25/8.75 and a talkative parrot on the patio. *Hotel España* (☎ 662 0378, Calle Dr Penado 3), half a block from the plaza, is a faded colonial-style inn with battered rooms around a leafy courtyard for US$7/14. Large bathrooms with shutter-style doors facing the courtyard offer limited privacy.

Of the food stalls on the central plaza's north side, *Pupusería Juanita* is the cleanest and busiest. Its chicharrón pupusas are quite spicy and flavorful. Stuffed chiles, steamed veggies and pig's-foot soup are among the comida a la vista options at popular *Comedor Margaritas*, at the intersection of 4a Avenida Norte and 4a Calle Oriente.

Getting There & Away

There are two terminals on opposite sides of the road, one for Zacatecoluca and San Salvador, the other for San Miguel and points east.

Bus No 373 travels to San Miguel every 15 minutes (1½ hours). Take the same bus to Laguna El Jocotal, 1km from the turnoff, or to Playa El Cuco – get off at El Delirio and catch bus No 320. Bus No 351 goes to Playa El Espino eight times daily (2½ hours, 22km). To Puerto El Triunfo and Bahía de Jiquilisco, bus No 363 runs every 15 minutes along 4a Calle Oriente (40 minutes); the last bus back is at 5:30 pm. To Alegría, bus No 348 leaves at 5:20, 6:20, 7:45 and 11 am (1¾ hours).

BAHÍA DE JIQUILISCO

The long Peninsula San Juan del Gozo hems in this bay studded with mangrove-fringed islands, habitat for gray egrets and many other water birds. The best beaches are at **Corral de Mulas** on the sea side of the peninsula, **Punta San Juan** on the peninsula's east end and **Isla Madre Sal**. Also called Isla Jobal, **Isla Espíritu Santo** has a community of 4000, endless coconut groves and a coconut oil processing plant, but the beaches are no big deal. There's no food or lodging on any of the islands; boatmen can arrange a room in a home, or you could pitch a hammock between palm trunks, though locals warn of crime.

Regular passenger service to Corral de Mulas and Isla Jobal leaves in early morning from the dock at Puerto El Triunfo (US$1.25). The last boat back is around midday, but check with the boatman to be sure. Alternatively, hire a boat: Standard rates for up to 10 passengers are US$17 roundtrip to Corral de Mulas, Jobal and Madre Sal, US$29 to Punta San Juan. Advance arrangements for these journeys or tours of the waterways can be made through the Puerto El Triunfo development committee (☎ 663 6035).

SAN MIGUEL
pop 245,426

San Miguel, the country's third-largest city, is the main hub for the eastern half of the country. Founded in 1530, it still shows signs of Spanish influence. The town has quite a few park areas, and its cathedral and theater are in better shape than usual, though like other Salvadoran cities it's choking on its own smog. The market burgeons out of its central area onto many streets, adding some excitement to the active town – active, that is, until the sun sets bright-orange, and then it's downright dead. When the center shuts down, make sure you're somewhere you want to be.

Looming over town is Volcán de San Miguel (2130m), also called Chaparrastique. The volcano's still active: It erupted at least 10 times in the last century, most recently in

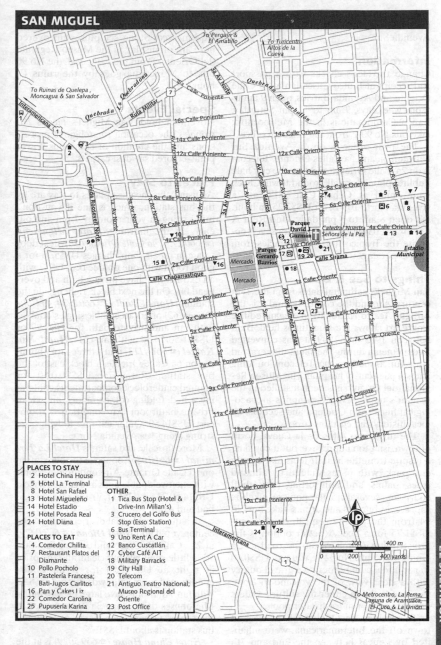

SAN MIGUEL

To Perquín &
El Amatillo

To Turicentro
Altos de la
Cueva

To Ruinas de Quelepa ,
Moncagua & San Salvador

Quebrada La Quebradona

Ruta Militar

Quebrada de El Borbollón

Quebrada

Interamericana

16a Calle Poniente

3a Av Norte

8a Calle Poniente

14a Calle Poniente

14a Calle Oriente

Monserrat Romero

12a Calle Poniente

12a Calle Oriente

10a Calle Poniente

10a Calle Oriente

8a Calle Poniente

8a Calle Oriente

Av Gerardo Barrios

6a Calle Oriente

4a Calle Oriente

Parque
David J.
Guzmán

Catedral Nuestra
Señora de la Paz

Estadio
Municipal

Parque
Gerardo
Barrios

2a Calle Oriente

Calle Sirama

Avenida Roosevelt Norte

Avenida Roosevelt Sur

Mercado

Mercado

Calle Chaparrástique

1a Calle Poniente

1a Calle Oriente

3a Calle Poniente

3a Calle Oriente

Av José Simeón Cañas

5a Calle Poniente

5a Calle Oriente

7a Calle Poniente

7a Calle Oriente

9a Calle Poniente

9a Calle Oriente

11a Calle Poniente

11a Calle Oriente

13a Calle Poniente

15a Calle Oriente

15a Calle Poniente

17a Calle Poniente

19a Calle Poniente

21a Calle Poniente

Interamericana

To Metrocentro, La Pema,
Laguna de Aramuaca,
El Cuco & La Unión

0   200   400 m
0   200   400 yards

PLACES TO STAY
2 Hotel China House
5 Hotel La Terminal
8 Hotel San Rafael
13 Hotel Migueleño
14 Hotel Estadio
15 Hotel Posada Real
24 Hotel Diana

PLACES TO EAT
4 Comedor Chilita
7 Restaurant Platos del
   Diamante
10 Pollo Pocholo
11 Pastelería Francesa;
   Bati-Jugos Carlitos
16 Pan y Cakes Liz
22 Comedor Carolina
25 Pupusería Karina

OTHER
1 Tica Bus Stop (Hotel &
   Drive-Inn Milian's)
3 Crucero del Golfo Bus
   Stop (Esso Station)
6 Bus Terminal
9 Uno Rent A Car
12 Banco Cuscatlán
17 Cyber Café AIT
18 Military Barracks
19 City Hall
20 Telecom
21 Antiguo Teatro Nacional;
   Museo Regional del
   Oriente
23 Post Office

EL SALVADOR

1976. To get there, take a Placitas bus from the corner of Calle Chaparrastique and 7a Avenida Sur.

Information

Change traveler's checks with a passport and receipt at Banco Cuscatlán at 4a Calle Oriente and Avenida Barrios, open 9 am to 5 pm weekdays, 9 am to 12 pm Saturday. Banco Credomatic is in the Metrocentro; take bus No 90-F from the Telecom office.

The post office is on 4a Avenida Sur between 3a and 5a Calles Oriente. Telecom is on 2a Calle Oriente, right by the city hall. Publitel phones are all around town. Check your email at Cyber Café AIT, at 2a Avenida Norte 103-B, for US$2.25 an hour. It's open 8 am to 8 pm daily. Uno Rent A Car (☎ 661 0344), on Avenida Roosevelt opposite the Tropico Inn, rents vehicles from US$43 per day.

Things to See & Do

San Miguel's **cathedral** dates from the 18th century. Around the corner behind it is the **Antiguo Teatro Nacional**, an elegant edifice where art shows are sometimes held. Built between 1903 and 1909, it was converted into a cinema during the silent film era and later functioned as the Telecom building and social security hospital. The **Museo Regional del Oriente** has been installed in the theater's upper level. It contains archaeological finds from Quelepa and sections on local history and customs (free).

The turicentro **Altos de la Cueva**, north of town, isn't too impressive, but it could be a respite from the heat. It feels like a large city park, with paths shaded by almond trees, palms, and poinsettias, basketball courts and several circular pools. A jukebox cafe serves burgers and drinks. Take bus No 94 from the parque central, or shell out US$1.75 for a taxi. A better option is the private **Club Aramuaca** on the road to La Unión (take bus No 324). You pay US$0.60 to get into a club bordering a gravel quarry with a clear view of the volcano in front. You can bathe in either the sulfuric waters of the lagoon or in freshwater pools.

The **Ruinas de Quelepa**, 8km west of town off the Interamericana, were inhabited by Lencas between the 2nd and 7th centuries AD. Evidence shows trade links with Copán in Honduras. Largely unexca-

vated, the site consists of around 40 ceremonial platforms dispersed over a ½-sq-km area. Stone sculptures uncovered here are on display in the Museo Regional del Oriente. From the cathedral, the No 90 bus to Moncagua goes by the ruins (½ hour).

Special Events

November holds San Miguel's *Fiestas Patronales*, the occasion for religious processions and the creation of enormous flower petal–colored sawdust carpets.

Places to Stay

As usual, the cheapest places to stay are by the bus station, which is fine if you don't mind being in your room by 7 pm and out early in the morning. **Hotel Migueleño** (☎ 660 2737, 4a Calle Oriente 610), next door to a gun repair shop, charges US$5.75 for a good room with one double bed, US$7 with an extra cot; all have private bath and overhead fan. On the next block, right beside the stadium, **Hotel Estadio** (☎ 660 2734, 4a Calle Oriente 62) offers acceptable singles/doubles with fan and private bath for US$7/9 or US$11.50/14.50 with air-con. **Hotel San Rafael** (☎ 661 4113) is in a three-story building on 6a Calle Oriente, a block east of the bus station. Rates are US$8/10.50 for painted cinderblock compartments containing a bed, folding cot, hammock and clean private bathroom. Air-conditioned rooms cost US$14.50. Other cut-rate lodgings are strung along 10a Avenida Norte.

More upscale, and safer, is **Hotel La Terminal** (☎ 661 1086), opposite the bus station on 6a Calle Oriente. Air-conditioned rooms with one/two double beds and cable TV cost US$14.50/21 or US$11.50 for one double bed and a fan.

In a quiet residential district south of the center, you'll find **Hotel Diana** (☎ 667 0429) at 21a Calle Poniente and 3a Avenida Sur. It's a little rundown but clean, and the price is right at US$11.50 for a large air-conditioned room with two beds or US$8.75 with fan. All rooms have large private baths. Microbuses drive along 3a Avenida Sur to the center. Otherwise, a taxi to or from the bus station is about US$1.75.

Hotel China House (☎ 669 5029) is at the junction of the CA7 and the Interamericana, across the street from the Esso station where buses to and from Honduras stop. Like a Salvadoran Motel 6, the hotel consists of a row of sterile, secure units you can park in front of. Small, air-conditioned rooms with private bath cost US$20/23. Microbuses to the center and Metrocentro pass right by.

For a few colones more, *Hotel Posada Real* (☎ 661 7174) offers a pretty good value. Modern rooms with TV, phone, sparkling bathroom and quiet air-conditioning go for US$20/25/37. It's the pink building that curves around the corner of 7a Avenida and 2a Calle Poniente, a few blocks west of the market.

Places to Eat

Pan y Cakes Liz, on 2a Calle Poniente near the market, has breakfast a la vista. Fill your tray with eggs, tamales, plantains, beans and coffee for under US$2. *Pastelería Francesa*, on 1a Avenida Norte between 4a and 6a Calles, offers a wide selection of sweet and savory pastries and some decent coffee. For intriguing fruit or vegetable juice cocktails, try *Bati-Jugos Carlitos* next door.

A number of comedores have comida a la vista for breakfast and lunch; show up early, when the trays are full, and the food is fresh. A local favorite is *Comedor Chilita* at the corner of 8a Calle Oriente and 6a Avenida Norte Bis. You can fill your plate here for around US$2.50, and meatless items like steamed veggies and beet salad are offered. After 4 pm, Chilita spills out onto 8a Calle Oriente and becomes a pupusería. *Comedor Carolina*, on Avenida José Simeón Cañas, is another popular spot.

San Miguel's bus station is one of the few worth considering for nourishment. There's a clean food court on the upper level, with coffee shops, ice cream stands and several comedores, as well as a Pollo Campestre. Nearby, on 6a Calle Oriente, *Restaurant Platos del Diamante* specializes in Spanish cuisine, with elaborate three-course lunches from US$4.50.

Chicken roasted in a huge wood-burning oven is the main attraction at *Pollo Pocholo*, an open-air restaurant on 4a Calle Poniente near Avenida Monseñor Romero. A combination platter includes a quarter chicken, pickled veggies, rice, salsa and tortillas for US$2.25. The restaurant at *Hotel China House* should satisfy a craving for

authentic Chinese food. The soups are especially hearty and loaded with vegetables (US$3). Both places are open till 9 pm. In the evening, *Pupusería Karina*, opposite Hotel Diana, mass produces pupusas de chicharrón.

La Pema is well known throughout the country for its mariscada. A bowl of this creamy seafood soup, served with a mallet to crack shellfish and two thick cheese tortillas, costs US$10. Don't be disappointed by the small bowl – it's positively bursting with shellfish. An *ensalada de fruta* costs about US$1 and is more like a dessert than a drink. La Pema is open 10:30 am to 4:30 pm daily. It's about 5km down the road to El Cuco.

Entertainment

Though the downtown is dark and deserted, the area around the Esso triangle is a throbbing nightlife zone, with discos, strip clubs and mariachis for hire. Most clubs have lots of pickups parked in front. You may have to dodge drunks in the mood to mess around with foreigners.

Getting There & Away

San Miguel's bus station is surely the nation's nicest. Among its unique features are clearly marked departure gates, clean tile floors, a bank, a pharmacy and a bright, clean food court on the upper level.

The following buses travel to and from San Miguel:

destination	distance	bus no	duration
El Amatillo*	58km	330	2 hours
El Cuco	37km	320	1½ hours
El Icacal	50km	385**	1¾ hours
El Tamarindo	65km	385	2¼ hours
La Unión	47km	324	1¼ hours
Perquín***	61km	332	3 hours
Puerto El Triunfo	70km	377	2½ hours
San Salvador	136km	301	2½ to 3 hours
Usulután	57km	373	1½ hours

*Honduran border

**Take No 385, get off at the fork in the road and walk down.

***Or take No 328 to San Francisco Gotera, from which there are frequent pickups to Perquín.

Crucero del Golfo leaves for Tegucigalpa at 3:30 pm (US$11.50, four to five hours) from the Esso station on the Interamericana. Reservations should be made 24 hours in advance; purchase tickets at the Tiger Market convenience store (☎ 669 5687). Tica Bus travels to Managua (US$25), San José (US$35) and Panama (US$60), departing at 7 am from the Hotel y Drive-Inn Milian's. Reservations should be made 72 hours in advance (☎ 669 5052). A taxi from the bus station to either departure point is about US$2.50.

PLAYA EL CUCO TO PLAYA EL TAMARINDO

The Carretera del Litoral swings south at El Delirio, almost reaching the Pacific before it turns abruptly east and parallels the coast for 25km or so. Along the way, tributary roads access the beaches of El Cuco, El Icacal, Las Tunas, Negras and El Tamarindo.

The most accessible eastern beach is **Playa El Cuco**. Take bus No 320 from San Miguel (two hours, 37km). No pristine paradise, El Cuco is a sad strip of seafood comedores, aguardiente shops and shacks. A few surfers scope out the waves. On the beach, you can rent *champas*, straw shacks for changing, for US$3. Buy freshwater showers along the beachfront. Three broken-down hospedajes are crunched together at the eastern corner of the town, charging US$4 to US$5 for a day or night in a concrete box with a straw pallet.

Decent restaurants are scarce, and even the stores don't seem well-stocked. **Restaurante Sofy** is the cleanest among the cluster of cheap comedores leading up to the beach, with mariscadas (US$6.50) and lunch specials. In the evening, **Comedor Vista Hermosa** has *panes de pollo* for US$1.50.

The beach improves eastward, but lodging prices go up. The best option is **Hotel Leones Marinos** (☎ 619 9015), 100m from town, with hammocks under tall palm trees and a pool. Beach access is via a tunnel that unsuccessfully attempts to block out the surrounding squalor. New cabañas with small bed and private bath are clean and comfortable, and better than the older rooms for the same price: US$11.50/23 for 12/24 hours. If you opt for 12 hours, you'll have to clear out by 8 am. For day use of the facilities, you pay US$5.75. Next door, **Motel Palmeras** charges similar rates, but the place is definitely in decline. **Hotel Cuco**

Chirilagua, Virginia

War and economics have scattered Salvadorans around the globe in a kind of diaspora, and hard-working 'Guanacos' can be spotted wherever there's employment, from Mexico City to Melbourne. A quarter of the population lives outside the country, sending nearly US$1.5 billion in earnings a year back home.

People from the same towns and villages tend to congregate in the same area, since these communities in absentia function as a support mechanism for their compatriots, helping new arrivals find a place to live or jobs on construction crews and in restaurants. Chalatenango natives settled in Boston, and a community called Chirilagua, after the town in southern La Unión Department, exists in the Washington, DC, suburb of Arlington, Virginia.

These Salvadorans maintain their home traditions and form hometown associations, pooling their remittances to finance public works projects in their communities of origin. Almost everyone in the *canton* of El Piche in La Unión Department, for example, has family in Los Angeles, and the village is now conspicuously more prosperous than neighboring communities. Wells have been drilled; kids can now study at the local school through the ninth grade (previously they could only get a sixth grade education); and the El Piche committee abroad has donated an ambulance to the clinic its salaries helped build.

Lindo, about 1km farther east, isn't bad but is overpriced at US$17.25/23 for 12-/24-hour stays in modest air-conditioned rooms with private bath. A small pool and meals are available. Still farther out, **Tropico Inn** (☎ 661 1800) has neat cabañas that can fit up to five people for US$35. For day use only, you pay US$7. The beach out this way is very nice, but public transportation is nonexistent.

To continue from El Cuco toward other beaches and La Unión, take the San Miguel bus and get off where the El Cuco road meets CA2. From there catch bus No 383 toward El Tamarindo or hop on a passing pickup. At Intipucá, there's a road down to **Playa El Icacal**. Farther east, **Playa Las Tunas** is an enticing rest stop just off the El Tamarindo road. Though primitive, the village is neat, with clean *palapas* edging a lovely beach. Order a beer and some shrimp at *Las Piedras*, also known as Rancho Rica Mar, while the surf splashes the rocks right below your table, then enjoy the view from a hammock. *Cabaña de Filomena Umaña*, left of Restaurant Roca Mar, has spartan rooms that are way overpriced.

At the small village of **El Tamarindo**, the main beach is cluttered with fishing boats and can become kind of messy when the villagers clean the catch, but a fine sandy beach to the east curves round the bay. Get written permission from the Ministerio de Trabajo in San Salvador (see Tourist Offices in that section, earlier in this chapter) to stay at the free *Centro Obrero Dr Miguel Felix Charlaix*, approximately 2km before town. It has 10 two-room cabins with four single beds and bathrooms. From the tree-lined grounds, gates open onto a calm, sandy beach. There isn't much around for eating. Near the bus stop, *Papi Pollo* serves unexciting fried chicken, burgers and shakes.

Small ferries cross the El Tamarindo estuary regularly (US$0.15). Bus No 382 from the other side makes a quick ride to La Unión. To get to the ferry landing, turn left at Blanca's Restaurant. Otherwise, bus No 383 takes the long route back around the bay past the other beaches.

LA UNIÓN
pop 40,578

The long-moribund port of La Unión, on Golfo de Fonseca, is experiencing a revival. Though the Cutuco dock is still officially closed, traffic has steadily increased over the past five years, as freighters from Ecuador, Venezuela and Spain unload their cargo at the nearby Complejo Pesquero, currently being converted into a free zone. The government has approved a US$100 million soft loan from Japan that will be devoted to the building of a container terminal and new docks and access roads at Cutuco. Up to 15 ships a month are expected to call here when the complex is complete in 2005.

Hot, seedy La Unión has an unusually lively market and is the primary embarkation point for the remote islands in the Gulf of Fonseca. For some respite from the heat, and views of the gulf, head to **Conchagua**, at the base of the imposing volcano of the same name. After dark, the streets exude an air of menace; know where you're heading and stick to well-lit areas.

Information
There's a 24-hour immigration office (☎ 604 4375) beside the post office. You need to stop by if arriving by boat from Nicaragua or Honduras.

Banco Cuscatlán, on the west side of the parque central, changes traveler's checks; check your guns, machetes and cameras at the door. It's open 8 am to 5 pm weekdays, till noon Saturday.

Places to Stay
Hotel San Francisco (☎ 604 4159), on Calle General Menéndez between 9a and 11a Avenidas Sur, is the best option in town, with large, clean and sunny rooms for US$9.25 with single bed and hammock or US$16 with two beds, hammock and chilly air-con. *Hotel Centroamericano* (☎ 664 4029) is a large, fenced-in hotel on 4a Calle Oriente between 1a and 3a Avenidas Sur. Though it's very clean and affords a nice view of the port from the upper level, the hotel nevertheless feels rather empty and creepy. Single/double rates are US$8.75/17.25 with fan or US$17.25/23 with air-con.

On 11a Avenida Sur between 2a and 4a Calles Oriente, *Hospedaje Night and Day* (☎ 604 3006) is small and family run. The 14 rooms have reasonably clean bathrooms (added plus – the toilets have seats). Rooms with one/two beds cost US$5.75/8.

Casa de Huespedes El Dorado (☎ 604 4724), a block west of the parque central, is built around a quiet courtyard with gardenias and mango trees. Though a little rundown, it's not bad for the price of US$7 for one-bed rooms with hammock, fan and private bath.

Places to Eat
If you're heading out to the islands, *Comedor Montecristo* at the ferry landing is a good place to start off the day, with big pots of eggs, sausage and *casamiento* on display. Bland but reassuring, *Pollo*

EL SALVADOR

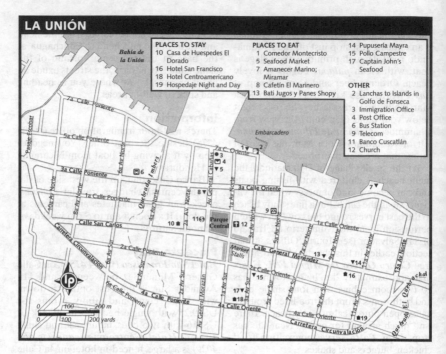

LA UNIÓN

PLACES TO STAY
10 Casa de Huespedes El Dorado
16 Hotel San Francisco
18 Hotel Centroamericano
19 Hospedaje Night and Day

PLACES TO EAT
1 Comedor Montecristo
5 Seafood Market
7 Amanecer Marino; Miramar
8 Cafetín El Marinero
13 Bati Jugos y Panes Shopy

14 Pupusería Mayra
15 Pollo Campestre
17 Captain John's Seafood

OTHER
2 Lanchas to Islands in Golfo de Fonseca
3 Immigration Office
4 Post Office
6 Bus Station
9 Telecom
11 Banco Cuscatlán
12 Church

Campestre, at the corner of 3a Avenida Sur and 2a Calle Oriente, has breakfast combos for US$2.

At the intersection of Calle General Menéndez and 9a Avenida Norte, *Bati Jugos y Panes Shopy* offers a variety of fruit shakes and licuados and, in the evening, big chicken sandwiches. *Pupusería Mayra*, opposite the Hotel San Francisco, is cheap and decent.

A popular hangout for foreigners doing business in the port, *Captain John's Seafood*, on 3a Avenida Sur at 4a Calle Oriente, offers fresh gulf fish at reasonable prices, plus a variety of Mexican dishes. A swordfish platter costs US$4 and a grilled fish fillet with shrimp is US$5.25. *Cafetín El Marinero*, at the corner of Avenida General Cabañas and 3a Calle Poniente, charges US$8 for a full plate of fish or shrimp.

For similar prices and late-afternoon views of the gulf islands, try *Amanecer Marino*, on the waterfront east of the center. Their *brocheta* is a shellfish feast (US$9.25). Nearer the inlet (a disadvantage at low tide) is *Miramar*, another seafood

restaurant with live Tex-Mex bands from 5 pm Thursday to Sunday.

If you can find a place to cook, you can buy a dozen lobsters for US$10 at the seafood market up the street from the post office.

Getting There & Away

The bus station is on 3a Calle Poniente between 4a and 6a Avenidas Norte. Bus service to nearby destinations includes the following:

destination	distance	bus no	duration
Conchagua	5km	382	½ hour
El Amatillo*	41km	342	1 hour
El Tamarindo**	45km	383	1½ hours
Las Playitas	8km	418	1 hour
San Miguel	47km	324	1¼ hours
Santa Rosa de Lima	45km	342	1½ hours

*Honduran border; take 342 toward Santa Rosa de Lima and pick up 330 at turnoff.

**Alternatively, take bus No 382 to Buenavista on the El Tamarindo estuary and catch a ferry to El Tamarindo (30 to 40 minutes).

EL SALVADOR

ISLANDS IN GOLFO DE FONSECA

In general, these islands remain oblivious to tourism. You'll get to see how the communities really live, but don't expect any services, and beaches are either trash-strewn or hard to get to. Take along food and water. **Isla Zacatillo**, the nearest island, has the largest community. Numerous coves with sandy beaches can be discovered, but it's no tropical dreamscape. The principal village has a few stores and lodging in a wooden shack over the bay. If you're looking for solitary beaches, head for **Isla Martín Pérez**, just south of Zacatillo. There's no regular ferry service, but you can hire a boat from La Unión or Zacatillo. More mountainous, **Isla Conchagüita** offers good opportunities for hiking. Fishing boats are neatly lined up under *enramadas* along the beachfront of the main village. Locals say there are prehistoric rock carvings on the way out to Playa Brava, a black sand beach an hour's walk from the village.

Isla Meanguera, the southernmost isle, was long the subject of territorial disputes with Honduras and Nicaragua, until an international court declared it part of El Salvador in 1992. It's the only island in the gulf with decent lodging. Perched over a peaceful cove, *Hotel El Mirador* (☎ 648 0072) has 13 small, clean rooms with double bed, fan, hammock and private bath for US$11.50. A restaurant serves fresh lobster and snacks. Owner, and former mayor, Julio César Ramos can shuttle you over to Playa Majahual for about US$1 per person. He can also take you to **Isla Amapala**, Honduras, or the port of Potosí, Nicaragua, for about US$35 roundtrip. To get to the hotel from the ferry landing, turn left and go uphill along a cobblestone path till you reach a pink house with lions on the doors. Turn left through a lot and down toward a white house. When the trail gets rough, get someone to point you to the hotel.

Lanchas ferry the locals out to the islands from the grimy little landing at the end of 3a Avenida Norte in La Unión. There's daily service to Zacatillo (20 minutes), Conchagüita (one hour) and Meanguera (two hours) for US$1.25 per person. Departure times may depend on tides. In general, though, the lanchas depart at around 10 am

and return the next day at 3 to 4 am (or from the islanders' point of view, they leave the islands early in the morning and return later in the day). Comedor Montecristo, at the landing, is a good place to get info on departures. Of course you can hire an 'express' lancha to anywhere you like, but it will cost you: In general, expect to pay US$35 to US$50 roundtrip to the nearest islands and up to US$70 to Meanguera. Agree on a price before the adventure commences, and pay in halves to ensure that someone will pick you up. Ferries for the islands also depart Las Playitas farther down the coast.

MORAZÁN

North of San Miguel, Morazán Department saw some of the heaviest fighting of the 1980s conflict. A war museum in Perquín and a memorial in El Mozote are sobering reminders of what atrocities befell fighters and families alike.

Indigenous traditions survive in villages around San Francisco Gotera, the capital of the department. The village of **Cacaopera** has a small ethnographic museum devoted to the local Ulúa tribe and an 18th century church. Dancers in feathered costumes perform during the patron saint's festival in February. The Lenca community at **Guatajiagua** produces a unique style of black pottery. Contact the indigenous organization ACOLGUA (☎ 644 0588) for more info.

Perquín
pop 3900

Perquín was the headquarters of the FMLN during the war, and leftover bunkers and bomb craters remain as evidence of the former guerrilla presence. Thus it's a fitting site for the **Museo de la Revolución Salvadoreña**. The war museum charts the causes and progress of the armed struggle with photos, posters, weapons and histories of those who died in action. Weapons range from high-tech hardware to homemade bombs and mines. Unfortunately, the exhibits aren't well-maintained and explanations are exclusively in Spanish. Behind the main building are the remains of the downed helicopter that carried Lieutenant Colonel Domingo Monterrosa, head of the notorious Atlacatl Battalion, to his death. The museum is open 8:30 am to 4 pm

Tuesday to Sunday (US$1.15). Local crafts, books and T-shirts are sold in the museum's shop.

Despite its devastating impact, the war may have actually benefited the natural environment, since rural inhabitants were forced to move to more populated zones, lessening the human impact on the more remote areas of the country. Orchids and butterflies are in abundance here, and Perquín is a prime birding zone – 12 varieties of oriole have been spotted along with the rare chestnut-headed oropendola. It's a 25-minute downhill hike through woods to the **Quebrada de Perquín**, a stream that's fine for swimming.

Places to Stay & Eat Perquín has two options for lodging, one budget, one upmarket. Both are along the southern approach to town about half a kilometer before the Perquín sign. *Casa de Huéspedes El Gigante* (☎ *661 5077 ext 237*) is in a converted lumber mill separated into cubicles, with space for little except a pair of single beds. Very clean common bathrooms are at one end of the building. The cost is US$5.75 per person.

Opened in 1999, *Hotel Perkin Lenca* (☎/*fax 661 5077 ext 246, perkin@netcomsa .com*) is a relaxed mountain lodge. Sunny, fresh cabins of oak and pine construction have attractive bathrooms with hot water, and porches with hammocks that provide superb views of the surrounding piney slopes. Two-bed cabins cost US$63. Rooms in the US$12 to US$15 range should be ready by 2001. Owner Ronald Brenneman, a Delaware native, did relief work during the 1980s, building low-income housing on both sides of the border. He is an avid naturalist and leads bird-watching walks in the area.

At the hotel, *La Cocina de Ma'anita* is a large country kitchen preparing hearty breakfasts for US$4 to US$5 and local favorites like chicken in *chicha* (US$5.75) and a stick-to-your-ribs bean stew (US$3.50). It's open 7 am to 8 pm daily. In Perquín, *Comedor La Montañona* is the most attractive option for lunch, served comida a la vista style. A plateful of food here costs about US$2. Open till 7:30 pm, the restaurant is in a circular pavilion near the church.

Getting There & Away The CA7 north of San Miguel to the Honduran border is in good shape. Bus No 332 runs from San Miguel to Perquín (three hours); departures are every one to two hours. Alternatively, take the more frequent No 328 to San Francisco Gotera, from which pickups go on to Perquín (one hour). The last bus back to San Miguel is at 2 pm; the last pickup to Gotera leaves at 4 pm, and buses from Gotera to San Miguel run until 6 pm.

There's daily bus service from Marcala, Honduras to Perquín via Sabanetas. The border is open, but El Salvador has not accepted the territorial boundary terms, so there is no customs post on the Salvadoran side. Once this border is established, it should be an excellent route for Tegucigalpa.

El Mozote

Once a town hidden in the lap of the northern hills, El Mozote is now a destination for those paying homage to the December 1981 massacre (see History in the Facts about El Salvador section, earlier in this chapter). A simple iron silhouette of a family is backed by a brick wall on which wooden boards hang with the names of the victims.

More evidence of the massacre was uncovered in April 2000, with the reinitiation of exhumations begun in 1992 then abruptly suspended in 1993 with approval of a blanket amnesty for war crimes. At that time, 143 victims were uncovered, 131 of them children. Families of the victims hope the discovery of more human remains will bring new pressure on authorities to reopen the case implicating 10 officers responsible for the atrocities here.

Locals are becoming used to the international presence; they've even set up snack bars for tourists, and cute kids may follow you around looking for handouts. Nevertheless, visitors should remain sensitive to the seriousness of the site and show restraint when snapping photos.

On the way to Perquín, turn right at the fork to Arambala, a village decimated by air raids. From there it's a 3km drive to El Mozote. A 7 am bus from San Miguel passes the site en route to Joateca and returns at 3:30 pm, making a day trip possible.

Northern El Salvador

The district of Chalatenango was the scene of intense fighting between the government army and the FMLN guerrillas. Villages bore the brunt of the military's *tierra arrasada* (scorched land) tactics, in which they would burn the fields and kill the cattle. The carnage precipitated an exodus, and it is not uncommon to run into locals who spent a dozen years in New York or Melbourne.

As the past's horrors recede, the region is struggling to rebuild. The main provider of water and hydroelectric power for El Salvador, Chalatenango Department faces grave environmental risks due to chaotic consumption of forest resources by impoverished rural populations. In response, the Comité Ambiental de Chalatenango (CACH), a coalition of some 95 NGOs and church groups, is providing leadership and training toward sustainable development of natural resources. Tourism is a key component in the development plan. Places like La Montañona, Arcatao and Cerro El Pital are being tapped for their natural beauty, and a plethora of new lodgings have sprung up in La Palma.

SUCHITOTO
pop 16,360

Suchitoto is an atmospheric place, 47km north of San Salvador and 380m above sea level. It's great for walking around – morning or evening – and welcomes outsiders. Come here to enjoy the colonial buildings, cobblestone streets, lake views and the forest reserves in the vicinity.

It is presumed that Yaquis and Pipils settled the area some thousand years ago. El Salvador's capital was established near here in the early 16th century, and the old city is being excavated. A cultural capital during the heyday of the indigo trade, it is now experiencing something of an arts revival. The February arts and culture festival brings in world-class music and dance groups, but events are held year-round on Saturdays at the Teatro de Las Ruinas.

Some of the earliest fighting of the civil war began in Suchitoto and went on for 13 years, accompanied by much destruction

and emigration. Since 1993, the city's colonial legacy has been impressively restored.

Suchitoto overlooks the Cerrón Grande, also known as Lago Suchitlán, a reservoir for hydroelectric power made by damming the Río Lempa. The project, undertaken by President Carlos Humberto Romero, displaced thousands of farmers from the fertile banks of the Río Lempa who became fishermen. The lake swells considerably in the rainy season. A beautiful 20-minute hike down to the lake heads out of town along 3a Avenida Norte. There are several pleasant lakeside cafes.

The area is a bird migration zone: As many as 200 species have been spotted. Thousands of hawks and falcons fill the skies as the seasons change. You can hire a lancha to Isla de las Garzas (US$11.50), a refuge for egrets, herons, cormorants and others.

Inquire about events and hiking opportunities at the Casa de la Cultura (☎ 335 1108), half a block left of the Santa Lucía church. The Casa de los Mestizos (see Places to Stay & Eat, below) organizes tours by Corsatur-trained local kids. There are plenty of Publitel card phones around town.

Places to Stay & Eat

Overnighters have two good options, a travelers' hotel and a colonial-style palace. *Casa de los Mestizos* (☎ 848 3438, casamestizos@ terra.com, 3a Ave Norte 48) has five clean singles with private bath for US$7 and one double for US$10.50 alongside a mango-shaded patio. There's a relaxed bar/cafe in front, with free concerts and movies on weekends. The Swedish-owned *Posada de Suchitlán* (☎ 335 1064), at the end of 4a Calle Poniente, was built to resemble a colonial hacienda. Rooms, from US$46, are a combination of antique splendor and modern convenience, and there's a fabulous pool on the tranquil grounds. The view from the restaurant may just be worth the US$2.50 for a large fruit drink. Lake fish dishes are around US$8.50. *La Fonda del Mirador*, on the way out to the lake, is another good restaurant with a view, specializing in *criolla* cuisine.

El Obraje, in an attractive old building left of the church, has well-prepared salads, seafood and chicken dishes for around US$2 to US$3. Off the plaza, *El Portal*

EL SALVADOR

makes good breakfasts and fruit salads. Weekends, you'll find various local specialties on the plaza, including *riguas* (sweet buttery corn tortillas wrapped in a corn husk) and *fogonazo*, sugarcane juice alcoholically enhanced on request. In the evening, after the day trippers have gone home, pupusas are served with the usual cabbage and pickled onions in the bright, clean *Pupusería Ciudad Vieja*, next door to the church.

Getting There & Away
Take bus No 129 from San Salvador's Terminal de Oriente; the last one back is at 5:30 pm. By car, go toward Cojutepeque on the Interamericana. When you get to San Martín, turn left at the Texaco sign.

Hourly ferries traverse the Cerrón Grande to San Luis del Carmen (US$0.60 or US$3.50 with vehicle); several continue to San Francisco Lempa, from which buses depart hourly for Chalatenango. Or you could pay US$3 for a lancha to take you directly to San Francisco.

CHALATENANGO
pop 30,220
The first thing you notice upon arriving in 'Chalate' is the huge military garrison on the plaza. FMLN guerrillas controlled the regional capital during the early part of the war, and the government established a major military presence here to rein in revolutionary activity. The scars have faded – at least on the surface – and Chalatenango hums with activity. It's not an unwelcoming place, but people are unfamiliar with the concept of foreign visitors. This very ordinary town is fringed by some impressive mountain scenery, making it a good base for exploring the natural attractions of the region.

Orientation & Information
As in other Salvadoran cities, two main streets meet at a central point by the main plaza. Avenida Fajardo/Avenida Libertad is the principal north/south thoroughfare, and the main street running east-west is Calle San Martín/Calle Morazán. The market sprawls from the church up Morazán and attenuates out near the departure point for buses to Arcatao and Las Vueltas.

Banco Cuscatlán, on 4a Calle Oriente, changes traveler's checks. The Comité Ambiental de Chalatenango (CACH; ☎ 301 0903), on the east end of Calle Morazán near the Iglesia El Calvario, can provide information about destinations throughout the department.

Things to See & Do
The blindingly white church, with its squat bell tower, sits on the east end of the plaza, a stone's throw from the military garrison. Follow Calle Morazán 400m to the east; you'll see a sign pointing north toward the turicentro, **Agua Fría**, a 15-minute walk from there. Picnic tables dot the pleasant park, kept cool by lush foliage. A cafeteria serves beer and meals. The pools are not replenished in the dry season, when groundskeepers simply chlorinate the hell out of what water's already there. A trail leads from the turicentro to **La Peña**, with panoramic views of the Cerrón Grande reservoir and beyond to Suchitoto. The hike takes about two hours; inquire at CACH for guides.

Places to Stay & Eat
There are a couple of perfectly good hotels in Chalate. The *Hotel California* (☎ 335 2170), on Calle Morazán between 2a and 4a Avenidas, is quiet and tidy. It charges US$10 for rooms with private bath, US$1.50 extra with TV. You must be out by 8 am, but the elderly caretaker will let you leave your luggage. *Hotelito San José* (☎ 301 0148) is in a safe area opposite the Cancha La Maraña basketball court, a popular evening spot in the Barrio San José. Rates are US$7/11.50 for freshly painted boxlike singles/doubles facing a cute patio. Clean toilets and showers are in a separate block.

Popular *Comedor Carmary*, on 3a Avenida across from the bus stop, serves excellent comida a la vista breakfast and lunch for around US$2.25. The fast food–style *Hamburguesas Camir*, on Calle Morazán just east of Fajardo, offers cool papaya licuados (US$0.60) in addition to the burgers (US$0.75 to US$1.25).

Several pupuserías are along 1a Calle Oriente east of the market. *Restaurant Campo Verde*, on 1a Calle Poniente beside the military garrison, has a lively jukebox ambience – it's a good place to chill out with a beer and a boca. The menu includes chicken (US$2.50), fish (US$4) and turtle eggs (US$0.60), but most folks go for the pupusas.

Getting There & Away
Bus No 125 runs regularly from San Salvador (two hours) and terminates on 3a Avenida Sur, a few blocks south of the church. To La Palma, take the 125 toward San Salvador and get off at Amayo, the junction with the Troncal de Norte highway (40 minutes); from there take No 119 north (1½ hours).

See Around Chalatenango for details on buses to local villages.

AROUND CHALATENANGO
The road to **Las Vueltas** ascends along the Río Tamulasco through a landscape of oddly shaped hills. The area was a battle zone; a 500lb bomb is part of the war memorial in the plaza behind the church, one of the few left standing in the area. Natural pools lie on either side of the bridge over the Río Sumpul near **San José Las Flores**. Beyond the river, **Arcatao** is a beautiful village in the mountains bordering Honduras. Make an appointment with the *directiva* (☎ 335 2263, ykd@bigfoot.com), or town council, for tours of the *tatus* (guerrilla cave hideouts), which attest to Arcatao's former role as an FMLN stronghold. A stay at the Jesuit retreat center costs US$9.50 per night including one meal.

To the northwest of Chalate, **Concepción Quezaltepeque** is a hammock-making center. The whole village is engaged in this activity. Hammocks made of woven cotton cost around US$40 (less for nylon), depending on size and rope thickness.

La Montañona is a pine forest reserve at 1600m offering excellent views, trees and animals and pre-Columbian rock carvings. It's a 5km hike from either La Laguna or El Carrizal, villages north of Quezaltepeque and Las Vueltas respectively. Camping is a possibility. Alex Zamora (☎ 335 2783) offers guide services.

The strenuous road up to **Dulce Nombre de María** takes you along cobbled roads through small villages painted in warm pastels. The small town of low red-tile roofs and white walls rests peacefully in the rolling hills. People are subdued but

friendly, and many hang out at the plaza during the hot afternoons.

North of Dulce Nombre is **El Manzano**, a cooperative of ex-FMLN combatants. The 10km road up hugs the hills, affording views of flat valleys dotted with volcanoes and the mountains leading into Honduras. When you get to the bombed plane, take the road down to your right.

Trails from El Manzano lead through woods and coffee plantations past some historic war sites to a waterfall. Climb to the top of El Pilón for more incredible views.

You can either camp up the hill at the soccer field (US$1.25) or stay in bunk-bed dorms, with the village's only shower and toilet, for US$5.75 per person. Another 10 cabins should be going up soon. Eat with local families or buy food from the store, which also serves as an information center. There's no phone, but reservations aren't necessary.

Getting There & Away
A 4WD high-clearance vehicle is required to make the journey from Chalatenango to Las Vueltas, but unnecessary for the paved road to Arcatao.

From the top of Avenida Morazán in Chalatenango, buses for Las Vueltas/Ojos de Agua (45 minutes to 1½ hours) leave at 9:30 and 11 am and 2:30 and 4 pm; the last bus returns at 2 pm. Buses for San José Las Flores/Arcatao (45 minutes to 1¼ hours) depart hourly from 7 am to 5 pm. Otherwise, take a pickup truck.

To Concepción Quezaltepeque, take bus No 300B from the 3a Avenida Sur terminal in Chalate. There is no direct service to Dulce Nombre de María; take No 125 to the turnoff, where you can pick up the No 124 from San Salvador. Two buses depart from Dulce Nombre to El Manzano, at 12:30 and 3:30 pm, or you may be able to find a pickup.

LA PALMA
pop 11,894
Surrounded by verdant mountains dotted with bright flowering plants and bathed in fresh mountain air, La Palma may be a long 84km north of San Salvador, but it's well worth the climb and a must if heading into Honduras via El Poy.

Fernando Llort moved to La Palma in 1972 and soon developed an art trend that still represents El Salvador around the world. Llort's childlike images of mountain villages, campesinos or images of Christ are painted in bright colors on anything from seeds to church walls. He taught some residents in La Palma how to create the same images and soon began a cooperative that churned out dozens of painted artifacts, from crosses to keyrings to napkin holders. Today 75% of the village makes a living by mass-producing this art, none deviating too far from the traditional drawings or colors.

The Casa de la Cultura (☎ 335 9090), on 1a Calle Poniente just off Delgado, is more tourist-oriented than elsewhere. They can tell you about hiking in the area. Publitel phones are easily found.

Things to See & Do

As you walk around town, peek into workshops to see families painting away. They'll let you in to observe, and of course, to buy their works. A number of shops are at the entrance to town on the road to the right. Semilla de Dios, on 3a Calle Poniente, has been recommended for its quality work. Some shops specialize in clothing embroidered with the Llort designs.

If hiking is of more interest, you'll stay busy. From the neighboring village of San Ignacio you can access **El Pital** (2730m), the highest peak in El Salvador. Camping is possible, but it gets very cold. From San Ignacio, bus No 509 to Las Pilas drops you off at Río Chiquito near the trail. Local kids can guide you to the top, a four-hour hike. To go to **Río Nunuapa** ('silent river' in the Nahua language), take the road leading to Los Horcones, past the Casa de Cultura. This walk takes about one hour.

Places to Stay & Eat

The long-established *Hotel La Palma* (☎ 335 9012) is a pleasant mountain getaway bordered by the Río La Palma. Rates are a very reasonable US$6.50 per person in fairly basic rooms with private bath and occasional hot water. You pay US$1.75 extra to use the pool. Salvador Zepeda, who owns this and several other hotels in the area, can set up excursions. A block farther up 2a Avenida Sur, the new *Hotel Posada Real* (☎ 335 9009) has narrow, log-beamed rooms with hot water and TV for US$11.50 per person. The up-

stairs terrace affords good mountain views, and the restaurant in front serves breakfast (US$1.75) and delicious bread pudding. *Quechelah* (☎ 305 9328) is a B&B in a beautiful adobe home perched atop a peaceful hill overlooking piney slopes. The price of US$25/38 for single/double occupancy seems high but includes all the comforts of home and a fabulous breakfast on the terrace. Quechelah is a 20-minute walk from the center of La Palma – phone ahead and they'll give you a ride up.

Off the highway 5km south of town, *Centro Obrero Dr Mario Zamora Rivas* offers 15 recently remodeled cabins and a couple of pools, and it's free with permission from the Ministerio de Trabajo in San Salvador (see Tourist Offices in that section, earlier in this chapter). Trails crisscross the forested grounds.

Additional options are in and around the neighboring village of San Ignacio. The friendly *Posada San Ignacio*, on the plaza, is a good deal: just US$4/8 for log cabin–style single/double rooms; clean showers and toilets are separate.

North of San Ignacio and 3km from the Honduran border, the *Hotel Cayahuanca* (☎ 335 9464) sits on a mountain-ringed plain. It's another good budget choice, charging US$9 per double room with private bath, US$11.50 in high season. All meals are served. Juan Ángel Deras, the helpful manager, can give you directions for hikes to Cerro Miramundo and Cayahuanca, the imposing rock formation that marks the frontier.

Down the road from Hotel La Palma, *Restaurante del Pueblo* serves a variety of soups and sandwiches for US$1.75 and a good plato típico (bananas, beans, cheese, cream) for US$3. On the next block over, *Cafetería La Estancia*, on Calle Barrios, offers breakfast and snacks for under US$2, and chicken and meat dishes for US$4 to US$5. For good inexpensive home cooking and hearty soups, go to *Comedor Rosita* opposite the Casa de la Cultura or *Comedor El Poyetón* one street north.

Getting There & Away

Bus No 119 runs every half hour from San Salvador's Terminal de Oriente to the Honduran border at El Poy, stopping at La

Palma (US$1, three hours) and San Ignacio, 3km to the north. The northern section of the road is paved but in poor condition; La Palma is only about 12km south of the border yet it's a 50-minute bus trip. From El Poy, you can take a taxi to Nuevo Ocotepeque, Honduras, from which you can catch buses to Tegucigalpa.

The last bus south from El Poy leaves around 3 pm.

Nicaragua

Political events of past decades have had a huge impact on many outsiders' perceptions of Nicaragua, and the country's natural, historical and cultural attractions remain largely undiscovered by tourists. First-time visitors to Nicaragua are often thrilled to find volcanoes, navigable rivers, colonial cities, Caribbean islands and deserted beaches – all without the floods of tourists seen elsewhere on the Central American isthmus. While it has a way to go in terms of tourism infrastructure, Central America's largest country is by no means a difficult place to travel, and those travelers who don't mind roughing it a bit will find Nicaragua surprisingly manageable.

The political scene remains as tumultuous as ever, but power conflicts are played out these days mostly in the National Assembly and the editorial pages – guns are rarely seen and the atmosphere is remarkably peaceful and open. In fact, the most interesting aspects of a visit here may be seeing how this postrevolutionary society is operating, and talking to people who have seen it all.

Highlights

- Stroll the streets of Granada and León, Spanish colonial cities with a richly preserved architectural heritage
- Seek out prehistoric rock art on Isla de Ometepe, an extraordinary island formed by a pair of volcanoes
- Peer into the smoke-billowing crater of Volcán Masaya, the centerpiece of a national park near the capital
- Swim and snorkel on the idyllic Corn Islands, Nicaragua's own little corner of the Caribbean
- Surf and savor seafood at San Juan del Sur, a magnificent bay on the southern Pacific coast
- Bask in the tranquility of Solentiname, an island chain at Lake Nicaragua's southern end populated by artists and poets

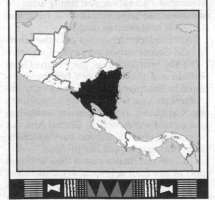

Facts about Nicaragua

HISTORY
Early History
The earliest traces of human habitation in Nicaragua are some 6000-year-old footprints found near the banks of Lago de Managua within the area occupied by the present-day capital. Pre-Columbian Nicaragua was inhabited by many indigenous groups, including the ancestors of today's Ramas and Sumos, on the Caribbean coast, and the Chorotegas and Nicaraos, who lived between the lakes and the Pacific. The Nicaraos, thought to have been descendants of groups who migrated from Mexico, spoke a form of Nahuatl, the language of the Aztecs. Many Nicaraguan places retain their Nahuatl names.

European Arrival
The indigenous inhabitants' first contact with Europeans was in 1502, when Columbus sailed down Nicaragua's Caribbean coast.

The first Spanish exploratory mission, led by Gil González de Ávila, came north from the Spanish settlement at Panama and reached Nicaragua in 1522. It found the southern shores of Lago de Nicaragua heavily populated by the Nicarao tribe. The Spanish derived the name 'Nicaragua' from the tribe's chief, also named Nicarao. The population under Nicarao interacted peacefully with the Spanish and were among the

NICARAGUA

MAP INDEX

CARIBBEAN
SEA

0   50   100 km
0   30   60 miles

HONDURAS

OTHER MAPS
Nicaragua pages 500-501
Parks & Protected Areas
page 507

Estelí
page 537

Matagalpa
page 533

León
page 543

Managua page 522
Área Monumental page 525
Barrio Martha
Quezada page 526

Big Corn Island
page 575

South of
Managua
page 549

Granada
page 555

Bluefields
page 572

Masaya
page 551

Isla de Ometepe
page 564

Moyogalpa
page 566

San Juan
del Sur
page 561

PACIFIC
OCEAN

COSTA
RICA

first indigenous Americans to voluntarily convert to Christianity.

Two years later the Spanish were back to colonize the region, led this time by Francisco Fernández de Córdoba, who founded first the city of Granada and then León in 1524. Both were established near indigenous settlements whose inhabitants were subjugated by the Spanish. The land around present-day Managua was also densely populated by a group dedicated to fishing, hunting and agriculture. They put up fierce resistance to the Spanish, who responded by destroying their city. For the next three centuries, Managua was but a village.

Colonial Settlement

The gold that had initially attracted Spanish settlers to Nicaragua soon gave out, but Granada and León remained. Granada, on the northwest end of Lago de Nicaragua, became a comparatively rich colonial city, its wealth due not only to surrounding agriculture but also to its importance as a trading center. The navigable Río San Juan, flowing out of Lago de Nicaragua, gave Granada a direct shipping connection to the

Caribbean and, from there, Europe. With its wealthy business class, Granada became the center for the Conservative Party, favoring traditional Spanish values of monarchy and Catholic authority.

Originally founded on the shore of Lago de Managua, León was destroyed by earthquake in 1610 and a new city was established some 30km west. It was poorer than Granada, but the Spanish made it the capital of the colonial province. León became the center for radical clerics and intellectuals, who formed the Liberal Party and supported the unification of Central America and reforms based on those of the French and American Revolutions.

The difference in wealth between the two cities, and the political supremacy of the poorer one, led to conflicts that raged into the 1850s, at times erupting into outright civil war. The continual fighting between them stopped only when the capital was moved to the neutral location of Managua, in 1857.

While the Spanish were settling the Pacific lowlands, the English were the dominant influence on the Caribbean side of Nicaragua. English, French and Dutch pirates plying the Caribbean waters repeatedly attacked the Caribbean coast in the 17th century, at times penetrating as far as Granada via the Río San Juan.

Early Independence

Along with the rest of Central America, Nicaragua gained independence from Spain in 1821, was part of Mexico for a brief time, then was incorporated into the new Central American Federation, and finally achieved complete independence in 1838. León and Granada continued to feud.

After independence, not only the Liberals and Conservatives were vying for power. With the Spanish out of the picture, Great Britain and the USA both became interested in Nicaragua and its strategically important passage from Lago de Nicaragua to the Caribbean. Both countries wanted to put a canal somewhere in Central America to connect the Atlantic and Pacific Oceans, and Nicaragua looked like the spot.

In 1848 the British seized the Caribbean port of San Juan del Norte, at the mouth of the Río San Juan, and renamed it Greytown. Meanwhile, the California gold rush had added fire to the quest for an interoceanic passage.

William Walker

The growing US interest in Nicaragua took a new turn in the person of William Walker, an adventurer intent on taking over Latin American territory. In 1853, he led a small party to attack Mexico, where he declared himself president of 'independent' Baja California and the state of Sonora before being ignominiously driven out.

In 1855, the Liberals of León asked William Walker to help them seize power from Granada's Conservatives. Walker entered Nicaragua with 56 followers, attacked Granada and prevailed. He soon had himself elected president of Nicaragua, and the US recognized his government. Three months later, he instituted slavery in order to gain favor with the Southern states of the USA. He declared English the country's official language, seized Cornelius Vanderbilt's transport company (Vanderbilt was one of the major US capitalists of the 18th century) and took out a large loan, putting the territory of Nicaragua up as collateral.

Walker then adopted the slogan 'five or none' and announced his intention to take over the remaining Central American countries. These nations, supported by Vanderbilt, united to drive him out. Walker fled Granada, leaving the city in flames. In May 1857, the Tennessean was defeated at Rivas and, to avoid capture by Central American forces, surrendered to the US Navy, which sent him back to the USA.

William Walker did not give up, however. Six months later, he landed at Greytown with another invading party, only to be arrested and deported again by the US Navy. In 1860, he embarked on yet another attempt to conquer Central America. Landing near Trujillo, on the coast of Honduras, he was captured by the British navy, who turned him over to the Honduran authorities. He was tried and executed by firing squad on September 12, 1860; his grave is in Trujillo's Old Cemetery (see Trujillo in the Honduras chapter).

The Late 19th Century

In 1857, the Liberals, disgraced as the party that had invited Walker into the country, lost power to the Conservatives and were not to regain it for the next 36 years. In the same year, the capital was transferred from León to Managua in an attempt to quell the rivalry between Granada and León. Managua was chosen largely because it lay between the two cities; it was then little more than a village.

In 1860 the British signed a treaty ceding the Caribbean region to the now-independent governments of Honduras and Nicaragua. The Nicaraguan section remained an autonomous region until the 1890s.

Zelaya's Coup & US Intervention

In 1893 a Liberal general, José Santos Zelaya, deposed the Conservative president and became dictator. Zelaya soon antagonized the USA by seeking a canal deal with Germany and Japan. Encouraged by the USA, which sought to monopolize a transisthmian canal in Panama, the Conservatives rebelled in 1909. After Zelaya ordered the execution of two US mercenaries accused of aiding the Conservatives, the US government forced his resignation. In 1912, the USA responded to another rebellion, this time against the corrupt Conservative administration, by sending 2500 Marines to Nicaragua.

For most of the next two decades the USA dominated politics in Nicaragua, installing presidents it favored and ousting those it didn't, using its marines as leverage. In 1914 the Bryan-Chamorro Treaty was signed, granting the USA exclusive rights to build a canal in Nicaragua and to establish US naval bases there. The USA had no intention of building such a canal, but it did want to ensure that no one else did.

In 1925, a new cycle of violence began with a Conservative coup. The Marines were withdrawn, but as political turmoil ensued, they returned the following year.

Augusto C Sandino & the Somoza Era

The Conservative regime was opposed by a group of Liberal rebels including Juan Bautista Sacasa, General José María Moncada and, most important in the long run, Augusto C Sandino, who led the movement to resist US involvement. Both Moncada and Sacasa, ironically enough, rose to the presidency with US support.

NICARAGUA

Sandino, however, fought on, inspiring rebels throughout Latin America. In 1933 the Marines withdrew from Nicaragua but left behind a new Nicaraguan Guardia Nacional (National Guard), which they had set up and trained, to put down resistance by Sandino's guerrillas. This military force was led by Anastasio Somoza García.

In February 1934, Somoza engineered the assassination of Sandino. From his mountain refuge, Sandino accepted a dinner invitation from Somoza, under the impression that he would be negotiating a peace agreement with Somoza's National Guard and the US Marines. After the dinner, Sandino was escorted to the Managua airport by National Guardsmen, who shot him and his brother Socrates. A couple of years later, Somoza overthrew Liberal president Sacasa. Fraudulent elections were held, and Somoza became president himself in 1937, beginning a four-decade Somoza family dynasty.

After creating a new constitution to grant himself more power, Somoza García ruled Nicaragua as an internationally notorious dictator for the next 20 years, sometimes as president, at other times behind a puppet president. He amassed huge personal wealth by corrupt means, and the Somoza landholdings grew to the size of El Salvador. Nicaragua was virtually the personal possession of the Somozas and their friends. Needless to say, the majority of Nicaraguans remained entrenched in poverty.

Somoza supported the USA (the CIA used Nicaragua as a staging area for both the 1954 overthrow of Guatemalan leader Jacobo Arbenz Guzmán and the 1961 invasion of Cuba) and was in turn supported by the US government. US president Franklin Roosevelt reportedly said of him, 'He may be a son of a bitch, but at least he's our son of a bitch.'

After his assassination in León in 1956, Somoza was succeeded by his elder son, Luis Somoza Debayle, and the Somoza family, with the help of the Guardia Nacional, continued to rule Nicaragua. In 1967 Luis died, and his younger brother, Anastasio Somoza Debayle, assumed the presidency.

Rising Opposition

In 1961, Carlos Fonseca Amador, a prominent figure in the student movement that had opposed the Somoza regime in the 1950s, joined forces with an old fighting partner of Sandino's, Colonel Santos López, and other activists to found the Frente Sandinista de Liberación Nacional (Sandinista National Liberation Front), or FSLN.

On December 23, 1972, at around midnight, an earthquake devastated Managua, leveling over 250 city blocks, killing over 6000 people and leaving 300,000 homeless. As international aid poured in, the money was diverted to Anastasio Somoza and his associates, while the people who needed it suffered and died. This obvious abuse dramatically increased opposition to Somoza among all classes of society. Over time, more and more moderate business leaders turned against Somoza as they saw their own companies being eclipsed by the Somoza family's corrupt empire.

By 1974, opposition was widespread. Two groups were widely recognized – the FSLN (also called Sandinistas), led by Carlos Fonseca, and the Unión Democrática de Liberación, led by Pedro Joaquín Chamorro, popular owner and editor of the Managua newspaper *La Prensa,* which had long printed articles critical of the Somoza regime.

In December 1974, the FSLN kidnapped several leading members of the Somoza regime, gaining ransoms and the freeing of political prisoners in exchange for the release of the hostages. The Somoza government responded with a campaign of systematic killings over the following 2½ years. Carlos Fonseca was assassinated in 1976.

Revolution & the FSLN

The last straw for the Nicaraguan public was the assassination in January 1978 of Pedro Joaquín Chamorro. Violence erupted and a general strike was declared. Business interests united with moderate factions in the Frente Amplio Opositor (FAO; Broad Opposition Front) and, with US backing, unsuccessfully attempted to negotiate an end to the Somoza dictatorship.

In August 1978, the FSLN occupied the Palacio Nacional and took over 2000 hostages, demanding freedom for 60 imprisoned Sandinistas. The government acceded, and the hostages were released. Nevertheless, the revolt spread, with spontaneous uprisings in many major towns. The Guardia

Nacional responded swiftly and ruthlessly, shelling those cities and exterminating thousands.

The FAO business alliance, having exhausted its negotiating efforts, threw in their lot with the Sandinistas, whom they now perceived as the only viable means to oust the Somoza dictatorship. This broad alliance formed a revolutionary government provisionally based in San José, Costa Rica, which gained recognition from some Latin American and European governments and military support in the form of arms shipments. Thus the FSLN was well prepared to launch its final offensive in June 1979. The revolutionary forces took city after city, with the support of thousands of civilians. On July 17, as the Sandinistas were preparing to enter Managua, Somoza resigned the presidency and fled the country. (He was assassinated by Sandinista agents a year later in Asunción, Paraguay.) The Sandinistas marched victorious into Managua on July 19, 1979.

The Sandinistas inherited a country in a shambles of poverty, homelessness, illiteracy, insufficient health care and many other problems. An estimated 50,000 people had been killed in the revolutionary struggle, and perhaps 150,000 more left homeless.

The FSLN and prominent anti-Somoza moderates (including Violeta Barrios de Chamorro, widow of the martyred Pedro Joaquín Chamorro) set up a five-member junta to administer the country. The constitution was suspended, the national congress dissolved and the Guardia Nacional replaced by the Sandinista People's Army.

However, the alliance between moderates and the FSLN did not last long. In April 1980, Chamorro and the one other moderate resigned from the ruling junta when it became clear that the FSLN intended to dominate the Council of State, which was being set up to serve as the nation's interim legislature. The junta thus was reduced from five members to three, with revolutionary commander Daniel Ortega Saavedra appointed coordinator.

Trying to salvage what it could of its influence over the country, the USA under President Jimmy Carter authorized US$75 million in emergency aid to the Sandinista-led government, but by late 1980 it was becoming concerned about the increasing numbers of Soviet and Cuban advisors in Nicaragua and allegations that the Sandinistas were beginning to provide arms to leftist rebels in El Salvador.

The Contra War

After Ronald Reagan became US president in January 1981, relations between Nicaragua and the USA took a turn for the worse. Reagan suspended all aid to Nicaragua and began funding the counterrevolutionary military groups known as Contras, operating out of Honduras and eventually out of Costa Rica as well. Most of the original Contras were ex-soldiers of Somoza's Guardia Nacional, but as time passed, their ranks filled with disaffected local people.

The Contra war escalated throughout the 1980s. As US money flowed to the Contras, their numbers grew to over 15,000 fighters. Honduras was heavily militarized, with large-scale US-Honduran maneuvers giving the impression of preparations for an invasion of Nicaragua. The Sandinistas responded by instituting conscription and building an army that eventually numbered 95,000. Soviet and Cuban military and economic aid poured in, reaching US$700 million in 1987. A CIA scheme to mine Nicaragua's harbors was revealed in 1984 and resulted in a judgment against the USA by the International Court of Justice.

Nicaraguan elections in November 1984 were boycotted by leading non-Sandinistas, who complained of sweeping FSLN control of the nation's media. (In fact, the Chamorro family's *La Prensa,* acknowledged to have been funded by the CIA to publish antigovernment views, had been allowed to operate freely by the revolutionary government, though as the Contra war escalated, a state of emergency was declared and censorship was implemented.) Daniel Ortega was elected president with 63% of the vote, and the FSLN won 61 of the 96 seats in the new National Assembly.

In May 1985, the US initiated an embargo on trade with Nicaragua and pressured other countries to do the same. The embargo lasted for the next five years and helped to strangle Nicaragua's economy.

After the US Congress rejected new military aid for the Contras in 1985, the Reagan administration secretly continued the funding through a scheme in which the CIA

illegally sold weapons to Iran at inflated prices and used the money to fund the Contras. When the details leaked out, the infamous 'Iran-Contra Affair' blew up.

Various peace plans were proposed by other countries throughout the years of conflict, but no agreement could be reached. The Costa Rican president, Oscar Arias Sánchez, finally came up with a peace plan that was signed in August 1987 by the presidents of Costa Rica, El Salvador, Nicaragua, Guatemala and Honduras. Though hailed as a great stride forward, it proved difficult to implement, as participating nations failed to follow through on their commitments while the USA took measures that seemed intentionally aimed at undermining the peace process.

The 1990 Election

By the late 1980s the Nicaraguan economy was again desperate. Civil war, the US trade embargo, falling world prices for leading Nicaraguan exports and the inefficiencies of a Soviet-style centralized economy had produced hyperinflation, falling production and rising unemployment. As it became clear that the US Congress was readying to reinvigorate the Contras with new aid, Daniel Ortega called elections that he fully expected would give the Sandinistas a popular mandate to govern.

The FSLN, however, underestimated the disillusionment and fatigue of the Nicaraguan people, who were tired of shortages, food rationing, buses that could not be fixed for lack of spare parts, censorship, political repression and having their sons conscripted to fight and die far from home. These problems came to eclipse the dramatic accomplishments of the Sandinistas' early years: redistributing Somoza lands to small farming cooperatives, reducing illiteracy from 50% to 13%, eliminating polio through a massive immunization program and reducing the rate of infant mortality by a third.

The Unión Nacional Opositora (UNO), a broad coalition of 14 political parties opposing the Sandinista government, was formed in 1989. UNO presidential candidate Violeta Barrios de Chamorro had the backing and financing of the USA, which had promised to remove the trade embargo and give hundreds of millions of dollars in economic aid to Nicaragua if UNO won. Enjoying such massive US support, the UNO handily took the elections of February 25, 1990, gaining 55% of the presidential votes and 51 of the 92 seats in the National Assembly, compared with the FSLN's 39.

Chamorro & the 1996 Election

Chamorro took office in April 1990. The Contras stopped fighting at the end of June with a symbolic and heavily publicized turning-in of their weapons. The US trade embargo was lifted, and US and other foreign aid began to pour in.

Chamorro faced a tricky balancing act in trying to reunify the country and satisfy all interests. General Humberto Ortega, Daniel's brother, remained as head of the army until early 1995. The FSLN split that same year into hard-line and moderate factions; the radical wing, mainly based on the Sandinista unions, remained a potent political and social force.

The promised economic recovery was slow in coming. Growth began in earnest only in 1994 and by 1996 had not nearly restored the economy to the level it enjoyed on the eve of the Sandinista revolution. Unemployment remained stubbornly high.

Against this background Nicaragua went to the polls again on October 20, 1996. The race quickly boiled down to a contest between the FSLN's Daniel Ortega and former Managua mayor Arnoldo Alemán of the Partido Liberal Constitucionalista (PLC), a center-right liberal alliance. The Nicaraguan people once again rejected the Sandinistas. In a massive voter turnout closely monitored by international observers, Alemán won 51 percent to Ortega's 38 percent (21 minor parties split the remaining votes).

The Pact

Alemán's achievements included investing heavily in infrastructure and reducing the size of the army by a factor of 10, but his administration was plagued by scandal. However, his tarnished image did not enhance that of the Sandinistas, who disgraced themselves by forming an unholy alliance with Alemán's PLC.

A 1999 investigation of Alemán's finances by Comptroller General Agustín Jarquín revealed that the corpulent president had illic-

itly amassed great personal wealth during his term as mayor of Managua. Jarquín was subsequently thrown in jail. Meanwhile, the Sandinistas had their own image problems, as the ever-present Ortega was accused by his stepdaughter of sexual abuse. In a gesture of mutual self-preservation, Ortega and Alemán struck a deal, popularly known as *el pacto* (the pact), aimed at nullifying the threat of the opposition.

The constitutional amendments the pact members proposed were approved by the National Assembly in January 2000, effectively removing any checks on the new alliance. Provisions changed the makeup of both the Supreme Court and Supreme Electoral Council by stacking them with partisan appointees; they also defanged the watchdog Comptroller General's office. Another provision awarded lifetime National Assembly seats to outgoing presidents, thus guaranteeing that Alemán would have parliamentary immunity from further investigation.

The most roundly criticized provision made it harder for small parties to obtain legal status. Though it was supposedly intended to remove 'frivolous' small-party candidates, many claimed its purpose was to exclude other parties. Furthermore, the percentage of votes needed to ensure a presidential victory was reduced, with an expected benefit for the Sandinistas.

A flagrant example of the new partnership's disregard for public opinion was demonstrated in the campaign for the 2000 Managua mayoral election, when Conservative candidate Pedro Solórzano, considered a shoo-in, was conveniently redistricted by the pacto parties to invalidate his candidacy.

Denunciation of the pact has been widespread and vehement, with critics saying it will end political pluralism in Nicaragua. Others, including former president Violeta Chamorro, believe that the participating parties have ensured a political backlash that will ultimately lead to the parties' own dissolution.

Though Sandinista diehards feel betrayed by Ortega's shenanigans, many still believe in their party. A rift has appeared between Sandinistas and 'Orteguistas,' those who follow the charismatic politician regardless of what many consider his betrayal of the party's basic tenets.

In the November 5, 2000, mayoral elections, only the Liberals appeared to be punished for the indiscretion of the pact members. Though the PLC won approximately two-thirds of Nicaragua's municipalities, the FSLN took 11 of 17 departmental capitals, and popular Sandinista Herty Lewites easily won Managua. A former minister of tourism and the creator of Hertilandia, an amusement park near Jinotepe, Lewites is seen as a conciliatory, pro-business representative of the FSLN. In retrospect, the pact seems to have been a deft political maneuver by the FSLN. The apparent recovery of the party as a political force has rekindled the hopes of Ortega to retake the presidency in 2001.

GEOGRAPHY

Nicaragua, comprising 130,688 sq km, is the largest country in Central America. It is bordered on the north by Honduras, the south by Costa Rica, the east by the Caribbean Sea and the west by the Pacific Ocean.

The country has three distinct geographical regions: the Pacific lowlands, the north-central mountains and the Caribbean lowlands, also called the Mosquito Coast, or Moskitia.

Pacific Lowlands

The Pacific coastal region is a broad, hot, fertile lowland plain broken by 11 major volcanoes. Some of the tallest are San Cristóbal (1745m), northeast of Chinandega; Concepción (1610m), on Isla de Ometepe in Lago de Nicaragua; and Mombacho (1345m), near Granada.

The fertile volcanic soil and the hot climate, with its distinct rainy and dry seasons (191cm annual rainfall), make these lowlands the most productive agricultural area in the country. This region holds three major cities – Managua, León and Granada – and most of Nicaragua's population.

The Pacific lowlands are notable, too, for their lakes. Lago de Nicaragua is the largest lake in Central America. Separated from the Pacific Ocean by the isthmus of Rivas, only 20km across at its narrowest point, Lago de Nicaragua is the only body of freshwater on Earth to be inhabited by sharks. It is linked to the Caribbean by the Río San Juan and to Lago de Managua, its smaller neighbor to the west, by the Río Tipitapa. The lake is studded with over 400 islands.

North-Central Mountains

The north-central region, with its high mountains and valleys, is cooler than the Pacific lowlands and also very fertile. About 25% of the country's agriculture is centered here. The region is not as heavily populated as the lowlands, but it hosts several major towns, including Estelí and Matagalpa. The highest point in the country, Pico Mogotón (2438m), is near the Honduran border, in the region around Ocotal. Lago de Apanás, an artificial reservoir on the Río Tuma near Jinotega, provides much of Nicaragua's electricity. North of Matagalpa, Selva Negra (Black Forest), a combination resort, coffee plantation and private nature preserve, is one of Nicaragua's best walking areas.

Mosquito Coast

The Caribbean region, or Mosquito Coast, occupies about half of Nicaragua's area. It is the widest lowland plain in Central America, averaging around 100km across. The 541km coastline is broken by many large lagoons, river mouths and deltas. Twenty-three rivers flow from the central mountains into the Caribbean. Some of the most notable are the Río Coco (685km), Nicaragua's longest river, which forms much of the border between Nicaragua and Honduras; the Río Grande Matagalpa (430km); and the Río San Juan (199km), which flows from Lago de Nicaragua and defines much of the border between Nicaragua and Costa Rica.

The Caribbean region is not quite as hot as the Pacific side and gets an immense amount of rainfall. It is sparsely populated and covered by tropical rain forest. The largest towns are Bluefields and Puerto Cabezas, both coastal ports.

Several small islands lie off the Caribbean coast, surrounded by coral reefs. The most visited are the Corn Islands, about 70km off the coast.

CLIMATE

Two factors dominate Nicaragua's climate: altitude and season. The entire Pacific lowland zone, including Managua, is hot year-round; the mountainous northern

NICARAGUA

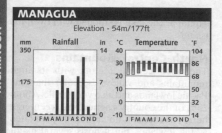

region around Matagalpa and Estelí is much cooler. The wet season in these two regions runs from May to November, when it can rain quite hard but rarely for more than a few hours at a time. The precipitation makes the countryside green and the air fresh, though humid. The dry season runs from December to April. By mid-January, the plains are parched and brown. March and April are the hottest, driest months, when the wind stirs up clouds of choking dust.

The Caribbean coastal lowlands are hot and much wetter than the rest of the country, with an annual rainfall anywhere between 330cm and 635cm. The dry season here lasts only from March to May, but even then it can rain heavily.

In October 1998, Hurricane Mitch caused catastrophic damage throughout northern and northwestern Nicaragua. At least 2800 Nicaraguans perished in the storm, which dumped more rain in seven days than the country normally sees in a year. Mitch crippled the economy, with damages to agriculture and infrastructure conservatively estimated at US$1.5 billion. Key export crops, including coffee and bananas, were destroyed, as were almost all roads and bridges in Chinandega, Nueva Segovia and Jinotega departments. Harder to measure were damages to colonial and pre-Columbian sites that had stood for hundreds of years alongside rivers. Ensuing international relief efforts helped the country to pick up the pieces, and foreign NGOs are still working to rebuild housing. By mid-2000 most of the damage had been patched up, leaving few obstacles to travel even in the most heavily impacted areas.

ECOLOGY & ENVIRONMENT

Like its neighbors on the Central American isthmus, Nicaragua is beset by grave envi-

ronmental problems. High on the list is inappropriate use of land. Forests are cleared to create ranches and farmlands, with consequent erosion, loss of soil quality and disappearance of species. The most deforested departments, León and Chinandega, remain dry most of the year but are flooded by torrential rivers during the brief rainy season. Equally distressing is the overuse of pesticides, which invade the water table and ultimately the food chain.

FLORA & FAUNA

Boasting the highest percentage of forest coverage of any Central American country, combined with the lowest population density, Nicaragua is one of the most biologically diverse regions in the Americas. According to Marena, over 1400 animal species dwell within its borders, as well as some 12,000 varieties of plants, 5000 of which are yet to be classified.

Flora

Nicaragua's plant life is at least as diverse as its animal life. The various types of ecosystems, ranging from dry tropical forest to cloud forest to rain forest, provide fertile territory for botanical exploration. Tree varieties include tamarind, kapok and fragrant frangipani and *palo de sal,* which adapts to its high-salinity coastal environment by excreting salt crystals. Orchids, including the nocturnally blooming *huele de noche,* flourish in the cloud forests of Mombacho and Selva Negra.

Fauna

Sea turtles make their annual nesting grounds along the extensive undeveloped beaches of Nicaragua's Pacific coast. Olive Ridley turtles and, in some areas, leatherbacks arrive in masses from July to January each year. Other reptiles and amphibians found in Nicaragua include green and black iguanas and numerous species of lizards and crocodiles.

Though many birds are elusive to the casual viewer, a patient observer may identify a wide variety of tropical species, as well as shorebirds and migrants. White-throated magpie jays *(urracas)* are found throughout the country, and green parakeets can be heard even in the trees of Managua, but scissor-tailed flycatchers, scarlet macaws and the colorful national bird, the *guarda-barranco* (blue-crowned motmot) may be more difficult to spot.

Mantled howler monkeys are easy to see and hear in the private reserve of Selva Negra and around the volcanoes of Ometepe, but Nicaragua also hosts Geoffrey's spider monkeys and white-faced capuchin monkeys.

Among the more curious aquatic species are the sharks of Lago de Nicaragua. These are generally referred to as 'freshwater sharks,' but genetically they appear to be the same as sharks found in the Caribbean, and some evidence suggests that they migrate up and down the Río San Juan. More sophisticated studies need to be conducted to determine if these sharks have

unique characteristics that allow them to make the transition from salt water to fresh water.

Parks & Protected Areas

The government has assigned approximately 17% of Nicaraguan territory to the Sistema Nacional de Áreas Protegidas (SINAP; National System of Protected Areas). Unfortunately, lacking the funds to staff or carry out research in these areas, such protection remains mostly on paper. Few reserves are actively managed and less than a third have any kind of supervision whatsoever.

Thus, the government is powerless to prevent illegal activities such as the settling of Bosawás, a 730,000-hectare rain

PARKS & PROTECTED AREAS

1 Parque Nacional Saslaya
2 Reserva Natural Miraflor
3 Reserva Natural Volcán Cosigüina
4 Reserva Natural Isla Juan Venado
5 Reserva Natural Volcán Momotombo
6 Reserva Natural Península de Chiltepe
7 Parque Nacional Volcán Masaya
8 Reserva Natural Volcán Mombacho
9 Parque Nacional Archipiélago Zapatera
10 Refugio de Vida Silvestre Río Escalante Chacocente
11 Refugio de Vida Silvestre La Flor
12 Reserva Biológica Río Indio-Maíz

forest in the as Región Autónoma Atlántico Norte (RAAN; Autonomous Region of the North Atlantic) that was certified as an international biosphere reserve by Unesco in 1997.

The Ministry of the Environment and Natural Resources (Marena) hopes to gain more control by getting better-financed nongovernmental organizations to comanage the protected areas in the system. Fundación Cocibolca, for example, has undertaken ambitious ecotourism and research projects at the Volcán Mombacho nature reserve and La Flor turtle nesting area, near San Juan del Sur; another group is promoting sustainable agriculture at the Miraflor nature reserve near Estelí. Other areas where Marena is working to promote ecotourism include the national parks of Volcán Masaya and Zapatera Archipelago, the Miskito villages of the RAAN, and the nature reserves of Volcán Cosigüina and Isla Juan Venado.

GOVERNMENT & POLITICS
Nicaragua is divided into 15 departments and two autonomous regions on the Caribbean coast.

The government is divided into four branches: executive, legislative, judicial and a Supreme Electoral Council, which runs voter registration and elections. The executive is headed by a president and vice president, jointly elected by popular vote to a five-year term and assisted by an appointed cabinet. The legislative branch consists of a 93-seat National Assembly, whose members are elected by popular vote to serve five-year terms.

The principal political parties are the ruling Liberal Constitutional Party (Partido Liberal Constitucionalista; PLC), the Sandinista National Liberation Front (Frente Sandinista de Liberación Nacional; FSLN), the Conservative Party (Partido Conservador; PC) and the Nicaraguan Christian Road (Camino Cristiano Nicaragüense; CCN).

Recent amendments to the 1995 constitution implemented as a result of the PLC-FSLN 'pacto' changed the makeup of the Supreme Court and Supreme Electoral Council by adding members of the pacto parties to the previously neutral bodies.

ECONOMY
While the Nicaraguan economy has demonstrated impressive growth in recent years, apparently overcoming the setbacks of Hurricane Mitch in the fall of 1998, it remains one of the poorest countries in the hemisphere, with at least 50% of the population estimated to be living below the poverty line.

Official figures show the economy expanded by 7% in 1999, reflecting growth in each principal sector, while inflation was brought under 8%. Unemployment decreased to 10.7% (down from 13.2% the previous year), though some estimates go much higher. Agriculture remains a key source of employment (42% of the labor force), but many Nicaraguans are forced to seek work picking coffee in neighboring Costa Rica.

The GDP reached US$2.24 billion in 1999, with farming, livestock and fishing making up 27.8%; manufacturing, construction and mining representing 28.8% and the remainder composed of commerce and services. Agricultural products account for two-thirds of exports, led by coffee, shrimp and lobster, cotton, tobacco, beef, sugar and bananas. Food processing, chemicals, textiles and petroleum refining are among the major industries. Tourism is an ascendant industry, earning US$105 million in 1999, and close to half a million foreign visitors are anticipated in 2002.

Nicaragua's massive US$6.3 billion external debt is a harsh burden on the economy, gobbling up 60% of export earnings – one of the highest ratios per capita in the world. The country has sought inclusion in the group of Highly Indebted Poor Countries (HIPC), which would erase a substantial chunk of the debt and free up national income for education and social programs. But approval hinges on demonstrating a commitment to reducing poverty and corruption as well as to openness of financial operations, requirements Nicaragua has been unable to satisfy.

POPULATION & PEOPLE
The population is projected to reach over 5.2 million by the end of 2001, with an annual growth rate of 2.2%. Mestizos, of mixed Spanish and indigenous ancestry, form the

majority, with 69% of the population; Spanish and other Europeans comprise 17%, blacks 9% and indigenous people 5%.

The great majority of the population lives in the Pacific lowland belt. The Caribbean region is sparsely populated; it makes up half the country's land area but has only 9% of its population.

Six ethnic groups inhabit the Caribbean. Indigenous people include the Sumos and Ramas, who speak their individual languages to this day, and the Miskitos. The Nahuatl-speaking Nicaraos have essentially been assimilated. There are two groups of blacks: those of West Indian (often Jamaican) descent, who are often English-speaking, and a small number of Garífunas (see the Honduras chapter). Still other Caribbean people are Spanish-speaking mestizos.

Nicaragua is a nation of young people: 72% of the population is under 30 years old, and 42% is under 15.

EDUCATION

Literacy increased under the Sandinistas, but subsequently receded as a result of a burgeoning population and scarce funds for basic education. According to a 1998 survey, one in five Nicaraguan adults lacks basic reading and writing skills. The most recent government statistics indicate that only 31% of primary-school children complete the sixth grade, and in 2000 less than a third of high-school-age kids were attending school.

ARTS

Poetry is one of Nicaragua's most important and beloved arts. Hispanic scholars rank the country with Spain, Mexico, Argentina and Cuba as a leader in literary achievements, and no other Central American nation can match Nicaragua's literary output. Rubén Darío (1867–1916), a poet who lived in León, was known as the 'Prince of Spanish-American literature.' His writings have inspired poetry movements and literary currents throughout the Latin world.

Three outstanding writers emerged soon after Darío, and their works are still popular: Azarías Pallais (1884–1954), Salomón de la Selva and Alfonso Cortés. In the 1930s the experimental 'Vanguardia'

movement came on the scene, led by José Coronel Urtecho, Pablo Antonio Cuadra, Joaquín Cuadra Pasos and Manolo Cuadra. The last two, each brilliant in his own way, died early. The work of these poets is widely read and quoted. A number of leading personalities in the Sandinista leadership, including Sergio Ramírez, Rosario Murillo and Ernesto Cardenal, were literary as well as political intellectuals.

The Caribbean coast, with its distinct culture, has its own art forms, too. In Bluefields, the calypso-influenced *palo de mayo,* or maypole, is the popular music.

A distinctive, colorful, primitivist style of painting is produced in the Solentiname archipelago, in the southern end of Lago de Nicaragua. The movement grew out of the creative collective-in-residence led by Sandinista Minister of Culture Ernesto Cardenal during the 1980s.

SOCIETY & CONDUCT

Though not excessively formal, Nicaraguans do value social rituals. Greetings are important, and it's considered rude to decline an offer of food or drink. While businesswear may seem casual by northern standards, Nicaraguans do pay attention to dress codes, especially on social occasions, when there is much shining of shoes and styling of hair. Going around shirtless marks you as a tourist and will certainly distance you from the local milieu.

There are no apolitical Nicaraguans, and political events are heatedly discussed on street corners and in bars and taxicabs, particularly in northern areas. Despite the country's historically turbulent relations with the USA, North Americans will encounter surprisingly little anti-US sentiment and are indeed welcomed by most Nicaraguans.

RELIGION

Roman Catholicism is the dominant religion in Nicaragua, claiming almost 95% of the population. A number of Protestant denominations also exist, notably the Pentecostals and Baptists. The Moravian church, a Protestant denomination that was introduced by missionaries in the days of British influence, is important on the Caribbean coast.

NICARAGUA

LANGUAGE

Spanish is the language of Nicaragua. On the Caribbean coast, which was under British influence for over a century, a Caribbean dialect of English is widely spoken, as are various indigenous languages. English is the language of the Corn Islands. See the Language chapter for more information.

Facts for the Visitor

SUGGESTED ITINERARIES

Travelers with just a few days in Nicaragua should consider making their base in the colonial city of Granada, near a host of interesting destinations such as Las Isletas, a chain of 365 tiny isles just offshore, Masaya and Mombacho volcanoes, the Pueblos Blancos, a series of colorful mountain villages south of Granada and the handicraft center of Masaya. Most travelers with a week to spend make it over to Ometepe Island and may spend a day or two in the Pacific resort of San Juan del Sur.

Those with a few weeks may additionally head for the idyllic Corn Islands, off Nicaragua's Caribbean coast, either by small plane from Managua or, more adventurously, by a two-day bus/riverboat journey to Bluefields, the main Caribbean port. From there, other boats sail out to Big and Little Corn. Alternatively, you could spend your second week exploring the mountainous north, including visits to the lively university city of León, the pleasant mountain towns of Estelí and Matagalpa, and protected forest areas such as Selva Negra or Miraflor. Another second-week option might be to continue from Ometepe by ferry to San Carlos, at the southeast end of the lake, from which you may travel down the Río San Juan to the historic El Castillo fort, or to the nearby archipelago/artists' colony of Solentiname (the latter trip requires careful planning because of limited public transportation).

PLANNING
When to Go

As detailed in the Climate section of Facts about Nicaragua, Nicaragua has two distinct seasons, the timing of which varies from coast to coast. The most pleasant time to visit the Pacific or central regions is early in the dry season (December and January), when temperatures are cooler and the foliage still lush. With the possible exception of the last month of the dry season (usually mid-April to mid-May), when the land is parched and the air full of dust, there is really no bad time to visit. Nicaraguans spend Semana Santa (the week leading up to Easter) at the beach; all available rooms will be booked for weeks or even months in advance.

Maps

Intur produces an excellent country map with blow-up sections of the most visited zones. Their sketchy Managua map is less useful. Up-to-date maps of other towns are difficult to find, except for León and Granada, whose Intur branches offer good maps. The Guía Mananic, available at Hotel Intercontinental and several *librerías* in Managua for US$10, includes foldout maps of every departmental capital, as well as a large Managua map. However, these are of little practical value, as they are out of date, lack street names and landmarks, and are often cluttered with logos of advertisers.

Ineter, the national geographic institute, produces 1:50,000-scale topographic maps covering the whole country (US$4) that are useful for hiking, though some sections are out of print. It is north of the Tenderí traffic light and opposite the immigration office in Managua, open 8 to 11:30 am and 1 to 4:30 pm weekdays.

What to Bring

Warm clothing is unnecessary unless you're planning to visit mountainous regions like Matagalpa, where a light jacket or sweater will suffice. Take rain gear if you're traveling during the wet season or to the Caribbean coast at any time of year. Mosquito repellent or netting is a must year-round.

Power outages are common, so pack a flashlight or candles. Carry your own toilet paper, which is rarely found in public facilities.

Pharmacies, found all over, carry most medications, including antimalarial chloroquine tablets. Tampons can be purchased in some pharmacies and in the major supermarkets in Managua, but there is no choice of brands.

TOURIST OFFICES

In addition to its headquarters in Managua near the Intercontinental Hotel, Intur (☎ 222 6652), the Nicaraguan tourist board, has extended its reach and now maintains branch offices in Bluefields, Chinandega, Granada, León, Masaya and Matagalpa (see those sections for details). With few exceptions, the Intur staff takes its mission seriously and demonstrates an impressive knowledge of assigned regions.

VISAS & DOCUMENTS

To enter Nicaragua every visitor must have a passport valid for at least the next six months.

Citizens of countries with which Nicaragua has a *libre visado* agreement may stay for up to 90 days without a visa. These countries include Belgium, Denmark, Finland, Germany, Greece, Hungary, the Netherlands, Norway, Spain, Sweden, Switzerland, the UK and the USA. Citizens of Australia, Canada and New Zealand do not need visas either but are permitted only a 30-day stay. Visitors from all of these countries are issued a tourist card for US$5 upon arrival.

Stays can be extended for up to three months for US$16 per month. Go to the Migración office in Managua (☎ 244 3989), 200m north of the Tenderí traffic signal near the Ciudad Jardín area. The office is open 8 am to 4 pm weekdays. There's a US$1.50-per-day fine for overstaying your allotted period.

CUSTOMS

Customs regulations are the usual 200 cigarettes, 0.5kg of tobacco and 3 liters of alcohol.

MONEY

The national currency is the *córdoba,* though you will often hear prices quoted in dollars.

With the rapid expansion of the banking system, traveler's checks have become easier to cash, but outside the capital only a handful of banks provide this service.

All over Nicaragua, moderately priced hotels and restaurants will accept Visa and MasterCard. However, they will add 6% to the bill for doing so. Credomatic, in Managua and León, and Banco de America

Central, in Granada, advance cash on Visa or MasterCard.

Automatic teller machines are becoming increasingly common, though they're rarely found at banks. Instead, look for them in shopping malls and at Texaco and Esso gas stations, usually on the highway at the edge of town. Obviously, ATMs are most easily found in Managua, but machines have been spotted in Masaya, Granada and Estelí. Those on the Red Total network accept Cirrus and American Express cards; others take Visa/Plus credit and debit cards.

Note that Nicaraguan córdobas cannot readily be changed in any other country. Once you cross the border, they're good only for souvenirs.

Currency & Exchange Rates

The córdoba is divided into 100 *centavos*. Bills are in denominations of 10, 20, 50 and 100 córdobas, and you may be handed the Monopoly-size 5, 10 and 25 centavo notes. Coins are issued in 50-centavo and 1- and 5-córdoba denominations. The term *peso* is sometimes used interchangeably with '*córdoba.*'

It is often difficult to get change for 100-córdoba notes, so break them into smaller bills when you can.

The Nicaraguan government devalues the córdoba by 6% annually against the US dollar in order to maintain stable relative prices despite local inflation. The rate is expected to reach 13.25 córdobas to the dollar by 2001. The following exchange rates are as of late 2000.

country	unit		córdobas
Australia	A$1	=	C$7.27
Canada	C$1	=	C$8.62
France	FF1	=	C$1.85
Germany	DM1	=	C$6.21
New Zealand	NZ$	=	C$5.78
UK	UK£1	=	C$19.22
US	US$1	=	C$12.90

Costs

You can usually find a cheap hotel room for around US$4 to US$5 per person and an inexpensive meal for under US$2. A 100km bus ride costs around US$1.50. Prices tend to be higher on the Caribbean coast.

Tipping & Bargaining

Nicaraguans do not generally tip in cheap restaurants. Better restaurants add a 10% service charge to the total, usually itemized on the bill.

As usual, be certain to bargain in large outdoor markets, especially when buying handicrafts (but not in the small indoor convenience stores known as *pulperías*). It is also standard practice to bargain over taxi fares.

Taxes

A 15% value-added tax (abbreviated IGV) is supposed to be applied to all business transactions, but this may be ignored at the cheapest businesses. As a general rule, places that provide a receipt will collect this tax.

Travelers departing by air must pay a US$25 departure tax.

POST & COMMUNICATIONS

Postal services, and increasingly phone and fax services, are handled by Correos de Nicaragua. The national telecommunications company, Enitel (often referred to as 'Telcor'), is is moving toward solely handling customer service for phone-line owners but is still the phone-calling center in many smaller towns.

Sending Mail

Airmail letters to the US cost US$0.60 and take at least a week to arrive. Rates to Europe and Australia are 30% and 60% higher, respectively, and delivery times are eight to 10 days.

Receiving Mail

You can receive mail at the central post office of any town by having it addressed to: (your name), Lista de Correos, Correos de Nicaragua, (town), (department). You'll need to show a passport as ID, and there's a charge of US$0.15 per letter.

Telephone

Card phones are being installed in many towns, though they are still hard to find in more remote areas. Chip cards, available in 50- and 100-córdoba denominations, can be purchased at most gas stations and pulperías. Insert the card to make a call; the phone will display the value remaining on the card. International calls can be made from these phones – simply dial ☎ 00 followed by the country code and number.

Where card phones are unavailable, make calls (or send faxes) from the post office or Enitel. The person at the desk will dial the number, then tell you which phone to pick up.

When calling between cities in Nicaragua, dial ☎ 0 before the seven-digit number; there are no area codes. For directory information, call ☎ 112. To call Nicaragua from abroad, use the international code (505) before the number.

Dial ☎ 116 to make collect calls to Australia, Belgium, Canada, Denmark, Holland, Italy, Japan, Norway, Sweden, the UK and the USA. In addition, the following access codes can be used for making collect calls abroad:

Canada	☎ 168
Germany	☎ 169
Holland	☎ 177
UK (BTI)	☎ 175
USA (AT&T)	☎ 174
USA (MCI)	☎ 166
USA (Sprint)	☎ 161

Email & Internet Access

Laptop owners seeking temporary access to the Internet will find half a dozen service providers, including IBW Communications (☎ 278 6328), 20m north of the Villa Fontana stoplight, and Telematix (☎ 278 3131), 50m north of the Centroamericana Shell station in Managua.

INTERNET RESOURCES

A wealth of information on Nicaragua is just a click away. The academically oriented Lanic, on the Web at www.lanic.utexas.edu/la/ca/nicaragua/, has a comprehensive list of links, arranged by topic: research resources, government, arts and humanities, news etc. IBW Internet Gateway (www.ibw.com.ni) catalogs everything from radio stations to real-estate agents and includes an exhaustive list of NGOs. The National Tourism Institute (Intur) Web site, at www.intur.gob.ni, is the electronic version of their glossy brochure: It provides some basic information on obtaining visas and lists car rental agencies, tour operators and pricey hotels.

To find out what's going on in San Juan del Sur – and there's a lot going on – have a look at www.sanjuandelsur.org.ni. For the news of the day, check the daily *La Prensa* Internet site (www.laprensa.com.ni), or for a left-of-center analysis of events (in English), check out www.ndtc.org/bmzp/ news_service/index.html#latestnews, compiled by the Brigada Maria Zunilda Pérez, a British group that supports projects in rural Nicaragua.

BOOKS

Political events and developments in Nicaragua have inspired a flood of books. Some informative or insightful ones include:

A Twilight Struggle: American Power and Nicaragua, 1977–1990, by Robert Kagan. An insider's view of the debate that raged within various branches of the US government on how to respond to the Nicaraguan revolution.

Comandos: The CIA and Nicaragua's Contra Rebels, by Sam Dillon. An analysis of the Contra war by a Pulitzer Prize–winning US newspaper correspondent. Out of print but worth looking for.

Culture and Politics in Nicaragua, by Steven White. Fascinating interviews and related material on the link between literature and revolution in Nicaragua.

Sandino's Daughters: Testimonies of Nicaraguan Women in Struggle, by Margaret Randall. First-hand accounts of the revolution by the women of the FSLN, some of whom later joined the Sandinista government.

The Naturalist in Nicaragua, by Thomas Belt. Insightful and entertaining observations on wildlife, written in the late 19th century by a British mining engineer during his travels through Chontales and Jinotega.

Oral History of Bluefields, by Hugo Sujo Wilson. Local characters reminisce, in unedited vernacular, about the customs, people and events of this Caribbean port.

Poetry is at the core of Nicaraguan culture and thus worth getting to know. Useful collections include:

A Nation of Poets: Writings from the Poetry Workshops of Nicaragua, translated by Kent Johnson. A bilingual anthology of revolutionary-era verse taken from the Sandinistas' ambitious program.

The Birth of the Sun: Selected Poems, by Pablo Antonio Cuadra. A judicious selection from the work of Nicaragua's outstanding contemporary writer, in Spanish and English.

Prosas Profanas, by Rubén Darío. For those whose Spanish is up to it, a slim volume by the country's celebrated poet.

MEDIA

The leading daily newspapers are the conservative *La Prensa,* owned by the Chamorro family, and *El Nuevo Diario,* run by a breakaway faction of the Sandinistas (*La Barricada,* the famous Sandinista newspaper, has folded because of dwindling readership). Both papers are available throughout the country. Other dailies include the business-and-finance-oriented *La Tribuna* and the sensationalist tabloid *El Mercurio.*

A few Managua radio stations stand out from the scores of pop and salsa purveyors. Radio Mujer (94.7 FM) addresses women's concerns and sometimes plays interesting folk, jazz and Caribbean music. Radio Pirata (99.9 FM), the 'pirate' station, broadcasts a mix of blues, reggae, '60s rock and local punk. Radio Sandino (107.5 FM) covers the news from a Sandinista perspective. For vintage Latin dance music and baseball games, tune in to Radio Nicaragua (88.7 FM).

PHOTOGRAPHY

One reliable source for film is the Kodak Express chain, with outlets at Metrocentro in Managua and in most large towns. A roll of 36-exposure color-print film costs US$5.30. Slide film is outrageously expensive; be sure to pack a few rolls. Kodak Express also provides one-hour processing.

LAUNDRY

Laundromats are scarce. If you want your clothes washed, you can sometimes get hotel staff to do it, often fairly cheaply, but make sure you get everything back. If it has been raining a lot, you may have to wait a few days.

HEALTH

Tap water is considered safe to drink in Managua, but outside the capital it's best to use bottled or boiled water. You should exercise the usual care about eating unpeeled raw foods and salads and food from unsanitary street stalls.

Malaria- and dengue-carrying mosquitoes are a problem, especially during the rainy season. Chloroquine, available in pharmacies, can be taken as a precaution against malaria, but there is no medication against dengue.

Hospital Bautista in Managua has been recommended as the country's top health-care facility (see the Managua section for details).

WOMEN TRAVELERS

Two organizations operate centers in Managua and throughout the country to provide health, legal and counseling services for women, especially those with limited resources. AMNLAE (☎ 277 0663), which started as the Sandinista women's organization but is now autonomous, runs several *casas de mujer*. Ixchen (☎ 244 3189, 248 4514) is a nongovernmental organization emphasizing women's health care. Visiting women are welcome to drop in at any AMNLAE or Ixchen women's center.

There are no special dangers for women traveling in Nicaragua, but the same advice applies as for the rest of Central America about dress and so on (see the Women Travelers section in the Facts about the Region chapter). In fact, with normal precautions, many women find Nicaragua to be a surprisingly pleasant country in which to travel.

GAY & LESBIAN TRAVELERS

A Nicaraguan statute forbids homosexual activity, but in reality the law is rarely enforced, except in cases involving a minor. Still, gay travelers should generally avoid public displays of affection.

For information on the gay community in Nicaragua, contact Fundación Xochiquetzal (☎ 249 0585, xochiquetzal@alfanumeric .com.ni), a gay and lesbian advocacy group.

DISABLED TRAVELERS

For those with special needs, travel in Nicaragua should be carefully planned. Where they exist, sidewalks are narrow and uneven. Outside the business-class hotels of Managua, accommodations provide little if any concession to those with limited mobility.

TRAVEL WITH CHILDREN

Long rides on crowded old school buses can be arduous for anyone, but especially for small children. However, in a society where child-rearing is a central concern, bringing the kids along can create opportunities for meeting the locals.

DANGERS & ANNOYANCES

Although the war is long over, regions once under Contra control have degenerated into perilous no-man's-lands roamed by bands of armed criminals. Though the government is reportedly making a concerted effort to rein in such lawlessness, the northern part of Jinotega department and the remote reaches of the Región Autónoma Atlántico Norte (RAAN) remain unsafe for travel, and there have been some reports of assaults in remote areas of Matagalpa and Nueva Guinea. It is best to check with local authorities before venturing into these sparsely populated regions. Worse still, most of the live land mines left over from the 1980s conflict are buried in these regions.

Crime is supposedly on the rise, especially in Managua. Official reports warn of increased gang violence, car-jackings and armed assaults. Nevertheless, the situation in Nicaragua is certainly less dire than in neighboring Central American countries, and Nicaraguans themselves don't seem overly concerned with security. Most crime falls under the category of petty theft and break-ins. Keep an eye on your things, especially when on buses or in open markets, and you won't run into any trouble.

While crime is unlikely to affect you, poverty is a fact of life that you'll confront on a daily basis. Nicaragua is a poor country. You'll be approached constantly by street kids asking for money, some of whom may pounce on the uneaten remnants on your plate.

Strong currents and riptides at Pacific beaches cause dozens of swimmers to drown each year. Lifeguards and rescue facilities are uncommon enough to warrant extreme caution when approaching the waves, particularly at Poneloya near León.

EMERGENCIES

In Managua, call ☎ 118 for police assistance, ☎ 128 for Red Cross ambulance, ☎ 115 for the fire department and ☎ 119 in highway emergencies. The numbers differ in other towns:

town	police	Red Cross	fire dept
Bluefields	822 2448	822 2582	822 2298
Estelí	118	119	713 2413
Granada	552 2929	552 2711	–
León	115	311 2627	311 2334
Masaya	522 4222	522 2131	522 5640
Rivas	453 3732	453 3415	453 3511

BUSINESS HOURS

Business and government hours are 8 am to noon and 2 to 5 or 6 pm weekdays. Many businesses are also open 8 am to noon Saturday. Banks are generally open 8:30 am to 4 or 5 pm, without a lunch break; some do business Saturday mornings.

PUBLIC HOLIDAYS & SPECIAL EVENTS

National holidays are as follows:

New Year's Day	January 1
Semana Santa (Holy Week)	Thursday, Friday and Saturday before Easter Sunday
Labor Day	May 1
Liberation Day	July 19
Battle of San Jacinto	September 14
Independence Day	September 15
Día de los Muertos (All Souls' Day)	November 2
La Purísima (Immaculate Conception)	December 8
Navidad (Christmas)	December 25

Liberation Day is the anniversary of the 1979 revolution. It is no longer an official holiday, but it is still observed with large commemorative events by the Sandinistas.

Every town throws an annual festival for its patron saint. Major celebrations include:

festival	location	date
San Sebastián	Diriamba	January 20
San Marcos	San Marcos	April 24
San Juan Bautista	San Juan de Oriente, San Juan del Sur	June 24
Santiago	Jinotepe	July 25
Virgen del Carmen	San Juan del Sur	July 16
Santa Ana	Chinandega, Isla de Ometepe	July 26
Santo Domingo	Managua	August 1–10
Virgen de la Asunción	Granada, Juigalpa, Ocotal	August 15
Virgen La Merced	Matagalpa, León	September 24
San Jerónimo	Masaya	September 30

ACTIVITIES

This section provides suggestions for activities in Nicaragua. For specific details for each area, please see the relevant regional sections, later in this chapter.

Hiking

Forests, volcanoes and beaches beckon travelers on foot. Trails crisscross Selva Negra near Matagalpa, traversing dense cloud forest inhabited by howler monkeys and toucans. The wooded slopes of old volcanoes are another invitation to roam. Hikers can spend days exploring the biologically varied heights of Volcán Mombacho with the option of overnighting at a research station. Magnificent crater lakes atop Maderas and Cosigüina volcanoes make good destinations. Less ambitious walks reach prehistoric rock carvings on the islands of Ometepe and Solentiname.

Diving

Reefs full of marine life near Little and Big Corn Islands offer outstanding opportunities for snorkelers and divers (though scuba-diving equipment rental is not available on the islands). A 17th-century Spanish galleon off the coast of Big Corn Island is shallow enough for snorkeling. The clear crater lakes of Xiloá and Apoyo can also be explored; both contain endemic aquatic species. Contact Proyecto Ecológico in Laguna de Apoyo (☎ 882 3992 cell phone) for information on diving expeditions.

Fishing

Expeditions sail out of San Juan del Sur in pursuit of blue marlin, swordfish and tuna; Puerto Cabezas is another deep-sea-fishing destination. In the Corn Islands, fly fishers cast for tarpon and bonefish. Fishing is also big in Lago de Nicaragua, with Ometepe and the Isletas de Granada being the best areas. Lodges along the Río San Juan and at Solentiname cater to the rod-and-reel crowd.

NICARAGUA

LANGUAGE COURSES

Estelí has the biggest selection of Spanish language schools, a holdover from its days as a haven for *internacionalistas,* but reputable institutes are also in Granada, San Juan del Sur and Laguna de Apoyo.

Unless otherwise noted, the following schools charge between US$150 and US$200 per week for 20 hours of instruction (weekdays four hours per day) and room and board with a local family. Excursions to lakes, volcanoes, beaches and cultural and historic sites, as well as meetings with community organizations, are generally included in the package. Prices may be reduced for longer stays. Programs usually run on a weekly cycle, with new classes beginning every Monday. Most schools can place students in volunteer social-service positions in the community.

Escuela Horizonte (☎ 713 4117), Apartado 007, Avenida 2, Calles 9 & 10 SE, Estelí. The well-established program utilizes its extensive contacts with local development groups to provide a deeper understanding of the sociopolitical milieu.
Web site: www.ibw.com.ni/~horizont/escuela.htm

Escuela de Español Estelí (☎ 713 4837, fax 713-2240), Apartado 72, Estelí. Allied with the Unemployed Women's Movement.

Asociación de Madres de Héroes (☎/fax 713 3753), Galería de Héroes y Mártires, Estelí. An organizatioin run by an association of mothers of fallen revolutionaries.

Casa Xalteva (☎/fax 552 2436), Calle Real Xalteva 103, Granada. Class sessions are augmented by seminars on Central American history, politics and culture.
Web site: www.ibw.com.ni/~casaxal/

Nicaragua Spanish Schools (☎ 805-687 9941, 800-211 7393 in USA), PO Box 20042, Santa Barbara, CA 93120, USA. Students can move between branch institutes in San Juan del Sur, Granada, León and Managua. US college credit available.
Web site: pages.prodigy.net/nss-pmc

Escuela de Español (☎ 278 3923 ext 188, 882 3992 cell phone), Laguna de Apoyo. Housed at the Proyecto Ecológico research station on the wooded banks of Apoyo crater lagoon, the school offers lodging in cabins, home-cooked meals and an opportunity to join diving research expeditions in the lagoon. Local teachers share their perspectives on community and campesino life.
Web site: www.guegue.com.ni/eco-nic

WORK

A number of Nicaraguan development organizations welcome foreign volunteers. Opportunities exist to work with homeless children, train women in employable skills and provide health education, among other programs. Casa Xalteva in Granada, Escuela Horizonte in Estelí (see Language Courses) and Amica (☎ 282 2325, amica@nicarao.org.ni), an indigenous women's association based in Puerto Cabezas, can set you up with women's centers, clinics and rural development groups.

International volunteer organizations operating in Nicaragua include Habitat for Humanity (☎ 266 6584, habinica@ibw.com.ni), which builds low-cost housing.

Because of a combined unemployment and underemployment rate of over 50%, it is difficult for foreigners to find any paid work. Teaching English remains an option, but the pay is minimal.

ACCOMMODATIONS

Most budget accommodations are in small, family-operated *hospedajes.* Usual costs are US$3 to US$5 per person for a minimally furnished room, with shared toilets and showers. You'll pay between US$5 and US$8 for your own bathroom. Spending US$8 to US$15 per person will yield substantial upgrades in space and comfort; accommodations in this price category are widely available. Adding air-conditioning usually doubles the price.

Costs for beach-resort lodging can increase by as much as 100% from December to April.

FOOD

A variety of restaurants can be found around Managua, serving some good, if pricey, international cuisine. Outside the capital, only León, Granada, and San Juan del Sur offer European fare. Vegetarians will eat well at a couple of specialty restaurants in Managua, or alternatively can find plenty to eat among the buffet-style *comedores* popular at midday.

While the proliferation of the standard pizza and burger chains remains refreshingly limited, Nicaragua has its own style of hearty, tasty fast food. The most typical (and inexpensive) fare is usually found in street stands and market stalls. Local favorites include *gallo pinto,* a blend of rice and beans often served with eggs for breakfast; *nacatamales,* banana-leaf-wrapped bundles of cornmeal, meat (usually pork), vegetables and herbs, traditionally served on weekends; *quesillos,* soft cheese and onions folded in a tortilla; and *vigorón,* yucca steamed and topped with fried pork rind *(chicharrón)* and cabbage salad, usually served on a banana leaf.

In the evenings, *fritangas* open up on street corners, at door fronts, and around the central plazas to grill up meat alongside a variety of fried treats. Try a hearty plate of *tajadas* – plantains thinly sliced lengthwise, served as a base for grilled beef or chicken and cabbage salad. A weekend treat is *baho,* a 'stew' of beef, various types of plantains and yucca steamed together for hours in a giant banana-leaf-lined pot.

Turtle eggs *(huevos de paslama)* show up on many menus, a sign of their popularity here. Locals say they collect only the ones that have been thrown out by turtles digging over existing nests. Without questioning the wisdom of exploiting endangered species to satisfy quirky appetites, it's safe to say these delicacies are sufficiently devoid of flavor to discourage their collection and sale.

DRINKS

Bottled water and soft drinks (gaseosas) such as Coca-Cola, Pepsi and Fanta are found nearly everywhere in Nicaragua. Many restaurants serve refrescos naturales, made from local fruits, herbs and seeds blended with water and sugar and poured over crushed ice.

These can be a delightful treat and an opportunity to sample some unusual fruits. Some common ones are pithaya, a bright purple cactus fruit; tamarindo, a brown, slightly sour drink made from the fruit and beans of the tamarind tree; and chía con limón, a mucilaginous seed usually blended with lemon. Tiste is a traditional drink made from cocoa beans and corn.

In spite of the importance of coffee farming, instant is what is most commonly served. Nicaraguan beers are Toña, Victoria and the more expensive but bland Premium. Rum is also produced in Nicaragua; the two major brands are Flor de Caña and Ron Plata. Connoisseurs consider Flor

de Caña superior to Cuban rum and other expensive brands.

ENTERTAINMENT

Managua offers the most varied nightlife, with bars and discos of every description dispersed around town, including some folk and jazz spots. Dancing is by far Nicaraguans' preferred after-dark pastime, and even the smallest towns have some kind of disco pumping out merengue, salsa and cumbias – or in the Caribbean, reggae and soca. In general, these are weekend venues that stay open very late, often till daybreak. Masaya, Granada and León each host their own boisterous weekly fiestas on Thursday, Friday and Saturday evenings respectively, with live music and barbecue grills taking over their plazas. See those sections for details.

SPECTATOR SPORTS

A legacy of the US Marine presence during the 1910s and 1920s, baseball is Nicaragua's national sport. (Former Montreal Expos pitcher Dennis Martínez, for whom the national stadium is named, is a local legend, and Nicaraguan players routinely show up on the rosters of US major league teams, whose games are closely covered by the local sports media.) Managua's Estadio Nacional attracts crowds of 20,000 or more to see its Bóer club play against the five other major league teams: Masaya (San Fernando), León, Estelí, Rivas and Chinandega (teams vary from year to year depending on who can raise the money to participate). In many smaller towns, recreational league play is avidly followed, with game results being reported by the local radio stations.

Soccer ranks second as a pro sport, though it does not receive nearly as much attention or national funding as does baseball. Basketball is gaining popularity.

SHOPPING

Distinctive Nicaraguan handicrafts include cotton hammocks, basketry, ceramics, and textile arts, wood carving, carved and painted gourds and leatherwork.

Masaya, 29km from Managua, is the country's principal *artesanía* center, with two major crafts markets. Its old market building has been restored and is now devoted entirely to quality work; the main market for everyday items houses a major crafts section as well. In Managua, the Mercado Central (also known as Mercado Roberto Huembes) also contains a subtantial artesanías department but the selection is not as vast as Masaya's.

Alternatively, you can go to the places where handicrafts are produced, see how they're made and buy them there. San Juan de Oriente, La Paz Centro and Somoto are known for their fine ceramics. The Monimbó neighborhood of Masaya is a center for production of leather goods, woodwork, embroidery and toys. Large baskets of bamboo or cane are made all over Masaya department, as are mats made of *tule* reeds.

Art aficionados can purchase canvases created in the unique primitivist style of the islands of Solentiname.

Getting There & Away

AIR
Augusto C Sandino international airport is 12km east of downtown Managua. There's a US$25 airport tax on departing flights.

Most airline offices are at Plaza España. Nica, the national airline, is one of four Central American carriers belonging to Grupo TACA (☎ 266 3136). Flights by Avi-ateca, Lacsa and TACA airlines are booked through the same office. Grupo TACA has daily flights to/from San Salvador (where there are connections to Tegucigalpa, Havana, Mexico City and many other Latin American destinations), San José and Guatemala City, as well as direct flights to/from Miami and Dallas/Fort Worth. Also serving Miami are American Airlines (☎ 266 3900) and Iberia (☎ 266 4440). Continental Airlines (☎ 278 2834) flies direct to Houston; Copa (☎ 267 5438) goes to San Salvador and Panama City.

During low season, roundtrip fares from Miami go for as low as US$350, from Los Angeles US$520. The one-way fare to San Salvador is US$144, to San José US$110.

LAND
Extensive international bus services are available to, from and through Nicaragua.

Tica Bus operates from Managua to the other five Central American capitals. The Tica Bus station (☎ 222 6094) is seven blocks west of the Intercontinental Hotel, in the Barrio Martha Quezada. Travelers are advised to purchase tickets at least a couple of days in advance. Non-Nicaraguans are required to pay fares in US dollars.

Across the street from Tica Bus is King Quality lines (☎ 228 1454), with daily departures for Tegucigalpa, San Salvador and Guatemala City. Their deluxe air-conditioned buses feature reclining seats, videos and toilets.

Border Crossings
Nicaragua shares borders with only two other Central American countries, Honduras and Costa Rica, but buses are also available to Panama, El Salvador and Guatemala.

Honduras
Border crossings between Nicaragua and Honduras are at Las Manos (near Ocotal), El Espino (near Somoto) and Guasaule, open 8 am to 5 pm daily. Local buses travel to all three locations.

Tica Bus and King Quality services to Tegucigalpa leave Managua at 4:45 and 4:30 am, respectively, both arriving around 1 pm and charging US$20/40 one-way/roundtrip.

Costa Rica & Panama
The Nicaraguan side of the main border crossing with Costa Rica is Sapoá (Peñas Blancas). Tica Bus leaves Managua daily at 6 and 7 am, arriving in San José around 3 and 4 pm, respectively, and costs US$10/20 one-way/roundtrip. Other lines traveling to San José include Nica Bus (☎ 228 1373), one block north and a half block west of Plaza Inter, departing at 6 am Tuesday to Sunday, and Trans Nica (☎ 278 2090), a half block east of Rotonda Santo Domingo, with departures at 7 and 10 am. The fare on either is US$10 each way. Tickets for the latter can be purchased from the Trans Nica agent (☎ 268 3220) a block east of the Montoya statue. Before reaching the border, Trans Nica buses stop in Rivas, where you can get on (paying the same ticket price as in Managua).

A cheaper option is to take a regular Nicaraguan bus to the border, walk across, and continue on the other side via Costa Rican bus to Liberia or San José. Local buses to the border depart frequently from Managua and Rivas.

Keep in mind that Costa Rica has an onward-ticket (air or bus) requirement, although it seems not to be rigorously enforced for non–Central American residents. Tica Bus advises that its bus drivers will sell passengers a roundtrip ticket to Managua if one is demanded by zealous border personnel. (If you are driving your own vehicle into Costa Rica, of course, no onward ticket will be required, but you will have to buy Costa Rican car insurance for around US$15.)

Tica buses to San José continue on to Panama at 10 pm, arriving in Panama City the next day at 2 pm. The fare is US$35/70 one-way/roundtrip.

El Salvador & Guatemala

Tica Bus service to San Salvador costs US$25 each way. Buses leave Managua at 4:45 am and reach the Salvadoran capital around 11 hours later. From there, a bus leaves for Guatemala City the following morning at 5:30 am – you could spend the night in the Hotel San Carlos over the Tica Bus station in San Salvador. The fare from Managua is US$33 each way.

King Quality buses depart for San Salvador (US$30) at 4:30 am, arriving at 4 pm. From there connections leave the same afternoon for Guatemala City (US$41). Al-

ternatively, travelers can spend the night at the hotel in the Puerto Bus terminal and catch a Guatemala-bound bus the following morning at 5:45 am.

RIVER

The Costa Rican border station at Los Chiles is reachable by boat from San Carlos up the Río Frío (see the San Carlos section, later in this chapter, for details). Those entering Costa Rica this way must get their passport stamped at the San Carlos immigration office.

Getting Around

AIR

Air connections between Managua and the Caribbean are provided by the two domestic carriers, La Costeña (☎ 263 1228) and Atlantic Airlines (☎ 233 2791). For current schedules and fare information see www.flylacostena.com/ing/coitinerarios.html#5 and www.atlanticairlines.com.ni/nicaragua.htm. The latter is the newer airline, with more comfortable planes, more reliable service and slightly more expensive fares. A US$1.25 domestic airport tax is charged on each flight, payable at check-in.

BUS

There are buses to most cities, towns and villages in Nicaragua. Intercity buses – most of which are former US school

Flights Within Nicaragua

Note that on some of the following routes, there may be fewer flights on Sunday. Fares indicated below are one-way/roundtrip.

route	La Costeña flights	Atlantic flights
Managua-Bluefields	4 (US$36/72)	3 (US$41/74)
Managua–Corn Islands (via Bluefields)	2 (US$46/92)	2 (US$52/95)
Managua–Minas	2 (US$36/72)	–
Managua–Puerto Cabezas	4 (US$40/80)	2 (US$49/86)
Managua–San Carlos	2 (US$31/62)	–
Managua–Waspan	1 (US$42/84)	–
Puerto Cabezas–Bluefields	1 (US$40/80)	–
Puerto Cabezas–Minas	1 (US$30/60)	–
Corn Islands–Bluefields	2 (US$29/58)	2 (US$32/62)

buses – are regular and frequent, albeit often crowded. There are also express vans between major cities that make fewer stops and are sometimes air-conditioned. Bus services usually start very early in the morning and finish in the late afternoon. See the Managua Getting There & Away section for specific routes and fares to/from the capital.

Nicaraguan buses are famous for their pickpockets, so take appropriate precautions. If you have luggage, watch it whenever there would be any possibility of someone either taking off with it or going through it. Many travelers stash their baggage somewhere safe and use only a day pack to carry essentials while traveling within the country, avoiding the problem of guarding belongings every minute. Some hotels may store baggage for you while you travel.

CAR & MOTORCYCLE
Nicaragua has no unusual traffic regulations. Drivers are urged to comply with speed limits, especially in towns, where there are many 'speed traps.' Roads are being improved on major routes, though potholed and even unpaved surfaces are not uncommon. Modern four-lane expressways move traffic quickly through parts of Managua.

Renting a car is neither particularly complicated nor exceptionally expensive. However, it's good to shop around, as rates vary. Sometimes downtown offices rent cars at slightly lower rates than their airport counterparts. Be sure to confirm kilometer allowances. Rentals of a week or more usually include unlimited kilometers, but for one to three days they may not. On average, a small economy car will cost US$20 to US$30 a day. There are several car rental agencies in Managua; see Managua's Getting Around section for details. Throughout Nicaragua, unleaded gasoline is widely available and is sold by the gallon.

BICYCLE
There's no reason why you couldn't bicycle through Nicaragua, except that it is hot, the roads are narrow and many drivers are careless. Bring any spare parts you might need with you.

HITCHHIKING
Hitchhiking is a common and accepted practice in Nicaragua. As elsewhere in Central America, it's polite to offer a little money when you're given a ride. See also the Hitchhiking section in the Getting Around chapter at the front of the book.

BOAT
Boats are the only way to get to some places in Nicaragua. On the Caribbean coast, boats go down the Río Escondido from Rama to Bluefields, from Bluefields to the Corn Islands, and from Bluefields to other places along the coast, including Laguna de Perlas.

Regularly scheduled boat services on Lago de Nicaragua include two routes from Granada: to Ometepe and to San Carlos via Ometepe and a couple of villages on the eastern lakeshore. A quicker service goes several times daily between Ometepe and San Jorge, near Rivas. Boats also depart from Granada for shorter day trips to explore Las Isletas and Isla Zapatera. The Archipiélago de Solentiname, in the southern end of the lake, can be reached from San Carlos.

Public boats regularly travel down the Río San Juan from San Carlos to El Castillo, an old Spanish fortress. There is also public boat service available to San Juan del Norte (Greytown). (See the relevant sections.)

LOCAL TRANSPORTATION
Taxis operate in all the major towns and cities of Nicaragua. They're not metered, so be sure to negotiate the fare before getting in. Fares are generally quite cheap, with short trips rarely exceeding US$1. Horse-drawn cabs are an alternative mode of local transport in Masaya and Granada.

ORGANIZED TOURS
The following operators provide a wide selection of tours all over the country.

Ecotourism International of Nicaragua (☎ 432 2484, 877-867 6540 toll free in North America) Web site: www.eco-nica.com/
Outdoor Expeditions (☎ 522 4281, 779 0909 cell phone)
Careli Tours (☎ 278 2572) Web site: www.carelitours.com

Oro Travel (☎ 552 4568)
Web site: www.orotravel.com

Tours Nicaragua (☎ 228 7063)
Web site: www.nvmundo.com/toursnicaragua

Managua

pop 1,011,235
The capital of Nicaragua, Managua spreads across the southern shore of Lago de Managua, known to indigenous inhabitants as Xolotán. Other lakes fill the craters of old volcanoes within and near the city.

One in five Nicaraguans lives in the capital, which is the national center for commerce, manufacturing, higher education and government. Only 50m above sea level, it is always hot: Daytime temperatures hover between 30°C and 32°C throughout the year.

Managua is perhaps the least accessible of the Central American capitals, and few travelers spend much time here. Aside from it's Área Monumental (monument zone), which stands aloof in what used to be the center, the capital holds little of interest for visitors, who become frustrated with its sprawling streets seemingly devoid of reference points. Consistent with Managua's new image of itself as a modern business landscape crisscrossed by freeways, a 'new center' is being developed around a shopping mall.

Nevertheless, Managua does present the country's cosmopolitan side, and those who have spent time in the hinterlands will appreciate its nightlife and diversity of restaurants, though these tend to be expensive and inconveniently dispersed.

History
At the time of the Spanish conquest, Managua was an indigenous settlement, stretching along the south shore of the lake as far as Tipitapa, whose inhabitants practiced agriculture, hunting and fishing. These early Managuans put up a vigorous resistance to the Spanish, who responded by destroying their city and establishing other urban centers at León and Granada. Managua subsequently remained a village until the mid-19th century.

The city rose out of obscurity in 1857 after conflicts between liberal León (the nation's capital from 1524) and conservative Granada had repeatedly erupted into civil war. Lying midway between the two, Managua was chosen as a compromise capital.

Since then, a series of natural disasters has thrashed the city. The colonial center was destroyed by earthquake in March 1931, then swept by fire five years later. It was completely rebuilt, only to be knocked down again by another earthquake in December 1972. When geologists found the downtown area to be riddled with faults, the decision was made to leave the site behind – only a handful of the abandoned 1930s-era buildings remain, some occupied by squatters. The new Managua is decentralized, with markets, shopping centers and residential districts built on the outskirts.

Orientation
The Interamericana (Pan-American Hwy) traverses Managua, entering from the southeast as the Carretera Masaya and heading out in the northeast as the Carretera Norte. Carretera Sur and the old and new León highways are the main roads on the west side of town.

Managua's former downtown district rests beside the lakefront in the northwest quadrant of the modern urban zone. Left as vacant land for decades after the '72 quake, the once-thriving center contains the city's few official attractions, including the ruins of the old municipal cathedral and the national museum.

Directly south of the old center, the pyramidal Intercontinental Hotel and Plaza Inter shopping mall stand on the east end of the main budget-hotel area. Farther south, the shopping centers on either side of the Rotonda El Güegüense contain banks, travel agencies and airline offices.

To the southeast is Managua's modern commercial center, a 2km strip of the Masaya highway extending from the shiny Metrocentro shopping mall past the five-star Hotel Princess, to the Zona Rosa nightlife zone. Managua's central market, Mercado Roberto Huembes, lies 2km east of Metrocentro; other major markets (and adjacent bus stations) are on the west, north and east ends of town.

Like other Nicaraguan cities and towns, Managua has few street signs, and only the

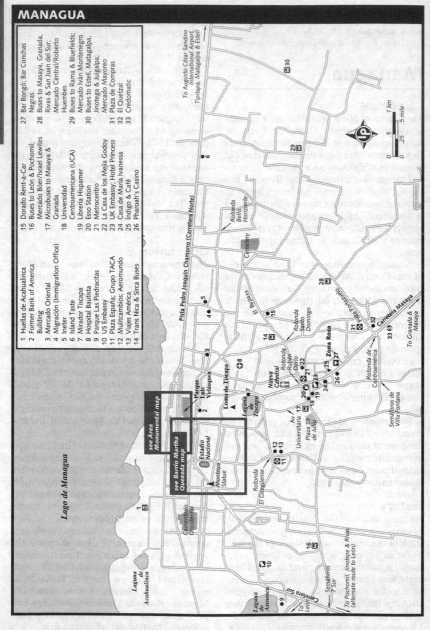

MANAGUA

1 Huellas de Acahualinca
2 Former Bank of America Building
3 Mercado Oriental
4 Migración (Immigration Office)
5 Ineter
6 Island Taste
7 Mirador Tiscapa
8 Hospital Bautista
9 Parque Las Piedracitas
10 US Embassy
11 Plaza España; Grupo TACA
12 Multicambios; Aeromundo
13 Viajes América
14 Trans Nica & Sirca Buses

15 Dorado Rent-a-Car
16 Buses to León & Pochomil; Mercado Bóer/Israel Lewites
17 Microbuses to Masaya & Granada
18 Universidad Centroamericana (UCA)
19 Librería Hispamer
20 Esso Station
21 Metrocentro
22 La Casa de los Mejía Godoy
23 UK Embassy; Hotel Princess
24 Casa de María Ivanessa
25 Indigo & Café
26 Pharoah's Casino

27 Bar Bongó; Bar Conchas Negras
28 Buses to Masaya, Granada, Rivas & San Juan del Sur; Mercado Central/Roberto Huembes
29 Buses to Rama & Bluefields; Mercado Iván Montenegro
30 Buses to Estelí, Matagalpa, Jinotega & Juigalpa; Mercado Mayoreo
31 Plaza de Compras
32 El Quetzal
33 Credomatic

major roads are named. Large buildings, *rotondas* (traffic circles) and traffic lights serve as de facto points of reference, and locations are described in terms of their direction and distance, usually in blocks, from these points. To make things more confusing, sometimes locations are given in relation to landmarks that no longer exist.

In addition, a special system is used for the cardinal points, whereby *al lago* (to the lake) means 'north' while *a la montaña* (to the mountains) means 'south.' *Arriba* (up) is 'east' and *abajo* (down) is 'west.' Thus one might hear: '*del antiguo Cine Dorado, una cuadra al lago y dos cuadras arriba*' ('from the old Cine Dorado, one block toward the lake and two blocks up').

Information

Tourist Offices The Nicaraguan Institute of Tourism (Intur; ☎ 222 6652, promo@intur.gob.ni), one block south and one block west of the Intercontinental Hotel, is open 8 am to 12:30 pm and 1:30 to 5 pm weekdays. Though understaffed and disorganized, the office does provide a good map of the country and a useful brochure with lists of hotels and tour operators. Intur also maintains an airport office (☎ 263 3176), open 7 am to 7 pm daily. Check out their Web site at www.intur.gob.ni.

Money Finding a bank in Managua to change US dollars is no problem. Street-corner 'coyotes' will also change dollars on the black market – they're often found in the Plaza España parking lot – but pay close attention to the transaction. They offer the same rates as the banks; the only real reason to use them would be if the banks were closed. Merchants throughout town gladly accept US dollars.

Traveler's checks remain difficult to cash in much of Nicaragua, so it's a good idea to change them before leaving the capital. Multicambios (☎ 266 8407), just south of Plaza España, changes all brands of dollar-denominated traveler's checks into US dollars (at a 3% commission) or córdobas (no commission). Banco de Finanzas (☎ 222 2444), opposite the Plaza Inter, changes American Express checks only.

The Banpro branch in the airport provides cash advances on Visa; Credomatic (☎ 278 0500), southeast of Rotonda Centroamerica, accepts both Visa and MasterCard credit cards.

Look for ATMs in gas stations and shopping malls. Plaza Inter, opposite the Intercontinental Hotel, has machines on both the Visa/Plus and MasterCard/Cirrus networks, as do the Texaco and Esso stations on Carretera Masaya near Metrocentro. The ATMs at Credomatic and Plaza Inter also take American Express cards. The airport ATM, on the Visa/Plus network, dispenses córdobas and US dollars.

The local affiliate of American Express is one block east of Rotonda El Güegüense in the Viajes Atlántida office (☎ 266 4050), open 8:30 am to 5 pm weekdays, till noon on Saturday. AmEx traveler's checks can be changed here.

Post & Communications The main post office is in the Palacio de Correos (the former Enitel building), two blocks west of the Plaza de la República. Postal services are available 7 am to 7 pm Monday to Saturday. The Lista de Correo (poste restante) window is open till 5 pm; mail is held for up to two months. An Express Mail office is also here, in addition to a philatelists' outlet.

International and domestic calls can be made from 7 am to 10 pm daily. Fax services are also available during post-office hours. The fax number is ☎ 228 4004.

Publitel card phones, from which local and international calls can be made, are sparsely distributed around town. One such phone is in front of the Tica Bus station. More are found at Plaza Inter, where a desk sells phone cards in various denominations.

Internet cafes in Barrio Martha Quezada include El Portal and Cyber Center (1½ and 4½ blocks south of the Casa del Obrero, respectively), both charging US$2 per half hour of access. Plaza Inter has an Internet 'kiosk' on the food-court level, with four PCs around a cubical module. Open 10 am to 8 pm daily, it charges US$1 per 15-minute block of access. Macintosh fans should head for the reasonably priced iMac Center beside the Universidad Centroamericana (UCA).

Travel Agencies Recommended travel agents include Viajes América (☎ 266 1130, vamerica@ibw.com.ni) and Aeromundo

(☎ 266 8725, aeromundo@ibw.com.ni), both south of Rotonda El Güegüense. They offer airline ticketing, auto reservations and visa processing. In the Nica bus terminal, Turismo Joven (☎ 222 2619, turjoven@ munditel.com.ni) specializes in student fares and issues ISIC cards.

Bookstores For a good selection of Nicaraguan and Latin American literature, history and poetry, plus local news and arts periodicals, head for the Librería Hispamer (☎ 278 3923), on the east side of the UCA. US newspapers, including the *New York Times* (US$4), are sold at the Hotel Intercontinental's gift shop.

Medical Services The Hospital Bautista (☎ 249 7070, 249 7277), 1km east of the Hotel Intercontinenetal, is recommended by the US Embassy, and some staff members speak English. Go to Emergencia for treatment. Pharmacies, found all over Managua, are usually open until 10 pm.

Emergency Emergency phone numbers in Managua are:

Police   ☎ 118
Fire   ☎ 115
Ambulance (Red Cross/Cruz Roja) ☎ 128

Things to See & Do
Managua's pre-earthquake downtown has been set aside as an area of monuments, museums and government buildings, though it remains eerily quiet and you're unlikely to see any other tourists around. Studded with mango trees and *flamboyanes*, **Plaza de la República** marks the center of the Área Monumental. On the northeast side rests the tomb of Sandinista commander Carlos Fonseca. An impressive fountain, sometimes seen dancing to Strauss waltzes or *cumbias* (Colombian dance tunes), is between the plaza and the ruins of Managua's old municipal **cathedral**. Built in 1929, the neoclassical cathedral was damaged by earthquake two years later, and again 41 years after that. The imposing shell that remains is worth a look for its frescoes and sculpted angels (US$0.75).

Adjacent to the cathedral, the **Palacio Nacional de la Cultura** (☎ 222 2905) has been impressively restored and now houses the

Museo Nacional, open 8 am to 5 pm daily ($0.75). The museum boasts the country's best collection of pre-Hispanic objects, including statuary from Ometepe and Zapatera islands and polychrome pottery, as well as an informative exhibit on the natural history of Lago de Nicaragua. Above the main staircase is a mural of revolutionary movements in the Americas by Mexican artist Arnold Belkin. Admission includes a guided tour of the exhibits. Upstairs are the National Library and Archives.

Opposite the Palacio Nacional is the brand new **Casa Presidencial**, the offices of Nicaragua's chief executive. Directly south of the plaza is the old Grand Hotel, now the **Centro Cultural Managua** (☎ 222 5291), which offers dance and art classes and stages the occasional university function.

On the lake side of the Plaza de la República, the **Monumento a Rubén Darío** pays homage to Nicaragua's foremost poet. Toward the lake, the oblong **Teatro Rubén Darío** (☎ 222 3630) sporadically hosts plays, puppet shows and concerts by the national orchestra in two auditoriums. The theater fronts on the **Malecón**, a lakeside promenade. Kiosks here serve drinks, beer and snacks such as globular sausages and *lechón asada* (roast pig). Unfortunately, the contaminated lake is absolutely unsuitable for swimming.

Inaugurated in July 2000, the **Plaza de la Fe Juan Pablo II** is the Área Monumental's latest addition. President Alemán's public work commemorates Pope John Paul II's appearances here in 1983 and 1996. On a little hill opposite is the *ranchito* that sheltered John Paul as he spoke to the masses of Nicaraguans assembled in the vacant lot now occupied by the plaza. A building atop this hill houses the **Sala de Exposición Fotográfica**, a modest collection of photos depicting some of Managua's notable edifices, pre- and post-earthquake.

The unabashedly political **Estatua al Soldado** stands on the west side of Avenida Bolívar, kitty-corner from the Centro Cultural. 'Workers and campesinos onward till the end,' reads the inscription below a bronze giant, who bears a pickax in his right hand and holds up an assault rifle with a Sandinista flag waving from the barrel in his left. As if in response, the **Parque de la Paz** three blocks west proclaims an end to conflict. Constructed in 1990, the site is recognizable by the symbolic lighthouse rising out of a circular pool. It was here that President Violeta Barrios de Chamorro gathered the weapons from the 1980s conflict to be destroyed and buried, and it is still possible to glimpse twisted gun barrels sticking out of the amorphous cement walls that encircle a burned-out tank. Behind the monument, a handful of abandoned buildings occupied by squatters reinforces the general air of neglect.

Under construction at the time of writing, the Ministry of Foreign Relations is being built with help from the Chinese government. The major project may signal the start of a development trend within the long-moribund area.

Some of the most ancient evidence of human habitation in Central America is preserved near the shore of Lago de Managua: a long line of footprints of men, women, children and animals running toward the lake. The prints, on display at the **Huellas de Acahualinca** museum (☎ 266 5774), are believed to be around 6000 years old and to have been made during a volcanic eruption, possibly of Volcán Masaya,

which buried them under a layer of ash and mud until their discovery in 1874. The museum, in the northwest corner of town, is open 8 am to 4 pm weekdays (US$1.20). Take a taxi or catch bus No 112 in front of the Plaza de la República.

The best view of the city is from **Loma de Tiscapa**, the hill that rises behind the Hotel Intercontinental and forms the north wall of the Tiscapa crater lagoon. Once the site of Somoza's Presidential Palace, it is now a national historic park, recognizable from around town by the silhouette of Sandino that stands at its edge.

South of Tiscapa along the road to the Rotonda Rubén Darío is another Managua landmark, the **Nueva Catedral** (☎ 278 4232). Most of the funds for its construction were provided by Tom Monaghan, owner of a chain of pizza restaurants. It is a modern but curious concrete structure. Some say its many small domes resemble a mosque; others see a nuclear reactor.

Organized Tours

Tours Nicaragua (☎ 228 7063), two blocks south, one block west of the Hotel Inter-

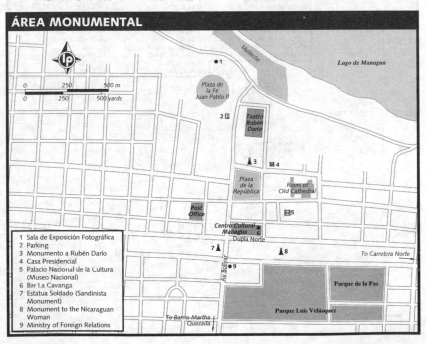

ÁREA MONUMENTAL

Malecón

Lago de Managua

Plaza de la Fe
Juan Pablo II

Teatro Rubén Darío

Plaza de la República

Ruins of Old Cathedral

Post Office

Centro Cultural Managua

Dupla Norte

To Carretera Norte

Av. Bolívar

Parque de la Paz

Parque Luis Velásquez

To Barrio Martha Quezada

0   250   500 m
0   250   500 yards

1 Sala de Exposición Fotográfica
2 Parking
3 Monumento a Rubén Darío
4 Casa Presidencial
5 Palacio Nacional de la Cultura (Museo Nacional)
6 Bar La Cavanga
7 Estatua Soldado (Sandinista Monument)
8 Monument to the Nicaraguan Woman
9 Ministry of Foreign Relations

NICARAGUA

continental, offers half-day tours of the capital with English-speaking guides, including visits to the cathedral and national museum, the Acahualinca museum and shopping at Huembes market. The price of US$45 includes entrance fees. Check out their Web site at www.nvmundo.com/toursnicaragua.

Careli Tours (☎ 278 2572) offers a similar package for US$30 per person (two persons minimum). For more information go to www.carelitours.com.

Special Events
The **festival of Santo Domingo**, held August 1 to 10, features a carnival, sports, a horse parade, cockfights and more. A procession with music and dancers takes the statue of the saint to its shrine at Sierritas de Managua, culminating in fireworks.

May Day (May 1), the anniversary of the 1979 Sandinista revolution (July 19) and Independence Day (September 15) are also celebrated in Managua.

Places to Stay
Barrio Martha Quezada, an eight-by-five-block residential district to the west of the Intercontinental, has many simple, cheap guesthouses and places to eat. International travelers have always tended to congregate here. Since the streets have no names, directions are usually given in relation to the Tica Bus station or the Workers Center (Centro del Obrero, also called CST, the initials for its Sandinista-era name).

BARRIO MARTHA QUEZADA

PLACES TO STAY
7   Hotel La Fragata
10 Casa Fiedler
13 Casa de Huéspedes Santos
14 Hospedaje Meza
22 Hospedaje El Dorado
24 Hospedaje El Viajero
25 Hospedaje Quintana
26 Hotel Casa Blanca
28 Hospedaje Carlos
29 Hospedaje El Molinito
31 Hotel Jardín de Italia
34 Hotel Los Felipe
37 Casa Vanegas
45 Casa Gabrinma
47 Hospedaje Solidaridad

PLACES TO EAT
5   Licuados Ananda
15 Bufet Comida Casera
21 Comida a la Vista
23 Doña Pilar; Rincón Marino
27 El Buen Sabor
35 Cafetín Mirna
39 Cafetín Goussen
40 Cafetín Tonalli
46 La Sazón

OTHER
1   Ruta Maya
2   Loco's
3   Montoya Statue
4   Casa del Obrero
6   Esso Station
8   Barraoke
9   Costa Rican Embassy
11 El Portal
12 Shell Station
16 Cat's Club
17 Nicabus Terminal; Turismo Joven
18 Banco de Finanzas
19 Plaza Inter
20 Former Cine Dorado
30 King Quality Bus Terminal
32 Tours Nicaragua
33 Intercontinental Hotel
36 Tica Bus Station
38 The Shannon Bar
41 Intur
42 Amatl Café
43 Bar La Loma
44 Cyber Center

Casa de Huéspedes Santos (☎ *222 3713*), a block north and 1½ blocks west of the Tica Bus station, is not too clean or well maintained, but nevertheless popular with backpackers, who gather in its large covered patio every evening. Rooms with private bath and fan cost US$3 per person. *Hospedaje Quintana* (☎ *228 6090*) has clean, well-kept rooms at US$4 per person. A block east, *Hospedaje Meza* (☎ *222 2046*) has singles/doubles with private bath that cost US$4/5.50. It's a basic concrete structure, but colorful murals brighten its appearance. *Hospedaje Carlos* (☎ *222 7946, fax 222 2554*) offers cell-like single rooms with fan and private bath at US$7 per person; air-con is available.

Up the street toward Tica Bus, friendly *Hospedaje El Molinito* (☎ *222 5100*) has neat and simple doubles/triples/quads with private bathroom and fans for US$12/18/24. Another good budget choice is the unsigned *Casa Vanegas* (☎ *222 4043*), a block east of Tica Bus, offering spotless little rooms beside an open-air lounge with hammocks. Singles/doubles with good tiled bathrooms are US$10/12, or pay US$6 for a single with separate bath. Bus travelers en route can stay at the *Tica Bus station* itself, where spartan quarters with two to four lumpy beds and private bathroom cost US$6 per person.

West of Tica Bus is a pair of adequate options: *Hospedaje El Viajero* (☎ *228 1280*), where singles/doubles with rattling fans and semifunctional fluorescent lighting cost US$7/10; and *Hospedaje El Dorado* (☎ *222 6012*), charging US$5 for dark, narrow singles with incredibly narrow showers. Three blocks south, *Hospedaje Solidaridad* (☎ *268 5227*) is run by a cooperative of disabled people. Very basic dormitories contain six to eight bunk beds sharing one bathroom for US$3 per person.

For a few córdobas more, you'll find more spacious and comfortable accommodations. Half a block north of Tica Bus is *Hotel Casa Blanca* (☎ *222 3178*) in a typical Managua home decorated with plants and handicrafts. It's quite decent for US$10/14 single/double with semiprivate bath and ceiling fan. Around the block, *Hotel Jardín de Italia* (☎ *222 7967*) charges US$10 per person (US$15 with air-con) for tidy rooms with private bath and single beds. Two

blocks south on the same street is the relaxed and homey *Casa Gabrinma* (☎ *222 6650*), run by a helpful Spanish couple. Rates are US$10/16/24 for very clean singles/doubles/triples alongside a garden, with rudimentary bedding, private bath, fan and large screened windows. A peaceful cottage at the rear is US$15/20/30. *Casa Fiedler* (☎ *266 6622, fax 266 3374*), on a quiet street in the El Carmen neighborhood west of Martha Quezada, is a cross between a budget guesthouse and a standard hotel. Rooms are functional, if minimally maintained, and there's a cavernous '60s-furnished lounge where breakfast is served. It's a good deal at US$12/17 for singles/doubles with fan.

The new *Hotel Los Felipe* (☎ *222 6501*), 1½ blocks west of Tica Bus, has a motel-style row of brightly painted doubles for US$20, including hot water and TV. Add US$5 for air-con. Parking, laundry service and Internet access are all available, plus a restaurant and playground. Those with more to spend might try the modern *Hotel La Fragata* (☎ *222 3403*), two blocks north and one block west of the Hotel Intercontinental, with all the standard comforts. Singles/doubles/triples are US$25/30/35, US$5 more with air-con.

The best deal in Managua's 'new center' is the *Casa de María Ivanessa* (☎ *277 3733, iva@datatex.com.ni*) often occupied by visiting NGOers. María charges US$25/35 for three spacious singles/doubles with fan, cable TV and private bath, plus a simple breakfast. It's 100m south of the Hotel Princess and has a remarkably peaceful garden and patio.

Places to Eat

Barrio Martha Quezada boasts a number of good cheap eateries where you're likely to run into other budget travelers. *Cafetín Mirna* is excellent for breakfast, with things like fresh fruit and pancakes along with the standard gallo pinto. Open by 6:30 am, it's one of the few places that operate on Sunday. Another good bet for a healthy breakfast is *Cafetín Tonalli*, serving yogurt and granola, soy milk and herbal teas. Open 7 am to 3 pm Monday to Saturday, they also do tasty lunch specials for US$1.50. Pick up a loaf of whole-wheat bread at the attached bakery, run by a women's association.

A number of places in the neighborhood are open only from 11 am to 3 pm, catering to workers on their lunch break. All serve buffet-style, filling your plate as you choose the items. Easily the best (and cheapest) of the lot is *Bufet Comida Casera*, also called Los Salvadoreños (a misnomer), though there's no name on the Pepsi sign one block east and 1½ blocks north of Tica Bus. During peak hours between noon and 2 pm (by which time the trays are almost empty), there's a line out the door and tables are communal. They serve a wide variety of salads and meatless entrées in addition to the usual beef and chicken. Exotic beverages vary daily, from papaya to *pithaya*. Other good lunch-buffet joints in Martha Quezada are *Comida a la Vista*, *El Buen Sabor* and *La Sazón*, the last of which features a pleasant, airy dining area.

Another place for mouthwatering *típico* Managua fare is *Doña Pilar*, open only in the evening, when it becomes a popular *fritanga*, or sidewalk grill. Chicken or enchiladas are served with gallo pinto, chopped pickled cabbage and plantain chips. On Sundays, Doña Pilar prepares a big tub of *baho*, which she portions out slowly into banana-leaf packages, making sure to include the requisite helpings of plantains, yucca and stewed beef. Show up during the appointed hours (noon to 2 pm) or you'll leave empty-handed.

The marine-themed *Rincón Marino*, next door to Doña Pilar, has hearty bowls of fish soup (US$3) and fresh bass and snapper (US$4). It's open daily till 10 pm. *Cafetín Goussen*, a local beer-drinking and sports-TV hangout, offers ceviche as well as shrimp and oyster cocktails for about US$1.

Outside of Martha Quezada, *Licuados Ananda*, an open-air vegetarian restaurant across from the Montoya statue, serves decent but unexciting salads, casseroles and fruit juices. Daily lunch specials are US$1.25. All the usual overpriced, mediocre fast-food franchises can be found at Plaza Inter and Metrocentro. If you go to the latter, try *La Cocina de Doña Haydee*, whose fast food at least resembles Nicaraguan cuisine and isn't bad at all. *Índigo & Café*, in Colonia Los Robles (on the east side of the Carretera Masaya) should take care of your cappuccino and café latte needs.

Entertainment

Managua is far and away the country's nightlife capital. Check entertainment listings in *Esta Semana,* a Thursday supplement to *El Nuevo Diario* newspaper.

Unwind with a Guinness and a game of darts at *The Shannon Bar*, a genuine Irish pub and travelers' meeting place in Barrio Martha Quezada. The outdoor *Bar La Loma*, popular with *universitarios,* plays an entertaining mix of rock and hip-hop till very late. It's on Avenida Bolívar south of the Intercontinental. Nearby, the vaguely bohemian *Amatl Café* attracts a more sedate thirty-something crowd. The open-air venue is a good place to relax and converse over a few beers and snacks. There's live music on Thursday nights; the US$3 cover includes one drink.

Three blocks north is *Barraoke*, where people take their karaoke seriously. Even if you don't fancy crooning before an audience, this is a fun spot to watch Managuans delivering tunes chosen from a binder full of ballads.

Revolutionary-era singers Carlos and Luis Enrique Mejía Godoy and their friends perform the Nicaraguan folk repertoire Thursday to Saturday night at *La Casa de los Mejía Godoy* (☎ 270 4928), in Colonial Los Robles, two blocks south of the Plaza del Sol Shell station. The cover varies from US$12 to US$15, US$4 of which goes toward drinks. Another good place to hear live folk, and jazz, is *Bar La Cavanga* (☎ 228 1098), a long-standing nightspot in the Centro Cultural Managua near the old cathedral. Shows are Thursday to Saturday night from 9:30 pm with an average cover of US$4. *Ruta Maya* (☎ 266 4912), 150m northeast of the Montoya statue, is an open-air cabaret with a varied musical program, from upstart rock bands to Caribbean *palo de mayo*. There's dancing Thursday nights to *son nicaragüense* combos.

More clubs are clustered in Managua's Zona Rosa district, notably *Bar Bongó* (☎ 277 4375), which features Cuban food and performers (US$2.50 cover Friday and Saturday night), and *Bar Conchas Negras*, with live music and tables spilling out onto the pavement. A little north, there's *Pharoah's Casino* for blackjack and slot machines. Mariachis wander in and out of the many bars, pizzerias and restaurants that encircle the Rotonda Bello Horizonte in the northeast of town.

There are dance floors all over town, and *El Quetzal* (☎ 277 0890), near Rotonda Centroamerica, has one of the largest and liveliest. Salsa, merengue and cumbias are in heavy rotation in this cavernous club, which attracts a local crowd. *Mirador Tiscapa* (☎ 222 5945) offers dancing under the stars on the eastern rim of the Laguna Tiscapa. *Cat's Club* (☎ 222 3232), one block north and a few blocks west of the Inter-continental, is a stylish disco popular with couples and groups. *Island Taste* (or Sabor Isleño) (☎ 240 0010), at Km 6.5 of the Carretera Norte, draws the Caribbean community with reggae and soca grooves. *Loco's*, west of the Montoya statue, is Managua's liveliest gay disco.

Multiplex cinemas at Plaza Inter and Metrocentro show subtitled versions of the usual Hollywood action, horror and sci-fi for less than you'd spend at home (US$3). More discriminating filmgoers should seek out *Coro de Ángeles* (☎ 267 0398) at Km 5½ on the Carretera Masaya, offering *cine de arte* (on video) nightly at 8 pm (US$2).

Spectator Sports

Managua's Bóer baseball team faces its first-division rivals from October to April at the Estadio Nacional (☎ 222 2021), just northwest of Barrio Martha Quezada. Weekend games start at 4 pm, weekday games at 6 pm.

Pro soccer action takes place at the Cranshaw stadium, adjacent to the National Stadium, from September to April. Games are at 3 pm on Sundays.

Shopping

Almost anything can be found in the huge Mercado Central, commonly known as Mercado Roberto Huembes. A large section is devoted to artesanías from around the country. Scores of vendors display hammocks from Tipitapa and pottery from San Juan del Oriente, as well as woodwork, leather bags and rocking chairs. The music shop here plays samples from its wide selection of Nicaraguan folk CDs and cassettes. Take bus No 119 from Plaza de España.

Other major markets, well-located around town, stock mostly food and household items. These include Israel Lewites (west), Iván Montenegro (east), Mayoreo (farther east) and Oriental (north). Intercity bus stations are attached to the first three.

Getting There & Away

Air For information on domestic air services, see the Getting Around section, earlier in this chapter.

Bus The principal bus stations for long-distance routes are at the city's major markets. Buses heading for southern destinations and the Costa Rican border depart from Mercado Roberto Huembes; for León and the border with Honduras from Mercado Bóer/Israel Lewites (☎ 265 2152); and for Matagalpa, Estelí and other northern destinations, including the Honduran border, from Mercado Mayoreo (☎ 233 4729). Buses for Rama, which connect with boat shuttles to the Caribbean coast, leave from both Mayoreo (☎ 233 4533) and Iván Montenegro (☎ 280 4561).

On the routes to Granada, León, Rivas and a few other large towns, you have a choice of riding either the standard old school buses or microbuses (vans that carry up to 20 passengers). The latter tend to be quicker and more comfortable and may have air-conditioning. Microbuses for Granada and Masaya depart from opposite the entrance to the UCA, others from their corresponding bus stations.

Some of the main routes are:

Chinandega (US$1.50, 2½ hours)
All buses leave Mercado Bóer. Expresos (US$1.50, 2½ hours) leave every 24 minutes. Micro-buses (US$2, 1¾ hours) leave as they fill.

Estelí (US$2, 2 hours)
Ten direct buses leave Mercado Mayoreo from 5:45 am to 5:45 pm.

Granada (US$0.50, 1 hour)
Ordinarios leave Mercado R Huembes every 15 minutes from 5:25 am to 9:30 pm. Microbuses (US$1, 45 minutes) leave from opposite UCA every 20 minutes from 5:40 am to 8 pm.

Jinotega (US$2.70, 3 hours)
Ten expresos leave Mercado Mayoreo from 5 am to 5:30 pm.

Juigalpa (US$2, 2½ hours)
Seven expresos leave Mercado Mayoreo from 5 am to 5 pm.

León
All buses leave from Mercado Bóer. Expresos (US$1.25, 1¼ hours) go via La Paz Centro every 30 minutes from 7:15 am to 4:45 pm. Microbuses (US$1, 1¼ hours) leave as they fill. Ruteados (US$1, 2¼ hours) go via the old highway every 20 minutes.

Masaya (US$0.40, 40 minutes)
Buses leave from Mercado R Huembes every 25 minutes. Expreso microbuses (US$0.60, 30 minutes) leave every 20 minutes from opposite UCA.

Matagalpa (US$2, 2 hours)
Eleven direct buses leave Mercado Mayoreo from 5:30 am to 6 pm.

Ocotal (US$2.75, 3½ hours)
Eleven direct buses leave Mercado Mayoreo from 5:10 am to 5:15 pm.

Pochomil, Masachapa (US$0.60, 1½ hours)
All buses leave Mercado Bóer. Ruteados depart every 20 minutes from 6:20 am to 7 pm. Expresos (US$0.75, 1½ hours) leave every 40 minutes from 6 am to 6 pm.

Rama (US$4.75, 7½ hours)
Transportes Vargas Peña departs Mercado I Montenegro 9:30 pm daily, connecting with boat to Bluefields. From Mercado Mayoreo, 6 ruteados leave from 4 to 11:30 am, and 1 expreso at 10 pm; alternatively, transfer in Juigalpa.

Rivas (US$1.25, 2¼ hours)
All buses leave from Mercado R Huembes. Ruteados depart every 25 minutes from 4 am to 6:30 pm. Microbuses (US$2, 1½ hours) go every 30 minutes from 5 am to 6:45 pm.

San Juan del Sur (US$2.75, 2 hours)
Microbuses leave Mercado R Huembes at 10:30 am and 5:30 pm, with a deluxe at 4 pm. Alternatively, take a Sapoá bus, get off at La Virgen, 10km past Rivas, and catch the bus from Rivas or hitchhike.

Sapoá (Costa Rican border; US$2, 3 hours)
All buses leave Mercado R Huembes. Ruteados go every 25 minutes from 5 to 8:40 am. Nine expresos (US$2.75, 2 hours) leave from 5 to 11:30 am.

For information on buses to San José, Costa Rica, and other Central American destinations, see the earlier Getting There & Away section in this chapter.

Getting Around

To/From the Airport Augusto C Sandino international airport is 11km east of Managua. Taxis at the airport charge up to US$15 for the ride into town, which is at least five times the fare charged by street taxis. To pay the normal fare, which should not exceed US$3 per person, walk the short distance through the airport parking lot, cross the highway and hail a cab.

Otherwise, you can catch any bus to Mercado Roberto Huembes (US$0.15), from which buses depart for all parts of town. In the reverse direction, from Mercado Huembes catch one of the frequent buses heading for Tipitapa and get off at the airport.

Bus Local buses are frequent and crowded. They're also notorious for their professional pickpockets, though the warnings are probably overblown – stay alert and you'll be fine. Routes run every 10 minutes from 4:45 am to 6 pm, then every 15 minutes until 10 pm. Buses do not generally stop en route – look for the nearest bus shelter. The fare is US$0.15.

Useful routes include:

No 109 – Plaza de la República to Mercado Roberto Huembes, stopping en route at Plaza Inter

No 110 – Mercado Bóer to Mercado Mayoreo, via the UCA, Metrocentro, Rotonda de Centroamerica, Mercado R Huembes and Mercado Iván Montenegro

No 116 – Montoya statue, Plaza Inter, Mercado Oriental, Rotonda Bello Horizonte

No 118 – From Parque Las Piedrecitas, heads down Carretera Sur, then east, passing Mercado Israel Lewites, Rotonda El Güegüense (Plaza España), Plaza Inter and Mercado Oriental on its way to Mercado Mayoreo

No 119 – From Lindavista to Mercado R Huembes, with stops at Rotonda El Güegüense and the UCA

Car Low rates are offered by Autoexpress (☎ 222 3816) near Plaza Inter, Lugo Rent-a-Car (☎ 266 4477), and Dorado Rent-a-Car (☎ 278 1825) at Rotonda El Dorado, charging an average of US$210 per week for a compact car, US$300 to US$400 for a 4WD vehicle, including basic insurance and unlimited mileage. Franchises at the airport include Budget (☎ 266 6226), Avis (☎ 265 0113) and Hertz (☎ 266 8399). Call around for the best deals.

Taxi Finding a cab is never a problem; many will honk as they pass to signal their availability. Drivers pick up additional passengers along the way, so you can hail a taxi even if it's occupied.

Taxis are not metered and fares should be agreed on before you get in. The standard rate for a short ride, for example, Plaza Inter to Plaza España, is around US$0.50 per person; longer journeys, such as Barrio Martha Quezada to Mercado Iván Montenegro, should not exceed US$1.50 per person. Fares go up 50% after dark.

Around Managua

DAY TRIPS
Among the places worth visiting near Managua, the most notable is Parque Nacional Volcán Masaya, but even Nicaragua's other principal cities are close enough to be comfortably visited in day trips from the capital. Masaya is only 45 minutes away by bus, Granada an hour and León 1½ hours. See the South of Managua and Northwest of Managua sections, later in this chapter, for details on these sites.

In Managua's hot climate, it's natural to seek out places to swim and cool off. Pacific beaches such as Pochomil and Montelimar are obvious destinations (see Around Managua). In addition, half a dozen *lagunas,* or volcanic crater lakes, lie within and just outside the city limits. Of these, the best for swimming is **Laguna de Xiloá**, on the Península de Chiltepe, about 20km northwest of Managua off the road to León. Xiloá is also suitable for diving; its clear waters provide the habitat for at least 15 endemic aquatic species. Though crowded on weekends, the site remains quite peaceful during the week. Unfortunately, the picnic areas and most of the bars and restaurants around the shore have been submerged since Hurricane Mitch.

Farther into the peninsula and less accessible is the picturesque **Laguna de Apoyeque**, deep within a steep crater. Small alligators can be spotted basking beside its sulfurous waters. It's a strenuous 30-minute hike from Xiloá. Take bus No 110 from the UCA to Ciudad Sandino, where you can catch another bus to the lagoons.

At **El Trapiche**, a *balneario* (thermal spa) 17km east of Managua, water from natural springs has been channeled into large outdoor pools surrounded by gardens and restaurants. Buses to Tipitapa, which pass by El Trapiche, depart from Mercado Central/ Roberto Huembes.

Even those who avoid zoos may want to check out the **Zoológica Nacional** (☎ 279 9073) for its variety of mostly indigenous animals, including peccaries, white-faced monkeys and some very large caimans. Though cages tend to be small, the animals appear healthy and well cared for. The zoo, open 9 am to 5 pm Tuesday to Sunday, is at Km 16 on the Carretera Masaya (US$0.75).

POCHOMIL, MASACHAPA & MONTELIMAR
One of Nicaragua's most popular vacation spots, **Pochomil** is a gorgeous swimming beach about an hour's drive (62km) from Managua. A kilometer-long promenade is lined with small bars, restaurants, picnic areas and a few hotels. People ride horses and dune buggies along the wide, smooth swath of sand, which extends southward beyond the weekend crowds.

At the south end of the beach, *Hotel y Restaurante Altamar* (☎ 269 9204) charges US$11.50 for decent rooms that accommodate up to three people, or US$15.50 with private bath. Altamar's restaurant, on an embankment over the beach, also has moderate prices. Up the beach, where the river cuts through, family-run *Hospedaje Johanna* offers a few clean, basic units with fan and fairly comfortable beds for US$7.50. For the same price, *Los Pelícanos* (☎ 886 4085 cell phone) has larger rooms but dumpier beds. Running water is sporadic at these hotels, and bucket showers are the norm. Lodging prices increase 10% during the dry season and double during Semana Santa.

Dozens of thatched-roof restaurants prepare fresh seafood. *Bar Jessenia*, next to Hospedaje Johanna, is one of the best, with red snapper from US$5 and lobster from US$7.

The fishing village of **Masachapa** is just 2km north of Pochomil. Not as clean or expansive as Pochomil, this beach attracts working-class crowds on weekends and holidays. *Hospedaje Bar Flipper* (☎ 269 7509), where the road branches off toward Pochomil, has concrete boxes with adequate beds, fans and basic showers for US$5.50.

Express buses from Managua for Pochomil and Masachapa depart every 40 minutes between 6 am and 6 pm from

Mercado Bóer (US$0.75, 1½ hours). Masachapa is the first stop. The last bus back to Managua departs at 5 pm.

About 5km up the coast from Pochomil, **Montelimar** is the former beach house of Anastasio Somoza. Expanded during the Sandinista period, it is now a world-class resort managed by the Spanish firm Barceló (☎ 269 6769, fax 269 7757, montelim@ ns.tmx.com.ni). If you can afford a splurge, this is the place. Rates at this 'all-inclusive' hotel are US$75/100 per night. The day rate of US$40 per person (higher during peak season) includes breakfast, lunch and dinner buffets and open bar all day long, plus volleyball and boogie-boarding on a 2km-long private beach. To get there from Pochomil, catch a bicycle taxi (US$0.40 per person).

LA BOQUITA, CASARES & HUEHUETE

Several other Pacific beaches are accessible by turning off the Interamericana farther south. **La Boquita**, 72km from Managua, is a clean, isolated beach, ideal for riding horses (which can be rented here). *Hotel Palmas del Mar (☎ 552 8715)* has OK doubles with a view, fan and private bath for US$30; the friendly owners can be persuaded to lower the price for shoestring travelers. French and English are spoken. Rooms with double bed, fan and separate bath cost US$20 at *Hotel Puertas del Cielo (☎ 552 8717)*. Both hotels have restaurants. The basic *El Pelícano* charges US$15 for doubles with shared bath. To get to La Boquita, take a bus from Mercado Bóer to the town of Diriamba and transfer for a coast bus. The same bus continues a little farther south to **Casares**, whose beach is often covered with fishing boats. Another 10km south is the pretty beach at **Huehuete** (not reachable by public transportation).

North of Managua

From Managua, the Interamericana runs north to the departments of Matagalpa, Estelí and Madriz, highland regions rich with coffee, tobacco and livestock. Cooler than the coastal lowlands, this part of Nicaragua has a distinct character that lures many travelers.

Estelí is the principal town between Managua and the Honduran border. South of Estelí, a turnoff at Sébaco (Route 3) leads to the pleasant mountain towns of Matagalpa and Jinotega and the Selva Negra, a farm and nature reserve managed by descendants of German coffee planters. North of Estelí, the road forks on its way to the border. The Interamericana route goes through Somoto, then crosses the border at El Espino into the southern lowlands of Honduras and continues to El Salvador. The right fork via Ocotal reaches the border crossing at Las Manos and proceeds through the mountains to Tegucigalpa. The remote regions of Jinotega department beyond El Cuá are regarded as a no-man's-land and are populated by marauding ex-Contras and peppered with land mines.

1998's Hurricane Mitch did some of its worst damage in this area, perilously elevating the Ríos Bocay and Coco over their banks, uprooting coffee plantations and destroying bridges from Managua to the border at Las Manos. Evidence of mudslide damage can still be spotted on mountain slopes around Selva Negra.

MATAGALPA
pop 76,503

Capital of the department of the same name, Matagalpa is blessed with a refreshing climate that somewhat compensates for its unkempt appearance. Surrounded by lovely green mountains, the relatively prosperous town spreads unevenly over hilly terrain. Just a trickle here, the Río Grande de Matagalpa is the nation's second-longest river, flowing all the way to the Caribbean.

Spanish conquistadores found several indigenous communities coexisting here, including the Nahuatl-speaking Molagüina, and the town's name can be traced to its tongue-twisting Nahuatl origin, Matlatlcallipan, meaning 'House of Nets.'

Orientation & Information

Bordered on its western edge by the river, Matagalpa's central zone lies between two principal plazas, Parque Morazán on the north side and the scruffier Parque Rubén Darío to the south. The municipal cathedral faces Morazán; budget accommodations are concentrated around Darío. Ten blocks west of the latter you'll find the market and

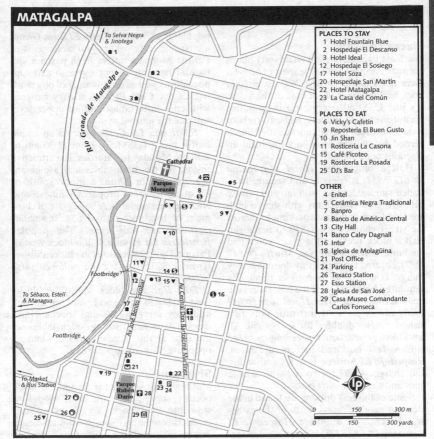

MATAGALPA

To Selva Negra
& Jinotega

Río Grande de Matagalpa

Cathedral

Parque
Morazán

Footbridge

To Sébaco, Estelí
& Managua

Footbridge

To Market
& Bus Station

Parque
Rubén
Darío

PLACES TO STAY
1 Hotel Fountain Blue
2 Hospedaje El Descanso
3 Hotel Ideal
12 Hospedaje El Sosiego
17 Hotel Soza
20 Hospedaje San Martín
22 Hotel Matagalpa
23 La Casa del Común

PLACES TO EAT
6 Vicky's Cafetín
9 Repostería El Buen Gusto
10 Jin Shan
11 Rostícería La Casona
15 Café Picoteo
19 Rostícería La Posada
25 DJ's Bar

OTHER
4 Enitel
5 Cerámica Negra Tradicional
7 Banpro
8 Banco de América Central
13 City Hall
14 Banco Caley Dagnall
16 Intur
18 Iglesia de Molagüina
21 Post Office
24 Parking
26 Texaco Station
27 Esso Station
28 Iglesia de San José
29 Casa Museo Comandante
     Carlos Fonseca

0   150   300 m
0   150   300 yards

bus-station complex. Only one street is signed: Avenida Central Don Bartolomé Martínez, named after an indigenous local who became president.

Matagalpa's Intur branch (☎ 612 7060), one block east and half a block north of the Molagüina church, is open 8 am to 5 pm weekdays with a break for lunch. The knowledgeable staff can suggest plenty of activities in the area. The post office is opposite the northwest corner of Parque Darío; Enitel is a block east of the cathedral. Public phones are easily found.

Things to See & Do
Matagalpa's **cathedral** is one of several 19th-century churches that grace the city. Construction was delayed during the years

when its Jesuit builders were expelled by a Conservative government.

Matagalpa is known throughout Nicaragua as the birthplace of Carlos Fonseca, martyr of the Sandinista revolution. His home has been converted to a museum, the **Casa Museo Comandante Carlos Fonseca**, open sporadically.

Special Events
The city's annual festival is held during the week of September 24, in honor of its patron saint, the Virgin of Mercedes. An agricultural fair, featuring horse processions and bullfights, coincides with the saint's-day festivities. A recently added event, the Festival of Polkas, Mazurkas and Jamaquellos, livens up the closing weekend celebration

with traditional dances from Nicaragua's five northern departments.

Places to Stay

The least expensive (and shabbiest) places are near Parque Darío. Cheapest of all is *La Casa del Común* (☎ *612 2692*), a circular brick building one block east of the plaza. It's just US$1.50 per person in primitive dormitories with rickety beds. Barrels of water constitute the bathing facilities. Funds earned by the Casa support the local indigenous community.

Half a block east, **Hotel Matagalpa** (☎ *612 3834*) is friendly and secure. Thin-walled singles/doubles with fan and private bath are US$6/10; rooms with shared bath are US$4 per person. A parking lot across the street charges just US$0.40 per night. Half a block north of the plaza you'll find the humble **Hospedaje San Martín** (☎ *612 3737*), entered through a tiny doorway. They charge US$2.50 per person in minimally ventilated boxes. At least the bathrooms are clean. Down by the river, *Hotel Soza* (☎ *612 3030*) offers clean, if institutionally furnished, singles/doubles for US$6/7.50. All units have private bath and ceiling-mounted fan. A few hundred meters upstream, **Hospedaje El Sosiego** is quiet and secure and charges US$7 for rooms with double beds and sloping mattresses.

Some of the best options are found in the pleasant neighborhood north of the cathedral. Perched on a hillside, **Hospedaje El Descanso** (☎ *612 3231*) is a rustic cabin featuring a front cafe/deck with sweeping views. Singles/doubles, at US$2.50/4, are sparsely furnished but comfortable and clean. A block downhill, **Hotel Ideal** (☎ *612 2483*) is a good deal at US$9 (US$11 with private bath) for simple, well-maintained doubles on two levels alongside a garden. Six or seven box turtles reside in the courtyard. Unquestionably the best in town is **Hotel Fountain Blue** (☎ *612 2733*) just across the bridge that leads to the Jinotega highway. Modern double rooms with large comfortable beds cost US$11.50, or US$15.50 with private bath and cable TV. Breakfast is included in the price.

Places to Eat

Opposite Parque Morazán, *Vicky's Cafetín* serves breakfast (US$2), snacks and sweet treats under a breezy pavilion. *Raspados* – crushed tropical fruit over shaved ice – are a popular dessert. **Repostería El Buen Gusto**, a charming cafe/bakery two blocks east of Parque Morazán, offers fresh pastries and natural fruit juices. For espresso and cappuccino, as well as donuts and po' boy sandwiches, try *Café Picoteo*, a cozy hangout with cute little tables and an upper level suitable for journal writing.

Rostiería La Casona serves an ample buffet lunch (US$1.50) from 11:30 am to 2:30 pm Monday to Saturday. The attractive restaurant has tiled tables and a pleasant rear patio. *Jin Shan*, a block south of Parque Morazán, prepares Chinese and Nicaraguan standards. A large plate of chow mein or fried rice costs US$4.50; smaller portions are half-priced. The popular **Rostiería La Posada**, half a block west of Parque Darío, specializes in chicken dishes (from US$3.50) – try the *pollo en salsa jalapeño*.

DJ's Bar, one block south, 2½ blocks west of Darío, is a good place to unwind, and they serve steaks and snacks. Hammocks, darts and rustic wooden tables set the tone at this pleasant open-air lounge, open late Monday to Saturday.

Shopping

Matagalpa is known for its unique black pottery; some pieces are small enough to stow into a backpack. Workshops are scattered throughout town. Cerámica Negra Tradicional, two blocks east of the cathedral, displays the work of Doña Ernestina Rodríguez, including jewelry and tiny tea sets.

Getting There & Away

The bus station (☎ 612 4659), as usual attached to the main market, is about 1km west of Parque Darío.

In addition to the following, Expresos del Norte (reservations ☎ 612 5927) runs a deluxe direct bus to Managua at 4:50 pm daily.

Jinotega (US$0.75, 1½ hours)
  Buses leave every 30 minutes from 5 am to 7 pm.
León (US$2.30, 2¾ hours)
  Buses leave at 6:20 am and 3 pm.
Estelí (US$0.75, 2 hours)
  Buses leave every 30 minutes from 5:15 am to 6:15 pm.

Managua (US$2, 2 hours)
Twelve direct buses leave from 5:20 am to 4:50 pm.

AROUND MATAGALPA
Selva Negra

This forest, 12km north of Matagalpa, was named after Germany's Black Forest (Schwarzwald) by German immigrants who came here in the 1880s to grow coffee by invitation of the Nicaraguan government. Eddy & Mausi Kühl, descendants of those immigrants, manage the 850-hectare Selva Negra estate, 300 hectares of which are devoted to coffee (and 50 of which were destroyed by Hurricane Mitch and subsequently replanted). Over half the area is protected rain forest, most of it primary growth. Howler monkeys, ocelots and sloths inhabit Selva Negra, which is also known for its bird life: You might see toucans, hummingbirds, wrens and the resplendent quetzal, best spotted during nesting season in April. Miles of trails meander through the forest, making it a fine destination for walkers and solitude seekers.

Featured at the **Selva Negra Hotel** (☎ 612 3883, selvanegra@tmx.com.ni), also managed by the Kühls, are 23 Bavarian-style cottages of varying size and 14 standard hotel rooms, as well as a chapel and a restaurant overlooking a small artificial lake. Rooms with private bath, hot water and porch are US$30/40 single/double; students and Peace Corps volunteers pay US$10 per person. Bungalows with fridge and TV start at US$50. Pick up a map from hotel reception showing the principal trails and monkey territory.

The Kühls take pride in their ecologically innovative farming methods, which include extracting methane gas for cooking from coffee byproducts, using rice husks as herbicides and planting heliotropes to prevent soil erosion. Mausi will gladly give you a pickup-truck tour of the farm.

Those on a tight budget may prefer to stay in Matagalpa and make a day trip of it. The US$2 admission fee is good toward a meal at the pricey restaurant, which serves a few traditional German dishes.

To get to Selva Negra, take any bus heading north from Matagalpa and get off at the signed turnoff, marked by an old military tank. From there it's a pleasant 1.5km walk.

Sébaco

The town of Sébaco, southwest of Matagalpa in a valley of the same name, was an important ceremonial center for the Chorotega, a powerful indigenous community. Its name is traced to Cihua Coalt (Serpent Woman), Chorotega goddess of the earth and humanity. In the nearby lagoon of Tecomapa are the ruins of a temple to the goddess. Sébaco's 19th-century church, declared a national historic monument, contains a small archaeological museum.

JINOTEGA
pop 37,001

Aptly nicknamed the City of Mists, Jinotega is a quiet town set in a valley amid a mountainous coffee-growing region. Murals on the plaza are testimony to the heavy fighting that took place here and in the surrounding areas during the war years.

The town saw more calamity in 1998, when Hurricane Mitch released its seemingly endless rains here. Rivers overflowed their banks, and streets became rivers. Massive flooding contaminated drinking-water sources, causing outbreaks of dysentery. Mud slides made roads impassable, cutting off access to food and supplies.

Apart from its recent status as a hub of disaster, Jinotega is the capital of the very large department of the same name that extends northeast to the Honduran border and the Autonomous Region of the North Atlantic (RAAN). The security situation in the remote areas is still unstable, with armed bands operating beyond the reach of the police and army.

The drive up from Matagalpa is one of the most scenic in the country and reason enough for a visit to Jinotega. Even during the dry season, when the rest of the country is parched and brown, these mountains remain green and cool. Roadside stands along the highway sell flowers and big bundles of carrots, beets and cabbages – a colorful sight that refreshes the spirit.

Things to See & Do

Though unremarkable from the outside, the **church** has a fine interior with a gilded altar and some splendid religious art and statuary. The most famous statue is the Black Christ of Esquipulas, but others are worth a look. The natural lighting and acoustics are also impressive.

A pair of fading murals on the walls of the old Somoza jail (now a youth center) serve as reminders of the revolutionary years. One portrays coffee pickers with rifles slung on their backs; another depicts young people at war. A monument to Sandinista leader Carlos Fonseca rests amid the tall trees of Jinotega's charming central plaza.

Places to Stay

The *Hotel Sollentuna Hem* (☎ 632 2334), an independent-travelers' favorite, is two blocks east, 4½ blocks north of the central plaza. The name refers to the suburb of Stockholm where the owner spent 15 years, and Swedish is spoken here. This clean, pleasant hotel has the feel of a country inn, and warm blankets are supplied. Room prices range from US$9 for basic singles to US$18 for homey doubles with cable TV, private bath and hot water. There's an enclosed garage and a small *comedor* where breakfast is served.

Alojamiento Mendoza, behind the church, isn't nearly as cheery, but it is cheap, charging US$2.50 per person for cinderblock cells without windows. Another budget-priced option is the *Hotel Central* (☎ 632 2425), on Calle Central half a block north of the church, with fairly bright singles/doubles for US$4/6; bathrooms are downstairs. There's an inexpensive restaurant at the entrance. *Hotel Tito* (☎ 632 2665), a block east and 2½ blocks south of the church, offers large neat rooms with four beds and attached bathroom for US$4 per person. A few rockers furnish the small patio. *Hospedaje El Tico* (☎ 632 4530), beside the bus station, has sterile singles/doubles with bathrooms behind Plexiglas partitions for US$5/8. The genial Costa Rican entrepreneur it's named after also owns a couple of restaurants in town (see Places to Eat).

Places to Eat

One block east, one block south of the plaza, *Soda El Tico* offers a filling buffet lunch for US$2.50, including fresh fruit drink, but show up before 1:30 pm or you'll find empty trays. Several open-air *cafetines* on either side of the bus station serve decent inexpensive fare. Also in this vicinity is *Restaurante El Tico*, a large, featureless dining hall serving all the standards for around US$5. Those low on córdobas can choose from a few 'junior' meals for US$3. The recently opened *Restaurante Trochez*, 1½ blocks east of the plaza, shows more character, with a handsome bar and clean tablecloths. It offers simple chicken or beef platters from US$3.

Getting There & Away

There are two bus stations. The terminal for Matagalpa, Estelí and Managua buses (☎ 632 4530) is near the town's southern entrance. Northbound buses depart from the main market beside the highway east of town.

Buses to Matagalpa leave every 30 minutes from 5 am to 6 pm (US$0.75, 1½ hours). There are 10 direct buses to Managua every day (US$3, three hours); the last departure is at 4 pm.

ESTELÍ
pop 88,045

The principal town between Managua and the Honduran border, Estelí is the center of an agriculturally rich highland valley and is capital of the department of the same name. Tobacco, grains, sesame and other crops, as well as livestock and cheese, are produced in the surrounding area. Equipped with a number of places to stay and eat, this pleasant town makes a good stopover on the way to or from the border.

Estelí saw heavy fighting during the revolution, and afterward the town remained one of the Sandinistas' strongest support bases. Along with León, it was one of only two important cities where the FSLN won a majority in the 1990 and 1996 elections.

Many *internacionalistas* arrived during the Sandinista years, contributing their efforts to the farming collectives established in the region. Their need to learn Spanish resulted in the creation of several politically oriented Spanish institutes, some of which still exist in some form, and Estelí remains a popular place for language study. (See this chapter's Facts for the Visitor section for more information on these schools.)

Orientation & Information

Avenida Central branches west off the Interamericana, then runs north some 25

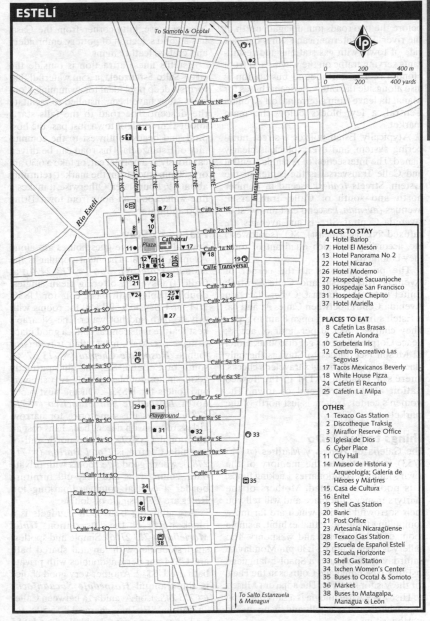

ESTELÍ

To Somoto & Ocotal

To Salto Estanzuela
& Managua

PLACES TO STAY
4 Hotel Barlop
7 Hotel El Mesón
13 Hotel Panorama No 2
22 Hotel Nicarao
26 Hotel Moderno
27 Hospedaje Sacuanjoche
30 Hospedaje San Francisco
31 Hospedaje Chepito
37 Hotel Mariella

PLACES TO EAT
8 Cafetín Las Brasas
9 Cafetín Alondra
10 Sorbetería Iris
12 Centro Recreativo Las Segovias
17 Tacos Mexicanos Beverly
18 White House Pizza
24 Cafetín El Recanto
25 Cafetín La Milpa

OTHER
1 Texaco Gas Station
2 Discotheque Traksig
3 Miraflor Reserve Office
5 Iglesia de Dios
6 Cyber Place
11 City Hall
14 Museo de Historia y Arqueología; Galería de Héroes y Mártires
15 Casa de Cultura
16 Enitel
19 Shell Gas Station
20 Banic
21 Post Office
23 Artesanía Nicaragüense
28 Texaco Gas Station
29 Escuela de Español Estelí
32 Escuela Horizonte
33 Shell Gas Station
34 Ixchen Women's Center
35 Buses to Ocotal & Somoto
36 Market
38 Buses to Matagalpa, Managua & León

blocks through Estelí's principal commerce and hotel district, paralleling the highway, before the two roads join up again north of the river. The Intermericana skirts the east side of town, with gas stations and restaurants serving traffic on the way to and from Honduras. The northbound bus station is also alongside the Interamericana; buses for Managua leave from a terminal off Avenida Central, a few blocks below the main market.

Atypically, Estelí utilizes a street numbering system, and every block is clearly signed. The intersection of Avenida Central and Calle Transversal is the center of the system. Streets (calles) ascend in number north and south of Calle Transversal; avenues (avenidas) ascend east and west of Avenida Central. Streets and avenues are suffixed 'NE' (northeast), 'SO' (southwest) etc, according to which quadrant of town they belong to.

The post office is at the corner of Avenida Transversal and Calle Central; Enitel is two blocks east. Cyber-Place, on Avenida Central between Calles 3a and 4a, is Estelí's Internet cafe, open 8 am to 8 pm. They charge US$3.50 per hour of access; Peace Corps volunteers get discounts. Hotel El Mesón (see Places to Stay) is the only place in town that changes traveler's checks. There's a Visa/Plus ATM in the Texaco station at the north end of town. The women's center, Ixchen, is just north of the market.

Things to See & Do

The **Galería de Héroes y Mártires** (☎ 713 3753) is devoted to the memory of the town's fallen revolutionaries. Lacking funds, it is poorly maintained. Mothers of the martyrs manage the place and will tell you their sorrowful stories, which are far more compelling than the actual exhibit: a single room of faded photos and weaponry. The gallery is open 9 am to 1:30 pm Monday to Saturday. It also houses a Spanish-language institute (see Language Courses in the Facts for the Visitor section). The adjacent Museo de Historia y Arqueología is a sad collection of potsherds and seashells and by no means worth visiting.

Around the corner, the **Casa de Cultura** functions mainly as an institute of theater, music and dance. It hosts an occasional *peña*

cultural, an evening of music and dance performed by its students. Artesanía Nicaragüense, kitty-corner from the Casa, has a good selection of pottery, embroidery and crafted leather items.

Estelí's finest attraction is outside the city – **Salto Estanzuela**, a 25m waterfall that forms a deep pool ideal for swimming. Concrete steps have been installed to facilitate the descent. The road to the falls starts about 1km south of town, just past the hospital, and heads southwest to the community of Estanzuela. This road can be driven cautiously in a normal car, or take a 6:30 am or 1:30 pm truck from the market, returning about 1½ hours later. Otherwise, it makes a fine walk, about an hour from town. Bring food and water.

Places to Stay

Several inexpensive guesthouses are along Avenida Central. The most popular is the friendly *Hotel Nicarao* (☎ 713 2490), at Calle Transversal, offering clean singles/doubles/triples with basic cots for US$6/7/11, or US$9.50/9.50/13.50 for rooms with private bath and hot water. The Nicarao's best feature is its central patio, a good place to have breakfast, meet other travelers or lounge. *Hospedaje Chepito* (☎ 713 3784), south of Calle 8a SE, has nine perfectly good singles/doubles sharing two showers and toilets for US$3/4. On the next block north, *Hospedaje San Francisco* (☎ 713 3787) charges the same price for narrow, airless rooms with decent beds. Fans cost an additional US$0.75. At the north end of Avenida Central is *Hotel Barlop* (☎ 713 2486), where good-size rooms with private bath, ceiling fans and very old furniture border a central courtyard/parking lot. Rates are US$9 single or double.

Arguably the best of the budgets is a block north of the bus station: *Hotel Mariella* (☎ 713 2166). Simple and spotless singles/doubles with fan and shared bath are US$4 per person; doubles with private bath are US$12. Another very good choice is the tranquil *Hospedaje Sacuanjoche* (☎ 713 2482), on Avenida 1a between Calles 2a and 3a SE. They charge US$5.50/8 for well-kept rooms with double bed, or US$5 per person in rooms with two or three single beds. All include private bath, and breakfast is just US$1.50. *Hotel El Mesón* (☎ 713

2655), at Avenida 1a and Calle 3a NE, has rather bare singles/doubles/triples with ceiling fan and private bath for US$8/10/14. There's a large, usually empty restaurant in front and a patio with odd little canopies over picnic tables.

Estelí's high-end lodgings tend to be overpriced. Singles/doubles at the *Hotel Panorama No 2* (☎ 713 5023) are very clean and comfortable but seem small and unexceptional for US$15/20 including cable TV, private bath and hot water. One unfortunate drawback: The hotel shares its rear wall with the recreation center, whose Saturday-night disco pounds relentlessly. Secure parking is available. Estelí's top choice is *Hotel Moderno* (☎ 713 2378, fax 713 4315), on Avenida 2a near Calle 1a SE, but it too seems overpriced at US$32 for cramped doubles with TV and private bath.

Places to Eat

Estelí has plenty of restaurants, though only a few manage to rise above the ordinary. One of those is *Cafetín La Milpa*, next to Hotel Moderno, whose menu is composed exclusively of corn-based fare – and that includes the desserts and drinks. Everything is nicely prepared and delicious.

The market, of course, offers the cheapest meals. There's a row of *food stalls* opposite the east side of the market building, but few are appealing, and sanitation is not a priority.

The exceptionally clean *Cafetín El Recanto*, on Calle 1a SO just west of Avenida Central, does a substantial breakfast, served fast. The municipally run *Centro Recreativo Las Segovias*, on the south side of the plaza, offers an inexpensive weekday buffet lunch. At *Cafetín Alondra*, a neighborhood joint north of the plaza, the food is fresh and well prepared. Dinner plates are US$2.

You'll find several fast-food options along Calle 1a behind the cathedral, including *Tacos Mexicanos Beverly* and *White House Pizza*, which serves a complimentary salad along with your pizza (from US$4). Between these two places are a couple of sit-down *fritangas*. For ice cream, head over to *Sorbetería Iris*, on the plaza's north side.

Cafetín Las Brasas, just off the plaza, serves the usual meat and chicken dishes for US$2 to US$4, as well as burgers and sandwiches. The food is nothing special, and the place is grubby – perhaps it's the waiters' beer-pouring skills that draw the crowds to this lively evening hangout.

Entertainment

The Peace Corps volunteers' choice is *Discotheque Traksig*, out on the highway by the Texaco station. Local youngsters flock to *Centro Recreativo Las Segovias*, which becomes a thumping disco every Saturday night. Next door is Estelí's quaint single-screen *cinema*, showing Hollywood hits.

Getting There & Away

Buses to and from Managua, Matagalpa and León use the market terminal (☎ 713 6162), where you can purchase tickets in advance. The 'Panamericano' terminal, alongside the highway, serves northern destinations, including Condega, Ocotal and the Honduran border, though it has service to Managua and Matagalpa as well.

Schedules refer to the market terminal unless otherwise indicated:

Jinotega (US$1.25, 3½ hours)
Buses leave at 5 and 8.30 am and 1:30 pm.

León (US$2, 2½ hours)
One bus leaves at 6:45 am. Alternatively, take the Matagalpa bus and change at San Isidro.

Managua (US$2, 2 hours)
Eight expresos leave from 5:45 am to 3:15 pm.

Matagalpa (US$0.75, 1¾ hours)
Buses leave every 30 minutes from 5:20 am to 4:20 pm.

Ocotal (US$0.60, 2 hours)
Buses leave every 30 minutes from 5 am to 6 pm.

Somoto (US$0.50, 1¾ hours)
Buses leave every 30 minutes from 5 am to 6 pm.

RESERVA NATURAL MIRAFLOR

Declared a nature reserve in 1996, Miraflor is named after the serene lake within its expanses. The reserve is actually in Jinotega department, 28km northeast of Estelí on the road to Yalí. Its 5675 hectares range from 800m to 1450m above sea level, covering a range of habitats from tropical savanna to dry forest to cloud forest, where orchids and begonias bloom amid mossy oaks and tall pines. Agoutis, monkeys and wildcats are among the varied species that inhabit Miraflor, and bird watchers may spot hummingbirds, toucans and quetzals.

The organization that manages the reserve, the Unión de Cooperativas Agropecuarias de Miraflor (UCA; ☎ 713 2971, miraflor@ibw.com.ni), is promoting sustainable agriculture among the resident communities who grow coffee, vegetables, flowers and livestock. Reforestation and reducing chemical use are key goals of UCA's plan. It is also hoped that ecotourism can provide alternative livelihoods. UCA has thus developed tours, trained local guides and built accommodations within the reserve.

UCA recommends making arrangements through them by phone or email. One-day guided hikes (US$8 per person) lead to the Laguna de Miraflor, caves, waterfalls or outstanding lookout points. Two-day tours focus on the organic agriculture, archaeology or bird life found here. Visitors can spend the night in solar-powered cabins with showers and latrines at US$10 to US$20 per person, or stay with local families. The UCA office is on Calle 9a NE in Estelí, one block west of the Interamericana.

NORTH TO HONDURAS

Of the two routes north to Honduras, the shorter one goes through Ocotal and on to the border crossing at Las Manos. From there, it's 132km (2½ hours by bus) to Tegucigalpa, via Danlí.

Alternatively, you can continue on the Interamericana into southern Honduras. This route goes through the town of Somoto, crossing the border at El Espino, and passes through the Honduran village of San Marcos de Colón on its way to Choluteca, the principal city in the southern Honduran lowlands (60km, one hour by bus from the border). Going this way, you could reach the Salvadoran border in three hours (plus waiting time for a connecting bus in Choluteca).

Honduras-bound travelers can take one bus to the border, go through, and catch a second bus on the other side. The border posts are open 8 am to 5 pm daily.

Ocotal

pop 31,331

The capital of Nueva Segovia department, Ocotal sits at the base of the Sierra de Dipilto, Nicaragua's highest mountain range. Boasting an imposing old church (under restoration) and one of the loveliest central plazas in the country, it's worth a stop on the way from Honduras (an hour away by bus), and there are plenty of reasonably priced hotels.

Ocotal displays its cowboy spirit during the Festival de La Virgen de la Asunción in mid-August, when its ranching gentry show off their horsemanship through the streets and around the plaza.

The bus station is beside the highway on the south end of town, just above the point where the road splits, the left branch bypassing town to the west and the right branch heading straight north through the center. Banpro, opposite the municipal market, reportedly exchanges traveler's checks.

Peace Corps volunteers rate **Hotel El Viajero** (☎ 732 2040) the best value in Ocotal. Three blocks north of the bus station, this clean, well-maintained place offers fresh-smelling singles/doubles with fans for US$4/6, or about twice that if you want a private bath. Rooms wrap around a tranquil patio with rocking chairs.

Around the corner is **Hospedaje Ruiz** (☎ 732 2438), perhaps the cheapest decent place in town. Rates are US$2.50 per person in cinder-block boxes that are noticeably cleaner than elsewhere. Male and female showers are in separate self-contained stalls.

Another good deal is **Hotelito San Martín** (☎ 732 2788), 1½ blocks east of the Shell station on the Interamericana. Run by helpful folks, the San Martín charges US$6/11 for big singles/doubles, all with private bath. Worth the extra córdobas, **Hotel Benmoral** (☎ 732 2824) is a large, pleasant establishment offering neat, comfortable doubles from US$12.50, each equipped with two fans, cable TV and private bath. Located on the main boulevard south of the center, it includes an inexpensive restaurant.

For places to eat, **Cafetín Del Bosque**, on the south side of the plaza, does grilled chicken; **Restaurante La Esquinita**, a few blocks south, offers a US$2 comida corriente; and **Restaurante La Cabaña**, next door to Hotel Benmoral, serves regional fare, with main courses in the US$5 to US$7 range.

All buses depart from the main terminal (☎ 732 3304). Border-bound buses stop to pick up passengers by the Shell station at the north end of town.

Estelí ($0.75, 2¼ hours)
Thirteen expresos depart from 4:45 am to 5 pm.

Las Manos, Honduran border (US$0.40, 1 hour)
Buses depart hourly from 5 am to 4:10 pm.

Managua (US$2.75, 3½ hours)
Ten expresos leave from 5 am to 3:15 pm.

Somoto (US$0.40, 1¾ hours)
Buses leave hourly from 5:45 am.

Somoto
pop 16,044
Somoto, 20km from the Honduran border at El Espino, is a quiet mountain town and capital of Madriz department. The colonial church on the plaza is Nicaragua's oldest.

Travelers crossing the border might want to spend the night in Somoto. *Hotel Panamericano* (☎ 722 2355), right on the plaza, is a good choice. Rates are US$4 per person, US$6 with private bath, US$8 with hot water and cable TV.

Somoto's bus station is on the Interamericana, a short walk from the center of town. Buses depart hourly for the border (US$0.40, 45 minutes) and every 40 minutes for Estelí (US$0.75, two hours). Direct buses bound for Managua depart at 5, 6:15 and 7:30 am, and 2 and 3:45 pm (US$2.75, 4½ hours).

Northwest of Managua

The main geographic feature of this area is the Cordillera de los Maribios, a chain of 10 volcanoes, some active, paralleling the Pacific coast from the northwestern shores of Lake Managua to the Gulf of Fonseca. Momotombo (1280m), the southernmost volcano, towers over Lake Managua; Cosigüina, the cordillera's northern endpoint, forms a peninsula that juts into the gulf. These volcanoes rise out of hot, agriculturally rich lowlands, where maize, sugarcane, rice and cotton are grown.

Two major cities rest at the base of the chain's eastern slopes: historic León, which was the capital of Nicaragua for over two centuries and is today the country's second-largest city and a center of university and cultural life; and the agricultural center of Chinandega, 37km farther north. A road leads southeast from Chinandega to Corinto, the principal Pacific port.

Catastrophe struck the region in 1998 when Hurricane Mitch hovered here for 10 days. Incessant rains destroyed every bridge from León to Chinandega and filled the crater lake of Volcán Casitas, precipitating the collapse of its eastern rim. The ensuing mud slides literally washed away two villages in the municipality of Posoltega, burying thousands of people. Reconstruction has been slow, but by mid-2000 most of the roads and bridges were functioning.

LEÓN
pop 142,569
León was founded in 1524 by Francisco Fernández de Córdoba at the site of the indigenous village of Imabite. Its location, at the foot of Volcán Momotombo, was 32km from where the present-day city stands. In 1610 the volcano's activity triggered an earthquake that destroyed the old city. It was rebuilt near the existing indigenous capital, Subtiava, where it remains.

León was the nation's capital from the colonial period until Managua took over the role in 1857. It was also the ecclesiastical center for both Nicaragua and Costa Rica. There are many fine colonial buildings and churches, including the impressive cathedral. Old Spanish-style houses, with stuccoed adobe walls, thick wooden doors and cool interior patios line the streets. The Universidad Autónoma de Nicaragua, Nicaragua's first university, was founded here in 1912.

Larger and livelier than longtime rival Granada, León is arguably Nicaragua's only true city, in the sense of a place that bubbles with cultural and intellectual activity. In addition, it's traditionally the most politically progressive of Nicaraguan cities. During the revolution, virtually the entire town fought against Somoza. Dramatic murals around town serve as vivid reminders of that period, though many are fading. Only in two cities – León and Estelí – was the FSLN victorious in the 1990 and 1996 elections.

Orientation

León is one of the few towns in Nicaragua that is clearly signed, and its street numbering system is easy to follow. Avenida Central and Calle Central Rubén Darío intersect at the northeast corner of the Parque Central, forming northeast, northwest, southeast and southwest quadrants. Calles ascend numerically as they go north or south of Calle Central; avenidas go up east or west of Avenida Central. Keep in mind, however, that the Leonese themselves rarely use this system when giving directions, preferring to use the old reliable '2½ blocks east of the Shell station.'

León's main market is behind the cathedral; other markets are found by the old railway station and near the bus station on the northeastern outskirts of town. The old indigenous town of Subtiava is a western suburb.

Information

The Intur office (☎ 311 3682), on 2a Avenida NE just north of 2a Calle NE, is open 8 am to 5 pm weekdays with a lunch break from 12:30 to 2 pm. The staff is unusually helpful (as long as you understand Spanish) and knowledgeable about León and other areas. Pick up their excellent city map (US$2).

Publitel phones are found outside the Enitel office just off the northwest corner of the central plaza. The post office is on 1a Avenida NE opposite the Iglesia de La Recolección. Check email for US$2 per hour at M&M, on Avenida Central. There are no ATMs, but Credomatic, on 1a Calle NE, can arrange cash advances for Visa and MasterCard holders.

Things to See & Do

Churches & Plazas León's **cathedral** is the largest in Central America. Construction began in 1747 and went on for over a hundred years. According to local legend, the city's leaders feared their original grandiose design for the structure would be turned down by Spanish imperial authorities, so they submitted a more modest but bogus set of plans. Among the magnificent works of art within are the *Stations of the Cross* by Antonio Sarria, considered masterpieces of Spanish colonial religious art.

The cathedral is a sort of pantheon of Nicaraguan culture. The tomb of Rubén Darío, León's favorite son, is on one side of the altar, guarded by a sorrowful lion. Darío's tomb bears the inscription 'Nicaragua is created of vigor and glory, Nicaragua is made for freedom.' Nearby rest the tombs of Alfonso Cortés (1893–1969) and Salomón de la Selva (1993–1959), lesser-known but important figures in Nicaraguan literature. 'Don Sal,' as the latter was called, wrote stinging verse in English during the various US interventions. Among the other illustrious persons buried here is Miguel Larreynaga, the pioneer of the Central American independence movement.

On the south side of the cathedral you'll find the **Colegio La Asunción**, the first theological college in Nicaragua; the attractive **Palacio Episcopal** (Bishop's Palace); and the **Colegio de San Ramón**, where Larreynaga was educated.

The refurbished **Parque Central de León** is notable for its simple lines and openness. Three blocks north of the cathedral, the 18th-century **Iglesia de La Recolección** has an interesting façade, with carved vines wound around stone pillars, and symbols in bas-relief medallions recalling events in the Passion of Christ. The **Iglesia de El Calvario**, another 18th-century building, stands at the east end of Calle Central. Its façade, between a pair of red-brick bell towers, displays biblical scenes that resemble comic-strip panels. Enter the building to admire its slender wood columns and ceiling decorated with harvest motifs. Other colonial churches worth visiting include **La Merced** and **San Juan**.

About 1km west of the central plaza is the church of **San Juan Bautista de Subtiava**, the oldest intact church in León. Built in the first decade of the 18th century and restored in the early 1990s with help from Spain, it features a typical arched timber roof upon which is affixed an extraordinary sun icon, said to have been put there by the Spanish to attract indigenous worshipers. The exquisite filigreed altar demonstrates the woodworking skills of the local builders. The church stands near the center of the indigenous village of Subtiava, which occupied the area long before the Spaniards arrived.

A few blocks west are the ruins of an even older church, **Veracruz**, built in the late 16th century as the original nucleus for the Spanish city that was transplanted here. The

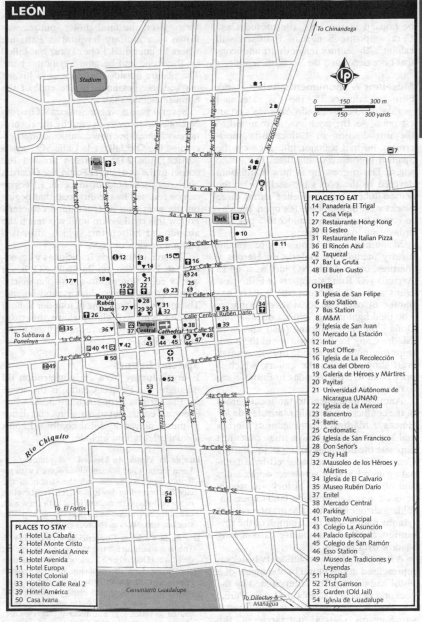

LEÓN

To Chinandega

Stadium

Park

To Subtiava &
Poneloya

Parque
Rubén
Darío

Parque
Central

Cathedral

Río Chiquito

To El Fortín

Cementerio Guadalupe

To Dilectus &
Managua

PLACES TO EAT
14 Panadería El Trigal
17 Casa Vieja
27 Restaurante Hong Kong
30 El Sesteo
31 Restaurante Italian Pizza
36 El Rincón Azul
42 Taquezal
47 Bar La Gruta
48 El Buen Gusto

OTHER
3 Iglesia de San Felipe
6 Esso Station
7 Bus Station
8 M&M
9 Iglesia de San Juan
10 Mercado La Estación
12 Intur
15 Post Office
16 Iglesia de La Recolección
18 Casa del Obrero
19 Galería de Héroes y Mártires
20 Payitas
21 Universidad Autónoma de
   Nicaragua (UNAN)
22 Iglesia de La Merced
23 Bancentro
24 Banic
25 Credomatic
26 Iglesia de San Francisco
28 Don Señor's
29 City Hall
32 Mausoleo de los Héroes y
   Mártires
34 Iglesia de El Calvario
35 Museo Rubén Darío
37 Enitel
38 Mercado Central
40 Parking
41 Teatro Municipal
43 Colegio La Asunción
44 Palacio Episcopal
45 Colegio de San Ramón
46 Esso Station
49 Museo de Tradiciones y
   Leyendas
51 Hospital
52 21st Garrison
53 Garden (Old Jail)
54 Iglesia de Guadalupe

PLACES TO STAY
1 Hotel La Cabaña
2 Hotel Monte Cristo
4 Hotel Avenida Annex
5 Hotel Avenida
11 Hotel Europa
13 Hotel Colonial
33 Hotelito Calle Real 2
39 Hotel América
50 Casa Ivana

building was destroyed by volcanic eruption in 1835. A planned **Museo de Arte Sacro**, to be housed in the long, tile-roofed Casa Cural opposite San Juan Bautista, will exhibit 17th-century religious art and icons that once decorated the Veracruz temple.

Museums & Monuments Rubén Darío, born on January 18, 1867, is esteemed worldwide as one of Latin America's greatest poets. As the poet most committed to the introduction of 19th-century modernism, he had a major influence on the Spanish literature of his time. The house where Darío grew up is now a museum devoted to the poet's life and works: the **Museo Rubén Darío**, on Calle Central, three blocks west of the plaza. It's open Tuesday to Friday 9 am to noon and 2 to 5 pm, Saturday 9 am to noon (free).

Monuments to León's more recent history include the **Galería de Héroes y Mártires**, on 1a Calle NO just west of 1a Avenida NO. Run by mothers of FSLN veterans and fallen heroes, the gallery has photos of over 300 local revolutionaries who died fighting the Somoza dictatorship. Doña Concepción Toruña (also known as 'Madre Cony') will tell you about the hardships the mothers continue to face. A small craft shop supports the gallery, which is open 8 am to 5 pm Monday to Friday, 8 am to noon Saturday.

Another monument to the local heroes of the conflict, the torch-lit **Mausoleo de los Héroes y Mártires** (Mausoleum of Heroes and Martyrs) rests within a small plaza just opposite the northeast corner of the Parque Central. This plaza is bordered by a fascinating mural, in which crosses, swords, tanks and other remnants of history are strewn across a series of desolate landscapes, unfolding chronologically in a sort of record of tyranny ending with the triumph of the revolution. Sandino's silhouette casts a long shadow over his era.

A key moment in revolutionary history is represented in this mural by the image of a pistol and a letter. The letter, signed by the poet and journalist Rigoberto López Pérez, declares his intention to assassinate Anastasio Somoza García, patriarch of the Somozas' four-decade dynasty. The house where he carried out his plan, the **Casa del Obrero**, is on 2a Avenida NO. On September 21, 1956, López Pérez, dressed as a waiter to gain entry to a party for dignitaries, fired the fatal shots; Somoza was flown to a military hospital in Panama, where he later died. López Pérez was killed on the scene and became a national hero. The plaque outside the house says his act marked the 'beginning of the end' of the Somoza dictatorship.

Several places where Somoza's Guardia Nacional were overpowered by the revolutionary fighters are now commemorated, including the **Old Jail** on 4a Calle SO (now a garden), the **21st Garrison** around the corner to the east, and **El Fortín**, the Guardia Nacional's last holdout in León. El Fortín can be reached by the dirt road that begins on the west side of Guadalupe cemetery. Follow this road 2½km until you reach the abandoned hilltop fort, which affords a panoramic view of León.

The small **Museo de Tradiciones y Leyendas** (☎ 311 2886), on 2a Calle SO, has a quirky collection of life-size papier-mâché figures from Leonese history and legend. The museum is the home of founder Señora Toruña, who will gladly share the story behind each figure. There are no fixed hours of operation.

Special Events

Every Saturday from early afternoon till midnight, the Parque Central is the scene for the Tertulia Leonesa, a big fiesta when everyone comes out to eat, drink and dance to music played by local combos. León's annual celebrations include:

Día de la Virgen de Merced – September 24. León's saint's day is solemnly observed with religious processions through the streets of the city. The preceding day is more festive: Revelers don a bull-shaped armature lined with fireworks, called the *toro encohetado,* then charge at panic-stricken onlookers as the rockets fly.

Día de la Purísima Concepción – December 7. This is a warm-up for the Día de la Concepción de María (December 8), celebrated throughout Nicaragua. It is the occasion for the *gritería* (shouting), in which groups wander around calling on any house that displays an altar and shouting, *¿Quién causa tanta alegría?* ('Who causes so much joy?') to receive the response, *¡La concepción de María!* ('The conception of Mary!'). The household then offers the callers traditional treats such as honey-dipped plantain slices and seasonal fruits.

La Gritería Chiquita – August 14, prior to the Day of the Assumption of Mary. This celebration began in 1947 as an erupting Cerro Negro threatened to bury the city in ashes. The volcano suddenly halted its activity after an innovative priest, Monseñor Isidro Augusto Oviedo, vowed to initiate a preliminary gritería, similar to December's but changing the response to *¡La asunción de María!*

Places to Stay

The best deal is *Casa Ivana* (☎ *311 4423)*, centrally located on Calle 2a SO beside the Teatro Municipal. It's a typical Leonese home, with a pretty interior garden, wicker rocking chairs and a photo gallery of old León. Neat and simple singles/doubles with overhead fans and decent bathrooms are US$5/7; rooms with separate bath are US$4 per person. There's no parking, but you can put your car in the lot around the corner for US$0.75 a day.

Hotelito Calle Real 2 (☎ *311 6510)*, on Calle Central and 2a Avenida, is a little cheaper but far less pleasant. Still, the creaky old building has character. Rates are US$6 for basic doubles, some with balconies. A block south is *Hotel América* (☎ *311 5533)*, another fading mansion, but a costlier one. Big, brooding singles/doubles with shabby furniture and private bath are overpriced at US$9/15. The cavernous cafe leads back to a jungly interior garden.

Several good options can be found along busy Avenida Pedro Arauz by the old railroad station. *Hotel Avenida* (☎ *311 2068)* charges US$5/7 for small, clean rooms around a flowery garden, all including fan and private bath. Its *annex*, just up the street, is slightly more basic at US$4 per person. Two blocks north, *Hotel Monte Cristo* offers well-maintained accommodations in a tranquil middle-class home. Singles with basic beds are US$5; doubles with much nicer beds are US$11. All rooms have private bath. The friendly owner lived in San Francisco for 30 years. Another block north and half a block west, *Hotel La Cabaña* (☎ *311 0467)* is a way from the center but quiet and in fairly good shape. They charge US$4 per person in basic rooms with foam-pad mattresses. Very clean separate-sex bathrooms are at the rear of each row of rooms.

Hotel Colonial (☎ *311 2279, fax 311 3125)*, 2½ blocks north of the plaza, is a stately old converted villa, with a delightful palm-lined inner courtyard. There are two classes of accommodations: comfortable air-conditioned doubles with TV and private bath for US$33, and run-down doubles with fan and poorly maintained separate bathrooms for about half that. Slightly more expensive, *Hotel Europa* (☎ *311 6041, fax 311 2577)*, on 3a Calle NE, is one of the top places in town. Here, too, air-conditioned doubles are in better shape than their fan-equipped counterparts and about twice the price.

Places to Eat

A León tradition, *El Sesteo* is a pleasant café on the plaza, with portraits of poets on the walls. The food is attractively presented and the service excellent. Here you can enjoy good coffee, ice-cold *refrescos* and regional favorites like *chancho con yuca* (US$2) – fried pork, yucca and pickled cabbage. It's open 11 am to 10 pm daily. For a traditional breakfast (Saturday and Sunday morning only), get scrumptious *nacatamales* at *Panadería El Trigal*, opposite the university.

Near the market, *Bar La Gruta* and *El Buen Gusto* have been recommended for cheap and hearty home-cooking. Both serve *comida corriente* for under US$1.

Taquezal, opposite the Teatro Municipal, is a stylish, relaxed bar/restaurant in a fine old building. They serve dinner salads and pastas (US$3.50), as well as cappuccino and cocktails. On the next block north, *El Rincón Azul* is a cool hangout with good music and colorful multilingual graffiti on the walls. Beer is their most popular item, but they also offer snacks, sandwiches and meals from US$2.50. It's open 3 pm 'until the last customer leaves.' Another bohemian haunt with food is *Casa Vieja*, open every evening except Wednesday.

Not only does *Restaurante Italian Pizza*, half a block north of the cathedral, make the best pizza in town, but the Lebanese-owned restaurant also serves great Middle Eastern dishes ($3 each). Around the block, *Restaurante Hong Kong* offers very cheap chop suey (US$1.50).

In Subtiava, one block south and 1½ blocks west of Iglesia San Juan Bautista, *Los Pescaditos* is a popular, moderately priced seafood restaurant. Two blocks west, the open-air *Las Caperas* serves very good food at reasonable prices.

Entertainment

The impressively preserved *Teatro Municipal* is León's premier venue for music, dance and theater, and most touring ensembles perform here. Check with Intur for current programs.

Don Señor's (☎ 311 1212), one block north of the plaza, is more than just a hot nightspot – it's three. There's a disco upstairs (US$1.50 cover), a relaxed bar (with dance floor) downstairs, and a restaurant/ pub called El Alamo around the corner. Kitty-corner from Don Señor, the afterhours drinking spot *Payitas* has a terrace with a view. *Dilectus* (☎ 311 5439) is an upscale dance hall on the highway to Managua. *Bar El Lobito* (☎ 311 4146), in Subtiava, is the place to hear great local musical combos, and there's tasty fare from the grill. It's not a late-night venue: El Lobito's peak hours are 5 to 10 pm nightly.

Getting There & Away

León's chaotic bus station is about 1km northeast of the center, on 6a Calle NE (☎ 311 3909). You can take a microbus to Managua (1¼ hours, US$1.30) or Chinandega (45 minutes, US$0.75) – these depart continually from the left side of the main platform, as they fill up.

Managua
Hourly expresos go via La Paz Centro (US$1.25, 1¼ hours) from 5 am to 4 pm. Buses go via Puerto Sandino (US$1, 1¾ hours) every 20 minutes from 4:30 am to 6:30 pm.

Chinandega/Corinto (US$0.50, 1½ hours)
Buses leave every 20 minutes from 4:30 am to 6 pm.

Matagalpa (US$1.75, 3 hours)
Buses leave at 4:30 am and 2:45 pm.

Estelí (US$1.75, 2½ hours)
Buses leave at 5:25 am and 3:10 pm.

For Matagalpa and Estelí, you can also take a bus to San Isidro, leaving every 30 minutes till 5:30 pm (US$1.25, 2½ hours) and change there for frequent buses to either destination.

Getting Around

Some local buses (US$0.12) and *ruleteros* (US$0.15) – canopied pickup trucks with wood-plank benches – leave from the central market for Subtiava, the bus terminal and Guadalupe and the Managua highway.

AROUND LEÓN
Beaches

Twenty kilometers west of León, **Poneloya** and its southern extension, **Las Peñitas**, are separated by a rock formation that offers a fine vantage point. Access is more restricted along Las Peñitas beach, with private homes taking up most of the beachfront. Crowds descend here on weekends and holidays, but during the week these beautiful beaches are practically deserted. Use extreme caution when swimming – people drown every year in Poneloya's strong currents.

Hotel Lacayo (☎ 887 6747 cell phone) is a large, rickety structure by the beachfront with a restaurant downstairs. They charge US$4 per person for big bare rooms with rusty cots and sea-view balconies. A block back from the beach, *Hotel La Posada* (☎ 311 4812) offers clean, spacious doubles with air-con for US$10, twice that with private bath.

The restaurant *Pariente Salinas*, on the main street, has great home cooking. Their *sopa de res con punche* – a big bowl of beef stew with crabs (served with a traditional gourd spoon) – is an outstanding value at US$1.25. You could lounge away the afternoon at *Bar Cáceres*, facing Las Peñitas beach, with tables under little thatched canopies. Seafood cocktails go for US$3 to US$4 and fish plates are US$4.

Around 2km south is *Hotel Suyapa Beach* (☎ 885 8345 cell phone), offering very clean double rooms with private bath and two fans for US$13; upstairs rooms have wraparound windows. A fine beach-view restaurant is on the rear terrace.

Buses to Poneloya depart every hour from early morning to 7 pm from El Mercadito in Subtiava, one block north and one block west of San Juan Bautista (40 minutes, US$0.40). Those arriving by car must pay US$0.75 admission to enter the community.

Another 40km down the coast is the broad sandy crescent of **El Velero** beach, virtually vacant during the week. There's a *centro turístico*, open Wednesday to Sunday, with cabins and a restaurant/bar.

Double rooms with private bath and air-con go for US$31; substantial discounts are offered during low season (reservations in Managua ☎ 222 6994). From León, take a Managua via Carretera Vieja bus and get off at the Puerto Sandino gas station, from which colectivo pickup trucks (US$0.50) run hourly to El Velero. Cars pay US$2.75 to enter the beach complex.

Reserva Natural Isla Juan Venado

This reserve, south of Las Peñitas, is a long, narrow barrier island extending 22km to Salinas Grandes. The 600m-wide island encloses a network of mangrove-lined estuaries, forming an ecosystem that sustains a variety of migratory birds, reptiles and amphibians. It is a nesting area for Olive Ridley and leatherback turtles between July and January. To visit, contact Raul Cruz (☎ 311 3776) at the Marena office in León. The reserve is accessible by boat from the fishing community at the south end of the Las Peñitas road, the end of the Poneloya bus route. The park ranger will meet you there and guide you through the estuaries; you'll pay around US$12 for gas.

León Viejo

At the foot of Volcán Momotombo are the remains of the original capital of the Spanish colonial province of Nicaragua. Founded in 1524, Old León was destroyed less than a century later by earthquake and subsequently buried under layers of ash spewed by Momotombo. The site was abandoned and the city moved to its present site.

It was not until 1967 that archaeologists from the Universidad Nacional managed to locate Old León, near the village of Puerto Momotombo on the southwest shore of Lago de Nicaragua. Excavations revealed the cathedral and the main plaza. Recent work has unearthed much more evidence, including the headless remains of Francisco Fernández de Córdoba, the founder of both León and Granada. It was here that Fernández de Córdoba was beheaded 'for treason against the crown,' on orders of Pedrarias Dávila, the first governor of Nicaragua. In fact he had probably just overstepped his bounds by demanding to govern the city he had established.

The remains of both men rest underneath the main plaza along with those of 21 other Spaniards. Farther along the main path are the ruins of some private homes and the church and convent of La Merced, where the explorer's skeleton was found in May 2000. Recognizing the archaeological significance of the recent discoveries, the UN has declared León Viejo a world heritage site.

While researchers of Spanish colonial history value León Viejo for its wealth of historical evidence, the setting may be the real attraction. Climb the hill on the eastern edge of the park for a marvelous view of the ruins, the lake, Momotombo and the other volcanic peaks that ring the village.

León Viejo is open 8 am to 5 pm daily. The US$0.75 admission includes a guided tour (in Spanish). The Museo Imabite, the archaeological museum adjacent to the park (named after the original indigenous settlement here), was damaged by Hurricane Mitch, and plans are underway to rebuild it nearer the center of Puerto Momotombo.

The turnoff for León Viejo and Puerto Momotombo is 3km east of La Paz Centro on the León-Managua highway (Rte 28). From there it's a 15km drive along a partially cobblestoned road (under construction at time of writing). Frequent León-Managua buses pass through La Paz Centro, from which buses leave hourly for Puerto Momotombo.

Volcán Momotombo

The perfect cone of Volcán Momotombo rises 1280m over the northwest shore of Lago de Managua. It is a symbol of Nicaragua and the subject of a notable poem by Darío. Momotombito, its miniature version, pokes out of the lake. Momotombo has erupted 14 times since the 16th century, when the Spanish began keeping track. The volcano roused in 2000 after a 95-year rest, registering hundreds of local tremors and igniting fears of an imminent eruption.

From Puerto Momotombo, you can see plumes of steam emanating from the geothermal plant on the volcano's south slopes, which supplies over a third of Nicaragua's electrical power. Ecotours de Nicaragua (☎ 222 2752, turismo@cablenet.com.ni) leads expeditions from Managua to Volcán

Momotombo, climbing a third of the way up by Unimog truck (a sort of mega-Jeep) and continuing on foot another two hours over a lava-strewn landscape to the crater. Fees are US$45 per person, with a minimum of seven participants.

NORTHWEST OF LEÓN

About 10km northwest of León, highway 26 branches east and cuts through the volcano corridor at **San Jacinto**, where hot springs and bubbling pools of mud provide glimpses of the forces at work within nearby Volcán Telica (1060m). Local kids will show you around for a few córdobas. Highway 26 then proceeds east another 100km to San Isidro, where you can catch buses to Matagalpa or to Estelí and on to the Honduran border.

Continuing northwest along the main highway (Rte 12), you reach **Chichigalpa**, the home of the Flor de Caña rum factory and the Ingenio San Antonio, the largest sugar mill in Central America. Fifteen kilometers farther is **Chinandega** (population 119,428), the center of a hot agricultural region where cotton and sugarcane are the principal crops. Intur maintains an office here at the Hotel Cosigüina (☎ 341 3636), open 8:30 am to 12:30 pm and 2 to 5:30 pm weekdays. Budget accommodations include *Hotel/Restaurant Glomar* (☎ 341 2562), a block south of the market, where adequate singles/doubles with fan and shared bath cost US$10/14; and *Hotel Chinandega*, opposite the Kodak outlet, charging US$4.75 for decent, simple rooms with fan and shared bath.

Northwest of Chinandega is **El Viejo**, the focus of several annual pilgrimages. Beyond looms **Volcán Cosigüina** (859m), at the end of a peninsula that extends into the Gulf of Fonseca. The volcano has been designated a nature reserve by Marena, but there is no infrastructure. Trails lead up through dry tropical forest to the edge of the crater, where you can peer down into the lagoon (the steep crater walls should be attempted only by experienced mountaineers). Climbers are rewarded with matchless views of the Salvadoran and Honduran gulf islands to the north and the extensive Pacific coastline to the south.

Aventuras San Cristóbal in Chinandega (☎ 341 3967) leads day/overnight journeys to Cosigüina (US$43/60 per person, four persons minimum), including van transportation to and from the village of Potosí. From there, you ascend for 2½ hours on horseback to within 150m of the crater. Bring mosquito repellent.

South of Managua

The area south of the capital boasts some of Nicaragua's most productive agricultural lands and most of its important towns and cities, including the handicraft center of Masaya and the beautiful colonial city of Granada. Both cities can easily be visited as day trips from Managua, though you can also find reasonable accommodations in either. Parque Nacional Volcán Masaya, west of Masaya, is one of the country's most visited destinations.

Southwest of Managua, the Pueblos Blancos (White Towns) of Catarina, San Juan de Oriente and Niquinohomo stand amid a highland coffee-growing region rich in pre-Columbian traditions. Continuing south toward the Costa Rican border (a four-hour journey), the only significant town is Rivas, where a turnoff leads to the lake port of San Jorge and ferries to Isla de Ometepe. Farther down the Interamericana at La Virgen is the turnoff for San Juan del Sur, a low-key beach resort and the jumping-off point for a string of Pacific beaches as well as a major turtle-nesting zone.

MASAYA
pop 110,524

Masaya traditionally attracts visitors in search of fine artesanías. Its recently restored Mercado Viejo carries quality work from all over the country; the market has also become a focus of the city's social and cultural life. Masaya is noted, too, for its myriad festivals held throughout the year.

In July 2000, a series of earthquakes in and around Masaya left much of the city's downtown area in ruins. Fissures marred nearly every church, and hundreds of old buildings collapsed, their unreinforced mud-and-pebble walls unable to withstand the repeated tremors. At least 30 people were killed and thousands left homeless. Although reconstruction should

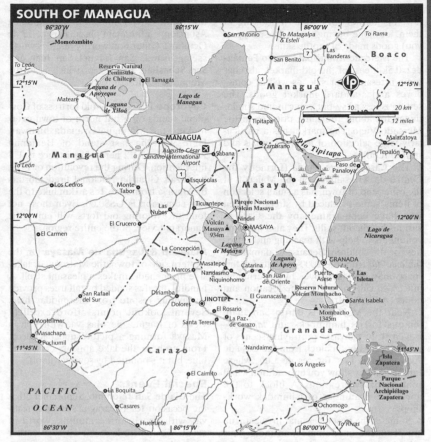

SOUTH OF MANAGUA

go on for quite a while, life goes on and visitors are welcome.

Orientation & Information

Masaya is just 29km southeast of Managua, with Granada another 16km down the road. The city sits at the edge of the Masaya crater lake, beyond which rises Volcán Masaya.

An Intur office (☎ 522 7615), open 8 am to 12:30 pm Monday to Saturday and 1:30 to 5 pm weekdays, is inside the Mercado Viejo, as is the post office and an ATM on the Visa/Plus network. Another ATM, which is on the MasterCard/Cirrus network, is inside the Esso Tiger Mart on the highway at the entrance to town. Banco de América Central, open 8:30 am to 4:30 pm Monday

to Friday plus Saturdays till noon, changes traveler's checks. Two doors down from Hotel Regis, Mi PC a Colores offers Internet access at US$4.50 an hour.

Things to See & Do

Artesanías Masaya's famous artesanías can be found in several places around town. The most concentrated place is in the original market, the **Mercado Viejo**, a block east of the main plaza, which was destroyed during the revolution and has been restored to serve as the main crafts market and a center for cultural activities. Here you will find a variety of neat, clean stalls selling excellent-quality cotton hammocks, colorful basketry and woven mats, carved and painted gourds, wood carvings, paintings, ceramics and pottery, marimbas, coral jewelry, leatherwork and (if looking at them, let alone buying them, doesn't upset you) goods made of reptile skins.

The **Mercado Municipal Ernesto Fernández**, 0.5km east of the old market, also has some artesanías for sale, as well as comedores and standard market goods. The setting is less artsy, but you can find similar things for about the same price as in the Mercado Viejo. The market has a particularly large selection of leather sandals and stuffed reptiles.

The **Casa de Ave María** (formerly the Centro de Artesanías), on the Malecón at the other end of town, has a small selection of items, some produced by street children who have been trained by the Casa in various handicraft skills. They also welcome volunteers to help with teaching and activities for the children. Because of damage to the *alcaldía* from the 2000 earthquake, this space may be taken over by government offices, so call to confirm the location and hours (☎ 522 2038).

Near the Malecón is **Barrio San Juan**, famous for its hammocks and *tapices* – woven straw canvases portraying scenes of village life. About a block from the Casa de Ave Maria is Los Tapices de Luis, where Luis will gladly show you his traditional and contemporary creations. A block to the north are a number of hammock workshops.

Some of the best artesanías in Nicaragua are produced in **Monimbó**, an indigenous suburb, the heart of which is around the Iglesia de San Sebastian about 1km south of the main plaza. The tourism office in the Mercado Viejo can give you a map showing the location of the many workshops scattered throughout this barrio. At first glance you won't see a lot, but if you walk around and ask, people will invite you into their homes to show you how the shoes, saddles, baskets, wood carvings and other crafts are made.

Churches & Plazas Many of Masaya's historic churches suffered significant damage in the earthquake of July 2000. Among the worst hit was the **Iglesia de San Jerónimo**, on the northern side of town between two plazas, though it remains open to visitors as rebuilding goes on. The Spanish government has infused funds for the reconstruction of the early-19th-century **Iglesia de La Asunción**, on the main plaza (Parque 17 de Octubre). Other noteworthy temples worth seeing include **San Miguel**, **San Juan** and **San Sebastián**, the last of which is in the Monimbó section of town.

Coyotepe The century-old fortress of Coyotepe stands on a hill north of town overlooking the Managua-Granada highway. Here was the last stand of Benjamín Zeledón, the 1912 hero of resistance to US intervention. During the revolution of 1979, Somoza's Guardia Nacional fired mortars on Masaya from here. It's a 1km hike to the top; admission is US$0.60. Even those not fond of exploring old forts will enjoy the panoramic view of the entire region.

Malecón & Laguna de Masaya On the western side of town, the Malecón, or lakeside promenade, makes a pleasant stroll. A handful of cafes shaded by tall trees provide an inviting respite from the midday heat. Several lookout points afford excellent views of Laguna de Masaya, with Volcán Masaya forming a picturesque backdrop. From up here, the lake appears crystalline blue, but it's polluted by sewage runoff.

Special Events

The **Día de San Jerónimo**, September 30, is the occasion for Nicaragua's longest festival, with nearly three months' worth of events. Festivities kick off 10 days earlier when the patron saint, in the form of a bearded campesino called 'Tata Chombó' (also known as the 'Doctor of the Poor') is taken from his usual perch on the San Jerónimo church altar. September 30 and October 7 are the main procession days, when the saint is borne on a flowery platform down to La Asunción and back home again. The festival continues each Sunday through November, with fireworks, dancing to marimbas in Plaza San Jerónimo and surreal parades, including the march of the 12-foot women. More costumed fun takes place the last Sunday in October as street performers reenact the indigenous legend of the tiger-slaying bull.

Other big festivals include the **Día de La Virgen de la Asunción** (March 16), when a statue of the virgin is taken to the lake for a

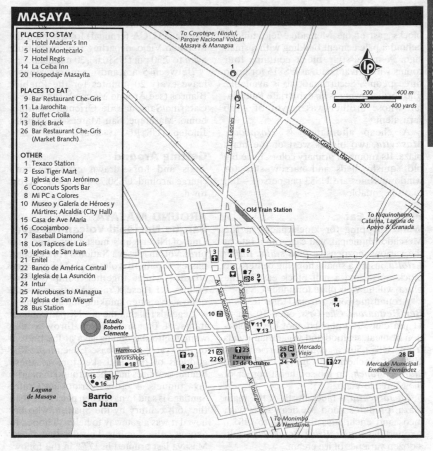

MASAYA

PLACES TO STAY
4 Hotel Madera's Inn
5 Hotel Montecarlo
7 Hotel Regis
14 La Ceiba Inn
20 Hospedaje Masayita

PLACES TO EAT
9 Bar Restaurant Che-Gris
11 La Jarochita
12 Buffet Criolla
13 Brick Brack
26 Bar Restaurant Che-Gris
(Market Branch)

OTHER
1 Texaco Station
2 Esso Tiger Mart
3 Iglesia de San Jerónimo
6 Coconuts Sports Bar
8 Mi PC a Colores
10 Museo y Galería de Héroes y
Mártires; Alcaldía (City Hall)
15 Casa de Ave María
16 Cocojamboo
17 Baseball Diamond
18 Los Tapices de Luis
19 Iglesia de San Juan
21 Enitel
22 Banco de América Central
23 Iglesia de La Asunción
24 Intur
25 Microbuses to Managua
27 Iglesia de San Miguel
28 Bus Station

To Coyotepe, Nindiri,
Parque Nacional Volcán
Masaya & Managua

Managua-Granada Hwy

Old Train Station

To Niquinohomo,
Catarina, Laguna de
Apoyo & Granada

Av Los Leones

Av San Jerónimo

Av Sergio Delgadillo

Av Insurgentes

Estadio
Roberto
Clemente

Hammock
Workshops

Mercado
Viejo

Mercado Municipal
Ernesto Fernández

Parque
17 de Octubre

Laguna
de Masaya

Barrio
San Juan

To Monimbó
& Nandaime

0   200   400 m
0   200   400 yards

---

blessing of the waters, and the **Día de San Lázaro**, a week before Palm Sunday, which includes a procession of costumed dogs.

In addition, every Thursday night is **Jueves de Verbena**, a lively fiesta held in the Mercado Viejo from 5 pm to midnight. There's plenty of food and music: Local restaurants set up tables offering grilled meats and beer, while marimba players and mariachis stroll around and folk combos perform on stage.

Places to Stay

The secure *Hotel Regis* (☎ 522 2300), 3½ blocks north of the main plaza, charges US$5 per person in small, tidy rooms alongside a pleasant courtyard, at the end of which are several clean bathrooms. The

elderly couple who run the place are especially helpful and glad to impart their abundant knowledge of the town. A generous breakfast is served for US$1.50. Doors close at 10 pm. *Hotel Montecarlo* (☎ /fax 522 2166, edgardjperezb@hotmail.com), on the next block north, is as charmless as the Regis is personable. Narrow, shabbily furnished doubles are US$8; larger triples cost US$12.50. The adjacent disco blares till late.

Just down the street from the Montecarlo is the new *Hotel Madera's Inn* (☎ 522 5825, hmaderas@ibw.com.ni), a good mid-priced place run by a congenial family. Interior doubles with powerful fans and private bath are US$15.50; small rooms with firm bunk beds and separate bath cost half that. There's a big TV lounge and Internet access. Another good choice is *La Ceiba Inn* (☎ 522 7632), two blocks north, 1½ blocks east of the Mercado Viejo, hidden behind a pale cement building with a small sign. A motel-style block contains four rooms with private bath at US$15 for up to three people. Secure parking is available. The cordial owner is an expatriate Palestinian whose brother was mayor of Arab Jerusalem.

A cheap alternative is *Hospedaje Masayita*, two blocks west of the main plaza. Its rooms, in primary colors, have big old squishy beds and narrow slits for windows. Rates are US$3 per person – but that's negotiable.

Places to Eat
While shopping for knickknacks at the Mercado Municipal, you can grab a bite at the various inexpensive *food stalls*. *Buffet Criolla*, inside a small shopping center one block north and a half block east of the plaza, will fill your plate for under US$2.

Around the corner from Hotel Regis is *Bar Restaurant Che-Gris*, open 10 am to 11 pm daily. The popular spot has a selection of meat, seafood and vegetarian meals from US$3.50; a comida corriente is US$2.50. Or check out Che-Gris' attractive *market branch*, on the southeast corner of the Mercado Viejo.

La Jarochita, a block north of the main plaza, prepares good Mexican fare, with tacos and enchiladas for US$2 to US$3. Around the corner, *Brick Brack* scoops up a dozen varieties of ice cream.

Entertainment
The disco *Cocojamboo* (☎ 522 6141), at the south end of the Malecón, is locally popular. *Coconuts Sports Bar*, across the street from Hotel Regis, is a relaxed hangout that draws a youthful crowd. It's open nightly except Tuesday. The last Friday of each month, open-air concerts at the Mercado Viejo feature some of the country's best-known singers.

Getting There & Away
Buses arrive and depart from the eastern side of the Mercado Municipal. There are departures for Managua every 20 minutes from 5 am to 7 pm (US$0.43, 45 minutes) and to Granada every 25 minutes from 5 am

to 6 pm (US$0.30, 40 minutes). Alternatively, take a more comfortable microbus to Managua (UCA terminal) from behind the Mercado Viejo, departing frequently from 5 am to 7:30 pm (US$0.60, 30 minutes).

Between 5 am and 6 pm, microbuses leave every 20 minutes for the Pueblos Blancos (see Around Masaya). The route is Catarina/San Juan de Oriente, Niquinohomo, Masatepe, San Marcos and finally, Jinotepe (US$1.60, 1¼ hours).

Getting Around
Taxis and horse-drawn carriages both charge around US$0.75 for a ride across town.

AROUND MASAYA
Parque Nacional Volcán Masaya
One of Nicaragua's most interesting features, Volcán Masaya National Park encompasses a pair of volcanoes, Masaya and Nindirí, which together comprise five craters. Of these, Cráter Santiago is still quite active, often smoking and steaming.

Legends tell that the pre-Hispanic inhabitants of the area would throw young women into the boiling lava at the bottom of the crater to appease Chaciutique, the goddess of fire, and skeletons of these human sacrifices have been found in nearby lava tunnels. A cross overlooking Cráter Santiago is said to have been placed there in the 16th century by the Spanish, who believed it was a gateway to hell and hoped to exorcise the demons who dwelled there. Masaya last erupted in 1772; in the following century, the Santiago and San Pedro craters were formed within the old Nindirí crater.

An interesting biological phenomenon is demonstrated by the *chocoyos,* parrots that nest beside Cráter Santiago apparently unharmed by its billowing toxic gases. Some speculate that this keeps them out of predators' reach.

From the summit of Volcán Masaya (632m), the easternmost volcano, you get a wonderful view of the surrounding countryside, including the Laguna de Masaya and town of Masaya beyond. The park has several marked hiking trails, including the self-guided Sendero Los Coyotes, which leads from a point before the visitors center 5.5km down through lava-strewn fields and dry tropical forest to the lagoon. You must be accompanied by a guide to view either the lava tunnels of Tzinancanostoc or El Comalito, a small steam-emitting volcanic cone. Purchase tickets for these tours at the visitors center.

The park entrance is just 23km from Managua off the Masaya highway. You can get there on any Managua-Masaya or Managua-Granada bus. A kilometer and a half from the entrance is the visitors center, picnic area and a substantial museum. From there it's 5km of paved road up to the Plaza de Oviedo, a clearing by the rim of the crater named after the Spaniard who explored the volcano in search of gold. There's no public transportation, but you may be able to hitch a ride. The lookout on the far side of Volcán Nindirí has been closed for a while because of the instability of the crater walls.

The park (☎ 522 5415) is open 9 am to 4:45 pm daily (US$4). Pick up a map and explanatory brochure at the entrance.

Laguna de Apoyo
The serene Apoyo crater lake is set in a picturesque valley noted for its biodiversity. Bird and wildlife watching are particularly fine in the dry tropical forest along the surrounding slopes – turquoise-browed motmot and montezuma oropendola can be spotted, along with some 60 species of bat, and howler monkeys dwell in the treetops. The pristine waters of the lagoon are good for swimming and diving.

The area is inhabited by both campesino families and former government officials, who have built opulent mansions near its shores. A series of earthquakes in July 2000 caused massive damage when avalanches sent boulders tumbling and homes sliding down the slopes.

The *Proyecto Ecológico* research station (☎ 278 3923 ext 188, 882 3992 cell phone, *eco-nic@guegue.com.ni*), which runs the Escuela de Español (see Language Courses in the Facts for the Visitor section), is tranquilly set amid woods near the lakefront. Lodging for nonstudents is available in the large ranch-style home or in adjacent cabins at US$18 for up to three occupants. The kitchen prepares great buffet-style meals, served on a pleasant deck shaded by native fruit trees. Bicycles and kayaks can be rented, and PADI-approved divers can join expeditions to research the lake's endemic fishes.

Four buses daily travel from the Masaya market to Valle de Apoyo, at the rim of the crater, from which it's a 25-minute walk down a paved road to the research station; turn left where the road forks at the bottom. From Managua, take any Masaya- or Granada-bound bus and get off at Km 37.5 to catch the Valle de Apoyo bus.

Pueblos Blancos
The mountainous coffee-growing region between the Managua-Masaya highway and the Interamericana is dotted with these pretty villages, so named for their typically white-stuccoed homes with brightly painted doors and window frames.

Pottery making is the main activity in **San Juan de Oriente** (population 1714). Many artisans feared they had lost their livelihood in July 2000 when earthquakes shattered their kilns, but Nicaraguan business groups came to their rescue, donating almost 200 new kilns to the community. You can shop at the Cooperativa Quetzalcóatl or at a number of workshops along the main road.

The nearby village of **Catarina** is known for its *mirador* (lookout), which offers incredible views of Laguna de Apoyo, Lago de Nicaragua and the city of Granada. It is said to have been the youthful Augusto C Sandino's favorite spot for meditation, and appropriately so, for this is also the grave site of Benjamín Zeledón, whose burial Sandino witnessed. There are a few cafes alongside the mirador.

Sandino was born and raised in **Niquinohomo**, aptly translated as 'Valley of the Warriors.' His boyhood home, in the house opposite the northwest corner of the main plaza, is now a library.

Carazo Towns
Southwest of the Pueblos Blancos, in Carazo department, **San Marcos** and the 'twin cities' of **Jinotepe** and **Diriamba** are set in a citrus- and coffee-cultivation area. The three towns celebrate a distinctive religious and folklore ritual known as 'Toro Guaco,' in which the Nicarao town of Jinotepe and Diriamba, its Chorotega rival before the European conquest, commemorate their relationship. Jinotepe's patron is Santiago (St

James), whose day is July 25; Diriamba's is San Sebastián (January 20). These two towns, along with San Marcos, carry out ceremonial visits to each other, livened up with striking costumes and masks displayed in dances, mock battles and plays that satirize their Spanish invaders. The pantomime figure of 'El Güegüense' is a symbol of Nicaraguan identity.

GRANADA
pop 84,773

Nicknamed 'the Great Sultan' in reference to its Moorish namesake across the Atlantic, Granada is Nicaragua's oldest Spanish city. Founded in 1524 by Francisco Fernández de Córdoba, it stands at the foot of Volcán Mombacho on the northwestern shore of Lago de Nicaragua. With access to the Caribbean Sea via the lake and the Río San Juan, Granada soon became a rich and important trade center and remained so into the 19th century. This same Caribbean passage made Granada an easy target for English and French buccaneers, who sacked the city three times between its founding and 1685.

From early on, conservative Granada was locked in bitter rivalry with liberal León, with which it vied for political supremacy. Their rivalry intensified after independence from Spain in 1821, erupting into full-blown civil war in the 1850s. To gain the upper hand, the Leonese contracted the services of American filibuster William Walker, who conquered Granada and ruled Nicaragua from there (see History in the Facts about Nicaragua section). When Walker was forced to flee in 1856, he had the city torched, with his retreating troops leaving only the infamous placard, 'Here was Granada.' In more recent times, Granada was the scene of brief street fighting between Sandinista and *Somocista* forces, but it was spared the shelling suffered by other Nicaraguan cities.

Today's Granada is a quiet town that retains its colonial character. Like León, its streets are lined with Spanish-style houses with stuccoed adobe walls and large wooden doors opening onto cool interior patios. Granada is a wonderful walking city, with most attractions within a six-block radius and the lake a 15-minute walk from the central plaza.

Granadinos have a reputation for being cliquish and stuck-up – it is said they drive around in the oppressive heat with their car windows up, just so onlookers will think they can afford air-conditioning. Nevertheless, it is perhaps the most visited of Nicaraguan towns, and justifiably so. Almost all independent travelers spend a few days here, and there's a small gringo expatriate community. The city has responded to this influx by offering accommodations and food to suit everyone's budget.

Orientation

The cathedral and plaza (Parque Colón) in front of it form the center of the city. The neoclassical market, built in 1890, is three blocks to the south. The main bus station is nearly a kilometer west of Parque Colón; other intercity buses can be caught near the market and plaza.

Calle La Calzada, one of Granada's principal streets with most of the budget lodgings, runs eastward from the plaza for 1km to the city dock, where boats leave for Ometepe and San Carlos. South of the dock, a lakefront park and beach extend toward Puerto Asese, where day cruises depart to the island chain known as Las Isletas.

Information

Granada's unusually helpful Intur office (☎ 552 6858) is just south of the cathedral. Open 8 am to noon and 2 to 5 pm weekdays, they distribute an excellent map identifying the city's historic buildings and churches.

Enitel, across from the plaza's northeast corner, includes a Sprint phone for collect calls. The post office, open 8 am to noon and 1 to 5 pm weekdays, 8 am to noon Saturday, is on Calle Atravesada opposite the Cine Karawala.

Compunet, in a stately old mansion on Calle La Libertad, charges US$3 per hour for Internet access and is open Monday to Saturday; the efficient Inter Café, just northwest of Parque Colón costs US$3.50.

To exchange traveler's checks or get cash advances on Visa or MasterCard (no commission charged), go to Banco de América Central, right on the plaza. The Esso station on the main highway had just installed an ATM as this was being written.

GRANADA

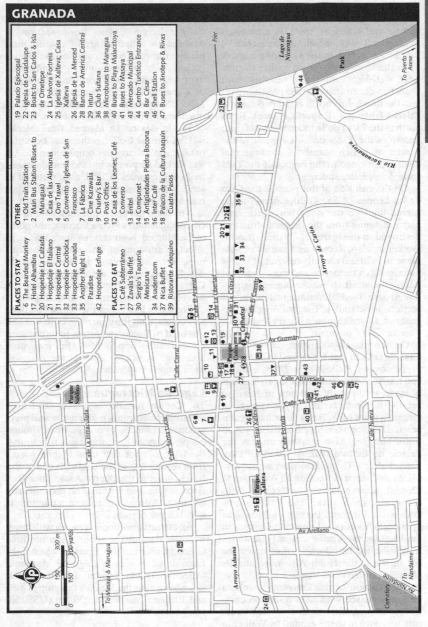

PLACES TO STAY
6 The Bearded Monkey
17 Hotel Alhambra
20 Hospedaje La Calzada
21 Hospedaje El Italiano
31 Hospedaje Central
32 Hospedaje Cocibolca
33 Hospedaje Granada
35 Another Night in Paradise
42 Hospedaje Esfinge

PLACES TO EAT
11 Café Subterráneo
27 Zavala's Buffet
30 Sergio's Taqueria Mexicana
34 Asadero.com
37 Nca Buffet
39 Ristorante Arlequino

OTHER
1 Old Train Station
2 Main Bus Station (Buses to Managua)
3 Casa de las Alemanas
4 Oro Travel
5 Convento y Iglesia de San Francisco
7 La Fábrica
8 Cine Karawala
9 Charley's Bar
10 Post Office
12 Casa de los Leones; Café Converso
13 Entel
14 Compunet
15 Antigüedades Piedra Bocona
16 Inter Café
18 Palacio de la Cultura Joaquín Cuadra Pasos
19 Palacio Episcopal
22 Iglesia de Guadalupe
23 Boats to San Carlos & Isla de Ometepe
24 La Pólvora Fortress
25 Iglesia de Xalteva; Casa Xalteva
26 Iglesia de La Merced
28 Banco de América Central
29 Intur
36 Club Sultana
38 Microbuses to Managua
40 Buses to Playa Malacatoya
41 Buses to Masaya
43 Mercado Municipal
44 Centro Turístico Entrance
45 Bar César
46 Shell Station
47 Buses to Jinotepe & Rivas

City Center

The nicely restored **Parque Colón**, with its mango and malinche trees, is a pleasant shady spot. The **cathedral**, on the east side of the plaza, was built in the early 20th century upon the foundations of an earlier church. The well-kept interior contains four chapels; a dozen stained-glass panels are set into the dome. Just north is the neoclassical **Palacio Episcopal** (Bishop's Palace). To its north is the **Plaza de la Independencia** (also known as the 'Plaza de los Leones'), at the center of which stands a monumental obelisk dedicated to the heroes of the 1821 struggle for independence.

On the east side of this plaza is the **Casa de los Leones** (☎ 552 4176), named for the carved lions on the stone portal, the only part remaining from the original structure, destroyed in the blaze set by the infamous Walker in 1856. Rebuilt as a stately private home in 1920 and recently renovated, it now functions as a residence and work space for international artists whose pieces are presented here (see Entertainment, later in this section, for details). The building houses galleries, an auditorium, a library and the attractive Café Converso.

On the plaza's southeast corner is the **Casa de la Gran Francia**, named for a former French owner. Rebuilt in 1997 from adobe and hardwoods, as used for the original, it is notable as the only building in town to retain the architectural style typical in Granada prior to Walker's destructive campaign. The caretaker, Virgilio, will let you in for a glimpse. Also worth seeing is the **Palacio de Cultura Joaquín Cuadra Pasos**, named after a Granadino poet who wrote *Canto de Guerra de las Cosas* (War Song of Things), a surrealist masterpiece of 20th-century Spanish verse. The Palacio now houses the Granada branch of Nicaragua Spanish Schools (see Language Courses in the Facts for the Visitor section) and an Internet facility, EB@Net. Farther down the colonnade is the Hotel Alhambra and its pleasant portico restaurant.

Construction of the **Convento y Iglesia de San Francisco**, with an entrance on Calle Cervantes, was initiated in 1585. The structure was burned to the ground by Walker in 1856 and rebuilt in 1867–68. The convent once served as Walker's headquarters, later as a university (shut down by Somoza in 1951). Completely restored, it is now the city's must-see museum, open 9 am to 6 pm daily (US$1.50). The front section is devoted to religious art of the colonial period; the rear court contains the Squier collection of pre-Columbian zoomorphic figures carved by the Chorotega inhabitants of Zapatera island between AD 800 and 1200. US diplomat Ephraim George Squier discovered the impressive statues in 1849.

The **Iglesia de La Merced**, three blocks west of Parque Colón, is the most beautiful of Granada's churches. Completed in 1539, it was sacked by pirates in 1655 and damaged by Leonese forces in 1854, then restored in 1862. It has a baroque façade and an elaborate interior. Ask the caretaker for permission to climb the bell tower for a view of the city. **Antigüedades Piedra Bocona**, just north of La Merced, is an antique store that is, in effect, a museum of 19th-century furnishings. Also noteworthy is the **Iglesia de Guadalupe**, at the east end of Calle La Calzada. Originally built as a fort, the church was converted to its current form in 1945.

Eight blocks west of the plaza, **Fortaleza La Pólvora**, a military garrison built in 1749, was used by Somocista forces to interrogate and execute opponents. The fort now houses an arms museum, but there are no fixed hours – just knock.

Lago de Nicaragua

The **Centro Turístico** is a 2km stretch of lakefront restaurants, picnic areas and playgrounds, all shaded by mango trees. Though people do swim here, the water is polluted. Boats depart for day trips to Las Isletas from restaurants at the southern end of the beach, or from the Puerto Asese dock (see Around Granada for more on these nearby islands). Admission to the complex is US$0.08 per person, US$0.75 per car.

An attractive swimming beach with clean water, **Malacatoya** is about 25km north of Granada, near the Río Tipitapa, which links Lago de Nicaragua to Lago de Managua. Colectivo trucks headed for this beach leave from near the Masaya bus stop at 8:30 and 10:30 am, noon and 1:30 pm (US$0.50, two hours).

Organized Tours

Oro Travel (☎ 552 4568, orotravl@tmx .com.ni), on Calle Corral half a block west of the San Francisco convent, leads city tours for US$33 per person, including lunch on one of the islands. They also offer reasonably priced excursions to Volcán Mombacho and Isla Zapatera (see Around Granada). Guides speak English, French and German.

Special Events
Granada is host to a variety of events and festivals throughout the year, including the following:

Fiestas Agostinas – third week of August. Granada celebrates the Assumption of Mary with fireworks, concerts in the park, a running of the bulls and major revelry by the lakefront.

Inmaculada Concepción, also known as 'Purísimas' – nine days leading up to December 7. Neighborhoods bear elaborate floats through the streets in honor of Granada's patron saint, the Virgen Concepción de María. Early-morning processions signal their arrival by blowing conch shells to drive the demons away.

Noches de Serenata – Friday nights from 6 pm to midnight. Throngs of Granadinos fill the Plaza de los Leones, where a stage is set up for local combos and grills mass-produce chicken and plantains.

Places to Stay
Granada offers a copious selection of budget lodgings, most found along Calle La Calzada. Heading east from Parque Colón, the first place you come to is *Hospedaje Central* (☎ 552 9500), a travelers' hostel with laundry services, book exchange and a popular street-front cafe. A bunk bed in the dormitory goes for US$2.50; clean, simple singles/doubles/triples sharing basic showers are US$5/8/11. A block and a half east is *Hospedaje Cocibolca* (☎ 552 7223, carlosgomez00@hotmail.com), a good deal at US$10 for clean, if unremarkable, doubles with fan and private bath; guests can use the kitchen.

Hospedaje Granada (☎ 552 3716) is the only budget hotel with a swimming pool, at the rear of a typical home with wicker rockers alongside the patio. Minimally maintained doubles cost US$7.50, or US$11.50 with private bath. *Hospedaje La Calzada* (☎ 552 6736), on the next block, features a leafy courtyard restaurant encircled by dark singles/doubles/triples with creaky beds for US$6.25/8/10. Next door is

the well-managed *Hospedaje El Italiano* (☎ 552 7047), appropriately owned by an Italian couple. They charge US$25/30 for very pleasant air-conditioned singles/doubles facing a quiet patio.

Beyond the Iglesia de Guadalupe, you'll find *Another Night in Paradise* (☎ 552 7113, donnatabor@hotmail.com) around the first corner on the right – look for the colorful mural. This US- and Danish-run establishment is a sort of upscale travelers' hostel, containing five airy, cheerfully painted rooms with comfortable beds and fans for US$11/16, with discounts for extended stays. Bathrooms are shared, as is the kitchen; a rear terrace has a hammock and cable TV.

The cheapest place is *The Bearded Monkey* (☎ 552 4028, thebeardedmonkey@yahoo.com), a recently opened hostel on Calle 16 de Septiembre, two blocks east of Parque Colón. Managed by a friendly Anglo couple, the cavernous colonial home contains coed dormitories with foam-pad bunks and clean, functional showers and toilets at US$2.50 per person. There's a pleasant cafe in the patio, a pool table, a message board and Internet access. The cordial *Hospedaje Esfinge* (☎ 552 4826), near the market, offers dim singles with shared bath from US$6, doubles with private bath and fan from US$14.

Hotel Alhambra (☎ 552 4486, fax 552 2035, hotalam@tmx.com.ni), on Parque Colón, is among Granada's top-shelf lodgings, featuring a restaurant, pool and 60 air-conditioned singles/doubles for US$33/42, or US$50/52 with balcony.

Places to Eat
An obligatory stop is the Parque Colón for ice-cold fruit juices and *vigorón,* a Granada specialty. Kiosks on the four corners of the plaza serve this tasty snack, consisting of yucca topped with fried pork skin and slaw; the kiosk on the northwest corner of the park is best.

Café Subterráneo, on the north side of Parque Colón, does excellent breakfasts, including waffles and French toast, for about US$3. It opens at 7 am. For a filling lunch, try *Zavala's Buffet*, on Calle Atravesada, where a big plate of beans, rice and various salads costs under US$2; or *Nica Buffet*, popular with expat retirees.

Sérgio's Taquería Mexicana, next to Hospedaje Central, produces huge Sinaloa-style tacos, filled with beef, chicken, pork or veggies for US$3 apiece. A couple of blocks east, *Asadero.com*, managed by the gregarious Chepe Cuadra, offers 'erotic' paellas, ratatouille, ceviches and other international fare, as well homemade sangria. The Sicilian-owned *Ristorante Arlequino*, on a quiet corner of Calle El Caimito, serves possibly Central America's best pizza in elegantly understated surroundings.

Entertainment
On Calle La Libertad, *La Fábrica* attracts a hip local crowd as well as a few travelers. A dimly lit bar furnished with simple wood tables and chairs, it's good for chatting with friends and listening to music, which tends toward alternative sounds. *Casa de las Alemanas*, on Calle Corral inside a mid-19th century building, is another atmospheric bar, featuring a pleasant outdoor terrace. *Charley's Bar*, upstairs from the Cine Karawala, is more of a neighborhood hangout, with a small dance floor. *The Bearded Monkey* (see Places to Stay) entertains nightly with videos of offbeat pictures.

Down by the lakefront, Friday to Sunday nights are busiest, but popular bars and discos such as *Bar César*, *Discoteca Centauro* and *Club Sultana* are open every night.

Getting There & Away
Bus The quickest way to Managua is by microbus (also called expreso). These depart every 20 minutes or so between 5:30 am and 7 pm from half a block south of Banco de América Central and arrive opposite UCA (US$1, 45 minutes). Ordinary buses (ruteados) to Managua's Mercado Central depart every 15 minutes in the morning, every half hour in the afternoon until 8 pm (US$0.50, one hour), from the main bus station on the west side of town. Either mode of transportation will also stop at the entrance of Masaya.

Buses to the center of Masaya (US$0.30, 40 minutes, 16km) depart every 15 minutes until 6 pm from a block west of the market. Rivas buses leave at 5:45, 9:30 and 11:20 am, 12:30 and 1:30 pm from a block south of the market (US$0.75, 1½ hours). From the same location, there are seven departures daily to the Carazo towns – Diriamba, Jinotepe and San Marcos (US$0.75, 35 minutes).

Boat Trans-lake boats leave from the dock at the east end of Calle La Calzada, departing for Altagracia on Isla de Ometepe on Monday and Thursday at 2 pm and on Saturday at noon (US$1.50, four hours). The Monday and Thursday boats continue on to San Carlos at the south end of Lago de Nicaragua, via Morrito and San Miguelito on the lake's north bank, arriving around 14 hours after departing from Granada (US$3). These return on Tuesday and Friday, departing from San Carlos at 2 pm, and from Altagracia at around 1:30 am. (See the Rivas section, later, for details on getting to Ometepe by the faster ferry from nearby San Jorge.) There are no sleeping arrangements.

The dockside ticket office (☎ 552 2966) opens at 10 am. As of this writing, hydrofoil service to San Carlos had been suspended indefinitely.

Getting Around
Granada's horse-drawn carriages, used routinely by locals, are a pleasant way to get around. A ride from the plaza to the lakefront can be bargained down to US$0.50 per person. Similarly priced taxis are also available.

AROUND GRANADA
Las Isletas & Isla Zapatera
Just offshore from Granada, Las Isletas are a group of 365 diminutive islands scattered along the edges of the Peninsula de Asese. Formed 10,000 years ago by an erupting Volcán Mombacho, the islands are well worth visiting and can be easily reached by motorboat. Many are inhabited, and quite a few are conveniently outfitted with restaurant/bars. Egrets, herons, cranes and other aquatic birds are commonly seen, especially around sunrise and sunset.

Boats may be rented from Cabaña Amarilla and other restaurants at the southern end of the Centro Turístico, or from **Puerto Asese**, 2km farther south on the other side of the peninsula. A covered boat holding up to 12 people costs US$8 per half hour, US$14 per hour. You can arrange to be dropped off at an island restaurant/bar and picked up later. At Puerto Asese itself, there's a deck restaurant by the harbor from which you can watch birds flitting among lilies or gaze at distant volcanic peaks.

On **Isla San Pablo**, a half-hour boat ride from Cabaña Amarilla, you can visit El Castillo, a small fort built in 1784 to guard against British incursions. Its rooftop observation deck affords great views of both Granada and Volcán Mombacho.

Hotel Isleta La Ceiba (☎ 266 1694, fax 266 0704, nir@nicaraolake.com.ni), on Isla La Ceiba, offers a package including a cabin, three meals, drinks, water sports and a roundtrip boat ride from Puerto Asese for US$49 per person.

Beyond Las Isletas is the much larger **Isla Zapatera**. Two hours away by motorboat from Granada, this island is one of Nicaragua's most important archaeological areas, though the giant pre-Columbian stone statues have been moved to museums in Granada, Rivas and Managua. Tombs and rock carvings remain on **Isla El Muerto**, off the northern coast of Zapatera. There's no regular boat service to the island, and hiring a *lancha* is expensive. Oro Travel (see Organized Tours in the Granada section) offers tours of Zapatera, combined with visits to Isla El Muerto and Las Isletas, from US$39.50 per person.

Reserva Natural Volcán Mombacho

Mombacho's jagged peaks – the highest is 1344m – stand guard over Granada. The slopes of the volcano form an island of biodiversity in a mostly deforested land. Vegetation and wildlife vary with altitude, and above 800m the climatic conditions are right for a cloud forest where ferns, mosses and bromeliads cling to the trees. Still higher, the landscape transforms to dwarf forest. The moisture-rich environment of the lower slopes is perfect for the cultivation of coffee.

The last recorded incidence of activity occurred in 1570, when a major tremor caused the wall of Mombacho's crater to collapse, draining the lagoon it held and washing away an indigenous village of 400 inhabitants. The volcano sends up a smoke ring now and then to remind you it's only sleeping.

Declared a protected area in 1999, the reserve is managed by the NGO Fundación Cocibolca (☎ 552 5858, fcocibol@ibw .com.ni), which maintains a biological research station and trains guides. Managua-Rivas buses can drop you at the reserve entrance at Empalme El Guanacaste, just south of where the Catarina road intersects the Granada-Nandaime highway. It's a 1½km hike to an information center, from which park rangers can drive you up in a 4WD 'ecomobile' to the biological station (US$3); phone ahead for departure times. From the station at 1100m, a self-guided trail traverses the cloud forest, with 20 informative signs along the way. By prior arrangement, you can spend the night at the research station. The mountain-lodge-style accommodations include eight beds and bathroom facilities. Sheets and blankets are provided. Rates are US$12 per person, and meals are available at US$3.

During the dry months, Oro Travel (see Organized Tours in Granada) conducts a half-day tour of the reserve on Saturday and Sunday for a reasonable US$10 per person, including lunch.

RIVAS
pop 24,108

Rivas is a crossroads town that has known moments of importance since its establishment in 1736. During the California gold rush, Rivas was a key stop on Cornelius Vanderbilt's trans-isthmian stagecoach route.

Today, Rivas is a departmental capital and center of an agricultural region where maize, beans, rice, sugarcane and tobacco are grown. Most travelers pass by here on their way to Isla de Ometepe. Buses go to San Jorge on Lago de Nicaragua, where boats depart regularly for the island. There are also frequent departures for Managua, Granada, the Costa Rican border at Peñas Blancas and the Pacific port of San Juan del Sur.

Though Rivas is not a compelling destination in itself, you might have a look at the old colonial church on the plaza. Among its curious artworks is a fresco in the cupola showing a battle at sea, with Communism, Protestantism and Secularism as burning hulks, and Catholicism as a victorious ship entering the harbor. Also worth visiting is the **Museo de Antropología**, four blocks northwest of the main plaza, with its collection of regional pre-Columbian artifacts. Rivas' Intur office (☎ 453 4914), open 8 am to noon and 2 to 5 pm Monday to Friday, is half a block west of the Texaco station on the Interamericana.

Places to Stay & Eat

The nicest budget lodging is *Hospedaje Lidia* (☎ 453 3475), opposite Intur. It's an amiable, family-run operation where well-scrubbed rooms with flimsy beds are US$4 per person, or US$5.50 with private bath. Meals are about US$2.

On the highway north of Texaco, *Hospedaje Internacional* (☎ 453 3652) is pretty basic, but the staff is most accommodating. They charge US$2.50 per person for clean, narrow rooms with shared bath, US$3 with private bath, plus US$0.40 for a fan. A few doors down, the slightly nicer *Hospedaje Coco* offers rooms with double bed and fan for US$4.50, with private bath for US$7.

In the center of town, behind the church, is *Hospedaje Hilmor* (☎ 776 7826 cell phone), a friendly and peaceful establishment. Clean rooms with cots and private bath cost US$4 per person; thin-walled cubicles with separate bath are US$3 per person.

If you're just here to catch a bus, grab a plate of food at the *market stalls* beside the open lot where the buses pull in. Those catching a ferry to Ometepe can get a huge bowl of fish or chicken soup for under US$4 at several lakefront eateries. On Rivas' central plaza, there's *Pizza Hot* and *Restaurant Chop Suey*, which serves both Chinese and Nicaraguan dishes for US$4 to US$5.

Getting There & Away

Rivas' bus terminal (☎ 453 4333) is adjacent to the market, about 10 blocks west of the Interamericana. Buses also stop at the Texaco station on the highway before leaving town, but it's best to walk the extra distance to the market if you want a seat.

Intercity buses from Rivas include:

Granada (US$0.75, 1½ hours)
Eight buses depart from 6:15 am to 4:25 pm; you can also take a Managua bus and change at Nandaime.

Managua (US$1.25, 2¼ hours)
Buses depart every 25 minutes from 3:30 am to 5:30 pm.

San Juan del Sur (US$0.50, 45 minutes)
Buses depart every 45 minutes from 6 am to 5:40 pm.

Sapoá/Peñas Blancas, Costa Rica (US$0.50, 45 minutes)
Buses depart every 30 minutes from 5 am to 4:30 pm.

If you're going to San Jorge for the Ometepe ferry, there's no need to go into Rivas; buses leave every 30 minutes from the Shell station on the highway (US$0.25). Collective taxis for the 4km trip cost US$0.40 per person.

Car/passenger ferries to Moyogalpa on Isla de Ometepe depart daily from the San Jorge dock at 10:30 am, 2:30 and 5:30 pm. The fare is US$1.50 per person for the one-hour crossing, US$11.50 for cars. Drivers should call ahead to reserve a space (☎ 278 8190), then show up at least half an hour early.

Other boats leave at 9:30 and 11:30 am, and 12:30, 2, 3:30 and 4:30 pm and cost US$1.25.

RIVAS TO COSTA RICA

Getting to Sapoá, the border crossing between Nicaragua and Costa Rica is a 45-minute ride. Remember that you may have to show a ticket out of Costa Rica when you arrive at the border crossing. See the Getting There & Away section, earlier in this chapter, for information on satisfying this requirement.

If you're in Rivas and still don't have your onward ticket from Costa Rica, you can buy one from the Trans Nica bus company, based at the Hospedaje Internacional (see Places to Stay in Rivas). You must purchase a Managua–San José ticket (US$12.50/25 one-way/roundtrip). Trans Nica buses leave Managua daily at 7 and 10 am, stopping in Rivas two hours later.

The border station at Peñas Blancas is open 6 am to 8 pm daily. Arrive well before closing time and expect delays. The border Intur office (☎ 454 0013) is open Monday to Friday.

SAN JUAN DEL SUR
pop 6484

Set on a stunning horseshoe-shaped cove with dramatic cliffs forming the far edges, San Juan del Sur is a fishing village most of the year, a busy resort and party center at

SAN JUAN DEL SUR

To Pizzería O Sole Mio

To Hotel Barlovento,
Bahía Majagual,
La Flor & Rivas

Beachfront
Restaurants
& Bars

Beachfront
Restaurants
& Bars

Bahía
San Juan
del Sur

0   50   100 m
0   50   100 yards

PLACES TO STAY
2 Casa de Huéspedes
   Mercedes
3 Hotelito Tairona
6 Hotel Beach Fun Casa 28;
   Mundo Skate 'n' Surf
7 Hospedaje Almendros
8 Hospedaje Nicaragua
11 Hotel Estrella
12 Casa Internacional Joxi
13 Hospedaje Elizabeth

PLACES TO EAT
4 Restaurante El Timón
5 Marie's Bar
10 Restaurante Josseline

OTHER
1 Ricardo's Bar
9 Bus Station; Market
14 Nicaragua Spanish Schools
15 City Hall
16 Church
17 Post Office; Entel

holiday times. The town's own beach is nice enough, but for real untamed beauty you must go up or down the coast (see Around San Juan del Sur).

During the California gold rush years of the mid-19th century, the town was the terminus of Cornelius Vanderbilt's transport company. Steamboats brought potential prospectors from eastern US ports up the Río San Juan to Lago de Nicaragua. They then traveled 20km by coach to the port at San Juan del Sur, where ships shuttled them on to California.

In the Sandinista era, San Juan was a favorite refuge for *internacionalistas* taking a break by the sea. It remains a leading beach town but is now more of a getaway for government officials and other wealthy Nicaraguans, many of whom have built luxury vacation homes along the bay's northern edge. The usually tranquil environment may change with its new status as the country's only cruise-ship port, inaugurated in 2000.

San Juan del Sur's most renowned fiesta is July 16, when a flotilla of fishing boats takes La Virgen del Carmen, patron of the town's mariners, for a cruise around the bay.

Information

Ricardo's Bar (ricardo@ibw.com.ni) functions as San Juan's information center, and

it's worth dropping by to pick up a town map and chat with owners Richard and Marie about surfing conditions, cheap hotels, bus schedules or the best hiking trails. They also rent flying discs and snorkeling gear (US$10 a day) and offer Internet access (US$0.15 a minute). Casa Internacional Joxi and Hospedaje Elizabeth (see Places to Stay) rent bicycles for US$5 a day, and Mundo Skate 'n' Surf, next to Hotel Beach Fun Casa 28, rents surfboards for US$20 a day.

Dale Dagger leads sunset tours of the area's beaches on his skiff *Masayita* (☎ 458 2492), setting off at 2 pm daily. The cost is US$15 per person, including supper and fishing gear. The vessel *Ivette* (☎ 458 2104, fishing@ibw.com.ni) can be chartered for guided fishing expeditions.

There's no bank in San Juan del Sur, but most businesses accept credit cards or traveler's checks. The post office/phone center, open 8 am to noon and 1 to 5 pm weekdays, 8 am to noon Saturday, is at the southern end of the beachfront drive.

Places to Stay

Accommodations run the gamut from humble guesthouses to luxury hotels. Expect widespread gouging at holiday times, when you're likely to pay double the prices listed here.

On the seafront is *Hotel Estrella (☎ 458 2210)*, a weathered building with a handsome downstairs bar. Spartan high-ceilinged rooms with balconies are US$4 per person. *Casa Internacional Joxi (☎/fax 458 2483, casajoxi@ns.tmx.com.ni)*, half a block from the beach, is operated by a friendly Norwegian-Nica couple. The most economical rooms have a pair of bunk beds and cost US$11.50 per person. Others have private bath, TV and air-con and cost US$21/33/41 for one/two/three occupants. Good breakfasts are served on the front terrace.

A favorite with surfers, *Hotel Beach Fun Casa 28 (☎ 458 2441)* offers adequate lodgings a block from the beach. Basic rooms sharing a central shower are US$4 per person. The friendly manager will provide mosquito coils or netting.

One of the best budget places is *Hospedaje Almendros (☎ 458 2388)*, a block east of the Joxi, with four well-maintained triples beside a quiet patio, two with private bath. Rates are US$5/9/14 for one/two/three people. Another good choice is the new *Hospedaje Nicaragua*, half a block north of the bus stop, with three freshly painted singles/doubles sharing a clean bathroom at US$5/7.50 and one room with private bath for US$6/11.50. East of the bus stop is *Hospedaje Elizabeth (☎ 458 2270)*, a friendly guesthouse popular with shoestring travelers. At US$4 per person, rooms vary in size and comfort; all have fans and easy access to shared showers. They serve a buffet-style lunch every day.

Two fine alternatives are side by side on the way out of town. *Hotelito Tairona (☎ 458 2318)*, run by a hospitable family, has neat, quiet rooms with screened windows and large hot-water bath at US$7.50 per person. *Casa de Huéspedes Mercedes (☎ 458 2564)*, entered through a plant-festooned patio, charges US$11.50/23 for comfortable rooms with one/two double beds and private bath.

Hotel Barlovento (☎ 458 2298), on a hill overlooking town, needs maintenance but still has the best view. Singles/doubles with picture windows and clunky air-con cost US$30/39.

Places to Eat

Loads of restaurants hug the beachfront and prepare fresh seafood at similar prices:
fish for US$4 to US$7, shrimp and lobster for US$9 or US$10. *Restaurante El Timón* and *Restaurante Josseline* are among the best; the latter does an outstanding *sopa de mariscos* (US$4.50). Service can be sluggish.

For breakfast, Casa Joxi offers omelets, pancakes and fruit crepes. *Ricardo's Bar* prepares good salads and tofu burgers. *Marie's Bar*, open Tuesday to Sunday, spices up the usual seafood platters with gourmet variations, and they make cappuccino and espresso. *Pizzería O Sole Mio*, on the northern end of the beach, has pizzas and pastas for US$4 to US$7.

The cheapest place to eat is San Juan's *market*, with a string of neat little kitchens, all serving hearty local fare. *Comedor Zapata* has been recommended.

Getting There & Away

Buses come and go from beside the market, two blocks from the beach. Expresos to Managua depart at 5 and 6 am daily (US$2.75, two hours). Buses for Rivas, with connections to Managua and the border, depart every 45 minutes from 5 am to 5:30 pm (US$0.45, 45 minutes, 29km). See the Refugio de Vida Silvestre La Flor section in Around San Juan del Sur for routes to area beaches.

AROUND SAN JUAN DEL SUR

Undeveloped beaches stretch south to El Ostional near the Costa Rican border. Few restaurants or facilities are found out this way, so bring food and water. The first beach to the south is **Playa El Remanso**, where tidal pools can be explored. To get there, head 5km down the dirt road that begins at the eastern outskirts of town, then 2km over to the coast. Farther south are Tamarindo, Hermosa and Yankee beaches, all great for surfing, and La Flor wildlife reserve.

North of San Juan del Sur, **Playa Marsella** is a beautiful untouched beach with good snorkeling, but beware of strong currents. At **Playa Majagual**, 12km north of town, is *Bahía Majagual Eco-Lodge (majagual@ibw.com.ni)*. Run by an Australian expat named Paul, it's more resort than ecological reserve – it may be hard to hear the howler monkeys over the rock and roll at the bar. Nevertheless, the setting is spectacular, and **Playa Maderas**, considered the finest surf beach in the area, is just a 10-minute hike north. Attractive cabins with overhead fans are US$45 double occupancy, plus US$15 for each additional person. There's also a rustic shared dorm with rudimentary exterior bathroom at US$4 per person. Prices are substantially higher during peak holiday periods. Reservations are by email only. Paul shuttles guests from Hospedaje Elizabeth in San Juan del Sur to the beach Monday, Wednesday and Friday at noon for US$2 per person.

Refugio de Vida Silvestre La Flor

Playa La Flor is one of the world's principal nesting areas for the endangered Olive Ridley turtle. Seven or eight times a year between July and January, thousands of these creatures emerge from the ocean during the night and dig holes above the tide line in which to lay their eggs, which start hatching a month and half later.

The widespread gathering of these eggs for profit has greatly reduced their numbers – Olive Ridley eggs still show up on menus throughout Nicaragua. The reserve, managed by Fundación Cocibolca (☎ 277 1681), is an attempt to protect the turtle population by reducing this practice.

The refuge is 20km south of San Juan del Sur by a rough road. At the turnoff, there's a large farmhouse where you pay the US$1.50 entrance fee. There are no facilities, but you can sleep on the beach; bring a tent or hammock and plenty of mosquito repellent. Park guards sell water but there's no food.

Getting There & Away

Buses to El Ostional via La Flor and other southern beaches leave from the market in San Juan del Sur at 1:15 pm daily, returning at 4 pm. To get to Playa Marsella and Majagual, take a 'La Chocolata' bus toward Rivas via the coast road, departing at 9:15 am daily. It returns from Rivas at 1 pm. However, bus times are subject to variation, so check at the market.

Jorge Zúniga (☎ 458 2116, baloy28@hotmail.com) offers rides to area beaches, charging US$12 per person each way.

Lago de Nicaragua

Lago de Nicaragua, also known by its indigenous name, Cocibolca, or 'the sweet sea,' is Latin America's third-largest lake: It is 177km long by an average 58km wide, covers 8624 sq km and reaches a depth of 70m. Forty-five rivers flow into it, including the Río Tipitapa, flowing from Lago de Managua, and it has an outlet to the Caribbean via the Río San Juan.

Separated from the Pacific by the Isthmus of Rivas, only 20km across at its narrowest point, the lake is home to many remarkable aquatic species, including freshwater sawfish and tarpon and some 20 varieties of ciclades. It is also said to contain the world's only freshwater sharks, though scientists have concluded that these creatures are not a distinct species but rather migrate up the Río San Juan from the Caribbean. They may have developed some adaptive characteristics that permit them to move between saline and freshwater environments. Although they are big – about 3m long – the sharks are rarely seen, and their numbers have greatly decreased, as they are trapped along with other fish.

An ancient indigenous story relates how the Chorotega and Nahuatl peoples were overpowered by the Olmecs in Mexico and forced to embark upon a massive migration south. Consulting their oracles, they were told that they would find a place to settle near a freshwater sea, where they would see an island with two high mountains.

There is ample evidence of ancient human habitation on the lake's 400 islands. Over 360 of these are in the group called Las Isletas, just offshore from Granada. Zapatera, the second-largest island in the lake, is just to the south of this group. The Archipiélago de Solentiname, near the south end of the lake, has 36 islands. The largest of all the lake's islands, Ometepe, is formed by two massive volcanoes. Lago de Nicaragua is, indeed, just as the oracle described it.

Among the ancient artifacts found on the islands are zoomorphic statues and rock-carved images of people, mammals, birds and geometric shapes. Many tombs have been found, too, notably on Zapatera and Isla del Muerto, beside it.

The lake's Caribbean connection was exploited for centuries by British and other pirates bent on attacking Granada and León. The possibility of using this link as part of a trans-isthmian sea crossing also lent the lake strategic importance, firing

NICARAGUA

imperial imaginations from the early 16th century on.

Lago de Nicaragua, its islands, and the people who inhabit them are memorialized in Pablo Antonio Cuadra's *Cantos de Cífar*, one of the most famous works of contemporary Nicaraguan literature.

ISLA DE OMETEPE

An ecological jewel, Ometepe is still sparsely developed for tourism, making the island all the more attractive for those who like unspoiled nature and don't mind expending extra effort to see it.

Ometepe (meaning 'between two hills' in Nahuatl) is formed by two large volcanoes: Volcán Concepción, which rises 1610m above the lake in an almost perfect cone, and Volcán Madera, 1394m high. Lava flowing from the two volcanoes created an isthmus between them to make a single island. Concepción is still active: Its last major eruption was in 1957.

With a population of 35,000, Ometepe is dotted by small coastal settlements where people live by fishing and growing bananas, citrus fruits, maize, sesame, beans and other crops in the fertile volcanic soil. Parts of the island are still covered in primary forest, which harbors abundant wildlife, including howler monkeys and green parrots. The gorgeous blue-tailed birds seen everywhere on the island are called *urracas* (white-throated magpie jays).

Ometepe is famous for its ancient stone statues and petroglyphs depicting humans, animals, birds and geometric shapes, especially spirals. These remnants of Chorotega settlement have been found all over the island, but they are most densely clustered along the northern side of Volcán Maderas, between Santa Cruz and La Palma.

A gravel road goes all around the part of the island formed by Volcán Concepción; at the isthmus of Istián it connects to a rougher road that skirts Volcán Maderas. Beyond Balgüe in the north and Mérida in the southwest, a 4WD vehicle is required to navigate the rutted surface.

The island's two major towns are Altagracia and Moyogalpa, both linked to the mainland by ferries. There are no banking services on the island, but credit cards are accepted by many hotels, traveler's checks by some.

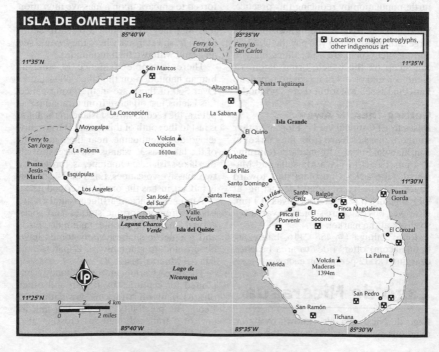

ISLA DE OMETEPE

Things to See & Do

Ometepe is great for walking, exploring and swimming. However, the terrain is rough, signage minimal and trails hard to follow. Even independent travelers are well advised to hire an inexpensive local guide (see Getting Around, later in this section, for details).

On the Volcán Concepción side of the island, excellent half-day **hikes** partially up the volcano begin at La Flor, La Sabana and San José del Sur. They offer breathtaking views and take you deep into the forest. If you really want a challenge, La Sabana is the recommended place to start the 10-hour hike to and from the summit crater. Lakeside destinations include **Punta Jesús María**, a nice swimming and picnic spot 5.5km south of Moyogalpa; **Playa Venecia** and **Laguna Charco Verde**, 12km southeast of Moyogalpa; the **Isla de Quiste**, a beautiful islet not far from Charco Verde; and **Punta Tagüizapa**, 2km east of Altagracia.

The coast south of Altagracia has nice wide beaches. The most popular is **Santo Domingo**, accessible via a rough 3km road that begins 6km south of Altagracia.

The road through Santo Domingo leads to the Maderas side of the island. There are some fine walks through forests full of wildlife and several hikes to see **petroglyphs**. The petroglyphs near the village of Finca El Porvenir are a 45-minute horse ride from Santo Domingo; ask hotel staffers for directions. Others are found at El Socorro, Finca Magdalena and El Corozal. If you are up to it, an eight-hour roundtrip climb starting at Balgüe leads to Volcán Maderas' exquisitely beautiful **crater lake**. Hire a local guide, who will provide the rope required for the final descent to the lake. On the south side of Maderas, a 35m-high **waterfall** is located a couple hours' hike above San Ramón.

A less strenuous way to see the island is simply to ride a bus around Volcán Concepción, across the isthmus and down to Balgüe, on the Maderas side, passing through many small villages and varied farming country.

Organized Tours

Most hotels in Moyogalpa and Altagracia will be happy to arrange tours, guides or horses, but these can be pricey. Typical rates are US$20 per person for a guided hike up Volcán Concepción, including transportation and lunch, US$15 per person for horse rides to the petroglyphs at Finca Porvenir.

Inexpensive local guides, called *baqueanos*, are available to lead groups on volcano or petroglyph hikes. They charge around US$15 to lead a group of up to four people to the summit of either volcano, excluding transportation. Daylong tours to Charco Verde or the Maderas petroglyphs are even cheaper. Casa Familiar in Moyogalpa and Hotel Castillo in Altagracia can hook you up with the baqueanos, who can also be found at the Finca Magdalena farmhouse near Balgüe.

Moyogalpa
pop 3483

The larger of the island's two principal villages, Moyogalpa has more hotels and restaurants than Altagracia. Ferries run several times daily to and from the mainland at San Jorge, near Rivas. You will spot Moyogalpa's top attraction before you even reach the dock: a **model of the island** that in more prosperous times had fountains jetting out of the two peaks.

The **Sala Arqueológica Ometepe** is worth a visit. The small museum, 3½ blocks from the dock, displays a modest collection of pre-Columbian pieces, including funerary urns carved with bat, snake and frog motifs. There's also an artesanías showroom and a good map of the island painted on the wall.

Moyogalpa's post office is housed in Hotelito Ally (see Places to Stay). There's a Publitel phone in front of the Enitel office, half a block east and 1½ blocks south of the Ally.

Places to Stay & Eat A women's organization in Moyogalpa, *Fundación Entre Volcanes* (☎ 459 4118, fev@ibw.com.ni), can set up homestays with families on the Concepción half of the island, including meals, for US$10 per person.

Right next to the dock, *Hospedaje El Puerto* (☎ 459 4194) charges US$2.50 per person for unkempt rooms with fans and shared bath, or US$4 with private bath. One block uphill from the dock, *Hotel Ometepetl* (☎ 459 4276, fax 459 4132) is the upscale choice. It offers small but well-kept doubles with private bath and air-con for US$25, less

NICARAGUA

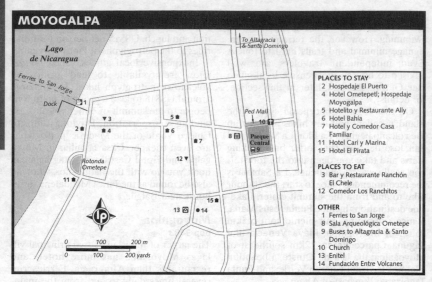

MOYOGALPA

Lago
de Nicaragua

Ferries to San Jorge

Dock

To Altagracia
& Santo Domingo

Ped Mall

Parque
Central

Rotonda
Ometepe

0   100   200 m
0   100   200 yards

PLACES TO STAY
2 Hospedaje El Puerto
4 Hotel Ometepetl; Hospedaje
   Moyogalpa
5 Hotelito y Restaurante Ally
6 Hotel Bahía
7 Hotel y Comedor Casa
   Familiar
11 Hotel Cari y Marina
15 Hotel El Pirata

PLACES TO EAT
3 Bar y Restaurante Ranchón
   El Chele
12 Comedor Los Ranchitos

OTHER
1 Ferries to San Jorge
8 Sala Arqueológica Ometepe
9 Buses to Altagracia & Santo
   Domingo
10 Church
13 Enitel
14 Fundación Entre Volcanes

if you don't turn on the air-con. The hotel features a good restaurant and a pleasant porch with hammocks and rocking chairs. Its cheaper annex next door, *Hospedaje Moyogalpa*, has simple singles/doubles with fan and shared bathroom for US$3.50/6.

One block up the same road, *Hotelito y Restaurante Ally* (☎ 459 4196) has a peaceful, attractive central patio with hammocks, trees and lots of plants. The friendly hotel, which also serves as Moyogalpa's post office, offers modest rooms with shared bath from US$2.50 per person; larger units with private bath are US$4 per person. Across the street, *Hotel Bahía* (☎ 459 4116) has fairly large rooms with cheap mattresses and private bath for US$4 per person. The rear balcony offers pretty good volcano views. A block east is *Hotel y Comedor Casa Familiar* (☎ 459 4240), a good budget choice. Rates are US$10 for clean and airy doubles with a couple of fans and bath behind a cement partition, or US$3 per person with private bath. Owner Gilberto is glad to share information on island hikes and can put you in touch with local guides.

South of the dock, *Hotel Cari y Marina* (☎ 459 4196) has the best setting of Moyogalpa's hotels and nicer rooms than the Ometepetl. Doubles with fan, private bath and windows facing the lake (views obscured by trees) are US$15, or US$25 with

air-con. There's a pretty lakefront lounging area shaded by palms where breakfast is served. *Hotel El Pirata* (☎ 459 4262), three blocks uphill from the Cari, has clean, spacious singles/doubles, all with private bath, for US$7.50/9.50; air-con is available.

One of the many lodgings that serve meals, Casa Familiar has a pleasant little *rancho* with exceptionally well prepared lake fish for US$3. *Comedor Los Ranchitos*, just down the street, offers inexpensive open-air dining. Portions are huge – a 'medium' fish served with rice and *tostones* will feed two. *Bar y Restaurante Ranchón El Chele*, underneath two thatched domes, is a cool place to enjoy lunch, and you can catch a game of pool after your meal.

Altagracia
pop 2157

Calmer and cuter than Moyogalpa, Altagracia makes an attractive base for exploring the island. It's also well placed for climbs up Concepción and forays to Maderas. The dock is 5km from town; from here, the ferry runs several times weekly to Granada (four hours) and to San Carlos (10 hours).

There is not much to see in town except for the ancient stone statues beside the church, which are quite fine, and the **Museo de Ometepe**, which displays a motley assortment of archaeological, geological and cultural artifacts. Most interesting is a painting depicting the legend of Chico Largo, a farmer who heads a mythical community underneath the lake. The museum is open 9 am to 5 pm daily; admission is US$0.60, including an obligatory spiel by the caretaker.

The post office is opposite the plaza's southwest corner.

Places to Stay & Eat The newest guesthouse in town is *Hospedaje Kencho* (☎ 552 8772), half a block south of the main plaza. Very clean, simple rooms are US$3 per person, slightly more with bath. There's a bamboo-paneled cafe, where you can get moderately priced meals and cold *refrescos* or play chess with hospitable owner Crecencio. A block south is the similarly priced *Hotel Central* (☎ 552 8770) with a pleasant lobby patio bar/restaurant serving comida corriente for around US$2.

Around the corner to the north is the most popular place to stay, *Hotel Castillo* (☎/fax 552 8744). Quiet, airy rooms with screened windows are US$3 per person, US$5 with private bath. Informative owner Julio César Castillo can help you arrange tours with local guides.

Istmo Istián & Other Areas

The Santo Domingo beach area has two small hotels. Though aged, the converted farmhouse *Hotel Finca Santo Domingo* (☎ 552 8751 in Altagracia) retains its charm, with a breezy porch facing the beach. A rickety spiral staircase (don't attempt after your third rum) leads up to some narrow wooden rooms with shared bath for US$5 per person. Doubles with private bath start at US$15. Nearby, the classier but similarly priced *Hotel Villa Paraíso* (☎ 453 4675, vparaiso@ibw.com.ni) offers pleasantly rustic rooms with shared bath. More elegant cabañas are US$30 with fan, US$40 with air-con. Both hotels have restaurants with meals in the US$5 to US$6 range; the Paraíso has tastier fare, including vegetarian options. Reservations are recommended for weekend stays.

A kilometer south of Santo Domingo at an equally pleasant beach is *Casa Istián*, priced at US$20 for cross-ventilated rooms with three or four beds and private bath. Outside, hammocks swing from large verandahs. Separate cabins are US$10 per person.

Meals (US$2 to US$3) are available. Make reservations with Nora at Hotel Ometepetl in Moyogalpa.

Travelers looking to climb Maderas might opt to stay at *Finca Magdalena*, near Balgüe, an old farmhouse with inexpensive dormitory-style accommodations. Simple meals are available. On the other side of Maderas near San Ramón is *Estación Biológica de Ometepe* (☎/fax 277 1130, ometepe@ibw.com.ni), a center for research in tropical ecology. Designed to house international university groups, the station also provides overnight accommodations for travelers, with double rooms for US$25, including three delicious home-cooked meals. Nearby is the trailhead for the riverbed climb to the waterfalls of Cascada San Ramón.

On the south side of Concepción is Valle Verde, a tranquil lakeside spot with enchanting views of both volcanoes. You can camp underneath tall ceibas at *El Tesoro del Pirata*, which rents two-person tents for US$7.50, or set up your own for half the price. A tall thatched dome shades a restaurant/bar and hammocks. Clean outhouses are provided. For more information, inquire at Hotel El Pirata in Moyogalpa.

Getting There & Away

El Ferry operates seven days a week, departing Moyogalpa at 6:45 am, 12:30 and 4 pm and reaching San Jorge an hour later (see the Rivas section for schedules from San Jorge). The trip costs US$1.50 per person, US$11.50 per auto. Vehicle owners must phone ahead to reserve a space (☎ 459 4284 in Moyogalpa). It's best to buy ferry tickets as soon as the dockside office opens, an hour before departure times. If the ferries fill up, they will depart ahead of schedule.

Smaller and cheaper boats (US$1.25) depart from Moyogalpa daily at 6, 6:30, 7 and 8 am as well as 1:30 pm, the last boat to catch if you hope to make the Rivas-Managua bus. Show up early and purchase tickets on board.

The boat from Granada to San Carlos, near the Costa Rican border, departs on Monday and Thursday at 2 pm. It arrives in Altagracia about four hours later and takes off for the 10-hour trip to San Carlos. Each leg of the journey costs US$1.50. The returning boat departs San Carlos at 2 pm Tuesday and Friday, calling at Altagracia between midnight and 1 am.

On Saturday, another boat leaves from Granada at noon bound for Altagracia and begins the return trip at 10 am Sunday. Travelers are urged to buy tickets ahead of departure time at the dockside ticket offices.

Getting Around

Bus service is frequent between Moyogalpa and Altagracia, less so to other places. Departing about once an hour from 5 am to 6 pm, Moyogalpa-Altagracia buses generally travel around the south side of Concepción, passing the turnoff for Charco Verde; a few take the north route via San Marcos. The trip takes 40 minutes (US$0.40). About six buses a day travel from Altagracia across the isthmus and down to Balgüe, on the Maderas side (one hour), two to Mérida and San Ramón. Both routes will let you off at Santo Domingo beach. Alternatively, take a Moyogalpa-Altagracia bus and hike from the turnoff at El Quino. Check departure times with hotels, some of which post schedules.

Marvin Arcia (☎ 459 4114) and Rommel Gómez (☎ 459 4112) provide pickup-truck taxi service to most of the island. You can also inquire at Comedor Los Ranchitos in Moyogalpa. The average roundtrip fare from Moyogalpa to Venecia beach is US$16, to Santo Domingo US$35. You can arrange for the driver to pick you up for the return trip at a set time.

If you want to explore on your own, you can rent a Suzuki jeep in Moyogalpa at Hotel Ometepetl (US$35 for 12 hours) and Hotel Cari (US$60). Also in Moyogalpa, Comercial Arcia, two blocks south of the church, has reasonable bike rentals at US$0.75 an hour.

ARCHIPIÉLAGO DE SOLENTINAME

The Solentiname Archipelago, in the southern part of Lago de Nicaragua, is a traditional haven for artists. Ernesto Cardenal, the poet and minister of culture during the Sandinista years, set up a communal society here for craftspeople, poets and painters. A distinctive school of colorful primitivist painting arose out of these revolutionary-era workshops.

Solentiname comprises 36 islands; the largest are Mancarrón, San Fernando and La Venada. The islands are great for hiking, fishing and taking it easy. A popular activity is to seek out prehistoric rock carvings amid the lush vegetation.

Albergue Solentiname (☎ 276 1910 in Managua, 283 0083 in San Carlos), on San Fernando island, has eight three-bed rooms sharing two bathrooms. Rates are US$20 per person including meals. The upmarket *Hotel Mancarrón* (☎ 265 2716 in Managua, zerger@ibw.com.ni), on the isle of Mancarrón, has comfortable rooms with bath at US$65/100/145 for one/two/three occupants (meals included).

Getting to Solentiname inexpensively takes some planning. A public boat departs San Carlos for Solentiname's principal islands on Tuesday at 1 pm (US$1.50, two hours) and travels back to San Carlos at 4 am on Friday. Additionally, boats between San Carlos and Papaturro (Costa Sur de San Carlos) stop en route at the islands. Ask around as well about boats to Papaturro, used by Nicaraguans on their way to work in Costa Rica, which may stop on the way. Otherwise, you can hire a *panga* (a small motorboat) at your own convenience. Boatman Armando Ortiz charges US$54 roundtrip for up to eight passengers. He can be found next to the Panadería La Católica in San Carlos.

SAN CARLOS

pop 6746

San Carlos is a hot and swampy port on the southeastern corner of Lago de Nicaragua beside the Río San Juan. Boats go from here down the river to the Caribbean coast, as well as to Archipiélago de Solentiname and the Costa Rican border.

While people usually visit San Carlos on the way to other places, the town features at least one point of interest: the ruins of an old fortress, built in 1793 by the Spanish to keep invading forces from entering the lake and gaining access to Granada's wealth.

Decent lodging can be found at *Hotel Carelhys* (☎ 283 0389) in a converted home near the church plaza (chimes at 4 am sharp). Breezy rooms with one or two double beds and private bath cost US$7.50 per person. As elsewhere, water is stored in big buckets as insurance against frequent outages. *Cabinas Leyko (☎ 283 0354)* offers clean, if musty, doubles with fan for US$14; rooms with private bath are US$16. *Hotel Azul (☎ 283 0282)*, near the market, and *Hospedaje Peña* both charge about US$2.50 for basic rooms with shared bath.

Stands at the corners of the plaza have their soup pots bubbling from early in the day. *El Mirador*, at the top of the hill, offers commanding views and good seafood from US$5.

Getting There & Away

Boats leave from Granada for San Carlos at 2 pm Monday and Thursday, heading back Tuesday and Friday at the same hour (US$3, 14 hours). Hydrofoil service has been suspended indefinitely.

La Costeña (☎ 283 0271 in San Carlos) has flights from Managua at 9 am Monday to Thursday and Saturday, at noon Friday and Sunday, returning at 10 am and 1:30 pm respectively (US$31/62 one-way/roundtrip). Alternatively, four buses run daily to/from Managua's Mayoreo terminal (US$5.50, nine hours) via Juigalpa (Juigalpa–San Carlos, four to six hours). The gravel-surface section between San Carlos and Juigalpa crosses over a number of single-lane bridges.

Small boats head to the Costa Rican border station at Los Chiles (US$3, 30 minutes) at 10:30 am and noon, and down the Río San Juan (see the next section). Costa Rica–bound travelers should get their exit stamp at the San Carlos immigration office, half a block west of the dock on the main street.

RÍO SAN JUAN & EL CASTILLO

The Río San Juan flows 199km from Lago de Nicaragua to the Caribbean, where it meets the port of San Juan del Norte (formerly Greytown). For much of its length, the river forms the border between Nicaragua and Costa Rica. Tensions arose in 1998, when Nicaragua, which has sovereignty over the waterway, prohibited Costa Rica from running armed patrols along the river to check border points. The dispute was apparently resolved two years later when the presidents of the two countries agreed that Costa Rica would be allowed to continue its patrols as long as it informed its northern neighbor beforehand.

Isolated stretches of uninterrupted forest line the riverbanks east of San Carlos, but most of this area has been converted to pastureland. About one-third of the way from the lake to the ocean is El Castillo, a fortress built by the Spanish in 1675 at a strategic bend in the river to try to halt the passage of English, French and other pirates heading for Granada. It was one of several fortifications designed for this purpose, including those at San Carlos and on San Pablo Island, near Granada.

Bitter battles were fought at El Castillo against flotillas of assailants. In 1762 the British and their Miskito allies attacked the fort, but Spanish forces, led by the daughter of their fallen commander, managed to hold off the invaders. The fort was besieged and briefly held by a British force in 1780 – a young Horatio Nelson was among their numbers – but the ill-equipped expedition succumbed to dysentery and once again had to retreat. The recently restored fort houses a good museum devoted to El Castillo's turbulent history (US$0.75).

Albergue El Castillo (☎ 267 8267 in Managua, 885 3679 cell phone), on the hillside below the fort, offers superior accommodations. The lodge contains 10 two- to four-bed rooms, some outfitted with riverview decks, sharing spotless communal bathrooms. Hammocks are strung along the broad wraparound verandah, from which there are tremendous views. Rates are US$10 per person including breakfast, or US$22 with all meals. Otherwise, there's *Hotel Richardson (☎ 552 8825)*, an old home that has been partitioned off into six narrow singles, bathrooms attached, for US$10 per person. They serve a hearty breakfast. The only other place to eat is a dockside restaurant catering to the river trade, with meals in the US$5 to US$8 range.

Farther downriver the contrast between the two sides becomes more marked, with steamy jungle along Nicaragua's banks and the Costa Rican side almost entirely cleared for ranches and farms.

This is because the Nicaraguan government has set aside a vast area between El Castillo and the coast as the **Reserva Biológica Indio Maíz**. At the mouth of the Río Bartola, which marks the western edge of the reserve, is *Refugio Bartola (☎ 289 7924* *in Managua, gme@tmx.com.ni)*, offering eight rustic rooms at US$45 per person with meals. Staying here may be the best way to see Indio Maíz: The lodge leads walking tours into the reserve (US$10 for groups of up to six people) and boat trips up the Río Bartola (US$5 per person).

San Juan del Norte, the Caribbean terminal of the San Juan waterway, has undergone explosive development recently, taking advantage of the beautiful beach that lies across the sandbar. Inexpensive guesthouses can be found for under US$10 per person.

Pangas depart San Carlos for El Castillo at 8 am daily (US$3.50, three hours), returning at 2 pm. In addition, cargo barges embark from San Carlos at 10 am Tuesday to Sunday; others leave El Castillo at 1 pm in the reverse direction (US$2.50, four to five hours). There is also service to San Juan del Norte, departing San Carlos at 6 am Tuesday and Friday only (US$12, at least 12 hours), stopping for bathrooms and food along the way. In the reverse direction, it leaves at the same time on Thursday and Sunday.

Caribbean Coast

The Caribbean coast of Nicaragua is a long (541km), wide, flat plain covered in tropical rain forest. In many places the virgin jungle is so thick that it's practically impenetrable, providing a home for abundant wildlife. The hot, sultry coast gets much more rain than the Pacific and inland regions: anywhere between 330cm and 635cm annually. Even during the March to May 'dry' season, rain is possible anytime.

Nicaragua's Caribbean coast is part of the larger Mosquitia region that extends well into Honduras. The Río Coco, which forms the border between present-day Honduras and Nicaragua, runs right through the traditional Mosquitia region, and the Miskitos, today numbering around 70,000, live on both sides of it.

Other ethnic groups in the region include the Sumo and Rama tribes, the black Creoles originally brought from other parts of the Caribbean by the British, a small number of other blacks known as Garífunas (see the Honduras chapter) and

mestizos from other parts of Nicaragua. The races have mingled a good deal over the centuries.

Unlike the rest of Nicaragua, the Mosquitia was never colonized by Spain. In the 18th century, leaders of the Mosquitia requested that it be made a British protectorate, as a defense against the Spanish. It remained British for over a century, with a capital at Bluefields, where the Miskito kings were crowned in the Protestant church.

The British signed treaties handing the Mosquitia over to the governments of Honduras and Nicaragua in 1859 and 1860. In Nicaragua, the region retained its autonomy until 1894, when it was brought under direct Nicaraguan government control.

The English language, and the Protestant religion brought by British missionaries, persist as important aspects of the regional culture. Timber, shrimp and lobster are key exports.

The only part of the coast much visited by international travelers is the city of Bluefields, where boats depart for the Corn Islands.

MANAGUA TO THE CARIBBEAN

The trip from Managua to Bluefields has long been a favorite with travelers. The easiest way to make the trip is to fly, but the journey overland is what many people like best about visiting the coast.

To go overland from Managua involves traveling 292km to Rama at the end of the highway, a journey of about seven hours, then taking a boat down the Río Escondido to Bluefields, on the coast, an additional five hours (or two hours if you take a speedboat). Most people find it a tiring but very enjoyable journey. You could make the trip in one big push, departing Managua on the 9:30 pm bus and arriving in Rama in time to transfer to a boat, but it's more relaxing to break up the journey by spending the night in either Juigalpa or Rama and then taking a boat the following day.

JUIGALPA

pop 41,641

Juigalpa, the capital of the department of Chontales, has an archaeological museum with a large collection of pre-Columbian idols excavated in the area. The museum, named after the local scholar Gregorio Aguilar Barea, is 1½ blocks behind the town's modern concrete church. It's open 8 am to noon and 2 to 5 pm Monday to Friday (US$0.15). A beautifully landscaped plaza is in front of the church. Juigalpa's *fiesta patronal*, honoring the Virgen de la Asunción, takes place in mid-August.

Hospedaje El Viajero (☎ 812 0291), a block southeast of the church, offers decent singles/doubles (with outhouses) for US$2.50/4. Other guesthouses are clustered behind the church. At the *Nuevo Milenio* (☎ 812 0646), six thinly partitioned rooms with overhead fans share a single bathroom. Rates are US$4 per person. The fancier *La Quinta* (☎ 812 2485), across from the hospital on the main highway, has singles/doubles with private bath, air-con and cable TV for US$13/15 (US$4 less with fan). It also has a restaurant and disco.

Besides the stalls in the dingy market, a couple of restaurants are around town. The cleanest place is *La Casita Country*, one block north of the museum.

Buses leave for the five-hour trip to Rama from Juigalpa's market, one block behind the church, at regular intervals from 4:30 am till 2:30 pm. Other buses journey to San Carlos from very early in the morning till 8:30 am, then depart hourly from the bus stop by the hospital till 3:30 pm (US$2.70, six hours).

RAMA
pop 7782
Rama is at the end of the highway heading east from Managua. There's not much to it – the town is just a few blocks square – and there's nothing in particular to do, but it's a peaceful place to spend the night while waiting for the boat to the coast. The simple, tropical-style church, with its stained-glass and patterned decorations, is worth a visit. Rama is at the confluence of two rivers, the Ríos Síquia and Rama. From here to the coast, the river is called the Río Escondido.

Places to Stay & Eat
Most of the places to stay are old wooden buildings offering basic rooms with fan and external bathrooms for around US$3 per person. The riverside *Hospedaje Gonzales* (☎ 817 0175) is the sturdiest choice. All-new rooms include windows, mosquito nets and

comfortable beds. *Hotel Johanna*, two blocks behind the church, has rocking chairs on a pleasant terrace, but with hookers in the downstairs bar it's not recommended for single women. *Hospedaje Jiménez El Viajero* (☎ 817 0156), a block from the dock, maintains rigorous admission standards for its windowless rooms. They serve decent meals. The friendly *Hospedaje Central* (☎ 817 0265), 1½ blocks farther inland in a nicer part of town, offers larger rooms with screened vents. There's a simple neighborhood cafe across the street. Another block up, *Restaurante Expresso*, open 11 am to 9 pm, is a pleasant open-air restaurant with good, inexpensive food.

Getting There & Away
Bus Buses take seven to eight hours to travel from Managua to Rama (US$4.75, 292km). Paved at the outset, the road surface begins to deteriorate beyond Juigalpa. From the Mayoreo terminal in Managua there are six departures between 4 and 11:30 am every day. Transportes Vargas Peña (☎ 280 4561 in Managua) operates a bus-boat package from Mercado Iván Montenegro (US$14, US$5 for bus only). Buses depart at 9:30 pm connecting with a 5 am motorboat that arrives in Bluefields two hours later. These buses wait at the dock in Rama to meet boats coming back from Bluefields, then leave immediately for the return trip to Managua. Transportes Aguilar has a similar deal leaving from Mayoreo at 10 pm.

If you miss the direct bus from Managua to Rama, you could take a bus to Juigalpa (2½ hours, 137 km) and take a second bus or hitch the rest of the way to Rama. The last bus leaves Juigalpa for Rama at 2:30 pm.

Boat The slow boat from Rama to Bluefields departs at noon on Tuesday, Thursday, Saturday and Sunday. Tickets go on sale at 9 am, but get there earlier if you want a good spot on the often-crowded boat. Tickets cost US$4 and the trip takes five hours. Pangas leave every day around 5 am and make the trip in two hours; the fare is US$9, plus a dock fee of US$0.25. Pangas sometimes are available later in the day as well. It's a good idea to go to the dock well in advance to verify departure times.

Food and drinks are sold at the dock; take some with you, as there is nothing available on the journey.

BLUEFIELDS
pop 39,208

Although Bluefields is Nicaragua's principal Caribbean port, the actual port is across the bay at Bluff. Bluefields was destroyed by Hurricane Joan in 1988 but has been rebuilt (including its beautiful bayside Moravian church). The town's economy is based on shrimp, lobster and deepwater fish; other food and merchandise are brought in from Managua and are consequently more expensive in Bluefields than in the capital.

Bluefields has no swimming beaches – the water here is murky, anyway – and it's not a particularly attractive town, but it's a fascinating place. There's a mix of ethnic groups, including indigenous Miskitos, blacks and mestizos from the rest of Nicaragua. Walking down the street you are just as likely to hear English as Spanish; music ranges from reggae to country & western. The people of Bluefields like to have a good time, and there is plenty of nightlife. In May there's a weeklong festival, with parades, music and dancing around the maypole. Bluefields celebrates its own birthday in early October.

The town gets its English-sounding name not from any nearby azure pastures, but rather from the Dutch pirate, Blewfeldt, who made a base here in the mid-17th century.

Orientation & Information

Most of Bluefields' commerce, hospedajes and restaurants are found in a nine-square-block area between Parque Reyes and the Caribbean. Enitel is on the southeast corner of Parque Reyes, and the post office is two blocks south, 1½ blocks east. The Intur office (☎ 822 0221), half a block south of the park, is open 8 am to 5 pm Monday to Friday with a break from noon to 1:30 pm. There are several banks; unofficial money changers are found near Banco Caley Dagnall. The airport is about 3km south of downtown.

Places to Stay

The **Hotel Hollywood** (☎ 822 2282), two blocks south of the Moravian church, charges US$5/7 for run-down singles/doubles separated by walls with gaps at the top, or US$9/13 for much nicer rooms with private bath around a shaded rear balcony. The pretty green house across the street is **Hotel Caribbean Dream** (☎ 822 0107), offering recently renovated rooms with private bath and fan for US$13/15. Despite

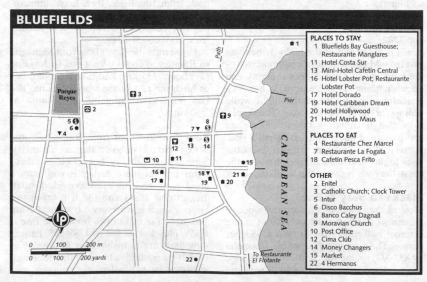

BLUEFIELDS

PLACES TO STAY
1 Bluefields Bay Guesthouse;
   Restaurante Manglares
11 Hotel Costa Sur
13 Mini-Hotel Cafetín Central
16 Hotel Lobster Pot; Restaurante
   Lobster Pot
17 Hotel Dorado
19 Hotel Caribbean Dream
20 Hotel Hollywood
21 Hotel Marda Maus

PLACES TO EAT
4 Restaurante Chez Marcel
7 Restaurante La Fogata
18 Cafetín Pesca Frito

OTHER
2 Enitel
3 Catholic Church; Clock Tower
5 Intur
6 Disco Bacchus
8 Banco Caley Dagnall
9 Moravian Church
10 Post Office
12 Cima Club
14 Money Changers
15 Market
22 4 Hermanos

Parque Reyes

Path

Pier

CARIBBEAN SEA

To Restaurante El Flotante

0   100   200 m
0   100   200 yards

a rough location opposite the market, *Hotel Marda Maus* (☎ *822 2429*) feels secure and charges just US$7 for clean, spacious doubles, or US$11.50 including private bath and cable TV.

A block and a half west, *Hotel Lobster Pot* is not the cauldron its name suggests but rather a decent budget guesthouse behind a seafood restaurant. Freshly painted singles/doubles with separate bath are US$5/6. Less attractive options in the same price range include the battered *Hotel Costa Sur* (☎ *822 2452*) with an interesting iron-railed balcony, and the dingy but hospitable *Hotel Dorado* (☎ *822 2452*) with a small dining room. *Mini-Hotel Cafetín Central* (☎ *822 2362*), at the rear of a lively cafe, offers very neat, if cramped, rooms with tiny private bath, cable TV and phone for US$10/15, or US$25 with air-con.

A block north of the pier, *Bluefields Bay Guesthouse* (☎/fax *822 2143, tiairene@ ibw.com.ni*), formerly Hotel Tía Irene, is efficiently managed by the regional university URACCAN. Its spacious, comfy rooms, all with air-con, go for US$26/45, including breakfast in the bayside restaurant.

Places to Eat

In Bluefields, you can eat shrimp and lobster that were caught a few hours earlier for prices lower than elsewhere in Nicaragua. *Restaurante El Flotante*, four blocks south of the Moravian church where the bayside street meets the water, has dining on a covered patio with a marvelous view of the bay. Meals start at US$4. *Restaurante Manglares*, attached to the Bluefields Bay Guesthouse, is a similar concept on the north side of town.

Less elegant but locally popular seafood places include *Restaurante Lobster Pot* and *Cafetín Pesca Frito*, both serving lobster for around US$6. Roasted chicken is the specialty at the clean and bright *Restaurante La Fogata*. For air-con and cloth napkins, go to *Restaurante Chez Marcel*, one block south of Parque Reyes, with meals from US$6.

Entertainment

Bluefields has an active nightlife. Dance to reggae, calypso and soca grooves at *4 Hermanos*, packed with moving bodies from Thursday to Sunday nights. *Disco Bacchus*,

just south of Parque Reyes, attracts a younger group and a few foreigners. A good place for a drink is the open-air *Cima Club*, with balcony seating and an excellent Caribbean sound track. You need go no farther than the Parque Reyes to find a crowd enjoying good music.

Getting There & Away

La Costeña (☎ *822 2500*) flies between Managua and Bluefields four times daily (US$40/80 one-way/roundtrip); Atlántico Airlines operates three daily flights (US$41/73). There's a Costeña flight from Bluefields to Puerto Cabezas at 12:20 pm daily except Sunday (US$40/80). Make reservations at Hotel South Atlantic II, a Costeña agent. A taxi to the airport costs US$0.75 per person. For information on flights to Corn Island, see that section.

Transportes Vargas Peña (☎ *280 4561* in Managua) offers bus/boat service all the way from Managua to Bluefields for US$14. Buses depart from Managua's Mercado Iván Montenegro at 9:30 pm nightly; at Rama, passengers continue by motorboat to Bluefields, arriving between 7 and 8 am. In the reverse direction, pangas depart Bluefields for Rama at 5:30 or 6 am. Check departure times and purchase tickets at the dockside office of Vargas Peña (☎ *822 1510*).

Slow boats from Bluefields to Rama depart at 5 am on Tuesday, Thursday, Saturday and Sunday; the five-hour trip costs US$4. Tickets are sold the morning of departure at the dockside office of Empresa Zeledón (☎ *822 2100*). Managua-bound buses wait at the dock in Rama to meet the arriving boats. If you want to take one, try to be first off the boat and make a flying run for a seat.

See the Laguna de Perlas and Corn Island sections for details on getting to and from these destinations.

LAGUNA DE PERLAS

The Laguna de Perlas (Pearl Lagoon), formed where the Río Kurinwas meets the sea about 80km north of Bluefields, is about 50km long and very wide in places. Miskitos living in the villages around the lagoon make a living from the abundant fish, shrimp and lobster. One can spend a few relaxing days in this peaceful multiethnic community talking to locals, observing aquatic bird life and visiting nearby indigenous villages. Within hiking distance is Awas, the best swimming beach in the area.

Places to Stay & Eat

At Laguna de Perlas village, travelers can find inexpensive lodging at *Bella Vista*, upstairs from the dock-front store, offering small, clean double rooms with shared bath for US$7.50. Another waterfront option in the same price range is the tidy *Sweet Pearly*, with its own restaurant. Even cheaper, *Green Lodge B&B* is more than just a pleasant guesthouse – manager Wesley is a knowledgeable source of information on local history and culture.

Laguna de Perla's premier lodging is *Casa Blanca*, a lively household headed by a Danish-Nica couple. At US$15, double rooms have screened windows and woodwork crafted in the proprietors' own shop. The kitchen serves creatively seasoned meals. To get there, turn left as you leave the dock and follow the signs.

You might have luck reaching any of these places by calling the local Enitel office, open 8 am to noon Monday to Saturday, 2 to 5 pm weekdays, at ☎ 822 2762 or 822 2355.

Getting There & Away

Pangas leave Bluefields for Laguna de Perlas every morning between and 7 and 8 am and later as they fill (US$5.50, 1½ hours). The last boat back leaves around noon; show up early to reserve a place, then be patient.

PUERTO CABEZAS
pop 29,601

Puerto Cabezas, on the northeast coast of Nicaragua, is the country's second-most-important Caribbean port. Banco Caley Dagnall changes dollars and traveler's checks.

The main interest here is the local inhabitants, who reflect an interesting mixture of indigenous and Hispanic cultures. It's possible to make excursions to nearby Miskito communities, though accommodations are scarce. Buses leave from Puerto Cabezas' main plaza to some villages, as well as to the river port of Lamlaya for boats to others. The Associación de Mujeres Indígenas de la Costa Atlántica (Amica; ☎ 282 2325, amica@nicarao.org.ni) arranges personalized excursions, including transportation, food and lodging with local families, and opportunities to learn local crafts or do volunteer work. Prices vary by program.

Most hotels and guesthouses have strict rules about drinking and visitors. An exception is *Hospedaje Tangni* (☎ 282 2379), which nevertheless has clean singles/doubles with shared bath for US$6.50/9.25. *Hospedaje El Viajante* (☎ 282 2263) is the best deal, with single rooms starting at US$4.75. Formerly Hotel Cayos Miskitu, *Hotel El Pelícano* (☎/fax 282 2336), with its sea-view patio, is quite comfortable, and owner (and former mayor) Rodolfo Jaentschke is happy to share his knowledge of the area with his guests. Singles/doubles with fan and private bath are US$9.25/10. The homey *Hotel Pérez* (☎ 282 2382) offers secure rooms with shared bath for US$9.25/10, or US$17/23 with private bath and air-con.

The best restaurant is *Kabu Payaska*, about 2km north of town. The impressive views from its cliffside location make it worth stopping for a beer and *tostones*, if not a plate of fish or lobster.

Getting There & Away

Air La Costeña flies between Managua and Puerto Cabezas four times daily (US$40/80 one-way/roundtrip); Atlántico has three daily flights (US$48/86). There is one Costeña flight a day between Puerto Cabezas and Bluefields. Tickets are sold at the airport, 2km outside of town. A taxi to the airport costs US$1.

CORN ISLANDS

Once a haven for buccaneers, Big and Little Corn Islands (Islas del Maíz) are now low-key vacation spots in an isolated corner of the Caribbean. The two isles retain all the magic associated with the Caribbean experience – clear turquoise water, white sandy beaches fringed with coconut palms, excellent fishing, coral reefs good for snorkeling and an unhurried, peaceful pace of life – without the crass development of better-known island 'paradises.' Little Corn in particular lives up to this elusive image.

Big Corn, 70km off the coast of Bluefields, measures about 6 sq km; its partner to the northeast is only about 1½ sq km and can be hiked across in half an hour. Most people on the islands are of British West Indian descent and speak English. Almost all live on the larger island, making a living from fishing, particularly lobster.

The Crab Soup Festival is held August 27, a date that marks the abolition of slavery.

Big Corn Island
pop 5970
Boats arrive at the north end of Brig Bay, which is just a 1km hike from the airstrip entrance. There's swimming and lodging at Brig Bay, but the best beaches are farther south at the Picnic Center. Snorkeling is good on the north and east sides of the island. Green vans provide public transportation around Big Corn, running every

40 minutes in either direction. Taxis are US$0.75 per person regardless of distance traveled.

Accommodations are scattered along Brig Bay south of the dock. *Casa Blanca* provides the best value. Rooms in this cozy family-run guesthouse cost US$9.50/11 with twin/double beds and mosquito nets. A little north, at a section of the beach wrecked by Hurricane Joan, is laid-back *Linda Vista*, with rudimentary lodging at similar prices. South of Casa Blanca, *Hotel Paraíso* (☎ 285 5111, 779 5979 cell phone) is Big Corn's top lodging, with circular thatched-roof bungalows from US$30. The French Canadian–run inn includes a lively bar/restaurant and rents snorkeling gear and horses. Secluded at Waula point,

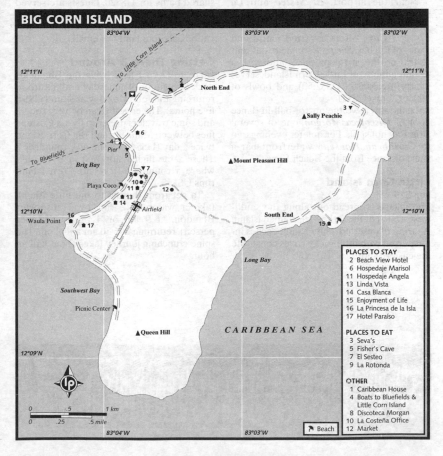

BIG CORN ISLAND

To Little Corn Island

North End

Sally Peachie

Mount Pleasant Hill

To Bluefields

Brig Bay

Pier

Playa Coco

Airfield

South End

Waula Point

Long Bay

Southwest Bay

Picnic Center

Queen Hill

CARIBBEAN SEA

PLACES TO STAY
2 Beach View Hotel
6 Hospedaje Marisol
11 Hospedaje Angela
13 Linda Vista
14 Casa Blanca
15 Enjoyment of Life
16 La Princesa de la Isla
17 Hotel Paraíso

PLACES TO EAT
3 Seva's
5 Fisher's Cave
7 El Sesteo
9 La Rotonda

OTHER
1 Caribbean House
4 Boats to Bluefields & Little Corn Island
8 Discoteca Morgan
10 La Costeña Office
12 Market

🏊 Beach

La Princesa de la Isla (☎ 285 5170) has more character. The Italian-run lodge offers stylish stone-and-timber rooms with shell showerheads for US$30. Meals are served in an intimate lounge or on an open-air terrace. Cheaper digs include *Hospedaje Angela*, beside the airstrip, and *Hospedaje Marisol*, near the dock.

On the edge of town is the oceanside *Beach View Hotel*, overpriced at US$20 for plain doubles with private bath and surf-side terrace, or US$10 for dark downstairs rooms with shared bath. At a palm-studded point on the north end of Long Bay, Ira Gómez' *Enjoyment of Life* has cabins for two with bath at US$30 and camping on shady grounds for US$15. There's country music in the Chill-Out bar.

Near the airport, *El Sesteo* and *La Rotonda* (evenings only) are good local eateries, with lobster for under US$5. *Fisher's Cave* offers a varied menu and views of the bay. *Seva's*, a simple restaurant at the northeast tip of the island with a distant glimpse of Little Corn Island, serves hearty breakfasts (US$2.50) and bowls of lobster soup (US$3).

Islanders crowd the mirror-ball-lit dance floor of *Discoteca Morgan*, one of several Brig Bay hot spots. For quieter evenings, go to *Caribbean House*, a waterfront bar a short distance from the Beach View.

Little Corn Island
pop 515
The village is spread out along the southwest stretch of the turkey-leg-shaped island. A string of deserted white-sand beaches interspersed with little rocky coves constitute the eastern shore.

In the village, *Doña Briggette* and *Doña Izayda* run guesthouses at US$7.50 per double. Camp and snorkel at *Derrick's*, an idyllic spot on the northeast corner of Little Corn. Derrick provides a tent or reed hut for US$5 per person, including a one-pot meal. To the south, *Doña Elsa* prepares a beachside picnic, served on primitive tables under the palms, and rents beds in stick huts for US$5 per person. Elsa's husband can take you out to the reefs.

Casa Iguana (*casaiguana@mindspring .com*), a largely self-sufficient eco-lodge, has more sophisticated facilities. Perched on a cliff with incredible sea views, its four cabins are equipped with flush toilets, showers and libraries and cost US$50 for two guests. It also has a couple of simpler cabins with shared baths for US$20. Guests are served fresh-cooked, family-style meals. It's often booked; don't expect to stay without reservations, accepted only by email.

Getting There & Around
Boats to Corn Island leave the Bluefields dock at 6 am on Wednesday and Saturday, returning the following day at 9 am (US$4, five hours). The crossing can be very rough, and some travelers prefer to fly. La Costeña flies between Managua and Big Corn Island twice a day (US$46/92 one-way/roundtrip). Those same flights stop first in Bluefields, where a roundtrip ticket to Corn Island runs US$58.

To get from the big to the little island, take a water taxi, run by Transportes Blandón, at 9 am or 4 pm (US$4 per person), returning at 6:30 am and 2 pm. The spine-crunching journey takes about half an hour.

Costa Rica

Costa Rica is famous for its enlightened approach to conservation. About 27% of the country is protected in one form or another, and more than 13% is within the national park system. The variety and density of wildlife in the preserved areas attract people whose dream is to see monkeys, sloths, caymans, sea turtles and exotic birds in their natural habitat. The adventurous traveler will find the opportunity in Costa Rica to hike through rain forest, peer into the smoking craters of active volcanoes, snorkel on tropical reefs and surf the best waves in Central America.

Costa Rica has had democratic elections since the 19th century and is now one of the most peaceful nations in the world. Armed forces were abolished after the 1948 civil war, and Costa Rica has avoided the despotic dictatorships, frequent military coups, terrorism and internal strife that have torn other countries in the region. Costa Rica is also the safest country to visit in Latin America.

Not only is it safe – but also friendly. Costa Ricans delight in showing off their lovely country to visitors, and wherever you go, you will find the locals to be a constant source of help, smiles and information.

Highlights

- Take a hike above the treetops and catch a glimpse of the elusive quetzal in the cloud forests near the small community of Monteverde
- Relax on beautiful beaches at the village of Montezuma and explore nearby wildlife reserves
- Climb Cerro Chirripó, the country's highest peak at 3820m
- Camp and watch wildlife in Parque Nacional Santa Rosa, the largest remaining tropical dry forest in Central America
- View spectacular lava flows and eruptions every few hours at Volcán Arenal, the most active volcano in Central America

Facts about Costa Rica

HISTORY

Costa Rica has been strongly influenced by the Spanish conquest. The pre-Columbian cultures put up little resistance to the Spanish. Few archaeological monuments remain, so our knowledge of Costa Rica's pre-Columbian history is scant. Despite this, a visit to San José's Museo de Jade or Museo del Oro Precolombino is worth your time.

Spanish Conquest

The first European arrival was Christopher Columbus, who landed near present-day Puerto Limón on September 18, 1502, on his fourth (and last) voyage to the Americas. During his 17-day stay, he noted that some of the natives wore gold decorations. Because of this, the area was dubbed *costa rica* (rich coast) by the Europeans, who imagined that there must be a rich empire lying farther inland.

Spanish King Ferdinand appointed Diego de Nicuesa as governor of the region and sent him to colonize it in 1506. The colonizers were hampered by the jungle, tropical diseases and small bands of indigenous peoples who used guerrilla tactics to fight off the invaders. About half the colonizers died, and the rest returned home, unsuccessful.

Further expeditions followed, but they were unable to form a permanent colony,

COSTA RICA

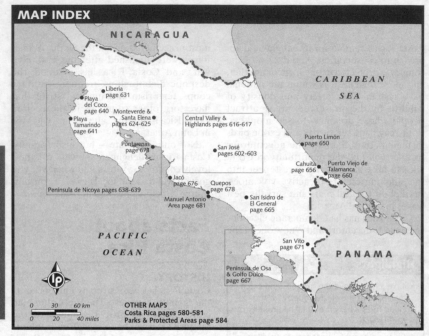

MAP INDEX

NICARAGUA

CARIBBEAN
SEA

Liberia
page 631

Playa
del Coco
page 640   Monteverde &
Playa   Santa Elena
Tamarindo   pages 624-625
page 641

Central Valley &
Highlands pages 616-617

Puntarenas
page 673

San José
pages 602-603

Puerto Limón
page 650

Cahuita   Puerto Viejo de
page 656   Talamanca
           page 660

Jacó
page 676   Quepos
            page 678   San Isidro de
Manuel Antonio   El General
Area page 681   page 665

Península de Nicoya pages 638-639

PACIFIC

OCEAN   San Vito
                                         page 671

                                                    PANAMA

Península de Osa
& Golfo Dulce
page 667

0   30   60 km   OTHER MAPS
0   20   40 miles   Costa Rica pages 580-581
                        Parks & Protected Areas page 584

and many Spaniards died of hunger and disease. Meanwhile, the indigenous population was decimated by European diseases to which they had no resistance. In 1562, Juan Vásquez de Coronado arrived as governor and founded a colony in the central highlands. Cartago was founded in 1563, and the healthy climate and fertile volcanic soil enabled the colony to survive.

For the next 150 years, the colony remained a forgotten backwater, isolated from the coast and the major trading routes and surviving only by dint of hard work and the generosity and friendliness that were to become the hallmarks of the Costa Rican character.

Eventually, in the early 18th century, the colony began to spread and change. Settlements were established throughout the fertile central highlands, including San José in 1737 and Alajuela in 1782. Much of the town of Cartago was destroyed in an eruption of Irazú in 1723, but the survivors rebuilt. Despite this incipient expansion, the colony remained one of the poorest in the Spanish empire.

Independence
Central America became independent from Spain on September 15, 1821. Costa Rica was briefly a part of the Mexican Empire, then became a state within the United Provinces of Central America. The first elected head of state was Juan Mora Fernández (1824 to 1833).

Coffee was introduced from Cuba in 1808, and was first exported during Mora Fernández's term. The rest of the 19th century saw a steady increase in coffee exports. Some of the growers became rich, and a class structure began to emerge. In 1849, a coffee grower, Juan Rafael Mora, became president and governed for 10 years.

Mora's presidency is remembered for economic and cultural growth and for a somewhat bizarre military incident that earned a place in every Costa Rican child's history books. In June 1855, the American filibuster William Walker arrived in Nicaragua to conquer Central America, convert the area into slaving territory and then use slaves to build a Nicaraguan canal joining the Atlantic and Pacific. Walker and his army defeated the Nicaraguans and marched south.

Costa Rica had no army, so Mora organized 9000 civilians to gather what arms they could and march north in February 1856. In a short but determined battle at Santa Rosa, the Costa Ricans defeated Walker, who retreated to Rivas in Nicaragua, followed by the victorious Costa Ricans. Walker made a stand in a wood fort, and Juan Santamaría, a drummer boy from Alajuela, volunteered to torch the building, thus forcing the North American to flee. Santamaría was killed in this action, and he is now remembered as one of Costa Rica's favorite national heroes.

Despite his defeat, Walker returned to Central America several more times, unsuccessfully, before finally being captured and shot in Honduras in 1860. In the meantime, Mora lost favor in his country (he and his army were thought to have brought back cholera, causing a massive epidemic in Costa Rica) and was deposed in 1859. In 1860 he led a failed coup against the government and was executed.

Democracy

The next three decades were characterized by power struggles among the coffee-growing elite. In 1889, the first democratic elections were held, although neither women nor blacks were allowed to vote. Democracy has been a hallmark of Costa Rican politics ever since, with a few lapses. One was between 1917 and 1919, when the minister of war, Frederico Tinoco, overthrew the democratically elected president and formed a dictatorship. After opposition from the rest of Costa Rica and the US government, the dictatorship ended and Tinoco was exiled.

In 1940, Rafael Angel Calderón Guardia became president. The reforms he introduced were supported by the poor but criticized by the rich. These included recognition of workers' rights to organize, minimum wage laws and a social security system. To further widen his power base, Calderón allied himself, strangely, with both the Catholic Church and the Communist Party to form the Republican Calderonista Party (PRC). This further alienated him from conservatives, intellectuals and the upper classes.

In 1948, Calderón again ran for the presidency and was beaten by Otilio Ulate. Unwilling to accept the result, Calderón fraudulently claimed victory. The tense situation escalated into civil war, with the opposing forces led by José (Pepe) Figueres Ferrer. After several weeks of warfare and more than 2000 deaths, Figueres emerged victorious. He took over an interim government, and in 1949 handed over the presidency to Ulate, who was not a member of Figueres' own Partido Liberación Nacional (PLN; National Liberation Party). The year marked the formation of the Costa Rican constitution, which is still in effect. Women and blacks received the vote; the army was abolished; presidents were not allowed to run for successive terms; and a neutral electoral tribunal was established to guarantee free and fair elections.

Although Costa Rica has more than a dozen political parties, the PLN has dominated since 1949, usually winning elections every other four years. Figueres remained popular and was elected to two terms of office (in 1954 and 1970). Another PLN president, Oscar Arias (1986 to 1990), received the 1987 Nobel Peace Prize for his peacekeeping efforts in Central America.

The Partido de Unidad Social Cristiana (PUSC; Social Christian Unity Party), the heirs to Calderón's 1940s alliance, has continued to be the favored party of the poor and working classes, and Calderón's son, Rafael Ángel Calderón Fournier, was elected president in 1990, succeeding Arias.

The 1994 presidential elections were narrowly won by PLN candidate José María Figueres (son of Don Pepe Figueres), who at age 39 became Costa Rica's youngest president ever. His presidency was unpopular, marked by price hikes, tax increases, bank closures and strikes.

In 1998, Miguel Ángel Rodríguez represented the PUSC against PLN candidate José Miguel Corrales. Rodríguez, a conservative economist, barely won the election. A 30% abstention level, notably higher than in previous elections, partly reflected a public that was disillusioned with the two-party dominance in Costa Rican politics. Rodríguez will lead the country until 2002.

The new president tried to promote a tough austerity plan, but he came under

COSTA RICA

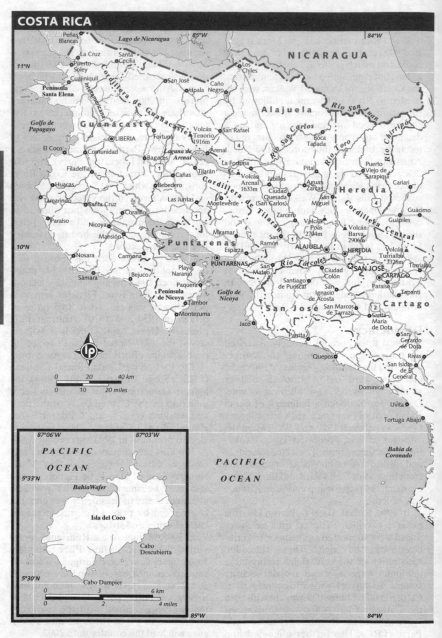

COSTA RICA

severe criticism after almost quadrupling the presidential annual salary, from US$70,000 to more than US$250,000. After widespread public outcry, Rodríguez apologized for his 'error' and returned the salary to close to its previous level. He continues to inspire little affection among Costa Ricans, and in 2000 he earned the dubious distinction of being Central America's least-popular leader, according to a Gallup poll.

GEOGRAPHY

Costa Rica is bordered to the north by Nicaragua, to the northeast by the Caribbean Sea, to the southeast by Panama, and to the west and southwest by the Pacific Ocean. It is an extremely varied country, despite its tiny size of 50,100 sq km.

A series of volcanic mountain chains run from the Nicaraguan border in the northwest to the Panamanian border in the southeast, splitting the country in two. The highlands reach 3820m, and changing altitudes play an important part in determining geographical and ecological variation.

In the center of the highlands lies a plain of fertile volcanic soil called the Meseta Central, at an altitude between about 1000 and 1500m. It contains four of Costa Rica's five largest cities, including the capital, San José. More than half of the population lives on this plain.

On either side of the volcanic central highlands lie coastal lowlands that differ greatly in character. The smooth Caribbean coastline is 212km long and is characterized by year-round rain, mangroves, swamps, an intracoastal waterway, sandy beaches and small tides. The 1016km Pacific coastline is much more rugged and rocky, with numerous gulfs and peninsulas. The northwest coast is bordered by tropical dry forests that receive almost no rain for several months each year, as well as by mangroves, rain forests and beaches. Tidal variation is quite large, and there are many offshore islands.

CLIMATE

The dry season is from late December to April and is called *verano* (summer) by Costa Ricans. The rest of the year is *invierno* (winter), the rainy season. The Caribbean coastal region is wetter than the rest of the country, and even its dry season has rainy days mixed with spells of fine weather. In

COSTA RICA

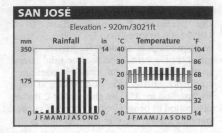

the highlands, the dry season really is dry, with only one or two rainy days per month. The north and central Pacific coastal regions have rain patterns similar to those of the highlands, and the southern Pacific coast can experience rain year-round, though the rain decreases in the dry season.

Temperature is mainly influenced by altitude. San José has average lows of 15°C, and highs are a pleasant 26°C. The coasts are much hotter: The Caribbean averages 21°C at night and 30°C during the day, and the Pacific coast is about 3°C warmer.

Like other nations on the Central American isthmus, Costa Rica is periodically whipped by hurricanes. In July 1996, Hurricane César left several dozen dead and an estimated US$100 million in damages. Two years later, the ill-famed Mitch caused more destruction, but the country managed to escape the catastrophes suffered by its neighbors to the north.

ECOLOGY & ENVIRONMENT

The major problem facing Costa Rica's environment is deforestation. Three-quarters of the country was covered by forests in the late 1940s; by the early 1990s, less than a quarter remained forested. The UN Food and Agriculture Organization estimates that between 1973 and 1989 Costa Rica's forestlands were cleared at an average annual rate of 2.3%, mainly for pasture or agriculture. Over the last decade, tree plantations have appeared, and the availability of commercially grown timber means there is less pressure to log the forests. Nevertheless, deforestation continues at a high rate, and there is now very little natural forest outside of the protected areas.

Deforestation has led to soil erosion. The topsoil is washed away, thus lowering land productivity and silting up watersheds. Some deforested lands become

banana plantations, which use pesticides and blue plastic bags to protect the fruit. Both pesticides and bags end up polluting the environment.

To try to control this deforestation and protect its wildlife, Costa Rica has undertaken the most progressive national park system in Latin America. A recent upsurge in nature tourism has in turn given new impetus to environmental protection efforts. The early 1990s saw a twofold increase in foreign visitors, many of whom came to witness Costa Rica's natural wonders. Of the more than 1 million foreign tourists who came to Costa Rica in 1999, 67% visited at least one national park, 60% had nature hiking on their itineraries and 41% did some bird watching.

New operations spring up daily eager to cash in on this boom, and 'ecotourism' has become the buzzword of the day. Though many hotels and tour operators are finding ways to prosper in environmentally responsible ways, some developers take advantage of Costa Rica's 'green' image to promote mass tourism and build huge hotels without regard for the adverse impact. Critics say such large-scale development would lead to severe environmental and cultural degradation, spoiling the country that people flock to see. The government has occasionally clamped down on violators – for example by ordering the demolition in 2000 of a hotel built illegally on protected coastline in Quepos – but the generally lax enforcement of environmental laws is what allows such hotels to be built in the first place. Furthermore, environmentalists complain that the revenues being collected in the tourism wave are not being sufficiently rechanneled into protected areas. Though Costa Rica is certainly at the forefront of ecotourism in Central America, some fear it lacks the commitment to deal with its own success.

FLORA & FAUNA

Costa Rica is a small country, yet its range of habitats harbor an extraordinarily wide variety of plant and animal species. This biodiversity attracts nature lovers from all over the world.

Flora

Some 10,000 species of vascular plant have been described and more are added every year. Orchids alone account for 1200 species, and more than 1400 tree species have been recorded.

Fauna

Birds Costa Rica's primary attraction for many naturalists is its birds, of which some 850 species have been recorded – more than in any one of the continents of North America, Australia or Europe. Many birders want to see the resplendent quetzal – Monteverde is a good place to do so, in season.

More than 50 species of hummingbird have been recorded from Costa Rica. Bird watchers will find scarlet macaws and 15 other parrot species; six different toucans, with their incredibly large and hollow bills; the huge and very rare harpy eagle, which is capable of snatching monkeys and sloths off branches as it flies past; and a large array of other tropical birds such as flycatchers (78 species), tanagers (50) and antbirds (30).

Mammals Costa Rica has more than 200 species of mammal. Visitors are likely to see some of the four monkey species found here and may encounter sloths, armadillos, coatis, agoutis (large rodents), peccaries (wild pigs), kinkajous, raccoons, skunks, otters, foxes, squirrels and bats. Others such as ocelots, jaguars and tapirs are extremely rare to glimpse.

Insects At least 35,000 species of insect from Costa Rica have been described to date, and many others still remain to be named. Among the thousands of butterflies are dazzling morphos with 15cm wingspans and electric blue upper wings. There are also many ant species in Costa Rica. One interesting type is the leaf cutter ants (genus Atta), which can be seen marching in columns along the forest floor, carrying pieces of leaves into their underground colonies. The leaves decompose and support a fungus that the ants eat.

Amphibians The approximately 160 species of amphibian include red, black, blue and yellow poison arrow frogs whose skin glands can exude a toxin capable of causing paralysis and death in other animals.

Reptiles Some 220 species of reptile are found in Costa Rica. About half are snakes, which are much talked about but seldom seen. Bright green basilisk lizards live near water. The males have huge crests along their head, body and tail, and reach almost a meter in length. The young are nicknamed Jesus Christ lizards for their ability to run across water. There are 14 species of freshwater and marine turtle. The latter nest in large numbers on sandy beaches – a spectacular sight. The largest are the leatherbacks, whose carapace (shell) can reach 160cm in length and average a stunning 360kg in weight. The smaller olive ridley turtles practice synchronous nesting, with thousands of females emerging from the sea on a single night.

Parks & Protected Areas

Created in the 1960s, the Costa Rican national park system now encompasses some three dozen parks and protected areas – about 13% of the country's area. In addition, various buffer zones and forest reserves boost the total area of protected land to about 27% (though these buffer zones allow farming, logging and other exploitation). Also, there are dozens of privately owned lodges, reserves and haciendas that are set up to protect the land.

A project is slowly developing to link geographically close groups of parks and preserves into a national system of conservation areas (Sinac; Sistema Nacional de Areas de Conservación), of which there are now 11. These 'megaparks' will eventually cover about a quarter of Costa Rica's land area, according to local conservationists.

Not all of the protected areas are accessible to travelers. Some reserves are closed to everyone except researchers with permits. Indigenous reserves are for the few remaining tribes in Costa Rica and have almost no infrastructure for tourism. Most visitors stick to the main national parks and a few reserves that have trails and other facilities. Only these are mentioned in the text.

National parks charge an entrance fee of US$6 per day. A few parks and refuges provide basic camping facilities or food and accommodations in ranger stations. Those most often visited by campers are Santa Rosa in northwestern Costa Rica (tropical

COSTA RICA

PARKS & PROTECTED AREAS

1   Refugio Nacional de Fuana Silvestre
    Isla Bolaños
2   Refugio Nacional de Vida Silvestre
    Bahía Junquillal
3   Parque Nacional Santa Rosa
4   Parque Nacional Guanacaste
5   Estación Experimental Horizontes
6   Parque Nacional Rincón de la Vieja
7   Refugio National de Vida Silvestre
    Caño Negro
8   Reserva Biológica Lomas de Barbudal
9   Zona Protectora Volcán Tenorio
10 Reserva Nacional Guatuso
11 Parque Nacional Arenal
12 Refugio Nacional de Vida Silvestre
    Barra del Colorado
13 Parque Nacional Tortuguero
14 Parque National Marino Las Baulas
15 Refugio Nacional de Vida Silvestre
    Ostional
16 Reserva Indígena Matambú
17 Parque Nacional Barra Honda
18 Parque Nacional Palo Verde
19 Reserva Biológica Isla de los Pájaros
20 Reserva Biológica Bosque Nuboso
    Monteverde
21 Refugio Silvestre Peñas Blancas

22 Parque Nacional Juan Castro Blanco
23 Parque Nacional Volcán Poás
24 Parque Nacional Braulio Carrillo
25 Zona Protectora
26 Reserva Natural Absoluta Cabo
    Blanco
27 Refugio Nacional de Vida Silvestre
    Curú
28 Reserva Biológica Isla Guayabo
29 Reserva Biológica Islas Negritos
30 Reserva Biológica Carara
31 Reserva Indígena Quitirrisí
32 Reserva Indígena Zapatón
33 Parque Nacional Volcán Irazú
34 Parque Nacional Tapantí
35 Monumento Nacional Arqueológico
    Guayabo
36 Reserva Indígena Barbilla
37 Reserva Indígena Barbilla
38 Reserva Indígena Alto y Bajo Chirripó
39 Parque Nacional Manuel Antonio
40 Parque Nacional Chirripó
41 Reserva Indígena Telire
42 Parque Internacional La Amistad
43 Reserva Indígena Tayní
44 Reserva Biológica Hitoy-Cerere
45 Reserva Indígena Talamanca-Cabécar

46 Reserva Indígena Talamanca Bribri
47 Parque Nacional Cahuita
48 Reserva Indígena Cocles/KéköLdi
49 Refugio Nacional de Vida Silvestre
    Gandoca-Manzanillo
50 Parque Nacional Marino Ballena
51 Reserva Indígena Ujarrás
52 Reserva Indígena Salitre
53 Reserva Indígena Cabagra
54 Reserva Indígena Térraba
55 Reserva Indígena Boruca
56 Reserva Indígena Curré
57 Zona Protectora Las Tablas
58 Reserva Biológica Isla del Caño
59 Humedal Nacional Térraba-Sierpe
60 Reserva Indígena Guaymí de Osa
61 Parque Nacional Corcovado
62 Parque Nacional Corcovado (Piedras
    Blancas Sector)
63 Refugio Nacional de Vida Silvestre
    Golfito
64 Reserva Indígena Guaymí de Coto
    Brus
65 Reserva Indígena Abrojo-Montezuma
66 Reserva Indígena Guaymí de Conte
    Burica
67 Parque Nacional Isla del Coco

dry forest, wildlife, beaches) and Corcovado in the Península de Osa (rain forest, wildlife).

GOVERNMENT & POLITICS

The Costa Rican government is based on the constitution of November 9, 1949. The president wields executive power, assisted by two vice presidents and a cabinet of 16 ministers. Elections are held every four years, and an incumbent cannot be reelected.

There are seven provinces, each with a governor appointed by the president. Fifty-seven *diputados/diputadas* (congressmen/women) are elected by direct popular vote to the Legislative Assembly every four years. This is where much of the power of Costa Rica's government lies.

The Legislative Assembly elects 22 Supreme Court judges for renewable eight-year terms. The Supreme Court in turn selects judges for the lower courts.

The vote is mandatory for all citizens over 18. Although there are about 30 political parties, only two groups have been in power since 1949: the National Liberation Party (PLN) and the Social Christian Unity Party (PUSC). Since 1998, the PUSC has been in power under the presidency of Miguel Angel Rodríguez.

There is no army in Costa Rica. Instead, there is a Fuerza Pública, a form of police force.

ECONOMY

Until the mid-19th century, Costa Rica was a very poor country with an economy based on subsistence agriculture. Then the introduction of coffee provided a product suitable for export. Bananas were introduced next, and today these two crops continue to be the country's most important agricultural exports, followed by pineapples and melons. In the early 1990s, nontraditional exports such as ornamental plants, pharmaceuticals, textiles, tires and furniture became increasingly important. Also in the '90s, tourism experienced an unprecedented boom. The numbers of foreign tourists rose from 376,000 in 1989 to more than a million a decade later, with revenues of more than US$1 billion in 1999.

After a mid-'90s slump, the economy bounced back toward the end of the decade, spurred largely by Intel, the multinational manufacturer of computer chips, which opened production facilities here in 1997. With Intel inside, the electronics industry soon became the country's top dollar earner, overtaking tourism in 1998. In early 1999, Intel products represented a staggering 40% of Costa Rica's total export revenues.

Costa Rica registered 8.3% growth in 1999, one of the few Latin American countries to perform so robustly that year. Exports continued to expand, totaling close to US$6.7 billion in 1999, about twice as much as in 1995.

Though Costa Rica's standard of living is high for Central America, the minimum wage was still only US$1.57 per hour in 1999, and average annual per capita income was US$3700. Unemployment hovers at a relatively benign 5% to 6%, but there is much underemployment. Inflation registered at more than 10% in 1999 and is expected to continue at that level.

POPULATION & PEOPLE

The estimated population of Costa Rica in 1999 was 3.67 million, with an annual growth rate of 1.9%. (A census was conducted in July 2000, the first in 16 years, but results were not available at this writing.)

Three out of five Costa Ricans live in the highlands, and 33% are younger than 15 years old. The average life expectancy is 66.7 years, placing it 40th in the world and fourth in Latin America (behind Cuba, Argentina and Uruguay), according to the World Health Organization.

Most people are white and of Spanish descent. Less than 2% of the population is black, most living in the Caribbean region and speaking a lively dialect of English. These black Costa Ricans trace their ancestry to immigrants from Jamaica who built the railroads and worked the banana plantations in the late 19th century.

Indigenous Costa Ricans make up about 1% of the population. Small tribes include the Bribri from the Talamanca area in the southeast and the Borucas in the southern Pacific coastal areas.

Costa Ricans call themselves *Ticos* (men and groups of men and women) or *Ticas* (females). Visitors are constantly surprised by the warmth and friendliness of the people.

COSTA RICA

EDUCATION

With the highest literacy rate in Latin America (94.8%), Costa Rica has an education system that appears to be in good shape. However, dropout rates are high beyond the ninth grade, the final year of legally mandated study, and in 1999 close to half of high school age Costa Ricans were not attending classes. This is blamed on various factors, including the need for conveniently located secondary schools, lack of student interest, lack of parental encouragement and a desire to enter the workforce.

ARTS

There is little indigenous cultural influence, and cultural activities of any kind have developed only in the last hundred years. Ticos consider San José to be the country's cultural center, and it is here that the most important museums are found as well as a lively theater scene. The Teatro Nacional (National Theater), in the heart of San José, is the venue for plays, performances by the national symphony, ballet, opera and poetry readings.

The biggest cultural event is the International Arts Festival, held in San José every March. Outside the capital, the Monteverde Music Festival brings in internationally recognized classical and jazz artists from January to April each year.

Most distinctive among Costa Rica's homegrown crafts are the replicas of gaily painted oxcarts, called *carretas,* which colorfully evoke rural life. Sarchí is the main center for carreta construction. Traditional pottery in the indigenous Chorotega style is produced in Guatil in Guanacaste Province.

SOCIETY & CONDUCT

Costa Rican society is the least diverse of any Central American nation, with the overwhelming majority of European descent.

Despite the apparent homogeneity, societal differences exist. Historically, a small noble class *(hidalgos)* led the colony's affairs, and since Costa Rica became independent, the descendants of three hidalgo families have provided the country with most of its presidents and congressional representatives. Nevertheless, the politicians take pride in mingling with the public and maintaining some semblance of a classless society. The distribution of land and wealth is uneven, but less so than in other Central American countries.

Until 1949, the small black minority was actively discriminated against; blacks were not allowed to vote or to travel into the highlands away from their Caribbean coastal homes. Now, racism is, officially, a thing of the past, and black travelers are unlikely to encounter problems in the main cities and on the Caribbean coast, although some racist attitudes might still be encountered off the beaten path. Indigenous people, with very few exceptions, remain a marginal element of Costa Rican society, and little is being done to change this.

Appearances are important to Costa Ricans. They usually dress conservatively and act in an agreeable and friendly manner, which has become a hallmark of Tico culture. Despite their conservatism, they tend to loosen up in certain settings. Flirtation and public displays of affection are often seen (but see Women Travelers in Facts for the Visitor). Though few Costa Ricans wear shorts in the highlands, once you get down to the coast, beachwear can become skimpy, though nudity or toplessness is inappropriate.

Prostitution is legal for women over 18. Professionals carry cards showing how recently they have had a medical checkup, though some don't bother with these cards. Sexually transmitted diseases can take months before they can be detected, so even an up-to-date health card doesn't guarantee that a prostitute is disease free.

RELIGION

Nearly 75% of the population is Roman Catholic, at least in principle. Religious processions on holy days are generally less fervent and colorful than elsewhere in Latin America. One exceptional display of faith occurs during the week leading up to August 2, when half the population of the country hikes great distances to the Basilica of Cartago to pay homage to the Virgen de los Ángeles. Semana Santa (Holy Week) is a national holiday in Costa Rica, and everything, including the bus system, stops from mid-Thursday until mid-Saturday.

The blacks on the Caribbean coast tend to be Protestants; various fundamentalist and evangelist groups, as well as Mormons, are slowly gaining some adherents. There is a small Jewish community.

LANGUAGE

Spanish is the official language. Those who want to try out the local lingo might pick up Lonely Planet's *Costa Rica Spanish Phrasebook*. English is understood in many hotels, airline offices, tourist agencies and along much of the Caribbean coast.

The following colloquialisms and slang are used in Costa Rica:

¡Adiós!	Hi! (used when passing a friend in the street, or anyone in remote rural areas; also means 'Farewell' but only when leaving for a long time)
bomba	gas station
buena nota	OK, excellent (literally 'good grade')
chapulines	a gang, usually of young thieves
chunche	thing (can refer to almost anything)
cien metros	one city block (literally 100m)
¿Hay campo?	Is there space? (on a bus)
macho/a	blonde person (male/female)
mae	buddy (pronounced **mah**-eh; mainly used by boys and young men)
mi amor	my love (used by both sexes as a friendly form of address)
pulpería	corner grocery store
pura vida	super, far out (literally 'pure life,' can be used as an expression of approval or even as a greeting)
sabanero	Costa Rican cowboy, especially from Guanacaste Province
salado	too bad, tough luck
soda	cafe or lunch counter
tuanis	cool!
¡Upe!	Is anybody home? (pronounced **oo**-pay; used mainly in the countryside, at people's houses, instead of knocking)
vos	you (informal, equivalent to 'tu')

Facts for the Visitor

PLANNING
When to Go

The dry season, December to April, is considered the best time to visit Costa Rica.

But beach resorts are busy during this period. They're often full on the weekends and holidays, especially Easter week, which is booked months ahead. Travel in the wet season may be difficult on the poorer roads, but there are fewer visitors and hotel prices may be lower, especially at the better hotels.

Maps

An excellent map is the 1:500,000 sheet by International Travel Map Productions, available around the world. The Instituto Costarricense de Turismo (ICT; see Tourist Offices) has published several useful maps, and they're free. Topographical maps, useful for hiking and backpacking, can be purchased at the Instituto Geográfico Nacional (IGN; ☎ 257 7798), Calle 9, between Avenidas 20 and 22, in San José.

What to Bring

The highlands can be cool, so bring a windproof jacket and a warm layer to wear underneath. Rainwear in tropical rain forests can make you sweat, so an umbrella is preferred by many travelers. A hat is indispensable.

Tampons are available but heavily taxed, so women should bring their favorite brand from home; the same applies for contraceptives. Bring insect repellent and strong sunblock (SPF 20 and above). For wildlife viewing, binoculars are recommended.

TOURIST OFFICES

The national tourism board (ICT) has an office in the capital (see Tourist Offices under San José). Elsewhere, locally run tourist offices or commercial tour operators provide information.

In the US, call ☎ 800-343 6332 for ICT brochures or information. In Germany, the ICT's public relations office is Tourismusbuero Costa Rica (☎ 0049 221 9 62 47 00, amik@mail.k.magicvillage.de). Citizens of other countries can ask their Costa Rican consulate for tourist information, or write to ICT in San José.

Alternatively, consult the ICT's flashy Web site (www.tourism-costarica.com) for some general information.

VISAS & DOCUMENTS
Visas

Passport-carrying nationals of the following countries are allowed 90 days' stay with no visa: most western European countries, Argentina, Canada, Israel, Japan, Panama, the UK and the USA. Citizens of Australia, France, Iceland, Mexico, Russia, South Africa, New Zealand and Venezuela are allowed 30 days' stay with no visa. Others require a visa from a Costa Rican consulate. These lists are subject to change. Check www.rree.go.cr/visa-ingreso.html for the latest restrictions.

During your stay, the law requires that you carry your passport or tourist card at all times. A photocopy of the pages bearing your photo, passport number, and entry stamp will suffice when walking around town, but the passport should be in the hotel you are staying at, not kept in a safe in San José.

Visa Extensions Extending your stay beyond the authorized 90 or 30 days is a time-consuming hassle. It is easier to leave the country for 72 hours or more and then reenter. Otherwise go to the Migración (Immigration) office in San José (☎ 220 0355), opposite Channel 6 about 4km north of Parque La Sabana. Hours are 8 am to 4 pm weekdays, and lines can be long. Requirements for stay extensions change so allow several working days.

If you inadvertently overstay your allotted time, you need an exit visa from Migración to leave the country. Some travel agencies will do the paperwork for you and charge a small processing fee; Tikal Tours is recommended (see Organized Tours).

Onward Ticket
Travelers officially need a ticket out of Costa Rica before they are allowed to enter, but the rules change and are enforced erratically. Those arriving by land can meet this requirement by purchasing an outward ticket from the TICA Bus company, which has offices in both Managua and Panama City.

Driver's License & Permits
If you plan to rent a car, your driver's license from your home country is normally accepted. If you plan to drive down to Costa Rica from North America, you will need all the usual insurance and ownership papers. In addition, you have to buy Costa Rican insurance at the border (about US$20 a

month) and pay a US$10 road tax. You can stay in the country 90 days. If you want to stay longer, you will need to get a Costa Rican driver's license. You are not allowed to sell the car in Costa Rica. If you need to leave the country without the car, you must leave the car in a customs warehouse in San José.

CUSTOMS
Three liters of wine or spirits and 500 cigarettes or 500g of tobacco are allowed duty free. Officially, you are limited to six rolls of film, but this is seldom checked or enforced. There's rarely a problem bringing in items for personal use.

MONEY
Currency
The Costa Rican currency is the *colón* (plural *colones*), normally written as ¢. Bills come in 50, 500, 1000, 5000 and 10,000 colones; coins are 1, 2, 5, 10, 20, 25, 50 and 100 colones.

Exchange Rates
These were the currency exchange rates at the time of publication:

country	unit		colones
Australia	A$1	=	¢172.71
Canada	C$1	=	¢208.43
euro	€1	=	¢283.87
Germany	DM1	=	¢145.03
New Zealand	NZ$1	=	¢134.56
Great Britain	UK£1	=	¢467.49
United States	US$1	=	¢317.07

Exchanging Money
In recent years the exchange rate has dropped steadily against the US dollar and in mid-2000 was hovering at 310 colones to US$1. Travelers should buy US dollars before they arrive. A few non-US currencies can be changed in San José, but rates are poor, and outside of San José, US dollars are the only way to go.

Traveler's checks in US dollars are readily exchanged, but at 1% or 2% lower than the rate for cash. Some banks will take only certain kinds of traveler's checks. Carry your passport when exchanging currency.

Banks can be slow in changing money, especially at the state-run institutions (Banco

Nacional, Banco Central, Banco de Costa Rica). Banking hours are generally 8:30 am to 3:30 or 4 pm Monday to Friday, later in San José. Banco de San José, Banco Cuscatlán and some others are open Saturday morning. Hotels and travel agencies sometimes give the same rate as the banks and are much faster and more convenient.

Changing money on the streets is not recommended, except possibly at land borders. Street changers don't give better rates, and scammers abound. Count your money carefully before handing over your dollars.

If visiting small towns, change enough money beforehand and be sure to get smaller denominations; changing large bills can be difficult in rural areas. Try not to leave the country with many excess colones; it's a hassle to buy back more than US$50 at the border or airport.

Holders of credit and debit cards can buy colones and sometimes US dollars in some banks. Visa and MasterCard are both widely accepted, American Express less so, and commissions are low. Cards linked to currencies other than US dollars get poor rates for cash withdrawal.

If you need money sent from home, you'll find the main branches of San José banks will accept cash transfers but charge a commission. Shop around for the best deal.

ATMs

It's increasingly easy to find ATMs, even in some smaller towns, especially those with a developed tourism industry. The Visa/Plus network is the standard, but machines that accept MasterCard/Cirrus and American Express can be found, and their presence is expanding. Some ATMs, such as those of Banco Nacional, will accept cards held by their own customers only. A handy Web site (http://economicos.nacion.co.cr:81/db/cajeros/list.cfm) will locate ATMs throughout Costa Rica by town and credit/debit card network.

Costs

Travel costs are higher here than in most Central American countries, but less than in the USA or Europe. San José and the most popular tourist areas are more expensive than the rest of the country, and prices are higher in the dry season (December to April).

Budget travelers will find the cheapest hotels start at about US$4 per person for a box with a bed. Fairly decent hotels with private bathrooms and hot water are US$10 per person and up. Cheap meals start at about US$2. Travelers can economize by eating at the lunch-counter places, called *sodas*, and by sticking to the cheaper set lunches offered in many restaurants. A beer will cost US$0.80 to US$2. Movie theaters charge up to US$3.50. National parks have a standard fee of US$6 per person per day.

Transportation is also cheap, with the longest bus journeys, from San José to the Panamanian border, for example, costing about US$8. A taxi, particularly when you're in a group, isn't expensive and costs US$1 to US$2 for short rides.

A budget traveler economizing hard can get by on US$12 to US$20 per day. If you want rooms with private baths and meals other than the daily special, expect to spend about twice that.

Tipping

Better restaurants add 13% tax as well as a 10% tip to the bill. In cheaper places where a service charge is not included, tipping is not expected (Ticos rarely tip) but is certainly appreciated. Taxi drivers are not normally tipped. If you take a guided tour, a tip of about US$1 to US$5 per person per day is about right – depending on the quality of the guide.

POST & COMMUNICATIONS
Sending Mail

Airmail letters to the USA cost about US$0.25 for the first 20g, to Europe and Australia US$0.30. Parcels can be mailed at the rate of US$2.50 per ½ kilo.

Receiving Mail

You can receive mail at the main post office of major towns. Mail to San José's central post office should be addressed 'c/o Lista de Correos, Correos Central, San José, Costa Rica.' Letters usually arrive within a week from North America; it takes a little longer from more distant places. The post office will hold mail for 30 days from the date it's received; there's a US$0.20 fee per letter. Avoid having parcels sent to you, as they are held in customs and cannot be retrieved until you have paid the exorbitant customs fees.

Telephone

Public phones are found all over Costa Rica and accept either coins – of 10 and 20 colones – or the far more convenient Chip telephone cards, available in 500, 1000 and 2000 colones denominations. Chip card phones can now be found even in small villages. Another kind of card in use works on any touch-tone phone by dialing a toll-free three-digit number and punching in the card's account number. There are two kinds: Colibrí (dial ☎ 197) for calls within Costa Rica, available in 100, 200, 300, 400, 500 and 1000 colones denominations, and Viajera (dial ☎ 199) for international calls, available in US$10 and US$20 denominations. A frustrating drawback of the Colibrí cards is that the toll-free number is continuously busy at peak hours. All of these cards can be purchased at Instituto Costarricense de Electricidad (ICE) telephone agencies, banks and at stores and newsstands.

There are no area codes; just dial the seven-digit number. For directory information, call ☎ 113. Hotels in remote areas sometimes receive messages on pagers, called 'beepers' in Costa Rica.

The cheapest international calls are direct-dialed using a phone card. Costs of calls per minute from Costa Rica are approximately US$0.55 to North America, US$0.80 to Europe and Australia. Cheaper rates are available from 10 pm to 7 am.

For collect calls, dial ☎ 116 on any phone for an English-speaking international operator. Countries having reciprocal agreements with Costa Rica will accept collect calls. You can also reach operators in 32 foreign countries by dialing the appropriate 800 number, after which you can call collect or use your credit card. Check the phone directory for a list of these, or dial ☎ 124.

To call Costa Rica from abroad, use the international code (☎ 506) before the seven-digit Costa Rican telephone number.

Email & Internet Access

Cybercafes are opening all over Costa Rica, particularly along the international travelers' circuit. In San José they've become as ubiquitous as sodas. Prices have standardized by geographical area: The normal rate

in the capital is US$1.75 per hour, slightly more in other large towns, and US$6 per hour in harder-to-reach places. The post office is investing considerable resources in the Internet wave via its Punto Com program, and it is already possible to log on at post office branches throughout the republic for a standard rate of US$1.75 per hour, regardless of location. Hotels, too, are increasingly offering Internet access.

INTERNET RESOURCES

A useful background site on many aspects of Costa Rica is www.lanic.utexas.edu/la/ca/cr/. The official country site is the memorably named www.cr, but it is mainly in Spanish. For links to anything from weather reports to gay nightlife to cosmetic surgery to the Costa Rica Chess Federation, try www.yellowweb.co.cr.

Though primarily aimed at well-heeled travelers, the following travel-oriented sites provide abundant information on domestic air service, car rentals, recreational opportunities and language courses: Costa Rica's Travelnet (www.centralamerica.com/cr/index.htm), Costa Rica Travelweb (www.crica.com) and ClickonCosta Rica.com (www.clickoncostarica.com).

BOOKS

Readers planning an extended visit to Costa Rica should pick up the comprehensive Lonely Planet's *Costa Rica*. The Tico Times' *Exploring Costa Rica* is an up-to-date traveler's sourcebook with plenty of color maps.

Costa Rica: The Ecotravellers' Wildlife Guide, by Les Beletsky, is the best book of its kind if you want just one guidebook for everything. *A Guide to the Birds of Costa Rica,* by F Gary Stiles and Alexander F Skutch, is an excellent, thorough book and the only one recommended for bird watching. Louise H Emmons' *Neotropical Rainforest Mammals – A Field Guide* describes and illustrates about 300 mammal species found in Costa Rica and other tropical countries. *The Butterflies of Costa Rica and Their Natural History,* by Philip J DeVries, is recommended for lepidopterists. The entertaining and readable *Tropical Nature,* by Adrian Forsyth and Ken Miyata, is recommended for the layperson interested in biology, particularly of the rain forest.

A book with a historical perspective on politics and social change in Costa Rica is *The Costa Ricans,* by Richard Biesanz. *The Ticos: Culture and Social Change in Costa Rica,* by Mavis Biesanz, is a more recent (1998) resource. Written by former Peace Corps volunteer Paula Palmer, *What Happen: A Folk History of Costa Rica's Talamanca Coast* and *Wa'apin Man,* portray the people of the south Caribbean coast. Though out of print, these still show up in bookstores.

Costa Rica – A Traveler's Literary Companion, edited by Barbara Ras, is a fine collection of 26 short stories by modern Costa Rican writers. *La Loca de Gandoca,* by Anacristina Rossi (EDUCA, San José), describes the struggle of a local conservationist trying to halt the development of a hotel in a protected area of the Caribbean coast, as well as problems with corruption at various levels of government. Although the characters are imaginary and any similarity to reality is coincidental, local cognoscenti will tell you that remarkably similar events happened here recently. It's available in Spanish only, but it's short and simply written, making it a good choice for those interested in local conservation issues, even if their Spanish is limited.

NEWSPAPERS & MAGAZINES

The best local daily newspapers are *La Nación* and *La República,* both fairly conservative. The former maintains a Web site (www.nacion.co.cr) where you can peruse the headlines in English. *La Prensa Libre* is an afternoon paper with a left-wing slant. *The Tico Times* (www.ticotimes.net), the English-language newspaper, is published Friday. You'll find some US and other newspapers (one or two days late) and magazines such as *Time* and *Newsweek* at Casa de las Revistas, on Calle 5 near Parque Morazán, and elsewhere.

RADIO & TV

Fifteen local TV stations broadcast an uninspiring mix of soap operas and standard US fare dubbed in Spanish, along with sports and local news. The Universidad de Costa Rica channel (15) airs some interesting cultural and current affairs programs. Many hotels and bars receive US cable TV.

Of the more than 100 local radio stations on the air in San José, Rock 107.5 FM has a 'classic rock' format with English-speaking DJs plus the BBC world news. Radio Universidad (96.7 FM) is the classical station, and Radio Sinfonola (90.3 FM) plays an intriguing variety of vintage Latin music. You can hear Costa Rican folk, classical, jazz and world music on Radio Nacional de Costa Rica (101.5 FM).

PHOTOGRAPHY

Camera gear is expensive in Costa Rica and film choice is limited. Film is easily developed, but serious photographers prefer to bring their film home to their favorite processing lab.

When taking photographs in the rain forest you will need high-speed film, flash or a tripod. The light penetrating the layers of vegetation is surprisingly dim.

If you're flying out of San José's international airport, carry all your film separately. The X-ray machine there is vicious.

See Photography in the Regional Facts for the Visitor chapter for more information on photography and equipment.

TIME

Costa Rica is six hours behind Greenwich mean time (GMT), the same as central time in the USA. There is no daylight saving time.

ELECTRICITY

Electricity is 110V AC at 60Hz (same as the USA). You will need a voltage converter if you want to use 240/250V AC-powered items. Outlets take US-style two-pronged plugs.

LAUNDRY

Self-service laundries are scarce in Costa Rica. A few exist in San José, but these charge the same rate whether you do your laundry yourself or they do it for you – between US$4 and US$5 a load wash and dry. Many hotels charge about US$1 per change of clothes; allow two or three days if it's raining and they can't be dried. Some cheaper hotels have sinks where you can hand wash your clothing.

HEALTH

Costa Rica has one of the highest standards of health care and hygiene in Latin America. The authorities do not, at present,

COSTA RICA

require anyone to have an up-to-date international vaccination card to enter the country, though you should make sure that your vaccinations are up to date.

Water is usually safe in San José and the major towns, though you should purify it or drink bottled drinks in out-of-the-way places, especially in the lowlands. Uncooked fruits and vegetables are best avoided unless they are peeled.

The social security hospitals in the major cities provide free emergency services to everyone, including foreigners. Private clinics are also available. An emergency phone number worth knowing is the Red Cross (Cruz Roja; ☎ 128, no coin needed) for ambulances in the San José area. Outside San José, the Cruz Roja has a different number in each province:

Alajuela	☎ 441 3939
Cartago	☎ 551 0421
Heredia	☎ 237 1115
Guanacaste	☎ 666 0994
Puerto Limón	☎ 798 1690
Puntarenas	☎ 661 1945

Also see Health in the Facts for the Visitor chapter, and see Dangers & Annoyances for other emergency numbers.

WOMEN TRAVELERS
Women are traditionally respected in Costa Rica (Mother's Day is a national holiday!) but only recently have women made gains in the workplace. Both vice presidents (Costa Rica has two) elected in 1998 were women, Astrid Fischel and Elizabeth Odio. Women routinely occupy roles in the political, legal, scientific and medical professions.

Despite this, Costa Rican men generally consider *gringas* to have looser morals and to be easier conquests than Ticas. They will often make flirtatious comments to single women, both local and foreign. Women traveling together are not exempt from this; women traveling with men are less likely to receive attention. Comments are rarely blatantly rude; the usual thing is a smiling 'mi amor' or an appreciative hiss. The best way to deal with this is to do what the Ticas do – ignore the comments completely and don't look at the man making them.

Costa Ricans are generally quite conservative in their manner of dress. Women travelers are advised to follow suit to avoid calling unnecessary attention to themselves.

GAY & LESBIAN TRAVELERS
The situation for gay and lesbian travelers is poor, though better than in most Central American countries. Most Costa Ricans are tolerant at a 'Don't ask; don't tell' level. Costa Rica's gays and lesbians made some significant strides during the 1990s. The Supreme Court ruled against police harassment in gay nightspots and affirmed the right of people with AIDS to receive state-of-the-art medical treatment. And in 2000 a prominent TV anchorman publicly announced his homosexuality. Despite the gains, this conservative society still frowns upon same-sex relationships, and gay and lesbian Costa Ricans face widespread discrimination in their daily lives.

Gay visitors to the capital can rely on an established support network and choose from a variety of social venues. Agua Buena Human Rights Association (☎ 234 2411, rastern@sol.racsa.co.cr) can recommend gay-friendly hotels, bars and meeting places in Costa Rica. The monthly newspaper *Gayness* is available at gay bars listed in the San José Entertainment section and at the Candy Shop, a newsstand beside the Gran Hotel in San José. Apart from the capital, the Pacific coast resort of Quepos has become the center of an expatriate gay community with several gay-oriented businesses and hotels.

DISABLED TRAVELERS
Although Costa Rica has an equal opportunity law for disabled people, its provisions are much less strict than those of similar laws in many other countries. Still, it is a small move in the right direction for disabled people. Unfortunately, the law applies only to new or newly remodeled businesses (including hotels and restaurants), so older businesses (built prior to the mid-1990s) are exempt. New businesses are required to have a barrier free entrance for disabled people.

Realistically, independent travel is difficult for disabled people. Very few hotels and restaurants, except for the newest, have features specifically suited to wheelchair use, for example. Many don't even have the basic minimum of a wheelchair ramp and room or bathroom doors wide enough to accommodate a wheelchair. Special phones for hearing impaired people or signs in Braille for blind people are very rare.

Outside of the buildings, streets and sidewalks are potholed and poorly paved, making wheelchair use frustrating everywhere. Public buses don't have provisions that allow wheelchairs to be carried.

Organizations
Vaya con Silla de Ruedas (☎ 391 5045, fax 454 2810, vayacon@sol.racsa.co.cr) translates into 'Go with Wheelchairs.' This company has a van specially designed to transport travelers in wheelchairs; equipment meets international accessibility standards and up to three wheelchairs can be transported. It can help with other arrangements such as bilingual guides, hotel reservations, and tours lasting anywhere from a few hours to a few days. Its Web site (www.gowithwheelchairs.com) has links to other sites of interest to disabled visitors to Costa Rica and Nicaragua.

La Fundacion Kosta Roda (☎/fax 771 7482, chabote@sol.racsa.co.cr), in San Isidro, is a nonprofit organization working with the ICT to list accessible sites of interest to disabled travelers.

DANGERS & ANNOYANCES
Tourist-oriented crime has increased recently, probably because there are many more visitors. However, you'll find Costa Rica is still less prone to theft than many countries. You should, nevertheless, take simple precautions, as recommended in the introductory chapters.

If you are robbed, police reports (for insurance claims) should be filed with the Organismo de Investigación Judicial (OIJ; ☎ 222 1365) in the Corte Suprema de Justicia (Supreme Court) complex on Avenida 6, between Calles 17 and 19, in San José.

Be aware of the dangers of riptides – strong currents that pull the swimmer out to sea – on both coasts. Few beaches have lifeguards. River rafting expeditions may be particularly risky during periods of heavy rain – flash floods have been known to capsize rafts. Reputable tour operators will ensure conditions are safe before setting out; some are listed in the Organized Tours section, later.

If you are caught in an earthquake, the best shelter in a building is in a doorframe or under a sturdy table. In the open, don't stand near anything that could collapse on you.

The general emergency number (☎ 911) is available in the central provinces and is expanding. Police (☎ 117) and fire (☎ 118) are, theoretically, reachable throughout the country.

BUSINESS HOURS
Government offices are open 8 am to 4 pm Monday to Friday, often closing between about 11:30 am and 1 pm. Stores are open 8 am to 6 or 7 pm Monday to Saturday, but a two-hour lunch break is not uncommon.

PUBLIC HOLIDAYS & SPECIAL EVENTS
The dates below are official national holidays when banks and businesses are closed throughout the country.

New Year's Day	January 1
Semana Santa (Holy Week)	Thursday and Friday before Easter
Día de Juan Santamaría	April 11
Labor Day	May 1
Día de Guanacaste	July 25
Virgen de Los Angeles	August 2
Día de la Madre (Mother's Day)	August 15
Independence Day	September 15
Día de la Raza (Columbus Day)	October 12
Día de Navidad (Christmas Day)	December 25

The week between Christmas and New Year's Day tends to be an unofficial holiday, especially in San José, celebrated with bullfights, equestrian events and a dance on New Year's Eve.

There are no buses at all on the Thursday afternoon and Friday before Easter, and many businesses close for the week preceding the holiday *(Semana Santa)*. From Thursday to Easter Sunday, all bars are closed and alcohol sales are prohibited.

ACTIVITIES
The wonderful array of parks and preserves and their attendant wildlife and scenery draw travelers from all over the

world. Outdoors enthusiasts will find many adventurous activities.

Wildlife Watching

Birding in Costa Rica is considered world class. Most visitors also see monkeys, sloths, leaf-cutter ants, blue morpho butterflies, poison arrow frogs, crocodiles and iguanas, to name a few. The national parks are good places for observation, but private areas such as gardens around rural hotels can also yield a good number of birds, insects, reptiles and even monkeys. Early morning and late afternoon are the best times to watch for wildlife, and a pair of binoculars will improve observation tremendously.

Have realistic expectations. It's hard to see wildlife in the rain forest because the vegetation is so thick. You could be 15m from a jaguar and not even know it is there. Walk slowly and quietly; listen as well as look.

Surfing

There are dozens of recognized surfing areas, most are uncrowded and have good waves. Places in Jacó, Quepos, Tamarindo and Puerto Viejo de Talamanca rent boards. Surf over to www.crsurf.com for tide and surf reports.

Rafting

One-day white-water trips on the popular Río Reventazón and the Río Pacuare, including roundtrip bus transportation from San José and lunch, start at around US$69 per person. Tour operators provide rafts, paddles, life jackets and guides for these adventures. Be sure to choose an operator with experienced guides, some of which are recommended in Organized Tours, later.

Scuba Diving & Snorkeling

The water in Costa Rica is warm, with plenty of marine life, though visibility is often low. Good places for diving are at Playa del Coco, Playa Ocotal and Playa Hermosa, where you can do a couple of boat dives for US$70 per person or learn to dive. The best snorkeling is at Manuel Antonio, Montezuma and Cahuita.

Hiking & Backpacking

Some of the best trips are at Parque Nacional Corcovado for rain forest backpacking,

Santa Rosa for tropical dry forest camping and Chirripó for highland hiking.

Windsurfing

Complete windsurfing equipment is available for rent in several hotels at the west end of Laguna Arenal, which is considered one of the best areas in the world for this activity. Consistently high winds attract experienced surfers – beginners will require expert instruction.

Horseback Riding

Wherever you go, you are sure to find someone renting horses or giving riding tours along the beaches or up into the mountains. Rates vary from about US$40 to US$100 a day, and overnight trips can be arranged. Avoid renting from unscrupulous outfitters who overwork their horses for a quick profit, an abuse often witnessed along the popular Arenal to Monteverde ride.

Rain Forest Canopy Tours

These give you the chance to survey the rain forest from above via ropes, cables and elevated platforms. The emphasis is on the sheer thrill of flying over the treetops rather than the opportunity to observe wildlife. Variations are found around Costa Rica, with several tours operating in the Monteverde area.

Sea Kayaking

Many places along the coast rent sea kayaks. Fun and easy to learn, this activity allows you to enter remote areas where wildlife may be easily spotted.

LANGUAGE COURSES

Spending a month learning Spanish in Costa Rica is an excellent and recommended way of seeing and learning about the country. Courses are offered mainly in San José, but they are also available in Alajuela, Dominical and a few other places. See the San José section for a list of language schools.

WORK

Getting a bona fide job necessitates obtaining a work permit, a time-consuming process. The most likely source of paid employment is as an English teacher in language institutes in San José, which advertise courses in the local newspapers.

Volunteer work in nature preserves or national parks is sometimes possible. Volunteers pay US$5 to US$12 per day toward costs, including room and board. Prospective volunteers must provide two letters of recommendation and should be able to speak some Spanish. For an application, contact the Asociación de Voluntarios para el Servicio en las Areas Protegidas de Costa Rica (ASVO); ☎/fax 233 4989, asvo89@sol.racsa.co.cr) or write to Apartado Postal 11384-1000 in San José.

ACCOMMODATIONS

There is a small youth hostel system that charges US$11 per night at the main hostel in San José, more elsewhere. Inexpensive camping facilities are available in many national parks.

Cheap hotels can be found in almost every town, ranging from about US$4 per person up to US$20 for a double room. Although the hotels are sometimes very basic, they can nevertheless be well looked after and can be an amazing value. You'll usually have to use communal bathrooms in the cheapest hotels, but you can sometimes find rooms with a private bathroom for as low as US$10 a double.

Cheap hotels may advertise hot water, but if water is supplied by an electric shower, it's usually tepid. These contraptions are not as dangerous as they appear. Used toilet paper should be placed in the receptacle provided – the plumbing cannot handle the paper.

Beach hotel choices may be limited during dry season weekends, and single rooms are generally scarce. *Cabinas,* as these hotels are typically called, are aimed at large families, so may have four to six beds in a room – a cheap per-person choice if you're traveling in a small group. High season (Christmas to Easter) rates are given in the text. Expect substantial discounts in the wet season.

FOOD

A good way to economize is to eat the set meal offered in most restaurants at lunchtime; it's usually filling and cheap. Another possibility is to try the inexpensive luncheon counters called sodas. There are reasonably priced Chinese and Italian restaurants in most towns. Better restaurants add a 13% tax plus 10% service to the bill.

Costa Rican specialties include the following items:

arroz con pollo – a basic dish of rice and chicken

casado – a filling and economical platter of rice, black beans, fried plantain, meat or fish, chopped cabbage and maybe an egg or an avocado; *casado vegetariano* is minus the meat

elote – corn on the cob

gallo pinto – a lightly spiced mixture of rice and black beans that is traditionally served for breakfast, sometimes with *natilla* (a form of sour cream) or fried eggs

palmitos – hearts of palm, usually served in a salad with vinegar dressing; *pejibaye* – a rather starchy tasting palm fruit also eaten as a salad

rondón – thick seafood based soup blended with coconut milk, found on the Caribbean side

tortillas – either Mexican-style corn pancakes or Spanish omelets, depending on what kind of meal you're having

Traditional desserts include:

cajeta – similar to dulce de leche, but thicker, like fudge

dulce de leche – milk and sugar boiled to make a thick syrup that may be used in a layered cake called torta chilena

flan – a cold caramel custard

mazamorra – a pudding made from cornstarch

queque seco – pound cake

The following are snacks, often obtained in sodas:

arreglados – little puff pastries stuffed with beef, chicken or cheese

ceviche – seafood marinated with lemon, onion, garlic, sweet red peppers and coriander; can be made with *corvina* (a white sea bass), *langostinos* (shrimps) or *conchas* (conch)

empanadas – Chilean-style turnovers stuffed with meat or cheese and raisins

gallos – tortilla sandwiches containing meat, beans or cheese

patacones – a Caribbean specialty consisting of slices of deep-fried plantain

tamales – boiled or steamed cornmeal filled with chicken or pork, usually wrapped in a banana leaf (you don't eat the leaf)

tamales asado – sweet cornmeal cakes

DRINKS
Nonalcoholic

Coffee, tea and herbal tea are easily found. The usual soft drinks are available. *Refrescos* are drinks made with local fruits. *Pipas* are green coconuts with a straw stuck in to drink the coconut milk – a slightly bitter but refreshing and filling drink. *Agua dulce* is boiled water mixed with brown sugar, and *horchata* is a rice-based drink flavored with cinnamon.

Alcoholic

Costa Ricans like to drink, though they don't like drunks. Most restaurants serve a variety of alcoholic beverages. Imported drinks are expensive, but local ones are quite cheap. There are five local beers, of which Imperial and Pilsen are the most popular. The local wines are cheap, taste cheap and provide a memorable hangover. Distilled liquor is made from Costa Rican–grown sugarcane. The cheapest is *guaro*, the local firewater, drunk by the shot. Also inexpensive and good is local rum, usually drunk as a *cuba libre* (rum and Coke). A locally made coffee liqueur is Café Rica.

Many bars traditionally serve *bocas*. These are little savory side dishes designed to make your drink more pleasurable – maybe you'll have another one! If you have several rounds, you can eat enough bocas to make a very light meal. Some bars charge a small amount extra for them, and a few don't have them at all.

ENTERTAINMENT

San José has the best selection of entertainment, though it is modest compared to many other capital cities. Traditionally, family get-togethers are what Ticos do to entertain themselves. There are plenty of cinemas, theaters, and nightclubs in San José (see details in that chapter), but relatively few elsewhere. Costa Rica is not a destination for travelers looking for nightlife.

SPECTATOR SPORTS

Fútbol (soccer) is the national sport, and Sunday games have a strong following of (mostly male) fans. Competition is fierce. The regular season is from August to May, but postseason play fills out the rest of the year.

Bullfighting is also popular (the bull is not killed in Costa Rican bullfighting).

SHOPPING

Coffee is excellent; many visitors take some freshly roasted coffee beans home.

Wood and leather crafts are well made and inexpensive. Wood items include salad bowls, plates, carving boards and other kitchen utensils, jewelry boxes and a variety of carvings and ornaments. Uniquely Costa Rican souvenirs are the colorfully painted replicas of traditional oxcarts *(carretas)* produced in the village of Sarchí.

Other souvenirs include jewelry, leatherwork and ceramics, some of which are replicas of pre-Columbian artifacts. Colorful posters and T-shirts with wildlife, national park and ecological themes are also popular.

Getting There & Away

AIR

Juan Santamaría, the main international airport, is 17km outside San José. There is a US$17 departure tax on international flights from San José, payable in cash US dollars or colones.

Lacsa, the international Costa Rican carrier (part of the TACA Central American airline group) flies to/from the USA, Mexico, Latin America and other Central American countries.

Other airlines serving Costa Rica include American, Continental, United and Delta in the USA, Mexicana, Iberia (Spain), Martinair (Netherlands) and Panama's Copa (for phone numbers and locations of airline offices, see the Getting There & Away section of San José). The main gateway cities from the US are Miami and Houston. At this writing, the lowest fare from Miami to San José was around US$320, flying midweek between August and November.

LAND
Border Crossings

Costa Rica shares land borders with Nicaragua and Panama. There are no problems crossing these borders, provided your papers are in order.

Nicaragua

Via Peñas Blancas The main border post is on the Interamericana at Peñas Blancas in northwestern Costa Rica. The border is open 8 am to 8 pm daily with a break from noon to 1 pm. The earlier in the day that you get there, the better. The Costa Rican and Nicaraguan immigration offices are 500m apart – within walking distance. On the Costa Rican side, Migración (☎ 677 0064) is next to Restaurant La Frontera. A Costa Rican tourist information office (☎ 677 0138) and a bus ticket office are also housed within the immigration building.

Money changers congregate at the Costa Rican post, but the border bank, open during border hours, will cash traveler's checks at better rates. Excess córdobas or colones can be sold at a small loss. The best place to sell córdobas is with the money changers at the Nicaraguan border post.

Travelers on transnational Sirca, Tica Bus, Nica Bus or Trans Nica buses between Managua and San José (and vice versa) should expect to wait at least two or three hours for all passengers to be processed. Alternatively, take a local bus to the border, walk across and then continue on another bus. From Peñas Blancas, there are eight buses a day to Liberia, six to San José (more on Saturday and Sunday), departing between 5 am and 4 pm.

Travelers leaving Costa Rica need no special permit unless they've overstayed their allocated time. Recently, citizens of the USA, UK and many European nations were allowed to enter Nicaragua for up to 90 days with a passport – see that chapter or check with the Nicaraguan Embassy in San José. There are frequent buses to the first Nicaraguan town, Rivas (37km), until 5 pm. Get to the border by early afternoon to get on a bus, and watch your luggage – many cases of pilfering on Nicaraguan buses have been reported.

Via Los Chiles This border crossing is rarely used by foreign travelers. It's reportedly hassle-free if your papers are in order.

Heading north from Los Chiles, a 14km 4WD road goes to San Carlos, Nicaragua, a town on the southeastern corner of Lago Nicaragua. Boats on the Río Frío go from Los Chiles to San Carlos every day. Boats from here go on to Granada, Nicaragua.

Panama

Panama's time zone is one hour ahead of Costa Rica's.

Via Paso Canoas This crossing on the Interamericana is the major border point with Panama. Hours (subject to change) are from 6 am to 9 pm with two breaks (from 11 am to 1 pm and 5 to 6 pm).

Visitors from the UK and some western European countries need only a passport to enter Panama. US, Canadian, New Zealand, Australian and some European citizens and others must buy a tourist card for US$5, which allows for a 30-day stay (the immigration office has been known to run out of tourist cards). Longer stays require a visa, not available at the border. Check with the Panamanian consul in San José (☎ 256 3241) about current requirements. On the Panamanian side, buses go to David about 1½ hours away, where there is a Costa Rican consulate. The last bus is at 7 pm.

Via Sixaola/Guabito This crossing is on the Caribbean coast. See Sixaola for details of how to get there and basic hotels. The border is open 7 to 11 am and 1 to 7 pm daily. From the border, minibuses and taxis make the 16km trip to Changuinola, Panama, where there are several moderately priced hotels and onward connections by bus and air.

Getting Around

AIR

Costa Rica's domestic airlines are Sansa (☎ 221 9414, fax 255 2176), now linked with Grupo TACA, and Travelair (☎ 220 3054, fax 220 0413). Flights on either airline can be booked through any travel agent or through their Web sites (www.flysansa.com, www.travelair-costarica.com).

Sansa services are with small aircraft (14 passengers), and passenger demand is high, so book ahead. The baggage allowance is 12kg. The Sansa terminal is to the right of the international terminal at Juan Santamaría Airport. Travelair flies from Tobías Bolaños Airport in the San José suburb of Pavas, about 5km from the city center. It tends to provide better on-time service and fewer canceled flights than Sansa but charges from 25% to 40% more for a one-way flight, though some Travelair flights are cheaper (La Fortuna, Tortuguero).

Fares given below are for high-season one-way/roundtrip flights from San José and are subject to change. Low-season fares are slightly cheaper. For destinations served by more than one flight daily, the number of flights is in parentheses.

destination	Travelair	Sansa
Barra del Colorado	–	US$55/110
La Fortuna	US$57/94	US$55/110
Golfito	US$84/144	US$65/130 (4)
Liberia	US$92/152	–
Neily/Coto	–	US$65/130
Palmar Sur	US$78/127	US$65/130
Playa Nosara	–	US$65/130
Playa Tamarindo	US$92/152 (3)	US$65/130 (4)
Puerto Jiménez	US$90/152 (2)	US$65/130
Quepos	US$50/80	US$45/90 (4)
Sámara/Carrillo	US$82/134	US$65/130
Tambor	US$60/109	US$55/110 (2)
Tortuguero	US$51/93	US$55/110

BUS

San José is the transportation center for the whole country (see the San José section for details). There is no central bus terminal in the capital, though some smaller towns have one. Larger companies with terminals sell tickets in advance, and companies with just a bus stop expect you to queue for the next bus, but normally there is room for everyone. The exceptions are the days before and after a major holiday, especially Easter, when buses are ridiculously full. Friday night and Saturday morning out of San José can be very crowded, as can Sunday afternoon and evening coming back.

Fares are generally cheap, with the longest journey out of San José running less than US$8.

Buses are of two types: *directo* and *normal* (or *corriente*). The directo buses are faster and about a quarter more expensive. Trips longer than four hours have a rest stop. Luggage space is limited, so leave what you don't need in San José. If you have to check luggage, watch that it gets loaded on the bus and that it isn't 'accidentally' given to the wrong passenger at intermediate stops.

You'll find up-to-date bus schedules, including fares and departure points, on the Web at www.yellowweb.co.cr/crbuses.html.

A reasonable alternative to the standard intercity buses are the van shuttle services provided by Fantasy Bus (☎ 800 326 8279) and Interbus (☎ 283 5573, info@ costaricapass.com). These run vans from San José to all of the most popular destinations, as well as directly between some of those destinations, avoiding the need to return to San José. Fantasy Bus charges a uniform US$19 fare for all journeys, and Interbus fares range from US$17 (San José–Playa Jacó) to US$45 (Monteverde-Papagayo).

CAR & MOTORCYCLE

San José is notorious for its narrow streets, heavy traffic and complicated one-way system. Outside the capital, most roads are single lanes, lack hard shoulders and are very windy – drive carefully. Speed limits are 100km per hour or less on primary roads and 60km per hour or less on others. Traffic police use radar and enforce speed limits. It is illegal to drive without using seat belts.

Unleaded fuel (super) costs about US$0.63 per liter (US$2.40 per US gallon) and costs the same at all fuel stations.

Rental

Most car rental agencies are in San José. Car rental is not cheap, around US$350 per week for a subcompact car in the high season, US$450 for a small air-conditioned Jeep, including mandatory insurance and unlimited mileage (*kilometraje libre*). Generally the insurance has a high deductible (as much as US$1500 in some cases).

Big discounts on rental prices can be found outside the peak tourism season; it's worth calling around. During periods of heavy rain, agencies may insist you rent a 4WD vehicle to drive on dirt roads.

To rent a car you need a valid driver's license, a major credit card and your passport. Your driver's license from home is acceptable for up to 90 days. The minimum age for car rental is 21.

Carefully inspect rented cars for minor damage and ensure it is noted on the rental agreement. Never leave valuables in sight even when you briefly leave the car. Always use a guarded parking lot at night and remove all your luggage.

Small mopeds and dirt bikes can be rented in a few places in San José and along the coast, but they aren't much cheaper than compact cars.

BICYCLE
Costa Rican roads don't have bike lanes, and traffic can be hazardous on the narrow, steep and winding roads. However, touring cyclists report that locals are very friendly.

Mountain bikes and beach bikes can be rented in most highland or coastal towns where there is a significant tourist presence, at the rate of US$8 to US$10 per day.

HITCHHIKING
Hitchhiking is not common on main roads that have frequent buses. On minor rural roads, hitching is possible. Vehicles pass infrequently; wave them down in a friendly fashion and ask for a ride (watch how the locals do it). If you get a ride, offer to pay for it when you arrive: *¿Cuanto le debo?* (How much do I owe you?) Your offer may be waved aside, or you may be asked to help with money for *gasolina*.

Travelers who hitchhike should understand that they are taking a small but potentially serious risk. Single women are urged to use discretion; it's safest to hitch with a friend. Talk to the occupants of the car to get an idea of their disposition. Hitch from somewhere (a gas station, store, restaurant, police post) that you can retreat to if you don't like the look of your prospective ride.

BOAT
Car and passenger ferries from Puntarenas cross the Golfo de Nicoya several times daily for Playa Naranjo and Paquera with bus connections to Montezuma. Another car ferry traverses the mouth of the Río Tempisque to the Península de Nicoya.

A daily passenger ferry links Golfito with Puerto Jiménez on the Península de Osa.

Motorized dugout canoes ply the Río Sarapiquí once a day on a scheduled basis and can be hired to the Río San Juan, which forms the Nicaraguan border. It is also possible to arrange boat trips up the inland waterway from Moín (near Limón) to Tortuguero.

LOCAL TRANSPORTATION
Taxis serve not only urban areas but also remote parts of the country. They may be an option for getting to destinations, such as national parks, where public buses are unavailable. An excursion from Liberia to Rincón de la Vieja National Park, for example, will cost less than US$50 roundtrip, not a bad deal if sharing with other travelers.

ORGANIZED TOURS
More than 200 tour operators are recognized by the Costa Rica Tourist Board, with the majority in San José. Most tours are beyond the budget of readers of this book, but a few reasonably priced options exist. Ecole Travel (☎ 223 2240, fax 223 4128, ecolecer@sol.racsa.co.cr), Calle 7, Avenidas Central and 1, specializes in budget travel, especially to Tortuguero. 'Budget' means that you might stay in rock bottom–priced hotels and that meals aren't included.

Many companies specialize in nature tours, with visits to the national parks and wilderness lodges. The biggest and longest running of these tours is Costa Rica Expeditions (☎ 257 0766, fax 257 1665), Calle Central, Avenida 3. Its guides are well-qualified naturalists and ornithologists. Also recommended are Horizontes (☎ 222 2022, fax 255 4513), Calle 28, Avenidas 1 and 3, and Costa Rica Sun Tours (☎ 255 3418, fax 255 4410) at Calle 36, Avenida 4. Tikal (☎ 223 2811, 257 1494, fax 223 1916), Avenida 2, Calles 7 and 9, has a wide variety of tours ranging from day trips to weeklong excursions.

Companies specializing in river rafting include Ríos Tropicales (☎ 233 6455, fax 255 4354), Calle 32, Avenida 2; Aventuras Naturales (☎ 225 3939, fax 253 6934), Avenida Central, Calles 33 and 35; and the aforementioned Costa Rica Expeditions. Rafting tours start at around US$70 a day including transportation from San José, use of equipment and meals. Iguana Tours (☎/fax 777 1262, info@iguanatours.com) does rafting and kayaking trips from Parque Nacional Manuel Antonio.

Canopy Tour (☎/fax 257 5149), in San José, has pioneered rain forest canopy tours near Monteverde and at Iguana Park near Orotina.
Web site: www.canopytour.com

San José

pop 330,000 • metropolitan area 900,000
Compared with other Central American
capitals, San José is more cosmopolitan,
even North American in character. There
are department stores and shopping malls,
fast-food restaurants and blue jeans. It
takes a day or two to get the real Tico feel
of the city. Perhaps the first sign of being in
Costa Rica is the friendliness of the people.
Asking someone the way will often result
in a smile and a genuine attempt to help
out. Inhabitants of San José are called
josefinos.

The city was founded in 1737, but little
remains from the colonial era. Until the
Teatro Nacional was built in the 1890s, San
José was not a notable city. Today the
capital boasts numerous fine museums and
restaurants, which combined with a pleasing
highland climate make for a worthwhile
visit. Costa Rica's road system radiates from
San José, and the capital is a good base from
which to visit the rest of the country.

Orientation

The city is at 1150m above sea level, in a
wide and fertile valley called the Meseta
Central.

The city center is arranged in a grid.
Streets are numbered in a logical fashion –
learn the system because all street addresses
rely on it. *Avenidas* run east to west and
calles run north to south. Avenidas south of
Avenida Central ascend by even numbers
(Avenida 2, Avenida 4), and those to the
north are odd. Similarly, calles west of Calle
Central are even-numbered, and those to
the east are odd. Avenida Central becomes
Paseo Colón west of Calle 14.

Street addresses are given by the nearest
street intersection. Thus the address of the
tourist office is Calle 5, (between) Avenidas
Central and 2. This is often abbreviated to
C5, A Ctl/2, or C5, A 0/2. The same system is
used in many other Costa Rican towns.

Ticos use landmarks to give directions or
even addresses; an address may be 200m
south and 150m east of a church, store or
radio station. A city block is called *cien
metros*, literally 100m, so if someone says
'250 metros al sur,' they mean 2½ blocks
south, regardless of the actual distance.

The center has several districts, or
barrios. Perhaps the most interesting to
downtown visitors is Barrio Amón, northeast of Avenida 5 and Calle 1, with the best
concentration of turn-of-the-century buildings. East of downtown is the semiresiden-
tial barrio of Los Yoses, followed by San
Pedro, a major suburb in its own right and
the site of the main university. West of the
center is La Sabana, named after the biggest
park in San José.

Information

Tourist Offices The main office of the Instituto Costarricense de Turismo (ICT;
☎ 222 1090, 223 1733 ext 277, fax 223 5452,
info@tourism-costarica.com) is on the Plaza
de la Cultura at Calle 5 and Avenida
Central, next to the Museo de Oro. It's open
9 am to 5 pm Monday to Friday, with a flexible lunch hour.
Web site: www.tourism-costarica.com

Money Any bank will change US dollars
into colones; some change other currencies
as well. Commissions, when charged, should
be small (1% or less); otherwise, go elsewhere. Banco Nacional de Costa Rica and
Banco de Costa Rica are very slow. The
private banks like Banco de San José (☎ 256
9911), Calle Central, Avenidas 3 and 5, and
Banco Metropolitano (☎ 257 3030), Calle
Central and Avenida 2, have faster service.
Most banks are open 8 am to 4 pm Monday
to Friday. Banco de San José also has Saturday hours.

The exchange house Compañía Financiera de Londres (☎ 222 8155), at Calle
Central and Avenida Central, gives good
rates, fast service and accepts currencies
other than US dollars.

Most of the major banks have 24-hour
ATMs. Some accept only locally issued
cards; those bearing the Cirrus or Plus logos
accept cards from foreign banks. Convenient ATMs are located at the western entrance of the Omni Center, inside the Banco
de San José and at the airport. Withdrawal
limits can vary significantly.

Credomatic (☎ 224 2155), with branches
in the Omni Center and inside the Banco de
San José, gives cash advances on Visa and
MasterCard. American Express (☎ 257
0846), in the same bank, sells US-dollar
traveler's checks to its cardholders.

Post & Communications The correo central (central post office) is on Calle 2, Avenidas 1 and 3. Hours are 8 am to 5 pm Monday to Friday. This is the best post office at which to receive mail. It also boasts a new Internet facility (see Email & Internet Access). You can make local and international calls from most public telephones, which are found all over town – several dozen are on the west side of Parque Central. Public phones accept 10- and 20-colón coins, Chip phone cards or Colibrí cards, which are sold at the ICE office near the Plaza de la Cultura, open 8 am to 8 pm daily, and at stores and newsstands. To make international calls for cash, go to Radiográfica, at Calle 1, Avenida 5, open 7 am to 9 pm daily. This facility also offers email, telex, and fax services.

Cybercafes are springing up all over; downtown it seems they're on every other block. Strong competition keeps access fees down to US$2 per hour or less. One of the cheapest options is the central post office, which charges US$1.75 per hour or US$1 per half hour. The facility, on the south side of the building, is open 8 am to 10 pm daily. Internet Café Costa Rica has two branches on Avenida Central – one at Calle 11, one opposite the Banco Central – another in San Pedro 75m west of Banco Popular and one more in the Centro Colón on Paseo Colón. Access is by the hour only (US$1.75), so if you're online 62 minutes, you'll be charged for two hours. All branches are open 8 am to midnight, except the San Pedro branch, open 24 hours. Other facilities include Internet Club (open 24 hours) on Calle 7 and Cybercafé search-costarica.com on Avenida 2 beside the Gran Hotel Costa Rica. In San Pedro, the well-designed Net Café, on Calle 3, charges just US$1.50 an hour, less for blocks of 15 hours or more.

Travel Agencies TAM (☎ 256 0203, fax 222 8092, info@tamtravel.com), at Calle 1, Avenidas Central and 1, has been recommended for airline ticketing and general sightseeing. Cosmos Tours (☎ 234 0607, fax 253 4707, cosmos@sol.racsa.co.cr), Avenida 7, Calles 37 and 39, is good for airline reservations and hotel and tour bookings.

Other agencies recommended by readers for general travel and tours include Central

American Tours (☎ 255 4111, fax 236 5270), with an office in the Cariari Hotel, and Camino Travel (☎ 257 0107, fax 257 0243), Calle 1, Avenidas Central and 1.

Two local agencies specializing in student and youth airline fares are OTEC (☎ 256 0633, fax 233 2321, otec@gotec.com), Calle 3, Avenida 3, and Viajes Sin Limites (☎ 280 5182, info@sinlimites.co.cr) on Avenida Central in Los Yoses.

Bookstores Seventh Street Books (☎ 256 8251), Calle 7, Avenidas Central and 1, has books in English and houses the budget agency Ecole Travel. Casa de las Revistas, Calle 5 just south of Parque Morazán, offers a complete range of foreign (mostly US) magazines and newspapers. Mora Books (☎ 255 4136) is a cluttered secondhand store in the Omni Center, specializing in guidebooks and comic books.

Librería Internacional (☎ 253 9553), north of the San Pedro Mall, offers a range of Latin American and world literature. Tienda de Libros Madre Natura (☎ 225 2385), in San Pedro off Calle Central by the railroad tracks, specializes in books on biology, the environment and nature, in Spanish and English, including an impressive array of wildlife and travel guides.

Laundry There are few laundromats in San José (though plenty of dry cleaners). Downtown, Lavandería Sixaola (☎ 221 2111), Avenida 2, Calles 7 and 9, charges US$4 a load (wash and dry) with same-day service. Lavandería Lavamex (☎ 258 2303), Calle 8, Avenidas Central and 1 (across from the mercado central), will wash and dry your clothes in about three hours at US$6 per load.

In San Pedro, Burbujas (☎ 224 9822), 50m west and 25m south of the Más x Menos Supermercado, has coin-operated machines.

Medical Services The free Hospital San Juan de Dios (☎ 257 6282) is centrally located at Paseo Colón, Calle 14. The best private clinic is the Clínica Bíblica (☎ 257 5252, press '2' for emergencies), on Avenida 14, Calles Central and 1, open 24 hours for emergencies. The hospital employs some English-speaking staff and carries out laboratory tests.

SAN JOSÉ

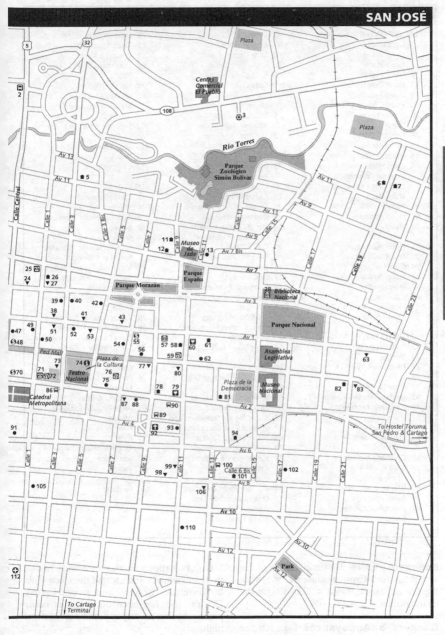

SAN JOSÉ

PLACES TO STAY
5   Casa Hilda
6   Hotel Aranjuez
7   Kap's Place
10 Hotel Marlyn
11 Hotel Don Carlos
12 Hotel Astoria
19 Hotel Compostela
20 Nuevo Hotel Central
21 Hotel Capital
26 Pensión Otoya
33 Hotel Boruca
35 Hotel Bienvenido; Meylin 2
46 Gran Hotel Imperial; Gran
    Imperial Restaurant;
    Lavandería Lavamex
58 Hotel Asia
61 Pensión de la Cuesta
66 Hotel Johnson
78 Hotel Avenida 2; Casa del
    Sandwich
81 Hotel Nicaragua
82 Hotel Bellavista
94 Casa Leo
96 Hotel Príncipe
97 Hotel Boston
101 Casa Ridgway
104 Hotel Ritz; Pensión Centro
    Continental

PLACES TO EAT
22 Soda Nini
24 Vishnu
27 Restaurant Yud Fad
38 Vishnu
41 Soda La Central
43 Restaurante Lung Mun
44 Pastelería Merayo
51 Vishnu
53 La Vasconia
63 El Cuartel de la Boca del
    Monte
68 Churrería Manolos
73 Café Parisien
77 Chelle's
80 Churrería Manolos
83 Restaurant Aya Sofía
87 Restaurante Pollo
    Campesino

98 Vishnu
99 Restaurante Tin-jo
103 Soda Castro
106 Restaurant Shakti
108 Soda Comilona #3
109 Soda Comilona #1

OTHER
1   Museo de los Niños,
    National Auditorium
3   Spirogyra Jardín de
    Mariposas
13 Casa Amarilla
23 Banco de San José;
    American Express;
    Credomatic
25 Radiográfica
28 Museo de Arte y Diseño
    Contemporáneo
36 Punto Com (Internet)
37 Costa Rica Expeditions
39 OTEC Travel
40 Salsa 54; Zadidas
42 Casa de las Revistas
47 La Casona
48 Compañía Financiera de
    Londres (Money Exchange)
49 Las Risas
50 TAM Travel Agency
52 Omni Center; Mora Books;
    Credomatic
54 Ecole Travel & 7th Street
    Books
55 Banco de Costa Rica
56 El Túnel de Tiempo Disco
57 Serpentario
59 Internet Café Costa Rica
60 Rico's Jazz Central
62 Más x Menos Supermercado
67 Internet Café Costa Rica
69 Teatro Melico Salazar
70 Banco Metropolitano
71 ICE Telephone Office
72 Cybercafé
    searchcostarica.com
74 ICT Tourism Information
    Office; Museo de Oro
    Precolombino
75 Bar La Esmeralda

76 Internet Club
79 Tiny's Sports Bar
84 Iglesia La Merced
88 Lavandería Sixaola; Tikal
    Tours
91 Los Cucharones
92 Iglesia La Soledad
93 Mercado Nacional de
    Artesanía
102 Supreme Court of Justice
105 La Avispa
110 Soda Blues
111 Deja Vú
112 Clínica Bíblica

BUS STOPS
2   Caribe Terminal
4   Puerto Jiménez
8   Atlántico Norte Terminal
9   Bejuco
14 Managua
15 Nicoya, Sámara, Tamarindo,
    San Vito & David (Panama)
16 Managua, Nicaraguan
    Border, Panama City &
    Changuinola
17 Playas Panamá & Hermosa
18 Upala
29 Tobias Bolaños Airport
30 Cañas, Playa Flamingo,
    Playa Panamá
31 San Isidro de El General
32 Cañas, San Isidro de El
    General
34 Playa del Coco
45 Escazú
64 Alajuela & Poás
65 Alajuela; Juan Santamaría
    Airport
85 Heredia
86 Irazú
89 Tica Bus (International)
90 San Pedro
95 Escazú
100 Turrialba
107 Puntarenas

Emergency Call ☎ 911 for all emergencies, ☎ 128 for Red Cross ambulance, ☎ 118 for the fire department and ☎ 222 9330 for the traffic police.

Dangers & Annoyances Take all the normal precautions you would in any large city. Pickpockets abound, so carry your money in an inside pocket. Most thefts from travelers happen in the area west of the mercado central and around the Coca-Cola bus terminal. The lively area around Parque Central, too, has been the scene of many pickpocketing attempts, particularly late at night.

Noise and smog are unavoidable components of the San José experience. Also, watch out for open gutters and potholes.

Museo de Jade

This is Costa Rica's most famous museum, housing the world's largest collection of American jade. Many pieces are backlit for full appreciation of the gem's exquisite translucent quality. There are also archaeological exhibits of ceramics, stonework and gold, arranged by cultural regions.

The museum (☎ 287 6034) is on the 11th floor of the Instituto Nacional de Seguros (which has good city views) at Avenida 7, Calles 9 and 11. Hours are 8:30 am to 3 pm Monday to Friday; admission costs US$1.75.

Museo Nacional

Inside the Bellavista Fortress, at Avenidas Central and 2, this museum (☎ 257 1433) exhibits Costa Rican archaeology, some jade and gold, colonial furniture and costumes, colonial and religious art, historical exhibits and natural history displays. Some pieces are labeled in English. The walls around the garden are pockmarked with bullet holes from the 1948 civil war. Hours are 8:30 am to 4:30 pm Tuesday to Saturday, 9 am to 4 pm Sunday and holidays. Admission costs US$0.70; students and children younger than 10 free.

Museo de Oro Precolombino

This museum houses a dazzling collection of pre-Columbian gold, a small numismatic museum and a display of Costa Rican art. The museum (☎ 243 4201) is in the basement of the Plaza de la Cultura complex on Calle 5, Avenidas Central and 2, under the ICT. Hours are 10 am to 4:30 pm Tuesday to Sunday; admission is US$5. Security is tight: You must leave your bags at the door.

Museo de Arte Costarricense

This small museum has a collection of Costa Rican art from the 19th and 20th centuries. The sculptures are especially worth a look. There are also shows of work by local artists.

The museum (☎ 222 7155) is in Parque La Sabana (San José's airport until 1955), at the west end of Paseo Colón. It's open 10 am to 5 pm Tuesday to Sunday; admission is US$1.30, free on Sunday.

Museo de Arte y Diseño Contemporáneo

This museum (☎ 257 7202) features changing exhibits by contemporary Costa Rican artists. It's next to the National Library on Avenida 3, Calles 15 and 17. It's open 10 am to 5 pm Tuesday to Saturday; admission is US$1, US$0.50 for students.

Serpentario

Live snakes and other reptiles, many native to Costa Rica, are on exhibit here. A bilingual (English and Spanish) biologist is sometimes available for explanations. The serpentarium (☎ 255 4210) is on Avenida 1, Calles 9 and 11. Hours are 9 am to 6 pm Monday to Friday and 10 am to 5 pm weekends; admission is US$5.

Museo de los Niños

This Children's Museum (☎ 233 2734, 223 7003) is inside the old penitentiary on Calle 4, north of Avenida 9. The hands-on displays allow kids to learn and experience science, music, geography and other things. There are exhibits about children's rights and lives in Costa Rica. Part of the old jail can be visited. Hours are 8 am to 3 pm Tuesday to Friday, 10 am to 4 pm Saturday and Sunday; admission is US$2/US$1.30 adults/children ages 3 to 17.

Parque Zoológico Simón Bolívar

The small national zoo (☎ 233 6701) is in Parque Simón Bolívar. The zoo claims to have shifted its focus recently to become more than simply an exhibit space for Costa Rica's animals, initiating a program to breed endangered species of the region. The gate is at Avenida 11, Calles 7 and 9 (go north on Calle 7 to get there). Hours are 8 am to 3:30 pm Monday to Friday, 9 am to 4:30 pm weekends; admission is US$1.75.

Museo de Ciencias Naturales

The Natural History Museum (☎ 232 1306) is in the old Colegio La Salle (high school) near the southwest corner of Parque La Sabana. The collection of stuffed animals and mounted butterflies is a resource for identifying species seen in the wild. There are also paleontology and archaeology exhibits. Hours are 7:30 am to 4 pm Monday to Saturday, 9 am to 5 pm Sunday; admission is US$1.75.

Museo de Insectos

This fine collection of insects is curated by the Facultad de Agronomía at the Universidad

COSTA RICA

de Costa Rica. The insect museum (☎ 207 5318) is incongruously located in the basement of the music building on the San Pedro campus. There are signs, or ask someone where it is. Hours are 1 to 4:45 pm Monday to Friday; admission is US$2.75. Ring the bell to gain admission.

Spirogyra Jardín de Mariposas
This garden offers close-up looks at Costa Rican butterflies near downtown San José. The garden is 100m east and 150m south of Centro Comercial El Pueblo. Spirogyra (☎ 222 2937) is open 8 am to 4 pm daily; admission is US$6.

Museo Postal, Telegráfico y Filatélico de Costa Rica
The stamp museum (☎ 223 9766 ext 269) is upstairs in the central post office, Calle 2, Avenidas 1 and 3. Hours are 9 am to 2 pm Monday to Friday; admission is free.

Teatro Nacional
The National Theater (☎ 221 1329) is considered San José's most impressive public building. Built in the 1890s, it is the center of Costa Rican culture. A columned façade and statues of Beethoven and Calderón de la Barca (a 17th-century Spanish dramatist) flank the entrance. Inside are paintings of Costa Rica; the most famous is a huge canvas showing coffee harvesting and export. (This painting is also printed on the old five colón note, which street vendors outside sell for US$1.) The marble staircases, gilded ceilings and parquet floors of local hardwoods are worth seeing.

The best way to see the inside is during a performance (see Entertainment). Otherwise, the theater may be visited 9 am to 5 pm Monday to Saturday; admission is US$3.

Mercado Central
The central market, at Avenidas Central and 1, Calles 6 and 8, is interesting to visit, although a little tame compared with those of other Central American countries. A block away is the similar Mercado Borbón, at Avenida 3 and Calle 8. Beware of pickpockets.

Parks & Plazas
The pleasant, shady Parque Nacional is between Avenidas 1 and 3 and Calles 15

and 19. The Monumento Nacional in the center depicts the Central American nations driving out William Walker. At the southwest corner is a statue of national hero Juan Santamaría. Important buildings surrounding the park include the Asemblea Legislativa (Congress Building) to the south, the National Library to the north and the National Liquor Factory (founded in 1856 and now the Museo de Arte y Diseño Contemporáneo) to the northwest.

The small Parque España has the tallest trees in San José and is a riot of birdsong just before sunset. The park is between Avenidas 3 and 7 and Calles 9 and 11. To the north is the Museo de Jade in the National Insurance Institute Building, which is fronted by a statue representing The Family, and to the northeast is the Casa Amarilla, home of the Ministry of Foreign Affairs.

Parque Morazán, covering four city blocks, is graced in the center by the domed Templo de Música. The northeast quarter of the park contains a small Japanese garden and a playground.

The Plaza de la Cultura, site of the Teatro Nacional, Museo de Oro and ICT office, is a good place to people watch. Street vendors wander around the plaza, especially at its western end by the terrace cafe of the Gran Hotel.

Parque Central, between busy Avenidas 2 and 4 and Calles Central and 2, is the place to catch many of the local city buses. To the east is the fairly modern (and not very interesting) Catedral Metropolitana.

Parque La Sabana, at the western end of the Paseo Colón, is home to both the Museum of Costa Rican Art and the National Stadium, where soccer matches are played. The sprawling park also contains tennis, volleyball and basketball courts and jogging paths.

Language Courses
Some excellent Spanish-language schools are in and near San José, but they're not cheap. In the usual arrangement, classes are given for several hours each weekday, with groups of two to five students; one-on-one instruction is available. Students are encouraged to stay with a Costa Rican family to immerse themselves in the language. Family homestays are arranged by the schools, as are the necessary visa extensions.

Many schools advertise in *The Tico Times*. Those listed below have been operating for at least five years or have received several reader recommendations.

Academia Costarricense de Lenguaje (☎ 221 1624, 800-854 6057 in the USA, fax 233 8670, crlang@sol.racsa.co.cr), in San Pedro, charges from US$10 per hour for lessons, US$100 per week for homestay.

Academia Latinoamericano de Español (☎ 224 9917, fax 225 8125, recajhi@sol.racsa.co.cr), Avenida 8, Calles 31 and 33, charges US$145 for 20 hours of tuition a week, plus family homestay for another US$135.

American Institute for Language & Culture (☎ 225 4313, fax 224 4244), in San Pedro has rates from US$300 per week for four hours of instruction daily.

Centro Cultural Costarricense Norteamericano (☎ 225 9433, fax 224 1480, acccnort@sol.racsa.co.cr), Calle 37, Avenidas 1 and 5, in Los Yoses, has all levels of classes at a wide range of costs, with or without homestays.

Universidad Veritas (☎ 283 4747), in the Edificio ITAN on Carretera a Zapote (a 20-minute walk southeast of San José) has a wide range of levels and courses.

Organized Tours

Numerous tour operators conduct English-language tours of the capital, which take in the Teatro Nacional, the Museo Nacional, the principal monuments and plazas and the embassy zone of Rohrmoser. Tours sometimes include a trip to the outlying district of Moravia for artesanía shopping. Expediciones Tropicales (☎ 257 4171), Swiss Travel (☎ 282 4896) and Fantasy Tours (☎ 220 2126, 800 326 8279), the Gray Line representative, charge US$20 to US$25 for a half-day tour and can pick you up at your hotel.

Places to Stay – Budget

Hostels The *Hostal Toruma* (☎ 234 8186, ☎/fax 224 4085), Avenida Central, Calles 29 and 31, is associated with Hostelling International (HI). Bunks in sex-segregated dormitories are US$11 for HI members, US$13 for nonmembers. Hot showers are sometimes available, and inexpensive meals are served in the cafeteria. There are laundry facilities, a message board and information, and reservations for other Costa Rican hostels can be made here. (Note that the San José hostel is by far the cheapest.)

Casa Ridgway (☎ 255 6399, ☎/fax 233 6168), Calle 15, Avenida 6 and 8, is operated by the adjacent Friends' Peace Center, whose stated mission is to promote understanding of international peace and justice issues. Guests are encouraged to use the library. Accommodations are US$10 per person in four-bed dormitory rooms with individual lockers or US$12/24 for a few singles/doubles. There are basic kitchen and laundry facilities, communal hot showers and quiet hours from 10 pm to 7 am.

Hotels Many budget hotels are found west of Calle Central. The areas around the Coca-Cola bus terminal, mercado central and Parque Central have had reports of occasional thefts and muggings. Though you're unlikely to encounter any trouble, keep your eyes open and use taxis at night.

The cavernous *Gran Hotel Imperial* (☎ 222 8463, fax 256 9650, granhimp@sol.racsa.co.cr), on Calle 8 opposite the mercado central, is popular with shoestringers. The hotel provides security, Internet and fax services and one of the best-value restaurants in town. Basic rooms with reasonably clean beds are US$4 per person, and the communal showers sporadically emit hot water. A few doubles/triples with private bath cost US$11.50/15. They'll hold a room until the afternoon if you call ahead.

Often full of travelers from other Central American countries, *Hotel Nicaragua* (☎ 223 0292), Avenida 2 near Calle 13, is family run, reasonably clean and secure, and charges just US$3.25 per person – perhaps the cheapest in town. Nearby is the basic but clean *Hotel Avenida 2* (☎ 222 0260, fax 223 9732, acebrisa@sol.racsa.co.cr), Avenida 2, Calles 9 and 11, which has communal hot showers and charges US$7.25/11.50.

The very secure *Hotel Marlyn* (☎ 233 3212), Calle 4, Avenidas 7 and 9, charges US$6 for a small single with communal cold showers, or US$13 with private bath and hot water. *Hotel Asia* (☎ 223 3893), Calle 11, Avenidas Central and 1, charges US$6.50/8.50 for spartan but clean rooms with hot water in the communal showers.

Hotel Boruca (☎ 223 0016), Calle 14, Avenidas 1 and 3, is convenient for buses, but the bus noise can be annoying in some rooms. The hotel is family run, friendly, secure and clean. Small rooms are US$5/10 and the communal showers are sometimes hot. Bags can be stored here for a small fee. **Hotel Astoria** (☎ 221 2174), Avenida 7, Calles 7 and 9, charges US$10 for austere doubles with wood floors or US$11.50 including private bath. Noise levels decrease toward the rear of the building. **Pensión Otoya** (☎ 221 3925), Calle 1, Avenidas 3 and 5, is clean, friendly and popular with foreigners. Security is tight, and there's free coffee and laundry service. Decent rooms are US$7.50/10.50 per person with shared/private hot water bathrooms.

The friendly **Hotel Boston** (☎ 221 0563, fax 257 5063), Avenida 8, Calles Central and 2, has big singles/doubles with private baths and tepid water for US$11.50/16.50. Ask for an inside room to avoid street noise. Note that nearby Calle 2 has a seedy red-light district, though the hotel is decent. A block north, the similarly priced **Hotel Príncipe** (☎ 222 7983, fax 223 1589) is secure, with good rooms and warm showers.

The popular **Pensión Centro Continental** (☎ 222 4103, fax 222 8849), Calle Central, Avenidas 8 and 10, has kitchen facilities and lukewarm communal electric showers. Rooms cost US$8/15, plus US$4 per extra person, up to four people. Upstairs, under the same ownership, **Hotel Ritz** (☎ 222 4103, fax 222 8849, ritzcr@sol.racsa.co.cr) charges US$26/31 for rooms with private bath and hot water.

Hotel Johnson (☎ 223 7633, fax 222 3683), Calle 8, Avenidas Central and 2, accepts credit cards and reservations. Reasonably sized rooms with phone and hot showers are US$15.50/16.50. Some 'suites' will take up to four people for about US$30. There's a mid-priced restaurant and bar on the premises, with music on Friday night.

Casa Leo (☎ 222 9725) is minimally signed. At the corner of Avenida 6 and Calle 13, follow the bend in the railroad tracks; it's the third house on the left. The German-run guesthouse charges US$9 per person for dormitories with attached hot showers or US$10 per person for double rooms with separate bath. The whole place is extremely neat and graced by hand-painted wall designs. Kitchen privileges and tourist information are available.

The friendly **Hotel Capital** (☎ 221 8497, fax 221 8583), Calle 4, Avenidas 3 and 5,

charges US$15 for simple, clean doubles with hot water, fans and TVs. Interior rooms are quieter (and darker). Weekend reservations are recommended. The secure **Hotel Compostela** (☎ 257 1514), Calle 6, Avenidas 3 and 5, charges US$14/16 for very clean singles/doubles. Each room has its own bathroom with hot water – across the corridor. Rooms with communal hot showers go for US$7/14. A reasonable choice is **Nuevo Hotel Central** (☎ 222 3509, fax 222 3231), Avenida 3, Calles 4 and 6, with large clean rooms for US$13/16.50 including private hot showers, slightly more with TV. Upstairs rooms are nicest.

Those staying in San José longer than a few days might consider **Casa Agua Buena** (☎/fax 234 2411, rastern@sol.racsa.co.cr), on a quiet street in the Barrio Lourdes just east of San Pedro. It's a group-house arrangement popular with visiting students and is equipped with a common kitchen, washing machine, cable TV and phone. Rates are US$60/75 per week for fairly comfortable rooms; large shared bathrooms have electric hot showers. The Casa is a gay-friendly establishment; all are welcome.

Places to Stay – Mid-Range

Hotel Bienvenido (☎ 233 2161, fax 221 1872), Calle 10, Avenidas 1 and 3, is secure and has helpful staff, a restaurant, and good clean rooms with hot water (sometimes). Rates are US$18 single or double. **Hotel Bellavista** (☎ 223 0095, 800-637 0899 in the USA, wimberly@racsa.co.cr), on Avenida Central 1½ blocks east of the Museo Nacional, is friendly and clean, with pleasant rooms with private baths and hot water for US$23/29. The attached diner is good and cheap.

Casa Hilda (☎ 221 0037, fax 221 2881, c1hilda@racsa.co.cr), Avenida 11, Calles 3 and 3 Bis, is in a renovated home in Barrio Amón. Nice rooms with private bathroom and hot water are worth the US$25/35. The owners are friendly, and tour services are available.

Pensión de la Cuesta (☎/fax 255 2896, ggmnber@sol.racsa.co.cr), Avenida 1, Calles 11 and 15, on a slope just east of the city center, is an attractive B&B popular with international travelers. Nine simple bedrooms sharing baths rent for US$23/33 including breakfast – some rooms seem small for the price. Guests can use the kitchen and laundry facilities or hang out in the bright, homey rear living room. The very helpful staff can arrange tours. *Hotel Aranjuez* (☎ 256 1825, fax 223 3528, info@ hotelaranjuez.com), Calle 19, Avenidas 11 and 13, is a lovely old rambling wood home, actually a series of houses connected by rain forest nooks and patios. Rooms of varying size, comfort and price (US$24/29 and up) all have polished wood floors, private hot showers, phone and cable TV. A few smaller rooms with shared hot showers are US$20/24. A buffet breakfast (included in the price) is served on a deck beside a tropical garden. There is plenty of parking and free email. Across the street, the new *Kap's Place* (☎ 221 1169, fax 256 4850, isabel@racsa.co.cr) is a homey guesthouse. Owner Karla Arias (who speaks Spanish, English and French) looks after guests, arranging airport transportation, tours and medical services if needed. Cozy rooms all have cable TV, phone and hot showers for US$20/30. A fully equipped kitchen, email, luggage storage and laundry are all available.

Places to Eat

Budget The *mercado central* has a variety of cheap sodas and restaurants inside. It's a great place to eat elbow to elbow with Ticos and has plenty of atmosphere. Typical fare includes black bean soup and tamales wrapped in banana leaves. Additional inexpensive places are on Avenida 1. The area around the market is not dangerous but is a little rough, and women may prefer not to go there alone.

Restaurant Pollo Campesino, Calle 7, Avenida 2, serves chicken rotisseried in a giant wood-burning oven, at about US$2.50 per half. It's open until midnight. *Restaurant Yud Fad*, Calle 1, Avenidas 3 and 5, is another *pollos a la leña* place, where a huge plate of food costs US$2.50.

La Vasconia, Avenida 1, Calle 5, is cheap but decent. A *pinto con huevo* (rice and beans topped with an egg) breakfast is about US$1.50 and lunch combos are less than US$3. The *Meylin 2*, attached to the Hotel Bienvenido, and the *Gran Imperial Restaurant* in the hotel of that name are both inexpensive and popular. *Casa del Sandwich*, at the corner of Avenida 2 and Calle 9, serves all kinds of grilled sandwiches for US$1.75.

Sodas These inexpensive snack bars are rather featureless, but they're popular with Ticos looking for a cheap meal. Catering to students and working people, they tend to close on weekends. A popular one is the *Soda La Central*, Avenida 1, Calles 3 and 5, where the empanadas are good and casados are US$3. *Soda Nini*, on Avenida 3 opposite the Banco Nacional, serves both Tico and Chinese food. *Chelle's*, at Avenida Central, Calle 9, is an unpretentious spot with good food and a full bar; it's open 24 hours. Other round-the-clock options are *Soda Comilona #1* and *Soda Comilona #3*, both on Avenida 10 in an area best approached by taxi at night. *Soda Castro*, also on Avenida 10, serves big ice cream sodas and fruit salads. This cavernous hall is an old-fashioned Tico family spot – notice the sign prohibiting public displays of romance.

Cafes & Coffee Shops These are good places for journal or letter writing. Prices are not necessarily cheap, but you can sit for hours without consuming much. A favorite place is the *Café Parisien*, the pavement cafe of the upmarket Gran Hotel Costa Rica, where you can watch the activity in the Plaza de la Cultura. Nearby, the Teatro Nacional houses the elegant *Café Ruisenor*. It isn't cheap, but it serves some of the best coffee in Costa Rica.

Churrería Manolos, with a pair of branches on Avenida Central, is famous for its cream-filled *churros* (hollow doughnut tubes) as well as other desserts and light meals. The first location, near Calle 2, is especially popular during breakfast time. *Pastelería Merayo*, on Calle 16 near the Coca-Cola terminal, is busy in the morning when locals fill the counter and booths. Stop in for excellent fresh pastries, fruit shakes and good coffee.

Las Delicias, in the mercado central, has been making its own cinnamon-spiced vanilla ice cream for a century. It's served in a small glass, and most patrons order cylindrical cookies on the side.

Vegetarian Vegetarians will find plenty of options in San José. One of the most popular is the *Vishnu* chain on both sides of Avenida 1, Calles 1 and 3. The daily set meal consists of bean soup, brown rice, soy ham, salad, fruit drink and 'a nutritionally balanced dessert' (US$3). Other Vishnus are at Avenida 3, Calles Central and 1, and at Avenida 8, Calles 9 and 11. The macrobiotic *Restaurant Shakti*, Avenida 8, Calle 13, has tastier fare – a good, filling lunch combo costs US$3.

In San Pedro, *La Mazorca*, on Calle 3 a block north of Avenida Central, adds creative flair to its substantial lunch specials, priced at US$2.50. An attached store sells fresh whole wheat bread and natural food products. On Calle Central, the next block over, is another fine veggie venue, *Comida Para Sentir* (Food for Feeling). It's crowded with gringo and Tico students and teachers at lunchtime. Felafel, whole-wheat pastas and salads are alternatives to the meatless lunch platters, and they serve great cappuccino.

Costa Rican For Costa Rican dishes in a relaxed pub setting, try *El Cuartel de la Boca del Monte*, on Avenida 1 a block east of Parque Nacional. The food is casually elegant, moderately priced and delicious. Main courses are around US$5, or you can fill up on a plate of cheese empanadas (US$3) or gallos (US$2.50).

International San José has its fair share of Chinese restaurants. In the center of town, *Restaurante Lung Mun*, Avenida 1, Calles 5 and 7, has large lunches for less than US$3.50. *Restaurante Tin Jo* (☎ 221 7605) offers a unique pan-Asian menu, serving everything from Szechuan tofu to Indian curries, all well-prepared and attractively presented. Main dishes run US$5 to US$10.

Students grab a pizza at *Pizzería Il Pomodoro*, 100m north of the San Pedro church near the Universidad de Costa Rica. This simple eatery serves some of the finest Italian food you're likely to find in San José and it's one of the few places in the zone that's open Sunday. Also in San Pedro, *Omar Khayyam*, on Calle 3 by the railroad tracks, has Iranian food, including Persian tacos (US$2.75). Or get authentic Turkish cuisine at *Aya Sofía*, at Avenida Central and Calle 21. Weekday lunch specials, served 11 am to 5 pm, are US$3.

Entertainment

Pick up *La Nación* on Thursday for a complete listing (in Spanish) of the coming week's nightlife and cultural events. *The Tico Times* also contains a comprehensive calendar of theater, music, museums and more cultural events in its Weekend section. Also have a look at the Web site www .entretenimiento.co.cr, which lists movies, theater and a few bars and clubs.

Bars & Discos A restaurant by day, *El Cuartel de la Boca del Monte* (☎ 233 1477), Avenida 1, Calles 21 and 23, is a popular nightspot for young people. The music is sometimes recorded, sometimes live (Monday and Wednesday nights), and often loud. The back room has a small dance floor – a good place to meet young Ticos. In San Pedro, Calle 3 leading to the university entrance – also known as Calle La Amargura (Street of Sorrow) – has perhaps the highest concentration of bars of any single street in town. *Mosaikos*, *Caccio's* and *Tavarua* are raucous, beer-soaked places packed with young people. *Taurus* is mellower, a good place to talk, listen to music, drink beer and munch on bocas. Another relaxed place is *La Villa*, in a great old wood house with a candlelit back patio. You can shoot pool at *Marrakech*, but no alcohol is served at this primarily adolescent hangout. A block west is *Copas*, the lone bar on the street, with tasty bar snacks and two-for-one beer nights.

More mature travelers may prefer the ambience at the stylish *Jazz Café* (☎ 253 8933) or *Bar Baleares*, both on Avenida Central east of Calle 3. More sedate than their counterparts for students, they're equally smoky and crowded. Costa Rica's foremost jazz and blues artists perform at Jazz Café Sunday to Wednesday nights (US$3.50 cover). Jazz fans can also check out *Rico's Jazz Central* (☎ 388 0062), on Calle 9 just south of Avenida Central in central San José, a venue featuring live music Tuesday to Saturday nights (US$5 cover).

Centro Comercial El Pueblo has a variety of pricey restaurants and nightspots – take your pick. The best-known dance club is *Infinito* (☎ 223 2195), with three *pistas de baile* (dance floors). Another is *Cocoloco* (☎ 222 8782), which charges a

US$5 cover. Other clubs within the complex are more intimate, such as the folk music grotto *Café Arte Boruca*. Opposite El Pueblo is *La Plaza* (☎ 257 1077), a dress-up disco (US$2.50 cover) featuring live music Wednesday and Thursday nights.

Downtown dance clubs include *El Tunel de Tiempo*, Avenida Central, Calles 7 and 9, with flashing lights and techno; *Salsa 54*, Calle 3, Avenidas 1 and 3, with Latin music and expert local *salseros*; and *Zadidas* next door, with a musical mix. All charge a US$2 to US$3 cover on weekends.

Tiny's Sports Bar, Avenida 2, Calles 9 and 11, is a favorite with ex-pats who come for the bar food and nonstop US sports TV. Ticos like *Las Risas* (☎ 223 2803), Calle 1, Avenidas Central and 1, in an attractive older building. There's a disco upstairs and rock videos in the bar. *Soda Blues* (☎ 221 8368), Calle 11, Avenidas 10 and 12, features live blues and blues karaoke. Also popular is *Bar Río* (☎ 225 8371), Avenida Central, Calle 39 in Los Yoses, with an outdoor verandah and occasional live bands. Just west of the fountain in Los Yoses, Centro Comercial Cocorí is another nightlife mall with four or five bars, including *Rock Bar Sand* (☎ 225 9229), which is popular with young black-clad headbangers, and *Reggae Bar Raices*, a dark, crowded lounge that typically attracts a racially mixed group. The well-known *Bar La Esmeralda* (☎ 221 0530), Avenida 2, Calles 5 and 7, is open all day and night (except Sunday) and is the city's mariachi center. At night, dozens of musicians stroll around.

Gay and lesbian bars and discos are found in the area south of Parque Central. *La Avispa* (☎ 223 5343), Calle 1, Avenidas 8 and 10, is a popular gay dance club, with Sunday and Tuesday being big nights. *Los Cucharones* (☎ 233 5797), Avenida 6, Calles Central and 1, is a loud disco frequented by young, working-class people. *Deja Vú* (☎ 223 3758), Calle 2, Avenidas 14 and 16, is known for spectacular, elaborately choreographed, drag shows on Friday and Saturday nights. This has become the place to be seen, and a dress code is strictly enforced.

Theater The local newspapers, including *The Tico Times*, advertise theaters. Most plays are in Spanish.

The most important theater is the Teatro Nacional (☎ 221 5341). The season is March to November, when National Symphony Orchestra concerts and other events take place every few days. Tickets are cheap by US and European standards. Other major performing arts venues include the restored 1920s *Teatro Melico Salazar* (☎ 222 2653), on Avenida 2 opposite Parque Central, and the *Auditorio Nacional* (☎ 249 1208) in the same building as the Museo de los Niños.

Cinemas Recent Hollywood films with Spanish subtitles are about US$3. The Sala Garbo (☎ 222 1034), Avenida 2, Calle 28, offers some interesting alternatives to the usual blockbusters.

Spectator Sports

International and national soccer games are played in the Estadio Nacional (☎ 255 0811) in Parque La Sabana. The regular season is from August to May, with games at 11 am on Sunday morning and sometimes on Wednesday evening.

Shopping

The government-run Mercado Nacional de Artesanía, Calle 11, Avenidas 2 and 4, offers a good selection of Costa Rican handicrafts at reasonable prices. La Casona, Calle Central, Avenidas Central and 1, is a complex with a wide variety of souvenirs, including imports from other Central American countries. Similar items can be found in the shops around Parque Morazán.

The mercado central has a small selection of handicrafts, and it's also the best place to buy fresh coffee beans at a fraction of the price you'd pay at home. Jewelry, cigars, clothing and hammocks can be found at the market on the western side of the Plaza de la Democracia. Also try the mock colonial village at Centro Comercial El Pueblo, where various small shops sell Costa Rican woodwork and leather, hammocks from Guanacaste and indigenous paintings.

Getting There & Away

Air The two airports serving San José are Aeropuerto Juan Santamaría (☎ 443 2942) near Alajuela, and Aeropuerto Tobias Bolaños (☎ 232 2820) in Pavas. The former handles all international traffic and Sansa domestic flights (a new terminal added in 2000 was not yet in use at time of writing). Tobias Bolaños is for domestic flights by Travelair.

Sansa can check you in at its city office, which it shares with Grupo TACA on Calle 42, Avenida 5, opposite the Datsun dealership. They provide transportation to the airport's domestic terminal.

Mexicana (☎ 257 6334, fax 257 6338), Calle 5, Avenidas 7 and 9

SAM (Colombia; ☎ 233 3066), Centro Colón

Grupo TACA (Central America; ☎ 296 0909), Calle 42, Avenida 5, across from the Datsun dealership

United (USA; ☎ 220 4844, fax 220 4813), Sabana Sur

Varig (Brazil; ☎ 290 5222, fax 290 0200), Sabana Oeste

Bus The Coca-Cola terminal, Avenida 1, Calles 16 and 18, is a well-known landmark in San José. A number of buses leave from within three or four blocks of the terminal. Two other terminals serve specific regions. The Caribe terminal, north of Avenida 13 on Calle Central, is for buses to the Caribbean coast. The Atlántico Norte terminal, at Avenida 9, Calle 12, serves northern destinations, including Monteverde, the Arenal area, and Puerto Viejo de Sarapiquí.

Buses are very crowded on Friday evening and Saturday morning, even more so during Christmas and Easter. Thefts are common in the area around the Coca-Cola terminal, especially when crowds are thick, so stay alert.

Many of the companies listed below have no more than a bus stop; some have a tiny office with a window opening onto the street; some operate out of a terminal. The following lists are for international buses. International bus companies are used to dealing with border procedures and will wait for passengers taking care of formalities. They are a bit more expensive than taking a bus to the border and changing there, but they're convenient and worthwhile. For more on border crossings, see the Costa Rica Getting There & Away section.

Managua, Nicaragua
Tica Bus (☎ 221 8954), Calle 9, Avenida 2 has buses to Managua (US$10, nine hours) leaving at 6 and 7:30 am. The Tica bus continues on to Tegucigalpa (US$29) or San Salvador (US$32) and Guatemala City (US$39, 2½ days). Sirca

(☎ 256 9072) has a bus (US$11.50, 7½ hours) leaving from the Hotel Cocorí, on Calle 16 between Avenidas 3 and 5, at 4:30 am. A Nica Bus (☎ 223 3816) for Managua (US$12, eight hours), leaves the Caribe terminal at 6 am. Trans Nica (☎ 223 4242), Calle 22, between Avenida 3 and 5, has a Managua bus (US$12.50, eight hours) at 5:30 and 9 am.

Peñas Blancas (border crossing)
Transportes Deldu (☎ 256 9072), Calle 16, Avenida 3, has buses to the border (US$5.50, 4½ hours) at 5, 7:45 and 10:30 am and 1:20 and 4:10 pm Monday to Friday, every fifteen minutes 3 am to 4 pm Saturday and Sunday.

Panama City
Tica Bus (☎ 221 8954), Calle 9, Avenida 2, has a bus to Panama City (US$23, 16 hours) leaving at 10 pm. Panaline buses (☎ 258 0022), Calle 16, Avenida 3, leave at 1 pm (US$20).

Changuinola (Bocas del Toro), Panama
Panaline buses to Changuinola (US$10, eight hours) leave from Calle 14, between Avenidas 3 and 5, at 10 am.

David, Panama
Tracopa (☎ 222 2666), Calle 14, between Avenidas 3 and 5, leave for David (US$8.25, nine hours) at 7:30 am.

For destinations within Costa Rica, consult the following lists.

For locations in the Central Valley:

Alajuela/Aeropuerto Juan Santamaría (US$0.50, ¾ hour)
Tuasa (☎ 222 5325), Avenida 2, Calle 10, has frequent buses between 4:45 am and 11 pm.

Cartago (US$0.40, ¾ hour)
SACSA (☎ 233 5350), Calle 5, between Avenidas 18 and 20, has frequent buses to Cartago.

Heredia (US$0.40)
Frequent buses for Heredia leave from Avenida 2, between Calles 10 and 12, from 4:40 am to 11 pm.

Turrialba (US$1.75, 1¾ hours)
Transtusa (☎ 256 7307), Calle 13, between Avenidas 6 and 8, has hourly directo buses from 8 am to 8 pm.

To southern Costa Rica:

Ciudad Neily (US$5.75, seven hours)
Tracopa (☎ 222 2666), Calle 14 between Avenidas 3 and 5, has five buses between 5 am and 6 pm. These buses continue on to the Panamanian border at Paso Canoas.

Golfito (US$5.75, eight hours)
Tracopa (☎ 222 2666), Calle 14 between Avenidas 3 and 5, has two buses at 7 am and 3 pm.

Palmar Norte Norte (US$4.50, six hours)
Tracopa (☎ 222 2666), Calle 14 between Avenidas 3 and 5, has seven buses from 5 am to 6 pm.

Puerto Jiménez (US$6.25, eight hours)
Blanco Lobo (☎ 257 4121), Calle 12 between Avenidas 9 and 11, has a bus leaving at 12 pm.

San Isidro de El General
Transportes Vargas Rojas (☎ 222 9763), Calle 16 between Avenidas 1 and 3, has five buses (US$2.75, three hours) between 6:30 am and 3:30 pm. Transportes Musoc (☎ 222 2422), Calle 16 between Avenidas 1 and 3, has nine buses (US$2.75) from 5 am to 5:30 pm.

San Vito (US$7, eight hours)
Tracopa (☎ 222 2666), Calle 14 between Avenidas 3 and 5, has four directo buses between 5:45 am and 2:45 pm.

To the Pacific coast:

Jacó (US$2, three hours)
Transportes Jacó (☎ 223 1109) has buses leaving from the Coca-Cola terminal at 7:30 and 10:30 am and 3:30 pm.

Puntarenas (US$2.75, 2¼ hours)
Empresarios Unidos (☎ 222 0064), Avenida 12, Calle 16, has 10 buses leaving from 4 am to 9 pm.

Quepos/Manuel Antonio (US$4.50, 3½ hours)
Transportes Morales (☎ 223 5567) buses depart the Coca-Cola terminal at 6 am, noon and 6 pm.

Uvita (US$4.75, seven hours)
Transportes Morales (☎ 223 5567) buses depart the Coca-Cola terminal at 3 pm daily, 5:30 am Saturday and Sunday.

To Península de Nicoya:

Nicoya
Empresas Alfaro (☎ 222 2666), Calle 14 between Avenidas 3 and 5, has five buses via Liberia (US$5.25, five hours) between 6:30 am and 5 pm and five buses via ferry (US$5, four hours).

Playa Bejuco (US$5.75, five hours)
Empresa Arza (☎ 257 1835), Calle 12 between Avenidas 7 and 9, has buses at 6 am and 3:30 pm.

Playa del Coco (US$5.25, five hours)
Pullmitan (☎ 222 1650), Calle 14 between Avenidas 1 and 3, has buses at 8 am and 2 pm.

Playa Flamingo (US$5.50, 5¼ hours)
Tralapa buses (☎ 221 7202), Avenida 3, Calle 20, depart at 8 and 10 am.

Playa Sámara (US$6.25, five hours)
Empresas Alfaro (☎ 222 2666), Calle 14 between Avenidas 3 and 5, has a bus at 12:30 pm.

Playa Panamá, Playa Hermosa
Buses Esquivel (☎ 666 0042), Calle 12 between Avenidas 5 and 7, has a bus departing for Playa Panamá and Playa Hermosa (US$4, 4½ hours) at 3 pm. Tralapa buses (☎ 221 7202), Avenida 3, Calle 20, depart for Playa Panamá (US$4) at 3:30 pm.

Tamarindo (US$5.50, five hours)
Empresas Alfaro (☎ 222 2666), Calle 14 between Avenidas 3 and 5, has a bus at 3:30 pm.

To northern Costa Rica:

Cañas
Tralapa (☎ 221 7202), Avenida 3, Calle 20, has hourly buses to Cañas (US$2.50, 2½ hours). Transportes La Cañera (☎ 222 3006), Calle 16 between Avenidas 1 and 3, has six buses (US$2.75, three hours).

Ciudad Quesada (US$2.25, 2½ hours)
Transportes San Carlos (☎ 255 4318), at the Atlantico Norte terminal, has hourly buses.

La Fortuna (US$3, 4½ hours)
Buses depart the Atlantico Norte terminal at 6:15, 8:40 and 11:30 am.

Liberia (US$4.50)
Pullmitan (☎ 222 1650), Calle 14 between Avenidas 1 and 3, has hourly buses to Liberia.

Los Chiles (US$3.75, five hours)
Buses depart the Atlantico Norte terminal at 5:30 am and 3:30 pm.

Monteverde (US$4.25, 4½ hours)
Trans Monteverde (☎ 222 3854) has buses departing the Atlantico Norte terminal at 6:30 am and 2:30 pm.

Puerto Viejo de Sarapiquí (US$2.25, two hours)
Eight buses depart the Atlantico Norte terminal between 6:30 am and 6 pm.

Tilarán (US$2.50, four hours)
Transportes Tilarán (☎ 222 3854), at the Atlantico Norte terminal, has five buses from 7:30 am to 6:30 pm.

Upala (US$5.50, four hours)
Transportes de Upala (☎ 221 3318), Calle 12, Avenida 5, has a daily bus at 3 pm and a bus at 2:40 Friday to Sunday.

To the Caribbean coast:

Guápiles (US$1.75, 1¼ hours)
Autotransportes Caribeños (☎ 222 0610), at the Caribe terminal, has buses every 40 minutes from 6:30 am to 7 pm.

Puerto Limón (US$3.25, three hours)
Autotransportes Caribeños (☎ 222 0610), at the Caribe terminal, has hourly buses from 5:30 am to 3:30 pm.

Sixaola
Autotransportes Mepe (☎ 257 8129) has buses via Cahuita (US$4.25, 3¾ hours) or Puerto Viejo de Talamanca (US$5, 4¼ hours), leaving four times a day.

Getting Around

To/From the Airport Taxis between Juan Santamaría Airport and San José should cost no more than US$11; establish the fare before getting into the cab. Alajuela–San José buses pass the airport every few minutes from 5 am to 11 pm (US$0.50, 40 minutes). The bus stop is just outside the terminal. From San José, catch the Alajuela bus at Calle 10 and Avenida 2, and tell the driver you're going to the airport. Interbus (☎ 283 5573) runs an airport shuttle service (US$5), departing from major downtown hotels – call to reserve a seat. Buses to Aeropuerto Tobías Bolaños depart every half hour from Avenida 1, 150m west of the Coca-Cola terminal; a taxi from downtown costs about US$3.

Bus Local buses run from 5 am to 10 pm, for US$0.30 to US$0.40. Patience is definitely not a virtue of San José bus drivers – you'd better have your change ready. Buses from Parque La Sabana head into town on Paseo Colón then jog over to Avenida 2 at the San Juan de Dios Hospital and head into the city center by various routes. In the reverse direction, catch a 'Sabana-Cementario' bus from Calle 11 between Avenidas Central and 2. Buses going east to Los Yoses and San Pedro travel along Avenida 2; they depart between Calles 9 and 11. Ask at the ICT office next to the Museo de Oro for routes to other destinations.

Taxi Red taxis can be easily hailed day or night. Downtown, *marías* (meters) are supposed to be used, but some drivers will pretend they are broken and try to charge you more. Make sure the maría operates when you get in, or hail another taxi. Within San José fares are US$0.65 for the first kilometer and US$0.35 for each additional kilometer. Short rides downtown should cost around US$1. There's a 20% surcharge after 10 pm. Taxi drivers are not normally tipped in Costa Rica.

Central Valley & Highlands

The local name for this area is La Meseta Central. Historically and geographically it is the heart of Costa Rica. To the north and east, the region is bounded by the Cordillera Central, which contains several volcanoes, including the famous Poás and Irazú. Between the Cordillera Central and the southern Cordillera de Talamanca lies the beautiful Río Reventazón Valley, San José's historical access to the Caribbean. To the west, the Central Valley drops to the Pacific. Four of Costa Rica's seven provinces have fingers of land within the Central Valley, and all four have their political capitals there. About 60% of Costa Rica's population lives in the region.

Many visitors use San José as a base for day trips to the other cities and attractions of the area. Along the way, they pass through rolling agricultural countryside dominated by the berries that made Costa Rica famous – coffee.

ALAJUELA
pop 172,000

This provincial capital is 18km northwest of San José; 200m lower, it has a slightly warmer climate. The international airport is 2.5km southeast of Alajuela.

Things to See & Do

Alajuela is the birthplace of the national hero, Juan Santamaría, for whom the international airport is named. The small **Museo Juan Santamaría** (☎ 441 4775) that commemorates him is in a former jail northwest of the pleasant, shaded parque central. Hours (subject to change) are 10 am to 6 pm Tuesday to Sunday; admission is free. Two blocks south of the parque central is the **Parque Juan Santamaría**, where a statue of the hero in action is flanked by cannons.

Places to Stay

Hotel La Central (☎ 443 8437), by the bus terminal (the entrance is off Avenida Central), is under friendly management. Basic rooms with shared cold showers cost US$6.50/10 single/double.

The *Villa Real Hostel* (☎ 441 4022), 100m south of the post office, is clean and congenial and popular with budget travelers. English is spoken here, and there's one hot shower in the shared bathrooms. Rates are US$10 per person, including kitchen privileges. The *Mango Verde Hostel* (☎ /fax 441 6330), Avenida 3, Calles 2 and 4, has all the amenities – hot water, a sitting/TV room, and kitchen privileges. Decent rooms cost US$14/24 with private baths.

Pensión Alajuela (☎ /fax 441 6251), four blocks north of the parque central, is a friendly place with a nice little bar. It charges US$20 for a double with shared bath or US$23 with private bath (no single rates).

Places to Eat
Most restaurants are near the parque central. *Señor Gazpacho* is a cheerful, popular place serving Mexican food. The pleasant *Bar Restaurant da Lucia*, upstairs at the corner of Calle 2 and Avenida 2, serves pasta and pizza for about US$5 and up. Some tables are on little balconies overlooking Parque Juan Santamaría.

For good inexpensive breakfasts, there's *Mi Choza*, Calle 1, Avenidas 1 and 3. Coffee and a variety of yummy desserts are the standby at *Café Almibar* on Avenida Central, Calles 1 and 3. *Wall's* on the corner of the parque central has good ice cream and snacks.

Nice places for a drink include *Bar La Hiedra* on the southeast corner of the parque central, and *Taberna Peppers*, Avenida Central, Calle 5. *La Troja*, a short distance south of the parque central, is a local favorite with live music.

Getting There & Away
Buses to San José leave from Avenida 4, Calles 2 and 4. Any of these will let you off at the airport (US$0.50), or you can take a taxi (US$2) from the parque central. The Alajuela bus terminal, off Avenida 1, Calles 8 and 10, is the departure point for buses to other towns and Volcan Poás.

SARCHÍ
Costa Rica's most famous craft center is Sarchí. It is commercial and touristy, but there is no pressure to buy anything and you can watch wooden handicrafts being made. The shopping area in the south part of town is modern, but the north is a more attractive area.

Among the best-known crafts are the *carretas,* gaily painted wooden carts, often used nowadays to decorate gardens; scaled-down versions are made for use as indoor tables, sideboards and bars, and miniature

models are available for use as indoor sculptures. All sizes come apart and fold down for transport. See them being made in *fábricas de carretas*; the most interesting part of the process is the painting of colorful mandala designs. Many other wooden items are for sale.

There are a couple of hotels, but most visitors come on day trips from San José.

The quickest way to get to Sarchí from San José is to take one of the frequent buses to Grecia from the Coca-Cola terminal and then connect with an Alajuela-Sarchí bus going through Grecia.

PARQUE NACIONAL VOLCÁN POÁS
This popular park, 37km north of Alajuela by road, is a must for anyone wanting to peer into an active volcano. It was closed briefly in 1989 after a minor eruption by Volcán Poás (2704m) sent volcanic ash more than a kilometer into the air and again in 1995 because of noxious fumes. However, the bubbling and steaming crater poses no imminent threat, and the park is usually open.

The crater is 1.5km across and 300m deep. Small eruptions take place periodically, with peaceful interludes lasting minutes or weeks.

A dwarf cloud forest near the crater has bromeliads, lichens and mosses clinging to the curiously shaped and twisted trees. Birds abound, especially hummingbirds. One of the nature trails leads through this forest to another nearby volcanic crater (extinct) containing a pretty lake.

The park's hours are 8 am to 3:30 pm daily, and admission is US$6. A visitor center shows videos every hour and contains an insect museum (US$0.50 extra). The park is crowded on Sunday.

The best time to go is in the dry season, especially early in the morning before the clouds roll in and obscure the view. If the clouds do blow in, wait a while – winds often blow the clouds back for intermittent views. It may be windy and cold during the day.

A coffee shop offers a limited menu, but it's best to bring your own food and drinking water – there are picnic areas. Though the park does not have hotels or campgrounds, there are several places to stay on the road up. The cheapest is the friendly

CENTRAL VALLEY & HIGHLANDS

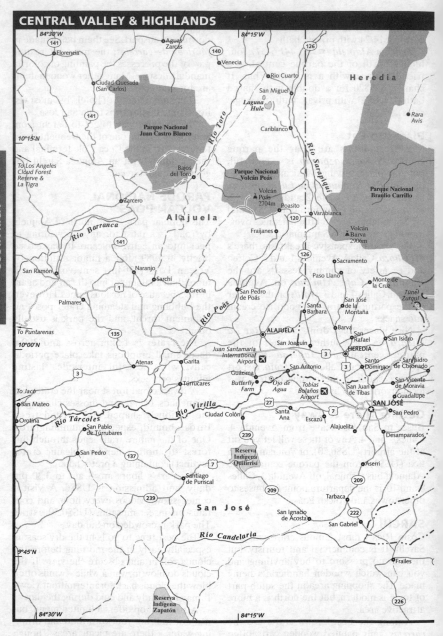

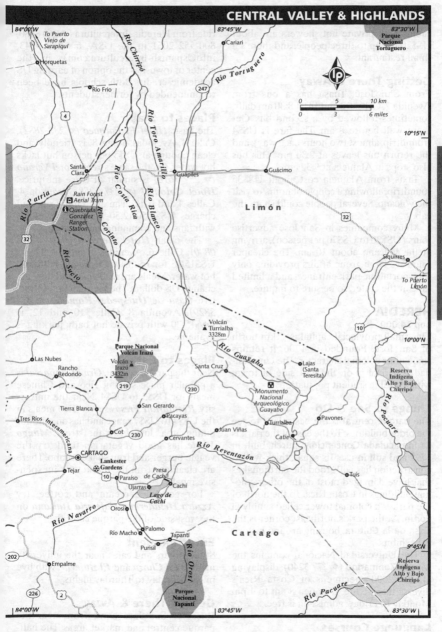

COSTA RICA

Lo Que Tu Quieres Lodge, just over 5km before the park entrance. Three basic little cabins with private hot showers are about US$20 for up to three people, and there's a small restaurant.

Getting There & Away
From San José, Tuasa has a bus from Avenida 2, Calles 12 and 14, at 8:30 am daily, sometimes followed by a second bus. Get there well before 8 am. The fare is US$4 (roundtrip, almost two hours each way), and the return bus leaves at 2:30 pm. This bus also stops in Alajuela at 9:30 am.

Taxis from Alajuela cost about US$35 roundtrip, allowing a couple of hours to visit the volcano. Several people could share the cab.

Many companies in San José advertise tours (US$20 to US$70 per person), arriving at the volcano about 10 am. The cheaper tours are large group affairs providing only transportation, park entrance, and a limited time at the crater, so be sure to inquire.

HEREDIA
pop 74,000
This small provincial capital is 11km north of San José. Founded in 1706, it retains some of its colonial character. The Universidad Nacional is on the east side of town, with a sizable student population.

Things to See & Do
The **parque central** is the best place to see the older buildings. To the east of the park is **La Inmaculada Concepción** church, built in 1797 and still in use. Its squat, thick-walled construction has withstood the earthquakes that have damaged most of the other colonial buildings in Costa Rica. To the north of the park is a colonial tower called simply **El Fortín**. At the park's northeast corner is the **Casa de la Cultura**, housing art and historical exhibits.

The Universidad Nacional contains the **Museo Zoomarino** (☎ 277 3240), displaying almost 2000 specimens of Costa Rica's diverse marine life. It's open 8 am to 4 pm Monday to Friday; admission is free.

Language Courses
These give the opportunity to stay near San José without being in the capital. The Centro Panamericano de Idiomas (☎ 265

6866, ☎/fax 265 6213, anajarro@sol.racsa .co.cr) is in a suburb about a 10-minute bus ride from Heredia. Intercultura (☎ 260 8480, 800-552 2051 in the USA, fax 260 9243, info@spanish-intercultura.com), in the center of town, has the option of earning US academic credit. Both schools have been recommended by former students.

Places to Stay
The basic **Hotel El Parqueo** (☎ 238 2882), Calle 4, Avenidas 6 and 8, is friendly and clean enough at US$5 per person but lacks hot water. On the same street, **Hotel Verano** (☎ 237 1616) is similar at twice the price. **Hotel Colonial** (☎ 237 5258), Avenida 4, Calles 4 and 6, is clean and family-run and charges US$7.50/12.50 for singles/doubles with fans and communal hot showers.

The clean **Hotel Heredia** (☎ /fax 238 0880), Calle 6, Avenidas 3 and 5, charges US$15/25 for rooms with private bath and hot water. Meals are available, and they exchange US dollars. The pleasant and attractive **Casa de Huespedes Ramble** (☎ 238 3829), Avenida 8, Calles 10 and 12, is US$15/30 with private hot bath; parking is available.

Places to Eat
Near the parque central, **Gran Chaparral** is a popular place serving Tico and Chinese meals for US$3 to US$4. Near the university, **Restaurant Fresas** serves Tico meals in the US$4 to US$7 range and has an outdoor dining area. Just down the street, **Mango Verde** has good vegetarian food; try the veggie burger and fruit shake combo. There are clean sodas in the market for inexpensive meals.

For good ice cream and coffee, try **Azzura Heladería y Cafetería Italiana** on the west side of the parque central.

Entertainment
Student bars and cafes near the university include **La Choza** and **El Bulevar**, with live music Monday to Thurday nights.

Getting There & Away
Buses to San José leave from near the parque central and market areas. The half-hour ride costs US$0.30.

Buses north for Barva leave from the Cruz Roja (Red Cross) on Calle Central,

Avenidas 1 and 3. Buses to San José de la Montaña depart every hour from Avenida 8, Calles 2 and 4. From the same stop, buses leave for Sacramento with access to the Volcán Barva in the Parque Nacional Braulio Carrillo.

BARVA

This colonial town, 2.5km north of Heredia, is a historic monument. It has a pleasant old-world ambience and is fun to stroll around in. To the southwest is the **Café Britt Finca** (☎ 260 2748, turismo@ cafebritt.com) which has 'coffee tours' for US$20 per person, including a plantation visit, a bilingual multimedia presentation explaining the historical importance of coffee and a tasting session. Tours are at 9 am and 11 am.

PARQUE NACIONAL BRAULIO CARRILLO

This national park protects the virgin rain forest that was threatened by the new highway between San José and Puerto Limón. The pristine areas on either side of the highway support many plants and animals, and no development is allowed. The extraordinary biodiversity of Braulio Carrillo is partly attributable to its wide range of elevations, from 2906m at the top of Volcán Barva to less than 50m in the Caribbean lowlands.

Most people see the park by driving through on one of the frequent buses between San José and Limón. The difference between this highway and other roads in the Central Valley is marked: instead of small villages and large coffee plantations, the panorama is one of rolling hills clothed with thick mountain rain forest, as much of Costa Rica looked prior to the 1950s.

Hiking

Access to the park is either off the main highway or via the Sacramento entrance near San José de la Montaña, the way to go if you want to climb Volcán Barva. The Quebrada González ranger station, on the right side of the highway about 22km beyond the Zurquí tunnel, is open 8 am to 3:30 pm Tuesday to Sunday (US$6 entry). There are a guarded parking lot, toilets, and two 1.5km walking trails. Buses bound for Guápiles can drop you off, but it's a 2km

walk back along the highway to reach the restaurant where returning buses stop, and assaults on tourists have been reported along this stretch.

From the Sacramento entrance, the trail up Barva is fairly obvious. A ranger station here is open erratically, and sometimes the rangers will take you up. A signed track climbs to the summit, about four or five hours' roundtrip at a leisurely pace. The slopes of Barva are one of the best places in the park to see the quetzal. Near the summit are several lakes. Camping is allowed anywhere you can pitch a tent, but no facilities are provided. The best time to go is supposedly the 'dry' season (December to April), but it's liable to rain any time. Night temperatures can drop below freezing.

Three buses a day leave Heredia for Sacramento, the last returning at 5 pm. Ask the driver to set you down at the track leading to Volcán Barva.

RAIN FOREST AERIAL TRAM

The aerial tram is designed to go silently through and just over the rain forest canopy, thus affording riders a unique vantage for viewing plant and bird life. It's on the right side of the San José–Limón road, just after leaving the national park. The 2.6km tram has 22 cars, each of which carries five passengers and a naturalist guide. The trip takes 45 minutes each way and costs US$49 (children 12 and younger, half price), including transportation to the tram (more than 3km from the parking lot). There's a restaurant and an exhibit/information area where you can see an orientation video, as well as several short hiking trails and a small visitor center. The tram is open 7 am to 3 pm daily. Those visiting independently must reserve a place – call ☎ 257 5961 (doselsa@ sol.racsa.co.cr). Buses bound for Guápiles can drop you at the entrance.

CARTAGO

pop 120,000

Cartago was founded in 1563 and was the colonial capital until 1823. Major earthquakes in 1841 and 1910 ruined almost all of the old buildings. The city is the capital of Cartago Province and lies at 1435m, between the Cordillera Central and the Cordillera de Talamanca. Volcán Irazú looms nearby.

COSTA RICA

Churches & La Negrita

The church, at Avenida 2, Calle 2, was destroyed by the 1910 earthquake, and **Las Ruinas** now contain a pretty garden.

East of the town center, at Avenida 2, Calle 16, is the most famous church of the Central Valley – **La Basílica de Nuestra Señora de los Angeles**. It was leveled by the 1926 earthquake then rebuilt in Byzantine style. The story goes that a statue of the virgin was discovered here on August 2, 1635, and miraculously reappeared after being removed. A shrine was built on the spot, and today the statue, La Negrita, represents the patron saint of Costa Rica. Miraculous healing powers are attributed to La Negrita, and every year on August 2 more than a million pilgrims arrive on foot from San José, 22km away. Inside the basilica is a chapel dedicated to her, where gifts from cured pilgrims can be seen, mostly metal models of body parts that have been miraculously healed.

Places to Stay & Eat

Decent budget accommodations are scarce. The family-run *Hotel Dinastia* (☎ 551 7057), 25m north of the market, charges US$10/23 per person in clean singles/ doubles, US$20/25 with private bath. The cheap dives near this hotel are not recommended. Restaurants are found along Avenidas 2 and 4 – *La Puerta del Sol* is probably the best for simple Tico food.

Getting There & Around

Buses arrive from San José along Avenida 2, going as far as the basilica. Frequent return buses run between 5 am and 11 pm, departing from Avenida 4, Calles 2 and 4 (US$0.40, 45 minutes).

Turrialba buses leave from in front of the Tribunales de Justicia on Avenida 3, Calles 8 and 10 (US$0.90, 1½ hours), departing every half hour until 10:30 am, then hourly until 10:30 pm.

Bus service to Volcán Irazú is limited to Saturday and Sunday, departing from the Iglesia de Los Padres Capuchinos (100m south of Las Ruinas) at 8:30 am. This blue-and-white bus originates in San José, leaving from Avenida 2, Calles 1 and 3 (opposite the Gran Hotel) at 8 am and returning at 12:30 pm (US$4.50). The schedule allows about two hours on the summit.

A taxi to Irazú costs US$25, including a short wait at the crater. The taxi stand is on the plaza west of the ruined church.

For Paraíso and the Lankester Gardens (see Around Cartago), buses leave from Avenida 1, Calles 2 and 4. Buses for Orosi depart from Calle 4 near Avenida 1. These buses run at least once an hour. For Tepantí park, take the early morning bus to Orosi that continues to Purisil, from which it is a 5km walk to the park. Alternatively, take a cab from Orosi (US$5 to US$10 each way). Montaña Linda can help you make arrangements.

AROUND CARTAGO
Lankester Gardens

Six kilometers east of Cartago, the university-run Lankester Gardens (☎ 551 9877) feature an extensive orchid collection, an arboretum and many plants. Any time of year is good for visiting the park, but February to April is best for viewing orchids in bloom. Free guided tours are sometimes given. Hours are 8:30 am to 3:30 pm daily; admission is US$3.50. Catch a Paraíso bus and ask for the turnoff to the gardens. From the turnoff, walk 0.75km to the entrance.

Río Orosi Valley

This river valley southeast of Cartago is famous for its pretty views, colonial buildings, hot springs, lake and national park. Many San José companies offer day tours to the valley, but you can visit cheaply by public bus from Cartago. The first village is **Paraíso**, 8km east of Cartago, with decent restaurants. Beyond Paraíso, you have the choice of going east to **Ujarras** and the artificial lake formed by the Presa de Cachí (Cachí Dam) or south to the village of **Orosi**. Ujarras, flooded and abandoned in 1833, features a ruined 17th-century church in a parklike setting. A short distance above the village is a good lookout point for the lake. The Virgen de Ujarras is honored the third Sunday in April with a procession, mass, music and local food.

Orosi (population 8000), named after a 16th-century Huetar Indian chief, is the center of an important coffee-growing region. The village boasts an early 18th-century church – one of the oldest still in use in Costa Rica. Hot springs are on the outskirts of town. *Albergue Montaña Linda*

(☎ 533 3640, mtnlinda@sol.racsa.co.cr) has a fun hostel environment. Rates are US$5.50 per person in dormitories or US$8/12 for a single/double room. Camping costs US$2.50 per person. Hot showers, kitchen privileges and inexpensive meals are offered. The hostel organizes tours and rents bicycles at US$6 per day.

Near **Purisil** village, 8km southeast of Orosi, is the private **Monte Sky** cloud forest reserve with good birding. Ask at Montaña Linda about guided walks (US$8), camping and overnight stays (US$25 per person including meals). Almost 3km farther east is **Parque Nacional Tapantí**, where waterfalls, trees and wildlife abound. However, there are few trails through the rugged terrain. The park is known for its birds, with at least 200 species spotted. Hours are 6 am to 4 pm daily; admission is US$6. There is an information center near the entrance. Camping may be allowed with a permit from the ranger. Dry season visits are recommended.

Parque Nacional Volcán Irazú

This is the highest active volcano in Costa Rica (3432m). A major eruption on March 19, 1963, covered San José and most of the Central Valley in a layer of volcanic ash more than 50cm deep in places. Since then Irazú's activity has been limited to gently smoking fumaroles.

A paved road leads to the summit, amid a bare landscape of volcanic ash and craters. The main crater is 1050m across and 300m deep. There are several smaller craters. From the summit it is possible to see both coasts, but it's rarely clear enough to do so. The best chance is in the early morning during the dry season (January to April).

The park is open 8 am to 3:30 pm daily; admission is US$6. There's a small information center and a cafe but no overnight accommodations or camping facilities. A 1km trail from the parking lot leads to a lookout over the craters. It tends to be cold and cloudy on the summit, so bring appropriate clothing.

TURRIALBA
pop 70,000

This pleasant, friendly and laid-back little town, near the headwaters of the Río Reventazón, is popular with river runners and kayakers. It's a good base for visiting the nearby agricultural station and archaeological site (see the Monumento Nacional Arqueológico Guayabo and Catie sections).

Places to Stay & Eat

On the south side of the old railway tracks is the best of the budget places to stay, *Hotel Interamericano (☎ 556 0142, hotelint@ sol.racsa.co.cr)*, popular with river runners. This bilingual establishment charges US$7 per person for decent rooms with shared baths or US$12/22 for singles/doubles with private bath. The nearby *Hotel Central* and *Hospedaje Chamango* are just a bit cheaper but not recommended.

Hotel La Roche (☎ 556 1624), Calle 4, Avenida 2 and Central, is basic but clean, with rates similar to the Interamericano's. Just across the street is another popular cheapie, *Whittingham's Hotel (☎ 556 8822)*, where large dark double rooms with private bath and hot water are US$8. Around the corner on Avenida 2, *Hotel Turrialba (☎ 556 6654)* has rooms with TVs, fans and private hot baths for US$12.50/18.50. The very basic *Hospedaje Hotel Primavera*, Avenida 2 at Calle 1, is about US$4 per person.

Restaurant Nuevo Hong Kong has reasonably priced Chinese food. *Pizzería Julian* is popular with young locals. *Bar/ Restaurant La Garza* sells a variety of meals for US$2 to US$6. All three are by the parque central.

Getting There & Away

Buses to San José (US$1.75, 1¾ hours) via Cartago leave every hour from Avenida 4, a block west of the parque central; buses for Siquirres (the transfer point for Puerto Limón) leave every two hours from the same place.

The terminal at Avenida 2 and Calle 2 has buses for nearby villages. The bus to Santa Teresita (also called Lajas), departing at 10:30 am and 1:30 pm, passes the turnoff for Monumento Nacional Arqueológico Guayabo (see the following section), from which it's a 4km walk to the monument. On Sunday, there's a direct bus to Guayabo at 9 am, returning at 4 pm, making a day trip to the ruins possible. On other days you could take an early taxi (US$15 one-way) and return by the daily 1 pm bus. These schedules are subject to change, so ask locally.

AROUND TURRIALBA
Catie

The acronym Catie stands for Centro Agronómico Tropical de Investigatión y Enseñanza (Center for Tropical Agronomy Research & Education). It's the most important center of its kind in Central America, with an extensive library and research facility. Guided tours (US$10) can be arranged in advance by calling ☎ 556 6431 or ☎ 556 1149. The grounds have pleasant paths and a pond that's good for watching waterbirds. The center is 4km east of Turrialba on the road to Limón.

Monumento Nacional Arqueológico Guayabo

This is the most important archaeological site in Costa Rica, although it is not as impressive as the Mayan sites of northern Central America. Excavations have revealed a number of cobbled roads, stone aqueducts, mounds, retaining walls and petroglyphs that visitors can examine. The area was occupied from about 1000 BC to AD 1400 and supported 10,000 inhabitants at its height. Archaeologists still don't know the exact significance of the site nor why it was abandoned.

The excavated section comprises about 10% of the monument. The remaining area is rain forest, with short trails for bird watching and wildlife observation.

Hours are daily from 8 am to 3 pm; admission is US$6. There's an information center at the monument entrance and maps are available. Rangers can show you around for a nominal fee. Excavation work may cause the ruins to be closed. Phone ☎ 556 9507 to check the situation.

Camping is permitted next to the information center and there are picnic areas, latrines and running water. See the Turrialba section for transportation to and from the monument.

Northwestern Costa Rica

Northwest of the Cordillera Central lie two mountain chains, the Cordillera de Tilarán and the Cordillera de Guanacaste. The former has rolling mountains that used to be covered with cloud forest. The Monteverde reserve is a popular destination for those wishing to see this tropical habitat. Separating the two cordilleras is Laguna de Arenal and the nearby Volcán Arenal – the most active in Costa Rica and the centerpiece of Parque Nacional Volcán Arenal. The Cordillera de Guanacaste is a spectacular string of volcanoes, some of which are also protected in national parks. West of the Cordillera de Guanacaste is the Península Santa Elena, with a rare, dry tropical forest habitat descending to remote Pacific beaches. This area is preserved in the splendid and historic Parque Nacional Santa Rosa.

MONTEVERDE & SANTA ELENA

Monteverde is a small community founded in 1951 by North American Quakers who bought about 1500 hectares and began dairy farming and cheese production. When the settlers arrived, they preserved a third of their property to protect the watershed above Monteverde. In 1972, about 2000 hectares were added. This became the **Reserva Biológica Bosque Nuboso Monteverde** (Monteverde Cloud Forest Biological Reserve). This reserve is just to the east of the community. The Monteverde Conservation League (MCL; ☎ 645 5003, acmmcl@ sol.racsa.co.cr), formed in 1985, continues to expand the protected area. In 1988, the MCL launched the International Children's Rain Forest Project, whereby school groups from all over the world raise money to save tropical rain forest adjacent to the reserve.

The Reserva Santa Elena was created in 1989 and relieves some of the heavy visitor pressure from Monteverde. Each year, these two cloud forest reserves attract many thousands of visitors. The area's elevation is 1200m to 1600m, and the cooler and cloudier climate here is a pleasant change from the tropical heat of the lowlands.

Orientation

The community of Monteverde is scattered along the several kilometers of road that lead to the reserve. Many better hotels are found along this road, and most of the budget hotels and the intercity bus stop are in the village of Santa Elena, at the west end. The Monteverde reserve is 6km southeast of Santa Elena, and the Santa Elena reserve is 5km north and then east.

Information

The office of the Reserva Santa Elena (☎ 645 5390, reserve@monteverdeinfo.com), at the public high school, can provide some general information and has a public notice board for tourist services. Jacques at the Pensión Santa Elena (see Places to Stay) is a seemingly inexhaustible supply of information about the area. See their informative Web site www.monteverdeinfo.com/, with links to many of the places mentioned here.

In Santa Elena, Banco Nacional (☎ 645 5027), open 8:30 am to 3:45 pm Monday to Friday, Hotel Camino Verde and Pensión Santa Elena (see Places to Stay) exchange money. The bank will advance cash on Visa cards. Supermercado La Esperanza has an ATM on the Visa-Plus network. Chip phones can be found in front of the supermarket and along Santa Elena's main street.

Chunches (☎/fax 645 5147) is a bookstore with travel and natural history guides and some US newspapers, as well as fax and laundry services. Internet access is provided by Desafío Expeditions (☎ 479 9464, fax 479 9463, desafio@sol.racsa.co.cr) at US$0.20 per minute and, theoretically, by the post office.

Reserva Biológica Bosque Nuboso Monteverde

Trails in the reserve are well maintained and clearly marked. The Sendero Bosque Nuboso is a 2km (one-way) interpretive walk through the cloud forest to the continental divide. From there you can return via El Camino Trail, from which a branch trail leads to a new 25m-high suspension bridge. This popular circuit takes two to three hours. No matter what time of year, the cloud forest is dripping, so bring rain gear. Rubber boots are needed only if you are venturing off the main trails.

Bird watching is good both in and around the reserve. More than 400 species have been recorded, but most visitors want to see the resplendent quetzal, best observed in March and April. Remember, it's hard to see wildlife in the cloud forest, a misty and mystical habitat. Don't go with unreasonable expectations.

You'll stand a better chance of seeing wildlife if you hire a guide. Half-day guided visits, in English, are arranged at the information office for US$15 per person (plus entrance fee). These start at 7:30 am and include a half-hour slide show and a three-hour walk limited to groups of nine. Call the day before to reserve a space. Night tours and birding tours can also be arranged. Most hotels can recommend local guides.

Camping is not permitted in the park. Backpackers can stay in one of three basic shelters, each containing at least 10 bunks and kitchen facilities; drinking water is available. You'll need to carry a sleeping bag, food and candles. The cost is US$3.50 to US$5 per night. Make reservations at least a week in advance. Also, dormitory-style accommodations near the park entrance are sometimes available for tourists at US$10 per night, including breakfast. Contact the reserve for information.

The information office (☎ 645 5122, fax 645 5034, montever@monteverdeinfo.com) at the reserve entrance is open 7 am to 4 pm daily. Admission is US$8.75 per day, US$4.75 for students with ID, and free for children younger than 12. Pick up a free trail map. You can rent binoculars and buy plant and wildlife guides here. There's a snack bar and a restaurant.

Reserva Santa Elena

This is a less-visited alternative to the Monteverde reserve, with similar habitat and wildlife. Almost 6km northeast of Santa Elena village, the reserve has a good trail system, where quetzals and other birds can be observed. One trail leads to a tower that affords views (weather permitting) of Volcán Arenal.

Reserve hours are 7:30 am to 4 pm daily; admission is US$7, US$4 for students. There's a small information center as well as a gift shop and coffee shop. Guided tours are given at 7:30 and 11:30 am and 7 pm daily (US$15/13 day/night plus entry fee). Make prior arrangements at the reserve office (☎/fax 645 5390, reserve@monteverdeinfo.com) in the Santa Elena high school. In the village, tickets are available at Pensión Santa Elena and Hotel Camino Verde.

Other Attractions

Several outfitters offer **horseback riding tours**. Apart from forest tours, day treks to the San Luis waterfalls and Volcán Arenal

MONTEVERDE & SANTA ELENA

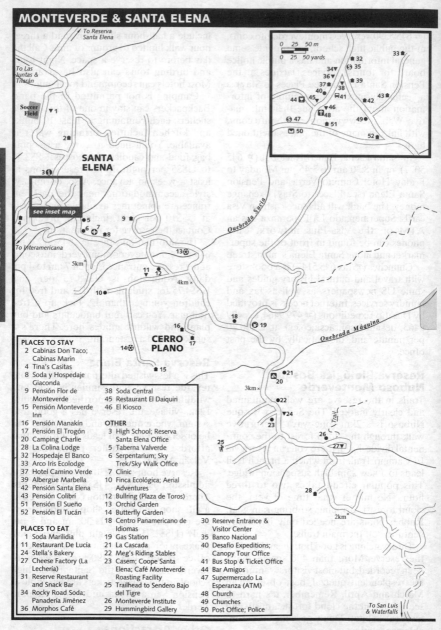

PLACES TO STAY

2 Cabinas Don Taco;
   Cabinas Marín
4 Tina's Casitas
8 Soda y Hospedaje
   Giaconda
9 Pensión Flor de
   Monteverde
15 Pensión Monteverde
   Inn
16 Pensión Manakin
17 Pensión El Trogón
20 Camping Charlie
28 La Colina Lodge
32 Hospedaje El Banco
33 Arco Iris Ecolodge
37 Hotel Camino Verde
39 Albergue Marbella
42 Pensión Santa Elena
43 Pensión Colibrí
51 Pensión El Sueño
52 Pensión El Tucán

PLACES TO EAT

1 Soda Marilidia
11 Restaurant De Lucía
24 Stella's Bakery
27 Cheese Factory (La
   Lechería)
31 Reserve Restaurant
   and Snack Bar
34 Rocky Road Soda;
   Panadería Jiménez
36 Morphos Café

38 Soda Central
45 Restaurant El Daiquiri
46 El Kiosco

OTHER

3 High School; Reserva
   Santa Elena Office
5 Taberna Valverde
6 Serpentarium; Sky
   Trek/Sky Walk Office
7 Clinic
10 Finca Ecológica; Aerial
   Adventures
12 Bullring (Plaza de Toros)
13 Orchid Garden
14 Butterfly Garden
18 Centro Panamericano de
   Idiomas
19 Gas Station
21 La Cascada
22 Meg's Riding Stables
23 Casem; Coope Santa
   Elena; Café Monteverde
   Roasting Facility
25 Trailhead to Sendero Bajo
   del Tigre
26 Monteverde Institute
29 Hummingbird Gallery

30 Reserve Entrance &
   Visitor Center
35 Banco Nacional
40 Desafío Expeditions;
   Canopy Tour Office
41 Bus Stop & Ticket Office
44 Bar Amigos
47 Supermercado La
   Esperanza (ATM)
48 Church
49 Chunches
50 Post Office; Police

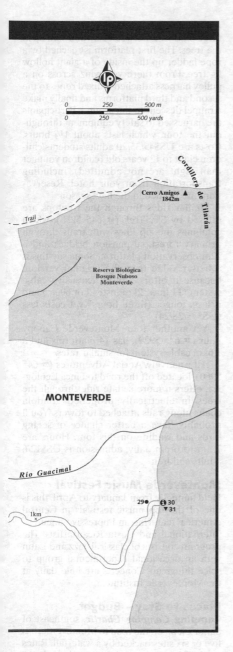

viewpoints are popular. Meg's Riding Stables (☎ 645 5560, rlaval@sol.racsa.co.cr), which charges US$10 per hour, has been recommended.

The interesting **butterfly garden** is open 9:30 am to 4 pm daily. Admission (US$7) includes an informative tour, led by a naturalist, of three butterfly-raising greenhouses, each representing a different geographic habitat.

The **hummingbird gallery**, near the Monteverde reserve entrance, has feeders attracting several species of hummingbird, creating great photo opportunities.

The **serpentarium** (☎ 645 5238), which shares a building with the Sky Trek office (see Canopy Tours, later), exhibits about 20 snakes and lizards with informative signs in English. Hours are 7 am to 5 pm; admission is US$3.

The **orchid garden** displays more than 400 species of the flowering plant, including the world's smallest orchid. It's open 8 am to 5 pm, and admission is US$5. The garden is part of an ongoing conservation and research project. The peak blooming period is November to February.

The local women's arts and crafts cooperative, **Casem** (☎ 645 5190), sells embroidered and hand-painted blouses, handmade clothing and other souvenirs. Profits benefit the local community.

Nature Trails & Hiking

Outside the reserves there are several other trails. The 3.5km **Sendero Bajo del Tigre** traverses a section of the Children's Eternal Rain Forest, which is managed by the Monteverde Conservation League. Vegetation is less dense here than in the cloud forest, so spotting birds tends to be easier. It's open 7:30 am to 5:30 pm; admission is US$5, US$4 for students.

The **Finca Ecológica** (☎ 645 5363) is a private property with four loop trails (the longest takes 2½ hours) through forest and coffee and banana plantations. Coatis, agoutis and sloths are often seen, and birding is good. Hours are 7 am to 5 pm; admission is US$6/4.

The **Hidden Valley Trail**, behind the Pensión Monteverde Inn (see Places to Stay), is free to inn guests and US$3.25 to others. A free hiking option is the 3km track leaving from behind the Hotel Belmar and climbing up to **Cerro Amigos** (1842m), with fine views of the surrounding rain forest.

As a way of getting up among the treetops, the new **Sky Walk** (☎ 645 5238) is a serene alternative to the various zip-wire tours offered (see Canopy Tours, later). Seven suspension bridges stretch high across valleys along a circular trail winding 3.5km through a 228-hectare private reserve. Gazing down through green layers of cloud forest from the bridges, birders can see their quarry dart beneath them. The walk is open 7 am to 4 pm; admission is US$12/6. Sky Walk provides Jeep transportation from the Santa Elena bank (US$1 per person) – check departure times at Pensión Santa Elena. For more information, see their Web site (www.skywalk.co.cr).

Courses

The Monteverde Studios of the Arts (☎ 645 5434, 800-370 3331 in the USA) provide the wonderful opportunity of taking classes with artists from the Monteverde community. Held in homes and studios, the classes include woodworking, photography, stained glass design, painting and drawing, cooking and storytelling. Classes last a week and cost US$235 plus materials fees. Food and lodging can be arranged. See their Web site (www.mvstudios.com).

The Monteverde Institute (☎ 645 5053, fax 645 5219) offers interdisciplinary courses in tropical biology, agroecology, conservation, sustainable development, local culture, Spanish and women's studies. Ten- to 14-day courses for high school and college students and adults are US$700 to US$1500, all inclusive from San José. You can also learn the crafts of batik, hammock weaving, papermaking and others in the newly opened community arts center. Their Web site has more information on classes and programs (www.mvinstitute.org).

The Centro Panamericano de Idiomas (☎/fax 645 5026) has established a Spanish language program in Monteverde with homestays available. See their Web site (www.cpi-edu.com).

Canopy Tours

The *Original* Canopy Tour (☎ 645 5243, see also San José) is on the grounds of the Cloud Forest Lodge and has an information office in Santa Elena. Their tour begins with a short hike through the forest to a series of three platforms between 20m and 33m up in the trees. The first platform is reached by a rope ladder up the inside of a giant hollow fig tree. From there you whiz across on a pulley harness attached to fixed ropes to the second and third platforms and finally make a rappel descent to the ground. Participants are harnessed to safety equipment throughout the tour, which lasts about 1¼ hours. Costs are US$45/35/20 adults/students/children eight to 12 years old (children younger than eight are not admitted), including transportation from your hotel. Reservations are needed in the high season.

Similar rides through the treetops are offered by Sky Trek (☎ 645 5238), which combines the zip lines with trails through primary forest, suspension bridges and a 22m observation platform. Some say this is a better value than the original version, because it offers a more extensive cable system (11 lines, 2km instead of 600m) and it lasts longer (three hours) yet costs less (US$35/28/24).

Yet another tour, Monteverde Canopy Tour (☎ 645 5929), has 14 platforms and a 1.6km cable system for similar rates.

Alternatively, Aerial Adventures (☎ 645 5960), located off the road to Finca Ecológica, offers a more sedate ride through the trees in electrically propelled gondola chairs along rails attached to towers. You'll probably have a better chance of seeing birds and wildlife on this tour. Hours are 7 am to 6 pm daily; admission is US$12/6 adults/children.

Monteverde Music Festival

Held annually from January to April, this is one of the top music festivals in Central America, featuring an impressive lineup of international and Costa Rican artists. The program consists of classical, jazz and Latin with an occasional experimental group to spice things up. Concerts are held daily at the Monteverde Institute.

Places to Stay – Budget

Camping *Camping Charlie*, southeast of Santa Elena on the road to Monteverde, has five or six sites backed by a waterfall. Rates are US$3 per tent, and there's a basic bathroom. Owner Charlie, a sculptor/welder, has his workshop in front.

Hotels Most budget hotels are in Santa Elena. Stiff competition has kept prices low: Unless otherwise noted, all of the following places charge US$5 to US$7 per person with shared bath, usually with warm water from electric showerheads, or US$7 to US$10 per person with private bath.

Pensión Santa Elena (☎ *645 5051, fax 645 6060, pension@monteverdeinfo.com*) is a full-service shoestringer's hostel with a message board, Internet (US$0.20 a minute), and a kind, knowledgeable host named Jacques. It contains 21 clean rooms of variable capacity, a common kitchen and a cozy lounge/dining area. The adjacent *Albergue Marbella*, run by the same people, is quieter, more comfortable and a little pricier. Down the street and up a quiet lane, *Pensión Colibrí* (☎ *645 5682*) feels like it's perched among the trees. Choose from small simple units with shared bath or larger rooms with private baths and little balconies overlooking the woods. *Hospedaje El Banco* (☎ *645 5204*), behind the bank, is basic but friendly, and laundry service and meals are offered. Homey, bilingual and popular with travelers, *Hotel Camino Verde* (☎ *645 5916*) is on the main street, but the interior feels reasonably distant from the noise. Rooms are clean and basic, and there's a common kitchen/dining area in back. The helpful *Pensión El Tucán* (☎ *645 5017*) has 14 small, clean doubles, half of which contain bathrooms. Hearty meals are prepared in its large aromatic kitchen. The family-run *Pensión El Sueño* (☎ *645 5021*) offers basic quads or slightly better doubles equipped with private hot shower, and meals on request.

About 50m above the Santa Elena high school, *Cabinas Marín* (☎ *645 5279*) and *Cabinas Don Taco* (☎ *645 5263*) offer mountain lodge–style accommodations. Both are tranquil and cordially managed. The Marín has neat cozy rooms of dark-hued wood, including a couple of small singles for US$10, while Don Taco features larger carpeted rooms alongside a balcony, some with good views.

On a hillside southwest of the center but close to everything, the friendly *Tina's Casitas* (☎ *645 5641*) is a terrific budget choice with pleasant variably-sized units around a pretty central garden. Larger rooms with bath contain three or four single beds; one room affords a sweeping view of the valley. Follow the signs from behind La Esperanza supermarket.

Heading out along the main road toward the cloud forest reserve, *Hospedaje Giaconda* (☎ *645 5461*) has four tidy little rooms in back of a soda that serves tasty meat or vegetarian casados (US$3). Farther out is the friendly *Pensión Flor de Monteverde* (☎ */fax 645 5236*), run by a former director of the Santa Elena reserve. Tours and transportation can be arranged and there's a meal plan.

About 1km southeast of Santa Elena in the Cerro Plano neighborhood, you'll find a pair of solid budget options side by side: *Pensión El Trogón* (☎ *645 5130; formerly El Pino*) and *Pensión Manakín* (☎ */fax 645 5080, fax 645 5517, manakin@sol.racsa .co.cr*). Both provide fresh, clean rooms in a homey setting, meals, laundry service, horse rental and local tours. Balconies on the Manakín's rear cabins (US$20/25 for one/two occupants) face the woods and are good vantage points for wildlife viewing; be prepared for simian visitors at dawn.

A quiet, remote location is the main attraction of *Pensión Monteverde Inn* (☎ *645 5156*), set in a private 11-hectare reserve. Rooms with two beds are simple and clean and have private hot showers. The owners can pick you up at the bus stop.

Places to Stay – Mid-Range

Six kilometers northwest of Santa Elena on the road to Tilarán is *Monte Los Olivos Ecoverde Lodge* (☎ *661 8126, 286 4203 in San José, cooprena@sol.racsa.co.cr*), which was developed by the Canadian WWF and other agencies. This grassroots ecotourism project aims to directly benefit small communities. Cabins with shared bathrooms are US$14/18 single/double, with private bathrooms US$35/45, including breakfast. Guided hikes and horseback rides are available.

On a peaceful hilltop a short distance from downtown Santa Elena, *Arco Iris Ecolodge* (☎ *645 5067, fax 645 5022, arcoiris@racsa.co.cr*) has beautiful hardwood cabins with terraces, a good value at US$35/60 with private hot water bath. One little cabin dubbed 'the doll's house' has a pair of bunk beds for US$20/30. The price includes a short orientation session on

Monteverde's bewildering array of attractions. A lavish buffet breakfast costs US$6.50. Trails and a sunset lookout point are behind the lodge.

La Colina Lodge (☎ 645 5009, 970-352 4767 in the US, info@lacolina.com) belongs to the same American family who run La Colina Bed & Breakfast in Manuel Antonio. Tastefully furnished rooms, some with balconies, are US$25/35 with shared bath or US$35/40 with private bath, including breakfast. Rooms with four bunk beds are US$15 per person. La Colina is 2km from the Monteverde reserve.

Places to Eat
Budget travelers eat in Santa Elena, where a casado can be had for US$3. The **Soda Central**, next to the bus stop, is clean and popular. Early bus travelers can grab breakfast at the small open-air **El Kiosco**, next to the church. Across from the soccer field, **Soda Marilidia** has delicious cold fruit drinks, breakfasts (US$2) and snacks.

The **Rocky Road Soda** (open only 10:30 am to 2 pm) prepares good hamburgers (US$2) and overstuffed hoagies (submarine sandwiches) on cheese bread (US$2.75). Their balcony overlooks 'downtown' Santa Elena. Below is **Panadería Jiménez** for baked goods. Next door, **Morphos Café** is a popular hangout, offering Tico fast food and some vegetarian dishes. It shuts at 9 pm. The cozy **Restaurant El Daiquiri** is open later and good for a beer, but the food is overpriced and nothing special. **Chunches** (see Information) has espresso and homemade snacks.

For picnics, **Stella's Bakery** offers a variety of pastries, delicious homemade bread and rolls. **La Lechería** – the Monteverde Cheese Factory – has fresh cheese. Or try the **Coope Santa Elena**, the grocery store next to Casem, then drop by the Café Monteverde roasting facility to sample a cup of locally grown coffee.

Restaurant De Lucía, on the road to the Finca Ecológica, is considered one of Monteverde's finest, and it's worth the splurge. Fresh fish and beef dishes are US$10, and a veggie lasagna with salad is US$5.

Entertainment
La Cascada (☎ 645 5186) is a popular dance club by a waterfall, open Thursday

to Sunday nights. Occasional live music is advertised by roadside banners. **Bar Amigos** in town is very much a local place with three pool tables in the backroom and live cumbia bands Friday night. The lively **Taberna Valverde** has a dance floor and attracts a healthy mix of visitors and locals.

Getting There & Around
Buses depart for San José (US$4.25, 4½ hours) from La Lechería at 6:30 am and 2:30 pm daily, stopping en route at the bus office (☎ 645 5032) opposite the Banco Nacional in Santa Elena.

Buses depart from the Banco Nacional at 6 am for Puntarenas (US$2, three hours) – from which there are connections to Quepos and Jacó (at 11 am) and the Nicoya Península.

There's a bus to Tilarán at 7 am daily (US$1.75, three to four hours). This connects with a 12:15 pm bus to La Fortuna and Volcán Arenal, arriving around 4 pm. Alternatively, Pensión Santa Elena offers a Jeep-boat-Jeep connection to La Fortuna (US$25, three hours).

Yet another alternative is to travel by horse. A number of operators can arrange this journey, which includes a four-hour horse ride to Laguna Arenal and onward transportation by ferry and Jeep. Keep in mind, however, that cutthroat competition has led some unscrupulous operators to overwork their horses. Expect to pay at least US$65 for a reputable operator – Arco Iris Ecolodge can help you find one – and don't travel this way during the rainy season.

Local buses for the Monteverde reserve depart from the bank in Santa Elena at 6:15 am and 1 pm, returning at noon and 4 pm (US$0.65). Collective taxis to Reserva Santa Elena leave from Pensión Santa Elena at 6:45 am, 11 am and 3 pm and return at noon and 3:30 pm (US$2 one-way), or take a regular taxi for US$6.50 each way.

CAÑAS
pop 23,500
This small, hot, lowland town is an agricultural center that travelers use as a base for visits to the nearby Parque Nacional Palo Verde and for Corobicí river trips. Cañas is

also the beginning and end of the Arenal back roads described later.

River Trips

The local outfitter Safaris Corobicí (☎/fax 669 1091, safaris@sol.racsa.co.cr) is 5km north of Cañas on the Interamericana. Daily two-hour float trips on the Río Corobicí are US$37 per person, a three-hour bird-watching float is US$43 per person, and a half-day saltwater estuary trip along the Bebedero and Tempisque Rivers, bordering Parque Nacional Palo Verde, costs US$60 per person, lunch included.

Places to Stay & Eat

Hotel Guillén (☎ 669 0070) and *Hotel Parque* on the south side of the parque central charge US$3.50 per person. The *Gran Hotel*, on the northwest side, is similarly priced, with a few basic doubles including bath for slightly more. *Cabinas Corobicí* (☎ 669 0241), Avenida 2 and Calle 5, is better, charging about US$6.50 per person with private bath. None of these has hot showers.

The best place downtown is *Hotel Cañas* (☎ 669 0039), Calle 2, Avenida 3, with a good restaurant. Singles/doubles with private cold baths and fan are US$15/21; with air-conditioning, it's US$28 for a double.

A couple of unremarkable Chinese restaurants are around the park, with meals in the US$2 to US$5 range.

Getting There & Away

Transportes La Cañera (☎ 669 0145) has six daily buses to San José from the main Cañas bus terminal, at Calle 1 and Avenida 11. Other San José–bound buses can be flagged down outside the San Carlos gas station on the Interamericana, which is also the departure point for buses en route to Liberia, Tilarán and Puntarenas (seven daily each).

Buses to Bebedero (near Parque Nacional Palo Verde) depart six times daily from the cemetery, while buses to Upala depart five times daily from the market, adjacent to the main terminal.

PARQUE NACIONAL PALO VERDE

This park on the northeastern banks of the mouth of Río Tempisque, 30km west of Cañas, is a major bird sanctuary. Several different habitats are found: swamps, marshes, mangroves, lagoons and a variety of seasonal grasslands and forests. Low limestone hills provide lookouts over the park.

During the dry season from December through March, much of the forest dries out. During other months, large areas are flooded. September to March see a huge influx of migratory and endemic birds – one of the greatest concentrations of waterfowl and shorebirds in Central America. When the dry season begins, birds congregate in the lakes and marshes, trees lose their leaves and the massed flocks become easier to observe. December to February are the best months for watching birds – bring binoculars.

Park admission is US$6 per day. Camping (US$2 per person) is permitted near the Palo Verde ranger station, where toilets and showers are available.

Limited information is available from the Area de Conservación Tempisque office (ACT; ☎/fax 671 1290) in Bagaces, 22km northwest of Cañas on the Interamericana.

The park is reached by a 28km road leaving the Interamericana from opposite the ACT office. There are no buses, but park rangers may be able to pick you up in Bagaces if you call ACT beforehand.

RESERVA BIOLÓGICA LOMAS BARBUDAL

This reserve, just north of Palo Verde, protects a tropical dry forest with riparian areas. Lomas Barbudal is locally famous for its abundance and variety of insects, including some 250 different species of bee – about a quarter of the world's bee species. Endangered birds seen here include the king vulture and scarlet macaw.

Information can be obtained from the ACT office in Bagaces (see Parque Nacional Palo Verde).

At the entrance is a small local museum and information center. The reserve is on the other side of the Río Cabuyo behind the museum – you have to wade across the river. There is no entry fee; camping is allowed.

The turnoff to Lomas Barbudal from the Interamericana is at Pijije, 2km northwest of Bagaces. The 7km road to the reserve is signed but in poor shape. Walk or use a 4WD.

LIBERIA
pop 40,000

Liberia, the capital of Guanacaste Province and Costa Rica's most important northerly town, is a ranching center and transportation hub. It's a good base for visiting the nearby national parks.

Information

A tourist office (☎ 666 4527), in a 19th-century adobe house on the corner of Avenida 6 and Calle 1, is open 8:30 am to 5 pm Monday to Saturday, with a break for lunch. It contains a small local museum.

The ICE telephone office has international phone and fax facilities. Cibermanía, on the north side of the parque central, charges US$1.60 an hour for Internet access, as does the post office. Banco de San José's ATM accepts Cirrus and American Express cards; Banco de Costa Rica is on the Visa-Plus network.

Places to Stay & Eat

The nicest budget choice is *La Posada del Tope* (☎ 666 3876), one of several 19th-century buildings along the historic Calle Real. Six simple, pleasant rooms with fans share one shower; rates are US$5 per person. The annex across the street, signed *Hotel Casa Real*, is similar and contains a courtyard restaurant. On the next block is *Hotel Liberia* (☎ /fax 666 0161) in another attractive old mansion, divided into basic singles/doubles for US$6/12, or US$9/17 with private bath. Rooms in the newer back wing are brighter. Both places can arrange excursions to Parque Nacional Rincón de la Vieja. Northeast of the parque central, *Pensión Golfito* (☎ 666 0963) has some spartan but acceptable rooms for US$4/10.

Several small family-run guesthouses are found in the quiet area south of Avenida 4. The best is *Hospedaje Lodge La Casona* (☎ /fax 666 2971), managed by English-speaking Alberto and María José. The pink wooden house contains seven basic rooms sharing three bathrooms at US$6/10/15 for one to three occupants; a newer annex has rooms with bath for US$9/15/22.50. Other decent but unexceptional places to stay in this neighborhood include *Hospedaje Anita* (☎ 666 1285) and *Hospedaje Condega* (☎ 666 1165), both charging US$5 per person.

The HI-affiliated *Hotel Guanacaste* (☎ 666 0085, fax 666 2287, htlguana@racsa.co.cr) is often full. Rates are US$14/25 with fan and bath, or US$10/20 for HI members. The hotel offers daily transportation to and from Parque Nacional Rincón de la Vieja. The good attached restaurant is popular with riders of the Trans-Nica bus, which picks up passengers here on its way to Managua (7 and 8 am, noon).

On the parque central, the modern *Hotel Primavera* (☎ 666 0464, fax 666 3069) offers bland but comfortable rooms with private bath, around an enclosed parking lot. Rates are US$16/23 with fan or US$28/36 with air-conditioning.

On the west side of the parque central, *Las Tinajas* is a good place to sit outside with a cold drink; meals are in the US$4 to US$7 range. You'll find cheaper fare at the Chinese restaurants along Calle Real: *Restaurante Elegante* and *Restaurante La Copa de Oro* both charge US$3 for an ample portion of chop suey or fried rice. *Pizza Pronto* is in a handsome hundred-year-old house with a clay oven, and the pizza's pretty good, from US$5 for a small pie.

Getting There & Away

Air The airport is 12km west of town, about 1.6km off the main highway to Nicoya. Sansa flies four times daily to and from San José (US$55/110 one-way/roundtrip), and Travelair flies San José-Tamarindo-Liberia at 8:20 am, returning directly to San José at 9:55 am (US$92/152). Schedules change often. The Sansa/Grupo TACA office (☎ 666 0306) is at Avenida Central and Calle 6.

Bus Pulmitan buses to San José depart 11 times daily between 4 am and 8 pm (US$4.50, four hours). The terminal (☎ 666 0458), Avenida 5, Calles 10 and 12, has a baggage check service for US$0.15.

Buses to and from other destinations use the terminal on Avenida 7, Calles 12 and 14:

Cañas (US$1, 1¼ hours)
Buses depart at 5:45 am and 1:30, 4:30 and 5:10 pm.

Nicaraguan border (via La Cruz; US$1.30, two hours)
Eight buses depart from 5:30 am to 8 pm.

Nicoya (via Filadelfia and Santa Cruz; US$1.25, two hours)
Frequent buses depart from 5:15 am to 8:20 pm.

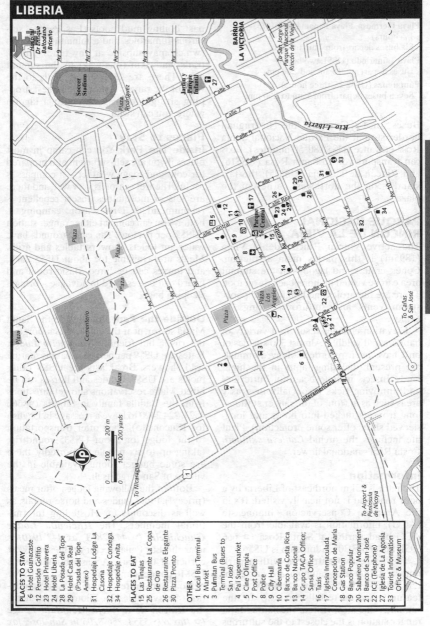

LIBERIA

To San Jorge &
Parque Nacional
Rincón de la Vieja

BARRIO
LA VICTORIA

Río Liberia

Jardin y
Parque Infantil

Soccer
Stadium

Plaza
Rodríguez

Cementerio

To Cañas
& San José

Interamericana

To Nicaragua

To Airport &
Península
de Nicoya

0   100   200 m
0   100   200 yards

COSTA RICA

PLACES TO STAY
6 Hotel Guanacaste
12 Pensión Golfito
23 Hotel Primavera
24 Hotel Liberia
28 La Posada del Tope
29 Hotel Casa Real
   (Posada del Tope
   Annex)
31 Hospedaje Lodge La
   Casona
32 Hospedaje Condega
34 Hospedaje Anita

PLACES TO EAT
15 Las Tinajas
25 Restaurante La Copa
   de Oro
26 Restaurante Elegante
30 Pizza Pronto

OTHER
1 Local Bus Terminal
2 Market
3 Pulmitan Bus
   Terminal (Buses to
   San José)
4 Pali Supermarket
5 Cine Olimpia
7 Post Office
8 Police
9 City Hall
10 Cibernmania
11 Banco de Costa Rica
13 Banco Nacional
14 Grupo TACA Office;
   Sansa Office
16 Taxis
17 Iglesia Inmaculada
   Concepción de María
18 Gas Station
19 Banco Popular
20 Sabanero Monument
21 Banco de San José
22 ICE (Telephone)
27 Iglesia de La Agonia
33 Tourist Information
   Office & Museum

Playa del Coco (US$0.75, one hour)
Six buses depart from 5:30 am to 6:15 pm.

Playa Hermosa, Playa Panamá (US$0.75,
1¼ hours)
Six buses depart from 7 am to 7 pm.

Playa Tamarindo (US$1, two hours)
Buses depart at 5:15 am and 2:30 pm.

Puntarenas (US$2.25, three hours)
Seven buses depart from 5 am to 3:30 pm.

Buses for La Cruz and the Nicaraguan
border stop at the Parque Nacional Santa
Rosa entrance (US$0.80, 50 minutes). Taxis
can transport you to Santa Rosa (US$16)
and Rincón de la Vieja (US$25); the taxi
stand is on the northwest corner of the
plaza.

PARQUE NACIONAL RINCÓN DE LA VIEJA

The active Volcán Rincón de la Vieja
(1895m) is this park's main attraction.
Cones, craters and lagoons in the summit
area can be visited on horseback or on foot.
There are fumaroles and boiling mud pools,
steam vents and sulfurous springs to
explore.

Elevation changes result in a variety of
habitats and wildlife. Almost 300 species of
bird have been recorded. Many mammals
are present, including tapirs in the highlands. Insects include beautiful butterflies
and annoying ticks (especially in grassy
areas such as in front of the ranger station –
long trousers tucked into boots and long-
sleeved shirts offer some protection). Plant
life includes the orchid *Cattleya skinneri,*
Costa Rica's national flower.

Information

The park is 25km northeast of Liberia by a
poor road and is not heavily visited. It's in
the Area de Conservación Guanacaste
(ACG); information is available from the
ACG headquarters at Santa Rosa (☎ 666
5051, fax 666 5020). Admission is US$6.

There are two entrances, with a park
ranger station and camping area at each.
Las Pailas, with trails past various volcanic
features and waterfalls and up to the
summit, is the most visited. The Santa María
ranger station is the closest to the sulfurous
hot springs (with supposed therapeutic
properties) and also has an observation
tower and a nearby waterfall.

Going east from the Las Pailas station, a
circular trail (about 8km in total) takes you
past boiling mud pools (Las Pailas), sulfurous fumaroles, and a miniature volcano
(which may subside at any time). North,
trails lead 8km (one-way) to the summit
area. There are several waterfalls to the
west of the ranger station, the largest dropping straight from a cliff into a lagoon
where you can swim.

Places to Stay

Inside the Park You can camp in most
places if you are self-sufficient and prepared
for cold and foggy weather – a compass is
useful. The wet season is very wet, and there
are lots of mosquitoes. Insect repellent is
recommended. Dry season camping is
better. You can camp at either ranger station
(US$2 per person). The campgrounds have
water, pit toilets, showers, tables and grills.
Meals are available for about US$3 each,
and horses can be hired. Basic room and
board can be reserved in advance – bring a
sleeping bag.

Outside the Park Just outside the Santa
María sector, near the village of San Jorge, is
the rustic but friendly *Rinconcito Lodge*.
Rates are US$9 per person in cabins sharing
cold showers. Breakfasts are US$3; other
meals are US$5. Guides and horses can be
hired. Make reservations and get directions
from the Badilla family in Liberia (☎ 666
4527, 224 2400 to leave a message in English
for Rinconcito). They offer transportation
to the lodge for about US$35 roundtrip,
taking up to six people. Reportedly, there
are some budget rooms available in the
village of San Jorge itself.

Both of the following lodges offer meals
(pricey!), tours, guides and horse rentals, as
well as discounts for Hostelling International members. The *Hacienda Lodge
Guachipelín* (☎ 442 2818, fax 442 1910) is
near the Las Pailas sector at the southwest
corner of the park. A basic bunkhouse is
US$10 per person; a dormitory is US$16 per
person, and more expensive accommodations are available. Five kilometers farther is
the *Rincón de la Vieja Mountain Lodge*
(☎ /fax 695 5553, 256 8206 in San José, fax
256 7290, rincon@sol.racsa.co.cr). It's about
2km from the mud pools and 5km from the
fumaroles. Dormitory rooms start at US$20,

and more expensive private rooms are available. Screens help keep out abundant insects in the wettest months. There is a canopy platform tour here.

Getting There & Away

Most hotels (or the tourist office) in Liberia can arrange transportation for US$18 roundtrip.

To Las Pailas Almost 5km north of Liberia on the Interamericana is a signed turnoff to the northeast onto a gravel road; from here, it is just a little more than 20km to the station at Las Pailas. The road passes through the grounds of the Hacienda Lodge Guachipelín (there are signs for the lodge along the way) and continues on to the Rincón de la Vieja Lodge (another 5km). The lodges can provide transportation. Frequent public buses from Liberia to Cañas Dulces can drop you at the turnoff if you want to walk up.

To Santa María Hike 25km or take a taxi (US$25) on the rough road that heads northeast out of Liberia through the Barrio La Victoria suburb. After 18km, the road passes San Jorge village and continues as far as the Santa María station. Sometimes a ride from Liberia can be arranged when a park service vehicle is in town.

PARQUE NACIONAL SANTA ROSA

The park covers most of the Península Santa Elena, which juts out into the Pacific at the far northwestern corner of the country. It is named after Hacienda Santa Rosa, where a battle was fought in 1856 between Costa Rica and the invading forces of William Walker. Santa Rosa protects the largest remaining stand of tropical dry forest in Central America, as well as important sea turtle nesting sites.

It's a good place to see wildlife, especially in the dry season, though the rainy months (especially September and October) are best for turtle watching.

Information

The park entrance is on the west side of the Interamericana, 35km north of Liberia. Hours are 7:30 am to 4:30 pm daily; admission is US$6.

It is 7km (no transportation) to the park headquarters (☎ 666 5051, fax 666 5020), where you'll find an information center, campground, museum, research station and nature trail. This is also the administrative center for the Area de Conservación Guanacaste (ACG) and has information about (and maintains radio contact with) Parque Nacional Rincón de la Vieja and Parque Nacional Guanacaste. Accommodations at the research station (US$20 per night) and meals (US$3 to US$4) can be arranged in advance through park headquarters.

The campground – one of the best-developed facilities of the nation's parks – has drinking water, picnic benches, flush toilets and cold showers. Large fig trees provide shade. Camping fees are US$2 per person.

A 4WD trail (closed from May to November) leads down to the coast, 12km away, where there are campsites with pit toilets. Ask the rangers if drinking water is available before heading down.

Buses between Liberia and Peñas Blancas will stop at the entrance. The ranger has a timetable for buses passing the park.

Things to See & Do

A **museum** is inside the historic Santa Rosa Hacienda. Exhibits describe the 1856 battle fought here and show Costa Rican life in the 19th century. Antique firearms, furniture and tools are on display. Another exhibit deals with the ecological significance and wildlife of the park.

Near the museum is a 1km **nature trail**, with signs explaining the relationships among the plants, animals and weather patterns of Santa Rosa. You will see a variety of plants and birds and probably, if you move slowly and keep your eyes and ears open, monkeys, snakes, iguanas and other animals. Bats are very common: Some 50 or 60 species have been identified in Santa Rosa.

The best turtle beach is **Playa Nancite**, and during September and October you may see as many as 8000 olive ridley turtles on the beach at once. Flashlights and flash photography are prohibited. Avoid nights near the full moon, as turtles prefer to lay their eggs in darkness. Nancite Beach is strictly protected and restricted, but permission can be obtained from the park service to see this spectacle.

Playa Naranjo, south of Nancite, has good surfing. There's a campground but facilities are limited.

PARQUE NACIONAL GUANACASTE

Separated from Santa Rosa by the Interamericana, the park is an extension of its neighbor's habitats, but the terrain soon begins to climb toward Volcán Orosí (1487m) and Volcán Cacao (1659m). The protected zone enables animals to range from the coast to the highlands, just as they have always done.

Places to Stay

Three biological stations in the park have dormitories for 30 to 40 people and bathrooms with cold water. A bed and three meals cost about US$20 a day, but researchers get preference and there's no public transportation. Camping near the stations costs US$2 per night. Contact ACG headquarters in Santa Rosa to camp or stay; they may be able to arrange transportation to the biological stations.

About 7km south of the park via the village of Quebrada Grande, the family-run *Santa Clara Lodge* (☎ *391 8766, 257 8585 beeper,* ☎ *666 4054 in Liberia, fax 666 4047)* offers clean, simple rooms for about US$9 per person. Electricity is available from 6 to 10 pm; showers are cold. Horseback and taxi tours are available to the national parks, as well as to local waterfalls and thermal springs.

PEÑAS BLANCAS

This is the border with Nicaragua, but there's nowhere to stay. See Costa Rica's Getting There & Away section, earlier. The nearest town is **La Cruz** (20km). The best budget hotel in La Cruz is *Cabinas Santa Rita* (☎ *679-9062)*, with clean doubles for US$8, or US$15 with private showers. Another economical choice is *Cabinas Maryfel* (☎ *679-9096)*, opposite the bus station. There are a couple of pricier hotels, too.

CIUDAD QUESADA
pop 31,000

Locals call this town San Carlos. It's not a major destination but is convenient for hotels en route to Arenal or the northern lowlands. Almost everything of importance

is on the parque central or close to it. It's known as a cowboy town, and there are several memorably aromatic saddle shops.

Places to Stay & Eat

The cheapest place to stay is the very basic and noisy *Hotel Terminal* (☎ *460 2158)*, in the bus terminal half a block from the parque central. West of the terminal, the clean *Hotel del Norte* (☎ *460 1959)* is better, at US$6.25 per person with shared hot showers. North of the parque central, the first two blocks of Calle 2 have several adequate budget hotels, including *Hotel Axel Alberto* (☎ *460 1423)*, at US$8 per double room with private bath, and *Hotel del Valle* (☎ *460-0718)*, which charges US$10/16/22 for one to three persons in rooms with private bath and cable TV.

Hotel El Retiro (☎ *460 0463)*, on the parque central, charges US$7.50/13 for basic, clean singles/doubles with electric showers. *Hotel Don Goyo* (☎ *460 1780,* ☎*/ fax 460 6383)*, a block south of the parque central, has small, clean, pleasant rooms with fans and private hot showers. Rates are US$12.50/19. Both places have parking lots.

Half a dozen restaurants around the park offer plenty of choice.

Getting There & Away

The Quesada terminal (☎ *460 0638)* is half a block south of the parque central. Direct buses to San José (US$2.25, 2¼ hours) leave hourly during the day until 6:15 pm – an attractive ride over the western flanks of the Cordillera Central. Buses to La Fortuna (1½ hours) leave six times a day; buses to Tilarán (4½ hours) leave at 6:30 am and 4 pm. Eastbound buses travel to Puerto Viejo de Sarapiquí (2½ hours) five times daily.

LA FORTUNA
pop 7000

La Fortuna is the nearest village to the spectacular Volcán Arenal (1633m), which looms 6km to the west. The volcano was dormant until 1968; in that year huge explosions triggered lava flows that killed about 80 people. The volcano retains its almost perfect conical shape, and with its continuing activity, Arenal is everyone's image of a typical volcano. The best nighttime views are from the north and west sides. The degree of activity varies from week to week; sometimes there is red-hot lava flowing and incandescent rocks flying through the air.

Information

There is no impartial tourist office, but any number of tour operators can answer your questions; Jacamar Tours' staff are helpful and speak English. Banco Nacional, Banco Popular and Banco de Costa Rica all have ATMs on the Visa-Plus network. Restaurante Las Jicaritas (see Places to Eat) charges US$0.15 per minute for Internet access; they also rent all-terrain bikes for US$10 a day. Chip phones can be found beside Rancho La Cascada restaurant and along the main street.

Volcán Arenal

Parque Nacional Volcán Arenal, 15km west of La Fortuna, is open 7 am to 10 pm daily; admission is US$6. From the 'Parque Nacional' sign off the main road, a 2km dirt road leads to the ranger station/information center. From there, trails lead another 3.4km toward the volcano. Though this route gets you close, it doesn't necessarily offer the best views of volcanic activity; many visitors prefer to gaze from a distance. Climbing the volcano is definitely not allowed; hikers have been killed by explosions. Most people arrive here on a tour, but you could take an 8 am bus toward Tilarán and catch the 2 pm bus back to La Fortuna.

Organized Tours

Many local hotels and operators will arrange tours to view the volcano. A popular option is a midafternoon departure, in which you take a short hike, watch the sunset and then observe nocturnal volcanic activity. Prices average US$25 per person. Note that there is no refund if it's cloudy and you don't see anything. Many of these tours include a dip in the Tabacón hot springs after the volcano visit, sometimes at additional charge.

Other tours include rafting on the Peñas Blancas river (US$45 to US$70 per person), mountain biking at Laguna Arenal (US$35), visits to Caño Negro (US$45) and horseback rides to La Catarata de Fortuna, an impressive waterfall. (You don't need a guide to reach the falls, a 6km walk along a signed road.) Various operators also offer full-day horseback rides to Monteverde (US$50 and up), but these are not recommended during the rainy season. Travelers have also complained of abuses by unscrupulous outfitters.

Of the numerous available tour operators, Sunset Tours (☎ 479 9415, ☎/fax 479 9099, mcastro@sol.racsa.co.cr) is one of the best established and most helpful, and Desafío Expeditions (☎ 479 9464, fax 479 9463, desafio@sol.racsa.co.cr) has been recommended by readers.

Places to Stay

Camping Six kilometers west of La Fortuna is *Jungla & Senderos Los Lagos (☎/fax 479 8000)*, also known as El Mirador, a resort on the northern flanks of the volcano. From the entrance, a 3km road leads to a pair of lakes where you can camp, the best site within view of the volcano. Rates are US$6 per person for one night and US$3 for additional nights. Drinking water, toilets and showers are available, as well as hiking trails and horse rentals.

Hotels Cheap rooms may be offered by entrepreneurial locals who greet you as you get off the bus. Otherwise, head for the west end of town, where low-cost lodgings are clustered. *Cabinas Adriana (☎ 479 9474)* charges just US$3 per person in cramped upstairs rooms with large fans. The riverside *Cabinas Jerry (☎ 479 9063)* has a quiet block of double rooms with clean private bathrooms and hot showers (not electric) for US$8 per person. *Cabinas Sissy (☎ 479 9356)* is US$6.50/10 for simple rooms with private electric showers and overhead fan. You can set up a tent in the yard for US$2 per person. All guests have kitchen privileges.

Going east along the river, you come to *Cabinas y Soda El Río (☎ 479 9341)*, which has a popular little restaurant and doubles for US$13. A block farther east is the pleasant *Mayol Lodge (☎ 479 9110)*, featuring a swimming pool and clean rooms with fans and hot water for US$15/25. *Hotel Fortuna (☎ 479 9197)* has decent rooms with electric showers for US$10 per person, and there's a good soda in front. Smaller rooms are across the street in the annex, *Hotel Monte de Sión. Hotel Las Colinas (☎/fax 479 9107, hcolinas@sol.racsa.co.cr)*, toward the center of town, offers clean rooms with hot water and fans for US$8/16.

Along the eastern approach, *La Posada Inn* (☎/fax 479 9793) is a welcoming place that's popular with young backpackers. Rates are US$5 per person in basic but clean rooms; hot showers are shared.

A block west of the soccer field is *Cabinas El Bosque* (☎ 479 9365), run by a friendly family. They charge US$7 per person for rooms with shared bath or US$8/14 for spacious rooms beside a tranquil rear garden.

Just down the street, *Cabinas Herví* (☎ 479 9100) has three or four small moldy doubles/triples that share two baths for US$10/13. The larger and fresher upstairs rooms with bath and fan are US$13/16.

Opposite the church is *Cabinas Carmela* (☎ 479 9010), with fairly large singles/doubles with hot showers and fan for US$20/25.

An excellent choice is the family-run *Cabinas Oriuma* (☎/fax 479 9111) on the northeast corner of the soccer field; reception is inside the veterinary supply store. Double rooms for US$20 have high ceilings, firm beds and sparkling bathrooms with hot water.

Places to Eat

Healthy breakfasts can be found at *Centro Natural San Rafael*, north of the soccer field, where a bowl of granola with soy milk is less than US$1, and a fruit salad costs US$2.

Both *Soda El Río* and *Las Jicaritas* are simple inexpensive eateries, with pleasant riverside seating, where casados cost around US$2.50. Only the latter serves beer.

On the west end of town, *La Choza de Laurel* is a very clean open-air restaurant with good service. La Choza's specialty is charcoal-broiled chicken served with homemade tortillas.

For first-rate espresso and cappuccino, head for *Lava Rocks Restaurant*, which shares the Jacamar Tours office opposite the church. The thatch-roofed *Rancho La Cascada*, on the northeast corner of the soccer field, is touristy, but a pleasant place to sip a margarita. Meals are in the US$4 to US$6 range.

A couple of blocks east is the recommended *Restaurante Nene's*, where a big steak costs US$6.

Getting There & Away

There are daily morning flights to and from San José by Sansa (US$55/110 one-way/roundtrip) and Travelair (US$57/94).

Direct buses from San José leave the Atlántico Norte terminal at 6:15, 8:40, and 11:30 am (US$3, 4½ hours), returning at 12:45 and 2:45 pm. In either direction, you have the option of taking a more frequent bus to Ciudad Quesada and changing.

All buses leave from the south side of the soccer field. Departures for Tilarán are at 8 am and 5 pm (3½ hours). The earlier bus connects with the 12:30 pm Monteverde bus (another three or four hours). A faster alternative is the daily Jeep-boat-Jeep connection offered by Pensión Santa Elena (☎ 645 5051 to reserve), which takes three hours (US$25).

TILARÁN

This small town, near the southwest end of Laguna de Arenal, is a ranching center. There's a rodeo the last weekend in April, popular with Tico visitors, and another fiesta in mid-June dedicated to patron saint Antonio – more rodeos and bullfights. The nearby lake (5km away) has consistently high winds that attract experienced windsurfers. Enjoying a pleasant climate and a rural atmosphere that's just lively enough, Tilarán makes a refreshingly tourist-free stopover between La Fortuna and Monteverde.

Places to Stay & Eat

The best deal is the capacious *Hotel Tilarán* (☎ 695 5043), on the west side of the parque central, with very clean rooms for as little as US$4.50 per person. Doubles with private bath and cable TV are US$11.50; those in the rear face a quiet garden. The park-view restaurant serves home-cooked meals. *Hotel Mary* (☎ 695 5479), south of the parque central, is friendly and has a recommended restaurant. Singles/doubles with private bath are US$8/15. Traffic noise reaches the parkside rooms; tiny interior singles are quieter. The similarly priced *Hotel Guadalupe* (☎ 695 5943, fax 695 5387), a block south and a block east of the cathedral, is better, with nine pleasant rooms with hot showers and TVs. *Cabinas El Sueño* (☎ 695 5347), over a restaurant near the bus terminal, offers dark-carpeted rooms with overhead fans, private bath and

TV for US$11.50/18.50. South of the church, *Hotel Naralit* (☎ 695 5393, fax 695 6767) – that's 'Tilarán' reversed – is the most comfortable central hotel. Rates are US$12/20 for modern accommodations alongside a tranquil court, including cable TV and hot water.

Cheap meals can be found in the market beside the bus station. *Restaurant Nuevo Fortuna*, opposite Cabinas El Sueño, whips up chop suey and fried rice for about US$2 or US$3.

The North American–run *La Carreta* (☎ 695 6654, *tilaran@hotmail.com*), behind the cathedral, is an obligatory stop for pizza made with Monteverde cheese (US$4), overstuffed sandwiches on homemade bread (US$5) and ice cold fruit *refrescos*. Gregarious owners Tom and Billie Jafek offer a book exchange, rent mountain bikes (US$20 per day) and organize lakeshore bike rides and tours of local coffee plantations.

Getting There & Away

Buses depart from the terminal, half a block west of the parque central. Baggage can be stored here for US$0.50 per item. Sunday afternoon buses to San José may be sold out by Saturday. The route between Tilarán and San José goes via Cañas and the Interamericana, not the Arenal-Fortuna-Ciudad Quesada route.

Buses offer regular service to the following places:

Arenal (US$0.40, 1¼ hours)
Five buses depart between 5 am and 4:30 pm.

Cañas (US$0.40, 45 minutes)
Seven buses depart from 5 am to 3:30 pm.

Ciudad Quesada (via La Fortuna; US$1.50, four hours)
Buses depart at 7:30 am and 12:30 pm.

Puntarenas (US$2.50, two hours)
Buses depart at 6 am and 1 pm.

San José (US$2.50, three hours)
Buses depart at 5, 7 and 7:45 am and 2 and 4:55 pm

Santa Elena (US$1.75, three hours)
Buses depart at 12:30 pm.

To reach Puerto San Luis, which is the nearest lakeshore point, take a Tronadora bus (there are six departures between 7:15 am and 4:30 pm) or any bus going east. Returning buses can be flagged down along the road.

Península de Nicoya

Some of Costa Rica's major beach resorts are on this peninsula, but with few paved roads, access remains difficult. There are several small wildlife reserves and parks, but generally people come here looking for relaxing beaches. Though public transportation is infrequent, it is possible to get around by bus if you have the time and patience. Hitching is a definite possibility; see the Hitchhiking section earlier in this chapter.

Hotels in the area tend to be expensive. If you want to cook for yourself, bring food from inland – stores are few and far between on the coast.

PLAYA DEL COCO

Thirty-five kilometers west of Liberia and connected by good roads to San José, Coco is the most easily accessible of the Península de Nicoya beaches. It is attractively set between two rocky headlands, with a small village and some nightlife, though the beach itself is not so inviting as others on the peninsula. Popular with Ticos in particular, foreign travelers to a lesser extent, the resort is not as pricey as most other beach towns. Beware of strong riptides.

Scuba diving is the main attraction, and this is the best place for it in the country. There are several competitively priced outfitters. Two-tank dives from a boat are typically US$70 (gear provided), and beginners' classes are available. Snorkeling trips are US$25 with gear. Rich Coast Diving (☎/fax 670 0176, dive@richcoastdiving.com) has been well reviewed by readers. Aqua Sport (☎ 670 0353), in nearby Playa Hermosa, rents kayaks, surfboards, snorkeling gear etc and can arrange excursions.

Papagayo Sport Fishing (☎ 670 0354, papagayo@infoweb.co.cr) offers information in English, whether or not you participate in their tours. The Banco Nacional will exchange cash US dollars and traveler's checks. Internet Café 2000 provides Web access (US$6 per hour, US$3.50 per ¼ hour) along with fax service, *The Tico Times,* fresh bagels and cappuccino.

The town's biggest festival is the Fiesta de la Virgen del Mar, celebrated in mid-July, featuring a vivid religious-themed boat procession in the harbor, plus a horse pageant, bullfights and fireworks.

Places to Stay

A *campground* just off the main road has basic bathrooms, showers and a kitchen for US$2.75 per person.

Cabinas Catarino (☎ 670 0156) is on the main road close to the beach. It's a small, tidy place charging US$8 per person. In a quiet area near the soccer field, *Cabinas Jibao* (☎ 670 0853) is designed for Tico families. Clean and simple rooms have four or five beds, overhead fans, a bathroom and a kitchen with fridge for US$8 per person. The adjacent *Cabinas Coco Azul* (☎ 670 0431), managed by the same family, has more comfortable doubles/triples that cost US$16/24.

Turn right at the beachfront park to find *Cabinas El Coco* (☎ 670 0110, fax 670 0167), popular with Tico weekenders. The sprawling place has singles/doubles/triples with fans for US$13/23/38, or with air-conditioning for US$20/32/49. Though nothing special, the 80-odd rooms are clean and have screened windows and private bathrooms. Only at the far end does the crashing surf override the thumping disco. There's a midpriced restaurant on the premises. Turn left at the park for *Cabinas Luna Tica* (☎ 670 0127, fax 670 0459), which has underventilated doubles/triples with private bath for US$19/26, or US$28/32 with air-conditioning. Rooms at the annex across the way seem breezier and better.

The motel-style *Cabinas Las Brisas* (☎ 670 0155) charges US$26 for airless doubles beside a row of almond trees. All rooms include showers and fans. A fine mid-range option is *Coco Palms Hotel* (☎ 670 0367, fax 670 0117, cocopalm@sol.racsa.co.cr)*, run by two German brothers. Rooms vary in size, but all are attractive and have air-con and hot water. Rates are US$15 per person, US$18 with breakfast, served inside a thatched *rancho* beside the pool.

Places to Eat

While visitors may not mind dropping some cash on vacation, economizing locals eat at *Restaurante La Casona*, with breakfasts for US$2 and fish platters for less than US$3, or at *Soda Teresita* beside the soccer field, with US$3 casados. Despite its Anglo name, *The*

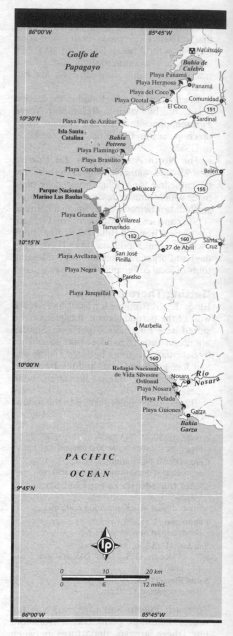

PENÍNSULA DE NICOYA

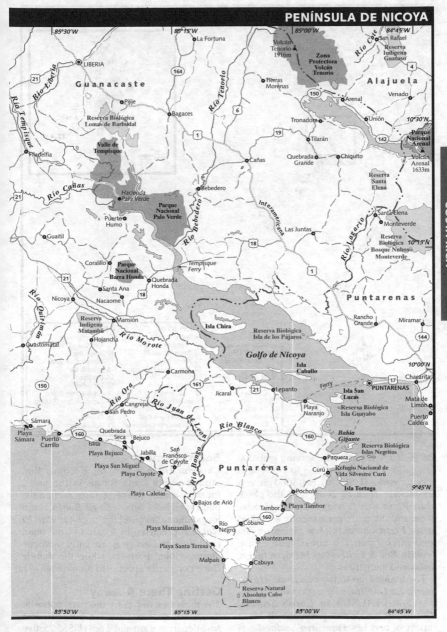

85°30'W

85°15'W

85°00'W

84°45'W

San Rafael

La Fortuna

Volcán
Tenorio
1916m

Zona
Protectora
Volcán
Tenorio

Reserva
Indígena
Guatuso

Río Cote

4

LIBERIA

Guanacaste

164

Río Tenorio

Tierras
Morenas

Alajuela

Venado

Arenal

150

Río Liberia

21

Pijije

Bagaces

6

Tronadora

Unión

10°30'N

Parque
Nacional
Arenal

142

Río Tempisque

Reserva Biológica
Lomas de Barbudal

1

19

Tilarán

Volcán
Arenal
1633m

Valle de
Tempisque

Quebrada
Grande

Chiquito

Filadelfia

Cañas

Reserva
Santa
Elena

Bebedero

Río Cañas

Interamericana

Río Bebedero

Las Juntas

Santa Elena

Monteverde

Hacienda
Palo Verde

Puerto
Humo

Parque
Nacional
Palo Verde

18

Río Lagarto

Reserva
Biológica
Bosque Nuboso
Monteverde

10°15'N

21

Guaitil

Coralillo

Parque
Nacional
Barra Honda

Tempisque
Ferry

1

Puntarenas

21

Santa Ana

Quebrada
Honda

Río Quirimán

Nicoya

Nacaome

18

Rancho
Grande

Miramar

Reserva
Indígena
Matambú

Mansión

Río Morote

144

Guastomatal

Hojancha

Isla Chira

Reserva Biológica
Isla de los Pájaros

Golfo de Nicoya

10°00'N

Carmona

Isla
Caballo

150

Río Ora

161

Jicaral

21

Lepanto

Ferry

Isla San
Lucas

17

Chacarita

PUNTARENAS

Cangrejal

San Pedro

Río Juan de León

Playa
Naranjo

Reserva Biológica
Isla Guayabo

Mata de
Limón

Sámara

Río Blanco

Puerto
Caldera

Playa
Sámara

160

Quebrada
Seca

Bejuco

Bahía
Gigante

Reserva Biológica
Islas Negritos

Puerto
Carrillo

Islita

Playa Bejuco

Jabilla

San
Francisco
de Coyote

160

Paquera

Playa San Miguel

Río Bongo

Puntarenas

Curú

Refugio Nacional de
Vida Silvestre Curú

Playa Coyete

Isla Tortuga

9°45'N

Playa Caletas

Pochote

Bajos de Arió

Tambor

Playa Tambor

Playa Manzanillo

Río
Negro

Cóbano

160

Montezuma

Playa Santa Teresa

Malpaís

Cabuya

Reserva Natural
Absoluta Cabo
Blanco

85°30'W

85°15' W

85°00' W

84°45' W

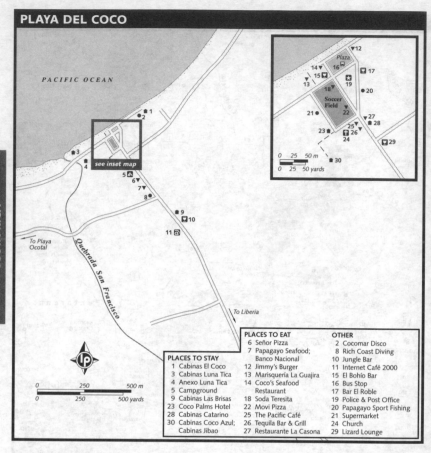

PLAYA DEL COCO

PACIFIC OCEAN

Plaza

Soccer Field

To Playa Ocotal

Quebrada San Francisco

To Liberia

PLACES TO STAY	PLACES TO EAT	OTHER
1 Cabinas El Coco	6 Señor Pizza	2 Cocomar Disco
3 Cabinas Luna Tica	7 Papagayo Seafood;	8 Rich Coast Diving
4 Anexo Luna Tica	Banco Nacional	10 Jungle Bar
5 Campground	12 Jimmy's Burger	11 Internet Café 2000
9 Cabinas Las Brisas	13 Marisquería La Guajira	15 El Bohío Bar
23 Coco Palms Hotel	14 Coco's Seafood	16 Bus Stop
28 Cabinas Catarino	Restaurant	17 Bar El Roble
30 Cabinas Coco Azul;	18 Soda Teresita	19 Police & Post Office
Cabinas Jibao	22 Movi Pizza	20 Papagayo Sport Fishing
	25 The Pacific Café	21 Supermarket
	26 Tequila Bar & Grill	24 Church
	27 Restaurante La Casona	29 Lizard Lounge

Pacific Café is pure Tico, serving empanadas, gallos, rice dishes (US$3 to US$4) and veggie casados (US$3.50). Fast food purveyors include *Jimmy's Burger* by the plaza, *Movi Pizza*, a truck body containing a pizza oven, and the more permanently anchored *Señor Pizza*, one of the few places serving food after 9 pm. The not-so-inexpensive *Tequila Bar & Grill* offers Mexican fajitas, tortas and margaritas.

For seafood, go to the beachside *Marisquería La Guajira*, whose specialty is shellfish chowder (US$6), or *Coco's Seafood Restaurant* beside the plaza, which has a variety of ceviches. *Papagayo Seafood* gets a mostly North American clientele lured by the Louisiana-themed menu. Main courses are in the US$7 to US$9 range.

Entertainment

Cocomar Disco, next to the Cocomar Bar, attracts young Costa Ricans in the mood for some action. The restaurants around the plaza double as bars, with *El Bohío Bar* a longstanding favorite; the open-air *Bar El Roble* is preferred by locals. On the main road, *Lizard Lounge* is currently in vogue among global partyers, while the *Jungle Bar*'s popularity appears to be waning.

Getting There & Away

The main bus stop is by the park opposite the police station. Pulmitan buses to San José depart at 8 am and 2 pm (US$5.25, five hours). Buses to Liberia leave six times a day during the dry season, less frequently off-season (US$0.75, one hour).

PLAYA TAMARINDO

A small community resides by this sprawling and attractive beach. Both surfing and windsurfing are good. Nonsurfers will find quiet stretches of ocean to play in (though watch out for riptides, especially at high tide) and a turtle nesting zone in the nearby marine national park. Tamarindo's varied attractions are well served by accommodations, restaurants, and equipment rental outlets.

Information

Any of the equipment outfitters will provide information. The Banco Nacional exchanges US dollars cash and traveler's checks. A new cybercafe, www.tamarindo .net, is open daily until 9 pm and charges US$3.25 per half hour.

Lavandería Mariposa, open Monday to Saturday, will do your laundry for US$2.50 per kilo.

Activities

Boat tours, snorkeling, diving, horse rentals, visits to turtle nesting areas and other activities can be arranged through Papagayo Excursions (☎ 653 0254, papagayo@sol.racsa .co.cr). The friendly Iguana Surf Aquatic Outfitters (☎/fax 653 0148, iguanasur@ aol.com), which operates a branch near the beach, rents kayaks, surfboards, boogie boards and snorkeling gear and also offers lessons and tours. At Tamarindo Aventuras (☎/fax 653 0108) you can rent scooters for US$32 per day, as well as water-sports equipment.

PLAYA TAMARINDO

PLACES TO STAY	PLACES TO EAT	OTHER
6 Cabinas Roda Mar; Restaurant Frutas Tropicales	4 Panadería de París	1 Boat Beach
7 Hotel Doly	5 Thai Restaurant; La Terraza del Chef	2 Supermercado El Pelícano
9 Cabinas Marielos; Iguana Surf Beach Outlet	10 Restaurant Blue Moon; Restaurant Copacabana	3 Travelair Office (Hotel Pueblo Dorado)
13 Big Bazar Beach Club	14 Pedro's	8 Sansa Office
18 Cabinas Zullymar	15 Bar Nogui	11 Supermercado Tamarindo; Banco Nacional; Papagayo Excursions
19 Cabinas Coral Reef	16 Restaurant Mambo	12 www.tamarindo.net
21 Tito's Camping	17 Fiesta del Mar	20 Tamarindo Aventuras
22 Cabinas 14 de Febrero	24 Smilin' Doc Taco Factory	25 Iguana Surf Aquatic Outfitters
23 Los Pelicanos Camping		26 Lavandería Mariposa
27 Hotel Mamiri		

Places to Stay

Tito's Camping (☎ 643 0549), on the beach at the south end of town, offers basic facilities for US$2 per person. During the busiest months, they serve inexpensive local food. *Los Pelícanos Camping* is slightly cheaper but not as close to the beach.

Cheap single rooms are at a premium during the high season, so budget travelers need to find a buddy. One of the least expensive places is *Cabinas Coral Reef* (☎ 653 0291), at US$8 per person in small rooms with fans. Bathrooms and kitchen are shared, and Swedish massage is available. The cordial *Cabinas Roda Mar* (☎ 653 0109) has some acceptably clean singles/doubles for US$6.50/13 with shared bath or US$13/16 with private bath. *Cabinas 14 de Febrero* (☎ 653 0238) is a good deal at US$15/20/22 for singles/doubles/triples. Cool high-ceilinged cabins, equipped with overhead fan and electric hot showers, encircle a pleasant garden.

Off to one side of the beach, the French-operated *Big Bazar Beach Club* (☎ 653 0307) is pleasantly laid-back, charging US$25 for jungle lodge–style doubles with shared hot showers. There's a beachfront bar/restaurant and pool table. Up the beach, *Hotel Doly* is a popular choice, containing small doubles with fans and private bath for US$25. Service is not a priority. Opposite, *Cabinas Marielos* (☎ 653 0141) provides comfortable rooms with firm beds, fans and bath for US$25/30, or US$30/37 with silent air-conditioning. Cabins have porches or balconies facing a tropical garden. Surfboards, boogie boards and bikes are available, and park visits can be arranged.

Accommodations at the rambling *Cabinas Zullymar* (☎ 653 0140) range from small, basic units with private bath and fan in the US$20s to large air-conditioned rooms with terraces in the US$40s. The swimming pool is a definite attraction. The peaceful *Hotel Mamiri* (☎ 653 0079) has a restaurant and nicely furnished doubles with private baths for about US$30. There are plenty of pricier places.

Places to Eat

Panadería de París has fresh pastries and croissants from 6:30 am. *Restaurant Frutas Tropicales* is a tourist-friendly soda with granola, fruit salads and good juices.

A number of places are around the circular park at the southwest end of town. *Pedro's* has the cheapest seafood, but unfortunately, the kitchen is not so adept at preparing it. *Fiesta del Mar* is an upscale alternative with reasonably priced lunch specials. *Bar Nogui* offers quiches and sandwiches for lunch, grilled fish and chicken for dinner. *Restaurant Mambo* makes real cappuccinos and has good lunch salads (US$4) and burger combos (US$5).

Northeast of the circle are a pair of French-owned beachside bistros. *Restaurant Blue Moon* serves hearty breakfasts and delicious fruit milkshakes, as well as inexpensive grilled fish and salads. The pricier *Restaurant Copacabana* prepares mouthwatering daily specials for US$6 to US$10.

Several new ethnic restaurants expand Tamarindo's culinary horizons. Tacos (US$1.75) and burritos (US$3.25) can be found at *Smilin' Doc Taco Factory*, open Wednesday to Sunday. *La Terraza del Chef* has Middle Eastern tabouli, hummus and felafel, and the unambiguously named *Thai Restaurant* offers meals for two at US$10.50. When the clock strikes 10 pm, the latter transforms into Discothai.

Getting There & Away

Air The airstrip is 2.5km north of town; a collective van picks up arriving passengers (US$3.25). Travelair (US$92/152) and Sansa (US$65/130) have several daily flights to and from San José. Travelair flights may stop at La Fortuna en route. Sansa (☎ 653 0012) has an office on the main road, and the Hotel Pueblo Dorado is the Travelair agent.

Bus Empresas Alfaro has a daily bus from San José at 3:30 pm, returning from Tamarindo at 6 am. There is an extra return bus on Sunday at noon (US$5.50, five hours). There are two or three daily buses to and from both Liberia (US$1, two hours) and Santa Cruz (US$0.70, 1¼ hours).

PARQUE NACIONAL MARINO LAS BAULAS

The park just north of Tamarindo village includes Playa Grande, an important nesting site for the *baula* (leatherback turtle). This is the world's largest turtle, weighing as much as 500kg. Nesting season is October to March, when more than a hundred turtles may be seen laying their eggs during the course of a night.

Visitors must watch the activities from specified areas, accompanied by a guide or ranger, and no flash photography or lights are allowed, as they disturb the laying process.

The park office (☎/fax 653 0470), open 9 am to 6 pm, is by the northern entrance. The US$6 entrance fee is generally charged only for the nighttime turtle-watching tours.

A good way to begin your tour is with a visit to El Mundo de la Tortuga (☎/fax 653 0471), an excellent exhibit about leatherback turtles near the north end of the park. Most of the tours offered from the exhibit itself are guided by reformed poachers who know the turtles well. The exhibit is open 4 pm until dawn, with tours running all night. A full tour costs US$18, including admission to the exhibit (US$5 for the exhibit alone).

PLAYA AVELLANA

This popular surfing beach is about 15km south of Tamarindo by road, but closer to 10km if you walk in along the beaches. The road may require 4WD in the wet season. The relatively difficult access means that this beach is frequented by those who appreciate it, mainly surfers.

Among the surfers' hangouts are the loosely organized *Avellanes Surf Ranch*, which has cabins, camping and a soda, and *Cabinas Gregorios*, which has three basic cabins, including private bath, for US$9 per person. Between Playa Avellana and Playa Negra to the south, *Mono Congo Surf Lodge* (☎ /fax 382 6926) is a large open-air ranch building surrounded by monkey-filled trees and gardens. Simple, well-designed rooms cost US$35 double. Bunkhouse beds are available for US$10 per person. There's an excellent vegetarian restaurant.

PLAYA JUNQUILLAL

This is a wide and wild beach, with high surf, strong riptides and few people. The beach is 2km long and has tide pools and pleasant walking. Ridley turtles nest here, but in smaller numbers than at the refuges. There is no village to speak of. Hotel rates drop by 20% to 40% outside the high season.

You can camp almost anywhere along the beach if you have your own food and water. *Hotel Playa Junquillal* (☎ 653 0432) will let campers use their showers for a small fee. Otherwise, stay in their basic but pleasant beach cabins with fans and private hot showers for about US$35 double (high season). *Hospedaje El Malinche* (☎ 653 0433) offers a few low-budget rooms and a camping area. There are several pricier places.

Tralapa has daily buses from San José (US$5.50, five hours) at 2 pm and from Santa Cruz (US$0.70) at 6:30 pm, both returning at 5 am. The latter may go only as far as Paraíso, 4km from the beach.

SANTA CRUZ
pop 15,000

This small town, 57km from Liberia, is a possible overnight stop for people visiting the peninsula. There is an annual rodeo and fiesta during the second week in January.

An interesting excursion is to the village of Guaitil, 12km away, where families make and sell attractive pottery in the pre-Columbian Chorotega style.

Places to Stay & Eat

Pensión Isabel (☎ 680 0173), 400m south and 50m east of the Plaza de los Mangos, has spartan rooms for US$5 per person. Basic wooden boxes are available for US$3 at *Hotel Anatolia* (☎ 680 0333), a boardinghouse-style place with a restaurant, 100m west and 200m south of the same plaza. Other inexpensive choices are *Cabinas Tauro* (☎ 680 0289), 100m west and 100m north of the plaza, and *Hospedaje Amadita*, 250m north. *Hotel La Estancia* (☎ 680 0476, fax 680 0348), 100m west of the plaza, has 16 clean rooms with fans, TV and private bath for US$11.50/23/29 single/double/triple.

Check out *La Fabrica de Tortillas*, 700m south of the Plaza de Los Mangos, for inexpensive Tico-style country meals.

Getting There & Away

Transportes La Pampa (☎ 680 0111) buses leave for Nicoya (US$0.40) from the north side of the Plaza de los Mangos 17 times a day from 6 am to 9:30 pm and for Liberia (US$0.90) 16 times a day from 5:30 am to 7:30 pm. Departing from the same point, Tralapa (☎ 680 0392) has eight buses a day to San José (US$5.20) between 3 am and 5 pm.

COSTA RICA

Additionally, Empresas Alfaro buses between Nicoya and San José stop in Santa Cruz en route. Their terminal is opposite the post office.

There are six buses a day to Guaitil. Buses for Playas Conchal, Brasilito, Flamingo and Potrero leave four times a day during the dry season, fewer in the wet. A bus leaves for Junquillal at 6:30 am and for Tamarindo at 6:45 and 8:30 pm. Some Tralapa beach buses also go via Santa Cruz.

NICOYA
pop 25,000

Nicoya, 23km south of Santa Cruz, is the most important town on the peninsula. It was named after the indigenous Chorotega chief Nicoya, who welcomed the first Spaniards in 1523. Locals are partly of Chorotega descent. The attractive white church on the pleasant parque central dates to the mid-17th century and is worth a look. Nicoya is now the commercial center of the cattle industry and the political capital and transportation hub of the peninsula. Banks here will exchange US dollars.

Places to Stay & Eat

The best of the budget bunch is the clean and popular *Hotel Chorotega* (☎ *685 5245*), two blocks south of the parque central, where decent singles/doubles with shower and fan are US$6/10. *Hotel Ali* (☎ *685 5148*), on the southwest corner of the parque central, has basic rooms for US$3.50 per person. On the north side, *Hotel Venecia* (☎ *685 5325*) charges US$3.25 per person in basic but clean rooms with shared cold showers, or US$7.25/10 for rooms with private showers. The adjacent *Hotel Elegancia* (☎ *685 5159*) is similarly priced.

Hotel Las Tinajas (☎ *685 5081, fax 685 5096*), 200m west and 100m north of the parque central, has decent rooms with bath and fans for US$10.50/14.50/20.50 single/double/triple. *Hotel Jenny* (☎ *685 5050*) is clean, popular and helpful. Air-conditioned rooms with bath and TV are US$14/18.50.

The three or four Chinese restaurants in the center of town are among the best places to eat. *Café Daniela*, a local favorite, serves breakfasts, burgers, pizzas and snacks. Next door, the Chinese-run Bar/Restaurant Nicoya is good for standard meals. Cheap snacks are available from various stands and sodas around the parque central.

Getting There & Away

Buses for Liberia (US$1.15) leave 18 times a day from Avenida 1 and Calle 5. Most other buses leave Nicoya from the bus terminal at the south end of Calle 5. Alfaro (☎ 685 5032) runs 10 buses a day to San José between 3:45 am and 5:20 pm, some by way of Liberia (US$5,25, five hours), others via the Río Tempique ferry (US$5, four hours). Buses to Playa Naranjo (US$0.60) leave at 5:15 am and 1 pm, connecting with the Puntarenas ferry. There is daily service to Playa Sámara, Playa Nosara and Santa Ana near the Parque Nacional Barra Honda.

PARQUE NACIONAL BARRA HONDA

Located midway between Nicoya and the mouth of the Río Tempisque, this park protects Costa Rica's most interesting cave system. Only 19 of a reported 42 caves have been explored, making Barra Honda of special interest to speleologists. A few of the caves are open to the public.

The dry season is best for caving. Permits to explore the cave system can be obtained from the headquarters of the Area de Conservación Tempisque in Nicoya (☎/fax 685 5667). Contact this office to reserve accommodations or guides.

The ranger station at the southwest corner of the park provides information and maps and takes the US$6 entrance fee. Near the station is a camping area with bathrooms and showers (US$2). Trails lead to the top of nearby hills – carry plenty of water and tell the rangers where you're going.

By the park entrance, the locally organized Proyecto Nacaome provides three small cabins, each with a shower and six beds, at US$5.50 per person. An inexpensive restaurant serves regional favorites. Local guides with gear charge US$40 per group to descend into the most popular caves.

Though no buses go directly to the park, a 12:30 pm bus travels from Nicoya to the village of Santa Ana (US$1, 45 minutes), 1km away. The last bus back to Nicoya is at 6:15 pm. A taxi from Nicoya to the park entrance costs about US$10.

PLAYA NOSARA

This attractive white-sand beach is backed by a pocket of luxuriant vegetation that attracts birds and wildlife. Foreign (especially North American) retirees live here year-round. Note that the airport and village of Nosara, with gas, basic food supplies and cheap lodging, are 5km inland from the beach.

South of Playa Nosara are a couple of other attractive beaches, Playa Pelada and Playa Guiones, the latter a long stretch of white sand with good snorkeling opportunities.

Places to Stay & Eat

You'll find inexpensive accommodations in the village. The basic *Cabinas Chorotega* (☎ 680 0836) is US$5 per person, US$7 with private shower. Similarly priced but not so well maintained is *Cabinas Agnel*, nearer the village.

Sodita Vannessa, on the main road by the public phone, is locally popular. There are other sodas and restaurants around the soccer field.

On the beach, camping is possible and there are shelters and water. Beach-area hotels start in the US$50s. *Olga's Restaurant* on Playa Pelada has US$3 casados.

Getting There & Away

Air Sansa has a daily flight from San José at 7:30 am, returning via Playa Sámara at 8:18 am (US$65 each way).

Bus Transportes Rojas (☎ 685 5352) runs a daily bus from Nicoya's main terminal at 2 pm, returning at 6 am (2½ to three hours). Empresas Alfaro departs from San José for Nosara at 6 am daily, returning at 1 pm.

REFUGIO NACIONAL DE VIDA SILVESTRE OSTIONAL

This refuge includes the coastal village of Ostional, 8km northwest of Playa Nosara. The reserve is 8km long but only a few hundred meters wide. The main attraction is the annual nesting of the olive ridley sea turtle, from July to November with a peak from August to October.

Apart from turtles, iguanas, crabs, howler monkeys, coatis and many birds can be seen. Some of the best birding is at the southeast end of the refuge, near the mouth

of the Río Nosara. At the opposite end, you'll find numerous tide pools teeming with life.

The villagers of Ostional are helpful and will guide you to the best areas.

Camping is permitted, but there are no facilities. In Ostional village, *Hospedaje Guacamaya* has a few air-conditioned rooms with bath at US$4 per person. *Cabinas Ostional* offers clean, basic rooms in a pleasant family backyard for similar rates. Neither one has a phone, but you can try leaving a message at the nearby pulpería (☎ 682 0267).

During the dry months, there are two daily buses from Santa Cruz (these may not run during the wet season, depending on road conditions). Hitchhiking from Nosara is reportedly easy; see the Hitchhiking section earlier in this chapter for tips.

PLAYA SÁMARA

This beautiful, gentle, white-sand beach is one of Costa Rica's safest and prettiest, and one of the most accessible on the peninsula. Former president Oscar Arias has a vacation house near here. Though it's still fairly tranquil, development has picked up since the paved road arrived in early 1996.

The village has a few stores and discotheques and several hotels, restaurants, and bars. Ciclo Mora, about 100m west of Cabinas Arenas, rents bicycles. Horse rentals can be arranged through the hotels.

Places to Stay & Eat

Behind the sign for *Coco's Camping* are several places to camp at about US$3 per person; ask around for the best price.

Popular with Tico weekenders, the basic *Hotel Playa Sámara* (☎ 656 0190) charges US$5.50 per person. A cheap soda and a loud disco are nearby. Other budget places include *Cabinas Magaly*, *Cabinas Stephanie* (☎ 656 0308) and *Bar/Cabinas Los Mangos* (☎ 656 0356); rates at the latter two are negotiable. *Cabinas El Ancla* (☎ 656 0254) has simple, clean rooms by the beach for US$7.50 per person, plus a restaurant and cheerful bar. Entrepreneurial surfers occasionally rent a house and put up a sign offering cheap rooms.

Inexpensive meals can be had at *Soda La Vaca Loca*. Campers can stock up on supplies at the *Pulpería Mileth* or *Super*

Sámara market. There are also cheap eateries on the beach. For seafood, *Marisquería Colochos* is a reasonably priced longtime favorite.

About 4km southeast of Sámara is the postcard-perfect **Playa Carrillo**, with basic *camping facilities*. Cheap rooms are sometimes offered by *Bar Restaurant Chala*, which has a hilltop view of the bay.

Getting There & Away
Air The Sámara/Carrillo airport is between the two beaches. Sansa flies from San José at 7:30 am daily, stopping in Playa Nosara (US$65/130 one-way/roundtrip); Travelair has a direct flight at 1 pm (US$82/134, 40 minutes).

Bus Alfaro in San José has a daily 12:30 pm bus to Sámara (US$6.25, five hours), returning at 4 am. Four buses travel daily between Nicoya and Sámara (US$1.25, two hours), fewer during the rainy season.

PLAYA NARANJO
This village is the terminal for the Puntarenas car ferry – the beach is not very exciting. Cheap lodgings are not available.

If you want to go to the south part of the Península de Nicoya, don't come to Playa Naranjo – take the ferry from Puntarenas to Paquera.

All transportation is geared to the arrival and departure of the Puntarenas ferry. Buses for Nicoya (three to four hours) meet incoming ferries. The ferry (☎ 661 1069) leaves Playa Naranjo at 5:10 and 8:50 am and 12:50, 5 and 9 pm daily (US$1.60 for passengers, US$11.50 for cars, 1½ hours).

PAQUERA
Four kilometers away from the Puntarenas-Paquera passenger ferry terminal, Paquera village is reached by a very crowded truck. In the village there are a couple of basic cabinas. However, most travelers take the bus from the ferry terminal to Montezuma (US$2.25, two hours). The bus is crowded – get off the ferry early to get a seat.

The passenger ferry (☎ 661 2830) leaves for Puntarenas at 7:30 am, 12:30 and 5 pm daily (US$1.50, 1½ hours). In addition, a pair of car/passenger ferries cross over to Puntarenas six times in all between 6 am and 8:30 pm (US$1.30 for passengers, US$10 for cars).

MONTEZUMA
This village, near the tip of the peninsula, has good beaches, friendly residents and a nature reserve a few kilometers away. Montezuma is very popular with younger gringo travelers who enjoy the laid-back atmosphere and affordable prices.

Information
Monte Aventuras (☎/fax 642 0025) provides international faxing, phone and email, and it can arrange tours. The most comprehensive tour agency in town is Rodel Tours/Nicoya Expeditions (☎/fax 642 0467). El Sano Banano (see Places to Eat) is a good source of local information and contacts.

There are no banks, but you can exchange US dollars or traveler's checks at Monte Aventuras. You might also be able to exchange cash dollars at either Chico's or El Sano Banano restaurants – if they have enough colones available.

Activities
Bicycle rentals are US$15 per day. Snorkeling gear and body boards cost about US$5 per day. Roger Rojas has been recommended for guided horseback rides; a half-day ride runs about US$25.

A 20-minute stroll to the south takes you to a waterfall with a swimming hole, reached by taking the trail to the right just after the bridge past the Restaurant La Cascada. A second set of falls is farther upriver. Beautiful beaches are strung out along the coast, separated by small rocky headlands and offering great beachcombing and tide-pool studying.

All-day boat excursions to swim and snorkel at Isla Tortuga are US$35 a person, including light snacks. It's 90 minutes to the island. Bring a sun hat and sunblock. Other boat trips are available.

Places to Stay
The high season (December to April) sometimes gets crowded, especially if you arrive late Friday afternoon, and single rooms are scarce. Low-season discounts are common.

Camping is permitted in a small area of the main beach, though some locals discourage the practice and there are no facilities.

Located on a hill that affords good sea views, above the soccer field, *Pensión Jenny* is a fair deal at US$5.50 per person in dormitories or US$11 for double rooms. All bathrooms are shared. Nearby, *Cabinas El Caracol* (☎ 642 0194) has large bare rooms with communal baths for US$6 per person; double rooms with private bath are US$16. An inexpensive restaurant is attached.

Pensión Lucy (☎ 642 0273) is just US$6/11 for breezy singles/doubles with shared showers. Its oceanview verandahs are a definite attraction. Just north of the soccer field, *Cabinas Tucán* (☎ 642 0284) is attentively managed by the cranky but benign Doña Marta. Rates are US$8/13 with communal cold showers. At similar rates, *Pensión Arenas* (☎ 642 0306) features private showers and a good beachfront setting, plus a family-run restaurant.

The central *Hotel Moctezuma* (☎ 642 0258, fax 642 0058) has a restaurant and popular bar with loud music. Large, clean rooms with fans and shower cost US$12/18, or US$8/11 with shared baths. Triples and quads are available.

About 100m up the road, *Cabinas Capitán* (☎ 642 0069) has clean, basic rooms with fans for US$10 single (shared showers) or US$15 double (private shower). Next door, *Cabinas Mar y Cielo* (☎ 642 0036) charges US$25 to US$30 for two to six people in rooms with private bath and fan. Upstairs rooms are breezy with nice views. Noise from nearby Chico's Bar, owned by the same family, may drift up this way after hours.

One of Montezuma's first hotels, *Hotel La Aurora* (☎ 642 0051, fax 642 0025) offers clean rooms with fans and mosquito nets for prices in the US$20s; some include private bath. Free coffee and tea, a library and lounging areas add to the place's appeal.

Travelers considering a longer stay might try the *Mochila Inn* (☎ 642 0030), which rents rooms equipped with fridge and gas range for US$100 to US$150 a week. It's on a quiet hillside at the entrance to the village.

Places to Eat

Some places charge 23% for tax and service on top of the bill; ask first if you are on a tight budget. Places that don't add tax and service include *Soda Las Gemelas* and *Restaurant El Parque*, the latter on the beach. A fish casado at either one is US$3.50, a little less with chicken, or around US$5 for a full fish dinner. They don't sell alcohol, but you can bring your own. Get there by 6 pm for the best choice of food and tables. The restaurant at *Cabinas El Caracol* is similarly priced; their fish soup (US$1.75) is sensational.

Other places that serve decent meals but are a little pricier include *Restaurant La Cascada*, pleasantly located next to a stream, and the popular restaurant/bar in the Hotel Moctezuma.

El Sano Banano (☎ /fax 642 0068) offers yogurt, juices and fruit salads, as well as vegetarian and seafood meals. It also shows films nightly (US$2.50 minimum consumption). The owners are a good source of local information.

Playa de las Artistas, on the way out to Pensión Lucy, has received rave reviews. Some claim the barbecued fish is the best they've ever eaten. A meal for two here will run less than US$10.

Entertainment

Soda Momaya, north along the beach, is the current hip hangout. There may be live music at *Luz de Mono*, and there is talk of a new disco opening; ask around. Otherwise, take in a 7:30 pm movie at El Sano Banano and go on to Chico's Bar for a beer.

Getting There & Away

The ferries from Puntarenas connect with the Paquera-Montezuma bus. The 3:15 pm ferry gets you into Montezuma well after dark.

Buses leave Montezuma for Paquera at 5:30, 8 and 10 am, noon, 2 and 4 pm, connecting with the Puntarenas ferry (US$2.50, 1½ hours). If you take the 2 pm bus, you can just catch the last Puntarenas–San José bus if you hustle.

MALPAÍS

This small village on the peninsula's west coast is popular with surfers. Horses can be rented for the 4km down to Cabo Blanco.

Frank's Place (☎ 640 0096), where the Cóbano road meets the beach road, has nice cabins at US$8 per person, or US$10 with private bath. Surfers camp near the *Mambo Café*, which serves veggie burgers and smoothies.

Heading south along the beach road from Frank's, *Malpaís Surf Camp & Resort* (☎ /fax 640 0061) has bungalows from US$25/35 for two/four people and a campground. The beachfront *Cabinas Atardecer* is a good budget option and allows camping. *Cabinas Bosque Mar* (☎ 640 0074) has big rooms with hot showers for US$25/28, slightly more with kitchenette. Overlooking a picturesque rocky headland, the friendly *Cabinas Mar Azul* (☎ 640 0075) offers decent cabins for US$15/20/25 for one to three people. The village is reached by two daily buses (one on Sunday) from Cóbano.

RESERVA NATURAL ABSOLUTA CABO BLANCO

This beautiful reserve, 11km south of Montezuma by dirt road, encompasses the southern tip of the peninsula. An evergreen forest, a couple of fine beaches and a host of birds and animals are among its attractions.

Just inside the park, south of Cabuya, is a ranger station (☎/fax 642 0093) with trail maps. Reserve hours are 8 am to 4 pm Wednesday to Sunday; admission is US$6. Camping is not permitted, and no food or drink is available.

A trail leads from the ranger station to the beaches at the tip of the peninsula. The hike takes a couple of hours, and you can return by a different trail. Look for boobies, pelicans, parrots and trogons.

A 4WD taxi (up to six passengers) from Montezuma to the park costs about US$15, or walk or cycle. Hitching is reportedly not bad.

Northern & Caribbean Lowlands

North of San José and beyond the volcanic ridges of the Cordillera Central, flat tropical lowlands stretch to the Nicaraguan border and beyond. The original vegetation of the northern lowlands was mixed tropical forest, but much of this has been replaced by cattle pasture. Population is sparse, with a few small towns, a skeletal road network, and limited tourist facilities. The climate is generally wet and hot. At the region's northern limit, the Río San Juan forms the border with Nicaragua and, in an earlier era, served as an important link with the Caribbean coast. Toward the Caribbean the dry season is shorter and not entirely dry.

Unlike the Pacific coast, the Caribbean is rainy year-round, though February to March and September to October are less wet. It has been developed more slowly than the Pacific side and has fewer roads. Half the coast is protected, with two national parks and two national wildlife refuges. The entire Caribbean coast belongs to Limón Province, which has 250,000 inhabitants, a third of them black. Most live near the coast and speak some form of English, providing a cultural diversity that is missing in the rest of Costa Rica. Also, several thousand indigenous Bribri and Cabecar people live in the south.

LOS CHILES
pop 8000

This small town is on the Río Frío, 3km from the Nicaraguan border (see Getting There & Away). Only 43m above sea level, it was originally designed to service river traffic on the nearby Río San Juan. Those arriving from Nicaragua will find the migración office 100m east of the parque central; the office is open 8 am to 5 pm daily.

Places to Stay & Eat

Hotel Onassis, on the corner of the parque central, and *Hotel Río Frío* (☎ 471 1127), near the immigration office, have rooms with shared cold bath for US$2 per person.

Cabinas Jabirú (☎ 471 1055) is the nicest budget option. The rate is about US$8 per person in spacious two bedroom units with sitting areas and hot shower. Parking is available.

Open 6 am to 9 pm, *Restaurant El Parque* serves Tico food and has a self-service coffee bar.

Getting There & Away

About 12 buses daily run between Ciudad Quesada and Los Chiles (US$2) from 5 am to 7:15 pm. Direct buses to San José (US$3.75) depart at 5 am and 3 pm. A bus to Upala, leaving around 5 am and 2 pm daily, passes through Caño Negro.

REFUGIO NACIONAL DE VIDA SILVESTRE CAÑO NEGRO

The Río Frío flows through the refuge, one of the country's best places for bird and wildlife observation. Most of the year it can be reached only by boat, but during the dry season it's accessible via horse trail from the village of Caño Negro. January to March is the best time for seeing large flocks of birds.

Boatmen can be hired at the dock in Los Chiles to take you up the Río Frío to the refuge for US$45 to US$80. Servitur, operating out of Cabinas Jabiru in Los Chiles, runs half-day tours to the refuge (US$20 per person, three-person minimum), as does Ecodirecta (☎/fax 471 1197), a Dutch-run reforestation project with an office near the docks in Los Chiles.

PUERTO VIEJO DE SARAPIQUÍ
pop 6000

Locally called Puerto Viejo, this shouldn't be confused with Puerto Viejo de Talamanca on the Caribbean. Located at the confluence of the Río Puerto Viejo and the Río Sarapiquí, it used to be an important port on the trade route to the Caribbean. Today the region is known for its nearby undisturbed premontane tropical wet forest, which extends from the northern arm of Parque Nacional Braulio Carrillo. The easiest access to the rain forest is from the local lodges and research station – all expensive but good.

Estación Biológica La Selva

This biological station (☎ 766 6565, fax 766 6335, laselva@sloth.ots.ac.cr), 5km southeast of Puerto Viejo, is run by the Organization of Tropical Studies (OTS). The place teems with researchers and grad students of tropical ecology. A well-developed trail system enables access year-round, and the birding is excellent.

Educational, guided 3½-hour walks are offered at 8 am and 1:30 pm (US$20, or US$30 for both hikes); reservations are required. Bring insect repellent and rain gear or an umbrella. Taxis from Puerto Viejo will take you to La Selva for about US$3.

Places to Stay & Eat

Budget travelers stay on the main street. Choice may be limited, since local workers often occupy the cheapest hotels long-term.

Cabinas Restaurant Monteverde (☎ 766 6236) charges US$6/8 for singles/doubles with private cold showers. The restaurant is popular and reasonable. The spartan *Hotel Gonar* (☎ 766 6196), above a hardware shop, charges US$3 per person, as does the rundown *Hospedaje Santa Martha*.

The nicest budget hotel is *Mi Lindo Sarapiquí* (☎ 766 6074), south of the soccer field. Simply decorated rooms with private hot shower rent for US$11/19. Downstairs is a decent locally recommended restaurant, open from 9 am to 10 pm.

Getting There & Away

Bus Direct buses for San José leave Puerto Viejo eight times a day from a stop on the main street. A nearby stop has buses for Ciudad Quesada and other destinations. About six buses a day head for Guápiles between 5:30 am and 6 pm.

Boat Motorized dugouts can be rented (at expensive rates) from the small port. A daily boat leaves around 12:30 pm for Oro Verde and Trinidad on the Río San Juan (US$3), returning the next morning at 7 am. Trinidad has a budget travelers' lodge with cabins for US$10 per person.

LA VIRGEN

This is the largest village between Puerto Viejo and San Miguel to the southwest, and it has one of the best budget options in the area, the friendly *Sarapiquí Outdoor Center* (☎/fax 761 1123, 297 1010 beeper). Simple rooms are US$8 per person – the draw is that behind the cabinas are lovely views of the river and landscaped grounds. You can camp here for US$3 per person; there is a communal kitchen and a covered terrace in case of rain. Meals are available. Boat trips (US$28) and horseback tours (US$25) can be arranged.

Other budget accommodations in La Virgen are *Hotel Claribel* (☎ 761 1190) and the slightly cheaper and simpler *Cabinas Tía Rosita* (☎ 761 1032), which gets a lot of truckers.

PUERTO LIMÓN
pop 76,000

Capital of Limón Province – locals simply call it Limón – this seedy but lively port has a mainly black population. Puerto Limón is not

COSTA RICA

COSTA RICA

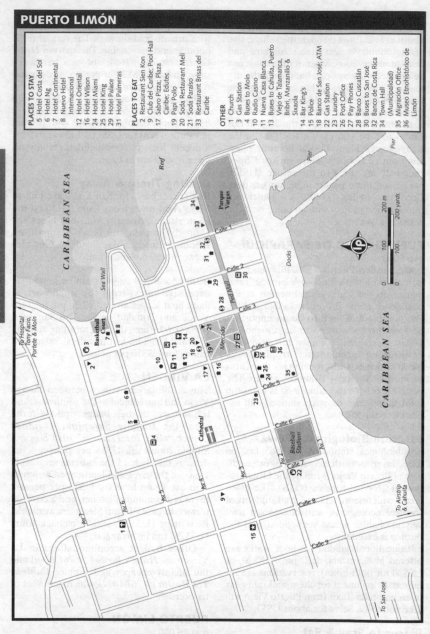

PUERTO LIMÓN

PLACES TO STAY
5 Hotel Costa del Sol
6 Hotel Ng
7 Hotel Continental
8 Nuevo Hotel
   Internacional
12 Hotel Oriental
16 Hotel Wilson
24 Hotel Miami
25 Hotel King
29 Hotel Palace
31 Hotel Palmeras

PLACES TO EAT
2 Restaurant Sien Kon
9 Club del Caribe; Pool Hall
17 Sabro Pizza; Plaza
   Caribe; Edutec
19 Papi Pollo
20 Soda Restaurant Meli
21 Soda Paraíso
33 Restaurant Brisas del
   Caribe

OTHER
1 Church
3 Gas Station
4 Buses to Moín
10 Radio Casino
11 Nueva Casa Blanca
13 Buses to Cahuita, Puerto
   Viejo de Talamanca,
   Bribrí, Manzanillo &
   Sixaola
14 Bar King's
15 Police
18 Banco de San José; ATM
22 Gas Station
23 Laundry
26 Post Office
27 Pay Phones
28 Banco Cuscatlán
30 Buses to San José
32 Banco de Costa Rica
34 Town Hall
   (Municipalidad)
35 Migración Office
36 Museo Etnohistórico de
   Limón

considered a tourist town, which means you may attract less negative attention here than in the more-visited villages. Note that the locals don't use street names, but only local landmarks like the *municipalidad* (town hall) on Parque Vargas, or Radio Casino.

Information
Banco Cuscatlán, open 9 am to 6 pm Monday to Friday, exchanges traveler's checks. The ATM at the Banco de San José accepts the widest variety of cards. Exchange facilities are sparse elsewhere along the coast.

There's a bank of pay phones on the south side of the market. Edutec, upstairs at the Plaza Caribe, charges US$2.30 per hour for Internet access; it's open 8 am to 10 pm Monday to Saturday. The post office is a cheaper alternative when the system is up.

The Hospital Tony Facio (☎ 758 2222), at the north end of the waterfront, serves the entire province.

Things to See & Do
The main attraction is **Parque Vargas**, on the southeastern corner of town by the waterfront. The park has tropical trees, flowers, birds and sloths hanging out (literally) in the trees. From the park, walk north along the sea wall for views of the rocky headland upon which the city is built. Another focal point is the colorful **mercado**. Also check out the **Museo Etnohistórico de Limón** (Limón Ethnography Museum), open erratically. The nearest beach is **Playa Bonita**, 4km northwest of town, which is OK for swimming.

On his fourth and final transatlantic voyage, Columbus landed at Uvita Island, 1km east of Limón, and **Día de la Raza** (Columbus Day) is celebrated enthusiastically in October most years. Thousands of Ticos stream into town for street parades: Dancing, music, singing and drinking go on for days. Hotels are booked in advance.

Places to Stay
Women traveling alone should avoid the cheapest hotels, which are a poor value and used by prostitutes.

Hotel Oriental (☎ 758 0117) is just US$7.50 a double with shared cold showers, but it's decent. *Hotel Ng* (☎ 758 3124) seems friendly, though its rooms, at

US$4/5 per person with shared/private cold shower, resemble jail cells. A good choice is the clean and cheerful *Hotel King* (☎ 758 1033), at US$4.50 per person for rooms with communal bath and US$11.50 for ·doubles with private cold shower. Most rooms have fans.

The ancient *Hotel Palace* (☎ 758 0419) charges US$6.50/10 for adequate singles/doubles or US$13 for better doubles with bath and fan. There's a huge birdcage in the patio. Near Parque Vargas, *Hotel Palmeras* (☎ 758 0241) has bare rooms with double bed and private cold shower for US$11.50, but the grimness is offset by the cheery balconies that overlook the pedestrian mall.

Hotel Costa del Sol (☎ 798 0707, fax 758 4748) is in better shape, with decent if cramped rooms for US$8/11, or US$9.25/13 with private bath. Credit cards are accepted and parking is available. The cordially managed *Hotel Wilson* (☎ 758 5028) offers neat rooms with private baths and fans for US$9/13. The clacking of domino games and TV create some noise.

Slightly costlier but far more comfortable, *Hotel Miami* (☎ /fax 758 0490) charges US$10.50/15.50/18 for clean, quiet singles/doubles/triples with private cold shower and industrial strength fans. Rooms with efficient air-conditioning and TV are US$17.50/23/26. Near the waterfront, *Nuevo Hotel Internacional* (☎ 798 0532) has clean fan-cooled rooms for US$7.25/10.50/13.50 or air-conditioned rooms for US$9/14/19.50, all with private hot showers. Across the street is the similar *Hotel Continental*, under the same management.

Places to Eat
The Chinese influence is evident: Almost every restaurant and bar has chop suey on the menu. *Soda Restaurant Meli*, on the north side of the market, typically serves fried rice (full or half portions) along with the usual casados. The best Chinese restaurant in Limón is *Restaurant Sien Kon*, with meals from US$5 to US$10.

There are plenty of snack bars and sodas around the mercado. *Soda Paraíso*, on the northeast corner, is an unpretentious joint where simple meals start at US$2. *Papi Pollo*, on the north side, specializes in rotisseried chicken (US$1.80 per quarter) and serves varied lunch platters.

Club del Caribe, next to a pool hall, is a soulful little eatery with a Creole flavor. There are two or three different dishes a day; a bowl of cow's foot soup and a cold beer cost US$2.40. In the Plaza Caribe's 'food court' is *Sabro Pizza*, which charges US$3 for a medium-sized pie. The *Restaurant Brisas del Caribe*, on the north side of Parque Vargas, is midpriced, pleasant and airy.

Entertainment

Scores of bars by Parque Vargas and a few blocks west are hangouts for various coastal characters and may not be appropriate for solo women travelers. If you really want to soak up some atmosphere, go to *Nueva Casa Blanca*, also known as Charlie's, which is packed from around 5 pm onward with a predominately black male clientele, though an occasional woman may join a domino game. Calypso bands perform here on Saturday night. *Bar King's* is more Latin in flavor and more relaxed. The spacious bar is cooled off by a dozen or so overhead fans, and a good sound system plays continuous salsa.

Getting There & Away

Autotransporte Caribeños express buses leave San José's Caribe terminal hourly from 5:30 am to 6:30 pm, returning from the Limón terminal a block east of the market (US$3.25, 2½ hours). (At the time of writing a new terminal was planned west of the baseball stadium, to be completed by mid-2001.) Avoid the slower competing line, Coopelimon.

Buses to Cahuita (US$0.90, 1½ hours) leave from a block north of the market 10 times a day from 5 am to 6 pm. All of these continue to Puerto Viejo, and most go on to Bribri and Sixaola (US$2.25, three hours). Three buses, at 6 am and 2:30 and 6 pm, go on to Manzanillo. These buses are crowded, so get advance tickets and show up early.

Buses to Moín, the embarkation point for Tortuguero boats, leave from Avenida 5 west of Calle 5 every half hour from 5:30 am.

Boats to Tortuguero leave from Moín (see above).

PARQUE NACIONAL TORTUGUERO

This coastal park is the most important Caribbean breeding ground of the green sea turtle. Of the eight species of marine turtle in the world, six nest in Costa Rica. Four nest in Tortuguero. Though the park has lately been encroached upon by loggers, banana plantations and tourism developers, you can still see more wildlife here than in many parts of Central America.

Information

Park headquarters (with information) is at the north end of the park, next to Tortuguero village. Admission is US$6 per day; camping is not permitted. There is a 2km loop nature trail, though it is often flooded during rainy months. Most visitors see the park by boat, as they arrive from the south or by hiring a boat in Tortuguero village.

The beaches are not suitable for swimming. The surf is very rough; the currents are strong; and sharks regularly patrol the waters. Rain gear and insect repellent are recommended.

Turtle Watching

Travelers are allowed to visit the nesting beaches at night and watch the turtles lay their eggs or observe the eggs hatching. However, camera flashes, VCRs, and flashlights are prohibited by law, as they disturb the egg-laying process. The best seasons to visit the beaches are from April 1 to May 31, when leatherbacks lay in small numbers, and July 1 to October 15, when green turtles lay in large numbers – most nest from late July to late August. Hawksbill turtles nest sporadically from March to October.

Guides (available by asking anyone in the area) must accompany visitors to the viewing areas. Park fees for two-hour night tours are US$5. Local guides charge US$10 and are knowledgeable.

Apart from turtle watching, Tortuguero has great opportunities for wildlife viewing and birding, either from trails in the park or on boat trips. Three species of monkey are frequently sighted, as are sloths, and many other mammals have been recorded. There are more than 400 species of bird in the area, including the magnificent frigate bird and royal tern. Caymans and crocodiles and a variety of snakes and amphibians are seen here. Freshwater turtles line up on logs by the riverbank, sunning themselves.

TORTUGUERO
pop 600

The inhabitants of this little village at the north end of the national park make most of their living from turtles and tourism. Generally speaking, a good balance has been struck between the interests of the local people, visitors and the turtles. Instead of harvesting the turtles, the people exploit them and the accompanying park in nondestructive yet economically satisfactory ways.

In the center of the village is an informative kiosk explaining the natural history, cultural history, geography and climate of the region. The Tortuguero Information Center, opposite the Catholic church (ask anyone), can recommend local guides and businesses catering to independent travelers.

Canoeing & Kayaking

Several places just north of the entrance to the park have signs announcing boats for hire. You can paddle yourself in a dugout canoe for about US$2 per person per hour, or go with a guide for a little more. Miss Junie's and the Manati Lodge (see Places to Stay & Eat) have plastic kayaks for rent, as do other places – ask around.

Organized Tours

For travelers with limited time, a rushed one-day tour is offered by Tucán Tico (☎ 260 6161, fax 261 6161, tucanti@sol.racsa .co.cr). This includes a dawn flight from San José to Tortuguero, a park tour with bilingual guide, breakfast and lunch in Tortuguero, a visit to the CCC museum (See Around Tortuguero) and a return along the canals by speedboat, continuing to San José by bus. This costs US$89, plus US$6 park and US$1 museum fees.

Tours of one, two or three nights are available, with the three-day/two-night option being the most popular. Ecole Travel (☎ 223 2240, fax 223 4128, ecolecr@sol.racsa .co.cr) offers two- and three-day tours, starting and ending at the Moín dock (Ecole gives you up-to-date instructions on how to get there by public transportation). The four- to five-hour boat ride through the canals to Tortuguero is part of the adventure. A night visit to the beach is added during the turtle nesting season, and a boat tour to the Caño Palma Biological Station is provided. The price of US$89/120 per person includes one/two nights at the Tortuguero Caribe Lodge (see Places to Stay & Eat). Meals and park entry fees are not included in the price.

Fran and Modesto Watson (☎/fax 226 0986, fvwatson@sol.racsa.co.cr) offer guided overnight tours, including transportation from San José to Moín by van, boat ride to Tortuguero, lodging at the Laguna Lodge, a turtle walk during nesting season, entry fees and meals, for US$185 per person. They can customize tours. See their Web site for more information (www.tortuguerocanals.com).

Independent travelers can stay in Tortuguero village and hire local guides.

Places to Stay & Eat

Budget travelers normally stay in the village. You might be able to bargain down the following prices if you're staying a few days. The friendly, family-run *Cabinas Mariscar* has basic, clean rooms with fans and shared bath for US$6 per person and a few more expensive rooms with private bath. *Cabinas Sabina* is the biggest place, with 31 no-frills rooms near the ocean at US$10/15 double/triple. The *Tropical Lodge*, just north of the park entrance, has a few basic cabins at US$5 per person. *Cabinas Tortuguero* is clean and good; the rate is US$10 per person. The similarly priced *Cabinas Joruki* (☎ 233 3333, leave message for Sherman Johnson) has been recommended. Rooms with bath are behind a riverfront restaurant serving reasonably priced meals.

A few rooms with bath and fan are found at *Cabinas Pancana* and the slightly better *Cabinas Aracari* (☎ 798 3059); the rate is US$13/20 for doubles/triples. *Miss Junie's* (☎ 710 0523) has 12 clean singles/doubles with fan and private bath for US$17/35, including breakfast. Tortuguero's best-known cook, Miss Junie serves meals for about US$5. If these hotels are full, ask around; you may be able to stay in someone's house.

The rustic *Tortuguero Caribe Lodge* (☎ 385 4676, 259 0820 in San José) is reachable by boat from the village – ask around for a ride to Marco Zamora's place. Simple cabins with shared/private bath are US$12/18 per person. Good home-cooked meals cost US$7.50 each. This includes a wide spread.

Restaurants in the village charge about US$3 for fairly basic meals. One of the best places is **La Caribeña**, across from the Super Morpho Pulpería.

Getting There & Away
Most travelers get to the national parks on organized tours with prearranged boat or plane transportation. These tend to be expensive, but it may be possible to pay for just the travel portion and then stay in cheaper accommodations in the Tortuguero area.

Air The airstrip is 4km north of Tortuguero village. Both Sansa (US$55/110 one-way/roundtrip) and Travelair (US$51/93) have daily flights from San José at 6 and 6:45 am respectively. The designated ticket-sales agent for Travelair in Tortuguero is the Paraíso Tropical Store (☎ 710 0323).

Boat The cheapest way to arrive and leave Tortuguero is to take an early bus from San José's Caribe terminal to Cariari (US$2, 1¾ hours), and from there a bus to La Geest (US$1.50, 1½ hours), a dock in a banana plantation on the Río Suerte. Here, you will be met by Bananero, who runs a daily boat at 1 pm to Tortuguero (US$10, one hour). Bananero will take you back in the morning in time to catch the bus from La Geest to Cariari and San José. His dock/office is just north of the national park at the south end of Tortuguero village.

Tucán Tico (see Organized Tours above) runs a bus-boat connection (US$30 oneway) from San José to Tortuguero (two-passenger minimum), departing at 6 am from opposite the Teatro Nacional.

Passenger and cargo boats leave most days from Moín, 7km west of Puerto Limón. The dock is about 300m to the left of the main port, through a guarded gate. Most travelers take a private boat; boatmen offer the roundtrip to Tortuguero for US$50 per person with a three-person minimum, or less with larger groups. Departures are normally between 7 and 8 am. The trip up takes about five hours (allowing for photography and wildlife viewing). After lunch and a brief visit to Tortuguero, the return trip is done in 2½ hours. Overnights and returns on the following day can be arranged.

You can make arrangements in advance with agencies in Limón. Laura's Tours (☎ 758 2410) has been recommended. Alfred Brown Robinson of Tortuguero Odyssey Tours (☎ 758 0824) offers US$75 overnight tours, including a cheap hotel and meals, or a day tour for US$50. Other boatmen include Willis Rankin (☎ 798 1556) and Modesto Watson (☎ 226 0986 in San José).

AROUND TORTUGUERO
Caribbean Conservation Corporation
The CCC (☎ 224 9215, 352-373 6441 in the USA, ccc@cccturtle.org) operates a research station about 1km north of Tortuguero and has a worthwhile visitor center explaining turtle conservation and research work. Hours are 10 am to 12 pm and 2 to 6 pm daily; admission is US$1. An 18-minute video on the history of local turtle conservation is shown on request. Volunteer opportunities are available for those interested in assisting scientists with turtle research. See their Web site for more information (www.cccturtle.org).

Cerro Tortuguero
This 119m hill, about 6km north of the village, is the highest point on the coast north of Limón. You need to hire a boat to get there. The path is very steep and usually muddy but has good views of the forest, canals, sea and birds. Howler monkeys can be seen hanging out in the trees below the trail.

BARRA DEL COLORADO
This is a village and also the biggest national wildlife refuge in Costa Rica. It is virtually an extension of Tortuguero National Park. The area has traditionally attracted visitors for sportfishing (tarpon and snook), but excellent birding and wildlife watching opportunities are beginning to draw nature tours.

Orientation & Information
The village lies near the mouth of the Río Colorado and is reached by air or boat. The airstrip is on the south side of the river (Barra del Sur), but more people live on the north bank (Barra del Norte). There are no roads, and travel is almost exclusively by boat.

A small ranger station is located on the south side of the Río Colorado near the village. Officially, US$6 is charged to enter the refuge, but this was not being enforced at time of writing.

Places to Stay

Camping is allowed in the refuge, but there are no facilities. Hotels, mostly sportfishing lodges, are expensive and can be reached only by boat. You may stay more cheaply with a local family (about US$8 per person) if you ask around – try C&D Souvenirs near the airstrip for information.

The cheapest hotel is *Tarponland Lodge* (☎ 383 6097) next to the airport. Basic rooms with bath and fan start at US$45 per person, including meals.

The German-run *Samay Lagoon Lodge* (☎ 284 7047 in San José, fax 383 6370, samaycr@sol.racsa.co.cr) is 8km south of the airstrip, with a beach a quarter kilometer away (swimming here is unsafe due to heavy surf and strong currents). Most visitors come on a three-day/two-night package, beginning in San José with a bus ride to Puerto Viejo de Sarapiquí and continuing with a 3½-hour boat ride down the Sarapiquí, San Juan and Colorado Rivers to the lodge. The second day includes a guided canoe trip and hike into the rain forest, and the third day you return the way you came. This costs US$278 per person from San José and includes meals, two nights' lodging in standard rooms with private hot showers, transportation and tour.

Getting There & Away

Air Sansa flies daily to and from Barra del Colorado at 6 am and 6:45 am (US$55 each way).

Boat A few of the boats from Moín to Tortuguero continue to Barra, but there's no regular service. Boats from Tortuguero charge about US$50; they'll take three to five passengers. If you have time, wait for a group of locals going to Barra and ride more cheaply.

Leaving Barra, you can also hire a motorboat up the Río Colorado to the small community of Puerto Lindo, less than an hour away. From there, 4WD taxis can be hired to the town of Cariari and bus service

to Guápiles and San José, though the road is often closed after heavy rains.

CAHUITA

This village, 43km southeast of Limón, is known for the attractive beaches found in Parque Nacional Cahuita, a small peninsula immediately to the south. Although only three hours by car from San José, the area has a provincial and unhurried ambience.

Creole culture lives on here, particularly in cooking, music and medicinal plants. Many of the 3500 inhabitants of the Cahuita district speak a Creole dialect.

Information

To orient yourself, have a look at the elaborate map painted on the wall next to Salon Sarafinas. Enrique and Wayne at Cabinas Safari articulately share their abundant knowledge of the area. They can also convert almost any currency into colones, and they cash traveler's checks.

The public telephone office is at Soda Uvita, and a few pay phones are along the main street. Cabinas Jenny charges a steep US$3.50 for 20 minutes of Internet access; alternatively, try Rainy Bay Cyber Café near the soccer field on Playa Negra.

Dangers & Annoyances The killings of two young North American women north of Cahuita in early 2000 sent shock waves through the area, and international coverage of the crime hurt tourism. However, the incident was clearly an isolated case and in no way indicative of any pattern of hostility or violence against visitors.

Nevertheless, visitors should take sensible precautions against petty crime. Don't leave your gear on the beach when swimming; don't walk the beaches alone at night; and be prudent in the local bars. Some locals do take advantage of tourists, but this is not a major problem. Beware of drug sellers who may be in cahoots with the police.

Single women travelers do get hassled by a few of the local men; travel with a friend. Nude bathing is not accepted, and wearing skimpy swimsuits in the villages is frowned upon. 'Safe sex' is rarely practiced here, and AIDS and other STDs are on the increase. If you are tempted by local sexual liaisons, bring your own condoms.

COSTA RICA

CAHUITA

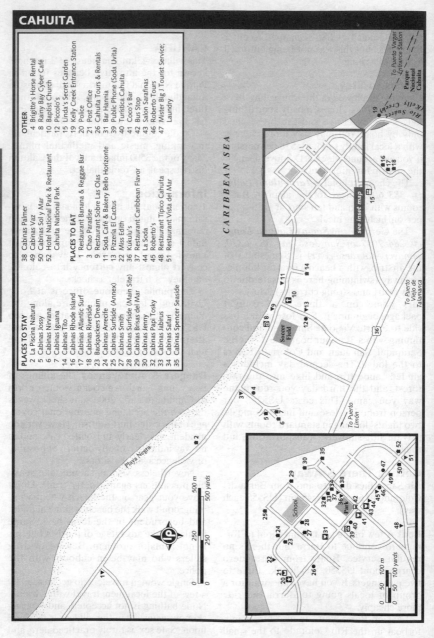

PLACES TO STAY
2 La Piscina Natural
5 Cabinas Jossy
6 Cabinas Nirvana
7 Cabinas Iguana
14 Cabinas Tito
16 Cabinas Rhode Island
17 Cabinas Atlantic Surf
18 Cabinas Riverside
23 Backpackers Dream
24 Cabinas Arrecife
25 Cabinas Surfside (Annex)
27 Cabinas Smith
28 Cabinas Surfside (Main Site)
29 Cabinas Brisas del Mar
30 Cabinas Jenny
32 Cabinas Papi Tosky
33 Cabinas Jabirus
34 Cabinas Safari
35 Cabinas Spencer Seaside
38 Cabinas Palmer
49 Cabinas Vaz
50 Cabinas Sol y Mar
52 Hotel National Park & Restaurant Cahuita National Park

PLACES TO EAT
1 Restaurant Banana & Reggae Bar
3 Chao Paradise
9 Restaurant Sobre Las Olas
11 Soda Café & Bakery Bello Horizonte
13 Pizzeria El Cactus
22 Miss Edith
36 Kukulu's
37 Restaurant Caribbean Flavor
44 La Soda
45 Roberto's
48 Restaurant Tipico Cahuita
51 Restaurant Vista del Mar

OTHER
4 Brigitte's Horse Rental
8 Rainy Bay Cyber Café
10 Baptist Church
12 Piccolo's
15 Linda's Secret Garden
19 Kelly Creek Entrance Station
20 Police
21 Post Office
26 Cahuita Tours & Rentals
31 Bar Hannia
39 Public Phone (Soda Uvita)
40 Turística Cahuita
41 Coco's Bar
42 Bus Stop
43 Salon Sarafinas
46 Roberto Tours
47 Mister Big J Tourist Service; Laundry

CARIBBEAN SEA

Playa Negra

To Puerto Limón

To Puerto Viejo de Talamanca

To Puerto Vargas Entrance Station

Parque Nacional Cahuita

Río Suárez (Kelly Creek)

Soccer Field

School

Park

see inset map

500 m
500 yards

100 m
100 yards

Beaches

At the northwest end of Cahuita is a long black-sand beach with good swimming. The white-sand beach at the eastern end of town is in the national park, and a trail in the jungle behind it leads to a third beach about 6km away. These last two beaches are separated by a rocky headland with a small coral reef.

Activities

A number of places rent equipment and arrange fishing and horseback tours, including Cahuita Tours (☎ 755 0232, fax 755 0082), Mister Big J Tourist Service (☎ 755 0328), Roberto Tours (☎/fax 755 0117) and Turística Cahuita (☎ 755 0071, dltacb@ sol.racsa.co.cr).

Shop around for the best deals. A mask, snorkel and fins usually rent for US$10 a day, bicycles for US$10, surfboards for US$6. Boat trips to the reef in a glass-bottomed boat, with snorkeling opportunities, are US$15 to US$20 per person for three or four hours. Day trips to Tortuguero are about US$70.

Brigitte (☎ 755 0053), a Swiss woman who has lived by Playa Negra for years, offers half-day guided horseback tours for US$25 to US$35 and horse rental (for unguided exploration) at US$10 per hour. Atec (see the Puerto Viejo de Talamanca section) can arrange reasonably priced visits to Parque Nacional Cahuita and birding walks with local guides.

Places to Stay

Hotels are concentrated in two areas: the center of town and northwest of town along Playa Negra. The latter zone tends to be more expensive, but good deals can be found. Cahuita's cheapest lodging is *Backpackers Dream*, with four basic fan-cooled rooms and one bathroom at the rate of US$6 per person. Also aimed at shoestring travelers, *Cabinas Jabirus* charges US$7 per person for bark-paneled cubicles along a narrow hallway. Inquire at Cabinas Safari around the corner. *Cabinas Surfside* (☎ 755 0246, fax 755 0203) has clean concrete-block rooms with fan, private bath and a guarded parking area. Rates are US$12 double. They have a couple of better cabins nearer the shore at US$25 for up to four occupants. The friendly *Cabinas Smith* (☎ 755 0068)

offers good clean singles/doubles with warm showers and fans for US$10/15. Recommended by travelers, *Papi Tosky* features cheerfully painted rooms with hot water for US$15/20. Inquire at Kukulu's restaurant around the corner. The oceanside *Cabinas Brisas del Mar* (☎ 755 0011) charges US$20/25 for clean double rooms with hot showers and good beds.

Cabinas Palmer (☎ 755 0243, 393 1670 cell phone) is owned by friendly locals. Tidy singles/doubles/triples with hot showers are US$15/20/25. Across the street, the hospitable *Cabinas Safari* (☎ 755 0078, fax 755 0020) has decent rooms with cold showers for US$20/25/30. Parking is available.

Right on the shore, *Cabinas Jenny* (☎ 755 0256, jenny@racsa.co.cr) charges US$15 for concrete doubles downstairs or US$25 for superior wooden cabins upstairs. These cabins include private bath and a seaview balcony. Next door, the equally pleasant and similarly priced *Cabinas Spencer Seaside* (☎ 755 0027, 392 2474 cell phone) is on the beach and has hammocks strung beneath the coconut palms.

Cabinas Arrecife (☎ 755 0081), on the northwest edge of the town center, offers clean comfortable rooms with screened windows, silent overhead fans and hot showers for US$15/20/25. Breakfast is served on a terrace overlooking the sea.

In the center of town, *Cabinas Vaz* (☎ 755 0218, fax 755 0283) has clean concrete-block rooms with bath and fan for US$10/15; street noise recedes toward the back. *Cabinas Sol y Mar* (☎ 755 0237) offers decent rooms with fan and hot shower for US$8.50/13.50.

South of the center of town, *Cabinas Rhode Island* (☎ 755 0237) has clean doubles with hot water and fan for US$12. Farther down the lane, *Cabinas Riverside*, managed by the helpful Louis Ferguson, features three rooms beside a quiet garden at US$15/20 for one/two occupants. Inquire about either of these at Cabinas Sol y Mar. Between the two, *Cabinas Atlantic Surf* (☎ 755 0086) is a two-level wood structure containing singles/doubles/triples with fans, cold showers and porches for US$7.50/ 12.50/14.50. Look for manager Mercedes in the green house opposite the Rhode Island.

Steps from the beach at the park entrance, *Hotel National Park* (☎ 755 0244)

COSTA RICA

has immaculate rooms with hot showers for US$15/20/25. A new beach-view wing may be ready soon.

Out toward Playa Negra, *Cabinas Tito* (☎ 755 0286) has six roomy bungalows on tranquil grounds, each equipped with attractive tiled bathroom and fan – a good value at US$20. About 700m farther up is a peaceful enclave of mostly European-run accommodations. *Cabinas Iguana* (☎ 755 0005, fax 755 0054, iguanas@sol.racsa.co.cr) has three neat double rooms with fans and porches for US$17, plus a swimming pool and book exchange. Built by a friendly Italian, *Cabinas Nirvana* (☎ 755 0110) charges US$14/25 for well-designed cabins with shared/private bath. Cheaper but still decent is *Cabinas Jossy* (☎ 755 0090), offering a couple of simple well-kept rooms and one clean bathroom at US$10 per person. Don't be put off by the growling dog.

Farther down the coast road is *La Piscina Natural* (the natural pool), named after a small inlet of clear water gracing the lush grounds. Worn but adequate rooms for up to four people, including private bath, cost US$17.

Places to Eat

Miss Edith is traditionally popular and has recently expanded. Meals are US$4 and up; alcohol isn't served. *Caribbean Flavor*, adjacent to Cabinas Safari, claims to make the best rondón around (US$10 for two), but the soulful stew must be ordered 24 hours in advance. Next door, *Kukulu's* is a stylish new addition that serves outstanding pizza. A 'personal' pie costs US$3 to US$5 but easily feeds two.

Restaurant Cahuita National Park, by the entrance to the park, is a little pricey but popular for all meals. *Restaurant Vista Del Mar*, across the way, has a Chinese menu in addition to seafood platters (US$4 and up). For breakfast and other meals, try *Soda Sol y Mar* (attached to the cabinas of the same name) or *La Soda*, both on the main street. The latter is more expensive, but its offerings are consistently fresh and well prepared. *Roberto's*, next to the tour company run by the same genial owner, is a relaxed place serving good, simple, Caribbean-inflected meals. *Restaurant Típico Cahuita* has a variety of local food – budget travelers should order the casado for US$3.

Del Rita sells homemade stews, beef patties and other snacks direct from the pot – weekends she's at the kiosk near the park entrance.

On a side road northwest of the center, *Pizzería El Cactus* has pizzas and pastas in the US$3 to US$6 range. Out toward the black-sand beach, *Soda Café & Bakery Bello Horizonte* makes delicious bread, cakes and pies. *Restaurant Sobre Las Olas* is a beachfront restaurant offering fresh sea bass (US$8.50), red snapper (US$7.50) and candlelit evenings. Continuing out along the coast, the laid-back *Chao Paradise* specializes in Caribbean cuisine, with coconut chicken for US$5. Still farther out, *Restaurant Banana* sells good local food.

Entertainment

This can be summed up in one word: bars. The liveliest option is *Coco's Bar*, Cahuita's undisputed nightlife center. Across the way, *Salon Sarafinas* claims its share of the soundscape with rap and techno beats. A block away is *Bar Hannia*, a more relaxed local hangout. Opposite Pizzería El Cactus, *Piccolo's* boasts a good pool table, direct TV and beer.

Cahuita now has a cinema: Linda's Secret Garden, down the lane opposite Restaurant Típico Cahuita, shows movies in the jungle Thursday to Sunday nights.

Getting There & Away

Express buses leave from the Caribe terminal in San José at 6 and 10 am, 1:30 and 3:30 pm. The trip takes about four hours (US$5). Alternately, take a bus from San José to Puerto Limón and change there for frequent buses to Cahuita. These buses go on to Puerto Viejo de Talamanca. Three continue from there to Manzanillo, and the rest go to Bribri and Sixaola (2 hours). These buses may stop only out on the highway, southwest of Cahuita; ask locally. All of them pass the Puerto Vargas entrance to Parque Nacional Cahuita.

Buses back to Limón and San José leave from the central crossroads in Cahuita at 7:30, 9:30 and 11 am and 4 pm.

PARQUE NACIONAL CAHUITA

This small park is one of the more frequently visited in Costa Rica. It offers easy access, nearby hotels, attractive beaches, a coral reef and a coastal rain forest. The main entrance is east of Cahuita village, through the Kelly Creek station. From here, a white-sand beach stretches 2km to the east. The first 500m have warning signs about unsafe swimming, but beyond that the waves are gentle. The rocky Punta Cahuita separates this beach from Vargas Beach, at the end of which is the Puerto Vargas ranger station (☎ 755 0302), 7km from Kelly Creek. A trail through the coastal jungle behind the beach links the two ranger stations. A river near the end of the first beach can be thigh-deep at high tide. Many animals and birds can be seen by an observant hiker.

The park stations are open 8 am to 4 pm Monday to Friday, 7 am to 5 pm Saturday and Sunday. Admission is US$6, though at the Kelly Creek entrance, the locals have set up a 'donate what you want' station because the US$6 fee was driving away travelers (and business). You can walk in and out after hours, though cars won't be able to get into Puerto Vargas.

Camping (US$2 per person) is at Vargas Beach, about 1km from the Puerto Vargas ranger station; campers must use that entrance. Outdoor showers and pit latrines are found at the administration center near the middle of the camping area. There is drinking water, and some sites have picnic tables. The area is rarely crowded. Camp close to the administration center for greater security; it's safe but don't leave your gear unattended.

A good day hike is to take the 8 am Cahuita–Puerto Viejo bus to the Puerto Vargas entrance road, walk 1km to the coast then 7km more back to Cahuita. Carry water, insect repellent and sunscreen.

PUERTO VIEJO DE TALAMANCA

This small village is known locally as Puerto Viejo (don't confuse it with Puerto Viejo de Sarapiquí). There is more influence from the local Bribri indigenous culture than in Cahuita. Lately, there has also been much more development, though mainly of an individual, low-key variety.

Puerto Viejo is more exposed to the sea than Cahuita, which encourages shoreside strolling (and partying). The area is a prime surfers' destination, with the country's biggest and most powerful waves. Snorkeling improves as surfing conditions decline in September and October.

Information

The Talamanca Association for Ecotourism and Conservation (Atec; ☎/fax 750 0191) is a nonprofit grassroots organization promoting local tourism in ways that enhance nearby communities and provide learning experiences for visitors. Office hours are 8 am to 9 pm daily, with a variable lunch break. You can check out its Web site at www.greencoast.com/atec.htm.

Atec serves as an information center about local issues and can arrange a variety of tours by local guides with an emphasis on native cultures, natural history and environmental issues (though it is not a tour agency). These trips are US$15 per person for half a day and US$25 for a full day and involve a fair amount of hiking. Overnight trips are possible.

The acceptance of credit cards and payment in US dollars is spreading to more hotels and cabinas, but the nearest bank is in Bribri; try to bring as many colones as you'll need.

The Ciber Café, open 8 am to 10 pm daily, charges US$10 per hour for satellite-connected Internet access. If that seems expensive, keep in mind that Puerto Viejo didn't even have electricity until a few years ago. Atec also has a few machines for public use and charges around US$6 per hour.

Indigenous Reserves

Atec is the most comprehensive source for those interested in visiting the area's indigenous reserves. Mauricio Salazar from Chimuri Nature Lodge (see Places to Stay) can guide you on day tours to the small KeköLdi reserve. Tours run twice a week for US$25 per person (six persons maximum); 10% of the tour cost goes directly to the reserve.

Activities

The waves are best for surfing from December to early March, with another season in June and July. Surfers praise Salsa Brava, outside the reef just east of town, but surfers with less experience may prefer the waves at Playa Cocles, 2km down the coast. The best snorkeling reefs are at Cahuita, Punta Uva and by Manzanillo.

Reef Runners (☎ 750 0480, reefrun@sol.racsa.co.cr) offers all levels of diving instruction and excursions. Atlántico Adven-

COSTA RICA

PUERTO VIEJO DE TALAMANCA

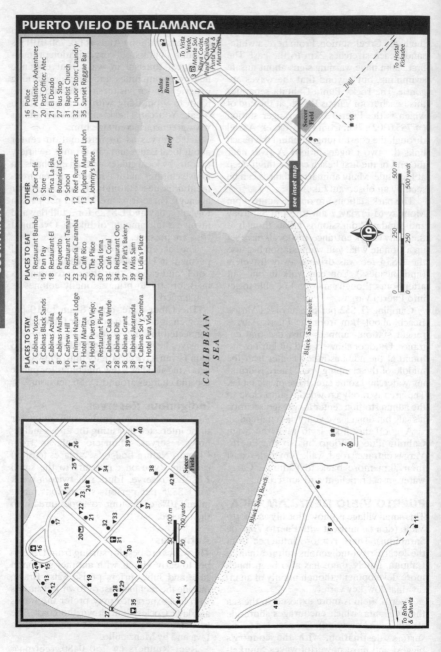

PLACES TO STAY
2 Cabinas Yucca
4 Cabinas Black Sands
5 Cabinas Maribe
8 Cabinas Azulia
10 Cashew Hill
11 Chimuri Nature Lodge
19 Hotel Maritza
24 Hotel Puerto Viejo;
   Restaurant Piraña
26 Cabinas Casa Verde
28 Cabinas Diti
36 Cabinas Grant
38 Cabinas Jacaranda
41 Cabinas Sol y Sombra
42 Hotel Pura Vida

PLACES TO EAT
1 Restaurant Bambú
15 Pan Pay
18 Restaurant El
   Parquecito
22 Restaurant Tamara
23 Pizzeria Caramba
25 Café Rico
29 The Place
30 Soda Isma
33 Café Coral
34 Restaurant Oro
37 Mr Pat's Bakery
39 Miss Sam
40 Lidia's Place

OTHER
3 Ciber Café
6 Store
7 Finca La Isla
   Botanical Garden
9 School
12 Reef Runners
13 Pulpería Manuel León
14 Johnny's Place
16 Police
17 Atlantico Adventures
20 Post Office; Atec
21 El Dorado
27 Bus Stop
31 Baptist Church
32 Liquor Store; Laundry
35 Sunset Reggae Bar

tures (☎ 750 0004) conducts tours up and down the coast from US$35. It also rents quality bikes for US$10 per day, as well as boogie boards and snorkel gear. Don Antonio (☎ 750 0342) rents horses for US$7 per hour and offers riding tours to Manzanillo and the Cordillera de Talamanca.

Places to Stay

Puerto Viejo has developed rapidly in recent years, so keep your eye out for new places and competition-induced bargains. High season weekend rates are given; discounts are available at other times. Most hotels provide mosquito netting or fans (a breeze helps keep mosquitoes away), and cold water showers are the norm. Ask around about camping on hotel grounds.

Cabinas Sol y Sombra, at the entrance to town, is a new budget choice. The French-run place is secure and tidy and charges just US$5 per bunk bed or US$7 per single room. Breakfast is served downstairs. A pair of recommended options are both on secluded hills southeast of town. *Hostal Kiskadee* (☎ 750 0284), a 10-minute hike up a steep, unlit path (carry a flashlight if arriving after dark), has dormitory-style accommodations for US$7 per person. *Cashew Hill* (☎ 750 0256) has two simple cabins for US$10/15 single/double, including kitchen privileges and shared warm shower. A larger room with private bath is US$15/20. *Hotel Puerto Viejo* (☎ 750 0465) is the biggest place in town and popular with surfers. Basic but clean upstairs rooms are US$6 per person; poorer downstairs rooms are a little cheaper. Doubles with private cold showers are US$14.

Cabinas Jacaranda (☎ 750 0069) has pleasant rooms with fans, mosquito nets and shared cold showers at US$10/15; a double with private hot shower costs US$18. A restaurant is attached. *Cabinas Diti* (☎ 750 0311) offers unexceptional rooms with private baths for US$8.50/12. The adjacent Tabu shop rents bicycles. *Hotel Pura Vida* (☎ 750 0002, fax 750 0296) charges US$15/19/24 for decent singles/doubles/triples and shared hot showers. Two rooms with private bath are US$25. There's a spacious lounge festooned with hammocks. *Cabinas Grant* (☎ 758 0292) has OK rooms with private cold bath and fan for US$13.50/20.

Steps from the ocean, *Hotel Maritza* (☎ 750 0003, fax 750 0313) is US$25 for pleasant doubles with fan, private bath and electric shower. A few basic older rooms over the restaurant, with shared cold showers, go for US$15. The clean, friendly, multilingual *Cabinas Casa Verde* (☎ 750 0015, fax 750 0047, atecmail@sol.racsa.co.cr) has pleasant rooms with warm communal showers for US$16/22 or US$30/34 with private bath.

West of town, by the black-sand beach, hospitable *Cabinas Maribe* (☎ 750 0182) has clean singles/doubles with cold showers and fan for less than US$10/17. Still farther west and right on the beach, the popular (and often full) *Cabinas Black Sands* (☎ 750 0124, bsands@sol.racsa.co.cr) is thatched in the local Bribri style and set in a pleasant garden. Five basic rooms with mosquito nets are US$10 per person with communal kitchen and bathroom facilities. *Cabinas Azulila* (☎/fax 750 0279), up the road to Cahuita, charges a reasonable US$16 for attractive hardwood double rooms with forest-view windows and private bath with hot water.

Chimuri Nature Lodge (☎/fax 750 0119, atecmail@sol.racsa.co.cr), run by Mauricio Salazar, who knows as much about indigenous culture as anyone in town, borders the KeköLdi reserve. Bribri-style A-frame cabins rent for US$20, one quadruple cabin for US$40. A dormitory with eight bunk beds is US$9 per person; students get discounts. Meals are provided on request. The cabins are set in a 20-hectare private reserve with trails and good birding.

A number of excellent European-run inns are just east of town. All charge US$20 to US$25 for a double with private bath, or about US$5 less in low season. *Cabinas Yucca* (☎/fax 750 0285) has well-designed rooms with back patios facing the sea and a wonderful *ranchito* where breakfast is served. Across the way, *Cabinas David* is also very nice, with scrubbed tile floors and a lush garden. *Vista Verde Jungle Lodge* (☎ 750 0014, michaelscharna@hotmail.com), run by a kindly German named Michael, has five rooms of varying size and access to a communal kitchen – a good place to meet people. Nearby, *Monte Sol* (☎/fax 750 0098, montesol@racsa.co.cr) offers simple, stylish rooms, some with imaginatively tiled

COSTA RICA

bathrooms. Co-owner Birgit runs a hair salon. Farther east, 800m from town, is the tranquil *Hotel Casa Blanca* (*☎/fax 750 0001*), a stone structure nestled in the woods. It contains five pleasant, fan-cooled rooms alongside a hammock-lined corridor.

Places to Eat
Several small places serve meals and snacks of the region. These include the reasonably priced *Miss Sam*, *Soda Isma* and *Lidia's Place*, all run by women who are long-term residents of Puereto Viejo. *Doña Juanita* and *Doña Guillerma* cook out of their houses near the entrance to town. Ask at Atec for other recommendations.

The *Café Coral* has yogurt, granola and homemade whole-wheat pancakes from 7 am to noon Tuesday to Sunday. Also popular for breakfast is *Café Rico*. *Mr Pat's* offers a variety of yummy cakes and fresh pastries, as does *Pan Pay*, whose specialty is chocolate croissants.

The *Restaurant Tamara* is good for Caribbean-style fish and chicken, starting at US$5, as well as baked goods. *Restaurant El Parquecito* offers decent meals for around US$4. *Restaurant Oro*, with its little open-air terrace, has good local food. *Restaurant Piraña*, in the Hotel Puerto Viejo, serves Mexican dishes, and *Pizzería Caramba* has Italian. *The Place*, near the bus stop, prepares healthy breakfasts and vegetarian and seafood meals, all reasonably priced; look for the chalkboard specials. *Restaurant Bambú* serves fruit shakes and sandwiches, within sight of the wave action at Salsa Brava. The 24-hour *Soda Cut-Back*, in an oceanside thatched hut east of town, offers Caribbean-style casados for US$3 as well as barbecued fish and lobster after 4 pm.

After checking your email at the *Ciber Café*, enjoy crepes and ice cream on its shore-view verandah.

Entertainment
The central evening hangout is *El Dorado*, featuring a pool table, microbrewed beers and good music. *Sunset Reggae Bar* is a locally popular establishment playing both Caribbean and rock music; Wednesday night there's an open jam session. Restaurant Bambu hosts reggae DJs Monday and Friday nights. *Johnny's Place* is the most happening dance club on weekends.

Getting There & Away
From San José, express buses leave at 6 and 10 am and 1:30 and 3:30 pm and cost US$4.75 for the four-hour trip. Otherwise, go from Puerto Limón, where buses leave from a block north of the market 10 times a day.

The following is a recent schedule of departures from Puerto Viejo; check with Atec for the latest.

Bribri/Sixaola (US$0.50/2.50, ½ hour/1½ hours)
  Buses depart at 6:15 and 9 am and 2, 5:30 and 7:30 pm

Cahuita/Limón (US$0.50/1.25, ½ hour/1½ hours)
  Buses depart at 6 and 9 am and 1, 4 and 5:30 pm.

Manzanillo (US$1.20, ½ hour)
  Buses depart at 7:15 am and 3:45 and 7:15 pm.

San José (US$4.75, four hours)
  Buses depart at 7, 9 and 11 am and 4 pm.

EAST OF PUERTO VIEJO
A 13km road heads east from Puerto Viejo along the coast, past sandy beaches and rocky points, through the small communities of Punta Uva and Manzanillo and sections of the Reserva Indígena Cocles/KeköLdi, ending up in Refugio Nacional de Vida Silvestre Gandoca-Manzanillo. It's paved as far as Playa Cocles and work is under way on the section extending to Punta Uva. This area is experiencing a minor boom in tourism, but the local people are trying to control development to ensure that the environment is not irreparably damaged.

Playa Cocles, 2km east of Puerto Viejo, has good surfing. The first lodging you'll find is *El Tesoro* (*☎ 750 0128*), with new hostel-style accommodations at US$8 per bunk bed, including use of communal hot showers. Private cabins are US$10 per person. Free morning coffee and email and a communal kitchen are among the services available at El Tesoro. The owners can find you short-term rentals for as little as US$250 a month.

Surfers stay at *Cabinas Garibaldi* (*☎ 750 0101*), where fairly basic doubles/triples with private bath and ocean views are US$8.50/11.50, and at *Surf Point* (*☎ 750 0123*), which has nicer rooms for US$10/20 with shared/private bath. Farther down the road, *Cabinas Roots* has a couple of thatched huts with private bath near the beach for US$20. The *Rinconcito Peruano* is a recommended Peruvian restaurant.

There are several places to stay along **Playa Chiquita**, a series of beaches about 4 to 7km east of Puerto Viejo. The clean little *Ranchita Blanca* has a few doubles with private bath for US$30 and bicycles for rent. *Kashá (☎ 750 0205, fax 283 7896)* charges US$32 for pleasant bungalows with private hot showers and satellite TV; there's a restaurant and bar on the premises. *Elena's Bar & Restaurant (☎ 750 0265)* is locally popular. *Soda Acuarius* bakes homemade bread and has a couple of basic rooms for rent.

Punta Uva is 7km east. The protected curve on the western side of this lovely point offers tranquil swimming. Near the beach is the long-standing *Selvin's Cabins*, which has basic double rooms and shared bath for US$16; another room with private bath and four-person capacity is US$30. Their popular restaurant is open Wednesday to Sunday. About 200m farther is *Walaba Cabinas*, offering basic rooms and dormitories from US$10 per person.

Manzanillo village is 12.5km east of Puerto Viejo, within the Gandoca-Manzanillo Wildlife Refuge (it already existed when the refuge was established). The road peters out about a kilometer beyond here. Footpaths continue around the coast through Gandoca-Manzanillo.

Near the bus stop in Manzanillo, the seaside *Cabinas Maxi* offers basic rooms for about US$15. The restaurant/bar serves excellent fish and lobster and there's dancing on weekends. On the way into the village, by the pulpería, is *Cabinas Las Veraneras (☎ 754-2298)*. It has clean singles/doubles for US$11.50/16.50. Several local women will prepare traditional Caribbean meals in their homes for travelers – ask around for details.

The **Gandoca-Manzanillo** refuge continues southeast as far as Panama. A coral reef is about 200m offshore and snorkeling is possible. The refuge contains a rain forest section and some of the most beautiful beaches on the Caribbean. A coastal trail leads 5.5km from Manzanillo to Punta Mona.

Atec in Puerto Viejo de Talamanca (see Information) offers a variety of tours into the refuge, including day and overnight trips on foot, horseback or by boat. Camping is permitted, but there are no organized facilities.

Getting There & Away
Buses leave Limón for Manzanillo (US$1.90, 2½ hours) at 6 am and 2:30 and 6 pm, passing through Cahuita and Puerto Viejo. Return buses leave Manzanillo at 5 and 8:30 am and 5 pm.

SIXAOLA
Sixaola is an unattractive border town with Panama. Most overlanders go to Panama via Paso Canoas on the Interamericana.

There are a few cheap and basic places to stay and eat, but better accommodations can be found on the Panamanian side. *Cabinas Sanchez (☎ 754-2105)*, at US$9 for a double, is one of the best places to stay.

Direct buses from San José leave from the Caribe terminal at 6 and 10 am and 1:30 and 3:30 pm, returning to San José at 5, 7:30 and 9:30 am and 2:30 pm (US$5.75, six hours). In addition, seven buses a day travel to/from Puerto Limón via Cahuita and Puerto Viejo (US$2.50, three hours).

Border Crossings
Panama The Panamanian town across the border from Sixaola is **Guabito**. There are no banks in Guabito, but stores accept colones, balboas and US dollars. Official border hours are 7 to 11 am and 1 to 7 pm. Frequent minibuses go from Guabito to Changuinola (16km), which has a bank, an airport with daily flights to David and buses to Almirante (30km), where there are cheaper hotels. From Almirante cheap public *lanchas* depart daily to Bocas del Toro. Set your watch an hour later when entering Panama.

Southern Costa Rica

The Interamericana reaches its highest point near the mist-shrouded 3491m peak of Cerro de la Muerte, about 100km south of San José. From there, the road drops steeply to the town of San Isidro de El General (702m), the entry point to nearby Parque Nacional Chirripó, which contains Costa Rica's highest mountains.

From San Isidro, the Interamericana continues southeast, through mainly agricultural lowlands, to Panama just a little more than 200km away. Towns in this area are small but offer an interesting view of Costa Rica off the main tourist trail and provide access to some of the more remote protected areas in the country.

The magnificent wilderness of Parque Nacional Corcovado and the popular Bahía Drake area in the Península de Osa are accessed farther south via Palmar or Golfito.

SAN JOSÉ TO SAN ISIDRO DE EL GENERAL

Two places along this stretch of the Interamericana are of interest to budget travelers. One is the **Finca del Eddie Serrano** (☎ 381 8456), where quetzals nest from November to early April. Bunk rooms are US$35 per person, including two meals and a guided hike to see the quetzals. The finca is 1km off the highway, near km marker 70 (south of San José).

Another place to view quetzals and other high-altitude birds is **Avalon Reserve** (☎ 380 2107, ☎/fax 771 7226), with 150 hectares of primary growth cloud forest and plenty of hiking trails. It's 3.5km west of the Interamericana from División, at km 107. Lodging is available from US$30 per night for rooms with double bed and shared hot showers. All meals are served.

SAN ISIDRO DE EL GENERAL
pop 40,000

Pleasant, bustling and fairly modern, San Isidro is the main town on the southern Interamericana. Set within the agriculturally rich valley of the Río General, San Isidro is a transportation hub and the commercial center for the coffee fincas, cattle ranches and plant nurseries that dot the surrounding slopes. Other than the small regional museum on Calle 2 and Avenida 1, there isn't much to see in San Isidro, but it makes a convenient gateway for Parque Nacional Chirripó and the Pacific coast.

Information

CIPROTUR (☎ 771 6096), the helpful tourist information center, is located on Calle 4, Avenida 1 and 3. A park service office (☎ 771 3155, fax 771 4836) on Calle 2, Avenidas 4 and 6, provides information on

the Parque Nacional Chirripó; it's open Monday to Friday. Several banks exchange US dollars and traveler's checks.

Special Events

The annual agricultural fair is held in early February. San Isidro is the patron saint of farmers, who bring animals into town to be blessed on May 15.

Places to Stay

The best budget option is **Hotel Amaneli** (☎ 771 0352). Clean rooms with private hot showers and fans are US$8.50 per person.

Shoestringers use **Hotel El Jardín** (☎ 771 0349), which offers clean, simple rooms (US$3.25 per person) and a cheap restaurant. The very basic **Hotel Lala** (☎ 771 0291) charges US$4 per person or US$10 a double with private cold shower. The friendly **Hotel Balboa** charges US$4/6 for spartan singles/doubles. **Hotel Astoria** (☎ 771 0914) has very basic boxes for US$4.25/7.50 or slightly better boxes for US$7/10.50 with private cold shower. The family-run **Pensión Eiffel**, near the bus terminal, is US$4.50 per person.

The modern **Hotel Chirripó** (☎ 771 0529) costs US$5.50/9.50 or US$8.50/15 for rooms with private electric shower. There's a decent restaurant on the premises. The best standard hotel in town is the clean and secure **Hotel Iguazú** (☎ 771 2571), charging US$10/15.50 for rooms with private hot shower, TV and fan.

Places to Eat

Plenty of inexpensive sodas are in the center of town and in the market/bus terminal area. **Soda El Bingo** serves decent casados for less than US$2. The restaurants at Hotel El Jardín and Hotel Chirripó are both good and reasonably priced. The latter features pleasant plaza views.

Restaurant El Tenedor has a balcony overlooking a busy street. Snacks and meals (including pizza) range from US$1 to US$5. For Chinese food, **Restaurant Hong Kong**, on the parque central, has been recommended. Across the parque central, **Panadería El Tío Marcos** offers good pastries and other baked goods.

Getting There & Away

The main bus terminal on Avenida 8 serves nearby villages. Long-distance buses leave

SAN ISIDRO DE EL GENERAL

PLACES TO STAY
6 Hotel Amaneli
7 Hotel Balboa
11 Hotel El Jardín;
    Restaurant El Jardín
12 Hotel Iguazú
14 Hotel Lala
15 Hotel Astoria
19 Hotel Chirripó; Hotel
    Chirripó Restaurant
25 Pensión Eiffel

PLACES TO EAT
9 Soda El Bingo
13 Restaurant El Tenedor
16 Restaurant Hong Kong
18 Panaderiá El Tió Marcos

OTHER
1 Gas Station
2 ICE Office (Telephone)
3 Transportes Vargas
    Rojas; Buses to San José
4 Transportes Musoc
    Buses to San José
5 CIPROTUR
8 Banco Nacional de
    Costa Rica
10 Museo Regional del Sur
17 24-Hour Gas Station;
    Buses to Puerto Jiménez
20 Tracopa Bus Terminal
21 Park Service Office
22 Banco de San José
23 Banco de Costa Rica
24 Buses to Uvita,
    Dominical & Quepos
26 Mercado Municipal
27 Main Bus Terminal
28 Post Office

COSTA RICA

from various points on or near the Interamericana. Frequent buses to San José (US$2.75, three hours) depart between 5 am and 5:30 pm from the north end of town.

Buses for San Gerardo de Rivas (and Chirripó) leave from the parque central at 5 am and from the main bus terminal at 2 pm (two hours).

Buses to Puerto Jiménez originate in San José, picking up passengers in San Isidro by a 24-hour gas station on the Interamericana at 9 am and 3 pm (US$4, six hours). Pacific coast buses travel via Dominical to Quepos at 7 am and 1:30 pm and to Uvita at 9 am and 4 pm.

Tracopa (☎ 771 0468), at Calle 3 and the Interamericana, has southbound routes.

Buses for Palmar Norte (US$2.50, three hours) and Neily (US$3, four hours) leave at 4:45 and 7:30 am and 12:30 and 3 pm. Buses to Buenos Aires and San Vito (US$2.75, 3½ hours) leave at 5:30 am and 2 pm. Buses from San José pass through San Isidro en route to Golfito, Paso Canoas, Palmar Norte, San Vito and David, Panama. Tickets are sold on a space-available basis.

SAN GERARDO DE RIVAS

This village is the base for climbing Chirripó. Buses from San Isidro stop outside the ranger station at the village entrance. A couple of kilometers north are thermal springs where you can soak all day for US$1.

Across from the ranger station, *Cabinas El Bosque* (☎ 771 4129 in San Isidro) has decent rooms for US$4 per person and a restaurant-bar. In the center of town, *Hotel y Restaurant Roca Dura Café* (☎ 771 1866) is a good deal at US$3 per person for simple two- to four-bed rooms with shared hot showers. There are other budget hotels.

Return buses to San Isidro leave from near the ranger station at 7 am and 4 pm (two hours).

PARQUE NACIONAL CHIRRIPÓ

This mountainous park is named for Cerro Chirripó (3820m), the highest peak in the country. In Central America, only Guatemala has higher mountains. Most of the park lies at more than 2000m above sea level. There are hiking trails and a mountain-top hostel. Camping is prohibited throughout the park.

Centro Ambientalista El Páramo, the new mountain hostel, sleeps up to 60 people. A solar panel provides electric light until 7 pm and sporadic heat for the showers; sleeping bags and cooking equipment can be rented.

To stay at the hostel, make a reservation with the central park office in San José (☎ 233 4160) or the office in San Isidro de El General (☎ 771 3155) or just show up at the ranger station near San Gerardo de Rivas, open 5 am to 5 pm daily, and ask for a space. During the busy dry season weekends (especially Easter), the hostel may be full. The park entrance fee is US$6 and staying at the hostel is US$6 per night.

The fascinating climb up Cerro Chirripó takes you through constantly changing scenery, vegetation, and wildlife. It's a steep 16km on a good, signed trail to the Chirripó summit area; there are signs. Allow seven to 16 hours to reach the hostel, and carry water – in the dry season only one place has water before the hostel. In emergencies, a small cave and a dilapidated hut are along the way. From Paramo it's an additional two-hour hike to the summit.

PALMAR NORTE & PALMAR SUR
pop 5200

Divided into north and south sections by the Río Grande de Térraba, this small town is a northern gateway to Parque Nacional Corcovado. Palmar Norte has a bank, buses and hotels; Palmar Sur has the airport.

Places to Stay & Eat

On the Interamericana, *Cabinas Tico Alemán* (☎ 786 6232) features clean rooms with private baths and fan for US$16 double or US$20 with air-conditioning, and *Cabinas & Restaurant Wah Lok* (☎ 786 6777) charges US$7/11 for singles/doubles with shower. In town, *Cabinas Casa Amarilla* (☎ 786 6251) offers clean secure units at US$3.25 per person or US$7.50 with private bath, and *Hotel Xenia* (☎ 786 6129) is even cheaper.

Bar/Restaurante El Puente serves Tico food and is popular with locals. There are several Chinese restaurants.

Getting There & Away

Air Sansa has daily direct flights to and from San José (US$60/120 one-way/roundtrip). Travelair may stop in Quepos en route (US$78/127).

Bus Tracopa has seven buses a day to and from San José (US$4.50, six hours), four buses to and from San Isidro (US$2.50, three hours) and southbound buses on a space-available basis.

Transportes Térraba runs six buses daily to Neily and hourly buses to Ciudad Cortés. Buses to Sierpe leave from the Supermercado Térraba four times a day.

Península de Osa & Golfo Dulce

The large Península de Osa has the best remaining stands of Central America's Pacific coastal rain forest, preserved in Parque Nacional Corcovado, the primary destination in the region for most visitors. This can be reached by boat via the Río Sierpe or by ferry across the Golfo Dulce to Puerto Jiménez, the peninsula's principal town.

SIERPE

This village on the Río Sierpe has boats to Bahía Drake from about US$15 per person (if there's a group). Sonia Rojas at the Pulpería Fénix (☎ 786 7311) knows boat operators and local hotels. *Hotel Margarita* has

PENÍNSULA DE OSA & GOLFO DULCE

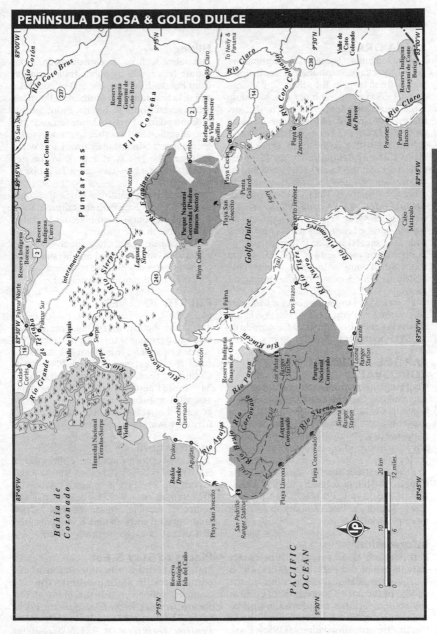

basic clean rooms for US$3 per person or US$11 for a double with private bath.

BAHÍA DRAKE

Several expensive lodges in the community cater to package vacationers. The cheapest places are in or near the village and charge about US$35 per person per day, including three meals, or about 30% less in the low season. The friendly *El Mirador Cabinas* (☎ *387 9138 cell phone*) has three rustic rooms, all with private bath and superb views. *Cabinas Bellavista* (☎ */fax 770 8012, leave message for Javier*) offers beachfront rooms with private or shared bath and can arrange cheap tours. The Canadian-run *Co-calito Lodge* (☎ *384 6369 cellular,* ☎ *225 4049 beeper,* ☎*/fax 519 782 3978 in Canada, BerryBend@aol.com*) has tents (with foam pads and sheets) at US$15 per person, or camp in your own tent for US$7. Recently renovated rooms with private bath cost US$55 to US$65 per person, including all meals.

From Bahía Drake it's about a five-hour hike to the San Pedrillo ranger station at the north end of Parque Nacional Corcovado or a US$15 boat ride to Sierpe and buses.

PARQUE NACIONAL CORCOVADO

Covering the southwestern corner of the Península de Osa, this rain forest preserve is home to Costa Rica's largest population of scarlet macaws and many other animal and plant species. Its great biological diversity has long attracted the attention of tropical ecologists.

Primitive trails lead to the four ranger stations. The hiking is hot, humid and insect-ridden, but it's a good way to see the rain forest. The dry season (January to April) is more pleasant.

Information

Park fees are US$6 per day. Three ranger stations are at the park boundaries, and a fourth is the headquarters at Sirena in the middle of the park. Camping costs US$2 at any station; facilities include water and latrines. Sirena and La Leona have basic bunkhouse accommodations (US$6); book in advance through the Puerto Jiménez office (☎/fax 735 5440). Meals can be arranged through the same office (about

US$3.25 breakfast, US$6.50 lunch or dinner). Most people bring their own food.

Hiking

It is safest to hike in a small group. From Carate (reachable by public transportation from Puerto Jiménez), it's a 90-minute hike to La Leona ranger station; from there it's six to seven hours to Sirena. From Sirena, hike inland for about six hours to Los Patos ranger station and another four hours to La Palma, from which buses travel to Puerto Jiménez (the last is at 2 pm). In the dry months, the rangers can call a Jeep-taxi to take you out.

Alternatively, continue along the coast from Sirena to San Pedrillo ranger station (eight to 10 hours), then hike out to Bahía Drake (five to seven hours).

The coastal trails often involve wading and may have loose sand and no shade. Be prepared. Ask about tide tables and don't get cut off. The rangers are helpful.

PUERTO JIMÉNEZ
pop 7000

This is the main town on the Península de Osa and the main entry town to Parque Nacional Corcovado. It is 76km (32 unpaved) from the Interamericana or 20km from Golfito by boat. Gold mining and logging have made Puerto Jiménez fairly important, and with improved access there's a burgeoning tourist industry. It's a pleasant and friendly town.

Information

The Corcovado information office (☎ 735 5036, fax 735 5276) is open 8 am to 4 pm Monday to Friday, with a lunch break. The Travelair agent (☎ 735 5062) is a good source of local information about lodges, land and air transportation. Banco Nacional de Costa Rica exchanges cash dollars.

Places to Stay & Eat

Hotels may fill during dry-season weekends, especially at Easter time. You can camp inexpensively on the grass at the *Puerto Jiménez Yacht Club* near the dock, with a basic bathroom but no lockers. *Pensión Quintero* (☎ *735 5087*), 200m south of the bus stop, has acceptable rooms and rustic shared bath facilities from US$3.25 per person. *Restaurant y Cabinas*

Carolina (☎ 735 5185), 100m west of the Banco Nacional, has five clean rooms with baths costing US$5 per person. Also try the similarly priced *Soda Katy y Cabinas*, a block south of the bus stop. The friendly *Cabinas Marcelina* (☎ 735 5007, osanatur@ sol.racsa.co.cr), on the main street 50m north of the church, has tidy rooms with fan and private bath for US$6.50/10/15 single/double/triple. Farther up the street is *Cabinas Oro Verde* (☎ 735 5241), which is in the same price range.

On the north side of the soccer field are *Cabinas Brisas del Mar* (☎ 735 5012) and *Cabinas Puerto Jiménez* (☎ 735 5090), both offering clean rooms with private bath and fan for US$7 per person. The noise from the nearby Bar El Rancho may be intolerable on weekends.

Restaurant Carolina is popular. By the main bus stop, *Soda Katy* and *Soda El Ranchito* are inexpensive and OK. *Restaurant Agua Luna*, near the boat dock, has seafood and sea views. Nearby, *Bar/ Restaurant El Rancho* serves meals, has a happy hour and has bands that play danceable music. It's also a good place to meet people.

Getting There & Away
Air Travelair has daily flights to San José (US$90/152), as does Sansa (US$65/130). Alfa Romeo Aero Taxi (☎ 735 5178) has local charter flights.

Bus Autotransportes Blanco Lobo leaves at 5 am daily for San José (US$6.25, eight hours) via San Isidro (US$4, six hours). Buy tickets in advance at Marly's Soda near the bus stop.

Buses to Neily (US$3, four to six hours) leave at 5:30 am and 2 pm, passing La Palma (23km away) for the eastern entry into Parque Nacional Corcovado. A Jeep/truck leaves the main street daily (except Sunday) at 6 am for Carate, at the south end of Corcovado (US$6).

Boat The passenger ferry to Golfito leaves at 6 am daily (US$3, 1½ hours).

GOLFITO
pop 13,900
Golfito is a former banana port now struggling to survive by tourism. It is strung out along a coastal road backed by the steep forested hills of **Refugio Nacional de Vida Silvestre Golfito**. Boats cross the Golfo Dulce to Puerto Jiménez, the point of entry to Parque Nacional Corcovado.

A good access road to the refuge is found 2km south of the town center, before you come to Las Gaviotas Hotel. This gravel road heads inland past a soccer field and up to some radio towers 7km away and 486m above sea level. Another possibility is to continue north along the road past the airstrip – there are trails. Camping is permitted in the refuge, but there are no facilities.

Places to Stay
Tico shoppers descend on the duty-free area on weekends, when cheaper hotels may fill up.

Budget options are clustered in the center of town. Near the ferry dock, *Hotel Uno* (☎ 775 0061) has windowless boxes without fans for US$2 per person. A better choice is the friendly *Cabinas Mazuren* (☎ 775 0058), north of the soccer field, featuring rooms with private bath for US$5 per person. English is spoken at *Hotel Delfina* (☎ 775 0043), where minimally ventilated rooms cost US$3.50 per person and doubles with private bath and fan are US$6.50 per person. Behind the Delfina, *Cabinas Melissa* (☎ 775 0443) overlooks the water and charges US$10/15/20 for two/three/four people in clean, quiet units. Another choice on the waterfront is *Hotel Golfito* (☎ 775 0047), which rents doubles with private bath and fan for US$10, US$20 with airconditioning.

In the quieter north end, several families take guests. The friendly *Cabinas El Vivero* (☎ 775 0217) charges US$5 per person in airy rooms with fans and shared baths. *Casa Blanca* (☎ 775 0124) has singles/doubles with fan and private bath for US$5/10. Nearby, *El Manglar* (☎ 775 0510), *Cabinas Wilson* (☎ 775 0795) and others are similarly priced.

More places can be found by the Tracopa bus terminal, including the personable *Hotel del Cerro* (☎ 775 0006, fax 775 0551), which has great bay views. Prices range from US$5 per person in dormitories ('backpacker rates') to US$8.25 per person in private rooms with fan and bath.

Places to Eat

Soda Muellecito, by the ferry dock, is good for early breakfasts. Popular with local gringos and Ticos, *Café Coconuts* serves a good casado for US$3 and a delicious avocado sandwich for US$2.50. The long-standing *Hotel Restaurant Uno* serves decent Chinese food, as does *Restaurant Cazuelita* in the northern zone.

Getting There & Away

Air The airport is 4km north of the town center. Sansa (☎ 775 0303) flies two or three times a day to and from San José, (US$65/130 one-way/roundtrip) in the high season; Travelair (☎ 775 0210) has a morning flight (US$84/144) via Puerto Jiménez.

Alfa Romeo Aero Taxi (☎ 775 1515) has light aircraft for charters to Corcovado and other areas.

Bus Tracopa buses (☎ 775 0365) to San Isidro and San José (US$5.75, seven to eight hours) leave at 5 am and 1 pm from the park at the north end of town.

Buses for Neily (1½ hours) leave hourly from outside the Club Latino near the same park. Buses for Pavones (three hours) and Playa Zancudo (three hours) leave from the Muellecito. Departures are in the early afternoon, but services may be interrupted in the wet season – ask locally.

Boat The daily passenger boat to Puerto Jiménez (US$3, 1½ hours) departs at 11:30 am from the Muellecito. Boats for Playa Zancudo leave from the same dock at 5 am and noon Monday to Friday, returning at 6 am and 1 pm (US$2). More expensive taxi boats serve other destinations; the dock is opposite the ICE building north of the center.

Getting Around

There are buses (US$0.15) and collective taxis (US$0.75) that travel up and down the main road of Golfito.

SOUTH OF GOLFITO
Playa Zancudo

This good swimming beach, 15km south of Golfito, is popular with locals, especially in the dry season when single rooms are scarce. There are several places to stay from about US$6 per person. One of the best is *Bar/Cabinas Suzy* (☎ 776 0107), which also serves decent casados and has a popular bar. Also good are *Restaurant & Cabinas Tranquilo* (tasty food) and *Cabinas Petier*. *El Coquito* is cheaper, with basic cabins including private bath for US$4 and a good inexpensive restaurant. The bus back to Golfito (three hours) leaves from El Coquito at 5 am in the dry season; boats leave at 6 am and 1 pm.

Pavones

Ten kilometers south of Playa Zancudo, Pavones has good surfing, especially from April to October. The popular *Esquina del Mar Cantina* has basic breezy rooms above the bar for US$5 per person. Ask around for other cheap places. The nicest hotel is *Cabinas La Ponderosa* (☎ 384 7430 message, ☎ 954-771 9166 in the USA), offering five clean rooms with ceiling fans and private bath for US$40 per person with three meals. The owners are helpful surfers. Check out their Web site at www.ccgnv .net/ponderosa).

Nearby, the *Impact Surf Lodge* provides decent rooms and meals at similar rates. There is a daily bus from Golfito (if the road is open) at 10 am and 2 pm, returning at 5 am and 12:30 pm from the Esquina del Mar Cantina.

NEILY

This hot but friendly agricultural center, 17km from Panama, is called 'Villa' locally. It is an important transportation hub but of little interest otherwise. Several banks exchange money.

Places to Stay & Eat

The following places are clustered in the area between the Interamericana and the main plaza. The basic *Pensión Elvira* (☎ 783 3057) is US$4.25 for a one-bed room with shared cold showers or US$6.50/10 for singles/doubles with private bath. The clean and secure *Hotel Musuco* (☎ 783 3048) offers small, simple rooms for US$4.50 per person or US$5 with bath and fan. Other cheap, basic places include *Hotel El Viajero* (☎ 783 5120) and the somewhat noisy *Hotel Villa* (☎ 783 5120).

North of the plaza are some other good possibilities, including *Cabinas Helga* (☎ 783 3146), which charges US$13.50/17 for singles/doubles with private bath and cable TV, and the plant-filled *Cabinas Heyleen* (☎ 783 3080), 3½ blocks west of the bus terminal. It charges US$7.50/12 for a room.

The best place to eat is *Restaurant La Moderna*, a block east of the plaza, with a variety of meals in the US$2 to US$6 range. *La Cuchara de Margot* serves ice cream and snacks.

Getting There & Away
Air Sansa (☎ 783 3275) has daily flights from San José to Coto 47, 7km southwest of Neily (US$65 each way). Local buses pass the airport.

Bus The bus terminal is next to the market. Tracopa (☎ 783 3227) has five daily buses to San José (US$5.75, seven hours); four to San Isidro; 19 to Paso Canoas; and two to Puerto Jiménez. Autotransportes Cepula runs six daily buses to San Vito (US$1.50, two hours), leaving from the market.

Buses for Golfito (US$0.50, 1½ hours) leave hourly from opposite the gas station just north of the Interamericana.

SAN VITO
pop 10,000
This pleasant town, 980m above sea level, offers respite from the heat of the nearby lowlands. It was founded by immigrants from Italy in the early 1950s, and you can still hear Italian spoken and eat Italian food. The steep and winding drive up from Neily is scenic, as is the route from San José.

Information
The Centro Cultural Dante Alighieri has tourist information. Two banks will exchange money.

Wilson Botanical Garden
These attractive and well-laid-out gardens are located 6km south (uphill) from San Vito and are well worth a visit. Thousands of plants are displayed in this world-class collection, including more than 700 species of palm. Short educational trails are named after the plants found along them, such as the Heliconia Loop Trail or the Bromeliad Walk.

The gardens (☎/fax 773-3278, lcruces@ ns.ots.ac.cr) are open 8 am to 4 pm daily; admission is US$6. A trail map is provided.

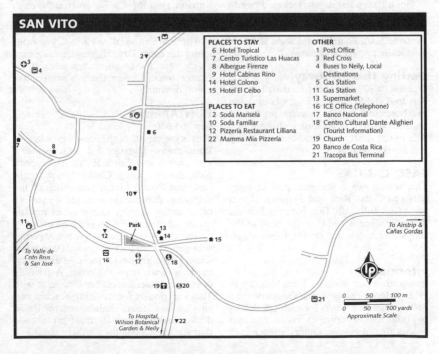

SAN VITO

PLACES TO STAY	OTHER
6 Hotel Tropical	1 Post Office
7 Centro Turístico Las Huacas	3 Red Cross
8 Albergue Firenze	4 Buses to Neily, Local
9 Hotel Cabinas Rino	Destinations
14 Hotel Colono	5 Gas Station
15 Hotel El Ceibo	11 Gas Station
	13 Supermarket
PLACES TO EAT	16 ICE Office (Telephone)
2 Soda Marisela	17 Banco Nacional
10 Soda Familiar	18 Centro Cultural Dante Alighieri
12 Pizzería Restaurant Lilliana	(Tourist Information)
22 Mamma Mia Pizzería	19 Church
	20 Banco de Costa Rica
	21 Tracopa Bus Terminal

To Airstrip & Cañas Gordas

To Valle de Coto Brus & San José

Park

To Hospital, Wilson Botanical Garden & Neily

0   50   100 m
0   50   100 yards
Approximate Scale

COSTA RICA

Fees go to maintenance and research. Students with ID can stay in dorms for US$32, including meals. Others pay US$80/130 for single/double rooms. Make arrangements with the Organization for Tropical Studies in San José (☎ 240 6696, fax 240 6783, reservas@ns.ots.ac.cr).

Some buses to Neily pass the gardens. Or you can walk or take a taxi (US$3).

Places to Stay & Eat

The *Hotel Tropical* is friendly and secure, though noisy. Basic rooms are US$3 per person. *Hotel Colono* (☎ 773 4543), another cheap and basic choice, is quieter.

Centro Turístico Las Huacas (☎ 773 3115) offers decent singles/doubles with private electric showers for US$5.50/9.50. *Albergue Firenze* (☎ 773 3206) is similar but charges less.

Hotel Cabinas Rino (☎ 773 3071, 773 4030 for late-night calls), open 24 hours, has five clean rooms with private hot showers and TVs for US$8.50/15. The recently renovated *Hotel El Ceibo* (☎ 773 3025) is the best in town at US$16.50/27 with TV, private hot shower, and a reasonable restaurant.

Good Italian restaurants include *Pizzería Restaurant Lilliana*, with meals for US$3 to US$4, and the fancier *Mamma Mia Pizzería*. *Soda Familiar* and *Soda Marisela* are locally popular and cheap.

Getting There & Away

Tracopa (☎ 773 3410) has four daily buses to San José (US$7, seven to eight hours) and two buses to San Isidro; the terminal is out on the road to Cañas Gordas. Other terminals in the center run local buses to Neily and nearby villages.

PASO CANOAS

This small town is the main port of entry between Costa Rica and Panama. Hotels are often full with Tico bargain hunters during weekends and holidays. Most of the shops and hotels are on the Costa Rican side.

Information

Banks are open 8 am to 5 pm Monday to Friday. Money changers near the border give better rates than banks for cash US dollars but rates for converting excess colones into dollars are not as good. Other currencies are harder to deal with. Traveler's checks can be negotiated with persistence.

Places to Stay & Eat

The hotel selection is poor. The best place to stay is *Cabinas Interamericano*, at US$12 for a double with bath. One of the better restaurants is attached. *Cabinas Hilda* is slightly cheaper. There are other budget hotels and some cheap sodas.

Getting There & Away

Tracopa buses (☎ 732 2119) make the journey to San José four times daily (US$6, eight hours). Sunday afternoon buses are usually full of weekend shoppers returning to San José, so make reservations.

Buses for Neily (with more connections) leave the border at least once an hour during the day.

Central Pacific Coast

The Pacific coast is more developed for tourism than the Caribbean coast, though you can still find deserted beaches, wildlife and small coastal villages.

There are marked wet and dry seasons along this coast. Dry (high) season rates are given here. Reservations are advised for Easter week. During the wet season, ask about discounts.

PUNTARENAS
pop 101,000

This is the capital of the coastal province of Puntarenas. During the 19th century, Puntarenas was Costa Rica's major port. Now, the new port at Caldera, 18km southeast, and Puerto Limón take much of the shipping. Puntarenas remains a bustling place during the dry season when tourists arrive. At other times it's much quieter.

The city is on the end of a sandy peninsula almost 8km long but only 100 to 600m wide – you're never more than a few minutes' walk from the coast. A friendly port, it has traditionally been popular with Tico vacationers for its sandy beaches and easy access to the capital. Indeed, the Paseo de los Turistas, the waterfront promenade that stretches along the southern coast, is a

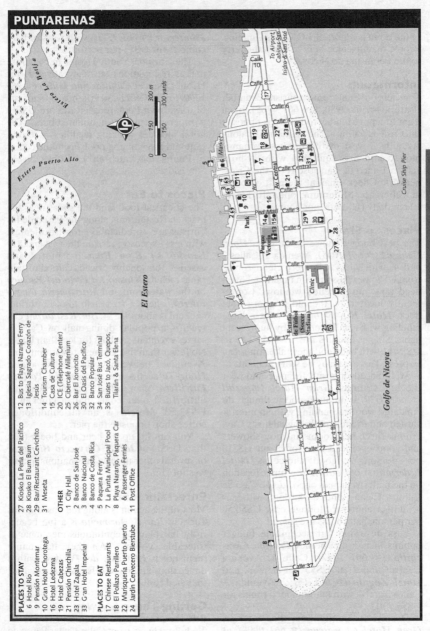

PUNTARENAS

PLACES TO STAY
6 Hotel Río
9 Pensión Montemar
10 Gran Hotel Chorotega
16 Hotel Ledezma
19 Hotel Cabezas
21 Pensión Chinchilla
23 Hotel Zagala
33 Gran Hotel Imperial

PLACES TO EAT
17 Chinese Restaurants
18 El Pollazo Parrillero
22 Marisquería Puerto Puerto
24 Jardín Cervecero Bierstube
27 Kiosko La Perla del Pacífico
28 Kiosko El Bum Bum
29 Bar/Restaurant Cevichito
31 Meseta

OTHER
1 City Hall
2 Banco de San José
3 Banco Nacional
4 Banco de Costa Rica
5 Paquera Ferry
7 La Punta Municipal Pool
8 Playa Naranjo, Paquera Car
   & Passenger Ferries
11 Post Office
12 Bus to Playa Naranjo Ferry
13 Iglesia Sagrado Corazón de
   Jesús
14 Tourism Chamber
15 Casa de Cultura
20 ICE (Telephone Center)
25 Cibercafé Millenium
26 Bar El Joroncito
30 El Oasis del Pacífico
32 Banco Popular
34 San José Bus Terminal
35 Buses to Jacó, Quepos,
   Tilarán & Santa Elena

pleasant place for a stroll. Unfortunately the water is polluted – though the south side of the point is reportedly OK for swimming. People mainly come here to catch the ferry to the Península de Nicoya.

Information

The helpful Puntarenas tourism chamber (Catup; ☎ 661 2980, fax 661 4705), open 8 am to 5 pm Monday to Friday, is opposite the Casa de Cultura. The major banks along Avenida 3 west of the market exchange money and are equipped with 24-hour ATMs. Banco de San José is on the Cirrus network. Check email at the post office, or at Cibercafé Millenium, open 10 am to 10 pm daily (US$2.60 per hour).

Places to Stay

The best budget choice is the calm *Hotel Cabezas* (☎ 661 1045), Avenida 1, Calles 2 and 4, which has relatively clean rooms from US$5 per person, with functional overhead fans and screened windows. Conveniently located by the old Paquera boat dock, *Hotel Río* (☎ 661 0331) is a large building with small rooms lit by fluorescent lights. Singles/doubles are US$4.50/7.25 or US$9/11 with bath, and they take American Express. This area may be scary at night.

Well-placed opposite the pier and near the bus stations, *Gran Hotel Imperial* (☎ 661 0579) is an atmospheric though dilapidated wooden building with an interior garden and friendly multilingual hosts. Cavernous three-bed rooms include showers and good overhead fans for about US$10 per person. A good choice is *Hotel Ledezma* (☎ 661 5014), in a quiet location on the pedestrian mall opposite the Casa de Cultura. Clean, rather dark rooms with fans around a courtyard/lounge cost US$6.50 per person; bathrooms are shared.

Less desirable but acceptable budget options include the homey *Pensión Chinchilla* (☎ 661 1047), Calle 1, Avenida Central and 2, at US$5 per person, and *Hotel Zagala* (☎ 661 1319), Avenida 2, Calles 2 and 4, with fan-equipped rooms for US$6.50/13.

Despite its penitentiary-like exterior, *Gran Hotel Chorotega* (☎ 661 0998), at Avenida 3, Calle 1, is an upscale choice, offering large decent rooms with clean tile floors, overhead fans and private bath for

US$13/21 or US$10/16.50 with shared bath. Next door is the extremely basic *Pensión Montemar* (☎ 661 2771), with rows of bare cubicles for US$5 per person.

The Toruma Youth Hostel in San José makes reservations (strongly advised) for HI members at *Cabinas San Isidro* (☎ 280 5200, fax 224 4611), near a beach 8km east of downtown Puntarenas. Rates are US$10 per person (more for nonmembers). The hotel includes cooking facilities, a restaurant and a swimming pool. From the center of Puntarenas, catch an 'El Roble' bus to San Isidro.

Places to Eat

The cheapest food is in the sodas near the market. Restaurants along the Paseo de los Turistas are – predictably – tourist-oriented, with less-expensive fare on the east end. Try *Kiosko El Bum Bum* for pintos and casados. Reasonably priced seafood restaurants include *Kiosko La Perla del Pacífico* on the waterfront and *Marisquería Puerto Puerto*, where a fresh fish fillet or shrimp cocktail is about US$4. *Bar/Restaurant Cevichito*, a popular dining hall on Calle 3, serves excellent sea bass for less than US$6. No fewer than five Chinese restaurants line Avenida 1 between Calle Central and 2; *Hong-Tu* seems the classiest. *El Pollazo Parrillero*, open until 10 pm, does chicken butterflied over coals; half a chicken is US$3.50. *Meseta* is an air-conditioned coffee shop opposite the pier.

You can fill up on beer and bocas (less than US$1) at *Jardín Cervecero Bierstube* or several other upscale international places west of Hotel Tioga.

Entertainment

Most of the action is along the Paseo de los Turistas. *Bar El Joroncito* is a fun beachfront bar playing continuous merengue at tolerable volume. Another happening nightspot is *El Oasis del Pacífico*, with a dance floor and good DJs underneath a big thatched roof.

Getting There & Away

Bus Frequent buses to San José (US$2.75, 2¼ hours) leave from Calle 2, near Paseo de los Turistas, from 4 am to 7 pm. Buses for the following destinations leave from around the corner on Calle 4:

Costa de Pájaros (US$0.40, 1½ to two hours)
Buses depart five times daily.

Jacó/Quepos (US$1.50/3, 1½ hours/three hours)
Buses depart at 5 and 11 am and 2:30 pm.

Liberia (US$2.25, 2½ hours)
Buses depart seven times daily.

Santa Elena, Monteverde (US$2, three hours)
Buses depart at 2:15 pm.

Tilarán (US$2.25, 1½ hours)
Buses depart at 11:45 am and 4:30 pm.

Boat The Conatramar car/passenger ferry (☎ 661 1069) sails five times daily from the northwest end of town to Playa Naranjo on the Península de Nicoya (1½ hours). Fares are US$1.60 for passengers and US$11.50 for cars (with driver). Foot passengers continue by bus to Nicoya. Naviera Tambor (☎ 661 2084) also has a car/passenger ferry from this dock to Paquera at 5 am and 12:30 and 5 pm (one hour). Another ferry to Paquera leaves at 8:45 am and 2 and 8:15 pm. The fare for either ferry is US$1.30 for passengers and US$10 for cars.

The old Paquera passenger ferry (☎ 661 2830) sails from the dock behind the market at 6 and 11 am and 3:15 pm (US$1.50, 1½ hours). Passengers continue to Montezuma by bus.

Getting Around
Buses marked 'Ferry' run up Avenida Central to the Playa Naranjo terminal (US$0.15). The initial departure point is Avenida 1, Calle Central and 1.

RESERVA BIOLÓGICA CARARA
This reserve is at the mouth of the Río Tárcoles, about 50km southeast of Puntarenas, or about 90km west of San José via the Orotina Hwy. The northernmost tropical wet forest on the Pacific coast, it is inhabited by an abundance of diverse wildlife. Scarlet macaws live here, but they can be difficult to spot without an experienced guide. Most tour companies offer day trips from San José for around US$75 per person. The dry season from December to April is the best time to go. Warning: Armed robbery has been reported in this area.

From the Río Tárcoles bridge, it's 3km south to the Carara ranger station, open 7 am to 5 pm daily, where there are bathrooms, picnic tables and information. Admission is US$6. You can get off at Carara

from any bus bound for Jacó or Quepos, though avoid weekends when returning buses tend to be full.

JACÓ
The closest developed beach resort to San José, Jacó is popular and crowded by Costa Rican standards. Hotels and restaurants are scattered along the road that parallels the long pretty beach, which is 2km off the coastal highway. The beaches are reasonably clean and swimming is possible, though be careful of rip currents.

Jacó is a popular surf spot with consistent waves and an annual tournament in August at **Playa Hermosa**, 5km south. Though it has a reputation as a 'party beach,' it's fairly sedate compared with its North American counterparts.

Information
Banco Popular exchanges traveler's checks and has an ATM on the Visa-Plus network. Surf-Net Jacó offers Internet access (US$1 per 15-minute block). You can call abroad from the international phone center, but Chip phones along the main street are cheaper.

Activities
Rent surfboards (US$8.50 per day), bikes (US$6) and mopeds (US$30) at Rad Rentals (☎ 643 1310) and others. La Chosita del Surf (☎ 643 1308) repairs boards and provides surfing information.

Places to Stay
Camping Friendly *Camping El Hicaco* (☎ 643 3004) is US$3 per person and has picnic tables, bathrooms and a lockup for your gear. The sandy campsites cut down on insects. North of the center of town, at an uncrowded end of the beach, *Camping Mariott* (☎ 643 3585) charges US$1.60 per person.

Hotels Reservations are recommended during dry season weekends. Single travelers on a shoestring won't find many deals, but low-season and surfer discounts are available.

On the south end of town, *Cabinas Calypso* (☎ 643 3208) has a pool and charges US$16 for adequate doubles with shared bath. At *Cabinas El Recreo* (☎ 643

COSTA RICA

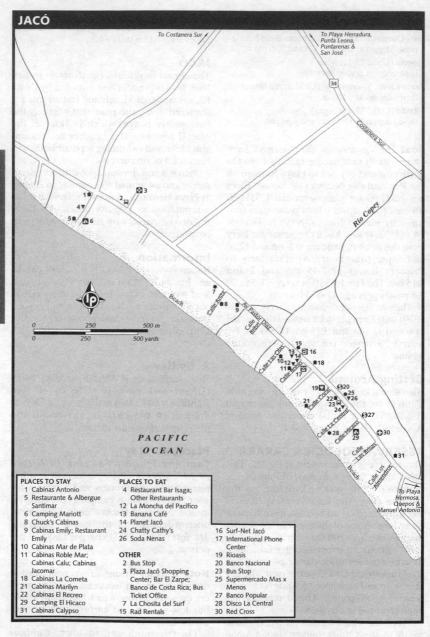

JACÓ

To Costanera Sur

To Playa Herradura, Punta Leona, Puntarenas & San José

Costanera Sur

Río Copey

Beach

Calle Anita

Av Pastor Díaz

Calle Las Olas

Calle Bribrí

Calle Bohío

Calle Cocal

Calle La Central

Calle Hicaco

Calle Las Briscas

Beach

Calle Los Almendros

To Playa Hermosa, Quepos & Manuel Antonio

PACIFIC OCEAN

0   250   500 m
0   250   500 yards

PLACES TO STAY
1   Cabinas Antonio
5   Restaurante & Albergue Santimar
6   Camping Mariott
8   Chuck's Cabinas
9   Cabinas Emily; Restaurant Emily
10 Cabinas Mar de Plata
11 Cabinas Roble Mar; Cabinas Calu; Cabinas Jacomar
18 Cabinas La Cometa
21 Cabinas Marilyn
22 Cabinas El Recreo
29 Camping El Hicaco
31 Cabinas Calypso

PLACES TO EAT
4   Restaurant Bar Isaga; Other Restaurants
12 La Moncha del Pacífico
13 Banana Café
14 Planet Jacó
24 Chatty Cathy's
26 Soda Nenas

OTHER
2   Bus Stop
3   Plaza Jacó Shopping Center; Bar El Zarpe; Banco de Costa Rica; Bus Ticket Office
7   La Chosita del Surf
15 Rad Rentals

16 Surf-Net Jacó
17 International Phone Center
19 Rioasis
20 Banco Nacional
23 Bus Stop
25 Supermercado Mas x Menos
27 Banco Popular
28 Disco La Central
30 Red Cross

3012), doubles with cold showers are set around a quiet yard but seem rundown for US$20. *Cabinas Marilyn* (☎ *643 3215)*, on Calle Cocal, has triples with double bed and bunks for US$16.50, including small bathroom and fridge.

The best value in town is *Cabinas La Cometa* (☎ *643 3615)*, which offers large fresh-smelling singles/doubles with shared cold showers for US$13/16.50 or US$8 more with private hot showers. The Canadian-run hotel is on the main street but feels calm and secluded.

A couple of more reasonably priced options are along Calle Bohío, a block up from the Cometa. The friendly *Cabinas Calu* (☎ *643 1107)* has good-sized clean doubles with cold shower and fans for US$20. *Cabinas Roble Mar* (☎ *643 3173)* has comfortable singles/doubles with showers and overhead fan for US$13/16.50. The similarly priced *Cabinas Jacomar* (☎ *643 1934)* offers well-scrubbed rooms alongside a garden. On the next street, *Cabinas Mar de Plata* (☎ *643 3580)* charges US$20 for tidy doubles with hot showers.

At the north end of town, *Cabinas Emily* (☎ *643 3513)* is popular with shoestringers. Small rooms with big beds and cool showers are US$10/13. Another 700m up the road, by the turnoff to the Costanera, is the pleasant *Cabinas Antonio* (☎ *643 3043)*, charging US$23 for comfortable doubles with private hot showers. Nearby, surfer-oriented *Chuck's Cabinas* (☎ */fax 643 3328, chucks@ sol.racsa.co.cr)* has simple rooms with high-powered fans and shared showers for US$7.50 per person. Owner Chuck Herwig runs a surf shop around the corner. The beachfront *Restaurante & Albergue Santimar* (☎ *643 3605)* offers four clean singles/doubles with shared cold showers at US$10/15. There are dozens of more expensive places.

Places to Eat

In the center, *Soda Nenas* has good casados for US$2. *Banana Café* prepares 100% natural breakfasts for US$2 – check out the banana pancakes. The Canadian-run *Chatty Cathy's* is a pleasant upstairs cafe serving whole-wheat sandwiches and self-serve coffee. *La Moncha del Pacífico*, a laid-back open-air restaurant, offers tropical fruit drinks, various salads and more at reasonable prices. Cosmic surfer murals set the tone at *Planet Jacó*, which is popular for snacks and US$3 casados until late evening.

North of the center, *Restaurant Emily* has great local food all day. Other inexpensive places are found near the Costanera Sur turnoff, including *Restaurant Bar Isaga* and *Restaurante & Albergue Santimar*, with a nice beachside patio and fresh, well-prepared seafood.

Entertainment

Ask around for the latest hotspots. *Rioasis* (the former Killer Munchies) is a hip evening hangout enhanced by listenable music and billiards. *Bar El Zarpe*, in the Plaza Jacó, has darts and satellite sports TV and attracts a mix of travelers and locals. *Disco La Central* sets the volume at loud, whether or not there's anyone on the dance floor.

Getting There & Away

Buses leave Jacó for San José at 5 and 11 am and 3 pm daily (three hours). Departures leave for Puntarenas (1½ hours) at 6 am, noon and 4:30 pm and for Quepos (two hours) at 6 am, noon and 3:45 pm.

The bus stop is opposite the Mas x Menos supermarket; buses for San José also stop at the Plaza Jacó mall north of the center.

QUEPOS

pop 13,300

Quepos, once a major port, is now known as a sportfishing center and the nearest town to Parque Nacional Manuel Antonio, 7km away.

Information

Banco de Costa Rica changes US dollars and traveler's checks; its ATM is on the Plus system. Lynch Travel (☎ 777 1170, lyntour@ racsa.co.cr) can make all local arrangements for your trip. Iguana Tours (☎ 777 1262, info@iguanatours.com) offers river rafting, sea kayaking and dolphin-watching tours.

Internet access is provided by Quepos Internet Café, open 9 am to 9 pm. The rate is US$7 per hour.

The beaches are polluted and not recommended for swimming.

COSTA RICA

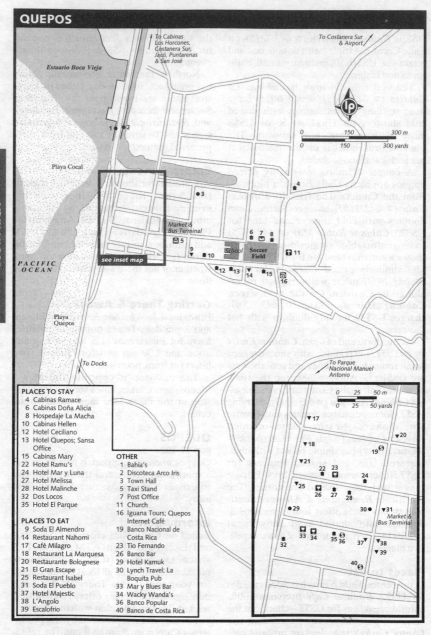

QUEPOS

PLACES TO STAY
4 Cabinas Ramace
6 Cabinas Doña Alicia
8 Hospedaje La Macha
10 Cabinas Hellen
12 Hotel Ceciliano
13 Hotel Quepos; Sansa
   Office
15 Cabinas Mary
22 Hotel Ramu's
24 Hotel Mar y Luna
27 Hotel Melissa
28 Hotel Malinche
32 Dos Locos
35 Hotel El Parque

PLACES TO EAT
9 Soda El Almendro
14 Restaurant Nahomi
17 Café Milagro
18 Restaurant La Marquesa
20 Restaurante Bolognese
21 El Gran Escape
25 Restaurant Isabel
31 Soda El Pueblo
37 Hotel Majestic
38 L'Angolo
39 Escalofrio

OTHER
1 Bahia's
2 Discoteca Arco Iris
3 Town Hall
5 Taxi Stand
7 Post Office
11 Church
16 Iguana Tours; Quepos
   Internet Café
19 Banco Nacional de
   Costa Rica
23 Tio Fernando
26 Banco Bar
29 Hotel Kamuk
30 Lynch Travel; La
   Boquita Pub
33 Mar y Blues Bar
34 Wacky Wanda's
36 Banco de Costa Rica
40 Banco de Costa Rica

Places to Stay

Rates listed are for high-season weekends; you can get substantial discounts at other times.

In the center of town, **Hotel Majestic** (☎ 777 1045) has no-frills boxes for less than US$4 per person. **Hotel El Parque** (☎ 777 0063), around the corner, charges US$5.50. Sharing a street with several bars, **Hotel Ramu's** (☎ 777 0245) exudes character. Singles/doubles/triples at US$6.50/10/15 are a bit dark but tidy and include bath and power fans.

Nearby, the friendly **Hotel Mar y Luna** (☎ 777 0394) is festooned with plants and charges slightly less. Across the street, **Hotel Melissa** (☎ 777 0025) has clean rooms with private bath for US$10 per person. Next door is the cordially run **Hotel Malinche** (☎ 777 0093), where singles/doubles with hot shower, air-conditioning and cable TV cost US$20/35; some older rooms with cold shower and fans are available for US$7 per person.

A number of good budget choices are clustered around the soccer field on the east edge of town. Cheapest among them is the basic but clean **Hospedaje La Macha** (☎ 777 0216). Rates are US$5 per person with shared bath, US$11.50 for rooms with double bed and private bath. Next door, **Cabinas Doña Alicia** (☎ 777 0419) has small dingy one-bed rooms for US$10 or larger rooms with three beds for US$16.50, all with private bath.

South of the soccer field, **Cabinas Mary** (☎ 777 0128) charges US$7 per person in clean acceptable rooms with private bath. Nearby is the similarly priced **Hotel Quepos** (☎ 777 0274). **Hotel Ceciliano** (☎/fax 777 0192) offers a little more comfort at US$10/16.50 for clean singles/doubles with private hot showers, or US$6.50/10 with shared bath. Across the way, **Hotel Hellen** (☎ 777 0504) has decent doubles with private showers and refrigerators for US$13.

Just off the exit for the highway south, the hospitable **Cabinas Ramace** (☎ 777 0590) offers doubles/triples with private hot bath, refrigerator, cable TV and multiple fans for US$16/20. There are some smaller less expensive doubles. **Cabinas Los Horcones** (☎ 777 0090), north of town, has good clean rooms with private bath for US$8.50 per person.

Places to Eat

Restaurant La Marquesa has good-value casados for less than US$2. One of several cheap eateries around the market/bus station, **Soda El Pueblo** offers good sandwiches and snacks and the chance to hear karaoke performed by some of Quepos' finest vocalists. It's open 24 hours, as is **Soda El Almendro** with Tico meals for around US$3. Cheap snacks are also available at **Restaurant Nahomi**.

Café Milagro makes great cappuccino, espresso and sandwiches; buy freshly roasted coffee beans here to take back home.

Pricier restaurants include **El Gran Escape**, a seafood place catering to gringo palates; **Restaurant Isabel** which has fish plates from US$8; and **Dos Locos** for good Mexican food. The **Banco Bar** has added a gourmet menu to its nachos and chicken wings. **Restaurante Bolognese** serves excellent Italian food in the US$4 to US$10 range. **L'Angolo** is an authentic Italian delicatessen – a good choice for picnic lunches. **Escalofrio** offers fine ice cream as well as the best pizzas around for US$4 to US$6.

Entertainment

Discoteca Arco Iris has dancing on weekends, as does **Bahías** just across the way. Bars include **Mar y Blues** for good music, **Banco Bar** for satellite sports TV, **El Gran Escape** for swapping fishing stories, **Wacky Wanda's** for cheap beer and air-conditioning, **La Boquita Pub** for a game of pool or **Tío Fernando** for a quiet drink. The **Hotel Kamuk** has a casino.

Getting There & Away

Air Sansa (☎ 777 0683) has four daily flights between San José and Quepos (US$45/90 one-way/roundtrip), and Travelair (☎ 777 0161) has a daily morning flight (US$50/80) and others that may stop in Quepos en route to Puerto Jiménez or Palmar Sur. The airport is 5km from town, and taxis to Quepos are US$3.

Bus Direct buses leave from San José's Coca-Cola terminal for Manuel Antonio (US$4.25, three hours) at 6 am, noon and 6 pm, and regular buses go to Quepos (four hours) at 7 and 10 am and 2 and 4 pm.

Regular services to San José are at 5 and 8 am and 2 and 4 pm daily. Direct buses to San José depart from Manuel Antonio at 6 am, noon and 5 pm (plus 3 pm on Sunday, more departures during high season) and pick up passengers at the Quepos bus terminal (☎ 777 0263). Buy tickets in advance.

Buses to Puntarenas (three hours) via Jacó leave at 4:30 and 10:30 am and 3 pm daily; to San Isidro via Dominical at 5 am and 1:30 pm (four hours); and to Uvita via Dominical at 7 pm daily plus at 9:30 am Saturday and Sunday (three hours).

Buses between Manuel Antonio and Quepos (US$0.25) run at least every half-hour between 6 am and 7:30 pm – less frequently after 7:30. The last bus departs Manuel Antonio at 10:30 pm. Taxis going back to Quepos may pick up extra passengers for about US$0.50.

MANUEL ANTONIO AREA
This village at the national park entrance is popular with younger international travelers. There is a good beach, but beware of rip currents. Take care not to leave your belongings unattended on any beach, and be sure to keep your hotel room locked even when leaving for brief periods.

Information
La Buena Nota (☎ 777 1002, buennota@ sol.racsa.co.cr) is an informal information center that sells maps, guidebooks, US newspapers, beach supplies and souvenirs. It also rents boogie boards.

Places to Stay & Eat
In the village, *Travotel Costa Linda* (☎ 777 0304) is reasonably clean. Basic rooms with shared showers are US$8 per person. *Cabinas Anep* (☎ 777 0565) charges US$5 per person but may be full on weekends.

Cabinas Irarosa (☎ 777 1089) has simple, clean single/double rooms with fan and private bath for US$20/25, or US$10 more with hot water and TV. Just outside the national park entrance, *Hotel Manuel Antonio* (☎ 777 1237) contains doubles with cold showers and fans for US$30. People camp outside for US$2 per person.

Cabinas Hermanos Ramírez (☎ 777 0003) is pretty basic at US$16.50 per person in rooms with private shower. The nearby disco may preclude sleep. *Cabinas Piscis*

(☎ 777 0046) is in a shaded compound with access to the beach. Rates are US$20/30 for clean rooms sharing a shower or US$40 for a double with private shower.

The pleasant *Hotel Vela Bar* (☎ 777 0413, fax 777 1071) charges US$30 to US$40 for double rooms of varying size, all including hot showers, ceiling fans and patios.

There are dozens of hotels between Quepos and Manuel Antonio. None are cheap, but prices are slashed in the rainy months. *La Colina Bed & Breakfast* (☎ 777 0231, info@lacolina.com) is one of the least expensive, with comfortable doubles for US$39 (US$29 from May to November), including a hearty breakfast on a deck that affords superb Pacific vistas. There's a lovely pool with swim-up bar.

The surfside *Restaurant Del Mar* serves fresh fish, octopus (US$7) and yummy mango cocktails. Just up the beach, *Restaurant Mar y Sombra* has casados for about US$3 and fish dinners for twice that. The place becomes a thumping disco on the weekends. A few inexpensive sodas are between there and the park entrance.

Getting There & Away
See the earlier Quepos entry for details on air and bus travel. Buses leave from near the national park entrance and will stop along the road to Quepos if you flag them down. Purchase your San José tickets in advance at the Quepos terminal, particularly on weekends. Interbus shuttle vans depart for San José at 1:30 pm daily (US$25); they'll pick you up at your hotel. Call ☎ 777 1170 to reserve a space.

PARQUE NACIONAL MANUEL ANTONIO
Manuel Antonio's obvious attractions – beautiful forest-backed tropical beaches, rocky headlands with ocean and island views, prolific wildlife and a maintained trail system – make it one of the most popular national parks. It's also the smallest. This has led to intense pressure on both the park and the area: too many visitors, too many hotels and too much impact on the wildlife and environment. Therefore the park is closed on Monday and limited to 600 visitors on other days. To avoid the crowds, go early in the morning, midweek, during the rainy season.

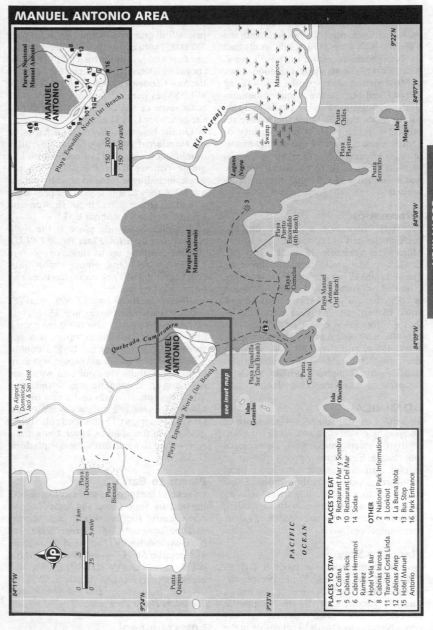

MANUEL ANTONIO AREA

Parque Nacional
Manuel Antonio

MANUEL
ANTONIO

Playa Espadilla Norte (1st Beach)

0   150   300 m
0   150   300 yards

Río Naranjo

Swamp

Mangrove

Punta
Chiles

Isla
Mogote

Playa
Playitas

Punta
Serrucho

Laguna
Negra

Parque Nacional
Manuel Antonio

Playa
Puerto
Escondido
(4th Beach)

Playa
Gemelas

Playa Manuel
Antonio
(3rd Beach)

Quebrada Camaronera

MANUEL
ANTONIO

see inset map

Playa Espadilla
Sur (2nd Beach)

Playa Espadilla Norte (1st Beach)

Punta
Catedral

Islas
Gemelas

Isla
Olocuita

To Airport,
Dominical,
Jacó & San José

Playa
Doctores

Playa
Biesanz

PACIFIC
OCEAN

Punta
Quepos

0   .5   1 km
0   .25   .5 mile

84°11'W

84°10'W

84°09'W

84°08'W

84°07'W

9°22'N

9°24'N

9°23'N

PLACES TO STAY
1 La Colina
5 Cabinas Piscis
6 Cabinas Hermanos
   Ramirez
7 Hotel Vela Bar
8 Cabinas Irarosa
11 Travotel Costa Linda
12 Cabinas Anep
15 Hotel Manuel
   Antonio

PLACES TO EAT
9 Restaurant Mar y Sombra
10 Restaurant Del Mar
14 Sodas

OTHER
2 National Park Information
3 Lookout
4 La Buena Nota
13 Bus Stop
16 Park Entrance

Cars are prohibited, and arriving on foot is a minor adventure. The estuary at the park entrance must be waded, and the water is thigh deep at high tide. Trails lead to three beaches within an hour's walk. Another trail climbs a cliff with good views.

Most visitors who spend a day walking around will see monkeys and sometimes sloths, agoutis, armadillos, coatis and raccoons. More than 350 bird species are reported for the park, and a variety of lizards, snakes, iguanas and other animals may be observed. There is a small coral reef off Manuel Antonio Beach, but the water is rather cloudy and the visibility limited.

Information

The park entrance is a little beyond the circle at the end of the road from Quepos. Maps are available here (US$1), and English-speaking wildlife guides can be requested (US$15 per person). Park hours are 7 am to 4 pm Tuesday to Sunday. Admission is US$6; have a guard stamp your hand if you'd like to exit and come back later. A visitor information center (☎ 777 0644) is near Playa Manuel Antonio. Drinking water is available, and there are toilets, beach showers, picnic tables and a refreshment stand nearby. Camping is prohibited. Carry sun protection and insect repellent.

DOMINICAL

This quiet coastal village is 44km south of Quepos by gravel road and 34km from San Isidro by steep paved road. Dominical's long beach has strong rip currents, so be careful. Surfers hang out here, and a small ecotourism industry is developing. Local tour operators are banding together in an effort to promote the area without spoiling it. Most places to stay are midpriced rather than budget options.

Places to Stay

On the main street, the basic but clean *Cabinas Coco* is US$6.50 per person; the adjacent disco may cause sleepless nights. *Cabinas Thrusters* (☎ 787 0127), opposite the Coco, is often filled with long-term occupants and it, too, tends to get rowdy in the evenings. Rates are US$20 for simple doubles with hot water. Nearby is the slightly less noisy *Sundancer Cabinas*

(☎ 787 0125), which offers basic double rooms in a pleasant family home for similar prices. Still quieter is *Posada del Sol* (☎ /fax 787 0085) with clean singles/doubles including fans and hot water for US$14/28. Basic rooms with shared bath can be found above the *San Clemente Bar & Grill* (☎ 787 0026) at US$8 per person. The San Clemente also rents some cabins on the northern end of the beach for US$30 double.

On the beach, the low-key *La Escuelita de Dominical* (☎ 787-0090, fax 787 0103, domini@sol.racsa.co.cr) offers Spanish language courses from about US$350 per week, including a place to stay. If space is available, they charge US$10 per person for a bed. Campers use their shower and kitchen facilities for about US$3.

Another beachside place is the well-maintained *Tortilla Flats* (☎ 787 0145). Rooms sleeping up to three people are US$35 with fans, more with air-conditioning. Their restaurant has been recommended by readers.

Hacienda Barú (☎ 787 0003, fax 787 0004, sstroud@racsa.co.cr), in a 330-hectare private nature reserve on the steep coastal hills north of Dominical, offers two and three-bedroom cabins for US$50 double, US$10 for each additional person, including breakfast. Cabins are equipped with fans, hot shower, kitchenette and refrigerator. Three interpretive trails and a new birding tower are available to guests and others (US$3 per person). The hacienda also offers guided rain forest hikes, kayak tours and a rope ascent to a rain forest canopy platform (US$35).

Places to Eat

Of several inexpensive sodas in Dominical, the best are *Soda Laura* and *Soda Nanyoa*, open early for breakfast and serving casados for about US$2. *Gringo Mike's* is a NYC-style deli with snacks and sandwiches. The popular *San Clemente Bar & Grill* has big breakfasts and US-style bar food, as well as sports programming via satellite TV. Just off the main road toward the beach, *Thrusters Bar* makes pizzas.

Entertainment

Saturday night, the dance floor at the *Hotel & Restaurante Roca Mar* fills up with weekenders down from San Isidro.

Getting There & Away

Buses for Quepos leave from Soda Nanyoa at 8 am and 2:30 pm (2½ hours); for San Isidro at 7:15 am and 3 pm (one hour); and for Uvita at 7 am and 4:30 and 7 pm (one hour).

In addition, buses from San José to Uvita pass through Dominical at about 9 pm daily (and at 11:30 am Saturday and Sunday). Buses from Uvita to Quepos and San José pass through Dominical at 2 pm (and at 6 am Saturday and Sunday).

UVITA

This hamlet, 17km south of Dominical, is a loose straggle of farms and houses and the entry point for Parque Nacional Marino Ballena. The beaches are locally referred to as Playa Uvita and, to the south, Playa Bahía Uvita. Both are popular with Ticos looking for a place to swim. This is not a surfing area.

Places to Stay & Eat

Some of the following can be contacted through Selva Mar (☎ 771 4582, fax 771 1903, selvamar@sol.racsa.co.cr), an agent in San Isidro. *Cabinas Los Laureles*, a few hundred meters to the left of the *abaste-cedor* (general store), has three cabins with bathrooms for US$12/20/25 for one/two/three people. They can arrange horseback tours. *Cabinas El Cocotico* has six simple, clean double rooms with private bath for US$8/12 single/double. A soda is attached.

Near Playa Bahía Uvita is the friendly *Cabinas Hegalva* (☎ 382 5780), run by Doña Cecilia, who cooks great food and charges US$10 per person for rooms with shared baths, including breakfast. Also in this area are *Cabinas María Jesús* and *Cabinas Betty*, both basic rural places charging about US$5 per person.

Students from Dominical-based La Es-cuelita's new Uvita institute stay at *El Chamán* (☎ 787 0090, fax 787 0103, domini@sol.racsa.co.cr), on a stretch of beach 1km south of town. Stand-alone cabins cost US$20 double. There's a pool and restaurant/bar decorated with indige-nous devil masks.

Getting There & Away

The daily bus to San José via Dominical and Quepos departs at 1 pm (US$4.75, seven hours); there's an additional departure on Saturday and Sunday at 5 am. Buses to San Isidro de El General, via Dominical, leave at 6 am and 2 pm. Three buses a day travel the road to Cortés; ask locally for times.

AROUND UVITA
Reserva Biológica Oro Verde

About 4km inland from Uvita along a signed rough road, this private reserve on the Duarte family farm is two-thirds rain forest. Their tours visit the forest, show you waterfalls and wildlife and give you a look at traditional rural Costa Rican life. Horse rental is US$5 per hour, and three- to four-hour hikes with a local guide are US$15 per person. A simple cabin has one room with a double bed and another with five bunk beds for US$10 per person. There is a kitchen, shower and patio. Homecooked meals are an additional US$10 per day.

Rancho La Merced

Opposite the Oro Verde turnoff is Rancho La Merced, a working cattle ranch, more than half of which is protected forest. Horseback tours include 'Cowboy for a Day,' where you ride with local cowboys and help on the ranch. They'll demonstrate what to do if this is your first time, dude. A three- to five-hour tour is US$20 (three person minimum) or US$30 (for one). Other horseback and hiking tours are offered. Lodging costs US$45/55 for doubles/triples sharing a bathroom and kitchen.

PARQUE NACIONAL MARINO BALLENA

This park protects coral and rock reefs in 4500 hectares of ocean around Isla Ballena, south of Uvita. The island has nesting seabird colonies and many green iguanas and basilisk lizards. Humpback whales migrate through the area from December to March. Also within the park's boundaries are 13km of sandy and rocky beaches, man-grove swamps, river mouths and rocky headlands to the southeast of Punta Uvita. Turtles nest on the beaches from May to November, with a peak in September and October.

The ranger station is in Bahía, the seaside extension of Uvita. From there you can walk out onto Punta Uvita and snorkel (best at low tide). Boats from Bahía to Isla Ballena can be hired for about US$15 to US$20 per hour; landing on the island and snorkeling are permitted. The still sparsely developed park lacks camping facilities and there is no entry fee.

Panama

Panama offers some of the finest natural scenery and ecotourism possibilities in Central America, yet most foreigners only know the country for its canal and the 1989 US invasion to depose General Manuel Noriega.

At the southern end of Central America, Panama is an 800km land bridge where the wildlife of North and South America meet and intermingle. Because of this geographical position, Panama is home to more than 940 bird species, more than in all of North America. Few countries offer such dramatic contrasts in such a small area: lush tropical rain forests in the central and eastern regions; cool, fresh volcanic mountains to the west; relaxing Caribbean and Pacific islands.

Panama is a crossroads not only of animals but of people as well. The country is an interesting combination of Spanish, Latin American, North American, Caribbean and indigenous cultural influences, with immigrants from Asia, Europe, the Middle East and other places that spice up the mix. Indian tribes are scattered across the country, and many have successfully maintained some of their traditional culture. The Kuna, in the San Blas Archipelago, are the most independent and politically organized of any native population in Central America. The Península de Azuero in central Panama is like a slice of Spain dropped into the Americas, with traditional Spanish festivals celebrated often and with great gusto.

Historically, Panama is a story of riches – of Peruvian gold carried by Spaniards across the isthmus, huge forts built to deter marauders and attacks by pirates. More recently, the US-built Panama Canal, one of the world's engineering wonders, has dominated political affairs since its construction. The 20th century began with Panama's independence from Colombia in 1903 and the triumphal completion of the canal in 1914, and it ended with another triumph: delivery of the canal from US to Panamanian control on December 31, 1999.

Panama isn't perfect for tourists. Information can sometimes be hard to find; tourism offices often run out of maps. Driving in Panama City is akin to practicing for a heart attack. Yet the roads outside the cities are some of the best in Central America, and buses can get you to almost any town on the map. Domestic flights can drop you in the middle of the jungle very cheaply.

The fact that tourists have often bypassed Panama is one of its appeals. You can spend days in some places without seeing another foreigner. You can spend hours walking in a rain forest or along a mountain trail without meeting another soul. There are beaches and beautiful snorkeling spots that are blissfully uncrowded. A peace like this probably cannot last, as travelers begin to discover the

Highlights

- Hike in the cool, green Chiriquí highlands along the Sendero Los Quetzales

- Snorkel, lie on the beach and soak up the island atmosphere in the laid-back Caribbean town of Bocas del Toro

- Visit the Kuna of the San Blas Archipelago, the most independent native people of Central America

- Watch huge cargo ships as they pass through the locks of the Panama Canal

- Celebrate a festival on the Península de Azuero, the heartland of Spanish culture in Panama

natural and cultural wonders of Panama, but for now, the untouristed roads of Panama offer the independent traveler adventure at a relaxed pace.

Facts about Panama

HISTORY
Pre-Columbian History

Archaeological evidence shows that people have been living in Panama for at least 11,000 years and that agriculture arose here as early as 1500 BC. Panama's first inhabitants lived beside the Pacific and fished in mangroves and estuaries, just as many of the country's native people do today.

Archaeologists divide pre-Columbian Panama into three distinct cultural zones – western, central and eastern – based on the types of pottery and other artisans found at various archaelogical sites. None of these zones was culturally isolated; evidence of trading shows ties among the zones and with Colombia, other parts of Central America and even Mexico and Peru. In addition to commercial trade and fishing, the economies of all Panama's early societies were based on extensive agriculture and hunting. It is believed that these societies were hierarchical and headed by chiefs and that war played a significant role.

In western Panama, on the slopes of the Volcán Barú, Barriles is an important archaeological center where finds have included unusual life-size stone statues of human figures, some with one figure sitting astride another's shoulders. Giant *metates* – flat stone platforms that were used for grinding corn – have also been found here.

Archaeologists estimate that the early civilization represented at Barriles was established around the 4th or 5th century BC, when settlers arrived from the west (now Costa Rica). This culture came to an abrupt end when Volcán Barú erupted violently in the 5th century AD. Later, the region was inhabited again, this time by two different groups whose archaeological remnants include a great variety of distinctive pottery.

Between Penonomé and Natá in the central region, Sitio Conte is an important archaeological zone and ancient ceremonial center where thousands of pieces of pottery, as well as tombs and other items of interest, have been unearthed.

Another central archaeological zone, Cerro Juan Díaz, near Villa de Los Santos on the Península de Azuero, is believed to have been inhabited from about 300 BC until the time of the Spanish conquest. Presently being excavated by the Smithsonian Institution, it is yielding evidence that pottery made here was traded for gold and other goods. Pre-Columbian pottery and other artifacts have also been found at sites in Parque Nacional Sarigua on the Península de Azuero.

Archaeologists have yet to conduct extensive studies of the eastern region of Panama. Most knowledge of the area's history and its peoples' hierarchical, tribal social structure has been gleaned from accounts by the first Spanish explorers.

Gold objects appeared in Panama suddenly, with a sophisticated and completely developed technology. Metallurgy was practiced in Peru as early as the 2nd century BC; by the 1st century AD it had arrived in Panama via Colombia. Colombia, Panama and Costa Rica all became metallurgic provinces, and objects of gold and other metals were exchanged all the way from Mesoamerica to the Andes. Gold was made into ornaments (necklaces, nose rings and so on) and animal, human and other figures. Gold was also used for ceremonial purposes; it probably did not connote wealth to the Indians in the same way that it did to the Spaniards.

Spanish Colonization

When Spaniards first arrived on the isthmus of Panama in the early 16th century, they found it inhabited by several dozen indigenous peoples. The population may have been as large then as it is now, but it was rapidly decimated by European diseases and Spanish swords. Only seven of the original tribes exist today.

The first Europeans in the area were led by the Spanish explorer Rodrigo de Bastidas, who sailed along Panama's Caribbean coast in 1501 with Vasco Núñez de Balboa and Juan de la Cosa as his first mates. Christopher Columbus, Diego de Nicuesa and Alonso de Ojeda each tried to settle along the Caribbean coast but were driven off by hunger or

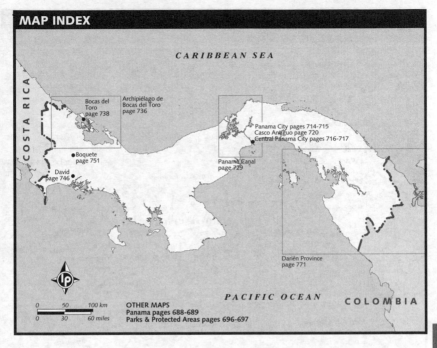

MAP INDEX

CARIBBEAN SEA

COSTA RICA

Bocas del Toro
page 738

Archipiélago de
Bocas del Toro
page 736

Panama City pages 714-715
Casco Antiguo page 720
Central Panama City pages 716-717

●Boquete
page 751

David
page 746

Panamá Canal
page 729

Darién Province
page 771

PACIFIC OCEAN   COLOMBIA

0   50   100 km
0   30   60 miles

OTHER MAPS
Panama pages 688-689
Parks & Protected Areas pages 696-697

PANAMA

by the native population. Balboa established the first successful European settlement on mainland America at Santa María la Antigua del Darién in 1510.

Native people told Balboa of a large sea and a wealthy, gold-producing civilization – almost certainly referring to the Inca empire of Peru – across the mountains of the isthmus. Balboa subsequently scaled the mountains and, in 1513, became the first European to set eyes upon the Pacific, claiming it and the lands it touched for the king of Spain.

In 1519 the cruel and vindictive Pedro Arias de Ávila founded the city of Panamá on the Pacific side, near where Panama City stands today. Pedrarias, as he was called, is remembered for beheading Balboa in 1517 and for ordering attacks against Indians, whom he roasted alive or fed to dogs.

Panamá (an Indian word for 'abundance of fish') became an important Spanish settlement, commercial center and the springboard for further exploration, including the conquest of Peru and expeditions north into Central America. The ruins of this old settlement, now known as Panamá La Vieja, can still be seen today.

When the world's major powers learned that the isthmus of Panama was the narrowest point between the Atlantic and Pacific Oceans, they focused attention on the region. The narrow isthmus became a crucial trade route. Goods from Panamá and Peru were transported by foot and boat to the town of Nombre de Dios on the Caribbean side. This route was called the Sendero Las Cruces (Las Cruces Trail, also known as the Camino de Cruces), vestiges of which can still be found. Goods moved between the two ports until late in the 16th century, when Nombre de Dios was destroyed by the English pirate Sir Francis Drake. The small nearby bay of Portobelo then became the chief Caribbean connection.

Peruvian gold and other natural products were also brought by mule train from Panamá to Portobelo along a series of trails known as El Camino Real (King's Highway). The products were held there for an annual trading fair that lured Spanish galleons laden with European goods.

All this wealth concentrated in one small bay attracted English, French, Dutch and other pirates who were plying the Caribbean.

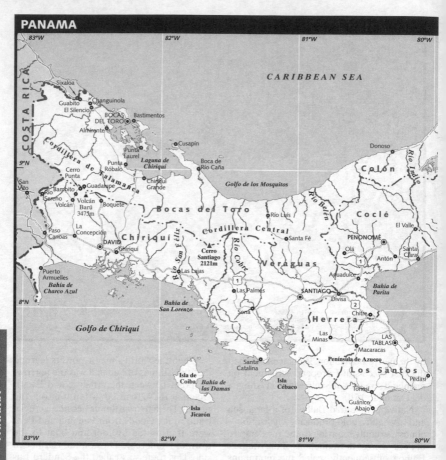

The Spaniards built large stone fortresses to try to ward off attack; the forts at Portobelo and at Fuerte San Lorenzo, on the Río Chagres, can still be visited today.

In 1671, the Welsh buccaneer Sir Henry Morgan overpowered Fuerte San Lorenzo, sailed up the Río Chagres and crossed the isthmus. His forces sacked the city of Panamá, made off with its entire treasure and arrived back on the Caribbean coast with 200 mules loaded with loot. The city burned during Morgan's stay there, but no one knows whether British pirates or fleeing Spaniards put it to the torch. The town was rebuilt a few years later on a cape several kilometers west of its original site, on the spot where the Casco Antiguo district of Panama City is today.

In 1739, the British destroyed Portobelo, finally forcing Spain to abandon the Panamanian crossing in favor of sailing the long way around Cape Horn to the western coast of South America. Without the trade route, Panama declined in importance.

Independence

In 1739, Panama became part of the Viceroyalty of Nueva Andalucía, later called Nueva Granada and thereafter Colombia. In 1821, Colombia, including Panama, gained independence from Spain. Together, Colombia, Panama, Bolivia, Ecuador, Peru and Venezuela formed Gran Colombia, the united Latin American nation that had long been the dream of Simón Bolívar. When Gran Colombia

PANAMA

split up, Panama remained a province of Colombia.

The Panama Railroad

In 1846, Colombia signed a treaty permitting the USA to construct a railway across the isthmus. The treaty guaranteed the USA the right of free transit across the isthmus and the right to protect the line with military force. This was a time of great political turbulence in Panama. Construction of the railroad began in 1850 and concluded in 1855; during that time Panama had 20 governors.

The California gold rush of 1848, which resulted in thousands of people traveling from the East Coast of the USA to the West Coast via Panama, helped to make the railway a profitable venture. It also spurred efforts to construct an interoceanic canal across Central America.

The Panama Canal & the French

The idea of a canal across the isthmus was first broached in 1524, when King Charles V of Spain ordered a survey to determine the feasibility of constructing such a waterway. In 1878, the Colombian government awarded a contract to build a canal to Lucien NB Wyse. He sold the concession to the French diplomat Ferdinand de Lesseps, who was then basking in his success as the contractor-builder of the Suez Canal.

Lesseps' Compagnie Universelle du Canal Interocéanique began work in 1881. Lesseps was determined to build a sea-level canal alongside the interoceanic railway, but the project proved more difficult than anyone had expected. Yellow fever and malaria killed 22,000 workers. Insurmountable construction problems and financial mismanagement drove the company bankrupt by 1889.

One of Lesseps' chief engineers, Philippe Bunau-Varilla, formed a new canal company, but at the same time the USA was seriously considering putting its own canal somewhere through Central America, possibly Nicaragua. The French, unable to complete the canal, agreed to sell the concession to the USA. In 1903, Bunau-Varilla asked for the Colombian government's permission to conclude this sale. Colombia refused.

Panama Becomes a Nation

Revolutionary sentiments had been brewing in Panama for many years, but repeated attempts to break away from Colombia had failed. In 1903 a civil war in Colombia created fresh discontent when it drafted Panamanian men and seized property for the war effort.

When the Colombian government refused to allow the transfer of the canal treaty to the USA, it thwarted US and French interests, as well as Panama's own. Bunau-Varilla, who had a lot to gain financially if the sale went through, asked the US government to back Panama if it declared independence from Colombia.

A revolutionary junta declared Panama independent on November 3, 1903, with the support of the USA, which immediately recognized the new government. Colombia sent troops by sea to try to regain control of the province, but US battleships prevented their reaching land.

The First Canal Treaty

An official Panamanian delegation was sent to Washington, DC, to negotiate a canal treaty, but Bunau-Varilla, already in the US as ambassador, preempted them with his own treaty. On November 18, before the delegation arrived, he signed the Hay-Bunau-Varilla Treaty with US Secretary of State John Hay. It gave the USA far more than had been offered in the original treaty rejected by the Colombian government. The treaty's 26 articles awarded the USA 'sovereign rights in perpetuity over the Canal Zone,' an area extending 8km on either side

of the canal, and a broad right of intervention in Panamanian affairs. The treaty was ratified over the Panamanian delegation's protests.

The treaty led to friction between the USA and Panama for decades, partly because it was overly favorable to the USA at the expense of Panama and partly due to lingering questions about its legality. Colombia did not recognize Panama as a separate nation until 1921, when the USA paid Colombia US$25 million in compensation.

The USA Builds the Canal

Construction began again on the canal in 1904 and took 10 years and more than 75,000 workers. The project remains one of the greatest engineering achievements of the 20th century, completed despite disease, landslides and many other difficulties. The first ship sailed through the canal on August 15, 1914.

The Canal Zone – the area surrounding the waterway – became a populous American military colony, with its own English-language schools, homes and businesses.

Rise of the Military

The US military intervened repeatedly in Panama's political affairs until 1936, when the Hay-Bunau-Varilla Treaty was replaced by the Hull-Alfaro Treaty. The USA relinquished its rights to use its troops outside the Canal Zone and to seize land for canal purposes, and the annual sum paid to Panama for use of the Canal Zone was increased.

With the new restrictions on US military activity, the Panamanian army grew more powerful. In 1968 the Guardia Nacional deposed the elected president and took control of the government; the constitution was suspended, the national assembly dissolved and the press censored. The Guardia's General Omar Torrijos Herrera emerged as the new leader.

Torrijos conducted public-works programs on a grand scale, including a massive modernization of Panama City, which won him the support of much of the populace but also plunged Panama into huge debt.

1977 Canal Treaty

US dominion over the Canal Zone, and the canal itself, were continuing sources of conflict between Panama and the USA. After years of negotiation that foundered in a series of stalemates, a new treaty was finally accepted by both sides in 1977. It was signed by Torrijos and US President Jimmy Carter.

The new treaty provided that US control of the canal would be gradually phased out, with Panama assuming complete ownership and control on December 31, 1999. It also called for the phasing out of US military bases in Panama. A separate treaty ensured that the canal will remain open and neutral for all nations during both peace and war. The US Senate attached extenuating conditions that granted the USA the right of limited intervention and rights to defend the canal beyond 1999.

Manuel Noriega

Torrijos was killed in a plane crash in 1981. In 1983, after a brief period of leadership by Colonel Rubén Darío Paredes, Colonel Manuel Antonio Noriega took control of the Guardia Nacional and then of the country itself.

Noriega, a former head of Panama's secret police and a former operative of the US Central Intelligence Agency (CIA), quickly consolidated his power. He enlarged the Guardia Nacional, expanded its authority and renamed it the Panama Defense Forces. He also closed down all media that criticized him and created a paramilitary 'Dignity Battalion' in every city and village, its members armed and ready to inform on any neighbor showing less than complete loyalty to the Noriega regime. In 1985, he removed from office the winner of the 1984 presidential election, Nicolás Ardito Barletta.

In early 1987, Noriega became the center of an international scandal. He was publicly accused of involvement in drug trafficking with Colombian drug cartels, murdering his opponents and rigging elections. Many Panamanians demanded Noriega's dismissal, protesting with general strikes and street demonstrations that resulted in violent clashes with the Panama Defense Forces.

Noriega's regime was now an international embarrassment, and relations with the USA deteriorated. In February 1988, the USA indicted Noriega for drug trafficking and involvement in organized crime. In the same month, Noriega deposed Barletta's successor as president, Eric Arturo Delvalle.

In March 1988, the USA imposed economic sanctions against Panama, ending a preferential trade agreement, freezing Panamanian assets in US banks and refusing to pay canal fees. Panama's international offshore banking industry, which the USA had asserted was deeply involved with international drug cartels and with laundering money for organized crime, buckled under the strain of the American sanctions. Noriega survived an unsuccessful military coup, and he responded by stepping up violent repression of his critics.

Presidential elections were held again in May 1989. When Noriega's candidate failed to win, Noriega declared the entire election null and void. Guillermo Endara, the winning candidate, and his two vice-presidential running mates were assaulted by Noriega's forces, a scene captured live on national TV and broadcast to a furious nation. Another attempted coup in October 1989 was followed by even more repressive measures.

On December 15, 1989, Noriega's legislature declared him president. At the same time, Noriega announced that Panama was at war with the USA. The following day, an unarmed US marine dressed in civilian clothes was killed by Panamanian soldiers.

Operation Just Cause

US reaction was swift. On December 20, 1989, aircraft, tanks and 26,000 US troops attacked Panama City in a mission called Operation Just Cause. US President George Bush said the invasion had four objectives: to protect US lives, to maintain the security of the Panama Canal, to restore democracy to Panama and to capture Noriega and bring him to justice.

On Christmas Day, Noriega went to the Vatican embassy for asylum and stayed 10 days. US soldiers set up loudspeakers in front of the embassy and blared rock music to unnerve those inside. Meanwhile, angry crowds near the blocked-off embassy demanded that Noriega be expelled.

Noriega surrendered to US forces on January 3, 1990. He was flown to Miami and convicted on eight charges of conspiracy to manufacture and distribute cocaine. In July 1992, he was sentenced to 40 years in prison.

PANAMA

Today he is serving his sentence in a Florida prison.

Post-Invasion Panama

After Noriega's ouster, Guillermo Endara, the legitimate winner of the 1989 election, was sworn in as president, and Panama City attempted to put itself back together. It had suffered damage not only from the invasion but from widespread looting. Many blocks of the residential district of Chorrillo, near the Panama Defense Forces headquarters, burned to the ground during the invasion. The invasion also left the country financially crippled for five years.

The death toll from the invasion was a subject of great controversy. The official toll was put at 540; a human-rights commission later determined that at least 4000 Panamanians had been killed.

Panamanian opinion of the US invasion remains divided. Nearly everyone is glad that Noriega is gone, and Panamanians had been unable to oust him. On the other hand, some continue to question the necessity of an invasion to achieve this, and many believe the invasion was badly handled. For example, US bombs killed hundreds of civilians in the poorest section of the city, where the Panama Defense Forces had its headquarters. US soldiers also did nothing to stop the post-invasion looting, dealing a death blow to an economy already crippled by economic sanctions. And Panamanians do not forget that the CIA helped Noriega amass the power that he eventually abused.

The Endara government did not turn out to be a panacea. Panamanians were concerned over what many considered Endara's excessive involvement with the USA, his handling of the military and his inability to create economic well-being for the country. In the 1994 presidential election, Ernesto Pérez Balladares won by a narrow margin. Under his leadership, the government improved transportation and communication infrastructure, joined the World Trade Organization, passed antimonopoly laws, and increased funding for education, health, farming and housing projects. On the downside, many Panamanians believed that he did not adequately address corruption and that his urban planning policies were disastrous, including many megatourism projects for the Canal Zone. Balladares lost a referendum that would have allowed him to run for a second term.

In 1999, Mireya Moscoso was elected as the country's first female president on a populist platform, including social development and reduction of poverty. Moscoso wants to expand the canal, embark on an ambitious road, school and health clinic building program, and use the proceeds from privatization to reduce the national debt. She has had a difficult time accomplishing her legislative objectives, however, because her party does not control the legislative assembly.

Panama's Canal

December 31, 1999 marked the completion of the transfer of the Panama Canal, the surrounding Canal Zone and US military bases to Panama. Some of the transferred area will be developed into tourist resorts, a high-tech village and container terminals.

The US military also left, taking with them an economic impact of up to US$350 million; 4000 Panamanians employed by the US military lost their jobs. Polls taken before the troop withdrawal showed that a majority of Panamanians did not want the US to pull out completely because of the economic consequences. This sentiment conflicted with the desire to cast off this last vestige of colonialism.

Operation of the canal presents ongoing challenges. Panamanians worry about possible political influence on the canal's operations, or that politicians will tap into the canal's income for pet projects. Excessive development in the Canal Zone could damage the watershed that the canal relies upon. Target practice by the US military left an estimated 105,000 unexploded bombs scattered throughout 7,800 acres of rain forest; the US claims that it cannot remove them without destroying the forest. Allowing ships laden with nuclear fuel to pass through the canal is an ongoing controversy. And an additional set of locks needed to accommodate larger ships will cost US$6 to US$8 billion.

Nevertheless, Panamanians are extremely proud that their country is fully independent for the first time in its history. There's no question that the Panamanians have the technical know-how to run the canal; more than 96% of the canal employees were

Panamanian before the transfer. Constitutional laws require operation of the canal independently of political concerns, and politicians are aware that the whole world is watching.

Finally, after nearly a century, the Panama Canal *is* Panama's canal.

GEOGRAPHY

Panama is the southernmost of the Central American countries. It is a long, narrow country in the shape of an S, bordered on the west by Costa Rica, on the east by Colombia, on the north by an 1160km Caribbean coastline and on the south by a 1690km Pacific coastline. The total land area is 78,000 sq km, roughly the size of Scotland or the US state of South Carolina.

The isthmus of Panama is the narrowest land mass between the Atlantic and Pacific Oceans. At the narrowest point it is less than 50km wide. The Panama Canal, which is around 80km long, effectively divides the country into eastern and western regions.

Two mountain chains run along Panama's spine, one in the east and one in the west. The highest point in the country is 3475m Volcán Barú in western Chiriquí Province. Panama's only volcano, it is dormant, although hot springs around its flanks testify to continuing underground thermal activity.

Like all the Central American countries, Panama has large, flat coastal lowlands, covered in places by huge banana plantations.

There are about 480 rivers in Panama and 1518 islands near its shores. The two main island groups are the San Blas and Bocas del Toro Archipelagos on the Caribbean side, but most of the islands are on the Pacific side. Even the Panama Canal has islands, including Isla Barro Colorado, which has a world-famous tropical rain forest research station.

CLIMATE

Like the rest of Central America, Panama has two seasons. The dry season (summer, or *verano)* lasts from around mid-December to mid-April, and the rainy season (winter, or *invierno)* lasts from mid-April to mid-December.

Rain patterns, however, differ markedly from one side of the country to the other, with the Caribbean side receiving much

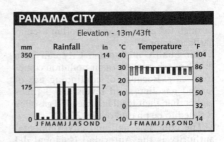

more rain than the Pacific side. The mountains that extend along the spine of the country form a barrier against the warm, moist trade winds blowing from the Caribbean. As the warm air rises against the mountains, the moisture it holds falls, frequently and heavily, as rain. The Caribbean coast receives around 1500 to 3500mm a year; of course, the rainy season is wetter, but downpours are possible at any time of year. There are lush tropical rain forests on the Caribbean side, along the Panama Canal and in the Darién Province.

Most people live on the Pacific side of the mountains. Here, the annual rainfall is only 1140 to 2290mm. This is still no small amount, but the rains are confined almost entirely to the rainy season. This seasonal weather pattern does not support tropical rain forest; the Pacific coast is lined with broad grasslands (savanna) and what remains of the deciduous forests.

Temperatures are typically hot in the lowlands (day/night temperatures around 32°/21°C) and cool in the mountains (18°/10°C). These remain about the same all year.

ECOLOGY & ENVIRONMENT

Panama has set aside more land – about 30% – for habitat protection than any other Central American country. Nevertheless, the country is plagued by environmental problems such as deforestation and soil erosion, stemming in part from poor enforcement of its laws. Mangroves, important for maintaining balance in delicate marine ecosystems, are being destroyed at an unsustainable pace. Coral reefs throughout the Caribbean are also endangered.

Water pollution is most evident around Panama City and Colón, where 90% of Panamanians live. Most of the sewage from these cities is discharged untreated directly into coastal waters or canals that flow through the cities. Rivers are often used as garbage dumps.

Air quality in Panama City can be a problem, where 90% of air pollution comes from cars. Because of continuing use of leaded gasoline, lead levels are 3 times higher than their legal limit; leaded gasoline is slated to be phased out by 2002.

The country's national environmental authority is the Autoridad Nacional del Ambiente (ANAM). Its responsibilities include managing the national park system.

The chief private environmental group is the Asociación Nacional para la Conservación de la Naturaleza (National Association for the Conservation of Nature, or Ancon; ☎ 314 0060, fax 314 0061, ancon@ancon.org). Ancon has played a major role in the creation of national parks and on many occasions has spurred ANAM into action. The Spanish-language Web site (www.ancon.org) includes its monthly magazine and information on its activities. Ancon provides nature guides and access to its nature lodges through its subsidiary Ancon Expeditions.

The Panama Audubon Society (☎ 224 9371, fax 224 4740, audupan@pananet.com) holds meetings at the Parque Natural Metropolitano' visitors center at 7 pm on the second Thursday of every month. The meetings are open to the public and often feature interesting speakers. Talks are usually presented in Spanish, but English is also spoken. These meetings provide an excellent opportunity to meet Panamanians and other birders, and to learn more about birds. The society takes part in an annual bird count. You can also go on birding expeditions for a small fee, generally far cheaper than an organized tour. Their useful Web site (www.pananet.com/audubon) contains their monthly newsletter, bird checklists and information on field trips.

Another wonderful organization dealing with environmental topics is the Smithsonian Tropical Research Institute (STRI; ☎ 212 8000, fax 212 8148), which conducts research on biological and conservation issues at locations throughout Panama. STRI's Tupper Center, near Avenida de los Mártires opposite the Legislative Palace in the Ancón district, features technical seminars in English every Tuesday at noon. The world-class library is open to the public and the bookstore has a good selection of nature and environmental books. Other STRI facilities that tourists can visit are the Marine Exhibit Center on the causeway near Panama City (see the Panama City section), and the research facility on Isla Barro Colorado (see the Panamá and Coclé Provinces section). For more information, see their Web site (www.stri.org).

FLORA & FAUNA

Panama's position as a narrow land bridge between two huge continents has given it a remarkable variety of plant and animal life. Species migrating between the continents have gathered in Panama, so that there are South American armadillos, anteaters and sloths along with North American tapirs, jaguars and deer. With its wide variety of native and migratory species, Panama is one of the world's best places for bird watchers.

Panama has more than 940 recorded bird species and more than 10,000 plant species, in addition to 125 animal species found nowhere else in the world. The country also has 105 rare and endangered species, including scarlet macaws, harpy eagles, golden frogs, jaguars and various species of sea turtle.

Tropical rain forest is the dominant vegetation in the canal area, along the Caribbean coast and in most of the eastern half of the country. The Parque Nacional del Darién protects much of Panama's largest tropical rain forest region. Other vegetation zones include grasslands on the Pacific coast, mountain forest in the highlands, alpine vegetation on the highest peaks and mangrove forests on both coasts and around many islands.

Parks & Protected Areas

Panama has 12 national parks, 2 national marine parks, 10 wildlife refuges and 18 other protected areas. Entrance fees are US$3 for the national parks and US$10 for the national marine parks. Camping costs US$5. Some parks have ranger stations where you can bunk for US$5 to US$10 per night. The fees can generally be paid at park headquarters or an ANAM ranger station near the park entrance, although these are sometimes closed.

Information about the parks and other protected areas can be difficult to come by. Some parks are described on a Web site (www.panamatours.com) operated by Panama's tourism board, the Instituto Panameño de Turismo (IPAT). The US$60 coffee-table book *Parques Nacionales Panamá (Panama National Parks)* features beautiful photos, bilingual information on flora and fauna and information on access; it is available in Panama City.

IPAT offices in Panama City and throughout Panama sometimes have information on some parks, but often not the ones you are asking about. ANAM operates an information center in Albrook, Building 804, where you can get copies of the few maps they have. ANAM also has several offices in Panama City, including in Albrook and near the old Terminal de Buses al Interior. However, they are not really organized to assist tourists; one office might send you to another office, which will then send you back to the first office without any helpful information.

Easily accessible parks in the Panama City area include the Parque Nacional Soberanía and the Parque Nacional Camino de Cruces, both with excellent hiking trails. Parque Natural Metropolitano at the edge of Panama City has trails that lead to a panoramic vista of the city.

In western Panama, Parque Nacional Volcán Barú contains the giant volcano, the resplendent quetzal and one of the country's best hiking trails. Parque Internacional La Amistad, shared by Panama and Costa Rica, has great biodiversity, numerous endemic species and several hiking trails. Three Indian tribes reside in this park.

Parque Nacional Marino Isla Bastimentos, on the Caribbean coast of western Panama in Bocas del Toro Province, conserves marine and coastal ecosystems including coral reefs, white sand beaches and more than 200 species of tropical fish.

Eastern Panama features Parque Nacional Darién, the country's largest park. A world heritage site and a biosphere reserve, the park contains the greatest tropical rain forest wilderness in Central America.

Details on these and other parks and reserves are contained in individual province sections.

GOVERNMENT & POLITICS

Panama is governed as a constitutional democracy. The executive branch is led by a president, elected by popular vote to a five-year term. The president is assisted by two elected vice presidents and an appointed cabinet. President Mireya Moscoso was elected to a five-year term in May 1999. Under the constitution, presidents may only serve one term.

The legislative assembly has 72 members, also elected by popular vote to five-year terms. The judiciary consists of a nine-member Supreme Court, appointed to 10-year terms by the president and approved by the legislature and various lower courts.

Panama has nine provinces, plus the autonomous region of Kuna Yala, which is governed by Kuna tribal leaders *(caciques)*. Each province has a governor appointed by the president, and each is divided into municipal districts.

ECONOMY

Panama has the highest per-capita income of the Central American countries, but still 37% of the population live below the poverty level, and 21% live in 'extreme' poverty. Unemployment hovers around 20%. Panama City, with its tall skyscrapers and international banking and trade, is a modern metropolis; but like other modern cities, it also has slums, crime and unemployment.

Finance and real estate account for about 15% of the country's gross national product, followed by commerce, restaurants and hotels (12%); government services (10%); agriculture (10%); manufacturing (9%); the Zona Libre (Free Trade Zone; 9%); the Panama Canal (8.5%); and utilities (3%).

Agriculture, including fishing, livestock and forestry, employs 27% of the workforce. Principal crops are bananas, plantains, sugarcane, rice, maize, coffee, beans and tobacco. Cattle, pigs and poultry are farmed; sea products include fish, shrimp and lobster. Industry and mining employ around 12% of the labor force; manufacturing employs about 9%.

Bananas, produced primarily around the Changuinola and Puerto Armuelles areas, account for almost 40% of Panama's exports; other important exports include shrimp (19%), coffee (5%), sugar (5%) and clothing (5%). The USA is Panama's main trading

PANAMA

PARKS & PROTECTED AREAS

1 Humedal de San San-Pond Sak	9 Monumento Natural Barro Colorado	17 Parque Nacional General de División
2 Parque Nacional Portobelo	10 Parque Nacional Soberanía	Omar Torrijos Herrea
3 Parque Internacional La Amistad	11 Summit Botanical Gardens & Zoo	18 Parque Nacional Altos de Campana
4 Parque Nacional Marino Isla Bastimentos	12 Parque Nacional Camino de Cruces	19 Refugio de Vida Silvestre Islas Taboga y
5 Área Recreativa Lago Gatún	13 Parque Natural Metropolitano	Urabá
6 Parque Nacional Chagres	14 Humedal Lagunas de Volcán	20 Refugio de Vida Silvestre Playa de La
7 Área Silvestre de Narganá	15 Parque Nacional Volcán Barú	Barqueta Agrícola
8 Bosque Protector Palo Seco	16 Reserva Forestal de Agua Fortuna	21 Refugio de Vida Silvestre Playa Boca Vieja

partner, taking 45% of its exports and providing 40% of its imports. Other important trading partners include Japan, Germany, Costa Rica, Ecuador and Venezuela.

Despite the hopes of nearly everyone in Panama, tourism remains a sluggish industry.

POPULATION & PEOPLE

Panama census takers counted 2,778,440 people in 2000. The majority of the population (62%) are mestizos of mixed indigenous and Spanish descent, but there are also a number of other sizable groups. About 14% of Panamanians are of African descent, 10% of Spanish descent, 5% of mixed African and Spanish descent and 5% are Indian.

Black Panamanians are mostly descendants of English-speaking West Indians such as Jamaicans and Trinidadians, who were brought to Panama as laborers. West Indians worked on banana plantations in Bocas del Toro Province, the transisthmian railway in the 1850s, the French canal project in the 1880s and the US construction of the canal in the early 20th century.

Of the several dozen native tribes that inhabited Panama when the Spanish arrived, seven now remain: the Kuna, the Ngöbe-Buglé (also known as the Guaymís), the Emberá, the Wounaan, the Bokatá, the Bribri and the Teribe (also known as the Naso). Each of these groups maintains its own language and culture. The Guaymís number about 125,000 and are Panama's

PANAMA

PARKS & PROTECTED AREAS

22 Reserva Forestal La Yeguada
23 Monumento Natural de Los Pozos de Calobre
24 Reserva Natural Isla San Telmo
25 Punta Patiño Wildlife Preserve
26 Reserva Hidrológica Serranía Filo del Tallo
27 Reserva Forestal Canglón
28 Parque Nacional Marino Golfo de Chiriquí

29 Área Natural Recreativa Salto de Las Palmas
30 Refugio de Vida Silvestre Cenegón del Mangle
31 Parque Nacional Sarigua
32 Corredor Biológico de la Serranía de Bagre
33 Parque Nacional Isla de Coiba
34 Humedal El Golfo de Montijo
35 Reserva Forestal Montuoso

36 Refugio de Vida Silvestre El Peñón del Cedro de Los Pozos
37 Refugio de Vida Silvestre Peñón de la Honda
38 Refugio de Vida Silvestre Pablo Arturo Barrios
39 Refugio de Vida Silvestre Isla Iguana
40 Parque Nacional Darién
41 Parque Nacional Cerro Hoya
42 Reserva Forestal La Tronosa
43 Refugio de Vida Silvestre Isla de Cañas

largest tribe; the Kuna, who govern their ancestral territory as the autonomous region of the Comarca de Kuna Yala and send representatives to the legislature, are the most politically organized.

EDUCATION

Panama's educational system is composed of elementary, secondary and university levels, each lasting six years. Officially, education is compulsory for six years between the ages of six and 15. Actual enrollment in elementary school is high (over 90%), but there's a drop off at the secondary level (about 50% enrollment). Education is free up to the university level. Panama has three universities, with regional campuses in the interior.

The 1990 illiteracy rate was reported to be 3.6% in urban areas, 19.7% in rural areas, and over 50% among the country's indigenous populations.

ARTS

Panama's arts reflect the country's ethnic mix. Traditional Panamanian products include wood carvings, weaving and textiles, ceramics, masks, straw goods and other handicrafts. Some of the more famous crafts include *molas* (colorful hand-stitched appliqué textiles made by Kuna women) and the *pollera,* the intricately stitched, lacy, Spanish-influenced dress of the Península de Azuero, which is the 'national dress' of Panama for festive occasions.

PANAMA

There is also a magnificent variety of music, dance, theater and other arts. Salsa is the most popular music in Panama. The country's most renowned salsa singer, Rubén Blades, has had several international hits, ran for president and has appeared in several movies. The jazz composer and pianist Danilo Pérez is widely acclaimed by critics, and Los Rabanes is the most well-known rock group in the country. Panamanian folk music (called *típico*), in which the accordion dominates, is well represented by Victorio Vergara and Samy and Sandra Sandoval.

SOCIETY & CONDUCT

Panama is home to widely different ethnic groups. The diverse Indian tribes, the various West Indian groups, the Spanish-Indian mestizos, the Chinese, Middle-Eastern, Swiss and Croatian immigrants, the North Americans and others – all have maintained their own cultures, and some elements of these cultures have mixed to form new combinations. Many come together in Panama City, where there's as much international variety as anywhere on Earth.

Despite the ethnic mix, class distinctions and racism exist in Panama. Whites, who make up only 10% of the population, control the majority of wealth and power. Some businesses will not hire blacks, and some nightclubs refuse admission to blacks or charge them more for admission. Still, outright racial violence is less common here than in many other countries.

Of the various indigenous groups, the Kuna and the Guaymí are the ones most often noticed by visitors. While the men of both tribes have adopted western dress, the women tend to dress in traditional costume.

The Kuna in traditional costume are striking, and tourists are often tempted to photograph them. If you wish to do so, be polite and respectful and ask their permission. Note that there is usually a US$1 fee for every photo you take of a Kuna, payable to the subject.

As elsewhere in the world, standards of conduct and dress are more relaxed in the big city than in rural areas. In Panama City, almost anything goes; in other parts of the country, it's important to be sensitive to local customs of behavior and dress. Panama is a conservative country. As elsewhere in Latin America, women should dress modestly, especially in rural areas. Even on very hot days, you'll rarely see a man working with his shirt off or a woman wearing shorts hemmed above the knee.

RELIGION

The major faiths are Roman Catholicism (85%), Protestant denominations (5%), Islam (5%) and Baha'i (1%). There are also a small number of Hindus, Jews and other believers. In addition, the various native tribes have their own belief systems, although these are fading quickly due to the influence of missionaries preaching Christianity.

Religion is especially mixed in Panama City, home to immigrants from all over the world. The city has many Catholic and Protestant churches, three synagogues, two mosques, and Hindu and Baha'i temples.

LANGUAGE

Spanish is the official language of Panama, but at least 14 other languages can be heard. The native groups still speak their own languages, and many immigrant groups do the same. You may hear Kuna, Chinese, Serbo-Croat, Hebrew, Creole French, German and Arabic.

Most of the descendants of the West Indian immigrants in Bocas del Toro still speak their original Caribbean-accented English. Other Panamanians grew up speaking English in the Canal Zone or learned it at school, and it is common in business, banking and some tourist activities. However, travelers will find it difficult to get by speaking only English, unless they are especially adept at miming. Taxi and bus drivers, hotel clerks (especially in less-expensive hotels), tourism board (IPAT) staff and restaurant servers often speak only Spanish.

Panamanian Spanish is distinctive and may be difficult to understand at first. It has a lot of slang and unusual words and a distinctive accent, and it is spoken very rapidly.

Facts for the Visitor

SUGGESTED ITINERARIES

One week
Hike in the cool Chiriquí highlands towns of Guadalupe and Boquete then snorkel in the Bocas del Toro Archipelago.

Two weeks
In addition to the Chiriquí highlands and Bocas del Toro, visit the Panama Canal area and the San Blas Archipelago.

One month
With a month, you can add Isla Boca Brava to your itinerary and explore Spanish culture, festivals and beaches in the Península de Azuero; Panama City and the Panama Canal area; and the jungles of the Darién.

PLANNING
When to Go

Panama's tourist season is during the dry season from mid-December to mid-April. The weather can be hot and steamy in the lowlands during the rainy season, when the humidity makes the heat oppressive. But it won't rain nonstop; rain in Panama, as elsewhere in the tropics, tends to come in sudden short downpours that freshen the air and are followed by sunshine. If you'll be doing any long, strenuous hiking, the dry season is the most comfortable time to do it; the Darién Gap can be crossed only at this time.

If you like to party, try to be in Panama City or on the Península de Azuero for Carnaval (Mardi Gras), held each year during the four days leading up to Ash Wednesday. Panama also has a number of other festivals worth catching, especially on the Península de Azuero; see that section for details.

Maps

ITM publishes an excellent 1:800,000 color map of Panama, showing the geographical features, cities, towns, national parks, airports and roads. It also publishes an excellent color map of Central America as a whole (see Maps in the Regional Facts for the Visitor chapter).

The Instituto Panameno de Turismo (IPAT) distributes a useful color map with the country on one side and Panama City on the other. Their other helpful maps include Bocas del Toro and Chiriquí Province. These are worth looking for, although there are some inaccuracies and the tourist offices often run out.

The Instituto Geográfico Nacional (Tommy Guardia) in Panama City sells topographical maps of selected cities and regions. During research for this book, however, many maps were out of stock and the map of Panama City was hopelessly out of date (though a new one was in production).

Various free tourist publications distributed in Panama also have maps.

What to Bring

You can buy anything you are likely to need in Panama and probably more cheaply than you can back home. But you may need to bring antimalarial medication, depending on which parts of Panama you'll be visiting (see Health).

TOURIST OFFICES

Panama has tourist representatives in the United States (☎ 305-629 3644, fax 305-823 6013), 5201 Blue Lagoon Drive, Penthouse, Miami, FL 33126; Germany (☎ 030 38 30 27 12, fax 030 382 42 16, ipat.de@gmx.de); and Colombia (☎ 571 626 6868, ajvallarino@hotmail.com).
Web site: www.panamainfo.com

The Instituto Panameño de Turismo (IPAT) has its main office in Panama City at the Centro Atlapa, with smaller information counters at the ruins of Panamá La Vieja, the Tocumen International Airport, the Albrook domestic airport and the pedestrian thoroughfare in Casco Antiguo. It also runs offices in Bocas del Toro, Boquete, Colón, David, Paso Canoas, Penonomé, Portobelo, Santiago, Villa de Los Santos, Las Tablas, and El Valle.

IPAT has a few useful maps and brochures, but often has a problem keeping enough in stock for distribution to tourists. Most offices are staffed with people who speak only Spanish, and the helpfulness of any particular office depends on the person at the counter. Some employees really try to help, but others are just passing the time. As a general rule, you will get more useful information if you have specific questions.

PANAMA

VISAS & DOCUMENTS

US citizens need a driver's license and a birth certificate (original or certified copy) to enter Panama, although a passport will ease your reentry to the US and is recommended. Everyone else needs a passport to enter Panama, but additional requirements vary by country.

Citizens of the UK, Germany, the Netherlands, Switzerland, Spain, Finland and Austria, as well as a few South and Central American countries, need only a passport. Most other nationals, including US, Canadian, Australian and New Zealand citizens, may enter with a US$5 tourist card, available from consulates, embassies and also from airlines, the Tica Bus company, at the airport or at some border posts upon entry. Those planning to enter Panama overland would be well advised to obtain a normal visa before showing up at the border, even though it is not technically required; the border post may run out of tourist cards, which has happened more than once (see Getting There & Away for more details).

Visas must be obtained before entering the country by nationals of many other countries. Visas are issued at Panamanian embassies and consulates and cost around US$20, depending on the nationality of the applicant.

If you are heading to Colombia, Venezuela or some other South American country, you may need an onward ticket before you'll be allowed entry or even allowed to board the plane out. A quick check with the appropriate embassy – easy to do by phone in Panama City – will tell you whether the country you're heading to has an onward-ticket requirement.

Visa Extensions

Visas and tourist cards are both good for 30 days and can be extended within Panama to 90 days. To extend your stay, go to an office of Migración y Naturalización in Panama City, David, Santiago, Chitré or Changuinola. You must bring your passport and photocopies of the page with your personal information and of the stamp of your most recent entry to Panama. You also must bring two passport-size photos, an onward air or bus ticket, and a letter to the director stating your reasons for wishing to extend your visit. You will have to fill out a *prórroga de turista* form and pay US$10. You will then be issued a plastic photo ID card.

If you have extended your time, you will also need to obtain a permit *(permiso de salida)* to leave the country. For this, bring your passport and a *paz y salvo* form to the immigration office. Paz y salvos are issued at Ministerios de Hacienda y Tesoro, found in towns with immigration offices, which simply require that you bring in your passport, fill out a form and pay US$1. You will not be able to leave the country if you are in Panama more than 30 days and do not obtain a *permiso de salida*.

There's always talk of making this process easier for tourists by extending the 30-day limit to 90 days. Nothing has happened yet, though.

In Panama City, the Migración y Naturalización office (☎ 225 1373) is on the corner of Avenida Cuba and Calle 29 Este in La Exposición and is open 8 am to 3 pm weekdays.

For a paz y salvo, go to the Ministerio de Hacienda y Tesoro in the Hatillo Building, on Avenida Cuba between Calles 35 Este and 36 Este.

In David, the Migración y Naturalización office (☎ 775 4515) is on Calle C Sur near Avenida Central. The office is open 8 am to 8 pm weekdays.

CUSTOMS

You may bring in up to two cartons of cigarettes and three bottles of liquor tax free. There are few restrictions on personal quantities of items taken out of the country. However, visitors who try to leave Panama with products made from endangered species – like jaguar teeth, ocelot skins and items made of turtle shell – will face a fine that is usually accompanied by jail time.

MONEY
Currency

Panama uses the US dollar as its currency. The official name for it is the *balboa*, but it's exactly the same bill, and in practice people use the terms '*dólar*' and 'balboa' interchangeably.

Panamanian coins are of the same value, size and metal as US coins; both are used. Coins include one, five, 10, 25 and 50 *centavos* (or *centésimos)*; 100 centavos equal one balboa.

Exchange Rates

Exchange rates at time of publication were as follows:

country	unit		balboas
Australia	A$1	=	B/.0.55
Canada	C$1	=	B/.0.66
Euro	€1	=	B/.0.93
France	1FF	=	B/.0.14
Germany	DM1	=	B/.0.47
Japan	100¥	=	B/.0.87
New Zealand	NZ$1	=	B/.0.44
UK	UK£1	=	B/.1.49
US	US$1	=	B/.1

Exchanging Money

The only bank that exchanges foreign currency is the Banco Nacional de Panamá counter at Tocumen International Airport. Once you have left the airport, the only place to change foreign currency for dollars is a *casa de cambio* (exchange house). There are several in Panama City but few elsewhere.

ATMs are readily available throughout Panama, except in the most isolated places. Traveler's checks are rarely accepted by businesses, although they can be cashed at a few banks. Credit cards are widely accepted at travel agencies, upscale hotels and pricey restaurants, but they can be problematic almost everywhere else. In short, carry enough cash to get you to the next bank or ATM. Finally, many businesses will not break $50 and $100 bills; those that do may require you to present your passport.

Costs

Accommodations tend to be more expensive in Panama than in other parts of Central America; a hotel room that might cost US$6 in Nicaragua or Guatemala might cost US$10 here. In Panama City, you can get a very basic room for US$7, but it will not be in the best part of town. Rooms in better areas start at US$10, and decent, modern hotel rooms start at US$20. Away from Panama City, accommodations are much less expensive; a fine room may cost around US$12. Die-hard shoestring travelers can still find a room anywhere in the country for around US$7.

In Panama, more modern lodgings and better food are available at lower prices than elsewhere in the region and are very good values. Prices for everything else – food, transportation, places to visit – are very reasonable.

Tipping & Bargaining

The standard tipping rate in Panama is around 10% of the bill; in small cafes and more casual places, tipping is not necessary. Taxi drivers do not expect tips. Haggling over prices is not the general custom in Panama.

Taxes

A tax of 10% is added to the price of hotel rooms; when you inquire about a hotel, ask whether the quoted price includes the tax. Hotel prices given in this book include the 10% tax. A 5% sales tax is levied on nonfood products.

POST & COMMUNICATIONS
Sending Mail

Airmail to the USA takes five to 10 days and costs US$0.35 (postcards US$0.25); to Europe and Australia it takes 10 days and costs US$0.45 (postcards US$0.40). Panama has neither vending machines for stamps nor drop-off boxes for mail. You may be able to buy stamps and send mail from an upscale hotel to avoid going to the post office and standing in line.

Most post offices are open from 7 am to 6 pm weekdays and from 7 am to 4:30 pm Saturday.

Receiving Mail

General delivery mail can be addressed to '(name), Entrega General, (town and province), República de Panamá.' Be sure the sender calls the country 'República de Panamá' rather than simply 'Panamá,' or the mail may be sent back.

Telephone, Fax & Email

Panama's country code is 507. There are no local area codes.

Telephone calls to anywhere within Panama can be made from phone boxes. Local calls cost US$0.10 for the first three minutes, then US$0.05 per minute. You can buy *Telechip* phone cards in denominations of US$5, $10, and $20 from vending machines at Cable & Wireless offices. Some public phones accept both cards and coins, but many accept only cards.

PANAMA

The public phone system was in disarray at the time of writing. Vandalism had damaged many phones, and occasionally a phone could not read the phone card. Generally, though, a phone card is easier to use than coins; more phones accept the cards, and they are less vulnerable to damage.

You can connect to a local international operator by dialing ☎ 106; this works from any public, residential or business phone. To use an international calling card or to connect with an operator in the USA, dial ☎ 00-800-001-0108 (MCI), 00-800-001-0109 (ATT), or 00-800-001-0110 (Sprint). During research for this book, MCI calling cards could not be used from a public phone using their 800 number.

Many hotels will not allow you to connect directly to the 800 numbers for international calls; this allows them to charge outrageous connection and per-minute fees.

Cable & Wireless offices throughout Panama offer international telephone, telegraph, fax, and sometimes email and modem services.

The telephone directory gives information on email connections, modem rental and other specialized services.

INTERNET RESOURCES

The tourist board, IPAT, has Web sites in English (www.panamatours.com) and Spanish (www.ipat.gob.pa) with some useful links. The IPAT USA representative also operates a site (www.panamainfo.com) that is a good starting point. The University of Texas Latin American Network Information Center Web site (www.lanic.utexas .edu/la/ca/panama) includes links to newspapers, universities and other sources of information.

BOOKS

Lonely Planet's *Panama* provides additional details on the country, including more information and history for places off the beaten track. It covers the full range of prices, including hotels ranging from the US$5-a-night backpacker's dream to the US$250-a-night millionaire's lodging.

The Sack of Panamá: Sir Henry Morgan's Adventures on the Spanish Main, by Peter Earle, is a vivid account of the British pirate's looting and destruction of Panama City in 1671.

The Path Between the Seas: The Creation of the Panama Canal, by David McCullough, is a readable and exciting account of the building of the Panama Canal. It's 700 pages long and reads like a suspense novel. *The Impossible Dream: The Building of the Panama Canal*, by Ian Cameron, is also good.

On a more recent note, *Inside Panama*, by Tom Barry and John Lindsay-Poland, is a look at the political, economic and human-rights scenes in Panama, with special emphasis on Panamanian society since the 1960s and on US-Panama relations from that time through the mid-1990s.

Our Man in Panama: How General Noriega Used the United States and Made Millions in Drugs and Arms, by John Dinges; *Panama: The Whole Story*, by Kevin Buckley; *The Noriega Mess: The Drugs, the Canal, and Why America Invaded*, by Luis Murillo; and *America's Prisoner: The Memoirs of Manuel Noriega*, cowritten with Peter Eisner, provide perspectives on Noriega and the US invasion.

A People Who Would Not Kneel: Panama, the United States, and the San Blas Kuna, by James Howe, is an absorbing account of the Kuna struggles between 1900 and 1925 that led to the level of independence they still enjoy today.

Birders should look for *A Guide to the Birds of Panamá*, by Robert S Ridgley and John A Gwynne Jr, a thick, heavy and expensive (US$40) but very comprehensive volume that also includes the birds of Costa Rica, Honduras and Nicaragua.

The expensive (US$60) coffee-table book *Parques Nacionales Panamá (Panama National Parks)*, by Juan Carlos Navarro Q, features beautiful photos of the country's protected areas. It provides bilingual information on flora and fauna, and information on access; it is available in Panama City.

NEWSPAPERS & MAGAZINES

La Prensa is the most widely circulated daily newspaper in Panama and is available on the Web (www.sinfo.net/prensa). Other major Spanish-language dailies include *La Estrella de Panamá*, *El Panamá América*, *El Universal*, and *Crítica*.

The Panama News is published in English every two weeks. It is distributed free in Panama City and is also on the Web (www.thepanamanews.com). *The Visitor*, written in English and Spanish and targeting tourists, is another free publication. The *Miami Herald International Edition* is available in some upscale hotels.

English-language magazines are available at Farmacia Arrocha and Gran Morrison stores in Panama City.

RADIO & TV
Local radio and TV stations broadcast only in Spanish; the English stations left with the US military. Many hotels have cable TV with Spanish and English channels. Nearly every kind of music can be found somewhere on the radio.

WEIGHTS & MEASURES
The metric system is the official system for weights and measures, but the US system of pounds, gallons and miles is also used. This book uses the metric system.

LAUNDRY
Laundromats *(lavamáticos)* are abundant and convenient; usually you drop off your laundry, they wash and dry it for you, and you pick it up a few hours later. Cost per load is about US$1.50 to US$2.50, a little cheaper if you do your own. Dry cleaners *(lavanderías)* are also widely available but considerably more expensive.

HEALTH
Tap water is safe to drink in all areas except in the Bocas del Toro region and in the smallest, most remote towns. This means that washed raw vegetables and ice are OK, too.

Malaria is not a problem in Panama City. A malaria risk exists in the rural areas of Chiriquí, Bocas del Toro, and Veraguas Provinces; the western side of the Península de Azuero; around the Lago Bayano and Lago Gatún areas; the Comarca de Kuna Yala; and the Darién province. The areas east of the canal are the only parts of Central America where a chloroquine-resistant strain of malaria is present. If you go to these areas, you should take special precautions; see the Health section in the Regional Facts for the Visitor chapter.

You can protect yourself against the sun's rays with a hat, long sleeves and a good sunscreen lotion. Panama is between 7° and 10° from the equator, so the sun is very strong.

Be sure to drink plenty of liquids, preferably water, to avoid becoming dehydrated.

WOMEN TRAVELERS
Female travelers find Panama safe and pleasant to visit. Some Panamanian men make flirtatious comments or stare at single women, both local and foreign. Comments are rarely blatantly rude; the usual thing is a smiling *'mi amor,'* an appreciative hiss or a honk of the horn. The best way to deal with this is to do what Panamanian women do – ignore the comments and don't look at the man making them.

Panamanians are generally quite conservative in dress. Women travelers are advised to avoid skimpy or see-through clothing. And although Emberá women in the Darién go topless, it would be insulting for travelers to follow suit.

GAY & LESBIAN TRAVELERS
Other than the gay float during Carnaval in Panama City, there are few open expressions of homosexuality in Panama. Even suggesting that gays and lesbians are entitled to basic human rights is viewed as an act of treason by most heterosexuals.

Panama City offers a few gay and lesbian clubs (not openly advertised, however). Outside Panama City, gay bars are few and far between. In most instances, gays and lesbians just blend in with the straight crowd at the hipper places and avoid cantinas and other conventional lairs of homophobia. And of course, Panama's natural wonders are open to everyone.

DISABLED TRAVELERS
Panama is not wheelchair friendly; with the exception of handicapped parking spaces, wheelchair ramps outside a few upscale hotels and perhaps a few dozen oversize bathroom stalls, accommodations for people with physical disabilities do not exist in Panama. Even at the best hotels, you won't find railings in showers or beside toilets.

SENIOR TRAVELERS
Senior Panamanians are legally entitled to a wide range of discounts. However, the law does not require – and Panamanian businesses do not offer – discounts to foreign tourists on the basis of age.

PANAMA

TRAVEL WITH CHILDREN

Children pay full fare on buses if they occupy a seat, but they often ride for free if they sit on a parent's knee. Children ages two to five pay 75% of the full fare on domestic airline flights and get a seat, and infants under two pay 10% of the fare but don't get a seat. Children's car seats are not always available from Panamanian car-rental agencies, so bring one if you plan on driving with a baby or toddler.

Visitors traveling with children are still a curiosity in Panama and will meet with extra, generally friendly, attention and interest.

DANGERS & ANNOYANCES

Crime is a problem in certain parts of Panama City. The city's better districts, however, are much safer than in many other capitals: Witness the all-night restaurants and activity on the streets at night. On the other hand, it is not safe to walk around at night in the Casco Antiguo district, where some of the cheapest accommodations are found; be careful in the side streets of this district even in the daytime. In general, stay where it's well lit and there are plenty of people around.

Most of Colón is a sad slum known for street crime. If you walk around there, even in the middle of the day, well-meaning residents will inform you that you are in danger. It's probably best to avoid the city altogether.

The Madden Dam has become a danger spot, with knife-wielding gangs assaulting tourists as they get off the bus, and machete-toting thugs robbing drivers who stop at the overlook.

Parts of the Darién Province, which borders Colombia, are extremely dangerous. Not only is it easy to get hopelessly lost, but parts of the province are used by guerillas from Colombia, the paramilitary chasing the guerillas, and even plain old thieves pretending to be guerillas. Particularly treacherous is the area between Boca de Cupe and Colombia, which is the traditional path through the Darién Gap.

Boats from Colombia plying the waters of the San Blas Archipelago sometimes carry drugs and other contraband.

Most other areas of Panama are quite safe.

Police corruption is no longer a big problem in Panama, but it's not unheard of for a police officer to stop a motorist and levy a fine to be paid on the spot. Your only option may be to bargain the fine down.

EMERGENCIES

Throughout Panama, the police emergency number is ☎ 104; for fire emergencies, call ☎ 103. Telephone numbers for hospitals and ambulances are found on the first page of the national phone directory. In the blue pages of the directory, you'll find lists of service providers that appear under English headings ('attorneys,' 'physicians' etc).

LEGAL MATTERS

Newspaper reports show that Panama's court and correctional system is marred by judicial delay, violations of due process, overcrowding, cruel and degrading treatment, and inadequate food and medical attention. If you are even accused of a crime, you may wait in jail a long time before you go to trial.

Penalties for even small amounts of illegal drugs are much stricter than in the USA, Europe, Australia and most everywhere else. Conviction is certain, and sentences are measured in years.

It's important, therefore, to avoid even the *appearance* of criminal activity, by not associating with people who use illegal drugs or shoplift, for example. Embassies will offer only limited assistance and will not bail you out.

Public drinking is not tolerated. The legal drinking age is 18.

You are legally required to carry a photographic ID at all times in Panama. This should preferably be a passport with a tourist card (if applicable).

BUSINESS HOURS

Business hours are normally 8 am to noon and 1:30 to 5 pm weekdays, and 8 am to noon Saturday. Government offices are open 8 am to 4 pm weekdays and don't close for lunch. Most banks are open 8:30 am to 1 or 3 pm weekdays; some have Saturday hours as well. Shops are generally open from around 9 or 10 am until 6 or 7 pm Monday to Saturday.

PUBLIC HOLIDAYS & SPECIAL EVENTS

New Year's Day	January 1
Martyrs' Day	January 9
Carnaval	February–March
Semana Santa (Holy Week)	March–April
Labor Day	May 1
Founding of Old Panama	August 15
All Souls' Day	November 2
Independence from Colombia	November 3
First Call for Independence	November 10
Independence from Spain	November 28
Mothers' Day	December 8
Christmas Day	December 25

Carnaval, the Panamanian version of Mardi Gras, is celebrated on the four days before Ash Wednesday, the beginning of Lent. A major holiday in Panama City, it involves costumes, music, dancing, general festivities and a big parade on Shrove Tuesday. Carnaval is also celebrated on the Península de Azuero at Las Tablas, Chitré, Villa de Los Santos and Parita.

Semana Santa (Holy Week, the week before Easter) is another occasion for special events throughout the country, including the reenactment of the events surrounding the crucifixion and resurrection of Christ; on Good Friday, religious processions are held all over the country.

Founding of Old Panama is celebrated in Panama City only.

The famous Corpus Christi celebrations at Villa de Los Santos, on the Península de Azuero, take place 40 days after Easter. Masked and costumed dancers representing angels, devils, imps and other mythological figures enact dances, acrobatics and dramas.

The Península de Azuero has a number of other notable festivals; see the Península de Azuero section for details. Other popular celebrations include the Festival of the Black Christ at Portobelo on October 21; the Festival of Nuestra Señora del Carmen on Isla Taboga on July 16; and Boquete's Feria de las Flores y del Café, held for 10 days in January.

Panama's many ethnic groups each have their own cultural events; the Kuna people and the descendants of West Indians and Spanish all have their own special music and dance. If you get a chance to attend any of these occasions, don't miss it.

ACTIVITIES
Hiking

Hiking opportunities abound in Panama, although access can be a problem; trails are not marked and maps are difficult to find. In the Chiriquí highlands, the Sendero Los Quetzales is a lovely day's hike through Parque Nacional Volcán Barú that leads from Cerro Punta to Boquete. Parque Internacional La Amistad also has some fine, short trails, starting near its Cerro Punta entrance.

From Boquete, you can hike to the top of Volcán Barú, Panama's highest peak and only volcano. Other walks on narrow roads around Boquete wind up and down the slopes among coffee plantations.

The little town of El Valle, nestled into the Valle de Antón about a two-hour drive west of Panama City, is a fine place for walking. Many trails lead into the hills around the valley.

Near Panama City on the shores of the canal, Parque Nacional Soberanía contains a section of the old Sendero Las Cruces used by the Spanish to cross between the coasts, as well as an easy but interesting nature trail, the Sendero El Charco. The Parque Natural Metropolitano, on the outskirts of Panama City, also has some good walks leading to a panoramic view of the city.

The most famous walk in Panama is the trek of a week or more through the Darién Gap, where the Interamericana comes to a dead end and a jungle wilderness stands between Panama and Colombia. This dangerous walk is not recommended due to guerrilla activity along the border. Safer treks in the Darién go to and from the Pirre ranger station in the Parque Nacional Darién.

Diving & Snorkeling

Panama has numerous islands where the snorkeling and diving are good. The Bocas del Toro and San Blas Archipelagos are prime snorkeling spots on the Caribbean coast. Dive shops on Bocas del Toro rent snorkeling and diving gear, and offer PADI-certified classes. On the Pacific coast, visitors can snorkel around the Archipiélago de las Perlas, a chain of islands near Panama City.

You can often rent equipment, but avid snorkelers should bring their own. Dive shops operate in Bocas del Toro and Portobelo. Scubapanama (☎ 261 3841, fax 261 9586, renegomez@scubapanama.com), based in Panama City, offers dives throughout the country. See their Web site at www.scubapanama.com.

Surfing
The best surfing beaches in Panama are Playa Santa Catalina, Playa Teta and Playa Río Mar, all on the Pacific side near the center of the country. Playa Venado on the southern edge of the Península de Azuero is also a good isolated surfing beach.

Fishing
Panama has 1518 islands, 2988km of coast and 480 rivers that empty into the oceans, so there's no problem finding a fishing spot. Possibilities include deep-sea fishing, fishing for bass in Lago Gatún on the Panama Canal, and trout fishing in the rivers running down Volcán Barú near the towns of Boquete, Volcán, Bambito and Cerro Punta.

White-Water Rafting & Sea Kayaking
White-water rafting trips are available on the Ríos Chiriquí and Chiriquí Vieja in Chiriquí Province. Trips are also offered on rivers near Panama City.

Boats and dugout canoes are used in Darién Province and in the islands as a primary means of transportation, and you can often rent a boat and guide for a river journey.

It's possible to rent sea kayaks in Bocas del Toro and a few other places. Mountain Travel-Sobek offers kayaking trips through San Blas, and the Nantahala Outdoor Center offers kayaking among the Bocas del Toro islands (see Organized Tours in the Getting There & Away section).

Bird Watching
Go birding in Panama, and you'll see more variety than anywhere else in Central America. All told, more than 940 species of bird – native, migratory and endemic – have been identified here. This diversity of species is due to a couple of factors: Panama's location relative to two continents and its narrow girth. Birds migrating between North and South America tend to be funneled into a small area.

The famous resplendent quetzal, symbol of Central America, is most abundant in western Panama. It can be seen around Volcán Barú, where it is common much of the year. Other birds of particular interest include the three-wattled bellbird, the harpy eagle, the brown pelican, the great green macaw and the king vulture.

To see birds in Panama, just get a good set of binoculars and get out on a trail. The Camino del Oleoducto (Pipeline Rd) trail near Panama City is a favorite with birders; more than 500 species were sighted there in a single day during a Christmas bird count. Most birds are seen around dawn, so avid birders should plan to arrive just before daylight.

LANGUAGE COURSES
Panama offers only two intensive Spanish-language programs: one in Panama City and the other in Bocas del Toro. See those sections for details.

WORK
It's difficult for foreigners to find work in Panama. The government doesn't want them to take jobs away from Panamanians, and the labor laws reflect that sentiment. Basically, the only foreigners legally employed in Panama work for their own businesses, possess skills not found in Panama or work for companies that have special agreements with the Panamanian government.

Small boats transiting the Panama Canal sometimes take on backpackers as deck-hands (line handlers) in exchange for free passage, room and food. Inquiries can be made at the Panama Canal Yacht Club in Colón; some boat owners post notices in pensions. The official rate for line handling is US$55 per day, but anyone who pays this fee hires experienced locals. Competing with the locals for this work could get you and the boat captain in trouble.

Restaurants that hire foreign staff are often shut down for immigration violations.

ACCOMMODATIONS

Prices cited in this book for accommodations are year 2000 high-season rates, and they include Panama's 10% tax on hotel rooms.

There is usually no shortage of places to stay in Panama, except during holidays or special events outside Panama City, when advance reservations may be necessary.

Budget lodgings typically range from US$5 per person to US$20 for a double room. Hotels in the 'mid-range' category usually charge about US$20 to US$40 for a double room.

There are only a few places with dormitory-style living (hostels). Camping facilities are available in some national parks but in only a few of the towns. B&Bs are starting to be introduced.

FOOD

In keeping with its international and ethnic character, Panama offers a variety of food, from *comida típica* served in small traditional restaurants to the finest international cuisine.

Panama's national dish is *sancocho,* a spicy chicken and vegetable stew. *Ropa vieja* (old clothes), a spicy shredded beef combination served over rice, is another common and tasty dish.

Other typical Panamanian dishes include:

carimañola – a roll made from ground and boiled yucca filled with chopped meat and boiled egg and then deep-fried

empanadas – corn turnovers filled with ground meat and fried

patacones – fried green plantains cut crossways in thin pieces, covered in salt and then pressed and fried

plátano maduro – also called *plátanos ententación*; ripe plantain cut in slices lengthwise and baked or broiled with butter, brown sugar and cinnamon; served hot

tajadas – ripe plantain sliced lengthwise and fried

tamales – made from boiled ground corn with spices, filled with chicken or pork, wrapped in banana leaves and boiled

tasajo – dried meat, cooked with vegetables

tortilla de maíz   thick cornmeal tortilla, fried

Seafood is excellent and abundant in Panama. Often the seafood is mixed with coconut sauce; coconut rice and coconut bread are other Caribbean treats.

In Panama City, men pushing carts sell *raspadas,* cones of shaved ice topped with fruit syrup and sweetened condensed milk. This is no world-class gourmet dish, but on these hot streets it tastes like heaven.

DRINKS

Fresh fruit drinks, sweetened and mixed with water, are called *chichas* and are the most common cold drinks in Panama. *Batidos* are fruit shakes made with milk or water. (There is no need to worry about the water here.) Soft drinks are called *sodas,* and all the usual brands are available.

Beer and rum are made in Panama. The national alcoholic drink is made of *seco,* milk and ice. Seco, like rum, is distilled from sugarcane, but it doesn't taste anything like the rum you know. This is the drink of campesinos.

ENTERTAINMENT

Panama City has the best selection of entertainment in Central America. On a typical weekend night, visitors have the options of hearing live jazz, rock, salsa or Panamanian music; seeing the newest Hollywood movies in English at any of a number of cinemas; dancing at classy, high-tech dance clubs; drinking in fancy bars, neighborhood pubs or traditional cantinas; gambling at casinos; or shooting pool.

The number of entertainment options drops off dramatically outside the capital city, although it's odd to come across a community that doesn't have at least one watering hole at which to pass the time with some friendly people.

SPECTATOR SPORTS

Panamanians are enthusiastic sports fans. As in all of Latin America, soccer is a favorite; in Panama baseball, softball and basketball are also all the rage. Boxing is another popular spectator sport; it has been a source of pride to Panamanians (and to Latin Americans in general) ever since Roberto Durán, a Panama City native and boxing legend, won the world championship lightweight title in 1972. He went on to become the world champion in the welterweight (1980), light middleweight (1983) and super middleweight (1989) categories.

PANAMA

SHOPPING

A remarkable variety of imported goods, including cameras, electronic equipment and clothing, is sold in Panama, mostly in Panama City. Panama City's Avenida Central is a mecca for bargain hunters.

The favorite handicraft souvenir from Panama is the *mola,* a colorful, intricate, multilayered appliqué textile sewn by Kuna women from the Archipiélago de San Blas. Small, simple souvenir molas can be bought for as little as US$5, but the best ones are sold on the islands and can fetch several hundred dollars.

Other handicrafts include replicas of *huacas* (golden objects from before the Spanish conquest), wood carvings (from the cocobolo tree, made by the Wounaan and Emberá), tagua carvings (from the egg-sized tagua nut, also made by the Wounaan and Emberá), baskets (Wounaan and Emberá), masks, ceramics and clothing (including the pollera).

Places to buy handicrafts are mentioned in the Panama City, El Valle and Península de Azuero sections.

Getting There & Away

Panama's geographic location between two large continents and two great oceans makes it a true crossroads of the world. Each year more than 300 cruise ships transit the Panama Canal. Major airlines serve Panama on a regular basis. Overland travelers are entering the country in increasing numbers, and international tour operators have begun offering Panamanian tours.

AIR

Panama has international airports in Panama City and David. Airlines have flights connecting Panama with all the other Central American countries, South America, North America and the Caribbean, and you can usually arrange a ticket with one or more free stopovers.

The main air connection points in North America for flights to and from Panama, with ballpark airfares as of summer 2000, are Miami (US$350); Houston (US$650); Newark, New Jersey ($600); New York (US$450); Washington, DC (US$600); Dallas (US$600); Los Angeles (US$500); and Atlanta (US$600). Fares may change seasonally.

Sample fares from across the oceans include US$1200 from London, US$850 from Frankfurt; and US$1750 from Sydney or Melbourne.

Panama City has dozens of travel agents, including one specializing in student travel (see Panama City).

COPA is Panama's national airline. The following are phone numbers in Panama for international airlines serving Panama:

American Airlines	☎ 269 6022
Continental Airlines	☎ 263 9177
COPA	☎ 227 5000
Delta Air Lines	☎ 263 3802
EVA Air	☎ 263 7589
Mexicana	☎ 264 9855
Grupo TACA	☎ 265 7814

See the regional chapters for toll-free numbers in the USA.

Grupo TACA flies from San José, Costa Rica, to Panama City for about US$300 roundtrip and to David for US$175. Roundtrip airfare on COPA from Panama City to Bogotá is about US$270.

There's a US$20 departure tax at the airport, payable in cash only.

LAND

If you plan to enter Panama overland, it's a good idea to get a visa or tourist card before showing up at the border; border posts occasionally run out of tourist cards. If a post is out of tourist cards, you can't get in (with the exception of Guabito). You may need to show an onward ticket, although this is not usually requested, and sometimes a show of cash is also required to cross land borders (US$500 per month of your planned stay is generally sufficient; traveler's checks should qualify toward the total amount).

The cheapest way to satisfy an onward ticket requirement is to buy a Tracopa bus ticket from David to San José, Costa Rica; alternatively you could buy a ticket from Panama City to San José with Tica Bus or Panaline. Of course if you plan to fly out of the country, an airline ticket will fit the bill, too.

Border Crossings

The main border crossings from Panama are to Costa Rica and Colombia. Colombia, however, is much more difficult to reach, because of the Darién Gap.

Costa Rica

There are three border crossings between Panama and Costa Rica. Paso Canoas on the Interamericana is the most frequently used entry and exit point. It's open 24 hours a day. IPAT has an office here, where you can get a tourist card during office hours (8:30 am to 4:30 pm).

The Río Sereno border crossing is rather remote and not as busy. It's open 7 am to 5 pm. Officials here are sticklers for formalities (passport, visa or tourist card if applicable, onward ticket and show of cash).

The northernmost crossing at Guabito (Sixaola on the Costa Rican side) is the closest to Bocas del Toro; it's an interesting option for overland travelers, and is open 8 am to 6 pm. Tourist cards are not available here. In lieu of a tourist card, you can go to the Banco Nacional de Panamá, near the airport in Changuinola and, for US$10, obtain a stamp, which you should then take to Changuinola's immigration office. The office will put the stamp in your passport along with an official signature; this will serve as your tourist card.

If you have overstayed your 30 or 60 days, you will need a *paz y salvo* and permission to leave. These cannot be obtained at the border. For details, see the Visas & Documents section earlier.

Bus At all three of these border crossings, you can take local buses up to the border on either side, cross and board the next country's local bus.

Two companies, Panaline and Tica Bus, also operate daily direct buses between San José and Panama City. Both recommend that you make reservations a few days in advance to ensure getting a seat.

At the time of writing, Panaline buses (☎ 227 8648, fax 227 8647) arrived and departed from Panama City at the Gran Hotel Soloy on the corner of Avenida Perú and Calle 30 Este, but they may depart from the new Terminal Nacional de Transporte by the time you read this. They depart every day at 12:30 pm, arriving in San José the following

morning around 4 or 5 am. These are good buses, equipped with air-con, bathroom and video; riders get free sodas, and students receive a 10% discount with ISIC card. The cost is US$25 one-way.

Tica Bus (☎ 262 2084, fax 262 6275) arrived and departed from Panama City at the Hotel Ideal, Calle 17 Oeste, a block west of Avenida Central, at the time of writing, but may now depart from the Terminal Nacional de Transporte. These buses depart every day at 11 am, arriving in San José the following morning around 4 or 5 am. The cost is US$25.10 one way. You must bring your passport when you reserve your ticket. Tica Bus also has buses continuing up through Central America as far as Guatemala; see the regional Getting Around chapter for additional bus information.

Direct international buses also operate between San José, Costa Rica and Changuinola, and between San José to David. See the Changuinola and David sections for details.

Colombia

The Carretera Interamericana (Interamerican Hwy) stops at the town of Yaviza. It reappears 150km farther on, far beyond the Colombian border. This break in the highway between Central and South America is known as the Darién Gap, where untamed jungles are a major obstacle to travel. Although a trickle of travelers have walked through this gap, the presence of Colombian guerillas, paramilitary, smugglers and bandits make this a foolishly dangerous trip.

The border can also be crossed at a rugged point on the Caribbean coast between rustic Puerto Obaldía (on the Panamanian side) and the resort of Capurganá (on the Colombian side). You can walk or boat between these two points. Walking to the first Colombian village, Sapzurro, takes about 2½ hours, but the track is indistinct in places, and the presence of bandits and smugglers in the area makes boating the better option. From Sapzurro, it's a two-hour walk to Capurganá. Be sure to obtain the entry procedures from the Colombian embassy or consulate in your home country.

SEA

Every year, some 300 cruise ships transit the Panama Canal. The vast majority do not offer shore excursions. Some ships make stops in the San Blas Archipelago, and some have just begun docking near Colón, offering tours of Caribbean sites. The tourism industry is working hard on increasing facilities for cruise ships and their hundreds of passengers. This is good news if you're a cruise ship passenger, perhaps less welcome news if you're not.

Merchant boats ply the Caribbean from Colón to San Blas and on to Colombia. This is a very unofficial (and potentially risky) way to go, but it can be done. See the Comarca de Kuna Yala section for more.

Some private yachts offer trips, usually at a cost, but sometimes in exchange for serving on the crew or line handling through the canal. Notices are often posted at the Panama Canal Yacht Club in Colón or in pensions such as the Voyager International Hostel in Panama City. Besides possible risks associated with boat safety and smuggling activity, a certain amount of schedule flexibility is necessary. One traveler we heard about paid for a trip from Colón to Colombia. After a couple of days, the captain decided to lay over near Portobelo to wait for more passengers, leaving the clients who had already paid stranded for a while.

ORGANIZED TOURS

Because of Panama's relatively young tourist infrastructure, many people have the impression that they can visit Panama only as part of a tour group. With perhaps the exception of the Darién Province, this simply isn't true. Panama has an excellent road system (even if the drivers are aggressive), and travelers can get just about anywhere they want by bus (except the San Blas Archipelago).

There are enough companies in Panama City to serve your specific goals without needing to commit yourself to a two-week tour booked outside the country. Many tour agencies outside Panama subcontract the actual field work to Ancon Expeditions anyway. Tour companies based in Panama City are covered in Organized Tours in the Getting Around section.

A few companies based in the US have unique offerings. Mountain Travel-Sobek (☎ 510-527 8100, 888-687 6235, info@ mtsobek.com) offers 'Kayaking with the Kuna Indians: Paddling the San Blas Islands

in Panama.' Costs for the guided 15-day adventure range from US$2200 to US$2700 per person, not including airfare.
Web site: www.mtsobek.com

Nantahala Outdoor Center (☎ 828-488 2175, programs@noc.com) offers nine-day intermediate and advanced kayak trips on the rivers in the Chiriquí Province in conjunction with Chiriquí River Rafting, based in Boquete. Costs are US$1275 to US$1350 per person. They also offer eight-day kayaking tours of Bocas del Toro for US$1525 to US$1575 per person.
Web site: www.noc.com

Getting Around

AIR

Panama is served by a good network of domestic flights on several domestic airlines. All domestic flights from Panama City depart from Aeropuerto Marcos A. Gelabert, in the former Albrook Air Force Station near the canal, on the opposite side of the city from the international airport. It is commonly referred to simply as Albrook airport.

One-way prices are given here; double these for roundtrip. The following table lists flights on the largest domestic carrier, Aeroperlas (☎ 315 7500 in Panama City, fax 315 7580, iflyap@aeroperlas.com).
Web site: www.aeroperlas.com

destination	frequency	fare (one-way)
Bahía Piña	three weekly	US$43
Bocas del Toro town	daily	US$50
Changuinola	daily	US$53
Chitré	daily	US$32
Colón	weekdays only	US$36
David	daily	US$57
El Real	four times weekly	US$39
Garachiné	twice weekly	US$36
Isla Contadora	daily	US$26
Jaqué	three weekly	US$43
La Palma	daily except Sunday	US$36
Sambú	three weekly	US$36
Santiago	daily	US$34

Other Aeroperlas routes include David to Changuinola or Bocas del Toro, three times daily, for US$25, and Bocas del Toro to Changuinola, daily, for US$11.

Aerotaxi (☎ 264 8644), Ansa (☎ 226 6881) and Aviatur (☎ 315 0311) fly between Panama City and the San Blas Archipelago, serving 20 destinations, from El Porvenir (nearest Panama City) to Puerto Obaldía (nearest Colombia), with daily early morning flights to El Porvenir and flights three times weekly all the way to Puerto Obaldía. One-way fares are US$30 to El Porvenir, US$47 to Puerto Obaldía. Fares to other islands fall somewhere in between. An airplane flying from Panama City to the district may stop at several islands before reaching your destination; be sure to ask the name of the island you're on before leaving the plane.

BUS

A good bus system serves all the accessible parts of the country. Intercity fares are typically within the US$2 to US$5 range, except for long-distance routes, which run from US$9 to US$15.

CAR & MOTORCYCLE

Road rules are generally the same as in the USA. Conditions are good on major highways. More remote areas are served by dirt roads. Driving in Panama City, however, is a shortcut to insanity: Locals obdurately resist road signs; few traffic lights exist; and buses are called *diablos rojos* (red devils) for good reason. The lack of adequate street signs ensures that you will get lost; the numerous one-way streets (sometimes unmarked) will confuse you; and the local habit of using the horn at every opportunity may leave you feeling flummoxed. This aggressive driving makes motorcycling an even worse idea.

Rental

Due to the low cost and availability of buses and taxis, it really isn't necessary to rent a vehicle in Panama unless you intend to go to places far off the beaten track. You can rent cars in Panama City, Colón, David and Changuinola. See the Panama City and David sections for rental companies' contact information in those cities.

Car rental in Panama is not cheap. Expect to pay US$45 per day for a car or US$100 per day for a 4WD vehicle; in Panama such a vehicle is called a '4 by 4' or a *'cuatro por cuatro.'* Rates include insur-ance and unlimited mileage *(kilometraje)*. With an American Express card, you can decline about US$10 worth of insurance per day, but the third-person liability coverage is mandatory. From October to April – the high tourist season for rental-car companies – discounts are often available, as the agencies are competing for your business.

Some companies will let you rent in one city and drop the car off in another for an extra fee. The drop-off charge between David and Panama City is typically US$85.

To rent a vehicle in Panama, you must be 25 or older and present a passport and driver's license; if you rent the vehicle using an American Express card, you need be only 23. Carefully inspect the car for minor dents and scratches, missing radio antennae or hubcaps and anything else that makes it look less than brand-new. These damages *must* be noted on your rental agreement; otherwise you may be charged for them when you return the car.

Taking Your Own Vehicle

There's a great deal of paperwork involved in bringing a car into the country. If you plan on driving down to Panama from points north, you will need all the usual insurance and ownership papers. If you are bringing a vehicle into the country, you must pay US$4 for a vehicle control certificate *(tarjeta de circulación)* and to have your vehicle fumigated. You and your vehicle can stay in the country for up to 90 days.

Remember that if you want to take a vehicle between Central and South America, you will have to ship it around the Darién Gap, as the Interamericana stops short of the Colombian border.

BICYCLE

You can bicycle through Panama easily enough, but using a bicycle to travel within larger Panamanian cities – particularly Panama City – is not wise. The roads tend to be narrow; there are no bike lanes; bus drivers and motorists drive aggressively; and it rains a lot, reducing motorists' visibility and your tires' ability to grip the road.

Outside the cities, roads tend to be in fine shape, although parts of the Interamericana are narrow, leaving little room to move aside should a car pass by. Lodging is rarely more than a day's bike ride away.

In Panama City bicycles are available for sale; see the Panama City section. A few tourist places throughout the country rent bikes on an hourly basis, including at the causeway in Panama City, Playa Santa Clara, El Valle, Bocas del Toro and Cerro Punta.

HITCHHIKING

Hitchhiking is not as widespread in Panama as elsewhere in the region; most people travel by bus, and foreigners would do best to follow suit.

BOAT

Boats are the principal means of transportation in several parts of Panama, particularly in Darién Province, the Comarca de Kuna Yala and the Bocas del Toro islands. You can almost always rent a boat and guide in those areas. You should negotiate fees first, and in the Darién, you may need to pay for gas separately.

Colombian and Kuna merchant boats carry cargo and passengers all along the San Blas coast between Colón and Puerto Obaldía, stopping at up to 48 of the islands to load and unload passengers and cargo. Occasionally these boats are used to traffic narcotics. Travel by these often dangerously overloaded boats is neither comfortable nor safe. Hiring a local boatman is a safer option. See the Comarca de Kuna Yala section and the Panama Getting There & Away section for further details.

Bocas del Toro town is accessible from Almirante by speedy water taxis.

LOCAL TRANSPORTATION

All of Panama's cities and towns are served by cheap local buses; a ride usually costs around US$0.15.

Taxis are usually reasonably priced; a ride within city limits might cost around US$1 to US$2. Taxis in Panama are not metered; always agree on a price for the ride before you get into the cab.

ORGANIZED TOURS

Tour agencies in Panama City offer many kinds of tours, ranging from local city tours to ecological excursions into remote regions of the country. While tours are not cheap, they can be the easiest way to explore many of Panama's natural wonders.

Travelers who don't speak an iota of Spanish may find that an arranged tour is necessary to get started. Others like tours simply for the convenience of having everything prearranged. Tours are also useful for getting you to places you could not get to otherwise (parts of the Darién, Barro Colorado Island, Isla de Coiba, some islands of the Bocas del Toro Archipelago), for seeing and learning about wildlife (for example, bird-watching tours), for undertaking an activity you cannot do on your own (diving, cruising the canal, deep-sea fishing) or learning more about the local culture.

Tourism in Panama is still relatively young, and the quality varies. Some companies have problems with picking people up on time. Tours are often priced depending on the number of passengers; unless you have a group of at least four, you may need to inform the company of your interests and cost constraints then wait for additional people to sign up. Because there are relatively few tourists in the country, you can't always expect just to show up and get on a 10-person tour.

Ancon Expeditions (☎ 269 9415, fax 264 3713, econopanama@sinfo.net) is on Calle 49 A Este in Panama City. Created by Panama's top conservation organization, Ancon Expeditions employs some of the country's finest nature guides. Tour agencies in the USA often subcontract to this company. Unique trips include forays into the Darién jungle and overnights at Ancon lodges.
Web site: www.anconexpeditions.com

Iguana Tours (☎ 226 8738, fax 226 4736, iguana@sinfo.net), on Avenida Belisario Porras opposite Parque Omar in Panama City, offers a number of competitive tours. These include a tour to Isla Iguana off the coast of the Península de Azuero and rafting, fishing and scuba trips.
Web site: www.nvmundo.com/iguanatours

Pesantez Tours (☎ 263 7577, fax 263 7860, pesantez@pop.net), on Avenida 6 Sur near the Centro Medico Paitilla in Panama City, is a more traditional operator with many years of experience. The company offers the greatest number and variety of one-day tours in the Panama City area.
Web site: www.pesantez-tours.com

Scubapanama (☎ 261 3841, fax 261 9586, renegomez@scubapanama.com), located in

El Carmen area of Panama City, is the country's oldest and most respected dive operator, and offers dives throughout the country.

Web site: www.scubapanama.com

The Panama Audubon Society (see Ecology and Environment, earlier) has frequent birding trips that are considerably less expensive than a tour through a traditional tour company.

Chiriquí River Rafting leads rafting tours in the Chiriquí highlands. See the Boquete section for details.

See the Panama City and Panama Canal sections for information on tours in those areas.

It is also possible to hire individual guides in various tourist areas.

Panama City

pop 700,000

The capital of Panama is a modern, thriving center for international banking, business, trade and transportation, with a cosmopolitan flair.

History

Panama City was founded on the site of an Indian fishing village by the Spanish governor Pedro Arias de Ávila (Pedrarias) in 1519, not long after Balboa first saw the Pacific.

The Spanish settlement quickly became an important center of government and church authority. It was from here that gold and other plunder from the Pacific Spanish colonies were taken along El Camino Real and the Sendero Las Cruces across the isthmus to the Caribbean.

This treasure made Panama City the target of many attacks over the years. In 1671, the city was ransacked and destroyed by the English pirate Henry Morgan, leaving only the stone ruins of Panamá La Vieja.

Three years later, the city was reestablished about 8km to the southwest in the area now known as Casco Antiguo (ancient compound). The Spanish believed that the new site, on a small peninsula, would be easier to defend. The sea lapped the city on three sides; a moat was constructed on the land side and a massive stone wall ran around the whole city. It was never successfully attacked again.

The overland trade route, however, was attacked repeatedly, and the principal Caribbean port at Portobelo was destroyed. In 1746, the Spanish stopped using the route altogether; Panama City subsequently declined in importance. Panama returned to prominence when the Panama Railroad was completed and gold rushers on their way to California flooded across the isthmus by train.

Panama declared its independence from Colombia on November 3, 1903 in Panama City's Parque de la Independencia; the city became the capital of the new nation. Since the Panama Canal was completed in 1914, the city has grown as a center for international business and trade.

Orientation

Panama City stretches about 10km along the Pacific coast, from the Panama Canal at its western end to the ruins of Panamá La Vieja to the east.

Near the canal are Albrook airport, the Fort Amador causeway and the wealthy Balboa and Ancón suburbs built for the US canal and military workers. The Puente de las Américas (Bridge of the Americas) arches gracefully over the canal.

The colonial part of the city, Casco Antiguo (also called San Felipe and Casco Viejo), juts into the sea on the southwestern side of town. From here, two major roads head east through the city. The main drag is Avenida Central, which runs past the cathedral in Casco Antiguo to Parque Santa Ana and Plaza Cinco de Mayo; between these two plazas, the avenue is a pedestrian-only shopping street. At a fork farther east, the avenue becomes Avenida Central España; the section that traverses El Cangrejo business and financial district is called Vía España. In El Cangrejo, the white French-Gothic style **Iglesia del Carmen**, on the corner of Vía España and Avenida Federico Boyd, is one of the city's most distinctive buildings. The other part of the fork becomes Avenida 1 Norte (José D Espinar), Avenida Simón Bolívar and finally Vía Transístmica as it heads out of town and across the isthmus toward Colón.

Avenida 6 Sur branches off Avenida Central not far out of Casco Antiguo and

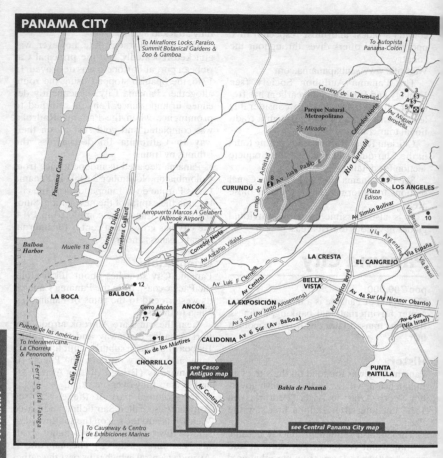

PANAMA CITY

To Miraflores Locks, Paraíso,
Summit Botanical Gardens &
Zoo & Gamboa

To Autopista
Panama-Colón

Camino de la Amistad

Parque Natural
Metropolitano

Mirador

Av Miguel
Brostella

Río Curundú

Corredor Norte

Camino de la Amistad

Av Juan Pablo II

CURUNDÚ

Plaza
Edison

LOS ANGELES

Av Simón Bolívar

Vía Brasil

Aeropuerto Marcos A Gelabert
(Albrook Airport)

Carretera Diablo

Carretera Gaillard

Panama Canal

Balboa
Harbor

Muelle 18

Corredor Norte

Av Ascanio Villalaz

Vía Argentina

Vía España

Av Luis F Clement

Av Central

LA CRESTA

EL CANGREJO

Vía Brasil

LA BOCA

BALBOA

Cerro Ancón

ANCÓN

BELLA
VISTA

Av Federico Boyd

Av 4a Sur (Av Nicanor Obarrio)

LA EXPOSICIÓN

Av 3 Sur (Av Justo Arosemena)

Av 6 Sur
(Vía Israel)

Puente de las Américas

To Interamericana;
La Chorrera
& Penonomé

Av de los Mártires

CALIDONIA

Av 6 Sur (Av Balboa)

Ferry to Isla Taboga

Calle Amador

CHORRILLO

see Casco
Antiguo map

Av Central

PUNTA
PAITILLA

Bahía de Panamá

see Central Panama City map

To Causeway & Centro
de Exhibiciones Marinas

undergoes several name changes. It is called Avenida Balboa as it curves around the edge of the bay to Punta Paitilla, on the bay's eastern point opposite Casco Antiguo; it then continues under various names past the Centro Atlapa to the ruins of Panamá La Vieja.

All three main roads are served by frequent buses.

The Corredor Norte is a toll expressway that loops over the northern side of the city from the Albrook domestic airport, through the Parque Natural Metropolitano, and to the Autopista Panama-Colón. The Corredor Sur is a southern toll expressway, running from Punta Paitilla, over Panama Bay, and to Tocumen International Airport.

Maps The Instituto Panameño de Turismo (IPAT) distributes a useful color map with the country on one side and Panama City on the other.

Various free tourist publications also have maps.

Information
Tourist Offices IPAT has its headquarters at the Centro Atlapa (☎ 226 7000, fax 226 3483, infotur@ns.ipat.gob.pa) on Vía Israel, open 8:30 am to 4:30 pm weekdays. The entrance is at the rear of the large building. There are also IPAT counters at Tocumen International Airport, Albrook airport, Panamá La Vieja and the pedestrian mall north of Casco Antiguo near Avenida Balboa.

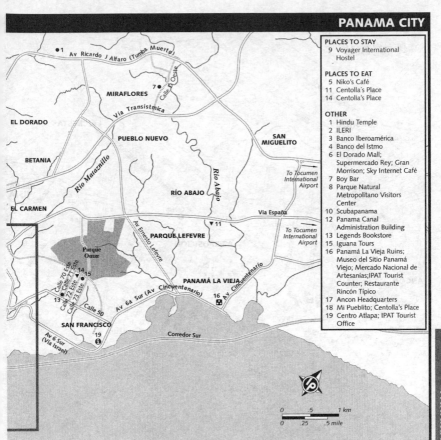

PANAMA CITY

PLACES TO STAY
9 Voyager International
   Hostel

PLACES TO EAT
5 Niko's Café
11 Centolla's Place
14 Centolla's Place

OTHER
1 Hindu Temple
2 ILERI
3 Banco Iberoamérica
4 Banco del Istmo
5 El Dorado Mall;
   Supermercado Rey; Gran
   Morrison; Sky Internet Café
7 Boy Bar
8 Parque Natural
   Metropolitano Visitors
   Center
10 Scubapanama
12 Panama Canal
   Administration Building
13 Legends Bookstore
15 Iguana Tours
16 Panamá La Vieja Ruins;
   Museo del Sitio Panamá
   Viejo; Mercado Nacional de
   Artesanías; IPAT Tourist
   Counter; Restaurante
   Rincón Típico
17 Ancon Headquarters
18 Mi Pueblito; Centolla's Place
19 Centro Atlapa; IPAT Tourist
   Office

PANAMA

All the IPAT offices give out free maps and, occasionally, information on things to see and do. The usefulness of a given office depends on the individual employees. The Atlapa headquarters does not necessarily have more information than the counters. During research for this book, the tiny information kiosk in the pedestrian mall was the most helpful and pleasant. Generally, more specific questions will yield more useful information. Few IPAT employees speak English.

The Autoridad Nacional del Ambiente (ANAM) operates an information center in Albrook, Building 804 (☎ 315 0855). ANAM also has several offices in Panama City, including in the Albrook area and near the old Terminal de Buses al Interior.

However, they are not organized to provide much assistance to tourists.

Money The only bank in Panama City that exchanges foreign currency is the Banco Nacional de Panamá counter at Tocumen International Airport. Panacambios (☎ 223 1800), on the ground floor of the Plaza Regency Building opposite Supermercado Rey in El Cangrejo, buys and sells international currencies.

Receiving cash advances against a credit card can be a headache, since some banks (eg, Citicorp) only honor their own cards. However, 24-hour ATMs are easy to find.

Post & Communications There's a post office on Vía España, in the Plaza Concordia

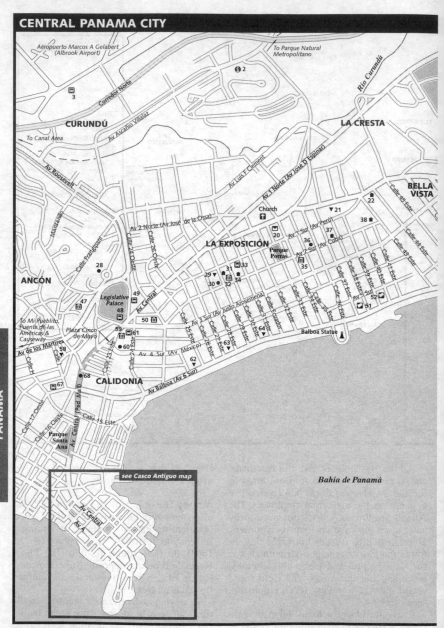

CENTRAL PANAMA CITY

PANAMA

Aeropuerto Marcos A Gelabert
(Albrook Airport)

To Parque Natural
Metropolitano

Río Curundú

CURUNDÚ

LA CRESTA

To Canal Area

Av Ascanio Villalaz

Av Roosevelt

Av Luis F Clement

Av 1 Norte (Av José D Espinar)

BELLA
VISTA

Church

22

Av 2 Norte (Av José de la Ossa)

LA EXPOSICIÓN

Parque
Porras

ANCÓN

Legislative
Palace

Balboa Statue

To Mi Pueblito,
Puente de las
Américas &
Causeway

Plaza Cinco
de Mayo

Av de los Mártires

CALIDONIA

Av Balboa (Av 6 Sur)

Parque
Santa
Ana

see Casco Antiguo map

Bahía de Panamá

Av Central

Av A

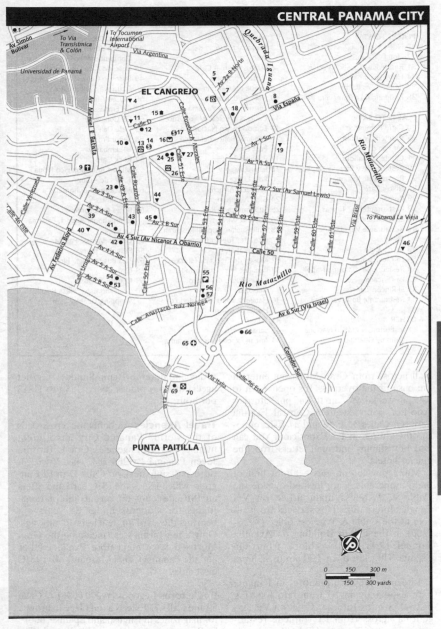

CENTRAL PANAMA CITY

CENTRAL PANAMA CITY

PLACES TO STAY
15 Hotel Marbella
22 Hotel California
31 Residencial Turístico Volcán
34 Hotel Lisboa
37 Pensión Las Palmeras
38 Residencial La Primavera

PLACES TO EAT
4 Caffè Pomodoro
5 Cafetería Manolo
7 Mr Pan
11 Cafetería Manolo
19 Restaurante y Pizzeria Napoli
21 Restaurante Vistamar
27 Niko's Café
29 Romanaccio's
39 Restaurante-Bar Tinajas
40 La Mexicanita
44 Restaurante Vegetariano
   Mireya
46 Niko's Café
56 La Mexicanita
58 Restaurante y Pizzeria Napoli
62 La Cascada
63 El Rincón Tableño
64 Restaurante Boulevard Balboa

OTHER
1 Instituto Geográfico Nacional
   (Tommy Guardia)

2 ANAM
3 Terminal Nacional de
   Transporte
6 Stratos Internet Café
8 Carretero Sports
9 Iglesia del Carmen
10 Flory Saltzman Molas
12 Turismo Joven Panamá
13 Cable & Wireless Main Office
14 Edificio Banco Nacional de
   Panamá; Banco del Istmo
16 Post Office
17 Panacambios
18 Libería Argosy
20 Post Office
23 Farmacia Arrocha
24 Gran Morrison
25 Supermercado Rey
26 Cable & Wireless
28 Smithsonian Tropical Research
   Institute; Tupper Center
30 Immigration Office
32 Museo de Ciencias Naturales
33 Panaline Buses to Costa Rica
35 Casa-Museo del Banco
   Nacional
36 Hatillo Building (Ministerio de
   Hacienda y Tesoro)
41 Tabou
42 Sahara
43 Ancon Expeditions of Panama

45 El Pavo Real
47 Museo de Arte
   Contemporáneo
48 Buses to Albrook Airport
49 Buses to Canal Zone,
   Causeway, Balboa Area
50 Museo Afro-Antilleano
51 US Embassy
52 US Consulate
53 Café Dalí
54 Señor Frogs
55 UK Embassy
57 Rock Café
59 Museo Antropológico Reina
   Torres de Araúz
60 Mercado de Buhonerías y
   Artesanías
61 Buses to Tocumen
   International Airport, Panamá
   La Vieja
65 Centro Medico Paitilla
66 Pesantez Tours
67 Tica Bus to Costa Rica
68 IPAT
69 Carretero Sports
70 Gran Morrison; Plaza Paitilla
   Shopping Center

mall across from Gran Morrison; enter at the base of the overpass. It's open 7 am to 5:45 pm weekdays, 7 am to 4:45 pm Saturday. Another is on Avenida Central España between Calles 33 Este and 34 Este, opposite the church in La Exposición. You can also buy stamps and mail letters from the fancier hotels.

Many pay telephones – about half of them inoperable – are located outside the Cable & Wireless main office on Vía España. International fax services are available at the Cable & Wireless office (☎ 264 6200) in the Dilido Building on Avenida Samuel Lewis, half a block from Vía España. They are open 7:30 am to 9:30 pm daily.

Internet cafes are plentiful in Panama City, especially in El Cangrejo banking district. Stratos Internet Café, on Vía Argentina across from El Trapiche restaurant, is open 10 am to 10 pm Tuesday to Saturday and 2 to 10 pm Sunday. The Sky Internet Café, located in El Dorado Mall, is open 9:30 am to 10 pm Monday to Sat-

urday and noon to 10 pm Sunday. Internet access at both places costs US$2 to US$3 per hour.

Travel Agencies As befits the 'crossroads of the world,' Panama City has a great number of travel agencies. One is Turismo Joven Panamá (☎ 264 2842, fax 264 0371, turjovpa@sinfo.net), on Calle D in El Cangrejo, which issues the ISIC card and offers an ISIC discount on certain international flights for students under 25 years old bearing the card or teachers of any age. Only a few businesses (including the Gran Morrison department store, Panaline buses and the Panama Canal Museum) offer ISIC discounts.

Bookstores Legends (☎ 270 0096), at Calle 50 and Calle 71 Este, is a fun place to browse for magazines in English and Spanish, books by Panamanian authors, art books and CDs. It has a few books in English.

The bookstore (☎ 212 8000) at the Tupper Center of the Smithsonian Tropical

Research Institute (STRI), near Avenida de los Mártires opposite the Legislative Palace in the Ancón district, has a nice selection of nature and environmental books. It also has books on research done by STRI and even a good selection of tagua nut carvings. It's open 10 am to 4:30 pm weekdays.

Gran Morrison department stores around the city carry a selection of books, magazines and postcards in English and Spanish, including Lonely Planet's *Panama*. Farmacia Arrocha, also with several smaller branches around the city, carries a smaller selection of magazines in English. Librería Argosy (☎ 223 5344), on Vía Argentina, is an expensive alternative for English and French books.

Libraries The Earl S Tupper Tropical Sciences Library (☎ 212 8113), at STRI's center in Ancón, is a world-class resource for information on tropical biology and conservation. It is open Monday to Saturday. The center also presents technical seminars in English every Tuesday at noon.

Universities Panama has three primary universities: the Universidad de Panamá, the Technological University and the Universidad Santa María la Antigua. Links to their Web pages can be found at www.lanic.utexas.edu/la/ca/panama.

Toilets Panama City does not have any public toilets. Neatly dressed tourists can usually use rest rooms in hotels and fast-food restaurants.

Medical Services Medicine in Panama, especially in Panama City, is of a high standard. Centro Medico Paitilla (☎ 263 6060), at Calle 53 Este and Avenida Balboa, has many well-trained physicians who speak English and Spanish.

Emergency Emergency phone numbers in Panama City are:

Police	☎ 104
Fire	☎ 103
Ambulance	☎ 228 2187

Dangers & Annoyances Casco Antiguo is a very interesting place, but it can be dangerous, especially at night. Stay where it's well lit and there are plenty of people around, and take taxis at night. Other high-crime areas include Curundú, El Chorrillo, Santa Ana, San Miguelito, and Río Abajo.

When walking the streets of Panama City, be aware that drivers do *not* yield to pedestrians. Be on the lookout for missing storm and sewer covers and high curbs.

The heavy volume of traffic and buses without mufflers make this a very noisy city. The air is often thick with vehicle exhaust.

Walking Tour

Colonial Casco Antiguo, previously called Casco Viejo, is one of the more interesting parts of the city. Sadly, nowadays many of the buildings are dilapidated. It's unsafe to walk here at night, and you must be careful walking down side streets even in the daytime, though you should be fine as long as you stick to the main streets. The area east of Plaza de la Independencia is less residential and feels somewhat safer.

This area is gradually being restored to be more tourist friendly. Current plans are to move the poorer residents to other areas of the city.

You could start a walking tour in Casco Antiguo at the **Teatro Nacional**, built in 1907. The ornate interior has been restored. It boasts red and gold decorations, a ceiling mural and a big crystal chandelier. Performances are still held here; to find out about them, or just to have a look at the theater, go around to the office door at the side of the building (US$1 entrance fee).

Walk south along the ocean, and you'll pass the **Ministerio de Gobierno y Justicia** building. Turn left at Avenida Central, where you'll see several restored buildings and a hollow ruin. This ruin is the former **Club de Clases y Tropas**, Noriega's old hangout, which was damaged heavily during the 1989 invasion. Some fresh paint was selectively applied in early 2000, when scenes from the movie *The Tailor of Panama* were filmed here.

An esplanade runs along the top of the sea wall built by the Spanish to protect the city. Walk south along this walkway then circle around north onto the **Paseo de las Bóvedas**. From here you can see the ships lining up to enter the canal and the Bridge of the Americas arching over the waterway.

PANAMA

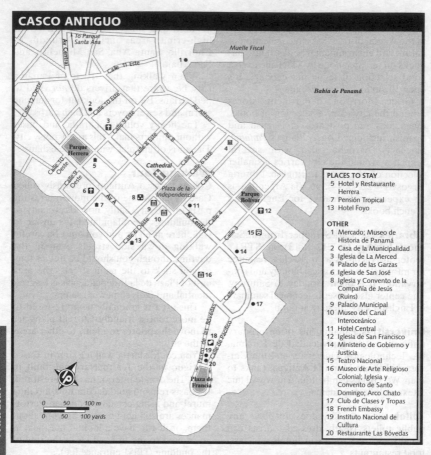

CASCO ANTIGUO

To Parque
Santa Ana

Muelle Fiscal

Bahía de Panamá

Parque
Herrera

Cathedral

Plaza de la
Independencia

Parque
Bolívar

Plaza de
Francia

PLACES TO STAY
5   Hotel y Restaurante
    Herrera
7   Pensión Tropical
13 Hotel Foyo

OTHER
1   Mercado; Museo de
    Historia de Panamá
2   Casa de la Municipalidad
3   Iglesia de La Merced
4   Palacio de las Garzas
6   Iglesia de San José
8   Iglesia y Convento de la
    Compañía de Jesús
    (Ruins)
9   Palacio Municipal
10 Museo del Canal
    Interoceánico
11 Hotel Central
12 Iglesia de San Francisco
14 Ministerio de Gobierno y
    Justicia
15 Teatro Nacional
16 Museo de Arte Religioso
    Colonial; Iglesia y
    Convento de Santo
    Domingo; Arco Chato
17 Club de Clases y Tropas
18 French Embassy
19 Instituto Nacional de
    Cultura
20 Restaurante Las Bóvedas

Below the wall, on the tip of the point, is the **Plaza de Francia**. Large stone tablets and statues tell the story (in Spanish) of the French role in the construction of the canal. The plaza is dedicated to the memory of the 22,000 workers, most of them from France, Guadeloupe and Martinique, who died working on the canal. Most were killed by yellow fever and malaria, and among the busts is a monument to Carlos J Finlay, who discovered how mosquitoes transmit yellow fever. His work led to the eradication of the disease in Panama.

On one side of the plaza are nine restored **dungeons**. Although they now contain an art gallery and a classy restaurant/piano bar (Restaurante Las Bóvedas), you can still see the dungeons' original

stonework. Also on the plaza are the Instituto Nacional de Cultura (INAC) and the French embassy.

Leaving the plaza to walk up Avenida A, you soon come to the **Museo de Arte Religioso Colonial**, beside the ruins of the **Iglesia y Convento de Santo Domingo** on the corner of Calle 3. Just inside the doorway of the ruins is the **Arco Chato**, a long arch that has stood here, unsupported, for centuries. It reportedly played a part in the selection of Panama over Nicaragua as the site for the canal: Its survival was taken as proof that the area was not subject to earthquakes.

Turning north along Calle 3, you pass the Teatro Nacional again. Opposite the theater is the **Iglesia de San Francisco**, facing onto the **Parque Bolívar**. In 1826, in a schoolroom opposite this plaza, Simón Bolívar held a meeting urging the union of the Latin American countries.

Around the block from this plaza, on Avenida Alfaro, is the **presidential palace**, called the Palacio de las Garzas for the great white herons here. The president of Panama lives on the upper floor. A few blocks farther west are the **muelle fiscal** (the port) and **mercado** (market).

Two blocks south of the palace, at the center of Casco Antiguo, is the central plaza, the **Plaza de la Independencia**, where Panamanian independence was declared on November 3, 1903. In addition to a **cathedral**, the plaza is fringed by several other historic buildings. On the southern side of the plaza, the **Museo de Historia de Panamá** is on the top floor of the palacio municipal (city hall). Next door is the **Museo del Canal Interoceánico** (Interoceanic Canal Museum), in the building that was once the headquarters of the original French canal company. Canal officials and other dignitaries stayed at the nearby **Hotel Central**, a very luxurious place in those days; this building closed as a hotel in 2000.

Half a block south of the plaza, on Calle 7, are the ruins of another church, the **Iglesia y Convento de la Compañía de Jesus**. Walk to the end of the block to rejoin Avenida A then walk a block west to arrive at the **Iglesia de San José**. Its famous **Altar de Oro** (Golden Altar) was about the only thing of value salvaged after Henry Morgan sacked Panamá La Vieja in 1671. When word came of the pirate's impending attack, according to local tales, a priest painted the altar black to disguise it. The priest told Morgan that the famous altar had been stolen by another pirate, and even convinced Morgan to donate handsomely for its replacement. Morgan is said to have told the priest, 'I don't know why, but I think you are more of a pirate than I am.' Whatever the historical fact, the altar was later moved from the old city to the present site.

A block farther west is another park, Parque Herrera. A block north, on Avenida Central, two blocks west of the cathedral, is the **Iglesia de La Merced**.

Walk out of Casco Antiguo along Avenida Central, past the **Casa de la Municipalidad**, and after a couple of blocks you'll come to the Parque Santa Ana, with its **Iglesia de Santa Ana**. This park marks the beginning of the Avenida Central shopping district; it is surrounded by restaurants and there are buses to the rest of the city.

Walk about five more blocks north on Avenida Central, past the big air-conditioned stores with hawkers outside, and you'll come to **Plaza Cinco de Mayo** and the **Legislative Palace**. Avenida Central between Parque Santa Ana and the Plaza Cinco de Mayo is a pedestrian-only shopping street. On Avenida Central opposite Plaza Cinco de Mayo is the excellent **Museo Antropológico Reina Torres de Araúz**, which focuses on the anthropology and archaeology of Panama; behind it is the handicrafts market, the **Mercado de Buonherías y Artesanías**.

Plaza Cinco de Mayo is a major bus stop. See the Getting Around section later for details.

Panamá La Vieja

At the eastern end of the city are the **ruins** of the first city the Spanish built here in 1519. The ruins cover a large area, and you can still see the cathedral with its stone tower, the plaza beside it, the convent of Santo Domingo, Iglesia de San José, the hospital of San Juan de Dios and the city hall.

The city's ruins are not fenced, and you can visit them any time; Panamá La Vieja buses coming from Plaza Cinco de Mayo will bring you here. There's the fine **Mercado Nacional de Artesanías** (National Artisans Market) beside the ruins; it is open 9 am to 6 pm daily. The Restaurante Rincón Típico serves local food.

Adjacent to the artisans market is the **Museo de Sitio Panamá Viejo**, which contains a rather impressive scale model of Panamá La Vieja prior to 1671 and colonial artifacts. All signs are in Spanish, and guides speak only Spanish; a brochure and tape recording recount the site's history in English. Admission is US$1.50, and it is customary to tip the guides US$1 or US$2. Hours are 8:30 am to 4:30 pm daily.

Causeway

At the Pacific entrance to the Panama Canal, a 2km *calzada* (causeway) connects the four small islands of Naos, Culebra,

Perico and Flamenco to the mainland. Solidaridad, the beach on Naos, is one of the most popular in the area.

Many people come to the causeway in the early morning and late afternoon to walk, jog, skate, bicycle or drive as a respite from the noise and pollution of the city. The causeway offers sweeping views of the city and, at some times of the year, flocks of brown pelicans diving into the sea.

Bicicletas Rali operates a booth at the causeway entrance where you can rent a bicycle for US$2.50 per hour or in-line skates for US$1 per hour; the booth is open 8 am to 6 pm weekends only.

The interesting **Centro de Exhibiciones Marines**, operated by the Smithsonian Tropical Research Institute (STRI), includes an informative marine museum with signs in English and Spanish, two small aquariums and a nature trail through a patch of dry forest containing sloths and iguanas. It's open 1 to 5 pm Tuesday to Friday and 10 am to 5 pm weekends; admission is US$1.

Food is available on the causeway. The orange SACA buses arrive from the Avenida Roosevelt bus stop across from the Legislative Palace and travel the entire length of the causeway.

This area is slated for some major resort projects to help attract free-spending tourists.

Parque Natural Metropolitano

Up on a hill to the north of downtown, this 265-hectare national park protects a wild area of tropical forest within the city limits. It has two main walking trails, the **Nature Trail** and the Tití Monkey Trail, that join to form one long loop. The 150m-high **mirador** (lookout point) offers a view over Panama City, the bay and the canal all the way to Miraflores Locks.

Mammals in the park include tití monkeys, anteaters, sloths and white-tailed deer; reptiles are represented by iguanas, turtles and tortoises. More than 250 known species of bird have been spotted here.

The park is bordered on the west and north by Camino de la Amistad; Avenida Juan Pablo II runs right through the park. The visitors center (☎ 232 5516), 40m north of the park entrance on Avenida Juan Pablo II, is open 8 am to 4 pm weekdays and 8 am to 1 pm Saturday. A pamphlet for a self-guided tour is available in Spanish and English. Rangers offer tours for US$6 per person, but you need to call in advance.

Mi Pueblito

At the foot of Cerro Ancón, on the western side of town on Avenida de Los Mártires, Mi Pueblito (My Little Village) features life-size replicas of rural villages found on the Península de Azuero, in Bocas del Toro and various indigenous villages. Its craft shops sell handicrafts from throughout the country. Kuna dances are presented on the weekends. Food stands and the restaurant Centolla's Place provide food.

Mi Pueblito is open 10 am to 10 pm Tuesday to Sunday. Admission is US$1. Note that there are two separate entrances to different exhibits.

Museums

A couple of museums have already been mentioned but there are several more. Here's a list:

Museo Antropológico Reina Torres de Araúz (☎ 212 3079), Plaza Cinco de Mayo on Avenida Central, is a fascinating museum of Panamanian anthropology, archaeology and pre-Columbian history. Limited exhibits were available at the time of writing due to renovation. It's open 10 am to 4 pm Tuesday to Sunday; admission is US$2 (children US$0.25).

Museo del Canal Interoceánico (☎ 211 1650), beside Plaza de la Independencia in Casco Antiguo, is widely known only as the Panama Canal Museum. It presents a detailed history of the waterway and railroad. Signs are in Spanish; English-speaking guides are available. It's open 9:30 am to 5:30 pm Tuesday to Sunday; US$2/1 adults/children.

Museo de Arte Religioso Colonial (☎ 228 2897), at Avenida A and Calle 3, in the Santo Domingo chapel, next to the church and convent of the same name in Casco Antiguo, shows colonial era religious artifacts. It's open 9 am to 4:15 pm Tuesday to Saturday, 1 to 5 pm Sunday; admission is US$0.75 (children US$0.25).

Museo Afro-Antilleano (☎ 262 5348), at Avenida Justo Arosemena and Calle 24 Este, has exhibits on the history of Panama's West Indian community. It's open 8:30 am to 3:30 pm Tuesday to Saturday; admission is US$1 (children and students US$0.25).

Museo de Arte Contemporáneo (☎ 262 8012), Near Avenida de los Mártires in the Ancón district, has permanent and changing exhibits. It's open 9 am to 4 pm weekdays, 9 am to noon Saturday, 9 am to 3 pm Sunday; admission is free.

Museo de Historia de Panamá (☎ 228 6231), in the Palacio Municipal, 3rd floor, beside Plaza de la Independencia in Casco Antiguo, has exhibits on the history of Panama from colonialism to 1977. It's open 8:30 to 3:30 pm weekdays; admission is free.

Museo de Ciencias Naturales (☎ 225 0645), on Avenida Cuba, between Calle 29 Este and 30 Este, has exhibits on natural sciences, flora, fauna, geology and paleontology of Panama. It's open 9 am to 3:30 pm Tuesday to Saturday, 1 to 5 pm Sunday; admission is US$1 (children US$0.25).

Casa-Museo del Banco Nacional (☎ 225 0640), at Calle 34 Este and Avenida Cuba, exhibits coins and bills circulated in Panama from the 16th century to the present and stamps and other objects related to the history of the Panamanian postal service. It's open 8 am to 12:30 pm and 1:30 to 4 pm Tuesday to Friday, 7:30 am to noon Saturday; admission is free.

Baha'i & Hindu Temples

On the outskirts of Panama City, 11km from the city center on the Transisthmian Hwy, the white-domed Baha'i temple sits on the crest of a hill. It looks much like an egg from the outside. The inside is surprisingly beautiful, with a fresh breeze always blowing through. This is the Baha'i House of Worship serving all of Latin America.

Information about the faith is available at the temple (☎ 231 1137) in English and Spanish; readings from the Baha'i writings (in English and Spanish) are held Sunday mornings at 10 am. The temple is open 10 am to 6 pm daily. Any bus to Colón can let you off on the highway, but it's a long walk up the hill. A taxi from Panama City costs around US$10.

On the way to the Baha'i temple is the magnificent Hindu temple, also atop a hill, open 7:30 to 11:30 am and 4:30 to 7:30 pm daily.

Language Courses

The only intensive Spanish-language school in Panama City is the Language & International Relations Institute (ILERI; ☎/fax 260 4424, espanolinst@cwp.net.pa), in Altos de Chase near El Dorado neighborhood. Classes include four hours of instruction per day. Costs range from US$300 for one week to US$999 for four weeks with homestay and from US$200 for one week to US$640

for four weeks without homestay. Fieldtrips and activities are also included. ILERI also offers Spanish classes at night. ILERI modifies the schedules for classes and activities during holidays, but may not voluntarily reduce the rate. Be sure that you receive written verification of the costs and schedule for all classes, field trips and activities. Web site: homepages.infoseek.com/~ileri _panama/index.htm

Organized Tours

A great number of tours are available in and around the city. City and canal tours are offered by nearly all tour operators. A two- to four-hour tour of the city and the canal's Miraflores Locks costs around US$25 to US$35 per person for two people, depending on the time, less for larger groups. Pesantez Tours offers an evening on the Chiva Parrandera, a bus with lively music and drinking, for US$20 per person.

Ancon Expeditions and Iguana Tours operate a variety of ecologically oriented tours near the city and farther afield. These naturalist-led tours can be a great way to learn about the tropical rain forests and their plants, animals, birds and human inhabitants. Trips from Panama City include rafting on the Río Chagres and Río Mamoni for US$95 to US$135 per person, and a visit to an Emberá village on the Río Chagres (US$85 to US$125 per person). Scuba and fishing trips are also offered.

Additional trips from Panama City are covered with specific destinations, and include transiting the Panama Canal, bird watching on Pipeline Rd in Parque Nacional Soberanía and visiting Barro Colorado Island and Natural Monument, Fuerte San Lorenzo, Isla Iguana and other places throughout Panama.

For more information, contact the tour agencies in the Getting Around section.

Special Events

Carnaval, on the four days preceding Ash Wednesday, is a lively festival in Panama City. Other events are listed in the arts section in the Sunday edition of *La Prensa* or the back pages of *The Panama News*.

Places to Stay – Budget

Hostels The only hostel in Panama is *Voyager International Hostel* (☎ 260 5913, *hostelpm@orbi.net)*, at Calle Arcangel and Calle 62 Oeste in the pleasant Los Angeles residential area. Rates are US$9 per person in a room with three bunk beds and US$10 per person in a room with two bunk beds. These rates include a continental breakfast (coffee, bread and fruit), use of the kitchen and common living area and Internet access. Rooms have fans, and one of the two showers has an electric heater. You can also wash and air dry your clothes here. Full services (banks, supermarket, restaurants) are nearby, and El Cangrejo banking district is within walking distance.

Casco Antiguo The historic Casco Antiguo area is home to some of the city's lowest-priced lodgings. These places are quite basic, though shoestringers will probably find them adequate. None of the hotels has hot water. It's dangerous to walk around this district at night; keep your eyes open in the side streets even in daytime.

Hotel Foyo (☎ 222 0434), a block and a half from the Plaza de la Independencia on Calle 6 Oeste, is among the cheapest at US$6/9 for one/two beds. Bathrooms are shared. Rooms are basic and look stained but are otherwise clean. Some of the rooms at the same price are better than others; ask to see several.

The *Pensión Tropical* (☎ 222 7634), on Calle 8 near Avenida A, charges US$7 for a room with shared bathrooms. There's only a bed and a fan in each room.

The architecturally attractive *Hotel y Restaurante Herrera* (☎ 228 8994), beside Parque Herrera on Calle 9, has single/double rooms for US$6/8 with shared bathrooms or US$11 with private bathrooms; rooms with air-con, fridge and TV cost US$16.

La Exposición & Bella Vista La Exposición is a newer part of town than Casco Antiguo, but still older than the banking district. Many government offices are located here. The area has many budget- and mid-range hotels, although food options tend to be limited to open-air corner cafes and hotels. Be alert walking to Avenida Balboa when the streets are deserted.

Residencial La Primavera (☎ 225 1195), simple but clean and well kept, is in a good location on Avenida Cuba near the corner of Calle 43 Este, in a residential neighbor-hood just a block from Vía España. All the rooms have private bathrooms and ceiling fans, and cost US$10 a night. We've been told that the hotel sometimes won't allow overnight guests to check in before 3 pm so that the rooms are available for their, uh, hourly customers.

Pensión Las Palmeras (☎ 225 0811), on Avenida Cuba near Calle 38 Este, is also simple but clean accommodation, with rooms for US$10/12 with shared/private bathrooms.

The *Residencial Turístico Volcán* (☎ 225 5275), on Calle 29 Este between Avenidas Perú and Cuba, is well maintained and clean. All rooms have private bathrooms and TVs. A room with double bed costs US$12/14 with ceiling fan/air-conditioning. A room with air-con and two beds costs US$16. You can use the lovely 24-hour rooftop pool at the Hotel Covadonga next door.

Places to Stay – Mid-Range
La Exposición & Bella Vista A couple of hotels in this area offer a higher standard of accommodations, at good value. The *Hotel California* (☎ 263-7736, fax 264-6144), on Vía España at the corner of Calle 43 Este, has good, clean rooms with private bathrooms, hot water, telephone and color TV with cable for US$20/33 for one/two beds, with a smoky restaurant/bar downstairs. Ask for a quiet, spacious room with a view of the bay. Members of the Peace Corps stay here for its value and safety.

The *Hotel Lisboa* (☎ 227 5916, fax 227 5919), on Avenida Cuba between Calles 30 Este and 31 Este, offers rooms for US$20/24 singles/doubles. It's a newer place, containing spacious rooms with quiet air-con, cable TVs, hot water and phones.

El Cangrejo Accommodations in the modern banking district are expensive. Many services are in this area, including banks, tour operators, restaurants, nightlife and Internet cafes.

The *Hotel Marbella* (☎ 263 2220, fax 263 3622), a modern hotel on Calle D, is a good value and a popular place. Every room has a writing/dining table, air-con, cable TV and good beds. The rate is US$38.50 for a room with a double bed.

Places to Eat

Panama City has hundreds of places to eat, with everything from fast-food joints to the fanciest gourmet restaurants.

Calidonia The *Restaurante y Pizzeria Napoli*, on Calle Estudiante a block south of Avenida de los Mártires, serves tasty pizzas and Italian food at reasonable prices. An 8-inch pizza costs US$3.75; pasta dishes are US$3.50 to US$5.50. It's closed Tuesday.

La Exposición The *Restaurante Vistamar*, on Avenida Central España between Calle 37 Este and Calle 43 Este, serves cheap, traditional Panamanian food in an air-conditioned atmosphere. A dinner with healthy proportions costs around US$2 to US$2.50. It's open 6 am to 8 pm Monday to Saturday.

El Rincón Tableño is another place serving cheap, traditional Panamanian food. It has several locations, including one on Avenida Balboa between Calles 27 Este and 28 Este, and another on Avenida Cuba at Calle 31 Este. The food is 100% working-class Panamanian. Set meals cost about US$2.25. They open early, at 5:30 am.

Restaurante Boulevard Balboa, on Avenida Balboa at Calle 31 Este, is popular with workers and businesspeople. It serves breakfasts, sandwiches, burgers and pasta for very reasonable prices. It's closed Sunday.

Romanaccio's, on Calle 29 Este just south of Avenida Perú, provides a welcome respite from the noise of the city in a quiet, air-conditioned atmosphere. Oh yeah, it serves food, too, with pizzas from US$3.25 and pastas from US$4.

La Cascada, on the corner of Avenida Balboa and Calle 25 Este, is a good place for a pleasant evening out. It has a large garden dining patio and a bilingual menu with many confusing choices. The meals are gigantic and very reasonably priced; for US$5.25 you can get an excellent steak or corvina fish, or try the giant seafood platter for US$9.25. The budget choice is roasted chicken, fries, salad and roll for US$3.

El Cangrejo On Vía Argentina 1½ blocks north of Vía España is *Mr Pan*, a good place to pick up cheap breads and pastries for snacking or walking about. Set meals are served for about US$3.

Cafetería Manolo has two restaurants in this area: on Vía Argentina two blocks north of Vía España, and on the corner of Calle 49 B Oeste and Calle D. It's a very popular restaurant with a varied menu and a specialty in pasta. Breakfasts cost US$3 to US$4, sandwiches US$2.50 to US$5, pastas about US$4.50, and larger meals start at US$7. Both restaurants have indoor and outdoor seating. Hours are 6 am to 2 am daily.

Niko's Café, on Calle 51 Este half a block south of Vía España, is a cafeteria-style restaurant popular with locals on a budget, serving gyros (US$3), sandwiches and burgers, pasta, and *sancocho* (US$1). It's open 24 hours.

Caffé Pomodoro, on Calle 49 B Oeste, is extremely popular for Italian food, with tables inside in an air-conditioned restaurant as well as outdoors in a pleasant courtyard. Pasta dishes run US$5 to US$10; sandwiches are also available for US$3 to US$5.

Restaurante Vegetariano Mireya, at the corner of Calle Ricardo Arias and Avenida 3 Sur, is a vegetarian budget traveler's delight, with scarcely any item over US$1.25. A typical meal (say, a vegetable empanada, cauliflower and potatoes, and a *chicha*) costs about US$3. Hours are 6 am to 8 pm Monday to Saturday.

The very casual and low-priced *La Mexicanita* has two locations: on Avenida 4 Sur near Calle Uruguay and on Calle 53 Este close to Calle Anastacio Ruíz Noriega. Tasty items on the long menu include three tacos of your choice (US$3), a burrito especial (US$4.50) and an enchilada con salsa roja (US$4.85). It's closed Monday.

A worthwhile splurge is *Restaurante-Bar Tinajas* (☎ 263 7890), on Avenida 3 A Sur near Avenida Frederico Boyd. Typical Panamanian dishes include pastel de yuca (country pie made with yucca, chicken, corn, capers and raisins; US$7.50) and gaucho de mariscos (fresh seafood stew, served with coconut rice; US$8.50). Tinajas is well known for its excellent and popular folkloric dance shows, offered at 9 pm on Tuesday, Wednesday, Thursday and Saturday nights; there's a US$5 entertainment fee on those nights, and reservations are highly recommended. The restaurant is closed Sunday.

Another branch of **Restaurante y Pizzeria Napoli** is on Calle 57 Este, 1½ blocks south of Vía España.

Other Areas *Centolla's Place* serves up seafood Bocas del Toro style at three locations: at Mi Pueblito, on Avenida Belisario Porras across from Parque Recreativo Omar, and on Vía España near Calle 94 Este. Popular dishes at this fun and casual place include pescado relleno (mackerel stuffed with onions, cilantro and garlic; US$6.50) and cambombia (conch with wine or garlic sauce; US$6.50).

Niko's Café has several other locations, including Avenida 4 Sur near Punta Paitilla and behind El Dorado Mall.

Entertainment

Check the arts section in the Sunday edition of *La Prensa* or the back pages of *The Panama News* for current information.

Dance, music, theater and other performances are presented at the historic *Teatro Nacional* (☎ 262 3525) in Casco Antiguo, and at the two modern theaters in the *Centro Atlapa* (☎ 226 7000). Other venues include *Teatro La Cúpula* (☎ 233 7516) on Calle F near Vía España in El Cangrejo, the *Teatro En Círculo* (☎ 261 5375) on Avenida 6 C Norte near Vía Transístmica in El Carmen neighborhood and *Teatro Balboa* (☎ 272 0327) across from the Avenida Balboa post office.

Many air-conditioned cinemas around the city show current US films, usually in English with Spanish subtitles (admission US$3).

A very popular new disco is *Señor Frogs*, on Avenida 4 A Sur. Other popular discos include *Café Dalí*, on Avenida 5 B Sur; *Rock Café*, which is patronized by many teenagers, on Calle 53 Este at Calle Anastacio Ruíz Noriega; and the long-time favorite *Sahara*, on Avenida 4 Sur near Calle Aquilino de la Guardia. *El Pavo Real*, on Avenida 3 B Sur, is a British pub with pool tables, live music on weekends and, of course, fish and chips. *Restaurante Las Bóvedas*, on Plaza de Francia in Casco Antiguo, is a former dungeon and classy restaurant offering live jazz on weekend nights. The *Boy Bar* (☎ 230 3128), known to taxi drivers as *El Garage* and located on an unnamed street in an industrial area north of downtown, is one of the city's few gay dance clubs. You could also try *Tabou*, a hopping place for straights and gays, across the street from Sahara.

Be forewarned that most clubs don't even open their doors until 9 pm.

Several of the larger hotels offer 'Noches Típicas,' featuring traditional Panamanian dancing and floor shows. Traditional dancing is also presented at the *Restaurante-Bar Tinajas* (see Places to Eat).

Gambling is legal; numerous casinos are scattered throughout the city. Horse races, soccer, baseball and boxing are all popular in or near Panama City.

Shopping

Merchandise from around the world is sold very cheaply in Panama. Walk along Avenida Central and take your pick.

Authentic handicrafts can be found at the Mercado de Buhonerías y Artesanías, behind the Reina Torres de Araúz anthropological museum; at Mi Pueblito, a life-size replica of a rural village at the foot of Cerro Ancón on Avenida de los Mártires; and at the Mercado Nacional de Artesanías, beside the ruins of Panamá La Vieja. Flory Saltzman Molas, on Calle 49 B Oeste near Vía España, has a large selection and perhaps the best quality you'll find outside the islands. The bookstore at the Tupper Center of the Smithsonian Tropical Research Institute (STRI), in Ancón, has a nice selection of tagua nut carvings.

Gran Morrison department stores sell a good variety of Panamanian handicrafts.

Getting There & Away

Air International flights arrive at Tocumen International Airport, 35km northeast of the city center. See the Panama Getting There & Away section for more information about flights to Panama.

Several airlines provide service between Panama City and other parts of the country. Domestic flights arrive at Aeropuerto Marcos A Gelabert, in the former Albrook Air Force Station near the canal. It is commonly referred to simply as Albrook airport. See the Panama Getting Around section for details.

Bus The Terminal Nacional de Transporte (☎ 314 6171) opened in 2000 near the

Albrook airport and is a convenient one-stop location for most buses leaving Panama City. The terminal includes a food court, banks, shops, a sports bar, storage room, bathrooms and showers. Please be aware that schedules quoted in this book were correct at the time of writing, but they may change as the terminal is broken in. It would be wise to verify schedules in Panama City.

Local buses from the city's major routes stop at the new terminal, and there are direct buses to and from Tocumen International Airport.

Some of the major bus routes are listed here. There are also buses to many small towns.

Chitré (US$6, four hours, 241km)
Buses depart hourly from 6 am to 11 pm.

El Valle (US$3.50, 2½ hours, 123km)
Buses depart hourly from 7 am to 6 pm.

Las Tablas (US$6.50, 4½ hours, 282km)
Buses depart every 1½ hours from 6 am to 6 pm.

Yaviza (US$14, 10 hours, 266km)
Buses depart hourly from 5 to 10 am.

Buses departing from other locations include the following:

Canal Zone
Buses to the Canal Zone (Miraflores and Pedro Miguel Locks, Paraíso, Gamboa and other locals) and the Balboa and Ancón areas depart from the bus stop on Avenida Roosevelt across from the Legislative Palace. A ride usually costs no more than US$1.

Changuinola & Almirante
The Union de Buses Panamericanos (☎ 758 8127) offers two buses a day, leaving at 7 am (US$23) and 11 pm (US$26). The 580km trip to Almirante takes 10 hours; Changuinola is 20km and 30 minutes farther. The buses depart from the Terminal Nacional de Transporte.

Colón
Regular bus service departs from the Terminal Nacional de Transporte every 20 minutes from around 5 am to 9 pm; the last bus departs at 1 am. Express buses depart hourly from 7 am to 8 pm. These are air-conditioned and cost US$2.

San José, Costa Rica
Panaline and Tica Bus offer direct services between Panama City and San José – see the Panama Getting There & Away section.

David
Buses leave the Terminal Nacional de Transporte every one to 1½ hours from 5:30 am to 8 pm. Express buses depart at 10:45 pm and midnight. Padafront (☎ 227 4210) departs for David every 1½ hours from 7 am to 8 pm, with express buses at 11 pm and midnight. Regular buses for both companies cost US$11; express buses cost US$15.

Car & Motorcycle Rental car companies in Panama City include:

Avis	☎ 264 0722, 238 4056 at the airport	
Barriga	☎ 269 0221, 238 4495 at the airport	
Budget	☎ 263 8777, 238 4069 at the airport	
Central	☎ 223 5745, 238 4936 at the airport	
Dollar	☎ 270 0355, 238 4032 at the airport	
Hertz	☎ 264 1111, 238 4081 at the airport	
National	☎ 265 2222, 238 4144 at the airport	
Thrifty	☎ 264 2613, 238 4955 at the airport	
Tico	☎ 229 5257	

Many car rental agencies have offices throughout the city. Several are located on or near Calle 49 B Oeste in El Cangrejo area. As always, it pays to shop around to compare rates and special promotions. At the time of writing, daily rates were about US$45 per day for the most economical cars, with insurance and unlimited kilometers.

Motorcycles cannot be rented in Panama City.

Boat Passenger boats between Panama City and Isla Taboga depart from Muelle (Pier) 18 on the canal; tour boats go along part of the Panama Canal. See the Panamá and Coclé Provinces section for details.

Cargo boats to Colombia depart from the docks near Casco Antiguo. See Dangers & Annoyances in the Facts for the Visitor section for a warning.

Getting Around
To/From the Airport Tocumen International Airport is 35km northeast of the city center. Buses to Tocumen depart every 15 minutes from the bus stop north of the Plaza Cinco de Mayo near the corner of Avenida Central and Avenida Justo Arosemena; they cost US$0.50 and take an hour to reach the airport. A taxi from downtown to the airport should cost US$12 for one, US$15 for two. There are also direct buses to and from the Terminal Nacional de Transporte, near Albrook airport.

When arriving at Tocumen, look for the *Transportes Turísticos* desk at the airport exit. Beside it is a taxi stand, with posted prices. Taxi drivers will assail you, offering rides into town for US$25, but you can take a *colectivo* for US$10 per person (for three or more passengers) or US$12 per person (for two passengers).

The Albrook airport north of Cerro Ancón handles domestic flights. Buses depart from the bus stop in front of the Legislative Palace. A taxi costs US$3 to US$4.

Bus Panama City has a good network of local buses, which run every day from around 5 am to 11 pm. A ride costs US$0.15 to US$0.25. Buses run along the three major west-to-east routes: Avenida Central-Vía España, Avenida Balboa-Vía Israel, and Avenida José D Espinar-Vía Transístmica. The Avenida Central-Vía España streets are one-way going west for much of the route; eastbound buses use Avenida Perú and Avenida 4 Sur; these buses will take you into the banking district of El Cangrejo. Buses also run along Avenida Ricard J Alfaro (known as Tumba Muerto). There are plenty of bus stops along the street.

Many of these buses stop at the Terminal Nacional de Transporte, the bus station near the Albrook airport.

The Plaza Cinco de Mayo area has three major bus stops. On the corner of Avenida Central and Avenida Justo Arosemena, buses depart for Panamá La Vieja and the Tocumen International Airport. Buses for the Albrook domestic airport depart in front of the Legislative Palace. Buses depart from the station on Avenida Roosevelt opposite the Legislative Palace for the Ancón area (including the causeway) and other destinations.

Taxi Taxis are plentiful. They are not metered, but there is a list of standard fares that drivers are supposed to charge, measured by zones. The fare for one zone is a minimum of US$1; the maximum fare within the city is US$4. An average ride, crossing a couple of zones, would cost US$1.25 to US$2, plus US$0.25 for each additional passenger. Always agree on a fare before you get into the cab. Taxis can also be rented for US$8 an hour.

Watch out for unmarked large-model US cars serving hotels as cabs. Their prices are up to four times that of regular street taxis. You can phone for a taxi:

Ama	☎ 221 1865
America	☎ 223 7694
El Parador	☎ 220 5322
Latino	☎ 226 7315
Union Servicio Unico	☎ 221 4074

Bicycle The only place to rent a bicycle in Panama City is Bicicletas Rali (☎ 220 3844), which operates a booth at the causeway entrance. You can rent a bicycle for US$2.50 per hour or in-line skates for US$1 per hour; the booth is open weekends only from 8 am to 6 pm.

The leading bike store, Carretero Sports (☎ 263 4137, comrali@sinfo.net), has three branches: in El Cangrejo on Vía España; on Vía Israel in Punta Paitilla; and in Los Pueblos shopping center. They do not rent bicycles, but they do arrange popular bike rides.

Panamá & Coclé Provinces

Panamá Province contains the largest population of Panama's nine provinces – 1,349,000 people, according to the 2000 census. Attractions include most of the Panama Canal, two island groups, wild jungle and lovely beaches.

Coclé Province is to the west of Panama City, and contains both mountains and coast. It's an easy day trip from Panama.

PANAMA CANAL

The canal is one of the world's most significant waterways, truly an engineering marvel, stretching 80km from Panama City on the Pacific side to Colón on the Atlantic side, cutting right through the Continental Divide. Nearly 14,000 ships pass through the canal each year. Ships worldwide are built with the dimensions of the Panama Canal's locks in mind: 305m long and 33.5m wide.

Ships pay according to their weight, with the average fee around US$30,000. The highest amount paid was US$184,114.80, paid in January 2000 by the M/V *Sisler,* a 950-foot US-registered container ship; the lowest amount was US$0.36, paid in 1928 by Richard Halliburton, who swam through.

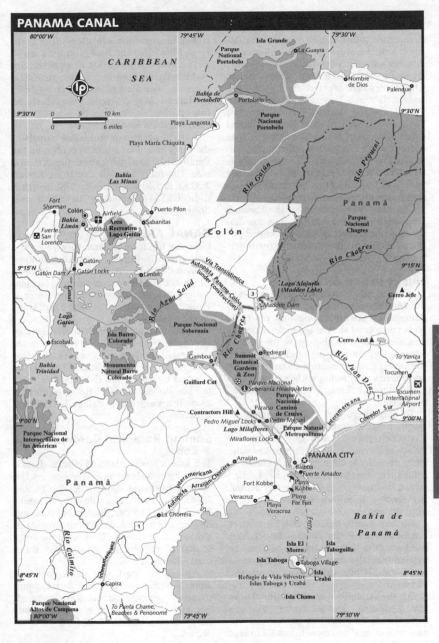

PANAMA CANAL

CARIBBEAN SEA

80°00'W
79°45'W
79°30'W

Parque National Portobelo
Isla Grande
La Guayra
Nombre de Dios
Palenque

9°30'N

0   5   10 km
0   3   6 miles

Bahía de Portobelo
Portobelo

Playa Langosta

Parque Nacional Portobelo

Playa María Chiquita

Río Gatún

Panamá

Bahía Las Minas

Parque Nacional Chagres

Fort Sherman
Colón
Airfield
Puerto Pilon
Bahía Limón
Cristóbal
Sabanitas
Fuerte San Lorenzo
Área Recreativa Lago Gatún

Colón

Gatún
Limón
Gatún Dam
Gatún Locks

9°15'N

Vía Transístmica
Autopista Panamá-Colón (under construction)

Río Agua Salud

Lago Alajuela (Madden Lake)
Cerro Jefe

Madden Dam

Canal
Lago Gatún

Escobal

Isla Barro Colorado

Parque Nacional Soberanía

Cerro Azul
To Yaviza

Río Chagres

Bahía Trinidad

Monumento Natural Barro Colorado

Gamboa
Summit Botanical Gardens & Zoo
Pedregal

Río Juan Diaz
Tocumen

Gaillard Cut

Parque Nacional Soberanía Headquarters

Tocumen International Airport

Parque Nacional Interoceánico de las Américas

Contractors Hill
Pedro Miguel Locks
Paraíso
Parque Nacional Camino de Cruces
Pedro Miguel

Interamericana
Corredor Sur

9°00'N

Lago Miraflores
Miraflores Locks

Parque Natural Metropolitano

PANAMÁ CITY

Panamá

Arraiján
Balboa
Fuerte Amador

Autopista Arraiján-Chorrera
Fort Kobbe
Playa Kobbe

Interamericana

Veracruz
Playa Far Fan

Playa Veracruz

Bahía de Panamá

La Chorrera

Isla El Morro
Isla Taboguilla

Río Caimito

Isla Taboga
Taboga Village

8°45'N

Interamericana

Capira

Refugio de Vida Silvestre Islas Taboga y Urabá

Isla Urabú

Isla Chama

Parque Nacional Altos de Campana

To Punta Chame, Beaches & Penonomé

80°00'W
79°45'W
79°30'W

PANAMA

The canal has three sets of double locks: Miraflores and Pedro Miguel Locks on the Pacific side and Gatún Locks on the Atlantic side. Between the locks, ships pass through a huge artificial lake, Lago Gatún, created by the Gatún Dam across the Río Chagres (when created they were the largest dam and largest artificial lake on Earth), and the Gaillard Cut, a 14km cut through the rock and shale of the isthmian mountains. A staggering 52 million gallons of fresh water is released to the ocean with the passage of each ship. Construction was an extreme challenge: In the wet climate the loose soil was subject to horrendous landslides even after the canal opened.

The more you learn about the Panama Canal, both in terms of the monumental construction project and the associated political intrigues, the more interesting it becomes.

Things to See & Do

The easiest way to visit the canal is to go to the **Miraflores Locks**, the locks closest to Panama City, where a viewing platform gives you a good view of the locks in operation as humongous ships pass through. A bilingual guide and bilingual illustrated pamphlets give information about the canal, and there's a museum with a model and film. Hours are 9 am to 5 pm daily; admission is free.

To get there, take any Paraíso or Gamboa bus from the bus stop on Avenida Roosevelt across from the Legislative Palace in Panama City. These buses, passing along the canal-side highway to Gamboa, will let you off at the 'Miraflores Locks' sign on the highway, 12km from the city center. It's about a 15-minute walk to the locks from the sign.

Farther north, beyond the Miraflores Locks, are the **Pedro Miguel Locks**. You will pass them if you're taking the highway to Gamboa. The only facilities here are a parking lot, from which you can see the locks.

On the Atlantic side, the **Gatún Locks** have a viewing stand for visitors. You can drive across the locks themselves; you will pass over them if you cross the canal to visit Fuerte San Lorenzo.

Argo Tours (☎ 228 4348, fax 228 1234) operates **partial canal transits** on Saturday

mornings. These boat tours depart from Balboa, a western suburb of Panama City, travel through the Miraflores Locks to Lago Miraflores and back, and then cruise out into the bay for scenic views of the city and the Pacific approach to the canal. The tours last about 4½ hours and cost US$90 (children US$45), including breakfast and lunch.

Web site: www.big-ditch.com

Argo Tours also operates **full transits** of the canal once a month, from Balboa on the Pacific side to Cristóbal on the Atlantic side. The tours take all day, from around 7:30 am to 5:30 pm; the cost is US$135 (children US$55), including all meals and drinks.

CANAL AREA

On a day trip from Panama City, you could visit the Miraflores Locks, the Summit Botanical Gardens & Zoo and the Sendero El Charco nature trail in Parque Nacional Soberanía, which is 25km from the center of Panama City but seems like a different world.

All of these places are along the highway that runs from Panama City to Gamboa, the small tropical town where the Río Chagres enters Lago Gatún. They can be reached by taking the Gamboa bus from the bus stop on Avenida Roosevelt across from the Legislative Palace in Panama City.

Summit Botanical Gardens & Zoo

Ten kilometers past the Miraflores Locks, on the highway heading to Gamboa, are the Summit Botanical Gardens & Zoo (☎ 232 4854). The botanical gardens were established in 1923 to introduce, propagate and disseminate tropical plants from around the world into Panama. They contain over 15,000 plant species, with 50 of them marked along a trail.

Also at the park is a small zoo with animals native to Central America; some cages are spacious, and others are cramped. The zoo's greatest attraction is its enormous harpy eagle compound and educational display.

The park is open 8 am to 4 pm daily. Admission is US$1; ask for a trail map of the park. The Gamboa bus stops here.

Parque Nacional Soberanía

The 22,104-hectare Parque Nacional Soberanía is one of the most accessible tropical rain forests in Panama. It extends much of the way across the isthmus, from Limón on Lago Gatún to just north of Paraíso. It features hiking trails, the Río Chagres, part of Lago Gatún and a remarkable variety of wildlife.

Hiking trails in the park include a section of the old **Sendero Las Cruces** (Las Cruces Trail), used by the Spanish to transport gold by mule train between Panama City and Nombre de Dios, and the 17km **Camino de Oleoducto** (Pipeline Rd), providing access (by driving or hiking) to Río Agua Salud, where you can walk upriver for a swim under a waterfall. A shorter, very easy trail is the **Sendero El Charco**, signposted from the highway, 3km past the Summit Botanical Gardens & Zoo.

The Pipeline Rd is a favorite with bird watchers. However, to enter, you need to stop by the park headquarters the day before to make arrangements with the park rangers. Tour agencies lead half-day bird watching tours here from Panama City for about US$45 to US$65 per person based on a group of four (see Organized Tours in the Panama Getting Around section).

Fishing is permitted in the Río Chagres and Lago Gatún.

Entrance to the park costs US$3, which you can pay at Soberanía National Park headquarters (no phone) at the turnoff to Summit. Maps, information about the park and camping permits are available here, including a self-guiding brochure for the nature trail.

Contractors Hill

On the western side of the canal, Contractors Hill was originally 123m above sea level. It was one of the highest points along the Gaillard Cut. There were landslides along the Cut, however, and in 1954 Contractors Hill was reduced to its present height of 111m in an effort to stabilize it.

Contractors Hill is one of the most accessible points from which to see the Gaillard Cut, but only if you have a private vehicle. The hill is pretty remote and is not served by public transportation.

ISLA BARRO COLORADO

This lush island in the middle of Lago Gatún was formed by the damming of the Río Chagres and the creation of the lake. It is managed by the Smithsonian Tropical Research Institute (STRI), which administers a world-renowned research facility here. It makes an interesting day trip from Panama City. The trip includes a boat ride down an attractive part of the canal, from Gamboa across the lake to the island.

STRI offers tours of the 1500-hectare island, but the number of tourists is strictly limited: 10 visitors on Tuesday and 30 on each weekend day. Children under 10 are not allowed on the island. A visit takes a full day and costs US$28 per person, which includes a bilingual guide, roundtrip boat transportation from Gamboa Pier and lunch at the research station cafeteria. The island has many ticks, so you should wear long pants, high socks and closed shoes and use insect repellent.

The Gamboa bus leaves from the bus stop on Avenida Roosevelt across from the Legislative Palace.

For reservations, contact STRI (☎ 212 8000, fax 212 8148, arosemo@tivoli.si.edu), log on to their Web site (www.stri.org) or stop by STRI's Panama City offices in the Tupper Research and Conference Center across Avenida de los Mártires from the Legislative Palace. Make a reservation as far in advance as possible; however, you can always call a day or two ahead to see if there have been any last-minute cancellations.

An alternative trip, but more expensive, is a visit to Monumento Natural Barro Colorado on the mainland bordering the canal, containing spectacular rain forest similar to that on the island. Some of these tours visit the island's coves by boat and go to the visitors center on the island, but not into the rain forest. Iguana Tours and Ancon Expeditions offer these tours for US$90 to US$99 per person.

ISLA TABOGA

About 20km offshore and an hour's ferry ride from Panama City, Taboga is a small, peaceful island with a good beach and swimming. It has an attractive village with only one narrow road and no traffic. It is known as the Island of Flowers, because at certain times of the year it is covered with sweet-smelling blossoms, the aroma filling the air. Taboga is a favorite retreat for city dwellers.

Taboga was settled by the Spanish in 1515, just two years after Balboa first sighted the Pacific and before Panama City was built. The village of Taboga has a small church, said to be the second oldest in the Western Hemisphere; the island's graveyard dates to the 16th century.

The island has a sheltered deep-water port from which Pizarro took off for Peru in 1524. Ships coming from South America anchored at this port during the colonial era; before the mainland port was built, large tidal variations prevented ships from anchoring too close to the mainland. Taboga also saw its share of piracy; Henry Morgan visited the island after sacking Panama City in 1671.

El Morro, the small island in front of the Hotel Taboga, is joined to Isla Taboga at low tide. In the 1860s it was the headquarters of the Pacific Steamship Navigation Company. The ruins of some of the walls and the wharf can still be seen, though no buildings remain. Some of the company workers are buried in a small cemetery there.

Information
ANAM has an office on Taboga near the ferry dock, open weekdays. It *sometimes* has a map and information on the island's natural features and snorkeling spots.

Things to See & Do
Most people come to Taboga for a day trip to the beach. There are fine **beaches** going in either direction from the ferry dock; they are all free to visit. Many visitors head straight for the Hotel Taboga, to your right as you walk off the ferry dock; the hotel faces onto the island's most popular beach, arcing between Taboga and the tiny Isla El Morro. A day entrance fee of US$5 includes vouchers for food and beverages at the hotel restaurant, dressing room and showers, and use of the large garden grounds. Hotel Taboga also rents paddleboats, beach umbrellas, hammocks, mats, snorkeling and diving gear and the like. There's no need to pay the hotel simply to use the beach, however; an easily overlooked walkway beside the hotel's gate entrance leads to the beach.

On weekends, when most people visit Taboga, you can find fishermen at the pier who will take you around the island, allowing you to see it from all sides and reach some good **snorkeling** spots. Caves on the island's western side are rumored (of course) to hold golden treasure left there by pirates. During the week, when the small boats aren't taking people around, you can still snorkel around Isla El Morro, which doesn't have coral but attracts some large fish.

The **church**, on the high road about 75m past the first beach to the left of the pier, was founded in 1550 and is the second-oldest church in the Western Hemisphere. Inside it is a handsome altar and lovely artwork. Farther down the road is a beautiful public garden. At the center of the garden is a statue of the island's patroness, **Nuestra Señora del Carmen**.

For a fine view, you can walk up the hill on the east side of the island, Cerro de la Cruz, which has a cross on the top. Another trail leads to a **mirador** (lookout point) at the top of Cerro El Vigia, on the western side of the island.

A wildlife refuge, the **Refugio de Vida Silvestre Isla Taboga y Urabá**, covers about a third of the island, as well as the island of Urabá just off Taboga's southeastern coast. This refuge is home to one of the largest breeding colonies of **brown pelicans** in the world. May is the height of nesting season, but pelicans can be seen from January to June.

Special Events
Taboga's annual festival takes place on July 16, the day of its patron saint, Nuestra Señora del Carmen. The statue is carried upon the shoulders of followers to the shore, placed on a boat and ferried around the island. Upon her return she is carried around the island while crowds follow.

Places to Stay & Eat
There are only two hotels on the island. The *Hotel Chu* (☎ 250 2035 on Taboga, 263 6933 in Panama City) has single/double rooms for US$20/25. It's a simple old wooden hotel with shared bathrooms, cold water and soft beds, but it's clean and well kept. The upstairs rooms have balconies overlooking the sea. The *Hotel Taboga* (☎ 250 2122 on Taboga, 264 6096 in Panama City, htaboga@sinfo.net)

is larger, more modern and more expensive, with rooms starting at US$66.

The Hotel Chu has an open-air restaurant overlooking the sea, and there are a few other restaurants, little shops and snack stands around town. The restaurant at Hotel Taboga is more expensive.

Getting There & Away

The boat trip to Taboga is part of the island's attraction. Two companies offer a one-hour ferry ride, and one company offers a half-hour boat trip. The roundtrip fare is US$8. All boats depart from Muelle 18 in the Balboa district of Panama City. They pass along the Balboa port, under the Puente de las Américas and along the last part of the Panama Canal channel on its journey out to sea. They also pass the Fort Amador causeway.

Between them, the *Calypso Queen* (☎ 232 5736) and Argo Tours (☎ 228 4348) ferries have three departures a day on weekdays and five departures on weekends and holidays. The first weekday departure is at 8:30 am; the first weekend departure is 7:45 am.

Expreso del Pacifico (☎ 261 0350) offers trips on faster, smaller boats. The voyage to Taboga takes about 35 minutes, but there's less time to enjoy the view. It has four departures per day on weekdays, with the first one at 6 am, and five departures on weekends and holidays, with the first boat leaving at 7 am.

To get to Muelle 18, take one of the squat little Balboa buses leaving from the bus stop on Avenida Roosevelt across from the Legislative Palace.

ARCHIPIÉLAGO DE LAS PERLAS & ISLA CONTADORA

The archipelago, about 70km out from Panama City, is named for the large pearls that were once found in its waters.

Contadora is the best-known island of the group and the easiest to get to. It is a lovely island with large vacation homes, white-sand beaches and turquoise waters. Activities include snorkeling, diving, fishing, bicycling, four-wheeling and windsurfing.

Places to Stay

Isla Contadora does not have any cheap places to stay. The least expensive is *Villa*

Ernesto (☎ 250 4112, fax 250 4029), a house whose owners rent a couple of rooms for US$30/50 singles/doubles, including breakfast. The owners speak German and a little English and Spanish.

Restaurante Romantic (☎ 250 4067) rents rooms for US$60 per couple and cabins for US$80 to US$100 a couple. The 354-room *Hotel Contadora Resort* (☎ 250 4033, fax 250 4038, islacont@sinfo.net) often seems deserted. The US$160 price for two people includes all meals and drinks.

Getting There & Away

Aeroperlas (☎ 315 7500) and Aviatur (☎ 315 0311) fly from Albrook airport to Isla Contadora several times a day for US$26 one way. Flight time is about 20 minutes. Another option is by boat. *Expreso del Pacifico* (☎ 261 0350) leaves Muelle 18 in the Port of Balboa at 7 am on Friday through Monday, returning at 3 or 4 pm. Because the trip takes about 1¾ hours, this option only gives you five or six hours on the island if it's done as a day trip. The roundtrip fare is US$40.

BEACHES

A popular beach, **Playa Kobbe**, is just across the canal from Panama City. Part of it is the Kobbe Beach Club (☎ 263 6885); at the entrance you pay US$7 for coupons good for food and drink at the club's restaurant/bar. The beach is safe and protected, and has lifeguards. Sailboards and boats are available for rent, and there are other recreation options. Buses to Kobbe Beach leave from the bus station at Plaza Cinco de Mayo.

About 1km past the entrance to Kobbe Beach is the signposted entrance to **Veracruz**, a free public beach. Food is available, and it is popular, especially on weekends.

San Carlos Area

A couple of hours' drive west of Panama City, a strip of excellent beaches stretches along the Pacific coast from **Playa Gorgona** to **Playa Farallón**. The beaches are quite similar to one another. All are wide and covered with salt-and-pepper sand. Playas Teta and Río Mar are two of the best **surfing** beaches in the country.

Near **Playa Santa Clara**, just north of the Interamericana, *XS Memories* (☎/fax 993 3096, xsmemories@hotmail.com), is a piece of Americana plopped onto Panama's Pacific coast. The sports-themed restaurant offers American food, with wonderful grilled cheese sandwiches for US$2. Lodging options include camping (US$3), with use of the pool and showers. Cabins, some of which are handicapped accessible, start at US$50. You can even park an RV here starting at US$8. Bicycle rentals are US$5 a day, good for going to the beach or exploring the surrounding tropical dry forest.

Cabañas Las Veraneras (☎ *993 3313 in Santa Clara, 230 1415 in Panama City)* has 12 two-story cabins set up on a knoll 200m from the ocean. Seven have ocean views. Rates at this romantic place start at US$55 for up to five people.

To get to any of these beaches, take any bus from the Terminal Nacional de Transporte heading west on the Interamericana.

EL VALLE
pop 6000
This picturesque town, 123km west of Panama City, is nestled in the crater of an extinct volcano. El Valle is best known for its Sunday handicrafts market – a popular event at which Indians trade vegetables and sell lovely baskets, painted clay figurines and carved serving trays. The town is also a superb place for walking.

Information
IPAT, the national tourist office, operates an information booth at the center of town next to the handicrafts market. It's open 8:30 am to 4:30 pm Wednesday to Sunday. It distributes a rudimentary map; a large map on the outside wall of the booth will help you find your way even when the booth is closed.

Things to See & Do
El Valle's main attraction is its Sunday **handicrafts market**, where local Indians – mostly Guaymí but also some Emberá and Wounaan – sell excellent quality fiber baskets and hats, woodwork, ceramics, soapstone carvings, flowers and plants (including orchids) and a variety of fresh produce. It's held in the marketplace in the center of town, starting at 8 am and running until early afternoon.

The one-room **Museo de El Valle**, at the church in the center of town, features ex-

hibits on the interesting geologic and human history of the valley. It's open 10 am to 2 pm Sunday only; admission is US$0.25.

El Nispero is a large, beautiful garden and zoo of exotic plants, birds and animals, located about 1km north of the town center. Most cages are large enough, but some of the larger animals and birds of prey could use more space. It's open 7 am to 5 pm daily; admission is US$2 (children US$1).

El Valle's famous **golden frogs** can be seen in grottos at El Nispero. The **square trees**, El Valle's other unusual native species, can be seen on a hiking trail behind the Hotel Campestre, east and north of the town center.

The hills around El Valle are excellent for walking and horseback riding. Trails are well defined, since they are used by locals. **Piedra El Sapo** ('toad stone'), west of town near La India Dormida (a mountain ridge that supposedly looks like a sleeping Indian girl), is said to have some of the most beautiful trails. Nearby, in the neighborhood of La Pintada, are some unusual ancient **petroglyphs** representing humans, animals and other shapes.

Chorro El Macho is one of the valley's most beautiful spots. The short hike to this 60m waterfall takes you through a lush rain forest that is protected as an ecological refuge. The waterfall is 2km northwest of town, reachable by the bus to La Mesa (US$0.35). Admission is US$2.

Near the entrance to Chorro El Macho is the **Canopy Adventure** (☎ 983 6547), an exciting, suspended ride that uses cables, pulleys and a harness to allow you a view of the rain forest from above. One of the platform-to-platform slides is above Chorro El Macho. The complete 1½-hour adventure costs US$40, or you can get a taste for US$10, consisting of one slide between two platforms.
Web site: http://canopy.mit.edu

You can rent **bicycles** at Jaque Mate, on the road to Hotel Campestre, for US$3 per hour. **Horses** can also be rented nearby, at Alquiler de Caballos, for US$3.50 per hour. A 3½-hour horseback tour into the mountains with a guide costs US$12.50.

Several tour agencies arrange day trips from Panama City to El Valle, including the Canopy Adventure.

Places to Stay

The **Restaurante Santa Librada** (☎ 986 6376), near the town center, has four clean rooms with cold water and private bathrooms for US$15/20 singles/doubles.

The **Motel-Restaurante Niña Delia** (☎ 983 6110), on Avenida Central five blocks east of the town center, has six basic rooms with shared cold-water bathrooms for US$15 and private bathrooms for US$20.

Cabañas Gysell (☎ 983 6507), 1.5km east of the town center, offers six comfortable cabins with private hot-water bathrooms for US$30/35. Owner Candida Carteret is fluent in English and Spanish, justifiably proud of the hotel's cleanliness and spends considerable effort on making every room unique. Unfortunately, sometimes there are strong smells of burning garbage from next door, which may be gone by the time you read this.

The **Cabañas Potosi** (☎ 636 7724), about 1.5km west of downtown, has five cabins on peaceful, parklike grounds with a view of the surrounding mountains. The rate is US$40.

The **Hostel El Valle** is a new hotel conveniently located in the center of El Valle. Rates for doubles range from US$25 to US$50. All 12 rooms have hot water and private bathrooms.

Places to Eat

The **Restaurante Santa Librada** serves local dishes, seafood and grilled food for reasonable prices. The **Motel-Restaurante Niña Delia** is a simple place with good, cheap food for US$2 to US$3. **Pinocchio's**, just west of downtown, serves cheap and tasty pizzas.

For a classy night out, try the **Hotel Rincón Vallero** or the hotel **Los Capitanes**.

Getting There & Around

Buses leave Panama City for El Valle from the Terminal Nacional de Transporte, if completed hourly from 7 am to 6 pm (US$3.50, 2½ hours, 123km).

The center of town is small, but many of El Valle's attractions are a distance from the center. Taxis within town cost no more than US$2. Buses to La Mesa run along El Valle's main street. They pass by the Canopy Adventure and Chorro El Macho (US$0.35).

PARQUE NACIONAL EL COPÉ

The forests in this nearly inaccessible national park – which is commonly known as Parque Nacional El Copé but is officially named Parque Nacional General de División Omar Torrijos Herrera, after former president Omar Torrijos Herrera, who died here in an airplane crash – are among the most beautiful in Panama and offer superb bird watching. Hiking trails have been built in the park, but nearby accommodations are few. You can camp here with permission from the park's ANAM office (☎ 993 9089). The road is paved as far as El Copé, but a washout on this road prevented further research for this book. The 8km between the town and park is suitable for a 4WD vehicle only. Buses from Panama City go as far as El Copé. Then you'll need to hike in or hitch a ride. Admission is US$3 per person; camping is US$5 more.

Bocas del Toro

Bocas del Toro Province is bordered by Costa Rica to the west, the Caribbean Sea to the north, Chiriquí Province to the south and Veraguas Province to the east.

The main reason travelers go to Bocas is to visit the islands of the Archipiélago de Bocas del Toro and the Parque Nacional Marino Isla Bastimentos.

More remotely, the Wetzo entrance to the Parque Internacional La Amistad, the large park shared by Panama and Costa Rica, is accessible from Changuinola.

ARCHIPIÉLAGO DE BOCAS DEL TORO

The archipelago, in the Laguna de Chiriquí just 32km from the Costa Rican border, consists of six large, mostly forested islands and scores of smaller ones.

Bocas del Toro
pop 6500

The town of Bocas del Toro, on the southeastern tip of Isla Colón, is the provincial capital and a pleasant, convenient base for exploring the Parque Nacional Bastimentos and other nearby sites. The town, the archipelago and the province all share the same name – Bocas del Toro. Isla Colón and Bocas del Toro town are often referred to as Bocas Isla.

PANAMA

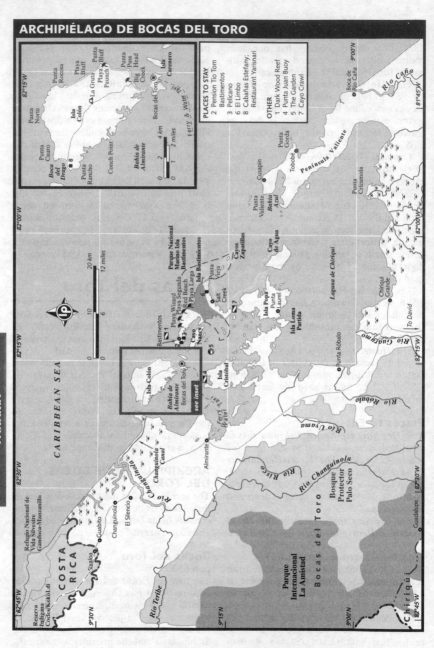

ARCHIPIÉLAGO DE BOCAS DEL TORO

PLACES TO STAY
2 Pension Tio Tom
   Bastimentos
3 Pelicano
6 El Limbo
8 Cabañas Estefany;
   Restaurant Yarisnari

OTHER
1 Dark Wood Reef
4 Punta Juan Buoy
5 The Garden
7 Cayo Crawl

Bocas del Toro town is where most of the archipelago's accommodations and restaurants are found. The town is a slow-paced community made up mostly of English- and Patois-speaking black people of West Indian ancestry. There are many Spanish-speaking Latinos as well.

Bocas is a great place to hang out for a few days. On the nearby islands and reefs are wonderful opportunities for swimming, snorkeling and diving, or lounging on white sandy beaches fringed by reeds and coconut palms. Readily available water taxis *(taxis marinos)* will take you to remote beaches and snorkeling sites. The town's relaxed, friendly atmosphere seems to rub off on everyone who visits; it's especially easy to meet locals and travelers here.

Although still relaxed, Bocas is experiencing a major development boom; land prices have skyrocketed since 1994, with foreign investors buying up land like crazy and building hotels and restaurants. The number of tourists continues to increase, so much so that travelers looking to get away from other tourists often stay at Boca del Drago, on Isla Bastimentos, or on Isla Carenero.

Visitors are sometimes disappointed in the unpredictable weather – it can rain for days, even in the 'dry' season.

Information The IPAT tourist office (☎ 757 9642, ipatbocas@cwp.net.pa) is in the new Centro de Facilidades Turísticas e Interpretación (CEFATI) on the eastern waterfront. A color map in English and Spanish is available. The center also houses an interesting display on the natural and human history of the area. It's open 8:30 am to 4:30 pm daily.

ANAM (☎ 757 9442) has an office on Calle 1. It's not really set up as a tourist information office, though they can answer questions about the national park or other protected areas. If you want to camp out in any of the protected areas, you must first get a permit from this or any other ANAM office.

Banco Nacional de Panamá, on Avenida F, exchanges traveler's checks; it's open 8 am to 3 pm weekdays, 9 am to noon Saturday. An ATM is also available next to Taxi 25 on the eastern waterfront.

An Internet cafe is on the main street (Calle 3), across from Parque Simón Bolívar. The Bocas del Toro Web site at www.bocas.com has useful information.

You can drop off laundry at the restaurant Don Chicho's, where they will wash and dry it for about US$3.

Unlike in most other places in Panama, tap water is not safe to drink in the Bocas del Toro area. Bottled water is readily available and costs about US$1.50 for a 1.5-liter bottle. Gallon jugs for US$2 are a better value if you can find them.

La Gruta Halfway across Isla Colón, 8km from town, is a **cave** known as La Gruta; it's also called the Santuario Natural de Nuestra Señora de la Gruta, for the statue of the Virgen del Carmen at the entrance. The cave is known for the **bats** that live there. You can walk through the cave and the guano; to see the bats easiest, walk around to the far side, where you only have to walk a few feet in before bats start swooping toward you.

Beaches There are plenty of beaches around Isla Colón, reached by a road that skirts up the eastern coast from town. There's no public transportation to them, but a taxi will take you there, and you can arrange for the driver to return at an appointed time.

Playa El Istmito, also called Playa La Cabaña, is the closest to town. It's on Bahía Sand Fly, and the *chitras* (sand flies) that live here have an itchy bite. Repellent is available in town. This is not the most attractive beach; better ones are farther north.

Farther up the coast are **Big Creek**, **Punta Puss Head** and **Playa Paunch**, which is dangerous for swimming but good for surfing. After you round Punta Bluff, the road takes you along the long **Playa Bluff**, which stretches all the way to Punta Rocosa. Endangered sea turtles nest on Playa Bluff during their nesting season, from around May to September.

Diving & Snorkeling Diving trips are offered by Starfleet Eco-Adventures (☎/fax 757 9630, scuba@vacationmail.com), on the Web at starfleeteco.hypermart.net; and by Bocas Water Sports (☎/fax 757 9541); and by Turtle Divers (☎/fax 757 9594, manginn@usa.net), www.bocas.com/mangrove.htm. Most diving trips cost about US$35 for a

PANAMA

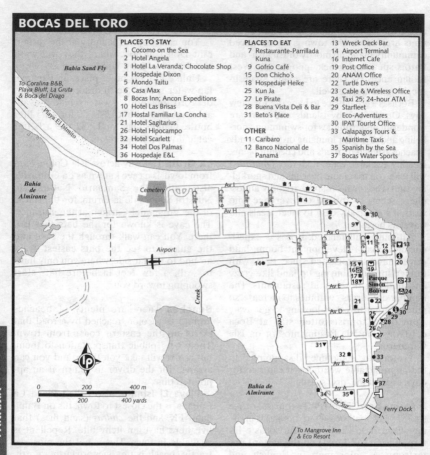

BOCAS DEL TORO

PLACES TO STAY
1 Cocomo on the Sea
2 Hotel Angela
3 Hotel La Veranda; Chocolate Shop
4 Hospedaje Dixon
5 Mondo Taitu
6 Casa Max
8 Bocas Inn; Ancon Expeditions
10 Hotel Las Brisas
17 Hostal Familiar La Concha
21 Hotel Sagitarius
26 Hotel Hipocampo
32 Hotel Scarlett
34 Hotel Dos Palmas
36 Hospedaje E&L

PLACES TO EAT
7 Restaurante-Parrillada Kuna
9 Gofrio Café
15 Don Chicho's
18 Hospedaje Heike
25 Kun Ja
27 Le Pirate
28 Buena Vista Deli & Bar
31 Beto's Place

OTHER
11 Caribaro
12 Banco Nacional de Panamá

13 Wreck Deck Bar
14 Airport Terminal
16 Internet Cafe
19 Post Office
20 ANAM Office
22 Turtle Divers
23 Cable & Wireless Office
24 Taxi 25; 24-hour ATM
29 Starfleet Eco-Adventures
30 IPAT Tourist Office
33 Galapagos Tours & Maritime Taxis
35 Spanish by the Sea
37 Bocas Water Sports

one-tank, one-site dive and US$50 for two tanks and two sites. PADI open-water and advanced-diver courses are also available. At Starfleet, a divemaster accompanies every trip.

The dive shops also offer snorkeling tours; the typical price for snorkeling trips, including gear, is US$15 per person per day. The farther from Bocas del Toro a trip goes, the more it costs. A trip to the distant Cayos Zapatillas costs US$40, including lunch, a laze on the beach and a jungle walkabout on Cayo Zapatilla Sur; these are very popular tours. Note that if you go into the marine park, there's a US$10 charge in addition to the tour fee.

Several other companies along the main street (Calle 3) offer snorkeling and other

tours, and hotels are also entering this business. Ancon Expeditions (at the Bocas Inn) offers an all-day snorkeling tour that includes Cayo Zapatilla, Punta Vieja, Coral Key, Red Frog Beach and Punta Hospital for US$15 to US$25, depending on the number of people. Another tour goes to Isla de los Pájaros, Boca del Drago and the Changuinola Canal, a 15km manmade waterway parallel to the Caribbean shoreline and connecting the Río Changuinola and Bahía de Almirante.

Many 'tours' are really little more than just boat transportation to a pretty spot. If you have your own snorkel gear (or if you rent it), you can also get the local boatmen to take you to many good snorkeling spots around the area in their small motorized canoes (botes). They know many good spots, and this option can be cheaper than the dive companies' trips. Agree on a price before you go.

Although the Cayos Zapatillas are within the boundaries of the national marine park, they're not a particularly good place to dive – currents there upset many divers. Better but not well-known sites include Cayo Crawl (a lovely reef with lots of fish, coral and lobster), south of Isla Bastimentos; Dark Wood Reef (with many nurse sharks and occasional hammerheads), northwest of Bastimentos; Hospital Point, a 50-foot wall off Cayo Nancy; and the base of the buoy near Punta Juan (with some beautiful coral) north of Isla Cristóbal. Of these, only the Punta Juan buoy and Hospital Point are also good for snorkeling. Another superior spot for snorkeling is the Garden, near Cayo Nancy, which has lots of coral.

Be forewarned that the archipelago's waters are notorious for poor visibility. Sometimes the visibility is very good; sometimes it's limited to 3m. More than 40 rivers empty into the bay around the islands, and they unload a lot of silt into the sea after heavy rains in the mountains. If it has rained a lot in recent days, don't expect good visibility.

Kayaking Sea kayaks can be rented from the Hotel Las Brisas for about US$1.50/10 per hour/day.

Sea Turtle Conservation Caribaro (☎/fax 757 9488, caribaro@cwp.net.pa), in an unmarked office at the school on the northern end of Calle 3, works to protect nesting sea turtles by patrolling the beaches and collecting information on nesting. Volunteers go to Playa Bluff on Thursday, Friday and Saturday nights from 8 pm to midnight, and again from midnight to 4 am. You can accompany them by paying a US$6 donation and sharing the transportation fee. Of course, your chances of seeing a turtle are much improved if you go during the primary nesting season, May to September. Only Spanish is spoken. Bring drinking water, as it's a four-hour walk through sand and usually hot and humid at night.

Language Courses Spanish by the Sea (☎/fax 757 9518, spanishbythesea@hotmail .com), on Calle 4 near Avenida A, offers Spanish classes for about US$6 per hour.

The school is accredited by ISLS, offers programs with homestays, and has a couple of rooms for rent. English, Spanish and Dutch are spoken.
Web site: http://spanishbythesea.tripod. com/index.html

Special Events Bocas celebrates all Panama's holidays, with a few enjoyable local ones besides. Annual events celebrated on Bocas and Bastimentos include the following:

May Day (May 1) – While the rest of Panama is celebrating Labor Day, the Palo de Mayo (a Maypole dance) is done by young girls in Bocas del Toro and on Isla Bastimentos.

Día de la Virgen del Carmen (third Sunday in July) – Bocatoreños make a pilgrimage to La Gruta, the cave in the middle of the Isla Colón, for a mass in honor of the Virgen del Carmen.

Feria del Mar (September 28–October 2) – The Fair of the Sea is held on Playa El Istmito, a few kilometers north of Bocas.

Fundación de la Provincia de Bocas del Toro (November 16) – Celebrating the foundation of the province in 1904, this is a day of parades and other events; it's a big affair, attracting people from all over the province, and the Panamanian president also attends.

Día de Bastimentos (November 23) – Bastimentos Day is celebrated with a parade and drums on Isla Bastimentos.

Places to Stay The town of Bocas has become a major tourist draw. Numerous new hotels have been opened by both expatriates and locals; many house owners have added a few rooms; and even more accommodations are under construction. You'd be wise to make a reservation during national holidays and local festivals.

Other places to stay are on Boca del Drago, Isla Carenero and Isla Bastimentos.

Mondo Taitu (☎/fax 757 9425, palmtop@ cwp.net.pa), on Avenida I, is popular with travelers and backpackers who like communal living: The bathrooms are shared; there's a ceiling fan in each room; and guests can use the kitchen. A dormitory bed costs US$5. A room with two beds costs US$6, and a single room is US$6. The owners speak Spanish, English, German, Italian and French.

Hospedaje E&L (☎ 757 9206), on the main street (Calle 3) near the southern side of town, is owned by locals Emiliano and Ligia Smith. Rates at this family-run place start at US$6 per bed or US$12 for a double room. Cold-water bathrooms are shared, and guests can use the kitchen.

Hotel Angela (☎ *757 9813, talleyco@cwp.net.pa*), on Avenida I, with a fine view of the bay, is run by an expatriate Californian. Rates for rooms with clean shared bathrooms (some have hot water) are US$12 for two people, or US$14 for a room with a view of the ocean. Guests can use the kitchen.

Another locally owned place in this price range is *Hostal Familiar La Concha* (☎ *757 9609*), on the main street, with dormitory rooms at US$5.50 to US$8 per person and rooms with two beds for US$20 to US$23. *Hospedaje Dixon* (☎ *757 9542*) has six rooms with private bathrooms, a double bed for US$12 and a kitchen for guests.

On the northern end of Calle 3, *Hotel Las Brisas* (☎ *757 9248, brisasbocas@cwp.net.pa*) is a popular spot, mostly for its terrace right over the water. The rooms all have private bathrooms with hot water, but they are worn and very basic; only some have windows. Doubles are US$12 with fan or US$22 with air-con. The hotel has recently constructed a new building nearby.

Hotel Sagitarius (☎ *757 9578*), on Calle 4, has downstairs rooms with fans and private bathrooms for US$15 to US$18 and upstairs rooms with hot water and air-con for US$25 to US$35. *Hotel Hipocampo* (☎ *757 9261*), on Calle 3, has double rooms with private bathrooms and air-con for US$18 to US$22; rates during holidays are significantly higher.

Casa Max (☎ *757 9120*), on Avenida H, offers large, cheerful rooms with ceiling fan, high ceilings, private bathrooms and hot water for US$15/20/27 for one/two/three people. The Dutch owner speaks English.

Hotel La Veranda (☎ *757 9211, heathguidi@hotmail.com*), on Avenida H, is a lovely renovated vintage home owned by a friendly Canadian woman. Many of the furnishings, fixtures and doors are early-20th-century Caribbean style. Rates range from US$18/20 for a double room with fans and immaculate, shared, hot-water bathrooms to US$35 for rooms with private bathrooms. Guests can use the kitchen. A bonus is the chocolate shop, operated on the ground level. The upstairs balcony is nice for relaxing and gathering.

Web site: www.explorepanama.com/veranda.htm

The local owners of the *Hotel Dos Palmas* (☎ *757 9906*), at Calle 6 and Avenida A, proudly proclaim the hotel to be '100% Bocatoreño.' The balcony provides a wonderful view of the bay. Rates for rooms with fans and private bathrooms with heated water are US$22/28 doubles/triples.

Hotel Scarlett (☎/fax *757 9290*), on Calle 4, has bright, big clean rooms with air-con and cold-water private bathrooms for US$20/22/27 for one/two/three people.

Cocomo on the Sea (☎/fax *757 9259*), on Avenida I, has a seaside terrace strung with hammocks and a gorgeous ocean view. The four comfortable, cozy rooms have air-con, private bathrooms and heated water. Rates for one or two people range from US$40 to US$45, one breakfast included.

The *Bocas Inn* (☎ *757 9226, bocasinn@hotmail.com*), near Calle 3 and Avenida G, is operated by Ancon Expeditions. This is another place with a wonderful view over the ocean. Rates range from US$40 to US$65 for rooms with private bathrooms, air-con and hot water. A restaurant is located on the premises, and Ancon Expeditions offers boat tours of the area.

Around the island, there are a couple more places to stay. On a hill overlooking the sea, *Hostal Familiar La Coralina* (☎/fax *684 2527*) is 4km north of town. There are parrots and monkeys on the once-elegant property. Extremely basic rooms are available for US$10; other rooms are US$20 to US$25; quality varies.

The *Mangrove Inn Eco Resort* (☎/fax *757 9594, manginn@usa.net*), a 10-minute boat ride from town, consists of five wooden cabins and a restaurant/bar (for guests only), all built on stilts over the water and connected by walkways. A reef right out front offers good snorkeling. Each cabin has a private bathroom and holds four to six people. The rates – US$85/60 based on double occupancy for divers/nondivers – include all meals, scheduled dives (or snorkeling tours for nondivers) and boat transportation to and from town.

Web site: www.bocas.com/mangrove.htm

Places to Eat The locals' favorite spot is *Don Chicho's*, on the main street, serving cafeteria-style Panamanian food; they even have ice cream. *Beto's Place*, on Calle 5, sells chicken by the slice and is open very late. *Hospedaje Heike*, on Calle 3, has a small but nice, popular restaurant.

Restaurante-Parrillada Kuna, on Avenida H, is a good place for a cheap breakfast. They also serve seafood lunch and dinner. *Gofrio Café*, at the northern end of the main street, is another good breakfast place, with delicious waffles built to your specifications. They also serve sandwiches and salads all day.

The *Buena Vista Deli & Bar*, on the eastern waterfront just behind Calle 3, is a truly American place, with sandwiches, margaritas and DirectTV tuned to US sporting events. The deck over the water is a good place to relax with a dessert (which can be very good but varies in quality) or a drink. It's closed Tuesday.

Le Pirate, on Calle 3, is a popular place for seafood; its bar is popular, too. *Kun Ja* on Calle 3 serves very good and cheap Chinese food.

Entertainment Many of the restaurants – eg, Le Pirate and Buena Vista Deli & Bar – are also popular as bars. The *Wreck Deck Bar*, on Calle 1 along the eastern waterfront, is popular with young travelers; they have a sunken boat and good snorkeling off the front of the bar. Locals frequent several bars along the main street.

Getting There & Away You can get to Bocas del Toro by road from David, Panama City or the Costa Rica border at Sixaola/Guabito to Almirante; by boat from Almirante; or by plane from David, Changuinola, or Panama City.

Bocas del Toro has a fine airport that's the pride of the town. Aeroperlas (☎ 757 8341 in Bocas town, 269 4555 in Panama City) offers daily flights connecting Bocas with Panama City (US$50 one way). A daily morning flight from David to Changuinola continues to Bocas. The cost from David to Bocas is US$25; from Changuinola to Bocas costs US$11.

Two companies, Taxi 25 (☎ 757 9062) and Galapagos Tours & Maritime Taxis (☎ 757 9073) operate frequent water taxis between Almirante and Bocas. Their offices/docks are near one another in both towns; you can easily walk from one to the other to ask which has a taxi leaving soonest. Taxis run between 6 am and 6 pm; the trip takes about 20 minutes and costs US$3.

A ferry (☎ 758 3731) operates between Almirante and Bocas on Wednesday, Friday, Saturday and Sunday. It leaves Almirante at 9 am and Bocas at 5 pm. The trip takes 1½ hours and costs US$1.50 per person and US$20 per vehicle.

Getting Around Bicycles can be rented from several places around town, including Galapagos Tours & Maritime Taxis, for about US$2 per hour, US$5 per half day or US$10 per day.

To go to nearby islands, Galapagos Tours & Maritime Taxis posts roundtrip rates of US$4 to the near side of Isla Bastimentos or US$7 to Red Frog Beach, on the far side. A trip to Isla Carenero costs about US$1. You could also hire any of the boatmen who operate motorized canoes from the dock beside Le Pirate restaurant on Calle 3.

Boca del Drago

Even though it's on Isla Colón, the pleasant, sleepy beach at Boca del Drago is farther from Bocas del Toro than beaches on other islands. Snorkeling and swimming are good here, and you can take tours to Isla de los Pájaros.

Cabañas Estefany (☎ 774 3168, code 2020) has small cabins with bathrooms and kitchen for US$28, suitable for up to four people; larger cabins for up to eight people cost US$55.

The only place to eat is *Restaurante Yarisnari*, which provides pleasant meals (usually involving fish), snorkel rental and tours. It's closed Wednesday.

A taxi from Bocas del Toro takes about 45 minutes and costs US$25 roundtrip. The driver can either wait for you or return at a specified time. You can also get a water taxi directly from Almirante; call Cabañas Estefany for more information.

A bus operates from Boca del Drago to Bocas del Toro on Monday, Wednesday and Friday, departing Boca del Drago at 7 am and leaving Bocas del Toro at 12:30 pm. The cost is US$1.50. If you depend on this bus for transportation from Bocas, you may need to stay at least two nights before you have a chance to catch the next bus back. For the trip back, you could call a taxi or get a ride with someone going that way.

Isla Bastimentos

Beautiful Isla Bastimentos is a 10-minute boat ride from the town of Bocas del Toro (see the Archipiélago de Bocas del Toro map). The small village of Bastimentos has no roads, only a wide, concrete footpath lined on both sides with wooden houses. The town has a lot of litter. There are a growing number of places to stay and eat here.

The island has beautiful beaches. You can walk across the island from the town of Bastimentos to **Playa Wizard** in about 15 minutes. Plenty of other beautiful beaches are along the northern side of the island, including **Playa Segunda** and the long **Playa Larga**, where sea turtles nest from April to August. Playa Larga and much of the eastern side of the island is protected by Parque Nacional Marino Isla Bastimentos, a national marine park.

On the southeastern side of the island is the remote Guaymí village of **Salt Creek**. Tropical forest covers the interior of the island; you can explore it, but go only with a guide, as it's very easy to get lost. There's also a lake, Laguna Bastimentos.

Parque Nacional Marino Isla Bastimentos

Established in 1988, this was Panama's first marine park. Protecting various areas of the Bocas del Toro Archipelago, including parts of Isla Bastimentos (especially Playa Larga) and the Cayos Zapatillas, the park is an important nature reserve for many species of Caribbean wildlife.

Its beaches are used as a nesting ground by four species of sea turtle. The abundant coral reefs support countless species of fish, lobster and other forms of sea life. The lagoons are home to other wildlife, including freshwater turtles and caimans, and there is still more wildlife in the forests. Unfortunately, hunting also occurs in the park.

You can get current park information from the IPAT or ANAM offices in Bocas del Toro. The park entrance fee is US$10.

The dive operators and boatmen in Bocas are also good sources of information about the park and its attractions. If you want to camp out anywhere in the park, you are required to first obtain a permit from ANAM.

Places to Stay & Eat Isla Bastimentos has a growing number of places to stay and eat.

Several beaches are suitable for **camping**. Bocas Water Sports in Bocas del Toro offers camping trips to lovely Red Beach.

The **Pension Tio Tom Bastimentos** (☎/fax 757 9831, tomina@cwp.net.pa) has five rooms with good cross-ventilation over the water. Rates are US$10 for a double room with shared bathrooms, and US$20/21/28 for two/three/four people in a big room with private bathrooms. The restaurant on the deck is a good place to relax. The owners – Tom and Ina Reichelt – offer tours and speak Spanish, English and German.

Pelicano (☎ 757 9830) has a restaurant/bar over the water and three cabins, with a couple more on the way. The cabins cost US$10/14 and have fans and private bathrooms with cold water. The restaurant serves good Italian food and seafood.

Several family-run pensions with basic, cheap rooms line the main walkway through town. **Hospedaje Sylvia** (☎ 757 9442) offers five rooms for US$10 for up to two people, with fans, clean shared bathrooms and a good common area. The rooms upstairs are the most cheerful. **Hostal El Caracol** (☎ 757 9444) has four rooms with small windows for US$5 per person. You can cook in the kitchen.

El Limbo (☎ 757 9888, fax 757 9591, ellimbo@hotmail.com) is a new, remote hotel right on the beach next to the Parque Nacional Marino Isla Bastimentos. The rate of US$40 per person includes breakfast, dinner and snorkeling equipment. Tours are also offered.

Web site: www.ellimbo.com

Getting There & Away To get to Isla Bastimentos from Bocas del Toro, just walk down to Galapagos Tours & Maritime Taxis or to the pier next to Le Pirate restaurant and ask a boatman to take you over. The ride will cost about US$2 to the near side of the island or US$4 to the far side, possibly more if there are fewer passengers.

Isla Carenero

Isla Carenero is a US$1 boat ride from Bocas del Toro. Some people stay here as an alternative to Bocas, and yet Bocas remains easily accessible. Isla Carenero has a marina, a path through the town strewn with litter and a couple of places to stay.

Doña Mara (☎ *757 9551*), on the far side of the island facing away from Bocas, is a hotel, restaurant and bar, with its own small beach. Rates for one of the six cabins are US$50, which can accommodate up to four people. Each room includes air-con, TV and a private bathroom with hot water.

Just across the water from Bocas, *El Pargo Rojo* (☎ *757 9649*) has five cabins built over the water. The rates are US$25 per cabin for up to four people, and include fans, heated water and shared bathrooms. The restaurant/bar serves delicious seafood dinners for US$7 to US$10 on a deck with a view of Bocas across the water. Call ahead for a free ride.

Other Islands

The archipelago has many other beautiful islands, all with good snorkeling spots. **Cayo Nancy** (also known as Isla Solarte), southeast of Isla Colón, has Hospital Point, named for the United Fruit Company hospital that was built here in 1900, when the company had its headquarters in Bocas del Toro. The hospital was established to isolate victims of yellow fever and malaria; at the time it was not yet known that these diseases, then rampant in the area, were transmitted by mosquitoes. It was here for only two decades, however; when a fungus killed the banana trees on the islands, the company moved its banana operations to the mainland and dismantled the hospital buildings. Forest reclaimed the site. There's good snorkeling and diving in front of the point.

Swan Cay, also called Isla de los Pájaros, is off the northwestern shore of Isla Colón, 20 minutes by boat from Boca del Drago. The island is home to red-billed tropic birds and white-crowned pigeons and is popular with bird watchers. Nearby are **Wreck Rock** and **Sail Rock**.

The **Cayos Zapatillas**, southeast of Isla Bastimentos, are popular destinations for snorkeling and diving trips, despite strong currents in the area. The two keys, Cayo Zapatilla Norte and Cayo Zapatilla Sur, have beautiful white-sand beaches that are surrounded by pristine reefs, plus forests for exploring. There is an ANAM station on the south key.

On the way to the Cayos Zapatillas, **Cayo Crawl**, in the long, shallow channel between Isla Bastimentos and Isla Popa, is a popular stopover. The key has an unpretentious restaurant, *El Paso del Marisco*. A beer or soda and a plate of fish with salsa and potatoes costs around US$3. The food's fine, and the location is perfect. From the restaurant, you can dive or snorkel in the tranquil channel, which is home to several coral reefs. Cayo Crawl is about a half-hour by fast boat from Bocas del Toro.

ALMIRANTE
pop 15,550

With the completion in 1999 of a road linking Chiriquí Grande and Almirante, the latter is now the sole jumping-off point for water taxis and ferries to Bocas del Toro. As long as you reach the Almirante water taxi docks by 6 pm, you can be in Bocas del Toro before dark.

Getting There & Away

The Union de Buses Panamericanos (☎ 758 8127) offers two buses a day from Panama City to Almirante, leaving at 7 am (US$23) and 11 pm (US$26). The station in Almirante is near the Accel gasoline station. Buses return to Panama City at 7:30 am (US$23) and 7:30 pm (US$26). The 580km trip takes 10 hours.

From David, buses depart for Almirante every 45 minutes from 5:15 am to 6 pm (US$10). Transporte de Teribe (☎ 758 9464) also has buses every one to 1½ hours for US$10. The coast-to-coast trip over the Cordillera Central mountain range is a beautiful journey.

Buses depart for Changuinola every 20 minutes from 6 am to 8 pm and cost US$1.

Boat service between Almirante and Bocas is frequent; see Getting There & Away under Bocas del Toro, earlier in this section.

CHANGUINOLA
pop 50,000

Headquarters of the Chiriquí Land Company, which brings you Chiquita bananas, Changuinola is a small, hot, rather dusty town surrounded by a sea of banana plantations. The blue bags you see everywhere are laden with pesticides to keep insects away from the bananas.

Changuinola is mainly a transit point to or from Bocas del Toro. It's also the access point for the Wetzo entrance to the Parque Internacional La Amistad. Although it's possible to enter the park from Changuinola, it's much easier to enter it from Chiriquí Province (see the Chiriquí Province section). Access is somewhat remote and expensive on the Bocas side, and entry is controlled by the Teribe tribe. Contact the ANAM office (☎ 758 8967) near the center of town for information on access and transportation to the Wetzo entrance.

Changuinola is the best place to stay overnight between Bocas del Toro and the border. The last water taxi from Almirante to Bocas del Toro departs at 6 pm; if you reach Changuinola after 5 pm, break your journey here.

The border crossing at Guabito (Sixaola on the Costa Rica side) is open every day from 8 am to 6 pm.

Places to Stay & Eat

Changuinola has several places to stay. *Hotel Changuinola* (☎ 758 8678, fax 758 8681), near the airport, is a decent deal. The hotel offers 32 clean, basic rooms with private bathrooms but has no hot water. Rates are US$12/16 singles/doubles with fan, and US$20/25 with air-con.

Hotel Carol (☎ 758 8731), on Avenida 17 de Abril, is less expensive, at US$11/14. It has air-con and private bathrooms, but its rooms are dark, worn, stained and depressing.

The *Restaurant/Bar Chiquita Banana* on the main road opposite the bus station is a good place for a moderately priced meal, with tables inside and out on the patio. Plenty of other places to eat are along the main road.

Getting There & Away

Air Aeroperlas (☎ 758 7521 in Changuinola, 210 9500 in Panama City) offers daily flights connecting Changuinola with Panama City (US$53) and David (US$25).

The morning flight coming from David continues on from Changuinola to Bocas del Toro for the same price.

Bus The Union de Buses Panamericanos (☎ 758 8127) offers two buses a day from Panama City to Changuinola, leaving at 7 am (US$23) and 11 pm (US$26). Buses return to Panama City at 7 am (US$23) and 7 pm (US$26). The 600km trip takes 10 hours.

From David, buses depart every 45 minutes from 5:15 am to 6 pm (US$10). Transporte de Teribe (☎ 758 9464) also has buses every one to 1½ hours for US$10.

Other routes leave from the bus station on the main road in the center of town:

Almirante (US$1, 35 minutes, 21km)
Buses depart every 20 or 25 minutes from 6:15 am to 9 pm.

Guabito (US$0.75, 30 minutes, 17km)
Buses depart every half hour from 6 am to 7 pm for the border with Sixaola, Costa Rica. The bus stops at the bridge at the border, where you transfer to another bus on the Costa Rica side.

San José, Costa Rica (US$8, 5½ to 6½ hours, 281km)
A direct express bus leaves at 10 am. In San José, the bus also departs at 10 am from the Coca-Cola terminal. Coming from San José, the bus arrives in time for you to continue on to Almirante and catch the water taxi for Bocas del Toro.

Taxi A taxi from Changuinola to Almirante takes about 20 minutes and costs US$12; if you're arriving in Changuinola by bus or plane, you can often find a few other passengers to share the ride and cost.

A taxi from Changuinola to the Costa Rican border at Guabito takes about 15 minutes and costs US$5. You can taxi all the way from the border to Almirante, passing through Changuinola, for about US$15; the ride takes around 45 minutes and saves a lot of waiting for buses.

Chiriquí Province

Chiriquí is Panama's beautiful and diverse southwestern province.

The giant Volcán Barú, Panama's only volcano, is protected as a national park; at 3475m, it's the highest point in the country. The flanks of the volcano, with rich black volcanic soil and a cool mountain climate, are home to a number of small farming communities, including Boquete, Volcán, Cerro Punta, and Guadalupe. Chiriquí also provides an entrance to Parque Internacional La Amistad, known for its pristine rain forests.

Chiriquí offers hot springs, beaches (Las Lajas is the best known) and opportunities for trout fishing, hiking, mountain climbing and bird watching. The Golfo de Chiriquí has a national marine park and a couple of islands accessible to visitors, including Isla Boca Brava.

While the climate of the provincial capital David tends to be hot, it's much cooler at the higher elevations around Volcán Barú, just a short distance away. Both the highlands and lowlands of Chiriquí are fertile and productive. The province's products include coffee, citrus fruit, bananas, sugarcane, rum, vegetables, livestock, thoroughbred racehorses and rainbow trout.

Chiriquí Province is also home to the Guaymí people (also called the Ngöbe-Buglé). Guaymí women are easily recognizable by their full, long, brightly colored dresses.

DAVID
pop 75,000
David is Panama's third-largest city, the capital of Chiriquí Province and the center of a rich agricultural region. It has plenty of places to stay and eat. Many travelers stop here overnight on their way to or from the Costa Rican border at Paso Canoas, 53km away. David is also used as a base to visit Boquete or Volcán, the Parque Nacional Volcán Barú and the islands in the Golfo de Chiriquí.

Orientation
David is halfway between San José (Costa Rica) and Panama City – about seven hours by road from either place. The Interamericana does not enter the town, but skirts around its northern and western sides. The city's heart is its fine central plaza, the Parque de Cervantes, about 1.5km southwest of the highway.

Information
IPAT (☎/fax 775 4120) has a tourist information office on the central plaza, upstairs in the Edificio Galherna, the building beside the church; a small sign is posted beside the stairway. It's open 8:30 am to 4:30 pm weekdays, and has information on the whole of Chiriquí Province, including maps of the province and of Boquete.

ANAM (☎ 775 7840, fax 774 6671) has an office near the airport, where you can get information and permits to camp in the national parks. It's open 8 am to 4 pm weekdays.

The post office is on Calle C Norte, a block behind the central plaza. It's open 7 am to 6 pm weekdays and 7 am to 4:30 pm Saturday.

Domestic and international phone calls can be placed from any public phone around town.

Cyber Zone Internet Café (☎ 774 7185), on Calle Central near Avenida 8 Este, provides Internet access for US$2 per hour. They are open 9 am to midnight daily.

Lavamática Cristal (☎ 775 9339), on Calle D Norte between Avenidas 1 Este and 2 Este, will wash and dry your laundry in a few hours for about US$2. It's open 7 am to 7 pm Monday to Saturday, 8 am to 1 pm Sunday.

Things to See & Do
Despite its size and role as a provincial capital, David doesn't offer much in the way of attractions. However, within an hour's drive are many good places to visit, including Boquete, Volcán, Cerro Punta, Guadalupe, Isla Boca Brava, Playa Las Lajas, the Caldera hot springs and the Hacienda Carta Vieja rum distillery.

David's small **Museo de Historia y de Arte José de Obaldía** is in a historic two-story house on Avenida 8 Este between Calle Central and Calle A Norte. The museum contains many fine examples of colonial-era religious art, photos from Chiriquí's past and displays explaining Panama's history (in Spanish).Hours are 8:30 am to noon and 12:45 to 4:30 pm Monday through Saturday; admission is US$1.

The **Pozo de Agua Sulfurosa** are off the road to the Universidad Santa María la Antigua. A **public market** is located at the junction of Avenidas Bolívar and Obaldía.

PANAMA

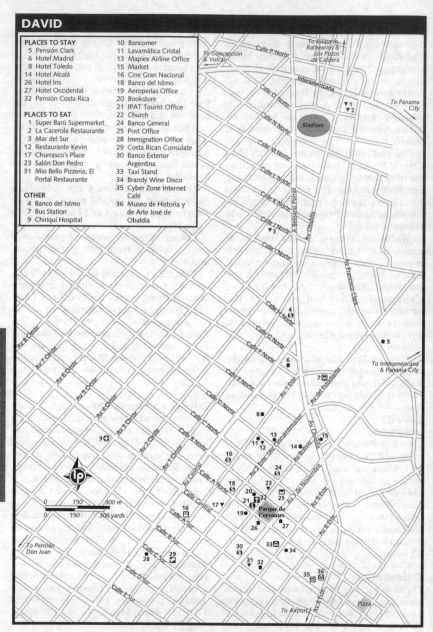

DAVID

PLACES TO STAY
5 Pensión Clark
6 Hotel Madrid
8 Hotel Toledo
14 Hotel Alcalá
26 Hotel Iris
27 Hotel Occidental
32 Pensión Costa Rica

PLACES TO EAT
1 Super Barú Supermarket
2 La Cacerola Restaurante
3 Mar del Sur
12 Restaurante Kevin
17 Churrasco's Place
23 Salón Don Pedro
31 Mio Bello Pizzeria; El
Portal Restaurante

OTHER
4 Banco del Istmo
7 Bus Station
9 Chiriquí Hospital

10 Bancomer
11 Lavamática Cristal
13 Mapiex Airline Office
15 Market
16 Cine Gran Nacional
18 Banco del Istmo
19 Aeroperlas Office
20 Bookstore
21 IPAT Tourist Office
22 Church
24 Banco General
25 Post Office
28 Immigration Office
29 Costa Rican Consulate
30 Banco Exterior
Argentina
33 Taxi Stand
34 Brandy Wine Disco
35 Cyber Zone Internet
Café
36 Museo de Historia y
de Arte José de
Obaldía

Special Events
The Feria de San José de David, held for 10 days each March, is a big international fair. Concepción, half an hour west of David, celebrates its saint's day every February 2.

Places to Stay – Budget
Pensión Costa Rica (☎ 775 1241), on Avenida 5 Este between Calles Central and A Sur, offers singles/doubles with fan for US$4/9 with shared bathrooms or US$6/11 with private bathrooms. This place can be suffocating when it's hot outside.

Three-story *Hotel Iris* (☎ 775 2251, fax 775 7233), beside the Parque de Cervantes, has 70 worn rooms with good beds and private bathrooms. Rates are US$12/15 for one/two people in a room with fan and one bed, US$15/18 with air-con and one bed and US$20 for air-con and two beds.

About a kilometer northeast of the plaza, *Pensión Clark* (☎ 774 3452) is on Avenida Francisco Clark, the fourth house from the corner of Avenida del Estudiante. It's a pleasant little family-run place, clean, quiet and respectable, with six rooms, four with private bathrooms, all priced at US$8. Ask for a room in the rear – each has a private balcony overlooking the lush green yard. At times, nobody is around to check you in.

Pensión Don Juan (☎ 774 6797), at Avenida 3 Oeste and Calle G Sur a block from the Mercado San Mateo, near the fairgrounds, is an upstairs hotel with clean but worn rooms, with one bed for US$7/10 with fan/air-con or a room with two beds and air-con for US$12. The private bathrooms only have a curtain for a toilet door.

Places to Stay – Mid-Range
The *Hotel Toledo* (☎ 774 6732, fax 774 6733), on Avenida 1 Este, an upstairs hotel built in 1995, has 28 clean rooms with air-con, private hot-water bathrooms, color TVs, firm beds and phones for US$17/22. Ask for a room with windows.

Hotel Madrid (☎ 775 2051, fax 774 1849), on Calle F Norte between Avenidas Obaldía and Domingo Diaz, has decent and clean but dark rooms with hot water and air-con for US$18/24. The upstairs rooms are newer.

Hotel Occidental (☎ 775 4068, fax 775 7424), on Avenida 3 de Noviembre beside Parque de Cervantes, has 40 rooms with air-con and private bathrooms for US$18/21/24 singles/doubles/triples. The rooms are a bit worn, but this place offers excellent value and is quite popular. There are a casino and a cheap, popular restaurant on the premises.

Hotel Alcalá (☎ 774 9018, fax 774 9021), on Avenida Bolívar three blocks northeast of Parque Cervantes, is basic but clean, modern and comfortable. Rooms with air-con and private bathrooms are US$20/24. There's a restaurant downstairs.

Places to Eat
The restaurant at the *Hotel Occidental* is the best value in town. It's hard to spend over US$2 at this popular cafeteria.

A block from the plaza, *Churrasco's Place* on Avenida 2a Este is popular with locals for its good, inexpensive food. Downstairs is a covered, open-air restaurant; a slightly more expensive air-conditioned bar/restaurant section is upstairs in the rear. Churrasco's is open 24 hours daily.

A pleasant little place for an inexpensive breakfast or lunch is the small open-air *Restaurante Kevin* in the front of the Hotel Saval. Service is friendly, and meals cost about US$2.

Mio Bello Pizzeria and the adjacent *El Portal Restaurante*, on Calle A Sur near Avenida 3 de Noviembre, share a menu and a kitchen. These places are popular with the college crowd on weekend nights, mainly because El Portal has a cozy, subterranean dining room that's quite hip. Pasta and seafood are the specialties of the house. A 12-inch pizza costs US$6. Fish and meat dishes run US$4 to US$6.

The *Salón Don Pedro*, on Avenida Bolívar near the northern corner of the central plaza, offers Chinese as well as Panamanian food, an economical 'meal of the day' (US$2) and some of the coolest air-con in town.

Mar del Sur, on Calle J Norte just west of Avenida Belisario Porras, is known for its Peruvian food and good seafood.

Among stores on the southern side of the Super Barú supermarket, on Avenida Obaldía near the Interamericana, is *La Cacerola Restaurante*, a popular buffet-style diner. Most dishes cost about US$2. Unfortunately, prices aren't posted, so you may get an occasional surprise.

PANAMA

The *Super Barú supermarket* has large deli and produce sections and a well-stocked pharmacy. There's even a small area where you can enjoy a dessert or cold beverage.

Entertainment

The cinema *Cine Gran Nacional* is on Avenida 1 Este between Calle Central and Calle A Sur. *Jorón Zebede*, 1km from the Interamericana on the road to Boquete, is a popular disco for dancing on weekends after 11 pm. In town, the *Brandy Wine Disco*, a couple of blocks south of the main plaza, is popular. There are also several casinos.

Getting There & Away

Air David's airport, the Aeropuerto Enrique Malek, is about 5km from town. There are no buses to the airport; take a taxi (US$3).

Aeroperlas (☎ 775 7779, 721 1195 at the airport) and Mapiex (☎ 721 0841) offer daily flights connecting David with Panama City (US$57). Aeroperlas flies to Changuinola and Bocas del Toro daily (US$25). Grupo TACA (☎ 265 7814) flies from San José, Costa Rica, to David for US$175.

Bus In Panama City, buses depart for David from the Terminal Nacional de Transporte near Albrook airport. Regular buses (US$11, 7 hours, 438km) leave every one to 1½ hours from 5:30 am to 8 pm. Express buses (US$15, 5 hours) leave at 10:45 pm and midnight. Padafront (☎ 227 4210) buses depart for David every 1½ hours from 7 am to 8 pm (US$11), with express buses at 11 pm and midnight (US$15).

The David bus station is on Avenida del Estudiante, about 600m northeast of the central plaza. It has a small office where you can leave luggage for US$0.50 a day, and a restaurant open 5 am to midnight.

David is a transportation hub for western Panama and has buses to many places:

Almirante (US$9, four hours, 170km)
Take the Changuinola bus.

Boquete (US$1.20, one hour, 38km)
Buses leave every 30 minutes from 6 am to 9:30 pm.

Caldera (US$1.50, 45 minutes, 20km)
Buses leave hourly from 8:15 am to 7:30 pm.

Cerro Punta (US$2.65, 2¼ hours, 79km)
Buses leave every 20 minutes from 5 am to 8 pm.

Changuinola (US$10, 4½ hours, 190km)
Buses leave hourly from 5 am to 6:30 pm.

Chiriquí Grande (US$6, three hours, 106km)
Take the Changuinola bus.

Guadalupe (US$2.65, 2½ hours, 82km)
Take the Cerro Punta bus, which continues on to Guadalupe.

Horconcitos (US$1.50, 45 minutes, 45km)
Four buses depart daily, at 11 am, noon, 4 and 5 pm.

Las Lajas (US$2, 1½ hours, 75km)
Four buses depart daily, from 11:45 am to 5:20 pm. The bus continues on to the beach for an additional US$1.50.

Panama City (US$10.60, 6½ to seven hours, 438km; express: US$15, 5½ to six hours)
The regular bus leaves every 45 minutes from 6:45 am to 8 pm. The express bus leaves at 10:45 pm and midnight.

Paso Canoas (Costa Rican border; US$1.50, 1½ hours, 53km)
Buses leave every 10 minutes from 4:30 am to 9:30 pm.

Puerto Armuelles (US$2.65, 2½ hours, 88km)
Buses leave every 15 minutes from 4:15 am to 9:45 pm.

Río Sereno (Costa Rican border; US$4, 2½ hours, 104km)
Buses leave every 45 minutes to an hour from 5 am to 5 pm.

Volcán (US$2.30, 1¾ hours, 57km)
Take the Cerro Punta bus.

Tracopa (☎ 775 0585) operates direct buses between David and San José, Costa Rica. Buses depart every day at 8:30 am from the David bus station and arrive in San José about eight hours later. From San José, buses depart for the return trip to David at 7:30 am. The fare is US$12.50 one-way.

You can buy your ticket up to two days in advance. The Tracopa office is open 7:30 am to noon and 2 to 4 pm Monday to Saturday, 7:30 to 8:30 am Sunday.

Getting Around

David has local buses and plenty of taxis. Taxi fares within the city are US$0.65 to US$1; the fare to the airport is US$3.

Rental car companies in David include:

Avis	☎ 774 7075
Budget	☎ 775 1667
Gaby's	☎ 777 0141
Hertz	☎ 775 6828
Hilary	☎ 774 6440
Mike's	☎ 775 4963

AROUND DAVID

The **Hacienda Carta Vieja** (☎ 772 7083), the largest and oldest rum distillery in Panama (established in 1915), is just off the Interamericana, 20 minutes' drive west of David. Carta Vieja gives tours in Spanish for parties of two or more. The distillery operates 7:30 am to noon and 12:30 to 4 pm weekdays. To get there, turn south at the intersection with the road to Boquerón, as if you're heading to Alanje.

The **Balneario Majagua**, 3.9km north of the Interamericana on the road to Boquete, is a cool place to swim in a river with a waterfall. There's also a dance floor and bar. Another place to cool off is the **Balneario La Cascada**, 8.4km from the Interamericana, also with a bar.

Los Pozos de Caldera are natural hot springs famous for their health-giving properties, especially for rheumatism sufferers. The springs are on private land near the town of **Caldera**. Admission is US$0.50.

Caldera is 14km east of the David-Boquete road; a sign marks the turnoff. There are hourly buses from David. The springs are reached by a bad dirt road that stems from the paved road through Caldera. The walk from the paved road to the springs takes about 45 minutes. In a 4WD vehicle, you can drive to within a 10-minute walk from the springs. You'll need to ask the way, as there are numerous turnoffs and no signs.

GOLFO DE CHIRIQUÍ

South of David, the Golfo de Chiriquí is home to the **Parque Nacional Marino Golfo de Chiriquí**, a national marine park with an area of 14,740 hectares protecting 25 islands, 19 coral reefs and abundant wildlife. Attractions include beaches, snorkeling, swimming, diving, surfing, bird watching and big-game fishing.

The 3000-hectare **Isla Boca Brava** is just off the coast. From here, you're a stone's throw from the national marine park. Sharing the island with you are three species of monkey, four species of sea turtle and lots of parrots. There are many coral reefs and picturesque beaches in the area, with excellent opportunities for snorkeling.

On the island, Frank and Yadira Köhler operate the *Restaurante y Cabañas Boca Brava* (☎ 676 3244). The lodgings consist of four comfortable rooms with private bathrooms for US$15 to US$22 for two people and five bamboo cabins for US$6 to US$10 with shared bathrooms. A hammock costs US$3 per person. Frank says he doesn't accept reservations for the cabins, but he can always find you a place to stay if you're willing to sleep in a hammock.

The breezy restaurant/bar features lobster for US$7; most other full meals are half as much. A water taxi will take you to a nearby island for US$2 to US$4 per person roundtrip, or you can arrange a tour through Frank (US$10 to US$70 for up to five people). He speaks English, German and Spanish.

To reach the island, drive or take a bus to the town of Horconcitos, south of the Interamericana and 45km east of David. Four buses run daily to Horconcitos from David, at 11 am, noon, 4 and 5 pm (US$1.50, 45 minutes). If you take the later buses, you'll reach the island after dark. You can also take any bus that runs along the Interamericana and ask them to drop you off at the Horconcitos road.

From Horconcitos or the Interamericana, you can take a 10km or 13km taxi ride to Boca Chica, a small fishing village. The ride costs about US$12 per group from Horconcitos and US$15 from the Interamericana. At the Boca Chica dock, hire a water taxi (US$1 per person) to take you 200m to the island.

Hint: Even if you're going only for the day, do not agree on a roundtrip price with the taxi driver; you may be able to find travelers to split the cost with you on the way back. Frank can arrange for a taxi to pick you up.

If you drive your own vehicle, you can safely leave it near the village dock, but at the time of writing, the road between Horconcitos and Boca Chica was quite rough. Plans were underway to repair and pave it.

PLAYA LAS LAJAS

Playa Las Lajas, which is located 62km east of David and 13km south of the Interamericana, is one of several long, palm-lined beaches along this stretch of the Pacific coast. With its broad expanse of white sand, Playa Las Lajas is quite popular and crowded on the weekends but often empty during the week. The waves are perfect for body surfing.

If you turn to the right at the end of the road to the beach, you'll come to *Las Lajas Beach Cabins* (☎ *690 7275, 775 4171 in David)*. These consist of seven bamboo cabins with shared bathrooms (US$6/10/15 for one/two/three people) and six concrete cabins with private bathrooms (US$18/23/36 for two/three/four people). The place is rustic but decent, and owner Roy is gradually adding more cabins and improving the bedding. He also plans to upgrade the restaurant/bar and add other conveniences such as a public phone. Roy speaks flawless English and Spanish; ask him about hiking to mangroves or renting horses.

Four buses a day run between David and the town of Las Lajas from 11:45 am to 5:20 pm (US$2, 1½ hours, 75km). You may be able to get the driver to continue on to the beach for an additional US$1.50. Alternatively, you can take any bus along the Interamericana and ask the driver to let you off at the turnoff for Las Lajas. From the turnoff or Las Lajas town, taxis will take you to the beach for US$4 to US$6.

PUERTO ARMUELLES
Puerto Armuelles is Panama's second Pacific port, used mainly for loading bananas from the area's plantations. There are some good beaches just south of town, or you can just amble around, but Puerto Armuelles is the end of the road and there isn't really much around here for visitors to do.

Puerto Armuelles has several restaurants and hotels. *Hotel Koco's Place* (☎ *770 7049)* offers rooms for US$17/28 with fan/air-con. In town at the eastern end of the oceanfront road is the family-run *Pensión Balboa*, which offers clean, fan-cooled rooms with shared bathrooms for US$6/8 singles/doubles and rooms with private bathrooms for US$12.

Close to the Pensión Balboa is the *Restaurante y Pizzeria Don Carlos*, which specializes in seafood and pizza.

Buses go to Puerto Armuelles from David every 15 minutes or so (US$2.65, 2½ hours, 88km).

Highlands

BOQUETE
pop 3000
Just 38km north of the hot provincial capital of David, Boquete is so different it feels like it's in another country. Nestled in a craggy mountain valley at 1060m, with the rocky Río Caldera running through it, Boquete is known for its cool, fresh climate and pristine natural environment. It's a fine place for walking, bird watching, and enjoying a respite from the heat of the lowlands.

Flowers, coffee, vegetables and citrus fruits are grown in and around Boquete. The navel-orange season, from November to February, is a popular time to visit. Boquete oranges, originally brought from Riverside, California, are known for their sweetness, and the coffee is widely regarded as the country's finest.

On some nights temperatures can drop to near freezing. Visitors should pack some warm clothes if they plan to do any camping.

Orientation & Information
Boquete's central area is only a few square blocks. The main road, Avenida Central, comes north from David, passes along the western side of the plaza and continues up the hill past the church.

An IPAT tourist office is on the main road about 1.5km south of town. You can pick up maps here and information on the sites. A balcony affords a wonderful view of the river valley.

The post office is on the eastern side of the plaza and is open 7 am to 6 pm weekdays, 7 am to 5 pm Saturday. International calls can be made from any pay phone around town.

The *lavamático* (laundry) is on Avenida Central, opposite and a little downhill from the church. They'll wash and dry your clothes (US$2 for a small load, twice that for a big load).

The CafeNet, on Avenida Central, half a block south of the plaza, provides Internet access for US$2 per hour.

For medical help, Dr Leonido Pretelt at Centro Medico San Juan Bautista (☎ 270 1881), on Calle 4 Sur a block east of the plaza, was highly recommended.

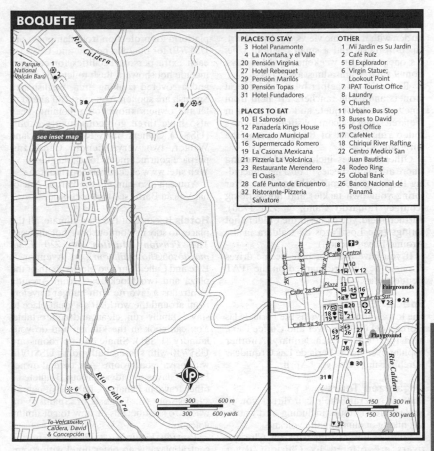

BOQUETE

PLACES TO STAY
3 Hotel Panamonte
4 La Montaña y el Valle
20 Pensión Virginia
27 Hotel Rebequet
29 Pensión Marilós
30 Pensión Topas
31 Hotel Fundadores

PLACES TO EAT
10 El Sabrosón
12 Panadería Kings House
14 Mercado Municipal
16 Supermercado Romero
19 La Casona Mexicana
21 Pizzería La Volcánica
23 Restaurante Merendero
   El Oasis
28 Café Punto de Encuentro
32 Ristorante-Pizzeria
   Salvatore

OTHER
1 Mi Jardín es Su Jardín
2 Café Ruíz
5 El Explorador
6 Virgin Statue;
   Lookout Point
7 IPAT Tourist Office
8 Laundry
9 Church
11 Urbano Bus Stop
13 Buses to David
15 Post Office
17 CafeNet
18 Chiriquí River Rafting
22 Centro Medico San
   Juan Bautista
24 Rodeo Ring
25 Global Bank
26 Banco Nacional de
   Panamá

The Instituto Geográfico Nacional (Tommy Guardia) in Panama City sells a topographical map of Boquete.

Things to See & Do

There is a lot to see and do around Boquete. Several good paved roads lead out of town into the surrounding hills, passing coffee plantations, agricultural and cattle farms, gardens and virgin forest. **Coffee plantations** include Café Sitton, one of the largest, with big processing barns, and Café Ruíz. You can visit to see how the coffee is grown and processed; at Café Ruíz, just north of town, you can see how flavored coffees are made.

Boquete is a great place for walking and hiking. Walk around the roads and trails, up the river, or, for the ambitious, climb to the summit of **Volcán Barú** (3475m), in the nearby national park. There are several entrances to the park, but the one with easiest access to the summit is from Boquete (see the section on Parque Nacional Volcán Barú). On the other hand, the Sendero Los Quetzales (Quetzals Trail) goes uphill from near here; it's easier to walk that trail from Cerro Punta.

The **Terrenos de la Feria de las Flores y Café** (Flower and Coffee Fairgrounds), on the eastern side of the river, is a large flower garden where you can take a peaceful stroll next to the river. Admission is US$0.50.

Mi Jardín es Su Jardín, just uphill from Café Ruiz, is a magnificent flower garden with painted animals surrounding a luxurious private estate. You're welcome to visit; there's no admission charge.

El Explorador, in a hilly area a half-hour walk northeast of town, offers a large flower garden with trails, fine views, quirky folk art, piped-in music and a small open-air cafe. It's open only on weekends and holidays, from 9 am to 6 pm; admission is US$1.

Rodeos, put together by a club of local farmers and cattle ranchers, are held from time to time in Boquete and other towns in the area. They welcome visitors. Boquete's rodeo ring is east of the river near the fairgrounds.

Other activities include **bird watching** (there are many species of bird here, including the quetzal), **trout fishing** in the river (bring your own tackle) and **horse riding** (contact Eduardo Cano, ☎ 720 1750). Further afield, you can visit the Caldera **hot springs** (see Los Pozos de Caldera in the Around David section).

If you have a car or bike, scenic drives through the hills are marked on the IPAT Boquete map.

Special Events
The town's annual festival is the Feria de las Flores y del Café (Flower and Coffee Fair), held for 10 days each January. Another popular event is the Feria de Las Orquídeas (Orchid Fair), held every April.

Organized Tours
Staff at several hotels can direct you to guides offering tours, including bird watching, hiking or climbing the volcano.

White-water rafting trips on Chiriquí rivers are offered by Chiriquí River Rafting (☎ 720 1505, fax 720 1506, rafting@panama-rafting.com), which has its office on Avenida Central just south of the plaza. This company has a great reputation for safety. All-day trips are offered for US$75 to US$100, depending on the river, with a minimum of four people. If you don't have four people, you can call the company, and they will try to team you with others to meet the minimum.
Web site: www.panama-rafting.com

Places to Stay
Camping A mountainside retreat 2.5km from town, *La Montaña y el Valle (☎/fax 720 2211, montana@chiriqui.com)* has large, attractive 2.5-hectare grounds on a working coffee farm, with nature trails and great views. Three tent sites, each on a concrete platform for protection from dampness, are US$7/10 for one/two people and US$3 for each extra person. Facilities for campers include hot showers, flush toilets, electricity and a covered cooking area. English and Spanish are spoken. You must call ahead to let the owners know you're coming. They also have three gorgeous luxury cabins (US$77). Owners Barry Robbins and Jane Walker, two very friendly Canadians, prepare gourmet meals for cabin guests.
Web site: www.executiveis.com/montana

You can also camp in the Parque Nacional Volcán Barú (see that section).

Hotels Because of the cool climate, all the places to stay in Boquete have hot showers. The *Pensión Marilós (☎ 720 1380, marilos66@hotmail.com)*, at Avenida A Este and Calle 6 Sur two blocks south of the plaza and two blocks east from Avenida Central, is a favorite with budget travelers from around the world. It's a great place to stay – family run, clean and comfortable. You can cook in the kitchen and do your laundry (US$1). Single/double rooms are US$7/10 with shared bathrooms, US$10/16 with private bathrooms. Ask cordial owner Frank Glavas for advice about Boquete or other travel in Panama – he's full of helpful suggestions (in English or Spanish) on where to see quetzals or how to get up the volcano.

Pensión Virginia (☎ 720 1260), on the central plaza, is an older hotel with rooms for US$8/10 with shared bathrooms or US$13/23 with private bathrooms.

Pensión Topas (☎/fax 720 1005), on Avenida Belisario Porras three blocks south of the plaza and one block east of the main road, has a swimming pool and five rooms, with two more scheduled to be built. Four rooms have private bathrooms and cost US$20/26. One room, with an outside, solar-heated bathroom, costs US$9/12. A wonderful breakfast is available for US$4. The gracious hosts speak English, Spanish, German and French and are planning to open additional rooms in Volcancito.

The *Hotel Rebequet (☎ 720 1365)*, opposite the Pensión Marilós, has nine attractive rooms each, with private bathroom, for

US$20/30. Each room has a TV and fridge; guests are welcome to cook in the kitchen, play billiards or use the TV room. It also has three smaller rooms with two single beds for US$10/15.

Hotel Fundadores (☎ 720 1298) on the main road charges US$24 to US$66 per room. The *Hotel Panamonte* (☎ 720 1327), at the northern end of town, is a beautiful old hotel, great for peace and quiet. Rooms start at US$49 to US$60.

Places to Eat

Boquete has many inexpensive restaurants to choose from. *Pizzería La Volcánica*, on the main road near the plaza, has pizza and Italian dishes for around US$5 and fruit drinks; the service is friendly and fast. *Ristorante-Pizzeria Salvatore*, two blocks south of Hotel Fundadores, offers better pizza in a pleasant environment, with tables inside and out. It also has pastas and seafood.

On the main road a block south of the plaza, *La Casona Mexicana* has tasty Mexican food and interesting decor. Entrees cost around US$4, and there are good vegetarian options.

El Sabrosón, on the main road two blocks north of the plaza, is a simple place that offers local regional food at incredibly low prices. Typical meals cost US$2.

The *Café Punto de Encuentro*, just east of the main road two blocks south of the plaza, serves breakfast and coffee from 7am to noon on a pleasant deck. It's a relaxing atmosphere with new-age music, service a bit on the slow side, and even an English-language book exchange.

The *Restaurante Merendero El Oasis*, with a wonderful location opposite the fairgrounds and next to the river, serves breakfast, lunch and dinner at reasonable prices. Sandwiches are US$1.50 to US$2; pastas are US$2 to US$5.50; and seafood dinners start at US$4.50.

The area's fresh produce is sold at the *mercado municipal*, on the northeastern corner of the plaza. *Supermercado Romero*, on Avenida A Este a block east of the plaza, has all your basic groceries. Among the several bakeries in town, *Panedería Kings House*, on Avenida A Este one block north and one block east of the plaza, is one of the best.

Getting There & Around

Buses to Boquete depart David's main bus terminal every 30 minutes from 6 am to 9:30 pm (US$1.20, one hour, 38km). Buses to David depart from the northern side of the Boquete's plaza every 30 minutes from 5 am to 6:30 pm (US$1.20, one hour, 38km).

Boquete is a small town and you can easily walk around the center in a short time. Walking is a great way to see the area.

The local *urbano* buses, winding around through the hills among coffee plantations, farms and forest, cost just US$0.50 to US$1 and are a good way to get oriented. They depart on the main road one block north of the plaza. There are also taxis; US$2 fares are the norm.

Getting around on horseback or bicycle is another option.

VOLCÁN TO GUADALUPE

A road branches off the Interamericana at Concepción (1200m) and climbs steadily through the towns of Volcán (1500m), Bambito (1600m), and Cerro Punta (1970m) until it stops at Guadalupe (2130m), on the western side of Volcán Barú. It's a good, paved road the entire way, frequently traversed by buses from David.

The climate up here is cool, and the air is brisk. The farmland around Cerro Punta has rich, black volcanic soil and it's a great area for walking. As you ascend toward Cerro Punta, everything starts to look European, with meticulously tended agricultural plots and houses with steep-pitched tin roofs. A Swiss colony was founded here (one farm is named Nueva Suiza). Later immigrants included Croatians, and you may still hear their language spoken in the area.

This area produces not only abundant cool-climate crops like vegetables, fruits, strawberries, flowers and coffee, but also trout, livestock and thoroughbred race-horses. You'll pass several *haras* (stables) along the Cerro Punta road, where race-horses are bred.

As on the Boquete side of Volcán Barú, there are accommodations that range from budget to expensive. And you can camp in the two national parks: Parque Nacional Volcán Barú and Parque Internacional La Amistad. Another option is to visit this area on a day trip from David.

PANAMA

Volcán
pop 9000

From Concepción, this little town, also called Hato del Volcán, is the first you'll come to, 32km uphill from the Interamericana turnoff. Clinging to the flanks of the giant Volcán Barú, it's almost dwarfed by its namesake.

Orientation & Information The road that links Concepción and Volcán forks in the center of town at the Shell gasoline station: One arrow points left toward Río Sereno, on the Costa Rican border (47km); the other points right toward Cerro Punta (16km).

Before you reach this fork, you'll see a small building marked 'Guias de Turismo' (☎ 771 4755) on the left. These friendly people, a cooperative of student guides, offer a number of inexpensive tours (in English and Spanish) around the area. You're also welcome to stop here just to ask for information about the area; they offer a map and plenty of helpful information.

Another tour cooperative is based in a small office beside the Shell station, marked 'Guias Ecológicas, High Lands Adventures' (☎/fax 771 4413, jcaceres@chiriqui.com). It too offers information, maps of the area, tours and guides. Rates range from US$30 to US$70 per person.

The CyberCafé, operated in conjunction with the Hotel and Restaurante Don Tavo, about 1.2km down the road toward Río Sereno, offers Internet access for US$1.50 an hour.

Things to See & Do The ruins of the pre-Columbian culture at **Barriles** are about a five-minute drive from the center of town. The ruins are on private land, but the family who lives there is very gracious, allowing visitors to see the ruins and answering questions about them. Major artifacts from the archaeological site, including statues, metates (flat stone platforms used for grinding corn), pottery and jewelry are displayed in the Museo Antropológico Reina Torres de Araúz in Panama City.

José de la Cruz González makes wood carvings, sculptures, furniture and etchings on crystal and glass at **Arte Cruz**, 3km south of Volcán. Small items are for sale, or he will make you a personal souvenir.

Just past Volcán, on the way to Bambito, is one of the entrances to Parque Nacional Volcán Barú; see the park's section, later, for details.

Other attractions around Volcán include springs, rivers, trout fishing, a botanical garden, coffee plantations (Café Volcán Barú or Cafetales Durán, with a million coffee bushes!), racehorse ranches and habitats of the quetzal and other exotic birds. Hiking trails in the area include one to the top of Cerro Punta; the Sendero Los Quetzales (the Quetzals Trail), which crosses the national park to Boquete (see the Parque Nacional Volcán Barú section); three trails in Parque Internacional La Amistad; the Sendero del Tapir (Tapir Trail); and a number of others. The lakes and the woodland around the nearby **Lagunas de Volcán** are excellent sites for bird watching.

Places to Stay Several places to stay are on the road to Río Sereno. Just past the turnoff, the *Motel California* (☎ 771 4272) has 15 clean, basic cabins with hot-water private bathrooms for US$22 for doubles, US$25 for families.

Farther along, about 800m from the turnoff, the *Hotel y Restaurante Don Tavo* (☎/fax 771 5144, volcan@chiriqui.com), has 17 nice rooms with private hot-water bathrooms for US$28/37/50 singles/doubles/triples. The hotel operates an Internet cafe.

Next you come to a turnoff to *Valle de la Luna* (☎/fax 771 4225), 1.6km from the center of town. This is a decent family-friendly place with 5 cabins for US$35 to US$48; more are under construction. Each cabin has a kitchen, and there's a small cafe.

About 2.3km from the turnoff are the very lovely *Cabañas Las Huacas* (☎ 771 4363), where five two-story A-frame cottages, each with a kitchen, six beds and hot-water bathroom, are set around attractive grounds that include a goose pond and gorgeous mountain vistas. Prices range from US$25 to US$85.

Farthest from town (2.8km from central Volcán), the recently remodeled *Hotel Dos Ríos* (☎ 771 4271, fax 771 5794) has the feel of a hunting lodge. The entire hotel is made of lightly stained oak, and all 16 rooms face a creek and the mountains. Rates at this attractive and peaceful place are US$50 for up to four people. The restaurant offers decent food at reasonable prices.

Places to Eat The *Café Cerro Brujo*, located next to the Shell gasoline station at the center of town, offers good food at reasonable prices, including pastas, free-range chicken, burritos and patacones. This eclectically decorated restaurant is becoming a popular meeting place in the evenings.

The *Biga Deli*, 1.5km from the center of town on the road to Río Sereno, is a good place for a meal. Offerings include pastas (US$7 to US$8) and pizza (US$4 to US$6). Soups, salads, sandwiches and bruschetta are also available. Even if you don't eat a meal there, if at all possible, stop for a treat from the bakery. A slice of wonderful pie is expensive (US$3) but humongous; you can wash down with an espresso.

Bambito
Seven kilometers past Volcán on the way to Cerro Punta, Bambito is barely a town at all. The only noticeable feature is the large Hotel Bambito (US$138/154 if you really need to know). Opposite this, the **Truchas de Bambito** rainbow trout farm is worth a stop. Thousands of trout are raised in outdoor ponds with frigid water from the nearby river. You can buy fresh trout here, or rent some tackle and catch your own. Admission is US$0.50.

Past the trout farm, *Cabañas Kucikas* (☎ 771 4245, fax 269 0623) has 17 spacious A-frame cottages that are set around 36 hectares of parklike grounds with children's play areas, barbecue sites and a river that provides decent trout fishing. Cottages of various sizes, sleeping two to 10 people, have kitchens and hot-water bathrooms. The cost is US$60 for two, but rates are not that much more for up to six people. This is a charming, romantic place.

Farther north, just past the bridge, is the *Bambito Camping Resort* (☎ 771 5126, fax 771 5127, eproject@chiriqui.com), in a lovely location next to Río Chiriquí Viejo. They offer tent camping for US$50 for four people (tent provided) and rooms from US$110. A range of activities is provided, including horseback riding (US$10 per hour), mountain bike rental (US$5 per hour), rock climbing and rappelling (US$25), river

tubing (US$10) and rafting (US$90), kayaking Lagunas de Volcán (US$30) and climbing Volcán Barú (US$90, overnight). You don't have to be a guest to participate in the activities.

Web site: www.bambito-forest-resort.com

Cerro Punta
pop 6000
At an altitude of 1970m, this town is only a few blocks long, but it's surrounded by beautiful, rich agricultural lands. About 7km north of Bambito, the village offers spectacular views across a fertile valley to the peaks of Parque Internacional La Amistad, a few kilometers away.

Visitors come here primarily during the dry season (November to April) to visit the two nearby parks (Volcán Barú and La Amistad) and to enjoy the beauty of the surroundings. During this time, quetzals are often seen right on the road; though they can be seen here year-round, they tend to live farther up in the mountains during the rainy season. Ask around to find the best places for quetzal spotting.

Other attractions in Cerro Punta include **Fresa Cerro Punta**, where strawberries are grown, and **Panaflores** and **Plantas y Flores**, where flowers are raised for commercial sale; you can visit all these places. Racehorse and prize cattle farms are also here.

The main road continues through Cerro Punta and ends at Guadalupe. Another road takes off to the west, heading for the Las Nubes entrance to Parque Internacional La Amistad, 6.8km away; the turnoff is marked by a large wooden sign (see the Parque Internacional La Amistad section, later in this chapter, for details on the park).

The *Hotel Cerro Punta* (☎/fax 771 2020, hotelcer@hotmail.com), on the main road, offers 10 decent rooms with big windows, nice views and good light. All rooms have private hot-water bathrooms; rates are US$22/28 singles/doubles. The hotel also has a good restaurant and bar.

La Primavera (☎ 774 1060 in David) is half a kilometer down the road to Las Nubes, opposite the Delca store. This family-run pension is much more basic, with just five rooms with hot-water private bathrooms. Rates are US$14 to US$16.

Guadalupe

Three kilometers beyond Cerro Punta, Guadalupe is at the end of the road. It's a beautiful area for walking among the meticulously tended farms and gardens, and enjoying the cool climate. The little community is full of flowers, and the agricultural plots curling up the steep, rich hillsides are as beautiful as any garden in the world. The **Jardín Botánico Dracula** offers tours of their orchid farm in Spanish for US$7.

Places to Stay & Eat In the center of town, the *Hotel Los Quetzales* (☎ 771 2182, *fax 771 2226, calfaro@chiriqui.com*) is the ideal place to enjoy this tranquil community. The hotel consists of 10 rooms, two dormitories, a restaurant, bar, lounge, bakery, pizzeria, spa with sauna and massages and an organic garden. Every room features a tall ceiling, cheerful decor and private hot-water bathrooms. Guests can use the trails around the Cabañas Los Quetzales inside the Parque Nacional Volcán Barú, less than an hour's walk from the hotel; the hotel can also provide transportation. Horses and bikes are available for rent. Owner Carlos Alfaro speaks fluent English and Spanish.

Space in a dormitory costs US$11 per person, a great deal considering you get use of the lodge for relaxing and the trails. Rooms start at US$44/55 without/with a bathtub. You can camp here for US$10.

Carlos also owns four chalets inside the Parque Nacional Volcán Barú (signs inside the park erroneously say 'La Amistad') called the *Cabañas Los Quetzales* (*same contact information as the hotel*). Each cabin has a fully equipped kitchen and separate bedrooms, hot water, a fireplace, kerosene lanterns and large terraces. Best of all, they're deep in the rain forest. Here you can stroll the jungle taking in all the sights – or just enjoy complete relaxation. Built in 1996, these lovely chalets are famous all over Panama.

The cabins hold from five to 14 people and cost US$66 to US$132 per night; the rates include transportation from the Hotel Los Quetzales, trail guides for exploring the forest, and use of horses, ponchos and boots. A good budget option is a geodesic dome, which sleeps several and costs US$44 (just be sure they remove the toilet from the center of the room before you agree to stay

here!). For a bit extra the hotel can provide you with food (cooked or uncooked). It's a good idea to reserve in advance, especially during the dry season (November to April). Web site: www.losquetzales.com

In addition to food at the hotel, Guadalupe has a couple of tiny restaurants.

Getting There & Away

The 'Cerro Punta' bus leaves David every 15 minutes from 5:30 am to 6 pm daily (US$2.65, 2¼ hours, 79km), stopping at Volcán and Bambito and continuing on to Guadalupe. You could catch this bus at the turnoff from the Interamericana in Concepción, if you're coming from Costa Rica.

PARQUE NACIONAL VOLCÁN BARÚ

Giant Volcán Barú is Panama's only volcano and the dominant geographical feature of western Panama. Its fertile volcanic soil and the temperate climate of its midaltitude slopes support some of Panama's most productive agriculture, especially in the areas around Cerro Punta and Boquete. Large trees dominate the volcano's lower slopes, giving way on the upper slopes to smaller plants, bushes, scrub and abundant alpine wildflowers.

Volcán Barú is no longer active, and there is no record of its most recent eruption. It has not one but seven craters. Its summit, at 3475m, is the highest point in Panama, and on a clear day it affords views of both the Pacific and Caribbean coasts.

The 14,300-hectare Parque Nacional Volcán Barú is home to abundant wildlife, including pumas, tapirs and the *conejo pintado,* a spotted raccoonlike animal. At lower elevations the mountain is good for bird watching; the resplendent quetzal is often seen in this park, especially during the dry season (November to April). The park provides ample possibilities for hiking, mountain climbing and camping.

The entrance fee is US$3, US$5 if you plan to camp.

Climbing the Volcano

There are entrances with summit access to the park on the eastern and western sides of the volcano. The eastern access to the summit, from Boquete, is the easiest, but it involves a strenuous (some say painful)

uphill hike along a 14km dirt/mud road that goes from the park entrance – about 8km northwest of the center of Boquete – to the summit. If you drive or take a taxi as far up as you can and then walk the rest of the way, it takes about five or six hours to reach the summit from the park gate; walking from town would take another two or three hours each way. It's best to camp on the mountain at least one night, and you should be prepared for cold. Camping will also allow you to be at the top during the morning, when the views are most likely to be clear.

Another park entrance is just outside the town of Volcán, on the road to Bambito and Cerro Punta. The rugged road into the park here – which soon becomes too rough for anything but a 4WD vehicle – goes only a short way off the main road, to the foot of the volcano. The view of the summit and the nearby peaks from this entrance is impressive, and there's a lovely loop trail that winds through secondary and virgin forest. The climb from this side is steep and technical.

Sendero Los Quetzales

The park's most accessible trail is the lovely Sendero Los Quetzales, near Cerro Punta. One of the most beautiful in Panama, this trail goes 8km between Cerro Punta and Boquete, crossing back and forth over the Río Caldera. The trail can be done in either direction, but is easiest from west to east: The town of Cerro Punta is almost 1000m higher than Boquete, so hiking east is more down hill. Also, a new, well-signed trail on the Cerro Punta side was recently constructed. This trail leads to a wonderful overlook after an hour of hiking, which makes a good half-day trip from Cerro Punta. The entire trail west to east takes about four hours. After the new section, the trail becomes much muddier and rougher.

To get to or from the trailhead will take another couple of hours of walking on either side. A 4WD taxi can take you to the start of the trail on the Cerro Punta side for about US$12; taxi drivers know the area as Respingo. The trail is 5km uphill from the main road and 2km from the last paved road. When you exit the trail, it's a two-

hour mostly downhill walk to Boquete. You can then stay overnight or take a bus to David and then Cerro Punta; note that the last Cerro Punta bus leaves David at 6:30 pm.

It's possible to send your luggage by bus from Cerro Punta to Boquete so that you need only to carry the minimum weight with you. Talk to the folks at the Hotel Los Quetzales in Guadalupe for details.

The US$3 entrance fee is payable at the ranger station near the trailhead on the Guadalupe side. A map is available when the ranger station is open.

Places to Stay

Camping is available in the park (US$5) on the trail to the summit from the Boquete side, along the Sendero Los Quetzales, or at the ranger station at the entrance to the Sendero Los Quetzales on the Cerro Punta side. You can also stay in bunk beds at the ranger station for US$5; bring your own food and bedding. If you plan to stay in the station, let them know you're coming by calling the ANAM office in David (☎ 774 6671, fax 775 3163) or stopping by the police station in Cerro Punta.

The *Cabañas Los Quetzales* are located inside the park on property with several hiking trails. See the Guadalupe section for details.

PARQUE INTERNACIONAL LA AMISTAD

This 407,000-hectare park, of which 207,000 hectares are in Panama and the rest in Costa Rica, has two Panamanian entrances: one at Las Nubes (near Cerro Punta on the Chiriquí side) and one at Wetzo (near Changuinola).

Three main trails originate at Las Nubes ranger station. One is a 1.4km trail that winds up to the Mirador la Nevera, a lookout point at 2500m. A second trail winds 1.7km to La Cascada, a 45m-high waterfall with a lovely bathing pool. A third trail, named Sendero El Retoño (Rebirth Trail), loops 2.1km through secondary forest.

Admission to the park costs US$3. Parking costs an additional US$1. The ranger station at Las Nubes has a dormitory room with bunk beds where tourists can stay for US$5 per night. Due to the

PANAMA

popularity of these beds among school groups from Canada and the USA, reservations are well advised. To make reservations, call the ANAM office in David (☎ 774 6671, fax 775 3163) or stop by the police station in Cerro Punta. Guests must bring their own bedding.

Permits to camp in the park cost US$5, payable at the ranger station.

If you plan to spend much time at Las Nubes, be sure to bring a jacket. This side of the park, at 2280m above sea level, has a cool climate. Temperatures are usually around 24°C (75°F) in the daytime and drop to about 3°C (38°F) at night. And be sure to bring your own food; there's none in the park.

Getting There & Away

The Las Nubes entrance is about 7km from Cerro Punta; a sign on the main road in Cerro Punta marks the turnoff. The road starts out good and paved, but by the time you reach the park, it's a rutted track suitable only for 4WD vehicles. A taxi will bring you from Cerro Punta for US$4 for up to two people, then US$2 per extra person.

RÍO SERENO

At Volcán a paved road turns off and heads west 47km to Río Sereno, on the Costa Rican border. The road winds through lush valleys sprinkled with coffee fields, teak plantations and stands of virgin forest. Travelers coming from the border crossing at Río Sereno usually have a very favorable first impression of Panama.

The border crossing at Río Sereno is open 7 am to 5 pm daily. If you need to stay over, the *Pensión Los Andes* above the pharmacy is OK; it has 14 rooms with shared bathrooms (US$9/14 for one/two people) and two rooms with private bathrooms (US$15 per room).

Buses from Río Sereno travel to Concepción and David; the last bus leaves the crossing at 5 pm daily.

On the Costa Rica side of the border, you can bus or take a taxi to San Vito, about a 15-minute ride (see the Costa Rica chapter).

FINCA LA SUIZA

If you travel along the paved road that crosses the Cordillera Central from the Interamericana to Chiriquí Grande, providing access to Bocas del Toro, you will pass a wonderful place for **hiking** and an overnight stay.

About 41km from the Interamericana is the lodge *Finca La Suiza* (☎ 615 3774, *afinis@chiriqui.com*), the accommodations with the best mountain view in Panama. The lodge has three clean, comfortable rooms with private hot-water bathrooms and large windows. On a clear day, you can see the islands in the Golfo de Chiriquí. The rates are a very reasonable US$28/35 singles/doubles. The enthusiastic and warm German owners – Herbert Brullman and Monika Kohler – will provide breakfast for about US$3.50 and dinner for US$5 to US$10. English, Spanish and German are spoken. Be sure to make reservations, as it's a long way to the next available lodgings in Chiriquí Grande or David. The lodge is closed June, September, and October.

Also on the property are several kilometers of well-marked **hiking trails**, which pass through primary tropical rain and cloud forest. The scenery features towering trees, hundreds of bird species and views of the Fortuna Park Forest Reserve, the Chiriquí mountains and the Pacific islands. Entrance to the trails, which are open all year, costs US$6. You don't have to be a guest to use the trails; however, you must start hiking between 7 and 10 am. The marked trails can take up to five or six hours. Children under 12 are not allowed.

To get to Finca La Suiza, take any Changuinola bus from David (hourly starting at 5 am) and ask the driver to drop you off. Coming from the Interamericana, the lodge is to the right just after the Accel gas station (the only gas station on this road). Coming from the north, the lodge is on the left 1.3km after a toll plaza for trucks. You can leave luggage with the caretaker near the entrance gate while hiking.

Veraguas Province

Panama's third-largest province, near the center of the country, is the only province that has both Caribbean and Pacific coastlines. It is home to 220,000 people, most of whom make their living farming or ranching. The varied landscape of this province ranges from lush forests in the Cordillera Central to deforested areas along the Pacific coast.

Santiago, Panama's fourth-largest city and capital of the province, is pleasant but offers little to the tourist. The town includes offices of IPAT, ANAM and immigration. You can catch buses from here to many places.

From Santiago, you can visit **Santa Fé**, a pleasant little mountain town 52km to the north. It's a great place for hikers and birders.

Santa Catalina, on the Pacific coast 115km southwest of Santiago via Soná, is one of the best surfing beaches in Central America. Surf booties are a must due to the volcanic rock beneath the surf and the long walk to the waves during low tide; for the same reasons, this isn't the best place for bodysurfing.

Off the Pacific coast is Panama's largest island, **Isla de Coiba**, which is oddly both part of a national park (Parque Nacional Isla de Coiba) and a federal penal colony. The diving and snorkeling around Coiba and neighboring islands are excellent, and the fishing is world class. However, it's an expensive place to get to. The only company with regular tours to the island is Coiba Explorer Panama (☎ 800-733 4743 in the US, info@coibaexplorer.com), which offers diving or fishing trips starting at US$3000 per week. Ancon Expeditions, based in Panama City, can also arrange tours (see the Panama Getting Around section). If you want to get there any other way, you will need to get permission from the ANAM office in Santiago (☎ 998 4271, fax 998 0615).

The **Parque Nacional Cerro Hoya** is yet another nearly inaccessible national park, containing some of the last remaining forest on the Península de Azuero. Access for the extremely adventurous is by a road subject to flooding along the western coast of the peninsula; from Cambutal by boat in a very rough sea; or by hiking or horseback riding from Tonosí. Contact the ANAM office in Santiago for more information.

Península de Azuero

The Península de Azuero hangs into the Pacific in a wide bulge. This area, settled by the Spanish in the 16th century, maintained many Spanish colonial traditions for centuries due to its relative isolation.

Today the region has an economy based on agriculture, but it is primarily known for its many traditional festivals and handicrafts. The intricate pollera dress is produced on the peninsula. The region is also famous for its excellent beaches.

Parts of the peninsula are still as isolated as they ever were, but a paved road now serves much of the eastern and southern areas. Turning south from the Interamericana at Divisa, the road passes through Chitré, capital of Herrera Province, and Las Tablas, capital of Los Santos Province.

Many other small towns are dotted around the peninsula. Founded by the Spanish four centuries ago, they are not much bigger now than they were then. Most still have their original, well-preserved colonial churches.

Very little English is spoken on the peninsula, and you won't see many tourists here.

Festivals

Festivals on the Península de Azuero are famous throughout Panama for their traditional costumes and celebrations. Some have survived intact for centuries; the 'dance of the little devils,' the 'penitent of the other life' and the 'peasant wedding' are dances and skits which show aspects of life in the times of the early Spaniards.

You can get details about these and other celebrations from any office of IPAT, the national tourist office. You may have problems finding a place to stay during a festival. Many hotels also increase their prices significantly.

Some of the peninsula's best known festivals, attracting visitors from all over Panama, include the following:

January 20 – Festival of San Sebastián, in Ocú

February/March – Carnaval, the four days before Ash Wednesday, in Las Tablas, Chitré, Villa de Los Santos and Parita

March/April – Semana Santa, in Villa de Los Santos and Pesé

Late April/early May – Feria de Azuero, in Villa de los Santos

May/June – Fiesta de Corpus Christi, Thursday to Sunday, 40 days after Easter, in Villa de Los Santos; one of Panama's most famous celebrations, with medieval dances and traditional costumes

June 24 – Fiesta de San Juan Bautista, in Chitré

June 29 – Patronales de San Pablo & San Pedro, in Pedasí and La Arena

July 20 – Fiestas Patronales de Santa Librada, in Las Tablas

July 22 – Fiesta de La Pollera, in Las Tablas

August 15 – Festival del Manito; Fiesta Popular, Matrimonio Campesino; El Duelo del Tamarindo; El Penitente de la Otra Vida – all celebrated in Ocú with traditional costumes

September 24–27 – Festival de la Mejorana, Festival de la Virgen de las Mercedes, in Guararé, with folkloric dance and music

October 19 – Founding of District of Chitré (1848), parades, historical costumes and celebrations in Chitré

November 10 – First Cry for Independence (1821), in Villa de Los Santos

November (date varies) – Festival del Manito, in Ocú

Artesanías

The Península de Azuero is also known for its traditional handicrafts, some of which have been made in the same places for hundreds of years.

Some of the best-known handicrafts, and the towns where they're made, include:

Polleras (dresses)
Santo Domingo (near Las Tablas); La Enea (near Guararé)

Masks
Parita, Villa de Los Santos

Musical instruments
San José de Las Tablas (near Santo Domingo, which is near Las Tablas)

Ceramics
La Arena (near Chitré)

Woven hats
Ocú, Los Pozos

Woven mats, carpets and wall hangings
Chitré

CHITRÉ
pop 40,000

Capital of the province of Herrera, Chitré is the largest town on the peninsula and a convenient base for exploring. It's also the home of some of the area's best-known festivals.

Information

The IPAT tourist office is in the Villa de Los Santos; see that section.

There are plenty of banks and ATMs in town, including a Banco Nacional de Panamá several short blocks west of the town square. MicroWorld Systems, across from the bank, provides Internet access for US$1 per hour.

Things to See & Do

Chitré has a wonderful **cathedral**. Unlike many cathedrals that impress through ornate overuse of gold, this one is striking for its elegant simplicity and fine balance of gold and wood.

The **Museo de Herrera** (☎ 996 0077), on Paseo Enrique Geenzier at Avenida Julio Arjona, is an anthropology and natural history museum. It contains many well-preserved pieces of pottery dating from 5000 BC until the time of the Spanish conquest, including some rather elaborate pieces that were used for trading. Also here are replicas of huacas found on the peninsula and photographs of archaeologists at work, Azuero residents, authentic folkloric costumes and religious artifacts of the region. The museum is open 9 am to 12:30 pm and 1:30 to 4 pm Tuesday to Saturday and 9 am to noon Sunday. Admission is US$1 (children US$0.25).

Ten kilometers north of downtown Chitré, **Parque Nacional Sarigua** is an unintentional monument to environmental devastation. The park's land is the end product of slash-and-burn agriculture, which created a tropical desert. It's morbidly fascinating as an example of environmental apocalypse. There *are* a few remaining stands of tropical dry forest. Admission is US$3, payable at the ANAM station at the entrance. Buses do not go here; a taxi from Chitré costs about US$20 roundtrip.

Ten kilometers northwest of Chitré is the beautiful and historic town of **Parita**. Its **church** is the only one in Panama that has its steeple located directly over its entrance rather than over a corner of the structure.

Playa El Agallito, 7km from Chitré, is not so much a beach as it is a mudflat, where migratory birds arrive by the thousands. These shorebirds are studied by Francisco Delgado and volunteers at the **Humboldt Ecological Station** (delgado_francisco@hotmail.com). You're welcome to stop by the station, where there are displays on the outside wall. If Francisco is not here, the staff at the restaurant/bar may know where to find him; they also have handouts explaining the work at the station and containing other information on the area.

The **Refugio de Vida Silvestre Cenegón del Mangle**, northeast of Parita, protects a mangrove forest at the mouths of the Parita and Santa María Rivers. An important wildlife area and nesting ground for herons, its primary attraction is bird watching. The refuge is about a 45-minute drive from Chitré.

You can see **ceramics** being made at the village of **La Arena**, 3km west of Chitré. One of the best pottery factories is Ceramica Calderón, where you can buy traditional painted ceramics at low cost.

Places to Stay & Eat
The *Pensión Herrerana* (☎ 996 4356), on Avenida Herrera 2½ blocks north of the cathedral, is a fairly clean but worn and very basic place with some of the cheapest rooms in town. Three rooms have private bathrooms; the rest have shared facilities. The cost is about US$7 per person, but stay here only as a last resort.

The *Pensión Chitré* (☎ 996 1856), on Calle Manuel Maria Correa near Avenida Perez, offers six worn, dusty rooms with ceiling fans and private cold-water bathrooms for US$8/10 singles/doubles. Some beds are better than others; ask to see several rooms.

The *Hotel Santa Rita* (☎ 996 4610, fax 996 2404), on the corner of Calle Manuel Maria Correa and Avenida Herrera, is a decent deal. Rates for the hotel's well-maintained rooms are US$11/16/18 singles/doubles/triples with fan and cold water and US$15/20/27 for air-con and hot water. All rooms have private bathrooms.

The *Hotel El Prado* (☎ 996 4620) is on Avenida Herrera just to the south of Calle Manuel Maria Correa. It's a clean, well-kept hotel with a 2nd-floor restaurant, sitting area and open balcony overlooking the street. The rooms are set back from the street, so they're not too noisy; each has a private bathroom, TV and phone. Rooms with air-con costs US$18/22 downstairs and US$22/33 upstairs; if you don't use the air-con, the rates are US$14/19.

The *Hotel Rex* (☎ 996 6660, fax 996 4310), with a good location beside the town square, offers 34 rooms with air-con, color TVs, phones and private hot-water bathrooms. The rates are US$20/25.

There are plenty of restaurants in the district around the cathedral. Facing the western end of the plaza, the *Restaurante y Refresqueria Aire Libre* is a pleasant open-air cafe with low prices.

Getting There & Away
Air Aeroperlas (☎ 996 4021, 210 9500 in Panama City) operates daily flights between Panama City and Chitré; cost is US$32 one way. A taxi to the airport costs around US$2.50.

Bus Buses depart for Chitré from Panama City's Terminal Nacional de Transporte hourly from 6 am to 11 pm (US$6, four hours, 241km).

Chitré is a center for regional bus transportation. Buses arrive and depart from the Terminal de Transportes de Herrera, 1km from downtown. To get to the station, take a taxi (US$2) or catch a 'Terminal' bus (US$0.25) at the intersection of Calle Aminta Burgos de Amado and Avenida Herrera. The terminal has a restaurant that's open 24 hours a day.

Tuasa (☎ 996 5619) buses depart Chitré for Panama City from 1:30 am to 6 pm, every 45 to 60 minutes. Transportes Inazun (☎ 996 4177) also has buses to the capital, departing hourly from 6 am to 3 pm. Both companies charge US$6 one way (four hours, 255km).

Other buses from Chitré operate from sunrise to sunset, and include the following:

Divisa (US$1, 30 minutes, 37km)
Frequent departures.

La Arena (US$0.35, five minutes, 3km)
Frequent departures.

Las Minas (US$1.50, one hour, 51km)
Buses depart hourly.

Las Tablas (US$1, 30 minutes, 31km)
Buses depart hourly.

Ocú (US$1.50, one hour, 46km)
Buses depart hourly.

Parita (US$0.50, 15 minutes, 10km)
Buses depart every 45 minutes.

Pedasí (US$2, one hour, 73km)
Buses depart hourly.

Pesé (US$1, 20 minutes, 24km)
Buses depart hourly.

Playa El Agallito (US$0.50, 12 minutes, 7km)
Buses depart hourly.

Playas Monagre and El Rompío (US$1, 30 minutes, 20km)
Buses depart hourly.

Santiago (US$1.50, 1¼ hours, 71km)
Buses depart hourly.

Tonosí (US$4, two hours, 103km)
Buses depart hourly.

Villa de Los Santos (US$0.25, 10 minutes, 4km)
Buses depart every few minutes.

VILLA DE LOS SANTOS
pop 7000

Villa de Los Santos (often called simply Los Santos) is 4km south of Chitré. This picturesque town, replete with many colonial structures, is where Panama's first 'cry for independence' from Spain was heard on November 10, 1821.

An IPAT office (☎ 966 8013) is located in the town center opposite Parque Simón Bolívar. They are very helpful if you have specific questions and speak Spanish.

The small **Museo de la Nacionalidad** (☎ 966 8192), next to the IPAT office, has been established in the house where Panama's Declaration of Independence was signed. It's open 9 am to 4 pm Tuesday to Saturday, 9 am to 2 pm Sunday; admission is US$1 (children US$0.25).

The 18th-century **Iglesia de San Atanacio** is a fine example of the Baroque style, with lots of intricately carved wood depicting cherubs, saints, Jesus and the Virgin, as well as ornate and colorful altars.

The Parque Simón Bolívar, IPAT office, museum and church are three blocks east of the Chitré–Las Tablas highway. Chitré–Las Tablas buses stop on the highway; frequent Chitré–Los Santos buses (US$0.25, 10 minutes, 4km) stop on the plaza.

The Smithsonian Institution has been conducting an excavation at **Cerro Juan Díaz**, 3km from Villa de Los Santos, where evidence shows people lived from approximately 300 BC until the time of the Spanish conquest. It's fascinating to watch the archaeologists unearthing pottery, shells and other items. However, this site is not always being worked.

You're welcome to visit the site, but you may have a hard time finding it on your own. A taxi from the taxi stand northwest of Parque Simón Bolívar can be hired for

US$2. Ask the driver to return for you, as there is no other transportation out there.

Playa Monagre and **Playa El Rompío**, 10km northeast of Los Santos, are popular with fishermen, families and bodysurfers. Buses to these beaches depart from Chitré hourly (US$1, 30 minutes, 20km) and pass Los Santos on the Carretera Nacional.

The anniversary of the 'cry for independence' is celebrated in Los Santos on November 10 every year. Other notable festivals include Carnaval, Semana Santa, the Feria de Azuero and Corpus Christi.

GUARARÉ
pop 3500

The tiny town of Guararé, on the main road between Chitré and Las Tablas, offers little to the tourist.

The single attraction is the **Museo Manuel F Zárate**. Zárate was a folklorist devoted to conserving the traditions and folklore of the Azuero region. The museum, in Zárate's former home, contains polleras, masks, *diablito* (little devil) costumes and other exhibits. It's two blocks behind the church, about six short blocks from the main road (turn off at the Delta fuel station) and is open 8 am to 4 pm Tuesday to Saturday and 8:30 am to noon Sunday; admission is US$0.75 (children US$0.25).

The **Festival de la Mejorana** is celebrated in Guararé on September 24–27.

La Enea, a small village near Guararé, is known for the fine **polleras** made there.

Just off the Chitré–Las Tablas highway, the ***Residencial La Mejorana*** (☎ 994 5794, fax 994 5796) is a large, clean, modern hotel. The rooms are in good condition; each has air-con, TV, telephone and private hot-water bathroom. Prices range from US$12 up to US$66, depending on the number of beds and the size of the room, but the cheaper rooms are just fine. There's a restaurant/bar here.

LAS TABLAS
pop 9000

Las Tablas is the capital of Los Santos Province. For information, a new IPAT office is located in the Casa de la Cultura Santeña, south of the town on the main road. A taxi here costs US$0.75.

Santa Librada, one of the finest colonial churches in the area, with its ornate gold-painted altar, has been declared a national historical monument. It's on the central plaza, in the heart of town.

The **Museo Belisario Porras** (☎ 994 6326), on the central plaza, is dedicated to the Las Tablas statesman who was president of Panama three times between 1912 and 1924. The museum is open 9 am to 12:30 pm and 1:30 to 4 pm Tuesday to Saturday, and 9 am to noon Sunday; admission is US$0.75 (children US$0.25).

In the countryside a few kilometers from town, **El Pausílipo** is Porras' former country estate. His surname means 'tranquillity' in Greek; it's easy to treasure the tranquillity here. El Pausílipo and its grounds are open 9 am to 4 pm Tuesday to Saturday and 8 am to noon Sunday. Admission is free.

Las Tablas hosts annual festivals including Carnaval and the Fiesta de Santa Librada, with its accompanying Fiesta de la Pollera.

The small town of **Santo Domingo**, about 10 minutes from Las Tablas, is known for its fine pollera dresses; polleras are also made in the nearby towns of San José, El Carate, La Tiza and El Cocal.

The best beach in the vicinity is **Playa El Uverito**.

Places to Stay & Eat

The *Hotel Hospedaje Zafiro* (☎ 994 8200), opposite the plaza, is an upstairs hotel – the entrance is around the corner from the plaza, on Calle Belisario Porras. It's clean and cheerful, with a balcony where guests can look out over the plaza. The nine rooms, all with private bathrooms, air-con and color TVs, cost US$15/19 singles/doubles. Larger rooms for up to five people are also available.

Several little restaurants are found around the plaza.

Getting There & Away

Frequent buses connect Las Tablas with Santo Domingo (US$0.50, 10 minutes, 5km), Chitré (US$1, 30 minutes, 31km), Panama City (US$6.50, 4½ hours, 282km), Pedasí (US$2, one hour, 41km), Tonosí (US$3, 1½ hours, 79km) and other places. There's also service twice a day to Playa Venado (US$3, two hours, 68km).

PEDASÍ

pop 3000

This pleasant coastal town, 41km southeast of Las Tablas, makes a good base for explo-

ration of area islands, beaches and wildlife. Pedasí's annual festival, the Patronales de San Pablo, is held on June 29.

Northeast of Pedasí, the **Refugio de Vida Silvestre Isla Iguana** (Isla Iguana Wildlife Refuge) is an important reserve, not only for the iguanas the 53-hectare island is named for, but also for its coral reefs, forest and bird life. The reef covers 15 hectares, contains 13 of the 20 eastern Pacific coral species and hosts over 200 species of fish. Swimming, snorkeling, diving, lazing on the white sandy beach, bird watching, hiking, fishing and camping are all possibilities here.

Humpback whales inhabit the waters around Isla Iguana from around June to November. These large sea mammals, 15 to 20m long, mate and bear their young here and then teach them to dive. The humpbacks are the famous 'singing whales' that you may have heard on recordings; occasionally if you're diving here, you can hear their underwater sounds.

The island is reachable by boat from Playa El Arenal, although it is difficult to reach this beach if you don't have a car. Some of the local hotels coordinate trips for about US$40.

Iguana Tours (see the Panama Getting Around section) operates skin diving and snorkeling tours to the island. Costs for a three-day, two-night tour of the Península de Azuero and Isla Iguana are about US$169 without transportation and US$289 with transportation from Panama City.

Playa Venado, 33km southwest of Pedasí, is one of Panama's finest surfing beaches. It's way off the beaten track but reachable by bus. There are *cabins* costing US$16 a night during the week, more on the weekend, but they're very basic. You can camp out on the beach for free, or hammocks may be available for very little. There's a simple bar and restaurant beside the beach with a nice, laid-back atmosphere.

A bus operates twice a day between Las Tablas and Playa Venado (US$3, two hours, 68km), although it sometimes fails to appear.

Places to Stay & Eat

The *Residencial Moscoso* (☎ 995 2203), near the center of town, has lovely rooms with cable TVs and cold-water private bathrooms for US$12/22 per room without/ with air-con.

The *Residencial Pedasí* (☎ 995 2322), near the northern end of town, has singles/ doubles/triples for US$17/22/28, all with air-con and cold-water private bathrooms. The rooms here are not as spacious as those at the Moscoso. There is a restaurant on the premises.

Hostal Dim's (☎/fax 995 2303), on the main road near the center of town, has a family atmosphere and offers a nice area to relax out back, with hammocks and a mango tree. Rooms have cold-water private bathrooms and cost US$15 to US$18 without air-con and US$23 with air-con.

If you've got a sweet tooth, be sure to try a slice of cake at the *Dulcería Yely*, across the street from the Residencial Moscoso. Slices of Mrs Dalila Vera de Quintero's delicious cakes sell for a mere US$0.25.

Getting There & Away
Pedasí is reachable by bus from Chitré (US$2, one hour, 73km) and from Las Tablas (US$2, one hour, 41km). Buses travel between these provincial capitals and Pedasí several times a day.

TONOSÍ
This cowboy town, 65km southwest of Pedasí, offers little of interest to the tourist. Its chief attractions are its scenery – the town is in a green valley ringed by tan hills – and its proximity to many isolated surfing beaches.

Playa Cambutal and **Playa Guánico** are two of the numerous beaches along the southern coast of the Península de Azuero that thrill surfers. Both beaches are reachable by dirt road from Tonosí and are served by bus.

At the end of August and all through September, thousands of green sea turtles come ashore at night to lay eggs in the sand on the broad beach of **Isla Caña**, about 22km east of Tonosí. The buses to Tonosí pass by the turnoff, a 5km trek to the beach. There are usually one or two boatmen here who will take you to the island for about US$7.

It's also possible to hire guides to the **Parque Nacional Cerro Hoya** or Isla Caña, although it's quite expensive unless you have a large group. Rates are around US$150 for up to eight people for a trip to Cerro Hoya,

and about US$40 to Isla Caña. Ask around at the hotels if you're interested.

Places to Stay & Eat
The *Hospedaje Irtha* (☎ 995 8316), on Calle Antonio Degracia, has seven very basic rooms with shared bathrooms for US$5/8 with fan, and US$10/15 with air-con. A common room with a TV is available to guests.

The *Pensión Rosyini* (☎ 995 8106), near the intersection of the Carretera a El Cacao and Avenida Central, has seven simple rooms with private bathrooms and mediocre beds. Rates are US$8/15 with fan/ air-con. The nearby *Pensión Boamy* (☎ 995 8142), near the church, has 11 rooms starting at US$16/18. It has air-con and hot-water private bathrooms.

The *Residencial Mar y Selva* (☎ 995 8153, fax 995 8185), on the main road into town, was built in late 1999. Its 10 clean, modern rooms have air-con and hot-water private bathrooms for US$16/20/24 singles/ doubles/triples. The owner offers local tours. On the ground floor, the *Restaurante Lindy* specializes in rural Panamanian food, which is good and cheap. Many meals are under US$3.

Getting There & Away
Hourly buses link Tonosí and points north all the way to Chitré. They operate only during daylight hours, from 7 am to 4 pm. The most expensive fare on the route, the fare to Chitré, is US$4 each way. The 103km ride can take two hours. Buses arrive from Pedasí three times a day (US$3).

Colón Province

The large Colón Province extends over 200km along the Caribbean coast from Veraguas Province in the west to the Comarca de Kuna Yala in the east. Most of the region is undeveloped and inaccessible.

Because of it's high crime rate, it's probably best to avoid the provincial capital of Colón, but Portobelo and Fuerte San Lorenzo, two historic Spanish fortresses, are impressive and worth seeing. On the way to Portobelo are a couple of good beaches. Just beyond it is Isla Grande, a beautiful little island just off the coast. It is busy on weekends and holidays; the rest of the time it's isolated, quiet and peaceful.

All of these places can easily be visited as day trips from Panama City, only a couple of hours away across the isthmus.

COLÓN
pop 59,000
On the Caribbean entrance to the Panama Canal, Colón is Panama's second-largest city and the country's principal Caribbean port.

Warning Colón is a dangerous slum, and if you don't have a pressing reason to come here, do yourself a favor and bypass it. Crime is a serious problem. It is not only possible but likely that you will get mugged, even in broad daylight, and even if you take every precaution. If you must go somewhere in Colón, take a taxi from the bus station; don't walk.

History
Colón was founded in 1850 as the Caribbean terminus of the Panama Railroad, and it grew rapidly to support the transisthmian travelers and, later, laborers on the French canal attempt. In 1885, a fire set by a Colombian hoping to spark a revolution burned nearly every structure in Colón and left 10,000 people homeless. The city was rebuilt in the architectural style popular in France at the time. Many buildings from that era, as well as ones built by Americans between 1904 and 1914 for Panama Canal workers, still exist today. Unfortunately, most are on the verge of collapse, with people still living inside them.

Things to See & Do
There are only a few reasons travelers would want to come to Colón.

One reason might be the **Zona Libre** (Free Zone), a huge fortresslike walled-off area of giant international stores selling items duty free; it's the world's second-largest duty-free port after Hong Kong. However, most of these stores only deal in bulk merchandise; they aren't set up to sell to individual tourists and simply window-shopping is not very interesting. Many travelers have been disappointed. When you *can* buy something, the store usually sends it to the Tocumen International Airport in Panama City, so you can't even wear your newly bought designer shoes until you leave the country.

Nevertheless, you can enter the Zona Libre by presenting your passport at the security office. The Zone Libre is open during regular business hours.

The **Panama Canal Yacht Club**, on Calle 16 in Cristóbal, is a safe haven for yachties heading through the canal. It has a restaurant, bar, showers and a bulletin board with notices from people offering or seeking positions as crew, rides to exotic places and passage through the canal, whether for the simple thrill of it or as a line handler. Boats heading along the coast past the San Blas Archipelago depart from the Coco Solo pier; see the Comarca de Kuna Yala section.

The **Gatún Locks** are accessible by taxi, bus or private vehicle. There's a viewing stand where visitors can watch the locks in action. You'll drive over them if you go to Fuerte San Lorenzo.

Getting There & Away
From Panama City, regular bus service to Colón departs from the Terminal Nacional de Transporte every 20 minutes from around 5 am to 9 pm; the last bus departs at 1 am. Express buses depart hourly from 7 am to 8 pm. These are air-conditioned and cost US$2.

Colón's Terminal de Buses is at the intersection of Calle Terminal and Avenida Bolívar. It serves towns throughout Colón Province, including the following:

La Guayra (US$2.25)
 Buses depart hourly 6:30 am to 6 pm. In La Guayra, you can catch the boat to Isla Grande.

Nombre de Dios (US$3, 66km)
 Buses depart hourly 6:30 am to 6 pm. Buses continue to Palenque.

Portobelo (US$1.30, 43km)
 Buses depart hourly 6:30 am to 6 pm.

These same buses can be boarded at Sabanitas, the turnoff for Portobelo, thus avoiding a trip into Colón.

FUERTE SAN LORENZO
On a promontory to the west of the canal, Fuerte (Fort) San Lorenzo is perched at the mouth of the Río Chagres. It was via this river that the British pirate Henry Morgan gained access to the interior in 1671, enabling

him to sack the first Panama City, today the ruins of Panamá La Vieja.

This Spanish fortress is built of blocks of cut coral and displays rows of old cannons. A British cannon among Spanish ones is evidence of the time when British pirates overcame the fort. Much of the fort is well preserved, including the moat, the cannons and the arched rooms. The fort commands a wide view of the river and bay far below.

There is no public transportation to Fuerte San Lorenzo. To get there, drive over the Gatún Locks and present identification at the checkpoint. Fuerte San Lorenzo is about 10km past the former Fort Sherman, a US military base that is now in Panamanian hands. Several tour operators in Panama City offer trips here.

PORTOBELO
pop 3300
Portobelo, 43km east of Colón, is one of the country's most important historic sites. The extensive ruins of Spanish stone fortresses erected centuries ago make for some interesting exploration.

There are no places to stay in Portobelo itself, but there are several dive shops with rooms on the Portobelo-Sabanitas road.

History
Portobelo, the 'beautiful port,' was named by Columbus in 1502, when he stopped here on his fourth New World voyage. It was the principal Spanish Caribbean port in Central America for around 200 years, until the 18th century. Gold and other treasure from Peru were shipped to Panama City and carried overland by mule. The goods were stored in fortresses at Portobelo until the annual trade fair, when galleons laden with goods from Spain arrived to trade for gold and other products from the New World.

British and other pirates made repeated attacks on all the strategic points of the Spanish treasure route; in 1739 Portobelo was destroyed by an attack led by the British admiral Edward Vernon. In 1746 the Spanish gave up and stopped using the overland Panama route altogether, instead sailing the long way around Cape Horn to and from the western coast of South America.

Portobelo was rebuilt in 1751, but it never achieved its former importance. In time, it became a virtual ruin. Much of the

outermost fortress was dismantled during construction of the Panama Canal and the stones used in building the Gatún Locks. There are still considerable parts of the town and fortresses left, however, and today Portobelo is protected as a national park and historic site.

Modern-day Portobelo consists of about 15 square blocks of – mostly rundown – homes and businesses interspersed with the ruins. Tourist officials plan to relocate the town's population to the west to allow the restoration of additional ruins and to create a more tourist-friendly atmosphere.

Information
IPAT has an office in the Alcaldía building, but it had absolutely no information about the town or area. A better bet is to go to the Customs House (see the next section).

Things to See & Do
The remnants of **Fuerte San Jerónimo** and **Fuerte Santiago** can still be seen near town, and the ruins of **Fuerte San Fernando** occupy a grassy flat across the bay. The ruins of Santiago, 500m west of Portobelo's center, include an officers' quarters, an artillery shed, a sentry box, a barracks and batteries. You can climb up a hill behind the fort for a beautiful view overlooking the ruins and bay. At the center of Portobelo, Fuerte San Jerónimo is a more complete fort than Santiago.

The restored **Real Aduana de Portobelo** (Customs House), also known as the contadoría (counting house), has interesting exhibits of Portobelo's history as well as a three-dimensional model of the area. Sometimes they have brochures. Admission is US$0.50.

Another notable feature of Portobelo is its large **colonial church**, built in 1776. It contains a famous life-size statue, the *Black Christ,* said to have miraculous powers. On October 21 each year, the **Festival of the Black Christ** attracts hundreds of pilgrims, many dressed in the same royal purple color as the statue's clothes. The statue is paraded through the streets starting at 6 pm, and street festivities follow.

Several **dive shops** west of town offer trips in the area. Scubaportobelo (☎ 461 3841, fax 461 9586) has a solid reputation.

All the dive shops also offer rooms starting at US$12 per person, as well as dining facilities. There are some food stands in town, but for restaurants you'll have to go west toward Sabanitas.

On the way to Portobelo, the black-sand **Playa María Chiquita** and the white-sand **Playa Langosta** are two attractive beaches.

Getting There & Away

Buses to Portobelo (US$1.30, 43km) depart from Colón's Terminal de Buses hourly from 6:30 am to 6 pm. If you're coming by bus from Panama City, take the bus heading for Colón and get off at Sabanitas, 10km before Colón, about a 1½-hour ride from Panama City. Then catch the bus coming from Colón to Portobelo when it passes through Sabanitas, thus avoiding a trip into Colón.

ISLA GRANDE

This island, 15km east of Portobelo, is a popular weekend destination for Panama City's party animals. About 300 people of African descent live on the island, most making a living from fishing and coconuts. Seafood and coconut milk are the principal ingredients of the island's food.

Things to See & Do

Some lovely **beaches** on the northern side of the island can be reached by boat (hire a water taxi at the dock in front of Cabañas Super Jackson) or on foot (a trail behind Cabañas Super Jackson crosses the island, and a water's-edge trail loops around it). The only beach on the southern side of the island is in front of Hotel Isla Grande.

The trail across the island leads to Bananas Village Resort, where US$25 will get you use of their facilities for the day, including the beach, snorkeling, kayaking, and excursions to other islands and beaches. Web site: www.bananasresort.com

Some fine **snorkeling** and dive sites are within a 10-minute boat ride of the island. The only surfing waves in the area are in front of Moon Cabins. The mangroves east of Isla Grande make for fun exploring, and you could also go snorkeling and take a picnic to a beach on the mainland or a small secluded island.

The Festival of San Juan Bautista is celebrated here on June 24 with swimming and canoe races. The Virgen del Carmen is honored on July 16 with a land and sea procession, baptisms and masses.

Carnaval is also celebrated here; the locals dance the conga with ribbons and mirrors in their hair, women wearing traditional pollera dresses and men in ragged pants tied at the waist with old sea rope. Along with the dancing, there are satirical songs about current events and a lot of joking in the Caribbean calypso tradition.

Places to Stay & Eat

You can find a place to stay without an advance reservation at any time of year except during busy holidays, when Panamanians might have reserved all the hotels weeks in advance. Hotels are presented west to east.

Hotel Isla Grande (☎ 225 6722, fax 225 6721), located on the western end of the island, charges US$50/55 for rooms with fans/air-conditioning. It has its own beach and activities such as snorkel rental and volleyball.

A 10-minute walk east is *Cabañas Super Jackson* (☎ 448 2311). Rates range from US$20 for simple rooms with two beds and fans to US$50 for four beds and air-con.

Five more minutes to the east is *Cabañas Cholita* (☎ 448 2962, fax 232 4561), which has rooms with a double bed for US$39 and rooms with two double beds for US$50. All rooms have air-con.

Next door is *Villa En Sueño* (☎ 448 2964), where the US$44 per person rates includes three meals a day.

Another 10-minute walk east, beyond the paved walkway, are the *Moon Cabins* (☎ 263 2783), an attractive-looking place. Cabins are US$66/77/125 for one/two/three beds. Beds in the surfer's dormitory go for US$25 a night.

The pickings are slim at the island's stand-alone restaurants. The restaurant at Cabañas Cholita has decent and reasonably priced food. *Bananas Village Resort* has good food, but it's more expensive.

Getting There & Away

Hourly buses from Colón go to La Guayra (US$2.25). A five-minute boat ride from there to Isla Grande costs US$1. Parking costs US$1 per day.

Comarca de Kuna Yala

The Comarca de Kuna Yala is a narrow, 226km-long strip on the Caribbean coast that includes the Archipiélago de San Blas. The islands of the archipelago are strung out along the coast of Panama from the Golfo de San Blas almost all the way to the Colombian border. The nearly 400 islands range in size from tiny, uninhabited sand cays to islands with so many people that there's only enough room for palm huts and the narrow walkways between them.

The islands are home to the Kuna, who run San Blas as a comarca – an autonomous region – with minimal interference from the national government, using their own system of governance, consultation and decision making. They maintain their own economic system, language, customs and culture, with distinctive dress, legends, music and dance. Given that their area has been in contact with Europeans ever since Columbus sailed along here in 1502, this is no mean achievement and has required remarkable tenacity by the Kuna, who zealously guard their traditional way of life. They have the greatest degree of political autonomy of any indigenous group in Latin America. Outsiders cannot own land in Kuna Yala.

The economy of the San Blas islands is based primarily on coconuts and fishing. Most of the coconuts are bartered to Colombian schooners for various products. Seafood caught includes fish, lobster, shrimp, Caribbean king crab and octopus; these are not usually sold for cash but are traded among the Kuna. Other food crops, including rice, yams, yucca, bananas and pineapples, are grown in plots on the mainland, a short distance away.

Most Kuna women continue to dress as their ancestors did. Their faces are distinguished by a black line painted from the forehead to the tip of the nose and by a gold ring worn through the nose. A length of colorful printed cloth is wrapped around the waist as a skirt, topped by a short-sleeved blouse covered in brilliantly colored *molas* (traditional Kuna textiles). The women also wrap their legs, from ankle to knee, in long strands of colorful beads. A printed head scarf and many necklaces, rings and bracelets complete the daily outfit. Kuna men usually wear Western dress, which in these warm islands often means shorts and a sleeveless shirt.

Molas are the most famous of Panamanian traditional handicrafts. Buyers come here from many countries. It takes a long time and a lot of skill to make the best molas, so they are not cheap. You can find a tiny, simple souvenir mola for around US$5, but a high-quality mola can cost anywhere from US$50 to several hundred dollars. Molas are also sold in handicrafts shops in Panama City.

Visiting Kuna Yala

The Kuna are a fascinating people with an interesting history (see the Books section for suggested reading). They can be particular about what outsiders do on their islands. On all the heavily inhabited islands, the Kuna require tourists to register and pay a visitation fee between US$3 and US$5. On smaller, privately owned islands, visitors must seek out the owner, receive permission and pay a fee (around US$2).

Visitors must also pay for any photo they take of Kuna. If you want to take someone's photo, ask his or her permission first and be prepared to pay at least US$1 per subject (some Kuna expect to be paid US$1 per photo). You may not be expected to pay for a photo taken of an artisan from whom you buy a mola, but it depends on the subject. Some islands may charge you US$50 just for possessing a video camera. Travelers who become especially bitter about these policies should perhaps leave their cameras tucked away. Other tourists are unsettled by the constant pressure to buy molas when they merely want to enjoy a bit of solitude or stroll about town.

Several islands are visited by cruise ships during season (November to April). When the ships arrive (up to 2 or 3 days a week), the number of people on an already congested island can triple, leaving barely enough room for anyone to turn around. Virtually two-thirds of the people (the tourists) are trying to photograph the other third (the Kuna).

Things to See & Do

Most hotels offer complete packages, where one price gets you a room, three meals a day and boat rides to neighboring islands for swimming, snorkeling and lounging on the beach. Before swimming off the shores of a heavily populated island, take a look at the number of outhouses built over the ocean – they may change your mind. Snorkeling is good in places, although many coral reefs are damaged. You can often rent snorkeling equipment from your hotel; serious snorkelers should bring their own gear. You can also make excursions to other populated islands.

Arranging activities outside the normal hotel offerings becomes trickier, because you need to negotiate boat rides between islands and find places to stay and eat. Of course, you'll need to speak pretty good Spanish or – better yet – Kuna to follow this route.

Places to Stay & Eat

Since there are no restaurants, each hotel provides all the meals for its guests. The meals are usually based on seafood, with lobster and fish the specialties. Quality varies, as some of the fishing stocks have been depleted through overfishing. Fresh coconuts make a good snack.

Near El Porvenir, the *Hotel San Blas* (☎ 290 6528) on the island of Nalunega is the best value and the most popular hotel in Kuna Yala. If you like the simple life, this is a great place to enjoy it. The ocean-side hotel consists of 31 simple but pleasant Kuna-style palm cabins with sand floors and more modern rooms with hard floors, all with shared bathrooms that could be cleaner. The daily rate of US$35 per person includes three meals a day and boat tours. Owner Luis Burgos speaks English and will meet you at the airport on El Porvenir.

The *Dormitory Cartí Sugdup*, on the crowded island of Cartí Suitupo, has basic rooms over the water with shared bathrooms for US$10 per person. Meals and boat transportation are not included in the price.

Other places to stay are farther east along the coast. On the heavily populated island of Nusatupo, *Hotel Kuna Yala* (☎ 315 0275) has four hot rooms with a shared bathroom, three daily meals and boat tours for US$40 per person. On the less-populated island of Kuanidup, the *Hotel Kuanidup* (☎ 227 7661, fax 227 1396) charges US$70 per person; the friendly

owner speaks English. This is a good place to get away from it all. To get to these two islands, you'll fly in to Río Sidra Island.

Many tour operators sell trips to the *Kwadule Eco-Resort* (☎ 263 0119, fax 263 0609), which is basically the only thing on the island of Kwadule. The hefty prices of US$236/378 singles/doubles for the first night includes roundtrip airfare from Panama City and meals; subsequent nights are US$168/190. The comfortable cabins have fans, hot-water private bathrooms, and an ocean view.

Also popular for those with money is the *Dolphin Island Lodge* (☎ 225 8435, fax 264 8384), on Isla Uaguitupo. Cabins cost US$115/190, including meals, boat rides to beaches and a trip to the very traditional island of Achutupu (which also has the nearest airport). Additional nights are less expensive.

If you want to camp on a relatively uninhabited island, US$5 a night per couple will usually do the trick. However, there's a risk of encountering narcotraffickers in the night. The Kuna do not allow the Panamanian coast guard or US antidrug vessels to operate in the archipelago, so the uninhabited islands are occasionally used by Colombian narcotraffickers running cocaine up the coast. If you're thinking about camping, you may want to check into one of the hotels for a day or two to get oriented, then ask around during the daily excursions for information.

Getting There & Away

Air Aerotaxi (☎ 264 8644), Aviatur (☎ 315 0311) and Ansa (☎ 226 6881) operate small planes between Panama City and the islands. The flight to El Porvenir departs from Albrook airport every day at 6 am, arriving at 6:30 am. Return flights leave El Porvenir soon after the incoming plane arrives.

Though El Porvenir is the principal stop, many other islands in the archipelago also have airports, and your plane may stop at a number of them while loading and unloading passengers or cargo. The airlines offer service to islands along the north coast all the way from El Porvenir to Puerto Obaldía, near the Colombian border.

Flying one way from Panama City costs US$30 to El Porvenir and US$47 to Puerto

Obaldía. Fares to other islands will fall somewhere in between.

Car Only one road leads into the district, the rugged El Llano–Cartí road that connects the town of El Llano, on the Interamericana 70km east of Panama City, to the coastal hamlet of Cartí. This road also goes to the very rustic Nusagandi Nature Lodge. The lodge is reachable only by a 4WD vehicle with a powerful engine, a winch and good off-road tires. The road beyond the lodge is barely passable by even a 4WD vehicle.

Boat Kuna merchant ships to the San Blas islands depart from Coco Solo Pier in Colón. Colombian merchant boats also travel the Caribbean Sea between Colón and Puerto Obaldía, stopping at inhabited islands to pick up and drop off people and goods. Other Colombian vessels visit the inhabited islands to take on coconuts. Some ships may be used for carrying contraband and/or for drug trafficking. Travel by these often overloaded boats is neither comfortable, safe, nor reliable, and it's always slow going. Some of these boats may not be willing to take outsiders or foreigners.

You may also be able to rent a boat in Palenque, east of Colón.

Darién Province

The large Darién Province occupies most of the eastern side of Panama. Unesco has declared this region of pristine tropical rain forest a world heritage site and biosphere reserve. Panama has established the 5790-sq-km Parque Nacional Darién, one of Central America's largest national parks and wilderness areas, to protect both the natural and cultural resources of the region. This park covers 90% of the border between Panama and Colombia.

A bridge between continents, this region is one of the most naturally diverse in tropical America, with many types of flora and fauna. The harpy eagle resides here, as do giant anteaters, jaguars, ocelots, howler monkeys, Baird's tapirs, white-lipped peccaries, caimans and American crocodiles. The Emberá, Wounaan and Kuna peoples inhabit the region, living traditionally, mostly along the rivers.

The Interamericana does not go all the way through Panama but terminates in the middle of the jungle near a town called Yaviza in the vast wilderness region of the Darién, before starting again 150km farther on in Colombia. This transportation break between Central and South America is known as the Darién Gap. It's literally the end of the road.

Despite occasional announcements by international authorities eager to improve transportation and trade between the continents, it is unlikely that the Interamericana will be pushed through the Darién Gap any time soon. Panamanians are concerned that a road could help Colombia's civil war spill over into Panama. A road could also increase illegal immigration and drug traffic, and help spread hoof-and-mouth disease in cattle, which is presently limited to South America. Finally, a paved road would make logging easier, leading to deforestation of the largest forested area in the country.

Dangers & Annoyances

Parts of the Darién Province are extremely dangerous. The greatest hazards are a result of the difficult environment. The Darién is hot and humid. Trails, when they exist at all, are often poorly defined and are never marked. The many large rivers that form the backbone of the Darién transportation network create their own hazards. Any help at all, much less medical help, is very far away. If you get lost out here, you are done for.

Areas of the Parque Nacional Darién are prime territory for the deadly fer-de-lance snake. The chance of snakebite is remote, but you should be careful; wear boots in camp and in the forest.

In addition to the natural dangers, the human threat to travelers must not be underestimated. Illegal immigrants heading north – including Colombians fleeing the civil war in their country – make their way through the jungle. Roaming bandits prey on jungle travelers. As an outsider, you may be viewed with suspicion, and some villages do not greet tourists with open arms. Narcotraffickers also use this way north and may not appreciate being surprised by travelers trekking through the woods. Police presence in the area south of Boca de Cupe is limited.

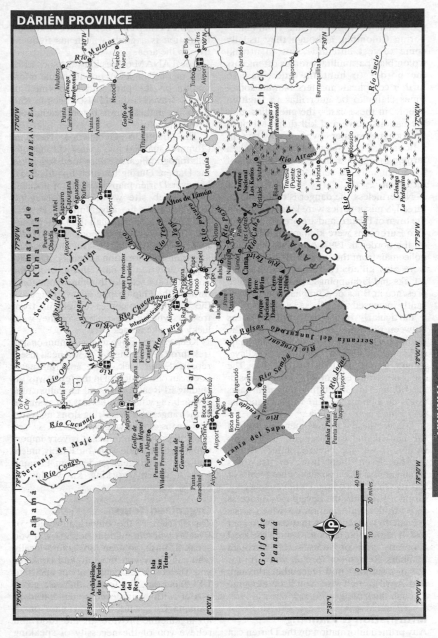

Parts of the Darién have also become areas of activity for guerrillas from neighboring Colombia, although they usually come to rest and hide, not to attack. Colombian paramilitary forces often cross the border to hunt the guerrillas. To further complicate matters, bandits sometimes claim to be guerrillas to frighten people; in these cases, the guerrillas hunt the bandits down and kill them. Much of the local newspaper coverage may be sensationalist. We've been told that a chicken farmer firing on a thief in the middle of the night may be reported as a guerilla incursion.

Nevertheless, the danger is real. In 1993, three US missionaries were kidnapped from the town of Púcuro, and are presumed dead. Two Europeans were kidnapped and killed on the border in 1997. A businessman and policeman from the town of Boca de Cupe were also killed. There have been other attacks and kidnappings as well. The police presence in Boca de Cupe has been significantly increased since these events.

Particularly treacherous are the areas between Boca de Cupe and Colombia, the traditional path through the Darién Gap, which includes the towns of Púcuro, Paya, Limón, Balsal and Palo de las Letras. The areas north and east of this are also considered dangerous, including the mountains Altos de Limón, the Río Tuquesa and the trail from Puerto Obaldía.

Despite these warnings, there *are* parts of the Darién that can be visited in relative safety; these are covered later in this section. Even then, however, travelers should always hire a guide – either locally or through the tour companies in Panama City. Using a guide has the advantages of access to up-to-date information on which areas are safe to visit, ensuring that you won't get lost. It also supports ecotourism in the local economy and provides safety through numbers. Remember to plan your trip for the dry season (mid-December through mid-April); otherwise, you'll be slogging through thick mud.

Information & Planning

Any printed information on the Darién can become rapidly outdated, as bandits, narcotraffickers and guerrillas change their bases of operation. Travelers should always seek out up-to-date information on local dangers. Perhaps the best source of this information is a guide who leads frequent trips to the area.

Local ANAM offices in towns such as El Real or La Palma can provide some information on the park and help you find guides. Travelers should also check in with the police in these towns before heading out into the jungle.

The Instituto Geográfico Nacional (Tommy Guardia) in Panama City usually sells topographical maps for some regions of the Darién. During research for this book, however, Darién maps were out of stock.

The Web site www.outbackofbeyond.com describes the adventures of Patricia and Loren Upton through the Darién Gap. They also sell the guidebook *Through the Darién Gap* for US$13. You should view any printed information as being potentially dangerously out of date. If you order the book, and are actually thinking about going through the Gap despite our warnings, ask the Uptons for copies of emails from trekkers who did the trip but said they were lucky to make it back alive.

Keep your baggage to a minimum on any trek through the jungle. You will need insect repellent, sunblock, a hat and rain gear. Food can only be found in the few towns, including El Real, Yaviza and La Palma; otherwise bring your own. Food is not available at the ranger stations. Bring drinking water or a means of purifying water.

As already mentioned, it is very important to bring a guide with you. Finally, unless you hire a bilingual guide from Panama City, a decent working knowledge of Spanish is a must.

Organized Tours

The Darién is the only major part of Panama where a guide is necessary. If you speak Spanish, you can hire guides locally who can show you the way and cook for you. The cost is reasonable, about US$10 to US$20 per day, plus food. Otherwise, go on a tour with a guide company based in Panama City, who will take care of all arrangements, provide all the food and relieve you of the necessity of speaking Spanish or one of the native languages.

Ancon Expeditions (see Organized Tours in the Panama Getting Around section) in

Panama City has by far the most extensive trips to the Darién. Their offerings include:

Trans Darién Expedition: A two-week trip that follows in the footsteps of Balboa on his journey across the isthmus in 1513 (US$2495).

Darién Explorer Trek: A two-week trip that includes Punta Patiño on the Pacific coast, El Real and the Pirre Station, and Cana (US$2400).

Cana: A four-day trip to Ancon's field station in Cana, an outstanding place for bird watching. The cost is US$700 (10 passengers) to US$1300 (2 passengers).

Coastal Darién Explorer: A three-day trip to Ancon's lodge near Punta Patiño on the Pacific coast. The cost is US$375 (8 passengers) to US$550 (2 passengers).

Other longer Ancon tours include parts of the Darién as one of the destinations.

YAVIZA
pop 3300

The Interamericana ends in Yaviza. There isn't much here, except a stretch of dirt where trucks, buses and cars park, one hotel and access to the Darién river network. Travelers can walk or boat from here to El Real or can boat up the Río Tuira as far as La Palma. You can't get to the national park from Yaviza without first going through El Real. There are a couple of restaurants and a hotel (US$8).

Hourly buses for Yaviza depart Panama City from 5 to 10 am (US$14, 10 hours, 266km). Driving a car takes about seven hours in the dry season, more in the wet. Note, however, that it's cheaper to fly to El Real than to rent a car and leave it sitting in Yaviza while you're hiking in the forest.

EL REAL
pop 3000

El Real dates from the days of the early conquistadores. Today this hot and humid town is one of the largest in the Darién. It doesn't offer much to the traveler except the airport closest to the Pirre Station, which is inside Parque Nacional Darién. You could also get access to the river system from here.

If you're headed into the national park (and why else would you be here?), you must visit the ANAM station in town to pay the US$3 entrance fee and learn about local conditions (both natural and human). Ask at the station for Narciso Bristan, who can put you in touch with guides or help you arrange river transportation. If you want to rent a horse, ask for Sebastian. Costs are typically US$10 to US$20 per day for a guide (plus food) and US$20 per day for a horse and guide.

Because of high gas costs, river transportation is expensive. Expect to pay US$120 to US$150 for a day on the water. You could conceivably hitch a ride with someone going in your direction for a lot cheaper.

The only hotel, *El Nazareno* has seven mildewy rooms with sagging mattresses and shared toilets that don't flush thoroughly for US$8 per person. The thought of staying here makes even the toughest jungle guides whimper.

Aeroperlas (☎ 315 7500 in Panama City) flies from Panama City to El Real four days weekly for US$39 one-way.

PIRRE STATION

Pirre is an ANAM· ranger station just inside the Parque Nacional Darién, 13km south of El Real. It is the most accessible part of the national park. The station has four **hiking trails** and opportunities for **bird watching** and **swimming** at the base of a forest waterfall.

The station has barracks with a dining area, several bunk beds and an outhouse. Flush toilets and showers were being installed when this book was researched. Bring a water purification system or tablets. If you plan on eating, you must bring your own food. You can stay here for US$10; pay this fee at the ANAM office in El Real, where you also pay the US$3 entrance fee. The rangers will cook the food you bring for a US$5 to US$10 tip.

Pirre Station can be reached by hiking, by boating and hiking or by tractoring and hiking. The hike from El Real takes three hours. You can also take a one-hour canoe ride from El Real to the Emberá village of Piji Baisal for US$75 per group and then make a one-hour hike from Piji Baisal to the Pirre Station.

You may also be able to catch a one-hour ride on a tractor that goes to Piji Baisal, and then hike from there. The tractor can go within a 15-minute hike of the Pirre Station. The cost is US$40 to charter the tractor, less

PANAMA

if you catch it on a normal run. Although the road to Piji Baisal and the trails to the Pirre Station are fairly well defined in the dry season, they are not marked. Get a guide in El Real for US$10 to US$20.

Ancon Expeditions in Panama City could also provide a naturalist guide to help arrange your trip, although the price will obviously be higher than using a local guide. At the time of writing, Ancon Expeditions was finishing plans to build a tent camp near Piji Baisal and the Pirre Station. This would provide ready access to the national park, as well as a higher standard of accommodations for visitors.

CANA

Cana, a valley nestled in foothills on the eastern slope of Pirre Ridge, is the most isolated place in Panama (the nearest town is several days away by foot) and home to some of the world's finest bird watching. About 60 Panamanian bird species can be found only in Parque Nacional Darién, and Cana is at the park's lush heart. The birds here include harpy eagles, golden-headed quetzals and four species of macaw.

During the early 16th century, Spaniards discovered gold in the valley. The gold mines soon brought 20,000 people to the town of Santa Cruz de Cana, which has long since been reclaimed by the jungle. A brief resurgence of mining occurred in the early 20th century.

The only signs of human habitation today are an airstrip at the eastern end of the valley, a border-police station, and an ANAM/Ancon field station. Three short trails begin near the ANAM/Ancon station and head off into the jungle. Two longer trails lead to a campsite on Pirre Mountain and to Boca de Cupe.

The valley's ANAM/Ancon field station is a basic wooden structure built by gold workers during the 1970s and enlarged in 1998 by the wildlife conservation group Ancon. Tourists are welcome to stay at the station, but to do so they must arrange their trips through Ancon Expeditions (see Organized Tours earlier in this section). Flights in and out are by charter only.

Warning

At the time of writing, the US embassy had issued a warning against travel to the Ancon nature preserve at Cana 'due to its proximity to the Colombian border and possible cross-border activity by Colombian rebels.' Embassy staff contacted for this chapter refused to provide additional details.

Staff at Ancon Expeditions, however, point out that the Cana area is geographically isolated from Colombia by the mountain ranges to the west and south. No trails lead to Cana from the Colombian border, and people on the move are more likely to use the established trails to the east. Furthermore, although Cana *is* near the Colombian border, there are no nearby towns on the Colombian side; even guerrillas in hiding need nearby facilities for supplies. There haven't been any incidents involving guerrillas in the immediate area, and no problems have surfaced at the Cana field station. The police station there helps discourage criminal activity.

Nevertheless, this is an area where it is best to check the latest conditions before you go, and to travel only with an established agency such as Ancon Expeditions.

LA PALMA
pop 4500

This provincial capital is the most populous town in the Darién. It's largely a government town and consists mostly of the descendents of slaves brought from Spain. The town itself offers little to see or do, except to serve as a gateway into the Darién coastal area.

La Palma is home to the only bank in the Darién. There are also a hospital, a port, a police station and an ANAM office, as well as two hotels, three bars and several food stands.

From La Palma, you can enter the Darién river transportation network via Río Tuira. Río Mogué, a couple of hours south along the coast, provides access to the Emberá village of Mogué. If you speak Spanish, you can usually find someone near the dock who owns a boat and is willing to take your group on an adventure for perhaps US$120 to US$150 per day, depending on the boat's gas consumption.

La Palma also provides access to Punta Patiño (see that section).

The better of the two hotels in La Palma is the *Hotel Blaquira Bacara* (☎ 299 6224). All the rooms are clean and have fans, and some have private balconies overlooking the wide Río Tuira. The rates are US$10 to US$15 for rooms with shared bathrooms and US$20 for rooms with private bathrooms. The nearby pension is a bit cheaper.

Aeroperlas (☎ 315 7500 in Panama City) offers flights from Panama City daily except Sunday for US$36 one way. Aviatur (☎ 315 0311 in Panama City) offers flights four times weekly. You can also boat in from Yaviza for US$120 to US$150.

PUNTA PATIÑO

Punta Patiño, on the southern shore of the Golfo de San Miguel, 25km from La Palma, is known mainly for its 26,315-hectare **wildlife preserve**, which is owned by the conservation group Ancon. Their private tour agency, Ancon Expeditions, operates a lodge here and offers trips from Panama City – this is the only way you can visit the preserve. (See the Darien Province Organized Tours section for prices.)

The preserve is a former cattle ranch that Ancon is allowing to return to its natural state. Both primary and secondary forest are represented here. You can **hike** on the trails or look in the meadows for capybaras, the world's largest rodents. The lodge's dining and viewing area, which is perched atop a ridge near the cabins, has a spellbinding panoramic view of the gulf.

The tour to this area includes a two-hour boat ride in the Golfo de San Miguel to Punta Patiño, perhaps visiting some mangrove areas on the way. The **Emberá village** of Mogué, 1½ hours from Punta Patiño on the Río Mogué, is home to about 400 people and remains fairly traditional. Be sure to bring small bills to buy baskets and other Emberá crafts, or to be painted with jagua-fruit juice in the local style. The community of **Punta Alegre** is a town of 500 or so, where you can stop for a cold drink. The beach of **Agua Bendita** is a nice place to investigate tide pools.

The Ancon lodge has pleasant cabins with good cross-ventilation and cold-water private bathrooms. The food here is quite good.

To reach Punta Patiño, fly into La Palma and take a boat from there. Since the only way to come here is through Ancon Expeditions, they will make all the arrangements. At the time of writing, the tour company was considering operating the lodge fulltime rather than only when they have tours. This would allow tourists to make their own transportation arrangements, select individual tours once they got to the lodge and reduce the overall cost of the visit. Check with Ancon Expeditions for their current offerings.

RÍO SAMBÚ

The mouth of the wide, brown Río Sambú is 1½ hours by fast boat south of Punta Patiño. Traveling it is a heart-of-darkness experience: You pass through spectacular jungle inhabited by jaguars and mountain lions and people who until recently did most of their hunting with blowguns. The river meanders for many kilometers toward the Colombian border, passing increasingly traditional Emberá villages along the way.

Boats and boatmen can be hired in La Palma, or you can travel with a guide. When you reach the Río Sambú, you will need to hire a dugout canoe to get farther upriver. During the rainy season, the river is navigable by dugout all the way to Pavarandó.

Today, traditional methods of agriculture are still practiced; the Sambú provides the Emberá with fish; and the Emberá still reside mainly in open-sided thatch-roof houses atop stilts. But western attire is replacing traditional dress; outboard motors are increasingly seen on the Indians' dugouts; and Christianity brought by missionaries is replacing traditional Emberá religious practices.

At night, you can camp where you please if you have a tent. However, unless you've brought a tent for your boatman, he will prefer an alternative – making a deal to sleep on the floor of an Emberá family's home. If you can speak Spanish, finding a family to move in with for the night isn't difficult, and even getting a hot meal is easy. Expect to pay US$10 per person for shelter and US$5 for food.

A trip far up the Río Sambú is not everyone's cup of tea. You will sit on a motorized dugout canoe loaded with leaking gasoline cans under a broiling tropical sun for a very long time. There are other minor hardships, like the lack of showers and toilets. But the Sambú offers you true adventure,

PANAMA

something that may not even be possible anywhere in the Tropics 50 years from now. Even if you travel deep into the Amazon, you'd be hard-pressed to find such wilderness and such people these days.

Getting There & Away

You can fly directly into Sambú from Panama City for US$36 one way. Or you can take a boat from La Palma, passing Punta Patiño.

Language

Spanish is the most commonly spoken language in Central America. English is the official language of Belize, although both Spanish and a local Creole are widely spoken. The patterns of British and US influence have left other English-speaking pockets in the region, most notably among the descendents of West Indian settlers on the Caribbean coast but also in Panama, particularly among residents of the Canal Zone. Groups of people throughout the region speak Mayan and other indigenous languages and dialects.

Every visitor to Central America will benefit from learning some Spanish, the basic elements of which are easily acquired (perhaps more so for speakers of English and Romance languages than for speakers of other languages). A language course taken before departure can go a long way toward facilitating communication and comfort on the road. Language courses are also available in Central America. Even if classes are impractical, you should make the effort to learn a few basic phrases and pleasantries. Do not hesitate to practice your new skills – in general, Latin Americans meet attempts to communicate in the vernacular, however halting, with enthusiasm and appreciation. For information on Spanish language courses, see Language Courses in the Regional Facts for the Visitor chapter and in the individual country chapters.

Central American Spanish

The Spanish of the Americas comes in a bewildering array of varieties. Depending upon the areas in which you travel, consonants may be glossed over, vowels squashed into each other, and syllables and even words dropped entirely. Slang and regional vocabulary, much of it derived from indigenous languages, can further add to your bewilderment. For example, a soft drink is called a *refresco* in Guatemala and Honduras but a *gaseosa* in El Salvador and Nicaragua and a *soda* in Panama. Because frequent travel among the small Central American republics is common, however, people are generally familiar with these

variations; you should have few problems with understanding.

Throughout Latin America, the Spanish language is referred to as *castellano* more often than *español*. Unlike in Spain, the plural of the familiar *tú* form is *ustedes* rather than *vosotros*; the latter term will sound quaint and archaic in the Americas. In addition, the letters 'c' and 'z' are never lisped in Latin America; attempts to do so could well provoke amusement or even contempt.

Phrasebooks & Dictionaries

Lonely Planet's *Latin American Spanish phrasebook,* by Anna Cody, is a worthwhile addition to your backpack. Lonely Planet also offers the *Costa Rican Spanish phrasebook* for those interested in the linguistic particulars of that destination. Another exceptionally useful resource is the *University of Chicago Spanish-English, English-Spanish Dictionary* – its small size, light weight and thorough entries make it ideal for travel. It also makes a great gift for any newfound friends upon your departure.

Pronunciation

The pronunciation of written Spanish is, in theory, consistently phonetic. Once you are aware of the basic rules, they should cause little difficulty. Speak slowly to avoid getting tongue-tied until you become confident of your ability. Of course, the best way to familiarize yourself with the pronunciation of the area you're traveling in is to chat with locals, keeping an ear out for regional variations.

Traditionally, there were three Spanish letters that did not exist in English: 'ch,' 'll' and 'ñ.' These followed 'c,' 'l,' and 'n' respectively in the alphabet, and had their own corresponding sections in the dictionary. However, in the mid-1990s, Spain's Academia Real de la Lengua Española abolished 'ch' and 'll' as separate letters; hence, newer Spanish dictionaries list them in their English alphabetical order. The practice varies from region to region, so look for a 'ch' section in the phone book if you can't find 'Chávez' under 'c.'

LANGUAGE

Vowels Spanish vowels are generally consistent and have close English equivalents:

a   is like the 'a' in 'father'
e   is somewhere between the 'e' in 'met' and the 'ey' in 'hey'
i   is like the 'ee' in 'feet'
o   is like the 'o' in 'note'
u   is like the 'oo' in 'boot'; it is silent after 'q' and in the pairings 'gue' and 'gui,' unless it's carrying a dieresis ('ü,' as in *güero*)

Consonants Spanish consonants generally resemble their English equivalents. The following are the major differences.

b   resembles the English 'b,' but is a softer sound produced by holding the lips nearly together. When beginning a word or when preceded by 'm' or 'n,' it's pronounced like the 'b' in 'book' *(bomba, embajada)*. The Spanish 'v' is pronounced almost identically; for clarification, Spanish speakers refer to 'b' as 'b larga' and to 'v' as 'b corta' or 'b chica'
c   is like the 's' in 'see' before 'e' and 'i'; otherwise, it's like the English 'k.'
d   is produced with the tongue up against the front teeth, almost like the 'th' in 'feather'; after 'l' and 'n,' it's pronounced like the English 'd' in 'dog.'
g   before 'e' and 'i' acts as a more guttural English 'h'; otherwise, it's like the 'g' in 'go.'
h   is invariably silent; if your name begins with this letter, listen carefully when immigration officials summon you to pick up your passport.
j   acts as a more guttural English 'h.'
ll   acts as a Spanish 'y,' although it is never a vowel; see Semiconsonant.
ñ   is like the 'ny' in 'canyon.'
r   is produced with the tongue touching the palate and flapping down, almost like the 'tt' of 'butter.' At the beginning of a word or following 'l,' 'n' or 's,' it is rolled strongly.
rr   is a very strongly rolled Spanish 'r.'
t   resembles the English 't,' but without the puff of air.
v   is pronounced like the Spanish 'b.'
x   is generally pronounced like the 'x' in 'taxi,' except in a few words in which it acts as the Spanish 'j' (as in 'México').
z   is like the 's' in 'sun.'

Semiconsonant The Spanish 'y' is a semiconsonant; it's pronounced as the Spanish 'i' when it stands alone or appears at the end of a word. Normally, 'y' is pronounced like the 'y' in 'yesterday'; however, in some regions it may be pronounced as the 's' in 'pleasure' or even the 'j' in 'jacket.' Hence, *yo me llamo* can sound like 'joe meh jahm-oh.'

Diphthongs Diphthongs are combinations of two vowels that form a single syllable. In Spanish, the formation of a diphthong depends on combinations of the two 'weak' vowels, 'i' and 'u,' or one weak and one of the three 'strong' vowels, 'a,' 'e' and 'o.' Two strong vowels form separate syllables.

An example of two weak vowels forming a diphthong is the word *viuda* (widow; pronounced **vyu**-tha). The initial syllable of 'Guatemala' is a combination of weak and strong vowels. In contrast, the verb *caer* (to fall) has two syllables (pronounced ca-**er**). Other examples of diphthongs and their approximate pronunciations include the following:

ai   as in 'hide'
au   as in 'how'
ei   as in 'hay'
ia   as in 'yard'
ie   as in 'yes'
oi   as in 'boy'
ua   as in 'wash'
ue   as in 'well' (unless preceded by 'q' or 'g')

Stress Stress is extremely important, as it can change the meaning of words. In general, words ending in vowels or the letters 'n' or 's' have stress on the next-to-last syllable, and those with other endings have stress on the last syllable. Thus *vaca* (cow) and *caballos* (horses) are both stressed on their penultimate syllables, but *catedral* (cathedral) is stressed on its last syllable.

To indicate departures from these general rules, Spanish employs the acute accent, which can occur anywhere in a word. If there is an accented syllable, stress is always on that syllable. Thus *sótano* (basement), 'América' and 'Panamá' have the first, second and third syllable stressed, respectively. When words are written in capital letters, the accent is often omitted, but the stress still falls where the accent would be.

Basic Grammar

Although even colloquial Spanish comprises a multitude of tenses and moods, learning enough grammar to enable basic conversation is not particularly difficult. In general, Spanish word order in sentences resembles that of English.

Nouns & Pronouns Nouns in Spanish are masculine or feminine. In general, nouns ending in 'o,' 'e' or 'ma' are masculine, and those ending in 'a,' 'ión' or 'dad' are feminine. Of course, there are scores of exceptions to this rule: Both *día* (day) and *mapa* (map) are masculine, and *mano* (hand) is feminine. To pluralize a noun, add 's' if it ends in an unaccented vowel – eg, *libro* (book) becomes *libros* – and 'es' if it ends in a consonant or accented vowel – eg, *rey* (king) becomes *reyes*. Fortunately for speakers of English, there is no declension of nouns as in Latin.

The personal pronouns are *yo* (I), *tú* or *vos* (you, informal), *usted* (you, formal; abbreviated Ud), *el/ella* (he/she), *nosotros/nosotras* (we), *ustedes* (you, plural; abbreviated Uds) and *ellos/ellas* (they). Note that to use the feminine plurals *nosotras* and *ellas,* the group referred to must be entirely composed of females; the presence of even one male calls for the masculine pronoun. In common speech, the personal pronoun may be omitted when it is the subject of a sentence, if the subject's identity is made clear by the verb ending: *estoy aquí* rather than *yo estoy aquí* (both mean 'I am here').

The possessive pronouns are *mi* (my), *tu* (your, informal), *nuestro* (our) and *su* (his/her/their/your, formal; singular and plural). As in English, possessive pronouns precede the noun they modify; however, they must agree in number and gender with that noun – not with the possessor. Thus we get *nuestro hombre* (our man), *nuestra mujer* (our woman), *nuestros novios* (our boyfriends) and *nuestras novias* (our girlfriends). *Mi, tu* and *su* do not change with gender, but add an 's' for plural nouns: *Mis libros* means 'my books.'

The demonstrative pronouns are *este* (this) and *ese* (that). Gender and number also affect demonstrative pronouns:

este libro	this book
estos cuadernos	these notebooks
esta carta	this letter
estas tijeras	these scissors
ese chico	that boy
esos muchachos	those guys
esa chica	that girl
esas muchachas	those gals

Articles, Adjectives & Adverbs The definite articles ('the' in English) are *el, la, los* and *las*. These four forms correspond to the four possible combinations of gender and number. Similarly, the indefinite articles ('a,' 'an' and 'some') are *un, una, unos* and *unas*. In Spanish, the definite article is used more extensively than in English, and the indefinite article is utilized less. As in English, the articles precede the nouns they modify, eg, *el papel* (the paper), *unas frutas* (some fruits).

In contrast, adjectives in Spanish usually follow the noun they modify. Those ending in 'o' agree with the noun in gender and number (thus *alto* means 'tall,' while *mujeres altas* means 'tall women'); those ending in other letters merely agree in number. To form a comparative, add *más* (more) or *menos* (less) before the adjective. For superlatives, add the *más* or *menos* as well as *lo, la, los* or *las* (depending on gender and number). For example, *pequeño* is 'small,' *más pequeño* 'smaller' and *lo más pequeño* 'the smallest.'

Adverbs can often be formed from adjectives by adding the suffix *-mente*. If the adjective ends in an 'o,' convert it to an 'a' before affixing the ending. Thus *actual* (current) becomes *actualmente* (currently) and *rápido* (rapid) becomes *rápidamente* (rapidly).

Verbs Spanish has three main categories of verbs: those ending in 'ar,' such as *hablar* (to speak); those ending in 'er,' such as *comer* (to eat); and those ending in 'ir,' such as *reir* (to laugh). Verbs are conjugated by retaining the verb's stem and altering the ending depending on subject, tense and mood. While most verbs follow a complicated yet predictable pattern of conjugation, scores of 'irregular' verbs, often the most commonly used, must be memorized. Refer to Lonely Planet's *Latin American Spanish phrasebook* for a more detailed explanation of verb conjugation.

LANGUAGE

Greetings & Civilities

In public behavior, Latin Americans are often cordial yet polite and expect others to reciprocate. Never, for example, address a stranger without extending a greeting such as *buenos días* or *buenas tardes*. The usage of the informal second-person singular *tú* and *vos* differs from country to country; when in doubt, use the more formal *usted*. You must *always* use *usted* when addressing the police or persons with considerable power.

Hello	*Hola*
Good morning/Good day	*Buenos días*
Good afternoon	*Buenas tardes*
Good evening/Good night	*Buenas noches*
(The above three are often shortened to *Buenos* or *Buenas*.)	
Goodbye	*Adiós* or *Hasta luego*
Please	*Por favor*
Thank you	*Gracias*
You're welcome/It's a pleasure	*De nada/Con mucho gusto*
Excuse me (when passing someone)	*Permiso*
Excuse me	*Discúlpeme* or *Perdón*
I'm sorry	*Lo siento*
What is your name?	*¿Cómo se llama usted?*
My name is …	*Me llamo …*
A pleasure (to meet you)	*Mucho gusto*

Useful Words & Phrases

yes	*sí*	I don't understand.	*No entiendo.*
no	*no*	I don't speak much Spanish.	*No hablo mucho castellano.*
and	*y*		
to/at	*a*	Is/are there …?	*¿Hay …?*
for	*por, para*	I would like …	*Me gustaría …* or *Quisiera …*
of/from	*de/desde*		
in/on	*en*	Where?	*¿Dónde?*
with	*con*	Where is/are …?	*¿Dónde está/están …?*
without	*sin*	When?	*¿Cuándo?*
before	*antes*	What?	*¿Qué?* (use *¿Cómo?* to ask someone to repeat something)
after	*después de*		
soon	*pronto*		
already	*ya*	Which (ones)?	*¿Cuál(es)?*
now	*ahora*	Who?	*¿Quién?*
right away	*ahorita, en seguida*	Why?	*¿Por qué?*
here	*aquí*	How?	*¿Cómo?*
there	*allí* or *allá*	How much?	*¿Cuánto?*
I understand.	*Entiendo.*	How many?	*¿Cuántos?*

Emergencies

Help!	*¡Socorro!* or *¡Auxilio!*	I've been robbed.	*Me han robado.*
Help me!	*¡Ayúdenme!*	They took my …	*Se me llevaron …*
Thief!	*¡Ladrón!*	money	*el dinero*
Fire!	*¡Fuego!*	passport	*el pasaporte*
police	*policía*	bag	*la bolsa*
doctor	*doctor*	Leave me alone!	*¡Déjeme!*
hospital	*hospital*	Go away!	*¡Váyase!*

Getting Around

plane	*avión*	motorcycle	*motocicleta*
train	*tren*	hitchhike	*hacer dedo* or *pedir*
bus	*autobús; bus; camión;*		*un ride* ('ride' pro-
	minibus		nounced as in
small bus	*colectivo; micro*		English)
ship	*barco; buque*		
car	*auto; carro; coche*	airport	*aeropuerto*
taxi	*taxi*	train station	*estación de ferrocarril*
truck	*camión*	bus terminal	*terminal de buses;*
pickup	*camioneta*		*central camionera;*
bicycle	*bicicleta*		*terminal terrestre*

I would like a ticket to …   *Quiero un boleto/pasaje a …*
What's the fare to …?   *¿Cuánto cuesta el pasaje a …?*
When does the next plane/train/bus leave for …?   *¿Cuándo sale el próximo avión/tren/bus para …?*
Are there student discounts?   *¿Hay descuentos estudiantiles?/¿Hay rebajas para estudiantes?*

first/last/next   *primero/último/próximo*
first/second class   *primera/segunda clase*
one way/roundtrip   *ida/ida y vuelta*
left luggage   *guardería de equipaje*
tourist office   *oficina de turismo*

Traffic Signs Keep in mind that traffic signs will invariably be in Spanish and may not be accompanied by internationally recognized symbols. Pay especially close attention to signs reading *Peligro* (Danger), *Cede el Paso* (Yield or Give Way; especially prevalent on one-lane bridges) and *Hundimiento* (Dip; often a euphemistic term for anaxle-breaking sinkhole). Disregarding these warnings could result in disaster.

Adelante	Ahead	*Mantenga Su Derecha*	Keep to the Right
Alto	Stop	*No Adelantar/*	No Passing
Cede el Paso	Yield/Give Way	*No Rebase*	
Curva Peligrosa	Dangerous Curve	*No Estacionar*	No Parking
Derrumbes en la Vía	Landslides or	*No Hay Paso*	No Entrance
	Rockfalls (in the	*Peligro*	Danger
	Road)	*Trabajos en la Vía*	Construction/
Despacio	Slow		Roadwork
Desvío	Detour	*Tránsito Entrando*	Entering Traffic
Hundimiento	Dip		

Crossing the Border

birth certificate	*certificado de*	immigration	*inmigración*
	nacimiento	insurance	*seguro*
border (frontier)	*la frontera*	passport	*pasaporte*
car-owner's title	*título de propiedad*	temporary vehicle	*permiso de importa-*
car registration	*registración*	import permit	*ción temporal de*
customs	*aduana*		*vehículo*
driver's license	*licencia de manejar*	tourist card	*tarjeta de turista*
identification	*identificación*	visa	*visado*

Accommodations

hotel	*hotel; pensión; residencial; hospedaje*
single room	*habitación single/sencilla*
double room	*habitación doble/matrimonial*
What does it cost?	*¿Cuánto cuesta?*
Can you give me a deal?	*¿Me puede hacer precio?/¿Me puede hacer promoción?/ ¿Me puede rebajar?*
per night	*por noche*
full board	*pensión completa*
shared bath	*baño compartido*
private bath	*baño privado*
too expensive	*demasiado caro*
cheaper	*más económico* or *más barato*
May I see it?	*¿Puedo verlo?*
I don't like it.	*No me gusta.*
the bill	*la cuenta*

Toilets

The most common word for 'toilet' is *baño*, but *servicios sanitarios* or just *servicios* (services) is a frequent alternative. Men's toilets will usually be signaled by *hombres, caballeros* or *varones*. Women's toilets will say *señoras* or *damas*.

Eating & Drinking

I (don't) eat/drink …	*(No) como/tomo …*	juice	*jugo*
I'm a vegetarian.	*Soy vegetariano/a.*	vegetables	*vegetales* or *legumbres*
water	*agua*		
purified water	*agua purificada*	fish	*pescado*
bread	*pan*	seafood	*mariscos*
meat	*carne*	coffee	*café*
cheese	*queso*	tea	*té*
eggs	*huevos*	beer	*cerveza*
milk	*leche*	alcohol	*alcohol*

Post & Communications

post office	*correo*	collect call	*llamada a cobro revertido*
letter	*carta*		
parcel	*paquete*	public telephone	*teléfono público*
postcard	*postal*	local call	*llamada local*
airmail	*correo aéreo*	long-distance call	*llamada de larga distancia*
registered mail	*correo certificado*		
stamps	*estampillas*	person to person	*persona a persona*
phone call	*llamada (telefónica)*	email	*correo electrónico*

Geographical Expressions

The expressions below are among the most common you will encounter in Spanish-language maps and guides.

avenida	avenue	*campo, finca, fundo, hacienda*	farm
bahía	bay		
calle	street	*carretera, camino, ruta*	highway
camino	road	*cascada, salto*	waterfall

cerro	hill, mount	*parque nacional*	national park
cordillera	mountain range	*paso*	pass
estancia, granja, rancho	ranch	*puente*	bridge
estero	marsh, estuary	*río*	river
lago	lake	*seno*	sound
montaña	mountain	*valle*	valley

Countries

The list below includes only countries whose names are spelled differently in English and Spanish.

Canada	*Canadá*	Scotland	*Escocia*
Denmark	*Dinamarca*	Spain	*España*
England	*Inglaterra*	Sweden	*Suecia*
France	*Francia*	Switzerland	*Suiza*
Germany	*Alemania*	United States	*Estados Unidos*
Great Britain	*Gran Bretaña*	Wales	*Gales*
Ireland	*Irlanda*	I am from	*Soy de...*
Italy	*Italia*	Where are you from?	*¿De dónde viene*
Japan	*Japón*		*usted?*
Netherlands	*Holanda*	Where do you live?	*¿Dónde vive usted?*
New Zealand	*Nueva Zelandia*		

Numbers

1	*uno*	40	*cuarenta*
2	*dos*	50	*cincuenta*
3	*tres*	60	*sesenta*
4	*cuatro*	70	*setenta*
5	*cinco*	80	*ochenta*
6	*seis*	90	*noventa*
7	*siete*	100	*cien*
8	*ocho*	101	*ciento uno*
9	*nueve*	102	*ciento dos*
10	*diez*	110	*ciento diez*
11	*once*	200	*doscientos*
12	*doce*	300	*trescientos*
13	*trece*	400	*cuatrocientos*
14	*catorce*	500	*quinientos*
15	*quince*	600	*seiscientos*
16	*dieciséis*	700	*setecientos*
17	*diecisiete*	800	*ochocientos*
18	*dieciocho*	900	*novecientos*
19	*diecinueve*	1000	*mil*
20	*veinte*	1100	*mil cien*
21	*veintiuno*	1200	*mil doscientos*
22	*veintidós*	2000	*dos mil*
23	*veintitrés*	10,000	*diez mil*
24	*veinticuatro*	50,000	*cincuenta mil*
30	*treinta*	100,000	*cien mil*
31	*treinta y uno*	1,000,000	*un millón*
32	*treinta y dos*	2,000,000	*dos millones*
33	*treinta y tres*	1,000,000,000	*un billón*

Ordinal Numbers

As with other adjectives, ordinals must agree in gender and number with the noun they modify. Ordinal numbers are often abbreviated using a numeral and a superscript 'o' or 'a' in street names, addresses, and so forth: Calle 1a, 2o piso, (1st Street, 2nd floor).

1st	*primero/a*	8th	*octavo/a*
2nd	*segundo/a*	9th	*noveno/a*
3rd	*tercero/a*	10th	*décimo/a*
4th	*cuarto/a*	11th	*undécimo/a*
5th	*quinto/a*	12th	*duodécimo/a*
6th	*sexto/a*	20th	*vigésimo/a*
7th	*séptimo/a*		

Days of the Week

Monday	*lunes*	Friday	*viernes*
Tuesday	*martes*	Saturday	*sábado*
Wednesday	*miércoles*	Sunday	*domingo*
Thursday	*jueves*		

Time

Eight o'clock is *las ocho,* while 8:30 is *las ocho y treinta* (eight and thirty) or *las ocho y media* (eight and a half). However, 7:45 is *las ocho menos quince* (eight minus fifteen) or *las ocho menos cuarto* (eight minus one quarter).

Times are modified by morning *(de la manaña)* or afternoon *(de la tarde)* instead of am or pm. Use of the 24-hour clock, or military time, is also common, especially with transportation schedules.

What time is it?	*¿Qué hora es?*
It's one o'clock.	*Es la una.*
It's two/three/etc o'clock.	*Son las dos/tres/etc.*
At three o'clock...	*A las tres...*

Glossary

aguardiente – a clear, potent liquor made from sugarcane; can also be referred to as *caña*

almuerzo ejecutivo – inexpensive set lunch

alquiler de automóviles – car rental

apartado – post office box

artesanías – handicrafts

Av – abbreviation for *avenida* (avenue)

ayuntamiento – municipal government

bahía – bay

balneario – public beach or swimming area

barrio – district, neighborhood

billete – bank note

bistec – grilled or fried beef

bocas – appetizers, often served with drinks in a bar

boleto – ticket (bus, museum, etc)

bomba – gasoline (petrol) station

bote – motorized canoe (Panama)

caballeros – literally 'horsemen,' but corresponds to the English 'gentlemen'; look for the term on bathroom doors

cabaña or **cabina** – cabin or bungalow

cacique – Indian tribal leader; provincial warlord or strongman

cafetería – literally 'coffee shop'; any informal restaurant with waiter service (not a self-service establishment as implied by the English 'cafeteria')

cafetín – small cafeteria

cajero automático – automated bank teller machine (ATM)

callejón – alley, or small, narrow or very short street

calzada – causeway

cama matrimonial – double bed

camarotes – smaller rooms

camión – truck; bus

camioneta – pickup truck

carretera – highway

Carretera Interamericana – Interamerican Hwy (also referred to as the Pan-American Hwy); the nearly continuous highway running from Alaska to Chile (it breaks at the Darién Gap)

casa de cambio – currency exchange office

casa de huéspedes – guesthouse

casa de la mujer – women's center

casado – a cheap set meal, usually served at lunchtime

caseta de larga distancia – long-distance telephone station, often shortened to *caseta*

catedral – cathedral

cay, caye or **cayo** – cay; small island of sand or coral fragments

cayuca – dugout canoe

cenote – large, natural limestone cave used for water storage or ceremonial purposes

cerro – hill

cerveza – beer

ceviche – seafood marinated in lemon or lime juice, garlic and seasonings

chamarras – thick, heavy woolen blankets (Guatemala)

chapín – a citizen of Guatemala; Guatemalan

chicha – fruit juice mixed with sugar and water (Panama)

cine – movie theater

ciudad – city

cocina – cookshop (literally 'kitchen'); a small, basic restaurant usually found in or near municipal markets

cofradía – religious brotherhood, particularly in highland Guatemala

colectivo – jitney taxi or minibus that picks up and drops off passengers along its route

comedor – a basic and cheap eatery, usually with a limited menu

comida corrida – meal of the day; a set meal of several courses, usually offered at lunchtime

comida corriente – a mixed plate of different foods typical of the local region

completo – complete, fully booked

conquistador – any of the Spanish explorer-conquerors of Latin America

Contras – counterrevolutionary military groups fighting against the Sandinista government in Nicaragua throughout the 1980s

cordillera – mountain range

correo aéreo – airmail

costa – coast

criollo – Creole; born in Latin America of Spanish parentage; on the Caribbean coast it refers to someone of mixed African and European descent (see also 'mestizo' and 'ladino')

cruce – a crossroads, usually where one makes bus connections; see also *tronque*

cuadra – city block
cueva – cave
curandero/a – traditional indigenous healer

damas – ladies; the usual sign on bathroom doors
dzul, dzules – Mayan for foreigners or 'townfolk'

edificio – building
empanada – Chilean-style turnover stuffed with meat or cheese and raisins
enredo – wraparound skirt

faja – waist sash that binds garments and holds what would otherwise be put in pockets
farmacia de turno – the 'on-duty' pharmacy in the revolving system by which designated pharmacies remain open at night and on weekends
finca – farm, plantation, ranch
fresco – drink made of fruit juice, sugar and water
fuerte – fort

gallo pinto – a common meal of blended rice and beans
galón, galones – US gallon (fluid measure of 3.79L)
Garífuna or **Garinagu** – descendants of West African slaves and Carib Indians, brought to the Caribbean coast of Central America in the late 18th century from the island of St Vincent; also referred to as Black Caribs
gaseosa – soda, soft drink
gibnut – small, brown-spotted rodent similar to a guinea pig; also called a *paca*
golfo – gulf
gringo/a – mildly pejorative term used in Latin America to describe male/female foreigners, particularly those from North America; often applied to any visitor of European heritage
gruta – cave
guacamole – a salad of mashed or chopped avocados, onions and tomatoes
guardaropa – cloakroom, place to leave parcels when entering an establishment
guaro – in Costa Rica, a local firewater made with sugarcane
guayabera – embroidered men's dress shirt, worn outside the pants

hacienda – agricultural estate, plantation; also treasury, as in *Departamento de Hacienda* (Treasury Dept)
hospedaje – guesthouse
huipil – long, woven, white sleeveless tunic, from the Maya regions, with intricate, colorful embroidery

iglesia – church
invierno – winter; Central America's wet season, which extends roughly from April through mid-December
isla – island
IVA – *impuesto al valor agregado,* or value-added tax

jejenes – sand flies
junco – type of basket weaving

ladino – a person of mixed Indian and European parentage, often used to describe mestizos who speak Spanish; see also 'mestizo' and 'criollo'
lago – lake
laguna – lagoon or lake
lancha – small motorboat
lempira – Honduran unit of currency
leng – colloquial Mayan term for coins (Guatemalan highlands)
libra – pound (a weight equal to 0.45kg)
licuado – fresh fruit drink, blended with milk or water
lista de correos – poste restante (general delivery) mail
lleno – full; can apply to a fuel tank

machismo – maleness, masculine virility; exaggerated masculine pride
malecón – pier or jetty; also a term for a waterfront promenade
manzana – literally 'apple,' but also a term for a city block
mar – sea
mercado – market
mestizo – person of mixed ancestry (usually Spanish and Indian; see also 'criollo' and 'ladino')
metate – flat stone on which corn is ground
migración – immigration; office of an immigration department
milla – mile (a distance equal to 1.61km)
milpa – cornfield
mirador – lookout point
mola – colorful hand-stitched appliqué textiles made by Kuna Indians

mordida – literally 'little bite'; a small bribe that's usually paid to keep the wheels of bureaucracy turning

muchacho – boy; also used as 'mate' or 'pal'

muelle – pier

municipalidad – town hall

museo – museum

Navidad – Christmas

NGO – nongovernmental organization

oficina de correos – post office

onza – ounce (a weight equal to 28.35g)

paca – see *gibnut*

PADI – Professional Association of Diving Instructors

palacio de gobierno – building housing the executive offices of a state or regional government

palacio municipal – city hall; seat of the corporation or municipal government

palapa – thatched, palm-leaf-roofed shelter with open sides

pan de coco – coconut bread

panga – small motorboat

parada – bus stop

parque – park; sometimes also to describe a plaza

peña – a folkloric club; an evening of music, song and dance

pensión – guesthouse

pie, pies – foot (a length equal to 0.3m), feet

pisto – colloquial Mayan term for Guatemalan money, quetzals

plato del día – plate (or meal) of the day

plato típico – a mixed plate of various foods typical or characteristic of a place or region

playa – beach

pollera – Spanish-influenced 'national dress' of Panamanian women, worn for festive occasions

pozos – springs

propina – a tip; gratuity

puente – bridge

puerta – gate; door

puerto – port; harbor

punta – point; traditional Garífuna dance involving much hip movement

pupusa – in El Salvador, cornmeal mass stuffed with cheese or refried beans (or a mixture of both)

quebrada – ravine; brook

refresco – soda, soft drink; in Costa Rica, a drink made with local fruits

río – river

rockola – jukebox

ropa vieja – literally 'old clothes'; spicy shredded beef and rice dish (Panama)

rosticería – restaurant selling roast meats

ruletero – jitney; public minibus

sacbé, sacbeob – ceremonial limestone avenue or path between Mayan cities

salchichas – sausages, like hot dogs

sancocho – spicy meat-and-vegetable stew, the 'national dish' of Panama

sanitario – literally 'sanitary'; usually means toilet

santos – saints

Semana Santa – Holy Week, the week preceding Easter

sendero – path or trail

servicios sanitarios – toilets

sierra – mountain range; a saw

soda – place that serves a counter lunch; soft drink (Panama)

sorbetería – ice-cream parlor

stela, stelae – standing stone monument(s) of the ancient Maya, usually carved

supermercado – supermarket, from a corner store to a large, US-style supermarket

tajaditas – crisp, fried banana chips

taller – shop or workshop

taller mecánico – a mechanic's shop, usually for cars

tamal, tamales – boiled or steamed cornmeal filled with chicken or pork, usually wrapped in a banana leaf

teléfono monedero – a coin-operated telephone

temblor or **terremoto** – earthquake

templo – temple or church

tico/tica – inhabitant of Costa Rica

tienda – small shop

típico – typical or characteristic of a region, particularly used to describe food; also a form of Panamanian folkloric music

traje – traditional handmade clothing

tronque – a crossroads where one makes bus connections; see also *cruce*

turicentro – literally 'tourist center'; outdoor recreation center with swimming facilities, restaurants and camping (term used in El Salvador)

Unesco – the United Nations Educational, Scientific, and Cultural Organization

vegetariano – vegetarian

venado – deer; venison

verano – summer; Central America's dry season, roughly from mid-December to April

viajero/viajera – traveler

volcán – volcano

Acknowledgments

THANKS

Thanks to the many travelers who wrote in with comments about our last edition and with tips and comments about Central America in general:

Anders Aarkrog, Genevieve Abbott, Jan Abu Kaulfuhs, C Adam Padd, Bob Agnew, Laura Ahrens, Louise & Charles Alexander, Ron Alldridge, Allison Allgaier, Vicente Alvarez, Arden Anderson, Lotta Andersson, Brian Andreasen, Paul Armstrong, Pat Ashley, Peter Balint, Grahame Bann, James Bardner, Jim Barnum Jr, Sue Barreau, Orlando Battle, Amelia Swan Baxter, Taylor Beavers, Rob Bell, Lou Bender, Edward Berkovich, Michel Bessette, Helle Bjerre, Carla Black, Joel Bleskacek, Jane Bode, Guillermo Bolanos, Claire Bonnet, Nicole Boogaers, Erik Botsford, Gery Bowerman, Roy & Audrey Bradford, Dirk Bremecke, Michel Brillet, Allison Brown, Dave Brown, Kenton Brown, Ben Budnitz, Lucky Burchett, Tim Burford, Astrud Burgess, Claude Bussires, Judith Butler, Jeannie Cain, Eva Calvo, Mark Camp, Luis Canas, Darsha & Mac Capaldi, Agustin Cardona, John Carlisle, Javier Castellon, Sara Castriota Scanderbeg, Ken Cavender, Phung Chain, E & J Chanecka, Jean-Francois Chariot, Eric Charlez, Mish Chillies, Colin J Churcher, Paolo Cicioni, Paula Cipolla, Robert Cisneros, Michael Clark, Debora Clawson, Steve Coats, Nina Cobos, Bess Cocke, Jodi Coleman, Joke Collewijn, Ben Colman, Glen Coming, David Connor, Karen Cooper, Michelle Cooper, Sonoe Kurimoto Corr, Megan Corrigan, Nicholas Couis, Bryce Coulter, Pascale Courrieu, Brenda Czaban, Dale Dagger, Zabelle D'amico, John Davison, Yorelle Dawes, Mark Dellar, Steven Dematteo, Willem-Henri den Hartog, Massimiliano Di Girolamo, Vanessa Dickson, Martin Dillig, Danny Dodd, Carol Doering, Daniel Drazan, Ilse Duijvestein, Brian Eggleston, Eve Eidelson, David Elderton, Ronald Ellerman, Kari Eloranta, Joeri Engelfriet, Laura Enridge, Christina Eriksson, Kaffanke Ernst, Carolyn Evans Nemia, Doron Ezra, Milena Fessmann, Gerhard Fiala, Michael & Patricia Filliol, A Firsimmons, Sandi Fisher Schmidt, A Fitzsimmons, Jamie Fleming, Tom Fletcher, Susan Foster, William F Frank, Steve Frankham, Tim Frodsham, Alison Frye, Marty & Laura Furlan, Andres Garcia, Terry S Gardner, Nathan Garneau, Irene E Gashu, Irene E Gashu, Fabrice Gendre, Tony Giardina, Simone Gisler, Nuala Glynn, Santiago Gonzalez, Jamie Gordon, Jamie Grant, Line Gregoire, Michael Greig, Luke Griffin, Jose Groothuis, Philip Grunow, Damian Guiney, Hubert Haas, Philip Habing, Niklas Hansson, Mabel Haourt, Dave Harralson, Langdon W Harris, Scott Hemphill, Janne Brunt Henriksen, John J Herd, Leah Mullet Hershberger, Amy Hewitt, Amy B Hewitt, Tony Hewitt, Anne Hinnegan, Charlie Hirst, Yvonne Hirt, Fried Hoeben, John Hoffman, Sophia Holtz, NH Home, Angie Hook, Carlos Hornstein, Katerina Horochowski, Katriona Hoskins, Ron Hoven, Viktor Hskansson, Camilla Hult, Marianne Hummel, Barbara Hunt, Cameron Hutchison, Andrew Hyde, Michael A Innis, Michael Irmer, Rie Ishii, Christian Iyer, Kerry Jackson, Karin Jacobsson, Christian Janout, Tim Jeffries, Donna Jessop, Catherine Johnson, Renee & Steven Johnson, Michael Jones, Catherine Joppart, Anne Jordan, Wolfgang Junesch, Marie Juul Petersen, Nik Katsourides, Nancy Keller, Anita Kelley, Carmel Kelly, Julie Kepner, Frank Khoo, Ginella Kirkland, Scott Kistler, Janet Kliches, RWJ Knight, Kristin Koehl, Leslie Korn, Daniela krause, Eckert Krebber, Raghu Krishnan, Marianne Friis Kristiansen, Randall R Krueger, Robert Kunstaetter, Bob Kurkijian, Brian Lacey, Johnathan Lalas, John Lea, Laura Lee Hartshorn, Peter Leedom, Guido Lehnen, Henriette Leifert, Kay Leissner, Michael Lemonds, Carrie & Hans Levenson-Wahl, Carolina Lindo Gonzalez, Iris Lohrengel, Ellen & Jos Lommerse, Christian Loncle, Adriana Lopez, Art Ludwig, Emma Lupin, William E Macauley, Jim Macgillis, Lachlan Mackenzie, Thomas Mader, Ole Madsen, Indrani Makhan, Jerry Makransky, Rob Manning, Paul Martin, Edwin Martinez, Oswaldo Martinez, Nancy Matson, Charles Mays, Amanda McCleery, Kevin McCord, Rhian McKee, Darryl McKenzie, Doug McKinnell, Alan Mead, Max Medina, Ralf Metzen, Savioli Micolino, Stephanie Mills, Jamie Monk, Darren Moody, Margarita Mooney, Frank Moore, Eduardo Morales, Kat Morgenstern, Kiran Morzaria, Martin Mowforth, Catherine Munier, Franklin Murillo, Roger Nash, Michael Newton, Fleming H Nielsen, Judy Night, Darrin Nix, Emilie Nolet, Michael North, Walter Novelly, Muireann O'Briain, Lars Olesen, Polly O'Loughlin, Lars Olsen, David Olson, Wayne Olson, Dean Oman, William Ormsbee, Louise Parlons, David Parrish, Erin Pass, Kip Patrick, Michael Patterson, Brendan Peace, Michele Pekovich, Deborah Pencharz, Javier Perez Vicente, Bart Peters, Edward Pilling, Alban Pilloud, Javier Pinel, Edward Pinto, Anne-Marijke Podt, Dries Poels, Alberto Pons Jr, Scott

Pope, Susan Pot, Louise & David Powers, Rosemary Pritchard, Aleesha Pruett, Ben Pughe-Morgan, Judy Quiros, Brett Rallings, John Randazzo, Nikolah Rasmussen, Andrew Redfern, George Redman, Caroline Redrup, Andrea Reigels, James Renn, Rod Reynolds, Roman Reznicek, Mike Richey, Tim Richey, Wolfgang Richter, Simon Roche, Sabine Rocholl, Steve Rogowski, Clive Rolfe, Howard Rosenweig, Howard Rosenzweig, Paul Rotheroe, Jeff Rothman, Ricardo Rubio, Anton Rupar, John Ryan, John F Ryan, N Saballos, Humberto M Salomon, Kevin Samarasingha, Per Samuelsson, Marietta Sander, Jarrod Sanderson, Greg Sands, Jennifer Sargent, Colin Savage, Steve Schmidt, Joke Schrijvershof, Taryn Schubert, Miriam Schumacher, Martin Schweinberger, Glenn Schwendinger, Diane Selkirk, Chad Sellmer, Arpna Shah, Teresa Shevchenko, Dr G Silvestro, Paula Simmons, Dean Simonsen, J Skeats, Carolyn Smith, Megan Smith, Nancy A Smith, Todd Smith, Victoria Snyder, Eliza Sorensen, Stan Spacey, Patrick Spanjaard, Paul Starkey, Roland Steffen, Julien Stern, Courtenay J Stevens, Janne Stolz, Anna Strongman, Christine Sutherland, Andrew Swift, Justin Synnott, Vivian Teubner, Robert Thiele, Raphadl Thiry, Gerry Thompson, Rachael Thompson, David Thomson, Ian Thurley, Walter Tibe, Gerald Timoney, Jerry Timoney, Lina Troendle, Michael Turinski, Martin Uzelac, Corstiaan van Aalsburg, Jeffrey van Fleet, Erik van Gilst, Danil van Grootheest, Marc van Maastricht, David van Moppes, Rian Van Schalwyk, Michael Vestergaard, H Viena, Johannes Vijlbrief, Herman Von Harten, Sally Wade, Clive Walker, Jeff Walker, Robert Walker, Moira Walsh, Martha Waring, Tom Waring, Tom & Martha Waring, Luis Wassmann, Tim Watson, Annemieke Wevers, Claire White, Paul white, Tara White, Tim White, Beth Whitman, Jerry Whitmire, John T Widdowson, Doekle Wielinga, Denise Williams, Pat Willyard, Eldon R Wilson, Tristram Winfield, Peter Wirth, Didier Wurster, mego Yamamoto, Gordon Young, Stephen Zaborowski, Magda Zupancic

LONELY PLANET

You already know that Lonely Planet produces more than this one guidebook, but you might not be aware of the other products we have on this region. Here is a selection of titles which you may want to check out as well:

Mexico
ISBN 1 86450 089 1
US$24.99 • UK£14.99

South America on a shoestring
ISBN 1 86450 283 5
US$29.99 • UK£17.99

Healthy Travel Central & South America
ISBN 1 86450 053 0
US$5.95 • UK£3.99

Diving & Snorkeling Belize
ISBN 0 86442 575 9
US$15.95 • UK£9.99

Read This First: Central & South America
ISBN 1 86450 067 0
US$14.99 • UK£8.99

Latin American Spanish phrasebook
ISBN 0 86442 558 9
US$6.95 • UK£4.50

Available wherever books are sold.

Guides by Region

Lonely Planet is known worldwide for publishing practical, reliable and no-nonsense travel information in our guides and on our Web site. The Lonely Planet list covers just about every accessible part of the world. Currently there are 16 series: Travel guides, Shoestring guides, Condensed guides, Watching Wildlife guides, Pisces Diving & Snorkeling guides, City Maps, Road Atlases, Out to Eat, World Food, Journeys travel literature and Pictorials.

AFRICA Africa on a shoestring • Cairo • Cairo City Map • Cape Town • Cape Town City Map • East Africa • Egypt • Egyptian Arabic phrasebook • Ethiopia, Eritrea & Djibouti • Ethiopian Amharic phrasebook • The Gambia & Senegal • Healthy Travel Africa • Kenya • Malawi • Morocco • Moroccan Arabic phrasebook • Mozambique • Read This First: Africa • South Africa, Lesotho & Swaziland • Southern Africa • Southern Africa Road Atlas • Swahili phrasebook • Tanzania, Zanzibar & Pemba • Trekking in East Africa • Tunisia • Watching Wildlife East Africa • Watching Wildlife Southern Africa • West Africa • World Food Morocco • Zimbabwe, Botswana & Namibia
Travel Literature: Mali Blues: Traveling to an African Beat • The Rainbird: A Central African Journey • Songs to an African Sunset: A Zimbabwean Story

AUSTRALIA & THE PACIFIC Auckland • Australia • Australian phrasebook • Australia Road Atlas • Cycling Australia • Cycling New Zealand • Fiji • Fijian phrasebook • Healthy Travel Australia, NZ and the Pacific • Islands of Australia's Great Barrier Reef • Melbourne • Melbourne City Map • Micronesia • New Caledonia • New South Wales • New Zealand • Northern Territory • Outback Australia • Out to Eat – Melbourne • Out to Eat – Sydney • Papua New Guinea • Pidgin phrasebook • Queensland • Rarotonga & the Cook Islands • Samoa • Solomon Islands • South Australia • South Pacific • South Pacific phrasebook • Sydney • Sydney City Map • Sydney Condensed • Tahiti & French Polynesia • Tasmania • Tonga • Tramping in New Zealand • Vanuatu • Victoria • Walking in Australia • Watching Wildlife Australia • Western Australia
Travel Literature: Islands in the Clouds: Travel in the Highlands of New Guinea • Kiwi Tracks: A New Zealand Journey • Sean & David's Long Drive

CENTRAL AMERICA & THE CARIBBEAN Bahamas, Turks & Caicos • Baja California • Belize, Guatemala & Yucatán • Bermuda • Central America on a shoestring • Costa Rica • Costa Rica Spanish-phrasebook • Cuba • Dominican Republic & Haiti • Eastern Caribbean • Guatemala • Havana • Healthy Travel Central & South America • Jamaica • Mexico • Mexico City • Panama • Puerto Rico • Read This First: Central & South America • World Food Mexico • Yucatán
Travel Literature: Green Dreams: Travels in Central America

EUROPE Amsterdam • Amsterdam City Map • Amsterdam Condensed • Andalucía • Austria • Baltic States phrasebook • Barcelona • Barcelona City Map • Belgium & Luxembourg • Berlin • Berlin City Map • Britain • British phrasebook • Brussels, Bruges & Antwerp • Brussels City Map • Budapest • Budapest City Map • Canary Islands • Central Europe • Central Europe phrasebook • Copenhagen • Corfu & the Ionians • Corsica • Crete • Crete Condensed • Croatia • Cycling Britain • Cycling France • Cyprus • Czech & Slovak Republics • Denmark • Dublin • Dublin City Map • Eastern Europe • Eastern Europe phrasebook • Edinburgh • England • Estonia, Latvia & Lithuania • Europe on a shoestring • Europe phrasebook • Finland • Florence • France • Frankfurt Condensed • French phrasebook • Georgia, Armenia & Azerbaijan • Germany • German phrasebook • Greece • Greek Islands • Greek phrasebook • Hungary • Iceland, Greenland & the Faroe Islands • Ireland • Italian phrasebook • Italy • Krakow • Lisbon • The Loire • London • London City Map • London Condensed • Madrid • Malta • Mediterranean Europe • Mediterranean Europe phrasebook • Moscow • Munich • Netherlands • Normandy • Norway • Out to Eat – London • Out to Eat – Paris • Paris • Paris City Map • Paris Condensed • Poland • Polish phrasebook • Portugal • Portuguese phrasebook • Prague • Prague City Map • Provence & the Côte d'Azur • Read This First: Europe • Rhodes & the Dodecanese • Romania & Moldova • Rome • Rome City Map • Russia, Ukraine & Belarus • Russian phrasebook • Scandinavian & Baltic Europe • Scandinavian phrasebook • Scotland • Sicily • Slovenia • South-West France • Spain • Spanish phrasebook • St Petersburg • St Petersburg City Map • Sweden • Switzerland • Tuscany • Ukrainian phrasebook • Venice • Vienna • Walking in Britain • Walking in France • Walking in Ireland • Walking in Italy • Walking in Spain • Walking in Switzerland • Western Europe • World Food France • World Food Ireland • World Food Italy • World Food Spain
Travel Literature: After Yugoslavia • Love and War in the Apennines • The Olive Grove: Travels in Greece • On the Shores of the Mediterranean • Round Ireland in Low Gear • A Small Place in Italy

LONELY PLANET

Mail Order

Lonely Planet products are distributed worldwide. They are also available by mail order from Lonely Planet, so if you have difficulty finding a title please write to us. North and South American residents should write to 150 Linden St, Oakland, CA 94607, USA; European and African residents should write to 10a Spring Place, London NW5 3BH, UK; and residents of other countries to Locked Bag 1, Footscray, Victoria 3011, Australia.

INDIAN SUBCONTINENT & THE INDIAN OCEAN Bangladesh • Bengali phrasebook • Bhutan • Delhi • Goa • Healthy Travel Asia & India • Hindi & Urdu phrasebook • India • Indian Himalaya • Karakoram Highway • Kerala • Madagascar • Maldives • Mauritius, Réunion & Seychelles • Mumbai (Bombay) • Nepal • Nepali phrasebook • Pakistan • Rajasthan • Read This First: Asia & India • South India • Sri Lanka • Sri Lanka phrasebook • Tibet • Tibetan phrasebook • Trekking in the Indian Himalaya • Trekking in the Karakoram & Hindukush • Trekking in the Nepal Himalaya
Travel Literature: The Age of Kali: Indian Travels and Encounters • Hello Goodnight: A Life of Goa • In Rajasthan • Maverick in Madagascar • A Season in Heaven: True Tales from the Road to Kathmandu • Shopping for Buddhas • A Short Walk in the Hindu Kush • Slowly Down the Ganges

MIDDLE EAST & CENTRAL ASIA Bahrain, Kuwait & Qatar • Central Asia • Central Asia phrasebook • Dubai • Farsi (Persian) phrasebook • Hebrew phrasebook • Iran • Israel & the Palestinian Territories • Istanbul • Istanbul City Map • Istanbul to Cairo • Istanbul to Kathmandu • Jerusalem • Jerusalem City Map • Jordan • Lebanon • Middle East • Oman & the United Arab Emirates • Syria • Turkey • Turkish phrasebook • World Food Turkey • Yemen
Travel Literature: Black on Black: Iran Revisited • The Gates of Damascus • Kingdom of the Film Stars: Journey into Jordan

NORTH AMERICA Alaska • Boston • Boston City Map • Boston Condensed • British Columbia • California & Nevada • California Condensed • Canada • Chicago • Chicago City Map • Florida • Great Lakes • Hawaii • Hiking in Alaska • Hiking in the USA • Las Vegas • Los Angeles • Los Angeles City Map • Louisiana & the Deep South • Miami • Miami City Map • Montréal • New England • New Orleans • New York City • New York City City Map • New York City Condensed • New York, New Jersey & Pennsylvania • Oahu • Out to Eat – San Francisco • Pacific Northwest • Rocky Mountains • San Francisco • San Francisco City Map • Seattle • Southwest • Texas • Toronto • USA • USA phrasebook • Vancouver • Virginia & the Capital Region • Washington, DC • Washington, DC City Map • World Food New Orleans
Travel Literature: Caught Inside: A Surfer's Year on the California Coast • Drive Thru America

NORTH-EAST ASIA Beijing • Beijing City Map • Cantonese phrasebook • China • Hiking in Japan • Hong Kong • Hong Kong City Map • Hong Kong Condensed • Hong Kong, Macau & Guangzhou • Japan • Japanese phrasebook • Korea • Korean phrasebook • Kyoto • Mandarin phrasebook • Mongolia • Mongolian phrasebook • Seoul • Shanghai • South-West China • Taiwan • Tokyo • World Food Hong Kong
Travel Literature: In Xanadu: A Quest • Lost Japan

SOUTH AMERICA Argentina, Uruguay & Paraguay • Bolivia • Brazil • Brazilian phrasebook • Buenos Aires • Chile & Easter Island • Colombia • Ecuador & the Galápagos Islands • Healthy Travel Central & South America • Latin American Spanish phrasebook • Peru • Quechua phrasebook • Read This First: Central & South America • Rio de Janeiro • Rio de Janeiro City Map • Santiago de Chile • South America on a shoestring • Trekking in the Patagonian Andes • Venezuela
Travel Literature: Full Circle: A South American Journey

SOUTH-EAST ASIA Bali & Lombok • Bangkok • Bangkok City Map • Burmese phrasebook • Cambodia • Hanoi • Healthy Travel Asia & India • Hill Tribes phrasebook • Ho Chi Minh City • Indonesia • Indonesian phrasebook • Indonesia's Eastern Islands • Java • Lao phrasebook • Laos • Malay phrasebook • Malaysia, Singapore & Brunei • Myanmar (Burma) • Philippines • Pilipino (Tagalog) phrasebook • Read This First: Asia & India • Singapore • Singapore City Map • South-East Asia on a shoestring • South-East Asia phrasebook • Thailand • Thailand's Islands & Beaches • Thailand, Vietnam, Laos & Cambodia Road Atlas • Thai phrasebook • Vietnam • Vietnamese phrasebook • World Food Thailand • World Food Vietnam

ALSO AVAILABLE: Antarctica • The Arctic • The Blue Man: Tales of Travel, Love and Coffee • Brief Encounters: Stories of Love, Sex & Travel • Chasing Rickshaws • The Last Grain Race • Lonely Planet...On the Edge: Adventurous Escapades from Around the World • Lonely Planet Unpacked • Not the Only Planet: Science Fiction Travel Stories • Sacred India • Travel Photography: A Guide to Taking Better Pictures • Travel with Children

Index

Abbreviations

B – Belize
C – Colombia
CR – Costa Rica

ES – El Salvador
G – Guatemala
H – Honduras

M – Mexico
N – Nicaragua
P – Panama

Text

Bold indicates maps.

Bold indicates maps.

Bold indicates maps.

Bold indicates maps.

Bold indicates maps.

Boxed Text

TROPIC 2012–

MAYA 2435–

MAP LEGEND

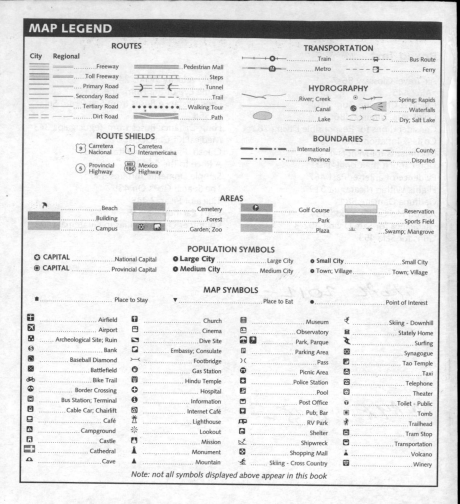

ROUTES

City **Regional**
- ....Freeway
- ....Toll Freeway
- ....Primary Road
- Secondary Road
- .... Tertiary Road
- ....Dirt Road

- ..Pedestrian Mall
- .... Steps
- ....Tunnel
- ....Trail
- ...... Walking Tour
- ....Path

ROUTE SHIELDS

- (9) Carretera Nacional
- (1) Carretera Interamericana
- (5) Provincial Highway
- (186) Mexico Highway

TRANSPORTATION

- ....Train
- ....Metro
- .... Bus Route
- .... Ferry

HYDROGRAPHY

- ......River; Creek
- ....Canal
- ....Lake
- .... Spring; Rapids
- ....Waterfalls
- .... Dry; Salt Lake

BOUNDARIES

- .... International
- ...... Province
- ....County
- ....Disputed

AREAS

- ....Beach
- ....Building
- ....Campus
- .... Cemetery
- ....Forest
- ...... Garden; Zoo
- ...... Golf Course
- ....Park
- ....Plaza
- ....Reservation
- ....Sports Field
- ...Swamp; Mangrove

POPULATION SYMBOLS

- ○ CAPITAL ....National Capital
- ◉ CAPITAL .... Provincial Capital
- ● **Large City** ....Large City
- ● **Medium City**................ Medium City
- ● Small City.........................Small City
- ○ Town; Village................ Town; Village

MAP SYMBOLS

- ▲ .... Place to Stay
- ▼ ....Place to Eat
- ● ....Point of Interest

- .... Airfield
- .... Airport
- ...... Archeological Site; Ruin
- .... Bank
- .... Baseball Diamond
- .... Battlefield
- .... Bike Trail
- .... Border Crossing
- .... Bus Station; Terminal
- ....Cable Car; Chairlift
- .... Café
- .... Campground
- .... Castle
- .... Cathedral
- .... Cave

- .... Church
- .... Cinema
- ....Dive Site
- ...... Embassy; Consulate
- .... Footbridge
- .... Gas Station
- .... Hindu Temple
- .... Hospital
- .... Information
- .... Internet Café
- .... Lighthouse
- .... Lookout
- .... Mission
- .... Monument
- .... Mountain

- .... Museum
- ....Observatory
- .... Park, Parque
- .... Parking Area
- .... Pass
- .... Picnic Area
- ....Police Station
- ....Pool
- .... Post Office
- .... Pub; Bar
- .... RV Park
- .... Shelter
- .... Shipwreck
- .... Shopping Mall
- ...... Skiing - Cross Country

- ....Skiing - Downhill
- .... Stately Home
- .... Surfing
- .... Synagogue
- .... Tao Temple
- ....Taxi
- .... Telephone
- .... Theater
- ....Toilet - Public
- ....Tomb
- ....Trailhead
- .... Tram Stop
- ....Transportation
- ....Volcano
- ....Winery

Note: not all symbols displayed above appear in this book

LONELY PLANET OFFICES

Australia
Locked Bag 1, Footscray, Victoria 3011
☎ 03 8379 8000 fax 03 8379 8111
email talk2us@lonelyplanet.com.au

USA
150 Linden Street, Oakland, California 94607
☎ 510 893 8555, TOLL FREE 800 275 8555
fax 510 893 8572
email info@lonelyplanet.com

UK
10a Spring Place, London NW5 3BH
☎ 020 7428 4800 fax 020 7428 4828
email go@lonelyplanet.co.uk

France
1 rue du Dahomey, 75011 Paris
☎ 01 55 25 33 00 fax 01 55 25 33 01
email bip@lonelyplanet.fr
www.lonelyplanet.fr

World Wide Web: www.lonelyplanet.com *or* **AOL keyword: lp**
Lonely Planet Images: lpi@lonelyplanet.com.au